ENCYCLOPEDIA OF THE RENAISSANCE

Leonardo da Vinci. *Virgin and Child with St. Anne.* Oil on wood; 1508; 168 x 130 cm (66 x 51 in.).

ENCYCLOPEDIA OF THE RENAISSANCE

Paul F. Grendler

Editor in Chief

PUBLISHED IN ASSOCIATION WITH
THE RENAISSANCE SOCIETY OF AMERICA

VOLUME 3

Galen – Lyon

CHARLES SCRIBNER'S SONS

An Imprint of The Gale Group

NEW YORK

Copyright © 1999 by Charles Scribner's Sons

Charles Scribner's Sons
1633 Broadway
New York, New York 10019

1 3 5 7 9 11 13 15 17 19   20 18 16 14 12 10 8 6 4 2

PRINTED IN THE UNITED STATES OF AMERICA

Library of Congress Cataloging-in-Publication Data
Encyclopedia of the Renaissance / Paul F. Grendler, editor in chief.
     p. cm.
   Includes bibliographical references and index.
   ISBN 0-684-80514-6 (set) — ISBN 0-684-80508-1 (v. 1) — ISBN 0-684-80509-X (v. 2)
— ISBN 0-684-80510-3 (v. 3) — ISBN 0-684-80511-1 (v. 4) — ISBN 0-684-80512-X (v.
5) — ISBN 0-684-80513-8 (v. 6)
   1. Renaissance—Encyclopedias.   I. Grendler, Paul F.   II. Renaissance Society of
America.
CB361.E52   1999
940.2′3′03—dc21   99-048290

The paper used in this publication meets the requirements of ANSI/NISO Z39.48-1992 (Permanence of Paper).

The typeface used in this book is ITC Garamond, a version of a typeface attributed to the French publisher and type founder Claude Garamond (c. 1480–1561).

CONTENTS OF OTHER VOLUMES

COMMON ABBREVIATIONS
USED IN THIS WORK

A.D.	*Anno Domini,* in the year of the Lord
A.H.	*Anno Hegirae,* in the year of the Hegira
b.	born
B.C.	before Christ
B.C.E.	before the common era (= B.C.)
c.	*circa,* about, approximately
C.E.	common era (= A.D.)
cf.	*confer,* compare
chap.	chapter
d.	died
D.	Dom, Portuguese honorific
diss.	dissertation
ed.	editor (pl., eds.), edition
e.g.	*exempli gratia,* for example
et al.	*et alii,* and others
etc.	*et cetera,* and so forth
f.	and following (pl., ff.)
fl.	*floruit,* flourished
HRE	Holy Roman Empire, Holy Roman Emperor
ibid.	*ibidem,* in the same place (as the one immediately preceding)
i.e.	*id est,* that is
MS.	manuscript (pl. MSS.)
n.	note
n.d.	no date
no.	number (pl., nos.)
n.p.	no place
n.s.	new series
N.S.	new style, according to the Gregorian calendar
O.F.M.	*Ordo Fratrum Minorum,* Order of Friars Minor; Franciscan
O.P.	*Ordo Predicatorum,* Order of Preachers; Dominican
O.S.	old style, according to the Julian calendar
p.	page (pl., pp.)
pt.	part
rev.	revised
S.	*san, sanctus, santo,* male saint
ser.	series

S.J.   *Societas Jesu,* Society of Jesus; Jesuit
SS.   *sancti, sanctae,* saints; *sanctissima, santissima,* most holy
Sta.   *sancta, santa,* female saint
supp.   supplement
vol.   volume
?   uncertain, possibly, perhaps

ENCYCLOPEDIA OF THE RENAISSANCE

GALEN (c. 129/130–c. 199–216 C.E.), Greek physician. For more than fifteen hundred years medicine in western Europe and in the Middle East was pervasively influenced, and to a greater or lesser degree dominated, by the medical philosophy developed from the writings of Galen of Pergamum. While very little is known of the life of Hippocrates, or even Aristotle, Galen's is well documented. He grew up in the Greek colony of Pergamum in Asia Minor and as the son of a prosperous architect was given an extensive education. As Galen later recalled it, the god Asclepius, whose great temple in Pergamum was then being constructed, came to his father in a dream and asked for Galen to be given to him. At sixteen, then, Galen became an apprentice to a local physician, and five years later he traveled to Smyrna, Corinth, and Alexandria to complete his medical education before returning home to take up the post of physician to the gladiators attached to the temple of Asclepius. In 161 he moved to Rome, as many provincials were doing, attracted by the emperor Marcus Aurelius's reputation for patronage. Galen had already produced several treatises by this time, most notably *On the Anatomy of the Uterus* and *On the Movement of the Chest and the Lungs,* and he later claimed this caused him to catch the eye of one of the consuls, Flavius Boethus. So with a patron, Boethus, who recommended him to wealthy Roman patients, and the publication of his two large anatomical works, *On Anatomical Procedures* and *On the Usefulness of the Parts of the Body,* Galen soon became a well-known physician and writer producing over three hundred volumes in modern terms.

Finally, at age forty he was appointed court physician to the Roman emperor himself, a post he held until his death.

Galen's Theory and Practice. To the Hippocratic and Aristotelian theories about the elements and the four fluids, or "humors," Galen added a discussion of "temperaments." He believed that each organ and each kind of tissue in the body had a unique mixture of humors; this qualitative mixture was its temperament, of which he insisted there were nine possible types. A patient's temperament was diagnosed from examining the skin of the palm of the hand, where the deviation from the ideal could best be seen. Galen upheld the Hippocratic belief that observation and experience were the keys to medical practice. Through his dissections and vivisections of Barbary apes, pigs, dogs, and once even an elephant, Galen established the function of a variety of nerves.

Diseases, he believed, were due largely to residues formed by an excess of humors becoming putrified or inflamed in specific parts of the body. Galen recommended prevention as the primary treatment for this situation. Overeating, drinking to excess, and particularly constipation were therefore to be avoided at all cost. He also advocated venesection (bloodletting) to both prevent and treat illness.

The Transmission of Galen's Medical Philosophy. Nearly all the works of Galen were translated by Islamic writers into Arabic by the ninth century. The Benedictine monk Constantine the African (c. 1020–1087) translated them into Latin from Arabic while at the monastery of Monte Cassino in southern Italy. Approximately 590 editions of works of Galen were published there between 1500 and 1600. In 1523 Thomas Linacre, an English humanist and medical graduate of the University of Padua, translated Galen's physiological treatise *On the Natural Faculties* into Latin, while Johann Guinter of Andernach published his Latin translation of an incomplete version of *On Anatomical Procedures* in 1531. Meanwhile, in 1525 the Aldine press in Venice published the complete works of Galen in the original Greek. Medical practitioners, however, largely unversed in Greek, continued to rely on Latin translations—often of the Aldine edition.

The new Galenic treatises quickly made an impact on the Italian universities, and they were significantly transformed by the movement known as medical humanism, with its ultimate goal to practice medicine in the manner of the ancient physicians as revealed in the newly recovered original texts of Galen. As the historian Jerome Bylebyl has noted, at the University of Padua new forms of botanical, anatomical, and clinical teaching were introduced into the medical curriculum. Bedside teaching was emphasized and the annual anatomy at Padua developed from a cursory event into an elaborate month-long ritual held every winter, in which two or three human bodies were dissected before medical students and interested civic dignitaries. The translation in 1531 of *On the Teachings of Hippocrates and Plato* was of particular importance, as in it Galen had used anatomical and vivisectional demonstrations to refute many of the central tenets of Aristotle's biology. Galen's stress on the theoretical and practical importance of anatomy to the physician also resulted in the elevation of anatomy as a subject. From being viewed as a minor adjunct to academic medical studies, anatomy as a teaching program based on dissections grew to be of crucial importance in university curricula.

Reaction to Galen in the Renaissance. In 1537 the Belgian Andreas Vesalius was appointed lecturer in surgery and anatomy at Padua. At the beginning of his career Vesalius read the newly published Latin translations of *On the Usefulness of the Parts of the Body* and *On Anatomical Procedures*. From these works he learned how to dissect and how to describe anatomical structures. After several years of teaching at Padua, however, Vesalius changed from being a skilled teacher of Galenic anatomy to becoming a critic of it as he observed that Galen's anatomical descriptions did not match what he found in the human body. Like Islamic and Christian readers before him, Vesalius mistakenly believed that Galen had dissected humans as well as animals. In 1543 he published *De humani corporis fabrica* (On the structure of the human body), which detailed over two hundred errors he had found. Yet, although Vesalius attacked Galen's anatomy, he continued to praise his authority and system by following Galen's outline of the body in his writings and using animals to illustrate human anatomy.

See also **Anatomy**; **Medicine**.

BIBLIOGRAPHY

Primary Works

Galen. *On Anatomical Procedures.* Edited by M. C. Lyons and B. Towers. Translated by W. L. H. Duckworth. Cambridge, U.K., 1962.

Galen. *On the Natural Faculties.* Translated by Arthur John Brock. Cambridge, Mass., 1963.

Galen. *Three Treatises on the Nature of Science.* Translated by Richard Walzer and Michael Frede. Indianapolis, Ind., 1985.

Secondary Works

Bylebyl, Jerome. "The School of Padua: Humanistic Medicine in the Sixteenth Century." In *Health, Medicine, and Mortality in the Sixteenth Century.* Edited by Charles Webster. Cambridge, U.K., 1987. Pages 361–363. The reception of Galen in the Renaissance.

Nutton, Vivian, ed. *Galen: Problems and Prospects.* London, 1981. Essays on the interpretation of Galen's impact on medicine from ancient to early modern times.

Temkin, Owsei. *Galenism: Rise and Decline of a Medical Philosophy.* Ithaca, N.Y., 1973.

LYNDA STEPHENSON PAYNE

GALILEI, GALILEO (1564–1642), Italian mathematician, physicist, and astronomer, foremost scientist of the Renaissance, the "father of modern science." Twentieth-century biographers consistently portrayed Galileo's work as based on modern scientific methods, paying little attention to the ways in which science was developing in his lifetime. Also, beginning around 1970 scholars made discoveries relating to Galileo's manuscripts that significantly altered hitherto accepted views of his scientific contributions. In what follows, account is taken of these findings as well as the Renaissance ambience of Galileo's work. The account unfolds in three stages: the early phase, from his birth to the publication of his *Siderius Nuncius* (1610; trans. *Sidereal Messenger*); the middle phase, leading up to the publication of his *Dialogo sopra i due massimi sistemi del mondo* (1632; trans. *Two World Systems*); and the final phase, which began with his trial in 1633 and ended with his death at Arcetri, near Florence, on 8 January 1642.

Early Phase (1564–1610). Galileo was born at Pisa on 15 February 1564, the first child of Vincenzio Galileo, a Florentine music teacher and lutanist of ability, and Giulia Ammannati of Pescia. The family moved to Florence in 1572; Galileo was tutored privately, then did his classical studies at the nearby monastery of Vallombrosa. He returned to Pisa in the fall of 1581 to enroll as a medical student at the university. There he studied under the philosophers Francesco Buonamici (1533–1603) and Girolamo Borro (1512–1592) and the mathematician Filippo Fantoni (d. 1591). Around 1583 Galileo became acquainted with Ostilio Ricci (1540–1603), a mathematician said to have studied under Niccolò Tartaglia (1499/1500–1557). Beginning in 1584 Ricci tutored Galileo in Euclid and Archimedes.

Teaching and writing. In 1585 Galileo dropped out of the university without a degree and began to teach mathematics privately at Florence, Vallombrosa, and Siena. He traveled to Rome in 1587 to discuss with the Jesuit Christopher Clavius (1537–1612) a work he was preparing on the center of gravity of solids. And in 1588 he was invited to give lectures at the Florentine Academy on the location and dimensions of hell in Dante's *Inferno*.

Fantoni relinquished his chair of mathematics at Pisa in 1589 and Galileo was chosen to replace him, partly because of the favorable impression he made on the Tuscan court with his lectures on Dante, partly on the endorsement of Clavius and other mathematicians who knew his work. In November 1589 Galileo began lecturing at the university along with the Aristotelian-Platonist Jacopo Mazzoni (1548–1598), who quickly became his friend.

While at Pisa, Galileo wrote three notebooks in Latin, one on logic explaining the Aristotelian concept of demonstration and proof (*Dialettica,* MS. 27), another exposing Aristotle's teachings on the heavens and the elements (*De caelo* and *De elementis,* MS. 46), and a third containing his "older treatise" on motion (*De motu,* MS. 71). The last treats gravity and levity, flotation, and bodies in motion, both in free fall and along inclined planes. MSS. 27 and 46 are basically theoretical expositions, but MS. 71 also mentions experiments (*pericula*) Galileo performed in attempts to formulate laws of motion.

Galileo taught at Pisa until 1592. The death of his father in 1591 put heavy financial burdens on him as eldest son, and he had to obtain a better salary than the 60 florins he was then being paid. He thus sought

Galileo Galilei. Portrait by Justus Austermans. GALLERIA DEGLI UFFIZI, FLORENCE/CORBIS/BETTMANN

and received an appointment with a salary of 180 florins at the University of Padua, where he delivered his inaugural lecture on 7 December 1592.

The next eighteen years Galileo spent in the republic of Venice; he later avowed these were the happiest years of his life. In this period he wrote treatises on mechanics (*Le Meccaniche;* c. 1600) and on the *Sphere* of Sacrobosco, which he titled cosmography (*Trattato della Sfera, overro Cosmografia;* c. 1604–1606) and which he used for teaching Ptolemaic astronomy. Between 1602 and 1609 he also made extensive manuscript notes and sketches of experiments he performed with pendulums, inclined planes, and bodies in natural and projectile motion (MS. 72). Particularly fruitful were those performed with inclined planes set on a tabletop near the edge, from which balls, rolling down the inclines from various heights and angles of inclination, when projected to the floor, follow paths that approach a semi-parabola. [For an illustration of Galileo's table-top experiment see Mechanics, in volume 4.]

Finally, in 1609, having heard of the invention of the telescope in Holland, Galileo perfected that instrument for the study of heavenly bodies. He made startling discoveries, including numerous stars in the heavens, mountains on the moon, and the satellites of Jupiter. In March 1610 he published these results at Venice in his *Sidereal Messenger* and soon won acclaim throughout Europe as the foremost astronomer of his day.

Manuscript discoveries. The foregoing chronology is based on research of the late twentieth century and is not that contained in the national edition of Galileo's *Opere,* edited in twenty volumes by Antonio Favaro (Florence, 1890–1909; repr. 1968). Favaro knew of MS. 27 but he thought it was an exercise Galileo copied from a monk at Vallombrosa, dated it around 1579, and did not include it in the national edition. He did transcribe and publish MSS. 46 and 71, but misdated the first and failed to order the components of the second correctly. The materials in MS. 72 were apparently intractable for him, for he left them out also. All four manuscripts are still conserved in the Galileiana collection of the Biblioteca Nazionale Centrale in Florence.

The Pisan manuscripts are indispensable for understanding Galileo's early period. MS. 27 was transcribed, edited, and published four hundred years after it was written and is available in English translation as his *Logical Treatises* (1992). These treatises were appropriated from the year-long logic course of the Jesuit Paulus Vallius (1561–1622) at the Collegio Romano ending in August 1588, and were probably composed by Galileo early in 1589. They contain exhaustive analyses of Aristotle's teachings on the foreknowledge required for demonstration and on demonstration itself, concluding with an explanation of the demonstrative regress.

MS. 46 is composed of the aforementioned two treatises on the heavens and the elements, plus a series of memoranda on motion that are related to the materials in MS. 71. These treatises have been translated as Galileo's *Physical Questions* (1977). The manuscript is written on paper with Pisan watermarks, presumes knowledge of the logic in MS. 27, and is similarly based on courses taught at the Jesuit Collegio Romano. Its composition is best located at Pisa around 1590, within a year after the questions on logic.

The story with respect to MS. 71 is more complex. Its five different components, all of which were original with Galileo, were written on folios with a variety of watermarks. His Latinity improved with each composition. Begun in 1588 and completed around 1592,

they were written in Florence and Pisa at different times. Their main teachings are contained in I. E. Drabkin's translation, *On Motion* (1960); complete details are given in Wallace (1998).

The final manuscript, MS. 72, provides abundant evidence of an experimental program carried out by Galileo at Padua between 1602 and 1609, which terminated in his discovery of the principles on which he later based his "new science" of motion. Starting around 1970 Stillman Drake developed a technique for dating the manuscript's folios on the basis of watermarks. From diagrams and calculations present on them, he and other investigators have been able to reconstruct and duplicate experiments Galileo actually performed at Padua but never reported in his published writings.

The import of this new manuscript evidence can best be seen by joining these experiments to the discoveries Galileo would soon make with his telescope, and considering both in light of the logical treatises in MS. 27. It is now clear that while at Padua, Galileo was able to secure strict demonstrations in the Aristotelian sense of the basic phenomena of the heavens and falling motion. By the end of 1610 he had discovered the phases of Venus, showed that it rotates around the sun, not the earth, and thus complemented the proofs offered in the *Sidereal Messenger.* The demonstrations in mechanics he reported only partially, and not until many years later, in 1638.

Middle Period (1611–1632). On the strength of his astronomical discoveries Galileo obtained the patronage of the grand duke of Tuscany, Cosimo II de' Medici. He gave up his teaching duties at Padua and moved to Florence to serve as "mathematician and philosopher" to the grand duke. In the spring of 1611 Galileo traveled to Rome, where he met with Clavius and was feted at the Collegio Romano by astronomers there who had verified his telescopic discoveries. He also talked with Cardinal Robert Bellarmine (1542–1621), himself a Jesuit, about the implications of his discoveries for resolving the differences between Ptolemy and Copernicus on the system of the world.

Controversies at Florence. At Padua, Galileo had taught Ptolemaic astronomy, but at Florence, armed with his new evidence, he became a convinced Copernican. This put him at odds with the Dominicans there who were concerned over how Copernicus's teaching that the sun is at rest and the earth moves could be reconciled with the Bible's statements to the contrary. He also entered into controversy with conservative Aristotelians there, notably Ludovico delle Colombe (b. 1565), about opposing Aristotelian and Archimedean explanations of the behavior of bodies in water.

In 1612 Galileo published his *Discorso . . . intorno alle cose che stanno in su l'acqua* (trans. *Discourse on Bodies on or in Water*) against Colombe. In that year he also got involved in a prolonged dispute with a German Jesuit, Christopher Scheiner (1573–1650), about the nature of sunspots. Scheiner and Galileo both discovered sunspots around the same time, and they attempted to explain them in different ways that favored the Ptolemaic and Copernican theories respectively, but without complete success.

In 1613 Galileo wrote a letter to a former student, the Benedictine Benedetto Castelli (1578–1643), on how the earth's motion need not be seen as opposed to scripture. A year later, Galileo was attacked from the pulpit by the Dominicans for his Copernican teachings. He was then queried by his patron's mother, the grand duchess Christina of Lorraine (d. 1637), who was a friend and was concerned over his orthodoxy. This elicited his *Lettera a Madama Cristina* (1615; trans. *Letter to the Grand Duchess*), an amplification of his earlier letter to Castelli that is still regarded as a masterpiece on reconciling biblical texts with scientific discoveries. At about the same time, and independently of Galileo, the Carmelite Paolo Foscarini (c. 1580–1616) wrote a letter to Cardinal Bellarmine explaining in similar ways how the Copernican system might be made consonant with scripture.

Developments in Rome.

Aware of these attempts at biblical exegesis, on 12 April 1615 Bellarmine wrote to Foscarini and Galileo that the Copernican system could be used for astronomical calculations, but that the earth's motion was as yet only a hypothesis and had not been conclusively demonstrated. Bellarmine cautioned that until such time as a demonstration was available, the commonly accepted interpretation of scripture was to be preserved. Alarmed by this development, Galileo prepared to defend himself. He sought Cosimo's permission to go to Rome and arrived there by the end of the year. He discussed with a young cardinal, Alessandro Orsini (1593–1626), a proof of the earth's motion based on the tides. Encouraged by Orsini, on 6 January 1616 Galileo wrote out his *Discourse on the Tides,* modeling his proof on the demonstrative regress but claiming for it only the status of a probable argument.

Shortly thereafter, on 23 February 1616, consultants to the holy office judged that holding the sun's rest was opposed to the literal sense of scripture and thus heretical, while holding the earth's motion, while not heretical, was at least theologically erroneous. Two days later, Pope Paul V asked Bellarmine to inform Galileo of this finding, and on 26 February, Bellarmine delivered a warning in the presence of officials of the holy office. The officials had prepared an injunction to be served on Galileo in the event that he not acquiesce. This injunction contained the wording that Galileo was to abandon his position on the sun's rest and the earth's motion and was "henceforth not to hold, teach, or defend it in any way whatever, either orally or in writing." Galileo gave his assent and the injunction was not served. It was returned instead to the files of the Holy Office.

Rumors began circulating that Galileo had abjured into Bellarmine's hands and had received a penance for his Copernican teachings. Galileo visited Bellarmine on 3 March 1616 and obtained certification from him that such was not the case, that Galileo had merely been notified of the church's teaching. Two days later the Congregation of the Index published a decree against Copernicanism, condemning Foscarini's work outright and suspending publication of Copernicus's *De revolutionibus* (Nürnberg, 1543; trans. *On the Revolutions of the Heavenly Spheres*) until its text was corrected.

Galileo then returned to Florence. In 1618 three comets appeared in the heavens, and a Jesuit astronomer, Orazio Grassi (1590–1654), gave a public lecture at the Collegio Romano on the paths and appearances of the comets. Informed of the lecture, Galileo attacked Grassi with a *Discorso sulle comete* (1619; trans. *Discourse on the Comets*), ostensibly authored by one of Galileo's students, Mario Guiducci (1585–1646), but composed mostly by Galileo. The latter's relationships with the Jesuits had soured during his dispute with Scheiner over sunspots, but they now verged on open warfare.

A new pope.

The year 1621 saw the deaths of three important figures: Pope Paul V, Bellarmine, and Galileo's patron, Cosimo II de' Medici. Fortunately, Paul V was succeeded by a Florentine cardinal, Maffeo Barberini, who had been sympathetic to Galileo during the troubles of 1616 and who generally took Galileo's side in his battles with the Jesuits.

When Barberini assumed the papacy in 1623 as Urban VIII, Galileo took the opportunity to dedicate

Sunspots. From Galileo's *Istorie e dimonstrazioni . . . intorno all macchie solari* (1613). BY PERMISSION OF THE HOUGHTON LIBRARY, HARVARD UNIVERSITY

the evidence and arguments for and against the Ptolemaic and Copernican systems, coming down heavily on the side of the Copernicans and making the Ptolemaists and Aristotelians look somewhat foolish in the process. Galileo caricatured their positions through a fictional character, the inept Simplicio, who found his philosophy in the text of Aristotle rather than in the book of nature.

Galileo had difficulty obtaining permission to have the *Dialogue* published. The Dominican Niccolò Riccardi (1585–1639), charged with censoring the work, was mindful of the decree against Copernicanism handed down in 1616. So Galileo added a new preface and a note at the end, disclaiming proof of the Copernican system and labeling it a pure mathematical hypothesis instead. Riccardi then gave his approval to the doctored manuscript and the book was printed at Florence in 1632.

The two world systems. In Renaissance style this work reports a reputed dialogue that takes place over four days among the fictional characters Salviati, Sagredo, and Simplicio, with a different series of arguments developed in the course of each day.

On the first day Salviati, Galileo's mouthpiece, argues that there is no clear dichotomy between the celestial and terrestrial regions, a central tenet of Aristotle's cosmology. He maintains that the world is one, probably constructed of the same kind of material (for example, mountains on the moon just like those on earth) and probably undergoing the same kinds of motion.

The main topic on the second day is the daily rotation of the earth on its axis. Here Galileo rebuts most of the proofs that the earth is at rest, such as the fact that a stone dropped from a tower always falls at its foot. He shows that, if one knows the principles of mechanics (which he had demonstrated at Padua but had yet to publish), the proofs offered yield the same results whether the earth is still or turning. These results, he admits, do not prove that the earth is turning; they simply destroy the proofs of his adversaries that it must be at rest. The earth's diurnal rotation is thus left an open question.

The third day is devoted to a more difficult problem: whether the earth is immobile in the center of the universe or actually travels in a large annual orbit around the sun. Here Galileo argues by analogy: since he has demonstrated that the other planets revolve about the sun, and that Jupiter carries its four moons along with it, the earth and its moon likely do the same. Further, earthly revolution can

to the new pope his definitive answer to Grassi on the comets, *Il saggiatore* (trans. *The Assayer*), which he had just completed. No doubt Urban VIII was pleased and flattered by this action, for he granted Galileo the favor of six audiences. Most scholars agree that Galileo secured some kind of permission from Urban to resume work on the Copernican system.

By 1630 Galileo had finished his great work, the *Dialogue on the World Systems*. In it he evaluated all

explain changes he has observed in the motion of sunspots.

Finally, on the fourth day Galileo reinforces the conclusions of the previous two days by showing how they provide a simple explanation of a universally observed phenomenon, the motion of the tides. His argument is essentially the same as he sketched to Cardinal Orsini in 1616, and was already known to Urban VIII, who had discouraged Galileo from using it. The proposal is that the combination of the earth's daily rotation on its axis with its annual revolution around the sun results in unequal forces being exerted on the waters on the earth's surface. These unequal forces give rise to the tides. The "proof" is one Galileo had worked on for years without being able to remove its flaws. In the preface to the *Dialogue* he himself refers to it as an "ingenious fantasy" (*fantasia ingegnosa*).

The trial (1632–1633). With the *Dialogue's* publication Galileo found himself in deeper trouble than he could have imagined. Pope Urban VIII was furious, probably because he felt Galileo had betrayed an earlier pledge that he would write impartially, almost certainly because he felt that Galileo had misused, and ridiculed, Urban's own answer to the Ptolemaic-Copernican controversy, namely, that it could not be definitively resolved by human intellect.

In August 1632 all further publication and sales of the book were prohibited by the Holy Office. Galileo was summoned to Rome from Florence to be tried by a tribunal of ten cardinals on the charge that he had willfully taught the Copernican doctrine despite its condemnation as contrary to scripture.

The charges and the defense. Galileo was in poor health in late 1632 and had to be brought to Rome on a litter, arriving there in February 1633. By that time all of the officials who had taken part in the investigations of 1615–1616 had died. The new commissary of the Holy Office, the Dominican Vincenzo Maculano of Firenzuola, had therefore to rely on the information in the Holy Office's file on Galileo. There he discovered the injunction of 1616 and decided to base the case against Galileo on that. When queried about the injunction, and particularly whether he was told "henceforth not to hold, teach, or defend it [Copernicanism] in any way whatever," Galileo replied that he did not remember those particular words. He did recall, however, a certificate sent him on 26 May 1616 by Cardinal Bellarmine, a copy of which he had brought with him. The cardinal's order was not to hold or defend the said opinion, but the expressions "not to teach" and "in any way whatever" are not in the certificate, which is probably why he did not remember them.

This information caught Firenzuola off guard, since he did not know about the certificate, no copy being in his files. (In 1984 the autograph copy was found in the Jesuit archives in Rome.) Firenzuola continued his interrogation nonetheless, asking Galileo whether he had obtained permission to write the book. Galileo's answer was ingenuous: he did not need permission to write it because in it he was not defending the Copernican opinion but actually refuting it. In fact, the injunction was irrelevant, because he showed in the book that Copernicus's arguments were invalid and inconclusive.

Nonplussed, Firenzuola had three consultants read the *Dialogue* to judge whether in it Galileo had actually "held, taught, or defended" the heliocentric system. All three concluded that without doubt Galileo had taught and defended Copernicus's opinion, but as to whether he personally held it, they were not sure, since there were many qualifications in the text. Yet two of them "vehemently suspected" that he did.

Obviously Galileo's first attempt at defense was irrational and would not work, so Firenzuola resorted to a plea-bargaining agreement with him. To head off the more serious charge that Galileo held the Copernican opinion, Firenzuola proposed that he admit to the lesser charge that he had defended the opinion, but he had done so without intending it, having gotten carried away when writing the book. Galileo accepted the offer and so was in a position to defend himself on that basis. He maintained that, as a devout son of the church, he would not personally believe anything that was contrary to scripture. He then denied any malicious intent, accused himself of "vain ambition and the satisfaction of appearing clever," and pleaded for clemency and pity.

The trial might well have ended there, but unfortunately it did not. At the insistence of Urban VIII, who remained unconvinced of Galileo's truthfulness, he was made to swear that he did not believe in the earth's motion and to abjure his former teachings. On this basis he was given a salutary penance and confined to house arrest, first at Siena and then in his villa at Arcetri. The *Dialogue* was banned, and Galileo was forbidden to write any more on Copernicanism.

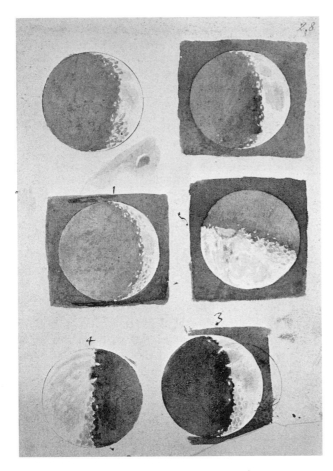

The Phases of the Moon. Painting by Galileo. BIBLIOTECA NAZIONALE, FLORENCE/SCALA/ART RESOURCE, NY

Last Years (1633–1642). At Arcetri Galileo recovered his early manuscripts and resumed work on his "new science" of motion, on which he had worked only intermittently after Padua, in 1618, 1627, and 1631. Now he projected a lengthy dialogue, again in four days and with the same discussants. The first two days focused on the science of mechanics, treating mainly the strength of materials; this Galileo completed by mid-1635. The third and fourth days then developed in systematic fashion the science of local motion, the third focusing mainly on naturally accelerated motion, the fourth on the motion of projectiles.

The resulting work, *Discorsi e dimostrazioni matematiche intorno a due nuove scienze,* now referred to as the *Two New Sciences,* was completed in 1637 and smuggled out of Italy to Holland, where

it was printed at Leiden in 1638. It was replete with references to the demonstrations on which the sciences were based, claims conspicuously absent in the *Dialogue* of 1632. But curiously it made no mention of the Paduan "tabletop experiments," which provided the main empirical foundation on which the new sciences were based. Galileo did append to the volume, however, his works on *Centers of Gravity* and *Force of Percussion* written fifty years previously.

The next few years Galileo worked on projected fifth and sixth days for these discourses. Despite his irrevocable opposition to Aristotelian physics, on 14 September 1640 he wrote to Fortunio Liceti (1577–1657) that in matters of logic he had been a peripatetic all his life. There is little doubt that his ideals of science and demonstration were Aristotelian and still inspired by the *Logical Treatises* of his early studies at Pisa.

In November 1641 Galileo developed a fever and palpitations of the heart that confined him to bed. After two months of illness he died peacefully at Arcetri on 8 January 1642. He was buried in a side chapel of the Franciscan church of Santa Croce in Florence. On 13 March 1736 his remains were moved to the main body of the church, close to the tombs of Michelangelo and Machiavelli.

The Aftermath. In 1820 the Holy Office revoked the condemnation of Copernicanism. It did so on the basis of discoveries of two little-known Italian astronomers. The first, Giovanni Battista Gugliel-mini, offered physical proof of the earth's rotation by measuring, in experiments performed at Bologna between 1789 and 1792, the slight deflection to the east of bodies falling from a high tower. The second, Giuseppe Calendrelli, measured the parallax of star Alpha in constellation Lyra and presented his results to Pope Pius VII in a work published in 1806. A dispute over an imprimatur to be given to an astronomy text in 1820 led the commissary of the Holy Office, the Dominican Benedetto Olivieri—who saw these findings as demonstrations of the earth's twofold movement—to revoke the decree of 1616. The next revision of the Index of Prohibited Books was not published until 1835, at which time Galileo's *Dialogue* was finally removed from its list.

On 10 November 1979, Pope John Paul II acknowledged that Galileo had suffered a great deal from the church and called for a frank reexamination of the famous trial. On 3 July 1981 he appointed a special commission to study and publish all available documents relating to it. The results of the commission's work he presented to the Pontifical Academy of Sciences on 31 October 1992. Its report made clear that in 1616 and 1633 astronomy was in transition and scripture scholars were confused about cosmology. Galileo had not demonstrated the earth's motion, and theologians had erred in their assessments of his teachings. But in the 1990s, the pope continued, science is so complex that it is almost impossible to certify scientific discoveries as absolutely true. The best one can hope for is that they be "seriously and solidly grounded." The function of the Pontifical Academy, he said, was to advise the church if the degree of probability of a discovery is such "that it would be imprudent or unreasonable to reject it." Had such enlightened advice been available to his predecessor Urban VIII, Galileo might have been spared his tragic end.

See also **Astronomy; Science; Scientific Method.**

BIBLIOGRAPHY

Primary Works

Finocchiaro, Maurice A. *The Galileo Affair: A Documentary History.* Berkeley, Los Angeles, and London, 1989. Edited and translated with an introduction and notes.

Galilei, Galileo. *Discoveries and Opinions of Galileo.* Translated with an introduction and notes by Stillman Drake. New York, 1957. Includes *The Starry Messenger* (1610), *Letter to the Grand Duchess Christina* (1615), and excerpts from *Letters on Sunspots* (1613) and *The Assayer* (1623).

Galilei, Galileo. *Galileo's Early Notebooks: The Physical Questions. A Translation from the Latin, with Historical and Paleographical Commentary.* Translated by William A. Wallace. Notre Dame, Ind., 1977.

Galilei, Galileo. *Galileo's Logical Treatises: A Translation, with Notes and Commentary, of His Appropriated Latin Questions on Aristotle's* Posterior Analytics. Translated by William A. Wallace. Dordrecht, Netherlands; Boston; and London, 1992.

Galilei, Galileo. *Galileo on the World Systems: A New Abridged Translation and Guide.* Translated by Maurice A. Finocchiaro. Berkeley, Los Angeles, and London, 1997.

Galilei, Galileo. On Motion and On Mechanics: *Comprising* De motu *(ca. 1590), and* Le meccaniche *(ca. 1600).* Madison, Wis., 1960. *De Motu* translated with introduction and notes by I. E. Drabkin. *Le Meccaniche* translated with introduction and notes by Stillman Drake.

Galilei, Galileo. *Sidereus Nuncius, or The Sidereal Messenger.* Translated with introduction, conclusion, and notes by Albert Van Helden. Chicago and London, 1989.

Galilei, Galileo. *Two New Sciences,* Including Centers of Gravity and Force of Percussion. Translated with introduction and notes by Stillman Drake. Madison, Wis., 1974.

Secondary Works

Biagioli, Mario. *Galileo Courtier: The Practice of Science in the Culture of Absolutism.* Chicago, 1993. A study of Galileo and patronage.

Blackwell, Richard J. *Galileo, Bellarmine, and the Bible: Including a Translation of Foscarini's Letter on the Motion of the Earth.* Notre Dame, Ind., and London, 1991.

Drake, Stillman. *Galileo at Work: His Scientific Biography.* Chicago and London, 1978. The best available account of Galileo's life and science.

Fantoli, Annibale. *Galileo for Copernicanism and for the Church.* Translated by George V. Coyne. 2d ed., revised and corrected. Rome and Notre Dame, Ind., 1996.

Feldhay, Rivka. *Galileo and the Church: Political Inquisition or Critical Dialogue?* New York and Cambridge, U.K., 1995.

Machamer, Peter, ed. *The Cambridge Companion to Galileo.* Cambridge, U.K., 1998.

Moss, Jean Dietz. *Novelties in the Heavens: Rhetoric and Science in the Copernican Controversy.* Chicago and London, 1993. Focuses on Galileo and the Jesuits.

Redondi, Pietro. *Galileo Heretic (Galileo Eretico).* Translated by Raymond Rosenthal. Princeton, N.J., 1987. A faulty thesis, but excellent historical background.

Wallace, William A. *Galileo and His Sources: The Heritage of the Collegio Romano in Galileo's Science.* Princeton, N.J., 1984.

Wallace, William A. *Galileo's Logic of Discovery and Proof: The Background, Content, and Use of His Appropriated Treatises on Aristotle's* Posterior Analytics. Dordrecht, Netherlands; Boston; and London, 1992.

Wallace, William A. "Galileo's Pisan Studies in Science and Philosophy." In *The Cambridge Companion to Galileo.* Edited by Peter Machamer. Cambridge, U.K., 1998. Pages 27–52.

WILLIAM A. WALLACE

GALLICANISM. Gallicanism is a term used broadly to designate any French Catholic opposition to Rome, and in particular the legal or theological defense of certain so-called liberties of the Gallican church under the old regime.

Origins. Clashes arose periodically between the French political or ecclesiastical authorities and those of Rome as the medieval French kings slowly built up the national monarchy. While these clashes were generally less serious than in England or Germany, there was a dramatic incident when Pope Boniface VIII attempted to depose Philip IV for disobedience, only to be militarily defeated and to die in captivity after mistreatment by Philip's henchmen (1303). This left the French with an abiding suspicion toward any papal claim of authority in their affairs. Otherwise, however, Franco-papal relations remained close, so that when the popes were driven out of Rome by factional fighting they took refuge in Avignon, an enclave in French territory (1309).

This move led to the Great Schism between rival popes at Rome and Avignon, which had a double influence on the development of Gallicanism. First, attempts to resolve it came to depend on the doctrine that a general council of the church could direct or overrule the pope. Widely supported in France (notably by the theologians Jean Gerson and Pierre d'Ailly), this doctrine implied that there should be strict limits on papal centralizing power. Second, for a time the French king recognized none of the contending popes, while the government took over some papal functions. Elements of this situation survived the final resolution of the schism at the Council of Basel and were formalized by the Pragmatic Sanction of Bourges (1438), a document promulgated by Charles VII in an assembly of lay and clerical notables, which, on the one hand, reiterated the decrees of Basel and, on the other, set forth an array of Gallican liberties.

By this time the list of those liberties was in substantially the form it would retain until the revolution, although the interpretation and relative importance of the different elements changed over time. Simplified, they were, first, that the pope had no direct authority in France in secular affairs; second, that the authority of a church council was superior to that of the pope; third, that the pope had the right only to confirm French bishops, who were to be selected within the kingdom (under the Pragmatic Sanction, they were to be elected by diocesan chapters); fourth, that the right of the pope to tax the French church was strictly limited; and fifth, that the judicial authority of the pope within France was likewise strictly limited.

The Concordat of Bologna.

Charles VIII's invasion of Italy in 1494, traditionally taken to mark the beginning of the French Renaissance, also opened a new chapter in the history of Gallicanism. Since Italian involvement could lead to open war with the papacy, a new urgency was added to the defense of the Gallican liberties. Popes had to be prevented from exercising influence in or drawing money from France, and the validity of any censures they might impose on France had to be denied. A very serious crisis arose in 1512 under Louis XII, who broke off relations with Rome, commissioned polemical Gallican tracts—by the theologian Jacques Almain and by the poet Jean Lemaire de Belges—and even convened a self-styled church council at Pisa to depose Pope Julius II.

The failure of this enterprise and Louis's death led his successor, Francis I, to try a different tack. A summit meeting between Francis and Pope Leo X produced the Concordat of Bologna (1516), in which the pope, as an act of grace, recognized some but not all of the liberties claimed in the Pragmatic Sanction and, crucially, gave the king the privilege of appointing bishops in France, subject to papal confirmation. Despite a poorly coordinated defense of the

Pragmatic Sanction by the Faculty of Theology and the Parlement (high court) of Paris, the concordat was swiftly implemented. Royal interest in the Gallican liberties thereafter tended to decline, since the concordat settled most outstanding issues between king and pope, while France was eventually excluded from Italy. The bishops' interests were tied more closely to those of the king, while the courts remained hostile to the new dispensation. Thus from this point one finds Gallicanism splitting into distinct and often competing legal, theological, and episcopal traditions.

Humanism and Reform.

French humanist literature showed a strong strain of hostility to Rome, portrayed as corrupt and as a distraction from true faith. This tendency, often described as "Gallican," drew upon older Gallican traditions, which in turn it served to ingrain more deeply into French culture. It had little immediate political impact, but in 1551 a dispute between Pope Julius III and Henry II over the duchy of Parma led to a revival of old-style royal Gallicanism and even fears of a schism. Quickly forgotten as the French completed their withdrawal from Italy, the incident had long-term importance because one of the weapons that Henry II mobilized for the struggle was a young, but destined to be influential, school of legal-humanist historiography. Treatises commissioned from Jean Du Tillet and Charles Dumoulin pointed the way toward a Gallicanism based on an erudite reading of the nation's political history and constitution. The gist of their doctrine was that the survival of both church and state depended on the careful preservation of customary arrangements that, they implied, legal historians were best able to understand and interpret.

The accelerating pace of Catholic reform soon allowed such ideas to gain prominence. The Council of Trent, especially its earlier sessions, was carried out with little French participation and little regard for French sensibilities or Gallican liberties. While the king and the bishops were inclined to overlook this fact in the interests of Catholic unity, the courts, which had never been reconciled to the abrogation of the Pragmatic Sanction and which were now strengthened by a new tract from Dumoulin and other similar works, set themselves firmly against the council. In successive meetings of the Estates General, the jurists managed to block the promulgation of the council's decrees in the face of a formidable royal, ecclesiastical, and papal coalition.

The Society of Jesus caused problems too. Attempts to establish the new order in Paris met fierce resistance from both theologians and humanists in the university. The issue made its way to the courts (1564), where the university was represented by a young lawyer named Étienne Pasquier who, besides being assisted by the inevitable Dumoulin, was rapidly becoming a major erudite historian in his own right. While the legal standing of the Jesuits was never properly resolved, Pasquier and his associates managed to turn them into a symbol of Roman excess and jurisdictional infringement.

Finally, papal attempts to combat the growing Protestant power in France further inflamed Gallican opinion. A sentence of excommunication and dispossession by the Roman Inquisition against Jeanne d'Albret, queen of Navarre and a French vassal (1561), aroused memories of Boniface VIII among the jurists; these were reinforced by papal support for the Guise faction of rebellious Catholics and eventually by the excommunication of Henry of Navarre, the Protestant heir to the French throne (1585). When Henry III was assassinated in 1589 and Navarre succeeded him in the face of massive ultra-Catholic resistance, Catholic defenders of hereditary monarchy turned to Gallicanism for ideological support. Though Henry IV eventually converted to Catholicism and was absolved by his own bishops in 1594—itself an act of Gallican defiance—France remained cut off from Rome until his papal absolution in 1595.

Henry IV and Louis XIII. It was thus during the civil war of 1588–1598 that the Gallicanism of the legal humanists became a major factor in French politics. A string of pamphlets set out a vision of the Gallican liberties, their historical justification, and contemporary relevance; the most influential was the "Libertez de l'église gallicane" (Liberties of the Gallican church) of Pierre Pithou. A formidable scholar, Pithou did little more than expand an earlier manuscript list of those liberties, but his eloquence, his reputation, and his strategic timing made the work a classic of French constitutional thought.

From 1595 on, treatises on the Gallican liberties and their history, and collections of documents to support them, flowed steadily from French presses and into the great manuscript collections of the erudite jurists, particularly Pithou's, which was inherited and vastly expanded by Pierre Dupuy. Among the most important were works by the lawyers Guy Coquille and Jacques Leschassier and the *avocat du roi* (attorney general) Louis Servin, as well as book 3 of Pasquier's *Recherches de la France* (Researches on France), which provided an enormously influ-

ential history of the French church, and the judge Jacques-Auguste de Thou's monumental, influential, and strongly Gallican-inflected *Historia sui temporis* (History of his time). In the peculiar political culture of old-regime France, where constitutional law was always up for grabs and—despite the king's absolutist pretensions—persuasion, tradition, and vested interest counted for a great deal, a well-articulated political and historical ideology such as legal Gallicanism had now become was a powerful force.

This fact was demonstrated in the struggle over the Gallican liberties, which pitted the courts against most of the French church from Henry IV's accession well into the seventeenth century. In this period the French church as a whole embraced the Council of Trent and the ideas of reform that flowed from it and, fearing local courts more than a distant papacy, entered an anti-Gallican phase. A theologian named Edmond Richer attempted to lead the Paris Faculty of Theology in an idiosyncratic revival of Gerson's conciliarism but was defeated and expelled from his posts. Henry IV, more concerned to placate his ultra-Catholic foes than to humor Gallican jurists whose support was firm, was inclined to side with the clergy. The jurists, on the other hand, collaborated to some extent with foreigners combating papal claims to secular authority, particularly Anglicans led by King James I and Venetians led by Paolo Sarpi.

The major issues in dispute were, first, the rights of the courts to interfere with ecclesiastical actions and dogma by the legal maneuver called *appel comme d'abus* (appeal to prevent abuse) or through legislation and, second, the vigor with which the church would repudiate the doctrine that kings might be deposed or assassinated as threats to Catholicism. The former question was fought out in innumerable local legal battles all over the kingdom and in largely unavailing attempts by the assembly of the clergy to have the *appel comme d'abus* restricted. The latter, part of an international debate, went through several phases. The Jesuits, portrayed as the principal defenders of the so-called tyrannicide doctrine, were expelled from most of northern France in 1595 on suspicion of involvement in assassination attempts against Henry IV. The king readmitted them in 1604, against strenuous opposition. When Henry actually was assassinated in 1610, calls for their expulsion were renewed, but without success. Instead the Parlement intensified a campaign to censor works perceived as soft on tyrannicide, though pro-papal forces limited its effectiveness. Finally, at the meeting of the Estates General in 1614–1615, the third estate, dominated by judges and lawyers, proposed that it should be proclaimed and enforced as religious dogma and a fundamental law of the kingdom that "there is no power whatever on earth, whether spiritual or temporal, which has any rights over [the French] kingdom" (Mousnier, *Assassination of Henry IV*, p. 382). The clergy, seeing a threat to its religious authority, lobbied effectively to have this proposal blocked, unilaterally implementing the decrees of Trent a few months later.

Later Developments. Despite these setbacks, the Gallicanism of the erudite jurists was too influential to be eliminated, and it remained a force into the 1760s. A more moderate episcopal Gallicanism was soon revived as well: its intellectual leaders were erudite bishops like Pierre de Marca and Jacques-Benigne Bossuet. At a low point in his relations with Rome, Louis XIV developed an enthusiasm for their thought and pushed the Gallican Articles of 1682 through an assembly of the French clergy. Both he and most of his bishops retreated from Gallicanism, though, when the quasi-heterodox and quasi-oppositional Catholic religious movement known as Jansenism came to seem a far more immediate menace than the papacy. Indeed, in the last century of the old regime, Gallicanism essentially merged with Jansenism as a single religious and political movement. In this form it was a major factor in eighteenth-century politics.

See also **Conciliarism; Concordats; Trent, Council of; Tyrannicide; Wars of Religion.**

BIBLIOGRAPHY

Primary Works

Burns, J. H., and Thomas M. Izbicki, eds. *Conciliarism and Papalism.* Cambridge, U.K., 1997. Includes much of the basic theological literature in translation.

Dupuy, Pierre, ed. *Traitez des droits et libertez de l'Eglise gallicane* (Treatises on the rights and liberties of the Gallican church). 4 vols. Paris, 1731. These four huge volumes contain the bulk of the theoretical and documentary basis for erudite Gallicanism. This is the last of six progressively larger editions going back to 1595.

Secondary Works

Kelley, Donald. *Foundations of Modern Historical Scholarship: Language, Law, and History in the French Renaissance.* New York, 1970. The classic study of the Gallican historians.

Martimort, Aimé-Georges. *Le gallicanisme.* Paris, 1973. There is still relatively little work on Gallicanism in English. For those who read French, this volume in the *Que sais-je?* series remains a good starting point.

Mousnier, Roland. *The Assassination of Henry IV: The Tyrannicide Problem and the Consolidation of the French Absolute Monarchy in the Early Seventeenth Century.* Translated by Joan Spencer. New York, 1973. Translation of *L'assasinat d'Henri IV: Le problème du tyrannicide et l'affermissment de la monarchie absolue* (1964). The standard survey of the tyrannicide question in France.

Powis, Jonathan. "Gallican Liberties and the Politics of Later Sixteenth-Century France." *Historical Journal* 26 (1983): 515–530.

Roelker, Nancy Lyman. *One King, One Faith: The Parlement of Paris and the Religious Reformations of the Sixteenth Century.* Berkeley, Calif., 1996. Strong on the political and emotional background of legal Gallicanism.

Salmon, J. H. M. *Renaissance and Revolt: Essays in the Intellectual and Social History of Early Modern France.* Cambridge, Mass., 1987. See "Gallicanism and Anglicanism," pp. 155–188. A study of Gallicanism's international connections.

JOTHAM PARSONS

GAMA, VASCO DA (c. 1469–1524), Portuguese explorer and discoverer of the maritime route to India. Most authors believe da Gama was born in the Portuguese fishing village of Sines in the Alentejo, probably in the late 1460s. His mother was Isabel Sodre. His father, Estêvão da Gama, had been a member of the household of Prince Fernando, younger brother of King Afonso V (ruled 1438–1481), and was a knight and commander in the Order of Santiago. Like his father, Vasco was a knight and a commander of Santiago, becoming a knight in 1488 and a commander in December 1495. About 1507 he transferred to the Order of Christ. Vasco served as a *fidalgo* (nobleman) in the royal household of King John II (ruled 1481–1495) and then in the household of King Manuel I (ruled 1495–1521), King John's first cousin, brother-in-law, and successor. Despite da Gama's own historical importance and that of his voyage to India, little else is known for certain about his career before 1497.

King Manuel named da Gama *capitão-mor* or leader of the armada of four ships—the *São Gabriel* (flagship), the *São Rafael,* the *Berrio,* and a supply ship whose name is not known—that sailed from the Tagus River on 8 July 1497 in search of a maritime route to India. Few details are known about the ships or the crew, which numbered about 150–170 men. Pilots included Pero de Alenquer (who had piloted Bartolomeu Dias's ships around the Cape of Good Hope in 1488), João de Coimbra, Pero Escobar, and Afonso Gonçalves.

By 27 July the small fleet reached the island of Santiago in the Cape Verde archipelago. On 3 August 1497 Vasco da Gama and his four ships continued on. The exact route is unknown. After more than ninety days at sea—the longest known voyage out of sight of land by a European to that date—da Gama dropped anchor on 8 November in the Bay of Santa Helena, one hundred miles north of the Cape of Good Hope. After resting and taking on wood and

Vasco da Gama. From a series of portraits of Portuguese viceroys and governors by Lizuarte de Abreu, c. 1558. THE PIERPONT MORGAN LIBRARY, NEW YORK/ART RESOURCE, NY

water, da Gama rounded the Cape on 22 November. Working his way up the east coast of Africa, with stops at Natal, the Quelimane estuary, Mozambique Island, and Mombasa, da Gama arrived in Malindi in April 1498. There he obtained the services of a Gujarati pilot in crossing the Indian Ocean. On 24 April da Gama departed for Calicut and on 18 May first sighted the Malabar coast of India. Two days later, he anchored several miles north of Calicut.

Da Gama and his men remained in India for more than three months, during which time the Portuguese attempted to trade for spices and precious stones but instead won the hostility of the local Hindu leader. On 5 October 1498 da Gama began the long, dangerous trip home. Two of the original four ships, the *Berrio* and *São Gabriel,* rounded the Cape of Good Hope on 20 March 1499. On 10 July 1499 the *Berrio* arrived in Lisbon, followed by the *São Gabriel* a few weeks later. Of the original 150–170 men to leave Portugal, only about one-third lived to return.

Upon his return to Portugal, Vasco da Gama was lavishly rewarded by King Manuel, who named him admiral of India with the same honors as the admiral of Portugal, appointed him to the King's Council, and granted him the title of "Dom" and a number of financial rewards for himself, his family, and his descendants. In 1519 King Manuel granted Vasco the title of first count of Vidigueira—a distinct honor since by 1521 only ten other men in Portugal held the rank of count as their highest title.

In the meantime, early in 1502, Vasco da Gama led the fourth Portuguese expedition to India. This expedition consisted of twenty ships and returned to Lisbon on 1 September 1503. In 1524 da Gama returned to India for a third and final time, this time as the viceroy of India. His administration, dedicated to ending corruption and restoring royal authority in Portuguese Asia, was an energetic but short one, lasting less than four months. He died in Cochin on Christmas Eve of 1524.

BIBLIOGRAPHY

The definitive biography of Vasco da Gama remains to be written. An important recent biography is Luís Adão da Fonseca, *Vasco da Gama. O homem, a viagem, a época* (Lisbon, 1997). An earlier account in English of da Gama's first voyage is Elaine Sanceau, *Good Hope: The Voyage of Vasco da Gama* (Lisbon, 1967). It is based largely on the sixteenth-century Portuguese chroniclers. The best short study in English is probably the chapter "The Indian Ocean Crossings" in John H. Parry, *The Discovery of the Sea* (Berkeley, Calif., 1981). A judicious summary in English of da Gama's career and contribution to world history is found in Bailey W. Diffie and George D. Winius, *Foundations of the Portuguese Empire 1415–1580* (Minneapolis, 1977). For da Gama's career in the Portuguese military orders, see Francis A. Dutra, "A New Look at the Life and Career of Vasco da Gama," *Portuguese Studies Review* 6, no. 2 (1997–1998): 23–28. The most important primary source for the first voyage is the diary of an anonymous eyewitness. It has been translated into English with excellent notes, introduction, and accompanying materials by E. G. Ravenstein, *A Journal of the First Voyage of Vasco da Gama, 1497–1499* (London, 1898). For an important perspective on the Portuguese context of da Gama's life and exploits, see the essays in Diogo Ramada Curto, ed., *O tempo de Vasco da Gama* (Lisbon, 1998).

FRANCIS A. DUTRA

GÀMBARA, VERONICA

(1485–1550), Italian poet and patron. Born to Giovanfrancesco, signore of Pratalboino, near Brescia, Gàmbara received a good classical education and in 1509 was married to Giberto X of Correggio. When Giberto died in 1518, she assumed control of his small estate and transformed it into a progressive center that quickly rose to a prestigious, if small, position in the intellectual life of the region.

As lady of Correggio, Gàmbara proved a thoughtful administrator and a good provider for the welfare of her family and subjects, making extraordinary efforts in times of war and famine. When, in the 1530s, the emperor Charles V became arbiter of Italian politics, Gàmbara made with him a pact of military and political alliance that sanctioned an exchange of obligations and privileges. She was also successful in maintaining friendly relations with the powerful Medici and Farnese families in the interest of her people and of her two sons, who pursued careers in the military and in the church bureaucracy.

Gàmbara began to write verse in her adolescence, and her reputation as a poet was established throughout Italy by 1530. Exhibiting a wide range of technical skill and a variety of moods and styles, her songs, sonnets, and madrigals were anthologized in many prestigious contemporary collections. While a few sonnets lament the anguish of love in a manner reminiscent of the *stil nuovo* poetry, others celebrate her requited love for Giberto in a graceful and limpid style. Some poems reveal the influence of musical rhythms—these were written for or later set to music. Still others rejoice in the beauty of the countryside. In the set of stanzas sent to Cosimo I, duke of Tuscany, the description of the fleeting season sets the mood for a meditation on the human condition, the disquiet of city life, and the wastefulness of mundane pursuits. Gàmbara employs pastoral conventions in celebration of conjugal love in the sonnets sent to Alfonso del Vasto and to his wife, Maria d'Aragona. Other verse, addressed to Charles V, commemorates the emperor's military and political victories.

While Gàmbara's poetic production attests to the formal literary training expected of a lady of the court, her correspondence offers a more direct insight into her character and provides a view of the more leisurely moments as well as the practical concerns of contemporary society. Besides a number of notes concerning everyday problems, letters exist addressed to politicians, literati, artists, relatives, and friends. Most interesting to the literary scholar are the letters addressed to Pietro Bembo, whose poetic and intellectual leadership Gàmbara was eager to follow, and those to Pietro Aretino, which testify to her dignity and dexterity in keeping at bay a dangerous opinion maker. Of greater appeal to the general reader, perhaps, are the letters sent to Lodovico de' Rossi; these give a glimpse of the full range of Gàmbara's poised and agreeable personality, her moral integrity, her intellectual independence, her playfulness and common sense, and her keen understanding of political events and human behavior. These personal qualities, combined with the cultural attainments of a sophisticated mind, all contributed to make Gàmbara the admired exemplar of the Renaissance lady.

BIBLIOGRAPHY

Primary Work
Gàmbara, Veronica, *Rime e lettere*. Edited by P. M. Chiappetti. Florence, 1879.

Secondary Works
Bozzetti, Cesare, Pietro Gibellini, and Ennio Sandal, eds. *Veronica Gàmbara e la poesia del suo tempo nell'Italia settentrionale. Atti del Convegno Brescia-Correggio, 17–19 ottobre 1985*. Florence, 1989.
Russell, Rinaldina. "Veronica Gàmbara." In *Italian Women Writers*. Edited by Rinaldina Russell. Westport, Conn., 1994. Pages 145–153.

RINALDINA RUSSELL

GAMES AND TOYS. *See* **Childhood.**

GANS, DAVID BEN SOLOMON (1541–1613), Jewish chronicler, astronomer, mathematician, pedagogue. David Gans was born in 1541 to a well-to-do Westphalia merchant family and received a fine rabbinical education, first in Bonn and Frankfurt and later in the renowned Cracow academy of Moses Isserles. In the mid-1560s Gans settled in Prague, where he befriended distinguished rabbis, preachers, printers, and lay leaders. In 1600 Gans met Tycho Brahe, Johannes Kepler, and others working at the imperial observatory in the Benátky summer palace of Holy Roman Emperor Rudolf II near Prague. He made three week-long visits to the palace observatory, praising it lavishly. He boasted of translating astronomical tables from Hebrew for Brahe.

Gans wrote prolifically, though little was published and much was lost. Only one book—his chronicle of Jewish and world history, *Zemah David* (Sprout of David)—was printed during his lifetime, in Prague in 1592. The section on world history displayed considerable admiration for Christian scholars and statesmen. In 1612 Gans published a prospectus for an epitome of astronomy called "Magen David" (Shield of David). The final version of the book was not published until 1743, when it was renamed *Nehmad ve-na'im* (Pleasant and agreeable). Though fundamentally Ptolemaic, as befit an introductory textbook in his epoch, Gans's epitome included terse, approving descriptions of the Copernican and Tychonic planetary systems.

Among Gans's unprinted works were mathematics and geometry texts called "Migdal David" (Tower of David) and "Prozdor" (Antechamber), a book on calculating the Jewish calendar titled "Sefer ha-'ibbur"

(The book of intercalation), and another about the moon, "Meor ha-katon" (The minor luminary). Gans also wrote a guide to using a quadrant, a geography textbook, and a Hebrew *Mappa mundi.* He may have written additional treatises on measurement, the lost Ten Tribes of Israel, and the kingdom of Prester John.

Together, Gans's books described recent developments in history, politics, mathematics, geometry, physics, astronomy, astrology, geography, natural history, and medicine, as well as signal inventions, discoveries, and marvels of his day. Gans hoped that educating Jews about such matters might increase their standing, at least among Christian scholars. Gans also believed that these subjects were particularly valuable because they represented "true wisdom" that was equally available to Jewish and Christian intellectuals. This persuasion reflected the unique background of the court of Rudolf II, in which the multiplicity of denominations encouraged a fitful spirit of peaceful coexistence.

Gans had little impact on his contemporaries. His goal of integrating natural philosophy and other liberal disciplines into academy curricula went unfulfilled. Gans's hope of promoting more companionable relations between Jewish and Christian intellectuals was also unrealized, owing largely to political, social, and cultural upheavals in central Europe—particularly the onset of the Thirty Years' War—and to the general deterioration of the standing of Jews in the region at the start of the sixteenth century. Equally important, Gans's ideals failed to resonate among his contemporaries. Only in the eighteenth century, with the start of the Jewish Enlightenment, or *Haskalah,* was Gans seen as an important exemplar of Jewish interest in knowledge of universal, rather than particular, appeal.

BIBLIOGRAPHY

Alter, George. *Two Renaissance Astronomers.* Prague, 1958.

Breuer, Mordechai. "Modernism and Traditionalism in Sixteenth-Century Historiography: A Study of David Gans's *Tzemah David.*" In *Jewish Thought in the Sixteenth Century.* Edited by Bernard Dov Cooperman. Cambridge, Mass., 1983. Pages 49–88.

Efron, Noah J. "Irenism and Natural Philosophy in Rudolfine Prague: The Case of David Gans." *Science in Context* 10, no. 4 (1997): 627–649.

Neher, André. *Jewish Thought and the Scientific Revolution of the Sixteenth Century: David Gans (1541–1613) and His Times.* Translated by David Maisel. Oxford, 1986.

NOAH J. EFRON

GANSFORT, WESSEL (cognomen *Lux mundi;* c. 1419–1489), northern humanist and theologian connected to the *Devotio Moderna* and the Brethren of the Common Life. Wessel Gansfort, sometimes erroneously called Johannes Wessel, attended Latin school at Groningen and studied at Zwolle with the Brethren of the Common Life. There he befriended Thomas à Kempis, the probable author of *The Imitation of Christ.* In 1452 Gansfort received a master of arts at Cologne. He also visited and taught at the universities of Louvain, Paris, Heidelberg, and Cologne, where he became acquainted with Johan Pupper van Goch, Gabriel Biel, and Johann Reuchlin. He traveled to Rome, becoming closely associated with Francesco della Rovere (Pope Sixtus IV) and Cardinal Bessarion. Around 1475 he returned to the Low Countries, staying at Groningen and Zwolle. He was a member of the humanist circle of Adwert, which included Rudolf Agricola, Rudolph von Langen, Paulus Pelantinus, Alexander Hegius, and his *famulus* (young servant) Goswinus van Halen. Gansfort also practiced as a medical doctor, treating among others the bishop of Utrecht.

Gansfort changed philosophical schools three times in his scholarly career. Some thus styled him *Magister Contradictionis* (master of contradiction), a name taken by some of his friends to signify his anti-Aristotelianism. This epithet also signifies his departure from Scholasticism. Gansfort knew Greek and Hebrew, and he applied especially the latter to interpreting scripture. Of Latin authors he admired Cicero for style and the art of memory and Virgil for his ability to evoke emotion. In Gansfort's biblical humanism, pious inner growth is central to a pedagogy that leads to moral action. The exact influence of Gansfort has not yet been traced. Protestants have often seen him as a forerunner of Luther, Erasmians as a proto-Erasmus.

Surviving works include *Scala meditationis* (Ladder of meditation) and a commentary on the Lord's Prayer. Other works treat church government, God's providence, penance, the communion of saints, and the Eucharist.

See also **Devotio Moderna.**

BIBLIOGRAPHY

Primary Work

Gansfort, Wessel. *Opera.* Groningen, Netherlands, 1614. Reprint, Nieuwkoop, Netherlands, 1966.

Secondary Works

Akkerman, F., G. C. Huisman, and A. J. Vanderjagt, eds. *Wessel Gansfort (1419–1489) and Northern Humanism.* Leiden, Netherlands, 1993.

Akkerman, F., A. J. Vanderjagt, and A. H. van der Laan, eds. *Northern Humanism in European Context, 1469–1625.* Leiden, Netherlands, forthcoming.

ARJO VANDERJAGT

GARCILASO DE LA VEGA

(c. 1501–1536), Toledan poet, soldier, courtier. Garcilaso de la Vega is credited with inaugurating Spain's literary renaissance, together with his mentor, the Catalonian poet Juan Boscán.

Garcilaso's literary production was modest in quantity, yet his Italianate poems, comprising thirty-eight sonnets, five *canciones* (songs), two elegies, one epistle, and three eclogues, set the standard for all subsequent cultured poetry and remain a source of inspiration for modern poets. Although Petrarchan rhyme scheme and hendecasyllabic meter were first attempted in Spain by Garcilaso's ancestor, the Marquis of Santillana, these forms were not fully assimilated in the Castilian vernacular until Boscán began to imitate Italian poetic forms. Boscán recommended the style to the younger poet, whose adaptations, successfully emulating the lyricism of their Italian models, surpassed his mentor's. First published posthumously in 1543 with Boscán's poetry, Garcilaso's own poems circulated separately in four major editions with commentaries by Francisco Sánchez de las Brozas, "el Brocense" (1574); Fernando de Herrera (1580); Thomás Tamayo de Vargas (1622); and José Nicolás de Azara (1765).

According to legend, at Charles V's wedding in Granada in 1526 to Isabella of Portugal, Garcilaso met the queen's Portuguese lady-in-waiting, Isabel Freire, fictionalized as Elisa in his lyrics. The enduring belief by numerous scholars in the sincerity of his love poetry demonstrates how well Garcilaso appropriated not only the Petrarchan form but its thematics of desire. In the *Rime sparse* (Scattered verses) Garcilaso transforms Petrarch's emotions for the elusive Laura into a prolonged poetic lament that relies on Ovidian myths of metamorphosis to emphasize both the lover's psychological instability and the impermanence of nature. Using diverse classical models, Garcilaso moves beyond Petrarch's obsessive desire for his lady and the limited formal aspects of his *canzoniere* (songbook), while still evoking the Tuscan's sense of frustrated love, mutability, and transcendence through art.

Scholars have attempted to establish a chronology for Garcilaso's poetry based on its increasing classicism and Neoplatonic tenor. It is likely, however, that he wrote most of his poetry after his forced departure to Naples in 1532, where he not only be-

friended the poets Bernardo Tasso, Luigi Tansillo, and Giulio Cesare Caracciolo, but was also exposed to the polemics on imitation that raged on from the previous century. Garcilaso clearly sided with those who favored an eclectic number of sources, of *omnes bonos* (all good men). His combinatory powers, drawing on his familiarity with an extensive range of Latin and Italian poets, are forcefully demonstrated in his three eclogues, his last and most finished poems. For example, *Egloga III* (Third eclogue) weaves three Ovidian myths of desire, loss, and transformation with the poet's own myth of lost love. Reprising the history of European poetics, the eclogue gathers together classical mythology, Petrarchist poetics, the Virgilian and Italian pastoral, and the Castilian *cancionero* (songbook) tradition.

A consummate courtier, Garcilaso dedicated his poetry mainly to Fernando de Toledo, third duke of Alba (1507–1582), who frequently came to his aid when the poet was reproved by the emperor. Unlike his older brother, Pedro Laso de la Vega, whose involvement in the 1521 comuneros (constitutionalists) rebellion earned him a lengthy exile, the poet from his youth onward dedicated his service to the emperor both as a soldier and diplomat. Charles V lavished rewards on Garcilaso: in 1520 he was made a member of the king's guard, in 1523 he was knighted into the Order of Santiago, and in 1525 he was wedded to Elena de Zúñiga, lady-in-waiting to Charles's sister, and endowed by the emperor with a substantial dowry. Garcilaso returned the favors by fighting against the comuneros, by spying along the Franco-Spanish border, and by accompanying Charles in his trip from Spain in 1529 to his coronation as Holy Roman Emperor, in 1530, in Bologna.

The poet's relations with the crown were nonetheless often tense. Risking the emperor's displeasure, he maintained close contact with his exiled brother. In 1531 his presence at the proscribed wedding of his nephew to a member of the powerful Alburquerque family resulted in his banishment to an island on the Danube—which inspired his *Canción III* (Third song)—and in his military deportation to Naples. Nevertheless, the poet's fealty to Charles finally won him an imperial pardon and governorship of the Reggio Calabria castle, which, however, he relinquished in order to take part in the battle at Tunisia. Garcilaso spent his last years on several military missions; in 1536, he was fatally wounded while leading an attack on Le Muy, near Marseilles, in the invasion of France.

See also **Boscán, Juan.**

BIBLIOGRAPHY

Primary Works

Gallego Morrell, Antonio, ed. *Garcilaso de la Vega y sus comentaristas.* Granada, Spain, 1966.

Vega, Garcilaso de la. *Obra poética y textos en prosa.* Edited by Bienvenido Morros with preliminary study by Rafael Lapesa. Barcelona, Spain, 1995.

Vega, Garcilaso de la. *Obras completas con comentario.* Edited by Elias L. Rivers. Madrid and Columbus, Ohio, 1974.

Secondary Works

Cruz, Anne J. *Imitación y transformación: El petrarquismo en la poesía de Boscán y Garcilaso de la Vega.* Amsterdam and Philadelphia, 1988. Studies influence of the Italian treatises of imitation in Garcilaso's appropriation of Petrarchist poetics.

Cruz, Anne J. "Self-Fashioning in Spain: Garcilaso de la Vega." *Romanic Review* 83 (November 1992): 517–538.

Fernández-Morera, Darío. *The Lyre and the Oaten Flute: Garcilaso and the Pastoral.* London, 1982. Investigates Garcilaso's classical background.

Heiple, Daniel L. *Garcilaso de la Vega and the Italian Renaissance.* University Park, Pa., 1994. Argues for an anti-Petrarchan, classical stance based on Neoplatonic and contemporary Italian influences.

ANNE J. CRUZ

GARCILASO DE LA VEGA, INCA. *See* Vega, Inca Garcilaso de la.

GARDENS.

The Renaissance garden had its genesis in Italy during the 1450s, reaching the height of its development in grand, terraced complexes of the late sixteenth century. Like the visual arts of this period, the garden was rooted in the classical world and therefore integral to the cultural phenomenon known as the Renaissance. Perceived by foreigners as the "garden of the world," Italy influenced garden design throughout Europe.

Reconstruction of the Renaissance garden is facilitated by the survival of several aristocratic examples into the twentieth century. Early prints, travel diaries, treatises, and manuscript sources document original plantings and design features. Major studies of the Italian garden first appeared in the 1920s and 1930s, and late-twentieth-century scholars, using the tools of formal analysis, iconography, botany, social and economic history, and cultural geography, have considerably enriched the field.

Origins. In the mid-fifteenth century a new type of garden took shape in Italy, gradually distinguishing itself from the gardens of the Middle Ages. Like their medieval predecessors, early Renaissance gardens were enclosed by walls and planted with herbs and flowers both ornamental and medicinal. The medieval garden was, however, untouched by humanism and the revival of antiquity central to the Renaissance. The gardens of the Villa Medici at Fiesole (1458–1461) or the Palazzo Piccolomini at Pienza (1459–1462), both in Tuscany, took their cue from learned humanist authors like Leon Battista Alberti (1404–1472). In his treatise on architecture, in circulation by 1452, Alberti showed a new preoccupation with the example of the ancients, with geometry and order in the garden, and with views of the larger landscape as integral to the ensemble of garden and residence.

Although a pronounced awareness of nature appeared in Italy with Petrarch (1304–1374), the idea of retreat to the countryside (*villeggiatura*) did not take hold until the mid-fifteenth century. At this time humanist translations of Latin writings on ancient Roman villa life by Pliny the Younger, Cicero, and Varro, among others, stimulated the renewal of villa culture and garden making in Tuscany, Rome, Naples, the Veneto, and elsewhere. Because the remains of ancient Roman gardens, such as those at Hadrian's Villa near Tivoli and on the Palatine Hill in Rome, were scant, patrons and designers seeking to create gardens *all'antica* (in the ancient mode) had to rely heavily on classical literary sources, the advice of Alberti, and a host of Renaissance treatises on agriculture and villa life.

Design and Planting. Common principles of organization and a distinctive attitude toward art and nature unified the gardens of Renaissance Italy despite significant regional differences, including differences of topography, climate, society, and circumstances of foreign occupation. Throughout the fifteenth and sixteenth centuries, the design of the Italian garden was based on a concern for order and geometry. Bilateral symmetry governed garden layouts in which grid patterns were formed on leveled terrain by low-lying compartments separated by straight paths. The units of the garden were measurable, its limits finite. Contemporaries understood the garden's regularity not as a demonstration of man's dominion over nature but as a reflection of the divine harmony of the cosmos, the order inherent in nature, revealed by the human hand.

The compartments took the form of geometric figures deemed perfect in the Renaissance, in particular squares and circles. Planted with herbs and flowers, their perimeters were lined with hedges and fruit trees. Although plants were chosen for medicinal reasons into the sixteenth century, ornamental plants were increasingly prized with the influx of rare and exotic specimens from the New World, Asia, Africa, and the Middle East. In addition to the compartments, the geometric garden featured orderly plantings of grapevines, orchards, and dense stands of trees planted in rows, known as *boschi*.

The protagonist of the garden was nature, whose raw materials were fashioned by human artifice into a work of art. Pergolas shaded garden paths, while trees and shrubs, carefully clipped, formed labyrinths and topiary inspired by classical descriptions. Some of the first topiary work appeared in the Rucellai family garden at the Villa Quaracchi near Florence (before 1459), the vegetation shaped into figural and geometric motifs. Other decorations sanctioned by antiquity included sculpture, fountains, and rustic grottoes, which likewise exhibited a witty intermingling of art and nature.

Contemporaries viewed art and nature in terms of a dialectic, each vying to simulate the other's effects, the garden a product of a relationship at once symbiotic and competitive. The lively interaction of art and nature generated a "third nature," as the garden was described, something partaking of each while belonging to neither realm. The notion of comparison (*paragone*) informed Renaissance artistic theory and culture in general. Artists and intellectuals discussed the relative merits of painting and poetry, sculpture and painting, ancients and moderns, art and nature. The spirit of debate mattered more than the declaration of a winner and was considered a stimulus to creativity. Virtually every ingredient of the Renaissance garden was inspired by the desire to rival the achievements of antiquity.

The essence of nature was conceived in terms of a duality. If nature's intrinsic order was reflected in the geometric garden, its wild and untamed aspect found expression in the park, which featured irregular terrain and plantings. These two aspects were juxtaposed in the grounds of the grand villa complexes of the sixteenth century, including the Villa Giulia (1551–1555) and the Villa Lante at Bagnaia (1568–1578), both near Rome. Occasionally an estate was designed as a large park, like the Villa Medici at Pratolino (1569–1586), near Florence, which embraced both the ordered and the untamed. An elevated site, furthermore, offered views of nature's own beauties in the larger landscape, an arrangement Alberti recommended, from Pliny's example, to villa builders.

The steep hillside became the position of choice in the sixteenth century. The finest aristocratic complexes exploited hilly topography in sequences of geometric terraces arranged on axis, a practice that overshadowed an earlier fashion for flat sites. Spacious terraces supported by massive retaining walls were connected by ramps and staircases. Inspired by ancient temple complexes and the contemporary example of Donato Bramante's Belvedere Court at the Vatican (begun 1504), Raphael envisioned the Villa Madama in Rome (begun c. 1518) in this way. Pirro Ligorio's design for the Villa d'Este at Tivoli (1550–1572) and Giacomo Barozzi da Vignola's design for the Villa Lante at Bagnaia followed. These were architectural gardens, defined by large architectural features and a geometry that controlled both garden and residence. Terraced gardens also appeared in the hills around Florence, Genoa, and elsewhere in Italy where topography permitted.

Function and Use. Early Renaissance gardens allowed no distinction between utility and pleasure. Plants were admired for aesthetic and medicinal properties; pleasure gardens produced fruit and wine for their owners. With its appeal to the senses and its cool, spraying fountains, the garden was conceived as a place for recreation—for strolling, conversation, and dining alfresco. In fifteenth-century Tuscany and in high Renaissance Rome humanists gathered in gardens to converse and to compose poetry in conscious emulation of the ancients. The garden was a healthful resort, a place of recuperation, where owners might escape noxious city air, as did the Medici at their villa near Castello (1537–1572), outside Florence.

The garden, a natural counterpart to the display of wealth, status, and culture in the owner's palace, furniture, tapestries, works of art, and antiquities, reflected the magnificence of the patron. With their collections of flora and fauna, often rare and exotic, gardens were considered an ideal locus for collections of classical statuary, as they had been in antiquity. The waterworks of the sixteenth-century central Italian garden offered lively testimony to the magnificence of the owner in the form of architectural fountains, cascades, and water chains, as well as water-powered moving figures (automata) and musical organs. These features depended on costly aqueducts and the expertise of hydraulic engineers, who learned from the technological feats of the ancients while endeavoring to surpass them. The gardens of Tivoli, Bagnaia, and Pratolino were noted by contemporaries for spectacular and ingenious water effects, while a distinctive sense of humor was betrayed in water jokes that doused unsuspecting visitors.

In the sixteenth century, figured fountains and statuary often conveyed iconographic programs that

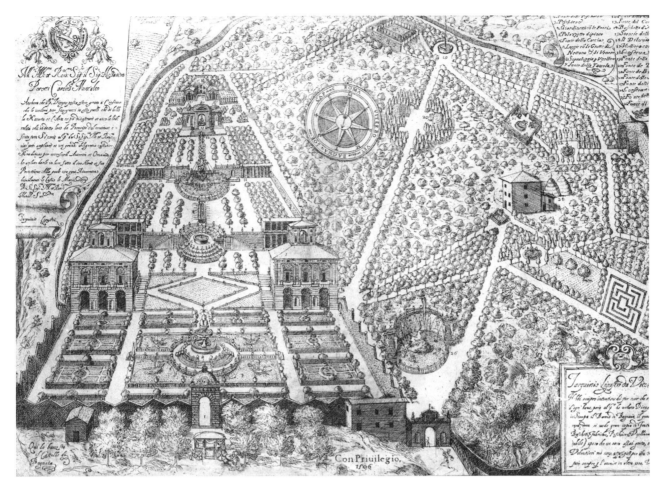

Gardens. Gardens of the Villa Lante at Bagnaia, near Viterbo in central Italy. Etching by Tarquino Ligustri, 1596. BIBLIO-THÈQUE NATIONALE DE FRANCE, PARIS. VB 132s

flattered the aristocratic patron. Classical mythology was employed to extol the patron's virtues by comparing him, for example, to Hercules or his garden to an earthly paradise. The garden of the Hesperides, the Golden Age, Mount Parnassus, and Arcadia were among the mythic realms most often invoked. The villas of central Italy incorporated geographic metaphors as well, their gardens making reference to fertile local settings and to the beneficence of the owner in bringing fresh water from mountain springs and rivers to the populace.

The sixteenth-century villas at Castello, Tivoli, and Bagnaia, while exhibiting both an attitude toward art and nature and a preoccupation with antiquity consistent with earlier gardens, developed on a scale not seen since ancient Rome. Serving the needs of aristocratic patrons for retreat from urban cares, these gardens also played host to important visitors and ceremonial entertainments. The moving of earth and construction of retaining walls were achieved at

enormous expense. Designed by leading artists for cardinals, popes, and wealthy patricians, these gardens were constructed and maintained by innumerable manual laborers. The Renaissance garden thus reflected within its borders the highly polarized nature of society.

Influence. By 1600 the design principles, scale, and planting of Italian gardens were changing. The idea of the Renaissance garden was, however, carried abroad by architects, sculptors, gardeners, hydraulic experts, and gentlemen traveling through Europe. Italian ideas about design and ornamental features—especially grottoes, waterworks, and statuary—were joined to the particulars of local topography, climate, and plant materials as well as to social needs throughout central and northern Europe. Notable Italianate gardens in France include those of Ancy-le-Franc, designed by the Italian architect Sebastiano Serlio in the 1540s, and Saint-Germain-en-

Laye (1597–1610) and in England Wilton House, which was laid out in the late 1630s.

BIBLIOGRAPHY

Coffin, David R. *Gardens and Gardening in Papal Rome.* Princeton, N.J., 1991.

Coffin, David R. *The Villa in the Life of Renaissance Rome.* Princeton, N.J., 1979.

Hunt, John Dixon. *Garden and Grove: The Italian Renaissance Garden in the English Imagination, 1600–1750.* Princeton, N.J., 1986.

Hunt, John Dixon, ed. *The Italian Garden: Art, Design, and Culture.* Cambridge, U.K., and New York, 1996.

Lazzaro, Claudia. "Gendered Nature and Its Representation in Sixteenth-Century Garden Sculpture." In *Looking at Italian Renaissance Sculpture.* Edited by Sarah Blake McHam. Cambridge, U.K., and New York, 1998. Pages 246–273.

Lazzaro, Claudia. *The Italian Renaissance Garden.* New Haven, Conn., 1990.

Lazzaro, Claudia. "Italy Is a Garden: The Idea of Italy and the Italian Garden Tradition." In *Villas and Gardens in Early Modern Italy and France.* Edited by Mirka Benes and Dianne Harris. Cambridge, U.K., and New York, 2000.

MacDougall, Elisabeth B. *Fountains, Statues, and Flowers: Studies in Italian Gardens of the Sixteenth and Seventeenth Centuries.* Washington, D.C., 1994.

MacDougall, Elisabeth B., ed. *Fons Sapientiae: Renaissance Garden Fountains.* Washington, D.C., 1978.

Masson, Georgina. *Italian Gardens.* London, 1961.

TRACY L. EHRLICH

GARIN, EUGENIO. *See* Renaissance, Interpretations of the, *subentry on* Eugenio Garin.

GATTAMELATA, ERASMO DA NARNI, IL (c. 1370–1443), Italian mercenary soldier. One of the few condottieri from a humble background, Erasmo—nicknamed "Gattamelata" (The honeyed cat) probably for his cunning, his sweet speech, or as an anagram based on his mother's name—was born the son of a baker in Narni. He began his training in the profession of arms under the command of Cecchino Broglio, the lord of Assisi (1398–1400), and later changed masters by joining the much more famous company of Braccio da Montone. He served with distinction in numerous campaigns in central and northern Italy. When Braccio suffered a heavy defeat at Aquila in 1424, Gattamelata escaped with the remnants of the Montone army, seeking refuge in Florence, where he served until 1427, when he passed to the service of Pope Martin V. He was a loyal soldier in the pay of a master, the pope, against whom he had often fought when in Montone's service. His allegiance to the pope ended when Martin's successor, Eugenius IV, was unable to pay Gattamelata. The condottiere was hired to serve the Republic of Venice in 1433 at the end of laborious negotiations in which Venice, an ally of the pope, agreed to pay Gattamelata the ten thousand ducats still owed him by Eugenius IV. He remained for another year, however, on loan from Venice to the papal forces. Gattamelata was in the republic's pay until his death. He received great honors and established a reputation of loyalty and bravery, which together with his caution suited perfectly the military policy of the Venetian state.

Several exploits made Gattamelata famous. In 1437 he attempted to attack the lands of the duke of Milan, which were defended by a former comrade, Niccolò Piccinino, who, like Gattamelata, had been part of Braccio da Montone's company. However, a sudden flood destroyed the bridge that Gattamelata had been building over the Adda River, leaving the condottiere stranded with a few soldiers on the enemy's riverbank. Legend says he escaped by crossing to the friendly shore while still wearing his armor. In 1438 Gattamelata brought an army of four thousand horsemen and one thousand foot soldiers to Verona after a perilous journey during which he was often nearly trapped by the forces of the duke of Milan, which had attacked Venetian territories. It is indicative of the republic's esteem for him that, about a month later, Venice appointed Gattamelata captain general, that is, commander in chief of the army of the republic. Finally, he is known for his attempt to use land and water transport to bring war to the viscount of Milan in 1439 by transporting thirty ships overland from the Adige River to Lake Garda.

Gattamelata died in Padua in 1443. The republic honored him with a state funeral. He was buried in the Church of Saint Anthony in Padua, in a tomb by Bartolomeo Bellano. Gattamelata's equestrian statue, which stands in front of the Basilica, is the work of the greatest sculptor of the early Renaissance, Donatello, and was commissioned apparently by members of Gattamelata's own family, not by the republic, as often claimed. Donatello completed his work ten years after the condottiere's death. The artist's creation, which was inspired either by the Roman statue of Marcus Aurelius or by the Hellenistic horses of San Marco in Venice, became the prototype of the equestrian creations of the following centuries.

BIBLIOGRAPHY

Ippolito, A. Menniti. "Erasmo da Narni, detto il Gattamelata." In *Dizionario biografico degli Italiani.* Vol. 43. Rome, 1993. Pages 46–52. Contains an excellent bibliography.

ANTONIO SANTOSUOSSO

GATTINARA, MERCURINO (Arborio di; 1465–1530), Habsburg administrator, chancellor of Charles V. Born near Vercelli, Piedmont, to a family of local, impecunious nobility but with relatives in the law and Savoyard ducal service, Mercurino Gattinara received his degrees in canon and civil law at the University of Turin sometime about 1493. Gattinara's command of Roman law recommended him to the highest circles of Habsburg affairs, serving Margaret and her father, the emperor Maximilian I, in a number of administrative and diplomatic capacities. He represented the emperor in Spain to Ferdinand of Aragon from June 1510 to April 1511 and was chief architect of the League of Cambrai against Venice. As president of the Parlement of Dôle, he became chief administrator and judge in Franche-Comté (1508–1518). His ascent culminated with the appointment as grand chancellor to the young Habsburg Charles I, on 15 October 1518 at Saragossa.

From his office at the ostensible bureaucratic center of a ramifying imperial government, Gattinara presided over many of the political developments of Europe as the confessional interests of the Reformation began to intrude upon the Renaissance. In Spain, Gattinara decisively supported the efforts of Bartolomé de Las Casas to reform the administration of the Indies to improve the treatment of the indigenous peoples. He promoted the election of his master as Holy Roman Emperor and presented the official justification for Charles's election. (At the Calais negotiations in 1521 he talked the English chancellor Thomas Wolsey and the French chancellor Antoine Du Prat to a standstill.) Back in Spain he was the driving force behind the conciliar reorganization of the central administration that would last down to the Bourbon (1700). In shaping a policy with messianic imperial overtones, Gattinara worked for the constriction or dismantling of France and for the European hegemony of Charles V, based upon Italy as Dante's *qiardin dell' imperio* (garden of the empire).

Gattinara's importance for the Renaissance itself stems from his efforts to construct out of Erasmian humanism an effective, moderating counterforce to the Lutheran menace and incipient confessional divisions. If faithful to Catholic unity, this statesman nonetheless saw the pope largely as simply another territorial ruler. Although he sought the ultimate extinction of Lutheranism, he hoped to be able to do it by accommodation. In framing his solution to this problem in the empire, he had by July 1526 claimed to find the Lutheran sect essentially based upon the truth of evangelical doctrine. Based on his reading of and dealings with Erasmus, after 1526 he began to articulate a religious policy of moderation in the empire. He tried unsuccessfully to get Erasmus to commit himself to the imperial cause by asking him to edit and publish Dante's *Monarchia*. Nevertheless their differences over monarchy and universal Christian polity did not prevent Gattinara from entertaining the idea of a third, middle group of Erasmians between the emerging confessional camps. Thus in his final years he and members of his chancellery drew ever closer to Erasmus, in whom Gattinara saw the paladin of orthodoxy and for whom he interceded successfully against the Louvain theologians in 1527. En route to the Diet of Augsburg, Gattinara died at Innsbruck. The absence of his moderation there came as a distinct disappointment to Philipp Melanchthon, among others.

BIBLIOGRAPHY

Primary Works
Gattinara, Mercurino Arborio di. "Historia vite et gestorum per dominum magnum cancellarium . . ." Edited by Carlo Bornate. In *Miscellanea di storia Italiana* 48 (1915): 233–568. Includes documents and important annotation as well as his autobiography.
Gattinara, Mercurino Arborio di. *Mercurino Arborio di Gattinara. Autobiografia.* Translated by Giancarlo Boccotti. Rome, 1991. An Italian translation also with valuable notation.

Secondary Work
Headley, John M. "Rhetoric and Reality: Messianic, Humanist, and Civilian Themes in the Imperial Ethos of Gattinara." In *Prophetic Rome in the High Renaissance Period.* Edited by Marjorie Reeves. Oxford, 1992. Pages 241–270. Analyzes his thought and policies.

JOHN M. HEADLEY

GAZA, THEODORE (c. 1415–c. 1476), Greek humanist and émigré to Renaissance Italy. Gaza's family hailed from Thessalonica, but he was born and educated in Constantinople. He came to Italy in 1440, the year after the Greeks had agreed to union with Rome at the Council of Florence. Unable to find employment at the University of Pavia, he worked first as a Greek copyist for the humanist Francesco Filelfo in Milan and then as an assistant in Vittorino da Feltre's school in Mantua. In 1446, now well trained in Latin, he began to teach Greek at the University of Ferrara while also studying medicine. Still extant are students' notes from the courses he taught at Ferrara on Demosthenes and Plato. In late 1449 he accepted an assignment in Rome engineered by the Greek cardinal Bessarion to participate in Pope Nicholas V's ambitious plan to translate into Latin the Greek literary heritage.

In Rome, Gaza established himself as a translator of scientific texts of the ancient Aristotelian tradition. First he translated into Latin Theophrastus's *On Plants* and Pseudo-Alexander of Aphrodisias's *Problems*. He then proceeded to translate Pseudo-Aristotle's *Problems* and had completed a translation of much of Aristotle's massive zoological writings when Nicholas V's death in 1455 deprived him of a patron for this work. He then transferred to the court of King Alfonso the Magnanimous in Naples, where he translated works more suited to his new environs, namely, Aelian's military manual, *Tactics,* and the sermons of Saint John Chrysostom.

After King Alfonso's death in 1458, Gaza stayed with Greek ecclesiastical friends in southern Italy before returning to Rome around 1463, where he enjoyed the support of Cardinal Bessarion. By the early 1460s he had completed his celebrated Greek grammar (written in Greek). Disappointed in his hopes for patronage from a former member of the Bessarion circle, Pope Sixtus IV (1471–1484), Gaza left Rome in 1474 (Bessarion had died in 1472) and spent the last year of his life at his benefice at San Giovanni in Policastro on the coast south of Salerno. It was in Sixtus IV's pontificate that he published his definitive version of Aristotle's zoological works. He also entered into the then-raging Plato-Aristotle controversy. He supported his patron Cardinal Bessarion, interpreting Aristotle in Neoplatonic fashion as mainly agreeing with Plato. Finally, he translated Cicero's *De senectute* (On old age) into Greek and wrote several opuscules in Greek, including one on the ancient Greek calendar.

Gaza's Aristotelian translations made him a cultural hero to younger humanists. By maintaining a strict classical vocabulary and by resorting to frequent paraphrase, glossing, and unacknowledged textual inventions, he was able to endow some of Aristotle's most difficult texts with an elegance and clarity that they had not before possessed. His fellow Greek émigré, George of Trebizond, who had translated these same texts, launched an invective against him (the *Protectio Aristotelis Problematum* [Protection of Aristotle's "Problems"] of 1456) for distorting Aristotle and for trying to undermine the medieval Aristotelian tradition, but to no avail; for the Renaissance and well beyond, Gaza's translations of the Aristotelian *Problemata* (Problems) and zoological works remained the standard versions and are still consulted as sources for modern critical editions of these texts.

See also **Greek Émigrés.**

BIBLIOGRAPHY

Primary Works

Gaza, Theodore. *Epistolae.* Edited by Pietro A. M. Leone. Naples, Italy, 1990.

Mohler, Ludwig. *Kardinal Bessarion.* 3 vols. Paderborn, Germany, 1923–1942. Reprinted, Aalen-Paderborn, 1967. See vol. 3, pp. 204–273. Contains some of Gaza's Greek and Latin opuscules.

Secondary Works

Perfetti, Stefano. " 'Cultius atque integrius': Teodoro Gaza, traduttore umanistico del *De partibus animalium.*" *Rinascimento,* series 2, 35 (1995): 253–286.

Trapp, Erich, et al., eds. *Prosopographisches Lexikon der Palaiologenzeit.* Vienna, 1977. See vol. 2, p. 139.

JOHN MONFASANI

GELLI, GIOVANNI BATTISTA (1498–1563), Florentine writer. Born into a modest family and a shoemaker by trade, Gelli believed in the value of education. He was a self-taught intellectual who advanced his fortunes to become a well-known translator and author. His literary activity was enhanced by participation in the learned conversations of the Orti Oricellari (Rucellai Gardens). In 1540 he was one of the first members of the Accademia degli Umidi, known since 1541 as the Florentine Academy. One of the goals of this academy was to translate into Tuscan all the knowledge recorded into classical language. Gelli declared himself in favor of the standard language of Florence in opposition to the humanist defenders of Latin. From this position resulted the *Ragionamento sopra le difficoltà di mettere in regole la nostra lingua* (Treatise on the difficulties of regulating our language; 1551) and the campaign in favor of the works of Dante.

Two prose comedies, *La sporta* (The bucket; 1543) and *L'errore* (The error; 1556), are dismissed because they are transparent adaptations of comedies by Niccolò Machiavelli. Fame was assured to him by his major works. *La Circe* (Circe; 1549) is a remake of the Homeric legend in which Ulysses persuades Circe to change the animals back into human beings. The refusal of the ten animals to return to their human form is a humorous reversal of the famous description by Giovanni Pico della Mirandola of humanity's potential to become either animal or angel. The elephant's decision to return to his former condition is celebrated in terms reminiscent of Marsilio Ficino's Neoplatonism. *I capricci del Giusto bottaio* (The whims of Giusto the cooper; 1546) is a playful treatment of some contemporary religious and cultural topics, such as the translation of the Bible into the vernacular.

BIBLIOGRAPHY

Primary Works

Gelli, Giovanni Battista. *Circe.* Edited by Robert Adams. Ithaca, N.Y., 1963.

Gelli, Giovanni Battista. *Letture edite ed inedite di Giovan Battista Gelli sopra la Commedia di Dante.* Florence, 1887.

Gelli, Giovanni Battista. *Opere.* Edited by Delmo Maestri. Turin, Italy, 1976.

Secondary Works

De Gaetano, Armand L. *Giambattista Gelli and the Florentine Academy: The Rebellion against Latin Florence.* Florence, 1976.

Migiel, Marilyn. "The Dignity of Man: A Feminist Perspective." In *Refiguring Woman: Perspectives on Gender and the Italian Renaissance.* Edited by Marilyn Migiel and Jiuliana Schiesari. Ithaca, N.Y., 1991. Pages 211–232.

Salman, Phillips. "Instruction and Delight in Medieval and Renaissance Criticism." *Renaissance Quarterly* 32 (1979): 303–332.

GIUSEPPE CANDELA

GEMISTUS PLETHO, GEORGE (c. 1355–1452 or 1454), Greek Neoplatonist, neopagan, educator, instigator of the Plato-Aristotle controversy of the Renaissance. Born into a family with numerous connections to the Orthodox church, Pletho is best known for his attempt to revive antique paganism. In the late 1430s he changed his last name in Greek from *Gemistos* (full) to *Plethon* (abundant) to associate himself with the two giants of the Platonic tradition, Plato and Plotinus. Pletho himself taught in Constantinople before transferring to Mistra in the Peloponnesus around 1409, where he reestablished his school and became a well-rewarded court official of successive despots. Pletho lived in Mistra for the rest of his life except for the trip he took in 1437–1440 as a member of the Greek delegation to the Council of Ferrara-Florence. His date of death is commonly given as 1452, but an argument can be made for 1454.

Inspired by Plato's *Republic,* Pletho was a political adviser as well as a philosopher. In a paper addressed to Despot Theodre of Mistra about 1415 and in another of 1418 to the emperor Manuel II he called for the wholesale reorganization of Greek society into three castes: peasants ("helots"), merchants, and rulers (consisting of soldiers, officials, and the king, supported by the taxes of the two lower castes), the elimination of mercenary troops, the firm suppression of all luxury, the prohibition of most agricultural exports, the replacement of money by barter for almost all purposes, and the ending of any subvention of monks ("philosophers"). He clearly despised Greece's large number of monks and had no use for a commercial economy, not to mention any sort of republicanism.

Pletho's most influential work was the comparison between Plato and Aristotle that he wrote while in Florence in 1439 for the Council. He argued that Plato's reasoning was superior to Aristotle's across a broad range of metaphysical, epistemological, scientific, and logical issues, and that Aristotle seemed even to have rejected the immortality of the soul and the sovereignty of God. For the next thirty years Greeks in Greece and Italy debated his assertion in the Plato-Aristotle controversy.

Pletho's largest work, *The Laws,* survives only in fragments, which include the blueprint of what Pletho hoped would be a restored neopagan religious regime, including a hierarchy of gods (each symbolizing philosophical principles), prayers, a calendar of feasts, and a moral code, all tied together by an overarching belief in an ironclad fate and eternal recurrence.

Pletho's Platonism was very different from that of the pious Marsilio Ficino in Florence one generation later. Nonetheless, he did influence Ficino; Pletho believed in an antique tradition of sages extending forward from Zoroaster through Plato to the later Platonists. Ficino took up this notion and molded it into the doctrine of the "ancient theology" characteristic of Renaissance Platonism.

See also **Greek Émigrés.**

BIBLIOGRAPHY

Primary Works

Legarde, Bernadette. "Le *De Differentiis* de Pléthon d'après l'autographe de la Marcienne." *Byzantion* 43 (1973): 312–343. An English translation based on this edition is available in Woodhouse, *Gemistos Plethon* (see below).

Pletho, George Gemistus. *Traité des lois.* Edited by C. Alexandre. Translated by A. Pellissier. Paris, 1858. Reprint, Amsterdam, 1966.

Secondary Works

Monfasani, John. *Byzantine Scholars in Renaissance Italy: Cardinal Bessarion and Other Emigrés.* Aldershot, U.K., and Brookfield, Vt., 1995. See article 10, "Platonic Platonism in the Fifteenth Century."

Monfasani, John. *George of Trebizond: A Biography and a Study of His Rhetoric and Logic.* Leiden, Netherlands, 1976. Pages 156–160, 170 (date of death), 201–209.

Woodhouse, C. M. *George Gemistos Plethon: The Last of the Hellenes.* Oxford, 1986.

JOHN MONFASANI

GEMS. *See* **Decorative Arts; Jewelry.**

GENDER. *See* **Homosexuality; Sexuality; Women.**

GENOA. [This entry includes two subentries, one on Genoa in the Renaissance and the other on Art in Genoa.]

Genoa in the Renaissance

Genoa is situated on the Ligurian coast of northwestern Italy at the center of a strip where the Apennines meet the sea. The entire Ligurian coast is characterized by the relative absence of flat terrain suitable for agriculture, and rugged mountains on the one side and the sea on the other. Good average annual rainfall and a natural harbor, combined with an easily defensible position, gave Genoa significant advantages as a port, despite the absence of a large river mouth typical of other major Mediterranean port cities. Renaissance Genoa also controlled, at one time or another, portions of the Lombard plain in what are today Piedmont and Lombardy, as well as the coast as far west as Monaco and east to La Spezia.

Government and Economy to 1528. The history of Renaissance Genoa can be divided into two periods, with 1528 as the dividing point. From 1339 to 1528, Genoa was governed by an often changing coalition of noble families and wealthy citizen clans. In practice, the noble clans, or *alberghi,* formed the nucleus of extended associations held together by patronage and economic ties, but *popolano* clans became increasingly important in this period as well. The noble clans had begun as neighborhood associations in the communal period and persisted into the Renaissance, long after similar associations in other Italian cities had been circumscribed. The endurance of the *alberghi* and their power to pursue their own political and economic interests unchecked by any institutional mechanisms are the most important characteristics of Renaissance Genoese politics. The lack of institutional controls over factional interests accounts, in part, for the consistent lack of political stability in the city. Between 1339 and 1528 there were forty-one successful bids to overthrow the government and another five that failed. Fifteen of these resulted in foreign rule, usually by the king of France or the duke of Milan.

The city was nominally governed by a council presided over by a doge, who was elected for life even though he rarely served out his term due to revolts or foreign rule. Unlike his Venetian counterpart, however, the doge was a member of the *popolo* who was ideally meant to safeguard the people's interests against the old aristocracy. In practice the Genoese doge was almost always selected from either the Adorno or the Fregoso families and attempted to rule like a prince by promoting factional conflict to augment his limited powers. When factional strife threatened to spiral out of control, the doge often ended up stepping down in favor of supposedly impartial foreign rule.

Constant political turmoil and civil war resulted in a crippling state debt. Attempts to restructure the debt through the sale of gabelles and colonies to powerful families generally failed because each successive revolt would lead to new debt and fairly consistent default on existing loans. This led to the founding by creditors of the state of the most important Genoese institution, the Casa San Giorgio. Established in 1405 to consolidate state debt through the sale of public shares, it was similar in character to the *monti* found in other Italian cities of this period. Unlike the *monti,* however, the Casa San Giorgio was controlled by the largest shareholders rather than an elected board and was used to force the state's hand in matters of policy. As such, it became a private government and provided the only real continuity in the ever-changing landscape of Genoese politics. It even acquired administrative functions of its own, including control of the mint, ownership of Corsica, and the power to inflict capital punishment on debtors.

In the high Middle Ages, Genoa had been the premier commercial power in the eastern Mediterranean. By the mid-fourteenth century Venice had displaced Genoa in the Levant by negotiating favorable commercial treaties, first with the Byzantines and later with the Ottomans, and by conquering Genoese possessions in the Aegean in a series of wars. The last of these, the War of Chioggia (1378–1381), ended in humiliating defeat for the Genoese after they had nearly captured Venice.

The War of Chioggia marked the end of Genoese pretensions to dominance in the eastern Mediterranean. It did not, however, mean the decline of Genoa as a commercial or maritime power. Despite the loss of most of its bases, Genoa retained many interests in Black Sea trade. These included alum concessions as well as slave trading. The bulk of Genoese economic interests, however, shifted to the western Mediterranean as the Genoese began to invest heavily in domestic manufactures and Spanish trade. The wool and silk industries figured most prominently among the growing Genoese industries in this period and enjoyed government protection.

The Republic after 1528. In the early sixteenth century, as the Habsburgs and Valois fought

Genoa. From Hartmann Schedel and Anton Koberger, *Liber chronicarum* (The Nürnberg Chronicle; 1493). RARE BOOK DIVISION, LIBRARY OF CONGRESS

for control of the Italian peninsula, Genoa's port became a major prize. The city passed back and forth between emperor and French king. This, along with continuing political and fiscal malaise, helped generate considerable sentiment for constitutional reform. By 1528 this had reached a boiling point, and reformers led by Andrea Doria successfully overthrew French rule and established a new republic. The events of 1528 are crucial for two reasons. First, a set of state institutions was created that provided the political continuity that had never existed under the old system. Second, Doria placed Genoa firmly in the imperial camp as a Spanish ally, but not as a subject, which also distinguishes the post-1528 Genoese state from earlier regimes that surrendered political control to foreign rulers.

The new Genoese republic, which would survive until 1798, finally brought the factional struggles that had plagued earlier regimes under control. The political class was defined and limited to the noble *alberghi*. Five important *popolo* clans were added to the nobility, bringing the definitive number of *alberghi* to twenty-eight. The members of these clans were theoretically eligible for service in the two councils (the Maggiore Consiglio and the Minore Consiglio) and executive positions, including the dogeship, which became a two-year office. The authority of the Casa San Giorgio was also circumscribed to keep power in the hands of official state institutions.

Still, the new regime relied heavily on the prestige and personal authority of Andrea Doria for its continuation, at least in the earliest years. In 1547 a failed coup, led by members of the Fieschi *albergo*, was narrowly averted, and drove home the need for further reform if the new regime was to survive beyond Doria's lifetime. The 1547 reforms were mainly aimed at controlling the election to the higher offices of the republic and guaranteed a measure of participation to all the *alberghi* that made up the political nobility as defined in 1528. The success of the 1547 reforms further stabilized the republic by curtailing the exclusion of some *alberghi* from higher office. It also convinced the Spanish to allow the republic to continue as an autonomous, if dependent, political entity. Finally, in 1576 the *alberghi* themselves were abolished in favor of a family-based aristocratic system that prevailed until the Napoleonic conquests of the eighteenth century.

See also **Doria, Andrea.**

BIBLIOGRAPHY

Costantini, Claudio. *La repubblica di Genova.* Turin, Italy, 1986. The standard general treatment for the post-1528 period.

Epstein, Steven A. *Genoa and the Genoese, 958–1528.* Chapel Hill, N.C., 1996. The only general treatment in English.

Grendi, Edoardo. *La repubblica aristocratica dei genovesi.* Bologna, Italy, 1987. A more detailed analysis of the post-1528 era.

Heers, Jacques, *Gênes au XVe siècle.* Paris, 1961. The classic treatment of the fifteenth century.

Lopez, Robert S. *Su e giù per la storia di Genova.* Genoa, Italy, 1975.

KARL APPUHN

Art in Genoa

The art historian Giorgio Vasari (1511–1574) popularized the idea that the Renaissance arrived in Genoa after the Sack of Rome in May 1527, when German and Swiss mercenaries of the Holy Roman Emperor Charles V (1500–1558) ravaged papal patronage, triggering a "diaspora of culture" throughout Italy and Europe. However, Genoa already had a vibrant Lombard Renaissance tradition. The prevailing view of Italian Renaissance history highlights the triumph of commune and individual over private family feudal groups. But in Genoa, landed, titled, military, and mercantile families took over the city and communal government, ruling from their local urban strongholds (the Genoese *alberghi*) and rural agricultural castle-villa estates, ever under the influence of Milan and France. Private family patronage distinguished medieval and Renaissance Genoa, creating powerful systems of representation of private over public communal space.

Lombard Influence. During the Lombard period of urban renovation from the mid-fifteenth to the early sixteenth century, prominent old noble family leaders commissioned finely carved classical portals as triumphal entryways to their tower palaces. These structures proclaimed the power and privilege of the families over their surroundings. Genoa was not a spatial continuum but a complex web, a labyrinth of private family enclaves in which architectural elements designated a family's associations and experiences. The sculpted portal became a heraldic emblem, a threshold to power, lineage, and the "antiquity" of a family. These triumphal entryways, placed on black-and-white marble palaces and church facades of old noble families, claimed private precedence over public space.

From the quarry region of Bissone on Lake Lugano, the Gagini and other Lombard stonemasons, sculptors, and builders (called Maestri Antelami) came to Genoa and set the Lombard Renaissance style. These artists followed medieval precedent, preserved by local guilds, which secured the Lombard presence in Genoa from the twelfth century, the great age of cathedral building and urban expansion. Sumptuous classical portals emblazoned with the crusading patron saint George killing the dragon or with family coats of arms on triumphal chariots; framing classical orders (pilasters and lintels) filled with paradisiacal vine-scroll decorations of Augustan golden age plenty; celebrant putti, cupids of love, peace, fertility, and abundance; Roman emperor medallions and allegorical virtues: all announced the stoic stature of a family in epicurean rhetorical style.

In the Genoa Cathedral, amid Muslim silver censers and Byzantine icon spoils from the Crusades, Domenico Gagini (c. 1425–1492) led his family workshop (from 1448 to 1457) in decorating the communal Chapel of St. John the Baptist, patron saint of baptism and of the port city of Genoa. The Gagini combined northern and central Italian influences to create an emporium of sacred images. From the Certosa of Pavia in Lombardy, a classical style overlaid Filippo Brunelleschi's Pazzi Chapel in Santa Croce in Florence. Gagini's Brunelleschian triumphal entrance arch displayed framed narrative, illusionistic bas-reliefs of the life of the Baptist, inspired by the sculptors Andrea and Nino Pisano, Lorenzo Ghiberti, and Donatello. Prophets and saints flanked the rich canopy of polychrome marble columns, enveloped by sacramental vine scrolls. This festive Genoese style honored the relics, sacred ashes, and stolen remains of the Baptist and other saints from the Crusades, while translating them to the new crusading, maritime City of the Saved, its reliquary chapel, and its central sepulchral altar. A genealogy of freestanding, *contrapposto* (opposing) Old and New Testament saints and virtues, supervised by the Lucchese sculptor Matteo Civitali (1436–1501), stood witness in niches around the chapel and altar. Heading these guardians were *St. John the Baptist* and the *Virgin and Child with Bird in Hand* (symbolic of salvation) of 1501–1503 by the Florentine sculptor

Chapel in the Cathedral of Genoa. Reliquary Chapel of St. John the Baptist in the Cathedral of Genoa by Domenico Gagini and family workshop; c. 1451–1504.
ARCHIVIO FOTOGRAFICO DEL COMUNE DI GENOVA/COURTESY OF GEORGE L. GORSE

Andrea Sansovino (c. 1467–1529), which completed the triumphal ensemble. Commissioned by the new "perpetual" doges of the Campofregoso family clan, with the support of the Doria family and the Confraternity of St. John the Baptist, classical inscriptions left the imprint of family even on this major communal monument.

The private also triumphed over public interest in the monumental palace of the Bank of St. George, located on the medieval harbor front, the center of trade. A series of seated and standing sculptural portraits of protectors (old noble governors) graced the central salon of this unique institution, which Niccolò Machiavelli called "the state within the state" for its control (after 1407) of Genoa's public debt, taxes, tariffs, and foreign colonies. A largely lost (but reconstructed in 1992) component of the urban scenography were the frescoed palace facades with patron saints, historical scenes, and allegorical figures, which were restored to celebrate Genoa's private wealth in rich tapestry-like foliage. These facades were integral to urban traditions of pageantry and procession, leading into sumptuous interiors of black-and-white marble decorations, paintings, sculptures, tapestries, and silver and gold, characteristic of the old noble-mercantile style.

Doria and the Habsburgs. In 1528 the Genoese admiral Andrea Doria (1466–1560) overthrew the new noble dogal government and French governor, founding an old noble republic led by a biennial doge and exclusive senate. The Genoese old noble families and their aristocratic republic became the rich bankers of the Habsburg empire, while a Roman Renaissance style articulated the Genoese-Habsburg connection in triumphal terms reminiscent of the Augustan Roman empire. The Lombard Renaissance influenced this style in its festive splendor, which was previewed in Roman triumphal entry ceremonies, then made permanent in church, palace, and villa decorations. Rich confections of stucco and painted classical decor became a hallmark of the Genoese nobility and republic during the Genoese golden age of the sixteenth century.

Strategically located on the harbor entrance, Andrea Doria's sea villa, designed in an "Augustan" Hellenistic style, became the new cultural, military, political, and economic center of the second Genoese Renaissance style. The villa, built in a Roman Maniera (late Renaissance or mannerist) style, transformed the city and reoriented Genoa from subservience to Lombardy and France to alliance with Rome and Spain.

After the Sack of Rome, the Florentine artist, Perino del Vaga (Pietro Buonaccorsi; 1501–1547), a principal in Raphael's Vatican workshop, came to Genoa to design the *all'antica* (in the ancient mode) Roman triumphal entry decorations for Charles V and to consolidate Andrea Doria's U-shaped, portico villa between 1528 and 1536. Temporary Roman triumphal arches on the streets blended with permanent villa architecture, formal gardens, and festive painted stucco, sculptures, tapestries, and decorative arts ensembles to construct a regal identity for the founder and restorer of the republic. Inspired by Suetonius's "Life of Augustus" and Pliny the Younger's description of Laurentinum (his sea villa near Ostia) as well as by ancient Roman remains—in particular, the "grottesque" (grotto-like) fantastic fusions of painting and stuccowork apotheosizing the emperor at the Golden House of Nero—Andrea Doria and his villa became synonymous with the city.

Complex mythological, historical, and allegorical programs marked this *all'antica* Roman triumphalist style. Learned panegyrics and portrait personifications identified Doria with ancient Roman defenders of the republic, such as Camillus, Lucius Aemilius Paulus, and Gaius Mucius Scaevola. Andrea was compared to Roman-style military heroes of the Doria family line, who were frescoed in the second-floor Doric loggia of the villa, a figural-architectural gallery of stoic virtue, overlooking the formal garden and harbor entrance. Doria became "Neptune Calming the Seas"; "Quos Ego," from the first book of Virgil's *Aeneid,* dedicated to the emperor Augustus; or "Jupiter Casting Down the Giants," the father of the gods restoring order to heaven and earth, mythic personifications of the early modern ruler-state. This type of triumphal entry—a linear sequence of public and private spaces ending in Ovid's *Loves of the Gods* in private bedroom chambers—was unique to Genoa.

Raphael's Stanze (rooms) and Michelangelo's Sistine Chapel at the Vatican influenced Perino del Vaga's workshop and succeeding generations of artists, who enriched this Roman festive style for Genoese patrician church, palace, and villa networks. The Genoese artist Luca Cambiaso (1527–1585) advanced Perino's mannerist style. For the ceiling fresco *Apollo Shooting Arrows at the Greeks before Troy* in the grand salon of Antonio Doria's painted-stucco block palace above Genoa (c. 1545–1550), Cambiaso's early, expressive Michelangelesque style dramatized Perino del Vaga's *Jupiter Casting Down the Giants* and Giulio Romano's *Stoning of St. Stephen* altar (1530) in the church of San Stefano. In 1551 Raphael's *grazia* (grace) triumphed during Cambiaso's collaboration with the Perugian architect Galeazzo Alessi (1512–1572) and the Genoese architect-decorator Giovanni Battista Castello, called Il Bergamasco (c. 1509–1569), the most refined followers of Raphael and Perino del Vaga. Cambiaso undertook a series of major decorative commissions with Alessi and Bergamasco, which defined the elegant third Genoese Renaissance style.

For the Alessi villa of the banker Luca Giustiniani in Albaro, a suburb east of Genoa, Cambiaso and Bergamasco decorated the refined mannerist painted-stucco loggia of this major Roman Vitruvian block villa, situated over the eastern entrance to the harbor. In the block Villa Pallavicino, above Genoa, Cambiaso reinterpreted Michelangelo's *Fall of Phaethon,* an appropriate golden age, Neoplatonic allegory of hubris for the banker. After 1550 Cambiaso's collaboration with Alessi and Bergamasco continued on the Renaissance axial palace street of the old nobility, the Strada Nuova, or Via Aurea, which was positioned above the medieval *alberghi* neighborhoods of Genoa. These monumental Roman palace blocks with "grottesque" decorations defined the Genoese patrician style during the late sixteenth and the early seventeenth century, celebrated by Peter Paul Rubens in his deluxe folio publication *Palazzi di Genova* (Antwerp, 1622) and John Evelyn's travel description of Genoa in 1644 as a highlight of the grand tour.

BIBLIOGRAPHY

Algeri, Giuliana, and Anna De Floriani. *La pittura in Liguria: Il Quattrocento.* Genoa, Italy, 1991.

Boccardo, Piero. *Andrea Doria e le arti: Committenza e mecenatismo a Genova nel Rinascimento.* Rome, 1989.

Conti, Graziella, et al. *La scultura a Genova e in Liguria dalle origini al Cinquecento.* Genoa, Italy, 1987.

Gavazza, Ezia. *La grande decorazione a Genova.* Genoa, Italy, 1974.

Gorse, George. "Between Empire and Republic: Triumphal Entries into Genoa during the Sixteenth Century." In *"All the world's a stage . . .": Art and Pageantry in the Renaissance and Baroque.* Pt. 1: *Triumphal Celebrations and the Rituals of Statecraft.* Edited by Barbara Wisch and Susan Scott Munshower. University Park, Pa., 1990. Pages 188–256.

Gorse, George. "A Classical Stage for the Old Nobility: The Strada Nuova and Sixteenth-Century Genoa." *Art Bulletin* 79 (June 1997): 301–327.

Kruft, Hanno-Walter. "La cappella di San Giovanni Battista nel Duomo di Genova." *Antichità viva* 9 (1970): 33–50.

Kruft, Hanno-Walter. *Portali genovesi del Rinascimento.* Florence, 1971.

Lotz, Wolfgang, et al. *Galeazzo Alessi e l'architettura del Cinquecento.* Genoa, Italy, 1975.

Magnani, Lauro. *Luca Cambiaso: Da Genova all'Escorial.* Genoa, Italy, 1995.

Magnani, Lauro. *Il tempio di Venere: Giardino e villa nella cultura Genovese.* Genoa, Italy, 1987.

Parma Armani, Elena. *Perin del Vaga: L'anello mancante.* Genoa, Italy, 1986.

Poleggi, Ennio. *Strada Nuova: Una lottizzazione del Cinquecento a Genova.* Genoa, Italy, 1968.

Poleggi, Ennio, and Paolo Cevini. *Le città nella storia d'Italia: Genova.* Rome, 1981.

GEORGE L. GORSE

GENTILESCHI, ARTEMISIA (1593–1652/53), Italian painter. Of the handful of women artists who achieved international stature in the Renaissance, Artemisia Gentileschi stands out for her progressive style, ambitious thematic range, and overtly feminist expression. Artemisia was born in Rome and trained in painting by her father, Orazio Gentileschi. She adopted Caravaggio's dramatic realism and strong chiaroscuro lighting but departed from his and other models in her preference for themes featuring biblical and historical women and in her humanizing and heroizing of female characters. In her first signed painting, *Susanna and the Elders* (1610), Artemisia presented the heroine as a protesting victim of the

Artemisia Gentileschi. *Self-Portrait.* THE GRANGER COLLECTION

lustful Elders. She constructed the first of four interpretations of the Judith theme (1612–1613; Naples, Capodimonte) as the gory decapitation of a helpless Holofernes by two powerful and determined women.

Artemisia's rare ability to dramatize credibly the acts and emotions of women was grounded in her experience of sexual intimidation. In March 1612 Orazio sued the painter Agostino Tassi, hired to teach Artemisia perspective, for the rape of his daughter. The seven-month trial resulted in Tassi's conviction and light punishment and Artemisia's arranged marriage to a Florentine artist in late 1612. In her eight-year stay in Florence, Artemisia received commissions from Michelangelo Buonarroti the Younger, contributing *The Allegory of Inclination* (1615–1617) to a gallery glorifying his famous greatuncle, and from Grand Duke Cosimo II de' Medici, for whom she painted a replica of her Naples *Judith* (c. 1620; Uffizi), a *Penitent Magdalen* (1617–1620; Pitti), and other works.

Artemisia's interest in female characters, fortified by her insider knowledge of female anatomy, was encouraged by her patrons, who typically regarded women artists and their paintings of women as twin specimens of female beauty. In 1616 Artemisia matriculated in the Accademia del Disegno, becoming the first female member of the prestigious Florentine academy. She befriended Galileo Galilei, then court mathematician to the grand duke; subtle tributes to the famous astronomer have been found in two of her pictures.

Artemisia returned to Rome around 1620 and is recorded in 1624 (presumably already separated from her husband) as head of a household that included a daughter and two servants. Lacking access to large church commissions, Artemisia found important private patrons. Her paintings were purchased or commissioned by the Genoese nobleman Pietro Gentile (*Cleopatra, Lucretia*), the Roman collector Vincenzo Giustiniani (*David,* lost), and the sitter who ordered her only surviving portrait (*Gonfaloniere,* 1622; Bologna). After returning to Rome, she abandoned the refined elegance that briefly marked her style at the still somewhat mannerist Florentine court and renewed her baroque realism and strong tenebrist lighting. The major work of this period is her third *Judith* (c. 1625; Detroit Institute), a large, grand painting that represents the suspenseful climax of the story, when the heroic tyrannicides pause, frozen by a sound that alerts them to danger. The picture's theatrical lighting and isolation of a dramatic moment can be connected with the popularity of the Judith theme in Roman Jesuit theater in this period. Perhaps also of the mid-1620s is the majestic *Esther and Ahasuerus* (New York, Metropolitan Museum).

About 1628 Artemisia moved to Naples. In 1630 she painted a self-portrait (one of several mentioned in the literature) for the Roman scholar-collector Cassiano dal Pozzo, probably identical with her *Self-Portrait as the Allegory of Painting* (London, Kensington Palace). This complex picture combines the traditionally female allegory with a prevalent Renaissance concern, the intellectual and social status of the artist, to convert a convention repressive for women into an image that celebrates both female capability and the intrinsic worth of artistic practice.

In Spanish-ruled Naples, Artemisia gained commissions for religious pictures. In this period, her style modulated from Roman Caravaggism to a more decorous classicizing now favored in Italy, and she began to hire collaborators to paint architectural and landscape backgrounds in her pictures. Other patrons in the 1630s included Francesco I d'Este, duke of Modena; Cardinals Francesco and Antonio Barberini; and Ferdinando II de' Medici.

In 1638–1641 Artemisia joined her aging father at the English court of King Charles I and Queen Henrietta Maria; together they painted ceiling allegories for the Great Hall of the Queen's House at Greenwich (1638–1639). King Charles's extensive Italian art purchases included six or more paintings by Artemisia; none is known today. The artist spent her final decade in Naples, where she painted for Dottore Luigi Romeo a *Bathsheba* (early 1640s; Columbus, Ohio, Museum of Art), *Susanna,* and *Lot and His Daughters* (1640s; Toledo, Ohio, Museum of Art).

Some of Artemisia's late paintings are overpainted or otherwise dubious; even the secure works tend toward a formal and expressive conservatism. An exception is *Corisca and the Satyr,* identified in the early 1990s, which, in a rarely depicted episode from Battista Guarini's *Il pastor fido,* presents a nymph gleefully outwitting a lustful satyr. In her last years, Artemisia produced for Don Antonio Ruffo of Sicily a *Galatea* (1649), *Diana and Actaeon,* and (in progress in 1651) *Andromeda Freed by Perseus* and *Joseph and Potiphar's Wife;* none has survived.

Artemisia's letters reveal both her acute consciousness of the presumed inferiority of women artists in a masculine art world and her own fierce determination to excel. Her success is partly seen in her demonstrable influence (in one or more instances) upon contemporary artists, including Bernardo Cavallino, Simon Vouet, Guercino, Rembrandt, and perhaps Velázquez. Resistance to Artemisia's achievement is reflected in the paucity of biographical accounts and in her persistent characterization in sexual terms. Many of her paintings were reattributed to her father, Orazio, her artistic identity nearly subsumed into his, before twentieth-century art historians began to reclaim her. Artemisia Gentileschi's singular achievement was her transformation of the image of females in art, from passive ciphers into autonomous agents.

[Gentileschi's *Judith and Holofernes* (c. 1620) appears in the color plates in this volume.]

See also **Women,** *subentry on* **Portrayal in Renaissance Art.**

BIBLIOGRAPHY

Bissell, R. Ward. *Artemisia Gentileschi and the Authority of Art: Critical Reading and Catalogue Raisonné.* University Park, Pa., 1999.

Cropper, Elizabeth. "New Documents for Artemisia Gentileschi's Life in Florence." *Burlington Magazine* 135 (1993): 760–761.

Garrard, Mary D. *Artemisia Gentileschi: The Image of the Female Hero in Italian Baroque Art*. Princeton, N.J., 1989. Includes an English translation of the artist's twenty-eight letters and testimony of the rape trial of 1612.

Hersey, George L. "Female and Male Art: *Postille* to Garrard's *Artemisia Gentileschi*." In *Parthenope's Splendor: Art of the Golden Age in Naples*. Edited by Jeanne Chenault Porter and Susan Scott Munshower. University Park, Pa., 1993. Pages 323–334.

MARY D. GARRARD

GEOGRAPHY AND CARTOGRAPHY.

During the Renaissance, Europeans became increasingly interested in understanding their world. Both geography, an academic discipline that described and explained the people and places of the globe, and cartography, a guild-based discipline that graphically illustrated those people and places, became more popular and more important to mercantile, political, and imperial ambitions.

Geography. Geography was a complex and wide-ranging discipline, providing a focus for both exploration and nation building. During the sixteenth and seventeenth centuries, geography was developing into a discipline distinct from the older study of cosmography. The subject of cosmography was the globe and its relationship with the heavens as a whole, picturing the earth as an integral part of the universe, while geography had a narrower focus, concentrating specifically on the earth itself. Although both terms continued to be used, sometimes interchangeably, the distinction became sharper. Geographers abstracted the globe from its surrounding cosmos and began to classify its parts by separation, rather than by union.

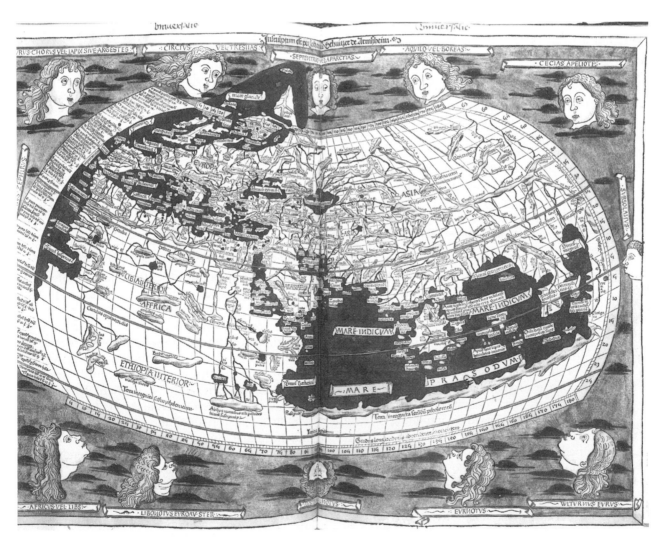

Ptolemy's Map of the World. From *Cosmographia* (Ulm, 1482). RARE BOOK DIVISION, LIBRARY OF CONGRESS

31

Three branches. Geography developed into three related branches: mathematical, descriptive, and chorographical geography, each with distinct practitioners and different topics of investigation. Mathematical geography had its roots in the *Geographia* of Ptolemy (c. 100–c. 170), which was translated into Latin in 1410—a late addition to the Ptolemaic corpus. It supplied Renaissance thinkers with the model of a branch of applied mathematics, which could be used to determine the exact positions of points and the figures and areas of large portions of the earth's surface, the shape and size of the earth, and the variations of terrestrial magnetism. Renaissance scholars who contributed to this branch of geography included two of the most popular authors of the early sixteenth century, Peter Apian (1495–1552) and Sebastian Münster (1489–1552). Apian's *Cosmographia,* first published in 1529, was essentially a popularization of Ptolemy, containing Ptolemy's method and theory of map projection and astronomical observation, and charts of longitude and latitude, as well as maps of the world, inspired by Ptolemy's work. Likewise, Münster's immensely popular *Cosmographia* (1544) began with Ptolemaic maps of the Old World, following them with more recent maps of the New (based, of course, on Ptolemy's technique). In fact, by the mid-sixteenth century, all major geographical treatises explicitly began with Ptolemy. Although they often scoffed at Ptolemy's lack of particular knowledge and demonstrated how much more of the globe modern men knew than the ancients, they all subscribed to the objective and geometrical framework established by Ptolemy.

Descriptive geography. Descriptive geography developed as a subdiscipline quite separate from mathematical geography. Using Strabo of Amaseia (c. 63 B.C.–c. A.D. 20) as its classical model, descriptive geography portrayed the physical and political structures of other lands. The most easily accessible of the three geographical subdisciplines, it encompassed everything from practical descriptions of European road conditions to outlandish yarns of exotic locales, providing intriguing reading and practical information alike. This form of geography helped people establish their own national and local identities against those of other European and non-European nations. Descriptive geographers included Giovanni Battista Ramusio (1485–1557), Joseph De Acosta (c. 1539–1598), Jan Huygen van Linschoten (1563–1611), Theodore (1528–1598) and Johann T. de Bry (1561–1623?), and Richard Hakluyt

(c. 1552–1616), all of whom wrote long and very popular compendia of travel narratives.

Chorography. The final type of geography, chorography, combined a medieval chronicle tradition with the Italian Renaissance study of local description. Chorography was the most wide ranging of the geographical subdisciplines, since it included an interest in genealogy, chronology, and antiquities, as well as local history and topography. Chorography thus united an anecdotal interest in local families and wonders with the mathematically arduous task of genealogical and chronological research. Two famous Renaissance chorographers were Joseph Justus Scaliger (1540–1609) and William Camden (1551–1623).

Cartography. The study of maps and map-making was related to mathematical geography, but depended more on craft traditions and so remained separate from the more academic discipline of geography. While geography gradually evolved during the Renaissance to create a detailed description and interpretation of the world and its inhabitants, cartography experienced a transformation far more revolutionary. The geographical consciousness of Europeans began to alter drastically in the fifteenth century, largely due to a cartographic change in projection and perception. This transformation was caused by the imposition of mathematical rules on global representation combined with the increased value placed on "objective" measurement and emplacement. This change, from subjective and vitalistic to objective and mathematical, began fundamentally to alter the attitude of Europeans to their world and their ability to control and exploit it.

From* mappae mundi *to Ptolemaic projection. The *mappae mundi* of the middle ages demonstrate that non-Ptolemaic representations of the world were constructed with very different criteria in mind from those of the more recognizable Ptolemaic or even Mercator depictions. *Mappae mundi* were of various types, with more than half in the tripartite form often known as the T–O map. These wheel maps, with Jerusalem often in the center, the earthly paradise at the top (east) and the Don River, the Nile, and the Mediterranean forming the T that divided the world into three continents, were not intended to be even crudely representational. Rather, their purpose was to indicate the larger significance of the world as a subjective and organic whole. They demonstrated the inherent order of God's plan, as well as the relationship between the microcosm of man and the macrocosm of the universe. The translation of

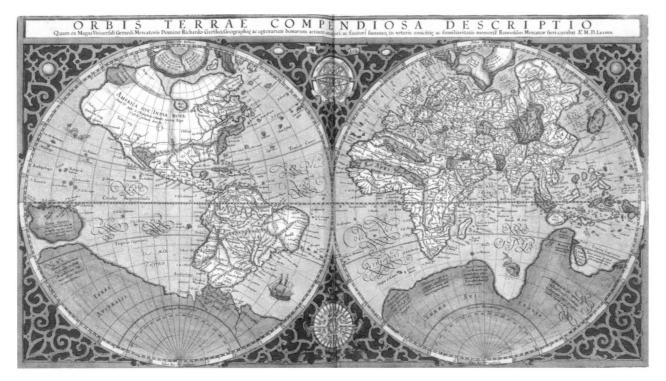

Mercator's Cartography. Map of the world by Gerard Mercator, 1582. BY PERMISSION OF THE BRITISH LIBRARY

Ptolemy's *Geographia* began to change this view of mapping. Ptolemy's work applied the same geometrical grid to the world that he has provided for astronomy in his more famous *Almagest*. He constructed a grid of latitude and longitude, and established methods for determining the exact location of geographical points on that grid. For Ptolemy and his followers, values of objectivity, realism and geometrical accuracy were far more important than subjective connections.

Ptolemy's *Geographia* was fundamental to cartography in the Renaissance, but had not interested scholars enough to translate with the rest of the Ptolemaic corpus in the twelfth century. A new Renaissance interest in this geometrical emplacement of the world was a result of a new emphasis in the European *mentalité* that affected every aspect of intellectual life—the new importance placed on the mathematical science of geometry. Geometry proved important for such aspects of Renaissance state-building as the development of artillery, new fortification designs, and navigation. In art, perspective, based on principles of geometry, developed as the most important new technique of the age.

In this drive to develop a measurable world, the *Geographia* was extremely important. The success of Ptolemy's conquest can be judged by the rapidity with which his method and world picture were assimilated. The *Geographia* itself was published in Latin in 1462, 1475, 1478, 1482, 1486, and 1490. Pierre d'Ailly (1350–1420) incorporated Ptolemaic techniques and maps into his *Compendium Cosmographiae* (1413) and his later versions of *Imago mundi*. The *Nürnberg Chronicles,* first published in 1493, contained among its beautiful woodcut illustrations a Ptolemaic map. By the sixteenth century, all cartographers were using a Ptolemaic framework, even as some developed more sophisticated mathematical projections.

Charts and portolan maps. While the revival of Ptolemy's schema was important for the popular consumers of cartography, a separate development was occurring in more practical maps. Sea charts, especially the portolan maps of the Iberian navigators, had long been constructed following a more pragmatic combination of observation, wind directions, and simple astronomical sightings. These were the maps used first to negotiate the Mediterranean and later to venture farther around Africa and to the New World. These charts were never published, often guarded jealously and passed from navigator to navigator. It was only in the course of the sixteenth century that the firsthand knowledge represented in these charts began to find its way onto published maps and globes.

Globes and atlases. Part of the revolution in cartography was the explosion of interest in the purchasing of maps and globes that occurred during the Renaissance. One of the earliest globes was made by Martin Behaim (c. 1459–1506) in Nürnberg in 1493; by the mid-1500s, many prosperous merchants and gentlefolk could purchase these marks of worldly familiarity. Likewise, the atlas developed as a completely new form of map ownership and one that achieved huge popularity in the early modern period. The geographers who most expertly took advantage of this trend were Gerhard Mercator (1512–1594) and Abraham Ortelius (1527–1598). Mercator produced a globe in 1541, for which he claimed objectivity, classical underpinning, and modern accuracy. Likewise, he developed a new world map in 1569, with a projection widening the latitudes of the north, that created a sense of the primacy of northern Europe and the Atlantic world Europeans were conquering. Ortelius, in 1570, published the first true atlas, *Theatrum orbis terrarum* (The theater of the world), from which all subsequent atlases took inspiration.

A Geographically Aware World.

The exploration of the world—both New and Old—provided an important impetus to the growing interest in geography and cartography. By the end of the seventeenth century, Europeans understood the social value of maps and had learned the lessons of the importance of geometry and objectivity. In fact, this geometrization of worldview could equally be called the objectification of the world, and carried with it implications about European attitudes to other peoples and places. Maps of other cultures, lacking this sense of objectivity, were usually dismissed by Europeans as they laid claim to other parts of the world. Geography and cartography were necessary preconditions for imperial expansion, as well as tools in creating the empires that were to come.

See also **Ptolemy.**

BIBLIOGRAPHY

Brotton, Jerry. *Trading Territories: Mapping the Early Modern World.* London, 1997. An excellent treatment of Portuguese geography and the use of cartographic experts in politics.

Buisseret, David, ed. *Monarchs, Ministers, and Maps: The Emergence of Cartography as a Tool of Government in Early Modern Europe.* The Kenneth Nebenzahl, Jr., Lectures in the History of Cartography. Published for the Hermon Dunlap Smith Center for the History of Cartography, the Newberry Library. Chicago and London, 1992. Especially interesting for its wide range of European locales.

Cormack, Lesley B. *Charting an Empire: Geography at the English Universities, 1580–1620.* Chicago, 1997.

Karrow, Robert W., Jr. *Mapmakers of the Sixteenth Century and Their Maps: Bio-Bibliographies of the Cartographers of Abraham Ortelius, 1570.* Chicago, 1993. Based on Leo Bagrow's *A. Ortelii Catalogus Cartographorum.* Excellent list of all maps, with extant copies, by the original cartographers listed and used by Ortelius.

Lestringant, Frank. *Mapping the Renaissance World: The Geographical Imagination in the Age of Discovery.* Translation by David Fausett of *L'atelier du cosmographe.* Cambridge, U.K., 1994. Discussion of the important Renaissance cosmographer André Thevet.

Livingstone, David N. *The Geographical Tradition: Episodes in the History of a Contested Enterprise.* Oxford, 1992. Best survey of geographical thought, although the Renaissance chapters are less well developed.

Mundy, Barbara E. *The Mapping of New Spain: Indigenous Cartography and the Maps of the Relaciones Geográficas.* Chicago, 1996.

LESLEY B. CORMACK

GEOLOGY. The passage from Paleolithic stone axe to early civilization in the river valleys of the Old World entailed a developing familiarity with earth materials and earth processes, as seen for example in irrigation and flood control. Already in the Bronze Age minerals were used as we use them today for pigments, preservatives and weapons, medicine and poison, ceramics, fuel, jewelry, plasters, mordants, and architecture. By the time of Pythagoras (c. 580–c. 500 B.C.), lead fallout from smelting silver for the coinage of Athens was extensive enough to reach the lakes of Sweden. As did the natural history of the earth and life, geology began with speculative philosophy when the Pythagoreans, in the conviction that the world was a rational evolution of pure spirit, turned their attention to the earth's crust, its materials, and their changing configuration over time.

Elements of so broad a science, ultimately traceable to Egypt and Mesopotamia, are found in nearly all of the literature available to the Greco-Latin world from the time of Pythagoras to the Renaissance. The scholarly physician Georgius Agricola (1494–1555), writing on minerals in *De natura fossilium* (1546), lists one hundred sources from Aelius Lampridius to Zoroaster. The spread of the printing press in the fifteenth century and the ensuing rapid dissemination of classical literature acted as major catalysts for Renaissance natural history. One hundred ninety editions of Pliny's *Natural History* were printed before 1500. In his *Metamorphoses,* printed in Italy in 1471, the Roman poet Ovid (43 B.C.–A.D. 17) has Pythagoras speak of the transformations on the earth worked by time:

Geology. *The Plain of Arezzo and the Val di Chiano* by Leonardo da Vinci, one of a series of aerial studies (viewed as from the flight of a bird) of the water resources above the Arno River for a proposed canal from Florence to the sea. Windsor MS. 12278. THE ROYAL COLLECTION © HER MAJESTY QUEEN ELIZABETH II

What once was solid earth turns into sea . . .
And I have seen earth made from water,
Far from any ocean, seashells strewn;
Old anchors found on mountain tops,
What once was field, the rush of water turns to valley.
The mountain leveled into plain by flood.
The marsh that was, become the desert sand . . .
Rivers stirred in ancient quakes burst forth or
    disappear . . . (Book 15, lines 262–268, 271, 272)

Macrocosm and Microcosm. Among the myriad sketches and notes, often incomplete, often contradictory, dispersed throughout his workbooks, Leonardo da Vinci (1452–1519) described the configuration of the earth's crust as the result of presently observable natural processes, principally fluvial, operating over immense periods of time. In Leonardo's geologic system, the highest peaks of the Alps and Apenines emerged as islands from an ancient sea. Mountains are continually eroded by winds and rains, and the debris is carried by the riv-

ers to the seas, constantly transforming the seas by advancing deltas into which the rivers carve their valleys. Thus, the Po will eventually fill the Adriatic and the Nile will fill the Mediterranean. To maintain the center of the earth at the center of the universe, mountains that have been lightened by erosion rise slowly, bringing up marine strata with their petrified fauna and flora, only to be carved into mountains in their turn—a concept of the world and time as an eternal series of renewals, a view foreshadowing the secular geology of the eighteenth century.

Leonardo's anticipation of modern ideas such as the organic origins of fossils, fluvial process and sedimentation, the association of folded strata with mountain belts, and his bird's-eye topographic constructions reflect the dissections of the earth that he carried out from 1482 to 1515 as architect-engineer of canals, irrigation systems, and roads. They also reflect his detailed studies of human anatomy based on dissection. He compared the movement of blood through the treelike network of veins in the body with the movement of water through the veins of the earth. The philosophy of Hermetism taught that man was a *microcosm* (little world) and a model of the *macrocosm* (great world). The universe was alive, a hierarchical organism connected by an all-encompassing web of harmonious influences and relationships, all discoverable. For Leonardo, as for his contemporaries, this Neoplatonic Hermetism set the framework of their debate with experience.

Mineralogy. The earliest mineralogies of the Renaissance were parts of illustrated *Kreutterbücher* (Herbals). Primarily glossaries in German, they were products of scholarship—compilations from the literature of the medicinal uses of herbs, animals, and minerals. Minerals were listed alphabetically with no attempt to classify or define them by their properties.

The *Nützlich Bergbüchlein* (Practical mining booklet), published anonymously, is of another order entirely. Beginning in 1496 and before the arrival of wealth from the New World, a series of rich strikes of silver in the ancient mining districts centering on the Erzgebirge (ore mountains) transformed the economy of all Europe. Ulrich Rülein von Calw, a physician, was sent to lay out new towns for the miners, first at Annaberg, and again in 1521 at Marienbad. He wrote the *Bergüchlein* around 1500 in vernacular German. It was in the form of a didactic dialogue based, he said, not only on the literature but also on the experience of practicing miners. The *Bergbüchlein* connected the origin of ore deposits with their mineralogy and structure and astrological orientation—all in twenty-four leaves. Citing Hermes (Trismegistus) and the thirteenth-century scholastic Albertus Magnus (c. 1200–1280), Rülein wrote that minerals originate in a birth and growth process brought about by the influence of the seven planets acting upon the earth's "moisture" and "exudations"—essentially an Aristotelian explanation incorporated into alchemical and Hermetic texts centuries before.

In defining the miner's terminology for the structures and the mineral associations of the ore deposits they worked, Rülein was summarizing the mining geology that had developed during the Middle Ages, for the ancients had no more idea of the structure or continuity of mineral assemblages than had their Stone Age predecessors.

The *Bergbüchlein* was followed in 1530 by Georgius Agricola's didactic dialogue on minerals, the *Bermannus,* and in 1540 by *De la pirotechnia* (On the technic of fire), by Vannoccio Biringuccio (1480–

c. 1539). Biringuccio arranged minerals in the order of their value, that is, gold came first. He described their physical properties, including appearance, taste, weight, texture, hardness, and cleavage, and he described six species by the geometry of their crystal forms. His own experience as a smelter of metals out of ores and as a producer of salts from brines left him skeptical of Aristotelian-astrological ideas of the generation of minerals. With Agricola, he scorned the use of the divining rod and dismissed the mystical paraphernalia of Kabbalists, alchemists, and Hermetists alike. Nevertheless, he drew from the Hermetists a Renaissance confidence in the power of the intellect, writing of men with knowledge of "all natural things that have been and are understandable in the world—descending to the center of the earth and ascending to . . . the heavens . . . ," a paraphrase of the characterization of man as miracle in a famous passage on the powers of man from the Hermetic treatise, the *Aesclepius* (chapter 3).

Agricola in *De natura fossilium* (On the Nature of Minerals, 1546) systematically divided minerals (then called "fossils") into classes, describing genera and individual species by their observable properties and recognizing what we currently call fossils as a separate genus, common stones with the same characteristics (*figured* stones in English). *Glossopetra,* he wrote, resembles the human tongue and takes its name from the resemblance. Some such stones, the ancients thought, were of marine origin, and some, called *cerauniae,* had fallen from the sky—an opinion of the ignorant, Agricola wrote.

In 1492, a three-hundred-pound meteorite had fallen from a spectacular fireball at Ensisheim in Alsace. Albrecht Dürer probably witnessed the fireball, for he painted it and later engraved it in *Melencolia I* (see the illustration in the Dürer entry in volume 2), along with a truncated rhombohedron (perhaps of Elba hematite). But specimens of the meteorite bore no resemblance to the miscellaneous figured stones called *cerauniae.* The enigmatic geometric block (a truncated rhombohedron), exemplifying the symmetry of crystals such as hematite from the mines of Elba, reflects Dürer's preoccupation with natural geometry and harmony—a prerequisite of crystallography.

Biringuccio (1540) and Agricola (1546) used the same phrasing in likening the networks of veins carrying blood through the animal body to the similar networks of veins carrying water through the earth. Agricola wrote that water could contain *succi lapidescens*—petrifying juices. Minerals grow from the *succi* under the influence not of Rülein's astrological influences but of heat or cold. Veins are the channels for the distribution of ground water originating from rain, rivers, and ponds, as well as the sea, and from a halitus (breath) formed by subterranean heat, the ultimate cause of earthquakes. The heat in turn was generated by the burning of bitumen (combustibles, including coal). Other scholars, such as the mathematician-physician Girolamo Cardano (1501–1576), attributed subterranean heat and violence to explosive mixtures of niter and sulfur with bitumen—a recipe for gunpowder.

Paleontology. In 1547 Cardano published *De subtilitate* (On subtlety), a Hermetic natural philosophy of encyclopedic scope, alternating naturalistic with animistic and astrological explanation. Using reasoning suggestively similar to Leonardo's, Cardano demonstrated the organic and marine origin of some species of *fossilia* and dismissed the possibility of their emplacement in mountains by the agency of the biblical deluge.

Conrad Gesner (1516–1565), city physician of Zurich, published *De omni rerum fossilium* in 1566. Gesner classified the fossils according to their shapes, as he conceived them to fit the Hermetic hierarchy of heavens to earth—an arrangement that separated out the two lowest classes of stones resembling marine and terrestrial animals. It was a first step toward the modern distinction of fossils as organic remains. Gesner described the properties of his specimens with care and employed artists to illustrate their shapes. His friend Johann Kentmann (1516–1574), city physician at Dresden, had assembled the first cataloged collection of minerals, and this catalog, with its classification derived from Agricola's, was published together with Gesner's work. With both the first illustrated identifications of fossils and Kentmann's catalog, *De omni rerum fossilium,* was as useful to the mineralogist as the *Kreutterbücher* were to the botanist.

The organic origin of many fossils was not doubted in the Paris circles of learned Huguenots and courtiers frequented by the royal potter Bernard Palissy (1510–1590) when he published *Discours admirables* (Admirable discourses; 1580). Palissy recognized the similarity between petrified shells in mountain strata and living species, even recognizing that some were extinct and noting their similarities. He planned to publish illustrations, but that honor fell to the naturalist Fabio Colonna (1567–1650) who, in 1616, was the first to illustrate fossils together with similar modern species and so to anticipate the biological classification of fossils.

Crystallography. The geometric forms of crystal were noted by the ancients. Biringuccio, Gesner, and Palissy, among others, described crystals geometrically. It remained for Johannes Kepler (1571–1630) in *The Six-cornered Snowflake* (1609) to match the striking symmetry of the snowflake to the hexagonal "closest pack . . . in three dimensions" of uniform pellets. Unable to conceive of a cause of the packing for the snowflake, however, he abandoned material necessity in favor of a Hermetic formative urge in the earth—a force, he wrote, learned in geometry.

The humanist doctors, artists, craftsmen, and engineer-architects, emboldened by their practical achievements, turned their attention to the gap between the Greco-Latin literature and the evidence of their own experience. From the chaos of classical literature, scholastic and Arabic glosses, kabbalism, alchemy, biblicism, and Hermetism, they drew the conviction of a natural world of patterned relationships, and they turned to their own daily practical experience to rewrite these texts. They described geologic structures and processes, erosion, sedimentation, and other phenomena; proposed rational explanations for the origins of minerals, for earthquakes, for volcanoes, for floods; solved the problem of the hydrologic cycle, for example, Palissy in 1560 and Pierre Perrault (1611?–1680) in his *De L'origine des fontaines* (1674); initiated systematic mineralogy; began the application of geometry to minerals; and separated the remains of once living creatures from other minerals. With the recognition of a continuum between living species and petrified shells, they enabled a new science of ancient life and laid the first bricks in what would become the geologic column and the concept of geological time.

See also **Mining and Metallurgy** *and biographies of Agricola and Cardano.*

BIBLIOGRAPHY

Primary Works

Agricola, Georgius. *De natura fossilium.* Ed. and trans. Bandy, M. C., and J. A. Bandy. *Special Paper No. 63.* Boulder, 1955. With comparative notes from Agricola's *Bermannus,* 1530.

Agricola, Georgius. *De re metallica.* Translated by Herbert Clark Hoover and Lou Henry Hoover. 1912. Repr., New York, 1950. Critical translation and study by the future U.S. president and first lady; includes extensive translations from Agricola's *Bermannus,* 1530, *De ortu et causis subterraneorum* (On underground origins and causes), 1546, and others, including the *Bergbüchlein* of Rülein von Calw.

Bergwerk und Probierbüchlein. A Translation from the German of the *Bergbüchlein* by Anneliese G. Sisco; and of the *Probierbüchlein,* a sixteenth-century work on assaying, by Anneliese G. Sisco and Cyril Stanley Smith. New York, 1949.

Technical, historical, and bibliographic study of the first modern work in earth science; profusely illustrated.

Biringuccio, Vannoccio. *The Pirotechnia of Vannoccio Biringuccio: The Classic Sixteenth-century Treatise on Metals and Metallurgy.* Translated and with an introduction by Cyril Stanley Smith and Martha Teach Gnudi. New York, 1990.

Kepler, Johannes. *The Six-Cornered Snowflake.* Ed. and trans. Colin Hardie, with essays by L. L. Whyte and B. F. J. Mason. Oxford, 1966.

Palissy, Bernard. *The Admirable Discourses.* Translated and edited by Aurèle La Rocque. Urbana, Ill., 1957.

Perrault, Pierre. *On the Origin of Springs.* Translated by Aurèle La Rocque. New York, 1967.

Pieper, W. *Ulrich Rülein von Calw und sein Bergbüchlein.* Berlin, 1955. Facsimile of the *Bergbüchlein* with translation to Neudeutsch; biographical, historical, and technical analysis with bibliography.

Secondary Works

Adams, Frank Dawson. *The Birth and Development of the Geological Sciences.* New York, 1954. Standard reference for history of geology from classical times to first publication in 1938.

Ellenberger, François. *History of Geology: From Ancient Times to the First Half of the Seventeenth Century.* Oxford and New Delhi, 1996. Translation of *Histoire de la geologie,* vol. 1.

La Rocque. Aurèle. "Bernard Palisy." In *Toward a History of Geology.* Edited by Cecil J. Schneer, 226–241. Cambridge, U.K., 1969.

Marvin, Ursula. "The Meteorite of Ensisheim: 1492 to 1992." *Meteoritics* 27 no. 1 (1992): 28–72.

Rudwick, M. J. S. *The Meaning of Fossils: Episodes in the History of Paleontology.* New York, 1972.

Schneer, Cecil J. "Origins of Mineralogy: The Age of Agricola." *European Journal of Mineralogy* 7 (1995): 721–734.

Yates, Frances A. *Giordano Bruno and the Hermetic Tradition.* Chicago, 1964. The authoritative reference on Renaissance Hermetism.

CECIL J. SCHNEER

GEORGE OF TREBIZOND

GEORGE OF TREBIZOND (1396–c. 1473), Greek émigré and humanist. Despite his English name, George was born in Crete into a family that had emigrated several generations earlier from Trebizond. His surname (Trapezountios in Greek, Trapezuntius in Latin) served him as a family name, not as an indication of his city of birth.

George arrived in Italy from Crete in 1416 as a Greek scribe. Under the tutelage of the famous teacher Vittorino da Feltre, who was then living in Venice, George made extraordinary progress in Latin. By 1420 he was appointed public teacher of Latin in nearby Vicenza and by 1426 he had converted from Greek Orthodoxy to Roman Catholicism. Forced out of Vicenza in 1427, he opened a school in Venice (1428–1436). In 1434 he published his first major work, *Rhetoricum libri V.* While teaching at the University of Florence (1438–1439, 1440–1442) he published his *Isagoge dialectica* (Introduction to logic). Together these two works made him one of the most influential humanists of the Renaissance. *Rhetoricum* innovatively combined Latin and Byzantine rhetoric in the analysis of Cicero and other Latin authors and remained a classic of Renaissance rhetoric into the middle of the sixteenth century. *Isagoge* was a short course in logic for orators. It became a best-seller in the sixteenth century when adopted in the schools of northern Europe as the manual in "judgment" for the widely embraced two-part logic (discovery and judgment) developed by the Dutch humanist Rudolf Agricola.

In Florence, George joined the papal court, which had come to the city for the council of union with the Greeks (Council of Ferrara-Florence). Initially only a scribe, he became a papal secretary in 1444 after the Curia had returned to Rome. Because of the needs and interests of the papal court, he also began a new career as a translator, first for various personages in the Curia, and then, with the accession of Nicholas V in 1447, for the pope himself. In this capacity George produced a stunning series of translations of Greek patristic and secular authors: Basil the Great, Gregory of Nazianzus, Gregory of Nyssa, Cyril of Alexandria, John Chrysostom, and Eusebius of Caesarea among the Fathers; Demosthenes, Ptolemy, Plato, and, most importantly, Aristotle, among the pagan authors. Some of his translations remained standard into the second half of the sixteenth century, making him one of the most important transmitters of Greek literature to the Renaissance.

A quarrel with the pope drove George to the court of King Alfonso of Naples in 1452. Only with Nicholas V's death in 1455 could he return to Rome and resume his position as papal secretary. He remained in Rome for the rest of life, save for two notable trips. One was to Venice in 1460–1462 to assume the chair in rhetoric at the public school of the Rialto, which he lost for obscure reasons. The years 1465 to 1466 he spent in Constantinople, where, compelled by a grand apocalyptic vision, he tried to convert Mehmed II, the conqueror of Constantinople, to Christianity. He failed, and upon returning to Rome spent a few months in jail under suspicion of treason.

The last major preoccupation of George's life was the Plato-Aristotle controversy. George was a great admirer of Aristotle and Latin Aristotelianism. Beginning with his *Protectio Aristotelis problematum* (Protection of Aristotle's "Problems") of 1456, he accused the circle of humanists around the Greek Platonist Cardinal Bessarion of subverting Latin Aristotelianism and theology. By January 1458 he published his major work in the controversy, *Comparatio philo-*

sophorum Platonis et Aristotelis (Comparison of the philosophers Plato and Aristotle), which was a Christianizing interpretation of Aristotle, a condemnation of Plato, and a warning against the pagan message of the contemporary Neoplatonic philosopher George Gemistus Pletho and the apocalyptic possibilities of a Platonist (such as Cardinal Bessarion) ascending the papal throne. In response, Cardinal Bessarion wrote his famous *Against the Calumniator of Plato.*

Most influential in the Renaissance as a cutting-edge teacher of rhetoric and humanist logic and as a translator of many Greek authors into Latin, George of Trebizond has remained best known as a passionate critic of early Renaissance Platonism.

See also **Greek Émigrés** *and biographies of Bessarion and George Gemistus Pletho.*

BIBLIOGRAPHY

Primary Work

Monfasani, John, ed. *Collectanea Trapezuntiana: Texts, Documents, and Bibliographies of George of Trebizond.* Binghamton, N.Y., 1984.

Secondary Work

Monfasani, John. *George of Trebizond: A Biography and a Study of His Rhetoric and Logic.* Leiden, Netherlands, 1976.

JOHN MONFASANI

GERMAN LITERATURE AND LANGUAGE.

German literature during the Renaissance was bilingual. Next to a substantial body of neo-Latin literature created by such brilliant humanists as Conrad Celtis, Desiderius Erasmus, Ulrich von Hutten, Johann Reuchlin, Willibald Pirckheimer, and numerous others, a multifaceted and rich literature in the vernacular was written. This article deals only with that vernacular literature and with the German language.

German Language.
What linguists now call Early New High German (ENHG; German: *Frühneuhochdeutsch*), the language spoken and written between around 1350 and 1650, was not a standardized language, but rather consisted of numerous regional dialects. The spelling was haphazard, the differences in morphology and phonology between the various dialects significant. Although a number of supraterritorial varieties of written German emerged gradually in the course of the sixteenth century, it was not until the end of the seventeenth century that a generally accepted written language developed. Three factors contributed to this gradual process of standardization: the influence of the language of the imperial and territorial chanceries, the invention of printing, and the translation of the Bible by Martin Luther.

The shift from Latin, the language in which most documents had been written during the Middle Ages, to German was gradual, occurring around the middle of the thirteenth century, and was in subsequent centuries especially promoted by the imperial and territorial chanceries. Of special importance was the chancery of the emperor Charles IV (reigned 1346–1378) in Prague, whose chancellor, Johann von Neumarkt (c. 1315/20–1380), not only created for the international correspondence a Latin modeled on the language of the early Italian humanists, but also developed a German characterized by flexibility, elegance, and rhetorical flourishes. Essentially a compromise of Upper German and East Middle German, it was in this language that one of the classics of early modern literature, *Der Ackermann aus Böhmen* (The plowman of Bohemia; c. 1400) by Johannes von Tepl, was written. The gradual move toward a standard German continued to be promoted by the imperial chanceries of the Habsburgs in Vienna under the emperors Frederick III (reigned 1440–1493) and Maximilian I (reigned 1493–1519). Because of the prestige of the chancelleries, the so-called *Gemeine Deutsch,* an essentially Upper German dialect, came to serve as the standard language of Austria and southern Germany. Later, the chancery of the electorate of Saxony during the coregency of Ernst and Albrecht (reigned 1464–1486) and Ernst's eldest son, Frederick the Wise (reigned 1486–1525), which used the regional East Middle German dialect, became increasingly important, especially since Martin Luther used the same dialect in his works.

A second powerful factor in the development of German was the invention of printing with movable metal types by Johann Gutenberg around 1445. This media revolution was to have far-reaching implications in many areas, including the development of German as a standardized language. The relative importance of the new print medium for the creation of a more standardized German is still debated, with some scholars claiming that printers served only regional markets, and others that printers aimed at a compromise between the regional dialects and a language free from explicitly dialectal features to ensure maximum distribution of the books. But it is obvious that printing played some role in the creation of a German *Schriftsprache* (written language), although printers did not create one standardized language but rather several distinctive *Druckersprachen* (printers' languages).

The third and probably most important factor in the creation of a German *Hochsprache* (standard language) was Martin Luther's translation of the Bible into German (New Testament, 1522; full Bible, 1534) and its subsequent wide distribution in German-speaking lands. It is estimated that up to his death in 1546, over three hundred editions with half a million copies of the German Bible appeared, an enormous number given the relatively low literacy rate at that time. Luther was not the first to translate the Bible into German, but the influence of the some twenty pre-Luther translations was small, not only because of their high price but also because of the obsolete language they employed. They were essentially meant only as an aid to understanding the Latin Vulgate, the only version acceptable to the church. That Luther, on the other hand, created a translation readable and comprehensible to the "common man and woman" was a consequence of two key theological concepts: the belief that the word of God (as revealed in the Holy Scriptures) was the only authoritative source of religious truth, and the notion of the "priesthood of all believers," which meant that the Bible had to be accessible to all.

Luther was not the creator of the modern German language, as has often been claimed, but through his translation he contributed significantly to the development and refinement of German as a literary tool. He created a language that was idiomatic, colorful, and earthy. With an ear for rhythmic balances and a gift for the telling phrase, using an abundance of images and phrases from everyday life, Luther forged a new idiom that had an enormous influence on German literary language from Friedrich Gottlieb Klopstock, Gotthold Ephraim Lessing, and Johann Wolfgang von Goethe to Friedrich Nietzsche, Thomas Mann, and Bertolt Brecht. Since his ENHG was based on the East Middle German dialect of the Saxon chancery in Meissen, it was this variety that had a great influence on the rise of the German *Hochsprache*.

Any survey of the emergence of a standard German must include the so-called *Sprachgesellschaften* (linguistic societies) of the seventeenth century. Modeled on the Florentine Accademia della Crusca and meant to stem the rampant use of French, the first and most important of those societies was the Fruchtbringende Gesellschaft (Fruit-bearing society), founded in 1617 by Duke Ludwig of Anhalt-Köthen. Because its aim was the purification and preservation of the German language, numerous "foreign words" were replaced by newly coined German words, many of which are still in use today.

While the influence of the *Sprachgesellschaften* on the courts, chanceries, and polite society was minimal, they had a lasting effect on the creation of a literary language, so that toward the end of the seventeenth century a more or less standardized language was adopted throughout the German lands. It was limited, however, to the educated classes. Those with less formal education continued to speak, as they still do, a German marked by local and regional dialectal features.

Literary Genres. Broadly speaking, three factors shaped the character of the German vernacular literature of the Renaissance: the emergence of a self-confident urban middle class with its own ideology and need for entertainment and guidance (which explains the didactic nature of much of sixteenth-century literature); the invention of printing, which, together with a gradual rise in the literacy rate, created new markets for reading material; and, most important, the Reformation, which touched all aspects of life after 1520, when Martin Luther, with a number of provocative treatises, challenged the authority of the church.

Pamphlet literature. Evidence of the importance of the new medium of print is the sheer number of pamphlets (*Flugschriften*) that flooded the German market in the wake of the Lutheran Reformation. It is estimated that between 1518 and 1526 three to five thousand of these works appeared. Drawing on a variety of literary genres or subgenres, these pamphlets could be couched in the forms of public letters, sermons, chronicles, satires, parodies, songs, dialogues, or fables. Often illustrated by a woodcut, they attempted to mobilize average citizens for or against the new ideas. For that reason the vast majority were written in the vernacular, which in itself was revolutionary since matters of faith had traditionally been debated in Latin, the language of the theologians.

By 1521 German had become the language of public discourse, and even humanists like Ulrich von Hutten (1488–1523) switched to the vernacular in their works. In 1521, for instance, Hutten published four antipapal dialogues which he had translated from Latin into German under the title *Gesprächbüchlein* (Book of conversations). Inspired by Hutten, who himself had modeled his dialogues on the Greek author Lucian, other writers adopted this genre, among them the cobbler-poet Hans Sachs (1494–1576). In four dialogues, published in 1524, Sachs lent support to the Lutheran Reformation. His seven-hundred-line allegorical poem, *Die Wittem-*

bergisch Nachtigall (The Wittenberg nightingale; 1523), in which he celebrated Luther as a nightingale and denounced Pope Leo X as the lion, became a huge success and made its author famous overnight.

Other known authors—most of the pamphlets were published anonymously—were Johann Eberlin von Günzburg (c. 1465–c. 1530), who in his *Fünfzehn Bundesgenossen* (Fifteen confederates; 1521–1523) eloquently advocated reforms, and Martin Bucer (1491–1551), who created the figure of the peasant in the dialogue in his popular *Neu Karsthans* (1521). Towering above all Protestant authors was Martin Luther. It is estimated that between 1516 and 1546 over three million copies of his works were sold, not including the various editions of the Bible. Catholics were slow to respond to the Protestant challenge and realize the potential of the new medium. For every Catholic treatise there were four Protestant ones. The only Catholic polemicist of note writing in German was Thomas Murner (1475–1537), the prolific Franciscan from Alsace.

Lyric poetry. Given the centrality of the Reformation in sixteenth-century Germany, it is not surprising that two of the most important developments in lyric poetry, the church hymn (*Kirchenlied* or *Choral* in German, never *Hymne*) and *Meistersang* (also *Meistergesang*), were placed in the service of the new reformatory ideas. Advocating the "priesthood of all believers," Luther assigned a central place in the worship to the communally sung hymns. While the radical reformer Thomas Müntzer (1490–1525) must be credited with having first introduced the vernacular hymn into the service, Luther is considered the actual founder of the evangelical hymn. Of the approximately forty hymns bearing his name, some are translations, others adaptations of folk songs or versifications of Psalms, and some are original compositions, like the well-known "Ein feste Burg ist unser Gott" (A mighty fortress is our God), the "Marseillaise of the Reformation," as Heinrich Heine called it. Luther was followed by a host of other authors and composers who wrote church songs that up to this day are part of the Protestant hymnals.

Largely forgotten, on the other hand, are the thousands of *Meisterlieder* (songs of the Meistersinger), which were written, composed, and performed by the Meistersinger (master singers). Were it not for Richard Wagner's opera *Die Meistersinger von Nürnberg* (1868), the *Meistersang* would be only a footnote in German literary history. Representing an urban lay culture and flourishing since the middle of the fifteenth century in numerous cities in southern Germany, the Meistersinger were usually artisans who met regularly (usually after the Sunday service) to perform their works. Their songs, sung solo and unaccompanied, were judged not according to their originality but according to their adherence to the strict rules laid down in tabulature. Whereas the *Freisingen* (free singing) allowed a great variety of topics, the *Hauptsingen* (main singing) was restricted to religious themes. With the advent of the Reformation, the Meistersinger focused on the dissemination of Luther's teachings on the basis of the Reformer's Bible translation, thus becoming important mediators of the reformatory ideas in their circles. Nürnberg became the center of the Meistersinger art, thanks largely to the genius of Hans Sachs, their undisputed leader for half a century, who contributed more than four thousand songs to the huge repertoire of the *Meistersang*.

Drama. Drama in sixteenth-century Germany can be divided into the German *Fastnachtspiele* (Shrovetide or carnival plays) and plays that were modeled on Latin humanist drama. There were no professional actors or theaters in Germany at the time. Plays were performed in schools, universities, and, in the case of the carnival plays, in inns, public squares, and private houses.

The *Fastnachtspiele* were linked to the pre-Lenten carnival. Before the most serious season of the year, Lent, the church allowed its believers to indulge in boisterous activities, to break taboos, to vent their pent-up anger, and to make fun of the authorities. Two well-known masters of the carnival play in Nürnberg of the fifteenth century were Hans Rosenplüt (c. 1400–c. 1470) and Hans Folz (c. 1450–not later than 1515). But it was the sixteenth century that saw a flowering of that genre, and the acknowledged master became, as in the *Meistersang,* Hans Sachs. Drawing more than his predecessors on literary sources and largely banning obscenities from his plays, Sachs created in his nearly 130 plays a colorful cast of characters and stock types: greedy merchants, simpleminded peasants, jealous and adulterous husbands and wives, cruel tyrants, nosy neighbors, and lecherous priests. Marriage with its large and small deceptions became an inexhaustible topic. Sachs's humor is good-natured, tolerant, forgiving; he laughs at human foibles and follies. Always ending with a pithy and reassuring moral lesson, these plays have retained much of their freshness and humor, and some, like *Der farendt Schuler im Paradeis* (The traveling scholar in paradise; 1550), *Das Narren schneyden* (Fool-ectomy; 1557), and *Der Kremer Korb* (The merchant's basket; 1554), are still performed today.

In contrast to Sachs, who, though a devout Lutheran throughout his life, seldom, if ever, voiced any anti-Catholic sentiments in his carnival plays, the Swiss Niklas Manuel (1484–1530), one of the most colorful figures of the Swiss Reformation, placed his militantly antipapal carnival plays squarely in the service of the Reformation. While *Vom Papst und seiner Priesterschafft* (Of the pope and his priesthood; 1523) portrays a bellicose pope, *Der Ablasskrämer* (The indulgence peddler; 1525), possibly Manuel's most powerful play, describes the violent humiliation the priest Richardus Hinterlist (Richard Deceitful) experiences at the hands of his villagers.

In contrast to the carnival plays, which grew out of the popular tradition, Protestant and later Catholic (Jesuit) drama received its inspiration from humanist drama, which in turn drew on the two Roman playwrights Terence and Plautus. Humanists thus provided German dramatists with models in structure, versification, and subject matter.

Important for the development of Protestant drama was the clear endorsement given by Luther in his treatise "An die Ratssherren aller Stotte teutsches Lands" (To the city councillors of all towns in German lands; 1524), in which he advocated the use of plays in schools to perfect the students' elocution and inculcate exemplary behavior found in the Bible. Although Protestant drama was written in both Latin and the vernacular, it was German that dominated in the biblical drama. Certain biblical stories were favored: the story of Susanna as the paragon of virtue and chastity, and the stories of Judith, Joseph, Cain and Abel, Lazarus, Judas, and the wedding at Cana. The story of the prodigal son, as a demonstration of the key Lutheran doctrine of justification by faith alone, was dramatized by several playwrights, among them Burkhard Waldis (c. 1490–1556) in his low-German *De Parabell vam vorlorn Szohn* (The parable of the prodigal son; 1527). Among the immense number and variety of biblical plays, Paul Rebhun's *Susanna* (1536) deserves to be singled out because of its skillful versification and topical treatment of its theme. While Rebhun (c. 1505–1546) wrote in German, the drama of the Strasbourg school under the leadership of Johannes Sturm (1507–1589) was written exclusively in Latin. As the rector of the Protestant gymnasium, Sturm favored not only Latin but also subjects from Greek and Roman antiquity at the expense of biblical topics. The fact that the plays were performed in Latin did not diminish their popularity with the general public. Records indicate that citizens attended in such large numbers that the performances had to be held in an outdoor courtyard that could accommodate over two thousand people. Jesuit drama, which began in the last decades of the sixteenth century and reached its apogee only after the Thirty Years' War, was a response to Protestant drama and was used as an instrument of confessional propaganda.

With his fifty-eight German tragedies and seventy comedies, Hans Sachs occupies a special position within the large Protestant drama production of the time. With little or no Latin, the Nürnberg cobbler had no firsthand knowledge of ancient or humanist drama. For that reason his plays show nothing of the refinement achieved by humanist drama. But he drew generously on the large stock of topics and themes from ancient, biblical, medieval, and modern literature available in German translation by the middle of the sixteenth century. At a time of insecurity and chaos, his plays were meant to provide moral guidance and convey the values of an urban middle class. They are therefore demonstrations of the paradigmatic behavior of representative types, not psychological explorations of individuals.

Toward the end of the sixteenth century, the German-speaking lands were frequently visited by groups of English players, called *Englische Komödianten*. Performing watered-down versions of English plays in their native language, they had to make up for the disadvantage of the foreign language by resorting to exaggerated gestures, buffoonery, and colorful costumes and music. This more demonstrative acting and the more sophisticated staging techniques represented a welcome infusion to the German theater of the time. The English players had an important influence on the plays of both Duke Heinrich of Brunswick (1564–1613), at whose court they were guests, and Jakob Ayrer (c. 1543–1605), who in his some seventy surviving plays attempted to graft onto the indigenous drama elements of the stagecraft of the English players.

Prose. German prose narrative of the fifteenth and sixteenth centuries received important impulses from abroad. In the fifteenth century two women of noble birth, Elisabeth von Nassau-Saarbrücken (1393–1456) and Eleonore of Austria (1433–1480), translated works from French into German. Of Nassau-Saarbrücken's four translations, *Hug Schapler* (printed in 1500), a rags-to-riches story of a young man of lowly descent who through his valor and virtue ends up marrying the queen of France, proved a great success, possibly because it reflected the bourgeois ideology that personal achievement and not noble birth is the key to success. Eleonore's *Pontus und Sidonie* (published in 1483), also a translation of a French verse romance into German prose, achieved great popularity and was reprinted until the eighteenth century.

In the second half of the fifteenth century a number of early humanists enriched German literature with their translations from Italian and Latin. Niklas von Wyle (c. 1410–1478), in his *Translatzen oder Tütschungen* (Translations or "Germanizations"; published 1478), introduced the German reading public to what we now would call the avant-garde literature of his time: Poggio Braccidini, Enea Silvio Piccolomini, Petrarch, Leonardo Bruni, and Giovanni Boccaccio. Wyle offered samples from a variety of literary genres, including model letters, dialogues, table talks, orations, treatises, and novellas. Albrecht von Eyb (1420–1475), a Bamberg canon who had spent more than ten years in Italy, composed a number of Latin works but was also the first to translate Plautus into German prose, a translation that was admired for centuries for its skillful and idiomatic German. Heinrich Steinhöwel (1412–1482) finally familiarized German readers with Boccaccio's *De claris mulieribus* in his *Von den synnrychen erluchten Wyben* (Of illustrious women; 1473) and introduced a collection of fables under the name of *Esopus*. All these translations took German literature out of its provincialism and gave it an infusion of fresh ideas, not only opening up an abundance of new themes, stories, and motifs but also contributing substantially to the formation of a German literary prose.

Popular with the reading public were the *Schwänke,* short humorous narratives in prose or verse. They were often published in collections, such as *Schimpf und Ernst* (Humor and seriousness; 1522) by the Franciscan Johannes Pauli or *Rollwagenbüchlein* (Carriage booklet; 1555) by the Alsatian Jörg Wickram (c. 1505–1561), a compilation of amusing stories meant for the entertainment of travelers. The immensely popular *Till Eulenspiegel* (1515), probably by the Brunswick tax and customs secretary Hermann Bote (c. 1460–c. 1520), also drew on the tradition of the medieval *Schwänke*. In ninety-six episodes the author follows the exploits of his main figure, who constantly outwits his victims. In the rich tradition of the *Schwankliteratur,* the *Lalebuch* (1597) tells the story of the citizens of Lalenburg, who in order to hide their wisdom pretend to be foolish and engage in all sorts of absurd activities, like constructing a building without windows or making a sausage too long to be cooked. In the end they burn down their village and disperse all over the world.

Jörg Wickram is usually credited with being the founder of the German novel in the sense that he wrote extensive prose narratives that, rather than consisting merely of a series of adventures revolving around one protagonist, had a plot and some psychological development of the main figure. *Der jungen Knaben Spiegel* (Manual for young boys; 1555) contrasts the poor farmer's son who becomes a virtuous young man with the son of a knight who resorts to drinking, gambling, and stealing, although in the tradition of the prodigal son he is forgiven in the end. A similar theme is sounded in *Der Goldtfaden* (The golden thread; 1557), in which the son of a shepherd rises to nobility through his own achievement and behavior. The most ambitious though least popular of Wickram's novels, *Von guten und bösen Nachbarn* (Of good and bad neighbors; 1556), follows the fortunes of a merchant family and their friends through three generations. Like his contemporary Hans Sachs, Wickram clearly articulated the ideology of the urban middle class: valued are hard work, obedience to parents, marriage, family, parsimoniousness, and good neighborliness; denounced are bad company, quarreling, and laziness.

The book that was to exert a worldwide influence, however, was the *Historia von D. Johann Fausten.* Published anonymously in 1587 by the Frankfurt printer Johann Spies, it was immediately translated into major European languages, and it formed the basis of narratives, plays, and operas by writers ranging from Christopher Marlowe to Lessing, Goethe, Charles Gounod, and Thomas Mann. In this *Volksbuch* (chapbook) Faust turns from theology to magic, makes a pact with the devil for a term of twenty-four years—during which time he lives richly and adventurously—and at the expiration of that time is carried off to hell. Originally meant as a cautionary tale against overweening pride and intellectual curiosity, the story of Faust has become, especially in its subsequent literary metamorphoses, a symbolic tale of humankind's insatiable but dangerous striving for knowledge.

See also biographies of figures mentioned in this entry.

BIBLIOGRAPHY

Burger, Heinz Otto. *Renaissance, Humanismus, Reformation: Deutsche Literatur im europäischen Kontext.* Bad Homburg and Berlin, Germany; and Zurich, Switzerland; 1969. Very readable story of German literature.

Edwards, Mark U., Jr. "Statistics on Sixteenth-Century Printing." In *The Process of Change in Early Modern Europe: Essays in Honor of Miriam Usher Chrisman*. Edited by Phillip N. Bebb and Sherrin Marshall. Athens, Ohio, 1988. Pages 149–163.

Füssel, Stephan, ed. *Deutsche Dichter der frühen Neuzeit (1450–1600): Ihr Leben und Werk*. Berlin, 1993. Thirty-six essays by different scholars on authors from the early modern period.

Hardin, James, and Max Reinhart. *German Writers of the Renaissance and Reformation, 1280–1580*. Dictionary of Literary Biography, vol. 179. Detroit, 1997. Forty biographical articles on individual authors with excellent primary and secondary literature. Best work in English.

Heger, Hedwig, ed. *Spätmittelalter, Humanismus, Reformation: Texte und Zeugnisse*. 2 vols. Munich, 1975–1978. Collection of primary texts with notes and translations of the Latin texts.

Könneker, Barbara. *Die deutsche Literatur der Reformationszeit*. Munich, 1975.

Michael, Wolfgang F. *Das deutsche Drama der Reformationszeit*. Bern, Switzerland, and New York, 1984. Very thorough survey of the drama of the Reformation.

Pascal, Roy. *German Literature in the Sixteenth and Seventeenth Centuries: Renaissance, Reformation, Baroque*. 2d ed. Westport, Conn., 1979.

Rupprich, Hans. *Die deutsche Literatur vom späten Mittelalter bis zum Barock*. 2d ed. 2 vols. Munich, 1994. Indispensable handbook of the literature of that time.

Schade, Richard E. *Studies in Early German Comedy: 1500–1650*. Columbia, S.C., 1988.

Schmidt, Wilhelm, ed. *Geschichte der deutschen Sprache*. 7th ed. Stuttgart, Germany, 1996.

Walz, Herbert. *Deutsche Literatur der Reformationszeit: Eine Einführung*. Darmstadt, Germany, 1988.

Watanabe-O'Kelly, Helen, ed. *The Cambridge History of German Literature*. Cambridge, U.K., 1997. See especially the article by Watanabe-O'Kelly "The Early Modern Period," pp. 92–146.

Waterman, John T. *A History of the German Language*. Rev. ed. Seattle, 1976.

Wells, C. J. *German. A Linguistic History to 1945*. Oxford, 1985.

ECKHARD BERNSTEIN

GERMANY. *See* **Holy Roman Empire.**

GERMANY, ART IN. The art of the German-speaking lands of the Holy Roman Empire exhibited remarkable diversity and inventiveness during the Renaissance. The period from 1400 to the late 1500s witnessed the advent of printmaking and book publishing, the rise of painting and sculpture to new levels of expression, and the emergence of artists, like Albrecht Dürer, who earned truly international reputations. More than ever before, art was available and, indeed, affordable. A simple woodcut cost just pennies. The growing mercantile class filled its churches with altarpieces, statues, stained-glass windows, tombs, and epitaphs, while portraits, goldsmith wares, and small collectible objects adorned their homes. Most of the art was religious. In a so-ciety steeped in images, religious art served simultaneously as a devotional aid and a physical embodiment of personal aspirations, both heavenly and earthly. An altarpiece might signal the patron's desire for salvation while reminding contemporaries of one's prominent social or solid financial status. Even the devastating blow of the Protestant Reformation with its iconophobia and iconoclasm provided opportunities for the industrious artist and patron.

In about 1500 Nürnberg cartographer Erhard Etzlaub published a road map of central Europe that provides a view of Germany's decentralized cultural landscape during the Renaissance. Oriented with Rome, the pilgrim's goal, at the top, the map charted the cities, rivers, forests, mountains, other topographic features, and major roads. Dozens of small dots indicate towns, including the Hanseatic cities, such as Lübeck, Hamburg, and Bremen, with their extensive trading ties throughout the Baltic and North Seas. The Rhineland is dominated by Cologne, the empire's largest town and the center of a wealthy archdiocese, and, farther south, by Mainz, Strasbourg, Freiburg im Breisgau, and Basel. Augsburg and Ulm in Swabia plus Nürnberg, Bamberg, and Würzburg in Franconia are each located on major trading routes. The artistic orbits of the painters and sculptors working in most towns were typically local or, at best, regional. Smaller locales looked to their episcopal seats or to nearby market towns for talented masters for important projects. Only a few of the biggest towns were able to sustain a critical concentration of artists who attracted patronage from across the German-speaking lands. Nürnberg, for example, was home to masters such as Albrecht Dürer, sculptor Veit Stoss, the Vischer family of metalworkers, and goldsmith Wenzel Jamnitzer. This decentralization meant that there was never a single German style at any point during these two centuries. Rather one finds a myriad of different manners that are individual, local, or, at best, regional, as in the case of the Danube school of landscape. This pluralism, while sometimes frustrating to define, embodies the wonderful richness of German art.

Cologne. The art of Cologne offers a good barometer for the changes that swept across Germany in the fifteenth century. As an important religious and commercial center, Cologne attracted a sizable community of artists. By 1400 the great age of church building was past, though work continued slowly on the cathedral and a few monasteries. Yet the city was poised to enter its finest era of painting as lay and clerical patrons alike sought to embellish both these monuments and their own residences. Situated on the Rhine River near the Netherlands, Cologne was exposed to a myriad of influences. The Master of St. Veronica, active from about 1400 until the 1420s, melded the naturalistic pathos of Franco-Burgundian art, notably André Beauneveu's, with a soft or lyrical style that had been popular earlier in Bohemia. In his small pictures such as the *Madonna with the Sweet Pea* (c. 1410; Nürnberg, Germanisches National-almuseum) or *St. Veronica* (c. 1410; Munich, Alte Pinakothek), he presents a beautiful young woman. Whether holding the Christ Child or the sudarium, the woman has a sad, introspective expression and a tender gentleness. The intense colors and rhythmic lines of the drapery are set off against the rich golden backgrounds with incised halos. Strongly iconic, these paintings are designed to promote memory and meditation.

This formula enjoyed a long life in Cologne where it was practiced by many masters including Stefan Lochner, originally from Meersburg, who was active between about 1440 and 1450. Lochner's clear understanding of space and the heightened expressiveness of some of his figures demonstrate his general familiarity with early Netherlandish art.

The artistic ties between Cologne and the Low Countries became even stronger after midcentury. Hans Memling (c. 1433–1494) of Seligenstadt probably trained in Cologne before settling in Bruges. Rogier van der Weyden's (c. 1399–1464) compositions as well as his portrait style greatly influenced subsequent generations of Cologne artists including the Master of the Life of the Virgin (fl. c. 1460–after 1480) and the Master of St. Bartholomew (fl. c. 1475–c. 1510), who hailed from Utrecht.

Fifteenth-Century Art. The general trends observed in Cologne can be found elsewhere. In Hamburg the simple, heavyset figures of Master Bertram (fl. 1367–1414/15), with their strong Bohemian influence, were followed by the highly expressive and intensely emotional art of Master Francke (fl. c. 1410–c. 1430). The softer style of the Master of St. Veronica directly affected the paintings of Konrad von Soest (fl. c. 1394–1422) in Minden and has its counterpart in Nürnberg's Master of the Imhoff Altar (c. 1420). Even more than Lochner, though without his inherent grace, south German painters Lukas Moser (fl. c. 1432), Konrad Witz (who worked in Basel from 1434 until about 1445), and the influential painter and sculptor Hans Multscher (fl. c. 1427–1467) in Ulm interjected greater realism into their settings and figures. In his *Altarpiece of St. Peter*

Martin Schongauer. *The Temptation of St. Anthony.* Anthony was an Egyptian hermit of the third and fourth centuries; he was considered the founder of Christian monasticism. Legend relates that he was tempted by the devil in the desert. Engraving; c. 1475. [For another depiction of the temptation of St. Anthony, see the painting by Hieronymus Bosch at the entry on Grotesque.] KUNST-GESCHICHTLICHEN INSTITUT DER PHILIPPS-UNIVERSITÄT MARBURG/BILDARCHIV FOTO MARBURG/ART RESOURCE

(1444), Witz offered a stunning vista of Lake Geneva and the surrounding Alps.

Nikolaus Gerhaert (fl. c. 1460–1473) of Leiden also transmitted Netherlandish, specifically Rogierian, ideas through the sculptures he carved in Trier, Strasbourg, Baden-Baden, Salem, Constance, and, at the end of his career, Vienna. Far more than his predecessors, Gerhaert skillfully brings life to his figures. In his *Epitaph of Conrad von Busnang* (1464; Strasbourg, Cathedral), the life-size canon prays before a vision of the Virgin Mary and Christ Child; his words are inscribed on the floating banderole. Gerhaert stresses Busnang's corpulence and the realism of the fabric of his robe that falls believably over the ledge. Although the actual audience for Gerhaert's carvings was primarily local, his figures were disseminated widely through the engravings of Master E.S. (fl. c. 1440–1467) and, less directly, Martin Schongauer of Colmar (c. 1450–1491), who had his own direct knowledge of the art of Rogier and of Dirk Bouts (c. 1420–1475).

Prints. The Rhineland and southern Germany were the foremost centers for the early printing and book publishing industry. Although woodcuts, especially those intended for printing on fabric, predate 1400, their popularity grew tremendously with the greater availability of paper. Most early examples, like the *Buxheim St. Christopher* (1423), depicted a saint or religious scene often with an accompanying prayer. During the course of the fifteenth century thousands of woodcuts and later engravings, many surviving today in unique impressions, revolutionized art by making it more accessible to a broader public. Artists explored new themes and developed new uses for the medium. Block books, with image and text on the same wood block, were soon supplanted by the illustrated book, with its movable type and flexible placement of scenes, that proliferated from the 1470s in Augsburg, Basel, and Nürnberg. Quickly these books became more ambitious. Michael Wolgemut (1434–1519) and Wilhelm Pleydenwurff (c. 1460–1494) collaborated with author Hartmann Schedel and publisher Anton Koberger to produce the *Weltchronik,* or *Liber chronicarum* (*Nürnberg Chronicle*) in 1493. Its 1,809 woodcuts (using 645 different wood blocks, many full page) depict the history of the world, its leaders, its great cities, and its curiosities.

Master E. S. and especially Martin Schongauer elevated the print to new qualitative levels. Their engravings, with varied descriptive lines, rich shadings, and highly pictorial effects, became increasingly sophisticated, rivaling painting in narrative and aesthetic possibilities. Prints by Schongauer also played a comparatively new role as models for other artists. His compositions may be seen replicated in sculpture, painting, metalwork, ceramics, and furniture, among other media. Israhel van Meckenem of Bocholt (1440/45–1503) exerted considerable influence. Many of the 624 engravings attributed to him are direct copies of prints of Master E. S., Schongauer, or the Master of the Housebook, the talented drypoint artist working in Heidelberg and along the Rhine in the last quarter of the fifteenth century.

Sculpted altarpieces. As the number of new churches grew so did the quantity and the variety of their altarpieces. These ranged from a very simple altar with a single statue or painting to monumental polyptychs combining both media. The most accomplished practitioners were Michael Pacher (fl. 1467–

1498), active in the southern Tyrol, Michel Erhart (fl. 1440/45–after 1522) of Ulm, Veit Stoss (fl. 1477–1533) of Nürnberg, Tilman Riemenschneider (c. 1460–1531) of Würzburg, and Hans Leinberger (fl. 1511–1530) of Landshut.

Dürer and His Contemporaries.
By 1500 Nürnberg and Augsburg emerged as Germany's most dynamic artistic centers. Both sustained sizable communities of painters, sculptors, printmakers, goldsmiths, and other artisans.

Albrecht Dürer. The young Albrecht Dürer (1471–1528), trained by Wolgemut and an admirer of Schongauer, helped bring Nürnberg to its greatest prominence. In 1498 he issued the *Apocalypse,* which was published with text as a book with the assistance of Anton Koberger (1440–1513), his godfather. Dürer's large woodcuts brilliantly captured the power of St. John's words whether illustrating the four horsemen terrorizing the world or the immateriality of an angelic apparition who seems to dissolve into clouds. Never have simple black lines been used so expressively and descriptively. Dürer's graphic skills are also evident in his *Adam and Eve* (1504) and *St. Jerome in His Study* (1514) engravings, one a commentary on ideal human form and the other a remarkable symphony of light. For Dürer, these prints presented the opportunity to disseminate his artistic ideas as well as to demonstrate his dazzling technical prowess. His fascination with the human body, inspired perhaps by his trips to Italy and his indirect knowledge of classical art, would preoccupy him throughout his career. Indeed, he wrote the first German theoretical treatises on art. As a printmaker, painter, designer, and teacher, Dürer broadened the scope of German art.

Germany and Italy. For many, Dürer bridged the arts of Germany and Italy. Into his own highly naturalistic style, he integrated humanistic themes, the spatial and figural studies of Andrea Mantegna (1431–1506), and, briefly, Venetian painting techniques. He translated north Italian art into an idiom more comprehensible to his peers. By 1530 a patron might specify whether he wanted a painting or sculpture done in the German or in the *Welsch* (Italian) manner. The former implied a particularized, late Gothic fashion; the latter meant a loosely classicizing style often with rounded arches, grotesques, and considerable ornamentation.

In Nürnberg, a younger generation of artists, including sculptors Hermann Vischer (1486?–1517) and Peter Vischer the Younger (1487–1528), Peter Flötner (1485–1546), Georg Pencz (c. 1500–1550), and the Beham brothers, Hans Sebald (1500–1550) and Barthel (1502–1540), embraced a more mature Italianate style. Augsburg's Hans Burgkmair (1473–1531) played a critical role in promoting Italian architectural forms and decorative motifs. He copied imperial Roman portrait coins for Konrad Peutinger and illustrated the projects of Conrad Celtes and other humanists. Early in his career Hans Holbein the Younger (1497/98–1543), under the influence of Andrea Mantegna, composed wonderfully inventive painted house facades that blend illusionistic architecture, triumphal arches, processional friezes, and antique figures with a liberal dose of whimsy.

Dürer's contemporaries. The Renaissance in Germany, however, was always far broader than the production of any single artist's career, even as inquisitive a master as Dürer. Although he worked briefly in Dürer's shop in Nürnberg, Hans Baldung Grien (c. 1484–1545) of Strasbourg explored the less rational side of human nature. Matthias Grünewald (Matthias Gothardt; c. 1480–1528), painter of the *Isenheim Altarpiece* (1510–1515; Colmar, France, Musée d'Unterlinden; see the color plates in volume 3), used explosive colors, bold strokes, and expressive poses as he mined a mystical strain that is deeply rooted in German art. Albrecht Altdorfer (c. 1480–1538) of Regensburg specialized in evocative landscapes in which nature more than man holds center stage. Altdorfer also pioneered landscape etchings of the Danube River countryside, a subject that he shared in common with Wolf Huber (1485–1553) of Passau, among others. Lucas Cranach the Elder's (1472–1553) early career, first in Vienna and then in Wittenberg in Saxony, produced evocative Danubesque landscapes, experimental chiaroscuro woodcuts, and conscious efforts to rival Dürer. Cranach's fate was intertwined with those of the electors of Saxony, who made Wittenberg an important university town, and Martin Luther, who shook Europe's religious landscape. For the elector Frederick III the Wise and his successors the artist painted innumerable altarpieces, portraits, and pictures often celebrating the nude female.

Art and the Reformation. As one of Luther's closest friends, Cranach was the Protestant Reformation's first great artist. Polemical anti-Catholic prints and paintings soon yielded to the challenge of shaping a new Lutheran art, one that avoided the potential for idolatry that the Reformers criticized in Catholic art. Cranach created pictures that juxtaposed Mosaic law with the salvific promise of Christ.

Other scenes stressed baptism and communion, two sacraments retained by the Lutherans.

The Reformation wrought drastic changes in German Renaissance art and damaged many careers. Protestant complaints about the idolatrous misuse of art resulted in widespread iconoclasm in many towns in the 1520s and 1530s. Even in Catholic regions, the demand for new altarpieces and other religious images waned dramatically. According to the humanist Desiderius Erasmus (?1466–1536), the arts "froze" in Protestant Basel so the ambitious Hans Holbein the Younger moved to England, where he became one of the Renaissance's most celebrated portraitists.

Since moving was not an option for most artists, many failed to adapt to the changing times. Yet others branched out into portraiture, notably in the form of small medals, or specializations such as landscape; Augustin Hirschvogel (1503–1553) and Hanns Lautensack (c. 1520–1564/66). Hans Daucher (c. 1485–after 1538) and Victor Kayser (before 1516–1552/53) in Augsburg, Peter Vischer the Younger and Peter Flötner in Nürnberg, and Loy Hering (c. 1485–after 1553) in Eichstätt crafted exquisite small-scale reliefs and statuettes for a growing number of patrons who collected art for its aesthetic, not merely religious, merits. Many of these objects were destined for the new residences and city halls that were erected across Germany during this period. Foremost among the palaces are those in Torgau and Heidelberg.

Wenzel Jamnitzer. The goldsmith Wenzel Jamnitzer (1508–1585) of Nürnberg capitalized upon this growing sophistication of the noble and patrician patrons within the Empire. Jamnitzer produced numerous sumptuous writing desks, jewelry boxes, cups, and other figurated precious ware. He also collaborated with sculptor Johann Gregor van der Schardt (?1530/31–after 1581) on a tall, allegorical room fountain for Emperor Maximilian II from 1568 to 1575.

Later Renaissance Art. Following the Peace of Augsburg (1555) and the last session of the Council of Trent (1563), with its official reaffirmation of the use of Catholic religious art, important new projects and buildings were initiated, beginning in the 1580s with the Jesuit church of Saint Michael's in Munich. Albert V, duke of Bavaria, commissioned his court painter, Hans Mielich (1516–1573), and others to produce the monumental *High Altar* (1572) for Ingolstadt's Liebfrauenmünster. Paulus Mair placed his *Mary Altar* (1571) in the Benedictine monastery of Saints Ulrich and Afra in Augsburg.

The decades between about 1540 and 1580 in Germany yielded very few masters of the stature of Dürer or Cranach. Certainly these later artists had far fewer opportunities than their earlier counterparts. Virgil Solis (1514–1562) or Jost Amman (c. 1539–1591), while very competent printmakers, are better known for the quantity of their productions. Foreign artists were often imported for major projects as in the case of the Netherlanders van der Schardt, who was briefly active in Nürnberg, and Alexander Colin (c. 1526–1612), who worked in Heidelberg and Innsbruck. By the late 1570s and 1580s a new and very gifted generation of German artists emerged. Sculptor Hubert Gerhard (?1540/50–?before 1621) and painters Christoph Schwarz (c. 1548–1592) and Hans von Aachen (1552–1615) worked in Augsburg, Landshut, and Munich alongside Friedrich Sustris (c. 1540–1599) and other skilled masters from the Netherlands and Italy. The arts in Germany flourished in the last years of the sixteenth and early seventeenth centuries before renewed religious strife and prolonged war proved to be devastating.

See also Austria; *subentry on* Art in Austria; *and biographies of figures mentioned in this entry.*

BIBLIOGRAPHY

Baxandall, Michael. *The Limewood Sculptors of Renaissance Germany.* New Haven, Conn., 1980.

Budde, Rainer. *Köln und seine Maler, 1300–1500.* Cologne, Germany, 1986.

Christensen, Carl C. *Art and the Reformation in Germany.* Athens, Ohio, 1979.

Gothic and Renaissance Art in Nuremberg, 1300–1550. Exhibition catalog, Nürnberg, Germanisches Nationalmuseum; New York, Metropolitan Museum of Art. New York and Munich, 1986.

Hayward, John F. *Virtuoso Goldsmiths and the Triumph of Mannerism, 1540–1620.* London, 1976.

Hitchcock, Henry-Russell. *German Renaissance Architecture.* Princeton, N.J., 1981.

Koerner, Joseph. *The Moment of Self-Portraiture in German Renaissance Art.* Chicago, 1993.

Landau, David, and Peter Parshall. *The Renaissance Print, 1470–1550.* New Haven, Conn., 1994.

Lehrs, Max. *Late Gothic Engravings of Germany and the Netherlands.* New York, 1969. The plates from Lehrs's *Kritischer Katalog,* with an introduction by A. Hyatt Mayor.

Smith, Jeffrey Chipps. *German Sculpture of the Later Renaissance, c. 1520–1580: Art in an Age of Uncertainty.* Princeton, N.J., 1994.

Smith, Jeffrey Chipps. *Nuremberg, A Renaissance City: 1500–1618.* Austin, Tex., 1983.

Snyder, James. *Northern Renaissance Art.* New York, 1985.

Stange, Alfred. *Deutsche Malerei der Gotik.* 10 vols. Berlin and Munich, 1934–1960.

Welt im Umbruch: Augsburg zwischen Renaissance und Barock. 3 vols. Augsburg, Germany, 1980–81.

JEFFREY CHIPPS SMITH

GHETTO. From the earliest days of the diaspora, Jews chose voluntarily to live close together, reflecting a practice commonly adopted by groups dwelling in foreign lands. Their quarters, often referred to as the Jewish quarter or street, were almost never compulsory or segregated, and they continued to have contacts on all levels with their Christian neighbors. However, the Catholic church looked askance at such relationships, and in 1179 the Third Lateran Council stipulated that Christians should not dwell together with Jews. This vague policy statement had to be translated into legislation by the secular authorities, and only infrequently in the Middle Ages were laws enacted confining Jews to compulsory segregated quarters. Even then, those laws were not always implemented. The few such Jewish quarters then established, such as that of Frankfurt, were never called ghettos, since that term originated in Venice and became associated with the Jews only in the sixteenth century.

The Venetian Ghetto. In the Middle Ages, the Venetian government permitted individual Jews to reside in Venice but never authorized Jews as a group to settle there, except for the brief period from 1382 to 1397. However, it did allow Jewish moneylenders to live on the Venetian mainland, and when they fled to Venice in the face of the invading armies of the League of Cambrai in 1509, the government granted them refuge. But Venetians were bothered by the fact that Jews lived wherever they wished, all over the city. Consequently, in 1516 the Senate enacted a compromise between the new freedom of residence and the previous state of exclusion, requiring all Jews to dwell on the island known as the Ghetto Nuovo (the new ghetto), which was walled up and had only two gates that were locked from sunset to sunrise.

Then in 1541, when visiting Ottoman Jewish merchants complained that they did not have enough room in the ghetto, the government ordered that twenty dwellings located across a small canal be walled up, joined by a footbridge to the Ghetto Nuovo, and assigned to them. This area was already known as the Ghetto Vecchio (the old ghetto), thereby strengthening the association between Jews and the word "ghetto."

Clearly, the word "ghetto" is of Venetian rather than Jewish origin, as is sometimes conjectured. The

Ghetto Vecchio had been the original site of the municipal copper foundry where iron was poured and cast into artillery; it was named from the Italian verb *gettare* (to pour or to cast), while the island across from it, on which waste products had been dumped, became known as "il terreno del ghetto" (the land of the ghetto), and eventually the Ghetto Nuovo.

Ghettos Elsewhere in Italy. The word "ghetto" did not remain confined to the city of Venice. The Counter-Reformation adopted a hostile attitude toward Jews, and in 1555 Pope Paul IV issued his restrictive bull, *Cum nimis absurdum*. Its first paragraph provided that the Jews of the papal states were to live together on a single street, or should it not suffice, then on as many adjacent ones as necessary, with only one entrance and exit. Accordingly, the Jews of Rome were moved into a new compulsory segregated and enclosed quarter, which apparently was first called a ghetto seven years later.

Influenced by the papal example, local Italian authorities established special compulsory quarters for Jews, and they spread to most places where Jews were allowed to live on the Counter-Reformation Italian peninsula. Following Venetian nomenclature, these new residential areas were already called "ghetto" in the legislation which established them, as in Florence in 1571, Siena in 1572, Padua in 1603, Mantua in 1612, Rovigo in 1613, Ferrara in 1624, and Modena in 1638.

Significantly, this new usage of the word "ghetto" for a compulsory Jewish quarter also came to be employed in Venice. In 1630 Jewish merchants there requested that the ghetto be enlarged to house some additional wealthy Jewish merchant families. Three years later, the Senate provided that an area located across the canal from the Ghetto Nuovo be enclosed and joined to it by a footbridge. This area almost immediately was referred to as the Ghetto Nuovissimo (the newest ghetto). Thus, the term "ghetto" had come full circle in its place of origin: from an original specific usage identifying a foundry in Venice, to a generic usage in other cities designating a compulsory, segregated, enclosed Jewish quarter with no relation to a foundry, and then to that generic usage also in Venice. Thus the oft-encountered statement that the first ghetto was established in Venice in 1516 is correct in a technical, linguistic sense but very misleading in a wider context, while to apply the term "ghetto" to an area prior to 1516 would be anachronistic. The most precise formulation is that the compulsory and exclusive separate Jewish quarter received the name "ghetto" as a result of developments in Venice in 1516.

Connotations of the Term. In later years, the Venetian origin of the word "ghetto" came to be forgotten, as it was used exclusively in its secondary meaning as referring to compulsory Jewish quarters, and then in a looser sense to refer to any area densely populated by Jews, even if they had freedom of residence and lived in the same districts and houses as Christians. Eventually, "ghetto" became the general designation for areas densely inhabited by members of minority groups, almost always for socioeconomic reasons, rather than for legal ones as had been the case with the initial Jewish ghetto.

To a great extent because of the negative connotations of the word "ghetto," the nature of Jewish life in the ghetto is often misunderstood. The establishment of ghettos did not lead, as shown strikingly in the autobiography of the Venetian rabbi Leon Modena (1571–1648), to the breaking off of Jewish contacts with the outside world on any level, from the highest to the lowest. Additionally, apart from the question of whether the ghetto succeeded in fulfilling the expectations of those who desired its establishment, from the internal Jewish perspective many evaluations of its alleged negative impact upon the life of Jews and their mentality require substantial revision. In general, the decisive element determining the nature of Jewish life was not so much whether Jews were required to live in a ghetto, but rather the nature of the surrounding environment and whether it constituted an attractive stimulus to Jewish thought and offered a desirable supplement to traditional Jewish genres of intellectual activity.

See also **Anti-Semitism**; **Jews**, *subentries on* **The Jewish Community** *and* **Jews and the Catholic Church**; **Venice**.

BIBLIOGRAPHY

Bonfil, Robert. *Jewish Life in Renaissance Italy*. Berkeley, Calif., 1994.

Calabi, Donatella. "Les quartiers juifs en Italie entre quinzième et dix-septième siècle." *Annales* 52 (1997): 777–797.

Concina, Ennio, Ugo Camerino, and Donatella Calabi. *La città degli Ebrei*. Venice, 1991

Ravid, Benjamin C. I. "From Geographical Realia to Historiographical Symbol: The Odyssey of the Word *Ghetto*." In *Essential Papers on Jewish Culture in Renaissance and Baroque Italy*. Edited by David B. Ruderman. New York, 1992. Pages 373–385.

BENJAMIN C. I. RAVID

GHIBELLINES. *See* **Faction**.

GHIBERTI, LORENZO (1378–1455), sculptor, goldsmith, draftsman, architect, writer, and the most acclaimed bronze caster of early fifteenth-century Florence. Many of the renowned artistic personalities of the age, including Donatello, Paolo Uccello, and Michelozzo di Bartolomeo, assisted him or trained in his busy, well-organized workshop. He was supremely versatile and, throughout his life, worked in a variety of media; in this respect he should be considered one of the greatest universal artists of the early Renaissance.

Early Activity (1400–1425): The North Doors.

In his youth Ghiberti trained as a goldsmith with his stepfather and in 1400 left Florence for Pesaro, where he collaborated with an unknown painter on decorating a room for the Malatesta family. Ghiberti rushed back to Florence in the winter of 1400–1401 so that he could participate in the competition, announced by the Arte di Calimala (guild of cloth dealers and refiners), to design bronze doors for the Baptistery. Seven artists reached the final stage, but only the trial pieces by Ghiberti and Filippo Brunelleschi of the *Sacrifice of Isaac* survive (Florence, Bargello). The young Ghiberti was given the commission, perhaps on the strength of his superior technical abilities in bronze casting, and executed twenty-eight partially gilded bronze reliefs on New Testament themes and saints by 19 April 1424. In the early panels, Ghiberti attempted to balance his compositions with the quatrefoil format (the framing device adopted by Andrea Pisano in the earlier Baptistery doors, the model for Ghiberti's work), and the elegant poses of the figures, spirited drapery forms, and graceful lines of these reliefs are in keeping with contemporary developments in Florentine painting, especially with the art of Gherardo Starnina and Lorenzo Monaco. Ghiberti's style evolved significantly in these years, and the later scenes display a more subtle use of the height of relief. The later figures, furthermore, emerge from the background almost in the round and are characterized by a heightened sense of movement. As time progressed, Ghiberti also took a greater interest in creating depth to the background of his panels, and the later designs appear more sophisticated in perspectival construction.

The Orsanmichele Statues (1413–1429).

In 1413 Ghiberti worked on the bronze statue of *St. John the Baptist* (Florence, Orsanmichele) for the Calimala. It was cast in one piece and testifies to Ghiberti's expertise with bronze. Enhanced by the finely chased details of its smooth surfaces, the figure is characterized by an air of rare elegance. Rich folds of fabric envelop the saint in a series of calligraphic curves, and these lyrical rhythms are a feature of what is sometimes called a late Gothic or International Gothic style. In 1419 the Arte del Cambio (guild of moneychangers) commissioned Ghiberti to execute the bronze statue *Saint Matthew,* completed in 1422 for the guild's niche on the facade of Orsanmichele. Compared to the *Baptist,* the Cambio sculpture exhibits a greater awareness of the structure and movement of the body (in line with developments in the oeuvre of Donatello and Nanni di Banco), and an obvious debt to antique art. The energized drapery forms of the earlier bronze statue are here replaced by calmer, more form-defining folds.

Ghiberti's third bronze statue for Orsanmichele, *Saint Stephen,* was commissioned by the Arte della Lana (wool guild) in 1425 and finished in 1429. The graceful pose, sweet expression, and fluid drapery forms of the statue contrast with the openly classicizing spirit of the earlier *Saint Matthew.*

The Siena Reliefs, the *Gates of Paradise,* and the Saint Zenobius Shrine (1417–1452).

Ghiberti executed fire-gilded bronze reliefs of *John the Baptist before Herod* and the *Baptism* for the font of the Baptistery in Siena by 1427. In these scenes he continued to develop his ideas on the placing of figures in space and on the organization of setting and background.

The pictorial relief of the *Baptism* is developed to the full in Ghiberti's second bronze door, commissioned by the Arte di Calimala for the Florence Baptistery in 1425. [See the color plates in this volume.] The rectangular format of the Siena reliefs is adopted for the scenes of the door, which comprises ten gilded bronze panels on Old Testament subjects. These larger sections present a greater illusion of depth and space and exhibit a wider range of detail in the shallow relief of their backgrounds. The style of the doors, apparently named *Porta del Paradiso* (Gate of Paradise) by Michelangelo, is enriched with classical influences; Ghiberti was also aware of contemporary developments in architecture, especially Brunelleschi's, and linear perspective. The sculptor is also responsible for the lyrical designs of floral ornamentation on the jambs and interior borders.

In 1432, as work progressed on the doors, the wool guild commissioned from him the bronze shrine *Saint Zenobius* for Florence Cathedral. Completed in 1442, the work includes some reliefs that display certain affinities in style and composition with the doors.

Lorenzo Ghiberti. *Jacob and Esau.* Detail from the Baptistery doors, Florence. As in Donatello's panel in the Baptistery of Siena, the perspective recedes from the figures in the
foreground through the arches at the back; the illusion of depth is enhanced by the combination of low and high relief. The panel illustrates the incident in Genesis 27. [For a view of the
entire doors, see the color plates in volume 3.] SUPERSTOCK

Other Activities and Legacy. Ghiberti was
also active as an architect, and he participated in the
planning of Florence Cathedral. From 1406 to 1408
and 1418 to 1436 he advised on the construction of
the dome, but his precise contribution to the final
project is not known. He also provided designs for
the building's stained-glass windows. Another of his
architectural projects is thought to be the facade of
Santa Trinità, Florence (1417–1424).

Around 1447 Ghiberti started writing the three
books of *I commentarii* (Commentaries), which
comprise a survey of the art of antiquity, a history of
the art of "modern times," including his autobiography, and notes on the sciences necessary to a
sculptor. His writing is characterized by a humanistic
belief in the preeminence of the art of antiquity, and
it draws on Vitruvius and Pliny the Elder. The second
book is particularly valuable for its astute observations on painters' styles and its appreciation of Sienese art. Ghiberti's suave figures and elegant drapery
forms, so different in character from Donatello's vigorous style, appealed to the artists of the later fifteenth century, from Benozzo Gozzoli to Andrea del
Verrocchio and Sandro Botticelli. The influence of
Ghiberti's lyrical art endured into the sixteenth century, as aspects of Benvenuto Cellini's work attest.

BIBLIOGRAPHY

Primary Work

Ghiberti, Lorenzo. *I commentarii.* Introduction by Lorenzo Bar-
toli. Florence, 1998.

Secondary Works

Finn, David. *The Florence Baptistery Doors.* New York, 1980.
Krautheimer, Richard. *Ghiberti's Bronze Doors.* Princeton, N.J.,
1971.
Krautheimer, Richard, and Trude Krautheimer-Hess. *Lorenzo
Ghiberti.* 1956. Rep., Princeton, N.J., 1982.

Lorenzo Ghiberti: materia e ragionamenti. Exhibition catalog, Accademia and San Marco Museum, Florence. Florence, 1978.

Lorenzo Ghiberti nel suo tempo: atti del Convegno internazionale di studi di Firenze (1978). 2 vols. Florence, 1980.

Schlosser, Julius von. *Lorenzo Ghiberti's Denkwürdigkeiten (I commentarii).* 2 vols. Berlin, 1912.

FLAVIO BOGGI

GHIRLANDAIO, DOMENICO.   *See* **Florence,** *subentry on* **Art of the Fifteenth Century.**

GIAMBOLOGNA.   *See* **Florence,** *subentry on* **Art of the Sixteenth Century.**

GIANNOTTI, DONATO   (1492–1573), Florentine intellectual committed to republican politics and theory during the decline and fall of the Florentine republic and the birth of the Medici principate. Donato Giannotti grew to manhood in the Florentine republic of 1494–1512, and after the return of the Medici he joined the young men whose discussions of politics, history, and literature centered on the Orti Oricellari (the Rucellai gardens). Most of them were *grandi,* offspring of the politically elite families that faced a historical dilemma from the 1430s to the 1530s between republican government—the form they preferred as long as they could dominate it, but in which they feared the preponderance of their social inferiors—and the principate of one family from among their number, the Medici. After the military defeat and collapse of the last Florentine republic (1527–1530), the majority of them embraced the Medici.

Donato Giannotti, unlike them, could not aspire to a political career in Florence, since no previous members of his family (artisans who had immigrated to the city) had held office, but his humanistic education gave him social and professional mobility. He served the last Florentine republic as secretary to the Dieci, the principal executive committee, then was exiled from Florence as an anti-Medicean. He remained, however, an intellectual in politics and a witness to history in the retinues of two of the most important members of the Roman Curia, Cardinals Niccolò Ridolfi and François de Tournon. His literary works include the dialogue *De' giorni che Dante consumò nel cercare l'inferno e 'l purgatorio* (On the days that Dante consumed in traversing Inferno and Purgatory) and the comedy *Il vecchio amoroso* (The elderly lover).

The political writings of Donato Giannotti are more valuable for his firsthand observations of politics, especially the behavior of the Florentine *grandi,* than they are for his constitutional proposals. The model for his ideal system was the republic of Venice, whose "mixed" constitution he described in *Della repubblica de' Viniziani* (composed c. 1526). His major work on the Florentine republic, *Della repubblica fiorentina* (or *Republica fiorentina*) was composed in the 1530s. The Florentine republics of 1494–1512 and 1527–1530 had both had the rudiments of a mixed constitution: a voting assembly comprising the male members of the politically entitled families; an intermediate council; an array of small interlocking executive committees; and a titular head of state. Since these institutions had failed, Giannotti had to account for their failure and suggest remedies. But there was no way in retrospect to make a clean analytical separation between individual actors and the institutions through which they had acted, and Giannotti's attempts to do so have all the thick texture and inconsistency of real history. He acutely portrayed the destabilizing effects of the ambition of the *grandi,* whom he compared to wolves and whom he blamed for their own ultimate defection. His proposals, in contrast, are purely institutional, a mechanism based on Venice which he believed would satisfy the needs of all groups, absorb conflict, prevent the arbitrary exercise of power, and produce optimal decisions. The utopianism of his political theories parallels the failure in actuality of the Florentine republic, but he was a precursor of the liberalism of later centuries.

BIBLIOGRAPHY

Primary Works

Giannotti, Donato. *Opere politiche. Lettere italiane.* 2 vols. Milan, 1974. With an introduction and very brief historical notes by Furio Diaz.

Giannotti, Donato. *Republica fiorentina: A Critical Edition and Introduction.* Geneva, 1990. A critical edition with text in Italian and an introduction by Giovanni Silvano in English, but with no notes to the text.

Starn, Randolph. *Donato Giannotti and His Epistolae.* Geneva, 1968. An edition with an introduction and detailed notes of previously unpublished correspondence.

Secondary Works

Bisaccia, Giuseppe. *La Repubblica fiorentina di Donato Giannotti.* Florence, 1978.

Viroli, Maurizio. *From Politics to Reason of State: The Acquisition and Transformation of the Language of Politics, 1250–1600.* Cambridge, U.K., and New York, 1992. See pp. 216–231 on Giannotti.

WILLIAM MCCUAIG

GIBBONS, ORLANDO   (1583–1625), English keyboard player and composer. Born into an Oxford musical family that was later active in Cambridge, Gibbons sang as a chorister at King's College, Cambridge (1596–1598), under his brother Edward, master of the choristers; he matriculated as a student at King's in 1599, receiving the bachelor of music degree in 1606. Gibbons joined the gentlemen of the Chapel Royal around 1603, probably as organist; he was coorganist with Edmund Hooper in 1615 and senior organist in 1625. He may have visited Heidelberg in 1613 in the entourage of the newly married Princess Elizabeth of England and Frederick V, elector Palatine (1610–1623), in whose honor *Parthenia* (1613), containing keyboard works by William Byrd, John Bull, and Gibbons, was published. In 1619 Gibbons became keyboard player of the king's privy chamber, a secular appointment unusual for a gentleman of the chapel. He was awarded the doctor of music degree at Oxford in 1622 and became organist of Westminster Abbey the following year. He died suddenly on Whitsunday 1625 at Canterbury, while the Chapel Royal awaited the arrival of Charles I's bride, Henrietta Maria.

Although none of Gibbons's comparatively small corpus of Anglican church music was published during his lifetime, it was among the most popular. His services included a four-voice, largely syllabic "short" service and another in the newer verse idiom, alternating sections for solo voices and organ with the full chorus. Particularly adept in this medium, Gibbons composed more than twice as many verse anthems (nineteen) as anthems for chorus alone (seven or eight). Both the full and verse anthems derive their expressive and dramatic effect from traditional, sixteenth-century imitative contrapuntal procedures rather than more overt contrasts and textual depiction. Gibbons's *First Set of Madrigals and Mottets* (1612) relies less on the lighthearted texts and variegated textures and word painting of the Italianate madrigal, recently in vogue, than on more serious verse, set in the sober, contrapuntal style of the older English part-song or song for voice and viols. Gibbons was the only important Jacobean composer to publish consort music for strings, the *Fantasies of Three Parts* (c. 1620); about thirty more works for three to six viols survive in manuscript. The consort music generally juxtaposes an imitative opening with a flexible succession of textures, note values, occasional meter changes, dance-like passages, and the odd popular tune. Gibbons's solo keyboard music includes several carefully wrought, expansive fantasias (freer works, following no fixed form) and pavannes and galliards (favorite sixteenth-century dance forms) that constitute his most significant contributions to the repertory, as well as shorter and less complicated "masks," almans, and corantos (lighter, early seventeenth-century dances).

BIBLIOGRAPHY

Primary Works

Buck, Percy, Alexander Ramsbotham, et al., eds. *Tudor Church Music.* Vol. 4, *Orlando Gibbons, 1583–1625.* Oxford, 1925.

Fellowes, Edmund, ed. *The English Madrigalists.* Vol. 5: *Orlando Gibbons First Set of Madrigals & Motets (1612).* Revised by Thurston Dart. London, 1964.

Harper, John. *Musica Britannica.* Vol. 48: *Orlando Gibbons: Consort Music.* London, 1982.

Hendrie, Gerald, ed. *Musica Britannica.* Vol. 20: *Orlando Gibbons: Keyboard Music.* London, 1962. 2d rev. ed., 1987.

Wulstan, David, ed. *Early English Church Music.* Vol. 3: *Orlando Gibbons: Verse Anthems.* London, 1964. Vol. 21: *Orlando Gibbons: II Full Anthems, Hymns, and Fragmentary Verse Anthems.* London, 1978.

Secondary Works

Dart, Thurston. "Two English Musicians at Heidelberg in 1613." *Musical Times* 111 (1970): 29–32.

Fellowes, Edmund H. *Orlando Gibbons and His Family: The Last of the Tudor School of Musicians.* 2d ed. Oxford, 1951.

Vining, Paul. "Gibbons and His Patrons." *The Musical Times* 124 (1983): 707–709.

CRAIG A. MONSON

GILBERT, WILLIAM

GILBERT, WILLIAM (1544–1603), English physician, important for his studies in magnetism and electricity. Born in Colchester, Gilbert studied at St. John's College, Cambridge, from which he obtained an M.A. in 1564 and an M.D. in 1569. He practiced medicine in London, where he was consulted by members of the English nobility, becoming physician to Elizabeth I in 1600 or 1601 and, on her death in 1603, to James I. Gilbert was a member of the Royal College of Physicians, to which he bequeathed his laboratory at Wingfield House, with his many books and instruments; but all were destroyed by the Great Fire of 1666.

Gilbert's most important work was his *De magnete, magneticisque corporibus, et de magno magnete tellure* (On the lodestone; magnetic bodies; and the great magnet, the earth; London, 1600). He also composed several essays expanding on the cosmological ideas in that work, which were collected by his half-brother, William Gilbert of Melford, and published under the collective title *De mundo nostro sublunari philosophia nova* (A new philosophy of the sublunar world; Amsterdam, 1651). Both of these works were known to Francis Bacon and Thomas Harriot, and *De magnete* was read carefully by Johannes Kepler and Galileo Galilei.

De Magnete. *De magnete* was an immediate success and a striking example of the new "experimental physics." In effect it was a laboratory manual wherein Gilbert marked his discoveries and experiments for their importance and gave full directions for readers to verify them for themselves.

Gilbert divided his treatment into six books. The first book is introductory in character. In it Gilbert recounted the sources on which the work was based, outlined the properties of the lodestone in a general way, and stated his goal: to explain all magnetic phenomena on the supposition that the earth itself is a giant lodestone.

In the remaining books Gilbert detailed various movements on the earth's surface. For Aristotle there were two, toward and away from the center. Gilbert replaced these with five—coition, direction, variation, declination, and revolution—to each of which he devoted a separate book. "Coition" is the term he preferred to "attraction," possibly to sidestep the problem of action at a distance. He began by differentiating magnetic from electric phenomena, the second of which are caused by substances that behave as amber does when rubbed. These he called *electrica,* thereby introducing the root term "electric" into the English language. Gilbert attributed electric effects to a material cause and magnetic effects to a formal cause—a "primal form" (*forma praecipua*) that generates an orb of virtue around the magnetic substance. For him, magnets approach each other, not because one pulls the other but because there exists in nature a harmonious action whereby they come together.

The next two motions, direction and variation, are seen in the sometimes erratic movements of a compass needle. Gilbert broke down such movements into two components, one a true direction whereby a directive force attempts to align the needle with the earth's north-south axis, the other a force that effects departures or variations from this direction. From experiments with small bars on the surface of an earth-like spherical magnet, which he called a *terrella* ("earthkin"), Gilbert argued that "true direction" is caused by the earth's acting on the compass needle as a large magnet. "Variation" he then attributed to inequalities of mass and magnetic purity among the earth's elevations. These cause departures from the true direction, which are constant at a given place on the earth's surface.

The two final movements are declination and revolution. "Declination" is another term for magnetic dip, already known in Gilbert's time, which he also attributed to the magnetic properties of the earth as

manifested by experiments with the *terrella.* Thinking, incorrectly, that the earth's magnetic pole coincides with its geographic pole, Gilbert planned to use measurements of dip to determine latitude at sea.

"Revolution" is taken up in the last book, wherein Gilbert draws out the cosmological implications of his doctrine. Relying on Petrus Peregrinus's *Epistola . . . de magnete* (Letter on the magnet; 1269), he became convinced that revolution or rotation is a magnetic movement that can be applied to the earth. Gilbert knew of Copernicus's *De revolutionibus orbium coelestium* (1543; *On the revolutions of celestial spheres*) and saw his explanation as consistent with that work. He admitted, however, that "we cannot assign with certainty any natural causes" of other astronomical phenomena.

De Mundo. Gilbert's second work is divided into two sections, "A new natural philosophy, against Aristotle," and "A new meteorology" against Aristotle's similar work. In the first, Gilbert replaced Aristotle's four elements with only one, the earth, which appears both with the magnetic property and without it in various degenerate forms. The moon, for him, is a miniature earth, with seas, continents, and islands. It is within the earth's orb of virtue, and thus there is a mutual attraction between them. The sun is the center for the orbits of the planets and causes their motions through its extensive orb of virtue. The fixed stars are not all equally distant from the earth, and he dismissed the third motion described in Copernicus's *De revolutionibus* as "no motion" at all.

Gilbert's meteorology contains discussions of comets, the Milky Way, clouds, winds, the rainbow, the origin of springs and rivers, and the nature of the sea and tides. These are all inconclusive, being based mainly on speculations of others, interspersed with Gilbert's own ideas.

Undoubtedly, the *De magnete* was the more important of Gilbert's works, and it had two major effects. The first was Gilbert's influence on Kepler, whose search for a "force" whereby the sun moves the earth was aided by Gilbert's speculations and led him to his laws of planetary motion, which in turn were a stepping stone to Newton's discovery of universal gravitation. The other was the stimulus he gave to others to experiment with magnetism and electricity, particularly Jesuit scientists, who made considerable advances in this field throughout the seventeenth century.

BIBLIOGRAPHY

Kelly, Suzanne. "Gilbert, William." In *Dictionary of Scientific Biography.* Vol. 5. New York, 1972. Pages 396–401.

Kelly, Suzanne. *The De mundo of William Gilbert*. Amsterdam, 1965.

Pumfrey, Stephen. "Neo-Aristotelianism and the Magnetic Philosophy." In *New Perspectives on Renaissance Thought*. Edited by John Henry and Sarah Hutton. London, 1990. Pages 177–189.

Roller, Duane H. D. *The De magnete of William Gilbert*. Amsterdam, 1959.

Wallace, William A. "Three Classics of Science." In *The Great Ideas Today: 1974*. Chicago, 1974. Pages 211–272. A guide to reading Gilbert's *De magnete* within a comparative setting provided by Galileo's *Two New Sciences* and William Harvey's *The Motion of the Heart and Blood*.

WILLIAM A. WALLACE

GILES OF VITERBO (1469–1532), Augustinian friar, scholar, reformer, cardinal. Born in Viterbo in central Italy, Giles's family name was Antonini, not Canisius as many historians state. Giles (Egidius, Aegidius) joined the Augustinians at Viterbo in 1488 and served as general of the order during a momentous period of its history, from 1506 to 1518. Appointed cardinal in 1517, he enjoyed the confidence of the popes during the tumultuous events of the early Reformation. While still only a student at Padua, Giles published, in 1493, an edition of three works of Giles of Rome (c. 1247–1316). As a scholar he drew most liberally from Plato, St. Augustine, and the Bible. Held in high regard in Renaissance literary circles, he became an outstanding member of the Academia Pontaniana at Naples. Giovanni Pontano (1426–1503) composed the dialogue *Aegidius* in his honor; Jacopo Sannazaro (1456–1530) based his *De partu Virginis* (1526) on a sermon by Giles. A skilled orator in the polished style of the Renaissance, Giles was perhaps the most sought-after preacher of his day. A memorable oration was his appeal for reform at the opening of the Fifth Lateran Council, 3 May 1512.

In 1503 he joined the observant movement within the Augustinian order and on 27 June 1506, to his own dismay, was appointed vicar-general of the Augustinians by Julius II. Thereafter, his main concern until he resigned from office (25 January 1518) was reform of the order. In 1508 he authorized the first printed edition of the constitutions of the order. He halted growing division between Augustinian observants and conventuals; early in 1511 he even won over the young German friar Martin Luther to the cause of unity. Giles insisted on a return to the full common life and greatly encouraged higher studies. To ensure reform he made personal visitations, demanded monthly reports, and did not hesitate to suspend or dismiss priors and provincials. His efforts were hampered, however, by general laxity in church affairs at the time.

Giles's intellectual versatility was astounding: he wrote Latin and Italian poetry, edited philosophical works, compiled a major theological commentary, attempted a survey of Christian history, and was indefatigable in scriptural studies, particularly Hebrew, the Kabbalah, and rabbinical literature. He defended Johann Reuchlin (1455–1522) and was the generous patron of Elijah Levita (1469–1549), who later became the leading Hebrew scholar of Renaissance Europe. A linguist of rare ability, Giles was even held, at one time, to be the only person in Europe with competent knowledge of Arabic. The first complete printed edition of the Bible in Greek, published at Venice in 1518, was dedicated to Giles. Most of his own works were unpublished; he suffered from intellectual meticulosity.

Giles was papal agent to Emperor Maximilian in 1515, was nominated cardinal in July 1517, and was sent as papal legate to Spain in 1518. He was a serious candidate for the papal tiara in 1521 and was appointed bishop of Viterbo by Clement VII in 1523. The remainder of his life he devoted mainly to scholarship, while making one notable political foray in May 1527, leading an army of two thousand soldiers to free Clement VII, then besieged by imperial troops in the Castel Sant'Angelo in Rome. To the end he continued to be an advocate for reform of the church.

BIBLIOGRAPHY

Primary Works

Egidio da Viterbo. *Giles of Viterbo OSA: Letters as Augustinian General*. Edited by Clare O'Reilly. Rome, 1992.

Egidio da Viterbo. *Lettere familiari*. Edited by Anna Maria Voci Roth. 2 vols. Rome, 1990.

Egidio da Viterbo. *Scechina e libellus de litteris hebraicis*. Edited by François Secret. 2 vols. Rome, 1959.

Secondary Works

Martin, F. X. "Egidio da Viterbo, 1469–1532: Bibliography, 1510–1982." *Biblioteca e società* (Viterbo) 4, nos. 1–2 (1982): 45–52.

Martin, F. X. *Friar, Reformer, and Renaissance Scholar: Life and Work of Giles of Viterbo, 1469–1532*. Edited by John E. Rotelle. Villanova, Pa., 1992.

Meijer, A. de. "Bibliographie historique de l'Ordre de Saint-Augustin." *Augustiniana* 35 (1985): 5–192; 39 (1989): 189–392; 43 (1993): 171–407; 47 (1997): 5–243.

O'Malley, John W. *Giles of Viterbo on Church and Reform: A Study in Renaissance Thought*. Leiden, Netherlands, 1968.

F. X. MARTIN, O.S.A.

GINÉS DE SEPÚLVEDA, JUAN (c. 1490–1573), Spanish humanist. Sepúlveda was born in the province of Córdoba, in southern Spain, to Ginés Sánchez Mellado (also called Ginés de Sepúlveda) and María Ruiz. He studied philosophy at the newly founded University of Alcalá from 1510 to 1513, earning his B.A. in 1512. In 1514 he was at the Colegio de San Antonio in Sigüenza, where he studied theology and probably took religious orders. In 1515 he entered the more prestigious Spanish College of San Clemente in Bologna with a scholarship in theology. He took doctoral degrees in arts and theology there in 1523. It was not as a theologian, however, but as a philosophical and political writer, and above all as a humanist translator and annotator of Greek philosophy, that Sepúlveda earned a reputation as one of the most learned Spaniards of the sixteenth century.

During his two decades in Italy Sepúlveda befriended powerful Italian and Spanish patrons who were indispensable in helping to launch his scholarly career. Among them were Alberto Pio, the prince of Carpi, and Giulio de' Medici (Pope Clement VII), who encouraged Sepúlveda's early Aristotelian studies. In the 1520s he also enjoyed the patronage of Ercole Gonzaga, Cardinal Tommaso de Vio (known as Cajetan), and Cardinal Francisco de Quiñones. In 1529 and 1530 he traveled with the entourage of the emperor Charles V through Italy and Austria. In 1536 Sepúlveda became the emperor's official chronicler and spent the rest of his life in Spain. He also served as royal chaplain, tutor to Prince Philip (later King Philip II), and occasional adviser to the Spanish Inquisition. In 1550–1551 he engaged in a famous polemic with the Dominican friar Bartolomé de Las Casas about the morality of the Spanish conquests in the Americas. He continued to publish until 1570 and died near his birthplace in Córdoba.

Sepúlveda's enduring reputation among scholars stems from his Latin translations of Aristotle's works, a project he conceived in the 1520s while studying in Bologna with the Aristotelian philosopher Pietro Pomponazzi. Between 1522 and 1532 he published translations of Aristotle's *Parva naturalia, De mundo* (On the world), *De generatione et corruptione* (On generation and corruption), *Meteorologica* (Meteorology), and *Historia animalium* (History of animals); and a translation of Alexander of Aphrodisias's commentaries on Aristotle. He later published a translation of Aristotle's *Ethics,* on commission from Pope Clement VII (1534), and of Aristotle's *Politics* (1548), which was considered by Sepúlveda and many later scholars to be his greatest achievement. It was also the basis for his famous dispute with Las Casas.

The debate with Las Casas was sparked by Sepúlveda's composition in the mid-1540s of a manuscript dialogue titled *Democrates secundus, sive de iustis belli causis apud Indos* (The second Democrates, or the causes for just war against the Indians), in which he defended the crown's policies of conquest in America. Sepúlveda made the Aristotelian argument that the Indians' cultural inferiority alone made them natural slaves and deprived them of the political rights belonging to civilized men. Outraged, Las Casas successfully blocked the publication of *Democrates secundus* in Spain and engaged in a highly publicized paper war with Sepúlveda, which culminated in inconclusive public debates held at Valladolid in 1550 and 1551. *Democrates secundus* was finally published in Rome in 1550 over Las Casas's protests.

Although this episode sealed Sepúlveda's popular reputation as an advocate of arrogant imperialism, he probably would have preferred to be remembered for his numerous other Latin works on an array of philosophical, political, and theological subjects, such as predestination (criticizing Luther), marriage and divorce (criticizing Henry VIII), Roman chronology, and the duties of kingship. Histories and chronicles make up the largest part of Sepúlveda's original works, but as a historian, he was mainly derivative and uncritical.

Sepúlveda's philological and literary pursuits made him a humanist in the most accurate sense of the term, but unlike some sixteenth-century humanists he valued philosophical precision over eloquence for its own sake. He criticized the vogue for rhetoric as detrimental to the more weighty disciplines (*graviores disciplinae*) of philosophy and theology and blamed rhetorical studies for helping to spread Lutheran ideas. In turn, some more rhetorically purist contemporaries criticized him for his use of scholastic, non-Ciceronian Latin. Sepúlveda's epistolary relations with the great Dutch humanist Erasmus of Rotterdam were characterized, like his attitudes toward the humanist movement in general, by muted respect.

See also **Las Casas, Bartolomé de; Vitoria, Francisco de.**

BIBLIOGRAPHY

Primary Works

Sepúlveda, Juan Ginés de. *Joannis Genesii Sepulvedae Cordubensis Opera, cum edita, tum inedita, accurante Regia historiae academia.* Madrid, 1780.

Sepúlveda, Juan Ginés de. *Obras completas.* 3 vols. Edited and translated by E. Rodríguez Peregrina. Pozoblanco, Spain, 1995–.

Secondary Works

Coroleu, Alejandro. "The *Fortuna* of Juan Ginés de Sepúlveda's Translations of Aristotle and of Alexander of Aphrodisias." *Journal of the Warburg and Courtauld Institutes* 59 (1996): 325–331.

Losada, Angel. *Juan Ginés de Sepúlveda a través de su "Epistolario" y nuevos documentos.* 2d ed. Madrid, 1973.

Pagden, Anthony. *The Fall of Natural Man: The American Indian and the Origins of Comparative Ethnology.* 2d ed. Cambridge, U.K., 1986.

KATHERINE ELLIOT VAN LIERE

GIOCONDO, FRA (Fra Giovanni Giocondo da Verona; Ioannes Jucundus; c. 1433–1515), Italian architect, engineer, and humanist scholar. Fra Giocondo was born under Venetian rule in or near Verona. Nothing is known of his family or the first fifty years of his life. It is uncertain whether he was a Dominican or a Franciscan, although most likely he was the latter. The first notices of him date to 1489, including praise by the humanist Angelo Poliziano for his knowledge of antiquities as "without any doubt most expert" in this field (Brenzoni, p. 109). Evidence of this is provided by his important manuscript collection, or *sylloge,* of ancient inscriptions, using both the work of earlier scholars and his own observations. Probably through a fellow humanist, Alessandro Cortesi, he dedicated the first recension of c. 1476–c. 1489 to Lorenzo de' Medici, and a second, of c. 1490 or c. 1497, to Ludovico Agnelli, archbishop of Cosenza.

Work in Naples, Paris, and Venice. Fra Giocondo's fame as an antiquarian seems to have been matched by his prestige as an architect and engineer. The first record of his activities, when he was referred to as a notable architect and engineer, is in Naples in 1489 working for Alfonso, duke of Calabria. He may have been involved in the design or construction of the famous suburban palace and gardens of Poggioreale, with their fountains and water games. In 1489 he was paid to examine ancient remains at Pozzuoli, Gaeta, and Formia. The first of these was with the poet Jacopo Sannazaro (1455–1530), and during Fra Giocondo's time at the Neapolitan court (certainly from the end of 1489 to the end of 1493) he was friends with other humanists and writers there, such as Giovanni Pontano. Fra Giocondo's knowledge of antiquity was also informed by time he spent in Rome, probably before and possibly during this period. By 1492 he was being employed to advise on military projects in various parts of the kingdom, and he was also sent to Formia to organize building for the duke of Calabria.

Fra Giocondo. *Roman Mausoleum at Capua.* THE STATE HERMITAGE MUSEUM, ST. PETERSBURG, RUSSIA

Perhaps in May 1495, maybe straight from Naples, Fra Giocondo went to the court of King Charles VIII in France, where he was recorded as a "deviseur des bastiments" (designer of buildings) in 1498. Various buildings have been attributed to him but have disappeared, including the Palais des Comptes and the Pont de Notre Dame in Paris. The bridge may have been his most notable construction if he was, as seems likely, employed on the project as designer or consultant between 1500 and 1505. He was responsible for an impressive feat of hydraulic engineering for waterworks in the garden of the royal chateau of Blois, and may also have been involved in work at the chateau of Amboise. Fra Giocondo's architectural skills seem to have lain in the area of technical expertise and were related to engineering projects, particularly in the design of fortifications and hydraulic projects.

In Paris in the first years of the sixteenth century he also acted as secretary to Filiberto Naturelli, Emperor Maximilian's legate in Paris, discussing mathematics, military matters, and the first-century B.C. Roman architect Vitruvius with him. But in November 1504 he provided information on the political activities of the French and the emperor to the Venetians, via their ambassador Francesco Morosini, who urged the Venetian Senate to employ Fra Giocondo as military architect to the republic. There were protracted negotiations for the job, and the Parisians wanted Fra Giocondo to stay in France, but he chose Venice and was eventually appointed architect to the Council of Ten on 28 May 1506 for a salary of three hundred ducats a year. For the Venetians, Fra Giocondo provided technical expertise on projects concerning canal and river systems, such as organizing the Brenta and Brentella canals, work on the river Adige, a scheme for the river Bacchiglione, rebuilding the Ponte della Pietra in Verona, and land reclamation in the Venetian lagoon and the *terraferma*. In addition he undertook military engineering work for the republic; he traveled to eastern parts of the Venetian empire, including Corfu and the Ionian islands, in order to advise on fortifications, and in the following years, during the war of the League of Cambrai, was involved in the fortification work on the *terraferma*, including at Cremona and Padua in 1509 and Treviso in about 1509–1511.

In Venice itself Fra Giocondo may have had some hand in building projects. Of doubtful attribution (although it first appeared in 1517, and given his position within the republic he may well have been consulted) is the residence and marketplace for the German merchant community in Venice, the Fondaco dei Tedeschi, which was rebuilt in 1505–1508 after a fire. There is more secure evidence that he was one of the engineers and architects whose proposals were considered for major rebuilding of the area around the Rialto Bridge, as well as the reconstruction of the bridge itself—in masonry instead of wood—after a fire in the area in January 1513. His plan was, however, rejected in 1514, perhaps as too radical.

New Saint Peter's, Rome.

After his return from France, Fra Giocondo indicated that it was Pope Julius II who had been instrumental in calling him back to Italy, possibly so that he could participate in designing the new Saint Peter's. He may have gone to Rome for this in the fall of 1505 and a plan (Gabinetto Disegni e Stampe degli Uffizi, Florence, 6A) may have been his contribution at this date. This design presented Saint Peter's in the form of a Latin cross articulated by seven equal-sized domes. It proposed large, apsed chapels radiating around the tomb of Saint Peter, as well as down the nave along the outside of broad outer aisles, closed off from the central nave and narrow aisles to form a U-shaped narthex—the latter element similar in plan to that of S. Marco in Venice.

Fra Giocondo's link to Saint Peter's was renewed under Pope Leo X. On 1 November 1513 the newly elected pope appointed Fra Giocondo architect of Saint Peter's alongside Donato Bramante, and they were joined by Giuliano da Sangallo on 1 January 1514. At Bramante's death, Raphael was appointed as architect on 1 April 1514. Fra Giocondo was certainly in Rome by the end of May, and Raphael wrote to his uncle on 1 July 1514 that the pope had given him Fra Giocondo as a colleague—a man of "great reputation, extremely wise"—and that Raphael hoped to learn his "architectural secrets" in order to perfect himself in the art of architecture (Brenzoni, p. 63). The position of all three architects was confirmed on 1 August, with Raphael as architect, Giuliano da Sangallo as administrator and aide, and Fra Giocondo as "master." His advanced age and experience resulted in a salary of four hundred instead of three hundred ducats a year. Fra Giocondo's input in the design and construction of the new Saint Peter's must have been fairly limited, as he died on 1 July 1515, but his knowledge of ancient and modern buildings as well as of Vitruvius's *De architectura* may well have been of significance in Raphael's desire to get to grips with both aspects of architecture.

Technical Skills and Interests.

Various sets of drawings, in the Hermitage and the Uffizi, have been attributed to Fra Giocondo, but none can be securely identified as either autographs or copies after Fra Giocondo originals. It is known that Fra Giocondo was a capable draftsman, since in Naples in 1492 he was paid for 126 drawings illustrating two manuscript treatises by Francesco di Giorgio Martini—one on architecture the other on military matters. Guillaume Budé also referred in 1508 to Fra Giocondo's use of images to elucidate the text of Vitruvius, and this would find expression in the woodcuts of Fra Giocondo's 1511 edition of Vitruvius.

Not only did Fra Giocondo's interests extend to technical engineering questions but also into the realm of mathematics and methods of measurement. In 1508 he was present when Luca Pacioli lectured in Venice on the ancient mathematician Euclid. In 1512 Fra Giocondo sought a license in Venice to publish a work on ancient arithmetic, which arose in part out of his study of Vitruvius and out of his desire to provide explanations for modern readers, but this book was probably never completed. Two of the manuscripts on mathematics that Fra Giocondo owned do survive. One of these, written in France, was largely composed of elements copied from elsewhere, but was extensively annotated and drawn on by Fra Giocondo. It focused principally on geometry and its applications, and on the connections between geometry and proportions. This is an issue that was also of importance in another manuscript treatise by Fra Giocondo on epigraphy and the forms of letters, for which he looked to classical inscriptions as models. He was also concerned in the French manuscript with technical issues, such as the practicalities of surveying and the forms of measuring instruments.

Editing of Classical Texts. During his time in France, Fra Giocondo seems to have developed his philological interests. He gave some lectures, such as on Vitruvius in Paris in 1504, and thus prepared the ground for subsequent publications. He shared these interests with French humanist friends like Jacques Lefèvre d'Étaples and Guillaume Budé, who admired his abilities as a scholar and architect, and his knowledge of antiquity. He knew the Greek humanist John Lascaris, probably in both Paris and Venice, and received some help from him with Greek. In 1504 Fra Giocondo published a work on Roman emperors, ascribed to Sextus Aurelius Victor. In France he found at least one classical manuscript, which contained previously lost letters from Pliny the Younger's *Epistolae* and the *De prodigiis* of Julius Obsequens. These were published by Aldo Manuzio in Venice in 1508, and Fra Giocondo provided manuscripts for other publications, like the Aldine Sallust of 1509. He also edited some classical texts for Aldo Manuzio—Nonius Marcellus's *De compendiosa doctrina* (1513), a partly illustrated edition of Caesar's *Commentaries* (1513), and *Libri de re rustica* (1514).

In Venice in 1511 the printer Giovanni Tacuino, or da Tridino, published for Fra Giocondo his greatest contribution to Renaissance architecture and scholarship—the first illustrated edition of Vitruvius's *De architectura*. It was a seminal publication: not only did it represent a high degree of scholarship in the creation of a comprehensible text, based on extensive knowledge of Vitruvius's manuscripts and Giocondo's skill in textual emendation, but also a profound study of antiquity, architecture, and engineering. The 136 woodcuts were later copied by others many times during the sixteenth century. Fra Giocondo's Vitruvius was immensely important for the development of the study of ancient architecture and its relationship to contemporary design in the Renaissance. This first-ever printing of proper illustra-

tions to *De architectura* provided a kind of graphic commentary, not only on *De architectura* but more broadly on classical architecture, which was of direct use and interest to architects and patrons engaged in transforming the forms and modes of ancient architecture for modern buildings. It also set a standard and model of interpretation for future editions. The technical achievements of Fra Giocondo as an engineer are also clearly evident in the plates illustrating and explaining machines, showing how classical scholarship and practical applications of such knowledge could be combined to great effect. Appropriately, the 1511 edition of Vitruvius was dedicated to the great builder, and to a fellow Franciscan, Pope Julius II, while the pocket-size version of October 1513, which included Frontinus's work on the aqueducts of Rome and four more woodcuts to Vitruvius, was dedicated to Giuliano de' Medici—revealing not only Fra Giocondo's link to the Medici but their importance as the new papal family.

See also subentries on **Architecture.**

BIBLIOGRAPHY

Brenzoni, Raffaello. *Fra Giovanni Giocondo veronese: Verona 1435–Roma 1515.* Florence, 1960.

Ciapponi, Lucia A. "Appunti per una biografia di Giovanni Giocondo da Verona." *Italia medioevale e umanistica* 4 (1961): 131–158.

Ciapponi, Lucia A. "Agli inizi dell'Umanesimo francese: Fra Giocondo e Guglielmo Budé." In *Forme e vicende per Giovanni Pozzi.* Edited by Ottavio Besomi et al. Padua, Italy, 1988. Pages 101–118.

Ciapponi, Lucia A. "Fra Giocondo da Verona and his Edition of Vitruvius." *Journal of the Warburg and Courtauld Institutes* 47 (1984): 72–90.

Frommel, Christoph Luitpold. "Fra Giocondo: Presentation Drawing of the Plan [of Saint Peter's, Rome]." In *The Renaissance from Brunelleschi to Michelangelo: The Representation of Architecture.* Edited by Henry A. Millon and Vittorio Magnano Lampugnani. London, 1994. Page 603.

Juren, Vladimir. "Fra Giovanni Giocondo et le début des études vitruviennes en France." *Rinascimento* ser. 2, 14 (1974): 101–115.

Michailova, Marie. "Bridges of Ancient Rome: Drawings in the Hermitage Ascribed to Fra Giocondo." *Art Bulletin* 52 (1970): 250–264.

GEORGIA CLARKE

GIOLITO PRESS. A prominent family dynasty of printers, publishers, and booksellers, the Giolito firm flourished in Venice from 1536 to 1606. Giovanni Giolito (d. 1540) operated a press in his native town of Trino (in Piedmont) from 1508 to 1523 and worked as a bookseller in Venice from 1523 to 1534 before moving there permanently in 1536. His eldest son, Gabriel (fl. 1538–1578), assumed principal control of the business; Gabriel's heirs, Giovanni (the younger) and Giovanni Paolo (fl. 1578–1591), and their children managed the firm until the end of the century.

The most prolific press in late-Renaissance Venice, the Giolito press produced 1,019 editions (527 originals and 492 reprints). Under Gabriel's superb direction the business enjoyed its greatest productivity. Working in a highly competitive industry—in Venice alone thirty to fifty publishers were active by the middle of the sixteenth century—Gabriel excelled by combining exceptional business acumen with a clearly articulated and original publication scheme designed to win over a broad reading market; he adapted production to suit the changing economic and cultural tastes of book consumers. Gabriel's first step in this direction was to adopt italic type (most printers still used larger roman type) which helped cut production costs. He also outfitted his shop with new cursive types, and thus his editions were greatly praised for their elegance as well as their clarity.

Even more significant for the firm's success, Gabriel aggressively manufactured and promoted a wide range of vernacular materials (and generally avoided Latin titles) in order to meet a growing demand. In this way the Giolito press contributed to the popularization the vernacular. It specialized in literature of all sorts: treatises and histories, as well as sermons and devotional materials. The firm published widely among the classic and contemporary best-sellers.

From 1542 to 1560, when the firm averaged just over thirty titles a year, Gabriel published twenty-eight editions of Ludovico Ariosto's *Orlando furioso,* twenty-two editions of Petrarch's *Rime,* twenty-six editions of Giovanni Boccaccio (including nine of the *Decameron*), and several works by such contemporary authors as Pietro Aretino, Ascanio Centorio, Anton Francesco Doni, Lodovico Dolce, Lodovico Domenichi, Paolo Giovio, Ortensio Lando, Girolamo Parabosco, and Bernardo Tasso. The breadth of the firm is obvious in other ways. Giolito published the works of 290 authors, and although many of the lesser-known writers published only one or two titles, the publishing strategy invigorated the demand for vernacular literature, brought greater respectability to Italian writers, and brought the firm into contact with literary circles, thus providing fresh business opportunities.

Gabriel's close association with leading authors helped him to introduce novelties into his books.

Most important in this regard was his collaboration until 1560 with Lodovico Dolce, the great doyen of Venetian editors and "poligrafi" (writers on many subjects). Dolce surely influenced Gabriel's decision in 1547 to complement an existing series of Petrarch's works in quarto with more compact editions in octavo and duodecimo, and it was Dolce who convinced Gabriel to experiment by adding ancillary materials (for example, collections of different authors, poems, commentaries, and letters to the readers promising new annotations and more perfection of the vernacular). These novelties were intended to attract readers to future Giolito editions.

By the middle of the 1550s, as the Counter-Reformation began to weigh on Venetian publishers with threats of confiscation and censorship of books considered heretical or immoral by the Catholic Church, Giolito shifted toward religious, devotional, and liturgical materials. By 1567 the firm was publishing more religious editions than works of secular literature. Gabriel published the titles of some of the most influential writers of the Counter-Reformation, such as Cornelio Musso (thirty-three editions), Antonio di Guevara (thirty-nine editions) and Luis de Granada (sixty-three editions). In 1559 Gabriel submitted prohibited books from his shop to the Inquisition in compliance with the Index of Prohibited Books, and in 1571 he was questioned about having more prohibited books and fined ten ducats by the Venetian Holy Office. During this period Gabriel inaugurated a publication scheme that, although not completed, was undoubtedly his most original venture. He conceived the idea of presenting translations of Greek and Latin classics in a uniform series of volumes. This so-called *Collana istorica* or historical necklace would be composed of twelve links or *anelli* (representing twelve authors) and embellished with a series of gems or *gioielli* of their writings. Giolito completed an analogous series for religious and devotional materials, called the *Ghirlanda spirituale* or "spiritual garland," in which various volumes formed the flowers.

The Giolito firm was located in the district of Sant'Apollinare near the Rialto at the center of the city. Gabriel also opened branch offices in Bologna, Ferrara, and Naples, primarily for the sale of books. The Giolito mark carries a phoenix rising from the flames, with various mottoes: "Semper eadem" (Always the same) and "De la mia morte eterna vita io viva" (From my death I live to eternal life).

See also **Italian Literature and Language; Printing and Publishing.**

BIBLIOGRAPHY

Bongi, Salvatore. *Annali di Gabriel Giolito de' Ferrari da Trino di Monferrato, stampatore in Venezia.* 2 vols. Rome, 1890–1895. Reprint, Rome, n.d.

Di Filippo Bareggi, Claudia. *Il mestiere di scrivere: Lavoro intellettuale e mercato librario a Venezia nel cinquecento.* Rome, 1988.

Dondi, Giovanni, "Giovanni Giolito editore e mercante," *La bibliofilia* 69 (1967): 147–189.

Grendler, Paul F. *The Roman Inquisition and the Venetian Press 1540–1605.* Princeton, N.J., 1977.

Richardson, Brian. *Print Culture in Renaissance Italy: The Editor and the Vernacular Text 1470–1600.* Cambridge, U.K., 1994.

Quondam, Amedeo. "Mercanzia d'onore/Mercanzia d'utile. Produzione libraria e lavoro intellettuale a Venezia nel Cinquecento." In *Libri, editori e pubblico nell'Europa moderna. Guida storica e critica.* Edited by Armando Petrucci. Rome, 1977. Pages 51–102.

KEVIN M. STEVENS

GIORGIONE (Giorgio da Castelfranco; 1477/78–1510), Venetian painter. Giorgione is among the most intriguing and enigmatic figures in Renaissance art. He was hailed by Baldassare Castiglione (1528) as one of the greatest painters of the age and claimed by Giorgio Vasari as the originator of "the modern style" (*maniera moderna*) of painting in Venice. But documentation of Giorgione's unusual, brilliant, and brief career is scanty. Mythification began soon after his death, and interpretation of his artistic personality is to some degree determined by subjective response to the hauntingly evocative, poetic works that have been associated with him. Consensus is lacking regarding which paintings should be considered autograph; the number of works assigned by individual scholars has varied widely. Dating of the majority of the most securely attributed pictures is problematic and further complicated by alternate views as to whether Giorgione's apparently earliest works were executed c. 1495 or c. 1500; the latter represents the traditional view.

Biography and Documentation. Giorgione's origin in the Venetian subject city Castelfranco is unquestioned; the birth date assigned him by Vasari, who names Giovanni Bellini as his teacher, is generally accepted. No signed works are known. A female portrait now entitled *Laura* (Vienna, Kunsthistorisches Museum) bears on the reverse an early sixteenth-century inscription with the date 1506 and an attribution to him. A *Portrait of a Man* (San Diego Museum of Art) is similarly inscribed with attribution and a no longer legible date. Documents record that in 1507–1508 Giorgione painted a now-lost canvas for the Sala dell'Udienza (audience chamber) in the Doge's Palace. In 1508 Giorgione received payment for frescoes decorating the facade of the Fondaco de' Tedeschi (German merchants' warehouse) in Venice. These depicted monumental, classicizing female nudes in niches. Already faded and damaged in the eighteenth century, when copied in engravings by Zanetti, the frescoes are lost except for fragments detached in 1937 (Venice, Galleria Franchetti, Ca' d'Oro). In October 1510, Isabella d'Este of Mantua requested that her agent in Venice acquire "a night" (*una nocte;* meaning "Nativity") by Giorgione; in November, the agent replied that the artist had died of plague.

Early Sources and Related Paintings. In notes compiled between 1521 and 1543, the Venetian patrician Marcantonio Michiel recorded several paintings—then in Venetian private collections—as by Giorgione. Three are now surely identifiable: *Boy with an Arrow; Three Philosophers in a Landscape* (both Vienna, Kunsthistorisches Museum); and *The Tempest* (Venice, Accademia). Identification of a fourth, the *Sleeping Venus* (Dresden, Gemäldegalerie), is usually accepted. The first three and the *Laura* share the feature of having uncommon subject matter, seemingly elusive of precise meaning. The latter three include landscapes of extraordinary beauty. The sleeping nude, the naked mother in the *Tempest,* the stately *Laura* exposing her breast, and the androgynous youth with the arrow are all subtly erotic. These pictures are stylistically cohesive. Although complicated by his statements that the Venetian painter Sebastiano del Piombo completed the *Three Philosophers* and that Titian completed the *Sleeping Venus,* Michiel's information is thus invaluable to establishing Giorgione's style and range of activity. Michiel (1530) locates *The Tempest* in the collection of Gabriele Vendramin; it appears in later Vendramin inventories (1567–1569; 1601), as does a picture of an old woman. This reference is now identified with *La Vecchia* (The old woman; Venice, Accademia), a painting inscribed *col tempo* (with time) and accepted as autograph.

An inventory (1528) of the collection of Domenico Grimani lists a *Self-portrait of Giorgione as David with the Head of Goliath.* An engraving by Wenceslaus Hollar (1650) records this work; a painted fragment of the same composition (Brunswick, Herzog Anton Ulrich Museum) is identified by some scholars as Giorgione's picture and thought by others to be a copy. In this picture, the San Diego portrait, *Boy with*

Giorgione. *Virgin and Child Enthroned with SS. Catherine and Francis.* Painted c. 1500–1501 or earlier. GALLERIE DELL'ACCADEMIA DI BELLE ARTI, VENICE/ALINARI/ART RESOURCE

an Arrow, and *La Vecchia,* the subject is presented startlingly close up, emerging from a dark background and looking out as if to engage the viewer in a penetrating psychological exchange. A close-up image of *Christ Carrying the Cross* (Venice, Scuola Grande di San Rocco), dated by document to 1508–1509, has been attributed to Giorgione and alternatively to Titian. In 1648 the Venetian art historian Carlo Ridolfi cited a work that is now universally attributed to Giorgione and placed near the start of his career: an altarpiece in the Cathedral of Castelfranco. Surprisingly, and except for St. Francis, the figures here do not look out or at each other but rather appear to be rapt in inward contemplation, their reverie enhanced by the soft, dusky modeling, golden light, and long shadows.

Other Works. Unrecorded works accepted by modern scholars and usually dated early in Giorgione's career include: *Judith* (St. Petersburg, Hermitage), which may reflect the classicism of the Venetian sculptor Tullio Lombardo; *Portrait of a Man in a Pink Quilted Jacket* (Berlin, Gemäldegalerie); and *Adoration of the Magi* (London, National Gallery). A *Nativity with Shepherds* (Washington, National Gallery) shares landscape and compositional features with the *Three Philosophers.* It is most often assigned to Giorgione, but has alternatively been attributed to Titian, as is also true of the later, large *Pastoral Concert* (Paris, Louvre).

Innovation and Influence. Many of the works associated with Giorgione indicate a taste for the sensual and the pastoral—equivalent to a contemporary revival of the classical genre by Venetian poets—among the humanistically educated patrons that must have constituted Giorgione's major clientele and may have encouraged his influential break with tradition in exploring landscape and mood as subject matter for "painted poems" (*poesie*). Most extraordinary is the *Tempest.* Despite numerous reasonable interpretations put forward for the subject as political allegory or mythological story, the eerie light and heavy air of the impending meteorological climax may be considered the essential subject.

In justifiably citing Giorgione's technique as revolutionary, Vasari stated that the Venetian eschewed drawing, sketching with brush on his canvas. X-radiography of his paintings confirms that Giorgione often made significant compositional changes in the paint layer. Recent observation, through infrared reflectography, of contours that are only loosely indicated by underdrawing has also tended to support Vasari's assertion. Giorgione's swift progression away from the precisely delineated and smoothly layered application of pigment characteristic of Giovanni Bellini toward an irregularly layered (*impasto*) application exploiting texture of canvas and brush was quickly taken up by a generation of Venetian painters and established not only the direction but also the renown of Venetian sixteenth-century painting. Vasari's suggestion that Leonardo da Vinci's stay in Venice (1500) inspired Giorgione's innovations, although dismissed by the early Venetian writers on art, has recently been reconsidered for stylistic and thematic analogies (as in the newly cleaned *Concert* or *Three Ages of Man;* Florence, Palazzo Pitti), as has the influence of the German painter Albrecht Dürer, who also visited Venice during the same decade.

BIBLIOGRAPHY

Primary Works

Michiel, Marcantonio. MS, Venice, Biblioteca Nazionale Marciana. Published as: *Notizia d'opere di disegno nella prima metà del secolo seidici* (manuscripts of 1521–1543). *Notizie d'opere di disegno* (manuscripts of c. 1520–1540). Edited by Jacopo Morelli. Bassano, 1800. *The Anonimo.* Translated by Paolo Mussi. Edited by George C. Williamson. London, 1903; reprint, New York, 1969.

Secondary Works

Anderson, Jaynie. *Giorgione: The Painter of "Poetic Brevity."* Paris and New York, 1997. A thoroughgoing review of works, copies, sources, and literature with pioneering analysis of historiographic questions, including those relating to conservation treatment. Also includes transcriptions of all relevant primary sources.

Ballarin, Alessandro. Two articles in *Le siècle de Titien.* Catalog of an exhibition held at the Grand Palais, Paris, 1993. Pages 281–347; 437–449. Reconsideration of Giorgione's chronology and influence.

Lucco, Mauro. *Giorgione.* Milan, 1996.

Torrini, Annalisa Perissa. *Giorgione: Catalogo completo dei dipinti.* Florence, 1993.

CAROLYN C. WILSON

GIOTTO DI BONDONE

GIOTTO DI BONDONE (1267/75–1337), Tuscan painter and architect. Little is certain regarding the details of Giotto's life, as sources are scarce and often unverifiable. According to a literary tradition, Giotto was born a peasant in the village of Vespignano, near Florence. The tradition dates at least to around 1447, when it appears in a passage of the Tuscan sculptor Lorenzo Ghiberti's *Commentaries* concerning the beginning of painting's rise in central Italy.

Giotto is mentioned in writings of fourteenth-century poets such as Dante Alighieri, Giovanni Boccaccio, and Petrarch (Francesco Petrarca), as well as in the Florentine chronicles of Filippo Villani. His renown among these authors attests to his early fame in Tuscany. Yet the Giotto lauded by these figures is a man of maturity and artistic accomplishment. The beginnings of his life became important only in later centuries, when he figured in laudatory histories written about artists and their works, such as Ghiberti's work and the Tuscan painter Giorgio Vasari's

Lives of the Artists (1550; revised 1568). Giotto is characterized as a boy of precocious intellect and artistic genius, qualities whose fruition is recounted in both texts. For both authors, Giotto's greatness as an artist was magnified by the story of his rise from rural poverty and obscurity to civic refinement and celebrity. The extent to which the narrative is factual cannot be ascertained.

Education. Both Ghiberti and Vasari relate that the Tuscan painter Cimabue (Bencivieni di Pepo) discovered Giotto as a boy in the countryside, drawing a nearby sheep on a slab of stone. As the story goes, the painter was struck by the boy's artistic abilities and obtained his father's permission to take Giotto as a student. After an unspecified amount of time, Giotto matched and surpassed his master's art. What Giotto then achieved and widely propagated, according to both authors, was a revolution of artistic style. His accurate drawing from life replaced what Vasari considered a derivative tradition of crude quality practiced by the famous Cimabue.

Giotto and Cimabue are associated already in literature of the early fourteenth century, during Giotto's lifetime. In the eleventh canto of his *Purgatory* (c. 1307–1321), Dante names both figures in an example of the transience of fame and the folly of vainglory. Giotto is here said to have replaced Cimabue in the field of painting. Toward the end of the century, Villani recapitulated Giotto's succession as an accomplished fact in his *Liber de origine Florentiae et eisdem famosis civibus* (On the origin of the Florentine state and its famous citizens; c. 1395). Yet Ghiberti was the first to use narrative to elaborate a process of artistic succession over time. The author's attention to Giotto's youth prepared readers to understand not only that Giotto was an artist worthy of highest praise, but also that the painter's achievement derived from a combination of innate talent and formal training by an artist who was exceptional in his own right. Vasari repeats and expands the details found in Ghiberti's image of Giotto, with some variation.

Importance and Reputation. Vasari amplifies Giotto's historical role, which was related as early as around 1353 in Giovanni Boccaccio's *Decameron.* The Giotto of Boccaccio resurrects a lost art of rendering objects naturalistically to the point of deceiving viewers. In Vasari, Giotto is the catalyst in a vaster and more complex history. Here Giotto ushers in art's rebirth or second rise to perfection, following a previous cycle that began in remote antiquity, culminated in ancient Greece and Rome, and

Giotto. *Kiss of Judas.* Fresco in the Scrovegni Chapel, church of S. Maria Annunziata dell'Arena, Padua. CAPPELLA DEGLI SCROVEGNI, PADUA, ITALY/SUPERSTOCK

declined during the twilight of the Roman empire. In this position Giotto is a hero who rescues and restores a lost art sought in vain by incompetent artists since the fall of Rome.

Career. Behind Giotto's triumph, according to Vasari, is the divine source of the painter's talent, an aspect highlighted through the biographical treatment of his youth. The preface of Vasari's *Lives* portrays God as the first artist and ultimate teacher of human artists, enabling them to perfect imperfect materials through the application of the same prin-

ciples by which God ordered nature. Giotto's talents are therefore understood not only as God-given, but also as instruments of God's will for the Tuscan people to reach divine perfection in the arts. The painter thus becomes both a Tuscan hero and a primary redeemer on a universal scale of absolute artistic value. In this capacity he is shown to have laid the foundation upon which subsequent artists discussed by Vasari built in persisting to use nature as a model to imitate and reproduce.

Vasari's scheme of progress in the arts culminated in the careers of the sixteenth-century artists Leo-

Giotto. *St. Francis of Assisi Preaching before Pope Honorius III.* Fresco in the church of San Francesco, Assisi. SAN FRANCESCO, ASSISI/CANALI PHOTOBANK, MILAN/SUPERSTOCK

nardo da Vinci, Raphael of Urbino, and Michelangelo Buonarroti. And while modern scholars have left behind the theological underpinnings of Vasari's history, Giotto's pivotal status in art history has remained: most of the thousands of Giotto studies written internationally in the twentieth century note how the art of Giotto anticipates the work of later Renaissance painters. Where they were concerned to show Giotto's importance in the history of painting, scholars in the twentieth century transformed the idea of Giotto as a historically pivotal figure in the

history of art. Vasari's focus on Giotto's naturalistic style was retained as a primary indicator of the fundamental change he effected in the art of painting, although modern studies approach his images with different notions of what constitutes the painter's style.

Many aspects of the painter's career, aside from claims made by Vasari, mark Giotto as an exceptional figure in his time. The works of art commonly attributed to him and his workshop, while vexed with questions of authorship, suggest an astonishing breadth of mastery in the media of fresco, tempera, gold leaf, and mosaic, as well as a conceptual inventiveness in meeting the demands of a variety of important projects. Giotto's artistic endeavors include diverse types of panel painting, from complex altarpieces to monumental crucifixes. He was also hired to paint church and chapel murals with dramatic narrative programs comprising several scenes—if not dozens of them—representing the lives of popular religious figures. In 1334, toward the end of his life, Giotto was appointed to oversee the fabric and workshop of the cathedral of Florence, and also received a commission to design its new tower. Such versatility was unprecedented for a single artist up to Giotto's time.

The patronage of these projects equally reveals the singularity of Giotto's career. The Florentine commune's appointment of Giotto to the works of its cathedral crowned a lifetime of prominent positions. Among Giotto's other employers in Florence were the Bardi and Peruzzi families, some of Italy's wealthiest bankers. He was also engaged by great religious orders in Florence, including the Dominicans at the church of Santa Maria Novella, the Franciscans at the church of Santa Croce, and the Umiliati at the church of Ognissanti. His other important patrons resided well beyond Florence. In Padua he painted for the commune of Padua and also for the private citizen Enrico Scrovegni, the wealthy son of a prosperous moneylender. Giotto's patrons south of Florence included a cardinal of old St. Peter's in Rome and Robert I, king of Naples. At the headquarters of the Franciscan order in Assisi, an extensive fresco cycle of the *Life of St. Francis* in the Upper Church of the Basilica of San Francesco stands as Giotto's most disputed attribution. Aside from issues of other possible patrons and the difficulties of attribution and dating of particular works, the cultural breadth of these examples is sufficient to suggest that Giotto's professional itinerary encompassed the principal centers of wealth, power, and artistic sponsorship in early fourteenth-century Italy. By contrast his followers, who included Taddeo Gaddi and perhaps Maso di Banco, worked mainly in Florentine milieus, such as the church of Santa Croce.

Significant Artistic Achievements. A prevalent current of American and British scholarship examines the painter's novel evocations of reality in the depiction of human drama. The ways in which Giotto depicted space through his rendering of architecture and figures, color and light have been shown to set him in advance of previous artists, as he forged new relationships between pictorial representation and visible reality. The painter's powers of observation emerge, for example, in the minute attention given to foliage and the distinctions made between birds in the fresco painting of *St. Francis Preaching to the Birds* in the Upper Church of San Francesco in Assisi [see the color plates in this volume], which scholars have dated variously from the 1290s to the 1320s. Moreover, the tonal contrasts and lines that define the friars' bodies contribute to an impression of spatial depth within the frame by giving the bodies volume. The disappearance of an elbow behind the left vertical frame suggests the extension of a unified space beyond the surface of the painted wall. *St. Francis's Sermon before Honorius III* in the same fresco cycle also conveys spatial depth through volumetric figures, but here spatial recession is defined by the architecture of a chamber rather than expanded laterally beyond the frame.

Where Giotto sets standards for painting illusionistic spaces, however, the character of spatial depth varies to amplify the particular subject represented. In the case of the Assisi frescoes, both the subjects and their spaces enhance the official image of the founder of a new and powerful religious order. *Preaching to the Birds* presents a rural space expressive of the wandering life of a radical figure who sought to reform the Church through dedication to material poverty and preaching beyond ecclesiastical walls. The *Sermon before Honorius III,* by contrast, takes place within a splendid interior. At the center, flanked by high clerics, sits Pope Honorius III, here depicted as a captive audience to Francis's preaching. Focus on the attentive pope affirms his supreme authority on church-related matters. This is the pontiff who formally approved Francis's Second Rule for his newly founded order of mendicant friars; his receptive posture in the Assisi fresco conveys a sense of inevitability to this crucial decision in the order's history. In sum, Giotto's art conveys both groundbreaking illusionism and spatial settings that recollect both the saint's commitments to itinerant preaching and his eventual attainment of papal recognition. Each of the remaining scenes in Assisi makes a similarly compelling point about Francis and his mission.

In addition to Giotto's attention to visible reality, modern observers of Giotto's work have been struck by a psychological realism in his human figures. A disturbing example is *The Kiss of Judas* from Enrico Scrovegni's chapel (Arena Chapel) in Padua, painted around 1303–1305. The scene, a highlight of Giotto's talent as a visual storyteller, follows upon a lengthy

Giotto. *Christ Entering Jerusalem.* Fresco in the Scrovegni Chapel of Santa Maria Annunziata all'Arena, Padua. Painted c. 1305–1306. CAPPELLA DEGLI SCROVEGNI, PADUA/ ALINARI/ART RESOURCE

narrative cycle representing Jesus's birth, childhood, and ministry. Throughout the story plots build against Jesus, and now reach a crescendo as dense groups of armed soldiers and Jewish men converge to surround him. His captors bear down with a hatred that becomes accute in a foreground confrontation between Judas's glare and Jesus's equanimity. The enveloping gesture dramatized by Judas's bright cape signals that Jesus has been overwhelmed. Yet Giotto's Christ shows by his calm expression that the capitulation is only physical, heightening the psychological tension between his figure and those of his adversaries.

The scene initiates a sequence of episodes representing the Passion, a popular subject of artistic and dramatic representation in this period. Here Giotto's introduction to the Passion with *The Kiss of Judas* is novel in the emotional charge that governs the attitudes of Jesus's persecutors, who appear at once as identifiable individuals and faceless hordes. With this image the painter magnifies anticipation of the expansive sequence of pictures that shows the

human God suffering at the hands of malevolent figures in the short time before his execution on the cross.

BIBLIOGRAPHY

Primary Work

Vasari, Giorgio. *Lives of the Artists.* 2 vols. Translated by George Bull. London, 1965. Translation of *Vite* (1550). See vol. 1.

Secondary Works

Belting, Hans. "Vasari and His Legacy: The History of Art as a Process?" In his *The End of the History of Art?* Translated by Christopher S. Wood. Chicago, 1987. Pages 65–94.

Falaschi, Enid. "Giotto: The Literary Legend." *Italian Studies* 27 (1972): 1–27.

Flores d'Arcais, Francesca. *Giotto.* New York, 1995.

Gardner, Julian. "Giotto: 'First of the Moderns' or Last of the Ancients?" *Wiener Jahrbuch für Kunstgeschichte* 44 (1991): 63–78.

Ladis, Andrew, ed. *Giotto and the World of Early Italian Art: An Anthology of Literature.* 4 vols. New York, 1998. A comprehensive collection of eighty-seven essays. Includes many of the twentieth century's fundamental English-language articles regarding Giotto.

Maginnis, Hayden B. J. *Painting in the Age of Giotto: A Historical Reevaluation.* University Park, Pa., 1997.

Murray, Peter. "Notes on Some Early Giotto Sources." *Journal of the Warburg and Courtauld Institutes* 16 (1953): 58–80.

Schneider, Laurie, ed. *Giotto in Perspective.* Englewood Cliffs, N.J., 1974. A practical anthology of thirty-three sources, which traces the history of Giotto's work and style. Dates of excerpted sources range from the fourteenth to the twentieth centuries. Includes a portion of Ghiberti's passage concerning Giotto.

Stubblebine, James H., ed. *Giotto: The Arena Chapel Frescoes.* New York and London, 1969. An anthology especially useful for the fourteenth-century sources it reproduces in English translation.

MATTHEW G. SHOAF

GIOVANNI DI PAOLO. *See* **Siena,** *subentry on* **Art in Siena.**

GIOVIO, PAOLO (1486–1552), Italian bishop and historian. Paolo Giovio was born into the urban patriciate of Como and given a humanistic education by his scholarly elder brother Benedetto. After receiving a doctorate in medicine and arts at Pavia in 1511, he migrated to Rome and secured an appointment as lecturer in philosophy at the Roman university. In 1517 he became physician to Cardinal Giulio de' Medici, whom he continued to serve when Giulio became Pope Clement VII. In 1527 he was appointed bishop of Nocera de' Pagani, near Salerno.

A versatile rather than a profound intellect, Giovio immersed himself in the culture of high Renaissance Rome and rapidly acquired a reputation for Livian style. His decision to become the historian of his times afforded him the opportunity of becoming acquainted with numerous leading figures of his day, from many of whom he received gifts and pensions, or at least up-to-date information. He had several interviews with the emperor Charles V and with Francis I of France. It was his commerce in the latest news, spiced with his own trenchant observations, that made him a figure to be reckoned with in the world of sixteenth-century Italy and led the influential historian of historiography, Eduard Fueter, to call him a "revolver journalist."

Service as courtier to Pope Paul III and his nephew Cardinal Alessandro Farnese assured Giovio's continuing at the Vatican after 1534. During the 1540s he became something of an arbiter of elegance for Cardinal Farnese, in which capacity he obtained commissions for his protégé, the artist Giorgio Vasari, whom he encouraged in the composition of his *Lives of the Artists.* Disappointed by the failure of Paul III to make him a cardinal, or even bishop of Como, Giovio retired to Florence, where he spent the last three years of his life as the guest of Cosimo I de' Medici and published his *Historianum sui temporis libri* (Histories of his own time; 1550–1552).

Giovio's virtue as a historian was that he revived the Greek tradition of contemporary eyewitness history and perfected the collation of eyewitness accounts in narratives that preserve much military history of the wars of Italy. His *Histories,* which cover the period 1494–1547, were supplemented by his biographies of Popes Leo X and Adrian VI, of the "Great Captain" Gonzalo de Córdova, and of the imperial commander Francisco d'Avalos, marquis of Pescara. Although Giovio's many friendships and pensions caused his history to be regarded as suspect, he in fact told his patrons "bitter truths." His real faults lay rather in his too-willing adherence to the canons of the declining humanist historiographical tradition and in his suppression of the political and diplomatic dimensions of history in the interest of narrative brevity and smoothly flowing Latin style. As a result, his work was soon eclipsed by the *Storia d'Italia* (History of Italy; 1561–1564) of Francesco Guicciardini, which covers the same period. His reputation as a historian was also diminished by the publication, against the advice of Cosimo I, of his highly rhetorical *Elogia* (1546 and 1551), short and lively character sketches of famous people that included apparent gossip. These were originally appended to the portraits of famous people that Giovio collected in his celebrated museum on Lake Como. His idea of bringing together a portrait and a brief biography was Giovio's most original contribution to Renaissance individualism, since the combination of portrait with text facilitated the "global" judgments made in assessing individual personality.

BIBLIOGRAPHY

Primary Works

Giovio, Paolo. *An Italian Portrait Gallery, Being Brief Biographies of Scholars.* Translated by Florence A. Gragg. Boston, 1935. Translation of *Elogia doctorum vivorum* (1546).

Giovio, Paolo. *Pauli Iovii opera.* 11 vols. Rome, 1956–.

Secondary Works

Cochrane, Eric. *Historians and Historiography in the Italian Renaissance.* Chicago, 1981. See chapter 13, "Contemporary History and Universal History," pp. 360–389.

Zimmermann, T. C. Price. *Paolo Giovio: The Historian and the Crisis of Sixteenth-Century Italy.* Princeton, N.J., 1995.

T. C. PRICE ZIMMERMANN

GIRALDI, GIAMBATTISTA CINZIO (1504–1573), Italian humanist nobleman who, following the fashion of the times, took on the classical pseudonym of Cinthio. Giambattista Giraldi taught philosophy and rhetoric at several Italian universities but spent most of his life in his native Ferrara, where he taught at the university and was for twelve years (1547–1559) the personal secretary of his patron duke Ercole II. Like most men of letters of the time, he wrote on a number of subjects, ranging from advice on how a gentleman may survive the perils and trappings of life at court, to chivalric poetry, drama, short stories, and literary criticism. He is mostly remembered for his *Ecatommiti,* for his contribution to the revival of tragic theater, and for his literary criticism. *Ecatommiti* (1565) is a collection of 113 short stories narrated by a group of ladies and gentlemen fleeing Rome during its 1527 sacking. On the ship to Marseille, they decide to combat the tedium of the ten-day voyage by telling stories, much in the way Giovanni Boccaccio's group tells the stories of *The Decameron.* Like *The Decameron, Ecatommiti* became a source of material for playwrights both in Italy and abroad. Among the best-known short stories in the English-speaking world are "Othello" (3.7) and "Measure for Measure" (8.5). Giraldi himself adapted some of his tales as the basic plotline for several of his dramas, including his widely known tragedy *Orbecche* (1541).

Though the ferocious vengeance and bloody scenes of this play bring to mind Seneca's *Thyestes* and Boccaccio's story of Tancredi (*Decameron* 4.1), the plot is actually an adaptation of *Ecatommiti* (2.2). The considerable critical attention that *Orbecche* received both in Italy and abroad contributed to the neglect of Giraldi's eight other dramas, which only began to attract the interest of scholars and publishers late in the twentieth century. The long-held view that Giraldi's bloody scenes, reminiscent of Senecan horror tragedies, strongly influenced the Italian stage is exaggerated, because he, after his initial experience with violent plays, turned to tragedies of *lieto fine* (with happy endings), which eventually gave rise to the popular tragicomedy of later centuries. Perhaps his most important contribution to the history of theater was his insistence on the possibility of staging tragedies at a time when they were viewed as poems to be read. His *Discorsi* (1554) on comedy and tragedy centers largely on the theatrical and spectacular dimensions of tragedy, which, he thought, may be fully appreciated only on the stage before an audience.

His critical insights were also influential in shaping the ongoing debate on the form and content of chivalric poetry. In his *Discorso* (1549; published 1554) on the subject, he proposed a reconciliatory alternative that would maintain the unity of action exemplified by Homer and Virgil while allowing for subplots that would ultimately tie in with the main story of the principal character, as in Ludovico Ariosto's *Orlando furioso.* Giraldi stands out as a keen literary critic and a major influence in the revival of classical tragedy.

BIBLIOGRAPHY

Primary Works

Giraldi, Giambattista. *Gli Ecatommiti ovvero cento novelle di Gio. Battista Giraldi Cinthio, nobile ferrarese.* Florence, 1832.

Giraldi, Giambattista. *Le tragedie di M. Gio. Battista Giraldi Cinthio, nobile ferrarese.* Venice, 1583.

Guerrieri-Crocetti, Camillo, ed. *Scritti critici.* Milan, 1973.

Secondary Works

Di Maria, Salvatore. "Blame-by-Praise Irony in the *Ecatommiti* of Giraldi Cinzio." *Quaderni d'italianistica* 6, no. 2 (1985): 178–192.

Horne, Philip Russell. *The Tragedies of Giambattista Cinthio Giraldi.* London, 1962.

Morrison, Mary G. *The Tragedies of G.-B. Giraldi Cinthio: The Transformation of Narrative Source into Stage Play.* Lewiston, N.Y., 1997.

Osborn, Peggy. "'Fuor di quel costume antico': Innovation versus Tradition in the Prologues of Giraldi Cinthio's Tragedies." *Italian Studies* 37 (1982): 49–66.

SALVATORE DI MARIA

GIULIO ROMANO (Giulio Pippi de' Gianuzzi; 1499–1546), Italian painter and architect. Giulio Romano has long been considered the most important pupil of Raphael (1483–1520), whose shop he entered at an early age. He assisted Raphael in frescoing the Vatican Stanze until the master's death, when Giulio was given free rein to complete the assignment according to his own aesthetic preference. Whereas Raphael's style had epitomized the most classical aspects of the Italian Renaissance, Giulio achieved in *Battle of Constantine,* an image completed in 1521 for which Raphael seems certainly to have left designs, the first grand statement of mannerism in Rome. Although Giulio did not wholly abandon Raphael's commitment to classicist form, he stressed the complexities rather than the clarity of the composition, exaggerating the separateness over the unity of the figural groupings. The distinct nature of spatial levels so favored by Raphael also loses its integrity under Giulio's hand, leaving the spectator lost and overwhelmed by such an ambiguous space.

With Raphael's death in 1520, Giulio emerged with a style that allowed for a free expression of his own innate inventiveness, thus transforming Ra-

Giulio Romano. Palazzo del Tè. Loggia di Davide in the Palazzo del Tè, Mantua, Italy. Built 1525–1535. ALINARI/ART RESOURCE

phaelesque precedents into a new visual language, mannerism. This can be seen not only in the frescoes for the Sala di Costantino but in the first altarpieces Giulio completed without guidance from his teacher. *The Stoning of St. Stephen* (Genoa, San Stefano), *The Holy Family* (Madrid, Prado), and *The Holy Family with St. Mark and St. James* (Rome, Santa Maria dell' Anima) all exhibit the spatial ambiguity, complex interrelationship of figures, elegance, and high artifice of *Battle of Constantine*.

In 1524 Giulio moved to Mantua to become court painter to Federico II Gonzaga. With the exception of the work of his predecessor, Andrea Mantegna (1431–1506), who had completed in the Gonzaga's ducal palace the first example of a room exhibiting a unified illusionistic structure, the so-called *camera picta,* or painted chamber (1465–1474), Mantua had seen little in the way of Roman art. Giulio was given absolute authority over all artistic decisions made in the small duchy. To aid him in this endeavor he es-

tablished in Mantua the shop system he had learned from Raphael in Rome. But whereas Raphael had had an abundance of competent pupils, Giulio had to settle for artists who had grown up in an artistically provincial environment, leaving room for the pupil-cum-master to dictate his ideas to those less talented.

One of the largest and most complex of Giulio's Mantuan projects was the Palazzo del Tè, completed largely between 1527 and 1530 with additional work continuing until 1534. The Palazzo del Tè originally functioned as a stable for the Gonzaga's horses. Federico, however, who was known for his amorous nature, wished to transform it into an elaborate trysting place and entrusted Giulio with both the architectural plan and its inside decorations. The palace is essentially based on classical prototypes, inspired by the work of the ancient Roman architect Vitruvius and Giulio's somewhat older contemporary, the architect Donato Bramante. Giulio, however, transformed such classicism, filling the exterior with subtle distortions and irregularities. The slipping triglyphs on the courtyard facade and the varied appearance of the rusticated surfaces are congruent with the mannerist conceit in the interior and animate the structure in a way that the sophisticated members of court must have appreciated with haughty delight.

In the interior, however, Giulio's genius is most strikingly displayed. Among the many rooms he designed, two stand out: the Sala di Psiche and the Sala dei Giganti (Room of the Giants). The Sala di Psiche (which tells of the marriage of Cupid to Psyche) was intended for use as a banquet hall. The room is a celebration of the senses, explicitly erotic and sensual in subject and tone, reflecting Federico's original, and admittedly lascivious, reason for refurbishing the palace. The Sala dei Giganti, on the other hand, offers a different form of entertainment. Here, the room seems about to collapse as a result of the battle between the gods and the giants, engulfing viewers and leading them to believe they are about to be unwilling participants in the fracas, an illusion that is not only entertaining but potentially frightening. Although Giulio's assistants aided in the execution of the interior decoration, the rooms were surely designed by the master, for they display his predilection for a form of fantasy and eccentricity that borders, at times, on the sadistically humorous.

Giulio's most controversial project was *I Modi*, or the sixteen pleasures. In the early 1520s Giulio made sixteen drawings displaying couples engaged in various forms of sexual intercourse that were initially circulated only to a select few. The drawings were heartily received, and therefore a set of engravings was made and circulated publicly. The engraver who executed the prints was Marcantonio Raimondi (c. 1480–c. 1534); ironically, he alone was imprisoned for taking part in this pornographic exercise, but Giulio was soon able to set him free. Pope Clement VII had declared the prints illegal; nonetheless, a second edition appeared, this time accompanied by lascivious sonnets written by the notorious author and pornographer Pietro Aretino (1492–1556). The popularity of these prints was such that they became the model for erotic art throughout the Renaissance.

Giulio's contribution to the development of the visual arts and architecture in the sixteenth century was, therefore, a varied and important one. Continuing Raphael's work in Rome, he moved beyond his master's classicism and helped to develop the style known as mannerism, an approach to image making that emphasized the most complex and esoteric aspects of both narrative structure and the vicissitudes of the human body. His decorations in the Palazzo del Tè exhibited his inventive illusionism; in this sphere he would remain highly influential not only for such slightly younger artists as Paolo Veronese, whose work in the area of overhead decoration shows marks of Giulio's tendency toward extreme foreshortenings, but also for artists of the seventeenth century, the period known as the baroque.

See also **Mannerism**; **Mantua**; **Pornography**; *and biographies of figures mentioned in this entry.*

BIBLIOGRAPHY

Primary Work
Ferrari, Daniela, ed. *Giulio Romano: Repertorio di fonti documentarie.* 2 vols. Rome, 1992.

Secondary Works
Carabell, Paula. "Breaking the Frame: Transgression and Transformation in Giulio Romano's Sala dei Giganti." *Artibus et Historiae* 36 (1997): 87–100.
Gombrich, E. H., and Sergio Polano, eds. *Giulio Romano.* Milan, 1989. Exhibition catalog.
Hartt, Frederick. *Giulio Romano.* 2 vols. New Haven, Conn., 1958.
Talvacchia, Bette. *Taking Positions: On the Erotic in Renaissance Culture.* Princeton, N.J., 1999.
Verheyen, Egon. *The Palazzo del Tè in Mantua: Images of Love and Politics.* Baltimore, 1977.

PAULA CARABELL

GIUNTI PRESS. The Giunti were prominent printers, publishers, and booksellers in Italy, France, and Spain from the fifteenth to the seventeenth century; they published numerous major Renaissance authors and professional works. Family members in these countries entered into formal partnerships among themselves or cooperated informally to publish and sell books and other goods.

Lucantonio (1457–1538), the first Giunti to engage in bookselling, began publishing in Venice in 1489; his list consisted largely of liturgical and medical works. In 1491 he formed a partnership with his older brother Filippo (1456–1517), who began publishing in Florence in 1497, producing primarily humanist titles, Greek and Latin classics, and a few Italian titles by Petrarch, Boccaccio, and Pietro Bembo. Filippo's sons, Bernardo (1487–1551) and Benedetto (1506–1562), continued the business in Florence, increasing somewhat their emphasis on Greek editions and Italian authors such as Niccolò Machiavelli, Baldassare Castiglione, Jacopo Sannazaro, and Luigi Alamanni. Giunti publishing in Florence declined in the 1530s and 1540s during the period of instability that followed the overthrow of the republic in 1530.

A Product of the Giunti Press. Ptolemy with astrological symbols from Sigismondo Fanti's *Triompho di fortuna,* printed by Giunti at Venice in 1527.

Transportation difficulties and the rise in prices caused by the struggle between Spain and France also contributed to disruption of the book trade.

Five of Bernardo's sons entered the book business either in Spain or in Italy. The oldest son, Filippo (II), took over the business in Florence with the help of his brother Iacopo (d. 1591). From 1551 to 1604 they published no fewer than twenty-eight first editions and many reprintings, among them *Ricettario fiorentino* (Florentine recipe book; 1567), Giorgio Vasari's *Vite* (Lives of the artists; 1568), and Alamanni's *Avarchide* (1570). In 1570 Filippo moved to Venice, where he established a press independent of Lucantonio's heirs. Iacopo's son Cosimo published in Florence until the firm's demise under a heavy burden of debt in 1618; he continued the bookselling business until about 1622, when he was evicted from his rented spaces.

In Venice, Lucantonio was succeeded in 1538 by his sons Tommaso (1494–1566) and Giovan Maria. The firm continued to emphasize legal, liturgical, and medical works in Latin, overcoming a bankruptcy in 1553 and a fire in 1557. Giovan Maria's son, Lucantonio (II; d. 1602), took over management of the press in 1566. Intensifying competition in the book trade and the prohibitions of the Index of Prohibited Books led him to diversify his investments. The continued emphasis on liturgical and professional books protected the firm somewhat from the losses that prohibitions of contemporary authors brought to other booksellers. The firm ultimately came under the control of the heirs of Filippo (II), one of the Florentine Giunti who had moved to Venice in 1570. The firm sought its last privilege for publication in 1654. The Venetian Giunti were the most successful members of the family, publishing about 1,450 titles.

A nephew of Lucantonio, Giacomo (Jacques) Giunti (1487–1547), entered in the booming book market in Lyon, a center of legal and medical education, after 1520; he also represented Lucantonio's press in France. Jacques became a leading member of the Grande Compagnie des Libraires, the booksellers' cartel. He published Latin works of canon law and medicine and no contemporary authors except those who commented on these works. At his death the prosperous firm passed into the hands of his daughters and their husbands, but differences between the daughters and difficult economic times hurt business. The firm was sold in 1598.

Giunti activity in Spain stemmed from two migrations some half century apart. Giovanni Giunti (Juan de Junta), a son of the Florentine Filippo, moved in 1520 to Salamanca, where he was an agent for Giunti businesses in Italy. He began publishing in Burgos in 1526 and in Salamanca in 1532, serving the students and masters at the University of Salamanca and the ecclesiastical, administrative, and mercantile communities of Burgos; by 1532 he had published more than twenty-five books, a substantial output for a Spanish publisher of the period. After his death, the Salamanca operation passed briefly to his son-in-law, Matías Gast. His son Felipe Junta inherited the Burgos operation, publishing the new breviary in 1575 and the folio edition of *Chronica del famoso cavallero Cid Ruy Diez Campeador* in 1593.

About 1570 two sons of Bernardo Giunti of Florence, Luca and Giulio, came to Salamanca. Luca published a few works there between 1580 and 1584. Giulio (Julio; d. 1619) was called to Madrid by Philip II to create an official (though unsubsidized) royal press. A nephew, Tomás de Junta (d. 1624), was named "Impresor del Rey" (printer to the king) in 1594; Julio retained responsibility for publishing and bookselling. Tomás printed liturgical and devotional works such as those of Teresa of Ávila. The press was supported by printing laws and the new missal. After 1624, Tomás's widow, Teresa Junti (his first cousin), managed the press until her death in 1656. The Junti name disappeared from Spanish publishing with the death of her son, Bernardo, in 1658.

BIBLIOGRAPHY

Camerini, Paolo. *Annali dei Giunti.* Vol. 1 in 2 parts. Florence, 1962–1963.

Pettas, William. "The Giunti and the Book Trade in Lyon." In *Libri tipografi biblioteche: ricerche storiche dedicate a Luigi Balsamo a cura dell'Istituto di Biblioteconomia e Paleografia Università degli Studi, Parma.* Edited by Leo S. Olschki. Florence, 1997. Pages 169–192.

Pettas, William. *The Giunti of Florence: Merchant Publishers of the Sixteenth Century.* San Francisco, 1980.

Pettas, William. *A Sixteenth-Century Spanish Bookstore: The Inventory of Juan de Junta.* Philadelphia, 1995.

WILLIAM A. PETTAS

GLORY, IDEA OF. In the eleventh canto of Dante's *Purgatory* the character Oderisi da Gubbio remarks the ephemeral nature of earthly glory, beginning with the exclamation "Oh vana gloria de l'umane posse!" (O vain glory of human powers!; line 91) and concluding with examples drawn from the figurative arts (the painter Cimabue is surpassed by Giotto) and from poetry (Guido Guinizzelli yields the field to Guido Cavalcanti, who, in turn, will yield to an unspecified poet, perhaps Dante himself!). In the Middle Ages glory—true glory—was understood to be the immaterial, eternal reward granted to individuals after death for their adherence to a life of moral virtue and spiritual righteousness, a reward that would consist of their being forever in the presence of God. In the great scheme of things, earthly glory—which may lead one to the sin of pride or *vana gloria*—is empty and ultimately without purpose, a diversion from the true divine path: *sic transit gloria mundi* (so passes away the glory of the world).

Because of its rather rigid moral formulation, the medieval conception of glory would come under increasing scrutiny in the course of the fourteenth century. For example, in many of his works Petrarch describes his internal conflict as one of being caught between earthly attractions and spiritual aspirations. This interior struggle is dramatized throughout the *Canzoniere,* as in poem 264, where he mentions the "duo nodi" (two knots), the two passions that overcome him: love for Laura and love for glory. In Book 3 of the intensely personal *Secretum,* Petrarch notes that the desire for glory is innate in all humans, who should therefore follow the natural order of things and strive for glory in this life. In his series of six allegorical poems, *Trionfi* (Triumphs), "Fame" follows "Death" and is superseded only by "Time" and "Eternity," an order that indicates Petrarch's high regard for earthly glory.

The problems implicit in reconciling the great desire for earthly glory with proper Christian humility, which the works of Petrarch disclose, were resolved in the fifteenth and sixteenth centuries, at least theoretically, by the humanists and their notion of the dignity and perfectibility of the human species. In the Renaissance, glory is associated with other terms—fame, praise, renown, grandeur, honor—all of which would suggest that earthly excellence transcends physical death and guarantees "immortality" for the person in question. Also important in this process of emphasizing and valuing basic human qualities is the rediscovery and interpretation of classical texts on their own merits, without the moralizing and/or allegorizing overlay of the Middle Ages. The characteristics of the idea of glory in the Renaissance are the quest for personal glory (as opposed to the collective honor associated with particular groups in the Middle Ages), the various forms of hero worship and emulation of ancient or chivalric models, and the significant commemorative power of poetry and funereal monuments. Indeed, poets believed in their ability to confer (or withhold) fame—hence immortality—on those whom they celebrated in their verses; similarly, artists fashioned tombs that honored the memory of great individuals, both past and present, and kept them and their achievements alive. The desire of famous men and women to be remembered in the more durable forms of art and literature encouraged patronage of the arts among the aristocracy and other wealthy persons. For the Renaissance the idea of glory and its artistic and literary manifestations represent the attempt to establish a stable and enduring monument to the supreme achievements of humanity within this changing world, as well as to proclaim victory over the relentless attacks of death and fortune.

See also **Petrarch.**

BIBLIOGRAPHY

Boitani, Piero. *Chaucer and the Imaginary World of Fame.* Cambridge, U.K., 1984.

Joukovsky, Françoise. *La gloire dans la poésie française et néo-latine du seizième siècle (Des rhétoriqueurs à Agrippa d'Aubigné).* Geneva, 1969.

Lida de Malkiel, María Rosa. *La idea de la Fama en la edad media castellana.* Mexico City, 1952.

Tenenti, Alberto. *Il senso della morte e l'amore della vita nel Rinascimento (Francia e Italia).* Turin, Italy, 1989. See chapter 1, "Il mito della gloria," pp. 3–29.

CHRISTOPHER KLEINHENZ

GLUECKEL OF HAMELN (1645–1724), German-Jewish businesswoman and mother of twelve, known for her multivolume autobiography, written "to while away the long and melancholy nights." Born in Hamburg to Judah Joseph, also known as Judah Leib, a trader, and Beila Melrich, a businesswoman, Glueckel was raised in the wake of the Thirty Years' War, in an unstable time that was especially difficult for German Jews, who had long been subject to official pressures and popular violence. At fourteen, Glueckel married Chaim of Hameln and settled into a life of child raising and active business collaboration with her husband. In 1689, however, Chaim—the "crown of her head"—died, and a bereft Glueckel began her journal while continuing to run a business and arrange important marriages for her children. Ten years later, at the age of fifty-four, she married Cerf Lévy, the foremost banker of Lorraine, but his eventual bankruptcy and death led her to a disappointing old age, dependent, as she had feared, on her children. She died at age seventy-nine.

Her autobiography—the first such work from a Jewish woman that is known to historians—tells a tale of varied fortune. Alongside the usual accounts of births, illnesses, deaths, and weddings are larger events that chronicle European Jewish life on the eve of the Enlightenment. The journal is also significant in revealing, through her interspersed fables and tales, a woman influenced by storybooks, popular pietistic works, Arthurian romances, histories, and works on arithmetic, medicine, and the care of children. The result is a unique work that resonates above all in the faith that a mother hopes to pass along to her children, as she laments and exalts a God who "slays and heals, may his name be praised."

BIBLIOGRAPHY

Primary Work

Glueckel of Hameln. *The Memoirs of Glückel of Hameln.* Translated by Marvin Lowenthal with introduction by Robert S. Rosen. New York, 1977.

Secondary Works

Davis, Natalie Zemon. *Women on the Margins: Three Seventeenth-Century Lives.* Cambridge, Mass., 1995.

Minkoff, N. B. *Glickel Hamel (1645–1724).* New York, 1952.

SARAH COVINGTON

GOES, HUGO VAN DER (c. 1440–1482), Flemish painter. Van der Goes was probably born in Ghent; it is not known where or under whom he trained. In May 1467 the painter Joos van Wassenhove sponsored his enrollment as master in the Ghent painters' guild, which van der Goes served as dean in 1474–1475. Van der Goes periodically furnished decorations for Ghent pageants between 1468 and 1474 and was among the artists summoned to Bruges in 1468 to provide adornments for the marriage celebrations of Charles the Bold and Margaret of York. About 1476–1477 he entered the monastery of the Rode Klooster in the Forêt de Soignes at Auderghem near Brussels as a lay brother. In his early sixteenth-century chronicle of the monastery, Gaspar Ofhuys states that van der Goes was allowed to continue painting at the Rode Klooster, where he also welcomed dignitaries, including Archduke Maximilian. Ofhuys also says that on his return trip from Cologne in 1481 van der Goes—who suffered from depression ("melancholia"), feared damnation, and was inundated with commissions—lapsed into madness, from which he briefly recovered before his death.

Van der Goes's few surviving works are not signed, dated, or documented as autograph paintings. However, the writers Giorgio Vasari, in 1550, and Lodovico Guicciardini, in 1567, mention a painting by "Ugo d'Anversa," or Hugo of Antwerp, at the hospital of Santa Maria Nuova in Florence. They are almost certainly referring to van der Goes and his painting the *Adoration of the Shepherds* (Florence, Uffizi), which was sent from Bruges by Tommaso Portinari and arrived at Santa Maria Nuova in 1483 [see the color plates in volume 4]. The central panel of the huge triptych ordered by Portinari for the high altar of the hospital's church of Sant' Egidio shows the vividly characterized Virgin, Joseph, angels, and shepherds encircling the nude Christ child lying on the ground as they adore him. The wings depict the donor and his family kneeling in the foreground, with their huge patron saints standing behind them, before a continuous landscape, with the *Flight into Egypt* on the left and the *Procession of the Magi* on the right. The central panel includes the *Annunciation to the Shepherds* in the top right. The exterior of the wings depicts the *Annunciation,* painted in gri-

saille, with simulacra of statues of Mary and Gabriel placed in separate niches. Van der Goes's remarkable powers of illusion are indebted to Jan van Eyck, while the monumentality and plasticity of his forms, their unexpected shifts in scale, the abrupt spatial transitions, and the nervousness of his compositions are his own highly expressive and original creations. The picture is dated about 1475, based on the birth dates of the donor's children.

The Adoration of the Magi (Berlin, Staatliche Museen, Gemäldegalerie), with its virtuoso foreshortenings, is generally dated several years before the Portinari Altarpiece, while the *Nativity* (Berlin, Staatliche Museen, Gemäldegalerie) and *The Death of the Virgin* (Bruges, Groeningemuseum) are usually dated after it, due to their greater spatial ambiguities, dramatic eloquence, and cooler coloring. In the unusually wide *Nativity* two half-length prophets in the immediate foreground draw curtains aside, offering a vision of shepherds bursting into the shed, where Mary, Joseph, and the angels adore the child lying in the manger. In *The Death of the Virgin* the apostles, beside themselves with grief, collapse around the Virgin's bed, as Christ appears above her—accompanied by angels in a halo of light—to receive her soul. Van der Goes's devotional paintings enjoyed tremendous appeal, and a number of lost works can be reconstructed through the many copies made after them.

BIBLIOGRAPHY

Dhanens, Elisabeth. *Hugo van der Goes.* Antwerp, 1998.

Pächt, Otto. *Early Netherlandish Painting: From Rogier van der Weyden to Gerard David.* Edited by Monika Rosenauer. Translated by David Britt. London, 1997. Pages 155–210. Based on the author's typescript of a series of lectures that he delivered at the University of Vienna in 1996.

Reynolds, Catherine. "Goes, Hugo van der." In *The Dictionary of Art.* Edited by Jane Turner. Vol. 12: New York, 1996. Pages 844–851.

Sander, Jochen. *Hugo van der Goes: Stilentwicklung und Chronologie.* Mainz, Germany, 1992.

MICHAËL J. AMY

GOLD. *See* **Decorative Arts; Jewelry.**

GÓMEZ DE SILVA, RUY (c. 1516–1573), Spanish courtier and statesman. The son of noble Portuguese parents, Ruy Gómez de Silva came to Castile in 1526. Capitalizing on his service as a page and, later, privy steward to the future Philip II, Ruy used his private access to the prince to become Philip's *privado* (favorite). In 1553 an advantageous marriage to the aristocratic heiress Ana de Mendoza y de la Cerda further enhanced the favorite's status.

In 1556 Philip became king, and Ruy Gómez, allied with the king's secretary Francisco de Eraso, became the chief figure in his government for the next ten years. For his services he was granted the Neapolitan title of prince of Eboli. By the mid-1560s, Ruy Gómez's influence had waned as the king favored the more aggressive policies of soldiers such as the duke of Alba and bureaucrats like Cardinal Espinosa.

In his final decade Ruy Gómez sought to ensure the continued prominence of his lineage. These dreams were realized when Philip raised Ruy Gómez to grandee status as duke of Pastrana one year before his death in 1573. He transformed the ephemeral glory of courtiership into the permanent privilege of aristocratic status, and was lauded as the "master of Favorites, and of the understanding of Kings."

BIBLIOGRAPHY

Primary Work

Pérez, Antonio. *Cartas de Antonio Perez, Secretario de Estado que fue del Rey Catholico Don Phelippe II, de este nombre. Para diversas personas despues de su salida de España.* Paris, n.d. (1598?).

Secondary Work

Boyden, James M. *The Courtier and the King: Ruy Gómez de Silva, Philip II, and the Court of Spain.* Berkeley and Los Angeles, 1995. Modern biography.

JAMES M. BOYDEN

GÓNGORA Y ARGOTE, LUIS DE (1561–1627),

poet of the Spanish golden age. Góngora was born in Córdoba on 11 July 1561 to a noble but impoverished family. Educated as a child by the Jesuits, he later studied at the University of Salamanca from 1576 to 1580, where he acquired a solid background in classical culture, although he never graduated. Not a religious man by nature, he nevertheless took minor orders out of financial necessity, and in 1585 he became a prebendary of the cathedral of Córdoba. In 1617 he was granted a royal chaplaincy, which required him to move to Madrid. Unable to find adequate patronage at the court, he suffered financial hardship and ultimately returned to Córdoba in 1626. He died in penury a year later on 23 May 1627 while preparing an edition of his works.

His earliest poetry dates from around 1580, and he would soon prove a prolific and versatile poet who cultivated a multiplicity of genres—popular forms, Italianate sonnets, pastoral poetry, burlesque (often scurrilous) or satirical compositions, parodies, and some religious verse. He also experimented briefly but unsuccessfully with drama (*Las firmezas de Isabela* [The constancy of Isabela] and the unfin-

ished *El doctor Carlino*). Góngora viewed poetry as an intellectual activity, and most of his compositions are characterized by great complexity and a desire to challenge strict definitions of genre and orthodox notions of literary decorum. The early sonnets were influenced by Petrarch, Torquato Tasso, Jacopo Sannazaro, Fernando de Herrera, and Garcilaso de la Vega; but even his earliest compositions suggest a desire to transcend conventional practice. His most admired sonnets are masterpieces of emulation and invention, in which typical Renaissance topics and tropes are transformed to forge a distinctive personal aesthetic.

At the same time as he cultivated Italianate poetry, he returned to traditional Castilian forms such as the *romance* or ballad (verses of eight syllables with assonance in alternate lines) and the *letrilla* (six- or eight-syllable lines, divided into stanzas ending with an *estribillo* or refrain). Indeed, he is credited—together with Lope de Vega (who would become a lifelong rival)—with revitalizing the *romance*. He fashioned this popular oral form into a genre that accommodates difficult metaphors, intricate wordplay, and sophisticated wit. Notable among his many ballads is his "Romance de Angélica y Medoro" (1602), an astonishing tour de force of imitation and originality. The *letrilla,* another minor genre, was virtually reinvented by Góngora through his combination of extreme artificiality and elaborate idioms within the lines, rhythms, and tone associated with the low style. Góngora gained immediate popularity with his *romances,* and many of his ballads would be adapted as songs and dances.

It was, however, as an erudite and *culto* poet that he would leave an indelible mark. Around 1613 his most influential and notorious poems were circulated in manuscript form: *Soledades* (Solitudes) and *La fábula de Polifemo y Galatea* (The fable of Polyphemus and Galatea). In these major works, he brings to fruition tendencies already apparent in earlier poems. *Soledades,* arguably the most original and controversial poetic work produced during the Spanish golden age, contains a plethora of themes and topics unified only by the central figure of the *peregrino* or wanderer. *Soledades* is in fact two separate poems, and there is speculation that Góngora may have planned to write four *soledades.* The two parts of *Soledades* are narrative poems of great linguistic difficulty that have defied traditional categories of genre. In them we find echoes of Horace, Catullus, Virgil, and Ovid, as well as some similarities to Sannazaro's *Arcadia* and the Byzantine novel. *La fábula de Polifemo y Galatea,* a pastoral poem writ-

Luis de Góngora y Argote. Portrait by Diego de Velázquez (1599–1660). Oil on canvas; 1622. COURTESY MUSEUM OF FINE ARTS, BOSTON, MARY ANTOINETTE EVANS FUND

ten in an elevated style, also shatters strict generic divisions and is a masterpiece of intertextuality and erotic discourse. Based on book 13 of Ovid's *Metamorphoses, Polifemo* is a complex and finely wrought parody not only of Ovid and Petrarch (among others) but also of Góngora's own poetic procedures. Góngora returned to the ballad form in his last major poem, *La fábula de Píramo y Tisbe* (The fable of Pyramus and Thisbe; 1618), in which he again eliminates the division between low and high poetic discourse. This poem, which Góngora himself considered his culminating achievement, is an ambitious and brilliant parody of yet another Ovidian tale.

Góngora attempted in his poems to give Spanish verse the versatility and prestige of classical poetry. To that end, he introduced Latinate constructions, neologisms, mythological allusions, and a multiplicity of tropes and figures of speech including the Greek accusative, periphrasis, hyperbole, hyperbaton (the inversion or rearrangement of normal word order), oxymorons, and especially an intensification of metaphoric language. Góngora's oeuvre would come to be considered a new type of poetry—a

"poesia nueva"—and he would ultimately give his name to a controversial poetic style that would be widely imitated, both reverentially and parodically. This style, *gongorismo,* became synonymous with *cultismo* (the practice of cultured, erudite poetry) as well as with *culteranismo,* a disparaging term which—with its echoes of *luteranismo* or Lutheranism—suggests poetic heresy. The term "gongoristic" is still used to describe a difficult hermetic style. Góngora is also associated with *conceptismo*—a term most readily applied to the poetry of his rival Francisco de Quevedo—which describes a style based on *agudeza* or wit achieved through unexpected conceptual analogies.

Góngora's poems, particularly *Soledades* and *Polifemo,* would have an immeasurable impact on poetic practice of the seventeenth century, notably in the New World. Of great importance also was the controversy that his poetry generated: a vigorous literary battle whose apologies, accusations, defenses, and counterdefenses constitute a significant corpus of literary theory and criticism in early modern Spain. The controversy also provides a vivid look at Góngora's polemical relationship and rivalry with his contemporaries.

Góngora's poetry and that of his followers fell out of critical favor in the eighteenth and nineteenth centuries. Nevertheless, the early twentieth century saw a powerful resurgence of interest thanks to the group of poets known as the Generation of 1927, particularly Dámaso Alonso, who provided the first modern edition and study of Góngora's poetry. Now universally recognized as one of the greatest Spanish poets of all time, Góngora's influence continues to be felt in the work of contemporary writers on both sides of the Atlantic.

BIBLIOGRAPHY

Primary Works

Góngora, Luis de. *Fábula de Polifemo y Galatea.* Edited by Alexander A. Parker. Madrid, 1983.

Góngora, Luis de. *Fourteen Sonnets and Polyphemus.* Translated by Mack Singleton. Madison, Wis., 1975.

Góngora, Luis de. *Letrillas.* Edited by Robert Jammes. Madrid, 1991.

Góngora, Luis de. *Obras completas de Don Luis de Góngora y Argote.* Edited by Isabel and Juan Millé y Giménez. Madrid, 1932.

Góngora, Luis de. *Romances.* Edited by Antonio Carreño. Madrid, 1982.

Góngora, Luis de. *Soledades.* Edited by John Beverley. Madrid, 1979.

Góngora, Luis de. *The Solitudes of Luis de Góngora.* Spanish text with an English translation by Gilbert F. Cunningham. Preface by Alexander A. Parker. Introduction by Elias L. Rivers. Baltimore, 1968

Góngora, Luis de. *Sonetos completos.* Edited by Birute Ciplijaus-kaite. Madrid, 1976.
Góngora, Luis de. *Teatro completo.* Edited by Laura Dolfi. Madrid, 1993.

Secondary Works
Alonso, Dámaso. *Estudios y ensayos gongorinos.* Madrid, 1955.
Alonso, Dámaso. *Góngora y el "Polifemo."* 3 vols. Madrid, 1967.
Alonso, Dámaso. *La lengua poética de Góngora.* Madrid, 1950.
Ball, Robert. "Poetic Imitation in Góngora's 'Romance de Angé-lica y Medoro.'" *Bulletin of Hispanic Studies* 57 (1980): 33–54.
Jammes, Robert. *Etudes sur l'ouvre poétique de Don Luis de Góngora y Argote.* Bordeaux, France, 1967.
Smith, Paul Julian. "Barthes, Góngora, and Non-sense." *PMLA* 101 (1986): 82–94.

MARÍA CRISTINA QUINTERO

GONZAGA, GIULIA (1513–1566), Italian noble-woman and reformer. Married at fourteen to Ves-pasiano Colonna, a mature widower and cousin of Vittoria Colonna, Giulia Gonzaga became the count-ess of Fondi, a small domain near Caserta. Widowed in 1528 after only a year of marriage, Gonzaga held court in her small principality, welcoming intellec-tuals and artists. Her charms, unsullied name, and intelligent conversation attracted admirers, as well as writers. In turn, she became a literary subject, cele-brated equally for her virtue and her beauty, person-ifying for many the period's ideals of chaste wid-owhood and feminine perfection.

Like many educated women of her day, Gonzaga dabbled in poetry in the Petrarchan style, although her work was not published. The legend of Gon-zaga's exceptional beauty spread far afield. In 1534 the Turkish pirate Barbarossa attempted to kidnap her, but she daringly escaped on horseback in the middle of the night. The corsair had intended her as a worthy gift for his sultan Suleyman I. About this time, Gonzaga retired to a convent in Naples, where she could pursue her profound spiritual calling. She was active in the Catholic reformist movement led by the exiled Spaniard Juan de Valdés; after his death, Gonzaga offered her patronage to his disci-ples. Active in the religious debates concerning theo-logical matters, alongside Vittoria Colonna and Pie-tro Carnesecchi, Gonzaga was tainted with accusations of Protestantism. Sought by the Inquisi-tion for heresy, Giulia Gonzaga died in the convent before she could be arrested.

BIBLIOGRAPHY
Thérault, Suzanne. *Un cénacle humaniste de la Renaissance autour de Vittoria Colonna, châtelaine d'Ischia.* Florence and Paris, 1968.

FIORA A. BASSANESE

GONZAGA, HOUSE OF. The Gonzaga family ruled Mantua from 1328 to 1707. They came to power in a coup d'état directed by Luigi I (Ludovico I; 1267–1360). The Gonzaga acted as *signori* (lords) of Mantua until 1433, when the Holy Roman Em-peror Sigismund invested Gianfrancesco Gonzaga (c. 1395–1444) with the loftier title of marquis of Mantua. By the reign of Ludovico II (1412/14–1478) they had become important Lombard princes and had successfully defended their small state from the ambitions of their larger neighbors, Venice and Milan. After Ludovico's death his widow, Barbara of Brandenburg (1422–1481), avoided rivalry and vio-lence within her family by dividing much of the mar-quisate among her younger sons while reserving the largest portion for the heir to the marquisate itself, Federico I (1441/42–1484). This resulted in greater peace among relatives and a large number of small Gonzaga lordships.

The Gonzaga achieved their greatest success un-der Francesco II (1466–1519) and his wife, Isabella d'Este (1474–1539). In addition to ruling Mantua, Francesco acted as a condottiere, or mercenary cap-tain. He served the Venetian Republic as well as the Papal States and played a crucial role in driving King Charles VIII of France (1470–1498) from Italy in 1495. During Francesco's numerous absences from Mantua, Isabella distinguished herself as a ruler of considerable talent.

The sixteenth century witnessed serious chal-lenges to Gonzaga power. During the Habsburg-Valois Wars of Italy, the Gonzaga allied themselves with the Habsburg emperors against the French. Federico II (1500–1540) struggled to maintain this alliance without jeopardizing his role as *capitano ge-nerale della chiesa* (commander of papal armies). The emperor Charles V in turn elevated Federico to the dignity of duke of Mantua in 1530. Upon Fe-derico's death a regency was established for his two sons, Francesco I (ruled as Francesco III; 1533–1550) and Guglielmo (1538–1587); the regents included Federico's widow, Margherita Paleologo, and his brothers Ferrante Gonzaga (1507–1557) and Cardi-nal Ercole Gonzaga (1505–1563). It was the cardinal, however, who effectively ruled Mantua between 1540 and 1556.

Under Duke Guglielmo and his successor, Vin-cenzo I (1562/63–1612), the Gonzaga presided over a splendid court, maintained the alliance with the Habsburgs, and fostered the piety of the Counter-Reformation in the court chapel of Santa Barbara. However, with the death of the last of the original line, Vincenzo II (1594–1627), the fortunes of the

Gonzaga became tangled in the diplomacy of the Thirty Years' War (1618–1648). The subsequent War of Mantuan Succession (1628–1631) pitted the forces of the Habsburg emperor, who supported one claimant, against the forces of the Bourbon, who supported Carlo I (1580–1637), scion of a French branch of the family, the Gonzaga de Nevers. The success of the French placed the duchy in the hands of Carlo, but not before Mantua was put to the sack by imperial troops in 1630. The extinction of the ducal line came in 1707 with the exile of Ferdinando Carlo (1652–1708) and the subsequent reversion of the duchy, an imperial fief, to the Habsburgs.

The Gonzaga made significant contributions to the arts and humanist culture during the Renaissance. Marquis Gianfrancesco assisted in the growth of Mantua as a center of humanism by inviting the humanist Vittorino da Feltre (1378–1446) to establish his school, the Casa Giocosa (House of joy), for the education of his children. Under Ludovico II Mantua emerged as a noteworthy center of art patronage. For many years he and Barbara of Brandenburg patronized Andrea Mantegna (1431–1506), whose frescoes in the Camera degli Sposi in the ducal palace celebrate the power of Ludovico and his family, and Leon Battista Alberti (1404–1472), architect of the Basilica of Sant'Andrea. Both Francesco II and Isabella D'Este were notable patrons although, as her correspondence demonstrates, Isabella was surely the more interested of the two. Federico II relied upon Giulio Romano (c. 1499–1546) as his chief architect, most importantly for the Palazzo del Te. Romano also worked for Federico's brother, Cardinal Ercole Gonzaga, in the renovation of the interior of the local cathedral. In the seventeenth century Vincenzo I employed Peter Paul Rubens (1577–1640), who created his *Most Holy Trinity* for the Jesuit church in Mantua. By the start of the Mantuan War the Gonzaga collection in the ducal palace, along with the paintings and buildings in other parts of the city, formed an impressive collection. However, the financial difficulties of Vincenzo II led him to sell much of the Gonzaga picture collection to Charles I of England (1600–1649). Most of the remainder of the art in Mantua was dispersed at the death of Ferdinando Carlo in 1708 or was carried off by Napoleon at the end of the eighteenth century. For the most part, only those works that were not transportable—architecture and frescoes—remain in Mantua.

The Gonzaga also played a prominent role in the church. Younger sons of the Gonzaga dukes usually held the offices of bishop of Mantua and cardinal.

The first of these Gonzaga cardinals was Francesco Gonzaga (1444–1483), Ludovico III's second son. Perhaps most notable was Cardinal Ercole Gonzaga, who was widely respected in his own day as a reformer of his diocese, an astute regent for his nephews, and a papal legate to the Council of Trent from 1562 to 1563. By 1707 ten Gonzagas had served as cardinals. A cadet branch of the family produced Saint Aloysius (Luigi) Gonzaga (1568–1591), an early Jesuit saint.

A number of remarkable women gave luster to the Gonzaga family. The role of Isabella D'Este has already been mentioned. Cecilia Gonzaga (1425/26–1451), the daughter of Gianfrancesco, was said to have mastered Greek as a girl and is numbered among the women humanists of the Italian Renaissance. Elisabetta Gonzaga (1476?–1526), daughter of Federico I, married Duke Guidobaldo of Urbino and gained renown as the leader of the dialogue in *Il cortegiano* (*The Book of the Courtier;* 1528) by the Mantuan humanist Baldassare Castiglione. Giulia Gonzaga, countess of Fondi (1513–1566), maintained a court that was frequented by outstanding literary and religious figures.

See also **Mantua.**

BIBLIOGRAPHY

Coniglio, Giuseppe. *I Gonzaga*. Milan, 1967.

Mazzoldi, Leonardo, ed. *Mantova: La Storia*. Vol. 2. Mantua, Italy, 1961.

Mozzarelli, Cesare. *Mantova e i Gonzaga dal 1382 al 1707*. Turin, Italy, 1987.

Simon, Kate. *A Renaissance Tapestry: The Gonzaga of Mantua*. New York, 1988.

PAUL V. MURPHY

GONZÁLEZ DE MENDOZA, PEDRO (1428–1495), archbishop of Toledo and cardinal of Spain. Fifth son of the marquises of Santillana, Mendoza received appointment as a parish priest and archdeacon at age twelve. After study in Salamanca, Mendoza became royal chaplain of John II, king of Castile, in 1452 and bishop of Calahorra in 1453. He resided at the royal court as the preeminent prelate for the rest of his life.

After his father's death in 1458, Pedro assumed leadership of the powerful Mendoza family, shaping its policies for his own benefit and profit in the succession disputes of the reign of Henry IV of Castile. Pedro supported the legitimacy of the king's infant daughter Juana until 1473, when he became a supporter of Henry's half-sister Isabella. His support was decisive for the success of the Isabelline party. Pedro and his troops took part in the Battle of Toro, on 30 March 1476, which turned back a Portuguese invasion in support of Juana. From that moment on he was the favorite counselor of the Catholic monarchs (King Ferdinand and Queen Isabella), especially in religious policy. He decisively influenced notable events of the reign: creation of the Inquisition; construction of new dioceses in territory captured from the Muslims; expulsion of the Jews; and support for Christopher Columbus. He was present when the ruler of Granada surrendered the city to the Catholic monarchs and, as Pope Alexander VI's legate *a latere,* created the archepiscopal church of Granada, on 23 January 1493.

Mendoza accumulated religious offices in and out of Spain. From his position in Calahorra, he was elevated in 1467 to bishop of Sigüenza, a coveted diocese near the Mendoza family estates. He accompanied Cardinal Rodrigo Borgia (the future Pope Alexander VI) during his Castilian legation in 1472. Thanks to Borgia, Pedro was elevated to the cardinalate of San Giorgio in Velabro, which he soon exchanged for that of Santa María in Domnica and, finally, for that of Santa Croce in 1478. Henry IV appointed him high chancellor and ordered that he be called Gran Cardenal. He became archbishop of Seville in 1474 and administrator of the diocese of Osma in 1482. Upon being named archbishop of Toledo on 13 November 1482, and patriarch of Alexandria, he resigned his other dioceses except Sigüenza, but not his many other benefices of lesser income.

Mendoza used his stupendous wealth to build new ecclesiastical institutions and reconstruct and embellish old ones. He founded and endowed two institutions that shaped Renaissance charity in Spain: the scholarship college of Santa Cruz in Valladolid in 1484 and the foundling hospital of Santa Cruz in Toledo (constructed 1514–1564). For these and other architectural projects, he hired Italian and Italian-trained artists. His sepulcher, on the Gospel side of the Toledo cathedral's main altar, set a new fashion for Renaissance funerary art among the royal family and aristocracy.

Mendoza had three sons, legitimated by popes and monarchs: Rodrigo Díaz de Vivar, marquis of Zenete; Diego de Mendoza, count of Mélito; and Juan Hurtado de Mendoza. Through them, Pedro was the progenitor of illustrious lineages in Spanish Renaissance politics and literature.

BIBLIOGRAPHY

Gonzálvez, R. "González de Mendoza, Pedro." In *Diccionario de historia eclesiástica de España.* Edited by Quentín Aldea, et al. 5 vols. Madrid, 1987.

Linaghan, Patrick. "Reinterpreting the Italian Renaissance in Spain: Attribution and Connoisseurship." *The Sculpture Journal* 2 (1998): 13–23.

Nader, Helen. *The Mendoza Family in the Spanish Renaissance, 1350–1550.* New Brunswick, N.J., 1979.

Villalba Ruiz de Toledo, F. Javier. *El cardenal Mendoza 1428–1495.* Madrid, 1988.

HELEN NADER

GOTHIC. The last two decades of the nineteenth century in French and English critical literature on architecture bore witness to formal stylistic definitions and the first widespread aesthetic acceptance of what architectural historians continue to refer to as Gothic architecture. This aesthetic appreciation of the pointed style developed two generations after the Gothic had been stylistically segregated and nominally distinguished from other medieval architectural styles such as the Romanesque, an appellation inaugurated as recently as 1819. This art historical consensus regarding naming was, however, nearly four centuries in the making.

The epithet "International Gothic" refers, for the most part, to a strikingly homogeneous and dominant pan-European style in painting, sculpture, and graphic arts such as woodcut and engraving, which developed and spread from a mid-twelfth-century French Gothic architectural matrix and evolved into both the Italian and Northern Renaissance styles of circa 1420. Turn-of-the-century works by Flemish artists who had settled in France—such as the sculpture of Claus Sluter at Dijon from c. 1385 to 1406, the manuscript illumination of the Limbourg brothers, the panel painting of Melchior Broederlam (active c. 1387–1409) and works from the south, as in the painting of the Italian Gentile da Fabriano (c. 1370–1427) and the sculpture of Jacobello and Pierpaolo dalle Masegne of the 1390s in Venice—all attest to an increasingly realistic, weighty, and volumetric artistic spirit accompanied by a fondness for intricate and abundant detail.

The construction and periodization of Gothic architecture was the work of Italian Renaissance criticism beginning with the segregation of Gothic architecture from that of the ancients and from Italy's revival of architecture *all'antica* (ancient style), which followed in the early fifteenth century. The contemporary notion of style as a transcendent principle, independent of the architecture, and of successive and unified stylistic periods, was not an intellectual possibility in the Middle Ages. Medieval historians generally favored a strict chronological and geographic ordering of events, basing their narratives on either biblical or classical theoretical and rhetorical models. Medieval commentary was generally restricted to inventory-like compilations or instructional treatises, unconcerned with formal criticism of a historical or stylistic character. While we have some examples of the medieval ability to differentiate stylistically between architectural types—for example, in the writing of Gervase of Canterbury (c. 1141–1210)—in general the theoretical framework of medieval narrative, for the most part chronologically and eschatologically based, did not employ incisive visual analyses and was not concerned with explaining any sense of stylistic innovation.

Italian Renaissance historians took on the task of blending medieval narrative techniques with a thematic overview to create history as an organic and cyclical narrative. Historiographical concepts born in the Italian Renaissance not only recognized a *media aetas,* or middle age, but also appraised that age in negative terms. The critical conviction that there were two kinds of architecture, an earlier and better (ancient) and a later and less refined (medieval)—and the corollary notion that there had been a decline or devolution in architecture—was perhaps the most significant and pregnant dictum of Renaissance art historical criticism.

It was primarily thanks to Giorgio Vasari (1511–1574) that the blanket term "Gothic" was applied to all medieval architecture by writers from the sixteenth to the early nineteenth century. Before Vasari, the adjective "Gothic" in Italy had generally been regarded as synonymous with "barbarian," and later came to signify foreign or non-Roman culture and people as well as architecture. In his *Lives of the Artists* (1550, rev. 1568), Vasari was the first to conflate the historical meaning (*I Goti,* the Goths, as a specific barbarian tribe) with the negative aesthetic evaluation of their work as barbarous. Vasari's formulation did not, however, spring *ex vacuo.* The same awareness of medieval architectural style as distinct from both ancient and modern can be seen in the writing of Filarete (Antonio Averlino) around 1460, in Antonio Manetti's *Vita di Brunelleschi* (Life of Brunelleschi; c. 1480), and in a letter by Raphael to Leo X (c. 1518). Although none of these works was published until after 1600, they were the common property of contemporary humanists, and Vasari drew on all of them to formulate his ideas.

See also **Renaissance, Interpretations of the,** *subentry on* **Giorgio Vasari.**

BIBLIOGRAPHY

Bizzarro, Tina Waldeier. *Romanesque Architectural Criticism: A Prehistory.* New York, 1992.

Frankl, Paul. *The Gothic: Literary Sources and Interpretations through Eight Centuries.* Princeton, N.J., 1960.

TINA WALDEIER BIZZARRO

GOULART, SIMON (1543–1628), French humanist. Simon Goulart, or Goulard, was a noted humanist scholar and follower of the Calvinist reform movement. His family lived in Senlis just north of Paris. What little is known of his youth suggests that his rearing and character closely parallel John Calvin's. Apparently self-taught in the classics, he studied law in Paris, where he was attracted to Reformed preaching. He became an intimate of the great Joseph Justus Scaliger, beginning his commitment to the classical tradition—that is, humanism, which stressed the mastery of languages and the ancient traditions. He also became interested in the Reformers' desire to restore a deep spirituality to the Christian church.

Arriving in Geneva in 1566, Goulart was ordained a pastor and put in charge of two churches in the environs; he eventually moved to the city parish of Saint Gervais. In 1570 he married Suzanne Picot of the Genevan bourgeoisie. This alliance gave him a strong voice in Genevan affairs. From 1607 to 1612 he acted as moderator of the Geneva Company of Pastors. His great equity of judgment was widely recognized, and he was often called on to mediate disputes. For example, he consulted with the fiery pastor Le Gagneulx, who had attacked the magistracy in his preaching. In these tasks Goulart was usually successful.

Goulart was a formidable linguist and prolific author, writing in the Swiss patois, Italian, German, and the ancient languages. He edited the famous collection of Protestant pamphlets responding to the massacre of Saint Bartholomew's Day titled *Mémoires de l'estat de France sous Charles IX* (Memoirs of the state of France under Charles IX; 1576), wrote and translated biographies of Protestant leaders, including Théodore de Bèze's *Les vrais pourtraits des hommes illustres en piété et doctrine* (True portraits of men illustrious in piety and doctrine; 1581), and pamphlets against Roman Catholic teaching, and translated Greek and Roman classics; but he was most celebrated for his oratorical skills, which he used to calm disturbances in Geneva.

See also **Humanism,** *subentry on* **France; Rhétoriqueurs.**

BIBLIOGRAPHY

Jones, Leonard Chester. *Simon Goulart, 1543–1628: Étude biographique et bibliographique.* Geneva, 1917.

Kingdon, Robert, et al., eds. *Registres de la compagnie des pasteurs de Genève.* Geneva, 1964–. See especially volume 4 and following for frequent references to Goulart.

BRIAN G. ARMSTRONG

GOURNAY, MARIE DE (Marie le Jars de Gournay; 1565–1645), French woman of letters and feminist. Gournay's family was noble but not wealthy, and financial difficulties stemming from her father's death in 1577 dogged her for the rest of her life.

Resisting her mother's pressure to marry and disdain for her intellectual ambitions, Marie de Gournay was a determined autodidact, first mastering the Latin language and its texts, then progressing to Greek. But her most profound literary inspiration was Michel de Montaigne's *Essays,* which she discovered at about the age of eighteen. When she encountered Montaigne in 1588, an intense pupil-mentor relation developed: he became her "second father," she his "adoptive daughter."

The latter role offered Marie de Gournay not only a counterweight to her mother's expectations but also a focus for her first literary endeavors. Yet it also kept her in the shadow of the great male author, and the resulting psychological conflict is unmistakable. Her single work of fiction, which sprang from their conversation during a stroll, was addressed reverently to him, and was eventually published as *Le proumenoir de Monsieur de Montaigne* (The promenade of Monsieur Montaigne; 1594). The plot, however, concerned a princess destroyed by both masculine treachery and her own reckless passion; the form was that of the tragic romance, which Montaigne despised; included was a long feminist digression doubtfully consistent with Montaigne's attitudes.

By 1594, Montaigne had been dead for two years, and the devastated "adoptive daughter" resolved to honor his memory with a new edition of the *Essays,* which she produced to an impressive scholarly standard in 1595. Several further editions followed. For the first, she wrote an extravagantly personal preface in which she equally championed Montaigne as a universal genius and herself as an intellectual woman combating male misogyny.

This document, at once sharply satirical and self-indulgently emotional, provoked the antifeminist hostility and ridicule that would be intermittently directed at Marie de Gournay for the remainder of her life, as she struggled—with remarkable success—to maintain a literary "salon" in Paris. Her reaction, too, was characteristic: she retracted the preface in the next edition, only to recycle it elsewhere. Beginning

with *Le proumenoir,* her substantial literary production, including autobiography, poetry, and explicitly feminist essays (most notably *Égalité des hommes et des femmes* [Equality of men and women; 1622]), was subjected to continual revision. The process was less one of refinement than of give-and-take, and it points to an ongoing negotiation of identity vis-à-vis a now purely symbolic father. Only after many years did she claim to cast a shadow of her own, with her first collected works, *L'ombre de la Damoiselle de Gournay* (The shadow of Miss de Gournay; 1626).

Largely neglected after her death until the nineteenth century, Marie de Gournay was then chiefly remembered, it seems, in order to be patronized: both her literary abilities and her feminism were depreciated. In the late twentieth century, however, she began to attract scholarly respect on both accounts. By the 1990s her work was taken more seriously than ever, with the support of a growing number of new editions and—for the first time—translations.

BIBLIOGRAPHY

Primary Works

Gournay, Marie le Jars de. *Les advis; ou, Les presens de la Demoiselle de Gournay: 1641.* Edited by Jean-Philippe Beaulieu and Hannah Fournier with the collaboration of Delbert Russell. 3 vols. Amsterdam and Atlanta, Ga., 1997–. Edition of Marie de Gournay's final collection of her works.

Gournay, Marie le Jars de. "The Equality of Men and Women" and "The Ladies' Grievance." Translated with a biographical introduction by Maja Bijvoet. In *Women Writers of the Seventeenth Century.* Edited by Katharina M. Wilson and Frank J. Warnke. Athens, Ga., 1989. Pages 3–29.

Gournay, Marie le Jars de. *Fragments d'un discours féminin.* Edited by Elyane Dezon-Jones. Paris, 1988. Useful collection of several texts in French with an extended analytical introduction.

Gournay, Marie le Jars de. *Marie de Gournay's 1595 Preface to Montaigne's* Essais. Translated and edited by Richard Hillman and Colette Quesnel. With an introduction by Richard Hillman. Tempe, Ariz., 1998. Includes French text as edited by François Rigolot.

Gournay, Marie le Jars de. *Le promenoir de Monsieur de Montaigne.* Edited by Jean-Claude Arnould. Paris, 1996. Text of 1641 with variants from all preceding editions.

Secondary Works

Horowitz, Maryanne Cline. "Marie de Gournay, Editor of the *Essais* of Michel de Montaigne: A Case-Study in Mentor-Protégée Friendship." *Sixteenth Century Journal* 17 (1986): 271–284.

Ilsley, Marjorie Henry. *A Daughter of the Renaissance: Marie le Jars de Gournay: Her Life and Works.* The Hague, Netherlands, 1963. The standard biography.

Regosin, Richard. "Montaigne's Dutiful Daughter." *Montaigne Studies* 3 (1991): 103–127.

Stanton, Domna C. "Woman as Object and Subject of Exchange: Marie de Gournay's *Le proumenoir* (1594)." *L'esprit créateur* 23, no. 2 (1983): 9–25.

RICHARD HILLMAN

GOVERNMENT. *See* **Political Thought.**

GRANADA, LUIS DE (Luis de Sarriá; 1504–1588), Dominican reformer and author. Luis de Granada was famous both as a preacher and as an important religious author of his time; his *Libro de la oración y meditación* (1554; Book of prayer and meditation) was by far the most published book in early modern Spain, and his guides to holy life and prayer were deeply esteemed by professional religious and secular readers alike.

After his father's death in 1509, Granada and his mother fell into severe poverty until the nobleman Luis Hurtado de Mendoza hired young Luis to accompany his son to school and so become educated as well. In 1529, four years after professing into the Dominican Order, he was selected to attend the famous Dominican college of San Gregorio in Valladolid, where he completed his studies in 1534. His request for a post in the New World was denied, and he was assigned the reform of the Dominican convent of Scala Coeli in Anadalucía. From this point forward, the reform of extant Catholic institutions and populations became his life's work.

While in Andalucía he met the ascetic preacher Juan de Ávila (1500–1569), whose penitential lifestyle and emotionally charged preaching method became the backbone of Granada's own reformist agenda. Granada quickly became renowned as a preacher and as a humble man, providing a vivid contrast with the increasing ostentation of the Counter-Reformation Spanish Church. He refused one high ecclesiastical post after another, striving instead to negotiate a delicate balance between the world and God. In 1546 he vowed to preach in the least attended zones of Spain, a mission he carried out until 1551 when he was assigned as chaplain to Cardinal Enrique, then Prince of Portugal, and settled in Évora. Five years later he was made Dominican Provincial.

Spain's Inquisitorial *Index* of 1559 included Luis de Granada's immensely popular *Libro de la oración,* his *Guía de pecadores* (Guide for sinners, approved by the Council of Trent in 1563), and also his *Manual de diversas oraciones y espirituales ejercicios* (Manual of diverse prayers and spiritual exercises). The conservative Catholic Church in Spain would not tolerate Granada's ideal of universal, unmediated access to the scriptures and to God. Undaunted, Granada rewrote his books to include even more scripture translations and added citations of other prohibited authors such as Erasmus.

When the revised *Guía de pecadores* was published in 1566, the tide had turned in Spanish religious politics and Granada received the open support of Philip II (1556–1598). In 1580, Philip tried to use him to advance Spanish designs on the Portuguese throne, but Granada maintained his alliance with Christ, temporarily alienating his king. Similarly, in 1583 he rejected a papal appointment to cardinal.

Luis de Granada's reputation, and some say his canonization, was compromised by his steadfast support of the visionary nun María de la Visitación, whose ecstatic experiences were determined to be a hoax in 1588. In his last work, *Sermón de las caídas públicas* (Sermon about public downfalls), dictated on his deathbed in 1588, he declared his error in spiritual discernment.

Luis de Granada was influential in both Catholic and Protestant reformist piety across western Europe. His twelve major works, widely translated, especially into Italian, together with three translations, sermon collections, Christian and classical compendiums, and several hundred extant letters are eloquent testimony to his commitment to the most basic and demanding principles of Christian faith.

BIBLIOGRAPHY

Primary Work
Granada, Luis de. *Obras completas.* Edited by Álvaro Huerga. 40 vols. Madrid, 1994–. Complete edition of Luis de Granada's works, with scholarly apparatus and including both pre- and post-*Index* editions.

Secondary Works
Huerga, Álvaro. *Fray Luis de Granada. Una vida al servicio de la Iglesia.* Madrid, 1988. A thorough study of Luis de Granada's life and times.
Moore, John A. *Fray Luis de Granada.* Boston, 1977. An introduction to the life and times of Luis de Granada.
Rhodes, Elizabeth. "Spain's Misfired Canon: The Case of Fray Luis de Granada's *Libro de la oración.*" *Journal of Hispanic Philology* 15 (1990): 43–63. Studies *The Book of Prayer* in light of political interests that form the literary canon.

ELIZABETH RHODES

GRANADA, CONQUEST OF. *See* **Moriscos.**

GRAND TOUR. Knowledge of classical antiquity and the Italian Renaissance was brought to England by the large number of young aristocrats and gentlemen who undertook the grand tour of the Continent. Beginning about the middle of the sixteenth century,

Grand Tour. Scenes from the life of Sir Henry Unton. Anonymous; 1596. BY COURTESY OF THE NATIONAL PORTRAIT GALLERY, LONDON

visits to the principal cultural and artistic sites of Europe became a virtually essential aspect of the education of the English elite.

Such tours nearly always included Rome and Florence. Sometimes they lasted two or three years. Sir Philip Sidney, for instance, left England in 1572, shortly after he graduated from Oxford, and did not return until 1575. He visited France, Germany, and the Netherlands in addition to Italy, learning languages and studying the ways of foreign courts as well as admiring scenery and great buildings. He was accompanied by a tutor (who was half Italian and thus fluent in that language) and several servants.

Queen Elizabeth occasionally subsidized such trips, anticipating that the returned travelers might serve her as diplomats or experts in foreign trade. Parents and educational institutions also provided funds. Fynes Moryson, who spent four years on the Continent during the 1590s, received an annual grant of twenty pounds from Peterhouse, Cambridge, where he remained a fellow while he traveled as far afield as Poland. Italy, as usual, was the main object of his tour; he wrote a book, the *Itinerary,* which describes the sights of Rome, Naples, Florence, Siena, Venice, and Genoa. Other famous tourists and writers were Sir Henry Wootton, Sir Francis Bacon, Theophilus Howard (the teenaged son of the earl of Suffolk), and Sir Kenelm Digby.

Inigo Jones's trip to Italy undertaken in 1613 in the company of Thomas Howard, earl of Arundel, was of special importance, for Jones was the first architect to bring to England the pure classical style of Vitruvius and Palladio. Arundel, for his part, acquired a fine collection of antique statuary; a surviving portrait depicts him proudly displaying this collection, as arranged in the long gallery of his country house. Another charming bit of visual evidence of the grand tour is the painting of Sir Henry Unton (d. 1596) now in the National Gallery in London. It shows us Unton's entire life, from the cradle to the grave; intermediate scenes represent him crossing the English Channel to France and the Alps to Italy.

Young men were frequently advised to avoid Douai and Reims, where they might be exposed to the temptations of Catholicism. Paris and Rome were thought to be dens of corruption, but few were willing to bypass them. Travelers were often robbed or assaulted on the roads, leading some to adopt disguises suggesting that they were poor peasants.

Occasional diplomatic problems and foreign wars provided temporary setbacks for English tourists, but the grand tour remained an important aspect of English society throughout the seventeenth and eighteenth centuries.

See also **Travel and Travel Literature.**

BIBLIOGRAPHY

Hibbert, Christopher. *The Grand Tour.* London, 1969. A popular work, but accurate and valuable.

Trease, Geoffrey. *The Grand Tour*. New York, 1967. Full of entertaining anecdotes.

STANFORD E. LEHMBERG

GRAPHIC ARTS. *See* **Drawing; Printmaking.**

GRAZZINI, ANTON FRANCESCO (1503–1584), Florentine writer. Grazzini, frequently referred to by his academic pseudonym, "Il Lasca" (the carp), was a Florentine comedy writer, burlesque poet, and author of one of the most important collections of sixteenth-century novellas, *Le cene* (The suppers). In 1540 he helped found the Accademia degli Umidi, a group dedicated to fostering the use of Tuscan as the literary language; the following year the academy was more formally organized under the patronage of the grand duke, Cosimo I de' Medici, and renamed the Accademia Fiorentina. In 1547 Grazzini was expelled from the academy because of several disagreements with his fellow members but was reinstated in 1566 through the efforts of Leonardo Salviati, with whom he then founded the Accademia della Crusca in 1582. Ironically, throughout his literary career, Grazzini's stance was essentially anti-academic in that he was constantly engaged in polemic with traditionalists and with those who espoused the use of highly formal language in literary compositions. His own writings, which reveal a deep interest in subjects of a very popular and often scabrous nature, employ the colloquial language of his fellow Florentine citizens.

Grazzini was an active editor of comic poetry; in 1548 he published an edition of the poetry of Francesco Berni (1498–1535) and in 1552 of Il Burchiello (Domenico di Giovanni, 1404–1449). He also edited an important collection of *canti carnascialeschi,* or carnival songs (1559), written by both anonymous and well-known poets for performance during public festivals. Grazzini was perhaps best known among his contemporaries as a poet who followed in the tradition of Berni and Burchiello, celebrating popular language and culture. *Municipalismo* or *campanilismo*—a sort of parochialism in the evocation of character and place—characterizes all of his writings from his burlesque poetry on popular themes to his comedies and collection of novellas. Grazzini's novellas, collected under the title *Le cene* (first edition, London, 1756), are, together with Matteo Bandello's (c. 1485–1561), among the most important in the sixteenth century and follow the tradition of Boccaccio's *Decameron* in their use of a frame structure (several young people take turns telling stories on three consecutive Thursdays) and of the *beffa,* or practical joke, which appears frequently in Boccaccio's collection and becomes a dominant motif in *Le cene*. The stories are particularly noteworthy for their representation of life in Florence, especially among artisans and tradesmen, and for their detailed description of Florentine locales. Grazzini's seven comedies (among the best known are *La strega* [The witch] and *La spiritata* [The possessed woman]) and one farce, *Il frate* (The friar), also take their inspiration from Florentine life and culture. Like most sixteenth-century comedies, they have a five-act structure with characters drawn from the stereotypes established by classical comedy and from comic characters of the novella tradition, although they also display the comic style of the *commedia dell'arte* that Grazzini championed for its freshness and vitality of language.

BIBLIOGRAPHY

Primary Works

Grazzini, Anton Francesco. *Le cene*. Edited by Riccardo Bruscagli. Rome, 1976.

Grazzini, Anton Francesco. *Le rime burlesche, edite e inedite*. Edited by Carlo Verzone. Florence, 1882.

Grazzini, Anton Francesco. *Teatro*. Edited by Giovanni Grazzini. Bari, Italy, 1953.

Secondary Works

Plaisance, Michel. "Culture et politique à Florence de 1542 à 1551: Lasca et les *Humidi* aux prises avec l'Académie Florentine." In *Les Écrivains et le pouvoir en Italie à l'époque de la Renaissance*. Edited by André Rochon. Paris, 1973. Pages 149–242.

Plaisance, Michel. "La structure de la 'beffa' dans les 'Cenes' d'Anton Francesco Grazzini." In *Formes et significations de la "beffa" dans la littérature italienne de la Renaissance*. Edited by André Rochon. Paris, 1972. Pages 45–97.

Rodini, Robert J. *Antonfrancesco Grazzini: Poet, Dramatist, and Novelliere, 1503–1584*. Madison, Wis., 1970. Only monographic study in English.

ROBERT J. RODINI

GRECO, EL. *See* **El Greco.**

GREEK ÉMIGRÉS. Although the myth that Greeks fleeing from the Fall of Constantinople in 1453 spurred the Renaissance in Italy no longer has any adherents, the fact remains that Greek émigrés to Renaissance Italy had an impact disproportionate to their number. The first of these Renaissance émigrés to exert important influence was Manuel Chrysoloras (c. 1349–1415), who arrived in Florence from Constantinople to teach Greek in 1397. However, he was certainly not the first Greek to come to Italy, and the history of the Greeks before Chrysoloras provides much insight into the Renaissance.

Greeks in Southern Italy. Into the twentieth century Greek-speaking villages could be found in southern Italy. These Greek-speakers were remnants not of ancient Magna Graecia or of any Renaissance migration, but rather of a large influx of Greeks into southern Italy fleeing the Slavic inundation of the Balkan Peninsula from the late sixth through the eighth centuries. These medieval Greek immigrants domesticated the Greek liturgy and Basilian monasticism in southern Italy. It was no accident that several Greek-speakers became popes in eighth-century Rome. Moreover, the Byzantine Empire controlled much of southern Italy until the Norman conquest in the eleventh century. Once under Latin control, southern Italy became the chief center of the translation of Greek texts in the Latin West. However, the amount of translating activity was moderate and limited mainly to scientific and philosophical texts, a focus that reflected the dominant interests of the medieval universities.

A Greek colony also existed in medieval Venice but did not become an important intellectual center until the Fall of Constantinople in 1453 swelled its ranks with educated refugees. In the 1340s in Avignon, Petrarch tried unsuccessfully to learn Greek from the learned south Italian monk Barlaam of Calabria. In the early 1360s in Florence, Giovanni Boccaccio persuaded his compatriots to hire another south Italian Greek, Leontius Pilatus, to teach Greek. Pilatus seems to have done little or no teaching, but he did complete a rather literal translation of Homer's *Iliad* and *Odyssey*. In 1380 and 1381 the scholarly Greek expatriate Simon Atumanus lived in Rome, where he probably gave Greek lessons; he also translated Plutarch's essay *De cohibenda ira* (On containing one's anger) into Latin. Atumanus's teaching had no significant resonance, but his translation of Plutarch interested the humanist chancellor of Florence, Coluccio Salutati, who revised it to improve its Latinity. Because Salutati knew no Greek, his revision was purely stylistic. Urged on by the young humanists in his circle, he was able eventually to persuade the Florentine government to hire at a generous salary the Greek diplomat and scholar Manuel Chrysoloras to teach Greek at the University of Florence.

Teachers of Greek, Learners of Latin. The arrival of Chrysoloras in Florence in 1397 was the decisive moment in the hellenization of the Renaissance. Although he taught there only three years,

he had a galvanizing effect. Salutati had gathered around himself a critical mass of humanists ready to learn Greek and set a standard for all humanists thereafter. Led by Leonardo Bruni, the most brilliant of Chrysoloras's students in Florence, humanists began the two-hundred-year Renaissance campaign to translate into Latin the whole of the extant antique Greek literary heritage. Chrysoloras taught Greek privately in Pavia, Milan, and Rome after he left Florence. In the early fifteenth century some Italian humanists, such as Guarino da Verona, went to Greece to learn the language of Homer. However, the only important Greek teacher in Italy in the decades after Chrysoloras was someone who specialized in Latin: George of Trebizond (1396–c. 1474). George had been summoned from his native Crete by a Venetian nobleman in 1416 to serve as a Greek scribe. He learned Latin with amazing rapidity and soon established himself as a successful teacher of Latin. He had accurately gauged the academic market; except perhaps for a place like Florence, there was not enough demand for Greek language and literature in the Italian society to make specialization in that field a viable career.

On the other hand, some Greeks wanted to learn from the Latins, not humanism (traditional Byzantine education was already humanistic and classical), but medieval scholasticism. George of Trebizond became a great admirer of Latin scholasticism. Another Greek, John Argyropoulos (1415–1487), received a degree from the University of Padua in 1444 and then returned to Constantinople, where he established a successful school. Still another Greek, Theodore Gaza (c. 1415–1475), arrived in Italy from Constantinople in 1440 and by 1446 seems to have begun to study medicine at Ferrara while teaching Greek. George Scholarios, destined to lead the opposition to union with Rome, learned Latin as a young man and even as leader of the antiunionists translated a great deal of Saint Thomas Aquinas into Greek. Bessarion (1403–1472), after Chrysoloras, the most important of all the Greeks who came to Italy, did not know Latin before he arrived. Nonetheless, he had already read Aquinas in the Greek translation made by a Greek Latinophile of an earlier generation, Demetrius Cydones.

Bessarion and Nicholas V. An event that brought a great number of Greeks to Italy was the Council of Ferrara-Florence in 1438 and 1439. There was a great deal of interaction between Greeks and Latins, much of it mediated by the Greek Nicholas Secundinus of Negroponte, given leave from his job as a Venetian civil servant to act as the council's main translator, but the only important participant who settled in Italy permanently as a result was the young bishop of Nicaea, Bessarion, who was made a cardinal by Pope Eugenius IV in 1439. For the next thirty years Bessarion's household became a refuge for Greek scholars and a point of encounter between Greek and Latin intellectuals, including scholastics as well as humanists. After the Fall of Constantinople, Bessarion saw it as his duty to gather as much as he could of Greece's literary remains. The result was the greatest Greek library up to that time in the West. Bessarion bequeathed it to Venice, the Republic of St. Mark, which he called a "second Byzantium," and it remains the historic core of the Biblioteca Marciana.

The Fall of Constantinople in 1453 did not result in any mass migration to the West mainly because so much of the Byzantine state had been lost to the Ottoman Turks long before then. Many of the elite did flee, however, including scholars. One of the refugees was John Argyropoulos. Because of his command of Latin, his degree from Padua, and his reputation among Italians, he landed well; in 1456 Florence gave him a chair in Aristotelian philosophy, and in the next fifteen years he became a major figure in Renaissance intellectual life. Many Greeks found a temporary safe haven with Bessarion, but eventually they had to make their own way in the West.

Even before the refugees arrived, one important avenue of advancement had been opened by Pope Nicholas V (1447–1455). Wishing to have Greek texts of every kind translated into Latin, Nicholas had made available papal monies to Greeks like his secretary George of Trebizond and the teacher Theodore Gaza, both of whom began dedicating themselves to translations, especially scientific and philosophical works, which because of their difficulty were apparently considered especially suitable for native Greek translators. Many of the post-1453 refugee translators, such as John Argyropoulos, Andronicus Callistus, Iohannes Sophianus, and Demetrius Chalcondyles, confirmed this assumption in the texts they chose to translate. Not all of these translations were successful, but many, such as those of Theodore Gaza, remained standard into the sixteenth century and beyond. Gaza, in fact, became something of a hero to future Italian Hellenists such as Angelo Poliziano and Aldo Manuzio.

Scribes and Publishers. The patronage the émigrés received was unreliable, however, especially after Bessarion, their great patron, died in 1472. What the Greeks needed was secure jobs. Some did well; Demetrius Chalcondyles became a successful teacher in Padua, Florence, and Milan; Constantine Lascaris was given a chair in Messina; and Athanasius Chalkeopoulos was made bishop of Gerace (in Calabria). Janus Lascaris thrived as a scholar and diplomat over a very long life. Marcus Musurus had a distinguished career in Padua. However, as Constantine Lascaris pointed out in a letter toward the end of the century, Andronicus Callistus could not establish himself in Italy and died trying to secure a position in England; John Argyropoulos was eventually reduced to selling his library to survive in Rome; Theodore Gaza died in virtual exile in a small south Italian monastery; the wandering teacher Demetrius Castrenus despaired and returned to Crete. We might add that others, like Callistus, went north: the querulous Andronicus Contoblacas simply disappeared, while George Heronymus made a living in Paris as a Greek tutor and scribe.

Copying manuscripts was in fact a major source of income for many Greek émigrés, whose hands in manuscripts modern scholars have identified. By the late fifteenth century, Greeks were also active in the new printing industry, the first being the Cretan Demetrius Damilas, who printed Constantine Lascaris's Greek grammar in Venice in 1476 before relocating his press to Florence. Another Cretan, Zacharias Calliergis, also first published in Venice before relocating his press to Rome in the early sixteenth century. Several Greeks participated in Aldo Manuzio's famous press in Venice as editors and proofreaders. Indeed, if we take Emile Legrand's bibliography as our guide, then as editors, proofreaders, and printers, Greek émigrés accounted for more than fifty first editions of Greek classical, patristic, biblical, and Byzantine texts before 1535.

In sum, a relatively small band of Greek émigrés exerted a far greater influence on Latin culture in the Renaissance than Greeks had exerted at any time in the Middle Ages. The Italian humanists desired access to the vast ancient Greek heritage; Greek scholars, many of whom admired the medieval Latin achievement, provided the humanists with the means to enter that literature.

See also **Chrysoloras, Manuel; Constantinople, Fall of; Gaza, Theodore; Gemistus Pletho, George; George of Trebizond; Lascaris, Constantine; Lascaris, Janus.**

BIBLIOGRAPHY

Geanakoplos, Deno. *Greek Scholars in Venice: Studies in the Dissemination of Greek Learning from Byzantium to Western Europe.* Cambridge, Mass., 1962.

Harris, Jonathan. *Greek Émigrés in the West 1400–1520.* Camberley, U.K., 1995.

Kristeller, Paul Oskar. "Italian Humanism and Byzantium." In *Renaissance Thought and Its Sources.* Edited by Michael Mooney. New York, 1979. Pages 137–150.

Legrand, Emile. *Bibliographie hellénique des quinzième et seizième siècles.* 4 vols. Paris, 1855–1906. Reprint, Paris, 1962.

Monfasani, John. *Byzantine Scholars in Renaissance Italy: Cardinal Bessarion and Other Émigrés.* Aldershot, U.K., 1995.

Weiss, Roberto. *Medieval and Humanist Greek: Collected Essays.* Padua, Italy, 1977.

JOHN MONFASANI

GREEK LITERATURE, CLASSICAL. *See* **Classical Scholarship.**

GREGORY XIII (Ugo Boncampagni, or Buoncampagni; 1502–1585), pope (1572–1585). Born to a merchant family of Bologna, Ugo Boncampagni studied law at the University of Bologna where he took his doctorate in canon and civil law (1530) and taught law (1531–1539). In the early 1540s he was ordained a priest and moved to Rome where he was appointed by Paul III as a judge in the civil tribunal of Rome, later as referendary in the Curia, and secretary (abbreviator) at the Council of Trent (1546). Under Paul IV he was made an assistant to a cardinal, secretary of state Carlo Carafa, under whom he served on papal missions to France (1556) and to the court of Philip II at Brussels (1557). Made bishop of Viesti (1558) by Paul IV, he was appointed to serve as a papal jurist in the last period of the Council of Trent (1561–1563). In 1565, he was made cardinal. In 1566, he was selected by Pius V for the Segnatura of Briefs.

In the conclave after the death of Pius V, he was strongly supported by Philip II and was elected pope on 14 May 1572; he took the name Gregory in honor of Pope Gregory the Great. Dedicated to the reforms of Trent and the restoration of Catholicism, he fostered clerical education, which he saw as crucial to this end; he supported both old and new religious orders, especially the Capuchins and Jesuits. He approved Filippo Neri's Congregation of the Oratory (1575), the new constitutions of the Barnabites (1577), and the reforms of Teresa of Avila's Discalced Carmelites (1580).

His vision of Rome as center of the universal church led him in 1573 to found colleges at Rome: for the Hungarians (1578, joined in 1584 to the German college), Greeks (1577), English (1579), Maronites (1584) and others. These colleges, or seminaries, educated the clergy of lands where the Catholic faith was threatened by Protestantism. Gregory sup-

Pope Gregory XIII. CORBIS/BETTMANN

ported numerous missionary efforts to India, Japan, China, Brazil, and the Americas.

He encouraged scholars such as Carlo Sigonio and Cesare Baronio to prepare ecclesiastical histories to demonstrate the truth of Catholicism and the church's jurisdictional claims; Gregory patronized many scholars who published editions of ecclesiastical texts. He launched a reform of the calendar in 1582 (revising the Julian calendar), a new edition of the canon law, and the Roman martyrology. He directed successful missions to the southern provinces of the Low Countries, Poland, and large parts of Germany, where he opened new nunciatures to work for Catholic restoration in Protestant areas; but missions to Sweden and Muscovy failed. In France, Gregory supported the Catholic Guise faction and Catholic League against the French Protestants, and promoted the activities of the English missionary-priests in England. Noteworthy are improvements to the city streets for the jubilee year of 1575; the building activity at the Collegio Romano, St. Peter's basilica, the Gregorian Chapel in St. Peter's, the Tower of the Winds at the Vatican, the Oratorian Church of S. Maria in Vallicella, the Greek college's church of San Atanasio, the fountains of the Piazza Navona, as well as restorations and adornments to many churches and religious sites. Gregory's many missions, building projects, and educational and artistic endowments continuously strained papal finances.

With a clear vision of papal leadership and an aggressive program for restoring lands lost to Protestantism, Gregory XIII marked the full development of a revived papacy in the Catholic Reformation. His patronage of the arts and major building programs in Rome continued the Renaissance popes' tradition of refurbishing the city while adding emphatic statements of papal authority.

BIBLIOGRAPHY

Ciappi, Marcantonio. *Compendio delle heroiche et gloriose attioni, et santa vita di Papa Gregorio XIII.* Rome, 1596. Microfilm, Rome, 1959.
Maffei, Giovanni Pietro. *Degli annali di Gregorio XIII, pontefice massimo.* Rome, 1742.
Pastor, Ludwig F. von. *The History of the Popes from the Close of the Middle Ages.* Nendeln, Liechtenstein, and St. Louis, Mo., 1938. Reprint, 1969. See vols. 19–20.

FREDERICK J. MCGINNESS

GREY, JANE (1537–1554), queen of England for nine days in 1553. Jane was born to Frances Brandon and Henry Grey, marquess of Dorset and future duke of Suffolk. Her maternal grandparents were Mary Tudor, the youngest sister of Henry VIII, and Charles Brandon, duke of Suffolk. In 1547 Jane entered the household of Katherine Parr, the widow of Henry VIII, who had married Sir Thomas Seymour. Following Katherine's death in 1548 and Seymour's execution in 1549, Jane resided with her parents at Bradgate, Leicestershire, where John Aylmer, future bishop of London, became her classical tutor. She was one of only a few noblewomen of her generation to receive this advanced education. In 1550, when Roger Ascham visited her home, he praised her considerable linguistic achievements. By then she knew Latin, French, Greek, possibly Italian, and was learning Hebrew. She also corresponded with two Swiss Reformers: John ab Ulmis, who lived in England under her father's protection, and Heinrich Bullinger, who was greatly impressed by her skills in classical languages.

It was her royal blood that caused her early death. Overcoming her reluctance, John Dudley, duke of Northumberland and chief minister of Edward VI, arranged her marriage to his son Guildford. Having persuaded Edward to name Jane his successor by executive decree (his "Device"), Dudley attempted to transfer it to her after the king's demise in 1553. But Edward's half-sister Mary, assisted by widespread public support, became queen and had Guildford and Jane imprisoned in the Tower of London. They were executed as traitors on 12 February 1554.

BIBLIOGRAPHY

Loades, David. *John Dudley: Duke of Northumberland, 1504–1553.* Oxford, 1996.
Luke, Mary. *The Nine Days Queen: A Portrait of Lady Jane Grey.* New York, 1986. This is a popular biography, but no modern historical study of Lady Jane's life is available.

RETHA M. WARNICKE

GRONINGEN. Groningen, a city in the northern Netherlands and a center for humanists, was first mentioned as "villa Groninga" in a charter of 1040. A prosperous market town with its own mint and tollage, Groningen developed trade links with England, the German Rhineland, Scandinavia, and Russia. In the fourteenth and fifteenth centuries it began to dominate the Ommelanden (the surrounding Frisian areas). The canals and roads of the north led to Groningen, the Aa River gave an outlet to the sea, and a sandspit, the Hondsrug, at whose very end the town stood, provided the only dry road through the swamps southeastward to Utrecht, Holland, and Germany. Thus Groningen was the natural staple town for butter, cheese, horses, colts, oxen, and cows, as well as wheat, rye, barley, oats, and buckwheat. At the end of the sixteenth century new products were flaxen, hemp, rape, and manuscripts written in local monasteries. Periodically Groningen was an active member of the Hanseatic League. By 1470 Groningen had about twelve thousand inhabitants. Groningen around 1500 was in effect a free imperial city at the apogee of its power. Its wealth is demonstrated by three ecclesiastical monuments: the late eleventh-century episcopal Saint Walpurgis Chapel (razed in 1627) and two parish churches dedicated to Saint Martin and to Saint Nicholas and Saint Mary. A pilgrimage site, Saint Martin's housed what was thought to be John the Baptist's left arm. Saint Martin's highly acclaimed Latin school drew many students.

In 1594 the town was "reduced" (*Reductie*) from Catholicism and Spanish-Habsburg rule to Protestantism and union with the United Provinces. Soon (1595) a law school was established for training governmental officials, and in a period of relative peace the university was founded (1614), "in order not to succumb to ignorance and barbarism." The university was closely linked with the learning of the Cistercian Saint Bernard Abbey of Aduard about six miles west of Groningen. One of the three richest monasteries in the Low Countries, it was surpassed only by Ten Duinen in West Flanders.

Aduard is especially important because a group of humanists regularly met there under the abbot Hendrik van Rees (1449–1485). Loosely syled an "academy," it included Rudolph Agricola, Wessel Gansfort, Rudolph von Langen, Alexander Hegius, Jacobus Canter, and Arnold of Hildesheim; closely connected to these men were Antonius Liber van Soest and Fredericus Moorman. There is little evidence here of what has usually been called the "biblical humanism" of the Renaissance in the Low Countries. Rather, their letters, poetry, and treatises emphasize a general literary love for classical scholarship and show a thorough command of Neo-Latin and humanist epistolography. Ubbo Emmius, first rector of the university, and his newly appointed colleagues sought to connect this learned humanism with the Protestantism that recently had been officially established. Toward the middle of the seventeenth century this amalgam was increasingly transformed into a kind of "Calvinist Scholasticism," which led to the famously fierce debate between a professor of philosophy at Groningen, Martinus Schoockius, and René Descartes on the foundation of human knowledge and the strength of the cogito (that is, thought or consciousness).

See also **Agricola, Rudolf; Humanism,** *subentry on* **Germany and the Low Countries.**

BIBLIOGRAPHY

Akkerman, F., and A. J. Vanderjagt, eds. *Rodolphus Phrisius Agricola (1444–1485)*. Leiden, Netherlands, 1988.

Akkerman, F., G. C. Huisman, and A. J. Vanderjagt, eds. *Wessel Gansfort (1419–1489) and Northern Humanism*. Leiden, Netherlands, 1993.

Akkerman, F., A. J. Vanderjagt, and A. H. van der Laan, eds. *Northern Humanism in European Context, 1469–1625: From the Adwert Academy to Ubbo Emmius*. Leiden, Netherlands, 1999.

Formsma, W. J., et al., eds. *Historie van Groningen. Stad en Land*. Groningen, Netherlands, 1976.

Gemert, G. A. van, J. Schuller tot Peursum-Meijer, and A. J. Vanderjagt, eds. *Om niet aan onwetendheid en barbarij te bezwijken: Groningse geleerden 1614–1989*. Hilversum, Netherlands, 1989.

ARJO VANDERJAGT

GROTESQUES. Renaissance artists and scholars applied the term grotesques, or *grottesche,* to the remnants of Roman painting that could be found still

Grotesque. *The Temptation of St. Anthony* by Hieronymus Bosch (1450–1516). Anthony (d. 356), the founder of Christian monasticism, was tempted in the desert by the devil. [For another depiction of the temptation of St. Anthony see the painting by Martin Schongauer at the entry Germany, Art in.] MUSEO NACIONALE DE ARTE ANTIGA, LISBON, PORTUGAL/SUPERSTOCK

preserved on the ancient buildings of Rome and its environs. Because most of these decorated ruins had been buried over the centuries, they tended to resemble caverns, *grotte;* and the paintings were accordingly described as "cave paintings." The most famous of all the *grotte* were to be found next to the Colosseum, in the ruins of the Golden House (Domus Aurea) built in 64 C.E. by the dissolute emperor Nero. However, the curiosity seekers who began to explore its rooms and passageways, perhaps in the 1470s, believed that they had found the ruins of the baths of a later emperor, Titus.

Nero built his Golden House in the aftermath of the great fire of 64, a blaze that consumed ten of the city's fourteen regions. Overcome by the dire spectacle, Nero was said to have seized his lyre and sung about the siege of Troy, "fiddling while Rome burned." Taking advantage of the huge tracts of newly desolate land, the emperor, a gifted architect in his own right, created a villa in the center of the city, designing an elaborate dining room with a revolving dome that sprayed guests with perfume. Pliny the Elder's *Natural History* reports that he engaged a painter, Fabullus or Famulus, to decorate the walls of the Golden House with frescoes executed in a fresh new style, with emphasis on quick, impressionistic effects. "At last I can begin to live like a human being," the emperor allegedly said of his new home.

After Nero's ruin and death in 68, subsequent emperors did their best to efface the memory of the Golden House, reopening its lands to the public. Vespasian sank the Colosseum's foundations into the bed of its artificial lake. Trajan incorporated the house itself into the foundations of his great bath complex on the Oppian Hill, filling its rooms with earth and rubble. Thus Renaissance explorers of the site crawled directly beneath the building's elabo-

Quentin Massys. *Grotesque Old Woman.* Oil on wood; c. 1525; 64 × 46 cm (25 × 18 in.). NATIONAL GALLERY, LONDON/SUPERSTOCK

rately painted and stuccoed ceilings. Although the domed dining room was not discovered until the twentieth century, the Golden House had spectacular sights to offer early visitors: room after room covered with vibrant frescoes and gilt stucco, all in the lively style that Famulus had made famous. As excavators began to clear some of Trajan's fill in 1506, they came upon a marble sculpture of Laocoön and his two sons being strangled by snakes, apparently another of the works of art mentioned by Pliny. It has been one of the prizes of the Vatican Museum ever since.

Explorers left their names inscribed on the ancient ceilings; hence we know that one of the earliest visitors to the *grotte* was the Umbrian painter Bernardino Pinturicchio (c. 1454–1513), whose close acquaintance with these ancient decorations quickly changed his whole sense of composition in addition to providing him with a rich repertory of new designs. The strong geometric forms by which the ancient Roman painters ordered their decorative schemes can be seen developing in Pinturicchio's ceiling frescoes for the Borgia apartments in the Vatican (1492–1495), but it was Raphael who truly absorbed the compositional sense of this ancient painting during the pontificate of Pope Leo X (1513–1521). The bathroom, or *stufetta,* he designed in the Vatican Palace for Leo's friend Cardinal Bernardo Dovizi da Bibbiena in 1514 directly imitated motifs from the Golden House; its adjoining Loggetta (1515–1516), however, already adapted the ancient style to Christian themes. But Raphael's real triumph as a master of grotesques depended on re-creation of ancient Roman stucco, and this was only achieved by his associate Giovanni da Udine for Pope Leo's Logge Vaticane, completed in 1518. Within the Raphael workshop, indeed, Giovanni da Udine, a superb miniaturist, made grotesques his specialty, notably in Cardinal Giulio de' Medici's Villa Madama.

Fanciful and endlessly inventive, the grotesque style had already inspired controversy in ancient times; the first century B.C.E. Roman architectural writer Vitruvius railed against it in the seventh of his *Ten Books on Architecture,* complaining that it failed to imitate nature. Renaissance critics renewed the debate, citing the ever-influential Vitruvius and Horace's *Ars poetica,* which advanced a similar argument in favor of imitating only what was possible in nature. Michelangelo felt the need to justify his own grotesques by insisting that they were allegorical; Raphael, like the ancient Roman artists before him, simply seems to have delighted in painting them. Meanwhile, the public adored the new style: it appeared on textiles, on ceramics, in painting, in sculpture, in wood inlay, in metalwork, jewelry, even reliquaries and religious paraphernalia, and although its greatest vogue had passed by the mid-sixteenth century, it persists to this day in the decoration of Italian majolica.

BIBLIOGRAPHY

Dacos, Nicole. *La découverte de la Domus Aurea et la formation des grotesques à la Renaissance.* London, 1969.

Dacos, Nicole. *Le logge di Raffaello: Maestro e bottega di fronte all' antico.* 2d rev. ed. Rome, 1986.

INGRID D. ROWLAND

GROTIUS, HUGO (Huigh de Groot, Hugeianus Grotius; 1583–1645), Dutch humanist. Theologian, historian, poet, playwright, philologist, statesman, and best known as a jurist, Grotius authored over 120 Latin and Dutch works; his correspondence comprises around 7,800 letters. His father, Jan, a well-connected official and versatile humanist in his own right, left a lasting mark on Hugo's education. In 1594, aged eleven, Hugo enrolled as a student at Leiden University, where Joseph Scaliger was among his teachers. Grotius never received formal teaching in law or theology; this was probably remedied by his uncle Cornelis, professor of law, and his landlord, the irenic Franciscus Junius, professor of theology. Brought to the notice of Johan van Oldenbarnevelt, the leader of the Seven Provinces (the Dutch republic), Grotius was part of a mission to France, where in 1598 he took his doctorate in law at Orléans.

By the time he set up as a barrister in The Hague, in late 1599, his reputation as a Greek and Latin poet and editor of classical texts had already been made. Further recognition of his talents came in 1601, when he was appointed historiographer of Holland—but his Tacitean *Annales et historiae de rebus Belgicis* (Annals and histories; 1657) were rejected in 1612 by the states of Holland and remained unpublished during his lifetime. In 1604 the Dutch East India Company ordered a defense of its capture of a Portuguese vessel, which became *De iure praedae* (The law of prize), Grotius's first discussion of divine, natural, and human law; only chapter 12 was published at the time, as *Mare liberum* (The freedom of the seas). After serving as attorney general beginning in 1607 Grotius was appointed city governor of Rotterdam in 1613, and entered the States of Holland, the leading province in the Dutch Republic.

In the religious conflicts of 1608–1618 between Remonstrants and Counter Remonstrants (Arminians and Gomarists) Grotius adhered to the former but,

Hugo Grotius. MANSELL COLLECTION/TIME INC.

more important, in several writings he staunchly defended rigorous control of the secular powers over the church and its ministers. When reasons of state made the Stadtholder Maurice of Nassau intervene, Grotius was arrested on 29 August 1618 and condemned to life imprisonment at Loevestein castle. Although Grotius never ceased to protest against the "illegality" of Maurice's coup d'état and his trial, Loevestein proved a blessing in disguise: there he prepared many later books. On 22 March 1621 he made a famous escape from prison in a book chest, a ruse devised by his energetic wife, Maria van Reigersberch (1589–1653).

An independent scholar in Paris, supported by an (irregularly paid) annuity granted by King Louis XIII, Grotius wrote his two most famous books. *De veritate religionis Christianae* (The truth of Christian religion; 1627) was a scholarly defense of Christianity, based on his Loevestein work, a favorite until the twentieth century with over 150 Latin editions, and translations into twelve languages. His monumental *De iure belli ac pacis* (The law of war and peace; 1625), is a systematic treatment of the law of conflicts. His resulting reputation as the father of international law, or as a pacifist, is now recognized as erroneous. Drawing on (especially Spanish) scholastic sources as well as ancient law and literature, Grotius formulates a comprehensive theory of legitimate force based on divine and natural law. Meanwhile he had one main preoccupation: unconditional rehabilitation. An ill-advised return from exile in 1631–1632 ended in his hurried departure as an outlaw to Hamburg, where he spent the next two years. In 1634 he accepted the post of Swedish ambassador in Paris, which he held until 1645.

The wane of Sweden's power and strained relations between Grotius and the French government interfered with his ambassadorship, and he gradually turned his back on the world to devote himself to his great theological projects: a commentary on the complete Bible, and the unification of Christendom. In his *Annotationes in Novum Testamentum* (Notes on the New Testament; 1641–1650) Grotius's lack of doctrinal concerns, his insistence on historical context, and his philological approach broke new ground. Having always advocated Protestant unification, after 1640 he openly voiced his desire for reconciliation between Geneva, Rome, and Constantinople. This earned him severe criticism from all sides. In 1645 Grotius was recalled and honorably discharged by the young Swedish queen Christina. On the way back he was shipwrecked, fell ill, and died on 28 August in Rostock.

Grotius was a Christian humanist scholar who was intimately familiar with classical literature. A devout Protestant, he was undogmatic and rational in the Erasmian ethical and irenic tradition, but was also a conservative patrician, a jealous defender of provincial sovereignty and local privilege, always looking back to his ideal period of humankind, the first three centuries of the Christian era. Characteristic are his exceptional talent with words, evinced by his poetry and translations and by his lucid, vigorous prose, imbued with an advocate's rhetoric; and secondly the sense of law as the God-given mainstay of human society that pervades his work.

BIBLIOGRAPHY

Primary Works

Annales et historiae de rebus Belgicis (Annals and histories: A Dutch history). Amsterdam, 1657. The most recent edition of the work by which Grotius hoped to gain immortality. Its only English translation (1665) is unreliable.

Briefwisseling van Hugo Grotius (The correspondence of Hugo Grotius). Edited by P. C. Molhuysen, B. L. Meulenbroek, P. P. Witkam, H. J. M. Nellen, and C. M. Ridderikhoff. The Hague, 1928–. The edition (annotated in Dutch) is in progress: vols. 1–15, published 1928–1997, comprise the years 1597–1644.

De dichtwerken van Hugo Grotius (The poetry of Hugo Grotius). Edited by E. Rabbie and others. Assen, Netherlands, 1970–. Critical edition of the lyric and dramatic poetry with commentary, in progress (temporarily suspended), 7 books in 10 vols. The volumes comprising the lyric poetry 1602–

1608 and the tragedy *Sophompaneas* (1635), have an English introduction, translation, and commentary.

De iure belli ac pacis libri tres. Edited by R. Feenstra and C. E. Persenaire. Aalen, Germany, 1993. Reprint of the 1939 Latin edition, with new notes on pp. 919–1074.

De iure praedae commentarius: Commentary on the Law of Prize and Booty by Hugo Grotius. Vol. 1, *A Translation of the Original Manuscript of 1604*. Translated by Gwladys L. Williams with the collaboration of Walter H. Zeydel. Vol. 2, *The Collotype Reproduction of the Original Manuscript of 1604 in the Handwriting of Grotius*. Oxford and London, 1950.

Meletius, sive, de iis quae inter Christianos conveniunt Epistola (Meletius; or, Letter on the points of agreement between Christians). Critical edition with translation, commentary, and introduction by Guillaume H. M. Posthumus Meyjes. Leiden, Netherlands, and New York, 1988.

Opera Omnia Theologica, in tres partes divisa (Complete theological works, in three parts). Amsterdam and London, 1679. Reprint in 4 vols. Stuttgart and Bad Cannstatt, Germany, 1972.

Ordinum Hollandiae ac Westfrisiae Pietas (1613). (The Religiousness of the States of Holland and Westfriesland). Critical edition with English translation and commentary by Edwin Rabbie. Leiden, Netherlands, 1995.

Secondary Works

Dunn, John, and Ian Harris, eds. *Grotius*. 2 vols. Cheltenham, U. K., and Lyme, N. H., 1997. Useful collection of thirty-nine articles (mostly) in English and in French on various aspects of Grotius, mainly his legal work.

Grotiana. Assen, Netherlands, 1980–. A journal published under the auspices of the Grotiana Foundation, including bibliographical surveys of primary and secondary works. Cumulative bibliography in Volume 11 (1990–1993): 78–123.

Haggenmacher, P. *Grotius et la doctrine de guerre juste* (Grotius and the doctrine of just war). Paris, 1983.

Nellen, Henk J. M. *Hugo de Groot, 1583–1645: De loopbaan van een geleerd staatsman* (Hugo de Groot, 1583–1645: The career of an erudite statesman). Weesp, Netherlands, 1985. The best short introduction to Grotius's life and works.

Nellen, Henk J. M., and Edwin Rabbie, eds. *Hugo Grotius Theologian: Essays in Honour of G. H. M. Posthumus Meyjes*. Leiden, Netherlands, and New York, 1994. With complete bibliography on Grotius as a theologian, 1840–1993, on pp. 219–245.

Ter Meulen, Jacob, and P. J. J. Diermanse *Bibliographie des écrits imprimés de Hugo Grotius*. The Hague, 1950 (Reprint, Zutphen, Netherlands, 1995). Full bibliography of Grotius's works printed before 1950.

The World of Hugo Grotius (1583–1645): Proceedings of the International Colloquium. Organized by the Grotius Committee of the Royal Netherlands Academy of Arts and Sciences, Rotterdam 6–9 April 1983. Amsterdam and Maarssen, Netherlands, 1984. Articles in English, French, and German on all aspects of Grotius.

HARM-JAN VAN DAM

GRUMBACH, ARGULA VON (1492–1554/69), Bavarian noblewoman, author, reformer. Born near Beratzhausen, not far from Regensburg, into an aristocratic and well-educated family, Argula, the daughter of Bernhardin and Katharina von Stauff, was orphaned in 1509 while being educated at the Munich court. In 1516 she married Friedrich von Grumbach, an administrator for the Bavarian dukes of the Franconian town of Dietfurt. She was probably drawn to her evangelical views by Paul Speratus, a scholar and cathedral preacher who was an ardent champion of reforming ideas. She also read the pamphlets of Martin Luther and other reformers and immersed herself in reading scripture.

After witnessing in 1523 the mock trial of a student, Arsacius Seehofer, which attacked his Lutheran views, Argula was provoked to challenge the Ingolstadt theologians to a debate in German about their coercive conduct. After their predictable refusal to participate, she wrote a vigorous pamphlet, which ran to a remarkable fourteen editions; the idea of a laywoman entering the theological fray had caught the popular imagination. In six open letters to German princes and to the cities of Ingolstadt and Regensburg, Argula outlined a reformist program for society as well as the church. She also published a poem to defend herself against vicious slander: she had been accused, without foundation, of having a sexual attraction to a certain Arsacius Seehofer. After 1524 she produced no more pamphlets but maintained personal and epistolary contact with Luther and Andreas Osiander and promoted the Reformation locally. In 1533, three years after the death of her Roman Catholic husband, she married Count von Schlick but was widowed again in 1535.

Her unpublished family papers illuminate early Protestant educational ideals; relationships with her four children; her network of friends, including Roman Catholics; the progress of the evangelical cause in Bavaria and Franconia; and the legal and financial difficulties of widows. Her main achievement was a fresh interpretation of scripture from a woman's perspective.

BIBLIOGRAPHY

Primary Work

Argula von Grumbach: A Woman's Voice in the Reformation. Edited by Peter Matheson. Edinburgh, 1995. Translation of her published writings.

Secondary Works

Classen, Albrecht. "Woman Poet and Reformer: The 16th-Century Feminist Argula von Grumbach." *Daphnis* 20, no. 1 (1991): 167–197.

Matheson, Peter. "Angels, Depression, and 'the Stone': A Late Medieval Prayer Book." *Journal of Theological Studies,* n.s., 48 (October 1997): 517–530.

Matheson, Peter. "Breaking the Silence: Women, Censorship, and the Reformation." *Sixteenth Century Journal* 27 (spring 1996): 97–109.

PETER MATHESON

GRÜNEWALD, MATTHIAS (Mathis Gothart Nithart; c. 1475/1480–1528), German painter. The painter and writer Joachim von Sandrart mentions a painter named "Matthaeus Grünewald," also known as "Matthaeus von Aschaffenburg," in his *Teutsche Academie der Edlen Bau-, Bild- und Mahlerey-Künste* (1675). This person is almost certainly the painter "Mathis Gothart Nithart" referred to in early sixteenth-century documents.

Earliest Evidence. Nothing is known regarding the training and early career of Grünewald, who was probably born in Würzburg. The *Mocking of Christ* (c. 1504–1506; Munich, Alte Pinakothek), is among his earliest surviving pictures.

Grünewald was recommended in 1510 as a hydraulic engineer. In 1511 he is recorded as a painter, stonecutter, superintendent of works, and architect at the court of Uriel von Gemmingen, archbishop of Mainz, at Aschaffenburg. Around that time, he painted four grisaille (gray-toned) *Saints* (Frankfurt, Städelsches Kunstinstitut, and Karlsruhe, Staatliche Kunsthalle), which became the fixed wings of Dürer's (lost) *Assumption and Coronation of the Virgin* (1508–1509), ordered by Jakob Heller in 1507 for the Dominican church of Frankfurt.

Isenheim Altarpiece. In 1512 the Antonite preceptor Guido Guersi commissioned three sets of painted wings from "Mathis Nithart" to complete the carved altarpiece on the high altar of the church of the monastery of Saint Anthony, near Isenheim in Alsace. The monumental polyptych dated 1515 (now disassembled; Colmar, Musée Unterlinden; see the color plates in this volume) shows in its closed state a *Crucifixion* rising above a *Lamentation* in the predella and flanked by fixed wings depicting *Saint Sebastian* (left) and *Saint Anthony* (right) as statues miraculously come alive. Once we open the first set of movable wings, we see: the *Annunciation* on the left, the so-called *Angels' Concert* and *Virgin and Child* in the center (above the *Lamentation*), and the *Resurrection* on the right. When the altarpiece is completely opened, we see Nikolaus Hagenower's polychrome wood sculpture group of c. 1505 depicting *Saint Anthony* enthroned between the standing *SS. Augustine* (left) and *Jerome* (right). Bust-length depictions of *Christ and the Twelve Apostles* carved by Desiderius Beichel appear in the predella

Matthias Grünewald. *Resurrection.* From the Isenheim Altarpiece, 1515 (detail). MUSÉE D'UNTERLINDEN, COLMAR, FRANCE/GIRAUDON/ART RESOURCE

below. Hagenau's ensemble is flanked by the interior of Grünewald's third set of painted wings, depicting the *Meeting of SS. Anthony and Paul the Hermit* (left) and the *Temptation of Saint Anthony* (right).

This altarpiece was presumably closed during most of the liturgical year; the first set of mobile wings was opened on Sundays and special feast days, and the second set was opened to uncover the sculpture within on the feasts of Anthony and other patron saints of the Antonine order. Grünewald's highly unusual imagery—comprising gruesome depictions of the dead Christ—has been interpreted in light of the fact that the monastery included a hospital. Christ's stiff, lacerated body harbors the promise of salvation (symbolized by the *Resurrection*) for those who suffer greatly—in "imitatio Christi"—and

repent. In addition, SS. Sebastian and Anthony were venerated by people seeking to ward off or cure diseases. However, Grünewald's pictures—with their accent on the mystery of Christ's incarnation, sacrifice, and resurrection, and on the trials of Anthony's ascetic way of life—also perfectly suited the monks' contemplative needs. Their expressive vocabulary goes back to certain types of German Gothic devotional images, such as the so-called Plague Crucifixes, as well as to the *Revelations* of the mystic Bridget of Sweden.

Additional Paintings. Grünewald returned to the theme of Christ's sacrifice in his harrowing *Crucifixions* (c. 1510–1520; Washington, D.C., National Gallery of Art; and c. 1525–1526; Karlsruhe, Germany, Staatliche Kunsthalle). His altarpiece dedicated to *The Virgin of the Snow* for a chapel of the (former) collegiate church in Aschaffenburg, is dismembered. Only the central panel depicting the *Madonna and Child in a Garden* (Stuppach, Pfarrkirche, near Mergentheim, Germany) and one side panel showing the *Miracle of the Snows* (Freiburg im Breisgau, Germany, Augustinermuseum) survive. This painting's frame bears the date 1519 and the artist's monogram MG (in ligature) beneath an N.

Grünewald was employed by the new archbishop of Mainz, Albrecht von Brandenburg, from c. 1516 to 1526, and completed *The Meeting of SS. Erasmus and Maurice* (Munich, Alte Pinakothek) for him by 1525. Several scholars suggest the artist was dismissed by Albrecht in 1526, either because of his (supposed) participation in the Peasants' War of 1525 or as a result of his (documented) enthusiasm for Lutheranism. Grünewald moved to Frankfurt and later to Halle, where he worked in his final year as a hydraulic engineer.

In his *Elementorum rhetorices libri duo* of 1531, Philipp Melanchthon ranked "Mathias" just after Dürer and before "Lucas" (Cranach). Grünewald conveys the emotional intensity and spiritual dimension of his religious subjects through his singular powers of invention, symbol-laden transformation of natural phenomena, and subtlety as a colorist and painter of ethereal light. Unlike Dürer, he appears to have been largely untouched by antique visual and literary sources, and hardly inspired by the achievements of the Italian Renaissance. His oeuvre proves the continued importance of medieval images, ideas, and modes of expression in some of the major cultural centers of Germany at the beginning of the sixteenth century.

BIBLIOGRAPHY

Andersson, Christiane. "Grünewald, Matthias." In *The Dictionary of Art*. Edited by Jane Turner. New York, 1996. Vol. 13, pp. 719–724.

Hayum, André. *The Isenheim Altarpiece: God's Medicine and the Painter's Vision*. Princeton, N.J., 1989.

Sitzmann, Karl, and Eugenio Battisti. "Grünewald, Matthias." In *Encyclopedia of World Art*. New York, Toronto, and London, 1963. Vol. 7, cols. 182–191.

MICHAËL J. AMY

GUARINI, GIOVANNI BATTISTA (1538–1612), Italian courtier, diplomat, poet, dramatist, literary polemicist. Guarini was trained in Ferrara and Padua, where he was a member of the famous Accademia degli Eterei. By 1567 he returned to Ferrara, where for the next fifteen years he would serve Duke Alfonso II d'Este as ambassador to Turin, Rome, and Poland. In 1581 he began the work for which he is best known, *Il pastor fido* (1590; trans. *The Faithful Shepherd*), writing it largely while in retirement at his modest estate of San Bellino. Although he eventually returned to Alfonso II's court as secretary, the late 1580s and 1590s are marked by his restless attempts to find patronage at other courts at Florence, Turin, Mantua, and Urbino. These years are also characterized by Guarini's efforts to have *Il pastor fido* performed, a goal not realized until 1596. In addition to his innovative pastoral tragicomedy, already in its twentieth edition by 1602, Guarini wrote madrigals (many set to music by the period's most notable composers, including Claudio Monteverdi); sonnets; a comedy, *La Idropica* (The dropsical lady; 1583); treatises on politics and the declining role of the court secretary; and three lengthy pamphlets defending *Il pastor fido* from attack. Guarini also published his lively and revealing letters during his lifetime.

Much of Guarini's writing, even while composed for a courtly audience, was vehemently anticourt. It is marked by deep contradictions that characterized late sixteenth-century Italy: a simultaneous loathing of and need for the court's patronage; appreciation for the peace his rustic estate could bring in contrast with the frustrated recognition that he was failing to make himself useful in public life beyond his estate; and his insistence that his literary writings were the work of an idle dilettante, which contradicted his desire, evident in the prodigious treatises he wrote on its behalf, that *Il pastor fido* occupy an important niche in the literary heritage of Italy.

Guarini's literary criticism quickly established itself as a major contribution to the ongoing quarrel of the ancients and the moderns. True to form, Guarini managed to anger many different camps. Even as he claimed a necessary autonomy of art from state and ecclesiastical censorship, he attacked the degeneracy of contemporary theater represented in the *commedia dell'arte*.

Indeed, *Il pastor fido* vehemently defends individual passion in opposition to social and political constraints, while it avoids the indecencies of improvised comedy and the excesses of tragedy. Far from being a timeless and tranquil setting, Guarini's Arcadia is beset by plague, harsh rules, and an inflexible priest who tries to subject the beautiful young shepherdess to the full weight of the law for her illicit love for the "faithful shepherd" of the play's title. Yet this love becomes the vehicle through which Arcadia's social and political excesses are cured, as potential tragedy is transformed into gentle comedy.

Il pastor fido was especially influential in Italy, Spain, France, and England, but it had a notable impact on several English works of the seventeenth century as well. Samuel Daniel's *The Queenes Arcadia* (1606) with its wily Corax owes more to Guarini's play than has generally been acknowledged. Written for Queen Margaret, the play also suggests the extent to which pastoral was used in England to cater to a specifically female audience. The most intensive engagement with *Il pastor fido* was that of Sir Richard Fanshawe, who in 1647 translated it for the recently exiled Prince Charles. Fanshawe's play is not only one of the finest translations of any Italian work into English, but it also represents a keen recognition of the political dynamics of *Il pastor fido*— a far cry from the romantics who would find in Guarini's play the expression of a strictly aesthetic and lyrical sensibility. That one of the offshoots of *Il pastor fido* is Handel's opera points to the lyric potential of both the pastoral genre and the play itself. Indeed, it is largely Guarini's elegant use of the many rhyme forms he had practiced in his youth that allows him to modulate skillfully between tragic and comic registers. Such modulations ultimately left their most profound mark on the seventeenth century's finest tragicomedies, including Pierre Corneille's *Le Cid* and the late plays of Shakespeare.

BIBLIOGRAPHY

Primary Works

Guarini, Battista. "The Compendium of Tragicomic Poetry." In *Literary Criticism: Plato to Dryden*. Edited by Allan H. Gilbert. Detroit, Mich., 1962. Pages 505–533.

Guarini, Battista. *The Faithful Shepherd*. Translated by Sir Richard Fanshawe. In *Five Renaissance Italian Comedies*. Edited by Bruce Penman. Harmondsworth, U.K., and New York, 1978.

Guarini, Battista. *Opere di Battista Guarini.* 2d ed. Edited by Marziano Guglielminetti. Turin, Italy, 1971.

Secondary Works

Henke, Robert. *Pastoral Transformations: Italian Tragicomedy and Shakespeare's Late Plays.* Newark, Del., and London, 1997.

Perella, Nicolas J. *The Critical Fortune of Battista Guarini's* Il Pastor Fido. Florence, 1973.

JANE TYLUS

GUARINI, GUARINO (Guarino Veronese; 1374–1460), Italian humanist and educator. Guarino Guarini was born in Verona, the son of an artisan. His father died in 1386, but Guarino's mother ensured that her gifted son received a Latin education. Guarino had a thirst for learning and left his native Verona in the 1390s to pursue it in Padua and Venice, in contact with scholars, teachers, and cultivated patricians; he may have trained as a notary. From 1394 to 1403 the Greek scholar and diplomat Manuel Chrysoloras was in Italy, and the instruction in the Greek language that he delivered in Florence from 1397 to 1400 sparked a fascination among the early humanists. This fascination, in conjunction with the discovery of many manuscripts of previously unknown Latin works from antiquity by Cicero and others, transformed the humanist community into a movement. Chrysoloras passed through Venice early in 1403, and Guarino was inspired to follow him back to Constantinople to learn Greek. A Venetian merchant, Paolo Zane, made this possible by hiring Guarino to accompany him to Constantinople as a secretary and paying for his schooling. Guarino spent five years there and was the first Renaissance humanist to study Greek in the Byzantine capital. Chrysoloras himself returned to Italy at the start of 1406.

Guarino's own return to Italy in 1408 or 1409 was followed by ten difficult years: he failed to attach himself to the papal Curia at Bologna in 1410, or to win substantial patronage in Florence in 1411–1414. Back in Venice in 1414, he opened a school, but the venture foundered. With his marriage in 1418 to Tadea Zendrata of Verona, the daughter of a wealthy family, Guarino's fortunes changed. He opened a humanistic boarding school in Verona that soon became successful, and when he was appointed by the commune of Verona in May 1420 to lecture on rhetoric and the newly discovered epistles and orations of Cicero, with a high salary and the privilege of continuing to teach his boarders privately, humanistic schooling received institutional status in Italy for the first time.

Guarino's final move was to the Este court at Ferrara in 1429. He became the tutor of Leonello d'Este, the son and successor of Duke Niccolò III, and proceeded to create a school whose fame was rivaled only by that of Vittorino da Feltre in Mantua and which attracted youthful boarders from northern Italy as well as other European countries. Guarino was made public lecturer in Ferrara in 1436 and professor when the city's university was revived in 1442. The youngest of his twelve children, Battista, took his father's place following the death of Guarino in December 1460. A fundamental resource for the study of Guarino's life and times is Remigio Sabbadini's collection of his correspondence (*Epistolario*), which includes many epistles intended to be read by the literate public, not just the addressee.

Guarino as Humanist Scholar. The most frequently cited letter of Guarino was written in 1452 (*Epistolario,* vol. 2, no. 862) to his son Niccolò, who had been surprised to find that his father's earliest writings failed to meet the humanist standard of good Latin. Guarino responded with an autobiographical account of his own schooling in late medieval Latin and of the humanist revolution. He named with scorn the school texts he had used as a boy, and gave an example, horrendous to cultivated ears, of what had then passed for eloquent composition. A striking fact is the absence of any mention of the role of Petrarch as precursor of the humanists: for Guarino the medieval darkness had remained virtually unbroken until the arrival of Chrysoloras, and it was knowledge of Greek that had made the rebirth of classical Latinity possible. Guarino's perception may be historically debatable, but it was sincere (the letter recounts his own transformation through contact with Chrysoloras), and the view that a rebirth of classical Latin was impossible without an influx of Greek is not absurd, for—as Guarino points out—ancient Roman civilization had been impregnated in the first place by Greek culture.

Like other humanists, Guarino faced the hostility of conservative ecclesiastics toward ancient literature, some of which is deliberately coarse, and all of which is pagan. He also exposed himself to their censure by praising *Hermaphroditus* (1425), the brilliant and lascivious collection of verse by Panormita (Antonio Beccadelli). On the first front he was able to hold his ground, but on the second he had to surrender abjectly. The Franciscan Giovanni da Prato, preaching at Ferrara in 1450, called for works of pagan literature to be burned—along with their owners. This was aimed directly at Guarino and the author he was teaching at the time, Terence. Guarino responded with a conventional humanist defense (*Epistolario,* vol. 2, no. 823): no modern Christian, not even a theologian, can understand the church fathers without a knowledge of the classical literature with which they were imbued; and the literary doctrine of decorum dictates that coarse matters be depicted coarsely. Such depictions have moral value and do not reflect the moral character of the author, for literature is autonomous. Guarino's earlier letter in praise of *Hermaphroditus,* dated February 1426 (*Epistolario,* vol. 1, no. 346), develops the same ideas more audaciously, and since it was added by copyists to manuscripts of the *Hermaphroditus,* it became notorious. Pressed by clerics and others to recant, Guarino did so in 1435, claiming that his earlier letter had been truncated and "restoring" passages that deplore the content of Panormita's verse (vol. 2, no. 666).

Though they were united against their critics, the humanists engaged in their own internal debates. One of the most important for the history of political thought began in the ancient world and has never really ended: Was Julius Caesar a vicious tyrant who corrupted republican liberty and deserved assassination, or was he a hero who laid the basis for the beneficial Roman empire? In a long letter of 1435 to an opponent, Poggio Bracciolini, Guarino was a strong defender of Caesar (vol. 2, no. 670). In defending Caesar, Guarino was defending the princely form of government established in Ferrara and other northern Italian courts against the republican form established, and endorsed, in Florence.

Two of the most important aspects of Guarino's activity can only be mentioned summarily here: his translations of Greek authors into Latin and his role in the rediscovery of Latin authors. Since only a very small number of humanists ever learned Greek well, the rest of the humanists and all readers in Europe depended on translators like Guarino for their knowledge of the Greek corpus. Two of the many authors whom he translated were the moralizing biographer Plutarch and the geographer Strabo. Guarino's role in the discovery, diffusion, and emendation of the manuscript texts of Latin authors was described by Sabbadini in his writings on humanism in general and Guarino in particular. Guarino has special importance in the history of the texts of the letters of Pliny the Younger, the commentary of Servius on Virgil, and the historical works of Julius Caesar and his continuators. Like Guarino's translations, his recensions of many Latin texts were reproduced in the earliest printed editions shortly after his death.

Guarino as Educator. Guarino wrote no pedagogical treatise, but he approved the one written by his son Battista that described the program of the school in Ferrara, and much incidental information survives about his teaching. Together with his colleagues Gasparino Barzizza and Vittorino da Feltre, Guarino had largely to invent a new style of education. Their model, which claimed to shape the boys—over whose lives they assumed control in their boarding schools—into free ("liberal") and fully realized human beings through instruction in classical studies, became dominant in Europe for centuries: this was the birth of the ideology of liberal education.

Guarino's practical aim was to make the students fluent in the classical Latin used by Cicero, knowledgeable about facts, personalities, and mythologies of the ancient world, and acquainted with Greek. The students' education began with the elements of Latin grammar, taught by intensive drilling and testing. Advanced grammar was taught from Guarino's own *Regulae grammaticales* (The rules of grammar), the first new Renaissance grammar of Latin. As the students expanded their reading into poetry and history, Guarino's lectures supplied a flood of detailed miscellaneous commentary. The senior students read the rhetorical works of Cicero and Quintilian, with their tincture of officious moral philosophy, assembled their own carefully indexed notebooks of information and quotations, and practiced extempore Latin composition and speech-making, aiming at fluency.

That this, Guarino's practical aim, was achievable and normally achieved, is demonstrable. The ideological claim that a human type of special excellence would necessarily emerge from such training is not subject to strict verification, but is certainly open to controversy and has been subjected to a sharply revisionist critique in the modern era.

See also **Humanism,** *subentry on* **Italy***; and biographies of figures mentioned in this entry.*

BIBLIOGRAPHY

Primary Works
Guarini, Guarino. *Epistolario.* Edited by Remigio Sabbadini. 3 vols. Venice, 1915–1919. Reprint, Turin, 1967. Letters to and from Guarino in Latin, Sabbadini's commentary (vol. 3) in Italian. Some additional letters have been discovered and published in scholarly journals since Sabbadini assembled this collection.
Prosatori Latini del Quattrocento. Edited by Eugenio Garin. Milan, 1952. Latin texts with Italian translations. Includes Guarino's letter in defense of Caesar, and the funeral oration for Guarino by Ludovico Carbone.

Thomson, Ian. *Humanist Pietas. The Panegyric of Ianus Pannonius on Guarinus Veronensis*. Bloomington, Ind., 1988. A panegyric on Guarino by one of his famous students, with detailed notes.

Secondary Works

Grafton, Anthony, and Lisa Jardine. *From Humanism to the Humanities: Education and the Liberal Arts in Fifteenth- and Sixteenth-Century Europe*. Cambridge, Mass., 1986. See chapter 1, "The School of Guarino: Ideals and Practice," pp. 58–82. Challenges the humanist claim for the value of liberal education.

Grendler, Paul F. *Schooling in Renaissance Italy: Literacy and Learning, 1300–1600*. Baltimore, 1989. Fundamental survey of the field; responds to Grafton-Jardine.

Sabbadini, Remigio. *Guariniana*. Turin, 1964. Repr. of *Vita di Guarino Veronese* (Genoa, 1891) and *La scuola e gli studi di Guarino Guarini Veronese* (Catania, 1896).

WILLIAM MCCUAIG

GUELFS AND GHIBELLINES.   *See* **Faction.**

GUEVARA, ANTONIO DE   (c. 1480–1545), Spanish writer and moralist. Guevara was born into a noble family in the town of Treceño (Asturias). At twelve he went to serve John, the crown prince, at the court of Ferdinand and Isabella, where he may well have been taught by the humanist Pietro Martire d'Anghiera (Peter Martyr). In 1504, after a spiritual crisis brought on, according to Guevara, by the deaths of Prince John and Queen Isabella, he abandoned his promising career to become a Franciscan friar. He nonetheless maintained close relations with the court throughout most of his life, since, alongside his religious calling, he participated directly in politics and the affairs of state. He served as adviser to don Gonzalo de Córdoba, the "Great Captain," and during the difficult political period of the war of the *comunidades* (1519–1521), he skillfully supported the imperial faction; this earned him the favor of the emperor Charles V, who was to honor him over many years with a series of distinguished posts.

Famous for his sermons and oratory style, he was named preacher of Charles V's court in 1521. In 1523 he was honored with the title of royal chronicler and later with that of royal counselor. In 1525 Charles V sent him to Valencia and in 1526 to Granada to convert the *moriscos* (Muslims nominally converted to Christianity). Guevara also played a role as consultant to the Holy Office in 1527 and was named bishop of Guadix (Granada) in 1529, a position he held until 1537, when he was appointed bishop of Mondoñedo (Lugo). His political activities nonetheless kept him far from his dioceses and close to the court. In 1535 he accompanied the emperor on the military expedition to Tunis, as well as on the lengthy and politically important return journey via Italy and France. Guevara's role as royal counselor and chronicler placed him at the forefront of the major events of his time. In the last years of his life he distanced himself from all political activity, retiring to his diocese of Mondoñedo, where he died in 1545.

Guevara's writings, widely read, often pose difficulties in their editorial history. Such is the case with his first very successful work, the *Libro áureo de Marco Aurelio* (Golden book of Marcus Aurelius), which was apparently written between 1518 and 1524, when Guevara presented the manuscript for the emperor to read. From then on adulterated manuscript copies proliferated and circulated in the court. When the work was published in Seville in 1528, it appeared without the author's name. The *Libro áureo* became widely known, and many editions appeared. In 1529 the *Relox de príncipes* (Dial of princes) was published, and that same year a second edition of the *Relox de príncipes* appeared under the title *Libro del elocuentísimo emperador Marco Aurelio con el Relox de príncipes* (Book of the most eloquent emperor Marcus Aurelius with the Dial of princes). Although this major work incorporates and rewrites many parts of the *Libro áureo de Marco Aurelio*, all in all it is a very different book.

These two works constitute magnificent examples of the Renaissance worldview. Guevara plays with the technique of the "found manuscript," incorporating aspects of the classical world, with the fictionalization of history, with intertextuality—mixing his own voice with voices from antiquity. Above all, he infuses a modern view that revitalizes the memory of the past for readers. In effect, these two texts are moral-didactic works written in the form of historical narrative. Guevara presents us with the emperor Marcus Aurelius as the perfect prince and rewrites his apocryphal history and his supposed letters as though they were authentic—the philosophic writings of the emperor had not yet been discovered. These texts display a wide variety of subject matter, including quotations, anecdotes, letters, interpolated episodes, and much textual material derived from ancient sources, mainly Valerius Maximus, Diogenes Laertius, and Plutarch. Both books were avidly read in Spanish and in many translations throughout Europe. The *Libro áureo* in Italian translation became a school textbook in Italy. Especially famous then and now is the episode of the "Danubian peasant" (in both texts, but more developed in the *Relox*), which criticizes Roman colonial practice and exalts the natural, uncorrupted way of life. This episode would later be retold in a fable by Lafontaine.

Another of Guevara's very successful works was the *Epístolas familiares*, written in the genre of the Renaissance epistle. It comprises a collection of letters of diverse subject matter addressed to famous people. In these letters Guevara gives advice, tells anecdotes about the courtly life of his time, and displays enormous erudition. This book arguably provides an early example of the genre of the essay. The *Epístolas familiares* were among Montaigne's preferred readings.

Other works by Guevara include the *Menosprecio de corte y alabanza de aldea* (Contempt for the court and praise for the village), which in Horatian manner glorifies the simple life as opposed to the artificiality of courtly life; *Aviso de privados y doctrina de cortesanos* (Advice to favorites and doctrine for courtiers), which concerns courtly manners; and *De los inventores del marear y de muchos trabajos que se pasan en las galeras* (On the inventors of sailing and on the many travails at sea), a treatise on navigation.

Marked by a rhetoric characteristic of sermons, Guevara's literary style is unique, both encumbered and ornate. Guevara shows a predilection for the *amplificatio*, quotations, anecdotes, learned references, and the like. In sum, Guevara incorporates into his texts every artifice that might dazzle and overwhelm his readers. He was an enormously influential prose writer, and his works are the reflection of a man who lived his epoch with great intensity.

BIBLIOGRAPHY

Primary Work

Guevara, Antonio de. *Relox de príncipes*. Edited by Emilio Blanco. Madrid, 1994.

Secondary Works

Hutchinson, Steven. "Genealogy of Guevara's Barbarian: An Invented Other." *Bulletin of Hispanic Studies* 74 (1997): 7–18.

Jones, Joseph R. *Antonio de Guevara*. Boston, 1975.

Redondo, Augustin. *Antonio de Guevara (1480?–1545) et L'Espagne de son temps: De la carrière officielle aux oeuvres politico-morales*. Geneva, Switzerland, 1976.

MERCEDES ALCALÁ-GALÁN

GUICCIARDINI, FRANCESCO (1483–1540), Florentine statesman and historian. Francesco Guicciardini was a statesman and administrator in Italy during the Italian Wars whose historical writings about his own times made him the greatest historian of the Renaissance period.

Life. As a scion of one of the leading families of Florence, Guicciardini received a broadly humanistic education before beginning a career in law. A politically advantageous marriage with Maria Salviati in 1508, combined with his evident abilities and family background, secured him an easy entry into public life, with the consequence that late in 1511, somewhat in advance of the statutory age, he was appointed ambassador to Spain. Having gained from the wily Ferdinand of Aragon an absorbing lesson in politics and diplomacy, Guicciardini was eventually recalled after the fall of the *gonfaloniere* (chief magistrate) Piero Soderini. But on reaching Florence in the winter of 1514 he found that old family loyalties made for an easy accommodation with the restored Medici regime, and in 1516, as part of Pope Leo X's policy of cultivating the Florentine patriciate, he was appointed governor of the city of Modena. The combination of forcefulness and tact that he exhibited in ruling a city rent with strife from having changed hands four times in six years led to the enlargement of his appointment with the city of Reggio, which he defended against the Ferrarese and French during Leo X's 1521 war to expel the French from Milan. Pope Clement VII subsequently promoted him to the presidency of the Romagna, a turbulent province that he governed with characteristic rigor.

In the aftermath of the emperor Charles V's stunning victory over King Francis I at Pavia on 24 February 1525, Guicciardini was summoned to Rome to advise the pope in the diplomatic negotiations among the papacy, France, Milan, and Venice that led to the League of Cognac of May 1526 for the liberation of Italy. Although appointed lieutenant general of the papal forces, he was unable, to his intense frustration, to persuade the senior officer of the League, Giovanni Maria della Rovere, the duke of Urbino, to persevere in relieving the citadel of Milan, where its duke, Francesco II Sforza, was besieged by the imperialists. Sforza's resultant surrender was followed by ineffectual maneuvering on the part of the allied army that failed to prevent the imperialists from crossing the river Po in November 1526. Guicciardini's one success, averting a sack of Florence by the rebellious imperial army nominally commanded by the duke of Bourbon, was gained at the cost of deflecting the attack to Rome, which was brutally sacked in May 1527.

In deep remorse for his share in the suffering of Rome and out of favor with the populists of the restored Florentine republic because of his service to the Medici, Guicciardini retired to his farm and later to his villa, just outside Florence at Santa Margherita in Monticci, where he engaged in rhetorical exercises of self-accusation and defense. He was subse-

Francesco Guicciardini. Portrait medal. © THE BRITISH MUSEUM, LONDON

quently banished by the republic, his possessions confiscated. The Prince of Orange arrived with the imperial army in the autumn of 1529 to recover Florence for the Medici, and Guicciardini had his revenge the following year when he presided with Baccio Valori over the punishment of the leaders of the last Florentine republic. The remainder of Clement VII's pontificate he spent as governor of Bologna.

Returning to Florence in November 1534, Guicciardini soon found himself enlisted as advisor by Alessandro de' Medici, whose position as duke had become less secure following the death of the pope. With his success in renegotiating Alessandro's marriage to the emperor Charles V's natural daughter, Margaret, Guicciardini enjoyed a short-lived preeminence as the duke's most trusted counselor. After Alessandro's assassination the night of 5–6 January 1537 he took a leading role in the negotiations that brought the scion of the cadet branch of the family to power, but once Cosimo de' Medici had won the approval of Charles V, Guicciardini was relieved of all significant responsibilities. In retirement at Santa Margherita, he turned to the commentaries on his lieutenant generalship that he had begun after his return from Bologna, a project that quickly grew into his *Storia d'Italia* (*History of Italy*). Into this great work he threw all his remaining energies, making such rapid progress that he was giving it a final revision when death overtook him on 22 May 1540.

Works. Guicciardini's outlook as a political thinker and historian was determined by his career as a statesman, his patrician heritage, and his pragmatic instincts. Although well-read in the classics, he did not have the theoretical bent of his close friend Niccolò Machiavelli, with whom he had many discussions on history and politics beginning in 1521. Not only in his unfinished *Considerazioni sui discorsi del Machiavelli sopra la prima Deca di Tito Livio* (Considerations on the "Discourses" of Machiavelli), but also throughout his later writings, there seems to be a running dialogue in which Guicciardini sustains the irreducibility of individual circumstances over and against Machiavelli's attempts to generalize about the historical process. While his unfinished *Storie fiorentine dal 1378 al 1509* (History of Florence; written in 1508–1509) had been critical of the Medici, especially Lorenzo the Magnificent, for undermining the traditional form of Florentine government, Guicciardini's *Dialogo del reggimento di Firenze* (Dialogue on the government of Florence; written in 1521–1524) analyzed both the strengths and weaknesses of Lorenzo's rule, arguing for a republic led by an elite of "wise citizens," more open than Lorenzo's government but more restricted than the republic of 1494–1512. Distrusting the political capacity of the populace, Guicciardini saw its role in government as mainly a check on tyranny. Acknowledging that political power rests on force, he accepted the pragmatic Machiavellian "reason of state."

Of the writings drafted after the Sack of Rome, Guicciardini's *Consolatoria* (Consolatory; 1527) gives the deepest insight into his inner nature. Lacking any deeply religious impulse, he took refuge in rationality, stressing the imperative of rational conduct despite ample evidence that irrational behavior is often successful. His ambition, for which he knew he was rebuked by his enemies, he defended with classical precedents as a worthy trait if directed toward constructive ends, this despite his growing sense of disillusion with the rewards of power. The unfinished *Considerazioni sui discorsi del Machiavelli,* begun in 1530, reveals Guicciardini's empiricism, his aversion to popular republicanism, his disagreement with Machiavelli's positive assessment of social conflict in the Roman republic, and his distrust for the theoretical and "prophetic" aspects of Machiavelli, including the latter's vision of a revival of civic virtue.

The same themes emerge even more clearly in the fascinating *Ricordi* (Maxims and reflections), which Guicciardini compiled in notebooks for his personal ruminations between 1512 and 1530, and which embody his relentless political realism and his historian's mistrust of Machiavelli's enthusiasm for Roman precedents and modeling of exemplars. It was by attempting to follow his father's example of 1479, Guicciardini observed, that Piero de' Medici, an inferior diplomat, came to grief in 1494. Less optimistic than Machiavelli about the possibility of controlling the role of chance, or Fortune, in human affairs, Guicciardini gave frequent vent to his disillusion with the efficacy even of rational statesmanship. On the personal level his *Ricordi* reveal a naturally aloof figure constantly reminding himself of the qualities necessary for success in public life.

Guicciardini's masterpiece, the *History of Italy,* grew out of a narrative begun about 1534 to explain his role as lieutenant general of the papal forces in the war of the League of Cognac, but he found that he could not adequately discuss the events of these years without returning to their origins in 1494. Intended for publication, the *History of Italy* was written in an elaborate periodic style, incorporating into the Italian vernacular many of the classically based conventions of humanist historiography, including rhetorical set speeches and even portents. But while classical in form, the *History* was brilliantly innovative in method. Not content with reading virtually all the available histories, chronicles, and memoirs of the period, to which he applied the humanists' methods of comparative criticism, Guicciardini moved to his villa the archive of the Florentine magistracy, the Ten of War, which gained him access to a network of diplomatic correspondence covering virtually the entire period of his *History.* His own memory and reading could thus be supplemented with confidential memoranda intended for the information and guidance of the rulers of Florence. From a historiographical standpoint, Guicciardini's use of the Florentine archives anticipated Leopold von Ranke's discovery of the Venetian archives in the nineteenth century, which is often held to be the beginning of modern diplomatic history. The sixteenth-century French theorist Jean Bodin was quick to note the significance of Guicciardini's innovation in his influential *Methodus ad facilem historiarum cognitionem* (Method for easily understanding history; 1566). Once Guicciardini had begun the systematic exploitation of archival sources, virtually all that remained to be laid of the foundations of modern historiography was a system of notation of sources.

But it was not only in method that Guicciardini advanced historiography; he also expanded its horizons with his focus on motive as a causal factor.

Following classical precedent, the humanists had seen character as a wellspring of action, but Guicciardini wove it into the fabric of his explanation, not only probing relentlessly for motive but patiently reweaving the intricate sequence of cause and effect. For Guicciardini history is a complex dynamic in which individuals are shaped by the very events they have initiated. It is, moreover, a vortex beyond the control of any individual. "The removal of causes," he cautions, "does not always remove the effects which those causes have given rise to" (*History of Italy,* book 1, chapter 3). Hence, while history is a human creation, it acquires an independent and often irrational nature of its own, the quality commonly personified as Fortune.

From meditation on the powerlessness of prudence to counteract blind ambition and shortsighted greed, seemingly the common motives of princes, came Guicciardini's sense of futility and deep pessimism as he narrated the demise of Italian liberty and the fall of much of the peninsula into foreign hands. The first chapter sets the tone for the whole, with its idyllic picture of late-fifteenth-century Italy flourishing in peace and prosperity owing to the wise statesmanship of Lorenzo the Magnificent, only to be plunged into the misery of continual warfare by the greed and ambition of its rulers. Although the pace of narration is slow owing to Guicciardini's exacting presentation of detail, his *History* is replete with brilliant historical portraits of popes and princes, dramatic events, and trenchant moral judgments on human wickedness and folly. Because of these judgments, Guicciardini's heirs delayed publication of the *History* until 1561, after which its stature quickly became apparent as the preeminent account of the Italian Wars and a milestone in historiography. Not until Edward Gibbon's eighteenth-century account of the fall of the Roman Empire was there another history with the sweep and narrative power of Guicciardini's.

See also **Historiography**, **Renaissance**, *subentry on* **Italian Historiography**.

BIBLIOGRAPHY

Primary Works

Guicciardini, Francesco. *Dialogue on the Government of Florence.* Edited and translated by Alison Brown. Cambridge, U.K., 1994.

Guicciardini, Francesco. *The History of Florence.* Translated by Mario Domandi. New York, 1970.

Guicciardini, Francesco. *The History of Italy* (abridged). Translated by Sidney Alexander. New York, 1969. Paperback ed., Princeton, N.J., 1984.

Guicciardini, Francesco. *History of Italy and History of Florence*. Translated by Cecil Grayson. Edited by John R. Hale. New York, 1964. Contains selections from *History of Italy*.

Guicciardini, Francesco. *Maxims and Reflections*. Translated by Mario Domandi. New York, 1965; 2d ed., Philadelphia, 1972. Translation of *Ricordi*.

Guicciardini, Francesco. *Selected Writings*. Translated by Margaret Grayson. Edited by Cecil Grayson. London, 1965. Includes *Ricordi* and *Considerations on the "Discourses" of Machiavelli*.

Secondary Works

Bondanella, Peter E. *Francesco Guicciardini*. Boston, 1976.

Cochrane, Eric. *Historians and Historiography in the Italian Renaissance*. Chicago, 1981.

Gilbert, Felix. *Machiavelli and Guicciardini*. Princeton, N.J., 1965.

Phillips, Mark. *Francesco Guicciardini: The Historian's Craft*. Toronto, 1977.

Pocock, J. G. A. *The Machiavellian Moment: Florentine Political Thought and the Atlantic Republican Tradition*. Princeton, N.J., 1975.

Ridolfi, Roberto. *The Life of Francesco Guicciardini*. Translated by Cecil Grayson. New York, 1968.

T. C. PRICE ZIMMERMANN

GUILDS. The corporations known as guilds played a significant part in the urban life of Italy and Europe throughout the Renaissance. They expressed the corporatist spirit of the commune and asserted the importance of horizontal social ties between practitioners of the same trade, which contrasted with the vertical hierarchy that characterized rural feudalism.

Character and Evolution. The origins of guilds remain obscure, since the term itself is Germanic, yet the corporation fulfilled social functions similar to those of the ancient Roman *collegium* (fraternity). However, from the thirteenth century onward, guilds proliferated throughout urban Europe. Their role was regulatory rather than productive. They controlled market conditions for foodstuffs, clothing, and construction as well as establishing the standards required in manufacture. While they were defensive of the interests of their members, particularly in ensuring the independence of the small-scale producer, there were also guilds for merchants. In certain cases, a formal distinction was made between the two types. Florence had its Arti Maggiori (greater guilds) and Arti Minori (lesser guilds), the former largely mercantile, the latter largely artisan. In other places, notably Venice, no such distinction existed, and guilds such as that of the mercers had a membership that included wealthy merchants and peddlers, people who might be respectable shopkeepers or very poor indeed.

Historians have generally not been kind to guilds, often holding them accountable for economic decline through restrictive and monopolistic practices and lack of competitiveness. In order to circumvent their regulations, merchants sought to "put out" work to the countryside. Some scholars consider such actions to be the early stages of industrialization, a development to which guilds would be opposed. The reputation of guilds also suffered in the Reformation, when their association with the cult of saints and with works rather than faith made them the focus of much criticism. However, although their economic functions claim obvious attention, it is of the utmost importance to note the wide range of their social, political, and religious activities, and the role that they played in cultural life.

Guilds and the "Social Economy." Guild regulations governed the production process and how people were trained in it. Yet the workshop was much more than a unit of production. The training of an apprentice, which usually lasted several years, was essentially an education, and provided the trainee not only with skills but also with shelter, board, and lodging, sometimes with care in the event of ill health, and even an incremented wage scale during the apprenticeship itself. Young, unattached males in particular were thereby kept off the streets and to some extent out of trouble. The guilds themselves offered some modest protection against illness and accident, and their insurance schemes might stretch to contingencies outside the city in which they were located. Municipal authorities continued to sanction such organizations as a protection against unrest. This contribution to the social economy helps to account for the durability of guilds in centers as distant and diverse in character as Venice and Leiden.

In many instances, guilds were also the basic unit of political life. In Florence and London, guild membership was essential to make a man eligible for office. The Revolt of the Ciompi (unenfranchised workers in the wool industry) in Florence in 1378 took as its slogan "long live the twenty-four guilds!" This represented a demand for an increase of three guilds in order to enfranchise unskilled workers in certain processes of textile production. In London, twelve great companies were distinguished from several dozen smaller crafts. In cities such as Siena and Venice, guilds played no part in politics, yet they still fulfilled important social functions.

Piety and Patronage. Although religious confraternities could, and often did, exist without the bond of a common occupation, all corporations had a devotional function. They met to celebrate their patron saint's festival, and members were guaranteed a funeral, at which attendance was compulsory for all. Such events usually took place in a chapel—or at least before an altar—in a parish church, and the guild maintained the premises through agreement with the resident clergy. The decoration of such a location often entailed patronage of the arts. Famously, the guilds of Florence were each expected to sponsor a sculpted figure in the niches at the church of Orsanmichele in Florence, and sought to outdo each other in works by masters such as Donatello and Ghiberti. The trade guilds and devotional confraternities of Venice commissioned cycles of paintings from, among others, the Bellini, Carpaccio, and Tintoretto. From 1535 onward, the guilds of London organized the pageant for the Lord Mayor's Show, responsibility resting with the guild of which the mayor was a member.

Corporate Traditions.

The persistence of guild organizations throughout the Renaissance is something of an inconvenience to those who identify that culture with the birth of modern "individualism," for guilds are an assertive reminder of the ways in which identities found collective expression. In the context of Renaissance culture, it is important to bear in mind that the term "masterpiece" derives from the piece of work that an apprentice submitted for admission to the rank of master within the corporation. The Florentines Lorenzo Ghiberti (a sculptor) and Filippo Brunelleschi (an architect) trained as goldsmiths, for instance. For many people outside the social elite, guild organizations may have acted as a sort of substitute family. As such, they were institutions that mediated between the public sphere of the state and the private world of domesticity. The relationship between the two seems to have begun to crystallize toward the end of the sixteenth century. The recording of complaints against sons of masters who were advancing their status in the guild without submission of a "masterpiece" was common in the history of guilds, but may have become overwhelming in the seventeenth century. The abandonment of quality control may yet prove to have been more important in the decline of guilds than what has traditionally been portrayed as their lack of economic competitiveness. In a curious way, tradition had served to maintain guilds rather than condemn them to ossification. Their eventual disappearance may have owed more to the hostility of the state than to the operation of economic forces.

See also **Confraternities**; **Industry**.

BIBLIOGRAPHY

Duplessis, Robert S., and Martha C. Howell. "Reconsidering the Early Modern Urban Economy: The Cases of Leyden and Lille." *Past and Present* 94 (1982): 49–84.

Goldthwaite, Richard A. *The Building of Renaissance Florence: An Economic and Social History.* Baltimore, 1981.

Humfrey, Peter, and Richard Mackenney. "The Venetian Trade Guilds as Patrons of Art in the Renaissance." *Burlington Magazine* 128 (1986): 317–330.

Mackenney, Richard. *Tradesmen and Traders: The World of the Guilds in Venice and Europe, c. 1250–c. 1650.* London, 1987.

Najemy, John M. *Corporatism and Consensus in Florentine Politics, 1280–1400.* Chapel Hill, N.C., 1982.

Unwin, George. *The Gilds and Companies of London.* 4th ed., London, 1963.

RICHARD MACKENNEY

GUISE-LORRAINE FAMILY. One of the most powerful aristocratic families in Renaissance France and newcomers to the French nobility, the Guise rose to prominence in the sixteenth century through their military ability, political skill, and uncompromising allegiance to the Catholic Church. Service to the French crown provided the house of Guise with lands, titles, provincial governorships, royal offices, and ecclesiastical and monastic benefices.

Origins. There was a close connection between the duchy of Lorraine and the house of Guise-Lorraine in France. The duchy of Lorraine was an ancient, illustrious house of independent princes who traced their descent from Charlemagne. After the death of duc René II de Lorraine in 1508, his eldest son, Antoine, inherited the duchy of Lorraine. Duc René's second son, Claude de Lorraine (1496–1550), was sent to be raised at the French court, where he became a naturalized French citizen in 1506. Claude inherited all his father's French seigneuries, including the territories of Guise, Aumale, Joinville, Elbeuf, Harcourt, Mayenne, Longjumeau, Boves, and other lands in Provence. Joinville, located in Champagne near the border between France and Lorraine, became the capital of the Guise family.

Claude de Lorraine, the founder of the French house of Guise-Lorraine, developed a close personal relationship with the future king of France, Francis I of Valois. Claude married Antoinette de Bourbon in June 1513, and they had twelve children. In 1527, Claude de Lorraine's loyalty and military service to the crown were rewarded when he was made the first duc de Guise. Upon the death of Francis I in 1547, Claude and Antoinette retreated to Joinville, leaving their children well established at the French court.

Guise-Lorraine Family

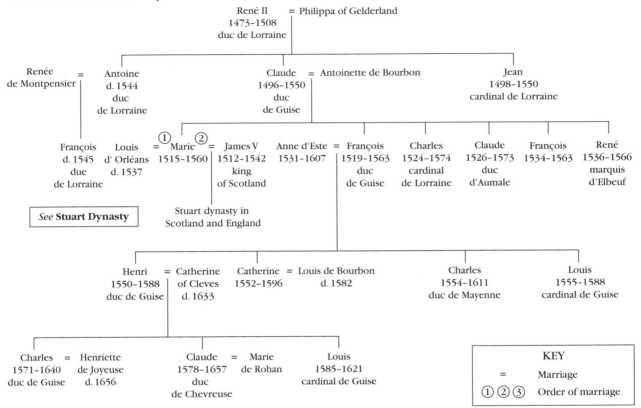

René II = Philippa of Gelderland
1473-1508
duc de Lorraine

Renée = Antoine
de Montpensier | d. 1544
duc
de Lorraine

Claude = Antoinette de Bourbon
1496-1550
duc
de Guise

Jean
1498-1550
cardinal de Lorraine

François   Louis   ①Marie② = James V   Anne d'Este = François   Charles   Claude   François   René
d. 1545   d' Orléans   1515-1560   1512-1542   1531-1607   1519-1563   1524-1574   1526-1573   1534-1563   1536-1566
due   d. 1537   king   duc   cardinal   duc   marquis
de Lorraine   of Scotland   de Guise   de Lorraine   d'Aumale   d'Elbeuf

See **Stuart Dynasty**

Stuart dynasty in
Scotland and England

Henri = Catherine   Catherine = Louis de Bourbon   Charles   Louis
1550-1588   of Cleves   1552-1596   d. 1582   1554-1611   1555-1588
duc de Guise   d. 1633   duc de Mayenne   cardinal de Guise

Charles = Henriette   Claude = Marie   Louis
1571-1640   de Joyeuse   1578-1657   de Rohan   1585-1621
duc de Guise   d. 1656   duc   cardinal de Guise
de Chevreuse

KEY		
=	Marriage	
①②③	Order of marriage	

In Royal Service.

A close friend and military companion to King Henry II, François de Lorraine (1519–1563) became the second duc de Guise after his father's death in 1550. His brother Charles (1524–1574), the archbishop of Reims, became cardinal de Lorraine that same year. A brilliant, skilled orator, the cardinal was a political adviser to Henry II, and eventually led the French delegation to the Council of Trent. The loyalty and talent of the younger Guise, Claude (duc d'Aumale), Louis (cardinal de Guise), François (grand prieur and general of the galleys), and René (marquis d'Elbeuf) also contributed to the Guise ascendancy in French society.

In 1548, François de Lorraine married Anne d'Este, daughter of Duke Ercole d'Este and Renée de France, and they had eight children. After the defeat at Saint-Quentin in 1557, Guise was named lieutenant general of France. In January 1558, he was responsible for the recovery of Calais from the English. This victory established him as a military hero in France and ensured the marriage of his niece, Mary Stuart, to the dauphin Francis. With the accession of Francis II in 1559, the duke and his brother, the cardinal, controlled royal policy. The preeminence of

the house of Guise at court, along with the spread of the French Reformed Church, created tensions among the French aristocracy during the reign of Francis II. François, duc de Guise, and his brother Charles, the cardinal de Lorraine, were the targets of the Conspiracy of Amboise in March 1560.

Catholic Leaders.

Unlike the houses of Bourbon and Montmorency, no members of the house of Guise converted to the French Reformed Church. By the reign of Charles IX, the duc de Guise and the cardinal de Lorraine were identified as champions of Catholicism in France. On 1 March 1562, François de Lorraine and his troops encountered a Huguenot congregation at Vassy. Although the massacre that ensued there was most likely unpremeditated, it is nevertheless considered the spark that set off the French Wars of Religion (1562–1598). The assassination of François de Lorraine on 18 February 1563 by Jean Poltrot de Méré created a Catholic martyr for France and for the city of Paris. Guise's widow, Anne, and his sons, particularly the third duc de Guise, Henri, held Admiral Gaspard de Coligny responsible for the assassination. This vendetta be-

Henry, Duc de Guise. Portrait of Henry de Lorraine, duc de Guise (1550–1588), by François Quesnel. MUSÉE CARNAVALET, PARIS/© COLLECTION VIOLLET

tween the Guises and Coligny led to Coligny's own death in the Saint Bartholomew's Day massacre in August 1572.

Unwilling to accept a Protestant succession to the French crown, the third duc de Guise, Henri (1550–1588), became head of the Catholic League in 1576. More popular in Paris and among Catholics than King Henry III of Valois, Henri de Guise gained control of the city of Paris in May 1588. In December 1588 at Blois, the duke and his brother Louis, the cardinal of Guise, were murdered on the orders of King Henry III.

Female Members of the House of Guise.

The women of the house of Guise contributed to the prominence of the family through their marriages, networks of clients, and preservation of church benefices for the family. The eldest daughter of Claude de Lorraine, Marie de Guise (1515–1560), married King James V of Scotland. Her daughter Mary Stuart, queen of Scots (1542–1587), wed Francis II of France. Antoinette de Bourbon (1494–1583) and Anne d'Este (1531–1607) exhibited the same intense devotion to family honor and Catholicism that was

characteristic of their spouses. Both women used their extensive network of clients to further the Guise at court. In the late sixteenth and early seventeenth centuries, the female members of the family played an important role in the French Catholic Reformation through religious patronage and the holding of monastic benefices as abbesses.

The Last Guise. While their political influence waned in the seventeenth century, the Guise remained a wealthy, noble family because of their ecclesiastical benefices. The last important duc de Guise was Henri's son Charles, who died in exile in 1640. His son Henri, the fifth duc de Guise (1614–1664), was better known for his scandals than his attempt to become king of Naples. The house of Guise was already in decline when the seventh duc de Guise, François Joseph, died in 1675. In 1688, with the death of Marie de Lorraine, great aunt of the last duke, the house of Guise came to an end.

See also **Wars of Religion.**

BIBLIOGRAPHY

Baker, Joanne. "Female Monasticism and Family Strategy: The Guises and Saint Pierre de Reims." *Sixteenth Century Journal* 28 (1997): 1091–1108.

Bellenger, Yvonne, ed. *Le mécènat et l'influence de Guise: Actes du colloque organisé par le Centre de Recherche sur la littérature.* Paris, 1997.

Bergin, J. A. "The Decline and Fall of the House of Guise as an Ecclesiastical Dynasty." *Historical Journal* 25 (1982): 781–803.

Bergin, J. A. "The Guises and Their Benefices, 1588–1641." *English Historical Review* 390 (1984): 34–58.

Constant, Jean-Marie. *Les Guise.* Paris, 1984.

Potter, David. "The Duc de Guise and the Fall of Calais, 1557–1558." *English Historical Review* 388 (1983): 481–512.

Sutherland, N. M. "The Assassination of François duc de Guise, February 1563." *Historical Journal* 24 (1981): 279–295.

SILVIA C. SHANNON

GUTENBERG, JOHANN (c. 1398–1468), inventor of the moveable type printing press. Gutenberg was the descendant of a socially prominent family from the area of Mainz, Germany, where he grew up. In 1434 he moved to Strasbourg, where he lived for eleven years. He returned to Mainz around 1448 and remained there until his death. Much of what is known about Gutenberg is derived from court records of lawsuits stemming from financial problems connected with the development of his printing press. A number of contemporary texts cite the importance of Gutenberg's work in the development of printing; these include Hartmann Schedel's *Nürnberg Chronicle* (1493) and Johann Trithemius's *Chronicle of Sponheim* (1509).

Gutenberg Bible. Two pages from a forty-two-line Bible printed by Gutenberg and Fust at Mainz, c. 1455. THE PIERPONT MORGAN LIBRARY/ART RESOURCE, NY

Gutenberg's Invention. The essence of Gutenberg's invention was his method of manufacturing moveable lead-based type that met the precise and exacting requirements for printed books. Gutenberg apparently experimented with many materials in his attempt to make printing more efficient. He worked out a system of typecasting each letter of the alphabet individually with an engraved steel punch and matrix box. His formulas for both lead type and ink are still viable. For the type he used an alloy of 80 percent lead, 5 percent tin, and 15 percent antimony; for the ink he used a mixture of linseed oil, varnish, and lampblack. Book pages were printed either on calfskin or on paper, which was cheaper. Trial and error experimentation and the construction of his printing equipment were expensive and Gutenberg was forced to borrow money from several sources, the most important being Johann Fust, a prosperous goldsmith and moneylender in Mainz, who loaned Gutenberg more than two thousand guldens, a small fortune in the fifteenth century.

The Forty-Two-Line Bible. Gutenberg's Mainz printshop may have contained as many as six printing presses. During 1454 and 1455 he printed more than two hundred copies of the Vulgate, thirty copies more than on calfskin (vellum) and the remainder on paper, each page composed of forty-two lines of print. Unfortunately for the history of printing, these Bibles were printed without an identifying colophon or date, but when Heinrich Cremer, vicar of Saint Stephen's Church in Mainz, finished with his own hand the illumination and rubrication on his newly printed Bible, he noted the year 1456. Probably a quarter of the original press run has survived the ravages of time.

One might expect that such an experimental "first book" would be crude and error filled; however, the forty-two-line Bible is a work of near perfection; the Gothic type is sharp and clear and the right-hand margins are straight. Many of the copies were beautifully hand illuminated in the spaces left by the printer for capital letters and headings—a process that had been honed to perfection in the production of medieval manuscripts. The cost of production apparently exceeded the profits from sales, and by the time the last copies of the forty-two-line Bible were printed, Gutenberg was being sued by Johann Fust. Court records in Mainz indicate that Fust and his son-in-law Peter Schöffer took possession of Gutenberg's printshop in lieu of loan repayment. Several other books have been attributed to Gutenberg, or at least his press, including a Latin grammar by Aelius Donatus, fourth-century teacher of St. Jerome (whose Bible translation Gutenberg printed), and an encyclopedic Latin dictionary, the *Catholicon*.

Gutenberg and the Renaissance. Gutenberg's work in the development of the printing press was in many ways a turning point in the history of Western civilization. The spread of printing had a limited effect on the Italian Renaissance of the fifteenth century, but on a broader scale influenced cultural and commercial developments in northern and western Europe in the sixteenth century. During the last half of the fifteenth century, printshops, often staffed with master printers of German origin, appeared in many of the cities and towns of western Europe. The availability of printed books fundamentally changed the methods by which students, scholars, and educated laypersons stored, retrieved, and disseminated information. Gutenberg's invention ensured that information could be reproduced accurately, quickly, and cheaply. The manuscript and oral culture of medieval Europe shifted to the visual world of the printed page. Handwritten or copied manuscripts without punctuation or visual clues for paragraph structure had to be read out loud or memorized. When the shift from hand-copied manuscript to the printed page occurred, there was less need to memorize texts or to read aloud.

One of the results of a broad distribution of printed materials was the censorship of books, a practice unnecessary in the limited world of the scribe but one which became common in the centuries following the birth of printing.

When considering the impact of Gutenberg on the Italian Renaissance it is worthwhile to note that many of the first books printed in the incunabular age (the first half-century of printing) were the works of ancient Greeks and Romans and the vernacular works of popular late-medieval and early Renaissance writers such as Petrarch and Giovanni Boccaccio. Writing and composing new and original works for the printing press became common in the first several decades of the sixteenth century. Another new use of printing was the production of maps relating to the discoveries of the new world; accurate maps were absolutely essential in the conceptualization by Europeans of the modern world.

Although knowledge of Gutenberg is scant, there is enough evidence to indicate that he deserved all the acclaim he has received from the beginning of the age of print to the present. Gutenberg focused on and solved many complex problems of printing. His first major effort of book printing with moveable type, the forty-two-line Bible, will remain a remarkable product of a seminal invention, the Gutenberg press.

See also **Printing and Publishing.**

BIBLIOGRAPHY

Primary Works

Fuhrman, Otto W. *Gutenberg and the Strasbourg Documents of 1439.* New York, 1940. Useful for the study of pertinent legal documents.

McMurtrie, Douglas C. *The Gutenberg Documents.* New York, 1941. Provides a broad survey of Gutenberg's court cases.

Secondary Works

Bühler, Curt F. *The Fifteenth-Century Book.* Philadelphia, 1960. The author provides some clear drawings of some technical aspects of typecasting.

Clair, Colin. *A History of European Printing.* New York, 1976. Contains an excellent bibliography on printing.

Cole, Richard G. "Reformation Printers: Unsung Heroes." *The Sixteenth-Century Journal* 15 (1984): 327–339. Examines the work of printers in the creation of a new print culture.

Kapr, Albert. *Johann Gutenberg: The Man and His Invention.* Translated by Douglas Martin. Aldershot, U.K., 1994.

RICHARD G. COLE

GYNECOLOGY. *See* **Obstetrics and Gynecology.**

HABSBURG DYNASTY.　During the course of the later Middle Ages and the Renaissance, the Habsburgs rose from relatively obscure origins to become the dominant political family of Europe in the sixteenth century.

The Rise of the Habsburgs.　The Habsburgs began as a local power in Swabia in southern Germany in the thirteenth century. By the sixteenth century, Habsburgs ruled the Holy Roman Empire and the powerful Spanish kingdom and its vast international empire. King Philip II of Spain (ruled 1556–1598) could claim rule over more of the earth's surface than any other prince. His cousin Maximilian II was the elected ruler of the Holy Roman Empire (1564–1576), the largest state in Europe.

The rise of the Habsburgs to international prominence began in 1246 when they took over Austria from the extinct Babenberg dynasty. They seemed to be just another ambitious noble house intent on expanding their domains through war and matrimonial alliances. But they had greater success than others, winning the imperial throne for a limited time under Rudolf I of Habsburg (1273–1291) and his son Albert I (1298–1308).

Albert II and Frederick III.　Given the family squabbles within their ranks, the ambitions of other families, and the general instability of political life in early Renaissance Europe, it is not surprising that the Habsburgs did not regain the imperial throne until 1438 when Albert II, an able military commander, secured power. Albert II (ruled 1438–1439) was the first of an unbroken succession of Habsburg

monarchs that lasted until 1740. After considerable difficulty, Albert was succeeded by his cousin, Duke Frederick of Steiermark, who ruled as Frederick III (1440–1493). Albert II's will had established a council of regency that included his influential widow, Elizabeth of Luxembourg, daughter of the emperor Sigismund (1433–1437). She hoped to hold the throne for her son Ladislas (d. 1457), born after the death of his father.

The situation for Frederick was further complicated by the fact that the Habsburg inheritance had been split in 1379 into two lines: the Albertine in Austria and the Leopoldine elsewhere. Even Frederick's own brother, Albert VI (1418–1463), did not want him to succeed to the thrones of Hungary, Austria, and Bohemia. Adding to the pressure of the situation was the growing power of the Ottoman Turks, who took Constantinople in 1453 and threatened the Habsburg patrimony in the east. Frederick's overwhelming difficulties and limited resources were part of the reason for his selection as Holy Roman Emperor. His preoccupation with securing his Habsburg possessions meant that he would have little time to interfere with the electors' various political initiatives inside Germany. It also meant that despite his long reign Frederick failed to establish the principle of regular taxation inside the empire. He ravaged the royal treasury by mortgaging incomes. Although he argued that Austria was carrying the empire on its financial back, Frederick found the wealthy German towns to be ready sources of cash, a situation that remained unchanged during the reign of his son, Maximilian I (1493 to 1519).

Habsburg Dynasty

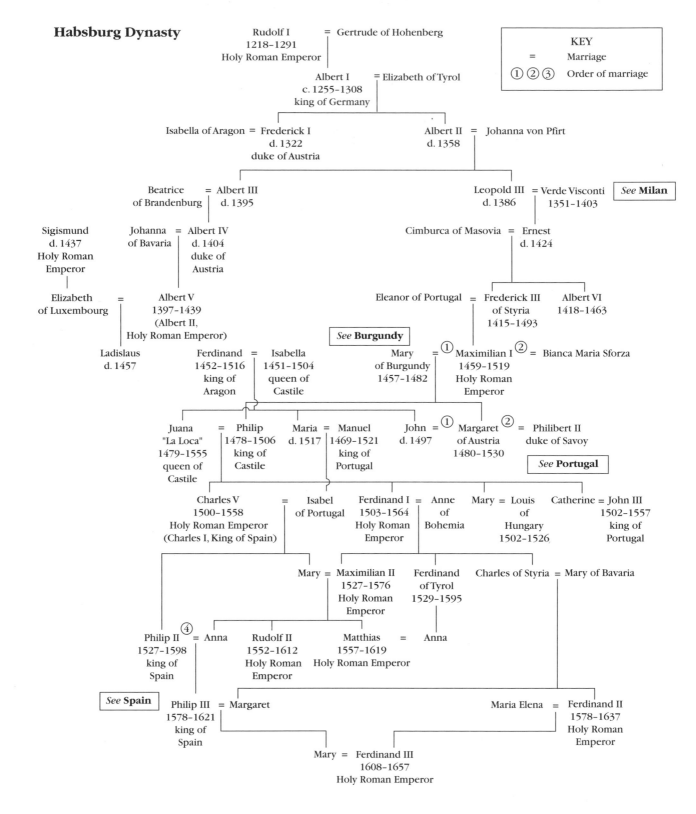

KEY
= Marriage
① ② ③ Order of marriage

Rudolf I 1218–1291 Holy Roman Emperor = Gertrude of Hohenberg

Albert I c. 1255–1308 king of Germany = Elizabeth of Tyrol

Isabella of Aragon = Frederick I d. 1322 duke of Austria

Albert II d. 1358 = Johanna von Pfirt

Beatrice of Brandenburg = Albert III d. 1395

Leopold III d. 1386 = Verde Visconti 1351–1403 **See Milan**

Sigismund d. 1437 Holy Roman Emperor

Johanna of Bavaria = Albert IV d. 1404 duke of Austria

Cimburca of Masovia = Ernest d. 1424

Elizabeth of Luxembourg = Albert V 1397–1439 (Albert II, Holy Roman Emperor)

Eleanor of Portugal = Frederick III of Styria 1415–1493   Albert VI 1418–1463

See Burgundy

Ladislaus d. 1457

Ferdinand 1452–1516 king of Aragon = Isabella 1451–1504 queen of Castile

Mary of Burgundy 1457–1482 = ① Maximilian I 1459–1519 Holy Roman Emperor ② = Bianca Maria Sforza

Juana "La Loca" 1479–1555 queen of Castile = Philip 1478–1506 king of Castile

Maria d. 1517 = Manuel 1469–1521 king of Portugal

John d. 1497 = ① Margaret of Austria 1480–1530 ② = Philibert II duke of Savoy

See Portugal

Charles V 1500–1558 Holy Roman Emperor (Charles I, King of Spain) = Isabel of Portugal

Ferdinand I 1503–1564 Holy Roman Emperor = Anne of Bohemia

Mary = Louis of Hungary 1502–1526

Catherine = John III 1502–1557 king of Portugal

Mary = Maximilian II 1527–1576 Holy Roman Emperor

Ferdinand of Tyrol 1529–1595

Charles of Styria = Mary of Bavaria

Philip II 1527–1598 king of Spain ④ = Anna

Rudolf II 1552–1612 Holy Roman Emperor

Matthias 1557–1619 Holy Roman Emperor = Anna

See Spain

Philip III 1578–1621 king of Spain = Margaret

Maria Elena = Ferdinand II 1578–1637 Holy Roman Emperor

Mary = Ferdinand III 1608–1657 Holy Roman Emperor

Frederick did have a number of successes in addition to eventually being able to take under control some of his claims to his eastern lands. He succeeded in marrying Eleanor of Portugal, which helped the dynasty's eventual acquisition of that kingdom (1580). He also reached an agreement with Pope Nicholas V in the Concordant of Vienna in 1448, which excluded Habsburg lands from external episcopal jurisdiction, granted the right of presentation of benefices, and shared ecclesiastical taxes. As a patron of the arts Frederick named one of his secretaries, Enea Silvio Piccolomini (1405–1464; later Pope Pius II, 1458–1464), as poet-laureate, a position that enabled him to introduce humanist learning to Germany. Although initially indifferent to the calls for imperial reform, Frederick III did lay the foundation for expanded Habsburg dynastic might by marrying his son, Maximilian, to Mary of Burgundy (1457–1482), sole heir to the prosperous lands of her father, Charles the Bold, duke of Burgundy (1467–1477).

The Last Knight: Maximilian I. Maximilian I (1459–1519) was one of the most remarkable princes to emerge during the Renaissance. In his youth he learned the seven liberal arts, astrology, carpentry, music, lute playing, mining, hunting, fishing, weaponry, painting, and drawing. An extremely congenial person, Maximilian acquired a speaking knowledge of seven languages, which greatly helped him in ruling his multilingual empire. He defended the Burgundian inheritance against the French kings Louis XI and Charles VIII by defeating Louis at Guinegate in Artois in 1479 and Charles at Salins in Franche-Comté in 1493. In 1486 Maximilian was elected king of the Romans and joined his father in the administration of the Holy Roman Empire. When Frederick died in 1493, Maximilian became the sole ruler of the empire and head of the house of Habsburg.

Maximilian faced a myriad of problems, including a fierce rivalry with the French over Italy; the continuing threat of the Ottomans to the eastern frontiers; and the internal problems of the empire, which included efforts by reformers to alter the political constitution of the empire, arguments over taxes, and a continual problem with robber barons. He eventually joined Spain, Pope Alexander VI, Milan, and Venice in a Holy League (1495) to drive the French out of Italy. In 1494 Maximilian married Bianca Maria Sforza (d. 1510), duchess of Milan and niece of Ludovico Sforza (Il Moro), to further his interests in Italy. In 1496, financed by Milan, he made an unsuc-

cessful expedition to Italy and was forced into a hasty withdrawal. His efforts to secure German support for a second expedition also failed, and he was forced to sign a peace treaty with Louis XII of France in 1504. Because of the opposition of the Venetians, Maximilian was unable to reach Rome in 1508 for his imperial coronation. He also failed to secure Milan from the French in 1515 or to achieve his dream of succeeding Julius II as pope. Maximilian was never without grandiose plans, even if most of them failed because of his continuing financial problems.

Maximilian did succeed in securing Austria for his father by driving the Hungarians out of Vienna in 1490. He got Ulászló II, king of Bohemia since 1471, to agree to pass the succession to both Bohemia and Hungary to the Habsburgs should Ulászló die without a male heir. Subsequent negotiations resulted in Ulászló's son Louis's betrothal to Maximilian's granddaughter Mary and his daughter Anna to Maximilian's grandson Ferdinand. As a marital diplomat, Maximilian had few equals. His greatest success was in marrying his son Philip (1478–1506) to Joan I of Castile (1479–1555), daughter of Isabella and Ferdinand of Spain. The result was that his grandson Charles inherited the Spanish crown as well as the inside track on succeeding Maximilian as Holy Roman Emperor. Later wags said of the Habsburgs, "Alii bellam gerant, sed tu, felix Austria, nube" (Others may wage war, but thou, happy Austria, marry!).

Maximilian attempted to bring greater cohesion and order to the administration of all the territories under his control. In the cases of his hereditary territories, he had to work with a regional administrative structure (*Regiment*) different from that of the Holy Roman Empire. Each region had separate diets dominated by the local nobility, which met in Graz Xand Linz. Maximilian used a series of separate administrative capitals: Vienna (Lower Austria), Innsbruck (Upper Austria), and Ensisheim (Alsace). Maximilian's imperial chancellery attempted to coordinate the activities of the three governments of the hereditary states. Maximilian attempted to integrate his rule by using his Aulic Council (*Hofrat*) for Austria and his Imperial Council (*Reichshofrat*) for the empire as the same institution. Therefore, one council was charged with the administration of justice in both the hereditary estates and the Holy Roman Empire.

Given Maximilian's own broad cultural interests and vanity, it is not surprising that he was a great success as a patron of the arts and literature. He utilized artists such as Albrecht Dürer and Hans Burgkmair on numerous projects, including illustrations for his own literary works. Seeking a reputation as a new Augustus, Maximilian helped support humanists such as Johann Cuspinian, Conrad Peutinger, and Johann Stabius. His own writings include *Theuerdank*, a political allegory describing his journey to claim Mary of Burgundy as his bride, and an unfinished autobiographical work of the young *Weisskunig* (white king).

Efforts at imperial reform came to naught during Maximilian's reign partly because his vision of reform was quite at odds with those of the princes led by Archbishop Berthold of Mainz (1442–1504). He did achieve a measure of prestige in the empire as a result of his victory in the 1504 dynastic war between Bavaria and the Rhenish Palatinate. His Italian policies, especially his eight-year war with Venice, were unpopular with German merchants, who were tired of Maximilian's incessant efforts to secure loans from them and the venality of many members of his court. At the Diet of Augsburg of 1518 Maximilian was unable to secure the election of his grandson Charles as king of the Romans. This was a final humiliation for the visionary emperor, who died at Wels the following year.

The World Empire of Charles V.

By the time of Maximilian's death, the Holy Roman Empire was already in the throes of a new crisis sparked by the Ninety-five Theses of the friar and university professor Martin Luther. Maximilian's grandson Charles had been proclaimed king of Spain following the death of his maternal grandfather, Ferdinand II, in 1516. With the help of huge loans from the German banking firms of the Fuggers and Welsers, Charles became the unanimous choice of the seven electors. His rivals for the imperial throne included Francis I of France and Henry VIII of England. By 1519 Charles held more than sixty royal and princely titles, including emperor, archduke of Austria, duke of Burgundy, king of Castile and Aragon, which included the rule of southern Italy and possessions in the New World, and king of Hungary. In addition to his titles, Charles of Habsburg inherited a host of problems.

A staunch Roman Catholic, Charles had to attempt to suppress the movement led by Martin Luther, which he considered a "dangerous and vile heresy." His efforts to suppress the Evangelicals in Germany were largely frustrated by his continuing dynastic rivalry with France, the Communero Revolt in Spain from 1520 to 1521, internal problems in Germany, and the great threat of the Ottoman Turks. Under the dynamic leadership of Sultan Süleyman I the Mag-

nificent (ruled 1520–1566), the Ottomans took Belgrade in 1521 and half of Hungary in 1526. In 1529 they threatened the walls of Vienna itself. Charles was aided considerably in his endeavors by his brother, Ferdinand (1503–1564), who served as his regent in the empire, and his aunt Margaret of Austria (1480–1530), who served as his regent in the Netherlands. Margaret had raised Charles during his youth in the Low Countries and contributed to his education.

Even relations with the papacy were at times strained after the death of Charles's old tutor Adrian of Utrecht, who became pope as Adrian VI in 1522, in part through the support of the young emperor. Rome itself was sacked in 1527 and Pope Clement VII was captured by rebellious troops of Charles V. Charles soon restored Clement to power, who in turn blocked the efforts of Henry VIII of England to secure an annulment of his marriage to Charles's aunt, Catherine of Aragon. This matrimonial crisis helped set off the English Reformation.

Charles did manage to hold his own against the Ottomans and the French. He staved off the Ottoman threat to the Habsburg lands in central Europe by 1532. Operating out of Spain in 1535 he captured Tunis in North Africa, but this did little to diminish the Ottoman's overall strength. Charles had been fighting the French over Italy since 1521. In 1525 at the Battle of Pavia, Charles defeated Francis I and took him prisoner. Francis later repudiated the Treaty of Madrid and hostilities resumed until the "Ladies Peace" of Cambrai (1529) negotiated by Louise of Savoy, the mother of the French king, and Charles's remarkable aunt, Margaret of Austria. While the Habsburg lands were technically patriarchies, Margaret and Charles's sister, Mary of Hungary (1505–1558), held great influence in the informal and sporadic family councils and the lands they administered.

New rounds of fighting between the Valois and the Habsburgs broke out again in 1536 after Francis made his shocking "devil's alliance" with the Ottomans and renewed his efforts to secure Milan. Finally, in 1544 Charles threatened Paris and Francis I agreed to the Peace of Crépy, which basically confirmed the status quo and at last ended the wars between them for the duration of Charles's life. Freed from both the Ottoman and French threats, the gout-afflicted emperor attempted to negotiate a peaceful settlement in the empire with the Protestants. When this failed, he tried military means to enforce a degree of religious uniformity. Despite winning the major battles of the Schmalkaldic War (1546–1547),

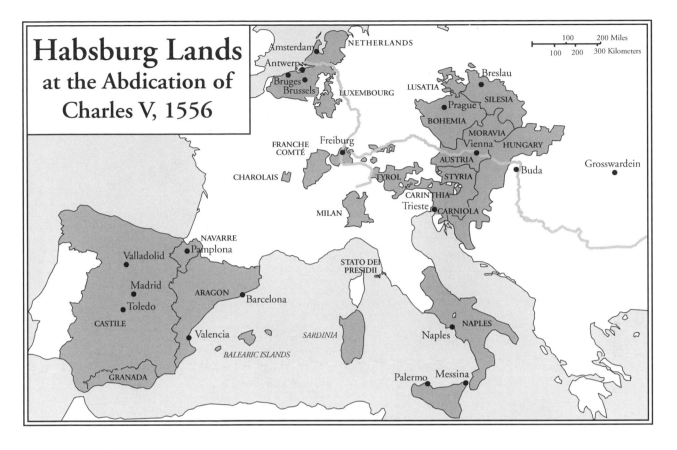

Habsburg Lands at the Abdication of Charles V, 1556

Charles was unable to eliminate the Protestants from the empire, and by the terms of the Peace of Augsburg (1555) he reluctantly followed Ferdinand's advice to allow Lutheranism to exist under a version of the old formula "he who has the rule, his religion."

Under Charles's sponsorship the Portuguese navigator Ferdinand Magellan (c. 1480–1521) began his effort to circumnavigate the globe. Hernan Cortés (1485–1547) completed his conquest of the Aztec Empire in Mexico and Francisco Pizarro (c. 1478–1541) his even more brutal conquest of the Inca Empire in Peru. Charles never fully appreciated the significance of his overseas possessions. The colonies existed to be exploited for their resources and to enhance the image of Habsburg power. Under Charles's rule they were never integrated into any overall imperial scheme. It was not until the 1550s that any significant amount of gold and silver reached Charles's Spain from the Americas.

Although Charles was overwhelmed with his administrative, financial, and political problems, he did extend important patronage to the great Italian artist Titian, who rendered several superb portraits of the emperor, including the well-known *Emperor Charles V at the Battle of Mühlberg* (Prado; see the color plates in this volume). Titian's *Gloria,* a magnificent rendering of the Trinity painted at Charles's order, was one of his most cherished possessions. He renewed the pension that his father had granted the Nürnberg artist Albrecht Dürer. Andreas Vesalius (1514–1564), after his revolutionary work in anatomy in Italy, became the emperor's personal physician. Petrus Apianus (1501–1552), a professor of mathematics at Ingolstadt, served as his court astrologer and dedicated his *Astronomicum Caesareum* to Charles. Charles also sponsored an important revision of the imperial criminal code, the Carolina, of 1532.

The Division of the Habsburg Inheritance. Impressed by the abilities of his talented son Philip and wishing to keep the Habsburg empire in the hands of one man, Charles in 1550 announced his plan to turn over his entire inheritance to Philip, thus bypassing his younger brother's claims to succeed as Holy Roman Emperor. At the Habsburg family council (an informal gathering of family members, which had no official status under the imperial constitution) at Arras, only Mary of Hungary supported the emperor in this decision. Ferdinand, who

Habsburg Dynasty. Bowl of a goblet depicting thirteen Habsburg emperors, made by J. B. Wienet, Augsburg, 1645.

had become king of both Bohemia and Hungary, was justifiably angry at his brother. It was Ferdinand who had taken the lead role in German affairs since 1521 and who had been the chief protector of the eastern lands from the depredations of the Ottomans. In order to avoid the threat of civil war, Charles signed an agreement in 1551 that Ferdinand would succeed him as emperor, to be followed not by Ferdinand's son, Maximilian, but by Charles's son, Philip. After Philip the imperial crown would pass to Maximilian, who like his father decided not to co-operate in carrying out this scheme when the time came to implement it. This arrangement pleased no one and added to the suspicions of many prominent Germans that the Habsburgs intended to turn the elective emperorship into a hereditary monarchy. Some of the Protestants had earlier attempted to

block Ferdinand's appointment as king of the Romans as a bargaining chip in religious negotiations.

Worn out by his exertions and troubled by ill health and insomnia, Charles decided to abdicate all his titles. In September 1555 he turned his imperial responsibilities completely over to Ferdinand, who was finally crowned emperor in 1558. The Netherlands was ceded to Philip in October 1555, and the following year he received Spain, the Italian lands, and the colonies. Charles V then retired to his country house at San Jerónimo de Yuste to prepare his soul for death, which came in 1558.

Ferdinand I spent much of his reign as emperor trying to settle the religious differences in Germany and pressing the war against the Ottomans more strongly. A dedicated Erasmian, his princely ideal was defined by the humanist's *Enchiridion militis*

Christiani (Handbook of the Christian knight; 1503), the second edition of which was dedicated to him. He kept Erasmians in his immediate circle, including his chancellor Bernhard of Cles. However, his toleration of diversity in thought went only so far. Before allowing his son Maximilian II to be elected king of the Romans, Ferdinand forced him to renounce his Protestant leanings. He opened the University of Vienna to the Jesuits in 1551.

With the death of Ferdinand I in 1564, the Habsburg lands were further split as all three of his sons were given crowns. Heartily disliked by the German princes and challenged by the difficulties of ruling his vast dominions, Philip II of Spain had renounced his claim to the imperial title even before the death of his father. Maximilian II followed Ferdinand I as Holy Roman Emperor and was also given the Bohemian lands and the surviving fragment of Hungary, plus Lower and Upper Austria. His brother Archduke Charles (1564–1590) received Inner Austria (Styria, Carinthia, and Carniola). Archduke Ferdinand (1564–1595) was given hereditary possessions in the Swabian Rhineland, Tirol, and the Vorarlberg.

Philip II of Spain, who had been named in 1564 as head of the house of Habsburg, was able to overshadow his cousins by ruling over what became the world's leading military power despite the loss of the Dutch Netherlands and the defeat of the Spanish Armada in 1588. Philip was more fortunate in his wars against the Turks, as his forces had successes in North Africa and won the great naval Battle of Lepanto in 1571. Both Maximilian and Philip succeeded greatly as patrons of the arts and sciences and possessed broad intellectual interests. Determined to make Vienna a center of European intellectual life, Maximilian brought to the city on the Danube such distinguished scholars as the botanist Carolus Clusius (Charles de L'Écluse) and the physician Johann Crato von Krafftsheim. Philip continued his father's patronage of the aging Titian, but also helped promote the career of one of the greatest female artists of the late Renaissance, Sofonisba Anguissola of Cremona (c. 1532–1625), among many others. The king established academies to promote mathematics and the sciences. He utilized the services of the brilliant architect Juan de Herrera (c. 1530–1597) on a number of major projects, including his great showplace the Escorial. Philip's expansive art and book collections established him as the foremost patron of the arts in late Renaissance Europe. This is certainly in keeping with the finer traditions of the Habsburgs.

The Later Habsburgs. Despite frequent intermarriages, the Habsburg patrimony remained divided between its Austrian and Spanish branches. Philip II was succeeded in Spain by his son Philip III (ruled 1598–1621). Ferdinand was followed by his son Maximilian II (ruled 1564–1576).

When Maximilian's largely unsuccessful reign ended, he was succeeded by his eldest son, Rudolf II (ruled 1576–1612). Rudolf was already king of Bohemia and Hungary. A lifelong bachelor, Rudolf is best known for his patronage of the arts and sciences. He made Prague a great cultural center by bringing such talents as the astronomers Tycho Brahe and Johannes Kepler to his court. John Dee, the English astrologer and mathematician, was a part of the emperor's large stable of occult specialists. Growing mental instability resulted in Rudolf's being forced to accept his brother Matthias as king of Bohemia in 1611. Following the death of Rudolf II, Matthias ruled as emperor from 1612 to 1619. Increasingly in ill health and indolent, Matthias devoted himself almost exclusively to his household and patronage of the arts. Government was for the most part left in the hands of Melchior Klesl (1552–1630), bishop of Vienna. Klesl's efforts to mediate between Catholics and Protestants were frustrated by the militancy of Matthias's cousin Ferdinand (1578–1637). Ferdinand II succeeded the childless Matthias as emperor in 1619, by which time the Thirty Years' War had already begun.

Conclusion. The Habsburgs were the preeminent political dynasty in the Renaissance era because members of the far-flung, yet cohesive family ruled the greater part of Europe at one time or another. The Habsburgs were the most important practitioners of dynastic rule, which transcended territorial and linguistic boundaries but could not overcome religious division and growing political division. The Habsburgs also greatly encouraged the artistic and literary Renaissance through their patronage of numerous major figures.

See also **Holy Roman Empire**; *biographies of figures mentioned in this entry.*

BIBLIOGRAPHY

Benecke, Gerhard. *Maximilian I, 1459–1519: An Analytical Biography.* London, 1982. Not a traditional biography, but very insightful.

Brady, Thomas A. *Turning Swiss: Cities and Empire, 1450–1550.* Cambridge, U.K., 1985. Lively study of the relations between the Habsburgs and the German towns.

Brandi, Karl. *The Emperor Charles V: The Growth and Destiny of a Man and of World Empire.* Translated by C. V. Wedgwood. Reprint, London, 1980. Still valuable for its treatment of the politics of the reign.

Du Boulay, F. R. H. *Germany in the Later Middle Ages.* New York, 1983. Worthwhile survey.

Evans, Robert J. W. *The Making of the Habsburg Monarchy, 1550–1700: An Interpretation.* Oxford, 1979. Erudite cultural synthesis.

Fernandez Alvarez, Manuel. *Charles V: Elected Emperor and Hereditary Ruler.* Translated by J. A. Lalaguna. London, 1975. Particularly good on Charles's political work in Spain.

Fichtner, Paula Sutter. *Ferdinand I of Austria.* New York, 1982. Best work in English on Ferdinand.

Hughes, Michael. *Early Modern Germany, 1477–1806.* Philadelphia, 1992. Valuable, concise survey.

Kamen, Henry. *Philip of Spain.* New Haven, Conn., 1997. Substantial biography of Philip II.

Kohler, Alfred. *Antihabsburgische Politik in der Epoche Karls V: Die reichsständischen Opposition gegen die Wahl Ferdinands I. zum römischen König und gegen die Annerkennung seines Königtums, 1524–1534.* Göttingen, Germany, 1982. Meticulous look at the interplay of religion and politics.

Press, Volker. "The Habsburg Lands: The Holy Roman Empire, 1400–1555." In *Handbook of European History 1400–1600: Late Middle Ages; Renaissance and Reformation.* Edited by Thomas Brady, Heiko Oberman, and James Tracy. Vol. 1. Pages 437–466. Leiden, Netherlands, 1994. Fine survey by a leading authority. See also the fine chapters on the Habsburgs in Iberia by Henry Kamen, pp. 467–498, and "The Burgundian-Habsburg Netherlands" by Hugo de Schepper, pp. 499–534.

Rodriguez-Salgado, M. J. *The Changing Face of Empire: Charles V, Philip II, and Habsburg Authority, 1551–1559.* New York, 1988. Important study of the succession crisis.

Russell, Joycelyne. *Peacemaking in the Renaissance.* Philadelphia, 1986. Has useful sections on Maximilian I, Charles V, and the Ladies' Peace of Cambrai.

Tapié, Victor L. *The Rise and Fall of the Habsburg Monarchy.* Translated by Stephen Hardman. New York, 1971. A useful popular history.

Wandruszka, Adam. *The House of Habsburg: Six Hundred Years of a European Dynasty.* Translated by Cathleen Epstein and Hans Epstein. Garden City, N.Y., 1964. Worthwhile introduction.

Wiesflecker, Hermann. *Kaiser Maximilian I: Das Reich, Osterreich und Europa an der Wende zur Neuzeit.* 5 vols. Vienna, 1971–1986. Monumental scholarship.

Zophy, Jonathan, ed. *The Holy Roman Empire: A Dictionary Handbook.* Westport, Conn., 1980. Provides concise sketches of all the Habsburg emperors until 1806.

JONATHAN W. ZOPHY

HADRIAN VI. *See* **Adrian VI.**

HAGIOGRAPHY.

Modern scholars use the word "hagiography" as a covering term to designate narratives about saints. During the Renaissance, however, hagiography (Latin, *hagiographa*) denoted something quite different: the historical books of the Hebrew Bible (Ketuvim), or commentaries on them. By the seventeenth century, the covering term for accounts of saints was "hagiology" (*hagiologia*), but this word fell into disuse in the eighteenth and nineteenth centuries, when the modern category of hagiography was formulated.

In denoting the literature on the saints, Renaissance authors followed medieval practices by acknowledging a variety of possible forms, including saints' lives (*vitae*, or more frequently, *vita sanctorum, res gestae*), martyrs' passions (*passiones*), histories (*historiae*), stories (*narrationes*), readings and offices (*legenda, officia*), miracle collections (*miracula*), and prayers to intercessory saints (*preces*). The word oration (*oratio*) indicated prayers, sermons (*sermones, homiliae*), and praise-filled speeches (*encomia, panegyrici*) informally, the reading of a life or passion, especially aloud, might also be called an oration (*oratio*). Thus, it is evident that to speak of medieval or Renaissance hagiography is to impose a single post-Enlightenment category on varied evidence; scholars disagree about the appropriateness of this imposition.

Textuality and Sanctity. Scholars also disagree on the nature of saintly virtue: Is it atemporal and transcendent, or historical and socially constructed? By the Renaissance, texts shaped the perception of sanctity both during and after the saint's lifetime; that is, the phenomena of sanctity were largely determined by the liturgical, literary, and documentary traditions within which authors, audiences, patrons, and potential saints found meaning. The result was a conservatism of narrative treatment that contradicts interpretations of the Renaissance as a period of radical change. As Eric Cochrane notes, lives of saints were among the "most recalcitrant of medieval literary forms" (p. 154). Nevertheless, between 1300 and 1700 several developments affected decisions about both the transcription or revision of existing accounts and the composition of new ones. Among these were the emergence of vernaculars, the development of scientific prose (as opposed to poetry), and the invention of movable type. Examples may be found of Renaissance hagiographers who rejected print as devaluing, who defended the authority of epic verse, and who retranslated vernacular versions back into Latin, but our evidence suggests that by the sixteenth century, printed vernacular prose lives had become the primary vehicle for the literature about saints (as opposed to liturgical collections such as metric breviaries and prose martyrologies). This impression is strengthened if the aural reception of printed sermons about saints is taken into account.

In content, Renaissance narratives of saints often reflected long-standing debates on the feminization of sanctity associated with late Medieval mysticism, the refeudalization of sanctity linked to the influence of powerful families in civic and national life, and the imitability of sanctity related to controversies raised in moral and natural philosophy concerning the possibility and evidence of human perfection. The complexity of these issues was belied by the brevity of most Renaissance accounts. The trend toward abbreviation derived from thirteenth-century Dominican hagiographic handbooks (new readings, *legendae novae*), in particular the *Legenda aurea* (Golden legend) by the late thirteenth-century Dominican master-general Jacobus de Voragine, who thus made a decisive contribution to the emergence of European encyclopedic and historiographical literature. The collection by John Foxe (1516–1587) of Reformation martyr narratives demonstrates, however, that encyclopedism and historiography throve on polemic. Indeed, the place of both Renaissance and Reformation in the literary history of hagiography is crucial: Reformers' arguments denying the authenticity of the cult of the saints forced Roman Catholic authors to take positions either strongly historical (thus contributing to the development of textual criticism and the study of church history) or strongly transcendent (thus contributing to the elaboration of post-Tridentine theology and a heroic model of virtue). These are the two poles of baroque hagiography.

Canonization and Miracle. Long-term trends toward rigor and bureaucratization in the making of saints had resulted, by the early Renaissance, in sharply increased attention to recording sanctity. Expressed in legalistic forms, for example the deposition of witnesses and the antagonistic stance of the devil's advocate, and aimed ostensibly at impartiality, these canonization trends have bequeathed to us records of several Renaissance processes, including some that failed or were left incomplete. We also have narratives submitted in hope of a process, or based afterward on witness reports. In this juridical atmosphere, the place of local intellectuals grew correspondingly more important, effecting a combination of the universal and the particular—to borrow Simon Ditchfield's formulation—that fed the emergence of the scientific study of saintly literature in the seventeenth century. It is also relevant to the development of hagiography that canonization was an area in which those with scholastic and those with humanist training might have

to cooperate to produce saints, or texts representing them. This cooperation meant that all sorts of curial officials, working with the often well-educated witnesses before them, recorded numerous miracles. Bonaventure's canonization in 1482 proceeded, for example, on the basis of extensive miracle collections and not a single contemporary life. It was overseen by Pope Sixtus IV, a supporter of humanists, and defended in print by two scholastically trained lawyers. A new life (no longer extant) was written by the Franciscan humanist Alessandro Ariosto (d. c. 1486).

The Contributions of the Humanists. Humanism had two contrary effects on the production of hagiographic literature, although both derived from the place of the classics in Renaissance pedagogy. On the one hand, humanists composed accounts of saints, especially orations, based not on scholastic subdivision of argument, but on classical models of panegyric. The earliest example may have been the oration on Jerome delivered by Pier Paolo Vergerio the Elder in 1408. Late medieval notions of saintly perfection, along with the humanists' rhetorical training, encouraged this reconceptualization of the sermon as a speech of praise, and since these orations were often part of an author's search for aristocratic patronage, the tendency to exaggerate was itself exaggerated. On the other hand, the sophistication of textual criticism associated with the editing of classical texts could be applied to hagiographic ones as well. This possibility, which has important parallels with the analysis of sacred texts sanctioned by late Scholasticism, could be formulated as criticism of the predominant panegyrics. Before the historical polemic associated with the Reformation, however, no authors published saints' lives that revealed the detailed application of new philological tenets.

The Scientific Literature on the Saints. Historical research that uses the tools of philology, distinguishes primary from secondary sources, and recognizes the intrusions of partiality is usually said to be scientific. In medieval monastic and mendicant hagiography we can find versions of these three features: an attention to the etymology of saints' names; a practice of compiling dossiers on subject saints; and an acute awareness, born of the decentralized nature of political power through most of the period, that competing interests could generate incompatible truths. Nevertheless, the medieval science of the saints differs fundamentally from the modern one;

the gradual, ambiguous transition from one to the other occurred in the Renaissance.

See also **Religious Literature**.

BIBLIOGRAPHY

Primary Work

Voragine, Jacobus de. *The Golden Legend.* Translated by William Granger Ryan. 2 vols. Princeton, N.J., 1993. A late-thirteenth-century Dominican collection that enjoyed great popularity in the late Middle Ages; criticized sharply but used by Renaissance humanists.

Secondary Works

Cochrane, Eric W. *Historians and Historiography in the Italian Renaissance.* Chicago, 1981. Includes a survey of Renaissance developments in hagiography, as well as brief discussions of the most important authors.

Ditchfield, Simon. *Liturgy, Sanctity, and History in Tridentine Italy: Pietro Maria Campi and the Preservation of the Particular.* Cambridge, U.K., 1995. An analysis of later Renaissance hagiographical scholarship in northern Italy, tracing the interplay of local interests with those of the Catholic Church in Rome; with valuable bibliography.

Dubois, Jacques, and Jean-Loup Lemaître. *Sources et méthodes de l'hagiographie médiévale.* Paris, 1993. A valuable guide for research in hagiographic literature, but lists works in many languages and covers some Renaissance developments.

Rice, Eugene, Jr. *Saint Jerome in the Renaissance.* Baltimore, 1985. A case study of change in the literary and artistic treatment of a saint.

Vauchez, André. *Sainthood in the Later Middle Ages.* Translation by Jean Birrell of *La sainteté en occident.* Cambridge, U.K., 1998. Perhaps the most important single book in the field to date.

Webb, D. "Eloquence and Education: A Humanist Approach to Hagiography." *Journal of Ecclesiastical History* 31 (1980): 319–339. The first publication in English to begin redressing the lack of scholarly works devoted specifically to Renaissance hagiography.

Weinstein, Donald, and Randolph M. Bell. *Saints and Society: The Two Worlds of Western Christendom, 1000–1700.* Chicago, 1982. A pathbreaking and controversial statistical study of the social construction of sanctity.

ALISON KNOWLES FRAZIER

HAKLUYT, RICHARD (1552?–1616), English geographer, propagandist for overseas enterprise, translator and compiler of voyage accounts. Richard Hakluyt was born in London and raised from an early age by his cousin, the elder Richard Hakluyt of the Middle Temple, from whom he got his interest in geography and overseas travel. He was educated at Westminster School and Christ Church, Oxford, where he lectured on geography. He completed his M.A. and took holy orders, thus making possible the series of ecclesiastical preferments from which he was to derive his primary income.

Hakluyt was an avid collector of geographical information. He corresponded with the great Flemish mapmakers Abraham Ortelius and Gerardus Mercator; got to know the mathematician and navigational theorist John Dee and such seamen as Sir Humphrey Gilbert, Sir Francis Drake, Martin Frobisher, and Sir Walter Ralegh; consulted the records of the London trading companies; and collected, edited, and often translated accounts of voyages undertaken by other travelers from European countries. But for all his interest in geography, Hakluyt was always more interested in promoting specifically English expansion. In 1580 he wrote "A Discourse of the Commodity of the Taking of the Strait of Magellan," in which he argued for a bold English effort to circumvent Spanish power in the New World. *Divers Voyages Touching the Discoverie of America,* a collection intended to establish England's New World claim and to prompt further activity, followed in 1582. And in 1584 he wrote a "Discourse on Western Planting" in support of Ralegh's Virginia project.

This patriotic impulse shapes Hakluyt's greatest work, *The Principal Navigations, Voyages, Traffiques, and Discoveries of the English Nation,* first published in 1589 and reissued in a greatly expanded second edition between 1598 and 1600. Though Hakluyt did everything he could to give English voyaging a pedigree stretching back some sixteen hundred years, by far the greatest bulk of the material he found concerns his own century. More evenhanded is the book's geographical distribution. The western voyages with which Hakluyt had been especially concerned occupy one full volume, but the other two volumes are given over to northeastern and southeastern voyages. Unlike the western voyages, which are dominated by such romantic figures as Gilbert, Drake, Frobisher, Ralegh, and Sir John Hawkins and are concerned with exploration, military confrontation, and settlement, the eastern voyages more often feature notably peaceable representatives of the English merchant community and concentrate on the practicalities of trade. This inclusion served Hakluyt's geographic aim of describing the whole of the known world and his patriotic aim of showing England active everywhere, but it also had the effect of promoting merchants to a position of prominence comparable to that of the gentlemen who had hitherto dominated accounts of England's greatness. In this and many other ways, *The Principal Navigations* has had a deep and lasting effect on England's self-understanding.

Hakluyt's work was continued by Samuel Purchas in *Hakluytus Posthumus* (1625) and has, since the mid-nineteenth century, been extended still further by the extensive publications of the Hakluyt Society.

BIBLIOGRAPHY

Parks, George Bruner. *Richard Hakluyt and the English Voyages.* 2d ed. New York, 1961.

Quinn, D. B., ed. *The Hakluyt Handbook.* 2 vols. London, 1974.

RICHARD HELGERSON

HANDWRITING. *See* **Calligraphy.**

HARRIOT, THOMAS (1560–1621), mathematician, astronomer, physicist. Harriot was born in Oxford, entered St. Mary's Hall, Oxford, and received his B.A. on 12 February 1580. He was subsequently employed by Walter Ralegh as a navigational instructor, and in 1585 served as scientist, cartographer, and surveyor on a colonizing expedition that Ralegh sent to Virginia. From his investigation of this uncharted territory (1585–1586) and the language and customs of its natural inhabitants, Harriot published his *Brief and True Report of the New Found Land of Virginia* (1588), the first original English book about the first English colony in America. He published no other work in his lifetime. In about 1598, Henry Percy, ninth earl of Northumberland, provided him with a residence and an annual pension. When Harriot died of a cancer in his nose in 1621, he left more than ten thousand folio pages, which testify to his numerous innovations in many fields. One other work, *Artis analyticae praxis ad aequationes algebraicas resolvendas* (a contribution to the study of algebraic equations), was published in 1631.

Harriot, an accomplished mathematician, investigated rhumb lines and binary number systems and devised elegant notation, including the signs of inequality, $<$ and $>$. His many scientific achievements include original discoveries in optics and ballistics. His study of reflection, refraction, and color display some of his innovations, as does his work on projectiles, falling bodies, and the theory of impacts. Before 1597, he discovered the sine law of refraction (Snell's law of 1621). He studied prismatic colors, and in 1604 computed the refractive indexes of green, orange, and extremely red light rays. His calculations of the specific weights of various substances (1603, 1604) are close to modern values. His correspondence with Johannes Kepler between 1606 and 1609 reveals that he assumed the existence of atoms and the vacuum. Independently of Galileo, he constructed telescopes, and in 1609 he was the first to map the moon from telescopic observations.

Between 1610 and 1613, he observed and diagramed Jupiter's satellites and sunspots. His influence was limited principally to his associates and disciples, for example, Walter Warner, Thomas Aylesbury, Robert Hughes, Sir William Lower, Lord Harington, and Robert Sidney.

BIBLIOGRAPHY

Primary Works

Harriot, Thomas. *A Brief and True Report of the New Found Land of Virginia: of the commodities there found and to be raysed, as well as marchantable, as others for victuall, building and other necessarie uses for those that are and shall be the planters there; and of the nature and manners of the naturall inhabitants.* London, 1588. Reprinted in Richard Hakluyt, *Principall Navigations.* 3 vols. London, 1598–1600. Vol. 3. Translated into Latin, German, and French. Facsimile reproduction, Ann Arbor, 1931.

Harriot, Thomas. *Artis Analyticae Praxis ad aequationes Algebraicas nova, expedita, & generali methodo, resoluendas: Tractatus e posthumis Thomae Harrioti Philosophi ac Mathematici celeberrimi schediasmatis summa fide & diligentia descriptus.* Edited by Walter Warner. London, 1631.

Secondary Works

Shirley, John W., ed. *Thomas Harriot: Renaissance Scientist.* Oxford, 1974. Collection of papers presented at the Thomas Harriot Symposium, University of Delaware, April 1971.

Shirley, John W., ed. *A Source Book for the Study of Thomas Harriot.* New York, 1981.

Shirley, John W. *Thomas Harriot: A Biography.* Oxford, 1983. Detailed biography with bibliography.

EMILY MICHAEL

HARVEY, WILLIAM (1578–1657), English physician. Harvey is important for his revolutionary discovery of the circulation of the blood based on anatomical observations.

Life and Career. Harvey was the eldest of nine children born to Thomas Harvey, and the only child of this family of merchants and landowners to become a doctor. He was educated at King's School, Canterbury, and from 1593 to 1599 at Gonville and Caius College, Cambridge. In 1600 he went to the University of Padua in Italy. There he studied anatomy and medicine with the professor of surgery and anatomy, Girolamo Fabricius of Aquapendente (1537–1619), and received his M.D. in 1602. On his return to England, Harvey began to practice medicine in London and in 1603 married Elizabeth, the daughter of Dr. Lancelot Browne. Browne was one of the court physicians to King James I.

In 1607 Harvey was elected a fellow of the College of Physicians, which oversaw professional medicine in London, and two years later he was made physician to St. Bartholomew's Hospital in London.

In 1615 Harvey was appointed Lumleian lecturer in surgery and anatomy to the College of Physicians. This was a stipendiary position that Harvey held until 1656, lecturing on anatomy to physicians and surgeons at the college every two years and holding a five-day dissection of a body every winter. Harvey reached the peak of his career in 1618 by becoming one of the royal physicians to James I. In 1625 he was appointed physician to James's son King Charles I. He supported the king against the parliamentary forces during the English Civil War (1642–1649). After the royalists were defeated and the king was publicly beheaded in 1649, Harvey quietly retired to live with his brothers in the countryside outside London.

Harvey as Anatomist and Physician.

Since many of Harvey's writings were destroyed in 1642 when his London lodgings were attacked by Parliamentary supporters, we have few records of his practice as a physician. Some of his gynecologic and obstetric cases have survived as part of the English translation of his work on generation, or reproduction of animals. These probably date from the late 1640s and in all take up less than thirty pages of *Anatomical Exercitations Concerning the Generation of Living Creatures, to which are added particular Discourses, of Births, and of Conceptions, etc.* (1653). However, we do possess the notes of his Lumleian lectures for 1616 on anatomy, along with annotations from later years.

From these it is apparent that Harvey may have come to some understanding of the circulation of blood before he published his full argument in 1628. The notes prove that he had repeated and confirmed, or modified, the work of early anatomists such as Realdo Colombo (c. 1510–1559) and Fabricius. Colombo had replaced the famous Andreas Vesalius (1514–1564) as professor of anatomy and surgery at the University of Padua (1543–1545), then taught at the University of Rome (1548–1559). Colombo's work on pulmonary circulation, *De re anatomica* (On anatomy), was published in 1559. Fabricius studied the structure and function of the venous valves. He argued that the valves existed to slow down the flow of the blood from the heart to the periphery so that all parts of the body could receive their share of nutrients.

Harvey concluded from his experiments that the heart acted as a muscle with the lower chambers or ventricles forcibly pushing the blood out into the arteries. The important movement of the heart was therefore contraction (systole) rather than expansion (diastole), as many previous anatomists including Galen had claimed. Harvey also came to the realization that venous blood was directed toward the heart and not away from it as Fabricius had assumed.

In 1628 Harvey finally published all his findings in a short book entitled *Exercitatio anatomica de motu cordis et sanguinis in animalibus* (An anatomical essay concerning the movement of the heart and the blood in animals; generally referred to as *De motu cordis*). He explained his delay in publishing as due to the fear that the novelty of his ideas might lead to repercussions by other physicians and predicted that no one under forty would understand his work. In fact Harvey's description of the circulation of the blood did initially meet with a mixed response—he reportedly told the famous diarist John Aubrey that after his book many believed him to be "crack-brained."

The blood's circulation.

Before Harvey the dominant theory of blood flow in Western medicine was that of Galen (c. 129/130–c. 199–216 C.E.). Food and drink were predigested in the stomach, according to this theory, and the resulting mixture, or chyle, was passed to the liver through the portal vessel. There it was transformed into venous blood by a "natural spirit." Some of the blood then flowed to the extremities while the rest went to the right ventricle of the heart. Here the blood was refined and the impurities extracted before they were passed to the lungs and exhaled. Once this was accomplished, the blood was divided again, and the majority ebbed back into the venous system while a small portion passed to the left ventricle through invisible pores in the cardiac septum. There this blood mixed with the life-giving "vital spirit" and was further purified. It then left the heart by the arteries, going to various parts including the base of the brain, or rete mirabile. In this area of the brain the blood and vital spirit were mixed with the "animal spirit" before its dispersal throughout the body in the nervous system.

In the first half of *De motu cordis* Harvey pointed out from his many dissections and vivisections of animals the inconsistencies of Galen's views of the movement of the air and blood to the heart. Harvey noted that he had solved the problem of seeing for himself the rapid and complex movements of the heart by vivisecting frogs and other cold blooded animals whose hearts were simpler and moved more slowly than those in warm blooded animals. He also used dogs and pigs bled almost to death so their heart moved lethargically.

In chapters six and seven Harvey acknowledged the work of Colombo and proved that the blood moves through the lungs. However, it is in the following chapter that Harvey makes his revolutionary announcement of the discovery of the circulation of the blood based on the fact that he had seen it. In this claim Harvey was reflecting the anatomist's stress on personal observation. This image of nature replacing words and books as the authority was a common one during the Renaissance. Throughout *De motu cordis* Harvey states that the reader had to see and repeat the experiments that demonstrated the circulation of the blood in order to have true knowledge of it. However, it is important to note that Aristotle and Galen had also praised the uses of the senses.

Harvey made quantitative experiments that showed that too much blood left the heart in a given time for it to have been absorbed by the body and replaced by blood made in the liver from the chyle. In other words he asked how much blood was sent into the body with each beat of the heart and concluded that the amount pumped out in an hour always exceeded the quantity of blood in the whole animal. He advised the reader to go to a butcher's shop and watch how quickly an experienced butcher can open an artery in a live ox and bleed it to death. Using only a magnifying glass, Harvey had demonstrated errors in Galen's theory and discovered all that could be seen of the cardiovascular system without the aid of a microscope.

One of the major gaps in Harvey's work was his inability to identify whatever joined the arteries to the veins as the blood made its circle. It was the Italian anatomist Marcello Malpighi (1628–1694) who would discover the capillary network with the aid of a microscope. However, in the meantime Harvey called these hypothetical structures anastomoses (pores in the flesh) and showed that a connection or circulation must exist by means of a simple experiment. He ligated, or tied a cord very tightly around, an arm so that no arterial blood could flow below the ligature down the arm. He then loosened the ligature so the arterial blood flowed down the arm but the ligature remained tight enough to stop venous blood from moving up above it. Harvey noted that the veins in the arm below the ligature now became swollen where before they had been normal. This demonstrated that blood moved down the arteries and then back up the arm inside the veins.

Harvey lived long enough to see his theory of the circulation of the blood largely accepted by the medical profession and the beginnings of a new experimental philosophy based on the questions raised by his work. Oxford physiologists such as Robert Boyle (1627–1691), Richard Lower (1631–1691), John Mayow (1641–1679), Christopher Wren (1632–1723; also the architect of St. Paul's Cathedral and many other buildings in London), and Robert Hooke (1635–1702) investigated the structure and function of respiration and also experimented with blood transfusions.

BIBLIOGRAPHY

Primary Works

Harvey, William. *Anatomical Lectures.* Translated by Gweneth Whitteridge. Edinburgh, Scotland, 1964. Two versions of Harvey's Lumleian lectures translated from the original Latin in which he first discussed the circulation of the blood.

Harvey, William. *Lectures on the Whole of Anatomy.* Translated by C. D. O'Malley, F. N. L. Poynter, and K. F. Russell. Berkeley, Calif., 1961.

Harvey, William. *On the Motion of the Heart and Blood in Animals.* Edited by Alexander Bowie. Chicago, 1962.

Secondary Works

Frank, Robert G., Jr. *Harvey and the Oxford Physiologists: Scientific Ideas and Social Interaction.* Berkeley and Los Angeles, 1980. Frank's work focuses on the influence Harvey's anatomical and physiological techniques had on some English doctors.

Frank, Robert G., Jr. "The Image of Harvey." In Jerome Bylebyl, ed. *William Harvey and His Age: The Professional and Social Context of the Discovery of the Circulation.* Baltimore, 1979.

French, Roger. *William Harvey's Natural Philosophy.* Cambridge, U.K., 1994. French examines the education Harvey received at the University of Padua and the impact it had on his work.

Wear, Andrew. "William Harvey and the 'Way of the Anatomists.'" *History of Science* 21 (1983): 223–249. An important article on Harvey's conception of the role of an anatomist.

LYNDA STEPHENSON PAYNE

HEBREW LITERATURE AND LANGUAGE.

From the late thirteenth to the early seventeenth century, Hebrew literature was being produced in several countries: in Spain and Provence until the expulsions of 1492 and 1502, respectively, and subsequently in the Ottoman Empire; in Amsterdam from 1600 onward; and in Italy during the entire period.

Much of that literature, to date largely extant only in manuscript, enjoyed distinct popularity in its time. In Italy it did not go unnoticed even by Christian scholars, who regarded Hebrew as a classical language, similar to Latin and Greek, and took lessons in Hebrew grammar, the Old Testament, and Kabbalah from Jewish teachers. Lorenzo de' Medici studied with Yohanan Alemanno, and Giovanni Pico della Mirandola with Elijah Delmedigo, to name just two examples. Prominent humanists not only promoted research on Hebrew grammar but composed Hebrew dictionaries themselves. University chairs for Hebrew studies were established in Bologna (1460) and Rome (1514). Italian Jews, too, regarded their language as part of the classical language group. Azariah dei Rossi composed dirges on Margaret of Savoy in Hebrew, Aramaic, and Latin. Hebrew authors, especially in Italy and Spain, felt at home with local culture. They composed works in the local languages, translated from them into Hebrew, and borrowed their literary conventions.

The Enterprise of Immanuel of Rome.

Italian norms and values were adopted early and successfully by Immanuel of Rome (c. 1260–c. 1328) in his *Mahbarot* (Notebooks; c. 1300), a volume of rhymed narratives interspersed with poetry. (A composition free of verse form and with a distinct rhythm was not considered poetry in Hebrew in the Middle Ages and Renaissance, but rather was referred to as rhymed prose or rhymed narrative.) In this work, in addition to classic Hebrew-Spanish verse, which was interwoven into the narrative according to custom, Immanuel inserted thirty-eight Hebrew sonnets, the first composed in any language other than Italian. These sonnets were a momentous step of Hebrew poetry on its way to becoming part of European Renaissance and baroque culture. In order to endow his sonnets with Italian musicality, Immanuel invented a new metrical system, combining the old quantitative Hebrew-Spanish meters (which measured rhythm by the duration of syllables rather than by counting accents), with new Italian syllabic metrical principles. That system was later employed in various verse forms adopted from the Italian. Immanuel's Hebrew sonnets served as models for generations of poets owing to their rich and grammatically correct Hebrew as well as to their "classic" or "Petrarchan" rhyme scheme (*abba abba cde cde*). Notably, Immanuel's intensive use of this rhyme scheme antedates Petrarch's birth.

Immanuel's sonnets represent a successful adoption of the elegant and highly Christian *dolce stil nuovo* (sweet new style) of Dante and his circle, as well as of the opposing, roughly realistic, nonconformist style of Cecco Angiolieri and his coterie. Some of his narratives may be considered Italian novellas, although they predate Giovanni Boccaccio. Immanuel's last *mahberet* is designed after Dante's *Divine Comedy*. Immanuel treats a broad range of subjects, including carnal, erotic love, and creates a colorful cast of characters attuned, in both sexes equally, to a wide range of traits, desires, and aspi-

rations. Immanuel's poetry was rejected after his death and banned by halakic order (rabbinic decree) in 1565.

Rhymed Prose. The tradition of rhymed narrative continued after 1300 in Spain and Provence, where it broke away from its classic form and moved closer to Christian literature, borrowing from it such conventions as the archetypes of the lascivious old man, the cuckold, and the malicious physician. The narratives included burlesque (*The War of the Pen and the Scissors* by Shem Tov Ardutiel), love intrigue (*Effer and Dina* by Don Vidal Benveniste), and satire and parody (compositions by Maimon Galipapa, *Masekhet Purim* [The tractate of the holiday of Purim] by Kalonymus ben Kalonymus, *Sefer Habakbuk ha-navi* [Book of the bottle the prophet] by Levi ben Gershom). Tales of adventure, didactic stories and proverbs, defenses of Judaism, humorous arguments, and more were all written in rhymed prose.

Poetry. The tradition of liturgical poetry (*piyyut*), mainly in short forms—*selihot* (poems on repentance), *geulot* (poems on redemption), *reshuiot* (poems to introduce certain prayers)—national in theme and mood, continued unbroken in Spain until the expulsion. In Italy it lived on after 1500 as well, but diminished after the introduction of printing, which essentially fixed the liturgy. Personal, nonliturgical pious poems, mainly self-accusatory in nature, were composed by Immanuel, by his contemporary Hebrew poets in Spain and Provence, and by later poets in Italy. Moses da Rieti, the author of the mystic-meditative *Mikdash Me'at* (The small sanctuary; c. 1410), earned the sobriquet "Dante Ebreo" for this poem's grasp of a whole spiritual world and descriptions of celestial journeys. In his *Mikdash Me'at* Rieti introduced into Hebrew the terza rima, the verse form employed by Dante in his *Divine Comedy*. Of interest also are religious sonnets by Joseph Zarfati, Judah Moscato, and other known and anonymous Italian poets of the sixteenth century.

However, the prominent body of contemporary religious lyrics was composed in the Near East by the masters of Kabbalah and their disciples: Isaac Luria (Aramaic Sabbath hymns), Solomon Alkabetz ("Lecha dodi" [Come my beloved]), Eliezer Azikri ("Yedid nefesh" [Soul-friend]), and, most important, Israel Najara, a prolific writer whose poems fill several volumes. The Venetian edition of his best-known work, *Zemirot Israel* (The melodies of Israel; 1592), is prefaced with a sonnet by Leone Modena. Its erotic imagery notwithstanding, Najara's poetry gained many enthusiastic followers, mainly in the

Near East and North Africa. Kabbalah-inspired religious poetry in Italy (such as Mordecai Dato's *Shemen arev* [Pleasant oil; Venice, 1570]), which was compiled in a quasi-"siddur" (prayer book), was intended to supplement regular prayers and for recitation during mystical meetings (*Ayelet ha-shahar* [Morning star; Mantua, 1612]).

While the rejection of Immanuel's poetics caused a general decline in secular Hebrew poetry, and the love lyric in particular, in fourteenth- and fifteenth-century Italy, in Spain such poetry was still being composed. The prominent poet Solomon Bonafed even endowed the theme of love with new realistic features. The publication of Immanuel's *Mahbarot* in 1492 marked a revival of his poetics, evidenced by the reappearance of Hebrew love poetry and Hebrew sonnetry, which had also declined when Immanuel fell into disfavor. During the sixteenth century, poets like Joseph Zarfati, Moses ben Yoav, Judah Sommo, Moses Anav, Samuel Archivolti, Leone Modena, others in Italy, and David Onkinerah and Saadia Longo in Salonika took the *Mahbarot* as their guide. Some of them used this work as a tool for adopting the fashionable Petrarchan mode.

Other secular Hebrew poetry of the fourteenth to sixteenth centuries was occupied with panegyric, friendship, ridicule and satire, polemic, parody, dirge, and historical description. Typical of the period are panegyrical poems addressed to Christians based on beliefs common to the monotheistic creeds. Samuel Archivolti, for example, while praising a Christian treatise on the soul's eternity, advises Philip II, the Spanish king who commissioned it, to fight for the Catholic faith by verbal means alone. Dirges bemoaned national tragedies such as the pogroms of 1391 in Spain, the burning of the Talmud in 1553 in Italy, or an auto-da-fé of Jews in Ancona (1556). Particularly outstanding is the dirge by the young fifteenth-century physician Moses Remos, bemoaning his fate on the eve of his execution in Sicily on a false charge of poisoning Christians.

Polemical poetry could be serious, like the poetic exchange on philosophical study between its opponent, Yehiel Nissim of Pisa, and its adherent, Moses ben Yoav; or it could be playful, like the long chain of controversial poems on the nature of women, initiated in the fifteenth century with a misogynous poem by Abraham of Sarteano. Poems on contemporary calamities were composed in pre-expulsion Spain by Solomon da Piera, among others. "Invective against Time," written in Naples in 1503 by Judah Abravanel (Leone Ebreo), describing the kidnapping and baptism of his infant son, is a rare example of Hebrew poetry on parental love—produced, not surprisingly, by the widely acclaimed author of the philosophical *Dialogues on Love* (1564).

In the late sixteenth century, poems for special occasions—weddings, circumcisions, deaths, the appearance of new books, or the awarding of doctoral degrees—became popular, attributable in large measure to Leone Modena's extensive contribution to this genre. These poems, either penned or printed on broadsheets, were distributed among the participants at these occasions. Poetry celebrated the invention of print: poetical blessings, introductions, and even dirges—if the author was recently deceased—adorned title pages of newly published books.

Poetic language underwent changes during the period, increasingly freeing itself from the traditional strictures of biblical purism, drawing upon rabbinical, philosophical, and non-Hebrew sources for vocabulary and syntax.

Hebrew poetry was measured by several meters: traditional quantitative meter, primarily used in classic Hebrew-Spanish verse; Immanuel's double system combining quantitative and syllabic meters, primarily used in verse forms adopted from the Italian; and a rather free non-Italian syllabic meter, mainly used in the East. Another short-lived syllabic meter, invented by Moses da Rieti, was used in the fifteenth century, mainly in terza rima. Religious lyrics, many of which were adapted to popular melodies, whether Turkish, Greek, or Italian, tended to use free rhythm. The representative verse forms were either traditional—strophic, originating in ancient liturgy, or nonstrophic, of Hebrew-Spanish origin—or of Italian extraction: terza rima, ballata, sestina, and quartina, which seem to have first emerged in fifteenth-century Hebrew religious poetry. After its revival around 1500, the sonnet enjoyed increasing popularity. The first Hebrew octaves, by Joseph Zarfati, are prime examples of High Renaissance refinement. Judah Sommo's series of *ballate* in defense of women, consisting of alternating Hebrew and Italian lines, is an elegant example of bilingual poetry, which may have served those unfamiliar with Hebrew, mainly women. Certain contemporary verse forms remain hard to identify or categorize.

Unrhymed Prose. Unrhymed prose principally served treatises, prefaces to poetry, and letters (which often contained poems). Samuel Archivolti composed a manual for elegant correspondence titled *Maayan ganim* (Fountain of gardens; 1553). However, we do have some nonrhymed belles lettres as well: David ha-Reuveni's sixteenth-century autobiography, in which he attempts to justify his messianic activity; an autobiographical chapter in Azariah dei Rossi's *Me'or einayim* (Light of eyes; 1574) describing his flight from Ferarra during an earthquake; and Abraham Yagel's autobiographical *Gei Hizzayon* (A valley of vision), which depicts a heavenly adventure, reminiscent of both Dante and Rieti, and contains novellas adapted from the Italian. Tales culled from various non-Hebrew sources are found in Solomon ibn Verga's pseudo-historical work, *Shevet Yehudah* (Rod of Judah; c. 1530), and Eliezer Halevi and Solomon Navarro related "The Terrible Tale of Joseph della Reina," a practitioner of Kabbalah who was entrapped by forces of evil.

Drama. Although the Talmud outlawed theatrical pursuits, contemporary drama was not alien to Jewish men of letters such as Joseph Zarfati, who provided an early Hebrew version of *Celestina,* the famous Spanish play by Fernando de Rojas. Only its prologue has survived. The first extant original Hebrew drama, *Is zahut bedihuta de-kiddushin* (A comedy of betrothal; 1550), was written by Judah Sommo, a noted sixteenth-century stage director who composed more than thirteen plays in Italian, as well as *Dialogues on Stagecraft* (c. 1565). This comedy of love intrigue was written in perfect non-rhymed Hebrew. While the complexities of the plot unfold in typical Renaissance fashion, its resolution relies on a resourceful use of halakah. *Zahut bedihuta* was designated for Purim, as were other plays existing, supposedly, in the sixteenth century. Moses Zacuto's play, *Yesod olam* (Foundation of the world; composed before 1630), whose final part is not extant, presents the life of Abraham. It is reminiscent of the Spanish *autos* that celebrate the victory of the faith. It employs a wide range of verse forms and includes complicated sonnet sequences.

Rhetoric, Grammar, and Poetic Theory. Jewish preaching in Italy aspired to rhetorical excellence. It could draw upon Judah Messer Leon's *Nofet tsufim* (The honeycomb's flow; Mantua, c. 1480), a systematic examination of biblical narrative based on Aristotelian, Ciceronian, and Quintillian rhetorical criteria, and upon Judah Moscato's collection of model sermons, *Nefutsot Yehudah* (The dispersion of Judah; Venice, 1589) delivered in Italian and translated into Hebrew for publication. Azaria Picho, Judah del Bene, and Leone Modena are prominent among the many gifted preachers of the period.

Regarding Hebrew as the mother language and the Bible as the origin of every knowledge, Hebrew scholars of the fifteenth century—Profiat Duran, Judah Messer Leon, Abraham Balmes, Moses ibn Haviv—composed Hebrew grammars and treatises on the Hebrew language. In sixteenth-century Italy, Elijah Levita wrote treatises on Hebrew grammar, composed Hebrew and Aramaic dictionaries, and examined the biblical text, proving, among other things, that the system for notating vocalization and cantillation (musical intonation) postdated the completion of the Talmud. Solomon of Poggibonsi composed a rhyme dictionary. Discussions of poetic theory were regularly included as chapters in grammar books. Most of the contemporary poetical treatises (by David ibn Yahyah, Moses ben Haviv, Solomon Almoli, and others) are concerned primarily with the old quantitative metrical system, ignoring Immanuel's all-important metrical innovations. Archivolti's *Arugat ha-bosem* (Fragrant garden bed; Venice, 1602) was the first to acknowledge that system. Citing by way of example a sonnet—the verse form in which the system originated—he explains its rules and allows wide liberty within the traditional quantitative system. Thus, Archivolti provided a means of preserving both the traditional quantitative system and Immanuel's half-quantitative one, keeping them alive for centuries. Archivolti's work served as a poetic manual until the end of the Italian school.

See also **Kabbalah**; **Preaching and Sermons**, *subentry on* **Jewish Preaching and Sermons**; **Rhetoric**; *and biographies of figures mentioned in this entry.*

BIBLIOGRAPHY

Primary Works

Bregman, Dvora. *Zeror zehuvim.* Jerusalem and Beersheba, Israel, 1997. See pp. 1–195.

Carmi, T., ed. and trans. *The Penguin Book of Hebrew Verse.* Harmondsworth, U.K., 1981. See pp. 421–491.

Schirmann, Jefim. *Mivhar ha-Shirah ha-Ivrit be-Italyah.* Berlin, 1934.

Schirmann, Jefim. *Ha-Shirah ha-Ivrit bi-Sefarad uve-Provans.* Jerusalem and Tel Aviv, 1960. See book 2, part 2, pp. 499–666, and the bibliography.

Yarden, Dov, ed. *Mahberot Imanuel ha-Romi.* Jerusalem, 1957.

Secondary Works

Bregman, Dvora. *Shevil ha-zahav.* Jerusalem and Beersheba, Israel, 1995.

Pagis, Dan. *Hidush u-Masoret be-Shirat ha-Hol ha-Ivrit: Sefarad ve-Italyah.* Jerusalem, 1976. See pp. 173–355.

Schirmann, Jefim. *Le-Toldot ha-Shirah veha-Dramah ha-Ivrit.* Jerusalem, 1979. See vol. 2, pp. 44–132.

Schirmann, Jefim. *Toldot ha-Shirah ha-Ivrit bi-Sefarad ha-Notsrit uvi-Derom Tsarfat.* Edited, supplemented, and annotated by Ezra Fleischer. Jerusalem, 1997.

Tietze, Andreas, and Joseph Yahalom. *Ottoman Melodies, Hebrew Hymns: A Sixteenth Century Cross-Cultural Adventure.* Budapest, Hungary, 1995.

DVORA BREGMAN

HELMONT, JOHANNES BAPTISTA VAN

(1579–1644), Flemish chemist, physiologist, natural philosopher. Born into an old and noble Flemish family, Helmont was linked to another influential family through marriage. Educated at Louvain, his university studies disillusioned him totally about the current state of knowledge and led him to refuse the M.A. conscious of his own ignorance. After ten years of study and European travel, he eventually returned to Louvain and became a doctor of medicine.

His first publication drew him into a controversy on spa water. Another was a publication at Paris, which Helmont insisted he had not authorized, concerning a weapon salve that it was claimed, cured a wound when applied to the weapon that inflicted it. Helmont's explanation of its efficacy drew unfavorable attention from Jesuits and the Inquisition in the Spanish Netherlands. Arrested and imprisoned in 1634, he was freed through family influence, but consigned to house arrest until the last six years of his life.

Although he had published only four works during his lifetime, their republication together with others by his son, Francis Mercurius, made Helmont's the most influential version of the iatrochemical philosophy founded by Paracelsus. It had many adherents in the Netherlands, Germany, and England, where it exerted an early formative influence on Robert Boyle.

Helmont rejected the Aristotelian four-element theory as well as the three-element theory of the Paracelsians. He argued that fire should be regarded as an agent rather than as a substance, and that earth was not elementary because experiments proved that it could be transmuted into water. Air was a repository for many vaporous substances but was not actively involved in changes in bodies. Water alone was truly elemental. When heated it did not turn into air as the Peripatetics believed, but rather into its own attenuated form. All bodies owed their origin to the action of a "ferment" transmuting the otherwise "empty" water into a specific substance.

Helmont used the balance extensively in researches supporting his conclusions. In a famous experiment he grew a willow tree from its stem over five years and concluded from careful weighing that the bulk of the material in the tree came from the water it had been fed. Actually he neglected to consider the role of carbon dioxide in the atmosphere. Yet it was Helmont himself who recognized gases as distinct entities, and identified what we now call carbon dioxide, which he called gas sylvestre. Helmont drew attention to other gases set free from bodies by combustion or fermentation.

His rejection of the early element theories, his use of the balance and quantitative reasoning in scientific inquiry, and his recognition of "gases" and "ferments" and their roles in nature were Helmont's accomplishments. Even more significant were his contributions to medicine. He recognized that acid in the stomach governed digestion of food and denied the Galenic theory of humoral imbalance as a cause of ill health. He leaned instead toward a conception of diseases as entities that invade the body and disturb its harmonious working. Nevertheless, Helmont did not embrace the corpuscular or mechanical view of nature but remained faithful to a monism that viewed matter and spirit as inseparable characteristics of all bodies. "Experience" for Helmont comprised not only laboratory experiments but also visions and illumination. He also placed great weight on evidence found in sacred scripture. For him, water had a superior claim to be considered an element since it was created on the First Day; if the waters of the Noachian Flood had turned into air, they would have choked all creatures when the earth was repopulated. As with other Renaissance figures, what seems modern and progressive to us in Helmont was the product of a basically mystical outlook.

BIBLIOGRAPHY

Primary Works
Francis Mercurius van Helmont's collected edition of his father's works, *Ortvs Medicinae* (Amsterdam, 1648), was translated into English as *Oriatrike, Or, Physick Refined* by John Chandler (London, 1662). There were two earlier and partial English translations: *Three Treatises* (London, 1650) and *Deliramenta catarrhi* (London, 1650) by Walter Charleton.

Secondary Works
Debus, Allen G. *The Chemical Philosophy: Paracelsian Science and Medicine in the Sixteenth and Seventeenth Centuries.* New York, 1977. Vol. 2.
Pagel, Walter. *Joan Baptista van Helmont: Reformer of Science and Medicine.* Cambridge, U.K., 1982. The most authoritative secondary work.
Partington, J. R. *A History of Chemistry.* London, 1961. Vol. 2.

P. M. RATTANSI

HELTAI, GÁSPÁR

(Caspar Helth; c. 1510–1574), Hungarian historian. Born to a family of Transylvanian Saxons, Gáspár Heltai did not speak Hungarian until he was in his mid-twenties. He studied in Wittenberg, and after his return, he married and was active as a Protestant pastor of the Saxon community in Kolozsvár (Cluj-Napoca, Romania). Living in that bilingual town, which in the sixteenth century had become an intellectual center of European Protestantism, Heltai soon moved from using German to Hungarian in his sermons and in his secular writings.

Heltai's real forte was the fable. In his *Száz fabula* (Hundred fables; 1566), a translation and reworking of Aesop's fables, his moral message is couched in ingeniously drawn animal characters, rich in Renaissance imagery. At least one piece, number ninetynine, is entirely Heltai's own.

A belletrist, parish priest, and the author of *Chronica az magyaroknak viselt dolgairól* (Chronicle of Hungarian history; 1575), Heltai was one of the first to use the vernacular to address the history of Hungary, which he presented from the alleged Scythian past until the Battle of Mohács (1526). While using earlier Latin works, some written by foreigners who had visited Hungary, Heltai had a clear editorial policy in mind for his magnum opus, as demonstrated by his additions, eliminations, and new emphases. He died, however, before its appearance, and the work was published by his widow.

Among his important compilations are *Cancionale* (1574), which included pieces by several authors, among them works by Sebestyén Tinódi. *Cancionale* also contains a treatment of the rule of Andrew II (1205–1235) and the murder of Queen Gertrudis (1213). The same regicide later formed the plot of nineteenth-century dramas in Austria and Hungary.

Heltai also published a work in Latin about Matthias Corvinus, *Historia inclyti Matthiae Hunyadis* (1565), in which he interweaves popular anecdotes about the king. In Heltai's case, history was deliberately "viewed from below"; his interpretation represents the ideology of the Protestant burghers, especially that of the townspeople who benefited from the crown's centralizing efforts.

Heltai's pamphleteering talents found expression in *Háló* (The net), published in 1570, a translation of Raimundo Gonzales de Montes (Reginaldus Gonsalvinus), in which the Spanish Protestant vividly describes Protestant suffering at the hands of the Inquisition. In this piece, Heltai openly confesses his anti-Trinitarian convictions (earlier he embraced Calvin's teachings). In other writings he attacks drunkards, the Catholic Church, and those who exploit the poor.

Heltai's seminal contribution to Renaissance civilization was his founding of a press in 1550 with Georg Hoffgreff. Together, they planned to translate the entire text of the Bible into Hungarian. After the death of Hoffgreff in 1559, Heltai continued alone in his remarkably prolific press. He published in Hungarian Stephan Werbőczi's *Tripartitum* (1517), the most important legal work regarding Hungarian laws, which remained in use until the mid-twentieth century. Heltai died, however, before he could complete his most ambitious work, the translation of the Bible.

BIBLIOGRAPHY

Primary Work
Heltai, Gáspár. *Válogatott írások*. Budapest, Hungary, 1957.

Secondary Works
Birnbaum, Marianna D. "Hungarian Literature." In *Renaissance Humanism: Foundations, Forms, and Legacies*. Edited by Albert Rabil Jr. Vol. 2, *Humanism beyond Italy*, 293–334. Philadelphia, 1988.
Lakos, Béla. *Heltai Gáspár reformátor és kora*. Budapest, Hungary, 1913.

MARIANNA D. BIRNBAUM

HENRY VII (1457–1509), King of England (1485–1509). Henry VII, the first of the Tudor monarchs, was born three months after the death of his father, Edmund, earl of Richmond, half brother of King Henry VI. Henry inherited a claim to the throne from his mother, Margaret Beaufort, great-granddaughter of John of Gaunt. He emerged as the principal Lancastrian pretender against the Yorkist king, Edward IV, following the deaths of Henry VI and his son in 1471. Forced to seek safety in exile in Brittany and France, Henry became a serious threat to the Yorkist dynasty after King Edward's death in 1483, when Richard III's usurpation and the disappearance of Edward's sons split the Yorkist affinity. Elizabeth Woodville, Edward IV's queen, cemented an alliance with Margaret Beaufort with an agreement for the marriage of Henry to Elizabeth of York, Edward IV's eldest daughter. Henry won the throne in August 1485, defeating King Richard at the Battle of Bosworth.

Yorkist Pretenders. The new Tudor regime was a mix of Lancastrians and members of Edward IV's affinity. Henry's marriage to Elizabeth of York in January 1486 did not prevent Yorkist insurgency. Henry put down insurrections in 1486 and overcame a more serious rebellion the following year, when he defeated the invading Yorkist army in a bloody battle at Stoke. By 1491 Henry was facing another serious conspiracy involving the impostor, Perkin Warbeck, who passed himself off as Richard, duke of York, Edward IV's missing son. This conspiracy included members of the king's own household. After receiving and then losing the support of Charles VIII of France, Maximilian I of Austria, and James IV of Scotland, Warbeck was captured following an attempted insurrection in the west of England in 1497. He was executed in 1499. A final conspiracy, involving the earl of Suffolk and his brother, who sought the support of Maximilian I and his son Archduke Philip, was ended in 1506, when Philip handed Suffolk over to Henry.

Foreign Policy. Dynastic security and acquisition of commercial advantages for English merchants were important components of Henry's foreign policy, but not always the paramount concerns. Between 1489 and 1491, Henry intervened militarily in Brittany against France, allying himself with Maximilian of Austria and Ferdinand and Isabella of Spain, perhaps with a view to recovering the lost Plantagenet lands. In 1492 he made peace with Charles VIII in the Treaty of Etaples, renewing it in 1499 with Charles's successor, Louis XII. Scotland was of more immediate concern in the 1490s. The murder of James III ended efforts to establish harmonious relations between England and Scotland. Under an increasingly hostile James IV, England and Scotland drifted toward war. Hostilities ceased with the Truce of Ayton in 1497, extended into the "Treaty of Perpetual Peace" in 1502, which included the marriage of James to Henry's daughter, Margaret.

Henry also linked his new dynasty with the established Trastamara dynasty of Spain in the treaties of Medina del Campo (1489) and London (1496) for the marriage of Prince Arthur to Catherine of Aragon, which took place in 1501. In the later years of his reign, after the deaths of his two sons and queen, Henry engaged in more ambitious dynastic politics. He tried to solidify his ties with the Habsburgs by proposing to marry Maximilian's daughter, Margaret of Savoy, and arranging the marriage of his daughter, Mary, to Maximilian's grandson, Charles of Castile, the future Emperor Charles V. While Margaret rebuffed Henry, the marriage of Mary and Charles was agreed in 1507. Had he lived to bring his policy of alliances through marriage to completion, Henry may have made England part of a greater Tudor-Stuart-Habsburg-Trastamara dynastic entity. Such an entity would have enhanced the security of the Tudors while isolating France.

Cultural Patronage. Henry was a modest patron of the Burgundian and Italian Renaissance. He patronized several poets and humanists. Bernard

Henry VII. Bust by Pietro Torrigiano (1472–1528). VICTORIA & ALBERT MUSEUM, LONDON

André of Toulouse was poet laureate, royal historiographer, and tutor to Prince Arthur. The Italian humanists employed in his household and government included Pietro Carmeliano, Giovanni de Gigli, Battista Boerio, Cornelio Viteli, Adriano Castellesi, and Polydore Vergil. Henry's benefaction extended to English poets Stephen Hawes and John Skelton, and to the humanist Thomas Linacre, who was also tutor to Prince Arthur and physician to the king. Henry left his cultural mark in stone as well. His Hospital of the Savoy, modeled on Santa Maria Nuova in Florence, no longer stands, nor does his impressive palace of Richmond. His greatest architectural monument is his splendid chapel at Westminster Abbey—one of the finest examples of the English Perpendicular style—wherein stands his tomb with the magnificent effigies of him and his queen fashioned by the Florentine sculptor Pietro Torrigiano.

Government. Traditionally, it has been thought that Henry's greatest talents were in administration and finance. Although he built upon the achievements of Edward IV, he added innovations of his own. Government by committees of his council became the hallmark of his rule, allowing the king to circumvent common law courts and procedures. Henry also furthered the recovery of crown finances. His first Parliament in 1485 bolstered crown revenues by granting tonnage and poundage—taxes levied on wine (in tons) and other imported and exported goods—for life. This source of income grew steadily through the reign, helped by the increase of trade and a new book of rates. Henry's attempt to finance his intervention in Brittany through a novel type of subsidy provoked the northern rebellion of 1489, and his heavy taxation for a war against Scotland sparked the western rebellion of 1497. He imposed forced loans in 1491 and 1496–1497 and ruthlessly exploited for money his feudal prerogatives.

In 1487 Henry tightened his control over the collection and disbursement of revenues by transferring from the Exchequer to his Chamber the receiving and auditing of receipts from crown lands, just as Edward IV had done. In 1495, in response to the treason within his own household, Henry established the Privy Chamber to insulate himself from his courtiers. Money received by the Privy Chamber was handled at the king's direction without any accounting to the treasurer of the Chamber.

Henry regarded most of the nobility and gentry of England with fear and suspicion. To control the abuses of magnates and check the corruption of justice, he expanded the powers of the justices of the peace and tightened legislation regulating retaining, a complex social relationship in which a man bound himself to a particular lord. Yet, spurred on by this mistrust, he abused his power and alienated many of the local nobility and gentry through whom he needed to rule. Henry employed a network of spies to keep watch on his subjects at home and abroad. Fearful of plots and hungry for money, he imposed bonds and recognizances on nobles, gentlemen, and his own courtiers in order to intimidate them and exploit them financially. As Henry grew older and sicker, his rule became harsher and more avaricious.

Henry's regime rested on a narrow base of trusted nobles, gentlemen, and crown servants. The king built up the wealth and influence of his favored few in the localities, counties in England directly governed by local nobility and gentry. In some regions, such as Warwickshire, his failure to act against the abuses perpetrated by his men led to local disorder. Resentment fed the treason of Lord Fitzwalter and Sir William Stanley in 1494, of Lord Audeley in 1497, and of Suffolk in 1501. But despite being loathed by many of England's ruling elite, he not only survived politically but also bequeathed to his heir, Henry VIII, a strengthened monarchy and a peaceful and stable kingdom.

See also **Tudor Dynasty.**

BIBLIOGRAPHY

Chrimes, S. B. *Henry VII.* London, 1972.

Gunn, S. J. *Early Tudor Government, 1485–1558.* Houndmills, U.K., 1995.

Kipling, Gordon. "Henry VII and the Origins of Tudor Patronage." In *Patronage in the Renaissance.* Edited by Guy Fitch Lyle and Stephen Orgel. Princeton, N.J., 1981.

Lockyer, Roger, and Andrew Thrush. *Henry VII.* 3d ed. London, 1997.

Thompson, Benjamin, ed. *The Reign of Henry VII.* Stamford, U.K., 1995.

JOHN M. CURRIN

HENRY VIII (1491–1547), king of England (1509–1547). Henry VIII was the second son of the first Tudor ruler, King Henry VII, and his wife, Elizabeth of York. Henry VIII's older brother, Arthur, was originally the heir to the English throne, but he died in 1502, only a year after his dynastic marriage to Catherine of Aragon, the daughter of Ferdinand and Isabella of Spain. Henry then became the heir apparent and succeeded upon his father's death in 1509. In the same year he married his brother's widow, anticipating that the benefits of a Spanish alliance could still be obtained.

Henry and Catherine remained happily married until 1527, but their union produced no male heir, despite the queen's repeated pregnancies. Only a daughter, Mary Tudor, lived more than a few days. During this period Henry remained devoted to the church and the papacy. He joined in Pope Julius II's Holy League, an alliance intended to prevent the French from acquiring territory in Italy, and in 1513 he invaded northern France. He personally commanded English troops at the famous Battle of the Spurs (near Thérouanne, in northern France, in 1513), so named because of the speed with which the French drove their horses in retreat. England then acquired control of two French towns, Thérouanne and Tournai, but when a peace treaty was signed Henry was not consulted and he benefited less than he had expected. As a result he dismissed his chief ministers, who had been carried over from his father's reign, and gave control of the government to Thomas Wolsey, a churchman who was also lord chancellor, archbishop of York, and a cardinal.

During this period Henry also supported the papacy against the Reformation doctrines of Martin Luther. In appreciation for his tract *The Defence of the Seven Sacraments,* the pope gave him the title "Defender of the Faith," still used by his successors.

The Divorce and the Reformation. By 1527 it had become apparent that Catherine would bear no more children, and Henry became concerned about succession to the throne. He was intent on the continuation of the Tudor dynasty and did not believe that the English people would accept a

Henry VIII. Portrait by Hans Holbein the Younger. Oil on panel; c. 1536–1537; 28 × 20 cm (11 × 8 in.). Museo Thyssen-Bornemisza, Madrid

female heir. He thus began to seek a divorce from Catherine of Aragon so that he could marry a younger woman who might bear a son. At about the same time he fell in love with Anne Boleyn, one of the queen's ladies-in-waiting, and determined to make her his wife.

Henry and Wolsey appealed to Pope Clement VII for an annulment and permission to remarry. Under ordinary circumstances the papacy would have granted such a request: Renaissance popes were political realists, and Henry had earned papal favor. But Catherine opposed the divorce, as did her nephew, Charles V, king of Spain and Holy Roman Emperor. The pope did not feel that he could oppose Charles on the divorce case because imperial troops had sacked Rome in May 1527, and because Clement wanted Charles's support in other diplomatic and political affairs. In the summer of 1529 the papacy did arrange to have the divorce tried by Wolsey and Lorenzo Campeggio, an Italian cardinal, sitting as a court at Blackfriars in London, but in the end the case was revoked to Rome and no verdict was rendered.

The irate king then dismissed Wolsey and summoned what came to be known as the Reformation Parliament (1529–1536). Wolsey was allowed to retain his position as archbishop of York but was forbidden to meddle in politics. When he was found to be corresponding with the French, he was summoned to London and would probably have been executed had he not died a natural death in 1530.

For several years the king and Parliament were content with measures that destroyed the independence of the English church (including the Submission of the Clergy in 1532) and put financial pressure on the papacy (through the Conditional Restraint of Annates, also enacted in 1532). By the beginning of 1533 Henry had a new chief minister, Thomas Cromwell, and a new archbishop of Canterbury, Thomas Cranmer. Cromwell conceived the idea of breaking England's ties with Rome, so that the archbishop rather than the pope might grant the divorce. Cranmer was eager to assist. So in January 1533 Henry married Anne. A few months later Parliament passed the famous Act in Restraint of Appeals, which said that no judicial decisions could be appealed from England to Rome, and in fact went much further, denying that the papacy had any jurisdiction in England whatever. In May, Cranmer granted the divorce and ratified the king's marriage to Anne. In September she bore him his second daughter, christened Elizabeth.

The English Reformation thus sprang from a political motive and was imposed from above. Parliament continued to determine the course of religion, passing acts naming Henry VIII the Supreme Head of the Church, absolutely cutting off payments to the papacy, regulating doctrine, and ordering the dissolution of all the monasteries and nunneries in the realm. Many subjects regretted these actions, some of which forbade the worship of popular saints and ordered the destruction of religious images, many of them objects of great beauty. Other subjects, some who were followers of the old Lollard movement (inspired by the fourteenth-century theologian John Wycliffe) and some who had accepted Lutheran doctrines, welcomed the reform of a church that they believed had become corrupt and superstitious.

Henry's Later Wives. In 1536 Henry came to believe that Anne Boleyn had not been faithful to him. She was charged with adultery and beheaded in the Tower of London, and he married his third wife, Jane Seymour. Jane did succeed in providing a male heir, Edward, born in 1537, but she died a few days later of the complications of childbirth. Grief-stricken, Henry remained single for several years. In 1540 Cromwell persuaded him to marry Anne of Cleves, the sister of a minor ruler in Germany, hoping to forge a Protestant alliance that could be useful if the papacy and the Catholic states of Europe decided to make war on England. One sight of Anne, however, convinced Henry that he had been deceived by reports of her appearance and by a portrait that he had commissioned; Cranmer had hardly completed the marriage ceremony before he began to arrange a divorce.

Henry's fifth wife, Catherine Howard, was a cousin of Anne Boleyn, and her career was much the same: she was charged with adultery and beheaded in 1542. Neither she nor the king's last wife, Katherine Parr, bore him children. At one time or another both Mary and Elizabeth had been declared illegitimate, but shortly before his death Henry drafted a will stating that the throne might pass in the normal order to all his children, Edward, Mary, and Elizabeth. When Henry died in January 1547 Edward VI was proclaimed king, although he was only nine years old. Both of his sisters were destined to succeed to the throne. Henry's wives Anne of Cleves and Katherine Parr survived him.

Henry's Last Years. Following the break with Rome, Henry and his advisers grew more and more fearful that the Catholic powers on the Continent would join in making war on England, hoping to eliminate both the king and his Protestant church. Vast sums of money were confiscated from the church, especially from the dissolved religious houses, but they proved inadequate for military expenses, and parliamentary taxation reached new heights in the 1540s. Expenditures on the navy and on new fortifications were unprecedented. A second invasion of France in 1543, coupled with a campaign against Scotland, was costly but brought no real benefits.

After about 1536 the government was divided into conservative and reforming factions. Those who opposed change in the church and in social policy were led by Catherine Howard's uncle Thomas Howard, duke of Norfolk, and Stephen Gardiner, bishop of Winchester. The leading reformers were Cranmer and Cromwell. Cromwell's execution in 1540, largely because of his involvement in the distasteful Cleves marriage, left Norfolk and his friends dominant, but the fall of Catherine Howard weakened the duke's position. Shortly before Henry died Norfolk was

found guilty of treason and sentenced to death, but his execution was delayed by the king's own death and eventually abandoned. Since Gardiner was also out of favor in 1547, the council of regents named by Henry to rule during his son's minority was dominated by reformers. It was actually Cranmer and Edward VI's uncle Edward Seymour, Protector Somerset, who assumed control of the government in 1547. Some religious reforms had been blocked by Henry, whose personal views were generally traditional, but Cranmer was engaged in compiling the English-language Book of Common Prayer at the time of the king's death and would bring it into use in 1549.

The marital and diplomatic troubles of Henry's later years were compounded by economic and social strains. The enclosure movement, in which open fields were converted into pasture for sheep, caused serious distress. Landlords profited, since wool was England's chief export, but many laborers were turned away from their homes and became unemployed vagrants or beggars. Henry met some of his financial obligations by debasing the coinage—minting coins from a larger proportion of base metals rather than gold or silver—but this led to an inflation of prices beginning in the 1530s. New poor laws were proposed in 1536 but were limited in their effectiveness, since the national government lacked the resources necessary to alleviate poverty. Individual parishes remained responsible for charity.

Henry VIII and the Renaissance. Ideas associated with the Italian Renaissance had begun to seep into England during the reign of Henry VII. Greek and classical Latin were taught regularly at Oxford and Cambridge from about 1500. The true impact of the Renaissance, however, was not felt until the earlier years of Henry VIII's reign. The writings of the ancient Greeks and Romans came more and more to dominate the curricula of the universities and schools, especially Saint Paul's School in London, founded by John Colet, dean of the cathedral, with the specific intent of instructing boys in classical languages and literature.

A circle of humanists associated with Sir Thomas More, Henry VIII's lord chancellor from 1529 to 1532, took the lead in spreading Renaissance learning. More himself was a fine scholar who left a large number of important writings, the most famous being his *Utopia* (1516), a description of an imaginary state newly discovered by seafaring explorers. Erasmus lived in More's home during much of his sojourn in England, and More was responsible for his appointment to teach at Cambridge. Thomas Linacre, who had studied medicine at Padua, translated the chief writings of Galen into Latin and published them so that they would be accessible to English doctors, and founded the Royal College of Physicians to enforce professional medical standards. Sir Thomas Elyot, who was for a time one of the king's secretaries, wrote *The Boke Named the Governour* (1531), a treatise that included Renaissance ideas about political thought, education, and virtue and illustrated them with examples from ancient history. He also popularized ancient medical teachings in his *Castel of Helth* (c. 1536) and compiled the first English dictionary of classical Latin. The great German painter Hans Holbein the Younger was also part of More's circle and painted portraits of its members as well as likenesses of the king and several of his wives.

The religious debates and divisions that followed the break with Rome inevitably drew attention away from humanistic studies. But Renaissance ideas had taken hold and grew in popularity and importance during the reigns of Elizabeth I (1558–1603) and the first Stuart monarch, James I (1603–1625). The works of Shakespeare, Milton, and the metaphysical poets show how fully the English world picture depended on classical allusions and concepts. The grand tour of the Continent, generally including visits to Florence and Rome, became virtually mandatory for young aristocrats and gentlemen. English architecture began to adopt classical motifs under Henry VIII; surviving examples are the busts of Roman emperors at Hampton Court. In the early seventeenth century Inigo Jones built perfectly proportioned classical buildings like the Banqueting House in Whitehall. Even speeches in Parliament, like Sir John Eliot's oration comparing the duke of Buckingham to Sejanus (1626), contained extended references to ancient history. But by the 1640s England had become caught up in governmental crises followed by the Civil War and the execution of King Charles I (1649). The influence of the Renaissance would never be lost, but its greatest days of glory had come under Henry VIII.

The Character of the King. In his younger years Henry VIII appeared to be the ideal Renaissance king. Handsome and dashing, fond of sport and pageantry, well educated, the patron of humanists and artists, he embodied many characteristics of the perfect monarch. Less attractive features became evident during the second half of his reign. His intellectual abilities were in fact limited, as was his willingness to attend to the details of government. He was often unfaithful to his closest friends, even

ordering the execution of two wives and his most able minister. He seems to have shed no tears over the deaths of Anne Boleyn and Jane Seymour but is said to have felt remorse at the loss of Thomas Cromwell. During the closing years of his life he did remain loyal to Katherine Parr and Thomas Cranmer, both of whom were accused of holding extreme religious views.

Henry had the ability to manage a council containing members of rival factions; if he appeared to vacillate, it was perhaps a conscious policy intended to keep all his ministers in line by keeping all in fear of losing the royal favor. Like his father and his younger daughter, he also had an innate understanding of his subjects. Unlike the Stuarts, he always knew how far he could go in advocating unpopular measures, and he always stopped short of disaster. Even at the end of his life, when he had become ill, obese, and arbitrary, he commanded the affection and respect of the English people.

See also **Tudor Dynasty.**

BIBLIOGRAPHY

Dickens, A. G. *The English Reformation.* 2d ed. London, 1989. The standard account of the Reformation, perhaps too favorable to the reformers.

Dowling, Maria. *Humanism in the Age of Henry VIII.* London, 1986. A useful summary, but brief and superficial.

Elton, G. R. *England under the Tudors.* 3d ed. London, 1991. For many years the best textbook for the Tudor period, written by the greatest Tudor scholar of the mid-twentieth century.

Guy, John. *Tudor England.* Oxford and New York, 1988. A fine newer textbook.

Hale, J. R. *England and the Italian Renaissance.* London, 1954. A provocative study of Renaissance influences in England.

Hoskins, W. G. *The Age of Plunder: King Henry's England, 1500–1547.* London, 1976. A social history of Henry's reign, perhaps excessively harsh on the king.

Lehmberg, Stanford E. *The Reformation Parliament, 1529–1536.* Cambridge, U.K., 1970. Describes administrative, legal, and social reforms as well as the legislation that enacted the Reformation.

Pollard, A. F. *Henry VIII.* London, 1902. A classic biography written by the earliest professional Tudor historian.

Scarisbrick, J. J. *Henry VIII.* Berkeley, Calif., 1968. The standard life; much fuller than Pollard.

Smith, Lacey Baldwin. *Henry VIII: The Mask of Royalty.* London, 1971. A psychological study, emphasizing the last decade of Henry's life.

STANFORD E. LEHMBERG

HENRY II (1519–1559), king of France (1547–1559). The second son of Francis I and Claude of France, at age seven Henry and his older brother were sent to Spain as hostages for Francis, who had been captured at Pavia in 1525. Henry felt that the

Spanish mistreated him during the four years he spent there and bore a grudge against both his father and Emperor Charles V. In 1533 he wedded Catherine de Médicis as part of Francis's attempt to build an alliance with the Medici pope, Clement VII. The pope soon died, ending the political value of the marriage, which also came under strain because of the lack of children during its first ten years. Henry and Catherine eventually had seven children who survived to adulthood. Henry's love for Diane de Poitiers further strained the marriage; he loved her until his death.

When Henry's older brother died in 1536, he became dauphin (title of eldest son of French king) and ascended the throne in 1547 at the death of his father. He had already formed a cadre of close advisers—the constable Anne de Montmorency, Francis, duc de Guise, and his brother Jean, cardinal de Lorraine, and Jacques d'Albon, marshal de Saint-André—who now dominated the royal council. Diane also wielded broad influence on her royal lover. In government Henry largely carried on trends begun under his father; his major innovation was creating the offices of the four secretaries of state, each having responsibility for a different area of administration. The selling of royal offices was already an important source of royal revenue, and Henry significantly increased the number of venal offices.

The war against the Habsburgs continued during Henry's reign, and he allied with the German Lutherans and the Ottoman Turks against them. With the approval of the Lutheran princes, he occupied the Three Bishoprics of Lorraine (Metz, Toul, and Verdun), and in cooperation with the Ottoman fleet he seized Corsica from Charles V's ally, Genoa, in 1553. Henry's alliance with the Lutherans prevented him from being as severe with the French Protestants as he wished, but he took seriously his oath to protect the Catholic Church. Shortly after becoming king, he created a new chamber in the Parlement of Paris to deal with heresy. Called the *chambre ardente* for its zealous pursuit of Protestants, it condemned thirty-seven persons to death in three years. The Catholic hierarchy's objections to the loss of jurisdiction over heresy persuaded him to close down the *chambre ardent* in 1550. The rivalry between the Parlement and the episcopate over heresy prosecution rendered ineffective such harsh edicts against heresy as the Edict of Châteaubriant in 1551. This problem, along with Henry's perception that heresy was lower-class sedition, leading him to overlook Protestantism among the French elite, allowed Prot-

Henry II of France. Equestrian portrait by anonymous sixteenth-century French artist. Gouache on wood; 2.7 × 2 m (9 × 6.5 ft.). MUSÉE CONDÉ, CHANTILLY, FRANCE/ GIRAUDON/ART RESOURCE, NY

estantism to flourish despite his resolve to rid his realm of "this Lutheran scum."

Under Henry the French monarchy continued to be a major patron of Renaissance culture, although he preferred to patronize French talent. He completed several projects begun by Francis, including the château of Fontainebleau and the reconstruction of the Louvre, while putting his own stamp on them. Henry assigned the architect Pierre Lescot and the sculptor Jean Goujon to the Louvre, and its Cour Carrée courtyard is probably the best example of their work. The major building project during Henry's reign was the château of Anet, done for Diane de Poitiers by Philibert de L'Orme. The two major portraits of Henry were done by Francesco Primaticcio and François Clouet. In literature Henry's reign saw something of a reaction against the emphasis on using Latin and a greater effort to use French. Joachim Du Bellay argued this in *La défense et illustration de la langue française* (Defense and illustration of the French language; 1549). Du Bellay was a member of the Pléiade, a group of poets who wrote in French. The most famous among them was Pierre de Ronsard. Étienne Jodelle's *Cléopâtre captive,* the first French tragedy, was performed for Henry in 1552.

The end of Henry's reign was shadowed by economic problems, a huge royal debt, an upsurge in religious dissent, and more intense war with the Habsburgs. When he sent an army under Francis of Guise to Italy to reclaim Naples and Milan, Philip II responded by invading northern France and defeated Montmorency at Saint-Quentin in 1557. Philip failed to push his forces on to Paris, and Henry used the army assembled for defending the city to take Calais in 1558. With the fortunes of war balanced, both rulers agreed to the Peace of Cateau-Cambrésis in 1559. Henry, jousting in the tournament celebrating the peace, was mortally wounded when his opponent's shattered lance struck him in the face. He left his fifteen-year-old son Francis II a realm beset with problems, most serious being the religious divisions. Henry's death led to the Wars of Religion.

BIBLIOGRAPHY

Baumgartner, Frederic J. *Henry II, King of France, 1547–1559.* Durham, N.C., 1988.
Cloulas, Ivan. *Henri II.* Paris, 1985. Especially strong on Henry's patronage of art and culture.

FREDERIC J. BAUMGARTNER

HENRY III (1551–1589), king of Poland (1573–1574), king of France (1574–1589). Christened Alexandre-Édouard but called Henry from his confirmation (1564), he was also known as Henry of Valois, duc d'Angoulême (1551–1560), duc d'Orléans (1560–1566), by the title of *monsieur* (1560–1574), and as duc d'Anjou (1566–1574). He was the favorite son of Catherine de Médicis, who engineered his election to the throne of Poland. As a youth, he showed intelligence, enhanced by his tutor, Jacques Amyot, and, under guidance, military flair. Appointed lieutenant-general of the kingdom in 1567, he was idolized as a hero after his victories against the Huguenots at Jarnac and Moncontour in 1569, and he was probably involved in the Saint Bartholomew's Day massacre in 1572. A reluctant king of Poland, he left Cracow by subterfuge on the death of his brother Charles IX of France. He married Louise de Vaudémont in 1575, two days after his coronation in Reims (his name had been linked with that of Elizabeth I). The instability of the Wars of Religion and a worsening economic climate characterized his reign. On his succession his policies were opposed by the "liberal" Politiques and Malcontents, who

Henry III of France. Portrait attributed to François Quesnel the Elder (1543–1619). Wood; 66 × 52 cm (26 × 20 in.). MUSÉE DU LOUVRE, PARIS/GIRAUDON/ART RESOURCE

later joined forces with the Protestants; in 1576 he became nominal head of the extremist Catholic group, the Holy League, which adopted a firmer line than the politiques against the "heretics" and was later identified with Guise family and, subsequently, Spanish interests.

Henry remained childless after the death in 1584 of his brother, François-Hercule, the duke of Anjou, and consequently his heir apparent was the Protestant Henry of Navarre. Hostile resistance to Henry, fomented by the Guise family and accompanied by a virulent and prurient propaganda campaign, reached its climax when Henry, who was trying to keep Navarre, the Guise, and Charles Emmanuel of Savoy at bay, was forced to flee Paris by a popular insurrection following the arrival of Henri de Guise in the capital on 9 May 1588. In an effort to restore internal peace, the king arranged the assassination of Henri de Guise and his cardinal brother, Louis, at Blois in December 1588. In 1589, after his mother's death, he joined forces with Navarre, and their combined armies laid siege to Paris in July. On 1 August

Henry was assassinated by a fanatical monk, Jacques Clément, at Saint-Cloud.

Henry's image has been tarnished by the polemical vituperation that prevailed during the closing years of his reign. His opponents attacked his sexuality and his beliefs and sought to prove he was an unworthy king and, hence, deposable. Of a sensitive disposition, he was weak but autocratic. Although he could not do what he wanted, he did what he could. He was endowed with a highly developed aesthetic sense and was interested in intellectual matters—a man of the Renaissance, he enjoyed pomp and festivities and supported the Palace Academy (especially in the early years) and men of letters, notably Philippe Desportes. He began the construction of the Pont Neuf and adopted the Gregorian calendar (1582). He proposed a number of governmental reforms, notably through an assembly meeting at Saint-Germain in 1583. He was devout, almost superstitiously so, founding religious orders (1583, 1585) and taking part in public displays of penance. He surrounded himself with young men (*mignons*) from relatively unknown families—a move to change the political balance and create trustworthy advisers, yet construed as perversity. In 1578 he founded the Ordre du Saint Esprit (Order of the Holy Ghost) to control the nobility and strengthen the Catholic Church. By acknowledging Navarre as his heir (Treaty of Tours, April 1589), the last of the Valois probably saved the institution of the monarchy and, through important monetary and legal reforms, provided France, albeit at the cost of excommunication by the pope and subsequent death, with the wherewithal for Bourbon government.

See also **Valois Dynasty**; **Wars of Religion**.

BIBLIOGRAPHY

Primary Work

L'Estoile, Pierre de. *Registre-journal du règne de Henri III.* Edited by Madeleine Lazard and Gilbert Schrenck. Geneva, 1992–.

Secondary Works

Bordonove, Georges. *Henri III: Roi de France et de Pologne.* Paris, 1988.

Cameron, Keith. *Henri III, a Maligned or Malignant King? (Aspects of the Satirical Iconography of Henri de Valois).* Exeter, U.K., 1978.

Cameron, Keith, ed. *From Valois to Bourbon: Dynasty, State, and Society in Early Modern France.* Exeter, U.K., 1989.

Crouzet, Denis. *Les guerriers de Dieu: La violence au temps des troubles de religion.* 2 vols. Seyssel, France, 1990.

Sauzet, Robert, ed. *Henri III et son temps: Actes du colloque international du Centre de la Renaissance de Tours, octobre 1989.* Paris, 1992.

KEITH CAMERON

HENRY IV (1553–1610), king of France and Navarre (1589–1610). Henry IV inaugurated the Bourbon dynasty that ruled until the French Revolution of 1789. His wit and impetuous nature endeared him to most of his contemporaries, and he remains to this day one of France's most popular rulers. Under his leadership, a generation of civil war ended and the groundwork was laid for France's rise as the most dominant power in Europe during the seventeenth century.

Family and Early Life. Henry was born on 14 December 1553 at the Château of Pau in Béarn. His father, Antoine de Bourbon, headed the powerful house of Bourbon-Vendôme, whose vast domains stretched from central to southwestern France. A prince of the blood, his lineage could be traced to Robert de France, count of Clermont, the sixth son of Louis IX. This remote royal ancestry assumed enormous significance later on as Henry II's sons each failed to sire an heir. Henry's mother, Jeanne d'Albret, queen of Navarre, ruled a tiny kingdom straddling the Pyrenees. Her conversion to Calvinism in 1555 brought her young son to the faith. Other members of the house of Bourbon-Vendôme also converted, most notably Louis, prince of Condé, who led the Huguenot movement until his death in 1569. Henry's tutors, Pierre Victor Palma-Cayet and François de La Gaucherie, reinforced these Protestant leanings in what was otherwise a typical Renaissance curriculum. Though not a deep thinker, Henry eventually became a keen judge of character and prone to decisive, frequently impulsive acts of will to overcome the many obstacles that challenged him during his eventful life. These traits served him well as the country slipped into the maelstrom of the Wars of Religion (1562–1598).

Huguenot Leader and Heir to the Throne. In an effort to reconcile the warring factions, the queen mother, Catherine de Médicis, arranged a marriage between her daughter Margaret of Valois and Henry on 18 August 1572. Rather than bringing peace, however, the wedding set the stage for the paroxysm of violence known as the Saint Bartholomew's Day massacre. Thousands of Huguenots perished, including the movement's leader, Gaspard de Coligny, admiral of France. Henry narrowly escaped death himself, but only at the price of renouncing his Calvinist faith. He remained a virtual prisoner of the Valois court until February 1576, when he escaped to reclaim headship of the Huguenot party— a position he consolidated during the course of three more civil wars he fought over the next eight years.

years before he was able to command the obedience of his rebellious Catholic subjects.

Winning the Kingdom. Henry's promise in the Declaration of Saint-Cloud (4 August 1589) to consider conversion to Catholicism, coupled with decisive military victories at Arques (21 September 1589) and Ivry (14 March 1590), shored up public support for him. However, the grueling siege of Paris (summer 1590) demonstrated that League resistance could not be overcome by sheer force. Three years later, while an Estates General met in Leaguer Paris to decide the election of a new French ruler, Henry converted to Catholicism amid much fanfare. The advice of both Maximilien de Béthune, duke of Sully, himself a Protestant, and Henry's mistress, Gabrielle d'Estrées, a Catholic, are thought to have heavily influenced the king's confessional change, though it is doubtful he ever uttered the famous phrase, "Paris is well worth a Mass." He was crowned in accordance with Catholic rite in February 1594 at Chartres and then triumphantly entered Paris. In 1595, Pope Clement VIII affirmed the converted king's standing as a Catholic by bestowing a papal absolution on him. Over the next three years, Henry IV gradually pacified the kingdom more by kindness than by force, winning the allegiance of former Catholic Leaguers through generous peace accords and by allaying Huguenot fears in 1598 with the royal guarantees enshrined in the celebrated Edict of Nantes. The year 1598 also saw the signing of the Treaty of Vervins, which brought to a favorable conclusion France's long war with Spain.

Recovery and Renewal. With peace finally at hand, Henry IV now embarked on a wide-ranging program to promote the recovery of not only his subjects but also the battered authority of the monarchy. The annulment of his marriage to Margaret of Valois in 1599 enabled him to marry Marie de Médicis, daughter of the grand duke of Tuscany, the next year. In 1601, Marie bore him a son, the future Louis XIII, thus securing the dynasty's future. With the aid of Sully, who served as superintendent of finances, the king put the crown's fiscal house back in order through prudent expenditures, an overhaul of municipal finance, and consolidation of the state's debt. By 1608, Sully estimated that the royal treasury had accumulated reserves totaling 32.5 million *livres*. Also introduced was a ministerial style of government that restricted the judicial prerogatives claimed by the parlements and the provincial privileges asserted by local representative assemblies. In 1604, Henry IV regularized the heritable nature of venal

Henry IV of France. Bronze bust, attributed to Mathieu Jacquet (d. 1610). 31 cm (12 in.). MUSÉE DU LOUVRE, PARIS/ GIRAUDON

Henry's position changed fundamentally when he became heir presumptive to the French throne as a result of the 10 June 1584 death of Francis, duke of Alençon. The dictates of the Salic law of succession clashed with the traditional Catholic character of the monarchy, rendering the question of Henry of Navarre's confessional allegiances the central issue of the day. Militant Catholics rallied to the Holy League revived in 1584 by Henry of Lorraine, duc de Guise, especially after Pope Sixtus V excommunicated Navarre the next year. The inability of Henry III to maintain order, particularly following his humiliating expulsion from Paris on the Day of the Barricades (12 May 1588), culminated in his calamitous decision on 24 December 1588 to order the murders of Henry of Guise and his brother Louis. Rather than restoring royal authority, the move sparked a general insurrection across the kingdom that eventually resulted in the king's own assassination at the hands of a fanatical monk on 1 August 1589. The regicide brought Henry of Navarre to the throne, though it was five

offices by the payment of a special fee known as the Paulette. He also cultivated close relations with the old nobility by showering them with pensions and titles; those aristocrats who conspired against him felt his full wrath, however, as demonstrated in the execution of Charles, duke of Biron in 1602.

Henry IV also encouraged the beginnings of Catholic reform among both churchmen and the lay public, working hard at the same time to uphold the protections recently granted to the Huguenots. On the economic front, the king entrusted Barthélemy de Laffemas to carry out innovative measures to restore commerce and living standards—a campaign reflected in the contemporary slogan, a "chicken in every pot" (*la poule au pot*).

With the restoration of the crown's finances and the country's general well-being, Henry IV felt the need to challenge Habsburg hegemony in Europe. An opportunity arose in 1609 in the lower Rhineland over the disputed succession to Jülich-Clèves. On the eve of his planned invasion in 1610, however, the king was cut down in the streets of Paris by an assassin's blade.

See also **Bourbon Family and Dynasty**; **Valois Dynasty**; **Wars of Religion**; *and biographies of figures mentioned in this entry.*

BIBLIOGRAPHY

Buisseret, David. *Henry IV.* London, 1984. An excellent biography that traces the course of Henry IV's life and contributions.

Greengrass, Mark. *France in the Age of Henri IV: The Struggle for Stability.* 2d ed. London and New York, 1995. A brilliant analysis of France's evolution under the first Bourbon king.

Thomas, Daniele. *Henri IV: Images d'un roi entre réalité et mythe.* Bizanos, France, 1996. A probing treatment of the images and myths associated with Henry IV.

Wolfe, Michael. *The Conversion of Henri IV: Politics, Power, and Religious Belief in Early Modern France.* Cambridge, Mass., 1993. Examines the struggles sparked by the issue of Henry IV's religion during the 1580s and 1590s.

MICHAEL WOLFE

HERALDRY. Heraldry is the art of properly designing and describing (blazoning) armorial bearings. These originated as identifying marks on shields, helmets, and banners in medieval warfare, and after the middle of the twelfth century the patterns and figures tended to become hereditary.

Terminology. It was literally a matter of life or death to be able to recognize heraldic devices at a distance, at least a bow shot away. Therefore, such devices had to be kept distinctive, simple, and in starkly contrasting tinctures. The basic rule of heraldry is that a correctly designed shield should contain one dark "color" (red, blue, black, green, with purple permitted) and one light "metal" (gold-yellow, silver-white). In the terms for the heraldic tinctures their origin with French-speaking crusaders is evident: or for gold (yellow), argent for silver (white), gules (from Persian *gûl*, a rose) for red, azure (from Arabic *azraq*) for blue, sable (from the black fur of the Asian mink) for black, and the French vert for green. In addition to these basic tinctures there are two "furs"—ermine and vair (from Latin *varius*, for the two-colored pelt of the Siberian squirrel)—stylizations of animal pelts once popular as the lining of clothing.

The term "heraldry" derives from Old High German *heriwalt* (arranger of an army), which points out the role of heralds as military intelligence and communications officers. In peacetime they became organizers of tournaments and masters of ceremony.

To add some flourishes in describing a champion's blazon (from German *blasen*, the trumpet signal announcing the entry of a jouster on the tournament field) the technical terms for the tinctures could be fancifully enhanced by substituting the names of precious stones. In the Renaissance erudite heraldists touted their humanist education in classical mythology, scientific lore, and astrology by introducing an increasingly stilted terminology, such as using the names of the planets and deities of classical antiquity, or even the days of the week (see "Erudite Heraldry" table in this entry).

Color is of the essence in heraldry—a lion gules in or is an entirely different coat-of-arms than a lion or in gules—and it was a major problem that woodcuts or engravings, and above all seals, did not show colors. Up to a degree this could be helped by "tricking," that is, inscribing initials or symbols in respective fields or charges (*a* = argent, *az* = azure, *g* = gules, *sa* = sable, *vt* = vert). German heraldists liked to draw a little linden leaf to indicate "green" and # for black, but their use of *g* for gold and *b* for *blau* (blue) added to the confusion since in Italy *b* meant *bianco* (white) and *a* stood for *azzurro* (blue). Therefore, it must have been a relief when in the late-sixteenth century an unknown engraver invented a simple system of hatching: horizontally for azure, vertically for gules, diagonally for vert, cross-hatched for sable, and dotted for or, while argent was simply left blank (see figure 1).

The description of a blazon starts with the color of the field, and if there are subdivisions, with the charges on the dexter side (the right side, as seen from the shield-bearer's point of view); the left side

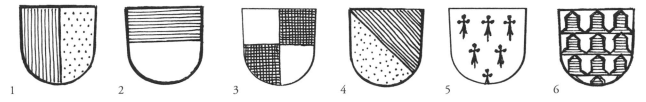

Figure 1. **Hatchments and Furs.** (1) Per pale, gules and or; (2) per fess, azure and argent; (3) quarterly, argent and sable; (4) per bend, vert and or; (5) ermine; (6) vair. COURTESY OF HELMUT NICKEL

is the sinister. Geometrical charges, called ordinaries, are pale, fess, bar, bend, chevron, pile, chief, canton, bordure, orle, and cross and saltire. Partitions of a multicolored field are, accordingly, per pale, per fess, per bend, per chevron, per cross or quarterly, and per saltire; multiple partitions are paly, barry, bendy, checky, lozengy, and gyronny (see figure 2).

Besides ordinaries, anything—animals, humans, celestial bodies, or inanimate objects—can be used as charges. Especially popular are so-called canting arms that represent a rebus or a pun on the bearer's name, such as *Argent, three staples sable* for Stapleton. Often the rebus is not so easy to decypher, as in *Or, a raven* (corbie) *sable* for Corbet, and *Sable, fretty or* for Maltravers, where the charge is a stylized grille "difficult to get through." Heraldry came into being at a time of very limited literacy, and therefore the pun might use a homophone without paying attention to etymology, such as *Argent, three cocks gules* for Cockburn, where the cocks' color indicates fire rather than that of a Scottish brook. Sometimes the pun is in a foreign language, such as *Azure, three strawberry blossoms* (fraises) *argent* for Fraser, or *Barry of argent and azure* for Grey, hinting at a flight of stairs (French *degré*, steps). Even Shakespeare's arms, granted in 1596, *Or, on a bend sable a lance of the field, its head argent,* have a "canting" crest: *A falcon* (saker) *argent holding* (shaking?) *a lance or,* that strains etymology quite a bit.

Some puns could get quite scurrilous; in 1531 a Peter Dodge of Kent had his arms confirmed: *Barry of six, Or and sable, a pale gules overall, charged with a woman's breast* (dugge), *spilling drops of milk,* while the condottiere Bartolommeo Colleoni (1400–1475) blatantly bore *Per fess of argent and gules, three scrota* (for *coglioni,* testicles) *counterchanged.* Much in the same macho spirit was the battle cry *Palle* (balls) by partisans of the Medici, whose canting arms were: *Or, six roundels* (pills) *in orle, five gules, the one in chief azure, charged with three fleurs-de-lis or.* The rival Strozzi faction countered with *Mezze* (wither), inspired by the three half-moons (*mezzelune*) in the Strozzi arms.

Uses of Heraldry. By the fifteenth century armorial bearings had become status symbols, and attempts were made to regulate them accordingly. In England the College of Arms was established in 1484 by Richard III, and checkups (visitations) were made at regular intervals between 1530 and 1686; the Holy Roman Emperors had officials called *Hofpfalzgrafen* for the granting of new arms and even for the confirmation of existing ones, when some armigers began to feel that having an officially signed, sealed (and paid for) *Wappenbrief* document was more dignified than mere customary use.

On the other hand, within the empire the custom continued that the adoption of arms was the privilege of any free man. Many burghers simply set their

Erudite Heraldry

Tincture	Precious stone	Planet	Metal	Day of the week
or	topaz	Sol	gold	Sunday
argent	pearl	Luna	silver	Monday
gules	ruby	Mars	iron	Tuesday
purpure	amethyst	Mercury	mercury	Wednesday
azure	sapphire	Jupiter	tin	Thursday
vert	emerald	Venus	copper	Friday
sable	diamond	Saturn	lead	Saturday

Figure 2. Ordinaries and Lines of Partition. (1) Pale (ordinary); (2) per pale (partition); (3) paly (partition); (4) fess (ordinary); (5) per fess (partition); (6) two bars (ordinaries); (7) barry (partition); (8) bend (ordinary); (9) per bend (ordinary); (10) bendy (partition); (11) chevron (ordinary); (12) per chevron (partition); (13) pile (ordinary); (14) saltire (ordinary); (15) per saltire (partition); (16) per cross or quarterly (partition); (17) gyronny (partition); (18) label (subordinary); (19) canton (ordinary); (20) checky (partition); (21) lozengy (partition); (22) fretty (subordinary); (23) chief (ordinary); (24) bordure (ordinary); (25) orle (ordinary). COURTESY OF HELMUT NICKEL

Figure 3. Renaissance Heraldic Motifs. *Left,* arms of Johannes Reuchlin (d. 1522); Roman altar with smoke; "canting": *Rauchlein* = a little smoke. *Right,* civic arms of the town of Glückstadt, 1617; "canting": *Glück* = luck, good fortune. COURTESY OF HELMUT NICKEL

Hausmarke—a geometric symbol identifying property, such as fire buckets—or their merchants' mark in a shield, but patricians (as the emerging city nobility), artists, and the new class of humanist scholars created their own (see figure 3). The canting arms of the humanist Johann Reuchlin (1455–1522) were a Roman altar with curling wisps of smoke (Räuchlein means "a little smoke"); Albrecht Dürer's (1471–1528), himself the foremost heraldic artist of the German Renaissance, were a gate (*Tür* means "door"). It seems that a certain amount of humor was appreciated, such as when the Nürnberg patrician family Tetzel bore *Gules, a cat argent, armed or* (*Tätzel* means "paws"), and the Igelbrechts whimsically bore a hedgehog (*Igel*) with three apples on its back. In order to distinguish arms of burghers from those of the nobility it was ruled that burghers should use the frog-mouthed tilting helmet for their crests, and noblemen the more prestigious barred helmet of the baston course (for shapes of helmets, see figure 4). Fought on horseback with blunt swords or specially designed clubs the baston course demanded superior horsemanship; the last baston course in the grand style was held at Worms, in 1487.

Civic arms too were often canting, as shown by the fleurs-de-lis of Florence and Lille, and the bears of Berne and Berlin. The goddess Fortuna in the arms of the little town of Glückstadt (*Glück* means "luck"), granted by King Christian IV of Denmark and Norway in 1617, is a fine, although late, example of Renaissance erudition.

Shields. By the middle of the fifteenth century the development of plate armor was complete, and the shield as a shock breaker in combat was no longer needed, as it had been, when tough but yielding mail armor was worn. (Armorial decoration on plate armor itself is surprisingly rare, and even then applied only as small elements within the overall ornamentation.) Heraldic shields (see figure 5) in the

Figure 4. Helmet Types. *Left,* "barred" baston-course helmet; arms of the knightly family Bock von Oeringen, c. 1550; canting: *Bock* = billy goat. *Right,* tilting helmet; arms of the artists' and painters' guild in Germany, with three shields indicating the main occupation of painters, painting shields; the crest is a *Leuchterweibchen,* a fancy chandelier made out of stag's antlers and a human figure. COURTESY OF HELMUT NICKEL

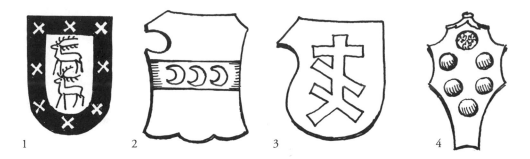

Figure 5. Shield Types. (1) "Spanish" form; arms of Miguel de Cervantes (1547–1616); "canting": *ciervo* = stag. (2) *Targe;* arms of the Strozzi family, c. 1490. (3) "Spanish" styled targe; *Hausmarke* of Wulf Blechschmidt, architect, c. 1540. (4) "Chanfron" form; arms of the Medici, c. 1520. COURTESY OF HELMUT NICKEL

fifteenth century were more or less U-shaped, because this allowed for a more pleasing display of figural charges than the old triangular battle shield. The U-shaped shield was called "Spanish"; although it was in use in Spain from the thirteenth century, it became widely fashionable only around 1500, when Spain through its dynastic connections with the Austrian and Burgundian Habsburgs became a power to be reckoned with even in central and northern Europe.

In the pageantry of the tournament, however, shields called targes were still in actual use. They were squarish in outline and had a cutout, the *bouche,* in the upper dexter corner, that was originally designed as a lance rest. Northern European heraldists liked to blend the eccentric outline of the targe with the rounded base of the "Spanish" shield. Often, for purely artistic reasons, Renaissance targes were given two symmetrical *bouches.* In Italy another bizarre form, the *chanfron* (shield) was preferred; it had been developed from the early medieval almond-shaped ("Norman") shield and was only for heraldic display.

Since shields were no longer borne in actual combat, multiquartered arms that could represent genealogical or, for princely arms, territorial claims came

in use. In German lands it became customary to place multiple helmets with the appropriate crests on top of a multiquartered shield (a custom abhorrent to English purists, who insist that more than one helmet could be used only by persons with more than one head; see figure 6). On the other hand, in France and to a degree in Italy, there was an increasing tendency to either omit crests altogether or replace them with panaches of ostrich plumes, usually in the colors of the shield.

Figure 6. Multiple Helmets and Orders of Chivalry. Bookplate of Florian Waldauf von Waldenstein, c. 1500, by Albrecht Dürer. The crests of the "barred" helmets repeat the charges of the quarterly shield of "Spanish" form, which is surrounded by the collar of the Brandenburg Order of the Swan; at the dexter is the Aragonese Order de la Jarra; at the sinister is the English collar SSS. COURTESY OF HELMUT NICKEL

Figure 7. Conquistador Heraldry. Arms of Francisco Pizarro (c. 1475–1541), conqueror of Peru, granted by the emperor Charles V on 19 January 1537. COURTESY OF HELMUT NICKEL

Quarters, Supporters, and Badges. In 1230 Spain had pioneered in introducing quartered arms, by combining in one shield the *Gules, a castle or* of Castile, and the *Argent, a lion purpure* of León, when these two Iberian kingdoms were united. The elegant quarterly design soon became popular all over Europe. A peculiarity of Spanish heraldry is the inclusion of mottos in the shield design, usually on the bordures, a custom that Cervantes mocks when Don Quixote blazons the arms of the champion Timonel de Carcaxona (in the episode of the two flocks of sheep on a collision course) as *Gules, a cat or, with the motto* MIAU. Aside from its fondness for bordures another typical feature of Spanish heraldry is to surround the shield with trophy banners. In the sixteenth century an unfortunate trend began of crowding too many elements on the shield. This is especially evident in the so-called conquistador heraldry, when existing or more often newly created coats of arms were overloaded with charges and augmentations without any regard for the traditional rules of clarity (see figure 7).

In the late fifteenth and the sixteenth centuries it became a fashion to add supporter figures to the shield. At first these were purely decorative, but soon they became seen as signs of rank and were regulated too, at least in Britain. Members of orders of chivalry started to have the shield encircled by the collars of their orders (or, in the case of the Most Noble Order of the Garter, by the Garter itself).

In western Europe, and particularly in England, badges were in use from the fourteenth century on. In the sixteenth century it became fashionable to have a badge or impresa in the classical spirit of the Renaissance; the best known example is the impresa of Emperor Charles V, the Twin Columns of Heracles with the motto PLVS VLTRA. [For Charles's coat of arms, see the illustration to the entry on Spanish Literature and Language.]

See also **Aristocracy; Chivalry,** *subentry on* **Knighthood and Chivalric Orders; Tournaments.**

BIBLIOGRAPHY

Boutell, Charles. *Boutell's Heraldry.* Revised by J. P. Brooke-Little. Rev. ed. London, 1973.

Brooke-Little, J. P. *An Heraldic Alphabet.* London, 1973.

Fox-Davies, Arthur Charles. *A Complete Guide to Heraldry.* Revised and annotated by J. P. Brooke-Little. London, 1969.

Gwynn-Jones, Peter. *The Art of Heraldry: Origins, Symbols, and Designs.* New York, 1998.

Hildebrandt, Adolf M. et al. *Wappenfibel: Handbuch der Heraldik.* 15th rev. ed. Neustadt an der Aisch, Germany, 1967.

Neubecker, Ottfried, and J. P. Brooke-Little. *Heraldry: Sources, Symbols, and Meaning.* New York, 1976.

Smith, Whitney. *Flags, through the Ages and across the World.* New York, 1975.

Woodcock, Thomas, and John Martin Robinson. *The Oxford Guide to Heraldry.* New York, 1988.

HELMUT NICKEL

HERBALS. *See* **Botany.**

HERBERT, EDWARD, LORD CHERBURY.
See **Poetry,** *subentry on* **Early Stuart and Metaphysical Poetry.**

HERBERT, GEORGE (1593–1633), English poet. If George Herbert cannot be said to have invented the Protestant devotional lyric in English, there is no doubt that he perfected it and made it a culturally viable and visible poetic form. His influence was immediate and widespread, transcending gender (he influenced many women poets), geography (the Atlantic Ocean), and even religious position (he influenced both "puritans" and Catholics), and this influence continues through the present, as testimony from W. H. Auden, Elizabeth Bishop, and Anthony Hecht suggests.

Authorities differ on whether Herbert was born in the (paternal) family castle on the Welsh border. As a younger son, he did not stand to inherit, and he was bound, from early on, by inclination as well as by material circumstances, for a life of scholarship. At Westminster School in London, Herbert began the study of Latin and Greek that eventually enabled him to become orator for Cambridge University seven years after his graduation from Trinity College. Scholarship and piety, as the young orator explained to his stepfather, Sir John Danvers (a future leader of the parliamentary opposition), did not preclude ambition and civic commitment. Former orators had become secretaries of state. But for reasons having to do with politics and patronage, Herbert's "court-hopes" failed. After taking deacon's orders in 1624 (which debarred him from civil office), he eventually secured an appointment at the tiny church of Bemerton, near Salisbury. Contemporaries were astonished at Herbert's social descent, and he died three years later.

Yet the period in which Herbert faded from social prominence was a period of extraordinary spiritual and artistic growth. His commitment to the *vita activa* metamorphosed into his vision of the ideal pastor described in his eloquent but straightforward manual, *The Country Parson* (published as *A Priest to the Temple*). We have none of his sermons, but we do have the volume of primarily lyric poems, *The Temple,* that he systematically worked on (revising, reordering, expanding) for his whole adult life and carefully prepared for publication without actually publishing himself. He became one of the great critics—in the first person—of pride and ambition, so that his ambivalence about publication fits in with his poetic themes. His lyrics might be seen as the most perfect instance of Protestant classicism. His control of tone, meter, stanzaic form, and colloquial elegance is astonishing and fully Horatian, but his central themes are the themes of the Protestant Reformation: the perverseness of man and the unmerited, stunningly "unmotivated" and irresistible grace of God. For Herbert, theology was psychology, and it is the combination of consummate artistic skill and penetrating psychological observation, including insights into the pride that skill generates, that made his lyrics the models for all later religious poets in the English-speaking world. Lyrics like "Love" (III), "The Collar," "The Temper" (I), "The Flower," "Artillerie," and "Affliction" (I) are unmatched for their mixture of daring, polish, immediacy, humor, and profundity. These qualities make George Herbert not only the greatest religious poet in English, but simply one of our greatest lyric poets.

BIBLIOGRAPHY

Primary Work
Herbert, George. *The Works.* Edited by F. E. Hutchinson. Oxford, 1945. The definitive edition, containing the prose as well as the poetry, with useful annotations.

Secondary Works
Charles, Amy M. *A Life of George Herbert.* Ithaca, N.Y., 1977. The most detailed biography.
Schoenfeldt, Michael C. *Prayer and Power: George Herbert and Renaissance Courtship.* Chicago, 1991. The importance of reading the poetry with an awareness of Herbert's political and courtly ambitions. New historicist approach.
Strier, Richard. *Love Known: Theology and Experience in George Herbert's Poetry.* Chicago, 1983. Detailed explications of many of the lyrics in the light of Reformation theology.
Summers, J. H. *George Herbert: His Religion and His Art.* Cambridge, Mass., 1954. A seminal study.

RICHARD STRIER

HERMETISM. The title "thrice-greatest" honored the god Thoth in ancient Egypt, and Greeks who knew Thoth as Hermes rendered this title as Trismegistos. Beginning in the fourth century B.C.E. (at the earliest), Hermes Trismegistus and other mythic figures—Asclepius, Isis, Tat, Ammon—became associated with a body of Greek texts later called "Hermetic." Although the home of all this literature, much of it now lost, was the turbulent religious world of Ptolemaic and Roman Egypt, later readers divided it into two types: technical works dealing with alchemy, astrology, magic, and other practical uses of occult wisdom; and theoretical works of pious philosophy or philosophical piety revealing the nature of the gods and the universe—the knowledge (gnosis) needed for salvation. Treatises of the second type, with their divinely revealed insights into theology, cosmogony, anthropogony, ethics, soteriology, and eschatology, achieved new prominence for Renaissance readers, who recognized their kinship with the sacred revelation of Moses and the secular wisdom of Plato. Salvation in the broadest sense—a better life based on gnosis—was the common aim of technical and theoretical Hermetica, but the former recommended recipes for the daily ills of the body, family, and society, while the latter preached a larger message about the gods, the other, and the self in order to secure a grander and enduring happiness.

The seventeen Greek treatises now known as the *Corpus Hermeticum,* along with most of twenty-nine related excerpts from an anthology composed by Stobaeus (John of Stobi) in the fifth century C.E., are the chief remains of the theoretical Hermetica. Technical Hermetica survive mainly in medieval Arabic or Latin works that translate lost Greek originals or derive from them. Some of the latter pseudo-Hermetica, most famously the alchemical *Emerald Tablet* of the ninth century and the eleventh-century wizard's manual called *Picatrix* in Latin, became notorious in the Middle Ages and retained their ill fame after the Renaissance. As the author of such infamous texts, the medieval Hermes Trismegistus was a mighty magician, a persona partly in keeping with his Greco-Egyptian pedigree. But the other Hermes, the theologian and philosopher, also revealed himself to the Middle Ages. The medieval *Book of Twenty-Four Philosophers* was a favorite of Bernardus Silvestris and other twelfth-century Christians who also admired the *Asclepius,* reading this originally Greek text in a Latin version known to Augustine.

Marsilio Ficino and Theoretical Hermetism. In both his avatars—the theologian of *Asclepius* and the sorcerer of *Picatrix*—Hermes was famous in later medieval Europe, long before Marsilio Ficino made the theological Hermes even more famous. In 1462, commissioned by Cosimo de' Medici to put all of Plato into Latin, Ficino interrupted that epochal task to translate the *Corpus Hermeticum*—or at least the fourteen treatises contained in the Greek manuscript that Cosimo supplied him. He finished the job in 1463, giving it the title *Pimander;* his translation, first printed in 1471, saw two dozen editions through the next century, while his Latin edition also inspired several vernacular renderings. When Adrien Turnebus produced the first printed Greek text in 1554, he included the treatises missing in Ficino's version. These had begun to circulate in Latin versions by 1507, when Symphorien Champier published Lodovico Lazzarelli's translation of the sixteenth treatise, *Diffinitiones Asclepii* (Definitions of Asclepius). Jacques Lefèvre d'Étaples had brought out the first extended commentary on the Hermetica even earlier, in 1494. When Lefèvre republished in 1505, his commentary connected Ficino's *Pimander* with the *Asclepius* for the first time in the same publication. Reprinted in later editions of Ficino's *Opera omnia,* Lefèvre's commentary has sometimes been mistaken for Ficino's.

In fact, Ficino wrote his most extensive commentary on a Hermetic text before he had seen Cosimo's Greek manuscript. For his short vernacular study *Di Dio et Anima* (Of God and the soul), the medieval *Book of Twenty-Four Philosophers* was a major focus. In this early work from the period after 1456, Ficino found Hermes agreeing with Plato (but not with Ar-istotle) on the power, wisdom, and will of God. A few years later, when he wrote a letter to introduce his *Pimander,* he described Hermes as a king, a priest, and—most of all—a theologian. He did not call Hermes a magus, however, nor did he mention magic in his letter, where Hermes is mainly the author of two theological works: *Asclepius,* which Ficino thought to be about God's will, and *Pimander,* which he read as an account of the power and wisdom of God. What Hermes the theologian said about this triad of divine attributes was enough to convince Ficino to turn briefly from his beloved Plato to this ancient Egyptian sage. He concluded that Hermes was nothing less than "the founder of theology," who passed his invention on to Orpheus and the other ancient theologians who prepared the way for Plato.

That Ficino preferred the theologian in Hermes to the magician is unsurprising: the theoretical Hermetica that he translated, unlike the technical treatises reflected in the medieval pseudepigrapha, have little to say about magic. What Ficino found in his *Pimander* and, for the most part, in *Asclepius* was a theology compatible with Christianity and dependent on Platonism. Later, when he published his philosophical theory of magic in the *Three Books on Life* of 1489, Ficino condemned Hermes for passages in the *Asclepius* on "god-making" or the magical animation of statues. He also reordered the ancient theology to put Hermes after Zoroaster, but Hermetic authority retained the force of its remote antiquity. Despite Ficino's role in promoting that authority, when the Sienese installed Hermes conspicuously among the Sibyls on the paved floor of their cathedral in 1488, they left no clue that a Florentine had given their Egyptian prophet a new voice. The Sienese Hermes is also *Hermes theologus,* the partner of Sibyls and Hebrew prophets in Christian revelation.

Hermetic Influences. Writing his celebrated *De hominis dignitate oratio* (Oration on the dignity of man) in 1487, Giovanni Pico della Mirandola cited *Asclepius* to praise man as "a great wonder" who shares the nature of the gods and other cosmic powers. But this passage of the *Asclepius,* while countering the pervasive Hermetic pessimism and exalting man as master of the elements, also depicts him as despising his human and earthly part in order to attain godhood. Since the *Oration* goes on to recommend an angelic rather than a human life and treats the death of the body as the good of the soul, Pico's ascetic intentions were in keeping with the world-denying Hermetica. The *Oration* also proposes a theory of natural magic and a program of theurgy, but not from Hermetic sources. The *Oration* never mentions Hermes as a magician, and nine of ten Hermetic theses in Pico's *Nine Hundred Conclusions* deal with theology or natural philosophy, only one with divination. Pico used Hermes neither to express original philosophical views nor to confirm the theory of magic announced in the *Oration* and elaborated in the *Conclusions*. He advertised his magic as Orphic and kabbalist, and he found its roots in Neoplatonic and scholastic philosophy.

For Pico and for later Renaissance readers—Francesco Giorgi, Giovanni Nesi, Agostino Steuco, Francesco Patrizi, Giordano Bruno, and many others—the strongest attractions of the Greek Hermetica translated by Ficino and later linked with the Latin *Asclepius* were their venerable age and their evident piety. As long as Christians believed that they came from the time of Moses, the vague religiosity of these badly preserved and sometimes incoherent writings was enough to sustain their author's reputation, even though Hermes had always been seen as a magician as well as a prophet.

The Hermetic literature as a whole—all the technical and theoretical texts, ancient and medieval, original and pseudepigraphal, in all their languages—presented an even more confusing picture, especially when enlarged by Renaissance interpreters. Hermetic influences detected in Philip Sidney, Edmund Spenser, Shakespeare, and others are hard to pin down because the possible sources—including the contemporary critic's imagination—go far beyond Ficino's *Pimander*. By the early seventeenth century, the English word "Hermetic" had come to refer to any kind of dubious occultism, but especially to alchemy. Marin Mersenne's attacks on Robert Fludd excluded this diffuse alchemical Hermetism from the history of philosophy, and Johannes Kepler relegated it to a new category—theosophy. Meanwhile, Isaac Casaubon had proved in 1614 that the surviving Greek Hermetica were of early Christian rather than Mosaic vintage, thus destroying the religious authority that Ficino had prized. But the broader historiographic framework of an ancient theology, which Ficino discovered in the church fathers and transmitted to Pico, Giorgi, Steuco, and others, survived the philological demise of Hermes, so that the doxography of the ancient theologians could still catch Isaac Newton's eye, however briefly, at the end of the seventeenth century.

See also **Magic** and **Astrology** *and biographies of Ficino and Pico della Mirandola.*

BIBLIOGRAPHY

Primary Work

Copenhaver, Brian P., ed. and trans. *Hermetica: The Greek Corpus Hermeticum and the Latin* Asclepius *in a New English Translation.* Cambridge, U.K., and New York, 1992.

Secondary Works

Allen, Michael J. B. "Marsilio Ficino, Hermes Trismegistus, and the *Corpus Hermeticum.*" In *New Perspectives on Renaissance Thought: Essays in the History of Science, Education, and Philosophy in Memory of Charles B. Schmitt.* Edited by John Henry and Sarah Hutton. London, 1990. Pages 38–47.

Copenhaver, Brian P. "Hermes Theologus: The Sienese Mercury and Ficino's Hermetic Demons." In *Humanity and Divinity in Renaissance and Reformation: Essays in Honor of Charles Trinkaus.* Edited by John W. O'Malley, Thomas M. Izbicki, and Gerald Christianson. Leiden, Netherlands, and New York, 1993. Pages 149–182.

Copenhaver, Brian P. "Hermes Trismegistus, Proclus, and the Question of a Philosophy of Magic in the Renaissance." In *Hermeticism and the Renaissance: Intellectual History and the Occult in Early Modern Europe.* Edited by Ingrid Merkel and Allen G. Debus. Washington, D.C., and London, 1988. Pages 79–110.

Copenhaver, Brian P. "Lorenzo de' Medici, Marsilio Ficino, and the Domesticated Hermes." In *Lorenzo il Magnifico e il suo mondo: Convegno internazionale di studi, Firenze 9–13 giugno 1992.* Edited by Gian Carlo Garfagnini. Florence, 1994. Pages 225–257.

Copenhaver, Brian P. "Natural Magic, Hermetism, and Occultism in Early Modern Science." In *Reappraisals of the Scientific Revolution.* Edited by David C. Lindberg and Robert S. Westman. Cambridge, U.K., and New York, 1990. Pages 261–301.

Dannefeldt, K. H. *"Hermetica philosophica."* In *Catalogus translationum et commentariorum: Medieval and Renaissance Latin Translations and Commentaries.* Edited by Paul Oskar Kristeller. Washington, D.C., 1960. Pages 137–164.

Festugière, A.-J. *La révélation d'Hermès Trismégiste.* 4 vols. Paris, 1944–1954.

Fowden, Garth. *The Egyptian Hermes: A Historical Approach to the Late Pagan Mind.* Cambridge, U.K., and New York, 1986.

Garin, Eugenio. *Ermetismo del rinascimento.* Rome, 1988.

Garin, Eugenio. *Il Ritorno dei filosofi antichi.* Naples, 1983.

Grafton, A. "Higher Criticism, Ancient and Modern: The Lamentable Deaths of Hermes and the Sibyls." In *The Uses of Greek and Latin: Historical Essays.* Edited by A. C. Dionisotti et al. London, 1988. Pages 155–170.

Grafton, A. "Protestant versus Prophet: Isaac Casaubon on Hermes Trismegistus." *Journal of the Warburg and Courtauld Institutes* 46 (1983): 78–93.

Hankins, James. *Plato in the Italian Renaissance.* Leiden, Netherlands, and New York, 1990.

Kristeller, Paul Oskar. "Lodovico Lazzarelli e Giovanni da Correggio, due ermetici del Quattrocento, e il manoscritto II.D.1.4 della Biblioteca Comunale degli Ardenti di Viterbo." In *Biblioteca degli Ardenti della città di Viterbo.* Viterbo, Italy, 1960. Pages 3–25.

Kristeller, Paul Oskar. *Studies in Renaissance Thought and Letters.* Rome, 1956

McGuire, J. E., and P. M. Rattansi. "Newton and the Pipes of Pan." *Notes and Records of the Royal Society of London* 21 (1966): 108–143.

Mahé, Jean-Pierre. *Hermès en Haute-Egypte.* 2 vols. Quebec, Canada, 1978–1982.

Nock, A. D., and A.-J. Festugière, eds. *Corpus Hermeticum.* 4 vols. Paris, 1946–1954.

Purnell, F. "Francesco Patrizi and the Critics of Hermes Trismegistus." *Journal of Medieval and Renaissance Studies* 6 (1976): 155–178.

Schmitt, Charles B. "Perennial Philosophy: From Agostino Steuco to Leibniz." *Journal of the History of Ideas* 27 (1966): 505–532.

Vasoli, Cesare. "Francesco Patrizi e la tradizione ermetica." *Nuova rivista storica* 64 (1980): 25–40.

Vasoli, Cesare. "L'hermétisme à Venise, de Giorgio à Patrizi." In *Présence d'Hermès Trismegiste.* Edited by Antoine Faivre et al. Paris, 1988. Pages 120–152.

Vasoli, Cesare. *Profezia e ragione: Studi sulla cultura del Cinquecento e del Seicento.* Naples, 1974.

Vasoli, Cesare. "Temi e fonti della tradizione ermetica in uno scritto di Symphorien Champier." In *Umanesimo e esoterismo.* Edited by Enrico Castelli. Padua, 1960. Pages 235–289.

Vickers, B. "Frances Yates and the Writing of History." *Journal of Modern History* 51 (1979): 287–316.

Walker, D. P. *The Ancient Theology: Studies in Christian Platonism from the Fifteenth to the Eighteenth Century.* London, 1972

Westman, Robert S., and J. E. McGuire. *Hermeticism and the Scientific Revolution: Papers Read at a Clark Library Seminar, March 9, 1974.* Los Angeles, 1977.

Yates, Frances A. *Giordano Bruno and the Hermetic Tradition.* London and Chicago, 1964.

Yates, Frances A. "The Hermetic Tradition in Renaissance Science." In *Art, Science, and History in the Renaissance.* Edited by Charles S. Singleton. Baltimore, 1968. Pages 255–274.

BRIAN P. COPENHAVER

HERRERA, FERNANDO DE

HERRERA, FERNANDO DE (1534–1597), Spanish writer. Fernando de Herrera spent his entire life in Seville, where he was a lay functionary of the church of San Andrés. He was a leading member of the group of writers and artists that met at the house of the conde de Gelves; Herrera's love for Doña Leonor de Milán, condesa de Gelves, was the chief inspiration of his poetry, and *Algunas obras* (Some works; 1582), the only volume of poems published in his lifetime, was probably conceived as a tribute to her memory. Apart from his poetry, he published two short historical works, an account of the Battle of Lepanto (1572) and a life of Sir Thomas More (1592), and the monumental *Anotaciones* (Annotations; 1580) to the poems of Garcilaso de la Vega. The enormous erudition and critical judgement displayed in the *Anotaciones* place Herrera among the great poet-critics of the Renaissance; his application of systematic linguistic criteria, reflected in the scrupulous revisions of his own poems, is a crucial step in the history of Spanish verse between Garcilaso and Luis de Góngora (1561–1627).

Herrera's love poems represent the highest and most original development of the Petrarchan tradition in Spain. Their intricate dialectic draws on many sources, from the psychological abstractions of the *cancioneros* (songbooks) and Ausiàs March to the Neoplatonic subtleties of Baldassare Castiglione and Leone Ebreo; the relationship they explore is conveyed in heroic terms. The lady addressed is given a poetic name—Luz (light) and its variants—which allows him the same kind of play with imagery and association that one finds in the works of Petrarch (for example, Laura, *l'aura,* and so on). Luz can be compared to the sun, to fire, and to the heavens in general: she both fits into the Petrarchan idiom and becomes a symbol of cosmic beauty. Herrera's achievement as a love poet has been obscured until recently by the excessive praise given to his patriotic odes, particularly those on the victory of Lepanto and the destruction of the Portuguese armies at the Battle of Alcázarquivir (1578). These, though they share the same concept of heroism as the love poems, lack the true religious and ethical content that would raise them above the level of accomplished rhetoric.

Herrera's poems exist in three collections: *Algunas obras;* the posthumous *Versos* (Verses), published by Francisco Pacheco in 1619; and the *Rimas inéditas* (Unpublished rhymes; 1578), published by José Manuel Blecua in 1948. These editions present a difficult textual problem that is still unsolved: some poems appear differently in all three volumes, and many only exist in the 1619 text. The question is fully discussed by Macrí, who defends the authenticity of the 1619 text against Blecua, who regards it as a mass of anomalies. Neither side has yet produced conclusive evidence of a definitive edition, and the fact remains that the 1619 edition is the only source for a large number of Herrera's poems, including some of the finest.

BIBLIOGRAPHY

Primary Work
Herrera, Fernando de. *Poesía castellana original completa.* Edited by Cristóbal Cuevas. Madrid, 1985.

Secondary Works
Coster, Adolphe. *Fernando de Herrera.* Paris, 1908.
Macrí, Oreste. *Fernando de Herrera.* Madrid, 1959.

ARTHUR TERRY

HERRERA, JUAN DE

HERRERA, JUAN DE (c. 1530–1597), Spanish architect, engineer, and intellectual. From modest origins and lacking the formal education and training of a master of the works, Juan de Herrera, favorite

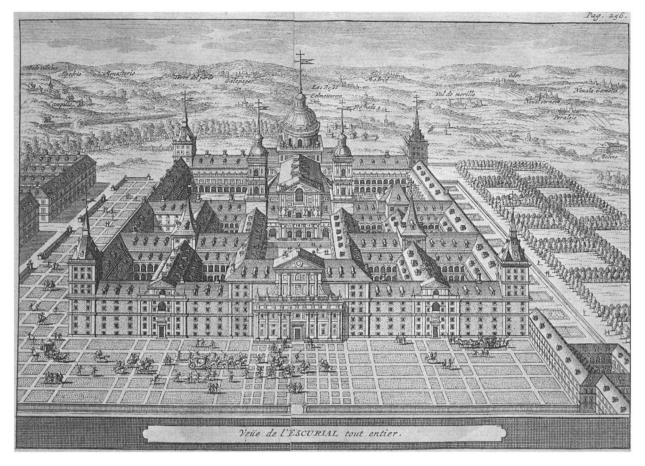

Pag. 256.

Veüe de l'ESCURIAL tout entier.

J. B. de Toledo and Juan de Herrera. Escorial Palace. Herrera succeeded Juan Bautista de Toleda as architect of the Escorial in 1567 and completed the palace in 1584. MUSEO DEL PRADO, MADRID/ORONOZ

of Philip II, became the most famous architect of sixteenth-century Spain. He abandoned the ornate Gothic form and defined a new architectural style, an austere classicism that emphasized geometry and the repetition of form and pattern.

Herrera most probably acquired his practical knowledge of building while in the army in the mid-1550s. Herrera refined his drafting skills and emerged as an architectural talent beginning in 1563 as assistant to Juan Bautista de Toledo, architect of Philip II's most ambitious undertaking, San Lorenzo el Real del Escorial (1563–1584)—a Habsburg mausoleum, a Hieronymite monastery and church, and a royal residence. Soon after Juan Bautista de Toledo's death in 1567, Herrera was charged with continuing the construction of the Escorial, which he brought to completion by 1584. Although he was involved in many components of the complex, such as the redesign of the main staircase (1573), Herrera's most significant contribution was the Basilica of San Lorenzo el Real, begun in 1574. This centrally

planned structure with rectangular transept arms and square-ended chancel has an interior dominated by massive piers supporting a dome above a square crossing, and by an elaborate retable behind the altar.

Herrera was also involved with a number of other architectural projects, most of them associated with the crown. He continued constructing the royal palaces at Aranjuez, the Alcázar in Toledo, and at Granada, the palace of Charles V in the Alhambra. However, his official positions as palace quartermaster and, following 1579, as architect to His Majesty, did not deter him from assisting the newly arrived Jesuits by reviewing plans and offering suggestions in structural matters. Although ecclesiastical commissions did not dominate his architectural works, his designs for rebuilding the cathedral at Valladolid (1578–1586) remain one of his greatest achievements. The building was only half finished, but the monumental rectangular piers of the crossing, the austerity of the interior, and the repetitive subdivision of the exterior massing are a testament to the overall power of Herrera's designs.

Civic commissions, engineering projects, and urban planning further occupied Herrera's professional life. Designs and instructions were provided for a new town hall in Toledo (1574), and in 1585 his advice was sought for a similar structure for Valladolid (1585). In 1582, plans were delivered for the Merchants' Exchange in Seville, a pivotal work, with construction completed in 1598. Herrera also constructed an elaborate water system for the Escorial (1576) and a municipal one at Valladolid (1580s). He was also active as a bridge designer and as a city planner.

Herrera was a true Renaissance man—architect, engineer, writer, philosopher, and mathematician. He found favor with the king and together they shared an intellectual approach to architecture that eliminated ornament and emphasized simple geometry. Although later generations admired Herrera's stark classicism, his architecture was too isolated from contemporary Italian design and too closely associated with a particular time and place in Spain's history ever to be precisely repeated.

See also **Architecture,** *subentry on* **Architecture in the Renaissance.**

BIBLIOGRAPHY

Primary Works

Herrera, Juan de. *Sumario y breve declaracion de los diseños y estampes de la fabrica de San Lorencio el Real del Escurial* (Summary and brief description of the designs and engravings of the building of San Lorenzo el Real del Escurial; Madrid, 1589). In *Las estampas y el sumario de El Escorial por Juan de Herrera.* Edited by Luis Cervera Vera. Madrid, Spain, 1954.

Herrera, Juan de. *Tratado de arquitectura y máquinas* (Treatise on architecture and machines). In *Juan de Herrera, arquitecto de Felipe II.* Edited by Agustín Ruiz de Arcaute. Madrid, Spain, 1936.

Herrera, Juan de. *Tratado del cuerpo cúbico, conforme a los principios y opiniones del 'arte' de Raimundo Lulio* (Treatise on the cube, conforming to the principles and opinions of the "Art" of Raymond Lull). Edited by Julio Rey Pastor. Madrid, Spain, 1935.

Secondary Works

Kubler, George. *Building the Escorial.* Princeton, N.J., 1982.

Wilkinson-Zerner, Catherine. *Juan de Herrera: Architect to Philip II of Spain.* New Haven, Conn., 1994.

MARIA ANN CONELLI

HESSE. The landgrave Ludwig I (1413–1458) made the Hessian house of Brabant a major power. Ludwig bridged the two core areas of Lower Hesse on the Werra River and Upper Hesse on the Lahn and laid claim to the counties of Katzenelnbogen on the Rhine (disputed until the Treaty of Frankfurt in 1557). Ludwig also renewed the important *Erbverbrüderung* (union of great noble houses) with the Saxon Wettin family, Hesse's most important alliance during the Renaissance. His heirs adopted Roman law to facilitate centralization of authority, while at the same time bringing Hesse into conformity with the emperor Maximilian I's policies to gain his support. By 1500 a powerful Hessian state emerged that roughly resembled the present federal state of Hesse. Connected to the world market by the Rhine and its merchants, Hesse produced wool and linen textiles for export as well as grains, raw wool, iron, and salt.

The landgraviate enjoyed its apex of power and prestige under Philipp the Magnanimous (1504–1567), who made it the major protector of the emerging Protestant churches and an opponent of Emperor Charles V's attempts to strengthen Habsburg power. After introducing Lutheran ideas at the Diet of Speyer and Synod of Homberg in 1526, Philipp sought an Evangelical political alliance to defend the new churches. In 1529 he held the Colloquy of Marburg to bring religious unity between the disputing Zwinglians and Lutherans. When Philipp's position was finally adopted in 1531, he played the leading role in the new Schmalkaldic League. However, Philipp's notorious bigamy in 1541 deflated his authority and, along with other factors, led to the defeat of the league and his imprisonment (1547–1552). During Philipp's imprisonment, Charles V imposed the Augsburg Interim, the only Counter-Reformation attempt undertaken in Hesse.

Philipp's testament split Hesse among his four legitimate sons. Growing religious discord and brotherly competition caused division between the regions. The major figures were Wilhelm IV, who ruled Lower Hesse until 1592, and Ludwig IV, who ruled in Upper Hesse until 1604. By 1604, a lack of male heirs resulted in the consolidation of the territory into two parts, Hessen-Kassel and Hessen-Darmstadt. Moritz of Hessen-Kassel (ruled 1592–1627), Wilhelm IV's son, played a prominent role in imperial affairs but led Hesse into the Thirty Years' War.

Many young Hessians attending the University of Erfurt in Thuringia during the early sixteenth century were associated with the prominent Hessian humanist Conrad Mutian (1471–1526), who advocated humanist reforms and involved them in the famous Reuchlin affair. Helius Eobanus Hessus (1488–1540) and Euricius Cordus (1486–1535) began as popular humanistic poets and later taught at Marburg. The major Hessian Reformer and theologian Adam Krafft (1493–1558) and Philipp's chancellor Johann Feige (served 1514–1542) were also associated with this group. Unlike Mutian, these younger men became associated with Martin Luther's teachings.

There were renowned schools in a number of pre-Reformation towns, such as Butzbach, where the nominalist theologian Gabriel Biel (1420–1495) taught prior to his professorship at Erfurt. Philipp promoted the establishment of Latin schools and founded the University of Marburg in 1527 to prepare people to serve in the state and the developing Protestant territorial church. As Hessians split into the hostile Reformed and Lutheran persuasions, the University of Giessen was founded (1605) to serve the latter group, while Marburg became Calvinist. Marburg excelled in the languages (philology), law, theology, and the emerging sciences, including medicine. Johannes Lonicerus (1497–1569) produced new editions of various ancient authors, including Demosthenes, Isocrates, Aristotle, and Galen, and he compiled ancient ideas and reports about meteors. Euricius Cordus conducted empirical studies in botany and pharmacology and attacked astrology. In 1609 Johann Hartmann (1568–1631) gained the first chair in the modern discipline of chemistry.

Wilhelm IV gathered mechanics, clock makers, mathematicians, and astronomers at his Kassel court to conduct empirical studies of the heavens. Such figures as Johannes Schöner (1528–1590), mathematician and son of the famous astronomer of the same name; Christoph Rothmann (1550–1597), a product of Wittenberg and a mathematician and astronomical observer; and Jost Bürgi (1552–1632), a clock maker, collaborated in building precise astronomical instruments and clocks. They improved star charts through rigorously accurate observations. Wilhelm IV's son Moritz drew Paracelsian and hermetic figures to the court to conduct alchemical studies.

The Hessian artistic Renaissance boasted Philipp Soldan of Frankenburg in Upper Hesse, a sculptor and form cutter, and Ludwig Juppe (c. 1460–1538), a Marburg sculptor. Soldan's decorative work in a late Gothic style may be found at the hospital of Haina. Juppe's relief of the coat of arms of the Hessian landgraves with St. Elizabeth may be seen at the entrance to the Marburg city hall. The Marburg University Museums for the Pictorial Arts and for Cultural History contain the best Renaissance collections. Marburg also provides examples of late Gothic architecture.

See also Reuchlin Affair.

BIBLIOGRAPHY

Hillerbrand, Hans J. *Landgrave Philipp of Hesse, 1504–1567: Religion and Politics in the Reformation.* St. Louis, Mo., 1967. The only study of the Hessian landgrave in English.

Moran, Bruce T. *The Alchemical World of the German Court: Occult Philosophy and Chemical Medicine in the Circle of Moritz of Hessen, 1572–1632.* Stuttgart, Germany, 1991. This book provides useful information on the politics and culture of the late sixteenth and early seventeenth centuries in Hesse.

Wright, William J. *Capitalism, the State, and the Lutheran Reformation: Sixteenth-Century Hesse.* Athens, Ohio, 1988.

WILLIAM J. WRIGHT

HESSUS, HELIUS EOBANUS (Eoban Koch; 1488–1540), German Neo-Latin poet, university professor. In his time Hessus was considered the foremost Latin poet in Germany. His linguistic virtuosity, his boldness in pioneering new literary genres, and his vast classical learning earned him such titles as "the German Ovid," "the German David," and "king of the poets."

Hessus's father was a peasant. Hessus himself was born in Halgehausen, Hesse, and enrolled in 1504 at the University of Erfurt. He received his B.A. in 1506 and his M.A. in 1509 and soon joined the circle of friends around Mutianus Rufus (1470–1526) in nearby Gotha. After writing two poems dealing with university life in Erfurt, Hessus entered the literary scene with the *Bucolicon* (Bucolic poem; 1509), a work that introduced the genre of the eclogue into German Neo-Latin literature. In eleven poems, shepherds—linked, by veiled allusions, to Hessus's Erfurt friends and to himself—discuss love, everyday concerns, and political events. Equally innovative for Germany was his *Heroidum Christianarum epistolae* (Letters of Christian heroines; 1514). Modeled on Ovid's *Heroides,* Hessus's work consists of twenty-two letters by female saints, some actual, some figures only of legend. Between 1509 and 1513, Hessus had been in the service of Hiob von Dobeneck, bishop of Pomerania in East Prussia. After brief stays at the universities of Frankfurt-an-der-Oder and Leipzig, Hessus returned to Erfurt, where he became the undisputed "king," as Johann Reuchlin called him, of the Erfurt humanists. Hessus together with some other Erfurt friends visited Erasmus, the hero of the German humanists, in Louvain. Within two years, however, his enthusiasm for Erasmus turned into ardor for Martin Luther, whose brief stay in Erfurt in April 1521 Hessus celebrated in a number of enthusiastic elegies.

In spite of his literary reputation, Hessus's economic situation always had been precarious. To improve his chances of providing an adequate standard of living for his growing family, he took up the study of medicine in 1523. Although he never obtained a medical degree, he produced a poem, *Bonae valetudinis conservandae praecepta* (Precepts to retain good health; 1524), that went into numerous editions. Economic reasons also prompted him to accept an invitation in 1526 to teach at the newly founded Gymnasium of Saint Aegidius in Nürnberg, where he stayed until 1533. During that time he published a masterful praise of Nürnberg, dedicated to the city council: *Urbs Noribergae illustrata carmine heroico* (Nürnberg glorified in heroic verse; 1532). After another three years in Erfurt, he was appointed professor at the University of Marburg. During that time his last major works were published: a Latin verse paraphrase of the entire Psalms (1537), a work that was to go through fifty reprints by the end of the century, and an admirably skillful metrical translation of the *Iliad* (1540).

Hessus left a large and multifaceted work. By the end of the sixteenth century, however, his fame, like that of the other humanists, began to be eclipsed by the rising vernacular literature.

BIBLIOGRAPHY

Primary Work

Hessus, Helius Eobanus. *Dichtungen der Jahre 1528–1537.* Edited and translated by Harry Vredeveld. Bern, Germany, 1990. See Vredeveld, "Eobanus Hessus" (below), for an excellent bibliography of primary sources.

Secondary Works

Kleineidam, Erich. "Helius Eobanus Hessus." In *Contemporaries of Erasmus.* Vol. 1. Toronto, 1985. Pages 434–436.

Krause, Karl. *Helius Eobanus Hessus, sein Leben und seine Werke: Ein Beitrag zur Cultur- und Gelehrtengeschichte des 16. Jahrhunderts.* 2 vols. Gotha, Germany, 1879. Reprint, Nieuwkoop, Netherlands, 1963. Classic study of Eobanus Hessus; still valuable.

Vredeveld, Harry. "Eobanus Hessus." In *Dictionary of Literary Biography.* Vol. 179, *German Writers of the Renaissance and Reformation, 1280–1580.* Edited by James Hardin and Max Reinhart. Detroit, Mich.; Washington, D.C.; and London; 1997. Pages 97–110. Best article in English, with detailed primary and secondary literature.

ECKHARD BERNSTEIN

HILLIARD, NICHOLAS (1547–1619), goldsmith and miniature painter from Exeter, son and grandson of successful goldsmiths. From age nine Hilliard was educated in the household of the wealthy Protestant merchant John Bodley (whose son, Thomas, founded the eponymous library at Oxford), with whom, under the Catholic queen, Mary, he fled to Geneva in 1557. In November 1562 Hilliard was apprenticed to Robert Brandon, Queen Elizabeth's goldsmith and jeweler. In July 1569 he became a freeman of the Goldsmiths' Company and established business with his brother. He gained access to the court, painting his first dated miniature, *Elizabeth I,* in 1572 (London, National Portrait Gallery).

In 1576 Hilliard married Brandon's daughter, Alice, and journeyed to Paris to make his fortune. He served François, duc d'Alençon, moved in the artistic circle surrounding King Henry II, painted miniatures, and created goldwork, but failed to become rich. He returned to London in 1578–1579, and from 1580 to 1584 painted miniatures for the queen and members of the court. In 1584 he was commissioned, together with Derick Anthony, graver of the mint, to make the second great seal for the queen, which engaged his skills as a portraitist and a goldsmith. Hilliard continued to serve the court under James I, who in 1617 granted him a monopoly for twelve years to make, engrave, and imprint royal portraits.

Hilliard's miniatures are usually circular or oval, and depict the sitter in three-quarter view. They are intimate objects, intended to be examined closely or worn as personal adornments. Created for an elite clientele, they often highlight the sitter's lavish costume and jewelry, and are themselves jewels, frequently encased in elegantly wrought goldwork embellished with gems. Hilliard likely made both pictures and frames—the *Armada Jewel* (c. 1588; London, Victoria and Albert) is probably his. The age of the sitter, date, and sometimes Hilliard's signature appear in the field in calligraphy. Hilliard also made jewelry proper—rings, medallions, gold tablets, and richly adorned cases for miniatures, some set with gems, others enameled—and apparently painted in oil. He acknowledged his artistic debt to Hans Holbein the Younger and Albrecht Dürer, whose linear style, fine detail, and strong lighting he echoed.

Hilliard received great praise from contemporaries at home and abroad, and enhanced his renown through *A Treatise Concerning the Arte of Limning* (miniature-painting), preserved in a posthumous manuscript copy of 1624. Hilliard's *Treatise* describes his working methods, life, and personality, and position vis-à-vis contemporary artistic developments in England and Europe. Hilliard reiterates that miniature painting is "fittest for gentlemen": a limner must paint in a well-lit room, in silk clothes to avoid shedding lint on miniatures, his aesthetic impulses quickened by fine perfume, good books read aloud, or music.

A superb artist, Hilliard was also a colorful personality, perpetually seduced by moneymaking

A Miniature by Hilliard. Portrait of Queen Elizabeth I, 1572. By courtesy of the National Portrait Gallery, London

schemes and questionable characters, and consistently failing to attain financial security or pay his debts promptly; indeed, he was briefly imprisoned in 1617 for standing surety on an unpaid debt.

Hilliard's most famous and successful pupils were Isaac Oliver, with whose work his has often been confused despite their distinct styles, and his own son Laurence, who followed his father's path as a goldsmith and "his Majesty's limner."

BIBLIOGRAPHY

Primary Work
Hilliard, Nicholas. *A Treatise Concerning the Arte of Limning.* Edited by Robert K. Thornton et al. Manchester, U.K., 1992.

Secondary Works
Auerbach, Erna. *Nicholas Hilliard.* London, 1961.
Edmond, Mary. *Hilliard and Oliver.* London, 1983.

MARINA BELOZERSKAYA

HIPPOCRATES OF COS (c. 450–c. 370 B.C.E.), Greek physician considered the father of Western medicine. Very little is known about Hippocrates himself except that he was born on the island of Cos and died in Larissa. His contemporary Plato (428–347 B.C.E.) says that Hippocrates became famous in his own lifetime for teaching medicine on Cos. Although few traces of his personal life remain, much

of what is known about the development of ancient Greek medicine is taken from about sixty treatises once traditionally attributed to Hippocrates. Today only a few can be directly linked to Hippocrates himself, but they are still referred to by historians as the Hippocratic Corpus, or body of writings. The treatises were largely brought together at Alexandria in Egypt around 280 B.C.E. and range broadly over such subjects as physiology, epidemiology, gynecology, and surgery. Included are the *Aphorisms,* or short sayings, of Hippocrates that may have been used in teaching, and the Hippocratic Oath that is still used in many Western medical schools today, with its famous advice to new physicians, "First, do no harm." (Hippocrates probably did not write the oath, but it does represent his beliefs.)

Several themes recur in the writings. They include the discounting of magical, theological, and mythological explanations of health and their replacement by rational ones. For instance, the author of one of the most famous treatises, *The Sacred Disease,* attacks popular superstitions about epilepsy, stating that it is not a disease sent by the gods, but one that is inherited. These writings also attach particular importance to the medical skill of prognosis—the ability to observe the signs of the body and recommend treatment based on these findings. The *Prognostics* addresses the necessity of observing the patient's entire body and examining samples of sputum, vomit, stool, and, in particular, urine, for signs of an imbalance of humors.

Later Development. The Hippocratic Corpus presents three conceptions of medicine: as a craft to be learned by apprenticeship or passed from parent to child; as a body of natural knowledge; and, as demonstrated in the Hippocratic Oath, as a moral way of life. These ideas were later incorporated, to a great extent, by the Greco-Roman doctor Galen of Pergamum (A.D. 129–199) into his enormous synthesis of the art and practice of medicine, which remained influential for centuries. Some Hippocratic treatises were translated from Greek into Arabic by Islamic writers from the eighth to the tenth century. They were then translated into Latin by a North African Benedictine monk, Constantine (fl. 1065–1085), at the monastery of Monte Cassino in southern Italy.

By the twelfth century, four works, *Aphorisms, Prognostics, On Regimen in Acute Diseases,* and *Epidemics,* were required study as part of the medical curriculum at the universities of Montpellier, Paris, and Bologna. Degree candidates were required to comment on (explain) passages from them as part of their oral examinations. Finally, in 1525 the first humanist Latin edition of Hippocrates was printed, and a year later a Greek edition was published by the Aldine Press in Venice. These were followed by numerous Latin editions of the commentaries by Galen on individual Hippocratic treatises and by other Renaissance authors.

The writings of Hippocrates influenced Renaissance medicine in several ways. He was praised by the German alchemist and physician Paracelsus (1493–1541) as a healer guided by clinical experience rather than by book learning. This image of Hippocrates as the great observer at the bedside was adopted and taught in the eighteenth century by Professor Hermann Boerhaave (1668–1738) at the University of Leiden in the Netherlands, then spread as his English, Scottish, and Irish students returned to their countries and practiced these teachings. The writings remained part of standard medical training until the beginning of the nineteenth century. By that time, the Hippocratic Corpus was slowly being eliminated from medical education and replaced by descriptions of patients' cases and clinical observations.

See also **Galen**; **Medicine**.

BIBLIOGRAPHY

Primary Works

Hippocrates. *Hippocrates*. 4 vols. Translated by W. H. S. Jones (vol. 3 by E. T. Withington). Cambridge, Mass., 1957–1959.

Lloyd, G. E. R., ed. *Hippocratic Writings*. New York, 1986. Translation of *Aphorisms* and selected treatises from the Hippocratic Corpus.

Secondary Works

Hanson, Ann Ellis. "Hippocrates: Diseases of Women." *SIGNS* 1 (1975): 567–584.

Siraisi, Nancy G. *Medieval and Renaissance Medicine*. Chicago, 1990.

Smith, Wesley D. *The Hippocratic Tradition*. Ithaca, N.Y., 1979.

Temkin, Oswei. *Hippocrates in a World of Pagans and Christians*. Baltimore, Md., 1991.

LYNDA STEPHENSON PAYNE

HISTORICAL THEMES IN RENAISSANCE ART.

In portraying the recent past, Renaissance artists sought less to record the details of a particular event than to convey its essence and historical significance. Usually commissioned and intended for a specific site or audience, their creations of necessity gave voice both to patrons' aims and to artists' wishes and styles. At the same time, they were also profoundly shaped by prevailing views about the purposes of representing history. Following the ancient Roman writers Cicero and Livy, Renaissance intellectuals valued history above all for the lessons it taught. Drawing upon stories of exemplary figures and their famous deeds, such as those that the classical authors Plutarch and Valerius Maximus had recounted, humanists and artists fashioned a conceptual vocabulary for celebrating contemporary heroes and their virtuous acts. Conversely, contemporary figures and events could be most edifying when dignified and magnified by association with glorious antecedents. Thus adorned, they could better inspire admiration and imitation. Such was the case for the various types of history painting: contemporary history, Roman history (which offered *exempla,* models of heroic action), and chivalric histories (which used simile to exalt contemporary heroes). Each genre evoked a different response, and the site of the painting may have helped determine the genre.

Ancient History and the Present. In part because of these priorities, verisimilitude was among the first casualties in Renaissance depictions of warfare. For example, in the three panels Paolo Uccello (1397–1475) painted (probably in the 1450s) of the Battle of San Romano in 1432 for the Medici, he displayed a genius for perspective. Technical expertise notwithstanding, however, he portrayed that encounter between Florentine and Luccan troops very unrealistically, almost as a chivalric pageant, including a ceremonial procession entering from one side. [For two of Uccello's panels, see the color plates in volume 6 and the entry on Warfare, also in volume 6.] In general, idealized depictions of skirmishes and of heroic personal encounters, exhibiting refinement and harmony and aimed at inspiring the viewer, triumphed over the inclination toward straightforward depiction of any given battle's actual strategy and tactics.

If the instructive purpose of history militated against depicting any enduring image of failure, so too did the exigencies of patronage. Following the Battle of Pavia (24 February 1525), in which an imperial army defeated an alliance including French troops and captured their leader, King Francis I, some of the victors commissioned elaborate works of art. Thus the marquis del Vasto, an Italian who had fought for the imperial side, commissioned a south Netherlands artist, Bernaert van Orley, to design a series of seven tapestries of the battle. The defeated, by contrast, gave Pavia scant artistic attention. More generally, the shifting alliances, military disasters, and dependency that marked Italian politics in the early sixteenth century narrowed the scope for heroic action that one could comfortably

The Pope Crowns the Emperor. Clement VII crowns Charles V at Bologna, 1530. Charles was the last Holy Roman Emperor crowned by the pope. Ceiling painting (1560s) by Baccio Bandinelli and Giovanni Caccini in the Salone di Cinquecento in the Palazzo Vecchio, Florence. PALAZZO VECCHIO, FLORENCE/ALINARI/ART RESOURCE

celebrate and commemorate. As a result, those years saw few Italian commissions for works of art that explicitly depicted contemporary battle scenes.

Even then, however, artists sought to dignify contemporary figures by depicting scenes of the distant past in ways that highlighted their relevance in the present. For example, Raphael's fresco of the *Expulsion of Heliodorus from the Temple,* properly a biblical subject, in the Vatican *stanze,* portrays his patron, Pope Julius II (reigned 1503–1513), as a witness to the scene, and the later fresco of the *Repulse of Attila,* completed by Giulio Romano, depicts Pope Leo I with the features of Julius's successor, Leo X (reigned 1513–1521). Whether or not such details were intended to allude to specific contemporary events (that is, in the latter instance, to the defeat of the French at the Battle of Ravenna in 1512), they bolstered with historical parallels the claims that Renaissance popes were making on behalf of the Papal States.

In representing historical events, Renaissance artists appropriated ancient and medieval exemplars and transformed their imagery so as to display the values and claims to power that characterized their own age. If classical Rome bequeathed to them its artistic celebrations of rulers' accomplishments (for example, the reliefs in the Arch of Constantine), the Middle Ages contributed a proliferation of saints' lives that offered alternative patterns for representing greatness. Renaissance artists drew upon and creatively modified these models and others in their works for private and for public sites, and on behalf of both ecclesiastical and secular patrons. By the latter half of the fifteenth century in Italy, painted narratives of recent events became commonplace in all of these contexts, which often overlapped or coalesced in ways that defy easy categorization.

Portraying Noble Deeds. Frescoes commissioned for patricians' residences came to focus upon a particular noteworthy deed or event in the patron's recent past, such as a military conquest or a royal visitation. For example, the Palazzo di Poggioreale in Naples, built after 1483 but no longer standing, contained numerous frescoes of the war of King Ferrante (Ferdinand I, reigned 1458–1494) with local barons. Such paintings not only recorded a regionally important event but could also promote a flattering interpretation of the patron's role in that event. Subsequently there developed cycles that narrated several discrete heroic moments in the patron's military career. For example, frescoes of Niccolò Orsini in his palazzo in Ghedi (executed c. 1506–1509) portrayed his appointment to prestigious commands by Pope Innocent VIII (1489), Alfonso II of Naples (1494), and a Doge of Venice (1495). A few decades later, Girolamo Genga designed a similar cycle for the Villa Imperiale in Pesaro to celebrate the career of the duke of Urbino, Francesco Maria della Rovere, calling attention to his prominent military appointments and to his distinguished position near the emperor Charles V at the latter's coronation ceremony in Bologna (1530). Clearly such images were intended not just to record events but to stimulate admiration and, in the case of heirs, emulation.

Two fresco cycles devoted to the biographies of popes broke with the above pattern: a series in the Ospedale di Santo Spirito in Rome that depicts the life of Sixtus IV and another in the Piccolomini Library in Siena that relates the biography of Pius II. [For two frescoes from the Piccolomini Library see the entries on Crusade in volume 2 and the Papacy in volume 4.] The former series, painted 1476–1480, appropriated the hagiographical tradition to depict the life story of Sixtus IV even as he reigned as pontiff. Beginning with his mother's dream in which Saints Anthony and Francis appeared to announce that her future son would become a Franciscan, it went on to detail various miracles from his youth before proceeding to his ecclesiastical career. After five frames left blank to accommodate further accomplishments, the cycle ended with two finished paintings, the final one showing St. Peter welcoming Sixtus into paradise. The less audacious frescoes of the life of Pius II by Pinturicchio were commissioned by Pius's nephew in 1502, decades after the pope's death. Designed in part by Raphael, the series emphasizes those scenes that could be depicted most beautifully. The accompanying inscriptions serve less to interpret the paintings than to provide critical information about Pius's life story that the frescoes have left out, such as his parentage and place of birth. Thus, a less miraculous narrative inspires through its beauty as well as through the deeds it portrays.

History in the Service of Politics. In 1519 or 1520, Pope Leo X (Giovanni de' Medici; reigned 1513–1521) commissioned a series of innovative historical frescoes for the Medici villa at Poggio a Caiano. Like other Italian art of the unsettled early sixteenth century, these paintings avoided the direct representation of current political events. Designed substantially by the humanist Paolo Giovio, the program cloaked Medicean dynastic pretensions in ancient garb that had been cut from whole cloth to serve present purposes. Thus a fresco by Franciabigio (Francesco di Cristofano) alluded to the return of Cosimo "il Vecchio" de' Medici from exile in 1434 by showing Cicero returning to Rome in triumph. In this fictitious account, the Roman statesman was portrayed with the physiognomy not of Cicero or even of Cosimo, but of Giuliano de' Medici, the duke of Nemours (1479–1516), who had re-entered Florence when the Medici returned to power there in 1512. Elsewhere in the cycle, Andrea del Sarto dignified Lorenzo "il Magnifico" de' Medici by depicting Julius Caesar receiving as tribute some exotic animals, a scene that recalled a similar gift in 1487 from Egypt to the Florentine government and to the person of Lorenzo. Painted not long before Leo X's death and at a point when the line of Medicean succession in Florence was far from clear (Giuliano, duke of Nemours, had died in 1516, and Lorenzo, duke of Urbino, in 1519), the cycle affirmed the continuity of Medicean genealogy and power at a point when both appeared to be in jeopardy.

Once ensconced as grand dukes of Tuscany, the Medici commissioned works of art that represented their grandeur and authority with a new explicitness and that overtly coopted public sites to portray the family's dynastic continuity. When Grand Duke Cosimo I de Medici hired Giorgio Vasari to decorate the Palazzo Vecchio in Florence, the artist and his workshop between 1555 and 1572 produced close to one hundred separate painted scenes that covered the walls of that public building, which had once been the nerve center of the Florentine Republic. Just as the frescoes appropriated the building's visual spaces on behalf of Cosimo I, so too the scenes that they portrayed arrogated Florentine history to the Medici and elided its story with the family's genealogy. The walls of the Salone dei Cinquecento, the sprawling room that had housed a new governing council after the Medici were exiled in 1494, were now devoted to chronicling episodes of war. Elsewhere in the building, entire rooms were given over to depicting the lives and deeds of exemplary Medici forebears, including the recent popes Leo X and Clement VII (Giulio de' Medici; reigned 1523–1534). In an effort to fix down the program's potentially confusing wealth of images, Vasari produced a guidebook that explained the "correct" readings of the frescoes. In sum, in this one sweeping project Vasari sought to commingle private and public historical themes and to encompass both sacred and secular forms of authority. He also attempted to harness the cultural resources at his disposal so as to glorify not only his patron, but also himself as the artist whose genius lay behind the iconographical program.

Unanswered Questions. Artists, like humanists, could at times sneak subversive subtexts past unsubtle patrons. Indeed, the intentions of Cosimo I and Vasari, the interplay between them, and the levels of meaning in the frescoes all remain open to scholarly debate. For example, in the room devoted to the biography of Clement VII, what is the meaning of the curiously unspecific fresco of Clement's "return" to Rome, which Vasari does not explicate very far? Clement's pontificate was disastrous, and although officially Vasari might have been glorifying it anyway, he might also have been subtly reminding viewers of its deficiencies.

When we know less of a painting's provenance and purpose, the complexities of possible interpretations only multiply. For example, Peter Brueghel the Elder's paintings of *The Massacre of the Innocents* have frequently been taken as a protest against Spanish oppression in the Netherlands and specifically against the duke of Alba, who tolerated or approved many atrocities. Some evidence suggests, however, that the paintings may have been done before the arrival of Alba's troops in Brussels in 1567. If that is correct, then what is the significance of the oppressive military presence they depict?

These questions serve to remind us that elaborate depictions of historical events in the Renaissance had multiple meanings. Shaped by patrons' and artists' ideological and aesthetic wishes, limited by material constraints, and executed with a particular audience in mind, they could incorporate a range of conflicting elements, express ambivalent messages, and at times even transform the cultural settings for which they were created.

See also **Armada, Spanish; Chivalry; Classical Antiquity, Discovery of; Crusade; Historiography; Lepanto, Battle of; Monarchy; Naval Warfare; Nepotism; Parades, Processions, and Pageants; Pazzi Conspiracy; Religious Themes in Renaissance Art; Republicanism; Ritual, Civic; Royal Iconography; Trent, Council of; Warfare; Wars of Religion.**

BIBLIOGRAPHY

Brown, Patricia Fortini. *Venice and Antiquity: The Venetian Sense of the Past.* New Haven and London, 1997.

Hale, J. R. *Artists and Warfare in the Renaissance.* New Haven, Conn., and London, 1990.

Kliemann, Julian-Matthias. *Gesta Dipinte: La grande decorazione nelle dimore italiane dal Quattrocento al Seicento.* Milan, 1993. An exceptionally valuable study of ancestral fresco cycles in Italian patrician residences during the Renaissance.

McGrath, Elizabeth. *Rubens: Subjects from History.* 2 vols. London, 1997. Chapter One, "Themes and Traditions," gives an overview of Renaissance appropriations of historical sources and *exempla.* Pages 33–54.

Rubin, Patricia Lee. *Giorgio Vasari: Art and History.* New Haven, Conn., and London, 1995.

Starn, Randolph, and Loren Partridge. *Arts of Power: Three Halls of State in Italy, 1300–1600.* Berkeley and Los Angeles, 1992. A theoretically sophisticated interpretation of the politics of representation and the representation of politics.

KENNETH GOUWENS

HISTORIOGRAPHY, CLASSICAL. [This entry includes three subentries:

Classical Historians (an overview)
Greek Historians
Roman Historians]

Classical Historians

In an age that prized the example of classical antiquity, the reading and appropriation of ancient historians combined, in the best classical tradition, utility and pleasure: edification, aesthetic and emotional enjoyment, political instruction, and scholarly reflection, as well as a solid training in Latin and Greek. The literary accounts of these historians were the principal sources for knowledge of the ancient world, especially in the spheres of government, diplomacy and warfare, customs, and religion. They provided education for private and public life and material for both critical studies and creative adaptations. From stories of noble deeds and heinous crimes, vividly described in the pages of ancient histories, readers learned patterns of conduct to emulate or shun. Speeches and letters, often extracted from the histories and collected in separate compendia, offered models for public orations and epistles, and vicarious experience for leisure reading. Portraits of famous men and women, heroes and villains, inspired works of Renaissance poetry, art, and drama, as well as conspiracies and tyrannicides.

If history was "philosophy teaching by example"—as Renaissance writers, quoting Dionysius of Halicarnassus, liked to repeat—nowhere was this exemplary role more important than in Renaissance historiography. The renewed interest in secular causation and the concern for making history memorable and persuasive fostered a sense of affinity between the "modern" authors and their ancient predecessors. Whether writing in Latin or the vernacular, Renaissance historians imitated, or emulated, format and style and adapted to their own ends the themes, character studies, and explanatory models of classical histories.

Transmission and Diffusion. Many of the Latin historical writers, who in a broad sense include authors of biographies, exempla, and military or technical manuals—Julius Caesar, Sallust, Livy, Valerius Maximus, Suetonius, Curtius Rufus, Florus, Frontinus, and Justinus—were familiar to Latin readers in the Middle Ages either directly or through florilegia (collections of excerpts) and short summaries of their work preserved in late antique epitomes and early Christian histories. As knowledge of the Greek language had virtually disappeared from most of western Europe, however, one could learn about Greek historians only through references in the Latin writers. Pliny the Elder and Aulus Gellius transmitted a wealth of material from the Greek historians, while Cicero and Quintilian discussed the style and merits of, among others, Herodotus, Thucydides, and Xenophon. Only the *History of the Jewish War* of Flavius Josephus and Eusebius's *Chronicle* were known directly, the first through late antique Latin translations and Hebrew paraphrases, the second in the influential Latin version of St. Jerome.

From the early fourteenth century onward, little-known texts of Latin writers, or missing portions of their work, were beginning to resurface. The humanist movement encouraged a return to the sources, and Renaissance manuscript hunters added substantially to the corpus of all Latin historians. Works that had not been independently transmitted also became the focus of scholarly attention. In the sixteenth century many fragments from Cato the Elder and the early Roman annalists, as well as from Caesar's *Commentaries* and Sallust's *Histories,* were assiduously culled from quotations and references in late antique grammarians and scholiasts (commentators).

The extraordinary efforts of Petrarch and Landolfo Colonna at Avignon in the late 1320s to reconstitute the text of Livy's history marked the beginning of modern scholarly studies of the Latin historians. In the following century, Lorenzo Valla added his own annotations to Petrarch's copy of Livy, while working at the court of Alfonso I of Naples, and composed emendations of Books 21–26. Florentine humanists, including Coluccio Salutati, Niccolò Niccoli, and Poggio Bracciolini, took an interest in the Beneventan codex of Tacitus, and Angelo Poliziano worked on Suetonius. In humanist circles of northern Italy, Angelo Decembrio, Guarino Guarini (Guarino da Verona), Gasparino and Guiniforte Barzizza, and Aulo Giano Parrasio copied and/or annotated the commentaries of Caesar. Closer reading of the texts in turn stimulated curiosity about the lives and characters of the authors. Petrarch wrote a biography of Julius Caesar (early 1370s), and brief vitae of Latin historians were included in the early humanist collections of *viri illustres* (lives of illustrious men) by Fra Giovanni Colonna (1330–1338), Guglielmo da Pastrengo (before 1350), and Sicco Polenton (c. 1437).

A revival of Greek studies was also under way. Petrarch probably knew the Greek historians he mentions (Herodotus, Thucydides, Xenophon, Polybius, and Plutarch) only through Latin writers. But in 1397, at the invitation of Coluccio Salutati, Manuel Chrysoloras began teaching Greek in Florence, and a number of his students, including Leonardo Bruni and Guarino Guarini, later translated works of Plutarch, Xenophon, Polybius, and others. The translation of Plutarch had a special place in Chrysoloras's school: if only for the sake of reading Plutarch, he believed, it was worth the effort to master the Greek language. The arrival of Greek manuscripts, brought into Italy from Constantinople and other parts of the Byzantine Empire from this time on, further encouraged the study of Greek historians. Biographical data for these authors, however, was less easily accessible than it was for the Latin historians: in the fifteenth century only a short life of Plutarch, based on the fictitious account in John of Salisbury's *Polycraticus* (completed in 1159), had some diffusion, notably through the encyclopedias of Domenico di Bandino (before 1418) and John Whethamstede (1439–1444).

An important impetus to the study of Greek historians came from the humanist pope Nicholas V (1447–1455), who commissioned several major translations: Appian's *Roman History* by Pier Candido Decembrio; the surviving books of Diodorus Siculus's universal history, *Bibliotheke,* by Poggio Bracciolini and Jacopo da San Cassiano; Polybius, Books 1–5, by Niccolò Perotti; and Herodotus and Thucydides by Lorenzo Valla. It was also thanks to Nicholas that the translation of Arrian, made by Pier Paolo Vergerio the Elder for the emperor Sigismund in Vienna in the 1430s, was copied and brought to Italy.

Closely associated with the art of translation was the practice of reconstructing lost accounts of ancient history from other, surviving sources or of summarizing a historical work. Bruni, for example, composed a history of the First Punic War from Polybius, Diodorus, and others to supplement the missing books in Livy, while his *Commentaria rerum graecarum* (History of Greece; 1439) was a Latin adaptation of Xenophon's *Hellenica.* Sir Henry Savile added a few introductory pages on Nero's downfall to his English version of Tacitus's *Histories* (1591) to fill in the part of the account missing from the *Annals*.

Printed editions. With the advent of printing, the Roman historians were among the first authors to go to press; indeed, throughout the Renaissance, they remained high on the list of most-published writers. Caesar's *Commentaries* and Livy's *History*, both printed in Rome in 1469 by Konrad Sweynheym and Arnold Pannartz, were followed by Sallust's monographs (Venice: Windelin of Speyer, 1470) and Tacitus's *Germania* (Bologna: Azoguido, 1472), *Histories, Annals* 11–16, *Germania* and *Dialogus* (Venice: Windelin, c. 1473), and *Agricola* (Milan: Zaroto, c. 1482). The year 1470 also witnessed the first edition of Plutarch's *Lives* in Latin translation (Rome: Ulrich Han). In the following decades, humanists supplied printers with newly discovered or what they considered to be better manuscripts and improved editions of the texts: Pomponio Leto for Sallust (1490), Marc'Antonio Sabellico for Livy (1491), Fra Giocondo and Janus Lascaris for Sallust (1509; printed by Aldo Manuzio), Filippo Beroaldo the Younger for Tacitus (1515), and Beatus Rhenanus for Velleius Paterculus (1515).

By the early sixteenth century the first printed editions of the Greek historians began to appear: Thucydides and Herodotus (1502); Xenophon, *Hellenica* (1503); Xenophon, *Anabasis* (1516); Plutarch's *Lives* (1517), published by the Giunti in Florence; Polybius 1–5, printed in Haguenau in 1530; and the *Excerpta antiqua* (surviving excerpts from Polybius, Books 6–18) in Basel in 1549. Aldo Manuzio not only produced a large number of Greek editions using the first serviceable Greek printing types (from 1495) but, with the collaboration of the Greeks Janus Lascaris and Marcus Musurus, his principal editor, he made his press an important center for Greek scholarship. It was only later in the sixteenth century, however, that significant contributions to establishing the texts of Latin and Greek historians were made by European scholars such as Johann Rivius (Sallust, 1539), Carlo Sigonio (Livy, 1555), Fulvio Orsini (Caesar, 1570), Ludovicus Carrio (fragments of Sallust's *Histories*, 1573), Justus Lipsius (Tacitus, 1574, 1579, etc., to 1607), Joachim Camerarius (Xenophon, 1543, 1556 and 1572; Thucydides, 1548), Johann Löwenklau (Xenophon, 1569), and Henri Estienne (Xenophon, 1561; Thucydides, 1564 and 1588; Herodotus, 1566).

Study of the texts. The study of Latin historians constituted one of the core subjects in humanist schools, closely linked to the study of grammar, po-

etry, moral philosophy, and rhetoric. According to Pier Paolo Vergerio the Elder, the study of history was indeed the first or central discipline among the liberal arts. As instruction in Greek was gradually introduced, the works of Greek historians also became part of the humanist curriculum. Commentaries designed for teaching typically included a simple explication of the text (especially important for Greek authors), brief explanations of historical facts and personages, moral lessons, and advice on the cultivation of classical discourse. More specialized philological commentaries, intended especially for fellow scholars and often accompanying critical editions of the text, became more prevalent in the sixteenth century. The notes identified sources, traced the etymology of words and literary parallels (for example, between Sallust and Cato the Elder or Thucydides or between Tacitus and Sallust), and debated variant readings and emendations. Other scholars introduced brief digressions or appendices on ancient laws, customs, religion, chronology, and military institutions. Editions and commentaries frequently included a brief biography of the author (often based on earlier manuscript vitae), summarizing aspects of his personal and public life and literary accomplishments.

The growing knowledge of ancient historians and interest in antiquarian and philological studies induced scholars to take a more critical view of evidence and to compare literary accounts with nonliterary sources (such as codes of law, coins, inscriptions, and archaeological remains), as well as with each other. At the turn of the fifteenth century, Coluccio Salutati rejected the traditional account of Caesar's foundation of Florence in favor of evidence for an earlier Republican dating in Cicero and Sallust. Leonardo Bruni, dissatisfied with Plutarch's "Life of Cicero," supplemented it with material from other sources, notably Sallust and Cicero's letters, in his immensely popular *Cicero novus* (New Cicero; 1415). The discovery in Rome in 1546 of the Capitoline Fasti (lists of Roman consuls and *triumphators*) sparked a learned debate between Carlo Sigonio and Heinrich Loriti (Glareanus) over Livy's chronology. A few scholars, however, like Annio da Viterbo, were also capable of producing forgeries or imaginative reconstructions of ancient historians, such as Fabius Pictor and Cato the Elder. Moreover, while historians frequently challenged medieval legends, they were usually more interested in annotating and publishing than in questioning the authorship of such classical texts as the *Invective against Cicero* and *Letters to Caesar*, attributed to Sallust, the books attached to Caesar's *Commentaries* of the Gallic and civil wars, or the *Institutio Traiani* (Education of Trajan) attributed to Plutarch in John of Salisbury's *Polycraticus*.

Vernacular versions. In the meantime, vernacular versions were introducing Latin historical literature to a broader, more diversified public. The earliest versions of Latin historians originated in France, notably the *Faits des Romains* (Deeds of the Romans; c. 1214), compiled from Suetonius, Sallust, Caesar, and Lucan (subsequently transmitted in the Italian *Fatti di Cesare*); the speeches of Caesar and Cato from Sallust's *Catiline* in Brunetto Latini's *Li livres dou tresor* (Books of treasure; 1260–1266); a late-thirteenth-century translation of Vegetius by Jean d'Eu; and an early-fourteenth-century version of Livy (before 1323). In the course of the fourteenth century, Italian scholars undertook their own vernacular versions based directly on the Latin sources and more attentive to language and style. Among these early *volgarizzamenti* were Fra Bartolomeo da San Concordio's version of Sallust's monographs (before 1313) and Giovanni Boccaccio's rendering of the third and fourth decades of Livy (1338–1346). In the fifteenth century, French, Spanish, and Italian humanists produced new versions not only of the classical historians but also of later Roman writers. With the spread of printing, a whole new crop of translations appeared, and by the end of the sixteenth century the works of Latin historians were available in all the principal European vernaculars, often accompanied by glossaries of ancient political, military, and geographical terms. Certain authors like Curtius and Suetonius had a larger following in the vernacular than in Latin, perhaps because of the popular appeal of their subjects, the deeds of Alexander the Great and the lives of the Roman emperors, respectively. Others, whose works appealed to national, or nationalistic, sentiment, appeared frequently in those particular languages: Caesar's *Gallic War* in French and his *Civil War* in Italian and Spanish; Livy's *Decades* and Tacitus's *Germania* and *Annals* 1–6 in German.

The process of turning the Greek historians into the vernacular was considerably slower. In the early stages of the Renaissance, humanists had devoted their energies to producing Latin translations, many of which were extremely popular and hence became the basis of the first vernacular versions. Among these were Battista Alessandro Jaconello's Italian translation of Plutarch's *Lives* (1482) and the French version of Thucydides by Claude de Seyssel (1527).

Again national sentiment was important; Plutarch's "Sertorius," the main events of which took place on the Iberian peninsula, was translated several times into Spanish and Portuguese. By the end of the sixteenth century, however, Greek historians were accessible in translations made directly from the originals into the principal modern European languages.

Interpretations and Influence. The cultural climate of the Renaissance assured an appreciative reception for all classical historians. Yet the popularity and influence of individual authors, or of particular writings within their corpus, varied considerably in accordance with changing interpretations and uses of their work. In the early stages of the Italian and northern Renaissances, especially in the context of civic or participatory humanism, interest centered on histories of the Roman Republic or on those historians who approached their work from a predominantly rhetorical and didactic point of view. The most admired Latin authors were Livy, the great patriotic moralist, who ascribed Rome's greatness to the noble deeds and public spirit of her citizens and leaders; Sallust, who traced the history of the Republic from an early golden age of liberty and *virtus* through the moral crises of the last two centuries; Suetonius, who viewed history as the unfolding of personality in a complex interplay of character and environment; and Valerius Maximus, compiler of nearly a thousand exempla of virtues and vices from the history and literature of antiquity. Tacitus was used by Bruni to support his republican arguments, but criticized, or avoided, by most humanists of the fifteenth century for the difficulties of his thought and style.

Among the Greeks, Polybius was appreciated for his account of Rome's rise to power and heroic struggle with Hannibal, but the early favorite was Plutarch, whose *Lives* of the great men of the Roman Republic were avidly read. His very subject (the comparison of Greeks and Romans) was especially well suited to bridge the cultural gap between the Latin and Hellenic/Byzantine cultures, and his descriptions of the characters of great men served the moral education of his readers. Although Xenophon was among the earliest Greek writers translated into Latin, interest centered on his philosophical works. His two historical works, *Anabasis* and *Hellenica,* received comparatively little attention at the time. Herodotus and Thucydides, known more widely after Valla's translations of 1452 and 1453, were often compared, respectively, to Livy and Sallust.

Authors of treatises on *ars historica,* attempting to define the aims and methods of their subject in relation to the other humanist disciplines, discussed history in terms of "prose poetry," moral philosophy, and particularly the genres of demonstrative and deliberative oratory. The theories of history and the precepts for historical writing were derived from a variety of Greek and Roman sources, including the treatise *On How to Write History* by the second-century author Lucian of Samosata (paraphrased by Guarino Guarini in a letter of 1446 to Tobia dal Borgo, historiographer at the Malatesta court of Rimini), and above all Cicero's rhetorical works, the *De oratore* (On the orator), *Brutus,* and *Orator,* and Quintilian's *Institutio oratoria* (The education of an orator). But humanists like Giovanni Pontano, author of the dialogue *Actius* (1499), also drew lessons from the proems of classical histories and illustrations from the practice of classical writers, especially the "two great lights" of Roman history, as he called them, Sallust and Livy.

In the wake of the political and religious crises of the sixteenth century and the trend toward authoritarian government, other classical models came into prominence whose subjects were more germane to contemporary conditions or whose thought and writing could help articulate the shift toward pragmatic politics and prudential ethics. Tacitus, historian of Roman emperors (and tyrants) and "master of prudence," seemed especially suited to times of discord, court intrigues, and political absolutism, and was read in conjunction with Seneca, the Stoic authority on private prudence. Polybius was now studied for his analysis of constitutional cycles, and both he and Caesar were recommended as authorities on military science and respected for their (apparently) objective reporting.

As the authors of treatises on historical method, such as Francesco Patrizi, François Baudouin, and Jean Bodin, turned to questions of research and interpretation, they in fact singled out classical historians such as Polybius and Caesar, Thucydides, Sallust, and Tacitus for their sharp powers of observation, personal experience in politics and war, and careful analysis of causes (the basis for a science of government). Among the classical authorities on historical writing, a number of the Greek treatises had, in the meantime, become increasingly popular. Aristotle's *Poetics,* used by Francesco Robortello (1548), stimulated discussions on the nature of historical knowledge; Lucian's *On How to Write History,* used by Robortello and other writers, stressed the importance of careful judgment and sound evidence; Dionysius of Halicarnassus's *On Thucydides,* first published in 1560 in a Latin translation by the German bishop Andreas Dudith, compared critically the subject matter, method, and style of Herodotus and Thucydides. Both of the latter treatises were included in the 1579 edition of Johann Wolf's *Artis historicae penus* (Storehouse of the science of history). Whereas Livy's "Asianic" style (characterized by rich and grand vocabulary and long periodic sentences) had appealed particularly to the early Renaissance, it was the more sober and acerbic prose of Caesar, Sallust, and Tacitus that helped shape the "neo-Attic" rhetoric of the later Renaissance, with its taste for brevity and conciseness.

The major classical historians nevertheless retained their popularity throughout the Renaissance, especially if they were read as curriculum authors or their works could be interpreted on different levels of meaning. Sallust could furnish moral precepts to students in both Catholic and Protestant schools and be used to bolster the tenets of public prudence just as he had supported a civic humanist ethic. Livy could offer a late-sixteenth-century English reader like Gabriel Harvey penetrating insights into politics and military science, as well as stirring accounts of Roman heroism and models of polished speech. For those who had neither the time nor inclination to read the full texts of the ancient writers, there was Florus's epitome, based chiefly on Livy, and collections of speeches from the Greek and Latin historians, addressed to popular audiences as well as to statesmen and generals. Plutarch provided examples of the effects of both democracy and authoritarian government, and his vivid studies of character inspired writers of drama and moral essays. Other ancient historians might have a comparatively small following, yet contribute to the work of highly influential authors, as Polybius and Thucydides did in Machiavelli's *Discourses.* Moreover, classical historians like Caesar, Livy, and Tacitus (along with such later historians as Ammianus Marcellinus, Paulus Orosius, the authors of the *Augustan History,* and the church fathers) could provide valuable material for national histories beginning with the formative stages of the nation's past or learned treatises on antiquarian topics.

The concern for making classical authors relevant to the present tended to overshadow any efforts by Renaissance readers to understand the works in their own intellectual context. Yet in comparison to the medieval concentration on *auctoritates,* there was a more discriminating approach and, in various aspects of reading and study, evidence of a growing historical consciousness: the reliance on ancient *testimonia* in appraising a historian's work (even if taken uncritically); a sensitivity to the distinctive features of his thought and writing and, in turn, an interest in comparing and evaluating historians of different epochs in terms of subject, style, and methods of research. By the end of the sixteenth century, the French writer Lancelot Voisin, sieur de La Popelinière, could treat ancient history as part of "l'histoire des histoires," the development of Western historiography, itself part of the history of civilization.

See also biographies of figures mentioned in this entry.

BIBLIOGRAPHY

Baron, Hans. *The Crisis of the Early Italian Renaissance*. Rev. ed. Princeton, N.J., 1966.

Burke, Peter. "A Survey of the Popularity of Ancient Historians, 1450–1700." *History and Theory* 5 (1966):135–152.

Cochrane, Eric. *Historians and Historiography in the Italian Renaissance*. Chicago, 1981.

Crawford, M. H., and C. R. Ligota, eds. *Ancient History and the Antiquarian: Essays in Memory of Arnaldo Momigliano*. London, 1995.

D'Amico, John F. *Renaissance Humanism in Papal Rome*. Baltimore, 1983.

D'Amico, John F. *Theory and Practice in Renaissance Textual Criticism: Beatus Rhenanus between Conjecture and History*. Berkeley, Calif., 1988.

Fryde, E. B. *Humanism and Renaissance Historiography*. London, 1983.

Grafton, Anthony. *Defenders of the Text*. Cambridge, Mass., 1991.

Grafton, Anthony. *Joseph Scaliger: A Study in the History of Classical Scholarship*. 2 vols. Oxford, 1983 and 1993.

Grant, Michael. *The Ancient Historians*. New York, 1970. See "Epilogue. The Survival of the Ancient Historians." Pages 387–409.

Grendler, Paul F. "Francesco Sansovino and Italian Popular History, 1560–1600." *Studies in the Renaissance* 16 (1969):139–180.

Grendler, Paul F. *Schooling in Renaissance Italy: Literacy and Learning, 1300–1600*. Baltimore and London, 1989.

Griffiths, Gordon, James Hankins, and David Thompson, trans. and eds. *The Humanism of Leonardo Bruni: Selected Texts*. Binghamton, N.Y., 1987.

Hampton, Timothy. *Writing from History: The Rhetoric of Exemplarity in Renaissance Literature*. Ithaca, N.Y., and London, 1990.

Ianziti, Gary. "Bruni on Writing History." *Renaissance Quarterly* 51 (1998):367–391.

Ianziti, Gary. *Humanistic Historiography under the Sforzas*. Oxford and New York, 1988.

Ianziti, Gary. "Writing from Procopius: Leonardo Bruni's *De Bello italico*." *Rinascimento* 37 (1997):3–27.

Kristeller, P. O., F. Edward Cranz, and Virginia Brown, eds. *Catalogus translationum et commentariorum: Mediaeval and Renaissance Latin Translations and Commentaries*. Washington, D.C., 1960–. See "fortuna" sections in articles on individual authors.

Lathrop, Henry B. *Translations from the Classics into English from Caxton to Chapman 1477–1620*. Madison, Wis., 1933.

McCuaig, William. *Carlo Sigonio: The Changing World of the Late Renaissance*. Princeton, N.J., 1989.

Momigliano, Arnaldo. *The Classical Foundations of Modern Historiography*. Berkeley, Calif., 1990.

Momigliano, Arnaldo. *Essays in Ancient and Modern Historiography*. Oxford, 1977.

Momigliano, Arnaldo. *Studies in Historiography*. London, 1966.

Monfrin, J. "La connaissance de l'antiquité et le problème de l'humanisme en langue vulgaire dans la France du quinzième siècle." In *The Late Middle Ages and the Dawn of Humanism outside Italy*. Edited by G. Verbeke and J. Ijsewin. Leuven, Belgium/The Hague, Netherlands, 1972. Pages 131–170.

Reynolds, Beatrice R. "Latin Historiography: A Survey, 1400–1600." *Studies in the Renaissance* 2 (1955):7–66.

Reynolds, Beatrice R. "Shifting Currents in Historical Criticism." *Journal of the History of Ideas* 14 (1953):471–492.

Reynolds, L. D., ed. *Texts and Transmission: A Survey of the Latin Classics*. Oxford, 1983.

Salmon, J. H. M. "Precept, Example, and Truth: Degory Wheare and the *ars historica*." In *The Historical Imagination in Early Modern Britain*. Edited by Donald R. Kelley and David Harris Sacks. Cambridge, U.K., and New York, 1997. Pages 11–36.

Witt, Ronald G. "Coluccio Salutati and the Origins of Florence." *Il pensiero politico* 2 (1969):161–172.

PATRICIA OSMOND *and* MARIANNE PADE

Greek Historians

The following profiles are devoted to the four most influential Greek historians in the Renaissance. They focus on the transmission of their work in translations and in the original, describing briefly the process by which they became an active part, once again, of the cultural heritage of western Europe.

Herodotus of Halicarnassus. Called "the Father of History," Herodotus (c. 485–c. 425 B.C.) wrote the *Histories* in nine books, each named after one of the nine Muses, in which he treated the events from the end of the Trojan War to Xerxes's campaign against Greece, ending with the battle of Mycale in 479 B.C. Interspersed with the historical narrative are long digressions on conditions in Egypt, Phoenicia, Mesopotamia, and Scythia, based on information collected during extensive travels in these regions; in the Renaissance these parts of Herodotus's work would be popular with travelers such as Ciriaco d'Ancona, who used Herodotus as a guide in Egypt. Commissioned by Pope Nicholas V, Lorenzo Valla's Latin translation of the *Histories* was probably left unfinished at his death in 1457. It remained, nonetheless, the standard translation in the following centuries, while a translation by Mattia Palmerio, completed before 1463, remained almost unknown.

From antiquity, Herodotus's reputation was not without blemishes. Plutarch had accused him of being unnecessarily malicious toward the protagonists of his account, and from Cicero, Quintilian, and Aulus Gellius he was known to be more of a storyteller, though a charming one, than a writer of history. It was said, moreover, that he was not always a reliable source. These judgments influenced Renaissance readers of the *Histories,* from Valla to Jean Bodin, and although many readers, such as Guarino Guarini (Guarino da Verona) and Giovanni Tortelli, found him delightful, scholars who appreciated Herodotus often felt the need to defend him. Henri Estienne, who edited Valla's translation in 1566, added an "Apologia pro Herodoto" (Apology for Herodotus) in which he refuted the charges of deliberate falsehoods and malice. As Herodotus's reputation improved, he became highly esteemed as a source for Greek and Oriental history and respected as a model for ethnographical treatises. A German translation by Hieronymus Boner was printed in 1531 and an English translation by Barnabe Rich in 1581.

Thucydides. Thucydides (c. 460–c. 400 B.C.) was the author of a contemporary *History of the Peloponnesian War* (431–404 B.C.), in which he himself participated on the side of his native Athens. From antiquity onward the style and form of the *History* became a model for innumerable historians, both Greek and Latin. The most celebrated and imitated passages of his work are the proem (1.1–23); the speeches, particularly Pericles's funeral oration (2.35–46); the description of the plague in Athens (2.47.3–54); and the description of the civil war in Corcyra (3.81–84).

The first modern translation we possess of any part of Thucydides dates from the end of the fourteenth century and consists of thirty-eight speeches from the *History* translated into Aragonese for the Spaniard Juan Fernandez de Heredia. Early in the fifteenth century, when the interest in Greek studies was gaining momentum in Italy, we have evidence that Thucydides himself was read. Leonardo Bruni drew upon Pericles's funeral oration for his own speech for Nanni Strozzi (1427–1428). In 1452 Lorenzo Valla completed his Latin translation of the *History,* commissioned by Pope Nicholas V. In his letter of dedication, Valla praised Thucydides's style and, quoting Cicero and Quintilian, compared him to Sallust. Indeed, as Sallust had imitated the style of Thucydides, so Valla often rendered the Greek historian in a Latin strongly reminiscent of Sallust's language. Valla's translation remained the standard Latin version for the next four hundred years and was rendered into French by Claude de Seyssel (1527) and into German by Hieronymus Boner (1533). Seyssel's translation was turned into English by Thomas Nicolls (1550); the next English version of Thucydides was the famous translation by Thomas Hobbes, published in 1629.

Thucydides's account of the Peloponnesian War also provided a useful model for contemporary history, and several historians, including Poggio Bracciolini, professed their intention of writing in the Thucydidean manner. As an astute political commentator, Thucydides influenced such writers as Niccolò Machiavelli and Francesco Guicciardini and was included in Jean Bodin's list of politically useful ancient historians. The speeches were attentively studied, as the many separate translations and commentaries indicate, among them Giovanni della Casa's Latin translations of the speeches from Books 1–3 (c. 1545–1546), which he undertook in preparation for his diplomatic duties as papal nuncio in Venice. During the sixteenth century Thucydidean scholarship moved north of the Alps. Important editions of the Greek text were published by Joachim Camerarius (1540) and Henri Estienne (1564 and 1588), and the first full-scale commentaries by Veit Winsheim (1569), Francesco Porto (1594), and Georg Acatius Enenckel (1598).

Polybius. Polybius (c. 200–c. 120 B.C.), from Megalopolis in Arcadia, wrote a universal history that originally encompassed forty books. His work aimed at explaining, especially to the Greeks, the causes of Rome's rapid and impressive rise to world dominion. We still possess the first five books and some longer passages from the later ones, the so-called *Excerpta antiqua.* Practically unknown during the Middle Ages, Polybius's work was not read in the Latin West until the fifteenth century. Books 1.7–2.34 (supplemented from other sources) were adapted by Leonardo Bruni for his *Commentarii de primo bello punico* (History of the first Punic War; 1418–1419), a substitute for the missing account of this war and the Gallic War in the lost second decade of Livy. In fact, in Bruni's very free version, Polybius often reads like the Roman historian. In 1454 the young Niccolò Perotti finished his translation of Polybius's Books 1–5, commissioned by Nicholas V, which in passages owes much to Bruni's version. Although severely criticized in the next century, it was an immediate success and widely read. The first known mention of Book 6, which contains chapters on the theory of *anacyclosis* (cycle of constitutions) and the mixed constitution (illustrated by Rome), as well as discussions of Roman army organization and castrametation (the art of laying out a camp), dates from the early years of the sixteenth century. The Florentine Bernardo Rucellai discussed it in his work *De urbe Roma* (On the city of Rome; before 1505), and it was used by Machiavelli in his *Discorsi* (c. 1513–c. 1517).

Polybius's popularity grew throughout the century, and he was praised for his firsthand knowledge of politics and warfare, his use of documentary sources, and his rational explanation of causes by such authors as François Baudouin and Jean Bodin. He came to be honored not least as an expert on Roman military organization. The relevant chapters from Book 6 were often translated separately, into Latin by Janus Lascaris (1537), and into Italian by Filippo Strozzi (1538) and Bartolomeo Cavalcanti (1539), who made use of Polybius in several of his works. Justus Lipsius's *De militia romana* (On Roman military affairs; 1594), formally a commentary on Book 6, was an enormously successful handbook meant to improve contemporary military organization. In the same year Francesco Patrizi published a treatise, also based on Book 6, treating parallels and differences between ancient and contemporary warfare.

In the sixteenth century several vernacular translations appeared: in French (1545–1546, Louis Meigret), Italian (1546, Ludovico Domenichi), English (1568, Christopher Watson), and German (1574, Wilhelm Xylander). The Greek text was considerably improved by Isaac Casaubon in his important edition (Paris, 1609).

Plutarch. Plutarch (c. A.D. 46–c. 120), from Chaeronea in Boeotia, was the author of the celebrated *Parallel Lives,* consisting of twenty-two pairs and four single biographies, as well as the *Moralia,* comprising seventy-two philosophical treatises of varying content. In the pairs of lives, celebrated Greeks and Romans are compared, including Alexander and Caesar, and Demosthenes and Cicero. Most of these pairs are then followed by a comparison discussing the merits of each hero. In the Middle Ages the historical Plutarch was unknown in the West, but by the end of the fourteenth century his works began to attract attention in cultural centers such as Avignon and Florence, and he soon became the most widely read Greek historian (in translation). His writings were proof of the close ties once uniting the Greek and Roman worlds, and his *Lives* preserved the fame of great Romans more eloquently than any book in Latin.

The Florentine chancellor Coluccio Salutati had an Aragonese translation of most of the *Lives,* com-

missioned by Juan Fernandez de Heredia in the 1380s, turned into Italian. When the students of Manuel Chrysoloras began to produce their own versions, interest centered initially on the Roman lives, especially those concerning the fall of the republic. The translations of "Brutus," "Cicero," "Pompey," "Mark Antony," and "Cato the Younger" by Jacopo Angeli da Scarperia and Leonardo Bruni (all before 1411) reflect the strong republican sentiments of Florentine humanists in these years. On other occasions as well, the choice of a particular text to render in Latin was influenced by ideological motives. The *Lives* were translated by some of the most eminent humanists of the fifteenth century: Guarino Guarini, Francesco Barbaro, Leonardo Giustinian, and Francesco Filelfo. More than five hundred manuscripts of these versions have survived, and the entire corpus was printed eight times before 1500 and frequently thereafter, until it was supplanted by the scholarly Latin editions of Wilhelm Xylander (1561), Hermann Crüser (1564), and the French translation of Jacques Amyot (1559), which was in turn the basis for Thomas North's English version (1579). From the Latin *Lives,* several vernacular versions were made, including those by Battista Alessandro Jaconello (Italian, 1482), Georg Spalatin (German, 1521), and Hieronymus Boner (German, 1534).

Plutarch's biographical form and method were widely imitated, and the *Lives* inspired fresco cycles in public buildings and private palaces, including the frescoes of Francesco da Siena, painted in 1547 for Fabio Colonna in Grottaferrata, and the cycle in Palazzo Massimo in Rome by Daniele da Volterra. The English translation by North was read by William Shakespeare, whose Roman dramas (*Coriolanus, Antony and Cleopatra, Julius Caesar*), as well as *Timon of Athens,* are largely based on the *Lives.*

See also biographies of figures mentioned in this entry.

BIBLIOGRAPHY

Herodotus
Momigliano, Arnaldo. *Studies in Historiography.* London, 1966. See chapter 8, "The Place of Herodotus in the History of Historiography," pp. 127–142.

Thucydides
Pade, Marianne. "Valla's Thucydides. Theory and Practice in a Renaissance Translation." *Classica et Mediaevalia* 36 (1985): 275–301.
Pade, Marianne. "The Manuscript Diffusion of Valla's Translation of Thucydides. Various Aspects of Its Importance for the Tradition of the Greek Text and for the History of Translation in the Renaissance." *Studi umanistici Piceni* 12 (1992): 171–180.

Tolbert Roberts, J. "Florentine Perceptions of Athenian Democracy." *Mediaevalia et Humanistica. Studies in Medieval and Renaissance Culture,* n.s. 15 (1987): 25–41.

Polybius

Momigliano, Arnaldo. "Polybius' Reappearance in Western Europe." In *Polybe: neuf exposés suivis de discussions.* Edited by Emilio Gabba. Geneva, 1973. Pages 345–372.

Reynolds, Beatrice R. "Bruni and Perotti Present a Greek Historian." *Bibliothèque d'humanisme et renaissance* 16 (1954): 108–118.

Plutarch

Fryde, E. B. *Humanism and Renaissance Historiography.* London, 1983. See "The Beginnings of Italian Humanist Historiography. The New Cicero of Leonardo Bruni," pp. 33–53.

McGrail, Mary Ann, ed. *Shakespeare's Plutarch.* Tokyo, 1997.

Pade, Marianne. "Guarino, His Princely Patron, and Plutarch's 'Vita Alexandri ac Caesaris.' An ineditum in Archivio di S. Pietro H 31." *Analecta Romana Instituti Danici* 17–18 (1989): 133–147.

Pade, Marianne. "The Latin Translations of Plutarch's Lives in Fifteenth-Century Italy and Their Manuscript Diffusion." In *The Classical Tradition in the Middle Ages and the Renaissance. Proceedings of the First European Science Foundation Workshop on "The Reception of Classical Texts."* Edited by Claudio Leonardi and Birger Munk Olsen. Spoleto, Italy, 1995. Pages 169–183.

MARIANNE PADE

Roman Historians

The following profiles are devoted to the most prominent Roman historians in the Renaissance. They aim to summarize significant aspects of their reception and point out influences within the political and intellectual context of the age.

Caesar. Gaius Julius Caesar (100–44 B.C.), author of two *Commentaries,* the *Gallic War* on his campaigns of 58–52 B.C., and the *Civil War* on the period 49–48 B.C., was known to the Renaissance not only as a historian but also as a protagonist of historical events in the late Roman Republic. In the fourteenth century, the increased manuscript production attests to the growing number of readers of the entire corpus, including the books by his continuators (on the Gallic War of 51–50 B.C., and on the Alexandrian, African, and Spanish Wars of 48–45 B.C.), although there were lingering doubts about the authorship of the *Gallic War,* often ascribed to a certain Julius Celsus.

In France, where the story of Caesar's campaigns in Gaul had a strong national appeal, the *Faits des Romains* (Deeds of the Romans; c. 1214), which recounted his "chivalrous" exploits, remained popular well into and beyond the fifteenth century. In Italy, Petrarch composed a biography, *De gestis Caesaris* (Deeds of Caesar; early 1370s), praising not only his

military valor but also his literary talents, and Pier Candido Decembrio prepared a vita, in addition to an Italian translation of the *Gallic War* (1438), for Duke Filippo Maria Visconti of Milan, an admirer of Caesar the "emperor." By this time, in fact, Caesar's political role as dictator was keenly debated in Renaissance controversies over monarchy versus republic. Dante and Coluccio Salutati had defended his position as dictator and condemned his assassins, but Leonardo Bruni argued that Caesar's autocratic rule had destroyed the Republic and marked the beginning of Rome's decline. In the 1430s Poggio Bracciolini and Guarino Guarini (Guarino da Verona), among others, compared the merits of Julius Caesar and the republican hero Scipio Africanus, victor of the war against Hannibal, and debated the implications of republican liberty and monarchical order for intellectual life and literary creativity.

Supporters of Guarino (who defended monarchy) might have found some justification in Renaissance historiography. It was in fact under monarchical forms of government that Caesar's literary work became a model for the writing of commentaries (histories of contemporary events focusing on the career or *gesta* of outstanding individuals) on King Alfonso I of Naples (c. 1455) by Bartolomeo Facio and on Duke Francesco Sforza of Milan (1473–1476) by Giovanni Simonetta. In the later Renaissance, Caesar's work was frequently recommended as a manual for the study of military science, especially in England; as a writer of Latin prose, he was also studied and imitated. His plain, unadorned manner of writing, which Cicero himself had admired, was praised by Jean Bodin and Roger Ascham, who spoke of the "unspotted propriety" of his language, and adopted by Michel de Montaigne as a model for his *Essays.* Translations of one or both of the commentaries appeared in print in French in 1488 and 1531, Spanish in 1498, German in 1507, and English in 1565 (Arthur Golding's version of the *Gallic War*) and 1604–1609 (Clement Edmondes's observations on and translations of the *Gallic War* and *Civil War*).

Sallust. Gaius Sallustius Crispus (86–35 B.C.), author of *The Conspiracy of Catiline, Jugurthine War,* and *Histories,* which survives only in fragments, and putative author of the *Letters to Caesar* and *Invective against Cicero,* was read, quoted, and imitated throughout the Renaissance. Manuscripts of the two monographs, the *Catiline* and *Jugurtha,* were plentiful (many of them still in circulation from the Middle Ages), and from the first printed edition of 1470 to the early 1600s, he was the most widely

Petrarch's Copy of Livy. The manuscript of the works of the Roman historian Livy (59 B.C.–A.D. 17) worked on by Petrarch, opened to a page in which Petrarch added in his own hand additional parts of Livy's history found in another manuscript. Petrarch's scholarship on Livy was an early example of the Renaissance interest in, and scholarship on, the classical historians. BY PERMISSION OF THE BRITISH LIBRARY. HARLEY 2493, PAGE 220V

thors imitated his character portraits, digressions on political and geographical topics, and dramatic battle scenes. Catiline had been a popular figure in early Tuscan chronicles, connected to legends of Florence and Fiesole, but it was his paradoxical personality, combining the heroic and criminal, that fascinated humanist historians and influenced later dramatists, including Ben Jonson.

In the history of political thought, Sallust's description of the early Roman Republic (*Catiline* 6–9) contributed key ideas to the development of a civic humanist ethic and the defense of republican government. The notion that political liberty stimulated the pursuit of *virtus* and *gloria,* and hence the growth and expansion of a state, was developed by Coluccio Salutati and especially Leonardo Bruni, while his defense of personal merit (particularly in *Jugurtha* 85) provided arguments for Renaissance debates on "true nobility." During the political crises of the late fifteenth and early sixteenth centuries in Italy, other aspects of his thought emerged. His sharp, critical analysis of party politics and the disillusioned attitude with which he exposed the hypocrisy of factional leaders appealed to historians and political thinkers like Giovanni Pontano and Bernardo Rucellai, also writing at times of crisis. According to Machiavelli, "everyone" had read Sallust's *Catiline;* he himself drew upon the monographs and the *Histories* (some fragments of which were transmitted in St. Augustine's *City of God*) for his own account of the rise and decline of the Roman Republic.

A politically conservative interpretation of Sallust already characterized the reading and adaptation of his work in fifteenth-century Italy, especially in circles attached to the papal court and to the Medici household in Florence, for his monographs (and other writings) could also be used to encourage obedience to established authority and discourage rebellion. Later in the sixteenth century, however, this approach became even more prevalent, both in Italy and northern Europe. Justus Lipsius found passages in his writings to support his arguments for *prudentia mixta,* an attenuated form of reason and state, and other political writers in France and England turned to Sallust's work, including the *Letters to Caesar,* to bolster the cause of absolute government. Occasionally Sallust's objectivity was questioned (especially when the critic was a supporter of Cicero), but Lipsius called him "the prince of the historical senate," and the German philologist Christoph Coler considered him superior even to Tacitus. Translations of one or both of the monographs appeared in print in Italian in 1518, French in 1528 and 1532,

published ancient historian. The two monographs were also familiar in the vernacular, while his poems, speeches, and letters were often collected in compendia.

Sallust's moralistic scheme of history and his style, famous for its epigrammatic brevity, made him a favorite curriculum author and a model for Renaissance writers. The monograph itself provided a format for treating contemporary events, especially Renaissance conspiracies and single wars, and au-

German in 1515, and English around 1520 (Alexander Barclay's *Jugurtha*) and in 1608 (Thomas Heywood's *Catiline* and *Jugurtha*).

Livy. Titus Livius (59 B.C.–A.D. 17 or 64 B.C.–A.D. 12), author of the *History of Rome from the Foundation of the City* (from 753 B.C. to the death of Drusus in 9 B.C.), originally in 142 books, was the chief source and inspiration for the Renaissance cult of "great men and noble deeds." In his native city of Padua, where his supposed tomb had been discovered, he was himself the object of a humanist cult. Thanks to Petrarch, working in Avignon in the late 1320s with Landolfo Colonna, the surviving books of the first, third, and fourth decades of the *History* were reunited. In 1527 Simon Griener (Grynaeus) discovered Books 41–45 of the fifth decade at Lorsch.

Petrarch, who lamented that he had not been born in Livy's own age, did more than anyone to popularize his history as a source of moral inspiration and model of elegant Latin prose. He himself drew upon the exempla of civic and military virtues for his biographies of famous Romans, his treatise on the cardinal virtues, the *Rerum memorandarum libri* (Memorabilia), and the *Trionfi* (Triumphs), and was inspired by Livy's account of the Hannibalic War to compose his epic poem *Africa*. In the fifteenth and early sixteenth centuries, Livy's history served as a model for humanist historians—Leonardo Bruni in Florence, Marc'Antonio Sabellico in Venice, and the Italian or native historians at the northern European courts, from England and France to Hungary and Poland—eager to celebrate the achievements of their city-states or nations and to emulate Livy's rich, flowing prose (according to Cicero, the most appropriate style for historical writing). The division into decades and annalistic format also furnished a framework for organizing long narratives "from the origins," while character portraits, speeches, and scenes of pathos offered edifying or entertaining diversions. Political commentaries on Livy began with Machiavelli's *Discorsi* (Discourses; c. 1513–1517 or 1515–1518), although the Florentine secretary was primarily interested in applying the lessons of ancient political and military history to the contemporary affairs of Italy and was not necessarily concerned with citing and interpreting his source accurately. The heroes and heroines of Livy's history reemerged in biographies of famous men and women and inspired literary works from Gian Giorgio Trissino's play *Sofonisba* (1514–1515) to Shakespeare's narrative poem *The Rape of Lucrece* (1594). The figure of Lucretia, personification of womanly honor, appeared frequently in painted *cassoni,* or marriage chests; Roman kings, magistrates, and military commanders populated the fresco cycles of *viri illustres* (illustrious men) in the Carrara Palace at Padua and in numerous private and civic halls.

In the *Divine Comedy*, Dante had reverently referred to the Roman historian as "Livio . . . che non erra" (Livy . . . who does not err), and most humanist scholars and historians considered his history generally reliable. Lorenzo Valla, however, questioned his account of the two Tarquins, and Carlo Sigonio cited new epigraphic and literary evidence to challenge his chronology. Printed translations of one or more sets of books from Livy's history appeared in French in 1486, German in 1505, and English in 1600 (Philemon Holland).

Tacitus. Cornelius Tacitus (c. A.D. 55–c. 120), author of *Annals, Histories,* the biography *Agricola,* the geographic-ethnographic account *Germania,* and *Dialogue on Oratory,* was the chief authority on Roman emperors and the Empire from the death of Augustus to the civil wars of 68–70. In the mid-fourteenth century, the manuscript of *Annals* 11–16, seen by Giovanni Boccaccio in the library of the monastery at Monte Cassino, was taken to Florence, perhaps by Zanobi da Strada, and later joined by the German codex containing Books 1–6, which entered the Medici library of the future pope Leo X in 1508. In the meantime, the minor works, also preserved in German libraries, arrived in Italy, where they were copied and studied by the early humanists. German scholars themselves, including Conrad Celtis, naturally cultivated the study of Tacitus, especially the *Germania,* which inspired early antiquarian studies and stimulated German patriotism. In the sixteenth century the figure of Arminius, known from the first books of the *Annals* as the "liberator Germaniae," also contributed to the growth of nationalistic sentiment.

In Florence, in the context of the early civic humanist movement, Leonardo Bruni drew upon the *Histories* to defend the ideals of republican liberty and denounce the corrupting effects of monarchy on moral and cultural life. But it was primarily in the sixteenth century, first in Italy and later in northern Europe, that Tacitus acquired greatest renown, or notoriety, especially as an exponent of political absolutism and as a master of pragmatic statecraft or "public prudence." Machiavelli saw in his work the principles that could explain the success of monarchy; Francesco Guicciardini introduced him as guide to tyrants and the "secrets of empire," and at the same time as guide to their subjects and the art of survival. In the later decades of the century, Marc-Antoine de Muret and Lipsius stressed his relevance to the troubled times of their own era, beset (like first-century A.D. Rome) by civil strife, persecutions, and the moral dilemmas experienced by those living under tyranny. Montaigne and Lipsius also appreciated the astringent quality and even the difficulties and ambiguities of his style, which earlier humanists had scorned, and read him in the company of Seneca and other Stoic philosophers. When the climate of the Counter-Reformation made it safer not to mention Machiavelli (whose work was now on the papal Index of Prohibited Books), Tacitus could be used as a substitute, whether to support or oppose monarchy, advocate or condemn Reason of State.

At times, his own writings might be considered subversive: Queen Elizabeth nearly charged Sir John Hayward with treason for his Tacitean account of the deposition of Richard II, and Ben Jonson's *Sejanus* (1605) aroused the suspicions of James I. Francis Bacon and others, however, drew frequently upon Tacitus, and his analyses of imperial politics and the psychological climate of Empire were generally acknowledged as the most sophisticated and subtle of any Roman historian and the best instruction for life at all times. Sir Henry Savile, in the address to the reader prefacing his translation of the *Histories* and *Agricola* of 1591, wrote: "he hath written the most matter with best conceit in fewest words of any historiographer ancient or modern." In 1598, this translation was reprinted together with Richard Greneway's English version of the *Annals* and *Germania*. In the meantime, Italian translations of the *Annals* and/or *Histories* had appeared in 1544, French in c. 1545 and 1582 and German in 1535. A German rendering of the *Germania* was printed in 1526.

See also biographies of figures mentioned in this entry.

BIBLIOGRAPHY

Livy

Dorey, Thomas A., ed. *Livy*. London, 1971.
Grafton, Anthony. "*Discitur ut agatur*: How Gabriel Harvey Read His Livy." In *Annotation and Its Texts*. Edited by Stephen A. Barney. New York, 1991. Pages 108–129.
McDonald, A. H. "Titus Livius." In *Catalogus translationum et commentariorum: Mediaeval and Renaissance Latin Translations and Commentaries* (henceforth abbreviated as *CTC*). Vol. 2. Washington, D.C., 1971. Pages 331–348.
McDonald, A. H. "Addenda et corrigenda." *CTC*. Vol. 3. Washington, D.C., 1973. Pages 445–449.
Ridley, R. T. "Machiavelli and Roman History." *Quaderni di Storia* 18 (1983): 197–219.

Ridley, R. T. "Machiavelli's Edition of Livy." *Rinascimento* 27 (1987): 327–348.

Caesar

Brown, Virginia. "Gaius Julius Caesar." In *CTC*. Vol. 3. Washington, D.C., 1976. Pages 87–139.
Brown, Virginia. "Portraits of Julius Caesar in Latin Manuscripts of the *Commentaries*." *Viator* 12 (1981): 319–353.
Ianziti, Gary. *Humanistic Historiography under the Sforzas*. Oxford and New York, 1988.

Sallust

McCuaig, William. "Bernardo Rucellai and Sallust." *Rinascimento* 22 (1982): 75–98.
Osmond, Patricia J. "Princeps Historiae Romanae: Sallust in Renaissance Political Thought." *Memoirs of the American Academy in Rome* 40 (1995): 101–143.
Osmond, Patricia J. "Sallust and Machiavelli." *Journal of Medieval and Renaissance Studies* 23 (1993): 407–438.
Osmond, Patricia J., and Robert W. Ulery Jr. "C. Sallustius Crispus." *CTC*. Vol. 8. Forthcoming.

Tacitus

Luce, T. J., and A. J. Woodman, eds. *Tacitus and the Tacitean Tradition*. Princeton, N.J., 1993.
Salmon, J. H. M. "Cicero and Tacitus in Sixteenth-Century France." *American Historical Review* 85 (1980): 307–331.
Salmon, J. H. M. "Stoicism and Roman Example: Seneca and Tacitus in Jacobean England." *Journal of the History of Ideas* 50 (1989): 199–225.
Ulery, Robert W., Jr. "Addenda et corrigenda." *CTC*. Vol. 8. Forthcoming.
Ulery, Robert W., Jr. "Cornelius Tacitus." *CTC*. Vol. 6. Washington, D.C., 1986. Pages 87–174.
Whitfield, J. H. "Livy > Tacitus." In *Classical Influences on European Culture, A.D. 1500–1700*. Edited by R. R. Bolgar. Cambridge, U.K., 1976. Pages 281–294.

PATRICIA OSMOND

HISTORIOGRAPHY, RENAISSANCE. [This entry includes six subentries:

Italian Historiography
French Historiography
British Historiography
German Historiography
Jewish Historiography
Spanish Historiography]

Italian Historiography

Italian Renaissance historiography originated with the humanist historians of the fifteenth century, whose return to classical prototypes replaced the year-by-year chronicles predominant in the Middle Ages with focused histories stressing coherent narrative, causal factors, and human agency.

Humanist Historiography. The study and imitation of ancient historians led to a more sophisticated sense of the differences between historical eras, a more critical attitude toward authority and evidence, a greater sense of individual character and motive, and a more rigorous grasp of causation. Adopting the classical view of history as "philosophy teaching by example," the humanists emphasized its rhetorical aspects, including the tradition of invented speeches, and they commended its utility because of the concrete examples of conduct it offered to someone confronted with the real-life dilemmas of statesmanship and civic life.

The first, and arguably the greatest, humanist historian was the Florentine chancellor Leonardo Bruni (c. 1370–1444), who patterned his *Historia florentini populi libri XII* (History of the Florentine people; 1610) on Roman models, particularly Livy. Bruni took as his theme the rise of Florence to the status of a great power through its resistance to Duke Giangaleazzo Visconti of Milan (1351–1402); he found the underlying cause of its rise in the city's republican form of government. Perhaps because of his familiarity with Greek historiography, Bruni displayed a critical spirit in his use of sources—a practice not always imitated by his successors, many of whom were more interested in Latin style and narrative presentation than in factual accuracy.

Bruni was followed by the Florentine chancellors Poggio Bracciolini (1380–1459) and Bartolomeo Scala (1430–1497) and by many humanists who wrote histories of the municipalities of Italy, among them the official historiographer of Venice, Sabellico (Marcantonio Coccio; 1436–1506), who also modeled himself on Livy. A pioneer in antiquarian research and the use of archaeological evidence was Flavio Biondo of Forlì (1392–1463), whose *Historiarum ab inclinatione Romanorum imperii decades* (Decades of history from the decline of the Roman empire; 1483) traced Rome's decline and the subsequent history of medieval Italy. Biondo's work embodied the new sense of anachronism that had originated with Petrarch (1304–1374), including a more sophisticated understanding of the nature of classical civilization and a rejection of the notion of its continuation in the Middle Ages through the ostensible "translation of empire" to Charlemagne. From the humanists' conception of the decline of Rome and the rebirth of civilization in their own day came the concept of discrete periods in history.

Owing to the patronage of rulers, much humanist historiography had a biographical orientation. Pier Candido Decembrio (1392–1477), Giorgio Merula (1430/31–1494), and Giovanni Simonetta (d. c. 1491) wrote histories of the Visconti and Sforza dukes of Milan; Lorenzo Valla (1407–1457), Giovanni Pon-

tano (1426–1503), and Antonio Beccadelli (1394–1471) wrote those of the kings of Aragon and Naples. The most widely read of the biographical histories was *Liber de vita Christi ac omnium pontificum* (Lives of the popes; 1479) by the Mantuan humanist Platina (Bartolomeo Sacchi; 1421–1481). Ironically (from the standpoint of their claim that history was moral philosophy) but understandably (from the standpoint of their livelihood), the humanists were seldom given to exploring the faults of their patrons, whether those were cities or princes. Humanist historiography culminated with Pietro Bembo's elegantly Ciceronian *Historia rerum Venetarum* (Venetian history; 1551) and *Historiarum sui temporis libri* (History of his own time; 1550–1552) by Paolo Giovio (1486–1552), a sweeping account of the Wars of Italy based largely on eyewitness testimony. By now, however, the cultivated public was wearying of Latin histories that reduced contemporary phenomena to the language and mind-set of Augustan Rome.

Vernacular History. The vernacular history of the sixteenth century was the heir not only of humanist historiography but of the critical disciplines—including philology and textual criticism, epigraphy, numismatics, and archaeology—that humanism had developed. The philologist and historian Lorenzo Valla disproved the "Donation of Constantine" (a medieval forgery purportedly granting vast temporal powers to the papacy) on philological and historical grounds; Biondo began to identify the different epochs in the building of Rome in contradistinction to the undifferentiated *Mirabilia Romae* (Marvels of Rome) of the medieval tradition; the philologist Angelo Poliziano (1454–1494) employed his new methods of analyzing manuscript sources to redate the founding of Florence. Vernacular history also profited from renewed interest in "pragmatic" Greek historiography—pragmatic because it stressed the utility of history less as moral philosophy and more as a means of explaining the workings of human society. The second-century Greek writer Lucian's short treatise on writing history became widely read, and the Greek historian Polybius (c. 203–c. 120 B.C.E.), with his intense interest in constitutional history, came to be considered a model. Interest revived, moreover, in the first-century Roman historian Tacitus, who was initially despised by the humanists on stylistic grounds but came to be admired for his analyses of psychology and motive and his focus on political power.

Sixteenth-century history also had roots in such vernacular traditions as the urban chronicles of the Middle Ages, family chronicles (of which Venetians were particularly fond), and the memoirs and diaries produced in great abundance in Florence since the late Middle Ages—such as those of Buonaccorso Pitti (1354–1431), Giovanni Morelli (1371–1444), Gregorio Dati (1362–1435), or Luca Landucci (1436–1516)—which sought in some way or other to make sense of the writer's experience and his role in the often stressful events of his city.

"The Calamity of Italy."

The immediate impetus for the great vernacular histories was an urgent need to explain Italy's subjugation to foreign powers in the course of the sixteenth century. Just as the wars with Milan and Naples had stimulated Florentine humanist historiography, so the invasion of Italy by Charles VIII of France in 1494 and the ensuing Wars of Italy stimulated a burst of historical production. Alessandro Benedetti (c. 1450–1512), physician to the Venetian army in 1495, published a diary of the "Caroline" war, and Domenico Malipiero (1428–1515) produced a long commentary on it in his *Annali veneti dall'anno 1457 al 1500* (*Venetian annals;* first ed. 1843–1844). The Venetian senator Marin Sanudo (1466–1535) not only wrote a commentary but in 1496 began keeping a diary of events, incorporating dispatches of ambassadors and texts of treaties to form a documentary basis for the formal history he projected. The Mantuan courtier Iacopo d'Atri chronicled the war as part of his *Croniche del marchese di Mantova* (Chronicles of the marquis of Mantua; first published 1879) and Bernardino Corio (1459–c. 1519) pondered the reasons for it in his extensive *Storia di Milano* (History of Milan, to 1499). The Florentine Bernardo Rucellai (1449–1514), a friend of Lorenzo de' Medici, produced an admirable Latin history, *De bello italico* (On the Italian War; 1724) in which he assigned responsibility for the invasion principally to the ambitions of Duke Lodovico Sforza of Milan (1452–1508) and of Pope Alexander VI (1431–1503), while a decade or so later Luigi Guicciardini (1478–1551) sought to explain the most dramatic event of the ensuing wars, the 1527 Sack of Rome.

Although humanist historians, notably Paolo Giovio, also responded to Italy's crisis, the future lay with the great vernacular histories of Niccolò Machiavelli (1469–1527) and Francesco Guicciardini (1483–1540). These combined the narrative and rhetorical traditions of humanist Latin historiography with the political and constitutional interests of Greek historiography and, especially in the case of Guicciardini, with the heightened sense of the value of documentary evidence created by philological and antiquarian studies. Machiavelli's *Istorie fiorentine* (History of Florence, to 1492; 1525) took one step further the humanist belief that history should be useful to the statesman: he attempted to abstract from it not moral precepts but general laws governing the behavior of human societies. Like Bruni an ardent republican, Machiavelli attributed the rise of Florence to its republican constitution, and in the growth of faction he found the cause of the city's having fallen under the dominance of the Medici.

Guicciardini had too keen a sense of the uniqueness of circumstances to want to generalize, but he too focused on explanation. An experienced diplomat and governor, he carried the humanist concern with character and motive to new levels, testing the actions of individuals against the generalizations about human conduct he had formulated as he sought to explain how the conflicting interests and selfish ambitions of Italy's princes had drawn, and continued to draw, the foreigner into Italy. What made Guicciardini's work a milestone in historiography was not only his relentless probing of motive and his detailed reconstruction of the causal chain of diplomacy but his use of documentary sources. Whereas Platina, although librarian of the Vatican, had not bothered to explore the Vatican archives, Guicciardini had whole sections of the Florentine archives moved to his villa so that he could reconstruct diplomatic maneuvers from contemporary documents.

Late-Sixteenth-Century Developments.

While theorists such as Francesco Robortello (1516–1567) and Francesco Patrizi (1529–1597) engaged in largely inconclusive discussions regarding the nature of history, later Renaissance historians continued to consolidate the achievements of the previous generations with a wide variety of historical writing. Although he was subjected to censorship by Counter-Reformation authorities, the Modenese historian Carlo Sigonio (1522/23–1584), one of the last to write in Latin, used the critical methods developed by humanism to revolutionize the study of medieval history, introducing new standards of accuracy and authenticity in his *De regno Italiae* (History of the kingdom of Italy; 1574). Under the tutelage of the man of letters Vincenzio Borghini (1515–1580), the artist Giorgio Vasari (1511–1574) perfected his historico-biographical approach to the study of the arts with the second edition of his *Vite de' più ec-*

celenti pittori scultori ed architteti (Lives of the artists; 1568). Municipal history continued to flourish under local patronage, as in Venice, where Paolo Paruta (1540–1598) wore the mantle of official historiographer almost to the end of the century, exploiting the archives that Bembo had scorned and eventually switching from Latin to Italian for wider readership. In Florence, the last heroic stand of the Florentine republic in 1529–1530 stimulated a whole school of vernacular historians, including Filippo Nerli (1485–1556), Iacopo Nardi (1476–after 1563), Bernardo Segni (1504–1558), Gian Michele Bruto (1517–1592), and Benedetto Varchi (1503–1565). Giovan Battista Adriani (1513–1579) wrote a continuation of Varchi's history, and at the end of the century Scipione Ammirato (1531–1601) produced a "definitive" *Istorie fiorentine* (History of Florence; 1641–1647) making use of the work of his many predecessors, the new critical methods, and the archives of Florence. Ecclesiastical history also achieved some notable monuments. Cesare Baronio (1538–1607) made a lasting contribution with his *Annales ecclesiastici* (Ecclesiastical annals; 1588–1607) and their vast collection of source materials for the history of the Catholic church, while in Venice the Servite friar Paolo Sarpi (1552–1623), an adviser to the Venetian government in its disputes with the papacy, utilized the explanatory methods of Guicciardini to produce his highly critical *Istoria del concilio tridentino* (History of the Council of Trent; 1619), an exposition of the political motives of the popes in their handling of the council.

See also **Classical Antiquity, Discovery of; Humanism,** *subentry on* **Italy; Middle Ages; Wars of Italy;** *and biographies of figures mentioned in this entry.*

BIBLIOGRAPHY

Primary Works

Benedetti, Alessandro. *Diaria de bello carolino* (*Diary of the Caroline War*). Translated and edited by Dorothy M. Schullian. New York, 1967.

Guicciardini, Luigi. *The Sack of Rome*. Translated and edited by James H. McGregor. New York, 1993. Translation of *Sacco di Roma*.

Landucci, Luca. *A Florentine Diary from 1450 to 1516*. Translated by Alice de Rosen Jervis. London and New York, 1927. Translation of *Diario fiorentino dal 1450 al 1516*.

Pitti, Buonaccorso, and Gregorio Dati. *Two Memoirs of Renaissance Florence*. Translated by Julia Martines. Edited by Gene Brucker. New York, 1967. Translation of *Cronica di Buonaccorso Pitti* and *Il Libro segreto di Gregorio Dati*.

Secondary Works

Bentley, Jerry H. *Politics and Culture in Renaissance Naples*. Princeton, N.J., 1987.

Breisach, Ernst. *Historiography, Ancient, Medieval, and Modern*. Chicago, 1983.

Burke, Peter. *The Renaissance Sense of the Past*. New York, 1969.

Cochrane, Eric. *Historians and Historiography in the Italian Renaissance*. Chicago, 1981.

Hay, Denys. *Annalists and Historians: Western Historiography from the Eighth to the Eighteenth Centuries*. London, 1977.

Ianziti, Gary. *Humanistic Historiography under the Sforzas*. Oxford, 1988.

Kelley, Donald R. "Humanism and History." In *Renaissance Humanism*. Vol. 3, *Humanism and the Disciplines*. Edited by Albert Rabil Jr. Philadelphia, 1988. Pages 236–270.

Wilcox, Donald J. *The Development of Florentine Humanist Historiography in the Fifteenth Century*. Cambridge, Mass., 1969.

Zimmermann, T. C. Price. *Paolo Giovio: The Historian and the Crisis of Sixteenth-Century Italy*. Princeton, N.J., 1995.

T. C. PRICE ZIMMERMANN

French Historiography

The Renaissance fascination with language shaped the development of sixteenth-century French historical thought in ways both intended and unintended. By proclaiming the power of rhetoric to inspire social and political action, Italian humanists had revitalized the classical conception of history as the *magistra vitae,* the "teacher of life." When imported to France, humanist historiography broke with the tradition of the medieval chronicle by emphasizing human rather than divine agency in history. And in distinction from those they derided as the "musty" chroniclers, French historians burnished with eloquence the virtues worthy of emulation.

But the rhetorical nature of humanist historiography unwittingly raised the specter of historical Pyrrhonism, that authors embellished accounts to suit the vanity of their patrons, thus threatening to render history an untrustworthy guide to life. In response, some scholars adopted the methods of the French legal humanists, using philology to create a new kind of history concerned with institutions rather than individuals. But here, too, the humanist fascination with language had unintended consequences. Philology fostered an awareness of fundamental differences between past and present, undermining the humanist conception of history as the *magistra vitae* while failing to provide a workable alternative.

Humanist Historiography and the Medieval Chronicle. The monk Robert Gaguin (c. 1433–1501) launched humanist historiography in France with the publication of his *Compendium de origine et gestis Francorum* (Compendium of the origins and deeds of the French) in 1495. This work recasts in a classical Latin mold the medieval vernacular chronicle, epitomized by the tradition of the *Grandes chroniques de France* (Great chronicles of France). The monks of the royal chapel of Saint-Denis had originated the *Grandes chroniques* in the thirteenth century, composing from Latin sources a vernacular chronicle that enfolds the history of the French kingdom within the broader scheme of a Christian universal history extending all the way back to the Creation. Subsequent generations of authors both lay and clerical carried this narrative forward to the sixteenth century, thus creating a quasi-official history of the kingdom. In addition to enshrining stories of divine intervention on behalf of the French, and tales of heroism and chivalry, the *Grandes chroniques* also inculcated the myth of the Trojan origins of the French as a race descended from Francus, a fugitive from the destruction of Troy.

Far from revising these myths and stories, Gaguin mainly tidied up the narrative as he transposed it into classical Latin, the language of enduring eloquence. He had written the *Compendium* in the vain hope of being appointed royal historiographer, a position subsequently attained by his rival Paolo Emilio (d. 1529), who broke decisively with the tradition of the *Grandes chroniques*. A native of Verona, Emilio followed Charles VIII back to France after the king's expedition to Italy in 1494. In his *De rebus gestis Francorum* (Deeds of the French), first published in 1517 and expanded in later editions, Emilio wrote history not only in classical Latin but also in the classical manner, emphasizing human over divine agency in the kind of political narrative that had become popular in fifteenth-century Italy. Although he based this narrative on a wide reading of sources, extending beyond the medieval chronicles to include ancient authorities as well as modern histories and scholarly works, Emilio did not so much write critical history as refabricate traditional tales from a political perspective.

Emilio established the humanist genre of royal historiography that would flourish well into the seventeenth century and would eventually include vernacular works in addition to Latin ones. But attacks on his immediate successors, Guillaume Du Bellay (1491–1543) and Pierre de Paschal (1522–1565), for being too credulous or too slavishly classical cast a shadow across the whole project of humanist historiography. Although motivated in part by professional jealousy, these attacks also reflect a growing concern for historical accuracy by some of the leading scholars and historians of the day. Writing in the preface to his 1571 account of the Wars of Religion in France, for example, Lancelot Voisin de La Po-

pelinière (1540–1608) brands humanist historians as "fly-by-nights" who sully an honorable profession with their distortions and lies. He echoes the historical Pyrrhonism of the Italian Francesco Patrizi (1529–1597) by arguing that most historians are biased in favor of their patrons, while the unbiased ones are too far removed from the councils of kings to render an accurate account of events.

The *Ars historica*. His own critique notwithstanding, La Popelinière still proclaimed history the *magistra vitae* and never doubted the utility of studying the past. Like many of his contemporaries, he drew confidence and inspiration from arguments put forth in the popular genre of the *ars historica*, or art of writing history. Arising with the humanist revival of political history in fifteenth-century Italy, this genre expounded classical commonplaces about the necessity for historical knowledge, the attributes of the good historian, and the qualities that imbue his writings. In the sixteenth century, however, French theorists expanded the genre to include not only the art of writing histories but also that of reading them. From the art of critical reading they intended to construct a new account of the past, detailing the customs, laws, and institutions of states.

In 1566 Jean Bodin (1530–1596) published the most famous and enduring of the *artes historicae*, his *Methodus ad facilem historiarum cognitionem* (Method for the easy comprehension of history). Here he maintains that histories cannot provide a prescription for human ills until their findings are reduced to a system, like the art of medicine. He suggests beginning one's study of history with an overview of the past that highlights the major peoples and affairs and then proceeds to elaborate these topics in ever greater detail through a systematic program of intensive reading and note taking. The latter task in particular underscored the need to choose historians carefully and to read them critically, lest one's notebook become filled with misleading and contradictory information.

In addition to showing how to distinguish good historians from bad ones, Bodin also proposed various methods of critical reading to resolve the inevitable contradictions within good histories and between reliable historians. Of special interest is his theory that climate affects the balance of "bodily humors," accounting for differences among peoples. By this and other means, such as astrology and numerology, Bodin attempted to provide readers with a critical standpoint for judging the accuracy of the historical record. This kind of theorizing reveals an implicit shift in the meaning of the term "history," from signifying a body of literature composed of "histories" to constituting a nascent conception of the past as a whole, what we would today call "history itself."

Legal Humanism and Historical Scholarship.

Foremost a jurist and legal thinker, Bodin owed his emerging conception of the past to his exposure to French legal humanism, which had pioneered the philological study of Justinian's *Corpus juris civilis* (Body of civil law), the sixth-century compilation of Roman law. In what became known as the *mos gallicus docendi,* or "French manner of teaching" Roman law, humanist legal scholars argued that the text of the *Corpus juris* needed to be purified of scribal errors before its universal principles could be applied to contemporary problems. This task fostered an awareness of historical as well as linguistic change and ultimately revealed that the *Corpus juris* was not the text of universal law but the law of a past society, promulgated in response to that society's own particular needs and circumstances.

The towering figure of legal humanism, Jacques Cujas (1522–1590), established the University of Bourges as the chief center for the "French historical school of law," influencing a generation of law students at a time when legal education was the passport to a career in the royal bureaucracy. Cujas's admirers—men like Pierre Pithou (1539–1596), Claude Fauchet (1530–1601), and Étienne Pasquier (1529–1615)—eventually constituted a scholarly circle of their own devoted to the study of French antiquities. In the routine performance of their professional duties to king and kingdom, these jurists handled countless documents, which they naturally came to view from the historical perspective acquired during their legal education. In this process, they developed a more critical appreciation of the French past, conceiving of the kingdom's customs, laws, and institutions as utterly distinct from Roman ones, as uniquely French.

An early casualty of the more critical view of the past was the myth of the Trojan origins of the Franks, by which the French had tried to graft their pedigree onto a Roman genealogical tree rooted in Trojan soil. Gaguin and Emilio had paid lip service to the story of Francus, but the brevity of their treatment bespoke their skepticism. Soon thereafter the redoubtable German humanist Beatus Rhenanus (1485–1547) began arguing for the Germanic origin of the Franks. Naturally, this possibility horrified the French, who generated competing theories, such as Bodin's con-

tention in the *Methodus* that the Franks were a Gallic people who eventually returned to their homeland after having migrated east of the Rhine.

Cujas's successor at Bourges, François Hotman (1524–1590), offered the most likely account of the origins of the Franks in his *Francogallia* (1573). Weaving together the best of ancient sources and modern research, Hotman contended that the name "Franks" appeared in Roman documents only after several Germanic tribes of long standing had joined forces to invade Gaul in the third century. Culminating decades of growing doubt, Hotman finally laid the centuries-old Trojan myth to rest, at least in learned circles.

Far from existing for its own sake, the new historical view of France served the various political agendas of its practitioners, who were active participants in the affairs of the kingdom rather than cloistered scholars. For example, Pithou, Fauchet, and Pasquier used their scholarship to bolster the relatively recent claim that a uniquely Gallican church had always existed independent of papal authority. Freely interpreting the historical record in support of this claim, Fauchet maintained that the Gallican church originated with the earliest kings of France, Pithou argued that its traditions stood apart from those of the church in Rome, and Pasquier fashioned a history of its ambivalent relations with the papacy.

Needless to say, the new scholarship became a ready weapon in the Wars of Religion that convulsed the kingdom from 1562 until the end of the century. The Protestant Hotman, for example, wrote the *Francogallia* not to resolve the scholarly problem of Frankish origins but to present a partisan view of French history. He ascribed the outbreak of the Wars of Religion to Louis XI's weakening of the Estates General in the late fifteenth century. According to Hotman, this assembly embodied the "ancient constitution" of the French, the vital heart of a polity born when the Franks established a council of notables charged with electing and, if necessary, deposing their kings. Under the guise of dispassionate inquiry, Hotman thus offered his coreligionists constitutional grounds for opposing the crown.

New versus Old Conceptions of History.

Forged in the philological mold of French legal humanism, the weapon of historical scholarship ultimately severed present from past. The polemical use of history generally turned upon arguments about the distinctiveness of French culture and institutions, thus calling into question the long-standing notion of history as the *magistra vitae.* How could the

French draw lessons relevant to the present from a remote past populated by different peoples and cultures? Bodin's response in the *Methodus* was to design a historical notebook that would organize ancient and modern examples topically in a wide range of categories, from which one could distill general lessons. True to his predilection as jurist, he sought universal principles underlying the newly revealed world of historical uniqueness.

Others among Bodin's contemporaries, juridically trained but more historically inclined, sought a different means of relating past to present. In his *Idée de l'histoire accomplie* (Idea of perfect history), published in 1599, La Popelinière outlined a new historiographical project that would reveal the "substance" of history, which devolved upon the "causes" shaping the different states and their distinctive institutions. His ideal of "perfect" or "complete" history was "scientific" in the Aristotelian sense, denoting a body of exact knowledge that disclosed the causes of things. Ultimately, La Popelinière sought to connect present to past by tracing all the causes of all the states back to the most remote past, potentially back to the ultimate cause, the very origin of mankind itself.

Hardly an original thinker, La Popelinière merely gave systematic expression to a conception of the past widespread among late-sixteenth-century scholars, as illustrated by Nicolas Vignier's compendious *Bibliothèque historiale* (Historical library) of 1587. In three massive folio volumes, Vignier (1530–1596) summarized all human history from the Creation to his own day on an enormous time line, dating each event with reference to many different chronological systems so as to give the most detailed and accurate presentation of the "substance" of history. The compulsive excess of Vignier's ponderous chronology underscores the impractical goal of perfect history. Even if one actually could achieve "completeness," anything approaching a systematic account of all events and peoples threatened to bury the reader under an avalanche of detail. Ultimately, perfect history proved too unwieldy a conception of the past to supplant the notion of *historia magistra vitae*.

Humanist Historiography and the New Scholarship.

Partially by default of readable alternatives, humanist historiography continued to flourish in the late sixteenth century, but it had to incorporate the results of the new scholarship in order to maintain respectability. Thus, for a short while, historical scholarship appeared on the verge of reshaping historical narrative. The royal histori-

ographer Bernard de Girard, seigneur Du Haillan (c. 1536–1610), utilized recent antiquarian research in the two editions of his *Histoire de France* (1576 and 1584), where he rejected the Trojan myth and wove an account of distinctive French laws and institutions into his humanistic narrative of political events. Even an unofficial history like *Les grandes annales,* a sixteenth-century continuation of the *Grandes chroniques* by the popularizer François de Belleforest (1530–1583), rejects the myth of the Trojan origins and subjects famous episodes in French history to more critical scrutiny than they had received at the hands of previous chroniclers.

Jacques Auguste De Thou (1553–1617) stands as the greatest humanist historian of the French Renaissance, combining refined scholarly sensibilities with a magisterial Latin eloquence worthy of the ancients. After studying law under both Hotman and Cujas, De Thou entered the Parlement of Paris, embarking upon an illustrious political career that brought him into contact with scholar-jurists like Pasquier and Pithou. The latter, a good friend of De Thou's, encouraged him to begin work on what would eventually become the *Historia sui temporis* (History of his time). De Thou conceived this project as a "universal history" in the Polybian sense of having broad geographical scope. It would weave together events in Germany, Spain, the Netherlands, England, and especially France, revealing the Europe-wide dynamics that underlay more than a half century of religious war. Having chosen his life's work, De Thou spent the next twenty years gathering the necessary documents and, in the course of time, amassed one of the largest private libraries in the kingdom.

The first volume of his monumental, and ultimately unfinished, history appeared in 1604, to almost immediate acclaim and censure. Adherents of both religious camps praised the Catholic De Thou's unflinching honesty, the very quality that excited the wrath of the powers that be. Placed on the Index of Prohibited Books in 1609, the *Historia sui temporis* garnered the admiration of subsequent generations, yet it found few imitators. By the mid-seventeenth century, humanist historiography had become little more than royal propaganda so divorced from the previous century's scholarly standards that even the myth of Trojan origins threatened a comeback. In the final analysis, the humanist mode of historical writing proved incapable of sustaining the new scholarship, which could not stand on its own for lack of a coherent conception of the past and its relation to the present. The new scholarship was thus relegated to little more than antiquarian status until the eighteenth century, when it finally revitalized the writing of history.

See also **Gallicanism**; **Humanism**, *subentry on* **Legal Humanism**; **Wars of Italy**; **Wars of Religion**; *and biographies of Jean Bodin and Beatus Rhenanus.*

BIBLIOGRAPHY

Bezold, Friedrich von. *Aus Mittelalter und Renaissance*. Munich, 1918. See in particular his pioneering essay, "Zur Enstehungsgeschichte der historischen Methodik."

Brown, John L. *The* Methodus ad facilem historiarum cognitionem *of Jean Bodin: A Critical Study*. Washington, D.C., 1939. A classic study not only of Bodin but also of the *artes historicae* in the sixteenth century.

Dubois, Claude-Gilbert. *Celtes et gaulois au XVIe siècle*. Paris, 1972.

Dubois, Claude-Gilbert. *La conception de l'histoire en France au XVIe siècle*. Paris, 1977. A compendious study emphasizing the relations between history and theology.

Franklin, Julian H. *Jean Bodin and the Sixteenth-Century Revolution in the Methodology of Law and History*. New York, 1963. An exceptionally cogent analysis encompassing other major figures in addition to Bodin.

Gilmore, Myron P. *Humanists and Jurists: Six Studies in the Renaissance*. Cambridge, Mass., 1963.

Huppert, George. *The Idea of Perfect History: Historical Evaluation and Historical Relativism in Renaissance France*. Urbana, Ill., 1970.

Kelley, Donald R. *Foundations of Modern Historical Scholarship: Language, Law, and History in the French Renaissance*. New York, 1970. By now the standard reference work on the topic.

Pocock, J. G. A. *The Ancient Constitution and the Feudal Law*. Cambridge, U.K., 1987. See especially chapter 1.

Ranum, Orest. *Artisans of Glory: Writers and Historical Thought in Seventeenth-century France*. Chapel Hill, N.C., 1980.

Schiffman, Zachary Sayre. *On the Threshold of Modernity: Relativism in the French Renaissance*. Baltimore, 1991. See especially chapters 1–2.

ZACHARY S. SCHIFFMAN

British Historiography

The changes that occurred in British historical writing between the late fifteenth and early seventeenth centuries are readily identified if one compares representative works from each end of the period. At the beginning, the late medieval chronicle, together with pseudohistorical hagiography and romances inspired by legends of Troy and Alexander the Great, dominated a relatively narrow field of historical works, which were read by few laymen in England, Wales, and Scotland. With some exceptions, principally biographical, chronicles were generally arranged in "annals," with all the events for a particular year recorded together without any overarching narrative structure. In contrast, by the early decades of the seventeenth century, the chronicle was in full decline, its place taken by a variety of other genres, including the humanist-inspired "politic history." Ecclesiastical history had been reenergized, if ideologically divided, by the debates of the Reformation; Catholic hagiography had been supplanted in large measure by Protestant and Catholic martyrology; and life-writing—biographical and autobiographical—was beginning to become a genre in its own right.

Early Surveys of History: Scotland. As elsewhere in Europe, the reading and writing of history in Renaissance Britain was intimately bound up with external developments in church and state, as well as with the expanded intellectual horizons opened up by humanism. Humanism came to Britain rather later than to other parts of Europe: by the time of John Major, or Mair (1469–1550), in Scotland and Polydore Vergil (1470–1555) in England, both of whom were active in the early part of the sixteenth century, humanist historiography had been in full flower in Italy for nearly a century. Moreover, the efforts of the early sixteenth-century British writers did not carry great weight in the first instance. Major was a first-rate thinker with a European orientation and a strongly ethnographic sense of his own nation's development, combined with a pan-British perspective, which led him to see Lowland Scots and English as more natural allies than the "barbarous" Highlanders whose culture and language were increasingly different from that of their neighbors to the south. Major's Britannic perspective had to wait a century or more to find a receptive audience; it was not popular in the era of continued Anglo-Scottish hostilities, and consequently his *Historia majoris Britanniae* (History of Great Britain; Paris, 1521) was much less widely read in Scotland than was the *Scotorum historiae a prima gentis origine* (History of the Scots from the origin of that people) written by his contemporary, Hector Boece (c. 1465–1536).

Published in 1526, Boece's work was a full-scale national history that reached back into the mists of remote antiquity. Boece rendered into elegant humanist Latin (subsequently put back into vernacular Scots by John Bellenden) a whole lineage of Scottish kings dating back to the mythical Fergus MacFerquhard, who had supposedly ruled about 330 B.C. Boece took his material largely from late medieval chroniclers such as Walter Bower, Andrew of Wyntoun, and above all John de Fordun (c. 1320–c. 1384); these writers had been inspired by patriotic feelings during the long struggle for independence from England that began in the 1290s, feelings expressed in medieval constitutional documents such as the 1320 Declaration of Arbroath. The medieval chroniclers had done for Scottish history what Geoffrey of Monmouth, a twelfth-century monk, had previously done for English history—namely, provide a mythical and legendary ancestry for the Stewart monarchs in an effort to proclaim Scotland's historical independence from the "auld inimie" to the south. Boece went further still, giving us much of the invented material on the foundation of the Mac-Malcolm dynasty in the mid-eleventh century, stories that Shakespeare would rework in *Macbeth* after the union of the Scottish and English crowns in 1603 under James I.

Early Surveys of History: England. In England the lines of humanist influence on historical writing came directly from Italy, or at least from peripatetic Italians in the service of English and foreign governments, beginning with Tito Livio Frulovisi of Ferrara (fl. 1437), retained by Duke Humfrey of Gloucester to write a biography of the duke's dead brother, King Henry V. Later in the century, the story of the Yorkist victory in the dynastic struggles of the 1450s and 1460s was told by the Brescian Pietro Carmeliano (d. 1527), who proved pliable enough to adapt his pen to the service of the first Tudor monarch, Henry VII. The first full-scale Renaissance history of England was the work of another Italian émigré, Polydore Vergil of Urbino, who arrived in England in 1502 as a minor papal official and stayed there for nearly half a century. His *Anglica historia* (first published at Basel in 1534) departed from previous chronicles by replacing annalistic writing with a connected story told reign by reign, modeled in good humanist fashion on the great histories of antiquity, especially those of Livy. Vergil's history was the closest equivalent in Britain to the sort of court-sponsored national history to emerge from the likes of Paolo Emili in France. But the importance of Vergil lay less in the humanist mold he established (which would not, in fact, be much imitated until very late in the century) than in his outsider's critical perspective on the myths of ancient British kings deriving from Geoffrey of Monmouth. Vergil cast particular doubt on two key figures in that lineage, the eponymous Brutus the Trojan, who had wrested Britain away from a race of giants and ruled the entire island, and Arthur, the British war leader whose historical reality had become completely buried in a morass of legend, oral tradition, and chivalric romance. Vergil's pro-Tudor perspective made him valuable to the dynasty in the early years of Henry VIII, when renewed struggles with France and the

protection of the dynasty from a perceived but negligible Yorkist threat took precedence; it was equally helpful after 1530, when England broke with Rome and the issue of establishing the nation as a sovereign "empire" became important. On the other hand, Vergil's skepticism toward the old legends outraged embryonic nationalist sensibilities, arousing native antiquaries like John Bale and John Leland, and especially the Welsh historians who traced their ancestry back to ancient Britons, such as John Price and Humphrey Llwyd, into heaping torrents of abuse on Vergil as a foreigner and, eventually, as a lackey of Rome.

Beginnings of Biography, Autobiography, and Diaries. During the first part of the sixteenth century biography began to emerge as a distinct historical genre, the outstanding examples being a life of Henry VIII's minister, Cardinal Wolsey, by his former servant, George Cavendish (1500–c. 1561), and an incomplete life of Richard III written in divergent English and Latin versions by the greatest figure among the early Tudor humanists, Sir Thomas More (1478–1535), the future lord chancellor and eventual saint. Cavendish would not be published until the seventeenth century, but More's work would turn up as an add-on to various longer histories, Vergil's included, throughout the period. Later in the century, the martyred More's own life would provide the subject for at least three biographies, the most famous being that by his son-in-law, William Roper (1496–1578). Although notions of "individualism" such as those formulated by Jakob Burckhardt as an explanation for Renaissance culture are often criticized, there is no good reason to doubt that a strong sense of the significance of individual lives, governed either by an overarching plan laid out by Providence or by the whim of Fortune, played an important role in the emergence of biography and, in the seventeenth century, autobiography. From the middle of the century onward, that sense of significance also led Scots and English alike to keep that most personal of historical records, the diary.

The inclusion of biographical elements in mid- and late-Tudor chronicles provides a warning against overemphasizing the degree of difference between the newer humanist history and the older medieval tradition. Edward Hall (d. 1547), the outstanding chronicler of Henry VIII's reign, would make use of Vergil (as Vergil himself, in his later editions, made use of Hall, first published posthumously in 1548), while the enormous multi-author chronicle assembled by Raphael Holinshed in 1577 (revised and expanded after Holinshed's death into a second edition of 1587) would show an awareness of England's overall history and a sense of national identity not radically different from that which emerges in Vergil.

Scottish Reformation Historiography.

A more decisive break with the historiographical practices of the past came in the second half of the century, and it was driven by religious and political forces as much as by intellectual change. In Scotland, the most celebrated neo-Latin poet of his age, George Buchanan (1506–1582), adapted material he found in Boece and Major into a revisionist history of the Scottish monarchy, the *Rerum Scoticarum historia* (History of Scottish affairs; 1582), and a political treatise, *De iure lure regni apud Scotos* (Of the law of kinship among the Scots; 1579). These works used history to provide an argument for constitutional limits on royal power and to establish what amounted to the sovereignty of the magistracy, or at least the right of the nobility to resist and even depose a tyrannical prince. In this Buchanan was inspired by the older tradition, dating back to the Declaration of Arbroath, of Scotland as a "community of the realm," as well as by Old Testament distinctions between godly and ungodly rulers and a presbyterian sense of the civil authority's separation from, and subordination to, the authority of the kirk, or church. As tutor to the young James VI, Buchanan would give that king both a dislike of attacks on royal prerogative and a strong sense of his own nation's past. Buchanan's Calvinist perspective would be given full form in the *History of the Reformation* written by the formidable John Knox (1505–1572), a disciple of John Calvin who, with aristocratic support, had turned Lowland Scotland Protestant in 1560 and then helped topple the country's last Catholic monarch of the sixteenth century, Mary, queen of Scots. In the writings of Knox and Buchanan, Scottish national consciousness was linked simultaneously to the history of the Scottish kirk and to the power of the nobility to enforce the Reformation on errant monarchs. That vision also placed Scotland in the wider divine plan for the ultimate redemption of humanity, since Knox in particular saw the Reformation he had enacted in Scotland as a model to be followed by other national monarchies. Knox established a strong tradition of Protestant ecclesiastical history writing that would be elaborated in different directions by early seventeenth-century historians such as David Calderwood (1575–1650) and Archbishop John Spottiswood (1565–1639)—the former taking the presbyterian line and the latter defending moderate episcopacy. Church history was thus, in many ways, the paradigm for all historical writing in Scotland for six or seven decades after 1580.

English Historiography after the Reformation.

In England, where the monarch from 1559 was "supreme governor" of the church, little such intermixture of the history of church and state took place. Indeed, those who wrote histories of particular reigns, especially of sixteenth-century rulers, tended to sidestep ecclesiastical matters and leave them to church polemicists like Richard Hooker, who made considerable use of history in their arguments. The principal exceptions to this rule were, not surprisingly, Catholic exiles such as Nicholas Harpsfield, Nicholas Sander, and, somewhat later, Robert Parsons and Richard Broughton, all of whom attacked the civil and ecclesiastical regimes of Elizabeth I and her successor, James I (James VI of Scotland). Beginning with attempts under Henry VIII to mine chronicles and records for evidence of English imperial status and for arguments on behalf of that king's divorce from Catherine of Aragon, the status of the English church, and especially its past, inspired considerable debates using historical sources. Throughout Elizabeth's reign, most of this activity, as noted above, did not take place in the form of proper histories. The single most widely read history book of the late sixteenth and early seventeenth centuries was the work of a former Protestant exile, John Foxe. His *Actes and Monuments* (1563) was republished several times during those centuries. Modeled on early ecclesiastical histories by Eusebius and Bede, but drawing also on martyrology and, somewhat perversely, on the very Catholic hagiography it was designed to supplant, Foxe's *Book of Martyrs*, as it became known—with its accounts of individual martyrdoms (especially those that took place under the Catholic Mary I) enlivened by colorful language and, for the illiterate, its many woodcuts—had an impact on English Protestants' sense of their national past that is impossible to overestimate.

Despite their sharing an attachment to differing myths of origins, England's historical culture developed quite differently from Scotland's in this and other ways. England had and continued to produce a much richer vein of chronicle writing than could be found in Scotland, sometimes informed by Protestant belief that injected a stronger sense of providentialism, and at other times rather more neutral on matters of faith. Certain chroniclers, like Thomas

Lanquet (1521–1545) or the printer-turned-chronicler Richard Grafton (d. 1572?), wrote from a Protestant perspective that would be echoed by Holinshed's various contributors in the 1570s and 1580s, especially the chronologer and minister William Harrison (1534–1593). Others, however, such as John Stow (1525?–1605), evinced pro-Catholic sympathies, a nostalgia for the lost medieval past, and a vigorous dislike of the iconoclastic destruction of books and monuments that occurred at various points in the Reformation. Stow in fact would be charged by the government with owning "popish" books in the late 1560s.

Stow's many historical works, published in different formats and lengths, each in several successive editions, dominated the expanding market for history books, principally an urban one centered in London, from the 1570s to the 1590s. They were reprinted at various points up to 1631, with continuations added after Stow's death in 1605 by Edmund Howes, about whom almost nothing is known. They formed a kind of middling-sized, middling-priced history between the bulk of a Holinshed and the slimmer volumes in small formats put out by Londoners such as the translator and dramatist Anthony Munday (c. 1560–1633), which were designed to service an even wider market. The late-Renaissance scholar Louis B. Wright has often been faulted for overstating the degree to which there was an identifiable and cohesive "middle-class" culture in late-Tudor England, but he was correct to note that the readership market for history had expanded considerably by the death of Queen Elizabeth in 1603, even if one concedes that that expansion was in turn dwarfed by the enormous explosion of historical works of various sorts that would occur in the second half of the seventeenth century.

Discussions of the Theory of History.
Beginning in Elizabeth's reign and continuing through the reigns of James I and Charles I, there was also some interest in theorizing about history, first expressed in frequent restatements in book prefaces of Cicero's discussion of history as *magistra vitae* (guide of life) and *lux veritatis* (light of truth) or as "philosophy teaching by examples." The importance of indigenous writings on the theory of history should not be overstated. There was no vigorous tradition of *artes historicae* of the sort that appeared in other European countries in the second half of the sixteenth century—though some late English imitations of these were produced by writers like Degory Whear, Peter Heylin, and Francis Bacon in the early

seventeenth century—but Thomas Blundeville (fl. 1561–1575) translated and revised works by two Italian *trattatisti* (essayists), Francesco Patrizi da Cherso and Giacomo Aconcio, in 1574. Jean Bodin's *Methodus ad facilem historiarum cognitionem* (Method of easily learning history; 1566), perhaps the most sophisticated of the European works, was widely read in England after about 1580. In the longer run, however, the most influential work on such matters was written by a man who was neither an historian nor especially well-disposed to history. Sir Philip Sidney's *Defence of Poesy* (1595) adopted an Aristotelian preference for the moral truths of fiction over the contingent knowledge of history. His concerns are symptomatic of the same sort of uncertainty over the status of the knowledge of the past, and the relationship between history and imaginative literature, that would drive the "Pyrrhonist" skeptical tradition in seventeenth-century Europe—an uncertainty that has continued to provoke debate down to our own day.

Antiquarianism. Antiquarianism must be mentioned here briefly because it ultimately had a significant impact on British historiography. The close philological study of documents and texts, including their language, handwriting, and physical appearance, which was the hallmark of Renaissance humanism from the time of Lorenzo Valla, had a rich history in Britain going at least as far back as John Leland's tours through England in the 1540s to rescue manuscripts from the libraries of dissolved monastic houses. The parallel archaeological side of antiquarianism that descends from Flavio Biondo emerges in Leland's *Itineraries*, a record of the monuments and landscape features that he encountered on his travels. This approach would culminate in William Camden's *Britannia* (1586), a much republished and widely read guide to the Roman and later antiquities of the whole island, and in similar studies of the monuments, landscape, families, and even customs of particular counties and cities. (The capital received exemplary treatment of this sort from John Stow in the former chronicler's 1598 *Survay of London.*) As practiced by heralds, expert in genealogical muniments, and especially lawyers, many of whom met in the short-lived Elizabethan Society of Antiquaries for two decades after 1586, antiquarianism maintained a distance from history proper for a while, eschewing its narrative form and preoccupation with great events. But by the early seventeenth century, antiquarian methods were beginning to influence narrative historiography more directly. The blurring of genres that this entailed can be seen at the end of the period in such works as John Selden's *History of Tithes* (1618), a controversial account that synthesized the best methods of late-Renaissance philology with a lawyer's sense of how to make an argument, producing what amounted to a full-scale revision of lay-clerical relations and the institutional history of the English church over several centuries.

The Displacement of the Chronicles. Little of this ferment derived from, or influenced, the chronicles, which had had their day by the 1590s. By then, authors and printer-booksellers alike were beginning to differentiate among subgenres of history in order to reach a market that was becoming increasingly socially stratified. The publication of Stow's London book in different forms was part of this trend, as were the mini-chronologies of the likes of Munday and the fictional "histories" by Thomas Deloney and others—early prose narratives or proto-novels with heroes drawn from the middling sort as in Deloney's *Jack of Newberry,* as well as older-style romances based on legendary local heroes like Sir Guy of Warwick and Sir Bevis of Southampton. But other sorts of history were also produced and sold, notably popular almanacs that increasingly featured little "chronologies" of major events (often including seemingly trivial facts, of interest to a more popular readership, such as the year in which boots were invented or particular buildings were erected). A socially heterogeneous audience was drawn to the history plays that began with early-Tudor efforts like John Bale's *King Johan,* continued with Thomas Sackville and Thomas Norton's *Gorboduc,* on the division of Britain in legendary times, and climaxed in the mature history plays of Christopher Marlowe, George Peele, George Chapman, Ben Jonson (especially on Roman history), and above all, William Shakespeare. The history plays reveal a deep insecurity about the status of the commonwealth in the waning years of Elizabeth I's reign, an uncertainty that recalls the anti-Yorkist thrust of early Tudor historiography rather more than the religious issues that dominated historical consciousness between 1530 and 1590.

The dramatists were not alone in evincing such concerns, for they had a prose counterpart in the so-called politic histories that began to appear in the 1590s amid a prolonged economic crisis and the great uncertainty surrounding the succession in the last years of the childless queen. These works looked back to Polydore Vergil's regnal structure (which offered a way out of further imitation of the chroniclers' annals) and also to biographical pieces such as More's *Richard III* for a pattern. But their real inspiration came from exposure to the still-proscribed writings of Niccolò Machiavelli and especially from an acute interest in Greco-Roman historians such as Polybius, Thucydides, Sallust, and above all Tacitus. That historian's terse, epigrammatic style, previously considered difficult, now came into fashion, spearheaded by English translations of his works by a distinguished classicist, Sir Henry Savile. Tacitus inspired this interest in part because his *Histories* and *Annals* of the early Roman emperors were pregnant with political advice for dark times—advice to rulers on how to govern and to subjects on how to survive the vicissitudes of politics. These teachings found their way into historical narratives. The vogue of the politic history lasted from 1590 to the early 1620s and witnessed a series of regnally structured histories, beginning with a work by the civil lawyer John Hayward, in 1598, and continuing into the next reign. The dangers of studying the deeds of monarchs too closely, in an age when the past was seen primarily as a mirror of the present rather than as its organic cause, were clear enough: Hayward's Tacitean study, *The First Part of the Life and Raigne of King Henrie the IIII,* which was really about the deposition of Richard II, was unwisely dedicated to the maverick courtier, Robert Devereux, earl of Essex, an alliance that nearly brought Hayward himself to the scaffold with his patron after Essex's abortive coup d'état in 1601.

Despite these difficulties, historians soldiered on. During the first two decades of the seventeenth century one also finds, in a similar vein, biographical studies of the middle Tudors (by Francis Godwin), Henry VII (by the disgraced former chancellor Francis Bacon, in 1622), Henry VIII (by Edward, Lord Herbert of Cherbury), and, most scholarly of all, a full-scale set of *Annales* (in Latin, soon translated by others) by William Camden on Queen Elizabeth, based on state papers made available to Camden by the Jacobean government. There were also general surveys of the history of England and (mainly in translation) of other nations, including a study of Anglo-Scottish history by Edward Ayscu (1549?–1617); general histories of England by John Clapham (1566–after 1613), John Speed (1552–1629), and William Martyn (1562–1617); and a *Collection of the Historie of England,* which was really an insightful study of the evolution of England's constitution and culture by the court poet Samuel Daniel (1562–1619). Finally, there was a curious but very popular

History of the World (1614) by Sir Walter Ralegh (1552–1618). Ralegh presented a dark vision of ancient history, suffused by providential judgments on the mighty, which he wrote during his long imprisonment under sentence of death. It was much read throughout the seventeenth century, proving especially popular among female readers and those of a millenarian disposition. The late-Renaissance histories proved remarkably durable and were reprinted and read well into the eighteenth century, long after the circumstances that had given rise to them had changed, and they completed the demotion of the chronicle into little more than a source for "proper" history, though it must be admitted that chronicle writing as a form of record keeping continued in many seventeenth-century towns.

There were limits to how many times each king's story could be told, and by the 1630s few new histories were being written. The end of Renaissance historiography in Britain may be said to have arrived in 1641, when the collapse of censorship, shortly followed by the outbreak of civil war throughout the British Isles, allowed for the same reenergizing of historical writing that had been seen in Italy in the 1490s during the French and Spanish invasions. From that point on, history ceased to be an instrument of advice for the ruler, or an account of mere facts for ordinary readers, and became instead a vehicle for the partisan debate that would infuse it throughout the next two centuries.

See also **Antiquarianism; Biography and Autobiography,** *subentry on* **England; Chivalry,** *subentries on* **Arthurian Romance** *and* **Romance of Chivalry; Chronicle, Elizabethan; Hagiography; Historiography, Classical,** *subentries on* **Greek Historians** *and* **Roman Historians; Machiavelli, Niccolò,** *subentry on* **The Political Theorist; Skepticism; Travel and Travel Literature.**

BIBLIOGRAPHY

Primary Works

Boece, Hector. *The Chronicles of Scotland, Compiled by Hector Boece, Translated into Scots by John Bellenden, 1531.* Edited by R. W. Chambers and Edith C. Batho. 2 vols. Edinburgh and London, 1938–1941.

Buchanan, George. *A Chronicle of the Kings of Scotland, from Fergus the First, to James the Sixth, in the Year 1611.* Edinburgh, 1830. Translation of Buchanan's *Rerum Scoticarum historia* (1582).

Camden, William. *Britain; or, A Chorographicall Description of the Most Flourishing Kingdomes, England, Scotland, and Ireland.* Translated by Philemon Holland (London, 1607) from the Latin *Britannia* (first published 1586).

Camden, William. *The History of the Most Renowned and Victorious Princess Elizabeth, Late Queen of England.* Edited by Wallace T. MacCaffrey. Chicago, 1970. Reprint of selected chapters from a seventeenth-century translation of Latin original, *Annales rerum anglicarum et hibernicarum regnante Elizabetha, ad annum salutis 1589* (London, 1615).

Daniel, Samuel. *The Collection of the Historie of England.* London, 1618. Facsimile edition, Delmar, N.Y., 1986.

Foxe, John. *The Acts and Monuments of John Foxe.* Edited by S. R. Cattley. 8 vols. London, 1837–1841. Readily available but unreliable; new critical edition under way under the editorship of David Loades.

Hall, Edward. *Hall's Chronicle.* Reprint, New York, 1965. Original publication 1548.

Holinshed, Raphael. *The First and Second Volumes of Chronicles.* London, 1587. Revised and expanded edition of work first published in 1577; a major source for Shakespeare's history plays.

Knox, John. *The History of the Reformation in Scotland.* Edited by David Laing. 2 vols. Edinburgh, 1846–1848. Volumes 1 and 2 of *Works of John Knox.*

Stow, John. *Annales; or, A Generall Chronicle of England.* London, 1631. The final edition of the longest of Stow's series of chronicles, as continued by Edmund Howes.

Vergil, Polydore. *Anglica historia, A.D. 1485–1537.* Edited with a translation by Denys Hay. London, 1950. Translation of portion of Vergil dealing with early Tudor history.

Vergil, Polydore. *Three Books of Polydore Vergil's English History.* Edited by Sir Henry Ellis. Reprint, New York, 1968. A partial English translation, made in the sixteenth century, of Vergil's Latin *Anglicae historiae libri vigintisex* (Basel, Switzerland, 1534).

Secondary Works

Allan, David. *Virtue, Learning, and the Scottish Enlightenment: Ideas of Scholarship in Early Modern History.* Edinburgh, 1993. Principally about later period, but has excellent introductory section on sixteenth-century Scottish scholarship.

Baker, Herschel. *The Race of Time: Three Lectures on Renaissance Historiography.* Toronto, 1967. Brief but interesting essays.

Ferguson, Arthur B. *Clio Unbound: Perceptions of the Social and Cultural Past in Renaissance England.* Durham, N.C., 1979. Insightful studies of the emergence of a perspective on the past, principally through the writings of polemicists and other nonhistorians.

Fussner, F. Smith. *The Historical Revolution: English Historical Writing and Thought, 1580–1640.* 1962. Reprint, Westport, Conn., 1976. Still a useful study, somewhat marred by anachronistically modern notions of historical truth and preoccupation with modernity.

Gransden, Antonia. *Historical Writing in England.* 2 vols. London, 1974–1982. Mainly about medieval writing, but the second volume has useful survey of early sixteenth-century chronicles.

Kelley, Donald R., and David Harris Sacks, eds. *The Historical Imagination in Early Modern Britain: History, Rhetoric, and Fiction, 1500–1800.* Washington, D.C.; New York; and Cambridge, U.K.; 1997. Studies of various historiographical topics by leading authorities.

Kendrick, Thomas Downing. *British Antiquity.* London, 1950. Best survey of myths of foundation and early antiquarian efforts to study them.

Kidd, Colin. *Subverting Scotland's Past: Scottish Whig Historians and the Creation of an Anglo-British Identity, 1689–c. 1830.* Cambridge, U.K., and New York, 1993. Mainly about eighteenth century, but has important opening chapter on Boece, Mair, Knox, and Scottish legends.

Levy, F. J. *Tudor Historical Thought*. San Marino, Calif., 1967. The definitive study of sixteenth-century historical writing.

McKisack, May. *Medieval History in the Tudor Age*. Oxford, 1971. Useful on the early development of antiquarianism but neglects its medieval origins.

Patterson, Annabel. *Reading Holinshed's Chronicles*. Chicago, 1994. Revisionist analysis of the major Elizabethan chronicles, arguing for the continued vitality of the chronicle tradition; valuable corrective to aspects of earlier works that privilege the humanist histories.

Pocock, J. G. A. *The Ancient Constitution and the Feudal Law: A Study of English Historical Thought in the Seventeenth Century: A Reissue with a Retrospect*. Cambridge, U.K., 1987. Expanded edition of a classic study, first published in 1957, principally about political implications of early seventeenth-century Scottish and English antiquarianism.

Williamson, Arthur H. *Scottish National Consciousness in the Age of James VI: The Apocalypse, the Union, and the Shaping of Scotland's Public Culture*. Edinburgh, 1979. Excellent study of historical consciousness at the end of the sixteenth century.

Woolf, D. R. *The Idea of History in Early Stuart England: Erudition, Ideology, and the "Light of Truth" from the Accession of James I to the Civil War*. Toronto, 1990. Special attention to relations between narrative history and antiquarianism, and to the role of ideology in historical writing during the early seventeenth century.

D. R. WOOLF

German Historiography

German historiography has medieval roots in the writing of universal and territorial histories and city chronicles, but self-conscious national history was more directly a product of the Renaissance. In order to defend themselves against the charge of "barbarism" brought by Italian humanists, German scholars such as Hartmann Schedel, Johann Trithemius, Jacob Wimpheling, Heinrich Bebel, Conrad Peutinger, and Conrad Celtis rejected classicist calumnies and began to fashion their own national tradition, so that protonationalist works like Flavio Biondo's *Italia illustrata* were rivaled by the *Germania illustrata* of Celtis (who like Petrarch was a poet laureate) and his colleagues.

German Antiquity.

Lorenzo Valla had famously praised the posthumous victories of Roman civilization, claiming that "ours [the Romans'] is Italy, ours Gaul, ours Spain, Germany . . . , and many other lands; for where the Roman tongue holds sway, there is the Roman Empire." To this challenge German humanists responded in kind. "Ours [the Germans'] are the victories of the Goths, Vandals, and Franks," insisted the Bavarian historian Johannes Aventinus, "ours the glory attached to the kingdoms that these peoples founded in the most illus-

trious provinces of the Romans, in Italy, and in the queen of cities, Rome herself."

Invoking a topos applied to the early Romans, Bebel lamented the neglect of ancient German glory and argued that "Germany can hold its own not only with attainments considered excellent in our own day but also with the greatest of the feats of antiquity." Wimpheling's *Epitome* was designed to fill just this gap, so that his readers

> might discover the antiquities of Germany, read the biographies of the emperors, learn to know their merits, intelligence, campaigns, victories, inventions, nobility, fidelity, courage, constancy, and love of truth of the Germans, and in order to encourage posterity . . . to try every day to add still greater achievements, thus augmenting Germany by new merits.

This was part of a rising chorus of tributes retrospectively bestowed on Germanic culture, with special emphasis on the new German invention of the printing press, which made it possible to celebrate the attainments of both ancients and moderns.

The locus classicus of the modern praise of barbarism was the *Germania* of Tacitus, which had been rediscovered in the early fifteenth century, was exploited thereafter by generations of historians, and was the center of a vast accumulation of commentary and interpretation. What Tacitus offered to his modern Germanist disciples was an "original image of Germany" and its "original manners." The Germanic virtues noted by Tacitus—*pudicitia, liberalitas, integritas, fides, libertas, constantia, fortitudo, ingenium, nobilitas,* and so on—were incorporated into historical works by Wimpheling, Albert Krantz, Ulrich von Hutten, and especially Erasmus's younger friend Beatus Rhenanus. "The German people have always lived in total liberty," wrote Beatus; and moreover they were racially pure—"indigenous" and "unmixed." "From all times the Saxons have been free," as Hutten declared, "and from all times invincible."

Periodization and Protestantism.

While humanists introduced new styles of scholarship and applied them to the study of medieval German "antiquities," older traditions were also preserved, especially in the form of universal chronicles. Among these were the works of Hartmann Schedel, Sebastian Franck, Johann Cario, and Johannes Sleidanus; in *De quatuor summis imperiis* (Geneva, 1559; later translated as *The Key to History*), Sleidanus rehearsed the old story of the Four World Monarchies (the passage of empire from the Medes to the Persians to the Greeks to the Romans) and the "Trans-

German Historian. Inspired by Venus (Cytherea) and other gods, Conrad Celtis (1459–1508) writes at his desk, the classics of antiquity on the bookshelves in front of him.

lation of Empire" to Charlemagne and his successors, including Charles V, the current ruler of the "Holy Roman Empire of the German Nation." In the wake of the Lutheran controversy, the Germanist line of argument was intensified, as historians attacked modern Romanist "tyranny" in the Lutheran struggle against the papacy and began to construct a new view of European and especially ecclesiastical tradition, culminating in Luther's break with the Roman church. Following a humanist as well as an evan-gelical line, Luther began the revision of the ortho-dox conception of the church by rejecting Scholas-ticism and the corrupt traditions of Scholasticism and canon law and by portraying ecclesiastical history as a process of falling away from the ideals of the "primitive church."

The larger patterns of history according to Prot-estant views were noted by Martin Bucer and elab-orated by Philipp Melanchthon in his oration on "Lu-ther and the Ages of the Church." The story was one of doctrinal expansion from the founding of the church, then medieval degeneration, and finally restoration. The first three ages were those of the "primitive church," of Origen, and of Augustine; then came the ages of monasticism and the new "barbarism" of Scholasticism; and lastly the age of the Reformation—of Luther. Not accidentally, this threefold periodization corresponded to the humanist scheme of a bright antiquity, a dark middle age, and a rebirth of "new learning" (a term usually reserved for evangelical religion). "Without history," Melanchthon repeated from Cicero and many others, "one remains forever a child"—referring to "continuous history from the beginning of the world, whence came the principles and sources of true religion."

The official historiographer of the German Reformation was Sleidanus, who was commissioned by the princes of the Schmalkaldic League (a Protestant alliance, 1531). Sleidanus devoted much of his life to telling the story of Luther's words and deeds and the program and efforts of the Protestant party, which gave its support to the new confessional movement. Sleidanus's book—*De statu religionis et reipublicae* (Strasbourg, 1555; translated as *The General History of the Reformation of the Church*) was both a "history of the restored religion" and a study of the "rise of modern Europe" in a political sense. In response to charges of error and partisanship, Sleidanus also published an "apology," a historiographical confession of faith, which affirmed the Ciceronian values of truth and impartiality as cornerstones of the story of the true religion.

The Lutheran interpretation of history was given further support in the publications of Matthias Flacius Illyricus: his *Catalogus testium veritatis* (Catalog of the witness of the truth), which constructed a proto-Lutheran canon of saints and martyrs; his treatise on biblical interpretation; and the *Centurias Magdeburgenses* (Magdeburg centuries), which was a vast collection of sources, from the time of the primitive church, gathered by Flacius and other collaborators to reinforce their confessional view of church history. Cardinal Cesare Baronio's *Annales* represented the countercollection endorsing the orthodox position. These efforts are part of the scholarly traditions connecting Renaissance and Reformation scholarship with the nineteenth-century "science of history" and modern hermeneutics.

See also biographies of figures mentioned in this entry.

BIBLIOGRAPHY

Primary Work

Bebel, Heinrich. "Oration in Praise of Germany." In *Manifestations of Discontent in Germany on the Eve of the Reforma-* tion. Edited and translated by Gerald Strauss. Bloomington, Ind., 1971.

Secondary Works

Borchardt, Frank. *German Antiquity in Renaissance Myth*. Baltimore, 1971. The mythical foundations of Germanism in classical and medieval literary and historical works.

D'Amico, John F. *Theory and Practice in Renaissance Textual Criticism: Beatus Rhenanus between Conjecture and History*. Berkeley, Calif., 1988. Study of Beatus's textual and historical scholarship.

Fraenkel, Pierre. *Testimonia Patrum: The Function of the Patristic Argument in the Theology of Philip Melanchthon*. Geneva, 1961. Melanchthon's efforts to trace the spiritual continuity between the early and the Reformed church.

Headley, John M. *Luther's View of Church History*. New Haven, Conn., 1963. Luther's revisionist ideas about and periodization of ecclesiastical history.

Kelley, Donald R. "Johann Sleidan and the Origins of the Profession of History." *Journal of Modern History* 52 (1980): 973–998. Reprinted in *The Writing of History*. Luther as official historian and his idea of history.

Kelley, Donald R. "Tacitus Noster: the *Germania* in the Renaissance and Reformation." *Tacitus and the Tacitean Tradition*. Edited by T. J. Luce and A. J. Woodman. Princeton, N.J., 1993. Pages 152–167. Tacitus as a major source of Renaissance Germanism.

Strauss, Gerald. *Historian in an Age of Crisis: The Life and Work of Johannes Aventinus 1477–1534*. Cambridge, Mass., 1963. Comprehensive study of a leading historian.

DONALD R. KELLEY

Jewish Historiography

Included in Moritz Steinschneider's comprehensive *Die Geschichtsliteratur der Juden* (The historical writings of the Jews) are ten substantial works written during the sixteenth century. Whether these texts, which with one exception were written in Hebrew, manifest the general, increasingly dominant preoccupation with history in all its guises in the Renaissance is a matter of scholarly debate. Several works are clearly written in the wake of and as a response to the expulsion of the Jews from the Iberian peninsula. However, this catastrophic event alone cannot account for the production of a variety of historical works, of which only some were written by first or second generation exiles. The extent to which these texts can be regarded as sharing the characteristics of Renaissance Latin or vernacular historical writings is difficult to ascertain in the majority of cases. Many are written in the form of chronicles or annals, which remained a popular genre throughout the Renaissance.

Chroniclers. The *Shevet Yehudah* (Rod of Judah; Adrianople, 1554) of Solomon ibn Verga (1450– after 1507), a Spanish exile who died in Flanders, recounts the persecutions of the Jewish people from the Second Temple until the author's own time. It contains a sociological analysis of exile, but it is also modeled on the notion that among the tasks of the historian are to entertain and to instruct. Many of its themes and motifs derive from Hispanic and particularly converso literary sources.

Joseph ha-Kohen (1496–1577), son of Spanish exiles, was born in Avignon but lived the greater part of his life in Piedmont and Lombardy, where he was intermittently subject to expulsions from the cities in which he was living. Only one of his works was printed in his lifetime, *Divre ha yamin le-Malkhe Zarefat u-Malkhe bet Ottoman ha-Togar* (The history of the kings of France and of the Ottoman Turkish sultans; Sabbioneta, 1554), which the author subsequently revised, adding extracts from Samuel Usque's *Consolation* and Sebastian Münster's *Cosmographia* (1544). Although the work contains forays into Jewish history, particularly accounts of persecutions, it mainly focuses on world events, such as the wars between the Christian West and the Moslem East and the struggle between the Habsburg Empire and France. At the beginning of the *History* ha-Kohen explicitly draws the reader's attention to the novelty of his work by the assertion that, after a period of some 1,400 years, he is a direct successor to the Jewish historian Flavius Josephus (37 C.E.–100). Ha-Kohen's other historical work, *Emeq ha-bakha* (Vale of tears; 1852), essentially composed of extracts from his world chronicle, lists Jewish persecutions from the destruction of the Temple to the author's own time.

Written in a different genre but on the same theme is the *Consolaçam as tribulaçoens de Israel* (Consolation for the tribulations of Israel; Ferrara, 1553), a Portuguese pastoral dialogue by the Portuguese converso Samuel Usque, about whom little is known. The book encompasses biblical, medieval, and contemporary Jewish history. Like Joseph ha-Kohen and many other writers of this period, Usque makes extensive use of the *Josippon,* the medieval paraphrase of Josephus.

The Cretan rabbi Elijah Capsali (1483–1555) wrote his *Seder Eliyahu zuta* (Minor order of Elijah) during the plague of 1523. It contains a history of the Ottoman Empire and an account of the expulsion of the Jews from Spain and Portugal that he claims to have based on oral and trustworthy evidence, as well as a separate work, *Sippure Venezia* (Annals of Venice), which also includes an account of his experiences in Padua from 1508 to 1515.

The noted Castilian astronomer Abraham Zacuto (1452–1515), who fled from Spain to Portugal and from there to North Africa, wrote his *Sefer yuhasin* (Book of genealogies) in Tunis. Written in the "chain of tradition" genre, its purpose is to outline the historical development of the Oral Torah and the chronology of the sages, while the last section of the work comprises a chronicle of world history. It was first published in Constantinople in 1566 by Samuel Shullam, who wrote an introduction and notes to the work and appended a Hebrew translation of Josephus's *Contra Apionem.*

The *Shalshelet ha-qabbalah* (Chain of tradition) by the Italian Jew Gedalyah ibn Yahya (1515–1578) was first published in Venice in 1587. Divided into three parts, it contains a substantial amount of historical and biographical material, often derived from unreliable sources. Where the author demonstrates more scholarly erudition, he has blatantly plagiarized from Azariah de' Rossi.

The chronicle form is also adapted by the Westphalian Jew David Gans (1541–1613) in his *Zemah David* (Sprout of David; Prague, 1592/93). For certain parts of his work Gans also used Azariah de' Rossi's data. He divided the work into two parts, separating Jewish from gentile history or, in his own words, "separating the holy from the profane since uninspired history should not be confused with the words of the living God." Each of the above texts contains some novel material or investigation of Jewish or gentile history, and all authors make some use of non-Jewish sources. Nevertheless, the annalistic form of literature is by its very nature restricted in scope and does not allow for extensive critical analysis or evaluation of source material.

Azariah de' Rossi. Of a completely different order is the *Me'or enayim* (Light of the eyes) written by the Italian Jew Azariah de' Rossi (1511?–1577), the first Jewish historiographer, according to the assessment of nineteenth-century Jewish scholars. On his own admission, de' Rossi chose to forgo traditional Jewish modes of writing in favor of the genre of miscellanea used by antiquarians, philologists, and encyclopedists of the time.

The book ranges over a wide number of topics, including the origins of the Septuagint, Philo of Alexandria, Jewish chronology, and the antiquity of the Hebrew language. For each inquiry, de' Rossi demonstrated outstanding erudition, using over 150 Jewish sources and over 100 non-Jewish sources. With these tools, de' Rossi was able to demonstrate the relevance of Jewish sources for certain areas of research which up to his time had been mainly the preserve of Christian scholars. On the other hand, de' Rossi also took as his starting point the problems and contradictions found in the rabbinic texts, which he attempted to solve on the basis of the most reliable evidence, Jewish or gentile (he did, however, use the fakes of Annius of Viterbo—purported to be lost works by ancient authors—as did many of his learned contemporaries). A major section of the book, entitled "Days of Old," is a critique of Jewish chronology in which he challenges the conventional *anno mundi* computation (the calculation of the age of the universe from creation). Using historical chronology, the calendar, Daniel's prophecy of the seventy weeks, and messianic speculation—which, like Joseph Scaliger, he debunks—de' Rossi shows himself to be at the vanguard of Renaissance historical scholarship.

BIBLIOGRAPHY

Primary Works

Capsali, Elijah. *Seder Eliyahu Zuta* (The minor order of Elijah). Edited by Aryeh Shmuelevitz, Shlomo Simonsohn, and Meir Benayahu. 3 vols. Jerusalem and Tel Aviv, 1975–1983.

De' Rossi, Azariah. *The Light of the Eyes.* Translated by Joanna Weinberg. New Haven, Conn., 2000. Translation of *Me'or Enayim* (1573–1575).

Gans, David. *Zemah David* (*The Sprout of David*). Edited with Introduction and Notes by Mordechai Breuer. Jerusalem, 1983 (1592/93).

Ha-Kohen, Joseph. *The Vale of Tears.* Translated by Harry S. May. The Hague, Netherlands, 1971. Translation of *Emeq ha-bakha.*

Ha-Kohen, Joseph. *Sefer Emeq Ha-Bakha (The Vale of Tears) with the Chronicle of the Anonymous Corrector.* Edited by Karin Almbladh. Stockholm and Uppsala, Sweden, 1981.

Ibn Verga, Solomon. *Shevet Yehudah* (Rod of Judah). Edited by Azriel Shochat. Jerusalem, 1946 or 1947.

Usque, Samuel. *Consolation for the Tribulations of Israel.* Translated by Martin A. Cohen. 2d ed. Philadelphia, 1977. Translation of *Consolaçam as tribulaçoens de Israel* (1553).

Secondary Works

Bonfil, Robert. "How Golden was the Age of the Renaissance in Jewish Historiography?" In *History and Theory Studies in the Philosophy of History* beiheft 27: *Essays in Jewish Historiography.* Edited by Ada Rapoport-Albert. Middletown, Conn., 1988. Pages 78–102.

Breuer, Mordechai. "Modernism and Traditionalism in Sixteenth-Century Jewish Historiography: A Study of David Gans' *Tsemah David.*" In *Jewish Thought in the Sixteenth Century.* Edited by Bernard Dov Cooperman. Cambridge, Mass., 1983. Pages 49–88.

Gutwirth, Eleazar. "The Expulsion from Spain and Jewish Historiography." In *Jewish History Essays in Honour of Chimen Abramsky.* Edited by Ada Rapoport-Albert and Steven J. Zipperstein. London, 1988. Pages 141–161.

Steinschneider, Moritz. *Die Geschichtsliteratur der Juden in Druckwerken und Handschriften.* Frankfurt am Main, 1905.

Weinberg, Joanna. "Azariah de' Rossi and the Forgeries of Annius of Viterbo." In *Essential Papers on Jewish Culture in Renaissance and Baroque Italy.* Edited by David B. Ruderman. New York and London, 1992. Pages 252–279.

Yerushalmi, Yosef Hayim. "Clio and the Jews: Reflections on Jewish Historiography in the Sixteenth Century." *Proceedings of the American Academy for Jewish Research* 46–47 (1979–1980): 607–638.

JOANNA WEINBERG

Spanish Historiography

The humanist concern with the writing of history was particularly acute in Renaissance Spain. At some point in their careers, most humanists, Spanish and Italian, working in the Iberian Peninsula during the sixteenth century embraced the writing of history. Important to this development was probably the increasing demand of the monarchy, especially in Castile, for ideological instruments able to support its claims to supremacy both among the unruly local powers and the other kingdoms competing in the international scenario of early modern Europe. History, and especially humanist history, seemed to fulfill this demand particularly well.

But as a closer analysis indicates, the radical transformations that Spanish historiography underwent from the second half of the fifteenth century were not exclusively carried out by humanists. The Latin works that the Castilian clergymen and diplomats Alfonso de Cartagena and Rodrigo Sánchez de Arévalo produced by the middle of the fifteenth century produced a radical breakthrough in medieval Spanish historiography. They did so by interrupting the tradition of vernacular chronicles and, more importantly, by setting up the ideological foundations of monarchic power in Spain until the advent of the Bourbon in the eighteenth century. Although both were acquainted with the innovative trends of Italian scholarship, they conceived their works within the intellectual framework of the scholastic tradition and explicitly adopted a controversial position against humanist ideas and methods.

Cardinal Joan Margarit (1421–1484), bishop of Girona and Aragonese chancellor in Rome, was the first to apply clearly humanist principles to the writing of history in Spain. His Latin *Paralipomenon hispaniae,* dedicated to King Ferdinand and Queen Isabella, records the history of Spain from its origins, replacing the traditional structure of the medieval chronicle with the models provided by Strabo, Ptolemy, Caesar, and Livy. Unlike his Castilian contemporary Sánchez de Arévalo, Joan Margarit did not insist on the Gothic origins of Spain. For him, the Roman legacy of Hispania was the true source of Spanish grandeur. The debate between these two visions of the past reappeared a few decades later in the heyday of the reign of King Ferdinand, this time having Antonio de Nebrija and Lucius Marineus Siculus as contenders.

Building an Official Historiography.

The unification of Aragon and Castile under Ferdinand and Isabella reinforced the interest of the crown in building an official historiography. The first historians officially attached to the royal chancellery were appointed by Isabella's father John II: the poet Juan de Mena and the humanist Alfonso de Palencia. The Catholic kings followed this tradition by also choosing distinguished members of the intellectual elite for the post: Alfonso de Palencia, Hernando del Pulgar, and Gonzalo de Ayora, a Castilian gentleman who had received humanist education in Pavia and Milan under the patronage of the Sforza. After Ayora's dismissal in 1507, King Ferdinand called the Sicilian humanist Lucius Marineus Siculus and the prestigious Latin scholars Antonio de Nebrija and Gonzalo de Santamaría to undertake several historiographical projects associated with the crown. The three were selected for their mastery in the new humanist style that Ferdinand required for the propaganda of his ambitious international policy. In this same context the Italian humanist Giovanni Nanni invented an ancient authority—Berosus—who wrote that the origins of the Spanish kingdom traced back to a direct descendent of Noah, thus making it possible for Spanish historians to claim that Spain was the first among European nations because the country's foundation predated that of Rome. Despite these efforts, King Ferdinand did not succeed in providing the Spanish kingdoms with a coherent historical discourse, as most of the historiographical projects he promoted remained either unfinished or unpublished.

The situation did not improve in the days of Ferdinand's grandson Emperor Charles V. The prestigious scholar Juan Ginés de Sepúlveda (1490–1573) attempted to apply Antonio de Nebrija's model of humanist history to the reign of Emperor Charles. However, his *De rebus gestis Caroli V* (*History of Charles V*) remained unpublished due to the unfavorable climate that followed Sepúlveda's confrontation with Bartolomé de Las Casas. Royal chronicles in the vernacular undertaken by Alonso de Santa Cruz and Pedro Mexía also were not completed.

A global account of Spanish history was still lacking by the middle of the sixteenth century. After constant requests of the Castilian courts, Florián de Ocampo (c. 1490–c. 1558) was officially entrusted in 1539 to write a general chronicle of Spain in the vernacular. He managed to finish only the first five books. During the reign of Charles's successor,

Philip II, the chronicle was continued by the erudite Ambrosio de Morales (1513–1591), who took it to the eleventh century. Contemporarily, the Basque historian Esteban de Garibay (1533–1599) published a summary of Spanish history that earned him an official appointment to continue Ambrosio de Morales's work after his death.

Ironically, the best-accomplished historiographical projects of the period did not result from the patronage of the new Spanish monarchy. Jerónimo de Zurita y Castro's (1512–1580) *Anales de la corona de Aragón* (Annals of the crown of Aragon; 1562–1580) provides an exhaustive account of the medieval kingdom of Aragon until the time of Ferdinand V. In 1592 the Jesuit author Juan de Mariana (1536–1624) published the definitive Renaissance history of Spain, *Historiae de rebus Hispaniae libri* XXV (History of the affairs of Spain in twenty-five books), which soon appeared in Spanish translation.

Simultaneous with the historical construction of Spain was an attempt to create a suitable portrait of its geography. In the first decades of the sixteenth century, the Italian humanist Lucius Marineus Siculus conceived the first systematic project of description of the Spanish territory. These early attempts were continued in the period of Charles V by Christopher Columbus's son Fernando Colón and by Pedro de Medina in his apologetic and patriotic *Libro de grandezas y cosas memorables de España* (The book of great and memorable things of Spain) in 1548.

Other historical genres developed parallel to these efforts toward a global history and description of Spain. In the second half of the fifteenth century Fernan Pérez de Guzmán and Hernando del Pulgar produced very successful accounts of illustrious contemporary Castilian men in the fashion of Valerius Maximus and Petrarch. After these early examples, the biographical genre almost disappeared in Spain. More successful were the histories of cities. First written in Latin after Flavio Biondo's model, these scholarly examples were soon outnumbered by works in vernacular during the sixteenth century. The vernacular histories set an enduring tradition of local historical writing that compensated for the ideological monopoly of the monarchy.

BIBLIOGRAPHY

Cuart Moner, Baltasar. "La historiografía áulica en la primera mitad del siglo XVI: los cronistas del Emperador." In *Antonio de Nebrija: Edad Media y Renacimiento*. Edited by Carmen Codoñer and Juan Antonio González Iglesias. Salamanca, 1994. Pages 39–58.

Kagan, Richard L. "Clio and the Crown: Writing History in Habsburg Spain." In *Spain, Europe, and the Atlantic World: Essays in Honour of John H. Elliott.* Edited by Richard L. Kagan and Geoffrey Parker. Cambridge, U.K., 1995. Pages 73–99.

Maravall, José Antonio. "Sobre naturaleza e historia en el humanismo Español." *Arbor* 18 (1951): 469–493.

Sánchez Alonso, B. *Historia de la Historiografía Española.* Vol. 2. Madrid, 1947.

Tate, Robert B. "El cronista real castellano durante el siglo quince." In *Homenaje a Pedro Sáinz Rodríguez.* Vol. 3. Madrid, 1986. Pages 659–668.

Tate, Robert B. *Ensayos sobre la historiografía peninsular del siglo XV.* Madrid, 1970.

JESÚS CARRILLO

HOLBEIN, HANS, THE ELDER (c. 1460–1534), German painter and draftsman, progenitor of the Holbein family of southern German painters, father to Ambrosius (b. 1494) and Hans (b. 1497). Primarily active in Augsburg, Hans Holbein traveled as commissions demanded to Ulm, Frankfurt, Alsace, and Lucerne. Nothing is known about his training. Many commissions for large-scale altars point to the establishment of a workshop by 1496 to accommodate them. These are mostly executed in the bright broad coloring typical of southern German painters of the late Gothic period. His inaugural work in Augsburg is an altarpiece commission from the church of SS. Ulrich and Afra. A joint commission in 1493 brought Holbein together with the sculptor Michel Erhart on the *Weingarten Altar* for the Benedictines in Ulm, which featured scenes from the life of the Virgin. These early works are broadly lit, vertically stacked compositions set in uncluttered stagelike spaces. The year 1500 marked another commission from SS.

Hans Holbein the Elder. *Martyrdom of St. Sebastian.* Oil on wood; 1516; 153 × 107 cm (60 × 42 in.). [For other depictions of St. Sebasian, see the entries on Correggio and Mantegna.] ALTE PINAKOTHEK, MUNICH/ARTOTHEK

Ulrich and Afra, a *Passion* sequence largely in grisaille (painted in shades of gray so as to resemble sculpture). While Holbein's *Deposition* in the gray *Passion* owes remarkable debt to Rogier van der Weyden's *Deposition,* the movement and individuation of the swirling array of tormentors in the other panels mark his growing departure from Netherlandish influence.

Holbein's next important set of commissions came from the Dominican St. Katharina Convent in Augsburg. With Augsburg painters Hans Burgkmair and the monogrammist LF, he helped execute a series of the seven original Roman basilicas to commemorate the jubilee year of 1500. While Holbein's contributions, *Sta. Maria Maggiore* (1499) and *S. Paolo fuori le Mura* (1504), maintain Netherlandish compartmentalization of space by means of fictive Gothic tracery, the agitated panoply of martyrdom and new conventions of recession developed to house it demonstrate the rupture with foregoing styles.

Holbein's growing popularity secured him commissions from Dominicans in Frankfurt and Kaisheim around 1501. Working again for the Augsburg Katharinenkloster in 1516, he executed the *St. Sebastian* altarpiece. *St. Sebastian* marks a powerful departure from his previous work; in it, Holbein opens out the cluttered figural tableaux of the gray *Passion* to clarify a focus on St. Sebastian. Architectural elements span the partitions of the altarpiece to unify the composition. Between 1517 and 1521, Holbein collaborated with his son on the facade decoration of Jacob von Hertenstein's house in Lucerne (destroyed) and on the *Oberried* altarpiece for the cathedral in Freiburg. In addition to altarpieces, Holbein also produced portraits, borders for single woodcuts, designs for glass painting, and patterns for sculptors and goldsmiths in the circle of Michel and Gregor Erhart. Holbein's output and breadth of influence are said to rival only Albrecht Dürer's, and the work of his son Hans the Younger bears out his legacy.

See also **Germany,** *subentry on* **Art in Germany.**

BIBLIOGRAPHY

Bushart, Bruno. *Hans Holbein der Ältere.* Augsburg, Germany, 1987.
Falk, Tilman. *Katalog der Zeichnungen des 15. und 16. Jahrhunderts im Kupferstichkabinett Basel.* Basel, Switzerland, and Stuttgart, Germany, 1979.
Die Malerfamilie Holbein in Basel. Exhibition catalog by Georg Schmidt and Hans Reinhardt. Basel, Switzerland, 1960.

STEPHANIE LEITCH

HOLBEIN, HANS THE YOUNGER   (1497–1543), German painter and draftsman, active in Basel and London as an altarpiece and portrait painter and woodcut designer. Independent until his 1532 return to London after which he worked primarily as a portraitist in the court of Henry VIII, Hans Holbein the Younger worked with his elder brother Ambrosius in their father's Augsburg workshop until he transferred to Hans Herbst's studio in Basel as a journeyman in 1516. One of his earliest commissions involved marginal illustrations to theologian Oswald Myconius's copy of Erasmus's *Praise of Folly,* dimly alluding to Erasmus's own sponsorship of the artist a number of years later. In 1516, Holbein completed a double portrait of the mayor of Basel, Jakob Meyer, and his wife. Several monumental commissions followed: in 1517, the illusionistic facade of Jacob von Hertenstein's house in Lucerne and, after his 1519 receipt into the Basel guild as master, works for the town council chamber and the facade of the Haus zum Tanz.

Holbein's 1521 *Body of the Dead Christ* testifies to his growing conviction that a new human form inhabit religious personages. This recumbent and decomposing Christ was probably suggested by the predella of Matthias Grünewald's *Isenheim Altar* (1512–1515), which he might have seen in 1516. In 1524, Holbein executed an eight-scene *Passion.* In part inspired by his father's 1502 altar in Kaisheim, its innovation lies in its use of dramatic lighting dictated by the unusual and predominant choice of night scenes.

Holbein's services as a portraitist were recommended to the humanist Erasmus of Rotterdam by Johannes Froben, Erasmus's publisher for whom Holbein had done some illustrative work. Erasmus actively commissioned portraits of himself as gifts for a network of colleagues, including the 1523 *Erasmus* for his protector, William Warham, the archbishop of Canterbury. A 1524 sojourn in France put Holbein in contact with French court styles and under the influence of Lombard painting prevalent there around the time of Francis I. Holbein's *Laïs Corinthiaca, Darmstadt Madonna,* and the *Last Supper* reflect such Leonardesque inspiration.

Holbein's first stay in England dates to 1526–1528. Recommendations from Erasmus won him commissions from Sir Thomas More and members of the Royal Court whose images Holbein aggrandized in frontal portraits. By the time he returned to Basel in 1529, the city was beseiged by anti-Catholic iconoclasts. He soon found untenable the practice of creating Catholic religious imagery while simulta-

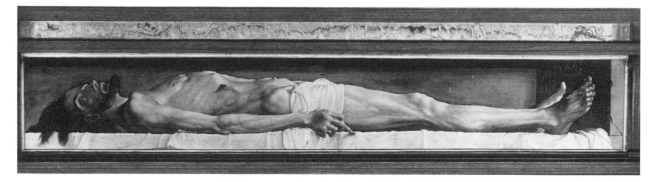

Hans Holbein. *Dead Christ.* Oil; 1521. KUNSTSMUSEUM, BASEL/GIRAUDON/ART RESOURCE

neously generating anti-Catholic woodcuts in the name of Protestant propaganda. By 1532, Holbein was back in London. *The Ambassadors* of 1533 is a double portrait of the French ambassador to England, Jean de Dinteville, and the bishop Georges de Selve. The table between them supports items of Byzantine iconography, topped by a foreground anamorphic image of a skull, which comes into focus only when the perspective system governing the rest of the picture drops away. Between 1532 and 1538, Holbein was retained by Henry VIII's court and executed numerous title-page and jewelry designs, miniatures, murals, and portraits. Henry's 1536 portrait by Holbein is perhaps that by which we know the king best. Holbein made some additional trips to the Continent to capture the likenesses of Henry's potential wives. He died in London in 1543. Holbein remained a great influence on the next generation of English portraitists and miniaturists, particularly Nicholas Hilliard, as well as Flemish painters Peter Paul Rubens and Anthony van Dyck. The Dutch painter and writer Karel van Mander gave the first real biographical account (1604) of Holbein as a northern foil to the idea of Italian genius propagated by Giorgio Vasari.

See also **Germany, Art in.**

BIBLIOGRAPHY

Bätschmann, Oskar, and Pascal Griener. *Hans Holbein.* London, 1997.

Hans Holbein d.J.: Zeichnungen aus dem Kupferstichkabinett der Öffentlichen Kunstsammlung Basel. Basel, Switzerland, 1988.

Rowlands, John. *The Paintings of Hans Holbein the Younger.* Boston, 1985.

STEPHANIE LEITCH

HOLY ROMAN EMPIRE. The Holy Roman Empire was a feudal state in central Europe. The terms "Holy" and "Roman" relate to the fact that in the Middle Ages history was grounded in theology. Based on the predictions of the prophet Daniel, four kingdoms were believed to precede the appearance of Jesus Christ as Messiah: these were the Babylonian, Medo-Persian, Grecian, and Roman empires. Thus the ancient Roman Empire was considered the last empire of the world, at the end of which the Last Judgment was to take place. In medieval belief, the Roman Empire lived on because in 800 the pope conferred the title of emperor on Charlemagne, king of the Franks. This theory was referred to as the translation of empire (*translatio imperii*). As a result of the imperial coronation of Otto I (962) the empire passed on to the eastern part of the former Franconian empire. The supra-national character, however, remained intact—the Holy Roman Empire consisted geographically of Germany, Burgundy, and Italy— as did the religious and institutional connections with the Roman Church. In the twelfth and thirteenth centuries, the final term Holy Roman Empire (*Sacrum Imperium Romanum*) was introduced. Thereby, the emperor's rule was elevated and took on the role of defender of the last monarchy, which was confirmed by God.

In the second half of the fifteenth century, the Holy Roman Empire covered central Europe from France in the west, to Denmark in the north, and to Poland and Hungary in the east. In Italy, all the territories north of the Papal States (except the Republic of Venice) were fiefs of the Holy Roman Empire. In the 1648 Peace of Westphalia, the Holy Roman Empire recognized the independence of the Netherlands and the Swiss Confederation. The empire existed in its reduced form until 1806, when the last emperor, Francis II, renounced the imperial crown.

Election of the King. The king of the Romans (*Rex Romanorum*) stood at the top of the Holy Roman Empire. Since Charles IV's Golden Bull of

1356 the king had been elected by the seven electors. Four of these were secular: the king of Bohemia, duke of Saxony, margrave of Brandenburg, and palatine of the Rhine; the other three electors were ecclesiastical princes: the archbishops of Mainz, Trier, and Cologne. Originally, the king of the Romans only became emperor once he had been crowned by the pope. This tradition was broken for the first time by Maximilian I, who had been hindered from passing through Italy to Rome by the Venetians (1508). As a result, he assumed the title "Elected Roman Emperor" (*Electus Imperator Romanorum*). Charles V was the last emperor to be crowned in Italy; his coronation, however, did not take place in Rome but in Bologna (1530). Although subsequent emperors of the Holy Roman Empire were still elected and crowned kings of the Romans by the electors, they assumed the title of emperor after the death of their predecessors without a separate coronation.

The Golden Bull regulated the election of the king in minute detail. The elector of Mainz convened the other electors to Frankfurt in his function as archchancellor of the Holy Roman Empire. Before the election proper, the electors discussed the terms of the electoral capitulation (*Wahlkapitulation*) to which the king would be bound. These negotiations could last for several weeks; after their termination the king was elected, then crowned in Aachen. During the Renaissance, this ceremony changed insofar as the election and coronation could also take place in other imperial cities. For example, Maximilian II was elected and crowned in Frankfurt (1564), Rudolf II in Regensburg (1576), but the privileges of Aachen and Frankfurt were confirmed again and again. The Holy Roman Empire was therefore an electoral monarchy, but between 1438 and 1740 the emperor was always a member of the Habsburg dynasty, in spite of the candidacy of other princes, such as the French king in 1519.

The Imperial Diet. The emperor did not rule over the empire autocratically but was bound to the resolutions of the imperial diet. This diet was summoned only when required. Sessions took place in one of the imperial cities, usually Augsburg, Nürnberg, Regensburg, or Speyer. Until the first half of the seventeenth century, the diet sat at irregular intervals. In general, the diet was attended by imperial princes and representatives of imperial cities. Only after 1663 did the imperial diet transform itself into a convention of representatives located permanently in Regensburg.

Rulers of the Holy Roman Empire

Albert II (1438–1439)
Frederick III (1440–1493)
Maximilian I (1493–1519)
Charles V (1519–1556)
Ferdinand I (1558–1564)
Maximilian II (1564–1576)
Rudolf II (1576–1612)
Matthias (1612–1619)
Ferdinand II (1619–1637)

Only the imperial estates had the right to participate in the diet. These consisted of those parts of the Holy Roman Empire that had received feudal tenure directly from the emperor. Since 1489 the diet was divided into three colleges: the college of the electors, in which the electors had a seat and vote; the college of the imperial princes; and the college of the imperial cities. The college of the imperial princes was divided into an ecclesiastical and a secular bench. The ecclesiastical bench was taken up by imperial bishops and some abbots; on the secular bench sat princes such as the duke of Bavaria. In 1521 the members of the college of the imperial princes included about fifty ecclesiastical and twenty secular imperial princes.

Imperial cities were different from other cities because their supreme lord was not an imperial prince but the emperor himself. At the beginning of the sixteenth century, the Holy Roman Empire included more than seventy imperial cities. As a result of their economic position, the imperial cities of Augsburg, Frankfurt, Cologne, Nürnberg, Regensburg, Strasbourg, and Ulm were the most important cities in the empire. Until 1582, the imperial cities had only two consultative votes at the imperial diet.

In Italy there were about three hundred imperial fees, or feudal estates, including Milan, Modena, Mantua, Florence, and Genoa. With the exception of Savoy, these fees were not represented at the imperial diet. Equally, the imperial knights were not represented at the diet, although they belonged to the imperial aristocracy.

The diet was summoned by the emperor. At the beginning of diets, the imperial proposition was read out. On the whole, this proposition was a report about the matters that were to be discussed. These matters were mainly questions about the military (for example, the defense against the Turks), the judicial system, the mint, and taxes. Apart from that function,

The Holy Roman Empire. Christ crucified on the imperial eagle, with emperor and estates below. Woodcut by Albert Kunne, 1487. SCHLOSSMUSEUM, SCHLOSS FRIEDENSTEIN, GOTHA, GERMANY

by all the members of the three imperial colleges. This procedure usually prolonged the sessions of the diet. Furthermore, the diets were complicated by the fact that the Reformation saw a nexus between political and religious problems. The Protestant estates often refused to negotiate tax levying unless resolutions on religious questions were brought about. Only in 1648, at the Peace of Westphalia, was a method found to treat religious questions separately from political ones.

Reforms during the Renaissance. In the fifteenth and sixteenth centuries reforms aimed at renewing the Holy Roman Empire and at remedying legal insecurity were introduced. Maximilian I vigorously promoted these reforms. At the imperial diet of 1495 in Worms, for example, an everlasting peace was pronounced through which feuds were to be restricted. In the same year, the imperial Chamber Court of Justice was founded as a supreme court of justice. From 1527 onward its seat was in Speyer, and its jurisdiction included cases of breach of public peace as well as civil and criminal litigation between the imperial estates. Furthermore, the imperial Chamber Court of Justice functioned as the appellate court for rulings of territorial courts of justice. The judge of the Chamber Court was appointed by the emperor, but the assessors were appointed by the imperial estates and the imperial circles respectively (see below). However, confessional or religious disputes, which started in the 1520s, generally caused one of the following to happen: either the Chamber Court of Justice was brought to a standstill or the Catholic majority judged disputes in a denominationally motivated way. Thus, during the entire period of the Reformation, the reform of the Chamber Court of Justice was a recurring demand, especially of the Protestant imperial estates.

As a result, the second judicial institution of the Holy Roman Empire, the imperial aulic council, enjoyed increasing popularity. This council had also been founded during the reign of Maximilian I, and had seen a reform under Ferdinand I. In 1559, it started to take over the duties of a supreme court of justice to an increasing degree. The sphere of jurisdiction of the imperial aulic council was not clearly defined. Originally concerned with disputes over feudal tenure, it had always been appealed to by Italian feudatories. The imperial aulic council sat in Vienna at the imperial court under the chairmanship of the emperor or its president. As the council's decisions were made much faster than those of the im-

diets served as the place where imperial princes were ceremoniously invested with a fief. The matters proposed by the emperor were negotiated separately by the three colleges. Not until the final resolutions of the colleges harmonized and the emperor had agreed to them, did the combined agreement become imperial law. The resolution was recorded solemnly in the so-called Recess of the Empire (*recessus imperii*), which had to be signed and sealed

perial Chamber Court of Justice, it was increasingly appealed to in criminal and civil litigation as well.

The construction of imperial circles also belongs to the reforms of the empire under Maximilian I; these were administrative bodies established in their final form at the beginning of the sixteenth century. Their main aim was the maintenance of peace; but later their responsibilities included the levying of imperial taxes, the supervision of the mint, the dispatch of assessors to the imperial Chamber Court of Justice, and, from 1555 onward, the execution of the Chamber Court's rulings. From 1512, the empire consisted of ten imperial circles: the Austrian and the Burgundian circles, the circle of the Rhenish electors, the Upper Saxonian, the Franconian, the Bavarian, the Swabian, the Upper Rhenish, the Lower Rhenish–Westphalian, and the Lower Saxonian circles. Not included in this organization into circles were the territories of the Bohemian Crown (Bohemia, Moravia, Silesia, Lusatia), the imperial knights, the Swiss Confederation, and the Italian imperial feudatories.

The Reformation. The Holy Roman Empire was not the only institution that had a great need for reform at the beginning of the sixteenth century; within the empire the Roman Catholic Church was also in a severe crisis. This was because most bishops and many abbots exercised secular authority and therefore belonged to the imperial princes. Because of their secular responsibilities, they very often neglected their pastoral duties. Martin Luther quickly found support among secular authorities, such as the elector of Saxony, in his demands for a reform of the Roman Catholic Church. Indeed, many princes of the Holy Roman Empire sided with and joined the Protestant religious doctrine; in 1530 they presented their newly worded confession of faith to the imperial diet in Augsburg. From that time onward, denominational and political disputes were the order of the day in the empire. The Protestant princes formed the so-called Schmalkaldic League. Although Charles V succeeded in militarily defeating the princes in the Schmalkaldic War of 1546–1547, his victory could not extirpate the Protestant confession of faith. Eventually, in 1555, a compromise was reached between the Protestant and the Catholic princes in the Peace of Augsburg: the territorial princes were to determine the religious denomination of their subjects (*cuius regio, eius religio*). This compromise succeeded in calming the empire's religious affairs for the next half century.

Population. As in the rest of Europe, the empire experienced a steady increase in population throughout the sixteenth century. While ten to twelve million people lived in the German-speaking territories of the empire in 1500, this number had grown to between seventeen and twenty million within a century. This near doubling of the population within one hundred years led to an abundance of social problems: the rise in population led to increased prices and a shortage of agricultural products, and a simultaneous drop in wages. It has to be stressed, however, that up to 90 percent of the population lived in the countryside, where the food supply was much better than it was for the lower classes in towns. Social unrest in large towns (around 1500 these included Cologne with thirty thousand inhabitants, and Strasbourg, Augsburg, and Nürnberg with about twenty thousand inhabitants each) was caused by the impoverishment of the urban lower classes and the rising food prices.

In the countryside, the majority of peasants lived in bondage with regard to both personal freedom and possessions. They were dependent on the aristocratic or ecclesiastical lord of the manor, to whom they were obliged to render certain service in money or kind. The lords of the manor limited the utilization and bequeathing of peasants' farms, controlled marriages, and had the power to allow or prohibit a change of place. In addition, an increase in rural dues can be observed throughout the Holy Roman Empire during the sixteenth century; this led to a deterioration of living conditions. The result, in 1524–1525, was the Peasants' War, one of the greatest rural revolts in the history of the empire. The peasants clamored for a reduction of service in money and kind, an abolition of personal bondage (serfdom), a modification of the judicial supremacy of the authorities, and a restitution of the ancient right of usufruct (regarding hunting and other uses of the forest, meadow, and pasture). By the summer of 1525 the revolt was crushed.

The aristocracy living in the countryside who did not have imperial status also suffered from these changes. Their duty to protect the rural population lost its meaning, as did that of the aristocratic chivalrous army to defend empire and emperor. A medieval army consisting of knights was increasingly replaced by mercenary troops. As a result, the nobility was reduced to landed aristocracy in the territorial states that were coming into being.

The cities, whether imperial or not, were distinct from their rural surroundings in their judicial system. The urban council, which had originally acted as a representative of its burghers, developed into an authority with claim to government. Theoretically,

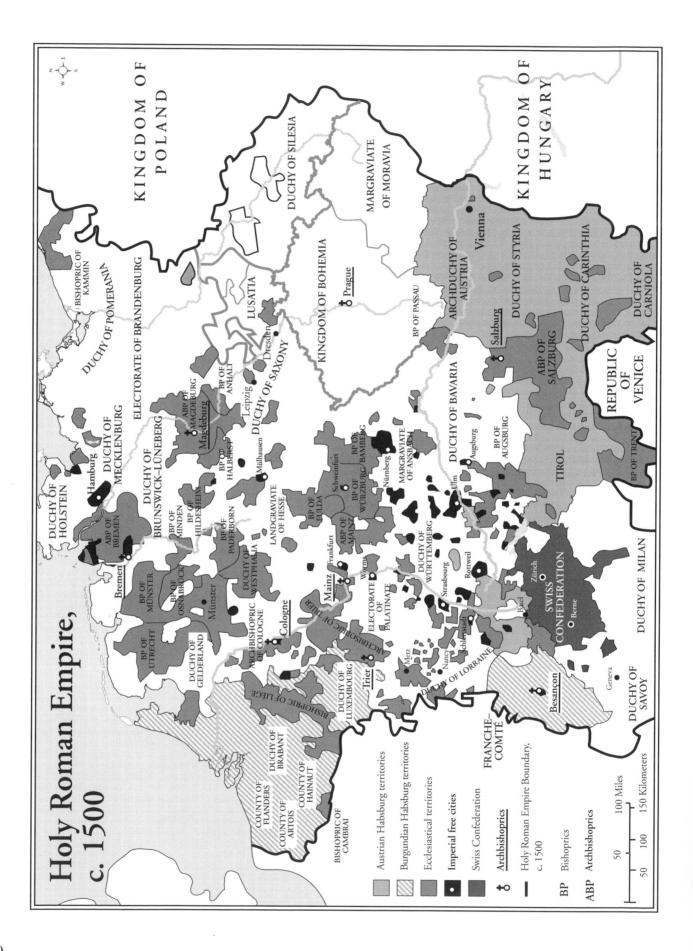

Holy Roman Empire, c. 1500

KINGDOM OF POLAND

KINGDOM OF HUNGARY

BISHOPRIC OF KAMMIN

DUCHY OF POMERANIA

DUCHY OF SILESIA

MARGRAVIATE OF MORAVIA

ELECTORATE OF BRANDENBURG

LUSATIA

KINGDOM OF BOHEMIA

• Prague

ARCHDUCHY OF AUSTRIA

• Vienna

DUCHY OF STYRIA

DUCHY OF CARINTHIA

DUCHY OF CARNIOLA

BP OF PASSAU

DUCHY OF MECKLENBURG

BP OF ANHALT

Leipzig
• Dresden

DUCHY OF BAVARIA

ABP OF SALZBURG

Salzburg

DUCHY OF HOLSTEIN

Hamburg

DUCHY OF BRUNSWICK-LÜNEBERG

ABP OF MAGDEBURG
Magdeburg

DUCHY OF SAXONY

Mühlhausen

REPUBLIC OF VENICE

BP OF HALBERST.

Augsburg

BP OF TRENT

ABP OF BREMEN

Bremen

BP OF MINDEN

BP OF HILDESHEIM

BP OF PADERBORN

LANDGRAVIATE OF HESSE

BP OF WÜRZBURG

Schweinfurt

MARGRAVIATE OF ANSBACH

Nürnberg

BAMBERG

BP OF AUGSBURG

Ulm

TIROL

BP OF MÜNSTER

BP OF OSNA-BRÜCK

Münster

DUCHY OF WESTPHALIA

BP OF FULDA

ABP OF MAINZ

Frankfurt

DUCHY OF WÜRTTEMBERG

Rottweil

DUCHY OF MILAN

BP OF UTRECHT

DUCHY OF GELDERLAND

ARCHBISHOPRIC OF COLOGNE

Cologne

ARCHBISHOPRIC OF TRIER

Mainz

Worms

ELECTORATE OF PALATINATE

Strasbourg

Zürich

SWISS CONFEDERATION

Berne

Basel

Schlettstadt

DUCHY OF LUXEMBOURG

Trier

Metz

Nancy

DUCHY OF LORRAINE

Geneva

DUCHY OF SAVOY

BISHOPRIC OF LIÈGE

DUCHY OF BRABANT

COUNTY OF HAINAUT

Besançon

FRANCHE-COMTÉ

COUNTY OF FLANDERS

COUNTY OF ARTOIS

BISHOPRIC OF CAMBRAI

Austrian Habsburg territories

Burgundian Habsburg territories

Ecclesiastical territories

Imperial free cities

Swiss Confederation

Archbishoprics

Holy Roman Empire Boundary, c. 1500

BP   Bishoprics

ABP   Archbishoprics

50   100   150 Kilometers

50   100 Miles

N   E   W   S

190

every burgher of the town had the right to vote for a representative of the urban council; in reality, however, the posts of the council remained in the hands of a very few rich patricians who could afford to accept such posts. Furthermore, the burghers were organized in guilds that held the privilege of monopoly. As elsewhere, the rich burghers constituted only a very small part of the urban population. Only up to 5 percent of the urban population were part of this rich upper class, while up to 80 percent belonged to the poor lower classes. The upper class, which had made its money trading with spices, textiles, and in credit transactions, continually tried to climb the social ladder by marriage. The money of the urban patricians not only financed the election of Charles V (1519), but also the military campaigns of the emperor.

Although the Holy Roman Empire experienced several crises during the Renaissance, its federalist infrastructure made it one of the strongest political systems in Europe.

See also **Habsburg Dynasty.**

BIBLIOGRAPHY

Asch, Ronald. *The Thirty Years War: The Holy Roman Empire and Europe, 1618–1648.* New York, 1997.

Blickle, Peter. *From the Communal Reformation to the Revolution of the Common Man.* Translated by Beat Kumin. Leiden, Netherlands, and Boston, 1998.

Evans, R. J. W. *The Making of the Habsburg Monarchy, 1550–1700: An Interpretation.* Reprint. Oxford and New York, 1985.

Eyck, Frank. *Religion and Politics in German History from the Beginnings to the French Revolution.* London, 1998.

Headley, John M. *The Emperor and His Chancellor: A Study of the Imperial Chancellery under Gattinara.* Cambridge, U.K., and New York, 1983.

Heer, Friedrich. *The Holy Roman Empire.* Translated by Janet Sondheimer. New York, 1968.

Kohler, Alfred. *Das Reich im Kampf um die Hegemonie in Europa 1521–1648.* Munich, 1990.

Moeller, Bernd. *Imperial Cities and the Reformation: Three Essays.* Edited and translated by H. C. Erik Midelfort and Mark U. Edwards Jr. Philadelphia, 1972.

Neuhaus, Helmut. *Das Reich in der frühen Neuzeit.* Munich, 1997.

Press, Volker. *Kriege und Krisen: Deutschland 1600–1715.* Munich, 1991.

Roeck, Bernd. *Lebenswelt und Kultur des Bürgertums in der frühen Neuzeit.* Munich, 1991.

Zophy, Jonathan W. *The Holy Roman Empire: A Dictionary Handbook.* Westport, Conn., 1980.

FRIEDRICH EDELMAYER

HOMILIES, BOOK OF. The *Homilies* are two books of official sermons published by the Church of England, the first in 1547, the second in 1563. The 1547 book responded to the twofold problem confronting the newly reformed English church in the first year of the reign of Edward VI: a poorly educated clergy and the widespread doctrinal conflict and confusion unleashed by the Reformation. Not only did the old religion still have numerous adherents, but Protestantism itself came in various shades and stripes (for example, Zwinglian, Lutheran, Anabaptist, Calvinist), with the result that, as a 1548 Royal Proclamation anxiously noted, "every man according to his zeal, some better, some worse, goeth about to set out his own fantasy, and to draw the people to his opinion." Except for those specially licensed to preach sermons they had written themselves, all ministers had to read the homilies in place of a sermon, lest the people be "tossed to and fro with seditious and contentious preaching."

Clerical education improved markedly during the Elizabethan period, with the result that more clergy were licensed (88 percent in 1601 London, up from 27 percent in 1561). While the Church's reliance on the *Homilies* declined, they remained crucial for establishing and enforcing doctrinal boundaries. Elizabeth prized them highly as a means of curbing troublemaking Puritans (who, in turn, extolled preaching). King James I valued preaching more than did Elizabeth, but in 1622, alarmed by the outpouring of sermons against his foreign policy, he forbade the clergy to treat matters of state in their sermons except as "presidented" in the *Homilies,* although he did not order ministers to read the homilies rather than preach.

The first book contains twelve sermons, all anonymous, although Thomas Cranmer (1489–1556) is known to have authored the key doctrinal ones (those concerning faith, works, justification, and scripture). The theology of these is Lutheran, but overall, the first book, with its social and ethical emphases, is as much derived from the thinking of Erasmus as from Protestantism as such. Neither book is Calvinist. Neither treats predestination. Besides doctrinal sermons, the first book's homilies deal with both social ethics ("Of Obedience," "Against Contention," "Against Adultery") and individual piety ("Of the Fear of Death"). The second book includes a long tract "Against Peril of Idolatry," probably by Bishop John Jewel (1522–1571); a series of festal sermons; and various homilies on topics ranging from Holy Communion to dress codes. In 1571 the "Homily against Disobedience" (composed in response to the 1569 Northern Rebellion against Elizabeth by Catholic earls) was added to the second book.

There were fifteen Edwardine editions of the first book; eight Elizabethan ones between 1559 and 1576. The second book went through twelve editions between 1563 and 1574. In 1582, 1587, and 1595, the two books were published conjointly in separate volumes. The first single-volume edition was in 1623; three subsequent editions (1633, 1635, 1640) adopt this format.

BIBLIOGRAPHY

Primary Works

"Certain Sermons or Homilies" (1547) and "A Homily against Disobedience and Wilful Rebellion" (1570): A Critical Edition. Edited by Ronald Bond. Toronto, 1987.

The Two Books of Homilies Appointed to Be Read in Churches. Edited by John Griffiths. Oxford, 1859.

Secondary Work

Wall, John N., Jr. "Godly and Fruitful Lessons: The English Bible, Erasmus' Paraphrases, and the Book of Homilies." In *The Godly Kingdom of Tudor England: Great Books of the English Reformation*. Edited by John Booty. Wilton, Conn., 1981. Pages 47–138.

DEBORA K. SHUGER

HOMOSEXUALITY. Sexual activity and passionate intimacy between individuals of the same sex were widespread in Renaissance society, and much acknowledged in literature and art, though notices of men far outweigh those of women. Victorian homosexual scholars who first pointed out this rich legacy invoked the era as a "silver age" when revival of the guilt-free pederasty and male comradeship of classical antiquity fostered tolerance of homosexuality and its cultural expression, but the reality was much more complex.

As urbanization accelerated, European cities developed a critical mass of men who desired men, and offered them increased opportunity for anonymous contacts. But these same cities gradually tightened the web of prohibitions against sodomy inherited from the Middle Ages, making it a civil crime as well as a sin. The central tension of the period was the attempt to reconcile Christian theology with the competing values of antiquity and the realities of urban life—an ultimately impossible task that enmeshed homosexuality in the broader debates out of which modern sexual patterns emerged by about 1700.

Male homosexuality, usually anal intercourse, is attested on all rungs of the social ladder, from kings and nobles to clerics, merchants, craftworkers, and sailors. The authorization for civil courts to pursue sodomy in Venice and Florence indicated mounting concern for public immorality through the four-teenth and fifteenth centuries; transcripts reveal that men met other men at public squares and taverns, schools, bathhouses, and private parties. Sex typically occurred between an adult and an adolescent, and at least in well-documented Florence many males passed through a series of roles as they matured from passive youth to active adult. Since most men outside the clergy married, these contacts were often part of a bisexual life, associated (at least by the elite) with libertine hedonism.

Opinions differ on the social and psychological identities attached to same-sex behavior. The dominant view stresses discontinuities between Renaissance and modern conceptions, arguing that no notion of "homosexual" as an innate or lifelong orientation opposed to "heterosexual" yet existed. Pointing out that sodomy remained a vague sin, embracing most nonprocreative sex, into which anyone might be sporadically tempted, these scholars argue that Florentine-style male sexuality, since it involved the majority of citizens at some time in their lives, was not so much a subculture as a pervasive component of the entire society: if everyone "did" it, no one "was" it. A cogent minority emphasizes a more evolutionary view, seeing the period as the "early modern" incubator of a separate subcultural identity that coalesced gradually before its full-scale emergence in about 1700. This school notes that philosophers like the Italian Neoplatonist Marsilio Ficino (1433–1499) penned defenses of male love, that terms like *ganymede* marked at least the passive partner as a psychological type, and that the unique status of sodomy as morally "unspeakable" forced its advocates to speak in coded terms.

Lesbian eros is less documented: few women were literate, female social networks were private, and both private and female behavior were generally of less concern to male public authorities. Prosecutions number only a handful, spread from Germany and France to Italy and Spain. But female passion, too, cut across all classes, from Queen Christina of Sweden, who abdicated to avoid marriage, to New England housewives, to nuns, whose passionate excesses were a favorite literary theme. In the 1620s, Italian church investigators sentenced Sister Benedetta Carlini of Pescia to life in prison for staging angelic visions that commanded her roommate to masturbate her.

Carlini was condemned not for lesbianism, but for blasphemy, revealing the frequent conflation of sexual deviance with heresy that led to the witchcraft persecutions of the fifteenth and sixteenth centuries, which occasionally included accusations of orgiastic sex. Moll Cutpurse in Jacobean London typifies the "passing women" who dressed as men for economic and social freedom, which sometimes included "marriage" with another woman. Unfortunately for our understanding of such women's desires and self-concept, we have only the testimony of male officials, who were less curious about women's own lives than about their usurpations of male privilege.

The Renaissance was a transitional period, developing distinctive forms of homosexual behavior and identity that, while they remained more fluid than later categories of sex and gender, were embryonic of the modern world. Period attitudes also affected global culture through exploration and conquest: Spanish colonists persecuted the crossdressing *berdaches* (shamans) of the Americas, and missionaries like Saint Francis Xavier preached against homosexuality in India, China, and Japan, much altering the sexual mores of those societies.

See also **Sexuality.**

BIBLIOGRAPHY

Bray, Alan. *Homosexuality in Renaissance England.* London, 1982.

Brown, Judith. *Immodest Acts: The Life of a Lesbian Nun in Renaissance Italy.* Oxford, 1986. Recounts the investigation of Benedetta Carlini.

Cady, Joseph. "The 'Masculine Love' of the 'Princes of Sodom'. . . ." In *Desire and Discipline: Sex and Sexuality in the Premodern West.* Edited by Jacqueline Murray and Konrad Eisenbichler. Toronto, 1996. Pages 123–154. Summarizes arguments for an evolutionary perspective on male identity.

Rocke, Michael. *Forbidden Friendships: Homosexuality and Male Culture in Renaissance Florence.* Oxford, 1996. Detailed study of court records, argues against separate subcultural identity.

Ruggiero, Guido. *The Boundaries of Eros: Sex Crime and Sexuality in Renaissance Venice.* Oxford, 1985.

Saslow, James M. *Ganymede in the Renaissance: Homosexuality in Art and Society.* New Haven, Conn., 1986.

Saslow, James M. "Homosexuality in the Renaissance: Behavior, Identity, and Artistic Expression." In *Hidden from History: Reclaiming the Gay and Lesbian Past.* Edited by Martin Duberman, Martha Vicinus, and George Chauncey. New York, 1989. Pages 90–105.

Simons, Patricia. "Lesbian (In)visibility in Italian Renaissance Culture: Diana and Other Cases of *donna con donna.*" In *Gay and Lesbian Studies in Art History.* Edited by Whitney Davis. Binghamton, N.Y., 1994. Pages 81–122. Also published as *Journal of Homosexuality* 27, nos. 1–2 (1994).

JAMES M. SASLOW

HONOR. The concept of honor was central to the ordering of Mediterranean societies. Closely linked with reputation, it was part of the value codes through which communities regulated conduct, social tensions, and conflict. Honor was a multidimensional, abstract idea represented with words, deeds, gestures, and analogies. It served to maintain hierarchy and to bind groups, lineages, clans, classes, guilds, and the sexes to a common culture that fostered personal as well as collective virtue, respect, and public esteem.

From antiquity to the Renaissance the ways people found to express their self-worth or respect for others remained fluid. Honor could be obtained by right of birth or through the acquisition of wealth, power, sanctity, and prestige. Codes of honor varied with social status, power, sex, and notions of gender—that is, what was considered acceptable behavior for members of each sex. The church related honor to Christian virtue and a conscience free from guilt. Nobles wielding military power relied on honor to maintain hierarchy and to defend their privileged status. The honor of a medieval knight, for example, depended on his military prowess, loyalty, largesse, courtesy, and Christian virtue. Ideally, Renaissance courtiers were expected to manifest many of the same attributes, though the fifteenth and sixteenth centuries greatly emphasized cultivating manners and a knowledge of the humanities and the arts. Nonetheless, gentlemen were required to avenge insult and injury in order to preserve their honor. Thus aristocrats turned cities and countrysides into theaters of war, defending their spheres of influence and redressing their injuries through blood feuds and duels rather than through formal systems of law and justice. At the same time urban power holders seeking to preserve and advance their status vaunted family antiquity, civic involvement, higher learning, and cultural patronage. Elite families strove to immortalize their glory and fame through literary and artistic patronage, while individuals sought to protect personal virtue by behaving with honesty and integrity, abiding by the norms and mores of the community, and performing worthy deeds. The behavior of individuals often affected the image of the entire group to which they belonged.

The concept of honor was applied differently to women than to men. A woman's honor depended on her chastity; thus she was expected to be modest, circumspect, and reserved. Because female honor affected marriageability in patriarchal societies, men controlled women's sexuality and powers of reproduction. Aware of the dire consequences of losing their honor by unwanted pregnancy or tainted reputation, women, too, enforced these values in their communities. Virtuous women were expected to be good Christians, expressing piety and humility.

Women who stepped outside these prescribed roles were perceived as a threat to the social order.

See also **Social Status.**

BIBLIOGRAPHY

Campbell, John Kennedy. *Honour, Family, and Patronage: A Study of Institutions and Moral Values in a Greek Mountain Community*. New York, 1974.

Muir, Edward. *Mad Blood Stirring: Vendetta and Factions in Friuli during the Renaissance*. Baltimore, 1993.

Peristiany, John G. *Honour and Shame: The Values of Mediterranean Society*. Chicago, 1966.

JOANNE M. FERRARO

HOOFT, PIETER CORNELISZOON (1581–1647), Dutch poet, dramatist, and historian. Hooft was a son of Cornelis Pieterszoon Hooft, merchant, burgomaster, and leader of the "Libertine" regents of the Amsterdam government that ruled after 1578. Hooft's father was probably not a member of the Dutch Reformed Church. His mother was Anna Blauw, cousin of William Johnson Blauw, the renowned printer and mapmaker to the States General. She was a Mennonite who attended the preaching of the liberal Jacobus Arminius. The elder Hoofts did not have their children baptized. Pieter Hooft thus grew up amid the wealth of the new Amsterdam merchant-oligarchy and the intellectual freedom of dissident Anabaptists and of civic leaders who had mounted anti-Catholic political dramas in Dutch in the Amsterdam chamber of rhetoric.

Hooft's thorough classical education was capped by a trip from 1598 to 1601 through France and Italy, where he was deeply impressed by the culture of Venice and Florence. He studied law at the University of Leiden from 1605 to 1607. Although his attention later turned to literature, he continued with his brothers in the family business.

In 1609 he was appointed bailiff and proprietor of the castle at Muiden (near Amsterdam) and given other responsibilities in the environs. He restored the neglected thirteenth-century fortress, turning it into his summer home and a gathering place for Holland's rising literati. Among them were the scholars Caspar van Baerle, Constantijn Huyghens, and Gerardus Johannes Vossius; the dramatist Joost van den Vondel; a governor general of the Dutch East Indies, Laurens Jacobszoon Reael; the organist and composer Jan Pieterszoon Sweelinck; and the poets Jacob Cats, Samuel Coster, Roemer Visscher, and Visscher's daughters Anna Roemers Visscher and Maria Tesselschade Roemers Visscher. The famed Muiderkring (Muiden Circle) probably never met as a group, but it symbolized and facilitated the circulation of new currents of literature as these visitors passed through. Hooft himself maintained his Amsterdam residence on the patrician Keizersgracht.

Hooft's first marriage (1610) to Christina Van Erp was saddened by the early deaths of all four of their children and by her own death (1624). In 1627 Hooft married Leonora Hellemans, widow of Jan Battista Bartolotti. Their two children lived to maturity.

In his youth Hooft drew on classical models to compose tender albeit erotic sonnets addressed to numerous young women of Amsterdam's regent society. Many consider them unsurpassed in refinement and ornateness of expression. The composition of sonnets in Dutch marked an advance in the sophistication of Dutch literature. In following his Latin and Italian models Hooft could be formal and mannered, but he reshaped the Dutch language into a fully poetic vehicle, a Northern flowering of the Italian Renaissance.

Taking Seneca as his model, he became one of the first to introduce classical tragedy into Dutch literature, an effort that bore more literary success than dramatic. In pastoral drama he wrote delightful poetry in such works as *Granida* (1605). His historical dramas, which were important for their cultural and historical insight, include *Geeraerdt van Velsen* (Gerard of Velsen; Amsterdam, 1612–1613) and *Baeto, oft Oorsprong der hollanderen* (The Batavi, or the origin of the Dutch people; written 1616; published 1626). His comedy *Warenar* (1617), after the example of Plautus's *Aulularia,* drew on the rich imagery of the common language of the time.

Later he turned to writing history, translating Tacitus over a period of years. During that time he wrote only one poetical work, the moving *Klaghte der Princesse van Oranjen over 't oorloogh voor 's Hartogenbosch* (Lament of the princess of Orange on the Battle for 's Hartogenbosch). His own first history was *Henrik de Grote* (Life of Henry the Great [Henry IV, of France]; 1626).

His major work, deemed the first Dutch history of literary distinction, was *Nederlandsche historien* (Netherlands history). Its first section, in twenty parts ending with the death in 1584 of William of Orange, appeared in 1642. From Hooft's estate another seven parts, incomplete, appeared in 1654. Where Pieter Bor and Emanuel van Meteren had written partisan Calvinist or Catholic chronicles of the Dutch wars of independence, Hooft covered the same events with a power of description and sense of purpose that elevated history to literature. Hooft viewed the war from the point of view of a liberal patrician defending Dutch liberty not only against a Spanish despot but also against mindless mobs and unscrupulous Calvinist fanatics. Thus, he was clearly in the camp of the religious and political figures who decried the actions of the Synod of Dort (1618–1619) and the execution of Johan van Oldenbarnevelt (1619).

Modern recognition is not lacking. A special P. C. Hooft literature prize is given annually in the Netherlands, and Hooft appeared on the first *euro* issued by the Dutch mint in 1999.

See also **Netherlandish Literature and Language.**

BIBLIOGRAPHY

Primary Work
Hooft, Pieter Corneliszoon. *Alle de Gedrukte Werken 1611–1738.* Amsterdam, 1972.

Secondary Work
Israel, Jonathan I. *The Dutch Republic: Its Rise, Greatness, and Fall, 1477–1806.* Oxford and New York, 1995.

CARL OLIVER BANGS

HOOKER, RICHARD (1554–1600), Elizabethan religious controversialist. Born in Heavitree, Exeter, England, in April 1554, Richard was the son of Roger Hooker, the younger son of Robert Hooker, mayor of Exeter in 1529, and of Joan, not otherwise known. The liaison may have been irregular. Roger Hooker left Exeter, serving as steward to Sir Thomas Chaloner in Spain from 1562 to 1565 and to Sir Peter Carew in Ireland as of 1569. Richard would thus have looked to his uncle John Hooker, prominent antiquary and chamberlain of Exeter, for support. He would have attended the Exeter grammar school. He matriculated at Corpus Christi College, Oxford, 1569, as a scholarship student. In 1574 he received a B.A., and in 1577, an M.A. He became probationary fellow of the college in 1577, then fellow in 1579. In the fall of 1584 he was presented the living of Drayton Beauchamp, Buckinghamshire, and he preached at London's Paul's Cross. In 1585 he was appointed Master of the Temple, where he preached and ministered to the legal establishment of the entire realm. His formal academic career came to a close with this appointment and with his marriage—fellows were expected to remain unmarried—to Joan Churchman, daughter of a prominent merchant tailor, by whom he had six children.

The Temple appointment, which was in the gift of the queen, was the fulcrum of Hooker's life and career. Upon his installation, he was challenged by his subordinate, Walter Travers, a prominent Puritan, on points of both doctrine and church order. The controversy, conducted in such a prominent venue, attracted widespread attention. Travers was silenced by John Whitgift, archbishop of Canterbury, and Hooker was provoked to compose the treatise *Of the Laws of Ecclesiastical Polity* (1593–1662), by which he is principally remembered. (Tracts by Hooker associated with the controversy itself were published in 1612.) In 1591 he resigned the mastership to become subdean of Salisbury and rector of nearby Boscombe, although it is doubtful that he moved there, preferring to live and write under the roof of his in-laws, the Churchmans. In 1595 he became vicar of Bishopsbourne, Kent, where he ministered as a parson and continued work on the *Laws* until his death, 2 November 1600.

Conceived of as a work of philosophic breadth and largeness of scale, the *Laws* appeared piecemeal. The preface and the first four books were published in 1593, book 5 late in 1597, books 6 and 8 posthumously in 1648, and book 7 in 1662. The preface skillfully situates the work in the contemporary agitation mounted by those within the Church of England who sought a more thoroughgoing reformation of its political structure ("polity") than had been provided by the Elizabethan Settlement (1559). They sought transfer to church consistories of legal jurisdiction traditionally vested in church courts (book 6), the elimination of the episcopate as a holdover from the Roman church, and the diminution of the secular monarch's authority as head of the church. Book 1, the most widely read, is a luminous exposition of the fundamental character of law as the ground of divine creation and of all human societies, whose particular laws are linked to prior divine law. Books 2–4 address general propositions set forth by the Puritans to sustain their political positions: book 2 discusses the overriding authority of scripture in human affairs; book 3, the specific authority of scripture in matters of church polity; and book 4, the corruption of the Church of England by "orders, rites, and ceremonies" of the Roman church. Book 5, the longest by far, supplies a detailed defense of the liturgy as set forth in the Elizabethan Book of Common Prayer (1559).

Scholars disagree as to why the treatise was not finished in Hooker's lifetime. In 1665 Izaak Walton, Hooker's first biographer, cited malicious vandals who destroyed completed versions of books 6–8. Walton's account still has supporters. Working from contemporary legal records, C. J. Sisson argues that Hooker himself never finished 6–8, a view substantially accepted by Hooker's twentieth-century editors. Book 6 at one time existed as a completed work

Richard Hooker. Portrait engraving by Wenceslaus Hollar (1607–1677). © THE BRITISH MUSEUM, LONDON

but was under revision at Hooker's death; book 7 survives complete but unrevised; book 8 is simply incomplete. Still, concerned as it is with the most explosive of political issues in the early seventeenth century, the authority of the monarch in the established church, book 8 circulated widely in manuscript after Hooker's death and before its publication in 1648.

Even unfinished, the *Laws* represent a uniquely constructive contribution to the religious polemic of the age, a debate that has largely dropped below the horizon of contemporary concern. Conceived of as a treatise of philosophic generality, comprehensiveness, and cohesiveness, it does in fact rise above the many other works contemporary to it, as has long been recognized; drawing on Walton's hagiographic portrait, writers continue to cite Hooker for his conciliatory treatment. More recent scholarship, however, has emphasized the incisive polemic underlying the philosophic fair-mindedness. And Peter Lake has argued that the inclusive, sacrament-based piety Hooker defends in the *Laws* distinguishes his view of the church not only from the Puritans' word-centered piety, but also from the views of contem-

porary conformist writers such as his own patron, Archbishop Whitgift.

Hooker's stature is evidenced by the publication record. Books 1–5 of the *Laws* appeared in seven editions before 1639. The collected works appeared in seven folio editions from 1662 to 1724 and in thirteen octavo editions from 1793 to 1890. John Keble's edition of 1836, itself reprinted eight times, claimed Hooker for the Tractarians. The Folger Library edition accords him full scholarly treatment, both of text and commentary.

Essential to Hooker's distinction as a polemicist was the training in Aristotelian logic and rhetoric he secured at Corpus Christi College, Oxford, a specifically humanist foundation, where he studied with John Rainolds, whose lectures in Aristotle's *Rhetoric* were then famous. Aristotle's *Politics,* which Hooker knew and cited, provided the literary model for the *Laws,* and humanist editions of the church fathers, such as those of Erasmus, underwrote Hooker's sophisticated historicism. In his passionate defense of the church, he may be considered a northern civic humanist whose "republic" was the Church of England as it had been established by the Elizabethan Settlement.

BIBLIOGRAPHY

Primary Works

Hill, W. Speed. *Richard Hooker: A Descriptive Bibliography of the Early Editions: 1593–1724.* Cleveland, Ohio, and London, 1970.

Hill, W. Speed, general ed. *The Folger Library Edition of the Works of Richard Hooker.* Vols. 1–5. Cambridge, Mass., 1977–1990; Vols. 6–7. Tempe, Ariz., 1993–1998.

Secondary Works

Hill, W. Speed, ed. *Studies in Richard Hooker: Essays Preliminary to an Edition of His Works.* Cleveland, Ohio, and London, 1972.

Kirby, W. J. Torrance. *Richard Hooker's Doctrine of the Royal Supremacy.* Leiden and New York, 1990.

Lake, Peter. *Anglicans and Puritans? Presbyterianism and English Conformist Thought from Whitgift to Hooker.* London and Boston, 1988.

McGrade, Arthur Stephen, ed. *Richard Hooker and the Construction of Christian Community.* Tempe, Ariz., 1997.

Secor, Philip B. *In Search of Richard Hooker: Prophet of Anglicanism.* London, 1999.

Sisson, C. J. *The Judicious Marriage of Richard Hooker and the Birth of* The Laws of Ecclesiastical Polity. Cambridge, U.K., 1940.

W. SPEED HILL

HORACE (Quintus Horatius Flaccus; 65–8 B.C.), Roman poet and satirist. Horace was born in Venusia, Italy. His father was a freedman who amassed sufficient wealth as an auctioneer's broker to send his son to school in Rome and, in about 46 B.C., Athens. In Athens Horace was swept into the army of Brutus, with which he fought as a military tribune against Octavian (later Augustus) at the battle of Philippi in 42 B.C. After a disastrous defeat, during which Horace records he shamefully abandoned his shield, the poet attempted to establish himself in Octavian's Rome. Through the intercession of his friend Virgil he obtained the patronage of Maecenas and later of the emperor himself. Maecenas presented him with a farm in the Sabine hills northeast of Rome in about 33 B.C., where Horace spent most summers in retirement from the capital.

Horace's earliest verses were *Epodes* and *Satires,* which frequently counterpoint the bustle of life in Rome with the life of philosophical *otium* (leisure). His mature *carmina* (odes), of which three books were published in 23 B.C., brought a flavor of Greek lyric poetry to Rome through imitations of panegyrics and drinking songs by Alcaeus, Anacreon, and Pindar. After Octavian's success in the battle of Actium in 31 B.C. Horace aligned his verse increasingly with the imperial cause and with the emperor's moral reforms, although not without showing admiration for the victims of empire, such as Cleopatra in *Odes* 1.37. His later works are in general more philosophical. His *Epistles* (20–19 B.C.) contain meditations on the good life, as well as his extremely influential epistle to the Pisones, later known as the *Ars poetica.*

After the appearance of the editio princeps (first printed edition) of his works in 1471 Horace became one of the most influential poets in the Renaissance. His tactful dealings with Maecenas provided a model for poets who wished to praise their patron while enjoying a measure of independence. His advocacy of Epicurean retreat from political engagement also offered his imitators a means by which to escape from or to criticize political abuses. Ludovico Ariosto's Horatian *Satires* (1517–1525) voice the poet's dissatisfaction with his patron Ippolito d'Este; in Luigi Alamanni's *Satires* of the 1520s Horace becomes the vehicle for outright republicanism, and in the *Satires* of Sir Thomas Wyatt from the late 1530s a Horatian epistolary form is used to decry courtly abuses in favor of quiet of mind.

As the self-proclaimed importer of Greek lyric poems into Rome, Horace appealed to poets who wished to bring lyric forms of Greece and Rome into the vernacular. By 1550 Pierre de Ronsard (whose Horatian four books of *Odes* appeared in that year) was drawing on Horace's *Odes* to create an inspired role for the Renaissance poet. Ronsard's friend Joachim du Bellay's *Défense et illustration de la langue française* (1549) owes partly to Horace its picture of the poet as one who enriched the vernacular with classical presences. From the 1540s vernacular translations of the *Ars poetica* appeared throughout Europe, and Horace's own precept that translators should not slavishly follow their model enabled a vast number of free imitations and translations of his works. By the time of Nicolas Boileau's *Arte poetique* (1674) Horatian poetics, fused with those of Aristotle, had become identified with civilized classicism throughout Europe.

Horace's ironical self-portraits in his *Satires* also enabled Renaissance poets to fashion their own autobiographical images. John Donne's first satire (c. 1590; modeled on *Satire* 1.9) presents the poet as one who fights his way past bores on his progress through the streets of London. Ben Jonson's presentations of himself—as a poet fond of conviviality, jealous of literary rivals, and zealous in his defense of true classical principles—are founded on his lifelong admiration for Horace, whose *Ars poetica* he translated with a painstaking literalness.

It is, however, as political poet that Horace had the greatest influence in the later Renaissance. Since Horace had fought with Brutus on the republican side in the civil wars before he became a panegyrist of Augustus, his wary political poems could appeal to poets of all persuasions. The neo-Latin imitations of Horace by Maciej Kazimierz Sarbiewski in the 1630s advocated a Christian stoic pursuit of inner constancy in response to adverse political events. This form of Horatianism was adopted by poets such as Abraham Cowley, who lived through the English Civil Wars in the 1640s, as a means of consoling themselves for the loss of their cause. Andrew Marvell's exquisitely balanced "Horatian Ode upon Cromwell's Return from Ireland" (1650) draws on Horace's Cleopatra *Ode* reservedly to praise Cromwell while acknowledging the "helpless right" of the executed Charles I. For republican and royalist alike, Horace provided a model for negotiating a balance between public poetry and private emotions.

BIBLIOGRAPHY

Fraenkel, Eduard. *Horace.* Oxford, 1957.

Lyne, R. O. A. M. *Horace: Behind the Public Poetry.* New Haven, Conn., and London, 1995.

Martindale, Charles, and David Hopkins, eds. *Horace Made New: Horatian Influences on British Writing from the Renaissance to the Twentieth Century.* Cambridge, U.K., 1993.

COLIN BURROW

HOSPITALS AND ASYLUMS. Pilgrims, foundlings, widows, the poor, the aged, the sick, and the dying all had recourse to the medieval *ospedale,* or hospice. Originating out of the drive to give some institutional structure to traditional works of charity, these hospitals were established by civic and ecclesiastical authorities, guilds, confraternities, and private parties. The designation "hospital" is to some extent misleading, in that specialized medical care in the modern sense was seldom practiced: hospitals provided hospitality. Most offered passive palliative care and short-term shelter to the broad category of *pauperes Christi,* or poor in Christ. A few private or corporate institutions, such as Roman pilgrims' hostels set up for particular national groups or Florentine guild hospitals, which were available to the families within a particular craft, served a more strictly defined set of clients.

While these features continued to characterize many hospitals to the end of the eighteenth century, significant developments in specialized care, administration, and scale occurred in the Renaissance period. This was particularly the case in Italy, whose hospitals were widely considered the wonder of Europe, even if their example was seldom followed. Physical need, political ambition, developments in medical care, and the Christian-humanist drive for a more moral, humane, and orderly society directed these changes. From the fifteenth century, urban and territorial governments aimed to merge the many small institutions into consolidated hospitals (called *ospedali maggiori* in Italy) under closer political control; this was at once a response to charges of fraud, an effort to make medical services and poor relief generally more efficient, and a recognition that control of the charitable institution could help extend the power of governing authorities over subject territories and marginal groups. From the sixteenth century, smaller, specialized asylums proliferated both to serve the specific needs of more closely defined groups of the poor (syphilitics, male or female orphans, battered women) and to go beyond passive care to a more deliberate effort to rehabilitate the poor and so reform society at large.

A Community of Care. Traditional hospitals brought the needy and caregivers together into a residential community oriented as much to spiritual as to physical care. Monastic hospitality provided the earliest models for communal care, administration, and design, but from the fourteenth century laity took a greater role in initiating and running hospitals. The care of pilgrims was usually limited to one night's room and board, with meals served communally after a short religious service and before the travelers retired, two or three to a bed. Guild and confraternal hospitals recruited members and their spouses to administrate and to perform such daily tasks as laundry and food preparation. They hired a chief administrator, who, with his family, took up residence in the hospital and looked after the details of its day-to-day operation: purchasing food and drink, sending out alms collectors, screening entrants, and, in larger institutions, supervising staff. The staff were also resident and were largely drawn from among the clientele; the poor in Christ were typically both recipients and givers of care in the hospital community, with widows being particularly prominent. A priest oversaw the community's spiritual care.

Consolidation and Specialization. Hospitals varied widely in scale and wealth. The majority were small: in a 1543–1544 census of 104 rural Tuscan hospitals, most had one or two beds, and some had none at all. Early fifteenth-century Florence had roughly thirty-five hospitals, of which five were considered large (four had fifty to seventy-five beds, and one had one hundred beds for men and seventy for women). On average, communities had one hospital per thousand people in the fifteenth century. For most, hospital size was dictated by the size of endowment, though Rome's S. Spirito in Sassia grew significantly through ongoing papal subsidies. If a founder's legacy had been invested wisely and expanded through subsequent donations and civic or ecclesiastical grants (not uncommon during the plagues of the fourteenth and fifteenth centuries), a hospital could become one of the wealthiest charitable institutions in the city; as a consequence, some expanded their services to include banking. The endowments of small and proprietorial hospitals were more easily exploited by fraudulent administrators.

The inadequacies of smaller hospitals were thrown into sharp relief by the example of larger institutions, while the latter's growing wealth led political authorities to seek greater control. Pressure for consolidation under lay and/or civic boards grew from the early fifteenth century, particularly in northern Italy. The power of both civic and ecclesiastical authorities was typically required to overcome opposition by the patrons of smaller institutions, whose properties and endowments were absorbed into the newly styled *ospedali maggiori.* Milan's Ospedale Maggiore was typical. Projected in 1447 and constructed from 1456, it was governed by a council rep-

French Hospital. Scene in a sixteenth-century *hôtel-Dieu*. BIBLIOTHÈQUE NATIONALE DE FRANCE, PARIS, MS. EA 17 RES

resenting religious orders, constituent hospitals, and civic authorities and steered by a ducal appointee; it in turn supervised the appointment of hospital administrators throughout the duchy. Duke Cosimo I de' Medici effected a similar consolidation of Tuscan hospitals in 1542, with a magistracy empowered to review administrations and accounts and to steer surpluses to an orphanage in the capital. Though their authority was frequently contested, these centralized hospitals were effective agents in the creation of the regional state. From the sixteenth century, northern European Protestant governments routinely drew hospitals into state networks of poor relief. The French crown attempted the same in the name of greater efficiency but was stymied by local resistance and a proliferation of new specialized hospitals and asylums under lay and clerical control.

Hospital consolidation pooled resources for the greater articulation of charitable care. Civic authorities or governing boards promoted a rationalization (that is, a form of management that would increase efficiency) through which small, general hospitals began serving particular groups of needy poor, particularly those perceived as requiring segregation, such as orphans, plague victims, and syphilitics. As a result, the community of caregivers within the hospital became more specialized, more professional, and more often paid. Historians have spoken of the medicalization of care at hospitals dedicated to serv-

ing the sick; these typically came to have separate wards for distinct categories of patients, doctors and surgeons on retainer, resident pharmacists, and the inevitable variety of financial administrators. Care followed the Galenic notion of diet, embracing food, rest, warmth, exercise, herbal remedies, and minimal invasive therapies, though some hospitals experimented with new treatments, particularly those serving syphilitics. By the sixteenth century, hospitals in Bologna and Florence were training sites for doctors.

Architecture. The needs of travelers put most early hospitals on major pilgrimage routes. They were styled after monasteries, with separate dormitories for men and women (with high ceilings to minimize airborne contagion), a large common refectory, and living quarters for the staff, often grouped around a courtyard. Renaissance innovations affected the elevations, the plan, and the scale of hospital buildings, in part because larger hospitals provided an opportunity to demonstrate civic magnificence. Filippo Brunelleschi's design for Florence's Ospedale degli Innocenti foundling home, particularly its graceful portico, was a landmark of Renaissance architecture and of hospital design in particular; Leon Battista Alberti recommended such porticoes for all hospitals on both aesthetic and practical grounds, and they were widely adopted. The cruciform plan was a further development, adopted

199

in part to simplify oversight by staff and to allow many patients to witness a single mass at an altar placed at the crossing. Siena's S. Maria della Scala, Florence's S. Maria Nuova, and Bologna's S. Maria della Morte all had modified cruciform plans, but the most ambitious was Filarete's double-cruciform plan for Milan's Ospedale Maggiore. Separate wards, sophisticated sanitation systems, ample storage for food, water, ice, and drugs, and distinct quarters for upper-class patients made this a particularly progressive and influential model, imitated in Spain, France, and England. The drawback in these plans was their comparatively vast scale, suitable for wealthy civic governments and royal patrons but beyond the means of most guild, confraternal, and private patrons. Nonetheless, patronage of hospital buildings or beds became a popular means both of publicly demonstrating one's wealth and charity and of providing for one's retainers, clients, and infirm servants.

Asylums and Enclosure. From the sixteenth century, hospital specialization reshaped the notion of a community of care. The impulse both to protect and to improve the poor made nonmedical hospitals more selective of their applicants and more prescriptive in their efforts; it also meant that the length of time the poor remained in the hospital extended from days or weeks to months or years. Asylums multiplied for abandoned children, "reformed" prostitutes, unhappily married women, widows, and Jews converting to Christianity. Not all took readily to "reform," and the strict segregation projected in statutes found only approximate translation into reality. Confraternities remained strong proponents of the new asylums, and former charges continued to make up the bulk of the staff, but the clergy recovered the active role it had held until the fourteenth century, with the new religious orders of the Catholic Reformation proving particularly vigorous. The discipline of work, education, and spiritual exercises aimed to reintegrate the weak or errant individual into society, particularly when that person came from an artisan or merchant family. Yet this discipline could have a punitive edge, particularly when combined with strict enclosure, and some hospitals for the vagrant poor degenerated into little more than prisons.

See also Confraternities; Orphans and Foundlings; Poverty and Charity.

BIBLIOGRAPHY

Cavallo, Sandra. *Charity and Power in Early Modern Italy: Benefactors and Their Motives in Turin, 1541–1789.* Cambridge, U.K., 1995.

Cohen, Sherrill. *The Evolution of Women's Asylums since 1500: From Refuges for Ex-Prostitutes to Shelters for Battered Women.* New York, 1992.

Grieco, Allen J., and Lucia Sandri, eds. *Ospedali e città: Italia del centro-nord, XIII–XVI secolo.* Florence, 1997.

Hickey, Daniel. *Local Hospitals in Ancien Régime France: Rationalization, Resistance, Renewal, 1530–1789.* Montreal, 1997.

Spierenburg, Pieter. *The Prison Experience: Disciplinary Institutions and Their Inmates in Early Modern Europe.* New Brunswick, N.J., 1991.

Thompson, John, and Grace Goldin. *The Hospital: A Social and Architectural History.* New Haven, Conn., 1975.

NICHOLAS TERPSTRA

HOTMAN, FRANÇOIS (1524–1590), French jurist. François Hotman was a French legal scholar who served as an agent of and propagandist for the Huguenot party during the Wars of Religion. The eldest son of a family of the office-holding nobility originally from Silesia, Hotman received a humanist education at the University of Paris and took his law degree at the University of Orléans in 1540. He taught the humanities and law in the academies of Lausanne and Strasbourg and the Universities of Valence and Bourges, practicing *mos gallicus iuris docendi* (the French, or humanist, method of teaching law) as distinguished from *mos italicus,* the traditional medieval (Italian) method. In a distinguished scholarly career Hotman published many treatises and commentaries on classical authors, civil law, and legal history, including his *Antitribonian* (1567), which denounced the foreign intrusions of Roman law and celebrated medieval French customs of Germanic derivation as the native legacy on which French law and legal education should be based.

At the same time he pursued a professional career Hotman was converted to Protestantism (the so-called reformed religion) and, with his friend and colleague Théodore de Bèze, fled Catholic France and his own orthodox family to seek exile in Geneva in 1547. Here he joined his "new father," John Calvin, and served for a while as his secretary. From this time until his death Hotman was a faithful follower and lawyerly champion of the Calvinist cause. As a French patriot of Protestant convictions Hotman opposed Romanism in every form—both the authoritarian influence of civil law and the analogous tyranny of the Roman church. On the eve of the religious wars Hotman took part in the conspiracy of Amboise (1560) directed against the evil influence of the "foreign" Guise family. After this fiasco he published an anonymous pamphlet, *Epistre envoiée au tigre de France* (The tiger of France; 1560), attacking the cardinal of Lorraine, evil partner of the queen mother, Catherine de Médicis, whose Italianate and Machiavellian influence was equally foreign and objectionable.

In the first of seven religious wars, which began in 1562, Hotman entered into the service of Louis I de Bourbon, prince of Condé, the Huguenot leader, and began to formulate his ideas about the facts and the ideals of constitutional monarchy, in which the Estates General shared authority with the king. This political view—which for a generation was in effect the Huguenot party line—combined with Hotman's own antiquarian interests in French history, led to his major work, *Francogallia* (1573). The book was actually begun several years before the Saint Bartholomew's Day massacre of 1572, but this horrendous episode in the religious wars—which almost claimed Hotman's own life and led to another Genevan exile—gave urgency to his line of argument. For the Calvinist Hotman the massacres represented an assault not only on true religion but also on the French people and so (as Hotman wrote privately) demanded resistance to the false sovereignty of a king who could murder his own subjects.

In his Geneva exile Hotman wrote accounts of the life of the Huguenot leader, Gaspard II de Coligny, and of the events of August 1572, and the next year he published the first edition of his *Francogallia*, which set up a constitutional ideal analogous to the primitive church of the Protestants and formulated a number of subversive theses, including the originally elective character of French (Frankish) kingship, the central role of the Great Council (root of the Estates General), and the Germanic (and Protestant) "liberties" of the authentic (anti-Roman, Franco-Celtic) traditions of the monarchy.

In later editions of the *Francogallia,* which appeared after the new Huguenot leader, Henry of Navarre, became next in line to the French throne, Hotman moderated his views somewhat, especially about the elective character of monarchy. Nevertheless, he continued to believe in the theory of Cicero and the practice of the old "Francogallic" monarchy that the best form of government was a mixture of the three forms of government: monarchy, aristocracy, and democracy. Hotman also continued his anti-Roman polemic, especially in his *Brutum fulmen* (Brutish thunderbolt) of 1586, which attacked Pope Sixtus V's bull excommunicating Henry of Navarre and defended the Bourbon succession. Hotman also continued to serve throughout all the wars as a diplomatic agent to various German Protestant princes, and to publish works in legal scholarship. He did not live to see his leader ascend to the throne

as Henry IV and convert to Catholicism, or to see any of his own properties restored. François Hotman died in Basel in 1590, leaving his contested estate to his son Jean and his subversive and even revolutionary intellectual legacy, especially the *Francogallia,* to later generations of constitutional thinkers.

See also **Resistance, Theory of**; *and biographies of figures mentioned in this entry.*

BIBLIOGRAPHY

Primary Work

Hotman, François. *Francogallia.* Edited by Ralph E. Giesey. Translated by J. H. M. Salmon. Cambridge, U.K., 1972. Variorum edition of Hotman's most influential work.

Secondary Works

Kelley, Donald R. *François Hotman: A Revolutionary's Ordeal.* Princeton, N.J., 1973. Full biography based on primary sources.

Giesey, Ralph E. "When and Why Hotman Wrote the *Francogallia.*" *Bibliothèque d'humanisme et renaissance* 29 (1967): 41–76.

Saint-Charmaran, A. H. *L'Antitribonian dans l'oeuvre de François Hotman.* 2 vols. Paris, 1972. Annotated facsimile of Hotman's *Antitribonian,* written in 1567 and published posthumously, on the reform of French law and legal education.

DONALD R. KELLEY

HOUSEHOLD. During the Renaissance, the word most often used to denote household was "family." Although "family" also had other meanings, it was primarily a synonym for household.

Types of Households. By far the most common household structure was, as it is today, the conjugal or nuclear-family household, based on one married couple and their children. Another common type, found among peasants using a system of inheritance in which property passed to a sole heir, has been termed the stem-family household. In it only the heir remains in the household after he or she marries, forming a second conjugal unit that may produce a third household generation. Less common was a structure often referred to nowadays as the extended-family household but more accurately termed the joint-family household. It was based on a conjugal pair and their sons, all of whom remained in the household after they married, along with their children.

The conjugal household was generally the smallest in size. Joint-family households sometimes reached enormous size, as did one in early fifteenth-century Tuscany that included forty-seven members, all related by blood or marriage. This was unusual, however. The chief determinant of size was wealth.

There was a sharp contrast between the majority of households, whatever their structure, and the households of the economically and socially elite. Most households averaged five or six members. There were some households of one or two; households of moderate means might reach nine or ten. Elite households were large even if they were conjugal in structure, because parents and children were not the only inhabitants. Renaissance households almost always also included people who had no kinship ties with each other, usually categorized as servants. A peasant household might have at most two or three, but the household of a lord or a prelate might have forty or more. Elite households expanded in the fifteenth and sixteenth centuries and slowly shrank after that, remaining huge in comparison to most households.

Some members of households were hard to categorize, even for contemporaries. Orphans who lived in the households of aunts and uncles were sometimes considered servants. Elderly relatives might be in a similar ambiguous position. Stepmothers, half siblings, and children born out of wedlock further complicated household structure, as did lodgers, who were neither servants nor kin.

Household Activities. Households were centers of production. Most were engaged in agriculture. This was true at all social levels. Noble households were organized for the exploitation of the land, usually managed by the lords' officers, servants of relatively high status. Peasants produced for both the lord and themselves, selling surpluses on the local market when they could. Whether tenants, sharecroppers, or direct owners, peasants used the labor of their whole households—their children, servants if they had any, and wives.

Manufacturing was also a household activity. The shops of craftsmen in towns were the front rooms of their houses, often open to the street, and the journeymen and apprentices who worked there were usually members of the masters' households. The textile industry, which accounted for so much wealth in this period, was based on households.

Great households were also centers of political power, from the households of kings and princes down to the households of lords of small manors. Various levels of justice were administered by the household officers of manorial and territorial lords, including ecclesiastical lords like abbots. The main political function of lesser households was that they constituted the units that were ruled. Heads of households were taxed rather than individuals.

The consumption of goods and the care of children were rather different from today. Consumption in poorer households could hardly be separated from production, since so much production was for subsistence. By contrast, consumption in great houses was prodigal. The very size of the houses was a form of conspicuous consumption, and their external appearance proclaimed their power and wealth. Interior decoration was similarly calculated to impress, often with reminders of an owner's distinguished ancestry. Vast numbers of servants proclaimed an owner's status. All this lavish display was put to use primarily when wealthy households entertained their frequent guests.

The care of children was not at the top of most households' concerns. The household was nevertheless the setting in which children were educated in most of the skills they would use as adults. A household's children might include its young servants, pages, and apprentices. As a result of the Protestant and Catholic reformations, the religious training of children and religious worship at home received increased attention, but many great houses had long had their own chapels and chaplains.

Ideas about the Household. Most treatises on household management endorsed a power structure in which the master, or household head, was the supreme authority, and all other members were subservient and obedient. Very large households were supposed to be organized into hierarchical levels of delegated authority.

The household figured prominently in political theory. Most writers followed the lead of Aristotle in considering the household the origin of the state. Jean Bodin in the sixteenth century and Thomas Hobbes in the seventeenth saw its "natural" power structure as the model for monarchy. The German philosopher Johannes Althusius in his *Politics* (1603) developed a theory, suggested by his observation of contemporary reality, that households were the constituent units of the state—a theory earlier embodied in Thomas More's *Utopia* (1516) where, incidentally, households were required to contain between ten and sixteen members.

Notions about the household affected the way many other institutions were run. A monarchy was supposed to be little different from a well-run household. A major complaint against England's Richard II (ruled 1377–1399) was that he did not manage finances like a good housekeeper. Monastic institutions were organized like households. Schools and colleges also aped households, partly because some of them were schoolmasters' homes, partly because the model seems to have been inescapable.

BIBLIOGRAPHY

Baulant, Micheline. "The Scattered Family: Another Aspect of Seventeenth-Century Demography." In *Family and Society: Selections from the Annales: Economies, Sociétés, Civilisations.* Edited by Robert Forster and Orest Ranum. Baltimore, 1976. Pages 104–116. Pertinent to earlier centuries as well.

Goldthwaite, Richard A. "The Florentine Palace as Domestic Architecture." *American Historical Review* 77 (1972): 977–1012.

Herlihy, David, and Christiane Klapisch-Zuber. *The Tuscans and Their Families: A Study of the Florentine Catasto of 1427.* New Haven, Conn., 1985.

Mertes, Kate. *The English Noble Household 1250–1600: Good Governance and Politic Rule.* Oxford and New York, 1988.

Wall, Richard, Jean Robin, and Peter Laslett, eds. *Family Forms in Historic Europe.* Cambridge, U.K., 1983. An important collection of essays. See especially the introduction by Wall and contributions by Laslett and John Hajnal.

BEATRICE GOTTLIEB

HOWARD, HENRY. *See* **Poetry, English,** *subentry on* **Tudor Poetry before Spenser.**

HUARTE DE SAN JUAN, JUAN

(1529–1588), Spanish physician. Huarte was born of Jewish parents. His fame is almost exclusively due to a single book, *El examen de ingenios* (The study of learning skills), published in 1575. In the book, Huarte postulates that human souls are substantially identical and that individual differences in *ingenios,* or learning skills, depend exclusively on the body as affected by climate, diet, age, gender, geographical location, and seasonal changes. Huarte used Galen's theory of temperaments as the foundation of all his work. Individual temperament is determined by the different combinations of the four qualities (cold, hot, dry, and wet) and the four humors of the body (blood, phlegm, yellow bile, and black bile). Huarte assigns the brain as the central organ of our rational powers: humid memory, hot imagination, and dry understanding. The dominant humor defines the learning capacity of each individual toward any given discipline to the exclusion of others. The division of *ingenios* corresponds to the division of the arts and sciences. Thus, the learning of languages, the theory of the law, and positive theology, which treats theology as fact or history, are made possible by humid brains with a strong memory. Scholastic theology, logic, and the practice of the law are made possible by a dry understanding. A hot imagination makes possible poetry, eloquence, music, the art of warfare, painting, and the invention of "devices and engines." The theoretical and the practical are without exception incompatible: a legal expert does not make a persuasive barrister. Individual talent can be recognized by certain signs. The state is responsible for supervising the professional orientation of its citizens (particularly young boys).

Huarte also explains gender differentiation and human development in terms of the four qualities. In males, heat expands the genitalia out of the body, while in females a lower degree of heat keeps the sex organs inside. Childhood is hot and wet, youth is hot and dry, adulthood has moderate heat and excessive dryness, old age is cold and dry.

Huarte concluded that "girls, on account of the cold and moisture of their sex," cannot be endowed with a sharp intelligence. The "art" of having boys instead of girls is based on Huarte's theory that the right testicle is hotter and drier than the left one and that some foods, such as honey and white wine, make the semen hot and dry. Exercise, the timing of copulation (seven days before menstruation), proper diet, intensive sexual desire, and the posture of the woman after copulation (resting on her right side with her head down and her heels up) guarantee the conception of boys.

The Spanish Inquisition included the book in its *Index* for several reasons. They included its naturalistic conception of the body as the part of the universe that determines the rational capacity of the soul, Huarte's explicit fideism (an emphasis on faith over reason) about the proofs for the immortality of the soul, and his fuzzy statements on the connection between temperament and moral behavior and free choice. These same ideas explain why it was read with interest by, among others, Descartes, Montesquieu, Roger Bacon, and Gotthold Lessing (who translated it into German).

BIBLIOGRAPHY

Primary Works

Huarte, Juan. *Examen de ingenios para las ciencias.* Edited by Esteban Torre. Madrid, 1976.

Huarte, Juan. *Examination of Men's Wits.* Translated by M. Camillo. Gainesville, Fla., 1959.

Secondary Works

Iriarte, Mauricio de. *El Doctor Juan Huarte de San Juan y su examen de ingenios: Contribución a la historia de la psicol-*

ogía diferencial. 3d ed. Madrid, 1948. The most authoritative work on Huarte.

Read, Malcolm K. *Juan Huarte de San Juan.* Boston, 1981.

CARLOS G. NOREÑA

HUGUENOTS. *See* **Wars of Religion.**

HUIZINGA, JOHAN. *See* **Renaissance, Interpretations of the,** *subentry on* **Johan Huizinga.**

HUMAN BODY IN RENAISSANCE ART. The period from about 1300 to about 1600 in Europe saw many new contexts emerge for the depiction of the human body, as well as a marked series of transformations in how the figure was represented. The portrait, the heroic or erotic nude, the memorial effigy, even the anatomical illustration all existed before 1400, but thereafter they are distinguished by greater quantity, by visibility, by the range of markets and audiences, and by the rapid transformation of styles and artistic technologies. As long as historians have debated the notion of a Renaissance, this feature has offered seemingly unarguable testimony to the existence of a *period* with distinctive characteristics. The representation of the human figure has also been used to illustrate the Renaissance as a specific *cultural movement* centered on what Jakob Burckhardt in 1860 called the "rise of the individual" and the "discovery of man." For writers in the tradition of Burckhardt, the Renaissance body is held to be marked by a sense of heroic individuality, to manifest a particularized subjectivity not evident in medieval art; it is thought to affirm physical sensation and sensual experience and to be free of the bodily shame inherent in "medieval Christianity." It signified, essentially, the rebirth of a classical culture centered on *humanitas,* the centrality of man (less so of woman) in the order of creation.

Some scholars recently have taken a less celebratory view and attempt to relate visual representation, the emergence of the body (or "man") as an object of knowledge, and the expression of power in increasingly centralized and autocratic early modern states. The public monument is a characteristic political deployment of the body. By the mid-fifteenth century, images of princes and military leaders appear not only as effigies on tombs in sacred space, but as public, secular sculpture; these images function not only as memorials, but establish the presence of authority, embodying the power of the state. In Ferrara in 1454 the bronze statue of a living prince, Borso d'Este, was erected as a personification of Justice near the site of public executions. In other cities, such as Florence, enemies of the state received a negative commemoration and even a surrogate punishment through paintings of their hanged bodies on the facades of civic buildings. While images of the nude in monumental sculpture, domestic painting, and in religious art honored physical beauty, they also related to a tightening of religious and legal controls of bodily comportment, sexual activity, the regulation of gender, and even the experience of desire. From this point of view, by the mid-sixteenth century, the idealized body in art would be another instance of a prevailing concern with social norms and decorum. By this time, manuals of personal conduct for would-be gentlemen enjoined restraint and discretion. Painters like Titian produced erotic female nudes for the rulers of Europe, but also images of spectacular, excruciating punishment of famous mythological transgressors (*The Flaying of Marsyas, The Punishment of Tityus*). Comic, grotesque, or erotic imagings of the human form (for instance, Peter Brueghel's scenes of peasant life) manifest a new interest in a range of bodily functions and sensations, but also suggest an increasingly stratified society visible in behavioral norms of class and social boundaries for wealthy and aristocratic patrons.

Nudity in Christian Art. The increased appearance of the nude in Christian art after 1300 was a new visual expression of long-established theological principles that viewed the body as a sign of sinfulness and mortality, its redemption through Christ's assumption of human form (the doctrine of the Incarnation), and the afterlife as a resurrection of the body. In medieval art, the naked male and female forms had occurred in scenes that frame human history—the Fall of Adam and Eve, and the Last Judgment in which the damned and the elect recover their bodies to experience damnation or salvation physically. In the fourteenth and fifteenth centuries the drama of the body's fall, suffering, and redemption are presented with a new realism in the rendering of the figure and its sensations, as the spectator might actually see and think of people. Images of the *Last Judgment* by Giotto (1266/67–1337; Arena Chapel, 1300s) and Rogier van der Weyden (1399?–1464) (Beaune, Hôtel-Dieu, c. 1450), vividly emphasize pain and sinful abjection in the depiction of the nude figure. But renderings of the subject by Luca Signorelli (c. 1445/50–1523; Orvieto, cathedral, c.

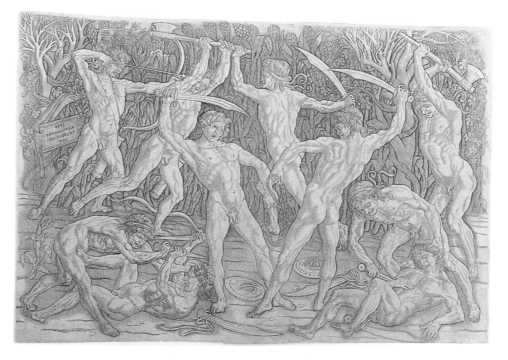

Antonio Pollaiuolo. *Battle of the Nudes.* Engraving; c. 1475. THE CLEVELAND MUSEUM OF ART, PURCHASED FROM THE J. H. WADE FUND, 1967.127

1500) and Michelangelo (Vatican, Sistine Chapel, 1541) emphasize more the doctrine of the resurrection of the body, through their use of robustly corporeal and emphatically muscular nude images.

The infant Christ had appeared wholly or partly nude from the early fourteenth century onwards, while in the fifteenth century the child's male sex is sometimes given prominence (see, for example, *Virgin and Child* by Robert Campin [c. 1378–1444; London, National Gallery] or *Virgin and Child* by Giovanni Bellini [c. 1430–1516; Bergamo, Academia Carrara]). Artistic realism again serves older doctrinal concerns: Christ's sexuality represents his human nature and thus signifies the redemption of the body in its most fallen and vilified features through a divine taking on of human nature that ennobles the flesh. Another characteristic visual theme that emerges in the fourteenth century, the *virgo lactans* (Mary nursing the infant Christ), places a new emphasis on the human and physical nature of the Virgin.

The theology of the Incarnation was expounded according to the canons of classical rhetoric in sermons preached at the papal court in the fifteenth century. Theologians such as Giles of Viterbo celebrated the beauty and dignity of man as a manifes-

tation of the divine image, a celebration that culminated in a work of monumental painting—the Sistine ceiling of Michelangelo, with its host of heroic male nudes who express divine grace and inspiration in terms of ecstatic bodily experience. The nude was charged with a theological significance, while its qualities of graceful animation could be identified with the virtue and inspiration of the artist. At the same time, the premium on artistic virtuosity manifest primarily in the rendering of the body did not easily coexist with the doctrinal sanction for the nude provided by incarnational theology, especially in the era of increased religious conformity following the Council of Trent, which began in 1545. The Protestant churches had proscribed the devotional use of images altogether, while the Catholic Church adopted a newly censorious stance, reviving and elaborating medieval polemics against "unchaste" images of Christ and the Virgin. Michelangelo's *Last Judgment* [see the frontispiece to volume 4] was attacked for its carnality and its "pagan" glorification of the flesh. Following the partial censorship and narrowly averted destruction of the fresco, any defense of the nude in Christian art became increasingly untenable. The nude becomes less prominent in religious art following the provisions on religious images by the Council of Trent (published in 1563), yet remains present in private painting on religious and secular themes.

The Influence of Antiquity. Civic art from the fourteenth century onwards, especially in Italy, aided the emergence of the nude figure in painting and sculpture. Works of art erected in the name of government and citizenry encompass both secular monuments and the adornment of churches, and a civic ideology promoting ancient Roman origins underlies the appearance of the classical, Herculean male nude, representing the virtue of Fortitude, in a marble pulpit for the Pisa Baptistery (Nicola Pisano, c. 1260) and the Porta della Mandorla of Florence cathedral (attributed to Jacopo della Quercia, 1390s). Antique sculptures had been collected throughout Europe and admired at Rome and elsewhere throughout the Middle Ages, yet were also regarded with a certain ambivalence, as dangerously seductive and contaminating relics of paganism. At the same time, to Renaissance observers, that such figures survived legitimated the ancient origins of their city and government. The sculptural decoration of the Fonte Gaia at Siena by Jacopo della Quercia (1415–1420) incorporated two freestanding near-nude female figures, among the earliest since antiquity. These figures both supplant and commemorate a pagan statue of Venus that once adorned the fountain, until allegations of its malign influence led to its destruction and burial in Florentine territory in 1357. The association of the female body with venereal temptation was now displaced by recasting the female form as a civic symbol of Charity or maternal nurture. Florentine sculptors absorbed technical lessons from the antique (such as the principle of *contrapposto* or weight-shift), but much fifteenth-century imagery of the nude eschews classical canons of proportion and physical idealization. The nudes in Masaccio's frescoes (Florence, S. Maria del Carmine; for the *Expulsion from Paradise,* see the entry on Masaccio in volume 4) portray tragically mortal flesh; such depictions suggest a "medieval" idea given a more striking and persuasive visual form, rather than a new world-affirming "humanism." In this generation, only Lorenzo Ghiberti's Isaac from his 1401 *Sacrifice of Isaac* relief [see the entry on Sculpture in volume 5] seems consciously antiquarian in its treatment of the naked body and does suggest a biblical figure cast as a classical hero.

The humanist and antiquarian culture of Padua fostered the emulation of classical sculpture by artists like Mantegna and Donatello by the middle of the fifteenth century, yet even in Mantegna's case, the encounter with antiquity suggests a dialogue with an adversary (antiquity) that had to be overcome. Thus, in Mantegna's *St. Sebastian* (Vienna, Kunsthistorisches Museum; see the entry on Mantegna in volume 4), the pagan sculpture on which the artist models his own work is shown in a ruined state, and hence contrasted with the corporeal integrity of the suffering martyr, the patron of recovery from plague. The carnal and pagan connotations of the nude always threatened to eclipse its positive identification with civic virtue and divine creation. The near-nudity of St. Sebastian from the fourteenth century carried a devotional message, the promise of physical healing in this life and corporeal resurrection in the next. Yet here too nudity at times crosses inappropriate boundaries; in early-sixteenth-century Florence a painting of the saint by the pious Fra Bartolomeo was deemed too lascivious for the community of nuns for which it was made and had to be removed from their convent church. The nudity of Michelangelo's marble *David* [see the color plates in this volume], the personification of masculine belligerence erected by the Florentine Republic in defiance of its enemies in 1504, *subsequently* offended propriety and was soon provided with a loincloth of gilded metal leaves; the aggressive male nude nonetheless continued to dominate Florentine civic space, especially under the princely government of the Medici that replaced the Republic in 1530 (examples include Cellini's *Perseus,* 1545–1554, and Giambologna's *Rape of the Sabine,* 1579–1583).

The nude appears in secular and domestic art by the mid-fourteenth century, especially in courtly environments where secular love poetry and romance literature formed part of a ritualized culture of civility, or *cortesia,* around the ruler. Pisanello, the preeminent court decorator of the early fifteenth century, made drawings of the nude after ancient sculpture, but his celebrated rendering of a dancing nude female figure is one of the earliest surviving examples of drawing from the live nude model. Northern European artists also contributed to this taste; Jan Van Eyck was celebrated by an Italian writer around 1450 for the painting of a naked female bather, in the collection of the king of Naples. At the courts and in the households of Florentine patricians, mythological painting emerges as a separate genre in the later fifteenth century. The definitive humanist art based on pagan and literary subject matter, mythology was understood as poetic meditation on nature and the psychology of love; sensuous and frankly erotic depictions of the body in mythologies by Botticelli, or later by Raphael and Titian, stood for the allure of pagan culture. In the case of Raphael and Titian, the female body becomes a kind of signature and a metaphor for the sensuous and ambiguous powers of poetry and painting itself.

Art Theory and Anatomy. Renaissance artistic culture is marked by the emergence of a theoretical literature, beginning with the humanist Leonbattista Alberti (*On Painting,* 1435) and the artists Cennino Cennini and Lorenzo Ghiberti, and continuing with Leonardo da Vinci (1452–1519) and the academic theorists of the sixteenth century. Following Alberti, the body in art theory observes a defined system of proportions and physiognomical attributes, appropriate to gender, age, and moral condition; through gesture and expression it expresses the "motions" of an inward propelling force, the mind or soul. The body is to be anatomically expressive, a clearly ordered system of interdependent parts, and the artist should conceive his compositions of figures as a system of layers, beginning with the skeleton and adding flesh and clothing. Extremes of motion and gesture are described, but these artists are enjoined to avoid depicting them for their own sake, to express virtuosity. Alberti prefers the sober visual narratives of Masaccio and Giotto, enacted by few figures who use explicit gesture economically. He was responding here to a belief in restraint that informed public and private life in the mercantile republics of the early Renaissance, breaches of which were regarded as signs of subversive individualism. His precepts are restated in the theoretical literature throughout the later Renaissance; they clearly engaged the attention of several artists (such as Mantegna, Dürer, Raphael, and Leonardo). In one fundamental respect, however, the injunctions against conspicuous virtuosity, manifest above all in the complex and difficult postures of the moving figure, were contrary to an increasing tendency to regard the body as the primary signifier of artistic expertise, of art as a distinctive form of humanistic knowledge grounded in anatomical study and the imitation of ancient sculpture. This accorded with a new premium on artistic mastery manifest in movement and expression, which reached its apogee in the art of Michelangelo and his contemporaries.

Alberti and Ghiberti had encouraged the artist to study the structure of the body by looking beneath its surface, at the arrangement of bones, muscles, and sinews. Ghiberti recommended attendance at the public anatomy lessons, which in Florence were held by the Faculty of Medicine and the Guild of Doctors and Druggists (to which artists also belonged). Although attitudes toward dissection or autopsy were more liberal in Italy than in Northern Europe, these public dissections were not held often, and no secure visual or documentary evidence exists of artists studying anatomy directly from dissected bodies until the early years of the sixteenth century, when Michelangelo and Leonardo made anatomical studies unrivaled in their sophistication before the era of Vesalius, who produced the most important anatomical work of the century, *De humani corporus fabrica* (Basel, 1543). Vasari claimed that Pollaiuolo and Andrea del Verrocchio carried out dissections, and Pollaiuolo's *Battle of the Nudes,* despite anatomical anomalies, suggests he was correct. In the sixteenth century Dürer, Leonardo, Michelangelo, Rosso Fiorentino, and Francesco Salviati had all engaged in or at least contemplated ambitious publications on human anatomy, and were followed by Bartolomeo Passarotti, Jacopo Ligozzi, and Alessandro Allori. In their ability to collect and to render empirical observations in a systematic manner, artists possessed the resources—but not the authority—to extend scientific knowledge of the body, and completed projects generally involved collaboration with university professionals. Vesalius's work was illustrated by a Flemish artist associated with Titian, Jan Stephan van Calcar; Charles Estienne's *De dissectione partium corporis humani* (Paris, 1546) based its illustrations on erotic and mythological prints by Italian artists.

The attainment of *maniera*—mannerism, or beautiful style—was conceived by Giorgio Vasari in 1550 as a composite process that required anatomical knowledge. The purpose was to train an artist's memory so that, independently of the model, he could mentally conceive and "assemble" figures more beautiful than life. Artists were praised for the degree to which their figures disclosed anatomical knowledge; artistic virtuosity and license had its signature in the body.

The Body as Artifact and as Text. The *signifying* aspect of the body, then, seems to operate as a common concern of social life, as well as of art theory and practice. In the literature of manners and deportment, the body is conceived as itself an elaborate and self-conscious act of representation. The face, the costume, even the exposure of the flesh evidence a concern with the human form as a surface that testifies to a truth that lies beyond the visible and tangible: that essence might be the intrinsic nobility or mental virtues of the sitter, the inspiration

Bartholomaeus Spranger. *Victory of Minerva.* Oil on canvas; 153 × 117 cm (60 × 46 in.). KUNSTHISTORICHES MUSEUM, GEMÄLDEGALERIE, VIENNA/ERICH LESSING/ART RESOURCE

of saints, the virtuosity of the artist, or the very existence of a problematic entity termed the *mind* or the *soul*. The quality of "psychological insight" in a Titian portrait might be less an actual power to discern "true character" through appearance than it is another manifestation of a prevailing concern of sixteenth-century aristocratic culture with the gestures, bodily performances, and adornments that can best depict depth *beyond appearances*. In their work Renaissance artists explore identity in terms of layers

and surfaces, and in which the indeterminacy of the layers from one another and from some fundamental ground of "true being" is creatively exploited.

See also **Anatomy** *and biographies of Vesalius and other figures mentioned in this entry.*

BIBLIOGRAPHY

Adler, Kathleen, and Marcia Pointon, eds. *The Body Imaged: The Human Form and Visual Culture since the Renaissance.* Cambridge, U.K., and New York, 1993.

Camille, Michael. *The Gothic Idol: Ideology and Image Making in Medieval Art*. Cambridge, U.K., and New York, 1989. Includes account of largely negative attitudes toward the nude in pre-Renaissance art, but with implications for the fifteenth and sixteenth centuries.

Campbell, Stephen J. *Cosmè Tura of Ferrara: Style, Politics, and the Renaissance City, 1450–1495*. New Haven, Conn., 1998. Includes chapter on the representation of the saintly body.

Carlino, Andrea. "Knowe Thyself: Anatomical Figures in Early Modern Europe." *Res* 27 (1995): 52–69.

Cazort, Mimi, Monique Kornell, and K. B. Roberts. *The Ingenious Machine of Nature: Four Centuries of Art and Anatomy*. Ottawa, Exhibition catalog. The National Gallery of Canada, 1996. The most useful survey of its kind, with abundant illustrations of Renaissance material.

Clark, Kenneth. *The Nude: A Study in Ideal Form*. New York, 1956. Reprint, Princeton, N.J., 1972. Discussion of the Renaissance body from a position influenced by Burckhardt.

Cropper, Elizabeth. "The Place of Beauty in the High Renaissance and Its Displacement in the History of Art." In *Place and Displacement in the Renaissance*. Edited by Alvin Vos. Pages 159–205. Binghamton, N.Y., 1995. Historiographically oriented account of one of the fundamental issues underlying the portrayal of the body.

Edgerton, Samuel Y. *Pictures and Punishment: Art and Criminal Prosecution during the Florentine Renaissance*. Ithaca, N.Y., and London, 1985.

Elkins, James. "Michelangelo and the Human Form: His Knowledge and Use of Anatomy." *Art History* 7, no. 2 (1984): 176–186.

Gent, Lucy, and Nigel Llewellyn, eds. *Renaissance Bodies: The Human Figure in English Renaissance Culture*. London, 1990. Includes essays on portraiture and on Renaissance anatomy.

Laneyrie-Dagen, Nadelije. *L'invention du corps: La representation de l'homme du Moyen Âge à la fin du XIXe siècle*. Paris, 1997.

Park, Katherine. "The Criminal and the Saintly Body: Autopsy and Dissection in Renaissance Italy." *Renaissance Quarterly* 47 (1994): 1–33. Presents evidence of widespread toleration of autopsy and dissection from the late Middle Ages.

Park, Katherine. "The Sensitive Corpse: Body and Self in Renaissance Medicine." *Fenway Court* (1990–91): 77–87. Contrasts attitudes to dissection in Italy with those of Northern Europe.

Sawday, Jonathan. *The Body Emblazoned: Dissection and the Human Body in Renaissance Culture*. New York and London, 1995. Problematic in its larger claims, but with useful local insights.

Steinberg, Leo. *The Sexuality of Christ in Renaissance Art and Modern Oblivion*. New York, 1983. 2d ed. Chicago, 1996. Controversial, provocative argument connecting the genital emphasis of numerous Renaissance images of Christ with the theology of the incarnation.

STEPHEN J. CAMPBELL

HUMANISM.

[This entry consists of nine subentries:

For discussion of civic humanism see Renaissance, Interpretations of the, subentry on Hans Baron.]

The Definition of Humanism

Humanism was the principal intellectual movement of the European Renaissance. It originated in fourteenth-century Italy and began to affect other countries shortly before 1500. Humanism was rooted in the belief that a specific body of learning, the humanities (*studia humanitatis*), based on the literary masterpieces of ancient Greece and Rome, could bring about a cultural rebirth (or renaissance): the study of ancient literary texts, some of them known throughout the Middle Ages but others newly rediscovered, would provide both general inspiration and specific knowledge useful for ending the alleged "barbarism" of the Middle Ages. These ancient texts included not only classical literature but also the Bible and the works of the church fathers. Although humanism began as a study of classical Latin literature, it reached its flowering after 1400 with the mastery of Greek language and literature, a part of the ancient heritage little known to medieval scholars. The distinctive trait of Renaissance humanism was not only increased knowledge of ancient texts but also the linking of that knowledge to the vision of cultural rebirth.

The term "humanism" is modern, but the concept of "humanistic studies" goes back to Renaissance authors who used it to designate five academic subjects they considered necessary for civilized life and placed at the center of the curriculum: grammar, rhetoric, moral philosophy, poetry, and history. The "humanist" was the teacher of these subjects. Most humanists rejected the theoretical, metaphysical, and scientific emphasis of medieval scholastic education as useless for ordinary life, where educated laypersons make daily choices in matters in which absolute truth remains uncertain and only probable choices are available, choices that have moral consequences. Thus humanism inspired an educational revolution in the Latin schools of fifteenth-century Italy.

The humanists' faith in the regenerative power of their studies assumed the existence of a symbiotic relationship between moral philosophy and rhetoric. They saw rhetoric—conceived as a system of choosing the more probable of two alternative courses of action and presenting them effectively in public discourse—as essential to participation in public life. Some modern scholars apply the term "civic humanism" to this political concept, which is exemplified in the works of Coluccio Salutati (1331–1406) and Leonardo Bruni (c. 1370–1444) and often associated with Florentine republicanism. Yet humanistic skills could also be applied to policy discussions at despotic courts, and this adaptability made humanism attractive to royal courts beyond Italy. Most historians agree that in both monarchies and republics, humanism became the preferred culture of political elites.

Humanists were always eager to discover and disseminate ancient texts, and from the 1450s the new art of printing greatly aided this goal. Humanist scholars from Lorenzo Valla (1407–1457) to Erasmus (c. 1466–1536) to Joseph Justus Scaliger (1540–1609) and Isaac Casaubon (1559–1614) developed skills in linguistic and historical criticism that laid the earliest foundations of modern classical philology and historiography. The humanists' aspirations also embraced the reform of religion through a return to the ancient biblical and patristic sources, an ideal associated with Erasmus and Jacques Lefèvre d'Étaples (c. 1455–1536) and often labelled "Christian humanism."

In the nineteenth century and since, "humanism" has often come to designate a secular philosophy of life, a viewpoint that was often anachronistically projected back onto Renaissance humanism; but this is a modern usage not valid for the "humanism" of the Renaissance.

See also Classical Antiquity, Discovery of; Classical Scholarship; Education; Renaissance, *subentry on* The Renaissance in Historical Thought; Renaissance, Interpretations of the, *subentries on* Hans Baron *and* Paul Oskar Kristeller.

BIBLIOGRAPHY

Baron, Hans. *The Crisis of the Early Italian Renaissance: Civic Humanism and Republican Liberty in an Age of Classicism and Tyranny,* 2d ed. Princeton, N.J., 1966. The classic presentation of the concept of "civic humanism."

Burckhardt, Jakob. *The Civilization of the Renaissance in Italy.* Translated by S. G. C. Middlemore. Reprint, New York and London, 1990. Translation of *Die Kultur der Renaissance in Italien,* the most influential book ever written about humanism and the Renaissance, first published in 1860 and much criticized in recent times, but still essential.

Garin, Eugenio. *Italian Humanism: Philosophy and Civic Life in the Renaissance.* Translated by Peter Munz. New York, 1965.

Grafton, Anthony. *Defenders of the Text: The Traditions of Scholarship in an Age of Science, 1450–1800.* Cambridge, Mass., 1991. An important account of the linguistic and philological heritage of humanism.

Grafton, Anthony, and Lisa Jardine. *From Humanism to the Humanities.* Cambridge, Mass., 1986. An arguable but stimulating interpretation of the historical significance of humanism.

Kristeller, Paul Oskar. *Renaissance Thought: The Classic, Scholastic, and Humanistic Strains.* New York, 1960. The views expressed in chapters 1, 5, and 6 have shaped all subsequent discussion of humanism.

Nauert, Charles G. *Humanism and the Culture of Renaissance Europe.* Cambridge, U.K., 1995.

Seigel, Jerrold E. *Rhetoric and Philosophy in Renaissance Humanism.* Princeton, N.J., 1968. A challenge to Baron's conception of "civic humanism."

Trinkaus, Charles. *In Our Image and Likeness: Humanity and Divinity in Italian Humanist Thought.* 2 vols. Chicago, 1970.

CHARLES G. NAUERT

The Origins of Humanism

Humanism slowly evolved in a series of steps from the mid-thirteenth century to 1400. French influences, poetry, and classical models, especially the writings of Cicero, all played roles in its development.

Compared to France, northern and central Italy in the twelfth century showed little interest in ancient Latin literature and history. Intellectual concerns were preeminently practical, focused on Roman and canon law and *ars dictaminis,* the technique of writing Latin formal letters tailored for easy learning. Grammatical training was largely limited to preparing the student for studying these disciplines. Significantly, almost no Latin poetry survives from this period in these areas.

The Medieval Background. The situation was changed after about 1180, however, when for a variety of reasons partly connected with the evolution of legal studies, Italy began to draw on contemporary French work in Latin grammar, particularly the newly developed speculative form. Also introduced were the rich corpus of Latin poetry produced by French poets heavily influenced by ancient literary writings, a highly wrought style of *ars dictaminis* replete with classical reminiscences, and a controversial conception of legal studies in which grammarians played a key role. Provençal poetry, French chivalric literature, and recently developed French handbooks called *artes predicandi,* or manuals of preaching, offering an innovative form of preaching, appear to have been eagerly sought by Italians.

By the 1190s Italians such as Bene of Florence (d. 1240) responded to the new grammatical material by producing the first grammar manuals securely datable to the century; and Henry of Settimello's Latin poem on fortune, *Elegia* (1193), broadly manifested the influence of both Provençal literature and the style of Latin poetry current in France. The late dictaminal writings of both Boncompagno da Signa (c. 1170–c. 1240) and Bene displayed a knowledge of ancient authors unparalleled in twelfth-century Italian *dictamen* treatises and in their own earlier writings. A judge and notary, Albertano da Brescia (c. 1200–c. 1270) was the first Italian north of Rome to reflect a knowledge of Seneca, who had enjoyed meteoric success in France from about 1150 and was the most important ancient author for the first two generations of Italian humanists.

The *Elegia,* however, remained an isolated event down to the mid-thirteenth century when, partly inspired by intense interest in vernacular poetry, a whole series of Latin poems appeared beginning with Urso da Genova's epic *De victoria quam Genuenses ex Friderico II retulerunt* (On the victory the Genoese won against Frederick II; c. 1245). Much of this poetry reflected a conscious decision of the poet to emulate ancient metric models rather than follow those of contemporary *ars poetica* (art of poetry). Among this group of poets Lovato dei Lovati (c. 1240–1309), a Paduan judge and notary, alone merited the title humanist in that his earliest surviving poetry (c. 1268) successfully captured not only the metrics but also the flavor of ancient poets.

Lovato's decision "to follow in the footsteps of the ancients" was made in conscious opposition to the current taste for French vernacular poetry in the Veneto region. In contrast to the few French poets of the twelfth century who had produced poems in classicized Latin, ancient style for Lovato was not merely one among various styles of composition, but rather the ultimate aesthetic ideal. His poetry reveals knowledge of a wide range of ancient writers, some perhaps unknown since late antiquity. Lovato's concern with ancient literature and history extended as well to the emendation of a variety of texts, the most significant being Seneca's tragedies.

Influence of Classical Models. While the new interest in composing Latin poetry at mid-century might have drawn inspiration from the popularity of vernacular poetry, the tendency to classicize that poetry had another source. Not coincidentally Brunetto Latini's translations of Cicero's *De inventione* and three of his orations occurred in the same decade as Lovato's earliest poetry. Moreover, the expanding number of humanists following Lovato who studied and imitated ancient Latin literature and history in their own writings found a parallel in the Tuscan translators subsequent to Latini (1212–1294), who rendered a large number of pagan works

in the vernacular. Such a wide and deep interest in antiquity, consequently, suggests that the return to pagan authors fulfilled a broadly felt need in Italian society.

Throughout the Middle Ages Italians had never forgotten their special relationship to Roman antiquity, but in the course of the thirteenth century they were coming to appreciate its significance for their way of life. Italian society, urban in orientation, institutionally republican, intellectually dominated by laymen, that is, lawyers and notaries, and characterized by a relatively high rate of social mobility, still remained largely governed by a constellation of values essentially rural, hierarchical, and clerical. Italy, moreover, was literally awash in influence from France, the society that perhaps best represented the medieval ideal. Socially, the French knight, romanticized in chivalric tales, constituted the ideal of conduct for most upper-class Italians.

Such a social model, however, fully justified the bitter party struggles that raged through most of the Italian city-states from the late twelfth century. Albertano da Brescia's citations of Seneca in his *ars dictaminis* prose, intended to reinforce a Christian ethic of civic peace and cooperation among citizens, perhaps reflected the first effort by an Italian to look to Rome's civic heritage as offering a set of values compatible with the republican institutions of the contemporary Italian city-state. Latini understood this function of antiquity more than any of his contemporaries, while, if less consciously, Lovato and his disciple Albertino Mussato (1261–1329), defenders of the failing Paduan commune, relied on classicized style to articulate their own patriotism.

Because humanism began in poetry, it should be considered as initially grammatical in character. The success of humanism in penetrating other genres of written expression related both to the character of Italian medieval education and the resistance of individual genre to change. All Lovato's classicizing efforts were made in poetry. His prose was either legal or an elaborate form of *ars dictaminis*. To the extent that schools in Italy in the thirteenth century relied on ancient writers for advanced instruction in grammar, only poets were studied. The study of prose was limited to *ars dictaminis*. Consequently, imitation of ancient prose required extreme effort and classicized prose did not appear until 1315 when Mussato published his *Historia augusta* (Imperial history), the account of the emperor Henry VII's abortive campaign in Italy (1310–1313). The same year marked the classicizing of drama when Mussato's Senecan tragedy, *Ecerinis,* was performed publicly in Padua. Only in the 1320s did Geri d'Arezzo initiate the reform of the private letter.

The last genres to be classicized were those properly belonging to rhetoric—the oration and the public letter, which traditionally was read aloud. All six surviving orations by Petrarch (1304–1374) are in medieval *ars predicandi* form, while of two orations by Coluccio Salutati (1331–1406), one is in sermon style and the other in a general form of *ars dictaminis*. Whereas in his private writings Salutati used classicized Latin, his public letters were composed in *ars dictaminis*. The reform of the oration, initiated by Pier Paolo Vergerio (1370–1444) in the last decade of the fourteenth century, was consummated in 1404 by Leonardo Bruni (1370–1444), whose *Laudatio urbis Florentinae* (Praise of the city of Florence) marked the rebirth of the Ciceronian oration. The public letter, however, fettered by rigid rules, continued to be written according to the prescriptions of *ars dictaminis* at least into the mid-fifteenth century.

Civic Humanism and Religious Humanism. Lovato and the second generation of humanists in Padua, Arezzo, and Bologna were overwhelmingly literary, civic, and scholarly in their humanistic interests. In the third generation Petrarch endeavored to Christianize the movement, reflecting to an extent his isolation from the communal origins of humanism and his immersion in the clerical world of Avignon, where he reached maturity. His ideas proved a complex inheritance for the fourth generation, who, almost all laymen, tried to reconcile his teachings with their daily experience. Less reverent than their predecessors, the next cohort of humanists, that of Bruni, returned humanism to its secular roots.

This insistence on Cicero points to a crucial aspect of the process of classicizing in early humanism. If any ancient author provided a stylistic model for the fourteenth century, it was Seneca. But as a matter of fact the eclectic approach taken by Petrarch dominated the conception of imitation: each writer should take the best elements from the best authors and create a personal style of his own. This attitude changed in the 1380s when teachers of rhetoric in Florence, Cino Rinuccini (d. 1417) and Giovanni Malpaghini da Ravenna (1343–1408), focused on Cicero's letters and orations as the principal sources for imitation. By the early fifteenth century, Cicero became the stylistic model in prose, not that contemporary writers slavishly imitated the ancient author (as did some later humanists), but rather each author, taking Cic-

ero as his model, negotiated his own position. While not the cause of the secularism of Ciceronians like Leonardo Bruni, Poggio Bracciolini (1380–1459), and Gasparino Barzizza (1360–1431), the style proved the ideal vehicle for expressing their ideas.

Almost certainly the religious emphasis of Petrarch's humanism rendered it congenial to northern Europeans. The second half of the fourteenth century witnessed the emergence of small groups of like-thinking learned men in France and Bohemia. The sustained religious interests of Coluccio Salutati made him the fitting heir of Petrarch and through him Italian humanism continued to exert its influence north of the Alps, especially on a circle of scholars in Paris among whom were Jean de Montreuil, Gontier Col, and Nicholas of Clémanges. The reversion of Italian humanism to its secular beginnings in the early fifteenth century, however, initiated a rupture in this contact and serves as a partial explanation for the delay which humanism experienced in striking its roots in northern countries.

See also **Cicero**; **Classical Antiquity, Discovery of**; **Classical Scholarship**; **Petrarchism**.

BIBLIOGRAPHY

Billanovich, Guido. "Il preumanesimo padovano." In *Storia della Cultura Veneta*. Vol. 2, *Il Trecento*. Vicenza, Italy 1976. Pages 19–110.

Weiss, Roberto. "The Dawn of Humanism." *Bulletin of the Institute of Historical Research* 42 (1969): 1–16. Originally published as a monograph (London, 1947).

Weiss, Roberto. *Il primo secolo dell'umanesimo*. Storia e letteratura 27. Rome, 1949.

Witt, Ronald. "Latini, Lovato, and the Revival of Antiquity." *Dante Studies* 112 (1994): 53–61.

Witt, Ronald. "Medieval *Ars Dictaminis* and the Beginnings of Humanism: A New Construction of the Problem." *Renaissance Quarterly* 35 (1982): 1–35.

Witt, Ronald. "Medieval Italian Culture and the Origins of Humanism as a Stylistic Ideal." In *Renaissance Humanism: Foundations, Forms, and Legacy*. Edited by Albert Rabil. 3 vols. Philadelphia, 1988. See vol. 1, pages 29–70.

RONALD G. WITT

Italy

During the Italian Renaissance *umanista* (humanist) referred to a practitioner of the *studia humanitatis*—grammar, rhetoric, history, poetry, moral philosophy, and in some cases also politics, or "civic humanism." The development of each discipline was based on the emulation of classical Greek and Roman models. This definition of Renaissance humanism is based on the work of Paul O. Kristeller, who regards humanism as a literary and rhetorical, not a philosophical movement, that flourished roughly from 1300 to 1600. This definition is adhered to here, though the focus will be on Italian humanism between 1350 and 1500.

Petrarch. Francesco Petrarca (1304–1374) was the central figure in the founding of Italian humanism; it was his accomplishments that attracted a following and created a self-conscious movement. As a young man Petrarch abandoned the study of law for literature. Literature meant for him classical Latin literature; Virgil was his favorite poet and Cicero his model for Latin prose. By 1341, when he was crowned poet laureate in Rome, he was the most famous private citizen in Europe, though known then primarily as a poet of Italian lyrics.

During the same year Petrarch wrote his famous letter to Giovanni Colonna pondering the ancient sites they had seen together when he was in Rome, leading him to make the rule of Constantine (rather than the birth of Christ) a great divide in history. He regarded as a "dark age" the period from Constantine to his own time. Petrarch is thus an important source for our historical periodization: ancient, medieval, modern. While always written with a larger audience in mind, his personal letters represent a return to the classical and early Christian practice of private letter writing and are a striking example of his own personal break with his age. He was overjoyed when he discovered Cicero's *Letters to Atticus* at Verona in 1345, though he discovered in them a Cicero not nearly as much to his liking as the Cicero who wrote philosophical dialogues. But Petrarch chastised himself as much as he did others. He began his autobiography, *Secretum* (Secret, or *The Soul's Conflict with Passion*), in 1342–1343 and uncovered all his sins in the presence of Augustine, his interlocutor, whose *Confessions* was his model, though not Augustine's vision of divine grace. Petrarch sought earthly fame through his writing, however, and that he refused to renounce. Thus, it should not be surprising that near the end of his life he was deeply stung by young men who gossiped that he was a good but not a learned man. In response Petrarch composed *De sui ipsius et multorum ignorantia* (On his own ignorance and that of many others; written in 1368), in which humanism and scholasticism face off in a dramatic confrontation. The text is a manifesto of sorts. Petrarch decries the impotence of knowledge: Aristotle's ethics describes what goodness is but is unable to make us better. Cicero and Seneca, on the other hand, inspire us to virtue. Their rhetoric (as opposed to Aristotelian logic and scholastic syllogisms) moves the will. In a

famous statement, Petrarch declares that he would rather will the good than know the truth, which in any case is unknowable. He identifies the Latin rhetorical tradition with Plato, whom he opposes to Aristotle, asserting that he owns a Greek manuscript copy of all the works of Plato, most of which, he chides his critics, the philosophers of his day do not know exist—which was true and remained so until Plato was translated into Latin by Marsilio Ficino (1433–1499) in the 1460s; Petrarch could not himself read the manuscripts he possessed since he had been unsuccessful in his attempt to learn classical Greek, although understanding the need to do so. Petrarch thus adumbrated in his own life many of the characteristics of the movement he inspired: emulation of classical style; recovery of the classical tradition, both Latin and Greek; a powerful sense of himself as an individual and a desire for personal earthly immortality; a realization of living at the end of a long dark age; and rejection of scholastic logic in favor of classical rhetoric, which elevates the will over the intellect.

Humanism in Florence. Humanism first emerged as a movement in the Florence of Coluccio Salutati (1331–1406), who became chancellor (chief administrative officer) of the city in 1375 and regarded himself as the guardian of the tradition begun by Petrarch. Salutati made two important contributions to the development of humanism. First, he expanded the community of humanists in the city by inviting others there, among them Poggio Bracciolini (1380–1459), whom he employed to copy manuscripts of classical texts, a precursor of Poggio's work as a discoverer of long unknown classical Roman works. Second, through the financial support of Palla Strozzi (1372–1462), he invited Manuel Chrysoloras (c. 1353–1415) to Florence in 1397 to teach Greek; during his three years there Chrysoloras taught outstanding students including Strozzi, Leonardo Bruni (c. 1370–1444), and the elder Pier Paolo Vergerio (1370–1444). Ambrogio Traversari (1386–1439) arrived in Florence in 1400 to join the Camaldolensian Order there, learning Greek, perhaps through the inspiration of Chrysoloras, to study the New Testament. Thus Salutati set the stage for the revival of all the classical traditions to which Italy was heir.

The generation of these disciples of Salutati is sometimes called the "heroic age" of humanism. While attending the Council of Constance (1414–1417), Poggio spent most of his time searching for manuscripts in nearby monasteries. He uncovered a number of Cicero's orations and a complete text of

Quintilian's *Training in Oratory*. Gerardo Landriani, bishop of Lodi, discovered in that city in 1421 Cicero's *On the Orator, Brutus,* and *Orator*. These texts constitute the principal sources for understanding the history of, training in, and practice of rhetoric. Humanists were elated; no complete copy of any of them had been known for centuries (and nothing at all had been known of Cicero's *Brutus*). They became the foundation of humanist rhetorical education. As texts were discovered they were indefatigably collected by Niccolò de' Niccoli (c. 1364–1437), who established the first lending library for scholars.

As Poggio, Landriani, and others were recovering the Latin classical past, Ciriaco d'Ancona (c. 1390–1455) was traveling to Greece, where in 1418 he collected manuscripts and epigraphs, the latter a source of knowledge of many artifacts subsequently destroyed. Also, in 1422 and 1423 Giovanni Aurispa (1369?–1459) purchased manuscripts in Greece, returning to Italy with 238 volumes (which ended up in Venice). He saved some texts that would otherwise have become lost in the sack of Constantinople in 1453. Cardinal Bessarion (1403–1472), who first came to Italy during the Council of Ferrara-Florence (1438–1445), which brought an end to the conciliar movement, later bequeathed his collection of more than eight hundred Greek books to the city of Venice, where they became the foundation of the collection in the Marciana Library.

Vergerio wrote the first humanist educational treatise, *De ingenuis moribus et liberalibus studiis adulescentiae* (On noble customs and liberal studies of adolescents; written in 1402–1403), in which the *studia humanitatis* is for the first time put forward as the basis of both a new educational philosophy and curriculum. Leonardo Bruni wrote a parallel tract on the education of girls in 1424. Traversari translated Basil of Caesarea's letter on education into Latin, as well as *De vitis philosophorum* (Lives of the philosophers), by Diogenes Laertius, a third century A.D. Greek writer. Bruni translated texts by Aristotle, Plato, Plutarch, and Xenophon into Latin and wrote polemically against "barbaric" medieval translations of Aristotle.

Bruni modeled his famous *Laudatio Florentinae urbis* (Panegyric to the city of Florence; written c. 1401 or later) on Aristides's *Panathenaic Oration*. His oration is among the documents on which Hans Baron based his thesis concerning the origins of Florentine civic humanism. According to Baron, Petrarch and his fourteenth-century humanistic followers preferred a life of scholarship and contemplation away from the cares of politics. But as a consequence of Florence's political and military struggle against Milan from 1390 to 1402, the Florentine humanists of the first years of the fifteenth century realized the value of their civic culture. They emphasized the union of classical studies with a commitment to republican values, thus creating "civic humanism," which greatly influenced the Renaissance and subsequent centuries, according to Baron. The thesis has been much disputed. A consensus seems to agree that, although the foundational status cannot be sustained, "civic humanism" does highlight a heightened focus on the "active life" appropriate to a citizen and an intense Florentine patriotism. From 1415 Bruni began, in Latin, a history of Florence from its foundation, with each volume translated into Italian as it appeared. His archival sources revealed that Florence was founded under the Roman republic, not the empire. Both Bruni (1427–1444) and Poggio (1453–1456), who also wrote a history of the city, served as chancellors of Florence after Salutati.

The development of humanism in Florence was closely connected to the Renaissance in art that occurred there between 1400 and 1440, associated with the names Alberti, Brunelleschi, Donatello, Ghiberti, and Masaccio. Donatello (1386?–1466) studied classical sculpture in Rome, and in his *St. Mark* (1411–1413) created the first freestanding statue since classical antiquity. Filippo Brunelleschi (1377–1446), best known for completing the cupola of the Florentine cathedral in the 1430s, earlier worked out one-point perspective mathematically, first employed in the *Holy Trinity with the Virgin and St. John* (1425) by Masaccio (1401–1428), and codified by Leon Battista Alberti (1404–1472) in *Della pittura* (On painting; written in 1436). Alberti, in the same text, developed the notion of *istoria,* that paintings should be narratives, and suggested that painters acquire a knowledge of history and poetry and associate with poets and orators. His book had a great influence on both artists and patrons and was instrumental in elevating painting from a craft to a liberal art by the end of the century. The *Doors of Paradise,* on which Lorenzo Ghiberti (c. 1378–1455) had been at work from the 1420s, changed under Alberti's influence as he continued work on them in the 1430s. Ghiberti also composed *Commentarii* (Commentaries), which presents a history of art based on Petrarch's historical divisions and uses Alberti's treatise as a basis of analysis.

Spread of Humanism in Italy. Humanists were able to adapt to the different political and cultural ambiances of the various Italian city-states without losing the essential core of humanism. In Florence, for example, the "heroic age" of Florentine humanism ended with the ascendancy in 1434 of the Medici family in Florentine politics, but humanists found in the changed setting new avenues of expression (Platonic philosophy, vernacular poetry, development of principles of criticism for historical and literary study). Ficino, Giovanni Pico della Mirandola (1463–1494), and Angelo Poliziano (1454–1494) are names that come readily to mind.

Adaptable to any political circumstance that favored the humanist program of the *studia humanitatis,* humanism spread rapidly among the elite in the northern and central Italian cities and courts, often initially with a direct connection to Florence. Antonio Loschi (1368–1441), for example, was a student of Salutati's before he entered the service of Milan, and the two remained friends even though they disputed against each other in behalf of their respective employers. Chrysoloras left Florence for Pavia in 1400 and resided in Lombardy until 1403, spreading the teaching of Greek. The first well-known Venetian humanist was Francesco Barbaro, whose *De re uxoria* (On wifely duties; written in 1415) is an outstanding rhetorical humanist text in its use of classical sources as well as a defense of the values of the Venetian patrician class—though similar values are expressed in Alberti's *Della famiglia* (On the family; written in 1436). Humanism developed more fully in Venetian territory outside Venice, including Padua and Verona, which Venice conquered between 1404 and 1406. Giovanni Conversino da Ravenna (1343–1408) taught many important humanists at the University of Padua, where he also served twice as chancellor. Gasparino Barzizza (1360–1430), professor of rhetoric at Padua (1407–1421), moved to Milan in 1421 at the behest of Landriani to copy and edit the Ciceronian oratorical texts that Landriani had recently discovered but could not decipher. Barzizza was succeeded in 1439 by Francesco Filelfo (1398–1481), who had lived in Florence from 1429 to 1434 but was forced to leave after he criticized the Medici; he became the center of cultural life in Milan until his final departure in 1475.

A number of women, about twenty of whom published letters and orations and learned classical Latin and in some cases classical Greek as well, sought to establish their credentials as humanist scholars. Sometimes they corresponded among themselves, but more often with male humanists, whose approbation they sought. Except for Alessandra Scala (1475–1506), these women were not Florentine;

most came from the Venetian and Milanese spheres of influence. Most notable was Isotta Nogarola (1418–1466) from Verona, perhaps the most learned woman of her century, who studied Latin and Greek at an early age with Martino Rizzoni, a pupil of Guarino Guarini (1370 or 1374–1460). Nogarola wrote to Guarino, whose approval she coveted and eventually received. Laura Cereta (1469–1499) from Brescia learned Latin from a nun and between the ages of fifteen and eighteen wrote in a unique Latin style a book of letters that also included an invective oration in praise of an ass. Cassandra Fedele (1465–1558) from Venice was also educated in Latin letters as a young girl. At the age of twenty-two she was invited by Queen Isabella to join her court in Spain, but according to tradition, was prevented by the Venetian senate from accepting on the ground that she was too great an asset to the state. She delivered a number of public orations, even one to inaugurate the year in a university she was not otherwise allowed to attend.

From northern Italy humanism spread south. Although both Bruni and Poggio had served as papal secretaries, Rome was not home for them as it was for another humanist émigré to the city, Flavio Biondo (1392–1463), who arrived in 1433 and remained until his death. He published the first substantial archaeological history of Rome, *Roma instaurata* (Rome restored; written in 1444–1446). Biondo was joined by many other leading humanists when Nicholas V (1447–1455), the first pope to favor and support humanists, enlisted some of their number, including Valla and Filelfo, to translate Greek texts into Latin. Eventually humanists in Rome developed a sodality of their own, the first under the leadership of Giulio Pomponio Leto (1427–1494) and Bartolomeo Platina (born Bartolomeo Sacchi; 1421–1481). After it was suppressed because of alleged subversion of the papacy, a second flourished under Paolo Cortesi (1465–1510).

Humanism began to flourish in Naples under King Alfonso I (1442–1458). Lorenzo Valla (1405–1457), perhaps the most outstanding humanist of the century, spent his most productive years in Naples. There he composed his *De falso credita et ementita Constantini donatione declamatio* (Declamation on the falsely believed and forged Donation of Constantine; written in 1440), in the cause of Alfonso's defense in his struggle against the papacy; *Dialectice* (Dialectical disputations; written in the 1430s and the 1440s); and *Collatio novi testamenti* (Collection on the New Testament; written in the 1430s)—the last being the basis of his later Roman redaction, *Adno-*

tationes novi testamenti (Notes on the New Testament; written in 1444). In Naples he also significantly revised two works begun earlier, *De voluptate ac vero bono* (On pleasure or the true good; written in 1431) and *De lingua latinae elegantiae* (Elegances of the Latin language; written in 1438–1444). The university was revived by Alfonso, but humanism in Naples as in many other places (including Florence) achieved greater vitality in an informal association of scholars called an academy. It was led by an indigenous Neapolitan, Giovanni Pontano (1422–1503), some of whose dialogues (*Antonius, Actius,* and *Aegidius*) provide us with a lively and varied picture of its gatherings. A number of outstanding poets participated in the academy, the most original among them being Jacopo Sannazaro (1458–1530).

Humanist Literature.   Reference has been made to the humanists' recovery, transcription (later publication), annotation, and translation of classical texts. The humanists used these texts as a basis for their own writings, which were more voluminous in comparison to their editorial labors. They wrote predominantly in Latin, though they also wrote in Italian; sometimes they wrote the same text in both languages (as with Alberti's *Della pittura*) or authorized their translation (as with Bruni's history of Florence). Initially they had to defend the *studia humanitatis*—after all, they were attempting a radical curricular change. The earliest polemics were in favor of reading pagan authors, notably *De genealogia deorum gentilium* (On the genealogy of the pagan gods; 1351–1360) by Giovanni Boccaccio (1313–1375); Traversari's translation of Basil's letter supporting the study by young men of pagan literature; and Salutati's use of this translation to respond to Giovanni Dominici's opposition to classical studies for Christians. This kind of defense proved unnecessary in the later 1400s. Quintilian, Plutarch's treatise on the education of children (translated by Guarino Guarini), and the prefaces to the various books of Valla's *De elegantiae linguae latinae* (Elegances of the Latin language; written in 1438–1444) reinforced humanist ideas of education and became the foundation for humanist schools that sprang up throughout northern Italy.

Two schools attained renown. That of Vittorino da Feltre (1378–1446) at Mantua (1423–1446, and continued by others after his death), established for the Gonzaga family, came to be known as the *casa giocosa* (house of joy). Vittorino taught all subjects (Latin, Greek, mathematics), kept strict but benign rule over his pupils, and maintained a balance between physical and mental training. Guarino Guarini established an equally famous school at Ferrara in 1430 for the ruling Este family and taught as well at the university there.

Humanists were best known as writers of prose, a favorite form being the letter. Petrarch recovered the idea of the personal letter. Some of his letters, like those of Salutati, are tracts. Later humanists followed the example of Cicero in keeping letters relatively brief and writing dialogues on ideas. Barzizza was the first to teach Cicero's epistolography as a model, though Salutati embodied it in his letters and other humanists imitated him. Poggio's letters to Niccoli from the Council of Constance on his manuscript hunts are among the best in the fifteenth century. His letters from England (also to Niccoli) are among the few in the century that are self-analytical. Collections have been made of the letters of Salutati, Bruni, Poggio, Vergerio, Guarino, and Barbaro. Women humanists shared particularly in this genre of humanist exchange.

The humanists were rhetoricians, not logicians, and their philosophy "moral," concerned with issues vital to them. Chief among these was the question of human dignity. Valla's *De voluptate* provoked a series of discussions on the subject. He argued that, apart from faith, the Epicurean value of pleasure was superior to the Stoic value of virtue, since the former was positive (enjoyment) while the latter was negative (endurance of suffering). Christianity, however, transforms both these natural values through faith, providing strength to face earthly suffering and looking toward eternal pleasure. The Genoese humanist Bartolomeo Facio, in *De vitae felicitate* (On the happiness of life; 1445–1446), attacked pleasure as a human value and defended the notion of the misery of temporal life. After reading Facio, Giannozzo Manetti (1396–1459) published a major work on the theme, *De dignitate et excellentia hominis* (On the dignity and excellence of man; 1452–1453). He emphasized positive human qualities in a divine dispensation: the superiority of human to animal bodies; the immortality of the human soul; the creative qualities of the human spirit (ingenuity, creativity, wisdom); and the pleasures of the body that compensate for its suffering. Poggio, a fellow Florentine, responded to Manetti in favor of human misery. The debate continued in Bologna with Giovanni Garzoni and Benedetto Morandi, and in Rome with Platina and Aurelio Brandolini. At the end of the century the discussion was taken up by the Florentine Platonists, Ficino and Pico, most notably in Pico's *De hominis dignitate oratio* (Oration on the dignity of man; published in 1486), which proclaimed human beings unique in being the only creatures who could rise or descend the scale of being.

Although these writers seem to have been expressing their own views, it was common for humanists to write on both sides of a question, a practice apparent in many of the themes they treated. An example is the nature of true nobility, the themes being whether it consists in individual achievement or in birth and wealth, the relative nobility of the various professions, the relation of the active to the contemplative life, the relative power of fate and fortune in human lives. Often these themes were treated in dialogue form and the issue examined from all sides without a resolution, a practice followed by Cicero in his philosophical dialogues and self-consciously emulated by the humanists.

Vergerio, in his treatise on education, wrote that "history is moral philosophy taught by example." History was the genre most exploited by the humanists. Petrarch's identification of the beginning of the "dark age" has been noted. Biondo, in his *Historiarum ab inclinatione Romanorum imperii decades* (History from the decline of the Roman Empire; written in 1439–1453), defined the "dark age" as having begun with the sack of Rome in 410 (Biondo mistakenly gave 412) and the "modern age" as having succeeded one thousand years later in 1412. This view broke with the notion that history is a perpetual decline from a pristine past. Thus, humanists gave expression to the feeling of revival in their own time, evident later in *Le vite de' più eccellenti architetti, pittori, et scultori italiani* (Lives of the most excellent Italian painters, sculptors, and architects; 1550), by Giorgio Vasari (1511–1574). Some humanist history approached modern canons of critical historiography, as with Bruni's attempt to prove that Florence was founded during the Roman republic, Poggio's work in gathering inscriptions, Valla's treatise on the Donation of Constantine and his notes on the New Testament, and Poliziano's rules for the critical reading of texts. Related to history was biography of famous persons of all kinds, corresponding to the emergence of portraits of individuals; neither is characteristic of the Middle Ages, as they both are of the Renaissance.

Humanism found its center of gravity at the turn of the century in Venice, where Aldus Manutius (1449–1515), trained as a humanist scholar, opened a printing press in 1493. The Aldine Press was the most important in Europe by 1500. Between 1495 and 1515 Aldus published 130 editions, the most important of which were Greek classical texts, about one-fourth of them being first editions of their authors. Manutius gave the public the new cursive script and he published a five-volume Greek edition of Aristotle (1495–1498). Aristotle's *Poetics* (published by Aldus in Greek in 1508) stimulated Italian humanists to write major works on poetic theory in the second half of the sixteenth century.

But the French invasion of Italy in 1494 and the sack of Rome in 1527 by imperial troops marked the end of Italian political autonomy. In the following generation the Council of Trent (1545–1563) deeply affected Italian cultural life. Humanism did not end; indeed, scholarship deepened, not only in poetics but also in the establishment of critical method in historical study, though that involved a struggle with the Inquisition. Perhaps the greatest accomplishment of humanists during the century, largely due to the impact of the Reformation, was the editing, translating, and publishing of the Bible and the works of the church fathers; the Christian classical tradition came fully abreast of the Greek and Roman literary traditions. But the political and cultural ambience that had produced fifteenth-century Italian humanism and its vast influence on art and literature was past.

See also **Greek Émigrés**; **Renaissance, Interpretation of the**, *subentries on Giorgio Vasari, Hans Baron, and Paul Oskar Kristeller.*

BIBLIOGRAPHY

Hans Baron, *The Crisis of the Early Italian Renaissance*, rev. ed. (Princeton, N.J., 1966); Jerry Bentley, *Politics and Culture in Renaissance Naples* (Princeton, N.J., 1987); Eric Cochrane, *Historians and Historiography in the Italian Renaissance* (Chicago, 1981); John F. D'Amico, *Renaissance Humanism in Papal Rome: Humanists and Churchmen on the Eve of the Reformation* (Baltimore, 1983); Eugenio Garin, *Italian Humanism: Philosophy and Civic Life in the Renaissance*, translated by Peter Munz (New York, 1965); Paul F. Grendler, *Schooling in Renaissance Italy: Literacy and Learning, 1300–1600* (Baltimore, 1989); Gary Ianziti, *Humanistic Historiography under the Sforzas: Politics and Propaganda in Fifteenth-Century Milan* (Oxford, 1988); Margaret L. King, *Venetian Humanism in an Age of Patrician Dominance* (Princeton, N.J., 1986); Margaret L. King, *Women of the Renaissance* (Chicago, 1991); Paul O. Kristeller, *Renaissance Thought: The Classic, Scholastic, and Humanist Strains*, rev. ed. (New York, 1961); Paul O. Kristeller, *Renaissance Thought II: Papers on Humanism and the Arts* (New York, 1965); David Marsh, *The Quattrocento Dialogue: Classical Tradition and Humanist Innovation* (Cambridge, Mass., 1980); Lauro Martines, *The Social World of the Florentine Humanists, 1390–1460* (Princeton, N.J., 1963); William McCuaig, *Carlo Sigonio: The Changing World of the Late Renaissance* (Princeton, N.J., 1989); Albert Rabil, Jr., ed., *Renaissance Humanism: Foundations, Forms, and Legacy*, 3 vols. (Philadelphia, 1988); Jerrold E. Seigel, *Rhetoric and Philosophy in Renaissance Humanism: The Union of Eloquence and Wisdom,*

Petrarch to Valla (Princeton, N.J., 1968); and Charles Trinkaus, *In Our Image and Likeness: Humanity and Divinity in Italian Humanist Thought,* 2 vols. (Chicago, 1970).

ALBERT RABIL

Spain

The idea of the Renaissance in Spanish historical thought of the last hundred years has not enjoyed as wide a reception as that encountered in other European national cultures. Having entered relatively late into the terminology of historians and literary critics, the term has been either subsumed under the category of the Golden Age (Siglo de Oro), which spans the sixteenth and seventeenth centuries, or slightly differentiated as the beginning of such a period. Because of the chronological overlapping with this older and widely accepted categorization, the newly formed concept of the Renaissance has never overcome the complementary role it had been assigned, and to this day its meaning within Spanish cultural history has never been fully clarified.

Fifteenth-century Beginnings.

The earliest manifestations of a cultural rebirth among Castilian men of letters can be dated from the second decade of the fifteenth century. The diffusion of some works of Dante, Petrarch, and Boccaccio and a growing need for more skilled secretaries and diplomatic representatives seem to have sparked a renewed interest in classical rhetoric. There were also at this time signs of a significant increase in the reception of works by classical authors and Italian humanists. Translations of these works into Spanish, together with adaptations such as Juan de Lucena's *Diálogo de vita beata* (Dialogue on the happiness of life; 1463), a reworking of Bartolomeo Facio's (1400–1457) treatise *De vitae felicitate* (On the happiness of life), give Spanish humanism a character of its own that can best be termed as "vernacular humanism." The dominant figure of the first half of the fifteenth century who combines this vernacular strain with the Latin humanism practiced by the Italians is Alonso (or Alfonso) García de Santa María, or Alphonsus Burgensis (1385 or 1386?–1456).

By the middle of the fifteenth century there was a growing awareness, particularly among Castilian men of letters, of cultural renewal. Many literary authors as well as moralists and thinkers of the time felt that they were living in a new age quite distinct from that of previous centuries, made possible, or so they thought, by their having dispelled the darkness of ignorance in the land or of having restored to Spain the peculiar classical culture it had enjoyed in

Roman times. In the second half of the fifteenth century, certain traits already discernible in Cartagena's learning and ideas were further pursued by the new generation of humanists such as Rodrigo Sánchez de Arévalo (1404–1470), Alfonso de Palencia (1423–1490), and Juan de Lucena (1430–1505?). The trends they followed, such as writing their works in Castilian or interest in national antiquities, in Spanish-born classical authors, and in historical figures, became the distinguishing characteristics of Spanish humanism. Unlike Italian humanists, fifteenth-century Spanish humanists were in general eclectic, concerned neither particularly with philological problems nor with a historical account of the development of Latin and the origin of the vernacular.

The Reign of Ferdinand and Isabella.

The year 1492, that annus mirabilis, is remembered for the discovery of the New World, the capitulation of the Islamic kingdom of Granada, and the religious unification of the kingdoms through the mass conversion or expulsion of the Jews and Moors. But 1492 also marks a perceptible divide in the intellectual life of Castile. Literary, ethical, and spiritual trends that had been forming since 1420, during the first phase of Castilian humanism, were swiftly being replaced by maturer, more assertive, and more internationally oriented currents that were better attuned to the outlook of the new generation of Spanish humanists.

The humanist who best characterizes this generation is Antonio de Nebrija (1444–1522), also known as Aelius Antonius Nebrissensis, after the Roman name of his birthplace (Nebrissa). Educated both in Spain and Italy, he dominated the intellectual life of Castile for decades with a constant outpouring of philological contributions and a relentless drive for academic and pedagogical reforms—endeavors that distinguished him from the learned men of the previous generations. Nebrija's writings indicate that his learning and scholarly pursuits may have evolved independently of Italian humanistic activities, particularly in the all-important method of classical philology. In an oration he delivered at the University of Salamanca, Nebrija advocated that the proper role of the modern teacher of the *studia humanitatis* (humanistic studies) should be that of the ancient *grammaticus* (grammarian). Nebrija's view predates by a few years the Italian Angeolo Poliziano's (1454–1494) formulation of the same concept as expressed in the final part of the *Lamia* (The witch; 1492). In attributing to the *grammaticus* knowledge of literature, philosophy, history, jurisprudence, medicine, and other sciences, both Nebrija and Polizano accorded the grammarian the highest critical faculty. Rather ingenuously, they relinquished to his authority absolute power to interpret and judge every possible writing, merely by virtue of a presumed encyclopedic knowledge.

Nebrija's textual emendations of the scriptures, together with his pioneering study of the pronunciation of Latin and Greek phonemes, on accentuation, lexicography, history, and cosmography, have earned him a place among the most distinguished European humanists of the time. But within Spain his most influential works were the *Introductiones Latinae* (Introduction to Latin; 1481), a Latin grammar, and his *Gramática de la lengua castellana* (Grammar of the Castilian language; 1492), the first vernacular grammar in a modern language.

Another achievement of the time was the new University of Alcalá, founded in 1508 by Cardinal Jiménez de Cisneros (1436–1517). Though the university's mission was predominantly religious, the university housed the Trilingual College for the study of the Bible in its original languages, and the various faculties were staffed by the most renowned humanists of the time. Their work culminated in the 1514–1517 publication of the Complutensian Polygot Bible. It was with this end in mind that Cisneros invited Erasmus to Alcalá; but the Dutch humanist, not particularly fond of Spain, declined the offer to collaborate in the edition of the Bible.

Humanism in Service of the Empire. Nebrija's generation of humanists was primarily concerned with the eradication of traditional ways of teaching and thinking. The following generation of scholars, literary men, and artists of a dynamic new world empire strove for an ideological expansion that would place them alongside the best minds of Europe at that time. The impressive cultural accomplishments of the first half of the sixteenth century, which provided the setting for the even greater artistic achievements during the next hundred years, are to be seen against the backdrop of a radical change in Spanish politics, the accession in 1516 of the Flemish-born Charles I (1500–1558; king of Spain, 1516–1556; Charles V, Holy Roman emperor, 1519–1556), who ruled the most extensive and powerful empire of the time.

Many distinguished humanists, especially those of the same generation as the young monarch, became the advocates of the emperor's programs. While the most influential poet in the new Italian style, Garcilaso de la Vega (1539/40–1615/17), died in battle in the emperor's service, other humanists and men of letters lent their professional support to defend the incipient absolutism of Charles V. In their capacity as diplomats (Diego Hurtado de Mendoza, 1503–1575), secretaries (Alfonso de Valdés, 1490?–1532), historians (Pedro Mexía; 1497–1551), confessors (Antonio de Guevara, c. 1481–1545), reformers (Juan de Valdés; 1490?–1541), Church dignitaries (Alfonso Manrique, general inquisitor), and academicians (Juan and Francisco de Vergara, Juan Luis Vives, 1492–1540; Juan Ginés de Sepúlveda, 1490–1572/73; Francisco de Vitoria 1486–1546), to name only a few, they all sought in their respective ways the same universalist objectives: the establishment of Christian unity in the world under Spanish hegemony, the eradication of abuses within the Church, the subjugation and conversion of Turks and Moors, and universal peace. Whether they wrote in Spanish or in Latin, their literary works and treatises were widely read in the Europe of the time, as attested by the popularity of Guevara and Mexía and many others.

It was among the humanists at the court of Charles V that the doctrines of the famous Dutch humanist, Erasmus of Rotterdam (c. 1466–1536), found many enthusiastic disciples. Some of his most widely read works—for example, *Enchiridion militis Christiani* (1503; trans. *The Manuell of the Christen Knight,* 1533)—were to have a lasting effect on the intellectual life of the sixteenth century, even after they were banned by the Inquisitor Fernando de Valdés in 1559. Since the publication in 1937 of Marcel Bataillon's study on Erasmus and Spain, *Erasme et l'Espagne,* specialists have tended to blur the distinction between Erasmianism and humanism in sixteenth-century Spain. By confusing a spiritual movement with a presumed "Christian" humanism, there has been a tendency to consider only religiously minded authors or reformists and to underestimate, for example, the significant linguistic contributions by such professional humanists as Francisco Sánchez de las Brozas (1523–1600).

The rapid dissemination of Erasmus's thought during the decade of the 1520s was due in part to the ability of his Spanish friends to promote his views and ideas, in part also to the favorable spiritual and intellectual atmosphere prevailing at that particular moment in Spain. Combining religion with politics, his followers used Erasmus and his widely accepted views to oppose their more conservative rivals, who still held considerable power, especially within the university and the church. The simmering conflict between humanism and scholasticism came to a head in 1527, when a council of Spain's most prominent theologians met in Valladolid to debate the humanist's orthodoxy. Thanks to the decisive intervention of General Inquisitor Alfonso Manrique, Erasmus and his followers were vindicated, but less than a decade later, with a new general inquisitor in charge, the most active defenders of Erasmus were tried and jailed by the Inquisition. The backlash against Erasmus and Spanish Erasmianism would ultimately succeed by having his works placed on the Index, thus driving Erasmianists underground.

A Spanish humanist who is frequently associated with Erasmus is Juan Luis Vives. Because of some general affinities with views and concerns of the Dutch humanist, the originality and contributions to Renaissance learning of this important thinker have generally been overlooked. The child of recent Jewish converts to Christianity who were burned by the Inquisition for apostasy, Vives studied at the University of Paris and never returned to Spain. His intellectual concerns were literally encyclopedic. In his relatively short life, he wrote extensively not only on moral, philosophical, pedagogical, and philological questions but also on the most pressing issues regarding society, politics, and religion. His pioneering essay, *De subventione pauperum* (On the assistance of the poor; 1526), added a new sociopolitical dimension to civic humanism and gave rise to a long series of treatises, both in Spain and Europe, dealing with the modern phenomenon of the urban poor. But it is *De disciplinis* (On disciplines; 1531) that synthesizes the mature philosophical thought of Vives. Written with a pedagogical end in mind, the treatise brings together many of his lifelong philosophical speculations. His anti-Scholastic polemic, his analysis of cultural decadence, the humanist reformation of learning, the new role assigned to the arts of discourse, the relation between classical and modern languages, questions of theoretical and historical linguistics, all stem from the study of the question of language. Vives valued the practical aspect of learning since the aim of all arts and sciences is always directed to be of service to human life (*usum vitae*).

The discovery and conquest of the New World is without doubt the most significant endeavor of the Spanish Renaissance. As humanists tried to assess this incredible feat, they became aware of the intellectual limitations of their own cultural tradition. In attempting to describe and explain the new cultures encountered there, many authoritative truths had to be questioned and overturned. Among these were the belief in the universality of Christianity and the supreme authority of Aristotle in scientific matters—an intellectual leap few were willing to take. At the University of Salamanca, Francisco de Vitoria concluded that what was needed was the establishment of a new world order based on natural law and on human experience, thereby setting the basis for international law and religious relativism. Ultimately, the many problems that the discovery posed as humanists tried to describe and explain the nature of the New World could only find a coherent explanation in a later generation of thinkers.

See also biographies of Cisneros, Nebrija, Vives, and other figures mentioned in this entry.

BIBLIOGRAPHY

Bataillon, Marcel. *Erasme et l'Espagne.* 3 vols. New ed. Geneva, 1991.

Di Camillo, Ottavio. "Humanism in Spain." In *Renaissance Humanism: Foundations, Forms, and Legacy.* 3 vols. Edited by Albert Rabil Jr. Philadelphia, 1988. Volume 2, *Humanism beyond Italy,* pages 55–108.

Elliott, John Huxtable. *Spain and Its World, 1500–1700.* New Haven, Conn., 1989.

Fernández-Santamaría, J. A. *The State, War, and Peace: Spanish Political Thought in the Renaissance, 1516–1559.* Cambridge, U.K., 1977.

Fernández-Santamaría, J. A. *The Theater of Man: J. L. Vives on Society.* Philadelphia, 1998.

Gerbi, Antonello. *Nature in the New World: From Christopher Columbus to Gonzalo Fernández de Oviedo.* Translated by Jeremy Moyle. Pittsburgh, 1985.

Lawrance, Jeremy N. H. "Humanism in the Iberian Peninsula." In *The Impact of Humanism on Western Europe.* Edited by Anthony Goodman and Angus MacKay. London, 1990. Pages 220–258.

Nader, Helen. *The Mendoza Family in the Spanish Renaissance, 1350 to 1550.* New Brunswick, N.J., 1979.

Nieto, José C. *Juan de Valdés and the Origins of the Spanish and Italian Reformation.* Geneva, 1970.

Noreña, Carlos G. *Juan Luis Vives.* The Hague, Netherlands, 1970.

Noreña, Carlos G. *Studies in Spanish Renaissance Thought.* The Hague, Netherlands, 1975.

Pagden, Anthony. *The Fall of Natural Man: The American Indian and the Origins of Comparative Ethnology.* Cambridge, U.K., and New York, 1982.

OTTAVIO DI CAMILLO

Portugal

Humanist influences came to be felt in Portugal by the early 1400s, peaked between 1527 and 1548, during the reign of John III, and were always impeded by Portugal's geographical distance from Italy and its strong adherence to conservative scholasticism. In the fields of navigation, cosmography, and botany, several groundbreaking, empirically based texts were written that rejected the hallowed authority of

Greek and Roman writers. However, these radical contributions to the natural sciences and, more fundamentally, to epistemology, were largely ignored within humanist activity in Portugal, although they were better known elsewhere in Europe through translations. By 1555 humanist inroads in Portugal had been largely appropriated by the Jesuit-led Counter-Reformation to advance its neo-scholastic, censored vision for thought and writing, thereby closing a window to new intellectual currents that had been only briefly open before.

Prehumanism. The earliest contacts between Portugal and Italy date from the 1100s and were mostly political and military in nature. By the early 1400s, while the infante, Prince Henry the Navigator, recruited Genoese shipbuilders and captains who would lay a foundation for Portuguese expansion and scientific advances, his brothers Pedro and Duarte made or sponsored translations of Cicero and Pliny. Works of Dante, Petrarch, and Boccaccio, as well as classical authors, were represented at the library of the monastery of Alcobaça. At the court of King Afonso V (ruled 1438–1481) Italian humanists, including Matteo Pisano and Giusto Baldini, tutored the king and made translations into Latin. Throughout the fifteenth century the Castilian converso Vasco Fernández de Lucena (1410?–1495) operated actively as humanist secretary and royal representative abroad. In 1485 the Sicilian Cataldo Parisio (b.c. 1453) became mentor and Latinist to King João II (1481–1495); his presence and writings (including *Opera,* 1500) heightened humanist activity among the native Portuguese at the court.

During this preliminary phase of Portuguese humanism, many Portuguese scholars studied and wrote abroad. In Genoa, Leão Hebreo (1465?–1521?), an expatriate Jew, wrote the Neoplatonic *Dialoghi d'amore* (c. 1502). Henrique Caiado (d. 1509), a student of Cataldo in Portugal, continued his studies in Bologna and Padua, taught in Ferrara, and was perhaps the first Portuguese to write Latin poetry (*Eclogae et sylvae et epigrammata* [Eclogues, miscellanies, and epigrams; 1501]). By the last decade of the sixteenth century Aires Barbosa (1456–1530) and several others had trained in Florence under Angelo Poliziano. Barbosa would distinguish himself as a professor of Greek studies at the University of Salamanca in Spain (influenced there by Antonio Nebrija), returning to Portugal only in 1520. Martinho de Figuciredo and Aquiles Estaço (1524–1581) wrote philological commentaries in editions of Latin classics, such as Pliny's *Natural History.* From

Ferrara and Dubrovnik, Diogo Pires (1517–1599) would write Latin poetry and correspondence.

Yet upon King Manuel I's death in 1521, humanism in Portugal seems to have been accepted more in form than in spirit. Scholars read and wrote in Latin but still avoided the application of humanist ideals to theology or education. While educational reforms in neighboring Spain were criticized by Spanish humanists such as Nebrija and Juan Luis Vives as lagging far behind those in Italy, Portugal was even slower to accept such changes. Aragonese and Castilian kings had, in fact, been forging cultural ties with Sicily and Naples since the late 1300s, and founded their humanist-oriented university at Alcalá de Henares in 1509. By contrast, at Lisbon's university, the Estudo Geral, a modern Latin grammar written by Estêvão Cavaleiro, *Nova gramatices ars* (New art of grammar; 1516), was ignored until well into the third decade of the century, in preference for an archaic version by the Spaniard Juan de Pastrana. Printing, normally a catalyst for the diffusion of culture, was introduced into Portugal only in 1487 and did not become well-established until a half century later.

Erasmian Influences. King Manuel I (ruled 1495–1521) had supervised the nation's imperial expansion, modernized the state's administration, and concentrated power in the monarchy. His son and successor, John III (ruled 1521–1557), used his royal prerogatives to promote culture. At his court a circle of erudite women included Luísa Sigea, a linguist, and the prodigy Públia Hortênsia de Castro. In 1527 fifty Portuguese scholars were sent to study at the Santa Barbara institute in Paris, which became the principal center for Portuguese students abroad during the next two decades. Universities in Padua, Bologna, and especially Louvain and Salamanca exposed Portuguese diplomats and clerics to humanist currents and to Protestant reforms. The influence of Erasmus was strong, not only through contact with his writings but also through personal friendships and correspondences. In his *Chrysostomi lucubrationes* (Meditations on Chrysostom; 1527) he dedicated advice to King John, who in turn invited him to teach at Lisbon's university (a project never realized). The Portuguese diplomat and historian Damião de Góis (1502–1574) spent months with Erasmus and also came to know Martin Luther, Philipp Melanchthon, and most likely, Thomas More. Góis's Latin writings include a Ciceronian tract, a defense of Ethiopian Christians, and a panegyrical description of Lisbon. André de Resende (1495–1573), a

Latin stylist deeply familiar with European intellectual life of the 1520s and 1530s, was another ardent defender of Erasmian humanism. He delivered a stirring denunciation of Portuguese academic conservatism in the speech "Oratio pro rostris" at the 1534 opening of classes at the University of Lisbon. Through Resende the Flemish scholar Nicholas Cleynaert was brought to Lisbon. Resende's plea for educational reform, imbued with the ideas of Nebrija, Vives, and Erasmus, bore fruit in the 1537 transfer of the university to Coimbra. Faculty turnover resulted in an updated curriculum that reflected a deeper study of classical grammar (Hebrew, Greek, and Latin) and rhetoric, though the academic facilities at Coimbra's Santa Cruz monastery impeded a distancing from scholastic theology. By 1544 the university found its own grounds at the Paço das Escolas.

Further modernization of education occurred in 1547 with the creation of an independent preparatory school, the Colégio das Artes, also in Coimbra. Its director, André de Gouveia, had earlier directed the Parisian institute of Santa Barbara and, dogged there by anti-Erasmian pressure from his uncle (a previous director), later moved to head the Guyenne school at Bordeaux. There, Michel de Montaigne hailed him as France's greatest principal. At Coimbra, over eight-hundred students enrolled at the Colégio das Artes in its first year, and plans were laid for expansion.

Literature and Science. Humanist influences in Portugal provoked new literary responses in the vernacular, among them Italian-style sonnets, letters, and an eclogue by Francisco de Sá de Miranda (1481–1558); the adaptation by António Ferreira (1528–1569) of classical tragedy to the Portuguese language and its setting (for example, *Castro;* 1557); the narrative elegance of João de Barros's (1497–1570) Portuguese-Asian history, the *Décadas* (Decades; 3 vols., 1553–1563); the Virgilian-style epic of Portuguese empire, *Os Lusíadas* (Lusiads; 1572), by Luiz Vaz de Camões (1525–1580); and the Neoplatonic dialogues of *Imagem da vida cristã* (Image of the Christian Life 1572), by Heitor Pinto (b. 1528).

Scientific literature accompanied Portuguese expansion, begun in 1415 with the capture of Ceuta in North Africa. Representative writings include Duarte Pacheco Pereira's *Esmeraldo de situ orbis* (Guide to terrestrial location; written 1505–1508), which affirmed the value of firsthand travel experience; the cosmographical observations in *Tratado da esfera* (Treatise on the sphere; 1537) by Pedro Nunes (b.

1502); the navigational charts and observations (*Roteiros,* 1538–1541) of João de Castro (1500–48); and the botanical-pharmacological dialogues, *Colóquio dos simples e drogas e cousas medicinais da Índia* (1563), by Garcia de Orta (d. 1568).

Decline during the Counter-Reformation. If King John III's reign encouraged humanism, it also nourished the conservative Catholic forces that would defeat it. The Inquisition was established and organized in Portugal in 1536 and 1547. Its first Index of prohibited books appeared in 1547; by 1561 all of Erasmus's works were banned, as in 1597 were all books written in English, Flemish, or German. The Jesuits entered Portugal in 1547 and, upon the death of André de Gouveia in 1548, initiated a series of maneuvers that unraveled the Erasmian outlook of the Colégio das Artes and won them control of the institution by 1555. The Jesuit University of Évora was founded in 1559, granting only the doctorate in theology. The measures decreed by the Council of Trent (1545–1563) reinforced Jesuit strength, resulting in the jailing of several humanists (Diogo de Teive, João da Costa, and George Buchanan in 1550; Damião de Góis in 1571) and the squelching of others, such as André de Resende. Perhaps the most paradigmatic Portuguese humanist, the diplomat and teacher Fernão de Oliveira (1507?–1581?), who had written both scholarly texts (e.g., *Gramática da linguagem portuguesa,* 1536) and a technical treatise on shipbuilding (*Livro da fábrica das naous*), was repeatedly imprisoned during the 1550s for Erasmian tendencies. The first auto-da-fé (the public procession and punishment of alleged heretics by the Inquisition) in Portugal took place in 1540; the remains of Garcia de Orta (who had been of Jewish descent) were disinterred and burned in 1580.

The fusion of church and state occurred from 1562 to 1568, when Cardinal Henrique (already the key figure in Portugal's Counter-Reformation) assumed the regency for John's young successor, his grandson Sebastian (ruled 1557–1578). Two years after Sebastian's total defeat at Alcacer Quibir (in modern Morocco) in 1578, Portugal fell under Spanish dominion for sixty years. The existing bilingualism among Portuguese intellectuals was intensified, eroding secular writing in Portuguese. The successful Spanish genres of novel and comedy found little counterpart at this time in Portugal. By 1600 the Jesuit plan of education was capped with an eight-volume classroom manual, the *Commentarii,* reaffirming the Aristotelian, neo-scholastic outlook that had transformed humanism in Portugal since the mid-1500s.

See also **Coimbra, University of; Portuguese Literature and Language**; *and biographies of Luíz Vaz de Camões, António Ferreira, Leone Ebreo, and Francisco de Sá de Miranda.*

BIBLIOGRAPHY

Cardim, Pedro. "Livros, literatura, e homens de letras no tempo de João de Barros." *Oceanos* 27 (July–September 1996): 27–47.

Hirsch, Elisabeth Feist. *Damião de Góis: Life and Thought of a Portuguese Humanist.* The Hague, Netherlands, 1967.

Lawrance, Jeremy N. H. "Humanism in the Iberian Peninsula." In *The Impact on Humanism of Western Europe.* Edited by Anthony Goodman and Angus MacKay. London, 1990. Pages 220–258.

Martins, José V. de Pina. *Humanisme et Renaissance de l'Italie au Portugal: Les deux regards de Janus.* Lisbon, 1989.

Mendes, António. "A vida cultural." In *No Alvorecer de Modernidade: 1480–1620.* Coordinated by Joaquim Romero Magalhães. Vol. 3 of *História de Portugal.* Edited by José Mattoso. Lisbon, 1994. Pages 374–421.

Rossi, Giuseppe Carlo. *A literatura italiana e as literaturas de língua portuguesa.* Translated by Giuseppe Mea. Porto, Portugal, 1973. Pages 2–75.

JEFFREY S. RUTH

Germany and the Low Countries

The marriage of Maximilian to Mary of Burgundy (1477) and his election to the imperial throne (1493) united Germany and the Low Countries under Habsburg rule. It was at this time that humanistic studies began to make inroads in northern Europe.

Origin and Dissemination.

According to Erasmus, Rudolf Agricola was "the first to bring a breath of better learning from Italy." Northern humanism was, however, not purely imitative of Italian culture. Filtered through the indigenous *devotio moderna,* the Christian humanism characterizing the region took shape. The religious movement, which emphasized inner piety, spread through the educational activities of the Brethren of the Common Life. Although their role in the dissemination of humanistic ideas has been disputed, it cannot be denied that their schools (especially Deventer) provided a training ground for an impressive number of humanist scholars.

However, the significance of indigenous elements pales by comparison with the Italian influence. Trade between Italy and commercial centers in Germany, Flanders, and Brabant provided a first conduit for the new learning. Scholars and students moving between Italy and northern Europe at the end of the fifteenth century were the most important carriers of

Italian civilization. Peter of Ravenna, the renowned Italian jurist who taught at Cologne and Mainz, and Rudolf Agricola, who taught in Groningen and Heidelberg, are representative of the two-way movement.

The Councils of Constance (1414–1418) and Basel (1431–1449) also played a role in the dissemination of humanistic ideas north of the Alps. Among the learned Italians in attendance were Poggio Bracciolini, Pier Paolo Vergerio, and Enea Silvio Piccolomini (later Pope Pius II). The presence of these scholars and their subsequent travels in northern Europe facilitated a cultural exchange.

Character.

In form and content, the *studia humanitatis* in Germany and the Low Countries reflected a pattern characteristic of transalpine Europe. Northern humanists, like their Italian counterparts, drew their inspiration from classical sources. The recovery of classical texts, their edition, annotation, and dissemination was one of their consuming passions. The desire to imitate and emulate classical models was another. In a significant shift of intellectual habits, humanists opted for a critical method that was historical or philological rather than logical. They disdained the scholastic method of disputation and regarded the textual glosses of medieval annotators as corruptions of the Aristotelian and Christian traditions. They made a determined effort, moreover, to impose classical idiom on scholarly discourse and to aim at didactic clarity. The educational philosophy of the humanists rested on a strong belief in the human potential for self-improvement and expressed their confidence in the power of nurture over nature. Humanistic educators proposed a curriculum focusing on classical languages and literature and advocated more humane and student-centered methods of instruction. By the sixteenth century these general trends were well established north of the Alps, and distinctive national features began to take shape. Humanism in Germany and the Low Countries was characterized by a strong academic focus, a pronounced religious dimension, and (in Germany) a nationalistic flavor.

Humanism in the schools.

It was not without a struggle that the new cultural program entered educational institutions. The rivalry between reform-minded humanists and advocates of the status quo spawned numerous polemics. The relative merit of rhetoric and philosophy-theology, the role of classical pagan authors in Christian education, and the place of philology in scriptural studies became subjects of intense debate. Among the controversies that

Humanism in Germany. After his studies in Italy, Albrecht Dürer embraced the classical revival and spread them in Germany. His engraving of Fortune (1500) demonstrates his use of perspective and mythological subject matter. STÄDTLICHE KUNSTMUSEUM, DÜSSELDORF, GERMANY/BILDARCHIV FOTO MARBURG/ART RESOURCE, NY

divided the protagonists along the lines of cultural affiliation, two transcended the national level: the cases of Johann Reuchlin and Desiderius Erasmus. Reuchlin, the leading Hebraist in Germany, defended the merit of Jewish literature and Hebrew language studies against critics who regarded them as dangerous to the Christian faith. The controversy resulted in a pamphlet war and produced one of the finest satires of the time: *Letters of Obscure Men* (1515), coauthored by Crotus Rubeanus and Ulrich von Hutten. Erasmus became the center of controversy after the publication of his critical edition of the New Testament (1516). When his writings were attacked by scholastic theologians, humanists in Germany, France, and Spain rallied to his defense.

Pedagogical tracts, curricular outlines, and orations in praise of the *studia humanitatis* proliferated in the early sixteenth century. They prepared the way for the acceptance of humanism at schools and universities. Northern humanists, moreover, produced an impressive number of textbooks that gradually edged out medieval manuals. Among the most important were Agricola's *De inventione dialectica* (On dialectical invention; composed 1479, printed 1515), Erasmus's *Colloquia* (Colloquies; 1519), and *Copia* (Foundations of the abundant style), the *Partitions* of the Strasbourg educator Johann Sturm, and the rhetorical and dialectical textbooks of Philipp Melanchthon, whose pedagogical zeal earned him the title "Preceptor of Germany."

Public expectations confined humanistic education largely to men. While some women of nobility and daughters of old patrician families received a Latin education (for example, the Pirckheimers of Nürnberg and the Blaurers of Constance), they did not match the scholarly ambitions of a Cassandra Fedele or an Isotta Nogarola. Anna Maria van Schurman (1607–1678), renowned for her knowledge of ancient languages and given the privilege of attending the University of Utrecht, was an exception.

Humanism and religion. The Christian character of humanism in Germany and the Low Countries was substantially shaped by Erasmus's vision of *docta pietas,* learned piety. He encapsulated the meaning of "Christian humanism" when he said that "one must study to become better no less than wiser." The long list of his patristic editions and translations and his edition of the New Testament were the beacons of a renaissance of Christian classics paralleling the earlier revival of pagan classics in Italy. Both Erasmus and Melanchthon connected the decline of learning with the corruption of the church and saw its revival as essential to a renewal of the faith and a return to sound theology.

The German Reformation subsumed many humanistic features. Bernd Moeller coined the famous phrase "Ohne Humanismus keine Reformation" ("No Reformation without humanism"). Although humanism played a facilitating rather than a necessary role in the Reformation, the perceived relationship between the two movements became a matter of reproach in the writings of Catholic apologists. In their opinion, humanistic philology had provided the underpinning for the new "heretical" doctrine. Humanist satires like Erasmus's *Praise of Folly* (1509) or Hutten's *Roman Triad* (1520) were used by the reformers as effective tools in the propaganda war. However, satire was also used as a weapon by Catholic writers such as Thomas Murner. Satirists on both sides built on a long-standing indigenous tradition of moralistic literature, which first merged with the humanist tradition in Sebastian Brant's famous *Ship of Fools* (1494). The educational program of the humanists came to play a role in the confessional struggle as well. Their call to take up the study of biblical languages was heeded first in Protestant seminaries. Soon, however, it was a standard requirement for theology students of both Protestant and Catholic confessions. Indeed, Jesuit schools in southern Germany and Austria became instrumental in reviving faith as well as humanistic studies.

Humanism and national pride. The nationalistic element characteristic of German humanism can be understood as a reaction to the condescension of Italian writers who routinely referred to Germans as "barbarians." It was also a protest against the financial exploitation of Germany by the Roman See. Ulrich von Hutten best exemplifies the nationalistic trend, which in his case translated into acts of violence and rebellion. In its more peaceful manifestation, cultural nationalism led to an interest in German history and geography and encouraged the collection of German antiquities. Among those who contributed to historiography and biography in Germany were the abbot Johannes Trithemius, Hartmann Schedel, Conrad Celtis, Jacob Wimpheling, Conrad Peutinger, and Johannes Aventinus. Regional and local history flourished in the Low Countries, especially in the seventeenth century. Among the principal contributors were Janus Dousa, Hugo Grotius, Antonius Sanderus, and Ubbo Emmius.

Patronage and Promotion.

The patronage of the imperial court contributed significantly to the dissemination of humanism in Germany and the Low Countries. Maximilian I founded one of the earliest humanistic institutes in Vienna. Like his father, Frederick III, he honored the achievements of leading German poets with the laurel crown. He sponsored historiography and personally collaborated on allegorical epics glorifying the Habsburg dynasty. A number of humanists (among them, Erasmus and Juan Luis Vives) dedicated works to Maximilian's grandson Charles V and were rewarded with pensions and positions of honor. The court of Margaret of Austria and her library at Mechelen became a center for the new learning in the Low Countries. At the end of the century Rudolf II, a scholar himself, provided patronage for artists, antiquaries, and scientists at his court in Prague.

Regional courts also supported humanistic scholars. Peter Luder, one of the earliest champions of humanistic studies, and the annalist Erycius Pu-

teanus enjoyed the support of the counts Palatine; the historian Johannes Aventinus was a protégé of Duke William IV of Bavaria. A number of universities received support from ducal courts (Wittenberg, founded in 1502 by Frederick the Wise; Marburg, in 1527 by Philip of Hesse; lectureships at Leipzig financed by George of Saxony). In the seventeenth century the bibliophile Duke August of Brunswick established a library at Wolfenbüttel, which contained some forty thousand volumes on his death in 1660. Town councils established and maintained important humanist schools in Schlettstadt, Strasbourg, Augsburg, and Nürnberg.

Private initiative also played a role in promoting the humanities. The Collegium Trilingue at Louvain (established 1517) was financed through a legacy from Jérôme de Busleiden. The printshops of publishers like Johann Amerbach and Johann Froben in Basel, Andreas Wechel in Frankfurt, or Christophe Plantin in Antwerp became meeting places for scholars, facilitating an exchange of information. A sense of camaraderie was fostered also by literary societies, notably in Heidelberg, Augsburg, Erfurt, and Strasbourg.

Chronological Patterns.

An atmosphere favorable to the reception of humanism developed at the end of the fifteenth century, but the first advances and curriculum reforms were threatened by the turbulent events of the Reformation. The climate of uncertainty led to a sharp decline in student enrollment during the 1520s, but progress resumed in the 1530s, and by the middle of the century humanism was firmly entrenched at the universities. Humanists began to enjoy public recognition as professional educators, editors, secretaries, and diplomats. In the seventeenth century the center of humanistic learning shifted to the Low Countries. The University of Leiden (established 1575) could boast a distinguished group of scholars in classical philology, history, and political thought: Justus Lipsius, Joseph Justus Scaliger, Daniel Heinsius, and Hugo Grotius. Germany, by contrast, went through a period of decline. The Thirty Years' War (1618–1648) interrupted cultural life. When peace and conditions favorable to learning were restored, humanism had lost much of its creative edge and driving force. Although it had left a permanent legacy and become an integral part of the cultural identity of Germany and the Low Countries, the importance of humanism was overshadowed in the second half of the century by the beginnings of modern science and the aesthetics of baroque.

See also **Brunswick-Wolfenbüttel; Education; Habsburg Dynasty; Reuchlin Affair;** *and biographies of figures mentioned in this entry.*

BIBLIOGRAPHY

Fleischer, Manfred P., ed. *The Harvest of Humanism in Central Europe: Essays in Honor of Lewis W. Spitz.* St. Louis, Mo., 1992. Focuses on the late Renaissance.

Goodman, Anthony, and Angus MacKay, eds. *The Impact of Humanism on Western Europe.* New York, 1990. A basic book with chapters on Germany and the Low Countries.

Moeller, Bernd. "Die deutschen Humanisten und die Anfänge der Reformation." *Zeitschrift für Kirchengeschichte* 70ᵉ (1959): 46–61. Translated by H. C. Midelfort and Mark U. Edwards in *Imperial Cities and the Reformation: Three Essays.* Philadelphia, 1972. A classic article.

Nauert, Charles G. *Humanism and the Culture of Renaissance Europe.* Cambridge, U.K., 1996. The second part of this lucid survey is dedicated to the northern Renaissance. Extensive bibliography.

Oberman, Heiko A., and Thomas A. Brady, eds. *Itinerarium Italicum: The Profile of the Italian Renaissance in the Mirror of Its European Transformations.* Leiden, Netherlands, 1975. Contains essays on Germany and the Low Countries.

Overfield, James H. *Humanism and Scholasticism in Late Medieval Germany.* Princeton, N.J., 1984. On academic controversies, especially the Reuchlin Affair.

Porter, Roy, and Mikulás Teich, eds. *The Renaissance in National Context.* Cambridge, U.K., 1992. Contains chapters on Germany and the Low Countries.

Rabil, Albert, ed. *Renaissance Humanism: Foundations, Forms, and Legacy.* 3 vols. Philadelphia, 1988. Volume 2 contains articles on Germany and the Low Countries.

Rummel, Erika. *The Humanist-Scholastic Debate in the Renaissance and Reformation.* Cambridge, Mass., 1995. Chapters 4–6 focus on humanism in Germany.

Spitz, Lewis W. *Luther and German Humanism.* Aldershot, U.K., 1996. Reprints of articles on the subject, conveniently gathered in one volume.

Spitz, Lewis. *The Religious Renaissance of the German Humanists.* Cambridge, Mass., 1963.

Tracy, James. "Humanism in the Reformation." In *Reformation Europe: A Guide to Research.* Edited by Steven Ozment. St. Louis, Mo., 1982. Pages 33–58. A bibliographical guide.

ERIKA RUMMEL

The British Isles

The humanist movement in England, as on the Continent, involved a new interest in classical antiquity. In order to read the writings of the ancient Greeks and Romans, it was necessary to know their languages, so the study of Greek and classical Latin began late in the fifteenth century. Once these tongues were mastered, it became possible to master ancient texts. The coming of printing to the British Isles about 1475 aided this enterprise greatly; translations and popularizations as well as scholarly editions of the texts themselves increasingly became available. Finally, the ideas of the ancient Greeks and Romans came to pervade the intellectual life of the British Isles, influencing not only academic curricula but also such areas as literary style, art, architecture, travel, pageantry, and parliamentary rhetoric.

Although several Englishmen, among them John Free, John Tiptoft, and John Gunthorpe, had studied classical languages in Italy during the fifteenth century, the first English scholar to teach Greek regularly at Oxford was William Grocyn (c. 1446–1519), who had spent three years abroad and had met the great printer Aldo Manuzio at Venice. John Colet (c. 1467–1519) also imbibed Italian humanism before becoming dean of Saint Paul's Cathedral. He was one of the greatest preachers of his day, and he delivered popular lectures on such topics as the books of Genesis and Romans in both Oxford and London, employing a historical approach to the texts rather than the scholastic analysis of medieval theologians. Colet was also interested in providing instruction in the classical languages for young men who would enter government service or the professions, not necessarily the church. As the only survivor of twenty-two children born to his father, a lord mayor of London, he was a wealthy man, and he gave his fortune to Saint Paul's School on condition that it offer a free classical education to promising boys. His friend William Lily, the first master of the school, wrote a Latin grammar for use there.

Sir Thomas More and His Circle. The greatest of the early humanists was Sir Thomas More (1478–1535). Although More was tempted to enter a religious order and spent some time living in the London Charterhouse (house of the Carthusian order), he ultimately followed his father into the legal profession. In 1529 he succeeded Thomas Wolsey as lord chancellor, but he did not approve of Henry VIII's divorce proceedings and resigned his office in 1532. He had hoped to live in quiet retirement, but in 1534 he was arrested and in 1535 he was executed on the grounds that he refused to swear the oath of supremacy demanded by statute following the king's break with Rome.

More's house in Chelsea became a home for many humanistic scholars. Erasmus lived with More during his first visit to England; it is likely that both Erasmus's *Praise of Folly* (1509; in Latin, *Moriae encomium,* a play on words involving More's name) and More's famous *Utopia* (1516) reflect their discussions of society and politics. In 1511 More was instrumental in securing Erasmus's position at Queens' College, Cambridge, and he corresponded with the Dutch humanist following his return to the Continent. Another member of More's circle was Thomas Linacre (c. 1460–1524), whose chief interest was ancient medicine. Linacre translated the works of Galen into Latin—not English, because he did not want ordinary people attempting to diagnose their ailments—and was the founder and first president of the Royal College of Physicians, which obtained a monopoly on medical practice, originally in London but eventually throughout England. As a result of Linacre's efforts, Galen's theory of the four humors (blood, choler, melancholy, and phlegm) and four complexions (sanguine, choleric, melancholic, and phlegmatic) became part of the intellectual framework that influenced English literature for centuries.

Galen's ideas were popularized by Sir Thomas Elyot (c. 1490–1546), whose *Castel of Helth,* published about 1536, made the medical theories of the ancients readily available in the vernacular. Elyot was another member of More's circle. He served for a time as secretary to the king's council and in 1532 was sent to the Continent as ambassador to Charles V, but when he failed to persuade the emperor to support Henry VIII's divorce from Catherine of Aragon (Charles's aunt), he was recalled and dismissed. He never again held government office, but in his retirement he wrote prolifically. His most important work, *The Boke Named the Governour* (1531), includes chapters about political theory, education, and the virtues appropriate for members of the governing class, all informed by ideas and anecdotes taken from classical writings. Elyot also wrote a number of political dialogues and compiled the first English dictionary of classical Latin.

Another member of More's household was the German painter Hans Holbein the Younger, who has left us likenesses of More and his family, Elyot, and More's friend Archbishop William Warham. Following More's fall, Holbein was accepted at court and became Henry VIII's official painter.

Later Humanism. Younger humanists included John Cheke (1514–1557), a noted Greek scholar who taught at Cambridge and was a tutor and secretary of Henry VIII's son, Prince Edward. Cheke was instrumental in introducing classical texts into the university curriculum but spent much of his energy arguing over the correct pronunciation of classical Greek. Roger Ascham (1515–1568) taught Latin and Greek to Elizabeth I while she was a young princess and wrote treatises on education (*The Scholemaster,* 1570) and archery (*Toxophilus,* 1545).

The earlier years of the reign of Henry VIII formed the golden age of English humanism. After the 1530s

scholars' attention was diverted to the Reformation and to the intellectual debate of religious issues. Renaissance ideas made the acceptance of the Reformation in England easier. Several of the humanists were reluctant to accept medieval religious traditions or papal pronouncements, preferring instead their own more skeptical and rational inquiries into history, theology, and biblical interpretation, and arguing for services in the vernacular and opportunities for laypeople to read and interpret the Bible themselves. The early humanists had planted seeds that germinated and grew during the later years of the sixteenth century and well into the seventeenth. The reigns of Elizabeth I (1558–1603) and James I (1603–1625) saw the fruition of Renaissance culture in England. The writings of Shakespeare, Sidney, Milton, and the metaphysical poets would have been impossible without a foundation in the classics. The grand tour of Europe came to be an essential part of the education of young aristocrats and gentlemen, and it almost always included extended visits to Rome and Florence, where ancient and Renaissance architecture could be admired. Classical details found their way into English architecture during the Tudor period—they are present in such buildings as Hampton Court and Longleat House—but it remained for Inigo Jones (1573–1652) to design pure classical structures like the Banqueting House in Whitehall and the Queen's House at Greenwich. Even the style of parliamentary oratory grew increasingly ornate and full of classical allusions, the most famous instance being Sir John Eliot's extended comparison of the duke of Buckingham (a favorite of James I and friend of Charles I) to Sejanus, the evil adviser to the Roman emperor Tiberius, in the Parliament of 1626, while Ben Jonson's play *Sejanus* was being performed in London.

Scotland and Ireland. Humanistic influences began to affect Scotland during the reign of James IV (1488–1513), who was married to Henry VIII's sister Margaret Tudor. A well-educated monarch, James was said to speak six languages as well as English and Gaelic. He encouraged the foundation of a new university at Aberdeen in 1495. The universities of Saint Andrews and Glasgow were already in existence, and another was established at Edinburgh in 1583. An education act of 1496 provided that the eldest sons of all substantial landowners should study Latin, law, and the arts. The first printing house in Scotland began operation in Edinburgh in 1507. Warfare and problems of succession sapped the energy of the Scots during much of the sixteenth century, but James VI had received a sound classical education in Scotland before ascending the English throne in 1603. Scottish education, law, religion, philosophy, medicine, astronomy, and literature were all influenced by Renaissance humanism, whose chief exponents were John Mair (Major), Gavin Douglas, George Buchanan, John Napier, and William Drummond; John Knox might also be included in this group.

Ireland was slower to accept the new learning. It was not until 1592 that a university was established, when Trinity College, Dublin, was founded on the site of a former Augustinian priory.

Continuing Influences of Humanism.
The political turmoil of the English Civil War (1642–1648) and Interregnum (1649–1660) brought an end to the English Renaissance. But the influence of humanism and classical antiquity continued to be felt throughout the eighteenth and nineteenth centuries. Many new country houses and government buildings were built in the classical style. Education was still based on the Latin and Greek languages and literatures. Tours of classical sites, especially Greece and Rome, remained popular. Only after World War II, with (among other things) the abandonment of Latin as an entrance requirement at Oxford and Cambridge, did humanist ideas come to seem a thing of the past.

See also biographies of figures mentioned in this entry.

BIBLIOGRAPHY

Caspari, Fritz. *Humanism and the Social Order in Tudor England.* Chicago, 1954. A good discussion of the social and political ideas of the humanists.

Chambers, R. W. *Thomas More.* London, 1935. The classic life, but now dated.

Dowling, Maria. *Humanism in the Age of Henry VIII.* London, 1986. A general survey of the topic, brief but useful.

Lehmberg, Stanford. *Sir Thomas Elyot, Tudor Humanist.* Austin, Tex., 1960. Describes Elyot's life and discusses his writings.

MacQueen, John, ed. *Humanism in Renaissance Scotland.* Edinburgh, 1990. Essays on various aspects of humanism by a group of Scottish scholars.

Simon, Joan. *Education and Society in Tudor England.* Cambridge, U.K., 1966. Includes material about humanism in the schools.

Weiss, Roberto. *Humanism in England during the Fifteenth Century.* 3d ed. Oxford, 1967. Traces the beginnings of humanist influences.

STANFORD E. LEHMBERG

France

One of the main points of contention in the historiography of humanism is the question of origins, and the origins of French humanism are usually debated in relation to the influence of Italian culture. According to Franco Simone's influential account, French humanism began in the course of the fourteenth century largely as a polemical reaction to Italian cultural hegemony, and many scholars have shown how national sentiment continued to inspire humanist research and rhetoric throughout the French Renaissance. Accordingly, we can begin our survey in the antagonistically intercultural domain of the papal court, which resided in the French city of Avignon from 1309 to 1377 before the Great Schism opposed the Roman Curia to the French antipapacy from 1378 to 1417.

The Early Stages. The presence of the papal court and its substantial Italian community made Avignon the center of contact between renascent Italian culture and French medieval tradition, and this contact, which was not exempt from rivalry, gave rise to the first expressions of French humanism. The papacy of John XXII (1316–1334) witnessed the expansion of the University of Avignon and the foundation of a pontifical library, whose collection of classical manuscripts had reached significant proportions by the time of the inventory commissioned by Pope Urban V in 1369. If Petrarch's residence in Avignon between 1326 and 1353 undoubtedly gave an important impetus to this enthusiasm for classical studies, his strident claims of Italian cultural primacy also directly provoked some of the inaugural texts of French humanism, including the invective of Jean de Hesdin, a courtier of Urban V, and the epistles of Nicolas de Clamanges (c. 1363–1437), secretary of the antipope Benedict XIII during the very last years of the Avignon papacy.

From Avignon, the center of French humanism moved to Paris and the Collège de Navarre, sometimes dubbed the cradle of French humanism. In the decades spanning the turn of the fourteenth to the fifteenth centuries, the Collège de Navarre numbered among its students and faculty such luminaries as the great theologian Jean de Gerson (1363–1429), the royal chancellor Jean de Montreuil (d. 1418), who was a friend and correspondent of Coluccio Salutati (1331–1406), and the defender of French eloquence, Nicolas de Clamanges, whose death is usually taken to mark a pause if not a rupture in the development of French humanism.

The most significant figure to emerge in the next generation of French humanists was Guillaume Fichet (b. 1433), who has been credited with having definitively introduced Italian humanism to the University of Paris. Beginning in 1453 Fichet taught the traditional scholastic disciplines of logic and theology while also expounding classical authors in keeping with the new humanist program of education. In 1470, with the collaboration of Jean Heynlin (1425?–1496), Fichet founded the first French printing press in the Sorbonne, where he printed editions and translations of classical authors, writings of Italian humanists, and works of scholastic philosophy. He also took the liberty of printing his own treatise on rhetoric, which has been recognized as the "first secure step of French culture toward the Renaissance" (Simone, 1968, p. 27), by virtue of its prefatory discourse on the pursuit of eloquence and the union of rhetoric and philosophy.

Among the disciples of Fichet the most prominent was Robert Gaguin (c. 1433–1501), who distinguished himself as a historian, translator, professor of rhetoric, and correspondent of Erasmus. Gaguin was the first French humanist to whom Erasmus wrote when he arrived in Paris in 1495, and Erasmus provided a laudatory epistle for Gaguin's most important work, *De origine et gestis Francorum compendium* (On the origin and deeds of the Franks; 1495) better known as the *Compendium*. Another leading figure from Gaguin's generation was Guillaume Tardif (b. c. 1400), whose treatises on grammar and rhetoric along with his translations of Lorenzo Valla and Poggio Bracciolini contributed to the diffusion of Italian humanism in France.

The Apogee. French humanism entered a new and more independent phase with the career of Jacques Lefèvre d'Étaples (c. 1460–1536), whose intellectual interests drew him more to the study of religion and philosophy than to the humanist cult of eloquence. Lefèvre first achieved widespread notoriety through his translations and commentaries on Aristotle's moral philosophy before establishing himself as a leader of Christian humanism through his translations of the Bible and his association with the reform movement of Guillaume Briçonnet, bishop of Meaux. Lefèvre's evangelical humanism earned him the enmity of the theological faculty of the Sorbonne as well as the patronage of Margaret of Angoulême, queen of Navarre, who counted among her protégés the leading French vernacular humanists of her era, including the poet Clément Marot (d. 1544) and the novelist François Rabelais (c. 1494–1553). Another aspect of Lefèvre's indefatigable activity that deserves mention is the interest he shared with Marsilio Ficino (1433–1499) and the Florentine Neoplatonists in the hermetic tradition. The editions that Lefèvre prepared of the writings of Pseudo-Dionysius in

1499 and of portions of the *Corpus Hermeticum* in 1505 gave a substantial impetus to the esoteric current of French humanism, which continued in the work of his disciple Charles de Bovelles (1479–1567) and in the mystic nationalism of Guillaume Postel (1510–1581) later in the century.

Any history of French humanism is likely to linger in greatest detail on the career of Guillaume Budé (1467–1540), who was the leading humanist in Renaissance France and the most prominent representative of a cultural class credited with effecting a "cultural revolution" during the reign of Francis I (1515–1547). Budé's career exemplifies the rise of the *noblesse de robe,* or those lawyers, magistrates, and notaries who were enriched and ennobled by service in the royal administration, which they entered primarily on the basis of their educational or cultural credentials. Budé was able to maintain an active career as a diplomat, royal secretary, and cultural adviser while composing his massive, encyclopedic studies of Roman civil law, *Annotationes in . . . Pandectarum* (Annotations on the Pandects; 1508); Roman coinage, *De asse et partibus ejus* (On the pound and its divisions; 1515); and Greek grammar, *Commentarii linguae graecae* (Commentary on the Greek language; 1529), as well as his vernacular treatise *De l'institution du prince* (On the education of the prince; 1519). Budé crowned his public career with the foundation in 1530 of the Collège Royal, which may not have assumed precisely the form that he advocated, of a sumptuous temple of the muses, but whose original faculty of four professors offering free public instruction in Greek and Hebrew gradually expanded to encompass the whole range of disciplines involved in the ideal of *encyclopaedia* that he espoused in a number of works, including his treatise *De studio literarum* (On the study of literature) and his dialogue *De philologia* (On philology), both published in 1532. Another enduring legacy of Budé's scholarship was the development of humanist jurisprudence, which brought to bear an acute sense of historical relativism on the study of ancient institutions. In France the main beneficiaries of this legacy were Jean Bodin (1530–1596), who proposed a comparative jurisprudence based on historical erudition, and François Hotman (1524–1590), whose *Antitribonien* of 1567 explored the furthest paradoxes of the modern revival of ancient law.

Sectarianism and Criticism. In the second half of the sixteenth century French humanism developed several new tendencies often in response to the sectarian pressures of religious conflict. Before the outbreak of religious warfare, Pierre de La Ramée (1515–1572), also known as Ramus, dominated the intellectual scene with his reform of logic and grammar and his dogged anti-Aristotelian polemics, which Rabelais commemorated in the prologue to his *Quart livre* (1548). However, Ramus's career came to an end in the St. Bartholomew's Day massacre of 1572 in the midst of the French Wars of Religion, which lasted from 1562 to 1598. During this period, Marc-Antoine Muret (1526–1585) championed the Counter-Reformation ideal of rhetorical humanism, Latin eloquence in the service of the papacy, while Guillaume du Vair (1556–1621) espoused the doctrine of Christian stoicism so characteristic of French baroque culture. Under Charles IX, Jean-Antoine de Baïf (1532–1589) founded an academy of music and poetry dedicated to the creation of harmony amid social strife, while under Henry III the Palace Academy tried to insulate itself from civil war through the lectures on moral philosophy delivered by Pierre de Ronsard (1524–1585) and other courtiers.

The final stages of French humanism have been interpreted as a "Renaissance of criticism" (Jehassse) due to the conspicuous role of textual criticism in the prolific output of Henri Estienne (1528–1598) and the humanist triumvirate of Joseph Scaliger (1540–1609), Isaac Casaubon (1559–1614), and Justus Lipsius (1547–1606). Their editions of classical authors and their exposure of postclassical forgeries transformed the canon of classical literature and dictated new literary modes and tastes. In particular, due to the efforts of the new critical humanism, the writings of Seneca and Tacitus began to eclipse the works of Cicero as the preeminent literary models of late-sixteenth-century Europe. This revision of literary taste corresponds to what Marc Fumaroli has called the transition from civic humanism to aulic humanism. While the civic humanists of fifteenth-century Italy often evoked the Ciceronian ideal of oratory in the service of the republic, humanism of the *aula*, or princely court, emphasized the political prudence and stoic fortitude taught by Seneca and Tacitus after the fall of the Roman Republic. In fact, the political and aesthetic eclipse of Ciceronianism is one way to measure the belated emancipation of French humanism from Italian influences.

Montaigne. The most problematic instance of humanist discourse at the end of the French Renaissance and the most important literary work of the time is Michel de Montaigne's *Essays,* which react against the pedagogical and rhetorical values of hu-

manism. While Montaigne (1533–1592) purports to disdain the professional orientation of the *studia humanitatis* and the verbal bias of humanism, he subscribes fully to the humanist tradition of communion with the past. In his essay "On Vanity," first published in 1588, Montaigne claims to have been brought up with the ancient Romans and to have remained their contemporary. He has befriended the heroes of the ancient republic and their acquaintance endures, "for even the present we hold only in our imagination." In this way Montaigne proposes a solution, or perhaps simply an epitaph, to the humanist dilemma of retrieving the classical past without superimposing it upon the present. Located within the tenuous grasp of the imagination, or *fantaisie,* the present can coexist vainly with the past.

See also biographies of humanists mentioned in this entry.

BIBLIOGRAPHY

Fumaroli, Marc. *L'âge de l'éloquence.* Geneva, 1980.

Gadoffre, Gilbert. *La révolution culturelle dans la France des humanistes. Guillaume Budé et François Ier.* Geneva, 1997.

Jehasse, Jean. *La Renaissance de la critique: L'essor de l'humanisme érudit de 1560 à 1614.* Saint-Étienne, France, 1976.

Levi, A. H. T., ed. *Humanism in France at the End of the Middle Ages and in the Early Renaissance.* Manchester, U.K., 1970.

Renaudet, Augustin. *Préréforme et humanisme à Paris pendant les premières guerres d'Italie (1494–1517).* 2d ed. Paris, 1953.

Rice, Eugene F. "Humanism in France." In *Renaissance Humanism: Foundations, Forms, and Legacy.* Vol. 2, *Humanism beyond Italy.* Edited by Albert Rabil. Philadelphia, 1988. Pages 109–122.

Simone, Franco. *Il Rinascimento Francese. Studi e ricerche.* Turin, Italy, 1961.

Simone, France. *Umanesimo, Rinascimento, Barocco in Francia.* Milan, 1968.

ERIC MACPHAIL

Legal Humanism

The encounter of humanism with law over the course of the sixteenth century bore fruit in both fields. It helped to weaken the view that law constitutes a body of timeless general principles in favor of a new understanding of laws as arising from problems and customs peculiar to specific peoples, times, and places. This recognition contributed ultimately to the weakening of the authority of Roman law in favor of a greater emphasis upon customary law. In humanism, it contributed to an increasingly sophisticated understanding of source criticism and scholarship, helped decrease the influence of the extreme classicism of many early humanists, and furthered the growth of institutional and political history.

Humanists confronted a tradition of scholastic criticism that stretched back to the late eleventh century. The Scholastics were thoroughly familiar with their major source, the *Corpus iuris civilis* (Body of civil law), the sixth-century compilation ordered by the Eastern Roman Emperor Justinian and edited by Tribonian. Unlike scholastic theologians, the legists did not often consciously allegorize. They suffered rather from an excessively literal approach to the *Corpus iuris,* which they combined with skill in logical analysis and synthesis to interpret problematic passages, resolve apparent contradictions, and "find" solutions to contemporary legal problems. They assumed that similar-appearing key terms and phrases expressed fixed, general meanings. Interpreters in this tradition, one that persisted through the Renaissance, showed little awareness of textual corruption or the importance of context or a particular author's usage in establishing the meaning of important legal terms. Still less did they appreciate mutability over time in the interpretation and application of laws. Humanists were distinguished not by a return to the sources but by their approach to them.

Lorenzo Valla. The humanist encounter begins with the pioneering critical work of the humanist scholar Lorenzo Valla (1407–1457) on the *Digest,* a compendium of excerpts from thirty-eight legal scholars (most of whom wrote in the early centuries of the empire) that constitutes the largest, most important section of the *Corpus iuris.* In his *Elegantiae linguae latinae* (Elegances of the Latin language; 1471) Valla ridiculed the entire tradition of legal interpretation and commentary. His finely tuned sense for word use led him to ferret out contradictory uses of important terms by different jurists. Thus he recognized the implications of the nature of the *Corpus iuris,* that in such an assemblage inconsistencies in use of key terms and in legal thought were inevitable. Furthermore, when he criticized some of the *Digest*'s jurists for contradictory usage of legal terms, he showed that law must be understood as existing and changing over time, rather than as a fixed body of truths arrived at through reason. He is among the first to recognize that the *Corpus iuris* distorted and misconstrued earlier Roman law.

Valla's criticisms arose from a program for cultural reform he shared with many early Renaissance humanists but that differed markedly from the assumptions of modern textual critics. First, he deeply believed that the Latin language (and indeed the culture) of the Roman Republic and early Empire was far superior to that of later times. Thus his

awareness of differences in usage was a consequence of his search for a purified Latin modeled upon that of the Roman authors he admired—whether legal scholars or not—and reflected his disdain for those who departed from the pure usage of his preferred authors. Second, he ridiculed the legal scholars of his own day, boasting that philological skill was not merely necessary but sufficient for a critical understanding of the law, and that in three years he could write glosses on the *Digest* "much more useful than those of Accursius," who wrote the standard gloss on the *Digest* in the thirteenth century. In practice Valla showed little interest in the substance of Roman law, either as it appeared in the *Corpus iuris* or in the thought of the earlier Western Roman scholars excerpted in the *Digest.*

Guillaume Budé. Valla's approach to Justinian inspired the French humanist Guillaume Budé (c. 1467–1540), the author of the first extensive humanist study of the *Digest.* Budé amplified Valla's methods and applied them to numerous passages in the *Corpus iuris.* His vast knowledge of Roman historical and literary writings enabled him to elucidate the meanings of many terms that had occasioned debates among earlier jurists. He too rejected the synthetic methods of the scholastic jurists and presented a list of contradictory passages, the *antinomiae,* which the Scholastics had long sought to resolve logically, as evidence rather of the corruption of the *Corpus iuris* and the inattention of its editor, Tribonian. Yet he shared Valla's classicizing approach to Latin, often criticizing as corruptions legal terms used by Roman jurists but rare or absent in nonlegal writings. And he shared Valla's aversion to the legal profession, showing little interest in the legal analyses preserved in the *Digest.* Thus the Roman jurists did not fully engage with the concerns of practicing legal scholars, even ones with humanist sympathies.

Humanist Legal Scholars. Professional jurists, most notably Andrea Alciato (1492–1550) and Ulrich Zasius (1461–1535) also applied humanist insights to Roman law. Zasius hoped to reconstruct the thought of the scholars whose works were excerpted in the *Digest,* and he rebuked Tribonian for having destroyed their original books. Alciato treated their pronouncements as responses to legal uncertainties arising in particular circumstances. He further made use of literary and historical sources to reconstruct pre-Justinian law and institutions (such as Roman magistracies) and showed acumen in restoring Greek sections of the *Digest.* Both he and Zasius also acknowledged a degree of uncertainty in their own interpretations.

Yet in defense of the authority of the *Corpus iuris,* an authority that was central to their profession's legitimacy, both Zasius and Alciato rebuked Valla's extreme classicism and indifference to legal concepts. To preserve the integrity of the *Corpus iuris* against Valla and Budé's challenge, they ironically allowed a greater role for figurative interpretation and reconstruction of the author's intention and relied less heavily on classical usage as a standard. But they often combined this more flexible interpretive approach with traditional, scholastic techniques of logical synthesis and the "discovery" of legal distinctions (often borrowed straight from medieval commentators) designed to overcome the textual problems their own critical work was highlighting.

Nevertheless, Alciato gave a great impetus to French humanist jurisprudence by initiating in 1529 humanist-influenced teaching in the faculty of law at the recently founded University of Bourges, then under the patronage of Margaret of Angoulême, duchess of Berry and sister of King Francis I. Although Alciato left Bourges in 1533, his teaching there marks the founding of the *mos gallicus* (French style), the school of humanist jurisprudence that flourished primarily in France, and which was counterposed to the more traditional *mos italicus* (Italian style). Indeed most later humanist-influenced legal scholars studied or taught at Bourges, including all the figures discussed below.

Later Approaches to Roman Law. François de Connan (1508–1551), François Douaren (1509–1559), Hugues Doneau (1527–1591), and François Baudouin (1520–1573) became increasingly aware that the *Corpus iuris civilis* was not consistent or fully coherent as it stood. Connan, Doneau, and to a lesser extent Douaren sought to rearrange the material of the *Corpus iuris* into a coherent system, thus showing the influence of Ramism but also perpetuating the systematizing habits of the medieval interpreters.

But Baudouin, Jacques Cujas (1522–1590), and Douaren were more interested in the laws and institutions of the Roman Republic and early Empire, and so were less concerned with rescuing Roman law from the destabilizing impact of humanist criticism. Baudouin noted that the *Corpus iuris* included laws and legal concepts from across a thirteen hundred year period, and that it contained incompatible laws and omitted or distorted much from the earlier period. Douaren also acknowledged the untrustwor-

thiness of the *Corpus iuris* for earlier Roman law. Cujas was especially important to the project of recovering pre-Justinian law. Little interested in contemporary politics, he concentrated rather on resurrecting classical Roman legal thought. Using manuscript sources when possible, he reconstructed earlier writings, such as those of the jurist Ulpian (d. 228) excerpted in the *Corpus iuris,* and published an edition of the Theodosian Code. These scholars were closer to Budé and Valla than to Alciato and Zasius in their sophisticated source criticism of the *Corpus iuris,* but far more interested in legal issues than Budé and Valla.

The Break with Roman Law. In the next generation, humanist-influenced legal scholars such as François Hotman (1524–1590), Louis Le Caron (1536–1617), Antoine Loisel (1534–1613), and Pierre Pithou (1539–1596) made a fundamental departure by challenging not only the possibility of reordering Roman law into a coherent system, but the very value of Roman law to contemporary French legal, institutional, and political problems. They adapted the philological tools of the earlier humanists to the study of medieval sources. Eguinaire Baron (1495–1550) had rejected the notion that French law was derived from Roman law, and he set forth a comparison of French and Roman law and institutions in which he was more cognizant than his contemporaries of differences between the two. Douaren, though concentrating on Roman law, had repudiated the tendency to see feudal law as derived from Rome and wrote one of the first sketches of canon law. Cujas made beginning forays into canon and feudal law and greatly influenced the next generation. Baudouin advocated a move away from the focus on Roman laws and institutions, argued that legal scholars should study the laws of their own nation as well as those of other peoples (with Rome but one among many), and asserted the value for the proper governing of a country of historical examples from all these traditions.

Hotman, Le Caron, Loisel, and Pithou carried these tendencies much further in the course of their research into early French and German legal and institutional history, and so extended humanist insights and developed more sophisticated approaches to the history of law and to history *tout court.* They were much more relativistic than the earlier humanist-influenced figures. Nevertheless, each writer pursued his inquiries with one eye on contemporary society, especially the crisis of the religious wars of the later sixteenth century. The ardent Huguenot Hotman argued that a body of laws must be constructed to serve a particular people, thus adopting a relativist view. But he used his research into Germanic law to argue that "Romanism," which for him encompassed both Roman and canon law, was responsible for the corruption of French law and the pervasiveness of "idolatry" in France, that France was rightly a mixed monarchy in which the estates general rather than the Parlement should have an important role, and that the early, unwritten laws of France manifested a purity lost with the later influx of Roman law. Loisel, Le Caron, and Pithou were more inclined to Politique sympathies, placing their hopes for compromise and reconciliation on a strengthened king and a Gallican church. Le Caron employed philology to show the Germanic sources of feudal law, but also idealized French law as simple and pure until corrupted by the complexities of Roman law. Pithou, who served Henry IV as procurer general in Guienne, and Loisel, who served as *avocat* for among others Catherine de Médicis and as *avocat général* for Henry IV, conducted less fanciful scholarship on French customs and practices. Yet Pithou's researches into French feudal law and church institutions were strongly colored by his desire to strengthen the king at the expense of both the nobility and the papacy. Loisel also explored French customs and church history, and sought to systematize French unwritten law in such works as the *Institutes coustumières* (Customary institutes; 1607).

Humanist and Scholastic Interpretation.

Despite the break with the *Corpus iuris civilis* and an increasingly sophisticated range of approaches, attempts to "rise above" historical change to universal principles—what Donald Kelley has called the "transcendent impulse"—resurfaced in manifold ways. Baron's comparative approach involved systematizing assumptions. Baudouin hoped to glean universal principles from the philological and historical study of many different legal traditions. Thus the synthesizing, generalizing habits dominant among prehumanist legal commentators did not disappear. Rather, in the work of many legal humanists they reappeared in new forms and in uneasy cohabitation with philological and historical criticism.

See also **Law** *and biographies of figures mentioned in this entry.*

BIBLIOGRAPHY

Franklin, Julian H. *Jean Bodin and the Sixteenth-Century Revolution in the Methodology of Law and History.* New York, 1963.

Gilmore, Myron Piper. *Argument from Roman Law in Political Thought, 1200–1600.* Cambridge, Mass., 1941.

Kelley, Donald R. *Foundations of Modern Historical Scholarship: Language, Law, and History in the French Renaissance.* New York, 1970.

Maclean, Ian. *Interpretation and Meaning in the Renaissance: The Case of Law.* Cambridge, U.K., 1992.

Monheit, Michael L. "Guillaume Budé, Andrea Alciato, Pierre de l'Estoile: Renaissance Interpreters of Roman Law." *Journal of the History of Ideas* 58 (1997): 21–40.

MICHAEL L. MONHEIT

HUMANITY, CONCEPT OF. Renaissance thinkers discussed the concept of humanity, that is, man and his nature, from a variety of perspectives. One source of Renaissance conceptions of humanity was Aristotle's *De Anima* (On the soul). Renaissance analyses of this text were influenced by interpretations of such medieval philosophers as Averroes (Ibn Rushd), Thomas Aquinas, John Duns Scotus, and William of Ockham, and, after the Renaissance Hellenistic revival, by Aristotle's ancient Greek commentators as well, such as Alexander of Aphrodisias, Philoponus, Themistius, and Simplicius. As Renaissance humanistic developments fostered a new respect for classic authors, they brought too a broader range of conceptions of humanity. These views went beyond the Aristotelian, and included Platonistic, Epicurean, Stoic, Ciceronean, and Augustinian perspectives, along with new ways of reconciling them. These developments fostered a new focus on the human predicament. Works or essays that examine particular issues of human interest—human dignity, human immortality, the human mind, and human free will—explore characteristic features of the nature of human beings. The discovery of America and its natives also raised controversy (such as that involving Bartolomé de Las Casas and Juan de Sepulveda) over the conception of humanity. During the Renaissance, these developments spurred new ways of understanding humanity that came into conflict with longstanding traditional conceptions.

Averroes's Monopyschism.

During the medieval period, Averroes was universally acknowledged as the authoritative commentator on Aristotle's works, and his commentaries retained a following, especially among natural philosophers in northern Italy. His continued importance influenced some to adopt Averroes's monopsychism. This is the view that the human intellective soul is a single, separate, eternal, substantial form, a distinct celestial intelligence. This human soul, operating like a great computer, processes sensory data of each individual and, in turn, assists each human being to formulate concepts and thereby to think abstractly. Human beings, each with a body, determined by a mortal sensitive soul called a cogitative soul, are defined as human by an association with the single separate and immortal human intellective soul or mind. Critics objected to this "communitarian" view that humans have no independent individual capacity to think abstractly and no personal immortality. The latter view moved the eighth session of the 1513 Fifth Lateran Council to proclaim the immortality of the individual human soul and to direct philosophers to demonstrate the personal immortality of the human soul.

Thomism. Many Renaissance thinkers followed the view of Thomas Aquinas (1225–1274). From this viewpoint, each substance, including human beings, has a single substantial form, which is its essence or nature and determines its species. Each substantial form is complete and fixed; each determines a particular kind of body and empowers its natural activities. All the substantial forms together constitute a hierarchical order in the universe, the great chain of being. The definitive substantial form of each human being is a rational soul, which, created by God and infused in the body, is the highest grade of substantial form of terrestrial beings. Aquinas devoted a lengthy section of his *Summa theologica* to a detailed study of the nature and powers of man, their relation to each other and to the divine, giving human beings a pride of place. Still, Aquinas presents a radical discontinuity between lower grades of being and human beings, who, by their distinctive nature (a like immortal spiritual substantial form) have natural dominion over all lower grades of being.

Naturalism and Human Reason. Distinctive Renaissance conceptions of humanity developed in reaction to these two views. A dramatic example is Pietro Pomponazzi (1462–1525), who, in his *De immortalitate animae* (On the immortality of the soul; 1516), contends, in opposition to the Averroists' collective conception of humanity, that a human soul, essential to humanity, must belong to each human being individually. But he also objected to the Thomistic supernaturalist conception of humanity, the ultimate end of which is beatitude (contemplation of God), which requires personal immortality. Pomponazzi claims instead that, according to Aristotle, human beings are continuous with the rest of nature, so man (not God) generates man. He argues further that humans, like nonhuman animals, must be mortal, since all terrestrial creatures are subject to the fundamental Aristotelian law of nature that

what is generated must be corrupted. Pomponazzi claims that human reason is what distinguishes humanity as a species. This is analogous to the distinctive intellective power of the celestial intelligences, which reason abstractly and reflect upon themselves. It makes man, relatively immortal in relation to his "angelic" rational capacity, though he is absolutely mortal. Human beings are elevated and ennobled by humanity's defining feature, the capacity to think. It is this superior power that permits human beings to direct their own will as moral agents. Pomponazzi argues further that immortality is not required for rewards and punishment, for the achievement of virtue is its own reward and vice its own punishment. His analysis points toward a new naturalistic Renaissance conception of the dignity of human beings.

Reason and Skepticism. Faith in the power of human reason to direct human action and to determine beliefs if correctly guided inspired new approaches to logic as a tool for investigating and communicating truth. This faith also prompted a claim by Protestants, that individual human beings can interpret scripture correctly. But closely following this concept of man were views of the degradation of human beings and skepticism. Some claimed that passions overtake reason too easily and too often. A contrary opinion came from Pierre Charron (1541–1603), a skeptic, who argues that natural powers common to all animals lead natural creatures aright. It is reason, he contends, distinctive to human beings and prone to error, that, in fact, inspires humans with inordinate desires and leads them astray. Although in Charron's view human reason is irreconcilably flawed, we find here another Renaissance theme of Pomponazzi, the continuity and common dignity of all of nature.

Naturalism, Body, and Mind. Jacopo Zabarella (1533–1589) also objected to Averroist monopsychism. Further, he rejected the Thomistic views that, like each living thing, each human being has a single substantial form, that is, a rational soul, and that the perfection of souls, where the higher contains all powers of the lower, defines grades of being. He argues, first, that this entails the absurd view that a plant reproduces by a vegetative soul, a cow by a sensitive soul, and a human being by a rational soul; but like powers must belong to like substantial forms. Further, all animals, including human beings, are living, sensitive creatures with some difference that places each in its species. From this viewpoint, Zabarella, stressing the continuity of nature, distinguishes in each animal common substantial forms of the body, such as blood, bones, flesh, and nerves, and three souls, a vegetative soul that makes a creature a living thing, a sensitive soul that makes it an animal, and a specific form or soul, which determines its distinctive nature and so places it in its species. The specific form of each human being is a human mind. This latter claim is tied to the view that humanity is determined, in each individual, by a mind that has in itself purely intellective powers, that is, abstractive, reflective, and reasoning powers that operate without the use of any bodily organ. The view espoused here that a human being has a *pluralistic* structure, a body that is essentially like that of other animals, and a supervening specific form or soul that is a purely intellective mind, was a common late Renaissance view of what a human being is. It was associated with a variety of pluralistic analyses of the composition of human beings. The most common view of Renaissance pluralists (for example, Gregor Reisch, Fillipo Fabri, Philipp Melanchthon, Francesco Piccolomini) was that humanity is identified with composite individuals, where each human being has an immortal soul caused by God, and a body that is caused by parents and that has a distinct corporeal form or a distinct organic soul.

All these Renaissance perspectives provided a foundation for seventeenth-century analyses that identify a human being as an entity composed of a body, continuous with other natural things, and a distinct purely intellective mind. This view was common, for example, to the very different theorctical accounts of René Descartes and Pierre Gassendi.

See also **Dignity of Man**; **Immortality of the Soul**; *and biographies of Pomponazzi, Zabarella, and Charron.*

BIBLIOGRAPHY

Primary Works

Cassirer, Ernst, Paul Oskar Kristeller, and John Herman Randall, eds. *Renaissance Philosophy of Man.* Chicago, 1948. Translated selections with commentary. Includes Pietro Pomponazzi, "On the Immortality of the Soul." Translated by W. H. Hay. Pages 257–381.

Davies, Stevie, ed. *Renaissance Views of Man.* New York, 1979. Translated selections with commentary.

Secondary Works

The Cambridge History of Renaissance Philosophy. Edited by Charles B. Schmitt, Quentin Skinner, Eckhard Kessler, and Jill Kraye. Cambridge, U.K., 1988. Discussion of Renaissance humanism, logic, natural philosophy, psychology, humanistic disciplines, etc. Extensive bibliography and biobibliographies.

Copenhaver, Brian P., and Charles B. Schmitt. *Renaissance Philosophy.* New York, 1992. Extensive bibliography.

Kristeller, Paul Oskar. *Renaissance Thought: The Classic, Scholastic, and Humanist Strains.* New York, 1961.

McConica, James, Anthony Quinton, Anthony Kenny, and Peter Burke. *Renaissance Thinkers.* Oxford and New York, 1993.

Schmitt, Charles B. *Aristotle and the Renaissance.* Cambridge, Mass., 1983.

EMILY MICHAEL

HUMOR. During the Renaissance the word "humor" referred to one of the four humors (blood, phlegm, choler, and melancholy) believed to determine the state of health and the temperament of a human being. This does not mean that "humor" in our sense of the word did not exist, or was not important; on the contrary, in some ways it was more important than it is today. But it is also extremely difficult to discuss, for a number of reasons.

Theory and Practice of Laughter. First, it is very difficult to generalize about humor in a period that covered several centuries, many parts of Europe, and numerous languages. No generalizations would suffice to cover the widely differing social groups involved. It would be highly misleading to say, for instance, "a Renaissance woman would have laughed if. . . ."

Second, the general assumption today seems to be that laughter is an agreeable condiment to, but not an essential ingredient of, human existence. Many Renaissance intellectuals would have taken exception; the Aristotelian definition of man as a being capable of laughter (from *De partibus animalium*) was frequently quoted, and the nature and function of laughter were discussed suprisingly often. Drama theorists attempted, with or without the support of Aristotle, to define comedy on stage; rhetoricians followed Cicero's lead in stressing the use of joking to disconcert an adversary and win over a judge or an audience. Princes, including Alfonso V of Aragon, Lorenzo de' Medici, and Louis XII of France, were portrayed as witty characters able to take, as well as make, a joke, and Baldassarre Castiglione's *Il cortegiano* (*The Book of the Courtier;* 1528), one of the sixteenth century's best-sellers, includes a long section, inspired by Cicero, on the kind of joking appropriate for a courtier. Medical theorists wrangled about the nature of laughter, its "seat" in the body (heart? brain? spleen?), and its physiological manifestations. The period produced, in both drama and fiction, some of the greatest comic writers ever, and many humanists agreed with Thomas More (who made a joke on the scaffold just before his execution) and Erasmus (one of whose favorite words was *festivitas,* or "gaiety") that laughter was an essential lifeline in a difficult and often distressing world.

There are other problems, the largest of which is terminology. We know, for instance, that to Lope de Vega *comedia* simply meant "play," but how do we translate the Latin *facetia,* the German *Schwank,* or the Italian *motto? Facetia* could mean "joke" (see below), but it could also designate a serious anecdote, a moral fable, a riddle, and even a ghost story, and such examples could be multiplied.

Evidence of what made people laugh is hard to come by, and evidence can be misleading. How can we tell if a given carnival monster was intended to cause laughter or shivers of horror? Bonaventure Des Périers (1500?–1544?) once used the verb "to laugh" meaning "to have sex," and some smiling characters in Italian paintings are expressing not amusement but Christian bliss. This article will attempt only to highlight some issues in each of the following areas: public and private laughter (the marketplace, the kitchen, the humanist's study); laughter in the visual arts; and laughter in literature.

Public and Private Laughter. We know, both from surviving texts and from archival material, that public festivities, from the Middle Ages until quite recently, tended to be more frequent, more communal, and more comic than they are today. The many celebrations found in the church calendar were for everybody; making a distinction between "popular" and "elite" Renaissance humor is no longer considered tenable. Some of these occasions are still famous today, like the Bavarian Fasching, the Florentine Calendimaggio (May Day festivities), and the Venetian Carnival, but there were many others, most notably in Germany, France, Spain, and Italy. Some involved masked revelers roaming the streets (King Henry III of France, at the end of the sixteenth century, loved to join them), while others featured races of people or animals, processions, plays, or feasting. It is impossible to tell how much of these communal celebrations would today be considered comic. We do know that the late fifteenth-century Florentine carnival songs contained satirical and obscene material, and that the French *sociétés joyeuses* put on comic and satirical plays (see below).

A more obvious need for humor was apparently satisfied by the institution of the "official" fool or court jester, with his fool's costume, bauble, cap, and bells, and license to denigrate and satirize everything and everyone. Some of these fools attained literary fame, like Triboulet in France and Will Kemp and Robert Armin in England. The fool was not confined to the courts of princes; Thomas More, in England, had one in his household. But again, we have no

means of knowing how much genuine hilarity he could generate. His appearances in literature are sometimes comic, as in Shakespeare, but more often, as in Sebastian Brant's *Der Narrenschiff* (Ship of fools, 1494) and in many sixteenth- and seventeenth-century emblem books, they serve heavily didactic, rather than comic, purposes.

We do not usually expect our food to make us laugh, but during the Renaissance people sometimes did. *De honesta voluptate* (Of honorable pleasure; 1475), the period's most often reprinted "cookery book" (the author calls it a health manual), was by Bartolomeo Platina, a fifteenth-century Italian humanist. It describes how to replace the skin and feathers on a cooked peacock before putting it on the table, so that it looks alive, and then how to make it appear to breathe fire, "to make the people laugh and wonder." Such marvels were commonplace in both medieval and Renaissance cookery. At a sumptuous banquet served on the Campidoglio in Rome in 1513, numerous deer, rabbits, other animals, and game birds were served with their skins on, and there were also live rabbits hopping about the room and on the tables, "a cause of much amusement and pleasure to the people." Should we then assume that laughter and surprise are close to synonymous?

We are on firmer ground when we move from the marketplace and the kitchen to the humanist's study, because unlike carnival organizers and cooks, humanists wrote voluminously, usually in Latin, so that national and class differences were outweighed by a common language. Starting with Petrarch in the fourteenth century, humanists were voracious collectors of passages and items from classical literature, often including *facetiae.* To Cicero and Petrarch, this word meant "laugh-provoking stories and remarks," but as already mentioned, it could have other meanings in the Renaissance. Most anthologies with *facetiae* or a vernacular equivalent in the title did contain at least a high proportion of comic anecdotes and witticisms.

Unfortunately, few compilers of joke collections explain on precisely what grounds they made their choice, or why they find comic the jokes they have included. Some, like Petrarch (*Rerum memorandarum libri* [Books of memorable things], c. 1344), follow Cicero's *De oratore* closely; others, like Poggio Bracciolini (1380–1459), in his *Facetiae* (1438–1452), never mention Cicero. Antonio Beccadelli (1394–1471), also called Panormita, a well-known humanist originally from Parma, produced in 1455 a "biography" of Alfonso V of Aragon (*Alfonso V: Regis dicta ac facta* [The words and deeds of Alfonso King of Aragon]; first printed 1485), which consists entirely of "memorable" remarks made by him, most of which are not funny. The 1538 edition has marginal comments which only add to the confusion; for instance, a saying can be labeled both *Facetè* (comically) and *Grauiter* (seriously).

Until about the middle of the sixteenth century, each *facetia* collection had its own individuality. After that date the anthologies become collective in most cases. The most influential were probably Heinrich Bebel's *Facetiae* (1508–1512), and Lodovico Domenichi's *Facetie, motti, et burle* (Funny stories, one-liners, and practical jokes), many times expanded and reprinted between 1548 and the end of the century.

Not only did humanists enjoy collecting humor, they also enjoyed creating it, especially for the purpose of satire. Erasmus, whose *Colloquies* (1524) include a brief *facetia* collection ("The Fabulous Feast"), was particularly good at using humor to make satire palatable. One of his most amusing dialogues ("The Abbot and the Learned Lady") ends with the peals of laughter of the witty, erudite lady who has out-argued the crass, ignorant, and prejudiced churchman. Erasmus is probably the author of the more virulent *Julius exclusus e coelis* (Julius excluded from heaven; written 1513–1514), a satirical attack on the corruption of the papacy.

In the early sixteenth century, German humanists produced some of the period's most effective polemical satire. The most comic is probably the brilliantly witty *Epistolae obscurorum virorum* (Epistles of obscure men; 1515), a jointly authored collection of letters making fun of Ortwin Gratius of Cologne and other adversaries of Johann Reuchlin, who was trying to protect Jewish books and the Jewish intellectual tradition from Catholic persecution. Unfortunately, the hilariously bad Latin of these letters cannot be adequately translated. A German dialogue probably written by Willibald Pirckheimer, the *Eccius dedolatus* (Eck beaten into shape; 1520), lampoons Johann Eck, an adversary of Luther, in a very funny mixture of reminiscences of classical poetry with obscenity and scatology. A similar technique was used at the end of the century by a French Protestant, Pierre Viret, in his *Satyres Chrestiennes de la cuisine papale* (Christian satires on the papal kitchen; 1544).

Laughter in the Visual Arts. Many humanists, from the Italian Andrea Alciati (1492–1550) to the Hungarian Johannes Sambucus (1531–1584), compiled emblem books, which curiously enough contain almost no humor. The occasional *pictura* which looks comic to a modern reader (a fool in "official" costume smiling out of the picture, or an industrious figure sweeping debris out of an oversized heart) turns out to be transmitting a stern Christian message. Only the Dutch, according to Karel Porteman, managed to infuse emblem books with a sense of humor.

However, the biting satirical wit characteristic of the German dialogues mentioned above was also employed in graphic art, especially in Germany, where pro- and anti-Reformation Flugblätter (single-sheet pamphlets) projected comic caricatures of Luther's adversaries as animals, or of the devil using a monk as a musical instrument. Graphic satire could be either specifically focused, as in these examples, or more generally didactic, as in the illustrations to Brant's *Der Narrenschiff,* or engravings by Hieronymus Cock and many others. Such visual moralizing appears characteristic of the northern Renaissance. The crowded canvases of Pieter Brueghel the Elder (c. 1530–1569), cluttered with peasants, children, or fools, are probably intended to transmit a faithful picture of contemporary life rather than to provoke laughter, and the charming lovers disporting themselves on the haywain or in the Edenic garden of Hieronymus Bosch (1450–1516) are delivering a stern warning about the evils of godlessness.

But there is plenty of playful, nondidactic humor in Renaissance art. Giulio Romano (1492/99–1546), decorating the Palazzo del Te in Mantua in the late 1520s, painted the walls of a small room with lifelike giant figures who appear to be pulling walls and pillars down upon the room's occupants, a striking example of the witty trompe l'oeil very popular at the time. After the discovery of ancient Roman wall painting in the early sixteenth century, there was a long vogue for "grotesques," decorative motifs for walls and ceilings which still delight visitors to Italian palaces and museums. Their fantastic human and animal figures, with leaves, flowers, and curlicues where we would expect limbs, are integrated into surreal but beautifully symmetrical designs.

Many Renaissance painters added witty touches to their basically serious compositions, and the occasional maverick enjoyed playing with the conventions he was using. In Italy, Giuseppe Arcimboldo (c. 1530–1593) composed portraits in which the face is built up entirely from fruit, or from flowers, fish, or books; from a distance, each gives the illusion of a conventional portrait. Sculpture, too, can be witty or grotesquely comic; the sixteenth-century Boboli Gardens in Florence contain a comic statue of a fat dwarf sitting astride a giant turtle, and an ingenious grotto, made entirely of concrete but looking eerily like an underwater cave with shells, seaweed, and sheep.

Figures who laugh outright are rare, in painting of this or any other period, but the Dutch painter Jan Steen (c. 1626–1679) depicted his own laughing face as a mockery on the painted scene in which he is taking part.

Humor in Literature. The period's great comic writers are treated in detail elsewhere in this encyclopedia, but it is worth stressing how much of the literature of the fifteenth and sixteenth centuries is comic. To take theater first, carnival-related dramatic performances had developed in all European countries by the sixteenth century: satirical *sotties* (fools' plays) in France; the Fastnachtspiel (Carnival play) in Germany; *komedia rybaltowska* (crude realistic comedy) in Poland; and so on. Some of this theater was politically oriented (Louis XII [ruled 1498–1515] in France encouraged it because he liked to know what was going on), while some of it was just variation on the perennial themes of trickster and victim; adulterous wife and deceived husband; or quarrels among barflies, fishwives, and assorted rogues. Most of these plays are anonymous, but a few well-known poets wrote farces, among them Guillaume Coquillart (c. 1450–1510) and Pierre Gringore (1475?–1538) in France, and John Heywood (1497?–1580) in England. In the sixteenth century a different kind of farce developed in Italy: the commedia dell'arte, whose actors improvised on schematic scenari, and whose plots varied from the fairly realistic to the wildly fantastic. Descendants of the characters Pantaleone, Zanni, and others can still be found in literature and cinema today.

Many humanists hoped this kind of theater, which they considered a regrettable survival of the Middle Ages, would be rendered obsolete by the new humanist comedy in imitation of the ancient Roman playwrights Plautus and (more often) Terence, but in fact the two continued to coexist quite happily. Humanist comedy, usually involving five acts and bourgeois characters, spread from Italy all over Europe, and produced some masterpieces, including Machiavelli's obscene and amoral *Mandragola* (1518?) in Italy, and Nicholas Udall's *Ralph Roister Doister* (1553?), a brilliant adaptation of Plautus's *Miles gloriosus* (Braggart soldier), in England. The great age of dramatic comedy, especially in England, France, and Spain, was the seventeenth century, but sixteenth-century theorists discussed its rules and conventions at length, and some sixteenth-century Italian and English plays are still performed today.

Comic poetry is another enormous topic. Mock-epic was a specifically Italian Renaissance genre. Luigi Pulci's *Morgante* (1481) has numerous burlesque elements, Ludovico Ariosto's *Orlando furioso* (1516) is a chivalric romance with isolated witty touches, and Teofilo Folengo's *Baldus* (1517), written in Macaronic (a mixture of Latin and Italian), is a strange combination of genuine epic adventure and pastiche. Jan Kochanowski (1530–1584), Poland's best-known Renaissance poet, wrote a mock-epic called *Szachy* (The chess game) around 1564, but there are no examples in England or France.

Burlesque poetry took various forms, from the Italian *capitoli* by Francesco Berni (1497/98–1535) and others, many of which are explicitly sexual, to the *Folastries* (Frolics; 1553) of France's star poet, Pierre de Ronsard (1524–1585), also largely obscene. Erotic poetry was also written in Latin, for instance by Janus Secundus (*Basia* [Kisses]; 1533), and in the seventeenth century John Donne and other "metaphysical" poets often combined wit with mild eroticism. The mid-sixteenth century saw a vogue for making fun of the conventions of Petrarchan love poetry; France's Joachim du Bellay wrote a long poem *Contre les Pétrarquistes* (Against the Petrarchans), and later in England Walter Ralegh made fun of Marlowe's pastoral poetry in "The Nymph's Reply," and Shakespeare contradicted Petrarch in several sonnets (130: "My mistress' eyes are nothing like the sun").

Most of this poetry is less well known than more "serious" productions like Ronsard's hymns and sonnets and Edmund Spenser's *Faerie Queene* (1590). Perhaps only in narrative fiction is Renaissance comedy valued as highly as its tragedy. Rabelais and Cervantes are still read today, although Rabelais's unique combination of riotous humor with a serious humanist message is not often appreciated. The picaresque novel originated in Spain, with the anonymous *Vida de Lazarillo de Tormes* (1554), which is only incidentally comic; later examples include the masterpiece of Elizabethan prose fiction, Thomas Nashe's *The Unfortunate Traveller* (1594), which is by turns comic, dramatic, and satirical.

Apart from Rabelais, France specialized in comic short stories rather than in full-length narratives. Numerous collections, most notably by Bonaventure Des Périers, Nicolas de Troyes, and Noël Du Fail, contain mostly humorous anecdotes, many from Italian sources; even Marguerite de Navarre, the pious sister of King Francis I, included several comic stories in her sixteenth-century *Heptaméron,* inspired by Boccaccio's *Decameron* (1353). In the early seventeenth century Béroalde de Verville produced an almost exclusively obscene collection, the *Moyen de Parvenir* (How to succeed; c. 1612).

Italy was also fond of the short story, which was not necessarily comic, but England seems to have preferred the "jest," or very short anecdote with a punchline. The so-called jestbooks grew out of both the humanist *facetiae* mentioned above, and the comic "biography," whose best-known representative is the German *Till Eulenspiegel* (1515), soon translated into many European languages, including Polish, and known in England as Howleglas. Eulenspiegel lacks charm for most modern readers, who find him crude and gratuitously scatological, but he was tremendously popular, and a model for later English jest "biographies" like those of Richard Tarlton and John Scogin in the seventeenth century. Jestbooks also flourished in Germany in the later sixteenth century, and there are a few Italian and Spanish examples.

This all-too-brief sampling of literary humor is not intended to gloss over the difficulties inherent in discussing literary genres in this period. How should we classify the (occasionally witty) Spanish *Celestina* (1499) by Fernando de Rojas, a narrative written in dialogue form and numerous acts? Or Anton Francesco Doni's *La zucca* (The gourd; 1551–1552), an unstructured mixture of proverbs, letters, stories, and jokes? Should we count Teofilo Folengo's *Baldus* (1517) as poetry or as narrative fiction? And it would not be possible to separate entirely satirical humor, black humor, wit, and simple playfulness, even if we all agreed on the definition of those terms.

We may have a general impression that Renaissance humor is more likely to be satirical, unkind, or even cruel than today's humor; Rabelais's readers are apparently supposed to laugh at scenes of torture and violent death, and in one of the Latin *facetiae* collections the spectators laugh when a condemned criminal is castrated instead of executed. But apart from the problems of knowing when we are expected to laugh, how are we to distinguish among the very different kinds of laughter provoked by Platina's fire-breathing peacock, Hans Holbein's depiction of Brant's foolish scholar, Romano's tumbling giants, and Don Quixote tilting at windmills? Much more research will be required before we can answer these questions.

See also **Bawdy, Elizabethan; Drama,** *subentry on* **Erudite Comedy; Facezie;** *and biographies of figures mentioned in this entry.*

BIBLIOGRAPHY

Primary Works

Best, Thomas W. *Eccius dedolatus: A Reformation Satire.* Lexington, Ky., 1971.

Bowen, Barbara C., ed. *One Hundred Renaissance Jokes: An Anthology.* Birmingham, Ala., 1988.

Erasmus, Desiderius. *The Colloquies of Erasmus.* Translated by Craig R. Thompson. Chicago, 1965.

Platina. *De honesta voluptate: The First Dated Cookery Book.* Translated by Elizabeth Buermann Andrews. St. Louis, Mo., 1967.

Zall, Paul M., ed. *A Hundred Merry Tales, and Other English Jestbooks of the Fifteenth and Sixteenth Centuries.* Lincoln, Neb., 1963.

Secondary Works

Bakhtin, Mikhail. *Rabelais and His World.* Translated by Hélène Iswolsky. Cambridge, Mass., 1968.

Barolsky, Paul. *Infinite Jest: Wit and Humor in Italian Renaissance Art.* Columbia, Mo., 1978.

Herrick, Marvin T. *Comic Theory in the Sixteenth Century.* Urbana, Ill., 1964.

Lavin, Marilyn Aronberg. "The Joy of the Bridegroom's Friend: Smiling Faces in Fra Filippo, Raphael, and Leonardo." In *Art the Ape of Nature: Studies in Honor of H. W. Janson.* Edited by Moshe Barasch and Lucy Freeman Sandler. New York, 1981. Pages 193–210.

Ménager, Daniel. *La Renaissance et le rire.* Paris, 1995.

Porteman, Karel. "The Emblem as 'Genus Jocosum': Theory and Praxis (Jacob Cats and Roemer Visscher)." *Emblematica* 8 (1994): 243–260.

Scribner, Robert W. *For the Sake of Simple Folk: Popular Propaganda for the German Reformation.* Cambridge, U.K., 1981.

Westermann, Mariët. "How Was Jan Steen Funny? Strategies and Functions of Comic Painting in the Seventeenth Century." In *A Cultural History of Humor: From Antiquity to the Present Day.* Edited by Jan Bremmer and Herman Roodenburg. Malden, Mass., 1997. Pages 134–178.

BARBARA C. BOWEN

HUNGARY. [This entry includes two subentries, one on the history of Hungary in the Renaissance and the other on artists active in Hungary.]

Hungary in the Renaissance

During the Middle Ages, the cultural centers of Hungary were the episcopal sees. From the fourteenth century on, Buda, though lacking a bishopric, became the real focus of cultural life because of the royal presence. This was most evident during the rule of Matthias Corvinus (1458–1490), whose splendid court became a center of Europe's scholarly and artistic elite.

The Circle of Vitéz. The concept of the "Hungarian Quattrocento," the fifteenth-century Hungarian Renaissance, which is frequently regarded as the most glorious period of Hungary's history, is closely tied to the name of Johannes Vitéz of

Zredna (1408–1472). First in his episcopal see in Várad, and later as archbishop of Esztergom and primate of Hungary, Vitéz was a fountainhead and a disseminator of humanist learning. His library was envied and imitated by Hungary's aristocrats. As a founder of the university in Pozsony (Academia Istropolitana) and a patron of artists and scholars all over Europe, Vitéz contributed to humanist learning far beyond the borders of Hungary. Born in Slavonia, Vitéz was the archetype of that Hungarian Renaissance personality who, whether originally Croatian, German, Italian, Polish, or Romanian, had made the Buda court flower. A wealthy prelate, Vitéz began sending his relatives and protégés (among them his nephew, Janus Pannonius, 1434–1472) to study in Italy at his own expense.

Vitéz, who had served under Johannes Hunyadi (c. 1387–1456), the national hero and regent of Hungary, was instrumental in the election of Hunyadi's son, Matthias Corvinus, to the Hungarian throne. He also can be credited with the development of the Royal Chancery, which, modeled on the papal court grew from a modest beginning to function much like the ones in Italy by the middle of the fifteenth century. Having served as envoy to a number of European courts, Vitéz knew and corresponded with, among others, Enea Silvio Piccolomini (later Pope Pius II) and Pope Nicholas V. His *Epistolae*, collected by Paulus Ivanich, in or about 1451, were famous for their tact and style. They are compelling evidence of a sophisticated humanist court in Buda.

The newly built royal palace and Matthias's famous library attracted such Italian historians as Galeotto Marzio (1427–1497?), who also excelled in astronomy; Antonio Bonfini (1425?–1502) and Pietro Ranzano (1428–1492), each of whom had written a history of Hungary; the German astronomer Regiomontanus (Johann Müller, 1436–1476); Giovanni Dalmata (Ivan Duknović, 1466–1514), the great Croatian sculptor; as well as dozens of lesser-known humanists, artists, and artisans. Many foreign authors dedicated their work to Matthias, who was considered a generous supporter of the arts. The royal court's fame at one point even tempted Marsilio Ficino to move to Buda.

The Role of Latin. In terms of local achievements, it must be remembered that in Hungary, literature, and in a broader sense, writing, from the tenth to the fifteenth century was in Latin; from the fifteenth to the seventeenth, it was bilingual. Although the majority of the population—having come from the Pontic steppes—spoke an Ugric language (related to Vogul and Ostyak, now spoken in western Siberia), for many centuries Hungary's religious, administrative, and cultural activities were conducted in Latin. Hungary was in fact the last in Europe to give up Latin as its acquired second language. Hungary was a multinational state, and Latin, no one's native tongue, successfully bridged the problems of administrative communication. As opposed to Italy, the vernacular was not practiced in humanist circles, probably because the humanists themselves belonged to different ethnic groups. Even during the high Renaissance, therefore, Latin works frequently surpassed the Hungarian ones, both in quantity and in quality.

The centers of Latin were the royal court, the episcopal sees, the monasteries, and, to a degree, the courts of the aristocrats. The Latin alphabet was found to be suitable for the notation of Hungarian sounds, and it was used in translating legends, hymns, and the like for beginners and for nuns whose education did not include Latin. (Beginning in the seventeenth century, Latin represented the language of national self-assertion against German.)

Ever since the twelfth century, students from Hungary attended Italian, French, English, and later, German universities. In fact, the first recorded undergraduate of Oxford was "Nicholao, Clerico de Hungaria," who studied there from 1193 to 1196. His expenses were defrayed by Richard the Lion-Hearted (1157–1199), who was distantly related to the Hungarian king. In the fifteenth century, one of the students, Janus Pannonius, achieved international fame as a poet and politician, and he contributed significantly to his European contemporaries' enthusiastic view of Hungary. The wealthier students attended the universities of Padua and Bologna, the rest chose Vienna and Cracow. After completing their studies, some students remained as faculty members at their alma maters; the majority, however, returned to Hungary and became part of the growing state and regional administration, or gained lucrative sees.

The beginnings of the Hungarian Renaissance go back to the rule of Sigismund of Luxembourg (1395–1437). It flowered during the reign of Matthias Corvinus, while the Jagiellon period, that is, the rule of Władysław II Jagiello (1490–1516) and his son, Louis II (1516–1526), was already marked by decline. Nonetheless, during the Jagiellon decades a much larger group came into contact with humanist learning than ever had before. Several young scholars joined the *Sodalitas Danubiana,* inspired by Conrad

Celtis (1459–1508), with whom some had studied in Ingolstadt. This group kept in touch with their humanist colleagues in Poland and in Austria.

The Effects of Mohács. The Battle of Mohács (29 August 1526), and the subsequent Turkish and Habsburg domination that split the country into three parts, changed the character of Hungarian Renaissance humanism. Six months after the defeat, Stephan Brodericus (Brodarić, 1470?–1539) published *De conflictu Hungarorum cum Turcis ad Mohatz verissima descriptio,* a vivid report of the events of that fateful day when Hungary lost its independence for many centuries to come. Excavations at the site of the battle, conducted in the twentieth century, proved Brodericus to be an astute observer and truthful narrator.

The Mohács disaster polarized the humanists. Many of them, having lost their feudatories or sees, joined their western colleagues in becoming paid decorations of individual feudal courts, or serving the simultaneously elected Hungarian kings, Johannes Zápolya (1487–1540) and Ferdinand I of Habsburg (1503–1564), often switching their loyalties from one to the other. Brodericus cast his fortune with Zápolya, while Nicholaus Olahus (1493–1568), chose the Habsburgs. After the death of Zápolya, the ensuing Habsburg reign of the parts free of the Turks lasted for four hundred years.

Already at the beginning of the Turkish occupation, the priceless volumes of the *Bibliotheca Corviniana* (Corvinus's library), hoarded on Suleiman's galleys, were shipped to Constantinople. The once fabulous capital city of Buda became impoverished and depopulated. Its previous splendor became the subject of authors in exile, as in Nicholaus Olahus's *Hungaria* (1536), written in the Low Countries.

Reformation and Counter-Reformation. The spread of Reformation ideologies gave birth to a broader use of the vernacular: from the 1530s, Latin and Hungarian works appeared side by side, frequently in the oeuvre of the same authors. The first *bella historia,* "Historia regis Volter" (The tale of King Volter), by Pál Istvánffy (d. 1553), was written in 1539. This verse epic treats Giovanni Boccaccio's tale number one hundred from the *Decameron,* but the author used Petrarch's Latin translation as his source.

Slowly, the traditions of Erasmus and Philipp Melanchthon (1497–1560) replaced Greco-Latin traditions. In addition, the country's fierce resistance to the Turks gave birth to a new literary genre, written in Hungarian: songs about battles. Its most famous

241

representatives were Bálint Balassi (1554–1594) and Sebestyén Tinódi (1505/10?–1556). A milestone in the development of Hungarian writing was Johannes Sylvester's *Grammatica Hungaro-latina* (published in 1539). Péter Bornemissza's translation of Sophocles's *Electra* (1558), an adaptation with many original features, testifies to the high level of the vernacular during that period.

In the sixteenth century, much of western writing was devoted to the discovery of the New World and to the scientific tasks connected to navigation, mapmaking, and the like. Although they did not participate in the western discoveries, the Verantius family should be mentioned. Antonius Verantius (Antun Vrančić, 1505–1573), of Dalmatian origin, spoke Italian, Hungarian, and German, in addition to Latin and his native Croatian. He became not just one of the most important primates in the history of the Hungarian church, but also a *locumtenens* (personal representative) of the king. Between 1555 and 1568, he made several ambassadorial trips to the Turkish court. He was a codiscoverer of the *Ancyranum monumentum* (the Ankara monument, a copy of the political testament of Emperor Augustus engraved on a column), a find usually attributed to the Flemish diplomat Augier Ghislain de Busbecq, although de Busbecq in his letters, published in 1589, credited the entire delegation with the discovery. Verantius's diaries were first published in his *Opera,* written in Latin and Italian, comprising twelve volumes.

Verantius's nephew, Faustus Verantius (Faust Vrančić, 1551–1617), bishop of Csanád, was, after Leonardo da Vinci, the most important inventor of his time. His *Machinae novae* (1596 and 1605) places him in the forefront in physics and engineering. The work contains forty-nine exquisite engravings, with detailed descriptions of fifty-six machines, mills, boats, bridges, and other technical devices. His *homo volans,* the flying man, features a parachute jump. Some scholars claim that Verantius actually tested his device by jumping off a tower in Venice. That would make him one of the pioneers of both flying and parachuting. The explanations in the volume are given in five languages: Latin, Italian, Spanish, French, and German. Verantius is also the author of *Dictionarium quinque nobilissimarum Europae linguarum, Latinae, Italicae, Germanicae, Dalmaticae et Ungaricae* (Dictionary of the five most noble European languages, Latin, Italian, German, Dalmatian, and Hungarian), second only to Ambrosio Calepino's famous Latin-Italian dictionary. Verantius's dictionary was expanded to contain eleven languages when published in 1590, eighty years after its author's death. It was published in Prague in 1605 because Verantius had served under Emperor Rudolf II.

In the second half of the sixteenth century, the Counter-Reformation, led by Nicholaus Olahus, then primate of Hungary and thus the head of Hungarian Roman Catholicism, reintegrated a part of Hungary into the Italianate world. However, in Transylvania, which enjoyed a quasi-independent status due to its provisional agreements with the Turks, Protestantism, in all its variants, gained ground rapidly. By 1557, the Diet at Torda asserted the freedom of religious practices, and the scale was tipping in favor of Protestantism. First Lutheranism, then Calvinism, and by 1571, Unitarianism, were recognized in Transylvania, whose constitution granted equality to Hungarians, Seklers, and Saxons living there. This liberal attitude was unparalleled in contemporary Europe.

In the sixteenth century, Hungarian texts were primarily composed for theological or political purposes. Also, the Protestants chose drama as a theologically potent genre. It is noteworthy that of the twelve Renaissance dramas written in Hungarian, all but one are in prose. They tend toward realism, each either a *comoedia* or *tragoedia,* designations that appear in the titles. A popular vehicle is the disputation, almost exclusively represented by Protestant authors. While the century also witnessed heated discussions over practical criticism, such as the language and style of Dante's poetry, Hungarian humanists, who a century before would have passionately joined the debate, were largely absent, owing to almost a hundred years of battles, raids, and impoverishment. The greatest Hungarian literary achievements of this period were translations into Hungarian, and, above all, the poetry of Bálint Balassi.

During the many decades of changing fronts, there was little chance to establish permanent printing presses, and most humanists had their works published in Italy, Poland, or Germany. Later, however, the Hungarian printing presses appeared as the crucial vehicles of Hungarian civilization. Serving various religious denominations, they also replaced the lost national institutions, and kept humanist ideas and letters alive in a dismembered country.

See also biographies of figures mentioned in this entry.

BIBLIOGRAPHY

Birnbaum, Marianna D. "Humanism in Hungary." In *Renaissance Humanism: Foundations, Forms, and Legacy.* Edited by Albert Rabil, Jr. Vol. 2, *Humanism beyond Italy.* Philadelphia, 1988. Pages 293–334.

Csapodi, Csaba, and Klára Csapodi-Gárdonyi, eds. *Bibliotheca Corviniana, 1490–1990*. Budapest, Hungary, 1981.

Matthias Corvinus und die Renaissance in Ungarn: Schallaburg '82 [Ausstellung], 8. Mai–1. November 1982. Schallaburg, Austria, 1982.

Vitéz de Zredna, Johannes. *Opera quae supersunt*. Edited by István Boronkai, Budapest, Hungary, 1980.

MARIANNA D. BIRNBAUM

Art in Hungary

The introduction of Renaissance art and culture into Hungary is primarily associated with the patronage of Matthias Corvinus, king of Hungary, and his humanistic court circles. During his reign (1458–1490), Hungary reached its largest territorial expansion, incorporating present-day Hungary, Upper Hungary (now Slovakia and western Ukraine), Transylvania, Slovenia, and parts of Austria. From the 1470s onward, its capital Buda evolved into an early center for the reception and dissemination of Italian Renaissance art, particularly of the Florentine quattrocento (fifteenth century).

The king's first major artistic project was the rebuilding of the royal palace at Buda (1476ff.). Directed by the Florentine architect Chimenti di Leonardo Camicia, the reconstruction included the creation of a series of grand courtyards partially enclosed by arcades surmounted by columned loggias, and featuring sculptures of Greek and Roman deities alongside those of Corvinus himself and members of his family. The sculptural decor was executed by a group of Dalmatian carvers supervised by Ivan Dukhovnić of Trogir, known in Italy as Giovanni Dalmata, and followed the style of the Florentine artists Bernardo Rossellino and Benedetto da Maiano. Contemporary accounts also mention a landscaped Renaissance garden accentuated by a fish pond, labyrinth, and marble villa. A few years later, the royal castle and summer palace at Visegrád, about thirty miles upriver from Buda, underwent similar modifications. Among the most significant artworks to survive from the now-ruined buildings are a fragmented fountain bearing the arms of the king, and initially surmounted by a figure of Hercules, and the so-called Madonna of Visegrád, a lunette-shaped tympanum from the castle chapel depicting the Virgin and Child (Esztergom, Museum of Christian Art).

During the last two decades of his reign Matthias Corvinus devoted a considerable part of his resources to assembling the so-called Bibliotheca Corvina, a library of approximately 1,000 codices, and one of the four largest in fifteenth-century Europe. The books were commissioned from both Florentine illuminators, such as Attavante Attavanti, Gherardo

Art in Hungary. Altarpiece by Andrea Ferrucci, Bakócz Chapel, Esztergom Cathedral, 1506–1519. COURTESY HUNGARIAN NATIONAL TOURIST OFFICE, BUDAPEST/PHOTOGRAPH BY ATTILA MUDROK

di Giovanni, and Boccardino Vecchio, and from a workshop of copyists established at the royal palace of Buda. The volumes bore witness to the king's aesthetic, humanistic, and dynastic interests and ambitions. On folio 1v of the so-called Philostratus-Codex, for example, a medallion of Corvinus appears in conjunction with those of Roman emperors and of Apollo defeating Marsyas. All frame a classicizing niche containing the dedication to the "invincible king," and surmounting a frieze of fighting centaurs, a possible allusion to Corvinus's recent victory over Austria (c. 1487–1490; Budapest, Oszágos Széchenyi Könyvtár, Cod. Lat. 417).

While some projects begun by Corvinus, including the royal palace at Buda, were continued after his death by his successor, Vladislav Jagiello II (1490–1506), all activities in the Bibliotheca Corvina were stopped and the local workshops closed. Probably the most important commission of the period of Jagiellonian rulership (1490–1526) was the Bakócz Chapel in Esztergom Cathedral, the first ecclesiastical building in Hungary designed entirely in Renaissance style and detail. The edifice was begun in 1506 by Thomas Bakócz, archbishop of Esztergom, and is built almost completely of red Hungarian marble. The interior space is articulated by fluted corner pilasters, a continuous entablature bearing the dedicatory inscription, and on the upper level, by lunettes featuring circular windows, as well as medallion-decorated pendentives that initially supported a now-lost coffered dome illuminated by a lantern. Among the original furnishings is an elaborate retable of Carrara marble, executed in 1519 by Andrea Ferrucci of Florence. In its centralizing design and use of a pendentive dome, the Bakócz Chapel is indebted to the chapel type first pioneered by Filippo Brunelleschi on the Old Sacristy in S. Lorenzo, Florence (1421ff.), and later emulated by Antonio Rossellino and Giuliano da Sangallo in the later decades of the Florentine quattrocento. During the sixteenth century, the Bakócz Chapel became the fountainhead of a whole series of similar buildings in central and eastern Europe, especially in Poland, with Bartolommeo Berrecci's Sigismund Chapel on the south side of Cracow cathedral as their most prominent example (1517–1533). Among the first patrons in the kingdom of Hungary to follow Bakócz in the commissioning of his own Renaissance-style mausoleum was the canon János Lázói, who in 1512 added a rectangular chapel to the north side of Alba Iulia (Gyulafehérvár) cathedral in Transylvania. The exterior decoration largely consists of motifs appropriated from Renaissance art in Lombardy, but its interior, featuring an elaborate Gothic net vault, testifies to the persistence of local building traditions in the solution of certain architectural problems.

Following the victory of the Ottoman Turks at Mohács (1526), and their subsequent capture of Buda (1541), the kingdom of Hungary was divided into three parts, with the central areas being integrated into the Ottoman Empire, and the northwestern regions falling under Habsburg rule (Royal Hungary), while Protestant Transylvania became a satellite principality of the Turks. The Renaissance style continued to be popular in both Transylvania and Royal Hungary well into the seventeenth century; works of art characteristic of these later years included funerary monuments, which were frequently accentuated by columned architectural frames. Because of the Turkish threat in both regions, considerable efforts were made to construct new castles or fortify old ones, often with the help of skilled Italian architects. Chief among the fortification specialists were Guilio and Ottavio Baldigara, who during the last decades of the sixteenth and the early seventeenth centuries built a series of centrally planned castles with corner bastions, including the pentagonal fort (1569–1573) at Szatmár (now Satu Mare, Romania) and a hexagonal example (1583–1588) at Érsekújvár.

BIBLIOGRAPHY

Feuer-Tóth, Rósza. *Renaissance Architecture in Hungary.* Budapest, 1977.

Matthias Corvinus und die Renaissance in Ungarn 1458–1541. Exhibition catalog, Schallaburg. Vienna, 1982.

Mazal, Otto. *Königliche Bücherliebe: Die Bibliothek des Matthias Corvinus.* Graz, Austria, 1990.

ACHIM TIMMERMANN

HURTADO DE MENDOZA, DIEGO (1504–1575), Spanish poet, historian, diplomat. Son of Count Iñigo López de Mendoza, the first captain-general of the newly incorporated Moorish kingdom of Granada (1492), the young Diego grew up in a multicultural environment of Spanish civilization, Arab culture, and the Greek and Latin classics. He entered the diplomatic service for Charles I of Spain (Charles V of the Holy Roman Empire) in the early 1520s, traveling for the emperor to Italy, North Africa, and England.

It was during these formative years (1526–1537) that Hurtado de Mendoza became close friends with Juan Boscán and Garcilaso de la Vega, two other famous poets from Spain's Renaissance. Although Boscán and Garcilaso are rightly credited with the introduction of Italianate meters (the royal octave, the canzone, the sonnet, and tercets) into Spanish poetry, Hurtado de Mendoza was also producing Italianate verses, as well as poetry of classical inspiration from the Greek Anthology (a collection of ancient Greek poems first compiled in the tenth century), Ovid, Claudian, and Virgil. His moral epistles in imitation of Horace are especially noteworthy, as are his renditions of poems by the neo-Latin writers Andrea Alciati, Michele Marullo, Celio Calcagnini, and Angelo Poliziano.

In 1538 Hurtado de Mendoza began a fifteen-year Italian sojourn that included representing the emperor at the initial sessions of the Council of Trent (1545–1546) and serving as military governor of Siena (1547–1552). He eventually lost this city to the French and was forced to flee the country. He returned to Spain in 1553 and entered the service of King Philip II, Charles's son.

In 1568 Hurtado de Mendoza traveled to Granada to chronicle the protracted rebellion (1568–1571) of the Moriscos, the Christianized Arab population that still formed the vast majority of Granada's inhabitants. His annals later became the famous history *Guerra de Granada* (War of Granada). The last years of his life were spent organizing his vast collection of Roman coins, Arab codices, and the classics, which he donated to Philip's new royal library at the Escorial. His own poetry did not appear in complete form until 1610, while *Guerra de Granada* was not published until 1627. Nevertheless, these printed versions of Hurtado de Mendoza's major works solidified his reputation as the most versatile Renaissance humanist in Spanish letters.

BIBLIOGRAPHY

Darst, David H. *Diego Hurtado de Mendoza*. Boston, 1987.
Spivakovsky, Erika. *Son of the Alhambra: Don Diego Hurtado de Mendoza, 1504–1575*. Austin, Tex., 1970.

DAVID H. DARST

HUTTEN, ULRICH VON (1488–1523), German humanist, neo-Latin poet, leading propagandist of the Lutheran Reformation. The life and work of Ulrich von Hutten are inextricably interwoven. Unlike most of his literary peers, he was a soldier, courtier, and politician, as well as an author of numerous works who used his pen to influence contemporary events, producing what in later eras would be termed *littérature engagé*.

Life and Career. Born in Castle Steckelberg into an old Franconian family of knights, Hutten was sent, at age eleven, to the school of the ancient abbey of Fulda, from which he fled six years later, in 1505. In the following years Hutten attended various universities, devoting himself to humanist studies. Mainz, Cologne, Erfurt, Frankfurt on the Oder (where he received his bachelor of arts degree in 1506), Leipzig, Greifswald, and Rostock marked the stations of these academic wanderings. His *De arte versificandi* (On the art of poetry; 1511), which would be reprinted sixty-six times before 1560, is evidence of his thorough knowledge of humanist poetics. The occasion to display these talents arose when the family of his Greifswald host, Professor Henning Lötze, had him robbed in a dispute over financial matters. In a language vibrant with passion and anger, Hutten denounces the Lötzes in the *Querelarum libri duo in Lossios* (Two books of complaints against the Lötzes; 1510), a collection of twenty poems. The last poem consists of fifty thumbnail sketches of German humanists that provide fas-

Ulrich von Hutten. KUPFERSTICHKABINETT, BERLIN

cinating snapshots of the literary scene around 1510. In this work, he summons his fellow poets to come to his aid, thereby elevating his personal mishap to the level of a national affair.

A brief stay in Vienna in 1511, where he came into the orbit of Emperor Maximilian I and the circle of patriotic humanists founded by the late Conrad Celtis, awakened Hutten's interest in political matters. Henceforth, the German knight became an ardent champion of Maximilian and an adversary of the emperor's opponents—in particular, the Venetians, the French, and the pope. All three subsequently became targets of the acerbic epigrams he penned during his two extended stays in Italy (1512 to early 1514; October 1515 to summer 1517).

Since 1511, intellectual discourse in Germany had been dominated by the so-called Reuchlin affair. Though it had begun as a debate between the eminent Hebraist Johann Reuchlin and the Cologne Dominicans about the value of Hebrew books, the disagreement had developed into an acrimonious controversy between humanists and Scholastics about the freedom of scholarship. The humanists not only supported the beleaguered Reuchlin in numerous letters but also responded with the satire *Epistolae obscurorum virorum* (Letters of obscure men; 1515, 1517), a fictitious correspondence allegedly written by Scholastics. In this brilliant work, the Scholastics are made to reveal all their academic pretensions, shallowness, and moral corruption. Although the satire was published anonymously, scholars believe that the humanist Crotus Rubeanus authored the first part and that Hutten was responsible for the second, more confrontational part.

No other work succeeded more in exposing the conservative theological establishment to laughter. German humanism was at its zenith. The mood of optimism and pride in the achievements of humanist scholars was articulated by Hutten in his famous letter of October 1518 to Willibald Pirckheimer: "O seculum! O literae! Iuvat vivere, etsi quiescere nondum iuvat, Bilibalde. Vigent studia, florent ingenia." (Oh century! Oh letters! It is a joy to be alive. It is not the time to keep quiet, Willibald. Studies thrive and minds flourish.) As evidence of this flourishing of letters, Hutten cites the works of his friends Desiderius, Erasmus Guillaume Budé, and Jacques Lefèvre d'Étaples, among others.

Hutten and the Reformation. In the following years, however, the conflict between humanism and Scholasticism was overshadowed by a more serious confrontation: Martin Luther's challenge to the Catholic Church. Hutten's two stays in Italy had reinforced his aversion to the Roman Curia. Incensed by fiscal exploitation and the alleged immorality of the priests, Hutten called for reforms even before Luther did so. Adopting the humanist genre of the dialogue, Hutten opened his literary campaign against Rome with four Latin dialogues: *Febris prima, Febris secunda, Inspicientes,* and *Trias romana,* or *Vadiscus* (The first and second fever, The onlookers, and The Roman trinity, or Vadiscus; 1520). *Trias Romana,* which Hajo Holborn called "the great manifesto of his campaign for German liberty," contains the most blistering attacks on the Curia. Realizing that his impact would be limited if he continued to write only in Latin, in 1520 Hutten began writing in the vernacular.

After initially dismissing the controversy over Martin Luther's ninety-five theses as a monkish squabble, Hutten after 1520 became Luther's ardent supporter. He was well aware, however, that their motivations and goals were different: Luther was prompted by religious and theological considerations, Hutten by national and political ones. "Shaking off the Roman yoke" became his declared goal; *alea iacta est* (the die is cast) his determined motto. Under papal ban from 1521 and physically threatened by his enemies, Hutten found refuge in his friend the knight Franz von Sickingen's Ebernburg Castle. From there he unfolded a flurry of activities, appealing—in Latin and German—in letters, poems, songs, invectives, and dialogues to his compatriots to take up arms against the church. By the time of the Diet of Worms (January–May 1521) he was considered one of Germany's most important (and dangerous) politicians. Realizing, however, the futility of his appeals, he subsequently resorted to a quixotic *Pfaffenkrieg* (war against the clergy). When von Sickingen's campaign against the archbishop of Trier, Richard von Greifenklau, ended in disaster in the fall of 1522, Hutten fled to Basel, then via Mühlhausen (Alsace) to Zurich, where Zwingli offered him asylum on the island of Ufenau. There he died in August 1523.

In later centuries, Hutten caught the imagination of his compatriots as did no other sixteenth-century figure except Luther. He was celebrated as a freedom fighter, a tragic hero, and a political visionary.

See also **Reuchlin Affair.**

BIBLIOGRAPHY

Primary Works

Hutten, Ulrich von, et al. *Letters of Obscure Men.* Translated by Francis Griffin Stokes. Philadelphia, 1964. Translation of *Epistolae obscurorum virorum* (1516).

Vlrichi Hutteni equitis Germani opera quae reperiri potverunt omnia. Edited by Eduard Böcking. 7 vols. Leipzig, Germany, 1859–1861. Reprint, Aalen, Germany, 1963.

Secondary Works

Bernstein, Eckhard. *Ulrich von Hutten.* Reinbek, Germany, 1988. Brief illustrated biography based on Hutten's letters and works.

Holborn, Hajo. *Ulrich von Hutten and the German Reformation.* Translated by Roland H. Bainton. Westport, Conn., 1978.

Mehl, James V. *Ulrich von Hutten.* In *Dictionary of Literary Biography.* Vol. 179, *German Writers of the Renaissance and Reformation, 1280–1580.* Detroit, Mich.; Washington, D.C.; and London, 1997. Pages 111–123. Concise article with bibliography of the most important works of primary and secondary literature.

ECKHARD BERNSTEIN

Plate 1. Lorenzo Ghiberti. Florence Baptistery Doors. The panels on the east doors of the Baptistery depict scenes from the Old Testament (*left to right*): Adam and Eve (*top left*), Cain and Abel (*top right*), Noah (*second tier left*), Abraham (*second tier right*), Esau and Jacob (*third tier left*), Joseph and his brothers (*third tier right*), Moses (*fourth tier left*), the fall of Jericho (*fourth tier right*), the battle with the Philistines (*bottom tier left*), and Solomon and the queen of Sheba (*bottom tier right*). Around the door are twenty-four statuettes of prophets and sibyls and twenty-four portrait medallions (Ghiberti's self-portrait among them). Michelangelo called the east doors the Gate of Paradise. The doors on the Baptistery are a copy installed in 1990; the original doors are in the Museo dell'Opera del Duomo, Florence. Bronze; 1425–1452. ALINARI/ ART RESOURCE, NY

Plate 2. Artemisia Gentileschi. *Judith and Holofernes.* The painting illustrates the incident in Judith 13:6–10. Painted c. 1618. [See the entry on Artemisia Gentileschi in this volume.] GALLERIA DEGLI UFFIZI, FLORENCE/ALINARI/ART RESOURCE, NY

Plate 3. Giotto. *St. Francis Preaches to the Birds.* The mural is in the church of San Francesco, Assisi. Fresco; c. 1296. [See the entry on Giotto in this volume.] SAN FRANCESCO, ASSISI, ITALY/CANALI PHOTO-BANK, MILAN/SUPERSTOCK

Plate 4. Giorgione. *Adoration of the Shepherds.* The painting is also ascribed to Titian. Oil on wood; c. 1505–1510; 90.8 x 110.5 cm (35.25 x 43.5 in.). NATIONAL GALLERY OF ART, WASHINGTON, D.C./SUPERSTOCK

Plate 5. Matthias Grünewald. *Crucifixion* From the *Isenheim Altarpiece.* Oil on panel; c. 1513–1515; 240 x 300 cm (94 x 118 in.). [See the entry on Grünewald in this volume.] MUSÉE UNTERLINDEN, COLMAR, FRANCE/SUPERSTOCK

Plate 9. Leonardo da Vinci. *Ginevra de' Benci.*
Ginevra de' Benci, the daughter of a wealthy
Florentine family, was sixteen years old when she
married Luigi Nicolini in 1474. Leonardo may
have painted her portait on the occasion of her
marriage or the painting may have been ordered
by Bernardo Bembo, a friend. The juniper bush
behind her symbolizes chastity; its Italian name,
ginepro, is also a pun on her name. Oil on wood;
c. 1474; 38.8 x 36.7 cm (15.3 x 14.5 in.). [See the
entry on Leonardo in this volume.] NATIONAL
GALLERY OF ART, WASHINGTON, D.C./SUPERSTOCK

Plate 10. Leonardo de Vinci. *Last Supper.* Mural in the refectory of the Convent of Santa Maria delle
Grazie, Milan. Mural; 1495–1497; 460 x 856 cm (181 x 337 in.). [See the entry on Leonardo in this volume.]
A.K.G., BERLIN/SUPERSTOCK

Plate 11. Leonardo da Vinci. *Mona Lisa.* Portrait of Lisa del Giocondo. Oil on panel; 1503–1506, 76.8 x 53.3 cm (30.2 x 21 in.). [See the entry on Leonardo in this volume.] MUSÉE DU LOUVRE, PARIS/THE BRIDGEMAN ART LIBRARY

Plate 12. Libraries. General view of the reading room of the Biblioteca Laurenziana (Laurentian Library), Florence, designed by Michelangelo and built between 1530 and 1534. [See the entry on Libraries in this volume and the entry on Michelangelo in volume 4.] SCALA/ART RESOURCE

ICONOGRAPHY, ROYAL. *See* **Royal Iconography.**

IGNATIUS LOYOLA (1491–1556), saint and principal founder of the Jesuit order (Society of Jesus). Ignatius Loyola was born into a noble family in the Basque territory of northern Spain. Baptized Iñigo, he began about 1537 to use Ignatius, probably because he mistakenly thought it was the Latin equivalent. He had the chivalric and academically limited education of his class, practically untouched by the new learning of the Renaissance. His brief military career ended in 1521 when he was wounded at the siege of Pamplona. During his long convalescence at the castle of Loyola, he underwent a series of profound religious experiences that utterly changed the course of his life. He became aware of the importance of attending to his feelings of "consolation" and "desolation," which would become a consistent point of reference in his religious teaching. At this time he also experienced a desire "to help souls," especially by assisting them in their inward spiritual journey. While passing a year in seclusion at the little town of Manresa outside Barcelona (1522–1523), he began to put his ideas on paper, the nucleus of his masterpiece, the *Spiritual Exercises,* not completed for two decades and not published until 1548.

After a pilgrimage to Jerusalem (1523–1524) he decided he needed a better education if he was "to help souls" more effectively. He began to study Latin at Barcelona, moved in 1526 to the recently founded university at Alcalá de Henares, where humanist influence was strong, and finally spent a short time at the University of Salamanca. He fell under the suspicion of ecclesiastical authorities in both Alcalá and Salamanca, which largely accounts for his decision to move on to the University of Paris, where he spent seven years (1528–1535). In 1533 he received his licentiate in philosophy, after which he devoted a year and a half to the study of scholastic theology without taking a degree.

At Paris he gathered around himself six disciples, whom he individually guided through the full course of his *Spiritual Exercises*. This group turned out to be the nucleus of the future Society of Jesus, and it included Francis Xavier (1506–1552), the great missionary to India and Japan, and Diego Laínez (1512–1565), later theologian at the Council of Trent and Ignatius's successor as head of the order. By 1534 the members of the group had decided they wanted to stay together, at least for a while, and to labor for the help of souls in Palestine. When the Palestine project failed, a now slightly larger group founded the new order in Rome in 1540. In 1541 the group elected Ignatius their superior, a position he held until his death.

With headquarters established in Rome, Ignatius, ordained a priest in 1537, set about governing the rapidly growing and geographically sprawling organization coming into shape before his eyes. From a handful of members it grew by the time of his death to a thousand, located in most countries of western Europe and in India, Japan, Brazil, and elsewhere overseas. He had a special gift for choosing assistants in this task whose training and talent complemented his own, many of whom had had a solid humanistic

Ignatius Loyola. Statue by Juan Martinéz Montañes, University Chapel, Seville. BILDARCHIV FOTO MARBURG/ART RESOURCE, NY

It is a paradox that the founder of an order that for centuries has been a major promoter of the humanistic curriculum and other values of the Renaissance was only superficially trained in them himself. His association with Polanco helps account for the unmistakably humanistic traits in his correspondence and in the *Constitutions* he wrote for the order. He legislated a humanistic program for the students in Jesuit schools and for younger members of the order itself. He thus became, in this somewhat curious way, an important figure in the history of humanism. He was canonized in 1622, and his feast day is 31 July.

See also **Religious Orders**, *subentry on* **The Jesuits**.

BIBLIOGRAPHY

Primary Works

Ignatius Loyola. *Ignatius of Loyola: The Spiritual Exercises and Selected Works*. Edited by George E. Ganss. New York, 1991. The best collection in English, and well translated. It includes the so-called autobiography, selected letters, and selections from the *Constitutions*.

Ignatius Loyola. *Letters to Women*. Edited by Hugo Rahner. Translated by Kathleen Pond and S. A. H. Weetman. New York, 1960. Rahner's extensive introductions make the book especially valuable.

Secondary Works

Dalmases, Cándido de. *Ignatius of Loyola, Founder of the Jesuits: His Life and Work*. Translated by Jerome Aixalá. Saint Louis, Mo., 1985. Succinct and factually reliable, although no fully satisfactory biography exists.

O'Malley, John W. *The First Jesuits*. Cambridge, Mass., 1993. Valuable for relating Ignatius to the general context of the early Society of Jesus.

JOHN W. O'MALLEY

education. Among them, most important were Juan Alfonso de Polanco (1517–1576), his secretary from 1547, and Jerónimo Nadal (1507–1580), invested by Ignatius in 1552 with plenipotentiary powers and sent to almost every Jesuit community in Europe.

One of the most striking characteristics of this new order was the high level of education attained by those who joined it or prescribed for those who lacked it. This was the precondition that led to the order's opening of a secondary school in Messina in 1548, after which many others followed in Europe and, soon, in other parts of the globe. Ignatius, founder of what has been correctly called the first teaching order in the Catholic church, unwaveringly promoted this development, even though it seemed somewhat incongruent with the strongly missionary, and even itinerant, features of the way of life the Jesuits at first envisaged for themselves.

ILLUMINATION. The Renaissance produced illuminated manuscripts that are as remarkable for their variety of content and technique as for their high artistic quality. Renaissance artists continued medieval traditions and also built on earlier experiments as they evolved new artistic styles. For example, Simone Martini illuminated the frontispiece of Petrarch's edition of Virgil (Milan, Ambrosian Library) about 1340, and features such as the antiquarian armor worn by Aeneas and the illusionistically painted *cartolino* (scroll) on which the *Aeneid*'s opening words *Arma virumque* are written anticipate aspects of later Renaissance illuminations.

One key change was the adoption at the beginning of the fifteenth century of humanistic script. The capital and minuscule alphabet based on Carolingian letter forms of the eighth century was developed in Florence by Niccolò de' Niccoli, Poggio Bracciolini, and Coluccio Salutati. It was immediately adopted by other scholars involved, like them, in rediscovering lost classical texts, in reforming the texts and orthography of those already known, and in teaching a more classical latinity to their pupils. With the new script came a particular form of initial known as "white vine" (*bianchi girari*), in which the plant scroll is reserved in the color of the membrane and the intervals between it are painted in red, blue, yellow, and green. This type of decoration, at first very simple in its forms and colors, was quickly adopted, with regional variations, throughout Italy for the decoration of humanist and classical texts.

Though the script and the white-vine initial were new and remained distinctive to Italy, there were many continuities in both artistic style and organizational practices from the previous century. First, the main manuscripts to receive extensive illumination were still those containing the liturgical and biblical texts of the Christian faith. There were continuities in subject matter, placement of illustration, and style of decoration of these manuscripts. For example, missals contain an image of the Crucifixion at the Canon of the Mass, and the forms of lush foliage and flower and fruit decoration retain generic similarities from the fourteenth to the sixteenth century.

Second, a network of individuals involved in the book trade existed in many cities: *cartolaii* (entrepreneurs who commissioned and sold manuscripts and the materials for their making), scribes, illuminators, and binders. Some religious institutions, such as the convent of the Angeli in Florence, continued to be involved in manuscript production, as the monasteries had been centuries earlier. Many scribes and some illuminators were priests or in religious orders.

Third, there was a continuity of patronage, not only of religious houses and owners but also of secular owners, the noble families who continued in power, such as the Visconti in Milan, and wealthy merchant patrons in cities like Florence and Venice. Secular patronage increased as the libraries of individuals grew in both size and scope under the influence of humanism.

The various regions of Italy developed recognizably different styles of illumination that were, however, always subject to cross-fertilization. Illuminators, including some of the most gifted, traveled to execute commissions. A notable example is Girolamo da Cremona, who worked successively in Ferrara, Siena, Florence, and Venice. Another is Matteo da Milano, who worked in Milan and, successively, in Bologna, Ferrara, and Rome.

Florence. Of the regional centers Florence undoubtedly was first in importance in the fifteenth century. A combination of causes included the patronage of Cosimo de' Medici and other members of the Medici family, the development of the university and the importance of humanist studies, and the impetus to the book trade of the Council of Florence (1438–1448), as emphasized by the city's premier *cartolaio,* Vespasiano da Bisticci. In artistic terms the achievements of the first generation of Renaissance monumental artists, among them Lorenzo Ghiberti, Donatello, and Masaccio, also were crucial. There had been a tradition of overlapping roles; for example, a major monumental artist of the previous generation working in the international Gothic style, Lorenzo Monaco (1370/71–1425/26), had on occasion worked as an illuminator. In the 1430s Fra Angelico, who had assimilated Masaccio's perspectival construction, is generally accepted as having illuminated a Gradual (the book containing the choral parts of the Mass) for the Dominican monastery of San Marco (Florence, Museo di San Marco). His pupil Zanobi Strozzi continued to work in his style.

The main Florentine illuminators include Francesco d'Antonio del Cherico (who signed one of his works), the priest Ser Riccio di Nanni, Francesco Rosselli, Mariano del Buono, and the brothers Monte di Giovanni and Gherardo del Fora, and Attavante degli Attavanti. Magnificent choir books were produced for the cathedral and other institutions such as the Badia church in Fiesole, the latter paid for by Cosimo de' Medici. Cosimo also funded the libraries at the Badia and San Marco; and his son, Piero di Cosimo, and grandson, Lorenzo the Magnificent, had large and important libraries. Lorenzo commissioned a famous series of books of hours illuminated by Francesco Rosselli for the weddings of his daughters. Medici patronage of Florentine illuminators continued into the sixteenth century under Cardinal Giovanni de' Medici (later Pope Leo X).

Northeastern Italy. In northeast Italy the patronage of the dukes of Ferrara resulted in a series of fine manuscripts that included the great Bible illuminated between 1455 and 1462 for Duke Borso d'Este (Modena, Biblioteca Estense). This, the most famous of all Italian Renaissance manuscripts, has, as stipulated in the surviving contract for the two volumes, a *principio* or illuminated opening for each book of the Bible. The director of the project, Taddeo Crivelli, worked with a group of illuminators and

Illuminated Printed Book. Illumination attributed to Girolamo da Cremona and assistants of a page from the works of Aristotle with commentary by Averroes. Printed at Venice by Andreas Torresanus de Asual and Barholomaeus de Balvis, 1483. THE PIERPONT MORGAN LIBRARY/ART RESOURCE

their assistants, including Franco de' Russi, Marco dell'Avogaro, and Girolamo da Cremona. Other illuminators working for the Este and known by name include Giorgio d'Alemagna, responsible for the duke's breviary, and his son, Tommaso da Modena, who worked on choir books for the churches of San Petronio in Bologna and San Giovanni Evangelista in Parma. Guglielmo Giraldi worked for the Este and also for Federico da Montefeltro, duke of Urbino, illuminating his famous Dante manuscript (Vatican

Library) in collaboration with his nephew, Alessandro Leoni, and a third artist. It was left incomplete at the duke's death in 1482. Artists working in the expressionistic style of the Este court painter, Cosmè Tura (who may have executed some historiated initials himself), include Fra Evangelista da Reggio and Jacopo Filippo d'Argenta. After the fall in 1499 of Duke Lodovico "il Moro" Sforza of Milan, Matteo da Milano came to Ferrara to work on a breviary (Modena) and a book of hours (Lisbon) for Duke Alfonso d'Este.

Venice. In Venice the leading illuminator of the second quarter of the fifteenth century was Cristoforo Cortese (d. before 1445). He had worked on the illumination of state documents and confraternity books, and on liturgical manuscripts, such as the choir books of the monastery of San Giorgio Maggiore. He also had illuminated some humanistic texts in the early 1440s with a version of white-vine scroll. Other illuminators active in Venice included Leonardo Bellini (nephew of the painter Jacopo Bellini), who worked on *dogali* and other state documents. He used some of the up-to-date stylistic features seen in the art of his uncle. The most innovative artists of the 1450s remain anonymous, however. One was responsible for a Petrarch manuscript written by Bartolomeo Sanvito of Padua (London, Victoria and Albert Museum), and others for the images of constellations in a copy of Hyginus (New York Public Library).

The first book to be printed in Venice (1469) issued from the press of Wendelin of Speyer (Vindelinus de Spira). His successors printed special copies on vellum, commissioned by patrons who either were among the Venetian patriciate or had been involved in putting up the capital; the outstanding example of the latter was the Nürnberg patrician merchant Peter Ugelheimer. A group of incunables (books printed before 1501) illuminated for Ugelheimer include an Aristotle edition of 1483 (New York, Morgan Library) and four law books (Gotha). Leading illuminators who worked on these printed books include Franco de' Russi, Benedetto Bordone, and Girolamo da Cremona. Other anonymous illuminators—the Maestro dei Putti, the Pliny Master, the Maestro degli Sette Virtu, and the Pico Master—found additional patronage from the new technology. The Pico Master and Bordone moved on to design woodcut illustrations for printed books.

Milan. Milan was already an important center under the first Visconti duke, Giangaleazzo (ruled 1395–1402), whose book of hours, started by Giovannino de' Grassi and his son Salamone, was completed after his death (1402) for his son Filippo Maria (ruled 1412–1447), by Belbello da Pavia sometime in the 1430s. In the period from about 1430 to 1460, anonymous artists in Lombardy continued to work conservatively in a version of the international Gothic style; the Master of the Vitae Imperatorum, the Master of the Franciscan Breviary, and the Master of Ippolita Sforza were the most important. The latter is named after his patron, daughter of Francesco Sforza and wife of Alfonso II, king of Naples (ruled 1494–1495) and son of Ferdinand I (Ferrante; ruled 1458–1494). Ippolita took to Naples in 1465 as part of her dowry a group of manuscripts that included an edition of Virgil containing her portrait (Valencia).

The great library formed by the Visconti and Sforza was housed in the castle at Pavia until it was removed to France following the conquest of the duchy of Lombardy by Louis XII of France in 1499. The Naples royal library is also well documented, giving us the names of the main illuminators, Cola Rapicano (Nicola Rubicano), Gioacchino de Gigantibus (or Gigante), Cristoforo Maiorana, and Matteo Felice, some of whom were on regular monthly salaries, others paid according to the number of miniatures or initials or borders they executed. The Naples library also was dispersed during the French invasions, some of the books being taken to France by Charles VIII after the capture of Naples in 1495, others being transported to Spain, where they were later given to the convent of San Miguel de los Reyes in Valencia.

Central Italy. In central Italy towns such as Pisa, Lucca, Prato, Perugia, and Siena employed illuminators. Some of the smaller courts were also important sources of patronage: especially those of the Gonzaga in Mantua and Duke Federico da Montefeltro in Urbino. The latter spent 30,000 ducats of his profits as a *condottiere* (mercenary soldier) on manuscripts for his library, according to Vespasiano da Bisticci, from whom he bought many of his manuscripts including his magnificent Bible illuminated by the main Florentine illuminators of the period and completed in 1478 (Vatican Library).

Wealthy monastic communities commissioned illuminated manuscripts, particularly sets of choir books for the sung parts of Mass and Divine Office. For example, the monastery of Monte Oliveto, near Chiusi, employed the illuminator Liberale da Verona to work on its *corali* (choir books). He then went on to Siena, where he worked with Girolamo da Cremona on the *corali* for the cathedral, beginning in

Illuminated Manuscript. Initial *S* with illumination showing the Madonna of Mercy by Fra Angelico, c. 1430. Museo di San Marco, Florence, MS. 558, fol. 156v. MUSEO DI SAN MARCO, FLORENCE/NICOLO ORSI BATTAGLINI/ART RESOURCE

1467. Twenty-nine volumes of this magnificent set are in the Piccolomini Library of the cathedral of Siena.

Choir books, antiphonals, and graduals are particularly prominent in Italian Renaissance illumination. Many survive in Italy, and many more were looted during the Napoleonic invasions, or acquired later by European and American collectors. Frequently large initials or whole pages have been cut out and survive in private collections, print rooms, and libraries, often awaiting identification. Sets of choir books for which illuminators' names are known include those in Cremona, Parma, Bergamo, Brescia, Verona, and Rimini.

Rome. With the end of the Western Schism after 1417, and especially under the rule of the humanist Pope Nicholas V (1447–1455), patronage was provided for illuminators by both popes and cardinals, who often used illuminators from their homelands. For example, Paul II (Pietro Barbo) employed Venetian artists, and Leo X employed Attavante from Florence. Some of the most splendid illuminated manuscripts executed in Rome in the second half of the fifteenth century were made for Pope Sixtus IV (1471–1484), and for two of his cardinals, Francesco Gonzaga (d. 1483) and Giovanni d'Aragona (d. 1485).

Bartolomeo Sanvito of Padua, perhaps the greatest of all Renaissance scribes, at this time resided with Cardinal Francesco Gonzaga in Rome. Sanvito had started his career in Padua and Venice, working for humanist patrons such as Bernardo Bembo. In Rome he collaborated with another artist employed by the cardinal, who may have been Gaspare da Padova, on a manuscript of Homer (Vatican Library). Gaspare executed magnificent architectural frontispieces for the classical and humanist texts written by Sanvito and decorated them with motifs drawn in the main from classical sculptural monuments. These paralleled the famous colored epigraphic capitals used by Sanvito, who was himself an illuminator. The architectural frontispiece, which originated in Padua and Venice in the 1450s, reached its full development in this group of manuscripts and came to be used all over Italy. Later it appeared in woodcut form in printed books, including those printed in northern Europe, into the sixteenth century and beyond.

The Rest of Europe. By the later fifteenth century patrons in northern Europe and in Spain—through links to the Curia in Rome, or through marriage alliances with the great Italian dynasties or under the influence of humanism—were buying or receiving as gifts manuscripts manufactured in Italy. An early example is Duke Humfrey of Gloucester (d. 1447) in England, who received decorated humanist manuscripts from Piercandido Decembrio in Milan. In some cases—the most important example being Matthias Corvinus, king of Hungary (d. 1490)—patrons persuaded scribes and artists to immigrate to their courts. Northern artists such as Jean Fouquet of Tours traveled to Italy, and when they returned home, they introduced stylistic or decorative features from Italian illumination. For example, native illuminators copied white-vine initials in manuscripts written in England for humanist patrons, and Renaissance architectural forms and frontispieces appear in French illuminations. Some French illuminators, the most noteworthy being the Master of the Theophylact (perhaps identifiable as Jacopo Ravaldi), worked for a time in Italy, adapting their native styles to a greater or lesser extent. On the whole, however, the areas north and south of the Alps remained remarkably separate in their styles. It is conventional to consider the northern production of the fifteenth and even sixteenth centuries under the heading of late Gothic rather than Renaissance.

By the early sixteenth century, printing was so established that the structure of the manuscript trade was withering away. The manuscript book thus became the exceptional artifact that it remains today. Illuminated manuscripts continued to be produced in two particular contexts. One was in Venice, where official state documents were still hand illuminated. The other was in Rome, where service books for the Sistine Chapel and for members of the Curia were illuminated by artists such as Matteo da Milano, who painted a missal for Cardinal Giulio de' Medici (later Pope Clement VII) in 1520 (Berlin); Vincenzo Raimondi (a Frenchman, Raimond de Lodève), who illuminated a psalter for Pope Paul III in 1542 (Paris, Bibliothèque Nationale de France); and Giulio Clovio, a Croatian born about 1498, who worked mainly for Cardinal Marino Grimani and Cardinal Alessandro Farnese. For the latter he executed the famous Farnese book of hours written in 1546 (New York, Morgan Library), and the Towneley lectionary (New York Public Library). Giorgio Vasari saw both of them and described them in his *Vite*. He called Clovio the "Michelangelo of small works"; indeed, Clovio both knew Michelangelo personally and collected and copied his drawings. Another influence, as on many later illuminators, was the prints of Albrecht Dürer. These commissions illustrate that the prestige of the illuminated manuscript continued and even as late as 1567 Pope Pius V commissioned a set of thirty-four choir books for the Dominicans at Santa Croce di Bosco (Alessandria).

BIBLIOGRAPHY

Jonathan J. G. Alexander, ed., *The Painted Page: Italian Renaissance Book Illumination, 1450–1550* (New York, 1994), contains entries for a representative selection of important Italian Renaissance illuminated manuscripts with good-quality color plates and an extensive bibliography. Older general surveys are Mario Salmi, *Italian Miniatures,* trans. E. Mann Borgese (New York, 1955); and Jonathan J. G. Alexander, *Italian Renaissance Illuminations* (New York, 1977). For Florence see Mirella Levi d'Ancona, *Miniatura e miniatori a Firenze dal XIV al XVI* seculo: Documenti per la storia della miniatura (Florence, 1962), and Annarosa Garzelli with Albinia C. de la Mare, Miniatura Fiorentina del Rinascimento 1440–1525, 2 vols. (Florence, 1985). For Milan see F. Malaguzzi Valeri, La corte di Lodovico il Moro, 4 vols. (Milan, 1913–1923); for Naples, Tammaro de Marinis, La biblioteca napoletana dei Re d'Aragona, 4 vols. (Milan, 1947–1952), and Supplemento, 2 vols. (Verona, 1969); for Venice, Girodana Mariani Canova, La miniatura veneta del rinascimento: 1450–1500 (Venice, 1969), and Lilian Armstrong, Renaissance Miniature Painters and Classical Imagery (London, 1981). Much important new research is included in exhibition catalogs, of which especially important recent examples are Laurence B. Kanter et al., Painting and Illumination in Renaissance Florence 1300–1450 (New York, 1994); Lorenzo Fabbri and Marica Tacconi, eds., I libri del Duomo di Firenze: Codici liturgici e Biblioteca di Santa Maria del Fiore (secoli XI–XVI) (Florence, 1997); Anna Maria Visser Travagli, Giordana Mariani Canova, and Federica Toniolo, La miniatura a Ferrara: Dal tempo di Cosmè Tura all'eredità di Ercole de' Roberti (Modena, 1998); and Giordana Canova Mariani, ed., La miniatura a Padora dal medioevo al settecento (Modena, 1999).

JONATHAN J. G. ALEXANDER

IMMORTALITY.

The controversy over the immortality of the soul caused a furor in sixteenth-century Italy and is significant for what it reveals about the culture of Renaissance Italy.

Background.

The roots of the controversy go back to the Middle Ages. In the thirteenth century the Latin Averroists of northern Europe had accepted the view of Averroes, the twelfth-century Arab commentator on Aristotle who taught that philosophy and science were synonymous with Aristotle and that therefore they contradicted religion on key issues. While readers of Aristotle know that he denied the eternity of the world, Averroes added that he also denied the immortality of the human soul. Averroes interpreted Aristotle to mean that there was one eternal intellect for all human beings while individual humans perished with their bodies. The Dominican theologian St. Thomas Aquinas (1225–1274) opposed the Latin Averroists. Thomas believed that faith and the supernatural perfected rather than negated reason and the natural. He argued that philosophy, when rightly conducted, led to the immortality of the human soul. By the middle of the fourteenth century, theologians and church authorities had successfully eliminated Latin Averroism from the universities of northern Europe. However, by then the Latin Averroists had found a home in Italy.

Italian universities lacked faculties of theology. They knew only a two-faculty system: law and arts. Since medicine held pride of place in the arts faculty and since theology was for the most part taught outside the universities in the monasteries of the mendicant orders, the interests of the twin secular professions of law and medicine dominated the Italian universities. Arab authors were the major authorities in medicine, philosophy, and science, so Italian professors appropriated Averroes's views on the immortality of the soul. Latin Averroism became domesticated in Italy in the second half of the thirteenth century and remained predominant there for the next three and a half centuries.

Opposition.

Opposition to the Italian Averroists built up slowly. Petrarch (1304–1374) condemned them as neopagans. But he had a disciplinary ax to grind: as the first great humanist, he used the charge of paganism to smear his cultural rivals. Moreover, Averroists who wrote on the subject stated that the soul was in fact immortal, but this knowledge derived from faith, not rational demonstration. Such a position might not have pleased Petrarch, but it was perfectly orthodox. The two most influential medieval theologians and philosophers after the death of Thomas Aquinas were the Franciscans John Duns Scotus (c. 1266–1308) and William of Ockham (c. 1285–c. 1349). Scotus was agnostic and Ockham was negative on the possibility of philosophical proof of the immortality of the human soul. Humanists after Petrarch abandoned his campaign to brand the Italian Averroists pagans.

Other countercurrents were also developing, including Platonism. The Florentine Marsilio Ficino (1433–1499), who founded Renaissance Platonism, made the immortality of the soul a core doctrine of the movement, as the title of his largest philosophical treatise, Theologia Platonica de immortalitate animorum (Platonic theology on the immortality of the soul; 1482), would suggest. Ficino condemned the Italian Aristotelians for denying the immortality of the soul. Ficino's intellectual heir in Florence was the teacher Francesco da Diacceto (1466–1522), who counted among his pupils and friends Giovanni de' Medici, the future Pope Leo X (reigned 1513–1521). In 1513, the first year of Leo's pontificate, the Fifth Lateran Council took aim at the Averroists by issuing the decree Apostolici Regiminis, which required all teachers of philosophy to argue for the immortality of the soul "as much as possible."

Other currents contributed to Apostolici Regiminis. In the later fourteenth and through the fifteenth century, a few theologians from the mendicant orders (mainly Dominicans and Franciscans, but also Augustinians) began to teach philosophy and theology in the Italian universities. These courses in themselves did not provide sufficient training for a degree in theology, but they did involve the theologians in the life of the universities. Furthermore, in the fifteenth century some Franciscan theologians accepted the Thomist position that philosophy should prove the immortality of the soul. Since by this time all Franciscan theologians were Scotists and since virtually all Dominican theologians were Thomists, and since the Franciscans and Dominicans dominated theology in Italy, a strong body of opinion was building against the Averroists. Not coincidentally, one of the most notable Franciscan opponents of the Averroists, the theologian Antonio Trombetta (1436–1517), was a member of the commission that drafted *Apostolici Regiminis*. Finally, church authorities were starting to take a jaundiced view of Averroism. They had long been suspicious of the astrological teachings associated with the medical curriculum, because they could lead to the opinion that celestial bodies determined Christ's birth and actions. In 1315 the Inquisition in Padua burned the exhumed corpse of the Aristotelian Pietro d'Abano for this reason; in 1327 the Inquisition in Florence burned at the stake the university professor Cecco d'Ascoli (b. 1269) for the same reason; and in 1396 the bishop of Pavia strictly warned the renowned Aristotelian Biagio Pelacani da Parma (c. 1347–1416) about his astrological views. In the fifteenth century Averroism also provoked some church authorities. In 1489 Pietro Barozzi (1441–1507), the bishop of Padua, threatened to excommunicate anyone at the University of Padua who publicly disputed on the Averroistic doctrine of the unity of the intellect. Nicoletto Vernia (c. 1420–1499), an Averroist professor at Padua, took the hint and in 1492 published the treatise *Contra perversam Averroys opinionem de unitate intellectus* (Against the perverse opinion of Averroes), in which he took back everything he had previously argued.

Pietro Pomponazzi.

In 1516, just when the anti-Averroists seemed on the verge of winning the day concerning the immortality of the soul, the most original of all Italian Aristotelians, Pietro Pomponazzi (1462–1525) of the University of Bologna, destroyed the illusion by publishing *De immortalitate animae* (On the immortality of the soul). Pomponazzi, who was not an Averroist, transformed the debate by using Thomas Aquinas to refute Averroes; but then he refuted Thomas. He argued that humans are necessarily mortal because they need matter both as the object of thought (i.e., images) and as thinking subjects (i.e., the imaginative faculty, which is tied to matter). Having thus established the mortality of the soul, Pomponazzi asked why we should ever do good or risk our lives for others. He answered: because only in that way are we truly human. We share abstract thought with angels and the ability to construct artifacts and social groups with animals. But of all creatures, only humans are continually faced with moral decisions. Pomponazzi argued a variation of the Stoic position that virtue is its own reward and vice its own punishment. To do evil, he said, is to become less human, and to do good, even while losing one's life in the act, is to become fully human. Pomponazzi ended with an affirmation that despite his philosophical analysis he believed in the immortality of the soul because it is an article of the Christian faith.

Reaction.

Was Pomponazzi sincere? Was he a cryptopagan? Those questions are disputed, especially since in a later treatise, *De incantationibus* (On incantations; completed 1520, published 1556), he denied the possibility of miracles, proposing instead a natural explanation for events attributed to the miraculous. He seems to have been a Christian determined not to confuse faith and reason. In any case, in his own time he set off a firestorm of controversy. His non-Averroistic denial of the immortality of the soul was too powerful to be ignored. The Venetian senate ordered the book burned and its sale forbidden. Pope Leo X sent a threatening letter but was persuaded not to proceed further by Pomponazzi's defender, Cardinal Pietro Bembo (1470–1547). Gasparo Contarini (1483–1542), the learned Venetian nobleman and future cardinal; Vincenzo Colzade of Vicenza, the chief of the Dominican school in Bologna; and others prepared extensive private criticisms, which Pomponazzi incorporated and answered in his *Apologia* of 1518. But the controversy only intensified. Agostino Nifo (1473?–1538?), perhaps the leading contemporary Aristotelian after Pomponazzi, published a lengthy *Libellus* against him in 1518, to which Pomponazzi responded in his *Defensorium* of 1519. Gasparo Contarini then wrote in 1518 a refutation of Pomponazzi's response, which appeared after he and Pomponazzi had died. In 1519 the Dominican theologian Bartolommeo Spina (1475–c. 1546) published critiques of Pomponazzi's *De immortalitate animae* and *Apologia*. That same year another Dominican theologian, Crisostomo Javelli (c. 1470–c. 1538), published two pieces on the controversy. Also in 1519 the Augustinian theologian and Platonist Ambrogio Flandino joined the fray with a large work against Pomponazzi. The traditionalist Averroist

Luca Prassicius chimed in with his own refutation in 1521, as did the physician Battista Fiera (1450–1540) in 1524 and the Paduan professor Marcantonio Zimara in an undated and unpublished opuscule. Finally, in 1533 (though not published until 1536), Javelli revisited the controversy with a treatise defending the immortality of the soul. Of all Pomponazzi's critics, Javelli was the most generous. He essentially conceded that on Aristotelian grounds Pomponazzi was right. What he, Javelli, did instead was to construct a philosophical argument based on Thomas Aquinas. Javelli could cite high authority for his position. The most prominent Thomist theologian of the day, the former master general of the Dominicans and, at the time Javelli wrote, cardinal, Tommaso de Vio (1469–1534; known as Cajetan), had expressed doubt about proving the immortality of the soul even before the controversy broke out.

In the end, therefore, Pomponazzi won. Aristotelian philosophy could not be made to conform to Christianity. But that meant that the Averroistic interpretation of Aristotle, though different from Pomponazzi's, was equally tolerable as a philosophical position. What destroyed Averroism in Italy was not *Apostolici Regiminis* or any fideistic backlash but the new science of the Renaissance, which by the later seventeenth century made Averroism untenable as science.

See also **Aristotle and Aristotelianism; Petrarch; Philosophy;** *and biography of Pomponazzi.*

BIBLIOGRAPHY

Primary Work

The Renaissance Philosophy of Man. Edited by Ernst Cassirer, Paul Oskar Kristeller, and John Herman Randall. Chicago, 1948. This anthology contains excerpts of Petrarch's letters about Averroists (pp. 140–143) and Pomponazzi's treatise *On the Immortality of the Soul* (pp. 254–381).

Secondary Works

Di Napoli, Giovanni. *L'immortalità dell'anima nel Rinascimento*. Turin, Italy, 1963.

Gilson, Étienne. *Humanisme et Renaissance*. Paris, 1983. This collection of articles by Gilson contains on pp. 133–249 his "Autour de Pomponazzi: Problématique de l'immortalité de l'âme en Italie au début du XVIe siècle" of 1961 and on pp. 251–281 his "L'affaire de l'immortalité de l'âme à Venise au début du XVIe siècle" of 1964.

Kristeller, Paul Oskar. *Studies in Renaissance Thought and Letters*. Vol. 1. 1956. See chapter "Francesco da Diacceto and Florentine Platonism in the Sixteenth Century," pp. 287–336.

Monfasani, John. "Aristotelians, Platonists, and the Missing Ockhamists: Philosophical Liberty in Pre-Reformation Italy." *Renaissance Quarterly* 46, no. 2 (1993): 247–276.

Nardi, Bruno. *Saggi sull'Aristotelismo padovano dal secolo XIV al XVI*. Florence, 1958.

Nardi, Bruno. *Studi su Pietro Pomponazzi*. Florence, 1965.

Pine, Martin L. *Pietro Pomponazzi: Radical Philosopher of the Renaissance*. Padua, Italy, 1986.

Poppi, Antonino. "L'Averroismo nella filosofia francescana." In *L'Averroismo in Italia*. Accademia Nazionale dei Lincei. Atti dei convegni lincei. Rome, 1979. Pages 175–220.

JOHN MONFASANI

INDEX OF PROHIBITED BOOKS. The compilation of lists of prohibited books is a practice that was already in existence in classical antiquity. In the Catholic Church the interdiction of books goes back to apostolic times and continued through the Middle Ages.

The First List of Prohibited Books. The extremely rapid diffusion of the Reformation thanks to the printing press provoked a reaction on the part of ecclesiastical and civil authorities, who sought at all costs to prevent the printing, sale, possession, and reading of the works of Martin Luther and his followers. Emperor Charles V ordered the publication of several edicts, principally in 1524, 1529, and 1540, outlawing Reformation books. Other European rulers quickly followed with their own ordinances against the heretical writings. Numerous interdictions were issued also by individual ecclesiastical authorities. A decree of the archbishop of Canterbury, dated 3 November 1526, prohibiting 110 titles, was followed by a score of others in the course of the first half of the sixteenth century. In Italy, both civil and clerical authorities reacted against the importation of Protestant books. In Milan, Duke Francesco Sforza, the Senate, and Inquisition together prepared in 1538 the first Italian catalog of prohibited books, containing 43 items, intended to be displayed in public places. This initiative was repeated by other Italian states Venice, Lucca, Florence, and Naples between 1530 and 1540.

In France, the monarchy, the Parlement of Paris, bishops, and the theology faculty of the University of Paris took various actions against suspect imprints. In the 1520s, the faculty drew up a list of prohibited books, to which it added considerably after 1541. The Spanish and Portuguese Inquisitions likewise were extremely vigilant and also published numerous edicts against Protestant writings and works by false mystics.

The First Printed Catalogs. The first printed Index of Prohibited Books was issued by the theology faculty of the University of Paris in 1544, containing 230 titles in Latin and French. The number of condemned books grew in subsequent editions published in 1545, 1547, 1549, 1551, and 1556.

This last version contains 528 interdictions, affecting principally Reformation authors and certain literary writings by humanists, especially Desiderius Erasmus and François Rabelais. Pursuant to orders issued by Charles V and Philip II, the theology faculty of the University of Louvain also issued catalogs of prohibited books in 1546, 1550, and 1558.

The first Index printed in Italy appeared at Venice in 1549, a cooperative effort of the Inquisition and the Venetian government, containing 150 prohibitions. The vigorous opposition launched against it by printers and booksellers led to its suppression, even before it could be officially published. Another catalog, containing six hundred interdictions, an official compilation of the Roman Curia but not an official Index, appeared in 1554 at Venice, Milan, and Florence. The Venetian imprint was withdrawn following vigorous protests.

Indexes of the Spanish and Portuguese Inquisitions.

The first catalog published by the Spanish Inquisition appeared in 1551. It reproduced the Index of the University of Louvain, with the addition of more than a hundred specifically Spanish condemnations. The *Cathalogus librorum* issued by the inquisitor general Fernando de Valdés, published in August 1559, eight months after the first Roman Index, is of special importance because it proclaimed the independence of the Spanish tribunal from the Roman Inquisition in matters of censorship. The roughly seven hundred condemnations are grouped by language: Latin, Castilian, Flemish, German, French, and Portuguese. The section on Castilian books reflects the censorship efforts of the Spanish Inquisition, which focused principally on works of piety and devotional books, Erasmian themes, and superstitious practices.

The Spanish Inquisition published its own catalogs during the whole of its long history. The Index of the inquisitor general Gaspar de Quiroga (1583) contains more than 2,000 interdictions. The following year, an Index of Expurgated Books was issued to complement the Index of Prohibited Books. By this procedure the Spanish Inquisition conformed to the policies of both the Roman and Spanish Index, which proposed that books should be allowed to circulate once the objectionable passages they contained had been expunged. This was a response to the pleas of intellectuals, university professors, professional men, and the complaints of printers and booksellers. The Indexes of 1583 and 1584 are cornerstones in the history of Spanish inquisitorial censorship.

The Portuguese Inquisition, drawing principally from the catalogs prepared in Paris and Louvain, compiled a printed catalog in 1551 containing almost five hundred interdictions. From the publication of the 1559 Roman Index, reprinted at Lisbon the same year, the Portuguese tribunal aligned itself with Roman censorship and appropriated its condemnations, but went beyond it by adding interdictions of its own in the catalogs of 1561, 1564, and 1581. The last Portuguese Index appeared in 1624.

Papal Indexes. In the mid-1550s Rome intensified considerably its battle against heresy and constituted a commission charged with preparing an Index of Prohibited Books. The papal Index of Paul IV includes over a thousand condemnations divided into three classes. The first, with more than 600 interdictions, contains authors whose complete writings are prohibited. The second, with 126 titles, lists individual works under the names of their authors. The third, with 332 titles, is reserved for books considered to be anonymous. This is followed by a list of forty-five editions of the Bible and the New Testament, along with the names of sixty-one printers known to have published heretical books. The Index of Paul IV stands out for its rigor: it contains an exceedingly high number of condemnations and promulgates certain draconian provisions such as, for example, the outlawing of all books produced by heretics. The papacy sought to attenuate its severity with modifications in 1559 and 1561.

The Index prepared by a commission established by the Council of Trent, published in 1564 by Pius IV, does not differ significantly from its predecessor in the number of condemnations it contains. It stands out, however, because it includes ten general rules which came to constitute the basic legislation of the Catholic Church in matters of censorship for four centuries. Prohibited absolutely were all books condemned previously by popes and councils; the complete works of heresiarchs (fomenters of heretical movements); the writings of other heretics that deal expressly with religion; lascivious and obscene writings; and writings dealing with astrology, divination, and the occult. To be permitted after proper examination and licensing by inquisitors or their delegates would be books by heretical authors that were not on religious subjects and works of controversy between Catholics and heretics in the vernacular. Similarly permitted, after expurgation, would be books containing objectionable passages that were otherwise sound, such as dictionaries, compendiums, and concordances compiled by heretics. The reading of

Index of 1559. Initial page of the letter *E* listing authors all of whose works are prohibited (Erasmus of Rotterdam among them) and authors of prohibited books whose names are not certain (Rome: Antonio Blado, 1559). BY PERMISSION OF THE BRITISH LIBRARY C107DE5

the Bible in the vernacular was permitted exclusively to persons who possessed a written license from an inquisitor or bishop. Before a work could be printed, permission had to be obtained, in Rome from the master of the Sacred Palace and elsewhere from bishops, inquisitors, or their delegates. The rules further enjoined the inspection of bookshops, cargoes imported from abroad, and books bequeathed by inheritance.

By order of Fernando Alvarez de Toledo, duke of Alba and governor of the Low Countries, the Tridentine Index was reprinted in Antwerp in 1569 and 1570 with an important appendix of more than eight hundred condemnations. A commission subsequently prepared a catalog of books to be expurgated, published at Antwerp in 1571.

In order to control the content and application of the Index, as well as to oversee the work of censorship, in 1571 Pius V created the Congregation of the Index, which became the permanent organ of government in the church entrusted with keeping the Indexes of Prohibited Books up-to-date. It possessed the authority to ban new writings, expurgate suspect works, permit the circulation of previously interdicted books no longer deemed objectionable, and exercise constant vigilance to prevent the diffusion of dangerous writings. This Congregation in theory enjoyed universal jurisdiction over the Catholic world. In practice, however, in Spain and in Portugal, which possessed their own Indexes, the control of the printed word was vested in the national Inquisitions.

In Rome efforts to prepare a new catalog ran into great difficulty because of the opposition of intellectuals, bookmen, and political authorities, especially the Venetian Republic. The Index finally published in 1596 by Clement VIII constituted a compromise among the various forces which vied all through the process of its preparation. The new compilation faithfully reproduced the Tridentine Index and added an appendix of 1,143 condemnations: 682 authors whose complete writings were prohibited, 185 individual works whose authors were known, and 276 anonymous items. A distinguishing feature of this Index, in relation to previous Roman catalogs, is that approximately half of the works in the second class, although condemned, would be allowed to circulate after expurgation.

Condemned Authors and Works. The sixteenth-century Indexes of Prohibited Books hit about two thousand authors with at least one condemnation. Three-fourths of those authors had all their works prohibited. The list of interdicted writings whose authors were known numbered about 1,660. Titles banned as anonymous surpassed a thousand, while editions of the Bible and of the New Testament totaled two hundred. Two-thirds of the condemned works were in Latin, the rest in various vernaculars. Some 20 works in the 1564 Roman Index and 116 authors and titles in Clement VIII's Index of 1596 were condemned only until they could be expurgated. Although the Congregation of the Index continued in this way temporarily to prohibit the circulation of certain writings until they could be reviewed, it never published an *Index expurgatorius* in the sixteenth century. In 1607 the master of the Sacred Palace, Giovanni Maria Brasichelli, published a solitary volume containing expurgations for fifty authors. There would be no others. After the appearance of the first Index of expurgations at Antwerp in 1571, all the publications of this genre, with the exception of Brasichelli's, were the work of the Spanish and Portuguese Inquisitions. In all, the sixteenth-century Indexes expurgated or designated for expurgation 290 authors and 20 anonymous titles.

The impact of the condemnation of a writing on its diffusion and use remains an open question. For authors such as Erasmus, for example, the effects of the interdictions were significant. But it will only be after systematic research on the authors, their works, and the often subterranean channels for the transmission of ideas that we shall know how successful the Indexes were in attaining their goals: to prevent the printing, circulation, and reading of outlawed literature. The Index of Prohibited Books was abolished in 1966.

See also **Censorship,** *subentry on* **Censorship on the Continent.**

BIBLIOGRAPHY

Primary Works

De Bujanda, J. M., ed *Index des livres interdits*. 10 vols. Sherbrooke, Canada, and Geneva, 1984–1996. Vol. 1, *Index de l'Université de Paris, 1544, 1545, 1547, 1549, 1551, 1556*. Vol. 2, *Index de l'Université de Louvain, 1546, 1550, 1558*. Vol. 3, *Index de Venise, 1549, et de Venise et Milan, 1554*. Vol. 4, *Index de l'Inquisition portugaise, 1547, 1551, 1561, 1564, 1581*. Vol. 5, *Index de l'Inquisition espagnole, 1551, 1554, 1559*. Vol. 6, *Index de l'Inquisition espagnole, 1583, 1584*. Vol. 7, *Index d'Anvers, 1569, 1570, 1571*. Vol. 8, *Index de Rome, 1557, 1559, 1564*. Vol. 9, *Index de Rome, 1590, 1593, 1596*. Vol. 10, *Thesaurus de la littérature interdite au seizième siècle*. Historical surveys, analyses of the expurgations, and critical editions of all sixteenth-century Indexes of Prohibited Books.

Secondary Works

Fragnito, Gigliola. *La Bibbia al rogo: La censura ecclesiastica e i volgarizzamenti della Scrittura (1471–1605)*. Bologna, Italy, 1997. Based on assiduous research in civil and ecclesiastical repositories, especially the Archive of the Holy Office in Rome, presents a detailed history of the prohibition and control of vernacular biblical translations and commentaries.

Grendler, Paul F. *The Roman Inquisition and the Venetian Press, 1540–1605*. Princeton, N.J., 1977. Influential study based on the large collection of Venetian Holy Office trials and other primary documents. Examines the impact of Inquisition and Index on the book trade and the reactions on all fronts to the invasive controls and prohibitions.

Higman, Francis M. *Censorship and the Sorbonne. A bibliographical study of books in French censored by the Faculty of Theology of the University of Paris, 1520–1551*. Geneva, 1979. Studies the works censored by the University of Paris in their political, religious, and cultural contexts.

Lopez, Pasquale. *Inquisizione, stampa e censura nel Regno di Napoli tra '500 e '600*. Naples, Italy, 1974. Uses the collection of inquisitorial documents preserved in the Archivio Storico Diocesano, Naples, to reconstruct censorship activity in the Italian *Mezzogiorno* (south).

Rozzo, Ugo, ed. *La censura libraria nell'Europa del secolo XVI*. Udine, Italy, 1997. Conference volume containing thirteen studies devoted to the Indexes, the activities of the congregations of the Inquisition and Index, and ecclesiastical censorship activity in various European countries.

Tedeschi, John. *The Prosecution of Heresy. Collected Studies on the Inquisition in Early Modern Italy*. Binghamton, N.Y., 1991. Collected studies by the author on aspects of the Roman Inquisition, ecclesiastical censorship and its enforcement.

J. M. DE BUJANDA

INDIVIDUALISM. "Individualism" is a quality of attitude or behavior attributed to persons living during the Renaissance. It denotes an increasing self-awareness and pursuit of self-interest in contrast to a supposed previous group-consciousness of various kinds. Jakob Burckhardt named part 2 of his *Civilization of the Renaissance in Italy* (1927) "The Development of the Individual." In the Middle Ages, Burckhardt says,

> Man was conscious of himself only as a member of a race, people, part, family or corporation—only through some general category. In Italy [of the Renaissance] . . . an objective treatment and consideration of this world became possible. The *subjective* at the same time asserted itself with corresponding emphasis; man became a spiritual *individual* and recognized himself as such.

Burckhardt and Cassirer. Burckhardt regarded this statement as central to his interpretation of the Renaissance as the first time and place that manifested a major characteristic of modern European (and Euro-American) civilization, namely, "individualism." Among the qualities he saw in Renaissance individualism were a striving toward universality, "the many-sided man," and the acquisition of fame and widespread admiration, or in some instances horror and awe—certainly qualities that are recognizable today.

To be sure, some of these characteristics of individualism existed in earlier times in the West, as in republican Rome, or in ancient Athens. And Christianity, as the dominant religion of medieval Europe, centrally emphasized individual salvation. But there is no doubt that there are striking examples of individualism in Burckhardt's Renaissance Italy. Burckhardt was much influenced by Vespasiano da Bisticci's *Vite di uomini illustri del secolo XV* (Lives of illustrious men of the fifteenth century; first published 1839). This collection describes the actions, accomplishments, personal attitudes, and self-concerned comments of rulers (many of whom had acquired power by their own actions), leading ecclesiastics, poets, humanists, and one woman, and is richly evocative of the qualities Burckhardt perceived and described. Many other narrative sources of this type, as well as the rich corpus of humanist writings, correspondence, and treatises contributed to Burckhardt's concept of individualism. However, documentary evidence to the contrary shows how firmly many leading figures of urban life retained a close sense of identity with their extended families (or clans), and also how incongruous these qualities of individualism would have been for the urban lower classes, not to mention the peasantry.

Burckhardt also depended heavily on the literary anecdotes of the lives of ordinary persons who were dramatized in the rich story collections of the period. Individualism, particularly in behavior, is hard to pin down except in such sources of historical or literary description, especially in the struggles for political power, which are graphically portrayed in part 1 of Burckhardt's work, titled: "The State as a Work of Art."

Renaissance individualism also refers to the idea, or ideal, of "individualism" that is examined in another famous and influential study: Ernst Cassirer's *The Individual and the Cosmos in Renaissance Philosophy* (1927). A philosopher in the German idealist tradition stemming from Kant and Hegel, Cassirer saw a new form evolving in the human spirit (meaning, of course, western European culture). It begins, he claims, in the Renaissance with Petrarch's criticism of Scholastic natural philosophy in his invective *De sui ipsius et multorum ignorantia* (On his own ignorance and that of many others; 1367). In this work, Petrarch (1304–1374) criticizes the enthusiasm of his young philosopher friends for Aristotle's philosophy of nature, and proclaims that in pursuit of salvation it is better to will the good than to know the truth.

Cassirer then presents, as a work of key influence in the Renaissance, Nicholas of Cusa's Christian theological and Neoplatonist work *De docta ignorantia* (On learned ignorance; 1440). Cusa argues that in order to reach toward divine infinity humans must realize their fundamental condition of finitude within the universe. Cusa's influence was greater in sixteenth-century Europe generally than in fifteenth-century Italy, and contrary to what Cassirer argues, his work was not well known to the Italian philos-

ophers Marsilio Ficino (1433–1499) and Giovanni Pico della Mirandola (1463–1494). Cassirer rightly identifies Ficino and Pico as stressing human capacity to achieve a position of dignity within the cosmos, but they did this through their own studies, not through Cusa's influence. Cassirer's further elaboration of the philosophy of Renaissance individualism is set forth in discussion of two basic themes of early modern European philosophy: human freedom emphasized as the capacity of the will as opposed to natural necessity, and the so-called subject-object problem, which he held experienced its fundamental breakthrough in René Descartes's *cogito ergo sum*.

The Individual and Moral Integrity. It is true that there was a marked increase of expression reflecting individualism—poetic, historical, rhetorical, and philosophical—in fourteenth- and fifteenth-century Italy, as well as in northern Europe of the late fifteenth and sixteenth centuries. But there had also been a notable earlier turn toward such attitudes in the twelfth century—as for example in Peter Abelard, or in Bernard of Clairvaux and others. In the thirteenth century the dominance of Scholasticism and its assimilation of Aristotle's writings tended to emphasize generalities and universals more than the individual and the particular. The scholastic followers of Duns Scotus and later of William of Ockham (both Franciscans) had a stronger interest in the particularities of life thus paralleling the developments in literature.

The Renaissance breakthrough toward individualism came in the third quarter of the fourteenth century with Petrarch's emphatic concern with the course of life of individuals. Interestingly, this was closely contemporary with Ockham's writings in Oxford and then Paris; Petrarch's activities were in Provence and northern Italy. Petrarch's work followed upon Dante's depiction in the early fourteenth century of the many sinners, ordinary Christians, and saints, and their otherworldly destinies in the *Commedia*. The enthusiastic reception of this work certainly was an important indication of the growth of interest in the lives of individuals, though within a predetermined ordering of human fates. In the case of Petrarch, his *Secretum* or *The Secret Conflict of My Cares* (completed 1347–1353) was a markedly individualistic work. The *Secretum* is a dialogue between "Augustinus," who represents the call to Christian piety and concern for the next life, and "Franciscus," who finds that call difficult to heed. Franciscus struggles to justify and determine his own life goals in relation to his personal experiences in the face of Augustinus's severe insistences. This imaginary conversation with St. Augustine intentionally recalls the saint's own *Confessions* and the individualism of Augustine's own struggles to attain a salvific life. Petrarch further manifested his individualism in his moral concerns over his own ways of life and those of his friends in his *Epistolae rerum familiarum* (Familiar letters). He debates the question of life paths even more explicitly in his *De vita solitaria* (trans. *Life of Solitude;* 1346), in *De otio religioso* (On the retirement of the religious; 1347), and in his work that was popular through the entire Renaissance and early modern period, *De remediis utriusque fortunae* (The remedies for both kinds of fortune; 1360).

The theme of all these works is that the individual necessarily goes through a struggle to achieve the kind of life that befits and fulfills a person's own moral sense and character. To attain this goal of moral integrity and transmit it to his readers and correspondents, Petrarch employs the vision of the poet, the flexibility of the rhetorician, the memory of the historian, and the moral responsibility of the humanist. Behind this for Petrarch was not only the paradigmatic figure of St. Augustine but the writings and imagined personas of the Roman pagans, Cicero, Horace, and Seneca, in their own pursuit of moral integrity. It was this that made Petrarch the model for subsequent generations of humanists.

In the emerging individualism of Petrarch's vision of life he reveals both his concern for the spiritual well-being of others and his ultimate concern for himself. In *Life of Solitude* he says,

> And certainly whoever is secure in himself . . . sins against the law of nature if he does not bring aid to the suffering when he can. As for me . . . I wish to be safe with others, or at least with many; but in the end what do you wish me to say? It is enough if I do not perish, nay more, it is abundant happiness.

Human Will and Divine Will. A central characteristic of the emerging Renaissance individualism was the emphasis on the human will in the context of the firmly established belief in divine will. The close successor and follower of Petrarch, Coluccio Salutati (1331–1406), wrestled with this problem of human and divine will in *De fato et fortuna* (On fate, fortune, and chance; 1399). Deeply religious, but also a vigorous affirmer of human capacities, he declared,

> And so God moves our wills in such a way that he does not force them at all. . . . We sin therefore in freedom of will when we do not do that which we ought. . . . To us, moreover, just as the mode and principle of existence is given, so also the rules of acting are prescribed as much by nature as by law and are certainly in our power so that if we transgress and do not fulfill them we sin through ourselves by our own freedom of choice.

And Lorenzo Valla (1407–1457), who stressed the great pleasure of life, found divine providence directed toward the well-being of mankind. In *De voluptate et vero bono* (On pleasure and true good; original edition 1431) he says, "That you might know how much more potent you are, for whom the whole world and all the heavens have been fabricated, I say that they are made for you alone. For although you have others sharing it with you, nevertheless, all things are made for the sake of individuals." Works like the *De dignitate et excellentia hominis* (The dignity and excellence of man) of Giannozzo Manetti also affirm the well-being of individuals, whereas others, like the *Demiseria humanae conditionis* (The misery of the human condition) of Poggio Bracciolini, stress the omnipresence of a destructive and competitive individualism. On the other hand, Leon Battista Alberti wrote the following in his *De Iciarchia* (On governing a household; 1470), a guidebook to living a useful and satisfying life that would make a person honored and respected for his contribution to his fellow humans:

> No worthy and no worthwhile thing ever happens to a person from laziness. From leisure and neglect many lose the most honored position among the citizens and their fortune and dignity. There is nothing so contrary to the life and condition of man as not to become active in some honorable task. . . . Man is born to be useful to himself and no less to others.

Certainly Alberti was expressing the notion of social participation as the road to success that became a key theme of the later economic individualism thought to originate in the Renaissance.

More fitting to the notions of Burckhardt and Cassirer, however, were the views of Ficino and Giovanni Pico della Mirandola. In book 13, chapter 3 of his *Theologia Platonica* (written 1469–1474), Marsilio Ficino gives a lengthy listing of the powers of humans in directing their lives in the world. Here his introductory statement will suffice to show the extent of his admiration for the achievements of individuals:

> The other animals either live without art, or have each one single art . . . The sign of this is that they gain nothing from time for the work of making things. On the

contrary men are the inventors of innumerable arts which they practice according to their own decision. This is shown by the fact that individuals practice many arts, change, and become more expert by extensive exercise, and what is marvellous, human arts make by themselves whatever nature itself makes, so that we seem not to be servants of nature but competitors.

Twelve years later Pico wrote his much admired *De hominis dignitate orationis* (Oration on the dignity of man; 1486). God had created the world in all its beauty and glory without a creature who might properly admire it. And all the other necessary functions had been provided for.

He therefore took man as a creature of indeterminate nature, and assigning him a place in the middle of the world, addressed him thus: "Neither a fixed abode nor a form that is thine alone nor any function peculiar to thyself have we given thee, Adam, to the end that according to thy longing and according to thy judgment thou mayest have and possess what abode, what form, and what functions thou thyself shalt desire."

Man was created, thus, with multipotentiality, and any given individual might become what he wished. This is a statement opening many possibilities of individual achievement and hence has been much admired by modern philosophers and historians. It is cosmic individualism, but is it social and civic? It can not be doubted that "individualism" played an important role in the ideas and ideals of the Renaissance but only a limited one in everyday practice.

See also Dignity of Man; Fortune; Moral Philosophy; Renaissance, Interpretations of the, *subentry on* Jakob Burckhardt; *and biographies of figures mentioned in this entry.*

BIBLIOGRAPHY

Primary Works

Alberti, Leon Battista. *Opere Volgari*. Edited by Cecil Grayson. 2 vols. Bari, Italy, 1966.

Bisticci, Vespasiano da. *Renaissance Princes, Popes and Prelates: The Vespasiano Memoirs. Lives of Illustrious Men of the Fifteenth Century*. New York, 1963.

Cassirer, Ernst, Paul Oskar Kristeller, and John Herman Randall Jr., eds. *The Renaissance Philosophy of Man*. Chicago, 1948.

Secondary Works

Burckhardt, Jakob. *The Civilization of the Renaissance in Italy*. Translated by S. G. C. Middlemore. New York, 1958. Translation of *Die Kultur der Renaissance in Italien* (1860).

Cassirer, Ernst. *The Individual and the Cosmos in Renaissance Philosophy*. Translated by Mario Domandi. New York, 1963. Translation of *Individuum und Kosmos in der Philosophie der Renaissance* (1927).

Morris, Colin. *The Discovery of the Individual, 1050–1200*. New York, 1972.

Trinkaus, Charles. *In Our Image and Likeness: Humanity and Divinity in Italian Humanist Thought*. 2 vols. Notre Dame, Ind., 1995.

Trinkaus, Charles. *The Poet as Philosopher: Petrarch and the Formation of Renaissance Consciousness*. New Haven, Conn., 1979.

CHARLES TRINKAUS

INDUSTRY. Despite the tradition of identifying the Renaissance with modernity, any discussion of this subject must set clear distance between twentieth-century notions of "industry" and the patterns of production that took shape in Italy and Europe between the fourteenth century and the seventeenth. The modern idea that industry involves the mass production of identical objects in factory locations within large urban agglomerations was then virtually unknown. The vast majority of the European population lived in rural areas. *Industria* as a term simply meant "hard work."

Urbanization, Capitalism, and the Reformation. Clusters of towns in a region stretching from Flanders through southern Germany to northern Italy had promoted trade and manufactures in the Middle Ages. The growth they helped generate was halted by the disasters of the fourteenth century, most notably the Black Death. However, a further phase of urban renewal opened around the middle of the fifteenth century and continued throughout the sixteenth. The emergence of a literate—and numerate—lay society in the towns of Italy and Europe might be seen as responsible for the liberation of Europeans from the constraints of the ecclesiological framework of medieval society, a process that was to culminate in the Reformation. The latter can also be regarded as an urban phenomenon, and Max Weber famously linked the "protestant ethic" with the "rise of capitalism" in articles published from 1904 to 1906. According to this thesis, people in control of industrial processes became impatient with the burdens of traditional religious practices that stood in the way of greater efficiency of production and pressed for their removal. Why should a feast day in the name of a particular saint necessitate closing the business when there was cloth to be stretched?

However, such interpretations are driven by a teleology that views European economic development as powering ineluctably toward the industrial revolution of the nineteenth century, and such a teleology is highly distorting. With regard to urbanization, any town of at least forty thousand inhabitants was large, and there may have been no more than forty towns of such proportions in Europe by 1600. Moreover, throughout the Middle Ages, the merchants of Italy and Flanders had developed advanced business techniques that did not necessitate a seismic break with the precepts of the medieval church. Put another way, the cities of Renaissance Europe were relatively small, and the capitalism they nurtured was commercial rather than industrial in character. Industry was subordinated to commerce, and depended heavily on the level of skill of the individual craftsman. Traffic in bulk was largely the preserve of unfinished commodities and did not involve large quantities of mass-produced goods.

Manufactures. The production of goods is perhaps better understood as "manufactures" since most items were handmade. The workplace was the workshop, not the factory, the supervisor and regulator was the guild, not the entrepreneur. These distinctions are necessary in order to underscore that the process of production was generally conducted on a very small scale throughout the period. This was the case even when a merchant controlled a scattering of workshops or processes. Francesco Datini (c. 1335–1410), the renowned merchant from Prato, controlled a cloth company that involved no more than a dozen employees. A substantial firm of cloth manufacturers in Florence in the early sixteenth century had personnel of no more than fifteen. However, the hard work of manufacturers within these small-scale units of production helped bring about some notable changes in material life. Many of these changes were the result of increased demand rather than of technological invention. The new patterns of demand began to make themselves felt around the middle of the fifteenth century and resulted from the recovery of population growth after the recurrent bouts of plague that began with the Black Death in 1348.

While it is important to exercise caution with regard to the notion that the Renaissance witnessed the birth of consumerism, it is unquestionable that there were significant changes in demand. Antwerp was to prove one of the great boomtowns of the sixteenth century, and its Beurs was the first stock exchange in Europe. When the Italian Lodovico Guicciardini recorded his impressions of the city in *Descrittione . . . di tutti i Paesi Bassi* (Description . . . of the Low Countries) published in 1581, his description conveyed the excitement of variety; he noted all kinds of cloth, tapestry, and metalwork—especially arms and armor. Then there was the decoration of clothing and furnishings through tanning, painting, dyeing, and gilding, as well as glassmaking like that of the Venetians. Moreover, there was haberdashery of every type, embellished with gold, silver, silk, and small wares in metal. He also recorded the impressive quantities of metal, wax, and sugar that were refined there. The combination of an abundance of inessentials and commodities in bulk is striking, and makes the point that factory-based industry was not the driving force of the new world of goods.

Large-scale Activities. It is important to acknowledge that there were three principal areas of economic activity that traditionally operated on a larger scale than that of workshop-based handicraft, and they were to assume new characteristics during the Renaissance. These were textiles, building, and mining. In some sense, these larger-scale activities complicate the picture still further because they reinforce the differences that separate modern notions of industry from the conditions that obtained in the Europe of the Renaissance. However, the changes in each of these sectors during the Renaissance were to give the culture of the age some of its most distinctive characteristics.

Textiles. Textiles purchased with money remained something of a luxury, and peasants working in subsistence agriculture often produced their own. Woolen cloth had been one of the mainstays of medieval manufacture. Production was complicated, and it involved the coordination of five principal stages: carding, spinning, weaving, fulling, and dyeing. Florence enjoyed the highest reputation for woolen cloth. Modern research has shown, however, that once again industrial expansion was the result of commercial expertise. The contacts that Florentine bankers had throughout Europe enabled them to establish what were the finest raw materials and the best production techniques, to bring both to Florence, and to produce a less expensive cloth. Demand fell dramatically as a result of the Black Death. In 1378, the uprising of the *ciompi* (unenfranchised workers in the cloth industry) in Florence included in its demands a minimum annual production of 24,000 cloths. Some sources suggest that the production level before the plague had reached 70,000. The long-term result was investment in silk manufacture. Higher-priced cloths, such as brocade, damask, and velvet, might maintain profits while reducing the scale of output. The invention during the fourteenth century of the silk-throwing machine had vastly simplified silk production. The flight of Lucchese artisans from their politically turbulent hometown spread production to centers such as Venice, Florence, Bologna, and Milan. The plague accelerated still further the tendency to invest in the production of small quantities of expensive cloth. When economic expansion returned around the middle of the fifteenth century, demand for luxury items also increased. Thus, Guicciardini noted that in Antwerp one might buy any kind of silk cloth—velvet, damask, satin, and so on—and that this extraordinary variety must be distinguished from wool, linens, or fustian (this last being a combination of cotton and linen).

Building. In examining building as an industrial undertaking, it is important to be aware that it was perhaps the most prestigious of the visual arts. Communes and princes sought to express their own identities in projects of ever more awesome scale. These in turn concentrated unusually large numbers of workers on the same site for extended periods of time. As has been shown in the case of Florence, a city's major buildings expressed not just the ingenuity of the designer, but also the managerial talents of the site manager. Filippo Brunelleschi was remarkable in combining both these talents to meet the challenges of the project to complete the Duomo. In the case of sixteenth-century Rome, the replanning of the city along classical lines was still more intensive, and the building of the new Saint Peter's demanded the presence of more than two thousand workers on site. The construction of comfortable dwellings for the social elite came to be replicated in the palaces of France and of the Spanish monarchy, and in the country houses of Tudor England. The declining importance of the fortified house also led to a considerable increase in demand for domestic comfort, notably in glass for windows.

One branch of the construction industry assumed still larger proportions than housing for the social elite. The numbers of workers called together to build palaces were exceeded by the concentration of personnel in the Venetian Arsenal. This complex of shipyards contained several thousand people—a considerable number of them women who worked as sail makers—but probably not the fifteen thousand recorded by the diarist Marino Sanudo around 1500. The Arsenal was the inferno of the poet Dante and the premier technological center of its age, the greatest industrial complex in the preindustrial world. In these surroundings, teams of workmen could fit out a galley in the time it took the king of France to have dinner (as happened in 1574 for the visit of Henry III). The Arsenal produced more than half of the two hundred galleys that won the battle of Lepanto for the Holy League against the Turks in 1571, a battle so destructive that it is said to have consumed the equivalent of half a million trees in lost shipping. The scale of industrial capacity devoted to warfare is a decidedly modern theme and one to which it will be pertinent to return.

Mining. The principal centers of mining in the Europe of the Renaissance were to be found outside of Italy. The mines of central Europe were, by then-existing standards, very large operations indeed. Silver was extracted from the Harz Mountains in northern Germany, copper was mined in the Tyrol, and rock salt in Poland. The extraction of materials from any depth required high levels of investment in machinery for crushing ore, for trip hammers and winches. In England, the scale of tin production was unusually large. A single entrepreneur in Cornwall in the fourteenth century employed around three hundred people. At the very end of the period, England also experienced a striking expansion in the use of coal as fuel. In the 1580s, London imported around eleven thousand tons, mostly from Newcastle; by 1606 the figure had risen to almost eighty thousand. And in the later Middle Ages, the blast furnace had greatly advanced the production of iron.

In a roundabout way, however, Renaissance Italy can be connected to the mining of precious metals. Through their sophisticated monetary arrangements, the Italians had become the leaders of the medieval business world. This was particularly true of the bills of exchange that did much to compensate for the comparative scarcity of precious metals; however, the situation was to change dramatically during the sixteenth century. The period witnessed a vast influx of bullion from the New World, which, by the middle of the seventeenth century, had probably tripled the amount of silver in circulation in Europe. It is important to consider the way in which the Spaniards in particular exploited the native peoples of Mexico and then Peru in order to accumulate gold and silver. The *encomienda* that granted land and native peoples to the conquistadores was a species of manorial fief. Yet, in various ways, the exploitation of the raw materials of newly acquired colonies set something of a standard for the later industrial era. First, the mining of gold and silver demanded the concentration of a dependent labor force. Second, the conquistadores held a singular control, confirmed by force, of the means of production. Finally, the ruthless reduction of overheads, in particular, the disregard for labor conditions, was a measure designed purely to maximize profits. Equally important, the end product that began with the mining process was coin. Until the end of the fifteenth century, coins were exceptional as identical items produced in relatively large quantities; in the sixteenth century, coins became much more common in the exchanges of everyday life. The greater availability of precious metals combined with the rising demand of the expanding population to generate inflation that was unprecedented.

War and Communication. The problems of currencies intensified immeasurably as a result of government tampering, often involving considerable reduction of the gold or silver content of coins. The reason that such debasements became necessary was overexpenditure—largely on warfare. Renaissance Europe experienced what has become known as a military revolution. The basic elements of this phenomenon involved, first, the construction of lower and thicker walls in fortifications to absorb the increasingly destructive fire of cannon, which made for longer sieges. The second element was the declining importance of the mounted knight and the increasing proportion of infantry. The third element was the use of firearms. The result was that much larger armies became engaged in longer lasting wars that were all the more destructive and expensive. These developments came into sharp focus in the wars that were fought in Italy in the early part of the sixteenth century. Warfare was to concentrate human and material resources in the hands of the state on a scale that no contemporary entrepreneur could ever have approached. Finding the means to pay for war on this new scale was beyond the capacities of most governments, and failure to do so was the downfall of the Spanish monarchy, despite all of its American treasure.

The vast increase in the scale of warfare during the Renaissance was certainly a feature of the age that anticipated the industrial era. A development of comparable proportions and more constructive consequences was the spread of printing with moveable type. Apart from coins, printed texts were unique in being reproduced as exact copies one after the other. The innovation in Europe was first made not in Italy, but in Germany. Indeed, Vespasiano da Bisticci (1421–1498), who supplied manuscripts to many of the Florentine humanists, was hostile to the printed word. However, Venice was to become the leading center of book production in Europe in the sixteenth century. The workshop of Aldus Manutius (c. 1450–1515) was the birthplace of two extraordinary developments: italic script and the pocket edition. The implications for the speed of circulation of new ideas

were truly revolutionary. As a result, Erasmus gained the sort of celebrity that was beyond any previous humanist, and Luther's ideas circulated at a velocity unimaginable to any previous Reformer. The new scientific knowledge of Andreas Vesalius and Nicolaus Copernicus reached an audience of vastly increased proportions. However, this advance must not be unduly exaggerated; books were to remain expensive even for the minority who could read them. All the same, Renaissance printing connects the preindustrial world with the postindustrial world. It can be misleading to link Renaissance industry to the age of coal, iron, and cotton. It is perhaps more useful to see the printed book as the beginning of a revolution in communications that has continued even though the industrial revolution has passed.

See also Capitalism; Cities and Urban Life; Mining and Metallurgy; Printing and Publishing; Warfare.

BIBLIOGRAPHY

Braudel, Fernand. *The Wheels of Commerce.* Vol. 2 of *Civilization and Capitalism, 15th–18th Centuries.* Translated by Sian Reynolds. London, 1983.

De Roover, Raymond. "A Florentine Firm of Cloth Manufacturers." In *Business, Banking, and Economic Thought in Late Medieval and Early Modern Europe.* Edited by Julius Kirshner. Chicago, 1974. Pages 85–118.

Eisenstein, Elizabeth. *The Printing Revolution in Early Modern Europe.* Cambridge, U.K., and New York, 1983.

Goldthwaite, Richard A. *The Building of Renaissance Florence.* Baltimore, 1980.

Goldthwaite, Richard A. *Wealth and the Demand for Art in Italy, 1300–1600.* Baltimore, 1993.

Hatcher, John. *English Tin Production and Trade before 1550.* Oxford, 1973.

Hoshino, Hidetoshi. *L'arte della lana in Firenze nel basso medio evo: Il commercio della lana e il mercato dei panni fiorentini nei secoli XIII–XV.* Florence, 1980.

Lowry, Martin. *The World of Aldus Manutius: Business and Scholarship in Renaissance Venice.* Oxford and Ithaca, N.Y., 1979.

Mazzaoui, Maureen Fennell. *The Italian Cotton Industry in the Later Middle Ages, 1100–1600.* Cambridge, U.K., and New York, 1981.

Miskimin, Harry A. *The Economy of Early Renaissance Europe, 1300–1460.* Cambridge, U.K.; London; and New York, 1975.

Miskimin, Harry A. *The Economy of Later Renaissance Europe, 1460–1600.* Cambridge, U.K., and New York, 1977.

Nef, John U. *Industry and Government in France and England, 1550–1640.* New York, 1957.

Parker, Geoffrey. *The Military Revolution: Military Innovation and the Rise of the West, 1500–1800.* Cambridge, U.K., 1986.

Ramsey, Peter H., ed., *The Price Revolution in Sixteenth-Century England.* London, 1971.

Thomson, David. *Renaissance Architecture: Critics, Patrons, and Luxury.* Manchester, U.K., and New York, 1993.

RICHARD MACKENNEY

INFANCY. *See* **Birth and Infancy; Childhood.**

INNS OF COURT. London's four inns of court—Gray's Inn, Lincoln's Inn, the Inner Temple, and the Middle Temple—took their titles from properties originally controlled by the Lords Grey, the earl of Lincoln (or a medieval lawyer of that name), and the knights Templar. From the fourteenth century onward groups of common lawyers ("men of the court") rented these hostels, town houses, or inns on London's western boundary as communal lodgings, convenient to the common-law courts of Westminster Hall. The medieval practitioner-tenants developed a complex system of legal instruction by oral "learning exercises" to supplement the would-be lawyers' private studies and observation of court sittings. The inns also increasingly attracted young men of good families and means who sought merely a basic acquaintance with the law of the land as well as some schooling in gentle accomplishments and manners.

The inns of court both contributed to and were influenced by the spread of humanism from the later fifteenth century onward. Expanding membership reflected their popularity as metropolitan, nonecclesiastical academies for the landed and mercantile elites of England and Wales as well as those of lowlier origins ambitious to rise in the world. Bringing together relatively large numbers of students in London's exceptionally lively urban environment, the Tudor and early Stuart inns inevitably fostered creative writing, patronage, and scholarship. While the future lord chancellor, Thomas More (1478–1535; who entered Lincoln's Inn in 1496), exiled all lawyers from his Isle of Utopia, professional lawyers were hardly isolated from these cultural developments. Together with More himself, the polymath essayist and philosopher Francis Bacon (1561–1626) and his brilliant young polyglot protégé John Selden (1584–1654) stand as exemplars of common lawyers whose learning was by no means limited to their profession. If humanists frequently deplored the common law's linguistic barbarism and unsystematic structure, such concerns also motivated attempts to clarify and rationalize its complexities, employing various dialectical and rhetorical techniques in order to make legal knowledge more accessible to laymen and students. Moreover, like their French and Italian counterparts, the lawyers of Renaissance England played a crucial role in fostering antiquarian pursuits and historical studies.

The inns of court also made a major contribution to the poetry and drama of the English Renaissance. Besides providing a congenial milieu for emerging authors such as Thomas Campion, John Donne, John Ford, John Hoskins, John Marston, and many more, the corporate life of the inns of court included a rich diet of interludes, plays, dancing, music, revels, and masques. Following traditional forms of entertainment at the royal court, these were originally staged by the members themselves, if increasingly supplemented by professional companies of players: Shakespeare's *Comedy of Errors* received its premiere at Gray's Inn during the Christmas revels of 1594, while *Twelfth Night* was staged in February 1602 at the Middle Temple. Inns of court men were also prominent in the audiences of Elizabethan and Jacobean playhouses. Indeed, after the first decade of the seventeenth century, their members increasingly tended to contribute to the arts and letters rather as consumers and patrons than producers.

See also **Drama, English**; **Law.**

BIBLIOGRAPHY

Baker, John H. *The Third University of England: The Inns of Court and the Common Law Tradition*. London, 1990.

Prest, Wilfrid R. *The Inns of Court under Elizabeth I and the Early Stuarts 1590–1640*. London and Totowa, N.J., 1972.

Richardson, Walter C. *A History of the Inns of Court*. Baton Rouge, La., 1975.

WILFRID PREST

INQUISITION. [This entry includes four subentries:

Roman Inquisition
Spanish Inquisition
Inquisition in the Americas
Portuguese Inquisition]

Roman Inquisition

The Roman Inquisition was a penal and judicial institution established in mid-sixteenth-century Italy as a response to the Protestant challenge in that country. It should not be confused with the earlier, decentralized medieval phase of the institution, which came into being in the first half of the thirteenth century, when the defense of the faith was placed in the hands of individual clerics appointed to investigate specific instances of heresy, nor with the Spanish version of this tribunal founded in 1478 and controlled by the crown, which had a separate history and operated in virtual independence of Rome.

The chief features of the reorganization set in motion by Pope Paul III with his bull *Licet ab initio* of July 1542 were: the centralization of authority for the pursuit of heresy in a supreme commission of cardinals that appointed and closely supervised the work of provincial inquisitors, over which the pope personally presided at weekly meetings; an expansion of local tribunals throughout the peninsula, the seats of which were usually Dominican and Franciscan convents; and the repeal of privileges exempting from prosecution regular clergy who previously had to answer only to their superiors in the religious orders.

Personnel. The authority vested in inquisitors was to be understood as emanating directly from the pontiff himself. Two future popes (Marcellus II and Paul IV) were among the first six cardinals appointed to the commission in 1542. And in the major reorganization of the Curia achieved in 1588 by Sixtus V, the Holy Office was ranked first among the fifteen Congregations into which papal government was divided. The uprooting of heresy, previously in the hands of both bishops and inquisitors, now became primarily the occupation of the inquisitorial courts; inquisitorial tribunals took precedence over all other courts, lay and ecclesiastical alike.

The customary provincial tribunal consisted of an inquisitor, his vicar (who could perform some of the lesser duties of the office and substitute for him in his absence), a notary, and such familiars as prison guards and messengers. Although the vicar was nominated to his office by the inquisitor, he was considered an apostolic legatee, since it was the Supreme Congregation in Rome that confirmed his appointment. A network of lesser officials, *vicari foranei* (external vicars), selected from the ranks of the regular clergy and parish priests, represented the parent tribunal in the small towns and hamlets under its jurisdiction. These external vicars were appointed by the inquisitor and required no further ratification on the part of Rome (although the Congregation kept a watchful eye even over these choices). Their judicial role was generally limited to conducting preliminary inquiries and receiving depositions.

The presence of a bishop or, more usually, an episcopal vicar was an indispensable requirement when the court wanted to proceed to such grave acts as the application of judicial torture or final sentencing. On the question of precedence, a bishop outranked an inquisitor, who in turn exceeded an episcopal vicar. Every court was further assisted in its deliberations by a body of consultors drawn from the ranks of prominent lawyers and theologians of the place. Except in the most ordinary cases, a local tribunal would not reach the point of final sentencing until the Supreme Congregation in Rome, which received and closely scrutinized copies or summa-

ries of trials in progress, had expressed its binding opinion.

Originally, inquisitors had to have reached their fortieth year (although the minimum age for bishops was only thirty, dispensable to twenty-seven), but this limit was waived when the appointment of inquisitors devolved to the pope and through him to the Congregation. Ideally, inquisitors would have degrees in both theology and law, but such highly trained individuals were rare, and in Italy the majority of appointees had theological backgrounds.

Jurisdiction and Trials. The effective jurisdiction of the reconstituted tribunal was essentially limited to the peninsula, excluding Sicily and Sardinia, where the Spanish Inquisition prevailed. It was also barred from exercising its functions openly in the Neapolitan *viceregno,* where Rome had to act under the cover of the episcopal courts. The island of Malta and the papal enclave of Avignon in France fell under Roman purview. As for the rest of Italy, although inquisitors were able to proceed in their duties freely in the states of the church, their activities were curtailed in varying degrees in independent principalities and republics, where arrests, incarceration, and extraditions to Rome were dependent on the approval of the local ruler. Lay functionaries appointed by the secular government sat on the tribunals as watchdogs to guarantee the correctness of the proceedings, although they had no official roles. Venice, perhaps more than any other state, limited the Inquisition by a series of special dispositions.

Beginning in the 1970s research overturned many long-standing assumptions connected with the Roman Inquisition. In terms of the jurisprudence of early modern Europe, it was not the arbitrary, oppressive tribunal of legend, a drumhead court, a chamber of horrors, or a judicial labyrinth from which escape was impossible. In trials conducted under its jurisdiction, loose allegations were not permitted, and accusers had to make their depositions under oath. To forestall charges stemming from personal animosities, since the names of prosecution witnesses were concealed for their own protection, defendants were asked in advance to provide the names of their enemies. The arraigned had the benefit of a defense attorney appointed by the court at a time when this figure did not exist in English law and had only a minor role in civil French and imperial legal codes.

Transcripts of the proceedings were provided to prisoners in writing and an appropriate interval, varying from several days to a few weeks, allowed for the preparation of counterarguments and the summoning of friendly witnesses. Judicial torture, which was carefully circumscribed, might be applied only after the defense had made its case and where the *indicia,* the evidence of heresy, were compelling. No properly conducted inquisitorial trial commenced with the *rigoroso esamine,* a euphemism for torture. The local bishop or his vicar, duly constituted members of a provincial inquisitorial court, had to concur in the decision and be present during the questioning.

Appeals could be and regularly were made to a higher court, namely the Supreme Congregation in Rome. First offenders were dealt with infinitely more leniently than recidivists. A sentence to life imprisonment (*carcere perpetuo*) by the Holy Office meant parole after a few years, generally three, subject to good behavior; and house arrest, often with permission to work outside one's domicile, was frequently imposed, especially given the lack of secure prisons outside Rome.

In witchcraft proceedings many other safeguards were in effect, especially from the end of the sixteenth century. Physicians were consulted to establish the corpus delicti—specifically, whether an illness or death might have had a natural cause—before jumping to the conclusion that a crime, a *maleficium,* had been perpetrated. Unlike the practice in secular tribunals, the search for the so-called Devil's mark was unknown in the inquisitorial process, and the failure of the accused to evince emotions or shed tears during the interrogation was considered of scant significance. Alleged participants at Sabbaths were not allowed, following a decision taken by the Supreme Congregation in 1588, to implicate accomplices, a measure that spared Italy (and Spain) the bloody persecutions that raged in northern Europe until well into the seventeenth century. Sentences pronounced by provincial tribunals were scrutinized by the Supreme Congregation of the Inquisition in Rome, and implausible confessions that contradicted the defendant's testimony during the trial were deemed invalid.

Punishment. Dramatic forms of penal procedure, such as the stake, incarceration, and galley sentences, are generally associated with inquisitorial practice. But a survey of the thousands of surviving sentences shows that milder forms of punishment prevailed. Most frequently encountered are public humiliation in the form of abjurations read on the cathedral steps on Sundays and feast days before the throngs of churchgoers; salutary penances, such as

fines or service for the benefit of charitable establishments; and a seemingly endless cycle of prayers and devotions to be performed over many months or even years.

Only a small percentage of cases adjudicated by the Roman Inquisitions concluded with capital punishment. The penalty of death by burning at the stake was reserved for three categories of offenders: the obstinate and unrepentant who refused to be reconciled to the church; the relapsed, namely those who had suffered a previous sentence for formal heresy; and, following bulls promulgated by Pope Paul IV in July 1556 and February 1558, persons convicted of attempting to overturn such central doctrines as the Virgin birth and the full divinity of Christ. In practice, an extraordinary number of defendants convicted of these specific transgressions received lesser penalties. Before being bound to the stake, gentlemen were beheaded, lesser mortals strangled. And even for those few who were condemned to the agony of being burned alive because they refused to the bitter end to recant their errors and be reconciled to the church, the moment of final release was often hastened with small sacks of gunpowder hung around their necks.

Although there are serious lacunae in the documentation, where long runs of trials and sentences are extant the available figures on those executed by the Inquisition suggest that the numbers fall far short of what has generally been believed. Only four of the first thousand defendants who appeared before the tribunal of Aquileia-Concordia (1551–1647) were put to death. A tentative calculation for Venice has counted fourteen executions between 1553 and 1588, plus four deaths occurring in prison and four extraditions to deaths in Rome between 1555 and 1593. Only twelve executions have been counted for Milan during the second half of the sixteenth century (but on the basis of incomplete records), and only one, in 1567, for religious heresy in Modena; and of the more than two hundred sentences contained in the Trinity College manuscripts for parts of 1580 to 1582, only three called for condemnations to the stake. The names of ninety-seven victims of the Holy Office in Rome for the period 1542 to 1761 have been extracted from the records of the Archconfraternity of San Giovanni Decollato (St. John Beheaded), which comforted victims in their final hours.

Records. The revisionist view is based on an assiduous examination of surviving inquisitorial sources, both printed and manuscript. Even before the formal opening (January 1998) to the scholarly public of the central archives of the old Roman Holy Office (the Congregation for the Doctrine of the Faith), there was no shortage of original inquisitorial documents. Among the most important printed materials are numerous legal manuals written between the early fourteenth and mid-seventeenth centuries, a significant number authored by Spaniards, even though printed in Italy. Although the Roman Holy Office never designated one as possessing exclusive authority in its tribunals, those most in use and frequently cited were Nicolas Eymeric's *Directorium inquisitorum* (Directory for inquisitors; 1585, 1587), edited and glossed by Francisco Peña; Jacopo de Simancas's *De catholicis institutionibus* (Catholic institutions; 1584); Umberto Locati's, *Opus quod iudiciale inquisitorum dicitur* (A judicial compendium for inquisitors); Prospero Farinacci's *Tractatus de haeresi* (Treatise on heresy; 1620); Eliseo Masini's *Sacro arsenale* (Sacred arsenal; 1625); and Cesare Carena's *Tractatus de officio sanctissimae inquisitionis* (Treatise on the Office of the Most Holy Inquisition; 1655) (all fully described in Emil van der Vekene's *Bibliotheca bibliographica*).

Large quantities of manuscript records are also available. The suppression of the Inquisition throughout the peninsula in the eighteenth century and the closing of many of the religious establishments that had housed provincial tribunals brought about the transfer of large numbers of inquisitorial records to public repositories and episcopal archives. Transcripts of thousands of trials have survived intact in Udine, Venice, Modena, Rovigo, Naples, Caserta, and elsewhere; extensive series of correspondence exist between the Supreme Congregation in Rome and some of its provincial outposts in Bologna, Modena, Naples, and Udine; and a large body of sentences spanning a century and a half (c. 1556–c. 1700) found its way in the nineteenth century to Trinity College, Dublin (part of the considerable archival material transported to Paris at Napoleon's orders from Roman depositories and which was never returned after the collapse of his empire). And in the Vatican library and Secret Vatican Archives (not to be confused with the Holy Office Archive), correspondence, decrees, manuscript inquisitorial manuals, handbooks, and memoranda, which had been copied for the use of cardinals of the Congregation of the Holy Office, can be found in abundance (described in detail by Patricia H. Jobe, "Inquisitorial Manuscripts").

The Roman Archive of the Holy Office holds an array of records. Researchers have unfettered access to the archive of the Congregation of the Index, which was transferred intact to the Holy Office in 1917; to the complete original trials of highly placed ecclesiastics such as Cardinal Giovanni Morone, Bishop Vittore Soranzo, and the protonotary Pietro Carnesecchi; to the long runs of the *Acta sancti officii,* namely the doctrinal, judicial, and administrative decrees coming out of the weekly meetings of the Congregation ranging in date from 1548 to the present (with lacunae); to the correspondence from provincial inquisitors to Rome, numbering some 225 volumes (previously only the letters *from* Rome were available); and, not least, to the records of the Sienese Inquisition, thought to be substantially complete, which were transferred to the Supreme Congregation in 1911 from the episcopal archive in Siena, which had housed them after the tribunal was suppressed by the grand duke Pietro Leopoldo in 1782. Although these records will help to fill in many gray areas, it seems safe to say that the new perspective on the Roman Inquisition will not be seriously impaired. The documentation coming to light will not bring back the Black Legend constructed by a bygone confessional age.

See also **Catholic Reformation and Counter-Reformation; Law**.

BIBLIOGRAPHY

Primary Works

Del Col, Andrea. *Domenico Scandella Known as Menocchio: His Trials before the Inquisition (1583–1599).* Translated by John Tedeschi and Anne C. Tedeschi. Binghamton, N.Y., 1996. The original Italian edition of the proceedings against the celebrated Friulan miller was published in 1990.

Firpo, Luigi. "Una relazione inedita su l'Inquisizione romana." *Rinascimento* 9 (1958): 97–102. Publishes an early-seventeenth-century account on the organization and routines of the Supreme Congregation.

Firpo, Massimo, and Dario Marcatto, eds. *Il processo inquisitoriale del Cardinal Giovanni Morone: Edizione critica.* 6 vols. Rome, 1981–1995. A monumental source for the study of the Reformation in Italy and the politicization of the Inquisition during the pontificate of Paul IV.

Pastor, Ludwig von. "Allgemeine Dekrete der römischen Inquisition aus den Jahren 1555–1597: Nach dem Notariatsprotokoll des S. Uffizio zum ersten Male veröffentlicht." *Historisches Jahrbuch der Görres-Gesellschaft* 33 (1912): 479–549.

Secondary Works

Borromeo, Agostino. "The Inquisition and Inquisitorial Censorship." In *Catholicism in Early Modern History: A Guide to Research.* Edited by John W. O'Malley. St. Louis, Mo., 1988. Pages 253–272. Bibliographical survey.

Del Col, Andrea, and Giovanna Paolin, eds. *L'inquisizione romana in Italia nell'età moderna: Archivi, problemi di metodo, e nuove ricerche.* Rome, 1991. The papers presented at an international symposium, Trieste, 18–20 May 1988.

Grendler, Paul F. *The Roman Inquisition and the Venetian Press, 1540–1605.* Princeton, N.J., 1977. Contains an excellent chapter on the organization and procedures of the Inquisition in Venice.

Henningsen, Gustav, and John Tedeschi in association with Charles Amiel, eds. *The Inquisition in Early Modern Europe: Studies on Sources and Methods.* De Kalb, Ill., 1986. Based on several papers presented at a Danish symposium, September 1978.

Jobe, Patricia H. "Inquisitorial Manuscripts in the Biblioteca Apostolica Vaticana: A Preliminary Handlist." In *The Inquisition in Early Modern Europe: Studies on Sources and Methods.* Edited by Gustav Henningsen and John Tedeschi in association with Charles Amiel. De Kalb, Ill., 1986. Pages 33–53. Detailed description of thirty-four manuscripts, especially useful because they are all available in microfilm at St. Louis University.

Peters, Edward. *Inquisition.* New York and London, 1988. A sweeping panorama of the Inquisition—medieval, Spanish, and Roman—in history and myth, with a comprehensive bibliographical essay.

Prosperi, Adriano. *Tribunali della coscienza: Inquisitori, confessori, missionari.* Turin, Italy, 1996. An original, provocative study of the affirmation of Catholic hegemony in Italy.

Romeo, Giovanni. *Inquisitori, esorcisti e streghe nell'Italia della Controriforma.* Florence, 1990. The best and most complete account of inquisitorial attitudes and procedures in regard to occult crimes.

Tedeschi, John. *The Prosecution of Heresy: Collected Studies on the Inquisition in Early Modern Italy.* Binghamton, N.Y., 1991. Revised and updated in an Italian translation: *Il giudice e l'eretico: Studi sull'Inquisizione romana.* Milan, 1997.

Vekene, Emil van der. *Bibliotheca bibliographica historiae sanctae Inquisitionis. Bibliographisches Verzeichnis des gedruckten Schrifttums zur Geschichte und Literatur der Inquisition.* 3 vols. Vaduz, Liechtenstein, 1982–1992. The standard bibliography listing both primary and secondary literature.

JOHN TEDESCHI

Spanish Inquisition

The system of inquiry (*inquisitio*) into heresy in the Catholic church dated from the thirteenth century and was associated principally with the countries of southern Europe, where the most famous of the inquisitions was that in Spain. In the Crown of Aragon, a medieval inquisition sanctioned by papal authority had been introduced in 1238 under the auspices of Ramon de Penyafort but had declined into inactivity by the fifteenth century; in the rest of the peninsula the medieval inquisition was unknown, and heresy when it occurred was tried in the bishops' courts.

Origins. Social pressure, dating from the fourteenth century, against converts of Jewish origin (conversos) led the late-fifteenth-century Spanish rulers Ferdinand and Isabella to ask the papacy to sanction the establishment of a tribunal in Castile to "inquire" into the converts' orthodoxy. The bull by Sixtus IV for an inquisition was issued in 1478, and it began functioning in 1480, first of all in Seville. Three years later (1483) the new tribunal was also established in Aragon, replacing the medieval tribunal there. After initial disagreements between Ferdinand and the papacy over its functions, the inquisition was given a firmer structure with the appointment of a Dominican prior, Tomás de Torquemada, as first inquisitor general of the united tribunals of Castile and Aragon, creating in effect a "Spanish" Inquisition. Torquemada drew up the first of the many Instructions that gave the Holy Office its working organization (1484–1485). In time, some sixteen permanent local tribunals were set up all over the peninsula (the last two were those of Galicia in 1574 and Madrid in 1640), and they were also extended (from 1571) to the American colonies of Spain. King Ferdinand's realms of Sardinia and Sicily also had the Spanish Inquisition (from 1500), but Ferdinand's attempts to introduce it into the newly acquired realm of Naples (1510) were firmly resisted. At no time thereafter did any king of Spain attempt to export the Spanish tribunal to other realms.

The Inquisition had jurisdiction only over baptized Christians who fell into error; it had no authority over Jews or Muslims. Those first prosecuted by the tribunal in the 1480s were almost exclusively conversos (over 90 percent of all the accused), but they did not necessarily suffer the death penalty: the early "edicts of grace," which encouraged conversos to confess their errors, guaranteed pardon, and the majority of death sentences were against absent accused. Though notoriously harsh in its early years, the Inquisition executed fewer people than is generally believed, possibly two thousand conversos during the half century 1480–1530; executions, for whatever offense, were few after those years. Though it has been widely believed that the conversos secretly persisted in practicing Judaism (a belief shared by the inquisitors when they justified the establishment of the Holy Office), the weight of the evidence indicates that they were convinced Christians who occasionally combined residual Jewish cultural practices with their normal Christian religion. A perception of social difference provoked conflicts with non-Jewish Christians, who therefore denounced conversos to the tribunal. The Inquisition gave respectability to anti-Semitic prejudices in Spanish society and perpetuated anti-Jewish attitudes, notably in the approval it subsequently gave to the blood-purity statutes that discriminated against people of Jewish origin. It was also the chief instigator of the expulsion of Jews from mainland Spain in 1492.

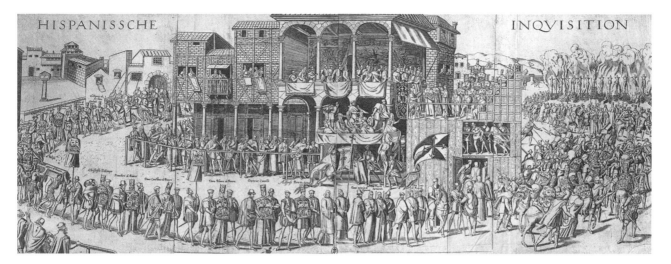

The Spanish Inquisition. German engraving; sixteenth century. BIBLIOTHÈQUE NATIONALE, PARIS/GIRAUDON/ART RESOURCE

Structure and Organization. The Inquisition derived its jurisdiction from the pope and could therefore claim to be an ecclesiastical court. But it was in practice dependent wholly on the crown, which paid salaries and also administered the tribunal through a central council, the Suprema (set up in 1488), consisting eventually of about six inquisitors (including the inquisitor general), a couple of judges from the royal council, and two secretariats, one for Castile and one for "Aragon." (The latter covered all the non-Castilian Spanish realms, including America.) It was therefore also a secular court. Its organization was based on that of the medieval papal inquisition as it had operated in France, and as in the earlier body the inquisitors were at the beginning all from the Dominican order. Inquisitors did not necessarily have to be clergy or theologians; the basic requirement came to be that they should have a university degree in law. Each of the permanent Spanish tribunals, with two or three inquisitors and a small administrative staff, was lodged in a suitable city building equipped with prison cells. It was assigned coverage of a large district, usually one or more provinces, and relied for its efficacy on a small network of assistants, the familiars (lay personnel who carried out bureaucratic tasks) and *comisarios* (local clergy).

The great period of inquisitorial activity was in the years 1480–1530, when conversos were its main objective and it initiated possibly three-fourths of all the prosecutions concluded in the course of its history. Decline of activity thereafter forced it to seek alternative funding, since it had been financed precariously out of confiscations from the property of those

arrested, and not until the 1560s did it obtain more reliable financing and also a more secure organization. The tribunal never became rich; the property of prisoners, for example, was usually partially used to maintain them during their confinement, and some income frequently went to the crown.

Though it constantly clashed with other jurisdictions, and was generally met with hostility outside Castile, with rare exceptions (notably the prosecution in 1592 of Aragonese who had supported the disgraced royal secretary Antonio Pérez) the tribunal was not used for political ends nor did it ever enhance royal power. It carried out prosecutions not on the basis of espionage by its familiars (as is often believed) but exclusively on the basis of denunciations made to each tribunal by members of the public, who were usually motivated by prejudice or animosity. The Inquisition therefore functioned actively in parts of Spain where community conflict was acute but received less support in non-Castilian areas such as Catalonia where it was considered a foreign institution.

Inquisition judicial procedures were based on secrecy, a practice alien to traditional Spanish law. In the early years denunciations were invited through an edict of grace, which allowed a month during which one could confess to heresy and repent and be pardoned. Inquisitors were also instructed to make periodic "visitations" through the towns to receive information. Before a person was arrested by the tribunal the evidence against him or her was examined by theologians to see if heresy was involved; if so, the person was detained and all property seized to pay for costs. The accused was then held in the inquisitorial prison and periodically examined by the inquisitors in sessions that constituted the "trial," during which advocates for the prosecution and defense were allowed to act. Torture was rarely used to extract information, and then only in cases involving heresy. Sentences were normally decreed not by the inquisitors alone but with the presence of lay judges and a legal representative of the local bishop.

The best known aspect of the tribunal was the *auto-de-fé,* a normally public ceremony which was given a more elaborate form in 1559 during the persecution of Protestants. Sentences were made public at the *auto;* executions, if any, were carried out subsequently in a different location and implemented not by the inquisitors, who as clergy were not allowed to shed blood, but by the local authorities, to whom the condemned were handed over ("relaxed to the secular arm"). In periods of great activity, such as the 1480s, *auto*s could be held annually, but outside such periods they were seldom held more than once a decade.

Prosecutions. Apart from interrogating the conversos, the Inquisition inquired also into the religious life of the large Islamic minority in Spain, the Moriscos, theoretically Christianized in Castile since 1502 and in Aragon since 1526. In the later sixteenth century Moriscos were a third of all those tried by the tribunal, though relatively few were executed and in practice the religious divergence of the Moriscos was tolerated as being incurable.

It is a common opinion, believed even in the sixteenth century, that the Inquisition saved Spain from going Protestant. This is unlikely, since the tribunal did not begin to act against suspected Protestants until the mid-sixteenth century; Spain's immunity from heresy until that date was due rather to its cultural isolation. When Protestants were identified in 1558, they were eliminated in a number of trials over the years 1558–1562 (about seventy were executed, considerably more imprisoned and penanced). However, Reformation heresy was a minor episode—after 1562 a few scattered cases occurred, but the bulk of arrests for so-called Lutheranism were of foreign nationals, such as sailors, who had strayed into the Inquisition's jurisdiction. Controversies of the Reformation period allowed the tribunal to carry out some of its most famous arrests, notably that of the archbishop of Toledo, Bartolomé Carranza, arrested in 1559 on suspicion of heresy and released into the hands of the papacy only in 1567.

As a convenient general court of justice, the Inquisition was allowed to extend its functions beyond the mere pursuit of heresy, tending to intrude into areas of minor administration (prosecution of those smuggling horses abroad) and morality (certain sexual attitudes and practices, in particular bigamy and sodomy, the latter an offense that was prosecuted only by the Inquisition of the territories in the Crown of Aragon). It also intervened from time to time in cases of witchcraft, an offense over which jurisdiction for the most part remained with secular courts. In a crucial decision of 1526, the Suprema decided to treat witchcraft as an imaginary offense and therefore not liable to prosecution. Occasionally thereafter some tribunals exceeded their authority and allowed witches to be executed, but after a famous case in Navarre in 1610 no witches suffered the death penalty at the hands of the Inquisition, though they continued to be executed in some number by Spanish secular courts.

The role of the Holy Office in censorship has led to unsubstantiated claims that it crushed free thought and destroyed culture. In fact, licensing and prepublication censorship were controlled by the state (since 1502 and particularly 1558) or by the church, not by the Inquisition, whose role was limited to two spheres: receiving denunciations of books (very few were made) and enforcing observance of the lists of condemned items issued as the Index of Prohibited Books in 1551, 1559, and 1583, with further editions in the subsequent two centuries. Items of Spanish literature were called in question primarily in the 1559 Index, which banned some works of literature and severely attacked well-known works of piety. Indexes published after 1559 relied in great measure on the technique of expurgation, by which books were allowed to circulate once offending passages had been deleted. In general, the Index irritated booksellers but had negligible impact on authors (who published freely both inside and outside Spain) and on readers. Objections to its role in censorship date mainly from the eighteenth century, when the Inquisition was largely inactive in matters of heresy and concentrated its energy on preventing French Enlightenment thought from entering Spain.

Abolition. In the late sixteenth and throughout the seventeenth century the Inquisition concentrated its attention less on formal heresy (rarely found among Spaniards) than on matters affecting social discipline (oaths, immorality, superstition); after the 1590s if conversos were prosecuted they tended to be recent immigrants of Portuguese origin.

During most of the eighteenth century after the 1730s, the tribunal was inactive; later in the century only ten people were condemned in *autos-de-fé* and only four were burned. The role of the Inquisition tended to be restricted to censorship of books and ideas (so-called Jansenism) coming in from France, especially during the period of the French Revolution. The tribunal was eventually abolished, first in 1808 by the French, who occupied the peninsula during the revolutionary wars, and then by the Spanish themselves in 1834. Because the documents of the Spanish Inquisition were always secret, no reliable information on its activities was available until after its abolition. The first thorough survey of its career was made by one of its own former officials, Juan Antonio Llorente, in his *Histoire critique de l'Inquisition d'Espagne* (4 volumes; Paris, 1817–1818).

See also **Anti-Semitism; Conversos; Index of Prohibited Books; Moriscos; Pérez, Antonio.**

BIBLIOGRAPHY

Bethencourt, Francisco. *L'Inquisition à l'époque moderne: Espagne, Italie, Portugal, XVe–XIXe siècle.* Paris, 1995.

Dedieu, Jean-Pierre. *L'administration de la foi: l'Inquisition de Tolède (XVIe–XVIIe siècle).* Madrid, 1989.

Kamen, Henry. *The Spanish Inquisition: An Historical Revision.* London, 1997.

Lea, Henry Charles. *A History of the Inquisition of Spain.* 4 vols. New York, 1906–1908. Reprint, New York, 1988.

Márquez, Antonio. *Literatura e Inquisición en España (1478–1834).* Madrid, 1980.

Monter, William. *Frontiers of Heresy: The Spanish Inquisition from the Basque Lands to Sicily.* New York, 1990.

Netanyahu, Benzion. *The Origins of the Inquisition in Fifteenth-Century Spain.* New York, 1995.

Pérez Villanueva, Joaquín, and Bartolomé Escandell Bonet. *Historia de la Inquisición en España y América.* 2 vols. Madrid, 1984–1993.

HENRY KAMEN

The Inquisition in the Americas

The Inquisition began in the New World with the erection of dioceses, since the power of inquisitor was one of the several powers canonically invested in the bishop. The religious orders, thanks to the papal bull *Omnimoda* (1522), were also empowered to conduct inquisitions in regions more than a two-day ride from a bishop. While rare, there are examples of these early forms of Inquisition, namely the trials of the native lord Don Carlos of Texcoco in Mexico in 1539, and the trials conducted by Bishop Landa in the Yucatán in 1562.

The more formal Holy Office of the Inquisition in the New World was established by royal order in 1569, when Philip II created two offices, one in Lima, Peru, and the other in Mexico. A third office was opened in Cartagena, Colombia, in 1610. With the establishment of these offices, local bishops ceased to exercise inquisitorial function but were urged to cooperate with the Holy Office in all matters relating to the suppression of heresy. In reaction to some of the earlier excesses, native peoples were exempted from the jurisdiction of the Holy Office. As a result, only Spaniards, other Europeans, and ethnically mixed populations were subject to the Holy Office.

The officers of the Holy Office consisted of two inquisitors assigned to each main office by the crown. Other principal officials included a prosecuting attorney, or *fiscal,* and a notary. The Holy Office also maintained a network of laypeople, or *familiares,* who assisted it in its work. In cities distant from the main offices, the Holy Office enlisted assistance from local ecclesiastical officials called *comisarios,* or commissioners. All these individuals enjoyed the *fuero inquisitorial,* an exemption from the civil courts and the right to have personal suits heard in the inquisitorial court.

The principal occupation of the Holy Office in the New World was to assure the doctrinal homogeneity of the faithful. As a result, individuals who were specifically targeted by the Holy Office included foreigners, especially French, English, and Portuguese. Also targeted were conversos, Jews recently converted to Christianity. In fact, the hunt for persons who continued to practice Judaism in a hidden form, crypto-Jews, was one of the major efforts of the Holy Office; this emphasis resulted in the famous trials of Luis de Carvajal and his family in Mexico in 1596.

The Holy Office also investigated violations of the sacraments, such as the profanation of the consecrated host. Among the other more common cases were the prosecution of priests who violated the sanctity of the confessional, using it as a guise for obtaining sexual favors from female penitents. Similarly, men who pretended to be priests were subjected to the scrutiny of the Inquisition.

The activity of the Holy Office peaked in the seventeenth century. By the end of the colonial period it was rarely used. In general the Holy Office in the New World was less rigorous than in Spain. The end of the Holy Office came with the victory of liberal forces in Spain in 1820, although it was not finally suppressed until 1834.

BIBLIOGRAPHY

Greenleaf, Richard E. *The Mexican Inquisition of the Sixteenth Century.* Albuquerque, N.Mex., 1969.

Lea, Henry C. *The Inquisition in the Spanish Dependencies.* New York, 1908.

Medina, José T. *Historia del tribunal de la Inquisición de Lima, 1569–1820.* 2d ed. Santiago, Chile, 1956.

Medina, José T. *Historia del tribunal del Santo oficio de la Inquisición en Mexico.* 2d ed. Santiago, Chile, 1952.

JOSEPH F. SCHWALLER

Portuguese Inquisition

The Inquisition was founded in Portugal during the reign of King John III the Pious (ruled 1521–1557), who wished to prevent religious pluralism in his domains and block the circulation of heretical works. He first established a censorship board under Frei Gaspar do Casal. In 1531 Pope Clement VII issued an inoperative papal bull, revoked two years later, establishing a Portuguese Inquisition.

Jurisdiction. Pressures were exerted in Rome by representatives of Portuguese New Christians to delay or prevent the setting up of a functioning Inquisition. In 1536 Pope Paul III, by the bull *Cum ad nil Magis,* provided for an Inquisition in the realms of the Portuguese monarchy and named the bishop of Ceuta, Diogo da Silva, as inquisitor general. In October 1536 an edict listing offenses under the jurisdiction of the Inquisition—among them Jewish, Protestant, and Islamic observances; witchcraft; sacrilege; and bigamy—was compiled. The first public ceremony of the act of faith (auto da fé) took place in Évora in 1536, and the first extant denunciation was received in the same city. The first act of faith in Lisbon occurred in 1540. The first burning of an individual condemned by the Portuguese Inquisition occurred in 1543 in Évora. The number of those sentenced to die during the period from 1536 to 1674 by the Lisbon tribunal was 593; in Coimbra the total was 454, and in Évora it was 468, for a total of 1,515. A few sentences may have been commuted at the ceremonies of the act of faith. The number of death sentences rendered by the Goa Inquisition, whose archives were burned in 1812, is less sure, but at least 103 individuals were condemned to die in Portuguese India between 1562 and 1605. Other Inquisition punishments included exile, terms as galley slaves, floggings, and property confiscations.

In 1539 the archbishop of Braga, later cardinal and king of Portugal, Henry (1512–1580), brother of King John III, was named inquisitor general; he retained that post until his death. The bishops of Coimbra, Lamego, and Ceuta were named in 1546 to head regional inquisitions; on 16 July 1547, however, a bull established tribunals of the Holy Office with inquisitors in Lisbon, Évora, Coimbra, Lamego, and Tomar in continental Portugal, and in Goa in Portuguese India. The Goa tribunal came into operation only in 1560, with jurisdiction over Portuguese possessions in Asia and east Africa, and the first act of faith was celebrated there in 1562. With the exception of Goa, no permanent tribunals sat in the Portuguese colonies, including Brazil. Inquisition business in the captaincies of Portuguese America was directly administered by correspondence between colonial agents of the Inquisition, both clerical and lay, and the Lisbon Tribunal. An umbrella General Council that sat in Lisbon produced revised bylaws of the Inquisition in manuscript in March 1570, by which time the Oporto, Lamego, and Tomar tribunals had been closed. The first printed version of the Inquisition bylaws appeared in 1613, and the second in 1640. During the joint monarchy of Portugal and Spain (1580–1640), the Portuguese tribunals retained their autonomy.

Operation and Personnel. The main purpose of the Inquisition was to ensure that converted Jews and their progeny, called New Christians, did not apostatize to Judaism. The Inquisition also sought to enforce Roman Catholic orthodoxy among gentiles. The offenses that were to be denounced to the Inquisition were enunciated in an edict of the faith, to be read annually in each parish church; the edict was revised occasionally. Christians knowing of individuals who committed the offenses were to denounce them. The accused could be tortured, and those found guilty could be flogged, imprisoned, exiled, and their property confiscated, or they could be turned over to the secular authorities for execution.

Denunciation of suspects was facilitated by the development of a system of local commissaries of the Inquisition, always ordained, and who were appointed after investigation into their suitability. Nominations of commissaries started toward the end of the sixteenth century and grew in number during the seventeenth. Commissaries were assisted in their investigations by auxiliaries called familiars of the Inquisition, usually laypersons. The numbers of familiars named by decade generally increased from 1571 to 1640; during that period a total of 1,618 men had been appointed for life. Their most common professions were those of farmer and merchant. A major review of the personnel and their performance in the central bureaucracy of the Lisbon Inquisition took place in 1571. The full implementation of the system, with agents of the Inquisition present in major centers throughout the Portuguese world, extended over decades but was substantially completed by

1600. The highest concentration of voluntary lay auxiliaries, the familiars, was found in the towns of Pernambuco, followed by Bahia and Rio de Janeiro, all in Brazil. (They were often overseas Portuguese immigrant merchants not of New Christian descent.)

An important means of maintaining contact between the tribunals was visitations, or inspections. The General Council ordered a series of inquisitorial visitations in response to reports of moral and doctrinal laxity in parts of continental Portugal, the Atlantic islands, parts of Africa, and Brazil. These visitations were concentrated between 1542 and 1637 and occurred less frequently than in territories under the jurisdiction of the Spanish Inquisition. The Azores and Madeira were visited in 1575 and 1576, 1591 through 1593, and 1618 and 1619. Angola was visited in 1561 and 1562, 1589 through 1591 and 1596 through 1598. Inquisitorial visitations took place in Asia in 1561 and 1562, 1589 through 1591, 1596, 1610, 1619 through 1621, and 1636. In Brazil, Father Heitor Furtado de Mendonça collected confessions and denunciations in Bahia from 1591 through 1593, and in Pernambuco from 1593 through 1595. Father Marcos Teixeira investigated three bishoprics along the Spanish frontier between 1578 and 1580, and was again a visitor in Bahia from 1618 through 1620. Inquisitorial investigations fluctuated in number in different years in accordance with the instructions sent by the General Council and the zeal of the agents. They were often assigned to junior members of the Inquisition bureaucracy to carry out and those individuals were often promoted to higher ranks later in their careers. Documentation from some of these visitations was published in the twentieth century and provides historians with information about social conditions and religious beliefs. Outside of the visitation periods, individual denunciations were forwarded to the seats of the tribunals with jurisdictions over the areas, which then instructed clerical commissaries to investigate and to arrest, if so instructed, those accused who were to stand trial.

Impact. In different parts of the Portuguese world the nature of the denunciations (many of which were not followed up), preliminary inquiries, and arrests by the Inquisition varied over time. For example, in a district south of Lisbon in 1624 and 1625, only 16 percent of denunciations resulted in a judgment. In Portugal proper, the percentage of New Christians among those denounced to the Inquisition was always higher than in neighboring Spain during the sixteenth and seventeenth centuries. Women appeared among the accused, especially New Christians. For the years from 1541 to 1580 in the Coimbra Inquisition, twice as many women were accused as men, but from 1581 to 1640 the numbers were approximately equal. Similar variations were found in other parts of Portugal. In Brazil the main business was the pursuit of converted and baptized Christians who were observing Jewish religious laws, but also investigated were cases of witchcraft, blasphemy, bigamy, and after 1562, of sodomy. Amerindians, Africans, and white women were rarely investigated before 1640. As a result of distance from the metropole and the relatively less effective colonial system of repression there, Brazil became a haven for New Christians, especially among sugar planters. Denounced individuals were transshipped to Lisbon if initial investigations showed sufficient grounds for a trial. In Goa, the Inquisition was primarily concerned with apostasy to Hinduism or Islam by baptized local Christians or the practice of non-Christian religious rituals, including Judaic ones by New Christians and other Europeans.

Contrary to its bloodthirsty image, the Portuguese Inquisition rarely imposed the death sentence. Between 1536 and 1674, a total of 32,675 individuals were tried by the courts; of these 1,618, or 5 percent, were executed in person or effigy.

Arrests and confiscations at the behest of the Inquisition damaged the economic life of Portugal and her colonies by disrupting the system of personal credit drawn on rich New Christian merchants. The inquisitors also played an important role in book censorship. Agents of the Inquisition searched foreign vessels for contraband forbidden books. A first list of prohibited books was made in 1547, and following the first Roman Index of 1559, the Portuguese catalogs not only promulgated it but added more books in 1564, 1581, 1597, and particularly in 1624. Since Portuguese books required prepublication authorization by the Inquisition, very few of them were listed in the catalogs of prohibited works.

The archives of the Portuguese Inquisition were deposited in the National Library under lay control in 1821. The most complete of any in Europe, they are now kept in the National Archives of Portugal in Lisbon.

See also **Index of Prohibited Books.**

BIBLIOGRAPHY

Bethencourt, Francisco. *História das inqusições: Portugal, Espanha, e Itália.* Lisbon, Portugal, 1994. The indispensable comparative study of Portuguese practice with that of Spain and Italy. A French edition has fewer illustrations.

Coelho, António Borges. *Inquisição de Évora: Dos primórdios a 1668.* 2 vols. Lisbon, Portugal, 1987. Gives an overview of a regional tribunal with jurisdiction over parts of eastern and southern Portugal.

De Bujanda, J. M. *Index de l'inquisition portugaise 1547, 1551, 1561, 1564, 1581.* Index des livres interdits, vol. 4. Sherbrooke, Canada, 1995. Lists the authors and books forbidden by the Portuguese Inquisition and includes reproductions of pages from banned books issued by various printers.

Farinha, Maria do Carmo Dias. *Os arquivos da inquisição.* Lisbon, Portugal, 1990. Provides an overview of the extant documentation and lists of inquisitors.

DAVID HIGGS

INTERNATIONAL RIVALRY.   *See* **Dynastic Rivalry.**

INTERPRETATIONS OF THE RENAISSANCE.

See **Renaissance,** *subentries on* **The Renaissance in Historical Thought, The Renaissance in Literary Intepretation,** *and* **The Renaissance in Popular Imagination,** *and the entry* **Renaissance, Interpretations of the.**

INVENTIONS.   *See* **Scientific Instruments; Technology.**

IRELAND.

In the fifteenth and sixteenth centuries Ireland had a population of approximately one million people. Most of the population was concentrated in the area known as the Pale, which consisted of the shires of Dublin, Meath, Westmeath, Kildare, and Louth. The Pale, along with the usually loyal corporate towns, was the only area of Ireland subject to English rule. The Pale itself was ruled by its lords and gentry, sometimes known as the "Old English," who were often able to trace their ancestry in Ireland back to the initial English invasion in the twelfth century. The leading figures in the Pale tended to regard themselves as English, and they generally supported the crown's initiatives in Ireland as long as those initiatives did not clash with their own goals.

Economy.   The Pale was the most fertile and prosperous area in Ireland. The aristocrats and gentry, who owned most of the land, made their money through collecting rents from their tenants and through a system of extortion sometimes called "coyne and livery," by which landlords exacted food and lodging from their tenants without payment in order to maintain private armies. While agriculture was the principal source of wealth, a rather primitive trading community was emerging in Dublin, engaged in the export of hides, tallow, linen yarn, and skins, along with the import of wine, salt, coal, and manufactured goods.

During this period Ireland was culturally divided. English influence prevailed in the Pale. Outside the Pale, Ireland was split between the English and Gaelic worlds. Much of the north and the western seaboard had more in common with Scotland and the Western Isles than with the Pale or England. At the same time much of the population in the lowlands of Leinster and Munster, geographically Gaelic, held stronger ties to the Pale and England.

Political Organization.   Power and lordship in Renaissance Ireland was overwhelmingly decentralized, based on the complex relationship between the overlord, his kinsmen, his vassal chiefs, and their kinsmen and clients. The maintenance of power depended upon the ability of a lord successfully to demand military service, rents, food, labor, lodging, and other forms of deference and tribute from those on his lands and prevent incursion from outsiders. Loss of land or loss of ability to control that land struck at the core of an Irish lord's power. Moreover, officeholding within the church hierarchy and Dublin bureaucracy gradually became the preserve and an additional source of power for the Old English aristocracy.

Governing Ireland presented many of the same problems that were posed by the governance of other English borderlands, such as Wales, the northern borders between England and Scotland, Calais, and the Channel Islands. The English wanted their peripheries ruled as inexpensively and inobtrusively as possible and were rarely willing to expend much money or devote much attention to them. For the most part, the English entrusted the rule of their borderlands to the authority of a local magnate. That magnate was expected to have enough power to enforce order, collect taxes, and raise a military force in times of emergency. Such a strategy was relatively cheap but entailed risks. A magnate with enough power to govern effectively could in the right circumstances use his power against English authority.

The most powerful of the Pale lords in Ireland in the early sixteenth century were the Fitzgeralds of Kildare, who maintained extensive holdings in the Pale and had successfully extended their authority into the Gaelic midlands. For most of the early Tudor period the Kildare earls represented the crown as the chief governors in Ireland, and they were capable of mustering considerable military support both on the crown's behalf and against it.

Ireland

common law was administered and taxes were collected with efficiency. During the early Tudor period, the crown's revenues in Ireland were actually increasing. Internal violence remained, but Ireland before the Tudors posed few problems for England. It was not until the late fifteenth century that the recovery of France and the political turmoil of the War of the Roses compelled English policy makers to pay more attention to Ireland. The recovery of France placed a powerful enemy across the channel from England. The War of the Roses and its aftermath included two attempts to seize the English throne by invading England from Ireland, both of which found Irish support and one of which was supported by the Irish Parliament and the English deputy in Ireland, Gerald Fitzgerald, the eighth earl of Kildare. The invasions were easily suppressed, but in 1494 the English decided to dispatch an English deputy, Sir Edward Poynings, to Ireland. Poynings punished the Irish lords who had supported the invasions and imposed Poynings's Law, which placed the Irish Parliament under the control of English authority.

English Policies in Ireland. The need to control Ireland became more evident during the 1530s and 1540s, when several changes in English government threatened the dominance of the leading families of the Pale. In the early 1530s several reformers called for new policies in Ireland, including the abandonment of coyne and livery and the appointment of English officials to Irish offices. Moreover, the break from the Roman Catholic Church and the establishment of the Protestant Church of England by Henry VIII (ruled 1509–1547), in addition to introducing unpopular divisions at home, complicated foreign relations. After the Reformation, religion played an important part in the construction of foreign alliances of both Catholic and Protestant countries, and Catholic powers quickly recognized that Ireland held an immense strategic value in dealing with schismatic England. With its extensive and craggy coastline, combined with the inability of the English to extend their influence much beyond the Pale, Ireland posed enormous logistical difficulties for the English policy makers charged with its defense. From Ireland an invasion of England could be launched, and in any event significant amounts of men, money, and resources would have to be expended to quash a rebellion in Ireland begun with foreign assistance.

Moreover, during the same period, English policy makers began trying to increase the amount of English control of the Dublin government, along the

Outside the Pale, authority was informal but still exercised by local magnates. In Ulster the most powerful overlords were the O'Neills of Tyrone, whose rivalry with the O'Donnells of Tyrconnell often defined Ulster politics. In Connaught the dominant lordships were held by the rival factions of the Burke families, the Burkes of Mayo and the Burkes of Clanrickard. By 1500 the Clanrickard Burkes had assumed control and the Ulster O'Donnells began a series of incursions into Connaught, forcing Clanrickard to seek allies among the O'Briens and the Ormonds.

Politics in Munster was shaped by the relationship between the Fitzgerald earls of Desmond and the Butler earls of Ormond. Both families were Old English normally loyal to English interests. But the scattered and rambling estates of the Fitzgerald earls of Desmond often intruded on those of the Butlers, and both sides occasionally entertained an interest in expansion, which resulted in increasing conflicts, border skirmishes, and military buildup.

Sporadic clashes between the various and transitory alliances of these groups were a constant part of fifteenth-century Ireland. But, despite this undercurrent of violence, English government in Ireland, in the hands of the Kildares, was often effective. The

lines suggested by the reformers. In the 1530s Thomas Cromwell, Henry VIII's closest adviser, asked the ninth earl of Kildare to give up the collection of coyne and livery and began appointing English officials to Irish offices. When Kildare balked, he was arrested and sent to the Tower in 1534. His son, "Silken" Thomas, repudiated Henry VIII's authority and rose in rebellion. Thomas's rebellion enjoyed some initial successes, and it took a force of twenty-three hundred men to quash it. The Kildare rebellion of 1534 was in large measure the response of the leading Pale family to perceived English incursions on its power. After the Kildare rebellion the English abandoned the practice of delegating a Pale lord as deputy and began appointing instead English-born deputies.

At the same time Ireland played a part in what historians have called "the British problem," which was compounded by the break from Rome. England's greatest defensive weakness was its borderlands, which were too varied and extensive to defend adequately, and several of England's nearest neighbors were Catholic or hostile in any event. By 1541 Henry had taken steps to reform government in Ireland, Wales, and in the north of England. But his attempts to control Scotland, an independent country as well as a borderland, compounded his difficulties in Ireland. In 1542 Henry invaded Scotland and inflicted a crippling defeat on the Scots at Solway Moss. Encouraged by his success, Henry invaded France, but failed wretchedly. French policy toward England then changed markedly, with serious consequences for English policy in Ireland. Earlier French kings had often been preoccupied with expansion in Italy. After Henry VIII's invasion of France, Henry II of France (ruled 1547–1559) was more concerned to prevent another English invasion. He did this primarily by exploiting English weakness along borderlands. With French agents dispatched to Scotland and Ireland to stir up trouble, the English were forced to begin a military campaign against Irish chieftains suspected of complicity with the French and of garrison construction along the borders of the Pale. By the mid-1550s English policy in Ireland was operated with two crucial but often contradictory goals. The traditional decisions about governing the Pale, which usually involved cutting costs and controlling the Pale lords, remained. But a new problem, sometimes more connected with events in Scotland, had emerged. This concerned developing a policy, often potentially expensive, that would protect Ireland from foreign intrigue.

The Tudor Conquest of Ireland. Between 1547 and 1565 the English pursued increasingly aggressive policies in Ireland. In 1556 Thomas Radcliffe, earl of Sussex, was appointed deputy. Sussex advanced a scheme to plant the areas of Leix and Offaly with loyal English subjects, expelling Scottish influence from Ireland, and bringing the rest of Ireland into obedience by building additional garrisons. He requested a larger army than earlier deputies had but proposed to pay for it by taxing the Pale community. Sussex, however, aroused the resentment of the Pale community and failed to control the Ulster chieftain Shane O'Neill, who plundered the borders of the Pale at will. In 1565 Sir Henry Sidney was appointed deputy. Sidney proposed to extend English control into Gaelic Ireland by implementing a series of provincial presidencies and placing different parts of western Ireland under the control of an English provincial president. Sidney also wished to wrest control of the land from Irish and Old English landowners and plant it with English settlers. Sidney's schemes met with considerable resistance, and his agents were forced to resort to violence, such as the burning of villages and the intimidation of the local population, in order to implement them.

At the same time English attitudes toward Ireland were changing. In the 1530s and 1540s English observers and officials often proposed "persuasive" strategies in Ireland to gain support for English policy, particularly in the introduction of the Protestant faith into Ireland. By the 1560s, the English in Ireland were faced with mounting foreign threats and seemingly unregenerate Old English and Irish populations. Influenced by these factors and by militant Calvinism, English writers began to advocate that the government implement aggressive policies toward Ireland and wrote tracts describing the inferiority and barbarity of the indigenous population. This spirit culminated in the writing of the most famous tract on Ireland, Edmund Spenser's *A View of the Present State of Ireland,* which appeared in 1596. Spenser proposed a grim final solution in which military rule would be imposed to confiscate Irish lands and destroy the native population by starving them to death. Spenser was by no means the first to advocate such a drastic solution, but he was one of the few who attempted to justify his exposition of it with a thin veneer of humanism. His solution for Ireland was not morally bankrupt; in his eyes it was virtuous, justified by the Irish abuse of earlier liberties granted them by the English.

Moreover, by the 1550s a steady stream of English officials, clergy, landowners, and settlers poured into

Ireland. Sir Turlough Luineach O'Neill (c. 1530–1595) submitting to Sir Henry Sidney (1529–1586), English deputy in Ireland. BY PERMISSION OF THE BRITISH LIBRARY. 1869c26

Ireland. The reliance of the English upon English-born deputies and officials in Ireland made it possible for ambitious courtiers, like Spenser, to make careers in Ireland and increased the number of the English officials seeking advancement in Ireland at the expense of the Old English families. The "New English" regarded Ireland as a colony and rejected the notion that they needed to share wealth and office with any part of the indigenous population. At the same time the tax demands of the English increased, through an exaction called the cess. The citizens of the Pale were expected, through the cess, to victual English garrisons, board soldiers, and supply horses, corn, and cattle to armies in the field. General cesses were held in 1556, 1563, 1566, and 1569, and there is evidence that cesses may have been held in other years as well. The English garrison in Ireland increased from about two thousand men in the 1560s to about six thousand men in the 1580s. These exactions and the bribery, fraud, and extortion that often accompanied them were bitterly resented. When key elements of the indigenous population, Old English and Gaelic, balked at the burden of the cess and exclusion from wealth and office, Ireland was transformed from a relatively insignificant part of the English polity to one that de-

manded regular attention and for which conquest became the most viable solution.

The tensions created by the entry of the "New English" into Ireland were made worse by constitutional confusions. After 1541 Irish policy increasingly was conceived in England by the sovereign and his council, with the Irish Parliament virtually ignored. This shift in government line clashed with the views of most of the Pale leadership, who expected some role in decision making. Thus, when confronted, particularly under the leadership of Sir Henry Sidney, the English deputy in Ireland for much of the 1560s and 1570s, who wished to change profoundly the nature of English rule in Ireland, the Palesmen held firmly to their constitutional claims, defending themselves as "commonwealth men," the real representatives of English interest in Ireland, in opposition to unjustified aggression.

International Pressures. Between 1565 and 1588 the tensions between England and Catholic powers, especially Spain, mounted. England and Ireland became caught in the power politics of the Counter-Reformation. English fears of an invasion from Catholic powers, possibly through Ireland, intensified. Security, rather than reform, became the principal consideration of English administrators in Ireland. The English demand for security and the requirement that the Palesmen should pay for it created an increasingly alienated Pale aristocracy, who felt they had no choice but to rebel and beg for assistance from foreign Catholic powers interested in weakening England. The rebellions of James Fitzmaurice Fitzgerald (1569–1573), the Baltinglass family, and the earl of Desmond in 1579 were primarily the expressions of a previously loyal Irish aristocracy that had been alienated by English policy. Foreign assistance for Irish rebels finally materialized in the Desmond rebellion. Even the defeat of the Spanish Armada in 1588 did not end English anxiety over Ireland. Throughout the 1590s the English continued to fear Catholic intervention in Ireland and, driven by this fear, strove to extend their influence into Gaelic Ireland. The rebellion (1595–1603) of Hugh O'Neill, earl of Tyrone, resulted from the English incursion into the territory and power of a previously loyal Gaelic lord.

Tyrone's rebellion was costly for the English. With Spanish assistance, Tyrone waged a guerilla war, largely eschewing direct confrontation with English forces, and it took nine years and an enormous amount of money to suppress the rebellion. Tyrone eventually surrendered at Mellifont in 1603, and in 1607 he and another leading lord, the earl of Tyrconnell, fled to the European continent.

Ireland in the Early Seventeenth Century. The flight of the earls and peace with Spain in 1604 reduced the importance of Ireland in English eyes. Subsequent deputies concentrated on the cultivation of English plantations in Munster and Ulster. The Ulster plantation was settled to a large extent by Scots immigrating into Ireland. In the 1620s Ireland resurfaced as an issue of importance when the possibility of English intervention on the Protestant side in the Thirty Years' War (1618–1648) again risked the possibility that English weakness in Ireland would be exploited by continental Catholic powers.

Ireland also became entwined in English domestic politics. In 1629, after several bitter quarrels over money with the English Parliament, Charles I (1625–1649) dissolved that parliament and ruled England without a representative body, even though he was deeply in debt. Dissolving parliament spared him the thankless task of asking them for money, but since taxes could only be raised with parliamentary consent, Charles was forced to seek other sources of revenue, which he found in several places. First, he and his ministers discovered laws still in the statute books that permitted them to collect certain kinds of taxes without parliamentary consent, even if those taxes had not been collected for decades or even centuries. Such measures were thus technically legal, but bound to offend. Second, he sent Thomas Wentworth, later the earl of Strafford, to Ireland. Wentworth sought to make Ireland profitable, and he did so by ruthlessly seizing for the crown those lands in which he found even the smallest defect in the title. Like Charles's taxes, Wentworth's measures were technically legal, but bound to offend.

By 1637 both Charles and Wentworth had succeeded in several senses. Charles's debts had been eradicated, and Ireland was profitable, which had contributed to Charles's improved fiscal status. But many had been offended by their actions. Moreover, an attempt to extend English religious practices to Scotland backfired when the Scots rose in rebellion against their imposition, launched a successful invasion of England, and refused to leave until Charles paid them for their troubles. With his surpluses exhausted by the war, Charles had no way to pay off the Scots and was forced to summon the body known as the Long Parliament to raise the money. Long Parliament was willing to raise the money to pay off the Scots but demanded a fearsome retribution in return. Among other things, Wentworth, who had been recalled from Ireland in 1639 to deal with the Scots, soon found himself convicted of treason by Long Parliament and was executed in May 1641. By the fall of 1641, Ireland, provoked largely by Wentworth's extortionate policies, was again in rebellion. Settling that rebellion would ultimately cost Charles I his throne and require the still more aggressive Oliver Cromwell to subdue.

Culture. The cultural achievements in other parts of Renaissance Europe were not matched in Ireland. Not only has little artistic achievement survived, but there is only minimal evidence that humanistic learning penetrated the island. Moreover, educational opportunities were limited. At the beginning of the English conquest, education in Ireland was primarily conducted by the church, with assistance from poets, legists, and other educated elements of society. In their efforts to control Ireland, English officials often clashed with the church, causing education to suffer. The dissolution of Ireland's monasteries further weakened education, driving many promising young Catholics to attend Catholic schools on the Continent.

In the 1540s several English officials, possibly influenced by humanist ideas, advocated a strategy for

English control of Ireland based on persuasion. This strategy was designed to anglicize Ireland by establishing the Protestant religion and by educating the indigenous population in English language and customs. Even those who pursued aggressive policies in Ireland saw the value in such a strategy. In the 1560s Sir Henry Sidney decided that if progress was to be made in the reformation of Ireland, politically and religiously, the state must assume control of education. As a result, an act was passed by Sidney's parliament that provided for the establishment of Latin grammar schools under the control of English officials.

English officials were also interested in the creation of a university to advance the Protestant faith. Although internecine squabbles delayed the approval of a charter until 1592, the College of the Holy and Undivided Trinity (later known as Trinity College) opened its gates in 1594. The creators of the college viewed it as an instrument for civilizing the native population and for the provision of educational opportunities for English settlers.

The most clearly articulated statement of the new settlers was, as we have seen, Edmund Spenser's *A View of the Present State of Ireland,* which argued that only the most coercive and draconian measures had a chance of success. One of Spenser's English contemporaries in Ireland, Sir John Davies, argued that the law could be employed as an instrument of conquest. In his tract *A Discovery of the True Causes why Ireland Was Never Entirely Subdued* (1612), Davies argued that the failure to extend English law to Ireland was the reason that the conquest had never been completed.

If Davies and Spenser represent the viewpoint of the English settler or official in Ireland, bardic poets may represent to a certain extent the viewpoint of the indigenous population. Despite the efforts of the English against them, poets remained important figures in Irish society. Powerful lords often employed poets to compose celebratory lines for special occasions and to conduct some of the lord's business. Since the poet depended upon the the lord's patronage for his survival, his poetry usually reflected what his lord wanted to hear. Not surprisingly, English officials regarded the poets as subversive and repeatedly tried to reduce their influence.

Several hundred manuscripts from these writers have survived. From such poets as Tadhg Dall O hUiginn and Eochaidh O hEodhusa, we can glean some idea of the native response to the English conquest of Ireland, though this response was varied. Most of the poetry remained fairly conventional, praising local potentates and displaying primary concern with local rivalries and factions. But there is some slight indication in the works of the poets that a limited sense of a national state was emerging. After the flight of the earls in 1607, Eochaidh O hEodhusa called for Hugh O'Neill to return home and restore the status of the Irish natural elite to its former station, though he blamed God's wrath against the lawlessness of Irish chiefs rather than the English for Ireland's plight.

In retrospect, the cultural and political history of Renaissance Ireland is pretty dismal. The highest cultural achievements came from English courtiers, and English adventurers eventually assumed control of Irish politics.

BIBLIOGRAPHY

Primary Works
Calendar of State Papers, Relating to Ireland. Edited by Hans Claude Hamilton, et al. 24 vols. London, 1860–.
Letters and Papers, Foreign and Domestic, of the Reign of Henry VIII. Edited by J. S. Brewer, et al. 22 vols. London, 1862–1932.

Secondary Works
Bradshaw, Brendan. *The Irish Constitutional Revolution of the Sixteenth Century.* Cambridge, U.K., 1979.
Brady, Ciaran. *The Chief Governors: The Rise and Fall of Reform Government in Tudor Ireland, 1536–1588.* New York, 1994. Much admired recent study.
Canny, Nicholas P. *The Elizabethan Conquest of Ireland: A Pattern Established.* New York, 1976. The trailblazing work on the nature of the English conquest.
Crawford, Jon. *Anglicizing the Government of Ireland: The Irish Privy Council and the Expansion of Tudor Rule, 1556–1578.* Dublin, 1993.
Ellis, Steven G. *Ireland in the Age of the Tudors: English Expansion and the End of Gaelic Rule.* London, 1999. The best, most up-to-date survey.
Ellis, Steven G. *Reform and Revival: English Government in Ireland, 1470–1534.* Woodbridge, U.K., 1986.
Ellis, Steven G. *Tudor Ireland: Crown, Community, and the Conflict of Cultures, 1470–1603.* Harlow, U.K., and New York, 1985.
Morgan, Hiram. *Tyrone's Rebellion: The Outbreak of the Nine Years' War.* London, 1993.
Palmer, William. *The Problem of Ireland in Tudor Foreign Policy, 1485–1603.* Woodbridge, U.K., 1994.
Perceval-Maxwell, Michael. *The Outbreak of the Irish Rebellion of 1641.* Montreal, 1994.

WILLIAM PALMER

ISABELLA OF CASTILE (1451–1504), queen of Castile (as Isabella I, 1474–1504). As the second child of the king of Castile, John II, and his second wife, Isabella of Portugal, Isabella of Castile's chances to reign were slim. They became even slimmer three years later when her father died and her

Isabella of Castile. Portrait by an unknown Flemish painter.
THE ROYAL COLLECTION © HER MAJESTY QUEEN ELIZABETH II

older half-brother, Henry IV, became king. Yet in the 1460s, dissident nobles, waging civil war, proclaimed Henry a tyrant, deposed him in effigy, and proclaimed her younger brother, Alfonso, rightful king. When Alfonso died suddenly in 1468, Isabella took up his claim, then made peace with Henry and pursued a more realistic path to the crown, as his heir. The following year, against Henry's wishes, she married Ferdinand, prince of Aragon and king of Sicily. Although Henry then renounced her, they subsequently reconciled, and at Henry's death in 1474 Isabella was crowned queen of Castile. The support of one powerful faction of nobles and the opposition of another led to renewed civil war, a contest Isabella had clearly won by 1478. The birth of a son that year and Ferdinand's succession to the crown of Aragon in 1479 promised actual Spanish unity.

Isabella the Queen. Isabella had little, if any, formal education, but a good mind and a strong will.

She exhibited high courage, a clear sense of royal vocation, and intuitive political skill. She understood that a woman could rule only with a strong man at her side. In Ferdinand she chose, sight unseen, not only her most attractive suitor but the only one who would reside in Castile and was acceptable to Castilians. Remarkably, their marriage brought love, trust, and lifelong partnership. In Castile, Isabella insisted the reign be represented as absolutely joint, although in principle and practice she never relinquished her role as proprietary queen. She also relied on highly capable ministers, notably Pedro González de Mendoza, archbishop of Toledo and cardinal of Spain; the Hieronymite friar Hernando de Talavera, who was both her chaplain and a principal financial adviser; and, after 1492, Francisco Jiménez de Cisneros, who took over the functions of both predecessors.

During her reign, the regions of Spain gained greater unity, society changed radically, international standing soared, and Spain embarked on what would become a global empire (under her grandson, Charles). In hindsight, the price was high, for in her time Spanish nationality received long-lasting definition, in ethnic and religious terms, as dedicated to eradicating divergent faiths and opinions. Isabella's reign instituted the Spanish Inquisition and expelled Spain's Jews in 1492 and Castile's Muslims in 1502.

As queen, Isabella—sometimes jointly with Ferdinand, sometimes in her own right—repeatedly drew on the time-honored and widely familiar language of holy war for a multitude of purposes: to justify her reign, define her political agenda, further social cohesion, enhance royal popularity and power, and effect a state-building consensus. War added urgency, a sense of crisis—even a sense of history—coming to a head and soon to end. And war dominated much of Isabella's life. Civil strife was followed by a decade of campaigns she oversaw against Granada, the last Muslim kingdom in Iberia. Granada's fall in 1492 completed Spain's reconquest, yet in that year the expulsion of the Jews, the sponsoring of Christopher Columbus, and a planned North African expedition signaled royal intent to continue pursuing religious exclusivity at home as well as carrying the crusade overseas. Even so, from 1492 her own activities were directed principally toward ensuring internal peace and order and arranging advantageous marriages for her son and four daughters, who wed the heirs to the crowns of the Habsburgs and of Portugal and England.

Isabella the Renaissance Patron. Just when the Renaissance came to Spain has been hotly debated. What is certain is that under Isabella its manifestations were fused with Christian humanism and an emphasis on religious reform. Her library, her art, and her chronicles and other documents point to her having been drawn to two Renaissance aspects: the emphasis on piety and good works of the northern humanists and the resurgence of Roman imperial precepts in law, government, and the expansion of the realm. She employed an Italian humanist, Pietro Martire d'Anghiera (1457–1526, known in Spain as Pedro Mártir), as court tutor and she comes most alive in his account of her later years. Members of the powerful family of Cardinal Mendoza, her chief minister, were preeminent patrons of southern Renaissance learning and culture and instrumental in Mártir's coming to Spain.

Her tastes in art leaned toward the northern Renaissance. She collected Flemish tapestries and paintings, notably works by Hans Memling and Rogier van der Weyden. She commissioned an altarpiece by Juan de Flandes, who also painted several portraits of her. Isabella also patronized German master builders, notably Juan Guas, who built in late Gothic style. Perhaps the most significant monuments to herself remain the church of San Juan de los Reyes in Toledo, originally meant as her pantheon, and the Cartuja de Miraflores outside Burgos, housing her parents' tombs. Her architecture and its iconography reflected her essentially medieval political theology—apocalyptic and millennial, conveying a personal, dynastic, and national sense of divine mission—if perhaps Renaissance in the imperial reach and vigor conveyed.

Isabella, from all surviving accounts, generally commanded respect, even awe, by her regal, virtuous, and no-nonsense demeanor, inspiring, as she wished, love and fear. During her reign, Spaniards chafed at royal exactions, greater central control, and wartime hardships; but, after years of internal strife, they also welcomed strong leadership, greater safety and security, and the opportunities for profit, upward mobility, and self-advancement accompanying war. Clearly wise in the ways of image-making, she was also highly respectful of the power of public opinion at all levels and adept in courting and molding it. Isabella and her court, selectively mining a stock of memories of the Spanish past, outlooks on the present, and visions of the future, gave to Castilians and bequeathed to Spaniards yet to come a compelling story about themselves and their country. At its center was the fiction of her absolutely joint reign with Ferdinand. Together they had in fact forged a working relationship so successful that by the 1490s their world automatically coupled them— as in the honorific title bestowed by the pope, *Los reyes católicos,* the Catholic monarchs.

See also **Ferdinand of Aragon**; **Queens and Queenship.**

BIBLIOGRAPHY

Fernández-Armesto, Felipe. *Ferdinand and Isabella.* New York, 1975.

Ladero Quesada, Miguel Angel. *Los reyes católicos: La corona y la unidad de España.* Valencia, Spain, 1989.

Liss, Peggy K. *Isabel the Queen: Life and Times.* New York, 1992.

Prescott, William H. *The History of the Reign of Ferdinand and Isabella, the Catholic.* 3 vols. New York, 1837. Reprinted many times since.

PEGGY K. LISS

ISLAM. Islamic civilization, from Spain to India, enjoyed a period of cultural revival and renewal that began in the fourteenth century and lasted well into the seventeenth century. Throughout this period Islamic civilization remained the great challenger and stimulator of the West.

Egypt and Syria. Until 1517 the chief city of this world was Cairo, where the Mamluks, military slaves of first Turkish then Circassian origin, created a powerful state that destroyed the European Crusader bases on the Syrian coast and kept the Mongols east of the Euphrates. As part of this policy, in 1261 the Mamluk sultan Baybars I (ruled 1260–1277) set up in Cairo a descendant of the 'Abbasid caliphs of Baghdad with the title Successor of the Messenger of God. Such a caliph was in legal theory the fountainhead of Islamic authority, and princes were held to derive authority through him. Eastern rulers still sent embassies to Cairo for decrees to legitimize their rule in the eyes of the religious legal scholars, the ulema, and their subjects. In the western lands the sultans of Granada, Fès, and Tunis claimed to hold caliphal powers in their own right, with the collaboration of the ulema of the Maliki legal school who predominated there. Renaissance sultans also depended on the goodwill of the ulema of their realms, and they built and endowed mosques, academies for scholars, and convents for the Sufi exponents of mystical Islam.

Mamluk sultans depended on the revenues of the rich spice trade from the Indies, which they monopolized due to their control of the Red Sea, on the wealth of merchants, and on the industry and productivity of their subjects. Inflated prices for Eastern luxuries in the fifteenth century led both Spain and Portugal to explore other routes to the Indies, with immense consequences for the Renaissance world.

وَمِنْهُمْ جَبْرَئِيلُ

The Koran. The Angel Gabriel is depicted in a page from the Koran, probably painted in Egypt or Syria in the early fourteenth century. BY PERMISSION OF THE BRITISH LIBRARY

Since the Mamluk military government, "men of the sword," was made up of imported slave stock, the native population chiefly advanced as religious scholars and bureaucrats, "men of the pen." Wholesale subsidy of scholarship in Egypt and Syria led to a blossoming of literary compilations, historiography, lexicography, and legal studies. Even the Black Death in the middle of the fourteenth century did little to undermine Cairo's prestige, since it continued to attract new population. The Muslim counterpart of Martin Luther, Ibn Taymiyah (1263–1328) of Damascus, campaigned against traditionalism and mystical excesses in Islam and preached a fundamentalist return to the Muslim scriptures (Qur'an and hadith). He died in a fortress for his activities, but his ideas are still active in the modern world. The great Ibn Khaldun of Tunis (1332–1406), a universal genius, historian, philosopher, sociologist, statesman, diplomat, and religious scholar, ended his days in the academies of Cairo.

Spain and North Africa. In Spain and North Africa the destruction of the Muwahhid caliphate led to the creation of four important kingdoms. The Spanish Muslims, militarily weak, were concentrated in the Kingdom of Granada, which survived by paying tribute to Castile. While militarily weak, Spanish Islam was the most highly developed Muslim culture of the West. It produced magnificent architecture (e.g., the Alhambra, an extensive group of buildings built between 1230 and 1354 as a citadel for the Moorish kings of Spain), men of letters, and an elegant culture, which was the envy of Christian Spain. It survived until 1492, when it fell to the combined forces of Aragon and Castile.

In North Africa were three important Berber kingdoms: Fès of the Banu Marin Berbers; its rival, the Kingdom of Tunis of the Banu Hafs, and between them the smaller Kingdom of Tlemcen of the Banu Zayyan. In all three there was a cultural flowering, assisted by talented émigrés from Muslim Spain, and a turn to the Maliki form of Sunnism, fostered through the madrasah academies, which educated the elite and supported the rulers in each major city. All these kingdoms suffered, however, from their rivalries and the divisive activities of Arab and Berber tribes. By the fifteenth century their weakness tempted Portugal and Spain to intervene militarily in North African affairs.

Iran and Iraq. In Iran and Iraq after 1258, the Mongol successors to Hülegü Khan (c. 1217–1265), the brother of Kublai Khan, were at first hostile to Islam and courted an alliance with Western Christians, holding out the prospect of conversion to Christianity. There were many Muslim Turks in the Mongol armies, and when the popes could not deliver the alliance, the Mongol rulers of Iran and Iraq converted in 1295 to Islam like their relatives in southern Russia. Forty years after the devastating Mongol invasion of Iran and Iraq (1256–1258), these rulers had become patrons of Muslim culture and learning, building up where they had once destroyed. Persian literature, architecture, arts, and commerce flourished, and Iranian Muslim culture benefited from exposure to new influences from China. Yet the House of Hülegü could not create a stable regime in Iran, and by 1340 successor states had replaced its empire.

A Muslim regime established by Afghan and Turk warriors at Delhi at the end of the twelfth century prevented northern India from being absorbed in a Mongol realm. Under several dynasties this Muslim state created a powerful and wealthy empire, extending deep into the central plateau and forcing the Hindu rajas to pay tribute to the sultans of Delhi.

Refugees from central Asia and Afghanistan brought needed skills to the administration, and Muslim Sufi mystics converted great numbers of Indians to their religion. Islam took firm root in India and has been profoundly tinged by a Sufi vision of the faith.

Ottoman Empire. In Anatolia the decline of Mongol authority saw the creation of a number of petty principalities, or *beyliks,* organized by Turkoman tribesmen. The most successful of these, the Ottomans, arose before 1300 among the *ghazis,* or warriors for the faith, on the Byzantine frontier. By 1326 their ruler had established his capital in Bursa, or Prusa, on the northern slopes of Mysian Olympus. The goal of the state was from the first to force non-Muslims to accept Muslim domination, though they were free to keep their own religion and customs; the culture of the Ottoman *beylik* was eclectic and syncretistic. Later, the weakened Byzantine state and its successors in the Balkans could neither oppose nor co-opt these aggressive neighbors. By 1346 the Ottoman Orhan Bey was established on the European side of the Hellespont, his warriors were raiding Thrace, and he was the son-in-law of the emperor of Byzantium, John VI Cantacuzenus, and allied with Genoa against Venice. Through marriage diplomacy he expanded Ottoman control in the Anatolian *beyliks.*

Battles at Kosovo in 1389 by a league of Balkan Christians under Serbian leadership and at Nicopolis on the Danube in 1396 by a new Western Crusade failed to stop Orhan's grandson Bayezid (ruled 1389–1402), who adopted the title sultan of Rum (sultan of the Romans) with the blessing of the Cairo caliphate.

Around 1369 a Turkish Muslim warlord, Timur (Tamerlane), rose in Transoxiana to rid the country of Mongol misrule with the support of the ulema and settled people. With a great army of central Asians, he went on to ravage and plunder the cities of Iran, Iraq, Syria, Anatolia, southern Russia, and India, always advancing zeal for Islam as his motive. Artists and artisans were carried off to beautify his capital of Samarqand.

After Timur's death in 1405, his empire fell apart, but in Herat his descendants patronized a Timurid renaissance of the arts and Persian and Turkish letters and made their capital a synonym for culture and elegance. In 1507 Herat fell to the Uzbek Mongols, but in 1526 Babur, a Timurid prince who was king of Kabul, conquered Delhi and became the first of the Great Mughal emperors in northern India.

The Ottomans reestablished their power in Anatolia and the Balkans after Timur's onslaught. They recruited Balkan Orthodox peasants' sons, who, once converted to Islam, could advance by merit to the highest posts in the military and administration. The Ottomans also adopted the new military technology of firearms, and in May 1453 Mehmed II (ruled 1451–1481) took Constantinople as his imperial capital. A new crusade summoned to Ancona in 1463–1464 by Pius II was an ineffectual episode in the long war Mehmed fought with Venice and Hungary, and only Mehmed's death on 3 May 1481 terminated the planned Ottoman march on Rome from Otranto in southern Italy and the siege of Rhodes was broken off. This was retaken by papal and Neapolitan troops on 10 September 1481.

By 1512 the Safavid dynasty, a Shiʿite empire that had risen after 1501 and gained command of Iran and Iraq, threatened Ottoman control of eastern Anatolia. Mehmed's grandson Selim I (ruled 1512–1520) massacred the Shiʿites of Anatolia and in 1514 defeated the cavalry of the Safavid Shah Ismaʿil (ruled 1501–1524) with Ottoman artillery and musketry. In 1516–1517 Selim conquered the Mamluk empire of Syria, Egypt, and western Arabia. The Ottomans were now the paramount rulers of the Islamic world, but the Shiʿite Safavids prevented Ottoman occupation of the Iranian plateau and even patronized a brilliant cultural revival, while after 1526 descendants of Babur the Timurid ruled over a magnificent Indo-Islamic empire.

The reign of Selim's son Suleyman I from 1520 to 1566 marked the pinnacle of Ottoman power and magnificence. Hungary was invaded in 1526; Austria was ravaged and Vienna besieged in 1529, and the Habsburgs had to agree to pay tribute in 1533; Iraq was taken from the Safavids in 1534–1535; and North Africa, up to the borders of Morocco, was added to the empire, while Turkish fleets with French aid campaigned in the western Mediterranean against the Habsburg navy. These successes masked the incipient disintegration of the empire's complex administration and society. The system depended on a strong and competent sultan at the center, and incompetent rulers such as Suleyman's immediate successors opened the way for abuses. The decline was accompanied by economic changes that were difficult for the ruling elite to understand or to control. Nonetheless, the decay was slow. Not until the end of the seventeenth century was it clear that the great empire was on the defensive and its culture essentially in stasis.

See also **Mehmed II; Ottoman Empire; Süleyman I.**

BIBLIOGRAPHY

Abun-Nasr, Jamil M. *A History of the Maghrib*. Cambridge, U.K., 1971.

Atiya, Aziz S. "The Crusade in the Fourteenth Century." In *A History of the Crusades*. Edited by Kenneth M. Setton. Vol. 3: *The Fourteenth and Fifteenth Centuries*. Edited by Harry W. Hazard. Madison, Wis., 1975. Pages 3–26.

The Cambridge History of Islam. Edited by P. M. Holt, Ann K. S. Lambton, and Bernard Lewis. 2 vols. Cambridge, U.K., 1970.

Encyclopaedia of Islam 2. Edited by H. A. R. Gibb et al. Leiden, Netherlands, 1960–. See entries on Baybars, Ibn Khaldun, Ibn Taymiyya, Mamluk, Mughals, Othmanli, and Safawids.

Geanakoplos, Deno. "Byzantium and the Crusades, 1261–1453." In *A History of the Crusades*. Edited by Kenneth M. Setton. Vol. 3: *The Fourteenth and Fifteenth Centuries*. Edited by Harry W. Hazard. Madison, Wis., 1975. Pages 27–103.

Julien, Charles A. *History of North Africa: Tunisia, Algeria, Morocco, from the Arab Conquest to 1830*. London, 1970.

Shaw, Stanford J. *History of the Ottoman Empire and Modern Turkey*. Vol. 1: *Empire of the Gazis: The Rise and Decline of the Ottoman Empire, 1280–1808*. Cambridge, U.K., 1976.

Williams, John Alden. "Urbanization and Monument Construction in Mamluk Cairo." *Muqarnas* 2 (1984): 33–45.

JOHN ALDEN WILLIAMS

ISLAMIC THOUGHT.

During the Renaissance in the West, there was a new contact with the ideas, science, and art of classical civilization, from which the West had been severed for some time. This was not the case for Islam, where Greek science and philosophy had been translated into Arabic and entered the mainstream of culture by the tenth century C.E. (classical art and mythology were regarded from the outset as unassimilable). By the twelfth century, however, among the great majority of Muslims, the Sunnis, the study of philosophy had come under heavy attack, mainly because the scholastic theologians of the East were opposed to Neoplatonism, and especially to the study of metaphysics. This they felt challenged revelation, and was not in any case necessary, since the Muslim majority, they believed, was divinely shielded from error. Since the study of philosophy had stimulated and encouraged systematic and rational investigation, scientific inquiry seems to have been adversely affected by this opposition. The Shi'a continued to use philosophy, which they felt they needed in order to understand a world which was not proceeding at all according to God's plan.

The Mongol invasions of the East and the breakdown of the Muslim caliphate in Spain and North Africa in the thirteenth century were harmful to nearly all aspects of Islamic culture. Yet by the fourteenth century there was a general recovery of power and patronage in the Muslim lands, and new expansion of Islam in south Asia and in sub-Saharan Africa. In the fifteenth and sixteenth centuries great new Muslim empires were created. It is this age that we may call a Muslim renaissance, certainly in art and architecture, but political success was rarely paralleled by a renaissance of Islamic science and philosophy.

As always in Islamic civilization, the best minds went to the study of Islamic law, deduced by different methods among varying schools from the Qur'an, the sayings of the Prophet, and (among the Shi'a) the teachings of the imams.

In Iran, the study of philosophy had been maintained by the Shi'i Nasir al-Din Tusi (1201–1274), who collaborated with the Mongol invaders after 1258 and was held in high esteem by them as a counselor and astronomer-astrologer. His *Akhlaq-i Nasiri* (Nasirean ethics), written in Persian (philosophical works had hitherto been largely in Arabic, which had developed the vocabulary and terms), reads badly but continues the late Aristotelianism of al-Farabi (c. 878–c. 950) and the Neoplatonist tradition of Ibn Sina (Avicenna; 980–1037). It is particularly notable for its political philosophy, always a major interest of Islamic philosophers.

The flowering of Persian as a language of ideas following the Mongol invasions included a splendid series of mystical poets, beginning with Jalal al-Din Rumi (c. 1207–1273) of Konya, through Shams al-Din Muhammad Shirazi (1325–1390), known as Hafiz, and ending with 'Abd al-Rahman Jami of Herat (1414–1492). These celebrated the themes of the unity of the lover and the beloved, often ambiguously, often most gracefully, and left their imprint on the literature of the Turks and the peoples of India.

Elsewhere in the Sunni world, the study of metaphysical philosophy gave way to mysticism and theosophy, following the renowned and prolific Muhyi al-Din ibn al-'Arabi (1165–1240) of Spain, who had taught in Anatolia and Syria and died in Damascus. He had many students and celebrants. However rich in spiritual insights this literature may be, it dispenses with logical proofs, and has been avidly studied and debated in Islamic circles both Sunni and Shi'i ever since. The powers of rare individuals who are "friends of God," and the divine unity of all existence are some of its controversial themes. The ideas of Ibn al-'Arabi and his followers have influenced both Spanish Catholic and Jewish mysticism.

The fear that the legal and ethical system of Islam would be dissolved in mystical speculation also brought about a fundamentalist reaction, introduced by Ibn Taymiya of Damascus (1263–1328) of the Hanbali legal school, which insisted that the goal of Islam is not to understand or love God but to obey him, and this can only be done by return to the Qur'an and the practices of the Prophet.

Through two channels, something of Islamic philosophy was reintroduced into Sunni Muslim culture in its renaissance. Ibn Khaldun of Tunis (1332–1406), who went to Morocco and was there introduced to philosophy by Muslim scholars who privately still studied it, argued that there are discernible laws governing human society and the life of states. His *Muqaddima* (Introduction to history) is a work of genius.

In Iran, the Sunni judge of Shiraz, Jalal al-Din Dawani (1427–1501/02), plagiarized Nasir al-Din Tusi's ideas to produce his own *Akhlaq-i Jalali* (Jalalian ethics) in an easily readable Persian style, palatable to lay and Sunni readers, stating, for example, that the ruler of a virtuous state is guided not by the angelic "Active Intellect," but by Islamic law. It became a textbook of practical political science for educated members of the elite wherever Persian was read: Turkey, Iran, central Asia, and India.

The creation of the Safavid Shi'i empire in Iran (1501–1736) meant that Shi'a scholarship could develop freely, and this included philosophy. The "School of Isfahan" in the seventeenth century produced several conspicuous figures, including Mir Damad (d. 1631/32), Baha'i al-Din 'Amili (c. 1546–c. 1622), and most notably, Mulla Sadra of Shiraz (c. 1571–1640). This latter laid the basis for a new synthesis of mystical philosophy referred to as "the Transcendent Wisdom;" a synthesis of the ideas of Avicenna, Yahya al-Suhrawardi (mystical philosopher executed by Saladin; c. 1155–1191), Ibn al-'Arabi, and others. Among other things, he argued that time is the fourth dimension of matter.

In the Muslim empire of India, the need to find some accommodation between the very different culture of the Muslim ruling class and their Hindu subjects had created an atmosphere of syncretism, in which the new religion of Sikhism took root, though it became an implacable enemy of Islam in north India in the eighteenth century. The "Universal Toleration" (*sulh-i kull*) of the Mughal emperor Akbar (ruled 1556–1605), gave way to the "Renewal" branch of the already existing Naqshbandi Brotherhood, which rejected syncretism and called for a purification of religion through return to the Qur'an and hadith, and spread its ideas into central Asia and the Ottoman empire in the seventeenth and eighteenth centuries.

BIBLIOGRAPHY

Primary Work
Tusi, Nasir al-Din. *The Nasirean Ethics.* Translated by G. M. Wickens. London, 1964.

Secondary Works
Fakhry, Majid. *A History of Islamic Philosophy.* London and New York, 1970.
Holt, Peter M., Ann K. S. Lambton, and Bernard Lewis, eds. *Cambridge History of Islam.* 2 vols. Cambridge, U.K., 1970.
Nasr, Seyyed H. *Sadr al-Din Shirazi and His Transcendent Theosophy.* Tehran, 1978.
Rahmany, Fazlur. *The Philosophy of Mulla Sadra.* Albany, N.Y., 1975.
Sharif, Mian M., ed. *History of Muslim Philosophy.* 2 vols. Wiesbaden, Germany, 1963; 1966.

JOHN ALDEN WILLIAMS

ISSERLES, MOSES (also known as Rema or Rama; c. 1530–1572), Cracow rabbi, judge, and academy master, authority on Jewish ritual law, community leader. Moses Isserles was born to an elite Cracovian Jewish family; his father was a wealthy, educated lay leader, and his relations included two renowned rabbis, Solomon Luria (1510?–1574) and Meir Katzenellenbogen (1473–1565). Isserles studied at the academy of Shalom Shachna, chief rabbi of Lesser Poland, and eventually married Shachna's daughter. Isserles was little older than twenty when he was invited to sit on the Cracow rabbinical court. Soon thereafter he established his own rabbinical academy, which grew to be one of the most highly regarded in Europe.

Isserles's greatest literary achievements concerned Jewish ritual law, or halakah. Most significant were his glosses on Joseph Caro's codification of Jewish law, the *Shulhan 'arukh* (Set table). By adding central European traditions to the book originally written in Safed, Isserles's glosses rendered the compendium authoritative for many Jews throughout Europe and the Levant. Isserles wrote other halakic works as well, including glosses on a seminal fourteenth-century legal code called the *Arba'ah turim* (Four columns), an essay on Jewish dietary laws, and many *responsa* (written decisions or rulings). His legal rulings drew generously upon French and German rabbinic sources, dating from the eleventh century and later. These rulings also took account of religious customs, sometimes elevating them to the status of obligation. Isserles's halakic compendiums were attacked by eminent contemporaries for various reasons. They attained great currency, however, which they have not relinquished to this day.

Isserles also wrote novellae (critical textual analyses) for portions of the Talmud, a commentary on the thirteenth-century kabbalistic classic the *Zohar*, an allegorical commentary on the Book of Esther, a mystical and philosophical exposition of Solomon's Temple and its rites, and glosses on Georg Peurbach's fifteenth-century cosmology, the *Theoricae novae planetarum* (New theories of the planets).

Isserles's writings reflect varied influences. He was much taken by medieval Jewish philosophy and its later interpretations. The impact of Maimonides's *Guide for the Perplexed* was especially great. Isserles was likewise influenced by kabbalistic literature, especially the *Zohar*. Intriguingly, Isserles often united his philosophical and kabbalistic interests, most obviously in his exegesis of Solomon's Temple. Indeed, Isserles wrote that "the ways of Kabbalah are [identical to] the ways of true, believing philosophers."

Isserles's impact was great in his day and has been enduring. His legal rulings were widely followed. His codifications are considered authoritative to this day and crucially legitimated the use of printed legal compendiums. Isserles's integration of philosophy and Kabbalah resonated among a circle of contemporary literati and inspired a brief revival of interest in philosophy and natural philosophy. Isserles trained an influential group of scholars whose work reflected extraordinarily broad interests and erudition. At least one of his students, David Gans (1541–1613), wrote that Isserles encouraged the study of natural philosophy and other liberal disciplines. Indeed, he was fiercely criticized by Solomon Luria for teaching Aristotle and other "Greek wisdom" in his academy.

Isserles died young, and his tombstone bears the epitaph, "From Moses to Moses, there were none like Moses," implying that Isserles was the greatest scholar since Maimonides. This aphorism reflected his exalted standing and acknowledged his efforts to revive rationalistic philosophy among central European Jews.

BIBLIOGRAPHY

Primary Works

Isserles, Moses. *Hagahot ha-Rama*. In Joseph Karo, *Shulhan arukh*. Jerusalem, 1993.
Isserles, Moses. *She'elot u-teshuvot ha-Rama*. Jerusalem, 1995.
Isserles, Moses. *Torat ha-hatat*. Jerusalem, 1977.
Isserles, Moses. *Torat ha-'olah*. Jerusalem, 1995.

Secondary Works

Ben-Sasson, Jonah. *The Philosophical System of R. Moses Isserles* [in Hebrew]. Jerusalem, 1984.

Fishman, David E. "R. Moses Isserles and the Study of Science among Polish Rabbis." *Science in Context* 10 (1997): 571–580.
Langermann, Y. Tzvi. "The Astronomy of Rabbi Moses Isserles." In *Physics, Cosmology and Astronomy, 1300–1700*. Edited by Sabetai Unguru. Dordecht, Netherlands, 1991. Pages 83–98.
Ziv, Asher. *Moses Isserles* [in Hebrew]. New York, 1972.

NOAH J. EFRON

ITALIAN LITERATURE AND LANGUAGE.

In Italy, renewed interest in the ancient world has important beginnings in the Middle Ages. The "Carolingian Renaissance," associated with the reign of Charlemagne, and the "Renaissance of the twelfth century" were focal points for the study of classical culture, an interest in philology, or textual analysis, and for attempts to reconcile the thought of ancient writers with Christian orthodoxy. However, it is Petrarch (1304–1374) who is most closely associated with the rebirth of classical culture in Italy and the restoration of classical values such as civic virtue and personal fame. He emphasized the importance of studying ancient texts as models of clarity of thought and rhetorical elegance as well as guides for modern living; he celebrated the study of classical languages and recommended the reading of ancient texts without the mediation of medieval commentaries. Throughout the Renaissance, an important result of Petrarch's devotion to classical learning was a passion for unearthing writings long neglected, submitting them to philological analysis, and editing and translating them into Latin or the vernacular.

Petrarch's legacy to the Renaissance was not confined to the revival of classical culture—the *studia humanitatis*—but also established a link between classical thought and Christian orthodoxy, between a renewed conviction of the value of secular life and the medieval Christian concept of the vanity of earthly pursuits. Anxiety and ambivalence mark much of Petrarch's writing. He has been called the "first modern man" in part because of an inherent sense of unease in his prose and verse as he grappled with the reconciliation of the secular with the spiritual.

The Renaissance Period. In Italy, the term "Renaissance" designates a span of about 250 years, from the late fourteenth century, when Petrarch and Giovanni Boccaccio (1313–1375) were active, until the early seventeenth century, when Giambattista Marino (1569–1625) published his early baroque epic, *L'Adone* (Adonis; Paris, 1623). Naturally, social, political, and economic factors brought about significant changes during this period of more than two hundred years, and these changes are reflected in customs, attitudes, political dynamics, and personal psychologies, as well as in language and literature, both of which can be used as barometers of changing social norms. In discussing literature and the other arts, it has therefore been convenient to divide the Renaissance into periods of particular cultural activity: for example, "humanism" is the term applied to the dawn of the Renaissance when activity centered on the *studia humanitatis* and the revival of antiquity; the "High Renaissance" is often used to designate the period from about 1490 to 1530, a period of considerable political, economic, and social upheaval, and, like so many similar periods in history, one of intense artistic productivity of the highest quality. The "late Renaissance," the last two-thirds of the sixteenth century and the early decades of the seventeenth century, is often further divided into artistic and literary "mannerism" and "early baroque," both of which felt the impact of the Counter-Reformation and of revolutions in scientific thought.

Importance of Dante, Boccaccio, and Petrarch.

Histories of Italian Renaissance literature usually begin with Petrarch as the first major figure but acknowledge both Dante and Boccaccio for their roles in the development of the early modern period. Oversimplifying, perhaps, we can say that Dante establishes in his *De vulgari eloquentia* (On the vulgar tongue; written 1303–c. 1304) the basis for one of the major literary preoccupations of the Renaissance, namely, the identification of the most effective and decorous means of writing in the vernacular. Dante's treatise is the most significant early document of what came to be known as the *questione della lingua* (debate over language). Boccaccio, too, left his mark on the Renaissance in especially significant ways: he encouraged the study of Greek, as well as Latin; introduced new literary genres (particularly the *romanzo,* or verse romance, and pastoral narratives); developed the basic stanza form for narrative in poetry, the *ottava rima* (octave rhyme); and was declared by Pietro Bembo in the sixteenth century to be the model prose writer in the vernacular (see *Prose della volgar lingua* [On writing in the vernacular]; Vinegia, 1525).

Upon his death in 1374, Petrarch left a literary patrimony of inestimable importance to the development of Renaissance thought and letters in Italy and throughout Europe. Convinced that he would establish his place in history by his works written in Latin (essays, formal letters, and an epic poem, *Africa*),

An Italian Text. First page of Petrarch's *Canzoniere* and *Trionfi,* printed by Wendelin of Speyer (Venice, 1470). BIBLIOTECA NAZIONALE MARCIANA, VENICE. INC. V. 546, FOL. 9R

Petrarch publicly dismissed his poetry in the vernacular as youthful indiscretions. However, modern critics such as Ernest Hatch Wilkins have amply documented the care with which Petrarch edited his *Canzoniere,* a collection of poems in the vernacular, essentially (but not exclusively) meditations on his love for a woman named Laura, a somewhat abstract representation of feminine beauty and perfection. In composing the poems of the *Canzoniere* (sonnets and *canzoni,* for the most part), Petrarch was indebted to a long tradition of lyric poetry, from classical poets such as Ovid and Catullus, through the entire medieval tradition of the Provençal love lyric, to the Sicilian school and the *dolce stil nuovo* (sweet new style), of which Dante, Guido Guinizzelli (c. 1230/40–c. 1276), and Guido Cavalcanti (c. 1259–

1300) were the best-known exponents. Nevertheless, Petrarch's collection of vernacular lyrics became the standard for the love lyric throughout Europe during the Renaissance. The *Canzoniere* firmly established the love lyric as a vehicle for the expression of the vagaries of love—and consequently of hope and despair—and, most important perhaps, as a mirror reflecting the psychology or emotional life of the poet himself.

The Humanist Period. During the decades immediately following Petrarch's death and well into the fifteenth century, the poet's fame rested essentially on his prose writings, which stressed the importance of the classical world and its culture. Fifteenth-century humanists often characterized their own era as a period of awakening from the oppressive scholastic tradition of the Middle Ages and cited Petrarch as an important harbinger of a movement toward renewed faith in the individual's potential for accomplishment in both the intellectual and civic arenas. The full impact of Petrarch's importance as a lyric poet, however, was not to be felt until the latter part of the century and especially the sixteenth century, when, with intellectuals such as Bembo, his poetry became the model for lyric composition. But the earlier part of the Renaissance, the humanist period of the fifteenth century, was dominated by intellectuals who, active in academic circles and government, expounded a philosophy of humanism that defined the individual's role as a rational being, free to make choices and of almost unlimited potential, as well as a civic being with social responsibilities. Major figures who represent the various strains of fifteenth-century humanist thought include Giovanni Pico della Mirandola (1463–1494), who celebrated human potential in his important tract *De hominis dignitate* (On the dignity of man); Leonardo da Vinci (1452–1519), whose notebooks underscore the importance of the empirical method in the development of human intellect; and Leon Battista Alberti (1404–1472), whose treatise on the family—*Della famiglia* (On the family, five books; written 1437–1441, published Florence, 1844)—concerns the civic and social responsibility of the individual.

The writings of the fifteenth-century humanists have important foundations in many philosophical traditions, especially Aristotelianism and Platonism, and in medieval patristic literature. Platonism enjoyed a particularly strong revival during this period and had its best-known exponent in the figure of Marsilio Ficino (1433–1499). Also of importance were concepts stemming from medieval theological thought; Saint Augustine and other figures central to the history of Christianity maintained a lively presence in fifteenth-century texts. For example, many fifteenth-century writings are concerned with such thorny problems as free will and predestination and with the struggle between the appeal of the secular and the responsibility to one's spiritual well-being.

The Later Humanist Period. If the first part of the fifteenth century witnessed the development of humanist thought in its abstract as well as its pragmatic aspects, the latter part of the century witnessed philosophical writings accompanying an abundance of literary works in prose and especially in poetry. In part, the development of literary genres, especially in the second half of the fifteenth century, evolved from the humanist interest in classical literary forms, but it was also caused by a variety of other factors, including the increasingly large numbers of classical texts unearthed, which then sparked imitations; the increasing importance of patronage in the court, the church, and in princely circles; and the invention of movable type (about 1440 in Europe) and, consequently, the easier dissemination of printed works to a more general public.

During the final decades of the century, four literary genres became central to the entire western European Renaissance: lyric poetry, the pastoral, comic theater, and the romance of chivalry. Petrarch's *Canzoniere* was a fundamentally important source for Matteo Maria Boiardo's collection of poems, *Amorum libri* (Books of love; integrated manuscript form, 1477), which narrates the vicissitudes of the poet's love for a certain Antonia Caprara, although the title of the collection clearly indicates its affinity with classical tradition and especially Ovid. Pastoral, which would have increasing importance in the later Renaissance and early baroque periods, especially for theater, has profound links with the classical works of Virgil and Theocritus. The pastoral mode influenced much of the lyric poetry of this period (for example, that of Lorenzo de' Medici and Angelo Poliziano) and inspired one of the most influential texts of the fifteenth century, Jacopo Sannazaro's *Arcadia* (Venice, 1502), a pastoral romance consisting of various kinds of pastoral lyric forms conjoined by a prose narrative. The writing of comedies, at first in Latin and in imitation of Terence and Plautus (many of whose plays were discovered during this period), and then in the vernacular, was also indebted to the medieval tradition of the novella for plots, characters, and situations, as well as to medieval religious theater. Finally, the romance of chivalry, best represented by Boiardo's unfinished *Orlando innamorato* (Roland in love; published 1482 or 1483) and Luigi Pulci's *Il Morgante* (first part, 1482; second part, 1483), reveals a particularly important characteristic of the literature of this period: the synthesis of many traditions, cultures, and genres. Whereas Boiardo's long poem has as its forebears the entire lyric tradition of the classical and medieval periods, the medieval romances of the Arthurian tradition, and the Carolingian cycles narrating the conflicts between the Christian and pagan worlds, Pulci's poem, while harking back to similar traditions, in particular the Carolingian, is also influenced by medieval comic and burlesque prose and poetry and their fascination with language, wordplay, and the creation of grotesque caricature-like figures.

The High Renaissance. While the end of the fifteenth century and the early sixteenth century were marked by political and social instability on the peninsula, with a major foreign invasion in 1494 and a lack of hegemony among political states, it was also a period of remarkable vitality in both the visual and literary arts. Among the many figures who were active during these decades were Raphael (Raffaello Sanzio), Michelangelo, Ludovico Ariosto, Niccolò Machiavelli, and Baldassare Castiglione. In many ways these artists and writers represent the full flowering of humanist culture and, in some cases, anticipate the moral dilemma, lack of certainties, and resultant anxiety that characterize the waning years of the Renaissance in Italy. Machiavelli, for example, is an exemplary product of humanism, as evidenced by his rhetorical skills, clarity of thought, and belief that the past can provide lessons for the present and future. At the same time, his writings document the societal, political, and military malaise of his day and his conviction that certain individuals are endowed with the potential for great accomplishments (*virtù*), although humankind in general is weak-willed, selfish, and mean-spirited. And Castiglione, in his *Il cortegiano* (*The Book of the Courtier;* written between 1508 and 1516), celebrates the refinement, decorum, and humanistic culture of court circles, while infusing the entire work with a sense of loss, a longing for a past time, and a distinct consciousness of the relative nature of all truths.

Literary Activity and the *Questione della Lingua*. The variety and wealth of both prose and poetry during the sixteenth century defies easy synthesis. It is a period that witnessed the culmination of the romance of chivalry with Ariosto's *Orlando furioso* (Mad Roland; first edition, Ferrara, 1516; revised editions, 1521 and 1532), a sequel to Boiardo's *Orlando innamorato,* and then, later in the century, Torquato Tasso's influential *Gerusalemme liberata* (Jerusalem delivered; completed 1575 and first published in Parma, 1581). Ariosto's and Tasso's poems were central to sixteenth-century polemics on the nature of epic poetry, polemics stimulated in part by renewed interest in Aristotle's writings on genre and in part by Counter-Reformation views on poetic decorum.

The sixteenth century was, in fact, marked by numerous debates and polemics, the most important perhaps being the debate over language, specifically, the appropriate vernacular for literary composition. The debate, or *questione della lingua,* which began, as noted above, with Dante, involved some of the most significant names in sixteenth-century letters, including Machiavelli, Castiglione, Sperone Speroni, Gian Giorgio Trissino, Ludovico Castelvetro, and Benedetto Varchi. Essentially, the debate pitted those who defended Tuscan Italian as the most decorous for composition in the vernacular against those who favored a literary Italian which reflected more closely the regional characteristics of a writer's language. The vital interest in the debate was reflected in the foundation of the Accademia della Crusca (c. 1582), the original function of which was to guarantee the pure Tuscan quality of Italian used for formal writing.

Treatises on language were matched in number by those written on a variety of other subjects, including the nature of love, feminine beauty, and social behavior. The treatise that perhaps had the most far-reaching effects in the world of Italian letters was Bembo's *Prose della volgar lingua* (1525), in which the author establishes Boccaccio as the model for prose writing in the vernacular and, more important perhaps, Petrarch as the model for poetry. In the wake of Bembo's proclamations, Petrarch's *Canzoniere*—its language, imagery, and structural elements—became the model for the love lyric both in Italy and abroad. Consequently, the vast production of lyric poetry in the sixteenth century is usually referred to as "Petrarchist": Petrarchism (or Bembism) infuses the poetic voice of all the major poets of the century to one degree or another, including Giovanni della Casa (1503–1556), Vittoria Colonna (1490–1547), and even Michelangelo (1475–1564), who was, however, noteworthy for seeking a new poetic voice unfettered by the dictates of Bembo.

It can be stated with confidence that all sixteenth-century Italian writers and many artists (Benvenuto

Cellini and Bronzino [Agnolo di Cosimo], for example) tried their hand at writing poetry even though their primary interest might have been in another genre or artistic medium. Many slavishly imitated Petrarch; others "negotiated" the Petrarchan legacy to accommodate their own particular situation. Especially important in this regard are the many women poets of the period who reversed the male-poet–female-object-of-desire paradigm and, consequently, adopted a distinctly feminine poetic voice; Gaspara Stampa (1523–1554) is one example.

It is important to note that, whereas one may regard the Italian Renaissance as a period of high literary and artistic achievement in court circles and academic communities, vital contributions were being made among individual writers and groups of writers who were at the periphery of or completely outside the elite world of intellectual circles. Often they were at odds with literary traditions they considered stifling to the creative spirit and not representative of linguistic or social realities. Two examples are Ruzzante (Angelo Beolco, c. 1495–1542), a Paduan playwright whose dialect comedies and barbs directed against many social and artistic traditions display one of the freshest voices of the sixteenth century, and Anton Francesco Grazzini (1503–1584), a Florentine who wrote burlesque poetry, comedies, and novellas that often celebrate the values and language of the lower classes and mock his tradition-bound contemporaries.

Ruzzante, like Grazzini, is associated with comic theater of the sixteenth century, a genre that flourished after the important initial ventures into vernacular theater made by Ariosto early in the century. The heritage of Italian comic theater from this period is extremely rich. Plays range from uninspired vernacular imitations of Plautine or Terentian comedies to little masterpieces such as Bibbiena's *Calandria* (The follies of Calandro; performed 1513), Machiavelli's *La mandragola* (The mandrake root, Florence?, 1518), and the anonymous *La Venexiana* (The Venetian woman; performed c. 1535–1537). Deriving their inspiration from classical models, the medieval novella tradition (especially Boccaccio's *Decameron*), and the jocose literature of the Middle Ages and early Renaissance, comedies of this period are fundamentally important to the development of comic theater throughout Europe. An irony of literary history is that the spark of originality burned only for a relatively brief moment in Italy; by mid-century such erudite comedies as those of Bibbiena or Machiavelli were supplanted in popularity by the improvised performances of the commedia dell'arte. It was to fall to the French and English to continue Italy's inspired theatrical tradition with the genius of Molière and Shakespeare.

The Late Renaissance. Literary activity of the latter part of the sixteenth century was influenced by the Counter-Reformation and the church's attempts to enforce orthodoxy in all aspects of life; also influential was the renewed interest in Aristotle's writings in the wake of mid-century translations and commentaries such as those of Francesco Robortello. Perhaps the work of Torquato Tasso (1544–1595) best exemplifies the combined influences of the Council of Trent and of Aristotelian poetics in his struggle to make his masterpiece, *Gerusalemme liberata,* not only reflect church orthodoxy but also conform to Aristotle's dictates on decorum and unity. If Tasso, both in his troubled life—he was committed to a mental asylum for many years—and in his writings, represents the moral and artistic confusion of the late Renaissance in Italy, a figure such as Galileo Galilei (1564–1642), persecuted by the church for his philosophical and scientific observations which took issue with orthodox positions, represents strength in the face of social and religious oppression and, in his writings, such as *Il saggiatore* (The assayer; Rome, 1623) and *Dialogo sopra i due massimi sistemi del mondo* (Dialogue on the two great world systems; Florence, 1632), a freedom from tradition and authoritarianism combined with a celebration of human potential.

The Renaissance in Italy, from Petrarch to Tasso and Galileo, represents one of the most vital, significant, and influential periods of Western civilization. For example, lyric poetry of the European Renaissance, especially in France, England, and Spain, has its roots in the Italian Petrarchan tradition; the development of the early modern novel harks back to the Italian romance tradition and to the work of writers such as Ariosto; Italian Renaissance theater and the novella tradition are the underpinnings of major dramatic writings of the European Renaissance, including Shakespeare's tragedies and comedies; and the thought of intellectuals such as Galileo set the stage for a scientific revolution that marks the beginnings of the modern era.

See also **Aristotle and Cinquecento Poetics; Chivalry,** *subentry on* **Romance of Chivalry; Commedia dell'Arte; Drama,** *subentry on* **Erudite Comedy; Epic; Humanism,** *subentry on* **The Definition of Humanism; Humanity, Concept of; Novella; Pastoral,** *subentry on* **Pastoral on the Continent; Petrarchism; Plato and Platonism; Poetry,** *subentry on* **Classical Poetry.**

BIBLIOGRAPHY

Baron, Hans. *The Crisis of the Early Italian Renaissance: Civic Humanism and Republican Liberty in an Age of Classicism and Tyranny.* Princeton, N.J., 1966.

Bergin, Thomas G. *Petrarch.* New York, 1970. Basic introduction to Petrarch and his works.

Brand, Peter, and Lino Pertile, eds. *The Cambridge History of Italian Literature.* Cambridge, U.K., and New York, 1996. Excellent articles on Renaissance literature.

Chabod, Federico. *Machiavelli and the Renaissance.* Translated by David Moore. New York, 1965.

Gilmore, Myron P. *The World of Humanism, 1453–1517.* New York, 1962.

Grendler, Paul. *Critics of the Italian World, 1530–1560.* Madison, Wis., 1969. Study of important marginal figures (*poligrafi*) of the Italian sixteenth century.

Haskins, Charles Homer. *The Renaissance of the Twelfth Century.* New York, 1957.

Kristeller, Paul O. *Renaissance Thought: The Classic, Scholastic, and Humanist Strains.* New York, 1961.

McLaughlin, Martin L. *Literary Imitation in the Italian Renaissance: The Theory and Practice of Literary Imitation in Italy from Dante to Bembo.* Oxford and New York, 1995.

Schmitt, Charles B., Quentin Skinner, and Eckhard Kessler, eds. *The Cambridge History of Renaissance Philosophy.* Cambridge, U.K., and New York, 1988.

Trinkaus, Charles. *The Poet as Philosopher: Petrarch and the Formation of Renaissance Consciousness.* New Haven, Conn., 1979.

Ullmann, Walter. *Medieval Foundations of Renaissance Humanism.* London and Ithaca, N.Y., 1977.

Weinberg, Bernard. *A History of Literary Criticism in the Italian Renaissance.* 2 vols. Chicago, 1961.

Weiss, Roberto. *The Renaissance Discovery of Classical Antiquity.* Oxford, 1969.

Wilkins, Ernest Hatch. *The Making of the "Canzoniere" and other Petrarchan Studies.* Rome, 1951. Essential study of the composition and dating of Petrarch's *Canzoniere.*

ROBERT J. RODINI

ITALIAN WARS. *See* **Wars of Italy.**

ITALY. Throughout the Renaissance, Italy was a divided country. The north—though not the sovereign city of Venice and its overseas territories—was legally, if nominally, part of the Holy Roman Empire, the kingdom of Italy. The center, north and south of Rome, was ruled by the papacy as the Lands of St. Peter or the Papal States. For much of the period, southern Italy—the kingdom of Naples, the Regno—and the islands of Sicily and Sardinia were ruled directly or indirectly by the crown of Aragon; they passed to the Habsburgs in the sixteenth century.

The Divisions of Italy. The divisions of Italy ran deeper than the description above. The reasons for this are partly geographical: the formidable Apennines—which should be understood as a series of mountain ranges—divide the peninsula for much of its length. The reasons are also geopolitical. Italy's central place in the well-traveled Mediterranean exposed it to influence, invasion, and settlement from Spain, North Africa, and the Balkans, as well as from northern Europe. Such forces were encouraged by the wealth of its greater cities and by the special significance of Rome, not a major commercial or industrial center but a city possessing unique spiritual and political associations. Moreover, the often competing commercial and colonial activities in the Mediterranean of the country's maritime cities—particularly Genoa and Venice—could result in conflicts abroad that intensified rivalry in Italy itself.

The divisions of Italy also were caused by social and economic factors, by the rise—earlier in the Middle Ages—of towns and cities. These tended to be of Roman, or pre-Roman, origin. Their growth was fueled by the commercial revolution in Europe from the tenth to the thirteenth century. And with growing population and wealth, Italian cities became increasingly self-governing communes, wresting power from distant or local overlords. This process was particularly marked in northern Italy from the eleventh century, and saw the emergence of city republics, recognized by the emperor Frederick I Hohenstaufen (Barbarossa) in the Peace of Constance (1183) and sustained in their growing independence by the natural resources of their hinterlands, as well as by their industrial, commercial, and financial activities. And economic conditions in the poorer areas of Italy—in the higher valleys of the Apennines, for example—contributed to the divisions of Italy by exporting mercenary soldiers.

Political divisions. Some of the factors in the formation of political divisions in Italy were common to the rest of Europe: disputes over successions, such as followed the death of the last Visconti duke of Milan, Filippo Maria (1447); disputes over territory, trade routes, and resources, such as between Venice and the Carrara lords of Padua over land, navigable rivers, and salt production in the Veneto in the late fourteenth century.

Other factors were more specific to Italy. The rivalry, in the Middle Ages, of the two powers that claimed the inheritance of the Roman Empire—the papacy and the Holy Roman Empire—had allowed local and regional autonomy to flourish. This situation had been further encouraged by the fact that neither power was hereditary, a fact opening the way for succession disputes; in the case of the papacy it was most damaging during the Great Schism (1378–1417). Second, neither power was consis-

Italy, 1500

tently based in the peninsula. In the Renaissance the emperors were occasional visitors, and though the popes were more often resident in or near Rome, they, too, had experienced periods of chosen or enforced exile, notably during their residence at Avignon (1305–1377). Again, as international powers neither popes nor emperors could devote all their energies to ruling Italy. The emperor Sigismund (ruled 1410–1437), for example, in the 1420s and 1430s was largely preoccupied with the Hussite rebellion and heresy in Bohemia, of which he was also king.

Finally, the rivalries and weaknesses of both powers added to the political divisions and diversity of Italy. For example, in the Middle Ages the emperors had established in the north of the country feudal principalities, some secular—like the county of Piedmont—and some ecclesiastical—like the prince-bishopric of Aquileia. The papacy had been forced to recognize Norman rule in southern Italy and Sicily in the eleventh century.

Many of the above points are illustrated by the way the papacy installed the French house of Anjou in the kingdom of Sicily (which embraced both the island of Sicily and part of southern Italy) in 1266 to thwart the imperial house of Hohenstaufen. This intensified and perpetuated the rivalry between pro-imperial (Ghibelline) and pro-papal (Guelph) factions throughout the peninsula. It also prompted the king of Aragon to accept the crown of Sicily in 1282, in pursuit of his own hereditary claims to the kingdom and to counter Angevin control of such a strategically and economically important island. The conquest of the kingdom of Naples by Alfonso V of Aragon in 1442 (which reunited the two kingdoms) was contested by both the papacy and Angevin claimants.

Cultural divisions. The divided condition of Italy can readily be illustrated. As the Florentine poet Dante Alighieri (1265–1321) pointed out in his account of the Italian language *De vulgari eloquentia* (On eloquence in the vernacular; begun c. 1304), the dialects of Italy revealed profound regional, even local, differences; foreign languages were also present: Spanish and Catalan in Sardinia, for example. In the courts of Italy, the style of dress varied. Italian merchants abroad habitually acted not as one but as several nations. The concept of *la patria* (native land, my home) was rarely applied to Italy as a whole, but rather to the local community. Civic patriotism, or *campanilismo*—loyalty to the local *campanile* or bell tower—was deeply rooted. The cult of local or adopted patron saints was intense, as in the cases of St. Petronius (Bologna) and St. Mark (Venice), whose shrines were protected and celebrated in magnificent churches.

In more secular terms civic identity was expressed—as at Siena—by the construction of communal palaces, law courts, bell towers, merchant halls (*mercanzie*), aqueducts, fountains, and *piazze,* as well as city walls and gates. Throughout Italy lords and communes, both urban and rural, jealously collected and guarded the letters and charters that were seen to spell out their liberties and privileges; for example, the communes of the strategic Val d'Aosta in Piedmont amassed privileges to document their wide-ranging autonomy, and lords in the States of the Church collected papal bulls and letters to establish their titles to property, fiefs, and vicariates.

Chroniclers and historians, even when claiming to write in general or even universal terms, tended to prioritize their native city or region. Thus the "universal chronicle" of Gaspare Broglio Tartaglia (1407–1483) gains much of its interest from what he has to say about the Malatesta lords of Rimini, whom he served. The description of Italy by the humanist Flavio Biondo, the *Italia illustra* of 1453, is slanted toward the author's native Romagna and those states with which he had close connections, like Venice. The *Lives of the Artists* by Giorgio Vasari, first published in 1550, highlights the achievements of artists from his native Tuscany and associated with his own patrons of choice, the Medici, at the expense of other Italian "schools."

Italian Identity.   If, however, Italy was divided politically and in many other respects, the extent of these divisions should not be exaggerated. Horizons were far from parochial. Indeed, in Sicily an awareness of Sicilian identity transcended the interests of its great cities and noble houses, fueled by the memory of past greatness and the struggle against foreign rule. Throughout the peninsula merchants and bankers traveled widely and often, setting up agencies "abroad" and acquiring multiple citizenships to facilitate their business interests. Mercenaries from the more impoverished areas of the Apennines sought military service with the wealthier states of the north. Students enrolled at such great universities as those of Padua and Bologna. Political exiles and outlaws found the boundaries of states conveniently porous.

All the cities of Italy needed immigrants to sustain their population; more specifically, skilled craftsmen and professionals were "head-hunted." Thus Venice imported silk workers from Lucca and the governments of university cities sought to attract teaching talent. The courts of Italy could recruit administrators and entertainers from abroad. Scholars and men of letters traveled in search of patronage—for instance, the learned but acrimonious Francesco Filelfo (1398–1481). So did artists; the talents of Antonio Pisanello (fl. c. 1415–c. 1455) were sought after in cities and at courts from Venice in the north to Naples in the south. Rome, where Pisanello also worked, became a magnet for artists and craftsmen of all kinds as the papacy set about reconstructing the city from the mid-fifteenth century on.

Finally, to achieve the appearance of impartiality in the administration of justice, communes imported—or had sent—their chief magistrate, the *podestà,* and his staff for short terms of office, thereby creating a peripatetic elite of well-traveled administrators. Such men were trained in Roman law, the legal system that informed the canon law of the church and the statutes of most Italian cities.

The broad influence of Roman law points to another powerful common denominator in medieval and Renaissance Italy: the legacy of Rome. This, of course, did more than influence legal systems. It encouraged a sense of Italian identity, indeed superiority, toward foreign "barbarians." The attitude was reinforced in the Renaissance by thinkers like Petrarch (1304–1374).

Hence the historian is faced with the paradox of a country that was at the same time both divided yet aware—albeit within an elite—of a cultural identity. That paradox was challenged perhaps only once in the Renaissance, by the Roman notary Cola di Rienzo (1313–1354). In 1347, steeped in the record of Italy's united past under Rome, as "tribune" of that city he summoned a meeting of Italian states to propose a federation. The initiative was poorly supported, however, and Cola was eventually overwhelmed by local jealousies and international suspicion.

Similarly, the Italian League, established in 1455 by the Peace of Lodi, was intended not to unite Italy but to acknowledge and preserve a balance of power between the principal and client states of the peninsula. Hence the political divisions and diversities of Italy, the lack of a central monarchy around which a history can be conveniently organized, can make the task of succinctly surveying the country's history in the Renaissance appear to be an almost impossible task. However, various themes have been identified to give some shape to Italy's history in the period.

Republics and Princedoms. One theme that exercised contemporaries like Niccolò Machiavelli and came to preoccupy historians of Renaissance Italy in both the nineteenth and the twentieth centuries, is the failure in most cities of communal regimes—republics—to survive, and their replacement by *signori,* or lords. Sometimes such lords were foreigners, installed by force of arms, as when Francesco Sforza took the duchy of Milan in 1450. But most *signori* were homegrown, sustained by property and retainers in city and countryside and by a network of local and regional alliances; their rise was often assisted by the communes' failure to eradicate faction and social unrest and to manage the burdens imposed by war and threats from abroad. The process was a long one, lasting from the thirteenth century to the sixteenth. It also was not invariable. In 1434 the Medici began to compromise the republican constitution of Florence; a republican regime was reintroduced in 1494, and it was only in 1530 that the lordship of the Medici was finally and formally recognized. Of the major republican cities of Renaissance Italy, only Venice survived.

For champions of republicanism the process was a disaster, a situation that explains why for many in the nineteenth century the Renaissance in Italy was seen in negative terms: heroic communal regimes were replaced by despots whose only saving grace was their patronage of the arts and letters and their maintenance of cultured courts.

However, to focus too narrowly on a confrontation between communes and despots would be to distort the picture in several ways. Most of Italy, throughout the Renaissance, was governed by forms of lordship ranging from the royal to the manorial. Access to communal government had always been restricted to a privileged minority, and such governments had always been dominated by powerful local families of lawyers, entrepreneurs, and landowners. If participation in government was certainly greater in fifteenth-century Venice than it was in contemporary Piedmont, the aims, methods, achievements, and failures of government were largely the same across the communal-despotic "divide." If *signori* could be denounced as tyrants by their enemies, their own propagandists could hail them as bringing peace, order, and justice to their subjects. Indeed, much of the significance of the confrontation between "communes and despots" lies in the world of ideas rather than of policies. The champions of republican Florence about 1400 sought inspiration from the spokesmen of republican Rome, while their adversaries, speaking for Giangaleazzo Visconti,

HOLY ROMAN EMPIRE

SWITZERLAND

OTTOMAN EMPIRE

DUCHY OF SAVOY

DUCHY OF MILAN

Trent

Milan

Turin

DUCHY OF MANTUA

MARQUISATE OF MONTFERRAT

DUCHY OF PARMA

Venice

DUCHY OF MODENA

MARQUISATE OF SALUZZO

REPUBLIC OF GENOA

Genoa

REPUBLIC OF VENICE

Oneglia

REPUBLIC OF SAN MARINO

Monaco

REPUBLIC OF LUCCA

Florence

DUCHY OF FLORENCE

Siena

ADRIATIC SEA

CORSICA (Genoa)

STATO DEI PRESIDI

DUBROVNIK

DUCHY OF PIOMBINO

PAPAL STATES

Rome

Pontecorvo

Benevento

KINGDOM OF SARDINIA

Naples

KINGDOM OF NAPLES

Cagliari

TYRRHENIAN SEA

Palermo

KINGDOM OF SICILY

AFRICA

Italy, 1559

Venetian Territory

Papal States

Boundary of the Holy Roman Empire

50   100 Miles

50   100   150 Kilometers

duke of Milan (ruled 1385–1402), drew on arguments from the imperial Roman tradition.

Foreign Invasions. The internal weaknesses of the Italian states, together with their failure to find a lasting political equilibrium, are revealed in a final theme in the history of Renaissance Italy, a theme that also brings the Renaissance period to a close: the foreign invasions of the peninsula beginning in 1494.

That these invasions were to have a considerable effect can obscure the fact that the motives behind them were fundamentally traditional and had been identified—and feared—in Italy long before the end of the fifteenth century. The French crown pursued dynastic claims to the kingdom of Naples (dating from the thirteenth century) and the duchy of Milan (dating from the fourteenth century). The Holy Roman Empire, revived in Habsburg hands, sought to defend and realize its rights in the kingdom of Italy. The crown of Aragon sought to retain its titles to Naples, Sicily, and Sardinia. The Swiss cantons had territorial ambitions in northern Lombardy and also sought profitable employment for their mercenary troops in the wars of the peninsula. But Italy's fate—becoming a battlefield for foreign powers—was intensified by the Europe-wide confrontation between France and the Habsburgs, especially when the latter, under Charles V, combined the crowns of Spain, Sicily, Sardinia, and Naples (from 1516) with the imperial title (from 1519).

For Italian contemporaries the wars that began with the invasion of Naples by Charles VIII of France in 1494 ushered in a period of disasters that made the forty years of relative peace following the Peace of Lodi appear as a golden age. The Italian states were unable to join forces to meet the threat; indeed, they habitually sought to exploit the actions of foreign powers to their own advantage, as when Pope Julius II joined in a coalition against Venice in 1509 to recover papal cities in the Romagna (including Ravenna, Rimini, and Faenza) from Venice. Reluctant subjects welcomed the arrival of foreign troops; the citizens of Pisa saw the French as their liberators from oppressive Florentine rule (1494). Long established regimes were exposed as weak, as when Charles VIII captured Naples in 1494, Louis XII took Milan in 1499, and the French crown occupied most of the lands of the house of Savoy in 1536.

The military reputation of the Italian states was undermined. The army of the Venetian Republic, hitherto the most effective in the peninsula, was soundly defeated at the battle of Aguadello (1509).

More generally Italian armies were seen, especially by disillusioned observers like Machiavelli, as inferior in their training, composition, commitment, and use of artillery. Still more generally the Italian sense of cultural superiority over the barbarian was punctured, especially when an ill-disciplined imperial army sacked Rome and took Pope Clement VII prisoner (1527). The Peace of Cateau-Cambrésis (1559) left the Habsburgs dominant in northern and southern Italy.

However, in some respects the impact of the invasions was exaggerated by both contemporaries and the nationalist historians of Italy's Risorgimento. Despite the arrival of imperial administrators, Italy did not become an occupied, garrisoned country, and for most Italians the political realities were, as ever, local and relatively unchanged. After centuries of political unrest, from 1528 Genoa experienced considerable stability, autonomy, and commercial opportunities under Habsburg rule. Although Venice had lost its mainland state in 1509, a combination of internal stability, skillful diplomacy, and military recovery saw that state virtually regained by 1517. The house of Savoy recovered its duchy in 1559. A number of small, exposed states succumbed to failures in the direct line of succession rather than foreign conquest, among them the Gonzaga marquisate of Mantua (1611) and the Della Rovere duchy of Urbino (1631).

Indeed, some regimes were strengthened as a result of the Italian Wars. The papacy continued a process begun in the fifteenth century and eliminated most of the lordships within the Papal States—for example, the Bentivoglio of Bologna (1512) and the Varano of Camerino (1540). It even extended its authority into northern Italy with the acquisition of Parma (1521). The Medici, driven from Florence in the aftermath of the French invasion of 1494, were reinstated by Spanish arms in 1512, and then definitively in 1530, subsequently acquiring the titles of duke of Florence (1537) and grand duke of Tuscany (1569).

But the Medici acquisition of Siena in 1537 was as a fief of the Habsburgs, a fact that helps underline the point that Italy had become dominated by foreign powers. Some states that had once ranked as great European powers, like the Visconti-Sforza duchy of Milan, no longer existed, and others, like the republic of Venice, survived through watchful neutrality. The Habsburgs ruled their lands in Italy not as a collection of states but as subject provinces under viceroys. In many respects, in political terms Italy had reverted to what it had been in the Middle

Ages, its own balance of power being subsumed within a greater balance of power. The surviving Italian states became the best informed in Europe about events taking place elsewhere.

See also **Republicanism** *and entries on individual Italian states.*

BIBLIOGRAPHY

Primary Work

Guicciardini, Francesco. *The History of Italy.* Translated and edited by Sidney Alexander. London and New York, 1968.

Secondary Works

Baron, Hans. *Crisis of the Early Italian Renaissance.* 1955. Reprint, Princeton, N.J., 1998.

Bentley, Jerry H. *Politics and Culture in Renaissance Naples.* Princeton, N.J., 1987.

Bueno de Mesquita, Daniel Meredith. *Giangaleazzo Visconti.* Cambridge, U.K., 1941.

Cochrane, Eric W. *Historians and Historiography in the Italian Renaissance.* Chicago and London, 1981.

Hay, Denys, and John E. Law. *Italy in the Age of the Renaissance, 1380–1530.* London and New York, 1989.

Kohl, Benjamin G. *Padua under the Carrara, 1318–1405.* Baltimore and London, 1998.

Larner, John. *Italy in the Age of Dante and Petrarch, 1216–1380.* London, 1980.

Mallett, Michael Edward, and John R. Hale. *The Military Organisation of a Renaissance State: Venice, c. 1400 to 1617.* Cambridge, U.K., and New York, 1984.

Martines, Lauro. *Power and Imagination: City-States in Renaissance Italy.* New York and London, 1979.

Partner, Peter. *The Lands of St. Peter.* London and Berkeley, Calif., 1972.

Prodi, Paolo. *The Papal Prince.* Cambridge, U.K., and New York, 1987.

Ryder, A. F. C. *The Kingdom of Naples under Alfonso the Magnanimous.* Oxford, 1976.

JOHN E. LAW

I TATTI. *See* **Villa I Tatti.**

JACOPO DELLA QUERCIA. *See* **Sculpture; Siena,** *subentry on* **Art in Siena.**

JAMES I (1566–1625), king of Scotland (as James VI; 1567–1625) and king of England (as James I; 1603–1625). The future James VI was born to Mary, queen of Scots, and her English husband, Henry, Lord Darnley, at Edinburgh Castle. Charles James Stuart's first year witnessed the tumultuous end of Mary's rule. Darnley was murdered, apparently at the hands of Mary and her new love, James Hepburn, earl of Bothwell. The Protestant lords revolted, forced their Catholic queen's abdication, and crowned the infant, renamed James, in 1567. A series of regents, sometimes in open conflict, handled governance until 1585, when James's personal rule effectively began. James married Anne of Denmark in 1589. Married life mixed affection, disagreement, and, finally, distant fondness, which produced three children who reached adulthood: Prince Henry (1594–1612), Princess Elizabeth of Bohemia (1596–1662), and the future Charles I (1600–1649). James successfully ruled Scotland until 1603 and enhanced royal authority at the expense of presbyterians in the church and often-fractious nobles.

Education. James received a Renaissance education. His studies were supervised by Peter Young and the renowned humanist George Buchanan, a favorite in English humanist circles. They set out to transform James into a godly Protestant ruler and surrounded him with the library of a virtuous prince. Young assembled Greek and Latin classics, among them Cato and Plutarch, the fables and aphorisms of Aesop and Phaedrus, histories, and theological tracts, including the Augsburg Confession and—naturally—the works of Protestant reformers. To these were added works of French and Italian poetry, logic, dialectics, mathematics, natural history, geography, and cosmography. Political treatises and manuals for the education of princes were plentiful: Roger Ascham's *The Scholemaster,* Thomas Elyot's renowned *The Boke Named the Governour,* and *Il cortegiano (The Book of the Courtier),* by Baldassare Castiglione. Buchanan was ill-tempered, cheerless, and intimidating, but James later valued his rigorous education, attributing to it his skills with languages and disputation.

Jacobean Court and Kingcraft. James loved conversation, and the boisterous Scottish court was the center of a competitive policy-making environment. James took counsel and advice widely, sometimes generating resentment among those who sought or believed they deserved predominant influence. While scholars have frequently viewed this practice as proof of James's malleability and lack of interest in government, the king knew his mind and jealously guarded his final authority in policy. The Scottish court's informality contrasted with court pretense and etiquette in England.

James constructed an Anglo-Scottish court and council upon his accession to the English throne, but administration soon reverted to his English ministers: Robert Cecil was chief minister and later lord treasurer (1603–1612); Henry Howard ran finance and the Privy Council after Cecil (1612–1614); Thomas Egerton presided over Chancery (1603–1617) and

James I of England. Portrait by Paul van Somer (c. 1576–c. 1622). THE ROYAL COLLECTION © HER MAJESTY QUEEN ELIZABETH II

was succeeded by Francis Bacon (1617–1621); the legal giant Sir Edward Coke served James in numerous capacities until relations between them became irreconcilable in 1621; and Sir Julius Caesar at the Exchequer (1605–1614) and Lord Treasurer Lionel Cranfield (1621–1624) were, perhaps, James's most able financial officers.

James's bedchamber, staffed by Scots, was a personal inner sanctum to which he retreated frequently following policy failures and strained relations with the English political elite before 1615. The most influential of the Scots were George Hume, who administered Scotland on James's behalf until 1610, and Robert Carr. Carr became James's favorite in 1610 but was eclipsed in 1615 by the English George Villiers. James expected Villiers to broker patronage and supervise administration while James Hamilton represented Scottish interests and acted as a Scottish favorite.

Major Events and Controversies in England. James succeeded Elizabeth I peacefully, for which the people were grateful and celebratory, but he inherited severe problems: war with Spain, reformist tensions within the church, a dearth of patronage, increasingly visible domestic corruption, financial decay, and the centuries-old enmity between Scotland and England. James proved successful with several matters. A peace treaty with Spain was signed in 1604 and the continuation of the peace proved a boon to British commerce and customs revenues. James stamped his own sense of uniformity on the church at the Hampton Court Conference in 1604. Thereafter, James successfully brokered reformist, conservative, and lay interests with his love of theological disputation, his clerical appointments, and his conformity initiatives. His support for a new translation of the Bible, which first appeared in 1611, is justly remembered. James met his subjects' pent-up demands for patronage and dispensed gifts, honors and titles, and positions within church and state like any bountiful Renaissance prince.

Royal largesse was a mixed blessing financially. Elizabeth's solvency had been dependent upon decades of parliamentary revenue, but James's pleas for taxation to, in effect, support patronage found less receptive ears than had Elizabeth's for military provision. Matters were exacerbated by James's resistance to calls for fiscal reform, especially his indifference to long-established peculation and dubious practices that functioned indirectly as patronage. English xenophobia was also important through the first decade. The political nation expected James to leave Scotland behind and become a thoroughly English king. Gifts to Scots were bitterly resented, as were James's moves to achieve some form of sociopolitical union of the two kingdoms. Matters came to a head in James's first English Parliaments (1604–1610 and 1614), when fiscal and patronage grievances were repeatedly disputed, the Great Contract to re-endow the crown collapsed, union was utterly rejected, and Scots were attacked in deliberately inflammatory speeches. Extraparliamentary fiscal projects were inadequate, and financial reform never consistently overcame the powerful vested interests that were accustomed to corruption, patronage, and James's willingness to give.

The Thirty Years' War (1618–1648) precipitated James's gravest political crisis. James had pursued an increasingly pro-Spanish foreign policy and dynastic marriages for Henry and Charles, tempted by large dowries and vague hopes of reunion between Protestant and Catholic powers. When Austrian Habsburg forces drove James's Protestant daughter Elizabeth and son-in-law Frederick from their homeland in the Rhenish Palatinate, James remained steadfast in his belief that only Spanish Habsburg intervention could settle the matter, but his subjects saw again the old specter of Spanish-Catholic hegemony. The initially productive parliament of 1621 collapsed over discussions of the Spanish match. After the final breakdown of the marriage project for Prince Charles in 1623, James emerged openly at odds with Charles, Villiers, and their war coalition in the Parliament of 1624. James died in March 1625, leaving his kingdoms and an unwanted, futile war in Charles's dubious care.

An Assessment of James as King.

James managed problems inherited from Elizabeth but—like her—did not solve them. His greatest failures were crown finance and union with Scotland. He and his ministers never found politically acceptable means to translate growing national wealth into solvency or to balance expenditures. Calvin's case (1608) was engineered as a test to demonstrate that Scots born after James's accession in 1603 were full citizens in England; it upheld the naturalization of Scots as full subjects in England, but political union never progressed past a union of the crowns in the person of the monarch. A peaceful foreign policy within the government's economic means was astute, but friendship with Spain fired the religious prejudices of James's Protestant subjects. Religious stability increasingly depended upon arbitration by the church's supreme governor, a responsibility for which James was well equipped but his son was not. Finally, the anglicization of the Stuarts left the London-based dynasty out of touch with Scotland, particularly in religious matters, with disastrous consequences under Charles I.

James and the Renaissance.

James considered himself a Renaissance prince; his distinctive italic handwriting is one self-conscious manifestation. But Buchanan singularly failed to convince James that the performance of his kingly office was under the judgment of subjects entitled to depose an ineffective monarch. James's refutation of that view was presented in his *Trew Law of Free Monarchies,* published (ostensibly anonymously) in Scotland in 1598. *Trew Law* stands as a seminal statement of divine right kingship, denying a monarch's accountability to anyone but God. However, James embraced his tutor's ideas of monarchical duty. His contribution to Renaissance thought rests in his reassertion of the maxim *salus populi suprema lex esto:*

in James's words, "A good king will not only delight to rule his subjects by the law, but even will conform himself in his own actions thereunto, always keeping that ground, that the health of the commonwealth be his chief law" (*King James VI and I, Political Writings,* Sommerville, ed., p. 75). James developed these ideas in *Basilikon doron* (Royal gift), an advice book for Henry written in 1598, privately printed in 1599, and published (in revised form) in Edinburgh in March 1603. James's parental and kingly counsel in matters of religion, kingship, and personal virtue shared much with the mirror-for-princes genre and earlier humanist tracts. Henry was advised to reflect daily on the virtues of his government, on his faith and devotion, his public and personal comportment, and even on the oppression of the poor. James also wrote political-theological rejoinders to Catholic resistance theorists, scriptural interpretation, poetry, a discourse on the authority of judges (1616), and parliamentary speeches and reflections. All of these served James's sense of kingship, and the publication of his *Workes* in 1616 enhanced his intellectual pretensions and reputation.

Jacobean artistic patronage was polycentric, and Jacobean culture reflected the diverse interests among its patrons and practitioners. The courts of Anne, Henry, and Charles were as influential as James's own, perhaps more so. The same can be said of numerous courtiers and individuals among the social elite, including Lucy Russell (countess of Bedford), Penelope Rich, Thomas Howard (earl of Arundel), Robert Cecil, Henry Howard, Dudley Carleton, and the king's favorites, Robert Carr and George Villiers. These individuals shared a mind-set that equated puissance and stature with the material magnificence of the king, his courtiers, and their entourages; this attitude inspired, among other things, the art collecting that came into vogue after 1604. Jacobean material and intellectual culture was eclectic, a vibrant admixture of late Renaissance styles from Flanders, Scotland, France, and Italy, of classicism, neomedievalism, and baroque ostentation. Country houses like Cecil's Hatfield House (1607–1612), Henry Hobart's Blicking Hall (1619–1622), and Thomas Howard's massive Audley End (1603–1616) were built simultaneously with Inigo Jones's classical masterpieces, the Queen's House at Greenwich (c. 1616–1630) and the Whitehall Banqueting House (1619–1622). Thomas Howard's passion for Italian art found its fullest expression in Arundel House's magnificent sculpture gallery, recorded in the Flemish Daniel Mytens's well-known portrait. The court masque was uniquely Jacobean, a spectacle acted and danced to music by aristocratic elites (including royalty) for the members of their exclusive social preserve. Inigo Jones and Ben Jonson were particularly adept writers, creating masques whose outward appearances hid remarkably complex references to "long-forgotten Renaissance codes of meaning," including classical mythology, scripture, and even James's political writings (*see* "The Masque of Stuart Culture," in Peck, ed., *The Mental World of the Jacobean Court*, pp. 209, 225–229).

The material abundance and corresponding fiscal burdens of the Jacobean court were not without critics. Passions for tapestries, jewels, and luxurious dress were countered by the plain attire of courtiers like Thomas and Henry Howard. Tacitean and neo-Stoic views of political corruption, factionalism, and favor-seeking in Roman history were a lens through which to analyze, criticize, and survive the apparent material and personal corruption of James's court. Taciteanism was especially welcome in the chivalric and assertively Protestant court of Henry and recurrently colored the work of Jacobean dramatists. Charles I's court was more materially robust, but an ethos of restraint, moral rectitude, and royal virtue was self-consciously cultivated after 1629 in court ceremony and iconography.

Portraits. There are numerous surviving portraits and depictions of James as a child and as an adult. There is an often-reproduced painting of James as an adult in the National Portrait Gallery of Scotland; a portrait at age eight, in the National Portrait Gallery, London; Jan de Critz's portraits (c. 1606) in the National Maritime Museum, London, and Sotheby's; those of Cornelius Janssen at Falkland Palace and Daniel Mytens (1621) at the National Portrait Gallery; the regally robed James standing before windows facing the Banqueting House, in the Royal Archives; and James as Marcus Aurelius (1621), in the Ashmolean Museum, Oxford. The most resplendent and iconographical depiction of James is Peter Paul Rubens's Banqueting House ceiling, commissioned by Charles and completed in 1634. Among its nine allegorical panels are those of an Augustan James ascending to heaven and another extolling James as Solomon, uniting Scotland and England, a depiction he would have found altogether pleasing.

See also **Bible,** *subentry on* **The English Bible; Scotland; Stuart Dynasty.**

BIBLIOGRAPHY

Primary Works
Goodman, Godfrey. *The Court of King James the First.* Edited by John S. Brewer. London, 1839.

James I. *King James VI and I: Political Writings.* Edited by J. P. Sommerville. Cambridge, U.K., 1994.
James I. *The Political Works of James I.* Edited by Charles Howard McIlwain. Cambridge, Mass., 1918.
Scott, Walter. *The Secret History of the Court of James the First.* Edinburgh, 1811.

Secondary Works
Bradshaw, Brendan, and John Morrill, eds. *The British Problem, c. 1534–1707: State Formation in the Atlantic Archipelago.* London, 1996.
Cuddy, Neil. "Anglo-Scottish Union and the Court of James I, 1603–1625." *Transactions of the Royal Historical Society* 39 (1989): 107–124.
Fincham, Kenneth, ed. *The Early Stuart Church, 1603–1642.* Basingstoke, U.K., 1993.
Ford, Boris, ed. *The Cambridge Cultural History of Britain: Seventeenth-Century Britain.* Cambridge, U.K., 1989.
Lee, Maurice, Jr. *Great Britain's Solomon: James VI and I in His Three Kingdoms.* Urbana, Ill., 1990.
Peck, Linda Levy, ed. *The Mental World of the Jacobean Court.* Cambridge, Mass., 1991.
Sharpe, Kevin, and Peter Lake, eds. *Culture and Politics in Early Stuart England.* Stanford, Calif., 1993.
Smuts, R. Malcolm, ed. *The Stuart Court and Europe: Essays in Politics and Political Culture.* Cambridge, U.K., 1996.
Sommerville, J. P. *Politics and Ideology in England, 1603–1640.* London, 1986.
Wilson, D. Harris. *King James VI and I.* London, 1956.
Wormald, Jenny. *Court, Kirk, and Community: Scotland 1470–1625.* London, 1981.
Wormald, Jenny. "James VI and I: Two Kings or One?" *History* 68 (1983): 187–209.

JOHN R. CRAMSIE

JAMNITZER, WENZEL. *See* **Germany, Art in.**

JAPAN. *See* **Asia, East.**

JEANNE D'ALBRET (1528–1572), queen of Navarre (1555–1572). As the daughter of Marguerite d'Angoulême, who was the sister of Francis I and of Henry of Navarre, one of the *grands seigneurs* of France, Jeanne's noble birth made her a princess of the blood on her mother's side and heiress to much of southwestern France through her father.

Jeanne was raised away from her mother and the Valois court in the rural atmosphere of Normandy at Lonray, on the lands of her governess Aymée de Lafayette. Her education was ostensibly supervised by the humanist Nicholas de Bourbon, who probably provided a curriculum of classical and French authors customarily read by educated French aristocratic women. Bourbon, like his patroness Marguerite, was interested in religious reform, leaving historians to conjecture about his influence and that of her mother on Jeanne's later uncompromising attitudes toward the Roman church and Calvinist reform.

In 1537 the king commanded Jeanne to come to court at Plessis-les-Tours, where she became a pawn in his political aims on the one hand and in her father's ambitions on the other, a situation that lends a poignancy to Clément Marot's famous epigram in which he addressed her as "la mignonne de deux rois" (the pet of two kings). By 1540 she was a virtual prisoner at Tours as her father negotiated to marry her to Philip of Spain, and Francis I accomplished his plan to cement a political alliance through her marriage to William de la Marck, duke of Clèves. Although Jeanne openly and defiantly objected, the marriage was celebrated in 1541. In 1545 the marriage was annulled when the political alliance disintegrated.

In 1548, Jeanne married Antoine de Bourbon, duc de Vendôme, a soldier and, as "first prince of the blood," next in line for the throne after King Henry II and his sons. On Christmas Day 1560 Jeanne publicly announced her conversion to Calvinism, and by mid-January, John Calvin sent her a letter congratulating her for her courage. According to her biographer Nancy Roelker, Calvinism provided the overriding source of energy and focus for Jeanne's life. She devoted her career to administering her lands in Béarn and promoting the Huguenot movement.

Jeanne entered into the factional struggles at court and on the national scene, and became a leader and diplomat of the Huguenot cause during the civil wars. Her positions conflicted with the aims of both Catherine de Médicis, who played a political balancing game between the Counter-Reformation and Huguenot parties, and Gaspard de Coligny, whose aim was to overcome the Spanish, papal-Guise faction in France and establish the Huguenots in power. Jeanne's concerns for the Huguenot cause remained secondary to her ambitions to assure her son Henry of Navarre's position as ruler of Protestant Béarn and heir to the French throne. She died in June 1572 without seeing the realization of her dreams through Henry's marriage to Marguerite de Valois, the Catholic daughter of Catherine de Médicis.

BIBLIOGRAPHY

Primary Work

Jeanne d'Albret. *Mémoires et poèsies de Jeanne d'Albret.* Edited by Alphonse de Ruble. Paris, 1893.

Secondary Works

Bordenave, Nicolas de. *Histoire de Béarn et Navarre.* Edited by Paul Raymond. Paris, 1873.

Roelker, Nancy L. *Queen of Navarre: Jeanne d'Albret, 1528–1572.* Cambridge, Mass., 1968. Definitive biography.

Ruble, Alphonse de. *Le mariage de Jeanne d'Albret.* Paris, 1877.

CHARMARIE J. BLAISDELL

JEROME (c. 347–419), church father. Jerome spent much of his youth in Rome (c. 357–367). He had further study in Trier and then went to Antioch in 372. There, in 374, he had a dream warning him against pagan studies and he became a hermit in the Syrian desert (374–376). He studied Hebrew in the desert and at Antioch and was ordained a priest in 378. He attended the Council of Constantinople in 381. In Rome between 382 and 385, Jerome began the revision of the Latin Bible at the request of Pope Damasus and advised the ascetic circle of women whose members included the Roman matron Paula. Made to leave Rome in 385, he returned to the Middle East. With Paula's help he erected a monastery and a convent in Bethlehem. He was the author of the (Vulgate) Latin translation of the Bible, several biblical commentaries, and translations of Origen, letters, and other works. He died in Bethlehem.

Jerome in the Middle Ages. Jerome's works circulated throughout the Middle Ages. By the eighth century he was known as one of the four original Latin Doctors of the church. In pre-1300 iconography he was frequently portrayed with a book, a pen, and a model of a church. Moreover, with the increasing prominence of the Roman cardinalate after 1179, he was frequently given the title of cardinal. After 1245, when the red hat was prescribed for cardinals by Innocent IV, Jerome was often portrayed wearing it. He was also frequently painted with a lion whose wounded paw he was supposed to have healed. By the late Middle Ages, Jerome was renowned as champion of asceticism and miracle worker.

Jerome and the Renaissance. The cult of Jerome became institutionalized in the late fourteenth century as several monastic congregations became dedicated to imitating his asceticism. The image of Jerome as penitent in the wilderness was invented in Italy around 1400 and became, together with the image of Jerome in his study, a typical Renaissance representation of the saint. Jerome the scholar began to be venerated by the fifteenth century: Ambrogio Traversari (1386–1439), the Camaldolese monk, found some previously unknown Jerome manuscripts, while the educator Pier Paolo Vergerio (1370–1444) became interested in the saint's eloquence, and Lorenzo Valla (1407–1457)

St. Jerome. *Jerome in His Study* by Albrecht Dürer. Engraving; 1514. MUSÉE DU PETIT-PALAIS, PARIS/GIRAUDON/ART RESOURCE

argued that Jerome's dream was a warning against excessive interest in pagan philosophy and not in pagan eloquence. Humanist orations delivered on Jerome's feast day (30 September) emphasized and exaggerated his virtue and his eloquence.

Erasmus (c. 1466–1536) collated manuscripts of Jerome's works and letters between 1490 and 1511. In 1514 he helped edit the Froben-Amerbach edition of Jerome's works in Basel. Working with his own collations and with a wide assortment of earlier editions, Erasmus eliminated, mainly on stylistic grounds, many inauthentic works. The 1516 Froben edition included Erasmus's *Life* of Jerome, which did away with the miracles, corrected the chronology of the saint's life, and showed that he could not have been a cardinal. Erasmus's portrait of Jerome otherwise emphasized the Renaissance gentleman scholar at the expense of the medieval monk.

During the Reformation, Jerome, although he never acquired the status of Augustine, was respected by all the reformers as an expert on the Holy Land and as a learned, albeit too allegorical, biblical commentator. Roman Catholic controversialists enlisted his aid in their defense of the cult of Mary, of penance, and of monasticism. Erasmus's edition of the complete works of Jerome was revised and reprinted seven times between 1520 and 1565. In 1565, the post-Tridentine Roman theologian and orientalist Mariano Vittori produced his own edition intended to replace Erasmus's work, which he corrected in fifteen hundred places. To his edition, Vittori added a new, more correct *Life* of Jerome. Vittori's approach was as critical as that of Erasmus and the Counter-Reformation iconography of Jerome was very sober: he now tended to be portrayed as hearing the trumpet of the Last Judgment.

Jerome's Bible translation (the Vulgate) came under criticism from the late fifteenth century onward: noting the uneven quality of the translation, scholars such as Jacques Lefèvre d'Étaples (c. 1455–1536) or the Hebraist Santes Pagnini (1470–1536) began to doubt that Jerome was the translator of the Vulgate, whereas conservative Catholic theologians defended his authorship. The Tridentine Decree on the Vulgate (1546) confirmed its authority without naming Jerome as translator.

BIBLIOGRAPHY

Backus, Irena. "Erasmus and the Spirituality of the Early Church." In *Erasmus' Vision of the Church*. Edited by Hilmar M. Pabel. Kirksville, Mo., 1995. Pages 95–114. Includes an analysis of Erasmus's *Life* of Jerome and of his preface (addressed to William Warham) to the 1516 edition of Jerome's works.

Backus, Irena, ed. *Reception of the Church Fathers in the West: From the Carolingians to the Maurists*. Leiden, Netherlands, 1997. Chapters dealing with the Renaissance and the Reformation contain much detail on Jerome's reception together with bibliographical information.

Olin, John C. "Erasmus and Saint Jerome: The Close Bond and Its Significance." *Erasmus of Rotterdam Society Yearbook 7* (1987): 33–53.

Rice, Eugene F., Jr. *Saint Jerome in the Renaissance*. Baltimore and London, 1985. Classic study, particularly helpful in its treatment of iconography; lacks a thorough examination of Jerome's theological influence.

IRENA BACKUS

JESUITS. *See* **Religious Orders,** *subentry on* **The Jesuits.**

JEWEL, JOHN (1522–1571), theologian, bishop of Salisbury under Elizabeth I. One of ten children of a Devonshire family, Jewel entered Merton College, Oxford, in 1535. In 1539 he moved to that Erasmian cradle of Christian humanism, Corpus Christi College, Oxford, where he was a student and then fellow. In the tradition of Renaissance Christian humanism, he acquired considerable skill in the biblical languages (later teaching Hebrew in Zurich) along with his studies of philosophy and theology. He received his bachelor of divinity degree in 1551 or 1552 and was awarded a doctorate of divinity in 1565. During the late 1540s he studied at Oxford under Peter Martyr Vermigli and developed moderate Protestant opinions. The accession of Mary Tudor brought elements of confusion and contradiction into Jewel's life. In 1553 he composed the University of Oxford's congratulations to the new queen, and in 1554, he signed an anti-Protestant document; but he also refused to attend the restored Mass at Corpus Christi and was deprived of his fellowship. In 1555 he went into exile in Frankfurt, where he reasserted his moderate Protestantism, now against John Knox and the more extreme Calvinists, and publicly repented his vacillation under Queen Mary. He then rejoined Peter Martyr in Strasbourg. They later spent time in Zurich and probably traveled to northern Italy. Jewel returned to England in 1559 after the coronation of Elizabeth I. In 1560 he was consecrated bishop of Salisbury. In the next years he was very active in disputations (especially with Roman Catholics), royal commissions, preaching, and episcopal visitations.

In 1562, partly in response to Roman Catholic attacks, Jewel published his *Apologia Ecclesiae Anglicanae,* the first major defense of the Church of England. He expounded the beliefs, polity, and

John Jewel. Nineteenth-century engraving by R. Graves.

practices of the official Church in England, grounded these in scripture and the church fathers of the first six centuries, and asked in what way these could be viewed as heretical. He both affirmed some of the reforms that Protestants had instituted and insisted on England's continuity with the catholic, orthodox, and especially patristic foundations of its church. There has been some debate, both in his own day and recently, about whether Jewel was the sole author of the *Apologia,* but no one doubts his principal responsibility for its shape and argument. The *Apologia* was translated into English in 1564 by Lady Ann Bacon. Archbishop Matthew Parker suggested that it be appended to the Articles of Religion, but it never received that official status. The *Apologia* provoked strong reactions from defenders of Roman Catholicism, both in England and on the Continent, notably by Thomas Harding, Henry Cole, and delegates to the Council of Trent. Jewel answered Harding's substantial attack with a lengthy exposition and rebuttal of his own. The main controverted issues included the papacy, the authority of "local [i.e., national] churches," and the Eucharist.

While Jewel battled with the church of Rome, he also suppressed extreme Protestant tendencies in his diocese, both in theology and in matters of liturgy,

vestments, and so on. In addition to the *Apologia* and its defense, Jewel published a number of sermons, a treatise on the scriptures, a commentary on the two letters to the Thessalonians, and an attack on the 1569 bull of Pius V. He personally supported the education of boys with potential, including Richard Hooker, who followed him to Corpus Christi College in 1567. His influence remained strong into the seventeenth century. In 1610 Archbishop Richard Bancroft instructed every parish to have a copy of Jewel's works. His collected works were published in 1609 and 1611, again in 1626, and often thereafter. Many would continue to cite the *Apologia* as the finest defense of the Christian tradition that would later come to be known as Anglicanism.

BIBLIOGRAPHY

Primary Works

Jewel, John. *An Apologie of the Church of England.* In *English Reformers.* Edited by T. H. L. Parker. Philadelphia, 1966. An abridgment of Jewel's treatise.

Jewel, John. *An Apology of the Church of England.* Edited by John E. Booty. Ithaca, N.Y., 1963. An edition of Lady Bacon's translation.

Jewel, John. *The Works of John Jewell, D. D., Bishop of Salisbury.* Edited by Richard William Jelf. 8 vols. Oxford, 1848.

Secondary Works

Booty, John E. *John Jewel as Apologist of the Church of England.* London, 1963.

Lytle, Guy Fitch. "Prelude to the Condemnations of Latimer, Ridley, and Cranmer: Heresy, Humanism, Controversy, and Conscience in Early Reformation Oxford." In *This Sacred History: Anglican Reflections for John Booty.* Edited by Donald S. Armentrout. Cambridge, Mass., 1990. Pages 222–242.

GUY FITCH LYTLE

JEWELRY. The quantity and variety of jewelry worn in the Renaissance reflects the wealth and personal ostentation of the age. Jewels had an importance disproportionate to their diminutive scale.

The Function of Jewelry in Society. As portraits document, the display of jewels was a highly visible mark of personal status. Juan Pantoja de la Cruz's painting of *Margaret of Austria, Queen of Philip III of Spain* (Royal Collection, London; 1605), for example, depicts the queen in a gown stitched with pearls and wearing a diamond and pearl combination called the *joyel de los Austrias.* Recognition of jewelry's power to reinforce status is also seen in numerous royal edicts. In 1530 Francis I, king of France, declared eight "jewels of the crown," preventing their dispersal during times of financial crisis for the inherent value of the precious stones and preserving these artistic creations as symbols of state. Sumptuary laws, enacted as early as 1362 in England, forbade lower classes from wearing gold and silver, legally preserving the distinction jewelry conferred.

Wearing jewelry was by no means limited to royalty or by sex. Men wore hat badges, rings, and gold chains. Women wore earrings, pendants, brooches, breast ornaments; these could be composed of cameos or encrusted with diamonds, emeralds, rubies, or pearls; they could be mounted on gold or silver and coated with enamel. Beyond social status, jewelry was often worn to mark political allegiance or religious faith. Some hat badges, for instance, bore likenesses of kings and emperors; others showed saints, more sumptuous versions of the base-metal badges worn by countless pilgrims. At many European courts monarchs favored courtiers with gifts of jewelry at New Year's celebrations to cement relationships. Armorial insignia enameled on the individual links of necklaces were among the more obvious displays of status. The nobility frequently commissioned special jewels to celebrate birth, baptism, or marriage, events that conferred family status.

The Making of Jewelry. Although few sources describe the techniques of Renaissance jewelry making, two Italian treatises, Vannoccio Biringuccio's *De la pirotechnica* (Concerning the use of fire in science and the arts; 1540) and Benvenuto Cellini's *Trattati dell'oreficeria e della scultura* (Treatise on goldsmith's work and sculpture; 1568), outline the preparation of materials and methods of production. As the making of jewelry was largely the domain of the goldsmith's guild, the regulations of this association of skilled craftsmen furnish information on their practice. Contracts or letters between patron and artist are other sources of study; a letter of 1571 from Catherine de Médicis, queen mother of France, to François Dujardin reveals how involved a patron could become with a commission and how knowledgeable patron and jeweler could be about the properties of stones. Surviving drawings indicate the process of design; even such well-known artists as Albrecht Dürer or Hans Holbein the Younger were sometimes engaged in designing jewelry. Finally the jewels themselves provide evidence of their making, though subsequent alterations due to changing tastes or needs require the historian to take care in determining the original form of an individual piece.

Artisans often began with a drawn design or incorporated motifs from one of many engraved pattern books circulating around Europe. Once the design was accepted by the patron, jewelers generally made three-dimensional models out of plaster, wood, or lead. These served as the basis of casting molds into which molten metals could be poured. The resulting gold or silver forms could be ornamented by embossing or chasing, painted with enamel decoration, or set with gems. During the Renaissance faceted stones gradually replaced cabochons, the smoothly rounded, highly polished precious stones preferred in the Middle Ages. Craftsmen cut stones into pointed octahedrons or table-cut stones, pyramidal forms with apex removed. As faceting revealed gems' color and luster, backing in metal foil was often added to enhance the effect. Different mounts such as the collet—a band of metal—were developed to best display and safely hold the precious stones.

The influx into Europe of precious stones and metals from the New World and the energetic pursuit of trade spurred the making of jewelry. Gold and emeralds came from South America, pearls from off the coast of Venezuela, diamonds from India, lapis lazuli from Afghanistan, and turquoise from Persia. Portugal and Spain, points of entry for wealth-laden galleons from the Americas, quickly developed a

Jewelry. "Hippocamp with Indian Rider," pendant; c. 1580. ©THE BRITISH MUSEUM, LONDON, WADDESDON BEQUEST

taste for rich materials in jewelry. International style spread the forms and types of jewels across Europe. Jewels were given as dowries or ambassadorial presents from one court to another. Guild practices required craftsmen to travel to different towns. By these means taste for jewelry spread throughout Europe. While regional techniques and preferences are sometimes apparent—for instance, German jewels show a taste for complex, curving patterns—jewelry style was so international in Europe that an individual piece's point of origin is often difficult to determine.

Types of Jewelry. Several types of jewelry were popular during the Renaissance. Since jewelry often responds to changes in fashion, these types tended to evolve with costume design. At the end of the fifteenth and beginning of the sixteenth centuries, men wore hat badges. These were large, often two to four inches in diameter, and strikingly sculptural, in order to be visible from a distance against then-fashionable black velvet headgear. Men and women wore multiple rings, often outsized, engraved or inset with stones. Among the most passionately collected ancient works, cameos—gems or hard stones carved in relief, often into multicolored layers of stone—were found in famous collections, such as that of Lorenzo de' Medici. In the Renaissance these were often reset as hat badges or pendants. Florentine, Milanese, and Prague artisans earned reputations for their revival of this ancient art and often chose subjects from Greek and Roman mythology. Although few jewelers are known by name, Alessandro Masnago of Milan was admired for his adroit integration of a stone's striations into his compositions. Renaissance patrons adored exotic materials, which were often incorporated into jewels. Bizzarely shaped pearls could be transformed into dragon pendants by the addition of enameled gold tails and heads. Some jewels, such as pomanders, functioned to contain rare spices. Others ensured that stones thought to have medicinal properties, such as topaz or sapphire, would be placed in contact with the wearer's skin.

As the necklines of women's dresses lowered, dangling ornaments, such as pendants, became increasingly popular. Pendants became heavier and more elaborate by the beginning of the seventeenth century. Enameling became an increasingly prevalent decoration of jewels' surfaces. Frankly decorative forms, such as ribbons, introduced the baroque era.

See also **Clothing**; **Sumptuary Laws**.

BIBLIOGRAPHY

Evans, Joan. *A History of Jewelry 1100–1870.* London, 1970. Second edition of the best general history of jewelry.

Hackenbroch, Yvonne. *Enseignes.* Florence, 1996. A recent study devoted to hat badges.

Hackenbroch, Yvonne. *Renaissance Jewelry.* London, 1979. An important survey arranged geographically.

Lightbown, Ronald W. *Mediaeval European Jewellery with a Catalogue of the Collection in the Victoria and Albert Museum.* London, 1992. A wealth of information on the medieval but also early Renaissance periods.

Muller, Priscilla E. *Jewels in Spain, 1500–1800.* New York, 1972.

Scarisbrick, Diana. *Jewellery in Britain 1066–1837.* Wilby, U.K., 1994. Useful chapter on Renaissance jewelry.

Victoria and Albert Museum. *Princely Magnificence: Court Jewels of the Renaissance. 1500–1630.* London, 1980. Important exhibition catalog.

IAN WARDROPPER

JEWISH LITERATURE AND LANGUAGES. *See* **Hebrew Literature and Language; Ladino Literature and Language; Yiddish Literature and Language.**

JEWISH MEDICINE AND SCIENCE. It is difficult to speak about Jewish involvement in medicine and science during the Renaissance and beyond without reference to Jewish traditions of medical and scientific activity in the ancient and medieval periods. Perceiving themselves as proud heirs of such medieval luminaries as the physician Moses Maimonides (1135–1204), the astrologer Abraham ibn Ezra (1089–1164), and the astronomer Levi ben Gershom (Gersonides; 1288–1344), as well as the biblical Abraham, Solomon, and the ancient rabbis, Jewish thinkers living in early modern Europe continued to believe that the study of nature was a supreme religious ideal and that the roots of magic and medicine, astrology and astronomy, were ultimately located in ancient Jewish sources.

The Study of Nature. Important differences in their approaches to the study of nature are also apparent due to a number of specific factors unique to the sixteenth and seventeenth centuries. Jews, like other Europeans, were profoundly affected by the more prominent role of science and technology in European culture and by the impact of printing on the dissemination of scientific information. Even more decisive were the new opportunities to study medicine in the universities as well as the integration of a new community of converso doctors into the Jewish community.

By the second half of the sixteenth century, certain scholars in central and eastern Europe pursued the study of astronomy and cosmology as a desirable supplement to their primary rabbinic pursuits. Moses Isserles (1525–1572) and Judah Loew ben Bezalel (the Maharal; c. 1525–1609) openly encouraged the study of the natural world. Their student David Gans (1541–1613) composed an original Hebrew compendium of geographical and astronomical information, even offering his readers a tantalizing report of his exchanges with Johann Kepler and Tycho Brahe in Prague.

In Padua, hundreds of Jews gained entrance to a great medical school for the first time, matriculated, and went on to practice medicine throughout Europe. Eventually, universities opened their doors to Jews elsewhere in Italy and in the rest of Europe. Through their medical studies, Jews received a prolonged exposure to the study of the liberal arts, to Latin studies, and to classical medical texts, as well as to the more recent scientific advances in botany, anatomy, chemistry, clinical medicine, physics, and astronomy. They were also afforded the opportunity for intense socialization with other like-minded Jews and non-Jews throughout Europe, maintaining intellectual and professional links with each other long after their graduation.

The writings of several illustrious graduates of Padua illustrate quite dramatically the impact the new medical education was having on Jewish religious and cultural sensibilities. Joseph Delmedigo (1591–1655) produced a highly sophisticated Hebrew compendium of physics, mathematics, and astronomy, and later attempted to integrate this knowledge with the latest cosmological theories of the Kabbalah. Tobias Cohen (1652–1729) published a comprehensive textbook of medicine, also in Hebrew, incorporating the most recent therapies of the chemical philosophers.

The ranks of this newly emerging Jewish medical community were swelled even more by hundreds of university-trained converso physicians who fled Spain and Portugal in the late sixteenth and seventeenth centuries, settling in Italy, Holland, Germany, England, and even eastern Europe and the New World. They served as clinicians and sometimes purveyors of scientific learning within the Jewish community while often wielding considerable economic and political power. While many of these physicians were indifferent to traditional Jewish practices and beliefs, their professional identity, as members of a highly successful but often racially maligned medical community, was frequently linked with their own personal quest to define their newly evolving relationships to Judaism and the Jewish community. The

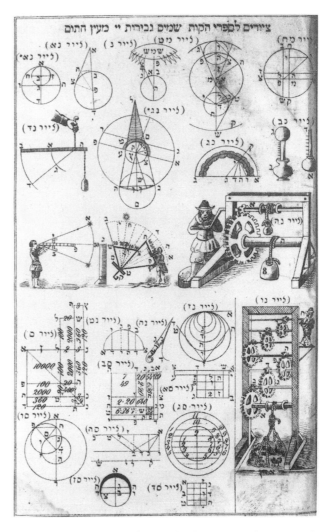

Jewish Science. Page of scientific illustrations from Joseph Solomon Delmedigo's *Sefer Elim* (Odessa, Russia, 1864) based on those from the first edition (Amsterdam, 1629).

biographies of such illustrious converso physicians as Amatus Lusitanus (1511–1568), Zacutus Lusitanus (1575–1642), and Rodrigo de Castro (1550–1627) and his son Benedict (1597–1684) reveal quite distinctly such linkages and, to a great extent, exemplify convictions shared by others with similar professional and ethnic backgrounds.

Jewish Theologies of Nature. Especially within these three subcommunities—rabbinic students in Prague and Cracow, graduates of Padua and other medical schools, and converso physicians—the study of natural philosophy was tolerated and even enthusiastically endorsed to a greater extent than in previous eras. Some Jewish religious thinkers in this period were increasingly willing to disentangle physics from metaphysics, the secular from the sacred, science from theology, and thus, in a manner similar to many of their Christian counterparts, to view scientific advances as positive resources to be enlisted in the cause of perpetuating the Jewish faith. By erecting carefully drawn boundaries between the domains of scientific activity and religious faith, they discovered a strategy whereby the two could live peacefully and harmoniously with each other, avoiding the often bitter acrimony between faith and reason of the medieval period.

Others found ways of integrating the new scientific information with Jewish theology, especially mystical theosophy, thus spiritualizing the former while reinvigorating the latter. And through the vehicles of greater mass communication available to the Jewish community—the pulpit sermon, Hebrew and Yiddish textbooks, and scientific literature in other languages—larger numbers of Jews were becoming aware and appreciative of the new scientific culture, whether or not they were literate in it. With the increasing secularization of European culture in the eighteenth century, these strategies of alliance between science and Jewish faith would become more tenuous and difficult to sustain.

Consumers, Not Creators, of Scientific Culture. Reflections on scientific activity among early modern Jewish thinkers, to be sure, are not the same as actual scientific performance itself. With few exceptions, the achievements of Jewish practitioners of science were unimpressive in comparison with those of the nineteenth and twentieth centuries. Probably the greatest achievements were related to the practice of clinical medicine. This lack of achievement, however, should not be attributed to any religious or theological inhibitions inherent in Judaism itself. More critical is the fact that Jews conspicuously lacked the institutional support of churches, courts, and especially scientific academies, and thus had little opportunity to "do" science other than medicine. The only avenue available to them in order to keep abreast of the latest scientific discoveries was through medical education or through their own reading of scientific literature. They consequently remained outside the scientific laboratory primarily because of social rather than religious constraints.

See also **Jewish Philosophy; Padua, University of.**

BIBLIOGRAPHY

Friedenwald. Harry. *The Jews and Medicine.* 2 vols. Baltimore, 1944. Reprint, New York, 1967.

Idel, Moshe. "Differing Conceptions of Kabbalah in the Early Seventeenth Century." In *Jewish Thought in the Seventeenth Century.* Edited by Isadore Twersky and Bernard Septimus. Cambridge, Mass., 1987. Pages 137–200.

Idel, Moshe. *Golem: Jewish Magical and Mystical Traditions on the Artificial Anthropoid.* Albany, N.Y., 1990

Langermann, Y. Tzvi. "The Astronomy of Rabbi Moses Isserles." In *Physics, Cosmology, and Astronomy, 1300–1700.* Edited by Sabetai Unguru. Dordrecht, Netherlands, 1991. Pages 83–98.

Levine, Hillel. "Paradise Not Surrendered: Jewish Reactions to Copernicus and the Growth of Modern Science." In *Epistemology, Methodology, and the Social Sciences.* Edited by Robert S. Cohen and Marx W. Wartofsky. Boston, 1983. Pages 203–225.

Neher, André. *Jewish Thought and the Scientific Revolution of the Sixteenth Century: David Gans (1541–1613) and His Times.* Translated from the French by David Maisel. Oxford, 1986.

Ruderman, David. *Jewish Thought and Scientific Discovery in Early Modern Europe.* New Haven, Conn., 1995.

Ruderman, David. *Kabbalah, Magic, and Science: The Cultural Universe of a Sixteenth-Century Jewish Physician.* Cambridge, Mass., 1988.

DAVID B. RUDERMAN

JEWISH MESSIANISM. Messianism among Jews in the Renaissance period generally entailed the expectation of an apocalyptic end of the world. The expectations of many messianic thinkers centered on the problem of the Marranos (forced converts in Spain and Portugal) and their return to Judaism, on the one hand, and the hope of finding the Ten Lost Tribes, on the other. Once part of the Twelve Tribes of Israel, constituting the northern Kingdom of Israel, the inhabitants of these ten tribes were exiled by the Assyrians when the kingdom fell in the eighth century B.C.E. They have been lost ever since. Very often messianic hopes stemmed from kabbalistic thought, although not all Kabbalists at that time had messianic expectations. Some of the messianic thinking also grew out of contemporary interest in magic.

Actual messianic movements are connected only with the names of Asher Lemlein and later with David Reuveni and Shelomo Molcho. In sixteenth-century Jerusalem and Safed, a messianic ferment can be noticed but not an actual movement.

Messianic Thinkers. After 1496 Isaac Abravanel (1437–1508), a statesman, a philosopher largely uninfluenced by Kabbalah, and a Bible commentator, wrote some treatises dedicated to messianic expectations, from a clear polemical and anti-Christian position. Redemption according to Abravanel would have two distinct aspects: eternal personal redemption—the immortality of the soul—and apocalyptic public redemption. The apocalypse would include a divine revenge against the Gentiles, the miraculous establishment of a messianic kingdom, and the resurrection of the dead. Thereafter an almost natural world would exist, one quite similar to ours, though better—people would live peaceful long lives in prosperity, without evil inclination and in search of knowledge.

In the first decade of the sixteenth century Asher Lemlein (Lammlin) preached repentance and the imminent coming of the Messiah. He was active in northern Italy, and his impact was felt mainly among Ashkenazic Jews. The grandfather of the chronicler David Gans "broke up the oven that he had for baking the mazzot, believing that next year he would be baking them in the Holy Land." Lemlein was influenced by the ecstatic Kabbalah of Abraham Abulafia from thirteenth-century Spain, medieval Ashkenazic Hassidism, and perhaps also by messianic ferment among Christians.

Before the expulsion of the Jews from Spain, Abraham ben Eliezer ha-Levi (1460–after 1528) was apparently part of the school known as the "Responding Angel," which tried to hasten redemption by magically "binding" the King of Evil, expecting redemption to start in 1492. After much wandering ha-Levi settled in Jerusalem in about 1514. While setting a new date for redemption which would not depend on human intervention, he organized public vigils to avert the dangers of the apocalyptic era. Ha-Levi also wrote a short treatise about Martin Luther, assigning him a messianic role as the man who came to pave the way for the Messiah by turning the Christians away from idolatrous customs and beliefs.

Messianic Figures. At the turn of the fifteenth and sixteenth centuries many tales about the Ten Lost Tribes were current, assigning them a messianic role. According to the tales mentioned, for example, in the writings of Obadiah di Bertinoro and Abraham ben Eliezer ha-Levi of Jerusalem, the ten tribes flourished in a strong independent kingdom beyond the legendary river of Sambatyon, living saintly lives without sin. David Reuveni (d. 1538) claimed to be their prince (being the son of their late king Solomon and the brother of Joseph, whom he held to be the presently ruling king) and commander in chief. He gave rise to messianic expectations revolving around his political and military skills and options in conquering Palestine. In his (legendary) diary he described the life of the Ten Lost Tribes in detail as well as his own adventures, the goal of which was propaganda for his messianic ideas. His first historically recorded appearance was in Venice in 1523. A year later he tried to convince Pope Clement VII to make an anti-Turkish alliance between the ten tribes and the Christian world. In 1525 he arrived in Portugal and was received almost as an official ambassador. Throughout his career many Jews doubted his story; nevertheless he found support, first among certain Jewish and Christian notables in Italy and then among the Marranos in Portugal.

Shelomo Molcho (1500–1532) was born a Marrano originally named Diego Pires in Lisbon and became a secretary of the king's council. After meeting David Reuveni in 1525 he circumcised himself and escaped to the Ottoman Empire. A few years later Reuveni too was ordered to leave Portugal. In spite of the danger, Molcho successfully attempted to meet Pope Clement VII. When the inquisitional court in Rome sentenced Molcho to death, the pope, probably believing in Molcho's spiritual powers, saved his life. His attempts to meet the emperor Charles V together with Reuveni were not as successful, and he died a martyr's death, refusing to convert to Christianity. Reuveni, on the other hand, was imprisoned, sent to Spain in chains, and perished sometime later.

Molcho successfully foretold a flood of the Tiber in 1530 and an earthquake in Portugal in 1531 and had several symbolic and messianic visions (recorded in *Sefer HaMefo'ar,* first published as *Derashot* in Salonika, 1529). In some of his texts he attributed a central messianic role to himself in the apocalyptical drama. His Jewish education included Kabbalah, possibly in the spirit of the school of the "Responding Angel." He might have been influenced by the Christian ideas of the Messiah, particularly regarding his death. Molcho left a considerable impression on his contemporaries as well as on the following generations. A messianic movement spread under his influence. His personal belongings were saved by the Jews of Prague and displayed long after his death, and the great halakist Joseph Karo wished that he might follow in Molcho's footsteps and be burnt at the stake. Still others, such as Hayyim Vital, viewed him negatively because of his espousal of magic.

Messianism in Palestine. A messianic ferment developed in Safed (in the upper Galilee, Palestine) in the second half of the sixteenth century. Some expected the messianic era to start in 1575, others in 1589. In its first phase this ferment is connected with Jacob Berab, who tried to renew rabbinic ordination as a prerequisite for the advent of the Messiah. In later phases much of the impetus for the ferment derives from kabbalistic thought. In most cases, such as in Moses Cordovero's thought, it did not focus on a specific personality, which might have been one reason why it never turned into an active movement (another reason might have been the quick physical collapse of the town). Only in its latest phase do we find two personalities who, together with their devotees, assigned a messianic role to themselves: Isaac Luria (1534–1572) and Hayyim Vital (1542–1620). Luria deeply impressed his contemporaries with both his appearance and his intellectual creativity, but his premature death after living in Safed for only two or three years seems to have hampered the development of a real movement. After Luria's death Vital kept trying to inspire a messianic movement revolving around his own personality, first in Safed and later in Damascus. His unattractive character and appearance must have been one reason why only a handful of devotees followed him. Others mocked him, but most people seem to have ignored him.

Luria's messianic theory (followed to a great degree by Vital) is based both on the messianic narrative found in *Sefer ha-Zohar* (Book of splendor; Spain, thirteenth century) and on the personalities of Vital and himself. It emphasized the spiritual powers and development of the messianic figure rather than mundane powers such as political or military skills. The Messiah was supposed to contribute to the "fixing" or "healing" of the "broken" divinity, to fight the evil forces, and to "draw" a new and pure messianic soul for himself from Heaven. His spirituality was supposed to mirror the immense productivity and strength of the cosmic sexual powers. His means were prayers and "spiritual death."

Modern Evaluations. The evaluation of the messianic activities in the Renaissance era has raised some controversy among researchers. The basic question under debate is whether the expulsion from Spain caused any rise in messianic expectations. Gershom Scholem argued that it did, pointing to the variety and wealth of messianic activities and writings after the expulsion and also to the presumably traumatic effect this event must have had over the Jews. Moshe Idel, on the other hand, points to the voluminous messianic writings of the school of the "Responding Angel" written earlier in Spain and observes that some of the most important messianic figures, such as Luria, did not even mention the expulsion and were not part of the exiled. Scholem's argument is supported by our knowledge of only one school with messianic ferment before the expulsion, compared with the wider strata of the Jewish population who embraced such hopes after the expulsion, especially in Jerusalem and in Safed.

Some scholars also see the messianic phenomena in a wider context, echoing similar expectations among Jews in Italy, Christians, and Muslims. This controversy is connected to another: whether any rise in messianic expectations should be conceived as a reaction to historical disasters, as a rise of positive hopes due to historical changes (such as the victories of the Ottoman empire), or as a response to the mystical experiences of individuals.

A third question is raised, namely whether messianism since the expulsion from Spain is bound to rise in the context of Kabbalah. Scholem answered this question affirmatively, thinking mainly of Abraham ha-Levi and Safadian Kabbalah. Idel opposes that view, pointing out that Isaac Abravanel, for example, cultivated messianic hopes without being a Kabbalist, whereas his son Yehudah, who was more devoted to Kabbalah, did not nurse such hopes.

See also **Kabbalah**; **Luria, Isaac**.

BIBLIOGRAPHY

Primary Works

Aescoly, Aaron Zeev. *Jewish Messianic Movements*. Jerusalem, 1987. In Hebrew.

Patai, Raphael. *The Messiah Texts*. Detroit, 1979.

Secondary Works

Cornell, Fleisher H. "The Lawgiver as Messiah: The Making of the Imperial Image in the Reign of Süleymân." *In Süleymân the Magnificent and His Time: Acts of the Parisian Conference, Galeries nationales du Grand Palais, 7–10 March 1990*. Edited by Gilles Veinstein. Paris, 1992. Pages 159–177.

Idel, Moshe. *Messianic Mystics*. New Haven, Conn., 1998.

Ruderman, D. B. "Hope against Hope: Jewish and Christian Messianic Expectations in the Late Middle Ages." In *Exile and Diaspora: Studies in the History of the Jewish People Presented to Prof. Haim Beinart*. Edited by A. Mirsky, A. Grossman, and Y. Kaplan. Jerusalem, 1991. Pages 185–202.

Scholem, Gershom. *The Messianic Idea in Judaism*. New York, 1971.

Tishby, Isaiah. "Acute Apocalyptic Messianism." In *Essential Papers on Messianic Movements and Personalities in Jewish History*. Edited by M. Saperstein. New York, 1992. Pages 259–286.

RONIT MEROZ

JEWISH PHILOSOPHY. The interest in philosophy and its related liberal arts and natural sciences was the hallmark of Jewish culture in Spain and the Jewish communities under its influence in Portugal, Provence, Italy, Crete, and North Africa. With the expulsion of the Jews from Spain (1492) and Portugal (1497), the exiles brought their philosophical heritage to the Ottoman Empire, where it was consolidated and popularized with the help of the newly discovered technology of printing. During the sixteenth century some interest in philosophy and the sciences was also evident among the Jews of Poland and Bohemia, especially in Cracow and Prague, but it remained marginal to the primary preoccupation with jurisprudence. With the establishment of the Jewish community in Amsterdam, composed of conversos who had fled the Inquisition and returned to Judaism, Jewish philosophy was cultivated again in western Europe. The philosophical interests of Amsterdam Jews, however, were shaped by European education and the existential concerns of the returning conversos rather than by the traditional themes of Jewish philosophy.

Jewish Philosophy in Spain, 1391–1492.

Aristotelianism was the dominant trend in medieval Jewish philosophy in Spain. Following Moses Maimonides (1135–1204), Jewish Aristotelians held that Judaism and philosophy are compatible because the prophet Moses attained the highest level of intellectual perfection available to humans. When properly understood, the divinely revealed sacred Torah of Moses and Greek philosophy (the philosophy of Aristotle as interpreted by medieval Muslim philosophers) teach the same truths, though they do so differently. Philosophy uses discursive reasoning and is thus accessible to the educated few, whereas the Torah of Moses teaches truth through figurative language in order to be accessible to the uneducated masses. The task of the Jewish philosopher is to remove the apparent contradictions between what human reason and divine revelation teach and to show their underlying compatibility. During the thirteenth and fourteenth centuries these assumptions undergirded the intellectual life of the Jewish elite in Spain.

The anti-Jewish riots of 1391 and the mass conversion of Jews to Christianity in their aftermath brought about a scathing attack on philosophy as Jews attempted to make sense of the crisis. Hasdai Crescas (c. 1340–1410/11), the rabbi of Saragossa, who was himself well trained in philosophy, considered the philosophic culture to be the cause for the failure of the Jews to uphold their ancestral faith. In his *Or ha-Shem* (Light of the Lord), completed in 1410, Crescas attempted to free Judaism from Aristotelianism by refuting Aristotle's physics, on the one hand, and by exposing the logical inconsistency of Maimonides's theory of knowledge and its ill effects on Jewish religious life, on the other hand. Crescas's alternative to Maimonides posited an infinite world held together by divine love and insisted on the will, rather than the intellect, as God's essence.

Notwithstanding his depth and originality, Crescas failed to displace either Aristotle or Maimonides. During the fifteenth century, thinkers such as Meir Alguades, Joseph ibn Shem Tov, his brother Isaac ibn Shem Tov and the grandson Shem Tov ben Shem Tov, Abraham Shalom, Abraham Bibago, Elijah Habillo, and Barukh ibn Yaish perpetuated Jewish Aristotelianism by writing supercommentaries on the commentaries of Averroes (Ibn Rushd) on Aristotle and by consulting the works of medieval Muslim philosophers such as Avicenna, Ibn Bajja, and Ibn Tufayl. In addition, Jewish philosophers became increasingly familiar with Christian Scholasticism and translated works by Albertus Magnus, Thomas Aquinas, William of Ockham, and Marsilius of Inghen into Hebrew. Consulting scholastic commentaries on Aristotle, Jewish philosophers also produced new translations of Aristotle's *Nicomachean Ethics* and commentaries on it.

Although Jewish familiarity with scholastic literature grew out of the intensifying polemics between Judaism and Christianity, it accounted for a new direction in Jewish philosophy. Considering themselves loyal to Maimonides and attributing their views to him, Spanish Jewish philosophers proposed a new model for the harmonization of reason and faith, one inspired by Aquinas's views. It recognized a formal distinction between natural philosophy, the domain of created human reason, and revealed theology, the manifestation of God's perfect, eternal wisdom. Philosophy and theology differ in terms of origin, scope, and aim, although they do not genuinely contradict each other. Rather, theology completes and perfects philosophy, as Aquinas has shown. In the case of some propositions, there is even an overlap between natural human reason and the truths of revelation, but only knowledge revealed by God is salvific. The task of the philosophically trained theologian is rationally to explicate the suprarational truths of divine revelation by employing philosophical arguments.

The rational exposition of Judaism was intended to prove its spiritual merits for Jews and Christians alike. Jewish philosophers attempted to show that the articles of Jewish faith are compatible with reason whereas the dogmas of Christianity are falsifiable. The definition and explication of Jewish dogmas were carried out by reference to Maimonides's list of Thirteen Principles and his still venerated *Guide of the Perplexed*. In the context of this discussion Jewish philosophers expressed their views on the standard themes of Jewish philosophy: God's essence and attributes, the origin and structure of the universe, divine providence and miracles, prophecy and revelation, and human perfection and redemption. Philosophically there was little novelty in these reflections, anticipating the eventual demise of Jewish Aristotelianism.

Within the category of revealed theology, Jewish philosophers included Kabbalah, whose theosophical and psychological doctrines had strong affinity with Platonism and Neoplatonism. Some Jewish scholars selectively absorbed kabbalistic views, incorporating them into the framework of their Aristotelian worldview, without becoming creative kabbalists. The most important influence of Kabbalah on philosophy concerns the esoteric meaning of the Torah. Contrary to Maimonides, who identified the esoteric dimension of the Torah with the physics and metaphysics of Aristotle, the fifteenth-century thinkers identified the esoteric Torah with the ideal order of the universe that preexists in the divine mind in a supereminent way. The structural affinity between the created universe and the revealed text entails that the more one studies Torah the more one is able to understand God and the created world.

Jewish Philosophy in Italy, 1290–1630.

The fusion of rationalist philosophy and Kabbalah was especially common in Italy, where Jewish intellectual life attests to a greater degree of contact between Jewish and Christian scholars than in Spain. Jewish rationalism was imported into Italy from Spain in the late twelfth century, about the time that Scholasticism entered Italy from France, and Jewish philosophers were instrumental to the dissemination of Aristotelianism in Italy. They translated works of Aristotle and the commentaries of Averroes from Hebrew and Arabic into Latin and cooperated with Christian scholars on the Latin translation of Maimonides's *Guide of the Perplexed,* which became one of Aquinas's philosophical sources. Conversely, Italian Jewish philosophers, such as Hillel ben Samuel of Verona (c. 1220–c. 1295), became familiar with Aquinas's works and employed some of his views in their interpretation of Maimonides. Judah ben Moses Romano (c. 1280–c. 1325) translated works of Aquinas, Giles of Rome, Albertus Magnus, and Alexander Alessandri into Hebrew, while his contemporary Shemaria of Crete translated the writings of Averroes into Latin, illustrating the cross-cultural interaction in the court of Charles of Anjou in the 1320s. From Latin sources, especially the *Liber de causis* (Book of causes), Jewish philosophers in Italy absorbed certain Neoplatonic themes that they grafted into the received Aristotelian tradition. The

Neoplatonized version of Jewish Aristotelianism was popularized in *Behinat olam* (The examination of the universe) by the fourteenth-century Provençal author Yedaiah Bedersi, which became a standard philosophical text among Italian Jews, and in the philosophical novel of Moses Rieti, *Miqdash Me'at* (Lesser sanctuary), which was composed in 1416 and modeled after Dante's *Divine Comedy.*

In the second half of the fifteenth century, Judah Messer Leon (c. 1425–c. 1495), a philosopher and physician who could grant doctorate degrees in medicine and philosophy to Jewish students, attempted to rid Jewish philosophy of its Neoplatonic tinge. Messer Leon introduced Jewish students to scholastic logic as taught by Paul of Venice and Walter Burley, thus marking a departure from the Judeo-Muslim logical tradition. Despite his commitment to the scholastic tradition, Messer Leon was also aware of Renaissance humanism and articulated the first polemical Jewish response to it. He composed a manual of Hebrew rhetoric, *Nofet tsufim* (The book of the honeycomb's flow), which fused the rhetoric of Aristotle with the newly discovered and admired rhetoric of Cicero and Quintilian, while arguing for the absolute perfection of the divinely revealed Bible.

Aristotelianism remained the dominant orientation among Jewish philosophers in sixteenth-century Italy. Jewish philosophers such as Elijah Delmedigo, Abraham de Balmes, Jacob Mantino, Obadiah Sforno, and Kalo Kalonymus translated texts by Aristotle and Averroes into Latin and were instrumental in the publication of the *editio princeps* (first printed edition) of Averroes's works in the 1550s, often dedicating their literary products to Christian clergymen and patrons of learning. With the admission of a small number of Jews to the medicine faculties of Italian universities, Jewish philosophers could become more familiar with contemporary academic debates, such as the debate on the nature of the soul and its immortality. Obadiah Sforno (c. 1470–c. 1550), for example, employed the subtle arguments of Agostino Nifo to advance a psychological doctrine that claimed the ontological superiority of Jews over non-Jews and their exclusive access to immortality not by virtue of intellectual perfection but through the voluntary performance of God's will in the performance of divine commands. His views, which were shared by his Italian Jewish contemporaries, echoed the insights of Hasdai Crescas. Fully aware of the polemical import of his work, Sforno had it translated into Latin and published in 1548. Italian Jewish philosophers, commonly trained as physicians, rose to defend Judaism, especially after the deterioration of Jewish political status in Italy in the 1550s.

Alongside the perpetuation of Aristotelianism, some Jewish philosophers were instrumental in the revival of Platonism among Renaissance humanists. Yohanan Alemanno (c. 1435–c. 1504), who received a doctorate in philosophy from Judah Messer Leon, disregarded his teacher's disdain toward Platonism and Kabbalah. Replacing Elijah Delmedigo as the tutor of Giovanni of Pico della Mirandolla, Alemanno introduced his Italian student to Jewish and Muslim medieval Neoplatonic sources as well as to Kabbalah. Alemanno expanded the scope of philosophy to include not only the sciences of the Aristotelian tradition but also alchemy, astrology, astral medicine, physiognomy, dream interpretation, and talismanic magic. In Alemanno's worldview, which admitted no meaningful distinction between the animate and the inanimate, bodies exert influences on each other through sympathies and antipathies. In this organically unified universe, the spiritual penetrates the physical, or more precisely, spiritual energy assumes material forms. On the basis of this view Jewish philosophers in the sixteenth century would change their approach to nature from a bookish learning about nature's structure to observation of nature's actual working, though they still believed that nature symbolically reflects the structure of God's revealed Torah.

The most original Jewish contribution to Renaissance philosophy was *Dialoghi d'amore* (Dialogues on love), composed by Leone Ebreo (1460–c. 1521) in 1502. This Jewish courtier from Spain articulated a philosophy of love that expressed popular themes in Renaissance philosophy, such as the primacy of the value of beauty, the unity of truth, and the positive role of the imagination in the pursuit of truth. Scholars still debate the original language of the composition and its intended audience. What is clear is that Ebreo successfully integrated the diverse trends of Renaissance culture while articulating a distinctly Jewish point of view. Written as an allegorical dialogue between two Jewish courtiers, Philo and Sophia, *Dialoghi* not only argues for the superiority of the Torah over all other intellectual and religious traditions but also shows how Jewish philosophy can employ Greek and Roman myths to pursue the truth about the principle of cosmic love that links all levels of reality. Ebreo's philosophical dialogue had some influence on Italian Jewish philosophy, but his real success was with non-Jewish readers or with Jews of converso descent.

The Sephardi Diaspora, 1492–1650.

Ebreo's best-seller was also known to Jewish philosophers in the Ottoman Empire, the descendants of the refugees from Iberia who settled in the Ottoman Empire with the encouragement of the Ottoman government. Prior to the Ottoman conquest of Byzantium, the local Jewish communities had a flourishing intellectual life that included the study of philosophy and the natural sciences (medicine in particular) on the basis of Greek, Arabic, Persian, and Turkish texts. In the fifteenth century Jewish philosophers such as Mordecai ben Eliezer Comtino and Karaite scholars such as Elijah Bashyatzi and Kaleb Afendopolo were deeply immersed in medieval Aristotelianism and perpetuated Maimonides's intellectualism. They prepared abridged translations of Aristotle's works in logic and astronomy from the Greek originals for the benefit of Iberian scholars who did not master Greek. But very shortly, the local Jewish culture was overwhelmed by the culture of the Jewish immigrants from Iberia.

In urban centers such as Salonika and Istanbul, the Sephardi exiles consolidated and systematized the Jewish philosophy by writing philosophical digests and printing seminal philosophical texts. The philosophical encyclopedia of Solomon Almoli, entitled *Measef le-khol ha-mahanot* (The gatherer of all camps; 1530), illustrates the range of philosophico-scientific interests among Sephardi intellectuals. It summarized knowledge in a range of disciplines including grammar, logic, mathematics, music, geometry, measurements and weights, optics, astronomy, physics, medicine, talismanic magic and alchemy, ethics, and metaphysics. This encyclopedia was not intended as original philosophy but as a didactic tool in the education of the Jewish public. Since the community now included many ex-conversos, it was necessary to reintroduce them to Judaism in a philosophically sophisticated manner. For this purpose philosophically trained theologians like Moses Almosnino, Meir Aderbi, Solomon Halevi, Isaac Aroyo, and Joseph Taitatzak composed philosophical commentaries on the Bible and expounded on the philosophical meaning of the sacred texts in their public preaching. In its final phase Jewish philosophy ceased to be elitist and esoteric while becoming subordinated to theology and exegesis of the Bible.

The most important Jewish philosopher in the Ottoman Empire was Moses Almosnino (1515–1580), the spiritual and political leader of Salonikan Jewry. Studying philosophy with the ex-converso Aharon Afiya, Almosnino illustrates the perpetuation of Aristotelianism among the educated classes in the Ottoman Empire and the particular impact of Christian Scholasticism. His commentary on Aristotle's *Nicomachean Ethics,* entitled *Penei Moshe* (The countenance of Moses), demonstrates familiarity with the commentaries by Eustratius of Nicaea, Albertus Magnus, Thomas Aquinas, Gerladus Odonis, John Buridan, Walter Burley, and Jacques Lefèvre d'Étaples. On the basis of Scholastic sources, Jewish and Muslim philosophy, and Kabbalah, Almosnino articulated a Jewish moral philosophy. Its focus was attainment of perfection in this world and thereafter through action in the moral sphere in which the human will expresses the unconditional love of the believer to God. The reward is the return of soul, considered to be a particle of God's essence, to its divine source in a mystical union with God. The importance of Almosnino's commentary lies not in its philosophical originality but in its creative exegesis of biblical and rabbinic sources, displaying the influence of the humanist ideal of eloquence as well as the remythologization of Jewish philosophy.

By the end of the sixteenth century Jewish Aristotelianism ceased to be a creative intellectual tradition, facilitating the emergence of Kabbalah as the dominant expression of Jewish theology. Spanish kabbalists such as Moses Cordovero (1522–1570) in Safed, Palestine, systematized kabbalistic theosophy and argued its epistemic superiority over the philosophy of Jewish Aristotelians. In contrast, Jewish philosophers of converso descent, such as Abraham Herera (d. c. 1630), were instrumental in translating the mythical doctrines of Lurianic Kabbalah back into philosophical parlance. His rationalist rendering of Kabbalah was based on the fusion of Platonic, Neoplatonic, and Thomistic elements, and facilitated the diffusion of Kabbalah among European intellectuals during the seventeenth century.

Jewish philosophy in the Renaissance was highly eclectic. While Aristotelianism remained the basis of philosophical training among Jews, Jewish philosophers did not ignore the emergence of alternative philosophies, especially Renaissance Platonism. Platonic philosophy was perceived to be more consonant with Jewish religious beliefs than was Aristotelianism, and Platonic themes were incorporated into the Aristotelian framework of Jewish philosophy. The growing Platonization of philosophy facilitated in turn the fusion of philosophy and Kabbalah and the reaffirmation of the myth of Judaism (especially in the form of Lurianic Kabbalah) among the Jewish philosophers of converso extraction. By the middle of the seventeenth century, Benedict de Spinoza dealt the final blow to the medieval synthesis of natural philosophy and religion by claiming that religion is the product of human imagination and that the revealed texts of Judaism do not teach philosophic truths.

See also **Aristotle and Aristotelianism; Bible,** *subentry on* **Jewish Interpretation of the Bible; Kabbalah; Leone Ebreo; Plato, Platonism, and Neoplatonism.**

BIBLIOGRAPHY

Bonfil, Roberto. *Jewish Life in Renaissance Italy.* Translated by Anthony Oldcorn. Berkeley, Calif., 1994.

Cooperman, Bernard D. *Jewish Thought in the Sixteenth Century.* Cambridge, Mass., and London, 1983.

Kellner, Menachem M. *Dogma in Medieval Jewish Thought: From Maimonides to Abravanel.* Oxford, 1986.

Lasker, Daniel. *Jewish Philosophical Polemics against Christianity in the Middle Ages.* New York, 1977.

Ruderman, David B. "The Italian Renaissance and Jewish Thought." In *Renaissance Humanism: Foundations, Forms, and Legacy.* Edited by Albert Rabil Jr. Vol. 1. Philadelphia, 1988. Pages 382–433.

Ruderman, David B. *Kabbalah, Magic, and Science: The Culture Universe of a Sixteenth-Century Jewish Physician.* Cambridge, Mass., 1988.

Ruderman, David B., ed. *Essential Papers on Jewish Culture in Renaissance and Baroque Italy.* New York, 1992.

Sirat, Collete. *A History of Jewish Philosophy in the Middle Ages.* Cambridge, U.K., 1985.

Tirosh-Rothschild, Hava. "Jewish Philosophy on the Eve of Modernity." In *History of Jewish Philosophy.* Edited by Daniel H. Frank and Oliver Leaman. New York and London, 1997. Pages 499–573.

Twersky, Isadore, and Bernard Septimus, eds. *Jewish Thought in the Seventeenth Century.* Cambridge, Mass., 1987.

HAVA TIROSH-SAMUELSON

JEWISH THEMES IN RENAISSANCE ART.

Italian Renaissance artists seldom portrayed Jews in their works, and when they did, they often portrayed an event in which Jews were punished for alleged anti-Christian acts. Nevertheless, such works provide insight into Jewish life.

Contemporary Jews in Renaissance Art.

Italy and northern European countries exhibited major differences of attitude in their visual representation of Jews during the Renaissance. While anti-Semitic images continued to be popular in fifteenth- and sixteenth-century Germany, in Italy Jews were not, by and large, presented in the same pejorative manner. Moreover, the number of works of art dealing with Jews in Italy is considerably smaller, demonstrating that this issue was never central in Italian art of the Renaissance. Even the degrading "Jewish features," sometimes given in northern art to negative biblical figures (in particular Cain and Judas), are generally absent in Italy.

Portrait of Daniel Norsa. *Madonna and Child Enthroned with Saints and Donors* by anonymous artist (attributed to Andrea Mantegna) in the church of Sant'Andrea, Mantua, Italy. Painted after 1496. The Jewish banker Daniel Norsa and his family, whose house was confiscated and replaced by the church, are shown below. ALINARI/ART RESOURCE

The identification of Jews in Italian art is not always possible. Scholars have attempted to identify Jewish types in paintings that present contemporary events, such as *Procession of the True Cross* by the Venetian painter Gentile Bellini (c. 1429–1507), but it seems unlikely that Jews would be asked to participate in such a religious, festive ceremony. Similarly doubtful is the identification of the bearded, oriental-looking figure in the "Procession of the Magi" fresco painted in 1459 by Benozzo Gozzoli in Palazzo Medici-Riccardi, Florence, as the noted Jewish philosopher and talmudist Elijah Delmedigo (1460?–1497?), among whose Christian disciples was Giovanni Pico della Mirandola.

Positive identification of Jews is possible in the case of the few Italian paintings depicting anti-Semitic subjects. Such topics were extremely popular in late medieval European art and continued to be widespread in some countries, notably Germany, during the Renaissance and beyond. In comparison with contemporary German art, these topics are treated considerably more lightly by the Italian masters. A well-known example is the *Miracle of the Host* predella (Palazzo Ducale, Urbino) painted in 1468 by the famous perspectivist Paolo Uccello (c. 1397–1475). The subject, known also from Italian illuminated manuscripts, concerns a poor Christian woman who gives a Jewish pawnbroker a consecrated Host to redeem her cloak; the Jew burns the Host, and when this is discovered, he and his family are punished and burned at the stake. Uccello's serene work hardly evokes the drama of this gruesome story and actually affords a rare glimpse into the interior of a Renaissance Jewish pawnshop and a living room. Of a similar nature is the late fifteenth-century *Martyrdom of Simon of Trent* (Israel Museum, Jerusalem) by the Piedmontese artist Gandolfino da Roreto o d'Asti (active c. 1493). Based on a historical event, the story of the Christian infant Simon who was supposedly killed by Jews was used as a pretext for anti-Jewish persecutions. Despite the Italian origin of the case, it was far more widespread in German art, and Gandolfino's panel can hardly be compared with the numerous emphatically anti-Semitic popular German prints of the topic.

Painted portraits of known Jews are rare in Renaissance Italy. An exceptional example is that of the prominent Mantuan Jewish banker Daniel Norsa, his son, and their wives, painted by an unknown artist after 1496 at the bottom of a panel depicting the enthroned Madonna with Christian saints (Church of Sant'Andrea, Mantua). The curious panel commemorates the erection of the Church of Santa Maria della Vittoria, built on the site of Norsa's private house, which was confiscated and destroyed after Norsa removed (by permission of the bishop) an image of the Madonna and child that decorated its walls. Norsa was required to pay 150 ducats to fund a picture of the Madonna commissioned from the noted artist Andrea Mantegna (1431–1506). Mantegna's painting (1493–1496; The Louvre, Paris) was later replaced by the present work. Like the Jews in Gandolfino's panel, Norsa and his son are shown with the distinctive circular yellow badge sporadically imposed upon Italian Jews. At the top of the image appears the Latin inscription, "The temerity of the Jews subdued."

The earliest medals commemorating individual Jews were produced in Renaissance Italy. These personal medals were commissioned by well-off Jews who wished to imitate a parallel vogue among the Italian upper class. The idealized portraits, showing well-dressed, self-assured figures, were executed by the leading medalists of the time, such as Pastorino de' Pastorini. Significantly, the compulsory badges are not shown in these medals.

Hebrew Script in Renaissance Art. A byproduct of the Renaissance interest in the past and of humanistic attempts to study, understand, and even revive the ancient world is the phenomenon of Hebrew inscriptions in contemporary artworks. Along with Greek and Latin, Hebrew was viewed as one of the three culturally important languages of antiquity. Thus Hebrew letters and words were inserted into works of art, just as Roman and other archaeological elements were, whenever artists wished to demonstrate the "authenticity" of their work. But the inscriptions may also have been used to shroud some topics with hidden, sometimes mystical, messages (similarly to the parallel imitation of Egyptian hieroglyphs).

A neglected side of this phenomenon is the reality of Jewish-Christian relationships in Renaissance Italy. Undoubtedly, contemporary Jews, their culture, and their involvement with their Christian neighbors contributed to the interest in and creation of such inscriptions. The bulk of works with Hebrew inscriptions clearly emanate from regions and towns with major Jewish communities, such as Venice and Rome. Printed Hebrew books, initially issued for Jewish consumption, helped the artists in this process as well.

Hebrew inscriptions abound from the fifteenth century on, in both Italian and northern European art. They appear mainly in biblical paintings, where the text calls for them (such as on the tablets of the Law held by Moses or on the tablet atop the cross of the Crucifixion), but also in works depicting heroes of the past, especially early Christian saints. The inscriptions are not always exact. Some artists imitated Hebrew script, or copied letters that do not form actual words, while those who apparently consulted Jews or Hebrew books created more accurate inscriptions (such as the Venetian artist Vittore Carpaccio). In rare cases, artists invested much effort in creating new and meaningful inscriptions—notably Rembrandt in seventeenth-century Holland. Rembrandt was also the first major artist to show genuine interest in contemporary Jews, portrayed them favorably, and used them as models for his biblical and other paintings.

BIBLIOGRAPHY

Barash, Moshe. "Hebrew Inscriptions in Renaissance Works of Art." In *Scritti in memoria di Leone Carpi. Saggi sull'Ebraismo italiano.* Edited by A. Milano et al. Jerusalem, 1967. Pages 141–150. In Hebrew.

Friedenberg, Daniel M. *Jewish Medals from the Renaissance to the Fall of Napoleon (1503–1815).* New York, 1970.

Mellinkoff, Ruth. *Outcasts: Signs of Otherness in Northern European Art of the Late Middle Ages.* Berkeley and Los Angeles, 1993.

Sabar, Shalom. "Hebrew Inscriptions in Rembrandt's Art." In *Rembrandt's Holland.* Edited by M. Weyl and R. Weiss-Blok. Jerusalem, 1993. Pages 169–187. In Hebrew.

Schreckenberg, Heinz. *The Jews in Christian Art: An Illustrated History.* New York, 1996.

Zafran, Eric M. "The Iconography of Anti-Semitism: A Study of the Representation of the Jews in the Visual Arts of Europe, 1400–1600." Ph.D. diss. New York University, 1973.

SHALOM SABAR

JEWISH THOUGHT AND THE RENAISSANCE.

The relationship between Italian Renaissance thought and Jewish philosophy is still a matter of debate for researchers. While some scholars acknowledge a distinct category of Renaissance Jewish thought influenced by contemporary non-Jewish speculation, others argue that fifteenth- and sixteenth-century Italian Jewish philosophy has to be considered as a mere evolution of the medieval Judeo-Arabic legacy amplified and refined by Christian scholastic influences. The historical approach taken by Roberto Bonfil generally aims to show that Italian Jewish communities were never deeply affected by Renaissance thought: new forms of speculation, derived from contemporary humanism, are rare and may be perceived only in the works of very few scholars, who represent an elite within Jewish society. However, from this perspective the same can be held true also for the analysis of contemporary non-Jewish society: Christian humanists represented only a small group within a wider intellectual milieu that was still reasoning in terms of medieval categories of thought. Any analysis of such an issue should take into account the internal social dynamics of fifteenth- and sixteenth-century Italian Jewish communities as well as the patterns of their cultural relations with the Christian majority.

Italian Jewish Thought.

Since the thirteenth century Italian Jewish philosophers generally followed Judeo-Arabic Aristotelian speculation, which also comprised a rational study of mysticism. Philosophical systems derived from Moses Maimonides (1135–1204) and Averroes (Ibn Rushd; 1126–1198) represented for Jewish scholars a source of intellectual debate with Christian Scholastics. These cultural trends continued into the fifteenth and sixteenth centuries: Jewish Scholasticism remained the most common model of speculation, in a manner not unlike that of the contemporary Christian milieu, where scholastic debates still took place. The arrival of Jewish refugees carrying their distinct traditions from various European countries rapidly changed the static situation of Italian Judaism, stressing the differences between the Italian Jews and the newcomers: for example, those coming from Germany were not used to cultural exchanges with the Christian majority and tried to convince the Italians not to let themselves get involved in rationalistic debates with Christians, which they feared might weaken their religious identity. Jews fleeing from the Iberian Peninsula before and after the 1492 expulsion were convinced that their troubles were the result of their abandonment of the true faith due to their adhesion to Aristotelian philosophy. In order to restore a closer contact with God, most of them embraced irrationalist doctrines such as those embodied in Spanish theurgic Kabbalah (wherein the righteous Kabbalist is believed capable of influencing God and creation through prayer and the correct observance of the commandments) and reacted against the philosophical interpretations of this discipline current among Italian Jews. Jewish savants coming from France and Provence generally possessed a very wide philosophical and mystical knowledge parallel to the Italian cultural models. Most of these scholars either taught in yeshiva academies or were employed as private teachers within rich Jewish families. These two models of education engendered an opposition of values that characterized Renaissance Jewish society: since the figure of the private tutor was seen as related to the Christian milieu, the more orthodox rabbis advocated traditional Jewish education and supported the foundation of community yeshivas. However, in spite of their apparent refusal of a cultural dialogue with the majority, the leaders of these academies borrowed several elements of their study programs from contemporary non-Jewish schools.

This conflicting attitude toward Christian society, expressed in terms of both separation and attraction, seems to represent one of the most typical features of Jewish culture in Renaissance Italy. Intellectual cooperation between the scholars of the two faiths was fostered in part by Christian humanists who began studying the scriptures in a more philological way. Scholars such as Giannozzo Manetti, Marsilio Ficino, Giovanni Pico della Mirandola, Angelo Poliziano, Annio da Viterbo, and Egidio da Viterbo were searching for the *Hebraica veritas* (Hebrew truth), the truth revealed by the Hebrew text of the Bible, and needed the assistance of Jewish scholars. The latter lost their medieval role as mere counterparts in public religious or private philosophical debates and became teachers and revealers of occult disciplines. In fact, Jewish scholars such as Yohanan Alemanno and Abraham de Balmes did not limit themselves to teaching humanists Hebrew and the literal sense of the scriptures but convinced them of the necessity of interpreting the Bible as a text containing every form of human and divine knowledge, thus stressing the superiority of Jewish traditional exegesis, both allegorical and mystical. According to them, even the ancient Greek philosophers would have drawn their subjects of speculation from the Bible or from dialogues with the prophets of Israel. The theory of the superiority of Jewish culture due to God's direct revelation to his people dated to the rabbinic period; now it could be successfully used with humanists, since the latter were especially interested in seeking out the sources of the original wisdom of mankind (*prisca theologia,* on ancient theology).

Hermeticism and the Kabbalah. The intellectual relationships between Jews and Christians were not only concerned with a Jewish approach to biblical topics but also concentrated around important issues in cultural humanistic training that could be adopted by Jews and reshaped according to their own tradition: philology, rhetoric, and Aristotelian and Platonic thought reconsidered on the basis of the textual evidence. Thus we observe a parallel Jewish appraisal of Renaissance philology and rhetoric, as well as a reconsideration of Judeo-Arabic scholastic thought in order to interpret the humanist Aristotle and a revaluation of medieval Platonism and Islamic hermetic and magical-astrological speculation in order to interpret Kabbalah in a way that could be more easily understood by humanists. When Marsilio Ficino translated from Greek Plato's works as well as other writings attributed to semi-legendary figures such as Orpheus, Hermes Trismegistus, or Zoroaster, many Jewish scholars, mainly those living in Tuscany, followed this Neoplatonic-Hermetic trend from their own perspective. They had at their disposal medieval Judeo-Arabic texts in which Aristotle was read in Platonic garb, as well as the kabbalistic writings that had actually been influenced by Platonic thought but were dated to more ancient times, being mostly attributed to biblical patriarchs or prophets. By accepting a Platonic or Hermetic reading of Kabbalah, these intellectuals could show their Christian contemporaries that Jewish tradition was far more ancient than the Hermetic or the Platonic ones. What the humanists could find in texts written by historical or legendary figures could be found expressed in a similar way in writings directly or indirectly revealed by God.

In contrast, the philosophical interpretation of Kabbalistic secret doctrines and their diffusion in non-Jewish milieus was hardly accepted by non-Italian Jews. Elijah Delmedigo (c. 1460–c. 1493) pointed out that Christians' interest in Kabbalah didn't merely depend on their curiosity about the close resemblances between Plato and the Jewish esoteric doctrines: they wanted to get hold of kabbalistic lore in order to confirm the superiority of their own faith, using Jewish hermeneutical instruments. In his short treatise *Behinat ha-dat* (The examination of the faith), Delmedigo condemns Jewish philosophers adhering to Neoplatonism. In spite of his critical position against Kabbalah, Delmedigo informed Giovanni Pico della Mirandola about the fundamental texts and doctrines the humanist should study in order to delve deeply into this lore.

Averroism. The collaboration between the two philosophers dated to the period of Pico's stay in Padua, where Delmedigo probably taught philosophy in the context of the Studium, one of the most important late Averroistic centers in Europe. Pico asked the Jewish scholar to make available to him the Hebrew translations of the Arabic texts of Averroes, mostly unknown to his contemporaries. Delmedigo convinced Pico about the necessity of using the Hebrew versions of the Arab philosopher in order to reconstruct philologically Aristotle's writings and thought. Delmedigo was certainly influenced by humanist philology: his Latin versions of the Hebrew Averroes, still extant both in autograph manuscripts and in fifteenth- and sixteenth-century printed editions, are based on careful collations of the Hebrew texts.

Delmedigo strongly emphasized the role of rationalist speculation, taking part in the scholastic debates of his contemporaries—both Jews and Christians—by employing Averroes and Maimonides as his main authorities. He wrote Latin and Hebrew commentaries on Averroes that were still circulating in the sixteenth and seventeenth centuries. At the same time he violently attacked the irrationalist approach to religion represented by Kabbalah, denouncing the role this doctrine was playing in contemporary Italian communities. His negative approach toward this esoteric lore was motivated not only by his adhesion to rationalist medieval sources and his fears of an inappropriate use by Christians but also by his recourse to critical humanist methods applied to traditionally authoritative texts: in *Behinat ha-dat,* by using philological argumentation, Delmedigo established for the first time in Jewish history that the kabbalistic *Sefer ha-zohar* (Book of splendor), attributed to the second-century Palestinian rabbi Simeon bar Yohai, was a medieval forgery.

Another Averroist thinker, the leader of an important yeshiva in Mantua, Judah Messer Leon (c. 1425–c. 1495), addressed a letter to the Florentine community expressing his disapproval of the Platonic interpretation of Kabbalah by local Jews. Messer Leon, of Ashkenazi origin, was an excellent Averroist who based the study program of his academy on a scholastic approach to philosophy. He maintained that rational thought was subordinate to religion, yet he considered the study of Averroes as a necessary prerequisite to every form of superior knowledge.

Messer Leon wrote several commentaries on Averroes's writings, but his most famous work is *Sefer nofet tsufim* (The book of the honeycomb's flow; c. 1475), the first attempt in Jewish cultural history to read the Hebrew scriptures as a literary text based on Aristotelian rhetorical rules. He demonstrated that biblical prophets and sages would have employed the art of persuasion long before the Greek philosopher. During the Middle Ages, Judeo-Arabic thought had inherited the negative attitude of Aristotle's Greek interpreters against the discipline of rhetoric: Jews and Arabs considered it a valuable tool in order to convince the uneducated masses but totally useless for the instruction of the wise. In reaction to the more technical logical interests of the Scholastics, the humanists revived the ancient Roman ideal of the perfect orator combining an all-comprehensive wisdom, moral and political qualities, and a perfect linguistic style.

By printing *Nofet tsufim,* which enjoyed a wide circulation among Jewish scholars, Messer Leon directly participated in the debate between the Scholastics and humanists over philosophy and rhetoric, supporting the latter discipline from a Hebrew biblical instead of a Latin classical perspective. *Nofet tsufim* represents a model of Jewish Renaissance education, resulting from a compilation of classical sources (mainly Cicero and Quintilian) derived from medieval and contemporary non-Jewish traditions, together with Judeo-Arabic texts (mostly Maimonides and Averroes), all of them adapted to the Hebrew Bible.

Messer Leon's students, who included his son David, Yohanan Alemanno, and Abraham Farissol, were influenced by his views on rhetoric. Farissol (1452–c. 1528), of French origin, taught his yeshiva students in Ferrara the qualities of a good speaker, the four Aristotelian causes to address their audience, and all the parts of an oration—in Jewish terms, a *derashah,* or homiletic sermon. In Farissol's school, as in Messer Leon's, students began their study program with grammar, proceeding through the study of Averroistic-Aristotelian logic and rhetoric to metaphysics.

David ben Judah Messer Leon (c. 1471–c. 1536) received in his father's academy a medieval scholastic education, based on Judeo-Arabic and Thomistic philosophy. After a period spent in Naples, where he probably deepened his interests in Spanish Jewish thought (mainly that of Judah Halevi and Abraham Bibago), he moved to Florence, where he became the disciple of Alemanno and extended his kabbalistic and Platonic culture, against his father's will. In his works we find alchemical, astrological, and magical elements common in Florentine Renaissance culture, as well as an attempt to harmonize philosophy and Kabbalah within a homogeneous system of thought dominated by the concept that the fundamental principles of Judaism cannot be proved by rational analysis.

Yohanan Alemanno, Leone Ebreo, and Genazzano.

The most outstanding of the Jewish intellectuals working in Florence was Yohanan Alemanno (1435–c. 1504), of French origin, mostly renowned for his cooperation with Giovanni Pico della Mirandola. In Messer Leon's yeshiva he had studied rhetoric and Averroistic philosophy, but, as he declares in the introduction of his *Sefer sha'ar ha-heshek* (Commentary on the Song of Songs), dedicated to Pico, he was not satisfied with this learning and searched for something that could allow him to connect the Hebrew scriptures and kabbalistic tradition within a comprehensive system of thought, aiming to show the superiority of Jewish faith. He found in Florence, in Marsilio Ficino's academy, what he was looking for: Platonism could be considered the link between the Bible, Kabbalah, and Western thought. Ficino's translations of Plato and the *prisci theologi* (ancient theologians) were but the expressions of a divinely revealed tradition that had been first taught to the patriarchs and the prophets of Israel, later transmitted to the Greeks, and eventually lost after the Diaspora. Thus the recourse to Platonic (and medieval Aristotelian) philosophy partly restored this original knowledge.

As a private teacher working mainly for the rich and cultured da Pisa family, Alemanno considered the high role of biblical and classical rhetoric as a vehicle for establishing intellectual premises both in the minds of uneducated masses and in those wise men chosen by God to rescue the Jewish nation from corruption. The perfect man had to be an eloquent and righteous orator, teaching all the sciences in a simple way to the people. Alemanno's contacts with Pico convinced him to elaborate a complex system of thought in which practical Kabbalah, interpreted as a superior form of Neoplatonic magic, represented the higher level of man's knowledge. The cooperation with Pico may be responsible for Alemanno's peculiar interest in the ecstatic and intellectual mysticism associated with the thirteenth-century mystic Abraham Abulafia, which was the form of Kabbalah Pico had most thoroughly investigated, through the translations entrusted to the converted Jew Flavius Mithridates. Mithridates, who located the premises of Christian Kabbalah largely in the doctrine of Abulafia, can be considered the actual founder of the Christian Kabbalah that Pico adopted in his *Conclusiones* (Theses; 1486). The concept of two different levels of Kabbalah, a theoretical and a more powerful practical one, was developed by Pico in a way that does not greatly differ from Alemanno's. The two philosophers were adapting Kabbalah to Ficino's Neoplatonism: they found a kabbalistic support for Ficino's theory of cosmic love, considered as a force common to all created things, a medium connecting the entire world.

This theory became the central subject of speculation for Judah Abravanel, better known as Leone Ebreo (c. 1460–c. 1521), the son of the Spanish exile Isaac Abravanel (1437–1509). In his *Dialoghi d'amore* (Dialogues on love; published 1564), Leone seems to have followed Pico's and Alemanno's lessons: Platonic love is the force unifying the whole universe; Kabbalah is a symbolic doctrine dating to remoter periods than those of the *prisci theologi;* even the classical pagan myths can be interpreted as symbols and explained through the Jewish original wisdom. Since everything in the lower world is closely connected with its correlative in the upper world, man's main duty is to repair the corrupted links between the two worlds in order to restore the original harmony of the creation. Alemanno's and Leone's works reveal very significant influences of Renaissance thought. However, their experiments to unify all philosophical and theosophical doctrines in a comprehensive system of speculation, in a manner not unlike that of Pico, had no profound and lasting influence on Jewish communities. Leone's *Dialoghi,* written in Italian, were mainly diffused in non-Jewish milieus. Among the philosophers Leone influenced were Giordano Bruno and Benedict de Spinoza. Alemanno's works circulated to a small extent in late Renaissance Jewish encyclopedic culture (represented, for example, by Abraham Yagel), while his kabbalistic views continued to be accepted in the elite da Pisa circle throughout the sixteenth century (mainly in Yehiel Nissim da Pisa's writings). Some elements of Safedian (a kabbalistic trend that spread from the Galilean town of Safed during the sixteenth century) and later Hasidic Kabbalah reveal close affinities with Alemanno's views.

Not all of the Jewish savants working in Tuscany accepted the syncretistic approach to Kabbalah. Elijah Hayyim of Genazzano (c. 1440–c. 1510) strongly condemned any attempt by his contemporaries to contaminate true Kabbalah with rationalist doctrines. By founding his speculative system on medieval scholastic reasoning, he demonstrated in his *Iggeret hamudot* (Delightful epistle) the superiority of theurgic Kabbalah over rational philosophy. Genazzano admitted he knew the attempts of his Jewish and Christian contemporaries to maintain the superiority of Kabbalah by appealing to the theory of *prisca theologia,* but he stressed that human intellect is unable to perceive the divine world: thus neither Aristotelian nor Platonic philosophy can explain the inner meanings of the commandments. He refused both Alemanno's Neoplatonic Kabbalah and Delmedigo's and Messer Leon's Scholasticism by following the contemporary revaluation of theurgic Kabbalah common among Spanish exiles such as Isaac Mar Hayyim and Judah Hayyat.

Most of the Jewish scholars active during the fifteenth and sixteenth centuries in the most important Italian Renaissance centers had to confront the cultural models of the majority: either they tried to reconcile Jewish medieval thought with the classical tradition that was being rediscovered by contemporary humanists or they totally rejected any such synthesis; in both cases they were aware of the cultural contents of the Renaissance. However, even those who actually absorbed specific issues from contemporary humanist research always aimed to stress the superiority of the Jewish faith over rational philosophy.

See also **Kabbalah.**

BIBLIOGRAPHY

Primary Works

Alemanno, Yohanan. *Hay ha-'olamim (L'Immortale). Parte I: la Retorica.* Edited by Fabrizio Lelli. Florence, 1995.

Lelli, Fabrizio. *L'Iggeret hamudot (Lettera preziosa) di Eliyyah Hayyim ben Binyamin da Genazzano e la mistica ebraica in Toscana alla fine del XV secolo.* Forthcoming, 2000.

Lesley, Arthur Michael, Jr. The Song of Solomon's Ascents *by Yohanan Alemanno: Love and Human Perfection according to a Jewish Colleague of Giovanni Pico della Mirandola.* Ann Arbor, Mich., 1976.

Secondary Works

Cassuto, Umberto. *Gli Ebrei a Firenze nell'età del Rinascimento.* Florence, 1918.

Cooperman, Bernard Dov, ed. *Jewish Thought in the Sixteenth Century.* Cambridge, Mass., 1983.

Idel, Moshe. "Hermeticism and Judaism." In *Hermeticism and the Renaissance: Intellectual History and the Occult in Early Modern Europe.* Edited by Ingrid Merkel and Allen G. Debus. Washington, D.C., 1988. Pages 59–76.

Idel, Moshe. "Kabbalah and Ancient Philosophy in R. Isaac and Yehudah Abravanel." In *The Philosophy of Leone Ebreo.* Edited by Menachem Dorman and Zeev Levy. Hakibbutz hameuchad, 1985. Pages 73–112. In Hebrew.

Idel, Moshe. "Major Currents in Italian Kabbalah between 1560 and 1660." In *Italia Judaica.* Rome, 1986. Pages 243–262.

Idel, Moshe. "The Sources of the Circle Images in *Dialoghi d'amore.*" *Iyyun* 28 (1978): 156–166. In Hebrew.

Lelli, Fabrizio. "Yohanan Alemanno, Giovanni Pico della Mirandola e la cultura ebraica italiana del XV secolo." In *Giovanni Pico della Mirandola: Convegno Internazionale di Studi nel cinquecentesimo anniversario della morte (1494–1994).* Edited by Gian Carlo Garfagnini. Florence, 1997. Pages 303–325.

Ruderman, David B. "The Italian Renaissance and Jewish Thought." In *Renaissance Humanism: Foundations, Forms, and Legacy.* Edited by Albert Rabil Jr. Vol. 1. Philadelphia, 1988. Pages 382–433.

Ruderman, David B. *The World of a Renaissance Jew: The Life and Thought of Abraham ben Mordecai Farissol.* Cincinnati, Ohio, 1983.

Ruderman, David B., ed. *Essential Papers on Jewish Culture in Renaissance and Baroque Italy.* New York, 1992.

Tirosh-Rothschild, Hava. *Between Worlds: The Life and Thought of Rabbi David ben Judah Messer Leon.* Albany, N.Y., 1991.

Tirosh-Rothschild, Hava. "Jewish Culture in Renaissance Italy. A Methodological Survey." *Italia* 9, no. 1–2 (1990): 63–96.

FABRIZIO LELLI

JEWISH TRANSLATORS. *See* **Translation,** *subentry on* **Jewish Translators.**

JEWS. [This entry includes eight subentries:

The Jewish Community
Jewish Women and Family Life
Jewish Religious Life
Court Jews
Jews and the Arts
Jews and Music
Print and Jewish Cultural Development
Jews and the Catholic Church]

The Jewish Community

The Jewish community during the Renaissance, and that of Italy in particular, was a community in constant flux and of infinite variety, partly because so many communities were new ones. The Jewish community in Venice, for example, existed only from the sixteenth century; in Livorno, only from that century's end. Even the community in Florence became large only after the founding of a ghetto there in 1571. Jews in Padua drafted statutes only in 1630. The term "community," on the other hand, would be incorrect as a description of the scores of very small settlements, mostly comprising one or two families, that were established in northern Italy during the fourteenth and fifteenth centuries.

The one place we may confidently use as a gauge of communal life is Rome, not only because Roman Jewry was ancient, but because Rome is the one community whose life and organization have been well researched. This research has brought to light a large quantity of internal documentation of everyday life, revealing the interaction between principle and practice. Rome presents us with a paradigm, therefore, against which emerging documentation of other communities may be measured. It is also significant that by the end of the sixteenth century, about 60 percent of Italy's 20,000 Jews lived within the Papal States, concentrated after 1569, but especially after 1593, in Rome, Ancona, and Ferrara. Demographic growth in the Veneto and Tuscany occurred much later. By 1770 the Papal State contained only about one-third of the 27,000 Jews then in Italy. Yet we cannot possibly hope to understand communal life, even in Rome, unless we first know something about the underpinnings of Jewish communal life in Europe as a whole.

Defining Communities. In medieval and Renaissance Europe, community was defined geographically, as the semi- or quasi-autonomous body of Jews living in a particular (usually urban) district. Although a commonplace of Jewish historiography holds that this community was a corporation, this definition is inaccurate. The structures of Jewish governance and their theoretical justifications, especially in northern Europe, were erected from the tenth through the twelfth centuries, and it is doubtful that Jews conceived of their early communities in strict corporate terms. Nor did they conceive of them in such terms afterward, and for good reason. Whether in the Middle Ages or the Renaissance, Jews never enjoyed true autonomy, the hallmark of a corporation. Rulers, whether kings, popes, or even urban councils, viewed Jews as directly dependent on them, so that whatever the Jewish community did was always subject to interference. In sixteenth-century Rome, for example, the papal vicar, responsible for life, religion, and morality in the city, was constantly interjecting himself into matters such as the deliberation of Jewish tribunals of arbitration, even to the point of instructing these tribunals how to interpret Jewish law. In short, Jews and their rulers both perceived the Jewish community as a body with limited powers of self-governance. These powers, moreover, were mostly bestowed and retracted arbitrarily and on a piecemeal basis that usually required point-by-point and timely renewal.

What is more, the forms of Jews' communal institutions were never the same in any two locales, although they were sometimes similar. This variety was an effect of the diverse conditions of these institutions' emergence. But it was no less a function of the Jews' own limited sense of political theory, especially that of representation. Jews spoke theoretically of the community as a court of law headed by a scholar. The question raised in a (possibly) theoretical discussion from the twelfth century about whether all those involved had to be consulted (whether directly or indirectly through elected representatives) before a law could be considered validly enacted received no direct answer in a long set of responses. Universal consultation is the keystone of modern representative theory, which derives in a straight line from medieval political thought. Most Jewish authorities got bogged down in simple issues of majority as opposed to unanimous rule, which is not what the original discussions by medieval Jews were weighing. The communities of the Renaissance inherited this tradition. And even their proximity to the councils that governed the Italian communes, and their apparent imitation of them, did not help fully to develop a proper notion of representational rule. Decisions of Jewish communal councils were frequently disputed and treated as if they were made by individuals or factions, not by a sovereign body to which all communal members owed allegiance.

Likewise, Jewish political discussions often hinged on the relative power of rabbinic as opposed to secular forces. Jewish law, the halakah, does not provide for independent secular and religious spheres, as did the canon law and Roman law that formally governed relations among Christians, particularly in Italy. Rabbis were meant to interpret all law, but secular communal heads often exerted pressures affecting these interpretations. In Italy, during both the Middle Ages and the Renaissance, communities were headed by secular leaders, while most rabbis were contractually employed, and only a few gained great prestige by being the heads of academies of learning. By about 1500 in Germany, the positions of regional or even national rabbis as communal leaders were undermined through a combination of internal competition and governmental

instability and exploitation. So, moreover, was the stability of most German communities themselves, nearly all of which had sustained attack or expulsion, and a large number of which had been new foundations made by those expelled or fleeing other places. Speaking of well-structured Jewish communal life in Renaissance or Reformation Germany—until at least the mid-seventeenth century, when these communities began to grow and receive proper legal underpinning—is something of a contradiction in terms.

There were no Jewish communities in France or England during the Renaissance. Jews of the Low Countries lived under cover as Christians until the seventeenth century, when, coming out of hiding in such places as Antwerp, they entered Holland and soon founded open Jewish communities, most notably in Amsterdam. The Jews of Spain—where, as also for a brief period in Sicily, the communities had been headed by a figure called the *rab de la corte* (court rabbi) or the *dayyan kellali* (judge general), although neither was necessarily, if ever, a rabbi by training or profession—were expelled in 1492. The Jews of Sicily, under Aragonese dominion, were forced to flee as well, while those of the Kingdom of Naples were ousted by 1541. The Jews of Portugal were all forcibly converted in 1497.

When speaking of Jewish communities during the Renaissance, therefore, we are speaking exclusively of northern and central Italy—unless we want to include those preexistent and emerging ones in the Ottoman Empire, where indigenous Jewish communities were suddenly forced to contend, from the fifteenth century in North Africa and the sixteenth century in Turkey, with a wave of Sephardic exiles. Proud of their heritage, these Spanish-speaking (eventually Ladino-speaking) Jews resisted assimilating, and they sought, often successfully, to gain political control over their new communities, mostly thanks to their (governmentally appreciated) international commercial endeavors. Such endeavors often brought these Sephardim into contact with Jews in Italy, but these contacts were principally personal, not institutional. Contacts initiated by Italian Jewish communities, on the other hand, were mostly charitable, and sometimes educational. The communities of Ottoman Jewry thus really stood apart.

Communal Organization and Institutions. The Italian Jewish communities were essentially collections of individuals mildly empowered by outside rulers collectively to administer Jewish internal affairs—and to collect taxes. Unlike

Jewish Wedding. Illuminated page from Jacob ben Asher's *Arba'ah Thurim* (1436) showing a marriage ceremony. ©BIBLIOTECA APOSTOLICA VATICANA

Christians, Jews had difficulty perceiving their communal institutions as unified bodies or bodies politic, which helps explain why they had problems with the allied concepts of corporate and representational sovereignty. Indeed, outside authorities had no less difficulty than did the Jews themselves in defining the nature of the Jewish community and empowering it. Did the Jewish community have any real authority, was it merely a confraternity, an association of laypeople that traditionally exercised the function of organizing neighborhoods, providing social services, and preserving neighborhood peace, or was it a tool of convenience? How, moreover, were the various aspects of the community to be seen as working together? In Rome, in the early sixteenth century but as late as the 1560s, when communal statutes and modes of operation were formally defined with papal sanction, papal authorities called synagogues *universitates*—literally, corporations—just as the primary communal body was called the *universitas,* the corporation. Yet everybody, and the papal authorities in particular, knew that by law the Jewish community—much less a synagogue—could not be defined as a juridically empowered corporate entity. Nor did anybody want the Jews to have such power. When Venetian authorities discovered, in 1631, that Jewish communal statutes threatened Jews who turned to non-Jewish courts with excommunication, the Jews were accused of trying to operate a republic within the republic. Normally, Jews everywhere were able to excommunicate only with specific permission for cases immediately at hand, never as a constant right.

In any case, Jews themselves had always viewed the synagogue as a dependency of an essentially geographical body, the community as a whole. The emergence of the synagogue in sixteenth-century Italy as a unit of ethnic or even political clout, as Jews entered central and northern Italy from Germany, southern France (Provence), Spain, Portugal, Sicily, and the Italian south, required adjustments. In Venice, the Ashkenazic and Sephardic synagogues eventually became the principal forums of communal organization, with the formal community mostly an umbrella under which the synagogues operated. In Livorno, Sephardic ritual was forcefully maintained as the only legitimate one. Communities also had to deal with greater intracommunal confraternal organization, the slow but sure emergence of the Gemilut Hasadim burial societies, in particular. Intended to complement communal authority, these confraternities sometimes had well-guarded spheres of their own, such as the ownership and occasionally the distribution of plots in cemeteries.

Jewish communal organization and rights also had venerable precedent. The community of Rome, which dated back to the ancient period, meaning that it was unique among nearly all Jewish communities of the Diaspora in not being a community of immigrants, could display a set of papal privileges by no later than 1402. These privileges exempted Roman Jews from wearing special clothing in specific Roman urban districts, allowed them to collect funds from Jews throughout northern Italy, and, most importantly, considered them *cives Romani.* This designation was as prejudicial as it was beneficial. Though the status of *civis* guaranteed due process of law, it also meant that any and every Jewish institution must conform to the highly restrictive statutes of Roman law, *ius commune.* It is crucial to understand that all Jews, wherever they settled in Italy, were considered *cives* according to *ius commune,* whether verbalized or not. Christian legal manuals and opinion are unanimous on the subject.

The Roman example is also paradigmatic with respect to communal statutes and organizations. The statutes known as the *Capitoli* of Daniel da Pisa, drawn up in 1524, are said to have reorganized communal institutions in order to reduce alleged ethnic strife supposedly provoked by large-scale immigration into Rome by Jews coming from Spain, Germany, and Sicily following the late fifteenth-century expulsions. Yet these *Capitoli* must be seen more as a measure of continuity than of innovation. Their basic goal was to redistribute power according, first, to economic divisions and, only second, to ethnic ones—an issue that quickly receded, in any case, as marriage between ethnic groups increased rapidly throughout the sixteenth century. Membership in a given synagogue or subcompany of the Gemilut Hasadim confraternity also became a matter of voluntary ethnic identification rather than one fixed by birth.

The one true innovation of the *Capitoli* may have been the institution of concentric councils to run communal affairs, taking the place of entities such as the *VII bonos Judaeos* mentioned in earlier texts, a local mirror of the Talmudic *shev'a tovei ha'ir* (the seven good men of the city). Da Pisa also produced a correct definition of representative communal authority in the preamble to the *Capitoli.* But this definition went unheeded. In practice, the councils most often seem to have been forums for ratifying decisions taken unilaterally by the communal executive, the three *fattori.* Yet, typical of the absence of communal power, even the *fattori* did not "rule," for they had almost no powers of coercion except (capricious) communal accord; nor did papal officials hesitate to circumvent them, dealing directly with the various synagogues or confraternities like the Gemilut Hasadim.

It has been said that the only real functioning communal institution in Rome was the office of the *sofer meta,* the communal notary. Actually, the notarial art itself was relatively new among Jews. Christian notaries functioned like magistrates; their acts concerning issues such as matrimony or civil contracts were given juridical recognition. Jews had had scribes, to be sure, but not notaries (the only other record of such is in fifteenth-century Navarre). This novelty seems corroborated by the tentativeness, and only eventual sophistication, of notarial formulations produced in Rome in the mid-sixteenth century by the father and son, Judah and Isaac Piattelli.

Resort to the notary to establish boards of voluntary arbitration, the only real judicial tool Jews were permitted on a continuous basis, was common. These arbitrations maintained communal order and peace and resolved conflicts but also facilitated partnerships and rentals. They also resolved disputes over taxation, the only area where the *fattori,* through appointed representatives, were truly indispensable. So important did the Roman notaries become that in about 1640, the papacy, through its Roman vicar, replaced them with Christian notaries, most of whose acts still survive.

Precisely how paradigmatic were these structures, which preceded formal communal structuring elsewhere, remains to be seen. For example, communal registers have been published for Padua and Verona, but the latter, dating to about 1600, distinguishes sharply between the Jewish *sofer* (scribe) and the Christian notary. On the other hand, these registers reveal that, like Rome, the other major Jewish centers were operated in theory by an elected council and from three to five leaders called *parnasim, fattori,* or *gastaldi.* Aristocratic Livorno had a body of twelve sages. The power of these bodies was highly circumscribed, however. Bankers sometimes sought exemption from communal controls, at least from paying taxes as part of their communities.

New Communities. Many communities were new, with origins no earlier than the fifteenth and sixteenth centuries. Jews were kept out of most towns for centuries, and some towns never accepted them. The Jews settled in Venice proper only in 1516, and then only because a compromise was reached that these Jews, primarily Ashkenazi in origin, might live permanently in the city, but only within the quarter long known as the Ghetto Nuovo—hence the origin of the name "ghetto." The

Sephardim, many direct refugees from Spain, settled in 1541 in the Ghetto Vecchio. Eventually they were joined by Portuguese refugees, known as Ponentines, while the Sephardim were known as Levantines. It was this clear and visible distinction between specific groups of Jews in Venice that encouraged placing greater administrative responsibility in the various synagogues rather than in the formally constituted community.

The Ponentines (and in some cases the Spanish Jews) posed another problem. Were they really Jews? Like Jews admitted into Ancona by the popes, and to some extent those in Ferrara, they had been unquestionable victims of forced conversion in Portugal in 1497, or they were voluntary converts. In the 1530s the papacy, involved in a conflict with the Spanish and the Portuguese over the issue of forced conversion, issued charters of privilege allowing the Portuguese Jews to settle in the above cities in order to foster commerce and international trade. Eventually, between 1591 and 1593, the grand duke of Tuscany brought a similar group, to be known as the *nazione ebrea,* into Livorno. He did so with the full knowledge that it was only his determination to resist papal and papal inquisitorial pressures (which had begun to attenuate by this time) that would make his scheme work, as it ultimately did. Livornese Jewry handled a large percentage of Tuscan commerce with North Africa through the eighteenth century. At the same time, the strict rules of conformity enforced by the Jewish community there suggest that tensions were stirring below the surface. Especially at the start, success was not guaranteed. Only twenty years previous to the issuance of the "Livornina," the charter fixing the rules for Jewish life in Livorno, the Spanish had more or less forced the duke of Savoy to scrap a similar project for his domains in Piedmont.

Inquisition and Expulsion. Jewish communal life of all stripes was affected by the Roman Inquisition. At Rome the Inquisition formally administered Jewish discipline with respect to violations of church law. The tribunal in Modena, which tried Jews for such offenses as overfamiliarity with Christians, may have been intended both to control and ultimately to convince the Este dukes to establish what they had long resisted, a ghetto, which they did in 1638. More ominously, volumes of Venetian trial records contain many prosecutions for heresy and apostasy, although the results were mostly moderate. However, at Ancona in 1556, inquisitional prosecutions produced sheer terror. Pope Paul IV reversed the policy in force since the days of Paul III in 1534 and attacked Jews of clear Portuguese Christian origin, burning twenty-five of them at the stake. These Portuguese Jews had always lived, by charter, as a separate community, which explains in part the ambivalence toward their fate evinced by other Jews. Yet, if they were not touched by the Inquisition, these other Jews were affected by the papal institution of the ghetto in the Papal States in the summer of 1555 (the establishment of ghettos spread slowly, often not taking effect in Piedmont until the early eighteenth century).

Jews in many locations seem to have lost their moorings at this time. People fled to larger communities and many others converted, which was Pope Paul IV's goal. A second and even greater dislocation took place in 1569, when Pope Pius V forced the Jews of the Papal States to live solely in Rome, Ancona, and in the French papal possessions around Avignon. The flourishing Jewish community of Bologna came to an abrupt end. There were also expulsions from various small settlements in the Italian northeast, such as Vicenza, Treviso, and Cividale. The authors of these expulsions, however, were secular leaders, most notably in Udine, where the patriciate spoke of an opportunity to boot the Jews out, although it required Venetian permission to accomplish this.

Yet, in theory, these expulsions should not have occurred. Jews throughout Italy were recognized formally by Roman law, but in practice a great many Italian communities owed their origins to a *condotta,* a limited contract allowing small groups of Jews to settle in a city for the purpose of providing credit for the poor. (That was their primary function; loans to other groups were often small, suggesting short-term loans providing liquidity, whether to individuals or the town government, not large-scale, long-term loans as a means for capitalistic finance.) These contracts obligated the bankers to remain in the town for periods of five to ten years and were regularly renewed. The switch to commerce occurred only from the sixteenth and seventeenth centuries and was limited to such cities as Livorno, Venice, and Ancona and to their Sephardic settlers. At the same time, as seen most clearly in the privilege offered to Jews to settle in Piedmont in the 1570s, these *condotte* also smacked of the traditional charter of protection given to Jews throughout northern Europe, in which the Jew was legally attached directly to the local ruler. Such charters were easily annulled. The Ashkenazi and Levantine Jews of Venice were threatened with expulsion as late as the seventeenth century each time their respective charters needed renewal.

However sound the foundations of Jewish residence were, they were also subject to constant reexamination, whether because of civic anxiety, as at Udine or Venice, or more regularly through a conflation of economic and spiritual factors. The Franciscan preacher Bernardino da Feltre (1439–1494), for example, said Jewish lending corrupted civic and Christian well-being; both it and its practitioners were like a gangrenous limb that had to be cut off. Communal life might also be threatened, as at Trent in 1475, when all the males were executed on a charge of ritual murder and the women and children forced to convert. It should be no surprise that gradually Jewish settlement, and hence Jewish communities, became restricted for the most part to larger cities, where such charges could normally be kept under control or suppressed.

The end to small settlements also meant an end to a kind of joint Jewish *imprenditore*-communal (political) head. No other kind of organization would have been possible in the hundreds of very small settlements, composed mostly of bankers (lenders) and their dependents and families, which sprouted in the fourteenth and fifteenth centuries. It would probably be a misnomer to call these groupings communities, for they had no real formal organization. Their operation was probably most akin to what one finds in Turin in the eighteenth century, where individual bankers functioned as the hinge in a small network of family members and other related hangers-on who were directly or indirectly dependent on the banker for their financial well-being.

Women in the Community. In the fifteenth century, in the era prior to the larger settlements and more formal organization, women exerted influence directly as heads of families and households, sometimes even when male children had reached maturity. Admittedly, elective communal office was the prerogative of men. Yet to judge by Rome, which did have a tradition of formal organization and office, the existence of organized communal life did not necessarily imply a retrenchment of the position of women. Jewish women were and continued to be social protagonists whose opinions carried weight in communal affairs. Their powers derived largely from economic and legal privilege. Unlike Christian women, Jewish women were invested (and had been so since the Middle Ages) with the legal right of acting as independent agents.

They could sign contracts, represent themselves in court, and initiate legal actions.

Such empowerment encouraged economic endeavor. A number of women were bankers and full members of partnerships. In Turin, Jewish women were further empowered, albeit indirectly, when paternal wealth was funneled principally into dowries. The reasons for this practice were many, all intended to conserve wealth, but the woman holding the dowry occupied an enviable position. Finally, the uniformly middle-class status of most of Italy's Jews played a role in balancing power between men and women. When the most honorific titles in use among Jews were no more grandiose than *onorati, nobili, et da bene,* and when not even the richest banker could provide a dowry greater than twice the average, there were few grounds on which men could stake a claim to exclusive rule.

Evaluating the Ghetto. A number of factors contributed to the survival of the ghettoized Jewish community. At Rome, the papacy could not afford a bankrupt community, which already strapped papal agencies would have been forced to support. In Livorno and Venice, pragmatic commercial motives made it imperative for the rulers of Tuscany and Venice to sustain organized Jewish life. But likely most decisive were Jewish perceptions of themselves and of their communities. Jews sometimes viewed the ghetto as a mere administrative maneuver—the first references to the Roman ghetto were simply to a papal "order that the Jews live together." Jews throughout Italy also referred to the ghetto as their *ghet*—playing on the Hebrew (and sometimes writing the word in Hebrew letters) for the bill of divorce given by a husband to his wife, implying a separation from society, yet one tinged with ambivalence and perhaps hope. And sometimes the ghetto was viewed as a source of liberation, as embodied in the so-called Purim of the Ghetto, the celebration at Mantua and Verona of the erection of ghetto walls, auguring safety and an enclosed, exclusively Jewish space. A variation of this last view was to transfer the time of mystical prayer to night, a mystical device for achieving spiritual liberation, with the physical closure in the ghetto inverted into spiritual opening and peace.

This view of the ghetto was, to be sure, a kind of fiction, just as the Jews no doubt perceived the ghetto walls as setting the boundaries for their *kehillah kedoshah,* the holy assembly, the name Jews always used to refer to their communities. Not by accident, this concept paralleled the notion of the holy space which Catholics achieved through ritual processions known as rogations and the beating of bounds. The greatest asset of the Italian Jewish Renaissance community was its ability to present itself to itself dramaturgically as a unified public sphere that was exclusively the Jews' own. The outside could be let in, or kept out, at pleasure, or so Jews pretended. Of this ability their formalized institutions were a symbol. In fact, these institutions were little more than pale shadows of real sovereignty and power.

BIBLIOGRAPHY

Allegra, Luciano. *Identità in bilico: Il ghetto ebraico di Torino nel Settecento.* Torino, Italy, 1996.

Bachi, Roberto. "The Demographic Development of Italian Jewry from the Seventeenth Century." *The Jewish Journal of Sociology* 4 (1962): 172–191.

Bonfil, Roberto. *Rabbis and Jewish Communities in Renaissance Italy.* Translated by Jonathan Chipman. Oxford, 1990.

Calimani, Riccardo. *The Ghetto of Venice.* Translated by Katherine Silberblatt Wolfthal. New York, 1987.

Cassuto, Umberto. *Gli ebrei a Firenze nell'eta' del Rinascimento.* Florence, 1965.

Colorni, Vittore. *Legge ebraica e leggi locali.* Milan, 1945.

Cozzi, Gaetano, ed. *Gli Ebrei e Venezia.* Milan, 1987.

Esposito, Anna. *Un'altra Roma: Minoranze nazionali e comunità ebraiche tra Medioevo e Rinascimento.* Rome, 1995.

Foa, Anna. *A History of the Jews in Europe.* Los Angeles, 2000.

Horowitz, Elliott. "The Eve of the Circumcision: a Chapter in the History of Jewish Nightlife." *Journal of Social History* 23 (1989): 45–69.

Ioly Zorattini, Pier Cesare, ed. *Processi del S. Uffizio di Venezia contro Ebrei e giudaizzanti.* 12 vols. Florence, 1980–1994.

Israel, Jonathan I. *European Jewry in the Age of Mercantilism, 1550–1750.* Oxford, 1985.

Kaplan, Yosef. *From Christianity to Judaism: The Story of Isaac Orobio de Castro.* Translated by Raphael Loewe. Oxford, 1989.

Katz, David S. *Philo-Semitism and the Readmission of the Jews to England, 1603–1655.* Oxford, 1982.

Kriegel, Maurice. *Les Juifs a la fin du Moyen Âge dans l'Europe mediterraneenne.* Paris, 1979.

Luzzati, Michele. *La casa dell'Ebreo. Saggi sugli Ebrei a Pisa e in Toscana nel Medioevo e nel Rinascimento.* Pisa, Italy, 1985.

Milano, Attilio. *Il Ghetto di Roma: Illustrazioni storiche.* Rome, 1964.

Milano, Attilio. *Storia degli ebrei in Italia.* Torino, Italy, 1963.

Pullan, Brian. *Rich and Poor in Renaissance Venice: The Social Institutions of a Catholic State, to 1620.* Cambridge, Mass., 1971.

Ravid, Benjamin. "The Religious, Economic, and Social Background and Context of the Establishment of the Ghetti of Venice." In *Gli Ebrei e Venezia.* Edited by Gaetano Cozzi. Milan, 1987. Pages 211–259.

Segre, Renata. *The Jews in Piedmont.* 3 vols. Jerusalem, 1986–1990.

Simonsohn, Shlomo. *History of the Jews in the Duchy of Mantua.* 2 vols. Jerusalem, 1977.

Simonsohn, Shlomo. *The Jews in the Duchy of Milan.* 4 vols. Jerusalem, 1982–1986.

Stow, Kenneth R. *The Jews in Rome.* 2 vols. New York, 1995–1997.

Stow, Kenneth R. "Marriages Are Made in Heaven." *Renaissance Quarterly* 48 (1995): 445–491.

Toaff, Ariel. *Il ghetto di Roma nel Cinquecento: conflitti etnici e problemi socioeconomici.* (Hebrew.) Ramat Gan, 1984.

Toaff, Ariel. *The Jews in Umbria.* 3 vols. Leiden, Netherlands, 1992.

ANNA FOA *and* KENNETH STOW

Jewish Women and Family Life

A mistaken notion in general as well as in Jewish historiography is that the Renaissance had a liberating effect on women. This notion has been reinforced by a wealth of literary and documentary materials that suggest that more Jewish women of exceptional accomplishment lived during the Renaissance than during the Middle Ages. These sources confuse the benefits enjoyed by a few women, usually on behalf of their extended families, and especially in matters of business, with substantive changes for all women. Often, when women appeared and acted publicly, many voices protested against them.

The Inquisition. Rather than the Renaissance producing any changes in rabbinic values, forced conversions and Inquisition scrutiny destabilized rabbinic and communal authority. Under these circumstances, which undermined Jewish practice in the early modern world, it was often women who taught crypto-Jewish practices and led messianic movements, sometimes without the knowledge of their Catholic husbands. According to inquisitorial dossiers, and contrary to his autobiography, the heretic and former Portuguese crypto-Jew, Uriel da Costa (1585–1640), received knowledge of Judaism from his mother.

Crypto-Jewish women led their families, sometimes controlling vast fortunes and commercial networks. After the deaths of her husband and brother-in-law, Doña Gracia Nasi (1510–1569), the Portuguese New Christian Beatrice de Luna, managed the family's financial, charitable, communal, and cultural activities, escaping the Inquisition by journeying across Europe until she reached the Ottoman Empire. When, in Ancona in 1555, the pope allowed approximately twenty-five Judaizing New Christians, including one woman, to be burned, Doña Gracia organized a boycott of the city. A powerful lady (*Ha-Geveret*) with her own court and yeshivah, she summoned leading rabbis to appear before her for instructions on how to take vengeance

Slaughtering Animals. A woman peers through an archway as men slaughter fowl and an ox; another man looks through the entrails of the ox to ensure that it meets ritual specifications. Frontispiece to the second part of *Arba'ah Thurim,* a fourteenth-century law code by Jacob ben Asher. The second part, entitled *Yoreh De'ah* (Teacher of knowledge), deals with matters lawful and unlawful, including slaughtering. The image appears between folios 127 and 128. ©BIBLIOTECA APOSTOLICA VATICANA

against the pope. The boycott, nevertheless, soon collapsed. However, Doña Gracia was not the only Jewish woman who amassed influence at the Sultan's court, further evidence that it was not Renaissance values that were necessary for women to rise to positions of prominence.

Benvenida Abravanel (b. 1473), also a Portuguese New Christian, settled in Italy where she taught Leonora, the daughter of the Spanish viceroy, who became the duchess of Tuscany and wife of Cosimo de' Medici. Together in 1533 they succeeded in having the edict of expulsion of the Jews from Naples postponed by Charles V until 1541. As a widow, Abravanel ran a loan-banking business, served the Medici, ransomed captives, gave charity, fasted regularly, and supported the messianic pretender David Reuveni, bestowing upon him a banner, a gown, and much money. The playwright and poet Judah Sommo called her a "Princess" and noted that her daughter Doña Gioia "has a name among the mighty" (*Magen nashin*).

Religious Practices. Women adopted ascetic practices such as daily fasting, prayer, placing ashes on their heads, wearing sackcloth, denying themselves enjoyment of even the smallest earthly matters, and vowing to abstain from all pleasure, practices very much like those of Catholic penitents. Although Rabbi Abraham Yagel (1553–c. 1623) admitted that the intentions of these pious women were good and holy, he declared that their single-minded devotion to God constituted a dereliction of their duties to their husbands and their homes.

One defiant, unnamed Italian Jewish woman, according to her manuscript prayer book, began her morning blessings in Hebrew each day by reciting praise that God "had made me a woman and not a man" (Jerusalem Ms. 8* 5492), thus changing the traditional blessing in which a man expresses his gratitude. Other women made their grievances public by stopping the daily services and loudly cursing those men who had done them wrong and asking for vengeance.

As the exercise of royal prerogatives by Christian women produced a backlash in their community, so too did such advances elicit negative reactions among Jews. A polemical Jewish literature about the nature of women emerged, showing many similarities with the Christian *querelle des femmes* tractates, which explored the same subject. Some Italian rabbis even considered physical chastisement of one's wife necessary. Similarly, Rabbi Azriel Diena (d. 1536) expressed the view that "over his women, every man shall be ruler in his house and rebuke his wife" (*Sheelot u-teshuvot,* no. 6), making it clear that men did not always have their way.

Domestic Relations. Acts of cruelty by men in domestic relations mentioned in documents included broken engagements, unfavorable divorce settlements, abandonment, nonsupport, physical and verbal abuse, the taking of a mistress or a second wife, the seduction or impregnation of servants, the blackmail of an abandoned wife or of a dead brother's widow, and the refusal to acknowledge or support a child born out of wedlock. A woman might threaten to bring the child to the synagogue or to pressure the lay leaders to come to her aid. The rabbis of Catholic Europe were much less willing than the rabbis of Islamic countries to force a man to divorce his wife, a reflection of the Catholic belief in the indissolubility of marriage and evidence that the Renaissance environment did not provide rabbinic recourse for women to extricate themselves from bad marriages.

Education. Jewish women had to persevere against great odds to receive an education and be admitted into literary and spiritual circles. Rabbis expressed great ambivalence toward Jewish women receiving education beyond the literary that was necessary for domestic management, for fear that such education would inflame the passions of women and therefore endanger their honor. Scholarly Jewish women included, in the sixteenth century, Diana Rieti and her sister, Fioretta (Bat Sheva) Rieti Modena, who both knew Torah and Talmud, Midrash, Jewish law, Maimonides, and Kabbalah, and who late in life set out to live in Safed, a community of mystics in Palestine, the Jewish equivalent of entering a convent. Others served as teachers to young girls of Italian and even Hebrew, at least in the fundamentals of reading. Some Jewish women were called *Rabbanit,* a title of distinction for a woman who attained a significant level of learning, joined in rabbinic discussions, and also participated in healing and birthing. Educated Jewish women in Italy found opportunities to work as scribes and printers, and their contributions are preserved in the colophons of many books.

Writers. Debora Ascarelli of Rome and Venice gained recognition for her rhymed translations of liturgical poetry from Hebrew to Italian, completed in

about 1537 and published in Venice in 1601 and again in 1609, the first publication by a Jewish woman.

Sarra Copia Sullam (c. 1592–1641), born to a prominent Italian Jewish family in Venice, received an education that included instruction in at least Italian and Spanish. She gathered around her a salon of men of letters who gave her lessons in exchange for financial backing, intellectual conversation, and brilliant letters. After being accused of denying the immortality of the soul, Sarra Copia Sullam sat down and in two days wrote a strong defense of her views published as "The Manifesto of Sarra Copia Sulam, a Jewish woman, in which she refutes and disavows the opinion denying immortality of the soul, falsely attributed to her by Signor Baldassare Bonifaccio."

Jewish women in the Renaissance used the opportunities provided by law, custom, and sheer need to assert their common rights and social status and provide for their families. They controlled property and wealth, advanced their claims in public, and contributed to the religious, social, and intellectual communities of their day.

See also Querelle des Femmes; Women, *subentries on* Women in the Renaissance *and* Women and Literature.

BIBLIOGRAPHY

Baskin, Judith, ed. *Jewish Women in Historical Perspective.* Detroit, Mich., 1991, 1998.

Baskin, Judith, ed. *Women of the Word: Jewish Women and Jewish Writing.* Detroit, Mich., 1994.

Davis, Robert C., and Benjamin Ravid, eds. *The Jews of Venice: A Unique Renaissance Community.* Baltimore, 1998.

Waddington, Raymond, and Arthur Williamson, eds. *The Expulsion of the Jews: 1492 and After.* New York, 1994.

Whitehead, Barbara, ed. *Women and Education in Early Modern Europe.* New York, forthcoming.

HOWARD TZVI ADELMAN

Jewish Religious Life

Although scholars once tended to see religion as having "served as a kind of barrier" against the "excessive absorption" of Italian Jews in Renaissance culture (Shulvass, *The Jews in the World of the Renaissance,* p. 19), the religious lives of Italian Jews, like those of early modern European Jewry as a whole, have increasingly come to be seen as reflecting a rather complex interaction with their social and cultural environments. The importance of this interaction was hardly diminished by the introduction of the ghetto, beginning with that of Venice in 1516. Many scholars have noted the pietistic revival that took hold of Italian Jewry toward the end of the sixteenth century and continued into the seventeenth, a revival which owed much to the kabbalistic piety emanating from Palestine and especially Safed. But the view that linked this revival largely to the increasing hostility of the Christian environment, which forced the Jew "to resort to Jewish content in order to fill the vacuum that developed . . . following the severence of his contacts with the larger society" (*Jews in the World of the Renaissance,* p. 211), is less favored by contemporary scholars, who generally no longer regard the precepts and practices of the Jewish religion as having been inherently opposed to Renaissance culture.

The barrier that was once perceived between religious and social life has also been disappearing. Synagogues are no longer seen only as places of solemn prayer, but also as the sites at which "conflicts endemic within the Jewish community tended to come to a head . . . often with surprising violence" (Toaff, *Love, Work, and Death,* p. 95). Some scholars have argued that the formal removal of Italian Jews from Christian society during the period of the ghetto enhanced their readiness to absorb modes of piety that might otherwise have been rejected as disturbingly "non-Jewish." Thus it has been noted that in Renaissance Italy the rabbi's role "came to more closely approximate that of the priest . . . moving further and further away from that of doctor of Jewish law" (Bonfil, *Jewish Life,* pp. 227–228). During the sixteenth and seventeenth centuries pious confraternities began to spread among Italian Jews, in a manner strikingly similar to their proliferation in local Catholic society. Their statutes, although generally drawn up in rabbinic Hebrew, often reflected pious practices and religious trends then popular among Italian Catholics.

Changing Death and Funeral Rites. The 1552 statutes of of Ferrara's Gemilut Hasadim, probably the oldest of Italy's Jewish confraternities, stipulated that its officials were required, when visiting a member who had been ill for three days, "to encourage him to confess his sins before God and to deliver his final testament before his family." Although the confraternity used ritual as a means of both reflecting and intensifying the fraternal bonds between its members, this concern with confession went beyond the functional level, mirroring a basic shift with regard to this "sacrament" which had occurred in Catholicism after the Council of Trent. The growing concern with the soul and its salvation clearly displaced much of the confraternity's initial concern with the body and its interment—tasks increasingly relegated, during the sixteenth century, to the group's poorer underclass, who would perform them in lieu of paying membership fees.

This new stress upon predeath confession is evident in other northern Italian Jewish communities as well. In the early seventeenth century Gemilut Hasadim confraternities in Finale and Bussetto required all members to be present at the bedside confession of any seriously infirm person. The statutes of the latter went so far as to threaten that any sick person refusing to confess publicly in this manner would be denied funeral and burial services. Even the notoriously independent-minded Venetian rabbi Leon Modena testified that when he had once sensed his own death approaching he recited the confessional prayer "in the presence of ten men, three of whom were rabbis."

Upon Modena's death in 1648 the council of Venice's indigenous Italiani Jewish community paid for the torches that were used in his funeral, but early in the sixteenth century, when funereal torches were first introduced among Jews of the Veneto, their use aroused considerable controversy. The Cretan-born Elijah Capsali, who arrived in Padua to study in Judah Minz's yeshiva shortly before Minz's death in 1509, left an account of the revered rabbi's controversial funeral—the first such detailed account in Jewish literature. Minz died on a Friday, and on the following Sunday morning the entire community gathered in the courtyard outside his home. Shortly afterward, writes Capsali,

> forty enormous torches of white wax, each costing . . . nine *marcelli,* were brought out and distributed to all the rabbis and notables, and to the distinguished students of the yeshiva. Each stood with his partner. . . . And I, the humble, was also among those holding torches . . . and we positioned ourselves around the coffin and then lit them.

The "enormous torches of white wax" he refers to were apparently *doppieri*—torches formed of several wax candles fastened together, which were highly popular in Catholic religious processions and would normally be carried in juxtaposition with either a crucifix or a holy relic. When held aloft during the eulogies for Rabbi Minz, these torches could be perceived by those present as lending impressive dignity to the event but also as icons of an alien religion, which explains why Padua's Jews were so careful not to carry them aloft in procession. Capsali's account, with its detailed description of the successive kindling and extinguishing of the torches, provides a poignant illustration of the mixture of attraction and repulsion felt by the Jews of the Veneto in the early sixteenth century toward the impressive public processions of their Catholic environment.

Religious Practices in Northern and Southern Italy.

As in most things Italian, Jewish religious life in the south was quite different from the north. This difference became apparent to Rabbi Obadiah di Bertinoro during the 1480s after he set out from his home in Città di Castello on a pilgrimage to the Holy Land. Writing home from Jerusalem after his arrival, he described Jewish life in some of the places he had visited during his long journey. Particularly striking is his account of Jewish life in Palermo, Sicily. After describing the various occupations of the Palermitan Jews and their impressive synagogue, he comments on the rampant problem of informers and then adds laconically, "In the matter of menstrual purity they are also very lax, and most brides enter the marriage canopy already pregnant. They are extremely zealous and meticulous, however, in observing the prohibition regarding wine of the gentiles."

These two sentences, although ostensibly somewhat at variance with each other, actually form a coherent whole. Throughout his voyage from Italy to the land of Israel, Obadiah noted the stringent observance of *setam yenam* (wine of the gentiles) as one of the hallmarks of Jewish religiousness in the eastern Mediterranean: "In all the communities that I visited, except for Italy," he wrote to his father, "Jews are extremely careful to abstain from wine of the gentiles." Obadiah's testimony in 1488 is perhaps the earliest we have concerning a tendency which came to be recognized as a kind of structural fault line among northern Italian Jews of later generations, even among members of the rabbinical class.

Early in the seventeenth century, when a bitterly contested struggle developed among the Italian rabbis concerning the ritual bath in the northern town of Rovigo, Rabbi Abtalion of Consiglio, one of those who deemed the bath ritually unacceptable, was accused by an opponent of being "stringent in water and lenient in wine." Despite the tone of sarcasm in this accusation, it did reflect, if somewhat obliquely, the dominant religious tendency among the Jews of northern Italy, where the prohibition of *setam yenam* was observed largely in the breach, and yet much care was taken by women to immerse themselves in the ritually prescribed manner after menstrual impurity—even under the most challenging circumstances. More than seeking to praise Palermitan Jews for their stringency in one area or find fault with their laxity in another, Obadiah evidently sought to highlight the sharp differences between the two religious cultures.

Rites of Birth.

Like the Jews of the medieval Mediterranean before them, Italian Jews of the Renaissance strongly preferred male offspring over female, a preference that could be expressed in a wide variety of ways. For example, a highly literary letter of consolation, attributed to the noted sixteenth-century banker Ishmael Rieti of Siena, seeks to comfort a friend to whom a daughter had just been born. Similarly, in early 1556 Isaac de Lattes, who had earlier served as a tutor in Rieti's home, appended to the (limited) license he granted a young Mantuan woman to perform Jewish ritual slaughter (a common phenomenon in Italy) the invocation that in return for performing the commandment she be blessed with "male children who will teach Torah and faithfully observe God's commandments." Some three decades later the wealthy Cremonese banker Abraham Carmi, who had been tutored in his youth by Lattes's son-in-law, sadly recorded in his family diary the birth of an unnamed daughter who died after several days. Toward the end of the entry he added the wish, paraphrasing a well-known Talmudic phrase, that her birth would augur the future arrival of sons.

In the opening to his diary Carmi had entered the circumstances of his own birth and circumcision, giving not only the date but also the exact hour of his birth, as he was later to do for most of his children. He also entered the names of the two main participants in the circumcision ceremony: his father, the "officer" Saul Raphael Carmi, had performed the procedure, and the "greatly learned rabbi," Joseph Ottolenghi, a leading figure in the local Hebrew printing trade, served as *sandak,* or godfather, holding him on his knees. When a boy was born to Abraham in early 1589, the child's grandfather Saul Raphael again performed the circumcision, and Abraham himself served as *sandak.* But the wonderful image of three generations of Carmis united in the covenantal ceremony was soon marred by the boy's death, some sixteen months later.

When Leon Modena began to compose his autobiography nearly three decades later in Venice, he too named the major participants in his own circumcision, noting proudly that the "noted kabbalist Rabbi Menahem Azariah Fano" had performed the procedure and that his "revered father and Sarah, the daughter of my uncle Shemaiah, served as my godparents." The custom of having both a *compare* and *comare* was characteristic of indigenous Italiani Jews such as Modena but not of northern Italy's Ashkenazim, to which group the Carmis belonged. When Modena's wife, Rachel, gave birth to their first son, Mordecai, in 1591, both paternal grandparents served as the child's godparents. At the circumcision of his next son, Isaac, two years later, Modena's father-in-law and mother-in-law served in that capacity. And when in March of 1595 a third son was born, Rachel's uncle and aunt served as the child's godparents.

The high incidence of infant mortality only heightened the natural fears many parents harbored in anticipation of their son's circumcision and contributed to the popularity of festive vigils held on the eve of the ceremony, or sometimes over an entire week. In 1580 the largely Ashkenazic Jewish community of Padua reconfirmed a statute banning dance celebrations among its members except on specifically stated occasions, which included "the nights of the *veglia,* these being the nights preceding the circumcision of a male child." Dancing on these nights was permitted only "in the home of the mother," suggesting that only her female friends and relatives participated. In Cremona, by contrast, we learn of more masculine forms of festivity associated with circumcision. When in 1575 penitential decrees were issued by its Jewish community after news had arrived of an impending plague, it was decided to ban games of chance, except on special occasions. These included "the night of the *veglia* and the day of the circumcision . . . and only in the home of the child's father." In his *Riti* (1637), Leon Modena offered non-Jewish readers a rather tame description of the all-night vigil preceding the circumcision, omitting, for apologetic reasons, any mention of its antidemonic character or often raucous celebrations, asserting only that "the father's friends come and visit him, and the women go to the mother, and spend the evening in merriment and making good cheer."

Precircumcision vigils were not the only piously inspired form of nightlife in the Italian ghettos. Late in the sixteenth century predawn devotions known as Shomrim la-Boker were first introduced in Venice by Menahem Azariah of Fano. By 1622 there were three Shomrim la-Boker confraternities in Venice alone, associated with the Italian, Ashkenazic, and Levantine synagogues. By the late 1620s even such communities as Modena and Mantua could boast two competing confraternities for predawn prayer. Their popularity was a sign of the enormous influence exercised in northern Italy by the kabbalistically inspired piety of Safed. There, however, it had been the midnight rite of Tikkun Hazot which, with the aid of coffee—widely available in Safed and throughout the Middle East—had reigned supreme. Although Hazot societies were established in some early seventeenth-century Italian communities, the midnight rite did not attain popularity until late in that century, by which point the Italian night had been conquered with the aid of coffee. Limiting the availability of coffee to those who came to study, rather than dance or gamble, in the parental home on the eve of a circumcision also allowed Italian rabbis and community leaders, late in the seventeenth century, to transform the *veglia* into a more spiritual affair.

See also **Bible,** *subentry on* **Jewish Interpretation of the Bible; Preaching and Sermons,** *subentry on* **Jewish Preaching and Sermons; Rabbis.**

BIBLIOGRAPHY

Bonfil, Robert. *Jewish Life in Renaissance Italy.* Translated by Anthony Oldcorn. Berkeley, Calif., 1994.

Bonfil, Robert. *Rabbis and Jewish Communities in Renaissance Italy.* Translated by Jonathan Chipman. Oxford, 1990.

Cohen, Mark, ed. and trans. *The Autobiography of a Seventeenth-Century Venetian Rabbi: Leon Modena's Life of Judah.* Princeton, N.J., 1988.

Horowitz, Elliott. "Coffee, Coffeehouses, and the Nocturnal Rituals of Early Modern Jewry." *AJS Review* 14 (1989): 17–46.

Horowitz, Elliott. "The Eve of the Circumcision: A Chapter in the History of Jewish Nightlife." *Journal of Social History* 23 (1989): 45–69.

Horowitz, Elliott. "The Jews of Europe and the Moment of Death in Medieval and Modern Times." *Judaism* 44 (1995): 271–281.

Horowitz, Elliott. "Towards a Social History of Jewish Popular Religion: Obadiah of Bertinoro on the Jews of Palermo." *Journal of Religious History* 17 (1992): 138–151.

Shulvass, Moses. *The Jews in the World of the Renaissance.* Translated by Elvin I. Kose. Leiden, Netherlands, and Chicago, 1973.

Toaff, Ariel. *Love, Work, and Death: Jewish Life in Medieval Umbria.* Translated by Judith Landry. London, 1996.

ELLIOTT HOROWITZ

Court Jews

The phenomenon of the court Jew (designated officially in a wide variety of titles and appellations—*Hofjude, Hoffaktor, Hoflieferant, Oberhoffaktor*), individual Jews in the service of European political rulers from the end of the sixteenth century until the early nineteenth century, has intrigued historians, political theorists, economists, writers, artists, and political figures for several generations. Identified by his extensive economic and political activity, the court Jew loomed in the eyes of the modern period as an enigmatic personality. Heralded by some (like the twentieth-century German-Jewish author Lion Feuchtwanger) and denounced by others (such as Adolf Hitler in his *Mein Kampf*), the court Jew seems to have encapsulated the fears, excitement, attraction, and revulsion associated with the penetration of a minority group to a position of influence in society. For some, that influence was considered a high point in the Jewish "contribution" to European civilization; for others it was a sign that European society had fallen prey to the insatiable appetite of outsiders driven by self-glorification and animosity toward the local population. A phenomenon with an ambivalent pedigree, the court Jew raises a variety of problems intrinsic to the nature of baroque society, absolutism, and to the role of the Jew in modern times.

The evolution of absolutism in Europe wrought radical changes in European society. Driven by a desire to centralize the army and authority and develop political and administrative institutions, while wresting power from the established elements of society, absolutist rulers in central and eastern Europe occasionally showed a more open policy to previously rejected religious minorities. In their quest for power, authority, fiscal fluidity, and more efficient financial and bureaucratic mechanisms, Protestant and Catholic rulers of small and large states broke with prevalent feudal models and looked to private entrepreneurs with limited vested interests in the state structure. Absolutist rulers introduced important innovations in the state system of government that had far-reaching implications for the lives of European Jews. The emphasis on *raison d'état* and its concomitant policies of religious toleration and the encouragement of population growth figured prominently in this regard.

Through their connections with the Levantine trade and Jews in the Ottoman Empire, European Jews were ideally suited to provision armies with grain, timber, horses, and cattle as well as to supply rulers with diamonds, precious stones, and other goods for conspicuous consumption. The growing expenditure on court, army, and bureaucracy necessitated a more rational, bureaucratic structure. Relying on their organizational skill and wide international connections, rulers turned to individual Jews who were able to offer reliable, speedy, and extensive supplies of foodstuffs, cloth, and weapons for the army, the central instrument of the prince's power. Court Jews were often employed as tax purveyors and court minters and engaged in secret and delicate diplomatic efforts on the ruler's behalf. Op-

erating on the strength of their personal bonds with the ruler, the court Jews were entrusted with arranging transfers of credit and providing assistance to the ruler, overstepping the domains of the vested interests of society. Along with these services, the court Jews procured luxury items for the courts that engaged in the development of a baroque court culture.

Court Jews became a sine qua non in most of the principalities of the Holy Roman Empire following the Thirty Years' War (1618–1648). In a period when sovereigns sought out loyal elements, Jews with wide connections and versatile means were attractive figures. Some rose to positions of unique influence and affluence and were regarded as indispensable by their ruler. Samuel Oppenheimer (c. 1630–1703), who served as an imperial court Jew under Leopold I, the Habsburg emperor (ruled 1658–1705), was recalled to Vienna in the early 1670s to help provision the Habsburg army only a few years after the devoutly Catholic emperor had expelled more than three thousand Jews from Vienna. Awarded the title of imperial military factor, Oppenheimer developed an extensive operation that included many agents, contractors, and subcontractors throughout the Habsburg Empire and beyond, which enabled him to provide substantial supplies and foodstuffs to the Austrian armies and huge sums of money to the emperor, as well as engaging in diplomatic activity on the emperor's behalf. Oppenheimer's activity, like that of some other court Jews, was performed in the face of adversity, as various forces within the Habsburg court intrigued against him and tried to curtail his power. The most famous case of such conflict surrounded the court factor of Duke Karl Alexander of Würtemberg, Joseph Suess Oppenheimer (1699–1738). In the 1730s Oppenheimer assumed a wide range of governmental responsibilities, including procurement of military and other supplies, minting, and tax farming. He became a pivotal figure in Duke Karl's attempt to revamp state government. In these efforts, often oppressive to the populace, both Oppenheimer and the duke aroused much antagonism, exacerbated by Oppenheimer's Jewish origins and the duke's conversion to Catholicism in a predominantly Protestant country. Oppenheimer's embracing of an ostentatious and promiscuous lifestyle and his own economic intrigues combined to make him the prime target of resentments arising from the financial policies promulgated in the name of Duke Karl. Oppenheimer was publicly hanged in 1738 following the abrupt death of his patron a year earlier and an extensive judicial inquiry and trial.

Yet the several hundred court Jews employed by European rulers were not daunted by opposition and placed their faith and trust in the ruler they served. Privileges granted them and their entourage, financial success, social and political influence, the attractions of court life, and impact within the Jewish community were significant benefits of the functions they performed, functions that contributed to the development of the modern absolutist state.

BIBLIOGRAPHY

Israel, Jonathan I. *European Jewry in the Age of Mercantilism 1550–1750.* 3d ed. Portland, Ore., 1998.

Mann, Vivian B., and Richard I. Cohen, eds. *From Court Jews to the Rothschilds: Art, Patronage, and Power: 1600–1800.* Munich and New York, 1996.

Schnee, Heinrich. *Die Hoffinanz und der moderne Staat.* 5 vols. Berlin, 1953–1965.

Stern, Selma. *The Court Jew; a Contribution to the History of the Period of Absolutism in Central Europe.* Translated by Ralph Weiman. Philadelphia, 1950.

RICHARD I. COHEN

Jews and the Arts

Jewish art in the Renaissance and baroque Italy emphasized manuscript and printed book illustration, synagogue architecture and decoration, and religious objects for home and the synagogue. The Jewish involvement with the arts in Italy should be viewed against two backdrops: Jewish tradition (with its particular needs and attitudes toward the visual) and the life of Jews as a religious minority open to profound cultural influences from the host society.

The Problem of Jewish Art.

A widely held opinion stresses the limits of Jewish art or even questions its very existence due to the so-called Second Commandment (Exod. 20:4) and other relevant biblical texts, which forbid the making of "graven images." According to this view, the spiritual nature of Judaism, its emphasis on the invisibility of God and the meaning of His words, caused the Jews to develop an "aural" sense, while the "visual" was largely neglected. This orientation is commonly contrasted with the Greco-Roman world and its heritage, which developed the representational arts and the "worship" of beautiful images.

While the development of Jewish art was indeed subject to reevaluation of the original biblical and talmudic precepts concerning images, local sociocultural factors largely shaped the art of every Jewish community, East and West. Following the rabbinic precept of "the beautification of the commandment,"

Jewish works of art were generally limited to the religious realm—the synagogue, liturgical Hebrew books, and ceremonial objects for home and public rituals. The style and decoration of these objects varied from one land to another, reflecting the influence of the host cultures. Thus works of art created in Italy by or for Jews from the fourteenth to the seventeenth century demonstrate the spirit and style of the time and differ markedly from parallel objects produced among the Jews of Germany or Yemen, for example.

Under the tremendous impact of the visual arts in Italy and the spirit of Italian humanism, the local Jews adopted a rather lenient approach to the image and showed their deep affection for richly illustrated manuscripts and illustrated printed books, attractive synagogues, and ritual objets d'art for private and public life. The issue is properly summed up by Rabbi Leon Modena of Venice (1571–1648), who commented on the difference between Italian Jews and other Jewish communities in the observance of the Second Commandment: "However, in Italy a great many [Jews] take the liberty to keep draughts [designs] and pictures in their houses, especially if they are not in *relievo,* nor a whole body but only the face" (*Historia de' riti hebraici* [History of Jewish rites; Paris, 1637]).

Despite the influence of the rich visual milieu in which Italian Jews lived, art never occupied the place it had in the general society. Jewish children with artistic talents were not sent to be trained in an artist's studio as their neighbors were, and no single Jew could or did attain fame as an artist in this period. Only a few names of artists—or, more properly, skilled craftsmen—of Jewish descent are known (the painter and engraver Moses da Castelazzo, for example, who was active in early sixteenth-century Venice). Moreover, the number of works that can be safely attributed to them is meager. Some artists of Jewish descent converted to Catholicism in order to get commissions and achieve public recognition; most notable is the celebrated sword and dagger silversmith Salomone da Sesso (c. 1465–1519), who was baptized upon entering the service of the Ferrarese duke Ercole d'Este, with his name accordingly altered to Ercole dei Fideli.

The composition of the Jewish communities also played a decisive role in the shaping of Italian Jewish art. As Jewish immigrants from various countries, especially Germany and Spain, arrived in Italy throughout this period, they brought their artistic traditions with them. A notable example is the important scribe-artist Joel ben Simeon, who came to Italy from Germany and continued to produce manu-

Jewish Art. *Ketubbah* (marriage contract), Rome, 1627. COLLECTION ISRAEL MUSEUM, JERUSALEM

scripts in his new land. Thus the manuscripts he produced on Italian soil show a mixture of Ashkenazi (German-Jewish) and Italian-Jewish cultures.

Hebrew Manuscript Illumination. In the fourteenth and fifteenth centuries the most beloved field of artistic expression among Italian Jews was apparently manuscript illumination. Hebrew codices, written by skilled scribes in the typical square and cursive Hebrew script of Italian Jews, were enriched by attractive miniatures produced by both Jewish and gentile illuminators. The high achievement of the Italian-Hebrew illuminated manuscripts of this period becomes apparent when compared to the centers of contemporary Jewish illumination elsewhere in Europe (in particular Germany and

Spain): the Italian codices are richer, more elaborate, and artistically superior. Moreover, the texts selected and the topics of the miniatures accompanying them are more varied, ranging from biblical and halakic (legal) books to literary, ethical, scientific, and medical works. By and large, the miniatures in the costly codices reflect feelings of pride and joy of life that the upper-class Jewish patrons who commissioned them must have felt in Renaissance Italy.

The earliest extant illuminated Hebrew manuscripts from Italy, mostly Bibles with decorations limited to marginal embellishments and initial panel words, were apparently produced in Rome in the last decades of the thirteenth century. Slightly more elaborate illustrations appear in the fourteenth century. Thus, for example, halakic treatises contain scenes of daily life—mostly liturgical Jewish practices, such as the building of a sukkah or lighting a Hanukkah lamp. The production of some of the manuscripts in this period was initiated by noted patrons, whose fictitious coats of arms decorate the borders of the page in the same manner as in the codices of the general society. Furthermore, at times these patrons turned to the best workshop around, whether Jewish or gentile, such as that of Matteo di Ser Cambio in Perugia, which illuminated a *Mishneh Torah* codex by Moses Maimonides around 1400.

This trend was strengthened in the fifteenth century, during which the illumination of Hebrew codices in Italy reached its height. A relatively large number of richly illustrated manuscripts were produced in central and northern Italy, reflecting the styles of the local schools current at the time. The miniatures vividly portray the life and ideals of Italian Jews. Marriage scenes, such as the elaborate panel in the *Arba'ah turim* (four rows; Mantua, 1435) of the Jacob ben Asher codex, exhibit the influence of the Italian nobility on wealthy Jewish families. The spirit of gaiety and exuberance comes to life especially in the numerous miniatures filling the elegant manuscript known as the Rothschild Miscellany (Ferrara?, c. 1470). For example, two full-page miniatures are dedicated to the story of Job; but instead of showing him suffering, as was common in both Jewish and Christian art, they depict the final verses of the book: a rural landscape illustrates the wealth of Job, and the biblical figure, possibly modeled on the patron of the codex, appears seated in an elaborate Renaissance palazzo with all his sons and daughters.

The Ghetto Era. Though this period is characterized by the forced enclosure of the Jews in segregated quarters—the ghettos—the production of artistic objects and books was not interrupted. On the contrary, the period saw increased production in almost every field of the visual arts, possibly because the new living conditions, on the one hand, and the growing Catholic reaction, on the other, intensified the social activities inside Jewish society and reshaped its need for cultural symbols.

Synagogue architecture. Non-Jewish contemporaries who walked in the crowded streets of the ghettos would have some difficulty in recognizing a Jewish *scuola* ("synagogue" among Italian Jews) by its exterior. The facades of sixteenth- and seventeenth-century Italian synagogues were purposely simple, with the splendor of the structure reserved for the interior, away from unwelcome visitors. By and large, every community had a few synagogues, which were small and served the local Jews according to their country of origin. Thus, for example, Venice had five synagogues, which followed Italian, Spanish, German, and Levantine rites. Though the identity of the architects is usually unknown, they followed accepted architectural norms (for example, the interior of the Scuola Spagnola in Venice was modeled by a follower of the noted Venetian architect Baldassare Longhena).

Two elements determine the interior of a synagogue: the Torah ark, a cabinet for preserving the holy Torah scrolls, and the *bimah*, the platform from which the Torah is read. The norm in Italy was a bipolar plan, with the *bimah* at one end and the ark at the other, while the area between them remained free. Seating was arranged along the side walls. The alternative plan, namely a central *bimah*, was preferred in some regions, such as Piedmont. Due to their importance, the ark and *bimah* were attractively designed, employing Renaissance and baroque architectural elements and gilt stucco ornaments. The altar canopy designed by Giovanni Bernini in St. Peter's in Rome, for example, inspired the shape of the *bimah* in several Piedmontese synagogues.

Ceremonial objects. Partly because the spirit of the Counter-Reformation did not encourage Jews to join professional guilds, most of the ritual silver objects produced during the "ghetto era" were the work of Christian silversmiths. The most lavish were the silver objects centered around the holiest object in the synagogue, the Torah scroll: finials (*rimmonim*), crowns, shields, and pointers (to avoid touching the sacred text). In addition, the Torah scroll is "dressed" in costly textiles (Torah mantles and binders), which were embroidered by pious

Jewish Art. *Cofanetto* (silver casket) attributed to Jeshuran Tober, northern Italy, fifteenth century. DAVID HARRIS/COLLECTION ISRAEL MUSEUM, JERUSALEM

Jewish women and donated to the synagogue. The ark was adorned with an attractively embroidered curtain, sometimes depicting biblical scenes and symbols, and an elaborate silver eternal light was hung in front of it.

To a different category belong objects for the home. A prominent example that survived from the pre-ghetto era is a small silver casket (*cofanetto*) created for a Jewish woman in northern Italy (Ferrara?) in the fifteenth century, probably to hold keys (Jerusalem, Israel Museum). The cover of the box is inscribed in Judeo-Italian with names of linen types, and the nielloed front features three women engaged in performing the commandments incumbent upon Jewish women. The central figure, a woman immersed in a ritual bath, is surprisingly shown in the nude. The spirit of the Renaissance is also preserved in sixteenth- and seventeenth-century-bronze Hanukkah lamps, featuring nude putti, animal and human masks, sphinxes, tritons, centaurs, and at times even the coats of arms of Catholic cardinals whose protection the Jewish communities sought.

Printed books and manuscripts. Hebrew book printing actually began in Renaissance Italy (the earliest Hebrew books were printed in Rome, 1469–1475). Early on, members of the noted Soncino family printed books with great care for typography and introduced decorative woodcuts of initial letters and border ornaments. In the sixteenth cen-

tury, when Italy (Venice in particular) was the center of Hebrew printing, the ornamentation was concentrated on the title page, which was decorated with a wealth of motifs and the printer's device, set in an architectural background. These designs had tremendous influence on the shaping of Judaica throughout the Jewish world. In Italy, attractive silver bindings were prepared for the books on special occasions such as weddings.

Italian Jews continued to produce richly illuminated manuscripts long after the invention of printing. Moreover, new types of manuscripts became popular in the ghettos. Chief among these were Esther scrolls for the holiday of Purim and marriage contracts (*ketubbot*). The large private scrolls were crowded with biblical scenes as well as allegorical and symbolic representations. The illustrated *ketubbah* was introduced in Italy by Jewish exiles from Spain and reached the height of its artistic development in the seventeenth century. Families vied with one another over whose *ketubbah* was more elaborate, and the best craftsmen available (mostly Jews) were called upon to decorate the large parchments with colorful images that shed light on social, cultural, and artistic aspects of Jewish life in Italy.

See also **Jewish Themes in Renaissance Art.**

BIBLIOGRAPHY

Amram, David Werner. *The Makers of Hebrew Books in Italy.* London, 1963.

Benjamin, Chaya. "An Illustrated Venetian Esther Scroll and the Commedia dell'Arte." *Israel Museum News* 14 (1978): 50–59.

Fishof, Iris. "Renaissance Hanukkah Lamps from Italy." *Israel Museum News* 8 (1970): 65–74.

Gutmann, Joseph. *Hebrew Manuscript Painting*. New York, 1978.

Jewish Art and Culture in Emilia-Romagna. Exhibition catalog, The Jewish Community Museum. Venice, 1989.

Krinsky, Carol Herselle. *Synagogues of Europe: Architecture, History, Meaning*. Cambridge, Mass., 1985.

Mann, Vivian B., ed., *Gardens and Ghettos: The Art of Jewish Life in Italy*. Berkeley, Calif., 1989.

Metzger, Mendel. "The Earliest Engraved Italian Megilloth." *Bulletin of the John Rylands Library* 48 (1966): 381–432.

Nahon, S. U. *Holy Arks and Ritual Appurtenances from Italy in Israel*. Tel Aviv, 1970.

Narkiss, Bezalel. *Hebrew Illuminated Manuscripts*. Jerusalem, 1969.

Narkiss, Mordechai. "An Italian Niello Casket of the Fifteenth Century." *Journal of the Warburg and Courtauld Institutes* 21 (1958): 288–295.

Pinkerfeld, Jacob. *The Synagogues of Italy: Their Architectural Development since the Renaissance*. Jerusalem, 1954 (in Hebrew).

Roth, Cecil. *The Jews in the Renaissance*. Philadelphia, 1959. See especially chapter 9, "Art and Artists," pp. 189–212.

Sabar, Shalom. *Ketubbah: Jewish Marriage Contracts of the Hebrew Union College Skirball Museum and Klau Library*. New York, 1990.

Sabar, Shalom. "The Use and Meaning of Christian Motifs in Illustrations of Jewish Marriage Contracts in Italy." *Journal of Jewish Art* 10 (1984): 47–63.

Wischnitzer, Rachel. *The Architecture of the European Synagogue*. Philadelphia, 1964.

SHALOM SABAR

Jews and Music

Jewish music was largely monophonic (one-voice) and liturgical until relatively late in the Renaissance. Art music—usually taken to refer to polyphony, or music for two or more voices, in the European tradition—by Jewish composers began in Italy, particularly Mantua, in the later sixteenth century, then spread to Amsterdam and southern France in the later seventeenth and eighteenth centuries.

Jewish art music may owe its relatively late start to rabbinical antagonism to any kind of music that breaks with traditional song as practiced in the synagogue. With the destruction of the Second Temple the Jews were expected to be in perpetual mourning, hence not to display art. The rabbis (such as Maimonides) condemned secular music and the use of instruments; they frowned upon music as a source of entertainment. Synagogal chant, for prayers and the cantillation (musical recitation) of the scriptural readings, was not considered "music," but rather a melodic inflection of sacred texts; from a rabbinical standpoint it sufficed to fulfill the ritual needs of the community.

Yet there are other reasons for the late start: synagogal music itself, with its monophony, put a brake on other forms of music making; art music was associated with Christians, and Jewish authorities hardly encouraged the imitation of "Christian ways" (*ḥukkat haggoy*) in prayer services or communal activities; and the Jews lacked a practical tradition of music theory (Hebrew writings on music were concerned with its mathematical, ethical, or cosmological ramifications, not with how it should be composed). For art music to develop, a musical script, or notation, was needed (Hebrew is written from right to left, hence the problem of devising an adequate correlation of notes and syllables). Sixteenth- and seventeenth-century humanist writings on Hebrew grammar (such as Johann Reuchlin's from 1518) contained some examples of cantillation, but the earliest full-fledged notation for Hebrew polyphony was that in Salamone Rossi's sacred songs published in 1622–1623.

Development. The motivation for an art music tradition came from various quarters. One important element was the practice of hymn composition. Hymns, or *piyyutim*, were introduced into the synagogue as early as the fifth century, only to become associated after the tenth century with strophic metrical types. Three elements were crucial here: the iterative structures of the verse; its quantitative or sometimes qualitative measurement, and the melodies to which the verse was performed, some of them drawn from secular or non-Jewish sources, then wed to the Hebrew texts. The *piyyut* differed thereby from biblical cantillation, which had free rhythms, usually prose texts, and formulaic melodic motives. From the very beginning it was often the practice to cultivate "new" melodies in its performance; in the thirteenth century *Sefer ḥassidim* (Book of the pious) one reads "seek for melodies and when you pray employ a melody which will be beautiful and soft in your eyes." By contrast, the "melodies" of the cantillated texts were not to be tampered with, for they were thought, by legend, to have been delivered to Moses on Mount Sinai. With the gradual rise of the cantor (*ḥazzan*) to a position of prominence in the synagogue liturgy, there was a concomitant tendency to favor the introduction of a "new" repertory suited to displaying his increasingly professional skills.

Another element in the formation of an incipient polyphony was the *meshorerim* practice of the Ashkenazi rite from the sixteenth century (or perhaps even earlier) on: the cantor was supported at times by two assistants, one a boy with a higher voice, the other an adult with a bass; they punctuated various portions of the phrase, particularly its cadences, creating three-voice harmony. Still other elements may have been influential: the use of music as an adjunct to joyous holidays (Simhat Torah, Purim) and to private and communal festivities (banquets, weddings, circumcisions, the consecration of a synagogue, the inauguration of a Torah scroll); the efforts deployed by rabbis of a more liberal tendency, in particular the Venetian Leon Modena (1571–1648), to introduce part-singing into the synagogue; and the service of Jewish musicians in the courts (mainly Mantua, though also Turin), where they became acquainted with and eventually adopted the latest styles of Christian art music. (Jewish musicians also performed in the Mantuan Jewish theater, which, from the mid-sixteenth to early seventeenth centuries, provided theatrical entertainment, with musical interludes, for Christian audiences, especially during carnival season.) In justifying their concern with art music, the Jews were wont to cite the example of the glorious music practiced in the ancient Temple, which Rossi, for one, was thought to have resuscitated in his own day, according to the eulogistic prefatory matter to his Hebrew collection.

Composers. Art music by Jewish composers began in Italy, particularly Mantua, in the later sixteenth century, then spread to Amsterdam and southern France in the later seventeenth and eighteenth centuries. The practical remains of art music by Jewish composers are limited. Secular vocal music, such as madrigals and canzonette, is represented by collections of the Jewish composers David Sacerdote (one, 1575), Salamone Rossi (eight, 1600–1628), Davit Civita (one, 1616), and Allegro Porto (three, 1619–1625), though except for Rossi's the collections are all incomplete, lacking one or more voices. The only known instrumental works are those in four collections by Rossi (1607–1623; they contain sinfonie, sonatas, *gagliarde, correnti,* and more). Sacred art music to Hebrew texts seems to have been introduced into the synagogue in the first decade of the seventeenth century, spreading from Ferrara to Mantua, Venice, and other mainly northern Italian centers. It may have been largely improvised; only two early Italian collections are known, Rossi's *Hashirim asher lish'lomo* (Songs of Solomon; 1622–1623) and an undated, anonymous manuscript, extant in one of assumedly eight voices, probably from the late 1620s or the 1630s and apparently associated with Venice.

The major early Jewish composer was Salamone Rossi. Beyond his twelve secular collections he can be credited with the first polyphonic set of Hebrew sacred songs. His activity as an art music composer was paralleled by utterances of contemporary writers, among them Judah Moscato, who, in a sermon on music (printed in 1588), expanded on the symbolism of the number eight (the octave, hence perfection; Simhat Torah, the joyous eighth day of the Feast of Tabernacles; the *scientia divina,* or eighth science that completes the seven liberal arts); Leon Modena, who, in a responsum published in 1605 and reprinted in Rossi's *Songs,* debated the legitimacy of using art music in the synagogue; and Abraham ben David Portaleone, who, in his voluminous treatise *Shiltei ha-gibborim* (Shields of heroes; 1612), described ꞏusic in the ancient Temple after the example ui ꞏne forms, practices, and instruments of sixteenth- and seventeenth-century Italian art music. Modena was closely connected with the genesis and completion of Rossi's Hebrew *Songs:* in their extensive prefatory matter (such as prefaces and poems), of which Modena was the principal author, an important sociocultural statement is made on the functions and purposes of Jewish art music.

BIBLIOGRAPHY

Primary Works

Adler, Israel. *Hebrew Writings Concerning Music in Manuscripts and Printed Books from Geonic Times up to 1800.* Munich, 1975.

Rossi, Salamone. *Complete Works.* Edited by Don Harrán. 12 vols. Neuhausen, Germany, 1995. Volumes 1–8 include the composer's secular music in Italian and 9–12 his instrumental works.

Secondary Works

Adler, Israel. "The Rise of Art Music in the Italian Ghetto." In *Jewish Medieval and Renaissance Studies.* Edited by Alexander Altmann. Cambridge, Mass., 1967. Pages 321–364.

Birnbaum, Eduard. *Jewish Musicians at the Court of the Mantuan Dukes (1542–1628).* Translated by Judith Cohen. Tel Aviv, Israel, 1978. Translation of *Jüdische Musiker am Hofe von Mantua von 1542–1628* (1893). A short, still useful study of Jewish musical activity in Mantua.

Harrán, Don. "Jewish Dramatists and Musicians in the Renaissance: Separate Activities, Common Aspirations." In *Musicologia Humana: Studies in Honour of Warren and Ursula Kirkendale.* Edited by Siegfried Gmeinwieser, David Hiley, and Jörg Riedlbauer. Florence, 1994. Pages 291–304. Discusses certain general tendencies in the life and works of Salamone Rossi and the contemporary Jewish dramatist Leone de' Sommi as a paradigm for Jewish musical versus theatrical concerns.

Harrán, Don. "Jewish Musical Culture in Early Modern Venice." In *The Jews of Venice: A Unique Renaissance Community.* Edited by Robert C. Davis and Benjamin Ravid. Baltimore, forthcoming. Modena is discussed within the broader frame of Jewish music in Venice.

Harrán, Don. *Salamone Rossi, Jewish Musician in Late Renaissance Mantua.* Oxford, 1998.

Harrán, Don. "Tradition and Innovation in Jewish Music of the Later Renaissance." *Journal of Musicology* 7 (1989): 107–130.

Idelsohn, A. Z. *Jewish Music in Its Historical Development.* 1929. Reprint, New York, 1981. Though early, remains the standard volume on Jewish music in its art and synagogue traditions.

DON HARRÁN

Print and Jewish Cultural Development

The advent of print had an enormous impact on Jewish culture, generating a radical change in modes of literacy and cultural definitions. Print enabled the circulation and standardization of texts as well as the unification and canonization of previous traditions. It led to the emergence of new types of writing, reading, and learning, and enhanced the shaping of new collective identities and modes of communication among communities. The transition from manuscript to print culture manifested itself in different, sometimes contradictory, directions and consequently defined different communities of readers and new relations between elite and popular culture. These directions were integrated into the global transformation of Jewish identity and intensified previous and simultaneous cultural developments that represent and reveal the complexity of the process of modernization.

The evolution of Hebrew print should be considered part of the global transition from manuscript to print culture. The centers of Hebrew print were the centers of print in general—Venice and later Amsterdam—and the routes of distribution were similar to those developed during the rise of the print industry. Hebrew printed works were subjected to the same systems of control that were established by religious and secular authorities in the Christian world. Differences express the unique nature of Jewish literature and experiences.

Early Hebrew Printers. Hebrew print first appeared soon after the introduction of the new technology. By the end of the fifteenth century about two hundred Hebrew volumes had already been printed. The first stage of the development of Hebrew print was accomplished by Joshua Soncino and his nephew Gershom Soncino, who were the first printers to offer critical editions of some of the major Jewish books, based on several manuscripts. The Soncino family published prayer books, legal codes, biblical commentaries, and some Talmud tractates, products that would continue to characterize Hebrew print. Gershom also published non-Hebrew books.

The center of Hebrew printing in the sixteenth century was Italy, in presses that were established by Christians. The first and the most prominent among these printers was Daniel Bomberg (1470 or 1480–?1550), a humanist from Antwerp who had established a press in Venice in 1516. Bomberg was instrumental in designing the Hebrew book as we know it even today. The editions he produced of the main Hebrew books continue to define Jewish literature. Among these should be mentioned his two editions of the Hebrew Bible with rabbinic commentaries (*Mikraot Gedolot*) and later the Talmud with its main commentaries (1520–1523). His establishment of commercial relations between Italy and the Ottoman Empire created a new community of readers of the Hebrew book as well as new frameworks of cultural communication. After Bomberg's retirement in 1548 came other printers, in Venice and in other Italian cities. Meanwhile, modest Hebrew printing houses also operated in the Ottoman Empire and in Poland. In the seventeenth century the center of Hebrew printing moved to Amsterdam, where it played a constitutive role in the reshaping of the Portuguese community.

The role of Christians in the formative stage of Hebrew printing is significant and points to the link between the advent of printing and the rise of Hebraist interest among contemporaneous Christian scholars. The Christians who invested in printing Hebrew books were first and foremost financially motivated, but they were also driven by intellectual and theological interests. The printers employed Jews and converts as editors and proofreaders, and their shops became a meeting place in which Jews and Christians who shared the same humanistic values and methods worked together. The common interest of Jews and Christians is demonstrated in some of the products of the early print industry, such as biblical commentaries and grammar books. At the same time, Jewish scholars developed similar methods of interpretation and participated in the humanistic culture, in which terms they defined their difference from their Christian contemporaries.

The aim of the printers was to produce the best editions possible and at the same time to make them accessible for both Jewish and Christian readers. But the Jewish public remained the main market for the Hebrew print industry, and its products reflect first of all the cultural interests of that audience. The most popular books that were printed very soon after the advent of the printing press—prayer books, works of codification, and custom books—reshaped different aspects of the Jewish collectivity.

Important Categories of Books Printed.

Works of legal codification were obvious products of print culture. Though the famous examples of this genre were already popular in previous centuries, their impact increased and generated a change in modes of reading and religious practice alike. In the early stages, the most popular among these books were Jacob ben Arba'ah Asher's *Turim* (The four rows; 1475) and Moses Maimonides's *Mishne Torah* (Second Torah; 1475), but these were later replaced by Joseph Karo's *Bet Yosef* (House of Joseph; 1550–1559) and especially *Shulhan 'arukh* (The set table; 1565), which was composed in Safed, Palestine. After being glossed by Moses Isserles of Cracow, *Shulhan 'arukh* became authoritative throughout the Jewish world. These books expressed the tendency toward unification of the Talmudic law, while replacing the dialogical halakic discourse with a systematic organization of knowledge. Such codes were aimed at scholars as well as laypersons.

Karo (1488–1575) can be considered a "new author," since he wrote with a view to publication and with a style that reflected the rules of the printing press. His work thus created a common ground for later developments of halakah (Jewish law). Although the Talmud remained the main text of learning, these texts gained broad popularity.

While Karo's *Shulhan 'arukh* aimed at universalization of the halakah, books of customs compiled and reshaped regional customs and practices, creating and reorganizing local communities, especially in Europe. Like prayer books, these books enabled the process of unification of everyday life as well as the rise of local collective identities, limited to a concrete cultural-geographical context. For instance, Yiddish custom books that appeared in the sixteenth century defined the imagined community that included different social groups and also reflected the crystallization of the Ashkenazi (the central and eastern European Jewish communities, which share a common tradition). Meanwhile, Judeo-Spanish (Ladino) books, which were composed in Italy, the Ottoman Empire, and later in Amsterdam, defined the imagined community of the Iberian Jewish communities all over the world.

The Talmud, which was first published by Bomberg, was directed to a smaller readership. The complicated structure and the price of the multivolume set made it beyond the reach of most readers. However, the Talmud remained the source of learning of the elite. While traditional ways of learning continued to play a crucial role, the creation of a fixed version and the standardization of the text led to a systematic study of texts and the rise of new modes of reflection upon them (such as *pilpul,* a dialectical, rational method of studying Jewish oral law as codified in the Talmud).

Another issue that emerged during the formative period was the printing and canonization of kabbalistic literature. This process signified the turn of an esoteric knowledge into an exoteric one, consequently initiating controversies, such as whether—and in what version—to print the *Zohar,* the central work of the Kabbalah. This controversy emerged from the debate over philosophy versus Kabbalah and at the same time reflected an awareness of the impact of printing, which altered the accessibility of previously protected knowledge. But the exposure to a relatively large audience also led to the canonization of kabbalistic texts in a way that integrated printing and contemporaneous intellectual trends. The publication of kabbalistic works generated a long process in which Kabbalah received a prominent role in the definition of ritual and spiritual life in Jewish communities, as well as in the shaping of attitudes of Christian scholars such as Giovanni Pico della Mirandola and Johann Reuchlin.

Control over the Printing Press.

The controversy over the printing of the *Zohar,* as well as other compositions such as *Meor Einayim* (Voice of God) by Azariah de' Rossi, was associated with the institutionalization of new systems of control over the printing press, in order to prevent the publication of material considered heretical. The control over the printing press, and the rabbinic permission or recommendation accompanying the printed book, demonstrated the awareness of the cultural change.

Besides being subject to internal Jewish control over the print industry, Hebrew books were also subject to censorship by Christian authorities, first by the church and then by civil authorities as well. The church control over the Hebrew printing press was part of the overall control system that was established after the Reformation and should be considered as part of the transition to print culture. The main intention of that control was to prevent blasphemy and anti-Christian statements in Hebrew literature. In the 1550s the pope ordered the burning of the Talmud as part of a global struggle against heretical literature. This policy was later replaced by a systematic prepublication examination of books, which evidently led to the explicit permission to use Jewish literature. The examination of books did not necessarily compromise Hebrew texts, and to a certain extent it was part of the process of editing. It followed the internal inclination to define Jewish identity as autonomous, relatively separated from the theological disputation of the surrounding Christian community.

See also **Caro, Joseph ben Ephraim.**

BIBLIOGRAPHY

Baruchson, Shifra. *Books and Readers: the Reading Interests of Italian Jews at the Close of the Renaissance.* Ramat Gan, Israel, 1993. (Hebrew)

Benayahu, Meir. *Copyright, Authorization, and Imprimatur for Hebrew Books Printed in Venice.* Jersualem, 1971. (Hebrew)

Bonfil, Roberto. "Le biblioteche degli Ebrei nell'Italia nell'epoca del Rinascimento." In *Manoscritti, frammenti, e libri ebraici nell'italia dei secoli XV-XVI.* Edited by Guiliano Tamani and Angelo Vivian. Rome, 1981. Pages 137–150.

Friedberg, H. D. *A History of the Hebrew Print in Italy.* Tel Aviv, 1956. (Hebrew)

Griess, Z. "The Role of the Printing Press in Communicating Between Jewish Societies after the Expulsion from Spain." *Da'at* (1992): 5–17.

Habermann, A. M. *Studies in the History of Hebrew Printers and Books.* Jerusalem, 1978. (Hebrew)

Hacker, Joseph. "Constantinople Prints in the Sixteenth Century." *Areshet* 5 (1972): 457–493.

Marx, Alexander. *Ueber den Einfluss des ersten hebraeischen Buch-drucks auf den cultus und die Cultur der Juden.* Jehres-Bericht des Rabbiner-Seminars zu Berlin. 1893–1894.

Reiner, Elchanan. "The Ashkenazi Elite at the Beginning of the Modern Era: Manuscript Versus Printed Book." *Jews in Early Modern Poland.* Edited by Gershon David Hundert. Vol. 10. London, 1997. Pages 85–98.

Sonneh, L. "Expurgation of Hebrew Books." *Bulletin of the New York Public Library.* 46 (1942): 975–1014.

Tishby, Isaiah. "The Controversy over the *Zohar* in Sixteenth-Century Italy." In *Studies in Kabbalah and Its Branches.* Edited by Isaiah Tishby. Vol. 1. Jerusalem, 1982. Pages 79–130.

AMNON RAZ-KRAKOTZKIN

Jews and the Catholic Church

Just as the Catholic Church itself was challenged and restructured during the fifteenth and sixteenth centuries, so was its relationship with the Jews.

Tradition and Challenge. Two, if not three, challenges to the relationship between the Jews and the church arose in the fifteenth century. The first was the appearance of thousands of potentially insincere converts in Spain, a problem amplified by the Spanish laws of purity of blood and by the mass forced conversion of thousands of Portuguese Jews in 1497, the legitimacy of whose very baptism was in doubt. What position would the church, its orders, and its head take on the question of conversion, especially in the Italian peninsula? The second challenge was the preaching of Observant Franciscans on the subject of usury, again in Italy. Would the

church change an age-old position that tolerated this lending at a controlled (20 percent) rate of interest?

What is more, the mendicant position prescribed, as a corollary, the possible expulsion of Jews who threatened Christian life, whether through lending or any other potentially "polluting" activity. This position was bolstered by the increasingly restrictive stance of certain legists, doctors of Roman and canon law, who judged that the law existed to marginalize the Jews in order to avoid infecting the Christian faithful. Their stance departed from that of medieval canon lawyers, who had sought a balanced formula for coexistence with, and restriction of, the Jews. Would the church follow suit, establishing segregation as its motto, or would it continue its venerable policy of assent to a Jewish presence? These same legists were responsible for the blood libels (accusing Jews not only of killing Christian boys but of using their blood for ritual ends) that destroyed the Jewish community in Trent in 1475 and created havoc in other Italian cities shortly afterward. Would the church accept these charges, entrenching a policy of repression and exclusion?

Conversion. These challenges were, of course, potentially contradictory, especially when that which was sought out—converts—was summarily rejected on grounds of insincerity. Were it assumed that all converts were false, then they, too, must be repressed, as in fact they were, through the establishment of the Inquisition in Spain, in about 1478, and Portugal, in about 1536. But in both cases the papacy assented to the Inquisition only after a struggle, for the papacy never subscribed to exclusion as a policy, as the response of Pope Sixtus IV to the events of Trent in 1475 shows. Though bowing to various political and humanistic pressures in accepting the pernicious story of the purported homicide of little Simonino in Trent, Sixtus refrained from beatifying, let alone sanctifying, the child, and he reiterated that henceforth, as in the past, Jews were not to be denied due legal process. By doubting the validity of the forced baptisms of 1497, Popes Clement VII and Paul III were really expressing their confidence that true conversion could take place.

Encouraging a compromise between the two political extremes was the Reformation unfolding in Germany, which pressed the church toward renewal in every quarter. One road toward renewal was proselytism, which received added impetus from the discovery of "masses awaiting conversion" in the New World. The principal document of overall renewal, the *Libellus ad Leonem Decem* (Book for Leo X), written in 1513 by two Venetian nobles turned monks, Vincenzo Querini and Tommaso Giustiniani, placed conversion at the center of its program, including the conversion of the Jews. In the early 1540s Ignatius Loyola argued successfully for the establishment of a house for converts, principally for Jews, along with an edict (the bull *Cupientes iudaeos*) setting the ground rules for making conversion work.

But in the early 1550s the Jesuit Francisco de Torres revived an earlier position by arguing that conversion further necessitated ridding the Jews of the fantasies of the rabbinic Talmud, a position that resulted in the burning of the Talmud throughout Italy beginning in 1553. Also resurrected was the notion that conversion of the Jews could be stimulated by imposing financial burdens too heavy to bear, an idea first espoused by Pope Gregory the Great nearly a thousand years earlier. It was also deemed necessary to isolate the Jews, which Pope Paul IV accomplished in 1555 through the establishment of the Roman ghetto. This action responded to the prevailing sense that the Jews' presence was breeding perpetual conflict and danger, and that it had become impossible to live with Jews under the old rules. But Paul IV's principal impetus in establishing the ghetto was his conviction that converting the Jews required administering "pious lashes," the heavy limitations proposed by Querini and Giustiniani in their tract to Leo X, rather than adopting the "sweetness of lips" prescribed centuries earlier by St. Augustine.

Ancona and the Ghetto of Rome. The methodical enclosure of the Jews was complemented by Paul IV's actions against those Portuguese returnees to Judaism—actually living in Ancona in the Italian Papal States since the 1530s under explicit papal license and with full papal knowledge of their origins—whom Paul IV perceived as apostates. In his eyes, the 1497 conversion of Portuguese Jewry was irrevocable. To allow at Ancona the fiction of conversion that his predecessors had accepted would be to compromise his goal of making the borders between Jews and Christians sharp and clear. Thus Jews who remained Jews would live behind a physical barrier, under pressure to become Christians. Partial, incomplete, or denied conversion would be brooked under no circumstance.

This idea functioned better in theory than in practice. If only because of financial considerations—to keep the Jewish community from going bankrupt and burdening the papal treasury—Roman Jews were allowed to maintain their communal life and culture. Converts often remained ambivalent. Nor

did matters change with partial expulsions of Jews from all cities of the Papal State except Rome and Ancona. That the pope was a civil monarch must always be kept in mind. The ghetto thus became an instrument and arena of gradual debilitation, but not dissolution, and the popes largely reverted to their old ways, except for the 1584 edict requiring Jews to attend sermons. In 1682 Jewish lending banks at Rome were finally closed. By this time, these banks were in effect mere financial shadows, but their closure created impoverishment, for even these shadow banks offered employment to a large circle of Jews besides the bankers themselves. Everything else marched in place until 20 September 1870, the day Rome became the capital of the modern Italian monarchy—and what dissolved was not the Jews, but the Papal State itself.

See also **Anti-Semitism; Ghetto.**

BIBLIOGRAPHY

Baron, Salo Wittmayer. *A Social and Religious History of the Jews.* Vol. 14, *Late Middle Ages and Era of European Expansion (1200–1650): Catholic Restoration and Wars of Religion.* 2d. ed., rev. and enl. New York, London, and Philadelphia, 1969.

Foa, Anna. *A History of the Jews of Europe, From the Black Death to Emancipation.* Berkeley and Los Angeles, forthcoming.

Pullan, Brian. *The Jews of Europe and the Inquisition of Venice, 1550–1670.* Oxford, 1983.

Stow, Kenneth R. *Catholic Thought and Papal Jewry Policy, 1555–1593.* New York, 1977.

Stow, Kenneth R. "The Papacy and the Jews, Catholic Reformation and Beyond." *Jewish History* 6 (1992): 257–279.

Stow, Kenneth R. *Taxation, Community, and State: The Jews and the Fiscal Foundations of the Early Modern Papal State.* Stuttgart, Germany, 1982.

Vogelstein, Hermann. *Rome.* Translated by Moses Hadas. Philadelphia, 1940.

KENNETH STOW

JIMÉNEZ DE CISNEROS, FRANCISCO. *See* **Cisneros, Francisco Jiménez de.**

JOHN OF AUSTRIA (Don John; 1547–1578), Spanish commander and statesman. Born Jeromín, natural son of the emperor Charles V, in Regensburg, he belongs to the chivalric side of the Renaissance. Taken to Spain as a child, he was dubbed Juan (John) by his half-brother Philip II when formally recognized in 1559 at age twelve. Educated in statecraft alongside Philip's son Don Carlos and nephew Alexander Farnese, Don John showed his propensity for war when he tried to bolt court in 1565 for Philip's relief expedition to Malta. Philip made him

John of Austria. Portrait attributed to Alonso Sanchéz Coello (c. 1531–1588). MUSEO D'ESCORIAL/CORBIS

captain general of his Mediterranean armada in 1568 and in 1569 put him in charge of the suppression of the Granadine Morisco revolt. The revolt subdued, he became in 1571 supreme commander of the Holy League armada and victor in the Battle of Lepanto over the Turks. In 1572 the sculptor Andrea Calmech produced a magnificent bronze statue of him for Messina.

With his bravery, leadership talent, and blond good looks, he dazzled Europe. Cervantes sang his praises, and he was hero of Juan Rufo's epic *Austriada* (1584). The papacy urged him to consider the rescue of Mary, queen of Scots, putting her on England's throne and marrying her. Loyal to Philip, he persisted in the Mediterranean war, despite setbacks related to the defection of Venice from the League and Philip's financial straits. In 1576, Philip ordered Don John to the Netherlands as governor general in the hope that he might end the Dutch Revolt through diplomacy. He delayed his departure to gain Philip's qualified agreement to his plan to rescue of Mary of Scots. By the time he reached the Netherlands, the king's army had mutinied for want of pay and sacked Antwerp. For the Netherlanders to accept his government, he had to discharge the army and thus give up his rescue plan. For a few months in 1577 he seemed successful in the restoration of peace, and in Brussels he made a deep impression on Philip Sidney, Queen Elizabeth's envoy to him. Subsequent negotiations over religious toleration broke down, and Don John resorted to arms. After mixed successes, he fell ill in August 1578 and died near Namur. To all he seemed a gallant knight and crusader. Philip had his body brought to the Escorial for burial near Emperor Charles.

See also **Lepanto, Battle of.**

BIBLIOGRAPHY

Stirling-Maxwell, William. *Don John of Austria*. 2 vols. London, 1883. Though old-fashioned, it remains the best book on the subject.

Törne, Per Olof von. *Don Juan d'Autriche et les projets de conquête de l'Angleterre*. 2 vols. Helsinki, Finland, 1915–1928. Mines Vatican sources to focus on Don John and the papal scheme to rescue Mary, queen of Scots, and restore England to Rome.

PETER PIERSON

JOHN OF THE CROSS (Juan de Yepes; 1542?–1591), Spanish poet and mystic. John of the Cross was born in the small village of Fontiveros, near Ávila. His father and one brother died when he was still a child, and his mother, driven by poverty and hunger, eventually settled with her remaining two sons in Medina del Campo, a thriving commercial center. Some scholars have speculated that she may have had Jewish or Moorish blood. After attending a local orphanage school, John studied at the Jesuit college in Medina, paying his way by working in a local syphilis hospital. Having decided to join the Carmelite order, he was sent to the University of Salamanca to study first arts and then theology, but a crisis of vocation led him to abandon his studies after four years. He was persuaded not to leave the Carmelites for the Carthusian order by Teresa of Ávila, who recruited him to promote among the friars the reforms she had begun among the Carmelite sisters. This was to be the focus of his life's work. He and

Teresa are the founders of what came to be known as the Discalced Carmelites.

Internal tensions in the Carmelite order reached a climax on 2 December 1577, when unreformed friars removed John from his post as confessor to Teresa's sisters in Ávila and placed him in solitary confinement in a tiny cell in the Carmelite monastery in Toledo, from which he escaped eight months later. His first poems were composed during this period of intense suffering. During the next few years he continued to write poetry but also began to prepare a series of commentaries on some of them: *Subida del Monte Carmelo* (The ascent of Mount Carmel) and *Noche oscura del alma* (The dark night of the soul), both based on the same poem; *Cántico espiritual* (The spiritual canticle), based on his longest poem; and *Llama de amor viva* (The living flame of love). These commentaries enshrine his teaching on the way a soul may reach union with God. The first two were unfinished, and the others were subject to various revisions. Some critics have questioned the authen-

ticity of the second redaction of *Cántico espiritual,* but their doubts have been convincingly answered.

After his escape, John spent his life in the service of the Carmelite order, occupying a number of important positions, especially in Andalucía, as a prior of Discalced houses, rector of Discalced colleges, and in a variety of administrative positions. He traveled quite widely in Spain and assisted in the foundation of new Discalced houses. Further dissension in the order led to his virtual banishment to a remote community, where he fell ill in September 1591. Sent for treatment to Úbeda, he died there in December of that year.

His poetic output was small and remained largely forgotten for over three hundred years. During the twentieth century his reputation grew steadily in Spain and beyond, and he is now regarded as one of the major lyrical poets of the golden age of Spain. His poems are characterized by their richly sensuous imagery and mysterious and evocative language. They delight in the wonder of natural creation and use the language of human love with delicate eroticism as an image for the union of the Lover with the Beloved, inspired by the language of the Song of Songs and its traditional exegesis as the love song between the soul and God. They have been widely praised by twentieth-century poets and have inspired and influenced T. S. Eliot and Seamus Heaney, among many others.

John's most famous phrase, "the dark night of the soul," is a complex symbol for the whole of the spiritual journey, from the moment the soul sets out on the way of detachment, through its passage in the way of faith, to the darkness of its destination, God. Influenced by traditions of apophatic theology, he is nonetheless highly original in his treatment of the night, which affects the senses and the spirit in both active and passive ways. Because he wrote for a small, private readership, the theological principles behind his teaching are not systematically presented and, if missed, can lead to serious misinterpretation of his work. His other characteristic symbols of journey and ascent suggest a process of growth in which both human activity and divine grace participate, although the priority lies with grace. For all that John writes about detachment, he is not a hater of the physical world, as his poems clearly show; creation is good in itself, but human beings consistently misuse its gifts. He never negates except to affirm something better. At the end of the journey, in *Llama de amor viva,* he makes an important distinction between seeing God through created things (which leads only to an indirect knowledge of the divine)

John of the Cross. John in prayer before the image of Jesus.

and seeing created things through God (which allows the soul, in union with God, to enjoy them as God intends them to be).

His status as the greatest Western teacher of the mystical way took time to become established. He was beatified in 1675, canonized in 1726, and proclaimed a doctor of the church by Pius XI in 1926. His influence in the English-speaking world owes much to the pioneering translations and studies of his works by the English Hispanist E. Allison Peers and to the translations of his verse by the South African poet Roy Campbell. He is held in high regard outside the Roman Catholic Church and has become a fruitful point of ecumenical encounter.

See also **Teresa of Ávila.**

BIBLIOGRAPHY

Primary Works

Campbell, Roy. *Poems of St. John of the Cross.* London, 1951.

Kavanaugh, Kieran, and Otilio Rodriguez, trans. *The Collected Works of St. John of the Cross.* Washington, D.C., 1991.

López-Baralt, Luce, and Eulogio Pacho, eds. *San Juan de la Cruz: Obra completa.* 2 vols. Madrid, 1991.

Ruano, Lucinio, ed. *San Juan de la Cruz: Obras completas.* 11th ed. Madrid, 1982.

Secondary Works

Alonso, Dámaso. *La poesía de San Juan de la Cruz.* Madrid, 1942.

Brenan, Gerald. *St. John of the Cross.* Cambridge, U.K., 1973.

Ruiz, Federico, ed. *Dios habla en la noche.* Madrid, 1990. For an English translation of this work, see *God Speaks in the Night: The Life, Times, and Teaching of St. John of the Cross.* Washington, D.C., 1991.

Thompson, C. P. *The Poet and the Mystic.* Oxford, 1977.

Wilson, Margaret. *San Juan de la Cruz: Poems.* London, 1975.

COLIN P. THOMPSON

JONES, INIGO (1573–1652), Stuart court architect, stage designer, and painter. Inigo Jones's early training was as a "picture maker" to the Manners family, and according to George Vertue he worked as an apprentice joiner in Saint Paul's churchyard. From 1598 Jones toured Europe, visiting Italy probably with Francis Manners, Lord Roos (1578–1632). During the summer of 1603 he went with the earl of Rutland to Denmark, where he prepared designs for Christian IV (ruled 1588–1648). On Jones's return to England in 1604 he collaborated with Ben Jonson on masques for the queen, Anne of Denmark (Christian's sister). He was employed by Robert Cecil, first earl of Salisbury, on the design for a New Exchange in the Strand, London (c. 1608, rejected in favor of Simon Basil's design) and a new tower to old Saint Paul's Cathedral (unbuilt).

In 1610 Jones was appointed surveyor of works to Henry, prince of Wales (1594–1612), who employed Jones and the Vitruvian engineers Constantino de' Servi and Salomon de Caus to replan Richmond garden upon Renaissance principles. Following the prince's unexpected death, in February 1613 Jones traveled to Heidelberg with Thomas Howard, second earl of Arundel (1585–1646), as part of the wedding party of James I's daughter, princess Elizabeth, subsequently journeying once more to Italy. In Venice he and Arundel met Andrea Palladio's pupil Vincenzo Scamozzi, although Jones famously noted in his copy of Palladio's *Quattro libri dell'architettura* (1601 ed., now at Worcester College, Oxford) that "this secrat[ive] Scamozio being purblind understoode nott" (I.xviii, p. 50). Jones made a systematic study of ancient monuments, evident from his annotations to his Palladio, which informed his study of the theory of *all'antica* architecture (building in the antique manner) and particularly the relationship between architectural and civil decorum (his library included works on moral philosophy by Xenophon, Aristotle, Alessandro Piccolomini, and Plutarch).

On their return in 1615 Jones was commissioned by Arundel to remodel his house at Greenwich (1615; destroyed 1617) and to design a gallery (c. 1615–1617) at Arundel House (destroyed 1678) in the Strand for the earl's collection of antique statuary. In September 1615 James I appointed Jones to be surveyor of the king's works, with the expectation that he give shape to James's ambition to remodel London as a second Rome and new Jerusalem, the fitting capital to a monarch cast in court sermons as the second Augustus and Solomon. London was considered the seat of the Protestant faith, a worthy successor to Catholic Rome. James's triumphal entry in 1604, celebrating his coronation the year before, was marked by a series of arches designed by a joiner, Stephen Harrison, which for the first time in London employed the *all'antica* architectural language that Jones was to introduce in more permanent architecture. Indeed the new imperial city aspired to by the Stuarts was in part defined by the triumphal route from Whitehall Palace down the Strand to Saint Paul's, along which significant sites—the New Exchange (c. 1608, unbuilt), Covent Garden (piazza begun 1631), Somerset House (1638, unbuilt), and Temple Bar (arch of 1636–1637, unbuilt)—were the subject of designs by Jones. This strategy of placing new buildings at significant points in the city mirrored the replanning of medieval Rome by Sixtus V in 1586, while reflecting the wider aspi-

Inigo Jones. Banqueting House. Jones built Banqueting House in Whitehall, London, from 1619 to 1622. BILDARCHIV FOTO MARBURG/ART RESOURCE

rations of contemporary ideal cities such as that by Tommaso Campanella, *La città del sole* (trans. *City of the Sun;* 1602), and of Stuart masques such as Jonson's *Love's Triumph through Callipolis* (1631).

In order to justify their succession, the Stuarts developed the Trojan ancestry cultivated by Tudor rulers, which equally justified the patronage of Renaissance arts, thus transformed into national emblems. Reflecting this cultivation of a heroic past, which embraced Arthur and Saint George, in 1620 Jones was instructed by James to survey Stonehenge. The origins of the enigmatic monument became the subject of Jones's only (posthumous) publication, the royal surveyor concluding in *Stone-Heng . . . Restored* (1655) that the monument's supposed underlying harmony "proved" its Romano-British ancestry—neatly in line with the self-image of the court and indeed the origins of his own *all'antica* architecture.

On his appointment to the royal surveyorship Jones had been commissioned to design the queen's house at Greenwich (1616–1638) for Queen Anne. When the queen died in 1619 the project was halted, with only the rusticated base having been completed, but following the accession of Charles I and Queen Henrietta Maria in 1625 work began anew on the villa, which was conceived as a retreat from Somerset House, the queen's official residence on the Strand. At the king's residence, Whitehall Palace, Jones designed a new Star Chamber (1617, unexe-

cuted) and his famous Banqueting House (1619–1622). The Banqueting House, a double cube with ceiling painted by Peter Paul Rubens (c. 1635), was intended as the setting for the court masque, an illusionistic Neoplatonic drama in which the king's policy was enacted and for which Jones provided numerous designs (now at Chatsworth House). Jones's movable perspective scenery—comprising either pivotal boards (*scena versatilis*) or, later, sliding shutters (*scena ductilis*)—developed Sebastiano Serlio's famous fixed scenes, published in 1545, and pioneered the proscenium-arch type of theater in Britain.

The Banqueting House was intended as a mere fragment of a much larger palace at Whitehall. Jones's "Preparatory" scheme (c. 1638), with later designs by Jones's assistant John Webb (1611–1672), would have projected the Stuart monarch's claim to be a new Solomon while rivaling the Escorial in Spain and the Louvre in France. The project remained a royalist fantasy, but a scheme equally grandiose was realized from 1633 onward at old Saint Paul's Cathedral. For here Jones resurfaced the huge nave walls with *all'antica* ornament and added a giant Corinthian portico to the west front, paid for by Charles I, as a fitting conclusion to the projected royal triumphal route. Work was abandoned in 1642 on the outbreak of civil war, however, when Jones's career was itself virtually ended.

Jones's use of *all'antica* architectural principles in Britain was in the wake of a limited and incoherent use of the orders on Elizabethan buildings. His architecture was intended to consolidate Stuart authority, a physical counterpart to the lawmaking powers of monarchy so much disputed by contemporaries. In developing a unique architectural expression for the Arthurian antiquity cultivated by his royal patrons, Jones surely deserves his famous title "Vitruvius Britannicus."

BIBLIOGRAPHY

Bold, John. *John Webb: Architectural Theory and Practice in the Seventeenth Century.* Oxford, U.K., and New York, 1989.

Cerutti Fusco, Annarosa. *Inigo Jones, Vitruvius Britannicus: Jones e Palladio nella cultura architettonica inglese, 1600–1740.* Rimini, Italy, 1985.

Gotch, John Alfred. *Inigo Jones.* London, 1928.

Harris, John, and Gordon Higgott. *Inigo Jones: Complete Architectural Drawings.* New York, 1989.

Harris, John, Stephen Orgel, and Roy Strong. *The King's Arcadia: Inigo Jones and the Stuart Court.* London, 1973.

Hart, Vaughan. *Art and Magic in the Court of the Stuarts.* London and New York, 1994.

Orgel, Stephen, and Roy C. Strong. *Inigo Jones: The Theatre of the Stuart Court.* 2 vols. London, 1973.

Orrell, John. *The Human Stage: English Theatre Design, 1567–1640.* Cambridge, U.K., 1988.

Orrell, John. *The Theatres of Inigo Jones and John Webb.* Cambridge, U.K., 1985.

Palme, Per. *Triumph of Peace: A Study of the Whitehall Banqueting House.* London, 1957.

Parry, Graham. *The Golden Age Restor'd: The Culture of the Stuart Court, 1603–42.* Manchester, U.K., 1981.

Peacock, John. *The Stage Designs of Inigo Jones: The European Context.* Cambridge, U.K., 1995.

Strong, Roy. *Britannia Triumphans: Inigo Jones, Rubens, and Whitehall Palace.* London, 1980.

Summerson, John. *Inigo Jones.* Harmondsworth, U.K., 1966.

Tavernor, Robert. *Palladio and Palladianism.* London, 1991.

VAUGHAN HART

JONSON, BEN (1572–1637), English poet and playwright. Ben Jonson was born on 11 June 1572, probably in or near London. He was a close friend of John Donne, who was born early that same year, and was eight years younger than Christopher Marlowe and William Shakespeare, both born in 1564. It is not certain that Jonson knew Marlowe, who died in 1593 as Jonson's theatrical career was just beginning, but Marlowe's influence on Jonson's early work is clearly evident. Jonson and Shakespeare were close and friendly rivals. Stories of their mutual antagonism stem largely from the imagination of eighteenth-century editors. Jonson's poem "To the Memory of My Beloved, the Author, Mr William Shakespeare, and What He Hath Left Us," printed at the head of Shakespeare's first folio (1623), pays generous tribute to the genius of his greatest contemporary.

Jonson told the Scottish poet William Drummond of Hawthornden, that his grandfather came from Annandale in Scotland; a member of the powerful border clan of Johnstones, he may have been taken prisoner by the English after the battle of Solway Moss in 1542, and brought south to Carlisle. His father, so Jonson reported, suffered imprisonment and forfeiture of his possessions on account of his beliefs during the reign of the Catholic queen Mary (1553–1558), and finally became a minister of religion. He died just a month before his son's birth. Jonson's mother eventually remarried, to a bricklayer named Robert Brett, and the new family moved to live in Hartshorn Lane near Charing Cross.

After attending a small private school in St. Martin's Church, Jonson was sent to Westminster School, where he had the good fortune to study under the great antiquary William Camden, whose influence he gratefully acknowledges in an affectionate poem (*Epigrams*, 14) and in the 1616 folio dedication to *Every Man in His Humour.* Among his contemporaries at Westminster were future diplomats, churchmen, statesmen, poets, and scholars such as Dudley Carleton, John Williams, Brian Duppa, Hugh Holland, Richard Corbett, and Robert Cotton, with whom Jonson maintained important friendships in later years. Jonson apparently did not go on to either of the universities, although according to a persistent rumor he resided briefly at St. John's College, Cambridge, before joining his stepfather in bricklaying work on new buildings then being erected at Lincoln's Inn: an occupation "he could not endure." He enlisted, probably in 1591, for service in the Low Countries, where the English were assisting the army of the Estates General in their revolt against the Spanish; and here, "in the face of both the Campes Killed ane Enimie," and took his arms and possessions from him.

Early Works. On his return to England, Jonson resumed his studies, and seems to have worked for a time as a strolling player, taking the part of the mad Hieronimo in Thomas Kyd's *The Spanish Tragedy.* In 1601 and 1602 the theater manager Philip Henslowe payed Jonson for writing "additions" to this immensely popular work, which evidently left a strong, though not entirely positive, impression on Jonson's mind: humorous and parodic references to Kyd's play recur throughout his later work. By 1594 Jonson was married, and was established as an actor

Ben Jonson. Portrait by Gerrit Honthorst (1590–1656).
CORBIS-BETTMANN

at Paris Garden, the Rose, and Newington Butts. He joined Pembroke's Men early in 1597, and by the middle of that year was working as one of Henslowe's authors.

His earliest surviving play, *The Case Is Altered,* was performed early in 1597; modeled on Roman comedy, it has dramatic elements that Jonson later ridiculed but to which he returned in his final years: cross-wooings, lost children, happy reunitings. With Thomas Nashe he wrote a (now lost) satirical comedy entitled *The Isle of Dogs* that was performed by Pembroke's Men at the new Swan playhouse in July 1597 and seems to have reflected a little too daringly on recent events in the royal palace of Greenwich, situated downriver opposite the Isle of Dogs. It provoked a sharp response from the Privy Council, which ordered the immediate closure of all of the London theaters, and issued warrants for the arrest of three of the principal actors in the play, Gabriel Spencer, Robert Shaa, and Jonson himself, who were dispatched to Marshalsea Prison; Nashe meanwhile had prudently fled town. Of Jonson's other collaboratively written plays from this early period, little survives apart from their titles: *Hot Anger Soon Cold*

(1598, with Henry Porter and Henry Chettle), *Page of Plymouth* (1599, with Thomas Dekker), and *Robert II, the King of Scots' Tragedy* (1599, with Dekker and Chettle). Other plays, both collaborative and single-authored, no doubt existed; for in 1598 Francis Meres in *Palladis Tamia* included Jonson's name in his list of English dramatists who are "our best for Tragedie," and Jonson himself later informed William Drummond "that the half of his comedies were not in Print."

In the autumn of 1598 Jonson scored his first major dramatic success with *Every Man in His Humour,* an intricately constructed urban comedy wittily exploiting then-fashionable notions of "humors," or character types. The play was performed at the Curtain Theater, Shoreditch, by Shakespeare's own company, the Lord Chamberlain's Men, with Shakespeare himself and the great Richard Burbage in leading roles. Jonson later rewrote the play, shifting its setting from Florence to London in order to sharpen its local application, and placed it at the very beginning of his 1616 folio, to exemplify his chosen new style of comedy, "When she would shew an Image of the times, / And sport with humane follies, not with crimes."

Jonson's success was overshadowed by personal troubles. While the play was apparently still in performance in late September 1598 he was arrested and tried for manslaughter after killing Gabriel Spencer, one of the actors with whom he had recently been imprisoned. He escaped the gallows narrowly by reading the so-called neck-verse (Psalms 51:1), but was branded on the thumb with a hot iron as a convicted felon. During this period of imprisonment Jonson was converted to Catholicism, probably by Father Thomas Wright, a learned Jesuit who had studied in Rome and Milan. A number of Jonson's poems from this time are addressed to fellow Catholics, or bear other marks of his newfound faith.

Every Man out of His Humour, further exploring the vein of humors comedy, was presented by the Lord Chamberlain's Men at the newly built Globe theater in 1599. Two more plays were performed by the Children of Queen Elizabeth's Chapel at the Blackfriars theater: *Cynthia's Revels, or The Fountain of Self-Love* (late 1600), a comedy somewhat in the style of John Lyly satirizing court follies in a manner that Jonson developed with greater sophistication over the next decade in his court masques and antimasques; and *Poetaster, or The Arraignment* (1601), a bristling account of poetry and politics in the Rome of the emperor Augustus—and, by implication, in the London of Queen Elizabeth's final years. Dekker's *Satiromastix* (1601), responding to this piece, presents in the character of Horace a vividly hostile picture of the young Ben Jonson as a self-promoting, "self-creating" literary figure, shooting his quills like a porcupine and flirting "inke in everie mans face."

Maturity. Jonson's Roman tragedy, *Sejanus His Fall,* was performed some time between January 1603 and March 1604 (though whether before or after the death of Elizabeth in March 1603 is far from certain). Shakespeare took a leading role, probably that of the emperor Tiberius. The play was not a theatrical success and brought Jonson into further trouble with the authorities: he was now summoned by the Privy Council at the earl of Northampton's instigation to answer charges "both of popperie and treason." The basis for these charges cannot easily be deduced from the 1605 quarto and 1616 folio texts of *Sejanus,* which differ, on Jonson's admission, from the play as originally performed. It is likely that some of the play's lines about the behavior of princes and court favorites were more sharply pointed in the now-lost text used by the actors.

Princes and courts were nonetheless exercising a powerful attraction on Jonson at that very moment. In 1603 he warmly greeted the accession of James I with an entertainment, a panegyrical address, and a scatter of admiring epigrams. Over the following years he consolidated his place as semiofficial poet to the new Stuart court with a series of elaborate masques and entertainments, working in fruitful though sometimes tempestuous collaboration with the designer Inigo Jones. Jonson's work from these years includes *The Masque of Blackness* (1605), *Hymenaei* and *The Entertainment of the Two Kings* (1606), *The Masque of Beauty* and *The Haddington Masque* (1608), and *The Masque of Queens* (1609). In 1997 the text of Jonson's *Entertainment at Britain's Burse* was discovered. Jonson wrote the work to celebrate the opening of Robert Cecil's grand shopping mall, New Exchange, in the presence of the king and queen in 1609.

Throughout this busy period Jonson led a curious double life. Although he was a favored playwright of the court, he was simultaneously the subject of repeated surveillance, interrogation, and arrest. He was summoned on several occasions to appear before the Consistory Courts on charges of recusancy, and was required to meet regularly with the dean of St. Paul's and the archbishop of Canterbury's chaplain to discuss and explain his religious beliefs. In the summer of 1605 he was imprisoned along with

George Chapman and John Marston "for writting something against the Scots in a play Eastward hoe," a comedy that makes gentle fun of the Scottish accents and James's lavish distribution of knighthoods to his Scottish followers. The original version of *Eastward Ho!,* like the original text of *Sejanus,* must have contained more serious satire, for the three authors feared they would have "their ears cutt & noses," and were released only after persistent petitioning to influential members of the court.

Later in 1605 Jonson was somewhat mysteriously caught up in the events surrounding the Gunpowder Plot of Guy Fawkes and others to destroy the houses of parliament at Westminster. Shortly before the discovery of the plot, Jonson is known to have attended a Catholic supper party with Robert Catesby and many of the conspirators; afterward he wrote a congratulatory poem to the plot's discoverer, William, Lord Monteagle (*Epigrams,* 60), and seems to have assisted Robert Cecil in obtaining information concerning the conspiracy from an anonymous priest. It has been conjectured that the Gunpowder Plot may in some sense be "shadowed" in Jonson's tragedy of 1611, *Catiline His Conspiracy,* but the similarities are of a general rather than a particular kind.

The series of threatening events that Jonson experienced in 1605 may have left a shadow of another kind, however, on his greatest and fiercest comedy, *Volpone,* performed by the King's Men at the Globe theater early in 1606 and later at the universities of Oxford and Cambridge. This dazzling account of fraud, seduction, legacy hunting, and judicial corruption in Renaissance Venice pushes constantly at the boundaries of comedic experience. Its severe conclusion—Mosca is sentenced to be whipped and "live perpetuall prisoner in our galleys," while Volpone is to be chained in prison till he is "sicke, and lame indeed"—stands in stark contrast to the more genial endings of Shakespearian comedy.

Epicene, or The Silent Woman was staged by the Children of Her Majesty's Revels at Whitefriars late in 1609 or early in 1610. The play has justly been described as "the first West End comedy." Its leisured and wittily discursive style anticipates the manner of George Etherege (1635?–?1692) and William Congreve (1670–1729), while its complex plotting—the surprises unfold up until the final moments—was praised by John Dryden (1631–1700). *The Alchemist,* a comedy even more brilliant in conception and construction, was presented in the summer of 1610 by the King's Men at the Blackfriars theater, in the very district of London in which the play's three confidence tricksters ply their vigorous trade:

spreading news of the recent discovery by a local alchemist of the fabled elixir, with its powers to confer eternal life and turn base metals into gold.

Anti-Catholic legislation in England was further tightened in 1610 after the assassination in Paris of King Henry IV. English recusants now found themselves facing an even stiffer range of civil penalties and restrictions. Jonson chose to return in this year to the Anglican church, drinking the entire chalice of wine at his first communion "in token of true Reconciliation." Piety and exuberance were similarly blended during his visit to Paris in 1613, where he listened to a theological disputation between Protestant and Catholic champions, boldly informed the learned Cardinal Jacques Davy Duperron that his translations of Virgil "were naught," and was carted, intoxicated, through the streets of Paris by the pupil of whom he was supposedly in charge, the mischievous son of Sir Walter Ralegh. A trace of this last episode may perhaps be found in Jonson's next comedy, *Bartholomew Fair* (1614), in which the irascible Humphrey Wasp, "governor" to the feckless young Bartholomew Cokes, is discovered in similarly embarrassing circumstances, which undermine his supposed authority.

The folio edition of Jonson's *Workes* published in London by William Stansby in 1616 proudly reveals the scale and range of Jonson's literary achievements up until his middle years. The volume, which Jonson supervised through the press with unusual care, includes two substantial collections of poems, *Epigrams* and *The Forest,* eight plays, the "Panegyre" addressed to King James in 1603, and a collection of masques, entertainments, and "barriers." Each major work is strategically dedicated to a patron, friend, or institution: William Camden; the Inns of Court; Esmé Stuart, Lord Aubigny; the Universities of Oxford and Cambridge; Sir Francis Stuart; Mary, Lady Wroth; William Herbert, earl of Pembroke.

Some of Jonson's contemporaries expressed surprise that mere play-texts—not at that time an esteemed kind of publication—should have been included in a volume whose title, *Workes,* appeared to promise graver matter. Jonson wanted to give his plays the dignity of classical texts and allow them to be studied with the kind of attention that the conditions of theatrical performance seemed all too often to prevent. He was presenting himself moreover as no mere "playwright"—a word just entering the language, which Jonson used only with disdain— but as a true Renaissance scholar, as versatile in his literary and intellectual range as in his social connections, standing at a crucial intersection between

Jonson's Works. Title page of the edition of 1616.
HENRY E. HUNTINGTON LIBRARY AND ART GALLERY

the court and the playhouse, the universities and the Inns of Court, and speaking with confidence and authority to each of these constituencies.

Earlier in 1616 Jonson had been rewarded with a life pension from the crown of a hundred marks per annum, a gesture that effectively marked his recognition, in fact if not in name, as the nation's poet laureate. With the death of Shakespeare that same year, Jonson clearly emerged as Britain's greatest living writer.

The Later Years.   Between *The Devil Is an Ass* (1616) and *The Staple of News* (1626) Jonson apparently wrote no plays for the theater. For the best part of a year, from the summer of 1618 to the summer of 1619, he disappeared entirely from London, taking a long walk up into Scotland via the Great North Road to visit the country of his forebears. His curiosity to see Scotland may have been stimulated in part by King James's return visit to Edinburgh in the summer of 1617 in the company of a huge retinue that included several of Jonson's patrons. Jonson journeyed alone and on foot, closely observing the northern countryside. He may have wagered on his chances of successfully completing the journey. During the winter of 1618–1619 he visited William Drummond at his romantically isolated castle on the river Esk, seven miles south of Edinburgh, gossiping there about books and friends and himself; the so-called *Conversations with Drummond* are the fullest surviving record of Jonson's life and opinions. Jonson planned to write a versified account of his Scottish travels, entitled *A Discovery,* along with "a fisher or Pastorall play" set on Loch Lomond, but these and other works were evidently destroyed in a fire that damaged his library in 1623—an event Jonson humorously laments in his poem "An Execration upon Vulcan" (*The Underwood,* 43).

In 1619 Jonson received an honorary degree from the University of Oxford, and appears to have stayed on for some time at Christ Church with his old friends from Westminster School, Brian Duppa and Richard Corbett. It has been suggested that at some stage thereafter he served as professor of rhetoric at Gresham College, London, where he is known to have been resident in 1623, deputizing perhaps for Henry Croke, who held that office from 1619 to 1627. Sections of Jonson's commonplace book, *Discoveries,* may perhaps represent notes for lectures that he delivered at the college. During this same period Jonson probably revised his translation of Horace's *Ars poetica* and completed his *English Grammar.*

Jonson continued over these years to write court masques and royal entertainments, the most popular of which was *The Gypsies Metamorphosed,* a high-spirited piece that was performed on three occasions in the late summer of 1621 at Burley-on-the-Hill, Belvoir, and Windsor. During the last years of James's reign, however, and especially after Charles I's accession in 1625, Jonson felt increasingly pushed to the margins of the court. His sense of alienation is evident in "An Epistle Answering to One That Asked to Be Sealed of the Tribe of Ben" (*The Underwood,* 47), written in 1623 while elaborate preparations were afoot in London and Southampton for the reception of Prince Charles's intended bride, Infanta Maria of Castile. Jonson's archrival Inigo Jones was playing a central role in these events; Jonson was not. Jonson consoles himself by describing another and superior social group, the "tribe of Ben," which met convivially under his presidency in the Apollo Room of the Devil and St. Dunstan Tavern near Temple Bar, with rules of conduct and standards of friendship more rigorous and exacting (the poem suggests) than those of the court itself.

Jonson's first new play in a decade, *The Staple of News* (1626), a satire on newsmongering, was staged at Blackfriars by the King's Men just a year after James's death. Charles's coronation is indeed referred to within the play, which deals explicitly and somewhat daringly with problems of succession and inheritance: how sons contrive to manage, or fatally mismanage, their fathers' fortunes. New systems of financial dealing and commodity transaction—the establishment of monopolies, the selling of profitable schemes and inventions (for the draining of the fens, the introduction of table forks, the marketing of political gossip)—held a particular fascination for Jonson. In *The Staple of News,* as in *The Devil Is an Ass,* he explores the phenomenon of "credit," the manner in which trust may be created and wealth generated through fast talk and deft negotiation: a system upon which the economic prosperity of Renaissance Europe was coming increasingly to depend, but which might also—in ways Jonson inventively conceived—be turned to dishonest ends.

Jonson must have felt his own credit ebbing at times throughout this final period of his life, along with his (always exiguous, often depleted) financial resources. In 1628, he suffered a stroke, which restricted his mobility and his powers of earning. Later in the same year he was made city chronologer in succession to Thomas Middleton, and was required "To collect and set down all memorable acts of this City and occurrences thereof," a duty he discharged with such inefficiency that payment was withheld for four years. His court pension was increased in 1630 from 100 marks to £100 per year (with the additional bonus of a tierce—42 gallons—of Canary wine from Charles's cellars at Whitehall), but payment of the pension was often tardy. Many of Jonson's poems from this period speak wittily and touchingly of his disabilities and his financial needs.

None of the comedies performed in the last decade of his life—*The New Inn* (1629), *The Magnetic Lady* (1632), *A Tale of a Tub* (1633)—was a theatrical success. It was once common to share Dryden's view of these plays as "dotages," and to regard the final decade of Jonson's career as impoverished in a creative as well as a material sense. In the late twentieth century Jonson's last plays attracted closer and more sympathetic attention. His final shift toward more rural and romantic themes was viewed by one critic (Anne Barton) as curiously "Shakespearian," a possible consequence of his reimmersion in Shakespeare's work while assisting John Heminges and Henry Condell to prepare the 1623 first folio.

Jonson died in August 1637 and was buried in Westminster Abbey, attended by a crowd that included "all or the greatest part of the nobilitie and gentry then in town." His death was a more notable public event than that of Shakespeare at Stratford-upon-Avon in 1616, which attracted little immediate comment or commemorative writing. A collection of poems in memory of Jonson, entitled *Jonsonus Virbius,* was published early in 1638 under the editorship of his old friend Brian Duppa, and a large two-volume folio edition of Jonson's own writings, prepared by his literary executor, Sir Kenelm Digby, followed in 1640–1641.

Evaluation and Reputation.   Jonson was commonly regarded throughout the seventeenth century as a writer whose powers were equal, if not superior, to those of Shakespeare. The range of his work was arguably greater than Shakespeare's, for it included not merely his plays but prose writings of an historical, philological, and philosophical nature, along with a large number of court masques and entertainments, and a substantial body of poems and classical translations. Through his prologues, epilogues, inductions (introductions), intermeans (dialogues or interludes between the acts of a play), and dedicatory epistles, apologetical dialogues, and through extended passages in *Discoveries,* he developed the most searching and systematic body of literary criticism to be found in England before the time of Dryden. In the true spirit of Renaissance humanism, he modeled his work—and to some extent, his life—on the finest classical models. He wished to become, through the independence of his social position and satirical stance, "the English Horace," and expressed deep admiration for the work of Virgil, Martial, Juvenal, Quintilian, Tacitus, Cicero, and Pliny. A skillful linguist and one of the finest Greek scholars of his day, he chose to write almost exclusively in the vernacular, and his "purity of language" was widely praised by later English poets.

During the eighteenth century his star began to wane. Audiences found his plays too harshly satirical and densely topical, and his masques, prose writings, and longer poems were generally neglected. Nineteenth-century readers found pleasure in his shorter lyrics, but little else. Throughout the twentieth century Jonson's reputation was slowly but perceptibly redeemed. His work is nowadays more widely and intelligently read, and several long-neglected plays, such as *The Devil Is an Ass* and *The New Inn,* have returned, surprisingly and triumphantly, to the theater. The reevaluation continues.

BIBLIOGRAPHY

Primary Works
The standard edition of Jonson's works is still that of C. H. Herford and Percy and Evelyn Simpson, eds., *Ben Jonson,* 11 vols. (Oxford, 1925–1952). A new print and electronic edition of the entire canon is currently being prepared under the general editorship of David Bevington, Martin Butler, and Ian Donaldson, for publication by Cambridge University Press in 2005. Good single-text editions of many of the plays are available in The Revels Plays series, published by Manchester University Press. *The Complete Masques* have been edited by Stephen Orgel for the Yale Ben Jonson (New Haven, Conn., and London, 1969). The poems and prose writings and two plays have been edited by Ian Donaldson, *Ben Jonson* (Oxford, 1985).

Secondary Works
Barish, Jonas. *Ben Jonson and the Language of Prose Comedy.* Cambridge, Mass., 1960.
Barton, Anne. *Ben Jonson: Dramatist.* Cambridge, U.K., 1984.
Brady, Jennifer, and W. H. Herendeen. *Ben Jonson's 1616 Folio.* Newark, Del., London, and Toronto, 1991
Burt, Richard. *Licensed by Authority: Ben Jonson and the Discourses of Censorship.* Ithaca, N.Y., and London, 1993.
Butler, Martin. *Theatre and Crisis 1632–1642.* Cambridge, U.K., 1984.
Craig, D. H. *Ben Jonson: The Critical Heritage.* London and New York, 1990.
Donaldson, Ian. *Jonson's Magic Houses.* Oxford, 1997.
Dutton, Richard. *Ben Jonson: To the First Folio.* Cambridge, U.K., 1983.
Evans, Robert C. *Ben Jonson and the Poetics of Patronage.* Lewisburg, Pa., London, and Toronto, 1989.
Fish, Stanley. "Authors-Readers: Jonson's Community of the Same." In *Representing the English Renaissance.* Edited by Stephen Greenblatt. Berkeley, Los Angeles, and London, 1988. Pages 231–263.
Helgerson, Richard. *Self-Crowned Laureates: Spenser, Jonson, Milton, and the Literary System.* Berkeley and Los Angeles, 1983.
Jones, Emrys. "The First West End Comedy." *Proceedings of the British Academy* 68 (1982): 215–258.
Kay, W. David. *Ben Jonson: A Literary Life.* Basingstoke, U.K., 1995.
Loewenstein, Joseph. "The Script in the Marketplace." In *Representing the English Renaissance.* Edited by Stephen Greenblatt. Berkeley, Los Angeles, and London, 1988. Pages 265–278.
Orgel, Stephen. *The Jonsonian Masque.* Cambridge, Mass., 1965.
Peterson, Richard S. *Imitation and Praise in the Poems of Ben Jonson.* New Haven, Conn., and London, 1981.
Riggs, David. *Ben Jonson: A Life.* Cambridge, Mass., 1989.
Slights, William W. E. *Ben Jonson and the Art of Secrecy.* Toronto, Buffalo, and London, 1994.
Womack, Peter. *Ben Jonson.* Oxford, 1986.

IAN DONALDSON

JOOS VAN CLEVE.   *See* **Cleve, Joos van.**

JOSQUIN DES PREZ (family name, Lebloitte; c. 1450–1521), French composer active in Italy. Josquin was probably born in northern France and trained as a choirboy in Saint-Quentin. In 1466 his aunt and uncle named him as heir to their property in Condé-sur-l'Escaut. Once identified as Juschinus de Picardia, a singer at Milan cathedral (1459–1472) and in the chapel of Duke Galeazzo Maria Sforza (1473–1476), newly discovered documents reveal that this is another musician altogether. Josquin probably received training in the 1460s and 1470s in France under Johannes Ockeghem, for whom he composed a lament, *Nymphes des bois.*

His first documented employment was in Aix-en-Provence in 1477–1478 under René, duke of Anjou (1434–1480), in whose service he remained perhaps until 1480, when René died and his singers transferred to the court of King Louis XI (ruled 1461–1483). Contact with Louis is suggested by *Misericordias Domini,* a motet on psalm verses associated with the king. In 1483 Josquin returned to Condé, his first visit since the French Wars had begun in 1477. Subsequent patrons include Cardinal Ascanio Sforza in Milan and Rome (1484–1485), and probably Ludovico Sforza "il Moro" in Milan (c. 1485–1489). Josquin sang in the papal chapel from 1489 to 1495 (perhaps longer), and then in 1498–1499 he apparently reentered Ascanio Sforza's service. Around 1500 he returned to France to serve King Louis XII (ruled 1498–1515), for whom he composed the psalm motet *Memor esto verbi tui.* In 1503 he was hired by Duke Ercole I d'Este of Ferrara at an enormous salary of 200 ducats; after one year's service he retired to Condé as provost of the collegiate church of Notre Dame.

Josquin wrote eighteen masses, some fifty motets (another fifty are spurious), and seventy secular works, mostly French chansons, but also three Italian songs and some instrumental pieces. He mastered techniques developed by predecessors such as Guillaume Dufay and Ockeghem, but he also forged a new style that influenced composers for a century after his death. The old techniques emphasize musical structure over the words, and include strict canon, cantus firmus (a preexisting melody in long notes in the tenor), and fixed song forms. The new style reflects the influence of humanist thought by its streamlining of melodic lines so that they clearly declaim the words, and by the attempt to make the music express the affect of the text. The old manner occurs in *Missa "L'homme armé" super voces musicales,* which takes a French song as cantus firmus and features several complex canons. Josquin pro-vided a new twist on an old device in the *Missa "Hercules dux Ferrarie"* by deriving the tenor cantus firmus from the vowels in the duke of Ferrara's name (*e u e u e a i e = re ut re ut re fa mi re*). *Missa "Pange lingua"* represents the new style: here Josquin dispenses with a cantus firmus, opting instead for equal melodic importance by paraphrasing the chant in each of the voices, which enter one after the other in imitation.

Many of Josquin's motets feature texts in honor of the Blessed Virgin Mary, and some, such as *Stabat mater,* employ a cantus firmus, but his most progressive works are settings of the psalms. Among these, *Miserere mei, Deus* (Ps. 50), commissioned by Ercole d'Este in 1503, stands out. The lapidary melodies, frequent use of alternating duets, and emphatic refrain on the words "miserere mei, Deus" all unite to project the text with startling clarity.

Similar stylistic development appears in the secular works, an early example of which is the three-voice *Que vous madame,* based on a Latin cantus firmus and in the fixed song form of the bergerette. A late work is the four-voice *Mille regretz;* here, economy of melodic ideas, subtle contrasts of texture, and plaintive tonality create a memorable effect of melancholy. The song, a favorite of Emperor Charles V, suggests how Martin Luther came to single out Josquin as "the master of the notes."

BIBLIOGRAPHY

Primary Works
Werken van Josquin des Prez. Edited by Albert Smijers et al. Amsterdam, 1921–1967.
The New Josquin Edition. Edited by Willem Elders et al. Utrecht, Netherlands, 1987–.

Secondary Works
Charles, Sydney R. *Josquin des Prez: A Guide to Research.* New York, 1983.
Lowinsky, Edward E., ed. *Josquin des Prez: Proceedings of the International Josquin Festival-Conference.* London, 1976.
Osthoff, Helmuth. *Josquin Desprez.* 2 vols. Tutzing, Germany, 1962–1965.
Sherr, Richard, ed. *The Josquin Companion.* Oxford, 2000.

PATRICK MACEY

JOYEUSE, ANNE DE (1560–1587), admiral of France and mignon (favorite) of Henry III. Descended from a family of old noble lineage from the Vivarais in Languedoc whose parents belonged to the "secondary nobility" of provincial France, Anne de Joyeuse enjoyed a short, but meteoric, career at the court of Henry III.

After studying at the Collège de Navarre in Paris, he served in the royal armies, mainly in Languedoc, in the French civil wars of the 1570s. Like Jean-Louis de Nogaret Epernon, his rival and relative (Joyeuse's brother and sister would marry Epernon's siblings), he was rewarded for his expressions of total obedience and devotion.

Joyeuse was initially given the command of a cavalry company and made governor of Mont St.-Michel. Subsequently, he served in the royal army at La Fère in 1580 and was badly wounded in the face. The king responded by elevating his viscounty of Joyeuse into a ducal peerage in April 1581 and arranging his marriage to his own sister-in-law, Marguerite de Lorraine-Vaudémont. The king promised a huge dowry and gave the new duke a substantial landed fortune at Limours in Languedoc. The following year, the king purchased the admiralty for Joyeuse from the duke of Mayenne. In 1583 he obtained the government of Normandy and, in 1584, that of Le Havre and the duchy of Alençon. His relatives, particularly his brother François (who was made a cardinal), participated in the largesse. Jealousy between Epernon and Joyeuse surfaced at court in the beginnings of the Catholic League in 1585, and Epernon actively sought the command of the royal forces to fight the Protestants in the southwest. After some initial successes in 1586, Joyeuse was killed in cold blood by the forces of Henry of Navarre at Coutras on 20 October 1587, a major political reversal for the king in the face of the Catholic League.

See also **Epernon, Jean-Louis de Nogaret, duc d'.**

BIBLIOGRAPHY

Chevallier, Pierre. *Henri III.* Paris, 1985.

Vaissière, Pierre de. *Messieurs de Joyeuse.* Paris, 1926.

MARK GREENGRASS

JUAN DE ÁVILA (1499?–1569), Spanish preacher, educator, religious reformer, saint. The "apostle of Andalusia" Juan de Ávila was born in Almodóvar del Campo to a family of Jewish converts to Christianity. As a young man he studied at the University of Alcalá de Henares—sixteenth-century Spain's center of humanist learning—reading the work of the scholar Erasmus of Rotterdam and other Christian humanists who called for a simpler, internalized Christian faith. Juan de Ávila applied their ideas to a wide range of missionary endeavors during his long career as an itinerant preacher in southern Spain.

To Juan de Ávila, spiritual rejuvenation within the Catholic church depended above all upon the establishment of effective systems of moral education for laity and clergy alike. He was among the principal Spanish advocates of teaching prayers in the vernacular rather than in Latin, and he wrote a popular catechism in rhyming couplets for children.

Even more important to Juan de Ávila was training parish clergymen to be shining examples of Christian morality. Toward this end, he established fifteen schools for future priests throughout southern Spain. In their emphasis on humanistic studies and moral training, these schools profoundly influenced the subsequent development of Jesuit educational institutions both in Spain and across Catholic Europe. In addition, Juan de Ávila wrote two lengthy tracts to the Council of Trent (1545–1563) in which he proposed specific educational and institutional reforms, and his ideas provided much of the basis for the council's landmark 1563 decree mandating for the first time the establishment of seminaries in every Catholic diocese.

Spanish religious reformers of all sorts frequently sought his advice on educational and spiritual matters. His correspondents and advisees included the founder of the Society of Jesus, Ignatius Loyola; the Carmelite reformer and influential mystic Teresa of Ávila; and the popular spiritual author Luís de Granada. Juan de Ávila was among the key figures in the translation of Christian humanist spiritual and educational ideals into long-lasting institutions of the Catholic church. He was canonized by Pope Paul VI in 1970.

BIBLIOGRAPHY

Primary Work

Ávila, Juan de. *Obras completas del santo maestro Juan de Ávila.* Edited by Luis Sala Balust and Francisco Martín Hernández. 2d ed. 6 vols. Madrid, 1970–1971.

Secondary Works

Bilinkoff, Jodi. *The Ávila of Saint Teresa: Religious Reform in a Sixteenth-Century City.* Ithaca, N.Y., 1989. Includes detailed examination of the influence of Juan de Ávila's work on religious reformers in one Spanish city.

Coleman, David. "Moral Formation and Social Control in the Catholic Reformation: The Case of San Juan de Ávila." *Sixteenth Century Journal* 26 (1995): 17–30.

DAVID COLEMAN

JUDAH LOEW BEN BEZALEL. *See* **Maharal of Prague.**

JUDAISM. *See* **Jewish Messianism; Jews,** *subentry on* **Jewish Religious Life; Rabbis.**

JUDEO-ITALIAN. Jit, also called *latino* and *volgare* by native users, is a variety of Italian found in Jewish texts from the tenth to the seventeenth centuries in Italy, and from the sixteenth through the eighteenth centuries in the Jewish community of Corfu. In essence, Jit was a koiné, or standardized language, that the various Jewish communities throughout Italy employed as a common literary vehicle, and which underwent an evolution parallel to standard Italian. Its literary usage declined by the end of the sixteenth century, but it survived in the local dialects spoken in the ghettos. Although Jit does not emerge from any specific dialect, its features reflect the demographic and cultural trends of the Jewish population in medieval Italy, which was primarily located in the southern and south-central regions of the peninsula, with important centers in Rome and Puglia.

The earliest traces of Jit appear as glosses. Glossing (the use of vernacular words to define obscure terminology) was widely practiced in medieval Romance culture. The earliest known author to make use of Jit glosses was Shabbetai Donnolo (913–c. 982), who included them to explain philosophic terms in his *Sefer hakhmoni* (Book of the wise). In the eleventh century, Nathan ben Jehiel of Rome (1035–c. 1110) compiled a number of Jit glosses in his *Arukh* (Thesaurus), a lexicon of the Talmud. During the same century French authors such as Joseph Kara and Rashi, as well as the Provençal authors David Kimhi, Isaac ben Abba Mari of Marseilles, and Aaron ha-Kohen, began including Old French and Provençal glosses in their commentaries on the Bible and on Jewish law. Some of these glosses would later make their way into Jit translations of the Bible, suggesting a network of exchange between Romance-speaking Jewish communities.

An important body of glosses is found in philosophical literature. About 1250 Moses da Salerno compiled a glossary to Moses Maimonides's *Guide of the Perplexed*. Judah Romano (1292–1330?) was especially active in the field of philosophy. In addition to acquainting Jewish scholars with such authors as Averroes, Thomas Aquinas, Boethius, and Aegidius Colonna, Romano composed a Jit glossary of philosophical terms in Maimonides's *Mishneh Torah* and translated into Jit several philosophical sections of Dante's *Paradise*. Interestingly, Immanuel of Rome (c. 1260–c. 1328), who was cousin to Romano, composed a small corpus of poetry consisting mainly of sonnets written in the literary Tuscan of his time (Immanuel is also the author of a Hebrew work called *Mahbarot* [Notebooks], in which he parallels Dante's trip through Purgatory and Paradise). The *Mikdash me'at* (The lesser temple) by Moses da Rieti (1388–1460?), inspired by Dante's *Paradise* as well as Petrarch's *Triumphs,* and composed in Hebrew in

terza rima, is a parodic journey through the science and philosophy of Rieti's time. Manuscript copies of the work contain Jit glosses attributed to Rieti.

Manuscripts from the fourteenth and fifteenth centuries respectively carry Jit translations of the Song of Solomon and of the latter prophets. The Jit practice of glossing the Bible probably originated in the tenth or eleventh century. A number of compendia of Jit glosses exist, the earliest printed one being the *Makre Dardake* (Naples, 1488). Some of the glosses strongly suggest a knowledge of Judeo-French and Judeo-Provençal glossary traditions, but the Italian traditions differ in that they would develop into complete translations of the Bible. Such translations were calques, or word-for-word translations from Hebrew, and were typically used to introduce young children to both the Hebrew language and Bible studies. Containing passages from non-Jewish Italian versions dating from the first half of the fourteenth century, they probably originated during the same period. The first Jit prayer books, typically used by women, probably also come from this period. The earliest known and most significant original literary work in Jit is the *Elegy for the Ninth of Av,* which linguistically dates from the first half of the thirteenth century. The *Elegy* recounts the fall of Jerusalem and the subsequent exile of Jews into Babylonia, and is noteworthy not only as one of the earliest extant pieces of Italian literature but also for its metrical scheme, which is unlike those used elsewhere in Italian and Romance poetry.

From the first half of the sixteenth century on, Jewish vernacular literature underwent a linguistic shift. Literary Italian became the language of choice in terms of both grammar and vocabulary; only the use of Hebrew characters and, to a lesser degree, the use of calque in translations endured. The advent of the Renaissance brought a number of factors that caused this decline. As the writings of Immanuel of Rome and Moses da Rieti illustrate, Jews were in direct contact not only with Italian literature but also with contemporary linguistic trends. Perhaps the most significant of these trends is the debate on the Italian language, which began in the fifteenth century and attempted to unify and impose a linguistic standard on literary Italian. The *Hymn for the Sabbath* by Mordecai Dato (1525–1591/1601), and his epic version of the story of Esther, as well as the translations by Leon Modena of the *Haggadah* (Venice, 1609), are examples of Italian works transcribed in Hebrew characters. Indeed, the two works by Dato were composed in rima ottava, a rhyme scheme that was particularly popular in the works of

Ludovico Ariosto and Torquato Tasso, both of whom were employed by the Estense court in Ferrara, where Dato officiated as rabbi. By the turn of the seventeenth century, authors such as Deborah Ascarelli had abandoned even the practice of Hebrew transcription and composed original works and translations for the Jewish community entirely in Roman characters.

BIBLIOGRAPHY

Primary Works

Cassuto, Umberto. "Un'antichissima elegia in dialetto giudeo-italiano." *Archivio Glottologico Italiano* 22–23 (1929): 349–408.

Dato, Mordecai. "Un hymne sabbatique du seizième siècle en judéo-italien." Edited by Cecil Roth. *Revue des Études Juives* 80 (1925): 60–80, 182–206; 81: 55–78.

Dato, Mordecai. *La istoria de Purim io ve racconto.* Edited by Giulio Busi. Bologna, Italy, 1987.

Elegia giudeo-italiana (Judeo-Italian elegy for the ninth of Av). Vol. 1 of *Poeti del Duecento.* Edited by Gianfranco Contini. La Letteratura Italiana, Storia e Testi, no. 2. Milan and Naples, 1960.

Rieti, Moses da. *Filosofia naturale e Fatti de Dio.* Edited by Irene Hijmans-Tromp. Leiden, Netherlands, 1989.

Secondary Works

Massariello-Merzagora, Giovanna. *Giudeo-italiano.* Profilo dei dialetti italiani, no. 23. Pisa, Italy, 1977.

Wexler, Paul. *Judeo-Romance Linguistics: A Bibliography.* New York, 1989.

SETH JERCHOWER

Pope Julius II. Titian's copy of the portrait by Raphael.
PALAZZO PITTI, FLORENCE/ALINARI/ART RESOURCE

JULIUS II (Giuliano della Rovere; c. 1445–1513), pope (1503–1513). Giuliano della Rovere was born in Albissola, near Savona, probably in 1445. He owed his career to the patronage of his uncle Francesco della Rovere, who may well have arranged for his education at a Franciscan friary in Perugia. Four months after his uncle had been elected pope as Sixtus IV, Giuliano was made a cardinal, on 15 December 1471. Among the benefices he was granted by Sixtus was the major see of Avignon in 1474. This appointment led to his being sent as papal legate there in 1476, and in 1480–1482 he was sent as legate to France and the Low Countries; both legations gave him experience of the difficulties of diplomatic negotiations and of the imperfect protection and respect accorded to high dignitaries of the papal court outside Rome. Another legation, to repress factional fighting in Umbria in the Papal States in 1474, revealed his taste for soldiering. Physically robust and energetic, he yearned for action; this characteristic, exacerbated by his hot temper and lack of tact (and occasional lack of political judgment), brought down on him criticism and some mockery. Although his influence over his uncle was limited, even as pope he recalled with pride that he was the nephew of Sixtus IV.

He had far more influence at first over the succeeding pope, Innocent VIII (reigned 1484–1492), whom he encouraged into a war in support of rebellious Neapolitan barons in 1485. When the war went badly and Innocent agreed to peace in 1486, Giuliano della Rovere was no longer so dominant but remained on friendly terms with the pope. He was no friend to Innocent's successor, Alexander VI (reigned 1492–1503), and soon became the focus of opposition among the cardinals. By 1494 he felt unsafe in Rome and in April sailed for France. There he encouraged the young Charles VIII to press on with plans for an expedition to claim the kingdom of Naples. He accompanied Charles on his campaign in 1494–1495 and returned to France with him. He did not see Rome again during Alexander's lifetime, spending most of his time in northwest Italy.

The decisive factor in his election as pope on 31 October 1503 (after the brief pontificate of Pius III) was probably his strength of character and reputation for defending the interests of the church. His first concern was to recover lands taken in the Romagna by Venice, but he could wrest only some of them back. He also wanted to establish closer control over Perugia and Bologna, which had been dominated by the Baglioni and the Bentivoglio families, respectively. This he accomplished by an expedition that he led personally in 1506. To recover the remaining lands held by Venice, Julius joined Louis XII of France, Ferdinand of Aragon, and the emperor-elect, Maximilian I, in the League of Cambrai in March 1509. The hard-pressed Venetians came to terms with him in February 1510, restoring all the lands they still held in the Romagna. But the war continued, with Julius now fighting his former allies. To oversee the campaign, he based himself at Bologna; after he left in May 1511, the Bolognese rebelled. In October 1511, Julius concluded the Holy League with Venice and the Spanish king, Ferdinand. The crushing defeat of the league's forces at Ravenna on 11 April 1512 was a heavy blow for Julius, but the French troops were demoralized by their losses in the battle and soon withdrew from the Romagna and Bologna; and so Julius was triumphant. He died on 20 February 1513.

Julius's personal involvement in wars earned him his reputation as the warrior pope. He was portrayed in this guise in the anonymous satire *Julius Exclusus* (generally attributed to Erasmus), in which he arrives at the gates of heaven at the head of an army and is refused admission. Although he sincerely believed that he was acting in the best interests of the church, his military exploits damaged the spiritual prestige of the papacy. But he did successfully counter the threat of the Council of Pisa-Milan-Asti-Lyon, summoned by dissident cardinals at the behest of Louis XII and Maximilian I in 1511. This prompted him to convene the fifth Lateran Council, which opened on 3 May 1512.

Julius was one of the most important artistic patrons of the Renaissance. Among his major commissions was the Belvedere courtyard of the Vatican, designed by Donato Bramante and begun in 1505. From 1508 he had Raphael paint frescoes, including the *School of Athens,* in two of his new Vatican apartments, later known as the Stanza della Segnatura and the Stanza d' Eliodoro, and had Michelangelo paint the Sistine Chapel ceiling (1508–1512). He began the destruction of the old St. Peter's and the construction of the new one by commissioning Bramante to build a new choir. His portrait by Raphael (1511–1512) influenced the iconography of papal portraiture for centuries. The project for the tomb he commissioned from Michelangelo was never completed but gave rise to some of Michelangelo's finest sculpture, including *Moses.*

BIBLIOGRAPHY

Primary Work
Erasmus, Desiderius. *Julius Excluded from Heaven: A Dialogue.* Translated and annotated by Michael J. Heath. In *Collected Works of Erasmus.* Vol. 27. Edited by A. H. T. Levi. Toronto, 1986. Pages 155–197.

Secondary Works
Partridge, Loren, and Randolph Starn. *A Renaissance Likeness: Art and Culture in Raphael's* Julius II. Berkeley, Calif., 1980.
Shaw, Christine. *Julius II, the Warrior Pope.* Oxford, 1993.

CHRISTINE SHAW

JURISPRUDENCE. *See* **Law.**

JUSTICE. *See* **Crime and Punishment; Law.**

KABBALAH. The sixteenth-century Jewish spiritual renaissance expressed itself in a variety of religious literatures, most prominent among them being Kabbalah, the name used for a variety of mystical schools emerging in western Europe since the late twelfth century. While the beginning of this renaissance was concomitant with the destruction of the Spanish Jewish center when the Jews were expelled from Spain in 1492, it nonetheless was also contemporaneous with the Renaissance in Italy and then in Europe at large.

Different kabbalistic currents were active in Renaissance Italy. The first current was the Italian Kabbalah perpetuated in this period by Jews. The second one consisted of kabbalistic writings by Spanish Kabbalists, and of some Spanish Kabbalists themselves, who arrived in Italy immediately before and more after the 1492 expulsion. The third current was the Christian Kabbalah, which originated in the middle of the 1480s and grew dramatically during the sixteenth century. Somewhat later was the arrival in Italy of the Palestinian types of Kabbalah beginning in the second third of the sixteenth century. The developments of these currents and their interactions are the main factors in the history of Kabbalah in Renaissance Italy.

The Italian Kabbalah. The Jewish Kabbalah of Italian extraction had been committed to writing during the late thirteenth and fourteenth centuries. This Kabbalah consisted, initially, of the ecstatic Kabbalah of Abraham Abulafia and his followers, and of the theosophical-theurgical Kabbalah of Menahem Recanati. Most of their manuscripts were copied in Italy, and they constituted the basis for many of the kabbalistic writings among Jewish and Christian authors in the late fifteenth century. In the late 1470s some young Jewish intellectuals started to pay much greater attention to Kabbalah than anyone had in the previous century and a half. They studied Kabbalah from written documents, apparently because of the lack of accomplished Kabbalists. Characteristic of this type of Kabbalah since its emergence was its strong exoteric propensity, which differed from the esoteric thrust of Spanish Kabbalah: the initiators of this current assumed that the contents of Kabbalah should be taught in public, or at least committed to writing in a manner that a learned person would be able to understand without being initiated in an oral tradition or receiving restricted information.

This exoteric attitude was adopted by Renaissance Jewish authors like Yohanan Alemanno, David ben Judah Messer Leon, Abraham de Balmes, Isaac de Lattes, and Abraham Yagel. Like Abulafia and a few Spanish Kabbalists, they conceived Kabbalah as a philosophical discipline. This attitude was important for creating a discourse that facilitated the acceptance of the Jewish Kabbalah by some Christian intellectuals. Like the Christian Kabbalah, the Italian Kabbalah also emphasized the magical aspects of this lore, aspects found much earlier but accentuated by Renaissance thinkers like Yohanan Alemanno and Abraham Yagel.

The Spanish Kabbalah. To a great extent, the Italian Kabbalah can be described as much more universalistic than the second current, the Spanish Kabbalah. From the end of the fourteenth century,

Kabbalah in Spain moved toward an increasingly particularistic direction, which entailed a critique, sometimes very sharp, of philosophy, science, and Christianity. With the arrival in Italy of the expellees from the Iberian Peninsula, frictions between the exoteric-universalistic and the esoteric-particularistic forms of Kabbalah became explicit. So, for example, Judah Hayyat, one of the most important Kabbalists among the expellees, criticized the Italians' concern with the writings of Abulafia and other philosophically oriented Kabbalists. The arrival of the Spaniards introduced the *Sefer ha-Zohar,* (Book of splendor), the most important classic of Kabbalah, whose impact started to become more evident only in the second third of the sixteenth century. Spanish Kabbalists like Joseph ibn Shraga, apparently active in Agrigento, became teachers of important Italian Kabbalists, such as Moses ben Mordecai Bassola. The publication of kabbalistic books from the 1520s testifies to the growing impact of the Spanish writings. Although Recanati's kabbalistic writings were among the first printed, the share of Spanish Kabbalah among the printed kabbalistic books is quite conspicuous. Shem Tov ben Shem Tov's antiphilosophical *Sefer ha-'Emunot* (Book of beliefs), the double printing of *Sefer Ma'arekhet ha-'Elohut* (Book of the system of divinity) with the lengthy commentary of Yehudah Hayyat in 1558, and the printing of the book of the *Zohar* constitute the most powerful emblems of the massive reception of this current in Italy.

However, even the printing of the *Zohar* evinces some of the tensions between the two currents: the inclination of Italian Kabbalists to exotericism was instrumental in the decision to print those books, against the more esoteric Spanish propensity, and in the debate that accompanied the printing of the *Zohar,* the clash between the two attitudes is evident. Not surprisingly, one of those who encouraged the printing was Guillaume Postel (1510–1581), one of the most important Christian Kabbalists.

The Christian Kabbalah. Concomitant with the renewed interest in Kabbalah at the end of the fifteenth century was the emergence of the Christian Kabbalah in Florence with Flavius Mithridates's massive translations of kabbalistic material—a substantial part of it from Jewish Italian Kabbalah—into Latin. Giovanni Pico della Mirandola, and following him a host of other Christian intellectuals in Europe, started to appropriate significant parts of the kabbalistic literature, most of it studied in translation. Indeed, at the beginning of the sixteenth century,

this yearning for the allegedly ancient Jewish lore took special forms, as Menahem Elijah Halfan of Venice testified:

> Especially after the rise of the sect of Luther, many of the nobles and scholars of the land [namely the Christians] sought to have a thorough knowledge of this glorious science [Kabbalah]. They have exhausted themselves in this search, because among our people there are but a small number of men expert in this wisdom, for after the great numbers of troubles and expulsions, but a few remain. So seven learned men [Christians] grasp a Jewish man by the hem of his garment and say: "Be our master in this science!" (Ruderman, *Essential Papers on Jewish Culture,* p. 108)

The most obvious change introduced by the Christian Kabbalists was the Christological interpretation of some elements in the Jewish Kabbalah. The Christian scholars used several modes of Jewish, kabbalistic, exegetical devices, especially combinations of letters and symbolic exegesis. Their main intention was to show that Kabbalah was less a Jewish lore than a veiled Christian theology. Since Kabbalah was conceived by both Jews and Christians as an ancient tradition originating long before the emergence of Christianity—what is called a *prisca theologia,* or ancient theology—it became important, from the polemical point of view, to demonstrate that Christological hints can be found even in the most esoteric Jewish traditions.

Christological topics were introduced into Jewish material in two main ways, the theological and the linguistic. The former resorted to the concept of the Christ in order to interpret the realm of the ten *sefirot* (divine numbers), which is intermediary between the hidden deity and the created world. This realm was described already by the earliest of the Jewish Kabbalists as having an anthropomorphical structure better known as *adam qadmon* (primordial man) or *adam elyon* (supernal man). The Christian Kabbalists easily translated this anthropomorphic schema into a Christological structure, identifying the mediatory system of *sefirot* with Christ. Although the anthropomorphic imagery was part and parcel of the theosophical-theurgical Kabbalah from the beginning of this lore, Jewish Kabbalists have very rarely drawn the configuration of the ten *sefirot* in an anthropomorphic manner; none of the Jewish Kabbalists, at least until the Renaissance, used anthropomorphic designs, though such literary imagery occurs without any theological inhibitions. The system of the ten was apparently designed in an anthropomorphic manner for the first time in the Christian Kabbalah. Eventually, probably not until the seventeenth century, occasional use of this pattern entered Jewish Kabbalah.

Christian Kabbalists also decoded in Christian terms a major secret of Jewish esotericism, namely the nature of the divine name or tetragrammaton. In Jewish mysticism the secret of the tetragrammaton lies in the peculiar, but allegedly unknown, vocalization of the four known consonants of the divine name. The problem of the pronunciation of the tetragrammaton was a major issue, as it was part of the ancient ritual of the high priest on the Day of Atonement. The first Christian Kabbalists, especially Johann Reuchlin (1455–1522), solved the problem by introducing a "small" though decisive change in the Hebrew form of spelling the tetragrammaton so that it would point to the name of Jesus. The four letters were divided into two units by introducing in the middle the letter *shin,* so that the Hebrew tetragrammaton became a pentagrammaton, YHShVH, spelling Yehoshuah, or Jesus. Thus the secret of Jewish esotericism was construed as pointing to the Christ. Christian Kabbalah, therefore, began with identifying the main Christological themes in kabbalistic speculations, both in the sefirotic realm, which represents a mode of theological thinking characteristic of the theosophical Kabbalah, and in connection to the divine name, which is one of the major subjects of the ecstatic Kabbalah.

The second major metamorphosis of Jewish Kabbalah is related to an unprecedented emphasis—actually an overemphasis—on the importance of the Jewish exegetical devices already found in Jewish kabbalistic texts. From the late thirteenth century, Jewish Kabbalah employed a great variety of exegetical devices as part of a greater hermeneutical enterprise; the mystical reinterpretation of the Jewish canonical writings and rituals. The Christian Kabbalists focused their interest on Jewish hermeneutics because they viewed the exegetical techniques of Kabbalah as a way to read not only kabbalistic texts but also the Bible Christologically. For them, it was convenient to resort to these extraordinarily flexible exegetical devices in order to demonstrate issues important for Christian theology. Thus a reader perusing most of the important Christian kabbalistic texts will find lengthy discussions of hermeneutics, including the meaning of *notariqon* or acronym, *tzerufei 'otiyyot* or combinations of letters, and lists of kabbalistic symbols. Only by mastering the exegetical methods of the Jewish Kabbalists could the Christians hope to convince Jews of the veracity of the Christian claims.

When the kabbalistic hermeneutics was introduced into Christian circles, a plethora of Christian themes were injected into the Hebrew Bible—and into kabbalistic texts like the *Zohar.* The shift to conceiving hermeneutics as a major concern, rather than a secondary interest, as in Jewish sources, is characteristic of Christian Kabbalah. This emphasis is demonstrated by the largest, most detailed, and most illuminating treatise on kabbalistic hermeneutics, which was composed at the middle of the sixteenth century in France by Nicolas Le Fèvre de La Boderie.

Kabbalah in the Land of Israel. The fourth important current active in Renaissance Kabbalah is the different schools developing in the land of Israel. First in Jerusalem and then in Safed, numerous Jewish Kabbalists construed a variety of kabbalistic systems, which had a great impact beyond their immediate environment. Most, if not all, were aware of the developments in Italy, as Abraham ben Eliezer ha-Levi, a messianically oriented Kabbalist in Jerusalem, demonstrated in the early 1520s in his *Commentary on the Prophecies of a Child:*

> In my opinion there is a danger sending to you this commentary, since we were told that our brethren, the sons of Essau [the Christians], study Hebrew and these matters are ancient, and whoever will write anything there, it may, God forfend, fall in their hands. And despite the fact that those who study are faithful to us, nevertheless it is reasonable and compelling to conceal these matters from them and there is also a severe ban concerning it. In any case, I have refrained from sending to you these treatises constituting the *Epistle of the Secret of the Redemption* and you, my masters those who conceal the wisdom and the secret of the Lord are to the fearers of God, [who are] the participants in the covenant will contemplate it (namely the secret), but this will not be accessible to every gentile. (quoted in David, p. 59)

This passage is a fine example of the particularistic approach of the Kabbalists in the land of Israel, similar to and influenced by the Spanish Kabbalah. Nevertheless, exchanges between the Palestinian center and the Italian one were vigorous: Italian Kabbalists such as Mordecai Dato came to Safed in order to study Kabbalah, and they brought back the kabbalistic classics produced there, which they were instrumental in printing. Kabbalists in Safed were also aware of a major development taking place in Italy and elsewhere in Europe, which they undersood as having a negative impact: the emergence and the printing of the Christian kabbalistic books.

At the end of the sixteenth century, the Safedian forms of Kabbalah as represented by Moses Cordovero and his disciples, and by Isaac Luria, started to have a strong impact on the Italian scene. The system of the former group of Kabbalists was printed early and disseminated in numerous versions. Their impact can be detected in the writings of Mordecai Dato, Abraham Yagel, and Aaron Berechiah ben Moses of Modena. Luria's sort of Kabbalah, however, remained in manuscripts that enjoyed a specialized reception in Italy: its theosophical and particularistic system, especially as presented by Israel Sarug, were interpreted in accordance with Renaissance types of thought—primarily Neoplatonic, but also atomistic.

See also **Jewish Philosophy**; **Jewish Thought and the Renaissance**; **Postel, Guillaume**; *and biographies of figures mentioned in this entry.*

BIBLIOGRAPHY

Bland, Kalman. "Elijah del Medigo's Averroistic Response to the Kabbalahs of the Fifteenth-Century Jewry and Pico della Mirandola." *Jewish Thought and Philosophy* 1 (1991): 23–53.

Blau, Joseph. *The Christian Interpretation of the Cabalah in the Renaissance*. New York, 1944.

David, Abraham. *Chapters in the History of Jerusalem at the Beginning of the Ottoman Period*. Jerusalem, 1979. In Hebrew.

Idel, Moshe. "The Anthropology of Yohanan Alemanno: Sources and Influences." *Topoi* 7 (1988): 201–210.

Idel, Moshe. "Differing Conceptions of Kabbalah in the Early Seventeenth Century." In *Jewish Thought in the Seventeenth Century*. Edited by I. Twersky and B. Septimus. London, 1987. Pages 137–200.

Idel, Moshe. "Hermeticism and Judaism." In *Hermeticism and the Renaissance*. Edited by Ingrid Merkel and Allen G. Debus. New York, 1988. Pages 59–76.

Lelli, F. "L'Incontro culturale tra Ebrei e Christiani nel Medioevo e nel Rinascimento." In *Atti del VI Congresso internazionale dell'AISG*. Rome, 1988. Pages 183–207.

Novak, B. C. "Giovanni Pico della Mirandola and Jochanan Alemanno." *Journal of the Warburg and Courtauld Institutes* 45 (1982): 125–147.

Ruderman, David B., ed. *Essential Papers on Jewish Culture in Renaissance and Baroque Italy*. New York, 1992. See especially pages 107–169 and 324–368.

Ruderman, David B. *The World of a Renaissance Jew: The Life and Thought of Abraham ben Mordecai Farissol*. Cincinnati, Ohio, 1991.

Secret, François. *Les kabbalistes chrétiens de la Renaissance*. Paris, 1964.

Tirosh-Rothschild, Hava. *Between Worlds: The Life and Thought of Rabbi David ben Judah Messer Leon*. Albany, N.Y., 1991.

Wirszubski, Chaim. *Pico della Mirandola's Encounter with Jewish Mysticism*. Cambridge, Mass., 1989.

MOSHE IDEL

KARO, JOSEPH BEN EPHRAIM. *See* **Caro, Joseph ben Ephraim.**

KEPLER, JOHANNES (1571–1630), astronomer, mathematician. Kepler was born to a Lutheran family in the Catholic imperial city Weil der Stadt, and in 1576 his family moved to Leonberg in the Protestant duchy of Württemberg. The need for an educated clergy and civil service led the dukes to establish Latin schools providing a humanist education throughout the duchy; they also gave scholarships to promising but poor boys. Kepler began his studies in a local German school, but his teachers recognized his talent, and he was transferred to a Latin school and received a ducal scholarship. Subsequently he enrolled in the University of Tübingen in 1589 to prepare for the Lutheran ministry. There he studied mathematics and astronomy with Michael Maestlin, a confirmed Copernican who introduced Kepler to the new system and convinced him of its validity.

The Graz Years. In 1594, when Kepler was in his third year working toward his theology degree, the mathematics teacher in the Protestant seminary in Graz died. Although Kepler was not primarily a mathematician, the university senate decided to send Kepler as a replacement. Their decision may have been influenced by Kepler's heterodox theological writings, particularly his preference for the Calvinist over the Lutheran doctrine of the Eucharist. At the seminary Kepler also taught Virgil and rhetoric because he had so few pupils in mathematics. In addition, he functioned as district mathematician, which required that he use astrology to write yearly calendars predicting the weather and upcoming events. In his first calendar for 1596 he correctly forecast bitter cold, peasant uprisings, and a Turkish invasion. Kepler's success with these predictions gave him a privileged position in this Catholic stronghold.

In Graz, Kepler wrote his first book, *Mysterium cosmographicum* (Secret of the universe), which was published in 1596. His main thesis was that the distances between the planets in the Copernican system were proportional to the five regular Platonic solids; he saw this as proof of the essential correctness of the Copernican system. He also reflected on the question of what made the planets move in their orbits. Although the thesis was incorrect, this was nevertheless an important first book. It set forth many of the themes in astronomy that were to occupy Kepler, including the belief that the universe could be described by simple mathematics.

This book also established Kepler's reputation as an astronomer, and Tycho Brahe invited him to work in his astronomical observatory on Hven in Denmark. Kepler was eager to do so because Tycho had amassed the best astronomical data available, which he hoped to use to prove his thesis. Kepler began to work with Tycho in January 1600, after Tycho had left Hven and had become imperial mathematician at the court of Emperor Rudolf II in Prague. Tycho began work on the orbit of Mars, which was the most difficult planet to map because, as Kepler later showed, its eccentricity was the greatest.

Kepler returned to Graz in June and found that Archduke Ferdinand of Styria, the future Holy Roman Emperor, had redoubled efforts to enforce measures against Protestants, and Kepler had to leave despite his special position.

The Prague Years. In October 1600 Kepler again joined Tycho. Kepler was one of many intellectuals who gathered around Rudolf's court, and his time there was the most productive period of Kepler's life. Kepler wrote his first book there at Tycho's prompting; the work grew out of an unfortunate incident at Hven. Some years earlier, Kepler had written effusively about Tycho's predecessor as imperial mathematician, Ursus (Reymers Baer). Ursus had used Kepler's effusive comments about him against Tycho, and Tycho demanded that Kepler vindicate him. The result, *Apologia Tychonis contra Nicolaum Ursum* (Defense of Tycho against Ursus), became a defense of scientific realism, the belief that astronomers could portray the real universe. Tycho died a year later, and Kepler was named to replace him as imperial mathematician, a title he held under Matthias I and Ferdinand II as well. His task, like Tycho's, was to establish definitive planetary tables in honor of Rudolf.

Kepler continued the work on the orbit of Mars, which he had begun in Hven. By 1605 he discovered his first two laws of planetary motion: the first is that a planetary orbit is an ellipse with the sun as one of the foci and the second that the radius vector drawn from the sun describes equal areas in equal times. His *Astronomia nova* (New astronomy) was thus ready for publication, although it did not come out until 1609 because Tycho's heirs fought Kepler's use of the data. This book also continued his speculations on a motive force for the planets. At this point Kepler had given up the idea that he had expressed in the *Mysterium cosmographicum* that the celestial force was immaterial. Thus the *Astronomia nova* importantly establishes the idea of a celestial physics.

Kepler became interested in optics while observing a partial solar eclipse in Prague in 1600. His *Ad Vitellionem paralipomena* (Supplement to Witelo),

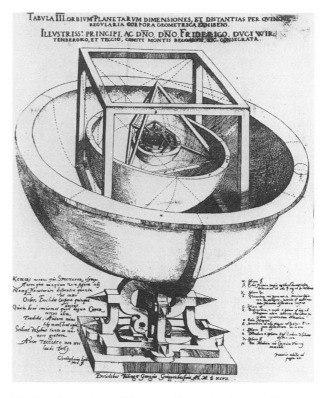

Kepler's Cosmological System. From *Prodromus dissertationum cosmographicarum* (1596–1631). AKG LONDON

published in 1604, describes the process of vision, including the function of the retina, and disclosed his inverse square law of refraction. He also discussed various astronomical phenomena—stellar parallax, astronomical refraction, and alterations in the apparent size of the sun. Kepler received news of Galileo's telescope and responded to Galileo's *Sidereus nuncius* (The sidereal messenger; 1610) with his *Dissertatio cum nuncio sidereo* (Conversation with the sidereal messenger) in 1610 and *Dioptrice* (Dioptrics) in 1611. These books discussed the optics of lenses, including the double convex lenses of the telescope.

During his years in Prague, Kepler also wrote two works on astrology. *De stella nova* (On the new star), published in 1606, was his reaction to a supernova that had appeared in 1604 close to a conjunction of Jupiter and Saturn. What he wrote was partly a meditation on astrology, accepting the significance of such events, but also trying to dampen what he considered the overzealous believers. (He was not an astrological determinist, but he believed that events on earth are influenced by planetary aspects, that is, the angles formed by two planets.) Chapters 8 and 9 are devoted to a respectful critique of Giovanni Pico della Mirandola's *Disputationes adversus astrologiam divinatricem* (Disputations against judicial astrology; 1496). In 1609 Kepler reacted against a physician, Philip Feselius, who had used Kepler's work to support his condemnation of astrology. Like Feselius's attack, *Tertius interveniens* (Third man in the middle; 1610) was written in German. In this book, Kepler tried to establish a middle way between zealots on both sides of the debate. He also tried to reform astrology in a way that would be more compatible with his new celestial physics. Finally, Kepler presented a Christmas gift to a friend in 1611. His *Strena seu de nive sexangula* (The six-cornered snowflake) was a pioneering study of crystallography.

The Linz Years. Kepler left Prague in 1612 after Rudolf's fall from power because he feared that the new regime would resume persecutions of Protestants. He had hoped for a position at Tübingen, but his support of the Calvinist doctrine of the Eucharist closed doors there. He landed a position as district mathematician in Linz, but he was denied communion by the local minister because of his well-publicized beliefs. His life was further disrupted when his mother was accused of being a witch, but because of his contacts with Tübingen he was at least able to prevent her from being tortured during the investigation, and she was later freed. In spite of these events, he continued to do important work. His musings on the quantity of wine that his barrels held resulted in *Nova stereometria doliorum vinariorum* (New stereometrics of wine casks) in 1615, a study of infinitesimals that was important in the development of calculus.

The work Kepler considered the culmination of his studies, *Harmonice mundi* (Harmony of the world), was published in 1619. In it he worked on theories of harmony in mathematics, music, astrology, and astronomy. Scholars have traditionally seen this emphasis on harmony as an example of Kepler's Neoplatonic mysticism, but recent interpretations have increasingly called this assessment into question. Kepler intended his vision of celestial harmony as a Copernican alternative to Ptolemy's *Harmonica*. *Harmonice mundi* contains Kepler's third law of planetary motion: the squares of the periodic times (that is, the time it takes to orbit the sun) of any two planets is proportional to the cubes of the mean distances from the sun.

Kepler's *Epitome astronomiae Copernicanae* (Epitome of Copernican astronomy) came out between 1618 and 1621. It was a textbook and became the means of disseminating his discoveries in astronomy. The work was much in demand because the *Tabulae Rudolphinae* (Rudolphine tables), which finally appeared in 1627, were so superior to earlier planetary tables.

Final Years. The last years of Kepler's life were unsettled. In 1626 the press where *Tabulae Rudolphinae* was being printed was destroyed during a siege in the Thirty Years' War. He joined the court of Count Albrecht von Wallenstein in the duchy of Sagan, Prussia, in 1628. Kepler had done a horoscope for Wallenstein in 1608 and a further elaboration in 1624, in which Kepler supposedly predicted Wallenstein's assassination in 1634. Wallenstein wanted Kepler's expertise in astrology, but Kepler was unhappy there. He left in 1630 to try to get the back salary Emperor Frederick II owed him for the *Tabulae Rudolphinae,* but he died on the journey.

Kepler's *Somnium* (Dream) is a forerunner of modern science fiction. He began to print it in Sagan, but it was not finally published until 1634, after his death. In it he describes how the solar system would appear to a person who took a trip to the moon. The idea of supporting the Copernican system in this novel way first came to him while he was a student in Tübingen, but the final version, which he first drafted in 1609, was based on an ancient model— Plutarch's *De facie in orbe lunae* (The face in the moon).

Kepler was a pivotal figure in seventeenth-century science. His discoveries in astronomy, optics, and mathematics spurred further developments, and many of his findings are still valid today. But his writings on theology, astrology, and celestial harmonies and his attempt at fiction show that he was very much a person of his times.

See also **Astronomy; Magic and Astrology; Optics.**

BIBLIOGRAPHY

Primary Works

Kepler, Johannes. *The Birth of History and the Philosophy of Science: Kepler's A Defence of Tycho against Ursus.* Translated by Nicholas Jardine. Cambridge, U.K., and New York, 1984. Translation of *Apologia pro Tychone contra Ursum.*

Kepler, Johannes. *Harmony of the World.* Translated by E. J. Aiton, A. M. Duncan, and J. V. Field. Philadelphia, 1997. Translation of *Harmonice mundi.*

Kepler, Johannes. *Johannes Kepler Gesammelte Werke.* Edited by Max Caspar et al. Munich, 1937– .

Kepler, Johannes. *New Astronomy.* Translated by William H. Donahue. Cambridge, U.K., and New York, 1992. Translation of *Nova astronomia.*

Kepler, Johannes. *The Secret of the Universe.* Translated by A. M. Duncan. New York, 1981. Translation of *Mysterium cosmographicum.*

Kepler, Johannes. *Somnium, The Dream*. Translated and edited by Edward Rosen. Madison, Wis., 1967.

Secondary Works

Caspar, Max. *Kepler*. Translated and edited by C. Doris Hellman. Annotated by Owen Gingerich and Alain Segonds. 2d ed., New York, 1993.

Field, J. V. *Kepler's Geometrical Cosmology*. Chicago, 1988.

Stephenson, Bruce. *The Music of the Heavens: Kepler's Harmonic Astronomy*. Princeton, N.J., 1994.

SHEILA J. RABIN

KING JAMES BIBLE.   *See* **Bible,** *subentry on* **The English Bible.**

KLONOWIC, SEBASTIAN FABIAN   (Acernus; c. 1545–1602), Polish poet, translator, satirist. Sebastian Klonowic's father, Jan, rented an estate in the area of Poznań. The patronym Klonowic is derived from the nickname *klon* (in Latin *acer*). It is not known where he received his education. After travels in Poland and Hungary, Klonowic settled in Lublin in 1574, where he held various municipal offices. He was also a lecturer at the Akademia Zamojska from 1589 to 1591.

Klonowic's major Latin work, *Roxolania* (1584), an epic poem written in elegiac distichs, concerns the topography, nature, and folklore of Ruś Czerwona (Ruthenia), a region of the contemporary territory of Poland between Lublin and Kamieniec Podolski. The poem describes many towns (such as Kiev), as well as the everyday life of the local people. Another work of Klonowic's, a poem in forty-four cantos, *Victoria deorum, in qua continetur veri herois educatio* (The victory of the gods, containing the education of a true hero; 1587?), deals with a poet's life experience. It concerns "true" (i.e., spiritual) nobility achieved through cultivating virtues rather than through birth. The victory mentioned in the title is moral success, for which Klonowic found a mythic allegory in Jupiter's victory over the rebellious Titans. The poem contains many digressions on the weaknesses and vices characteristic of the everyday life of particular social classes.

Klonowic's most significant Polish work is *Flis to jest spuszczanie statków Wisła i inszemi rzekami* (Boatmen on rafts floating down the Vistula and other rivers; 1595), which combines epic narration with the lyrical form of the sapphic stanza and deals with the shipping trade on the Vistula River. The boatmen described in the poem worked on boats that transport grain from southern Poland along the Vistula River and its tributaries. Klonowic's description of the boatmen's work includes numerous details concerning their way of life, their customs, and the places where they stopped. The poem is also full of comments on the vices of various social classes, particularly tradesmen who made their fortune on brokerage. Klonowic combines his moral reflections with the realistic description of a river journey by use of the *iter vitae* (journey of life) topos, which emphasizes the feebleness of human efforts.

Klonowic's talents as a moralist and a satirist are also clearly visible in another poem, *Worek Judaszów* (Judas's sack; 1600), which was received by readers with great interest and published several times. The title is an allusion to the bag in which Judas kept his "bloodstained" money. Because the bag, according to a medieval legend, was made of leather from four different predators—wolf, fox, lynx, and lion—it is also an allegory of four types of felons. Here Klonowic made use of his rich law experiences gained during his work as assessor, mayor, and member of a city council. The poem is a skillful depiction of a Renaissance town and its people, particularly various kinds of criminal circles.

Klonowic also worked as a translator. He began with a paraphrase of a Latin poem by Klemens Janicius, *Vitae regum polonorum* (Lives of Polish kings), entitled *Królów i książąt polskich . . . opis* (Description of the lives of Polish kings and princes; 1576). Toward the end of his life he published a translation of the so-called *Disticha Catonis* into Polish, *Katonowe wiersze podwójne* (Cato's distichs; 1598). Klonowic was also the author of a series of works dedicated to Jan Kochanowski, *Żale nagrobne na ślachetnie urodzonego męża . . . pana Jana Kochanowskiego* (Grieving at the grave of a nobly born husband . . . Lord Jan Kochanowskiego; 1585).

BIBLIOGRAPHY

Primary Work

Klonowic, Sebastian Fabian. *The Boatman*. Translated by Marion Moore Coleman. Cambridge Springs, Pa., 1958. Translation of *Flis to jest spuszczanie statków Wisla i inszemi rzekami*.

Secondary Works

Karpiński, Adam. "Sebastian Fabian Klonowic—Pisarz z przełomu epok." In *Przełom wieków XVI i XVII w literaturze i kulturze polskiej*. Edited by Barbara Otinowska. Wrocław, Poland, 1984.

Stankowa, Maria. "Sebastian Klonowic, pisarz i rajca miasta Lublina 1573–1602." *Archeion* 46 (1967).

ANDRZEJ BOROWSKI

KNOWLEDGE, PROBLEMS OF.   *See* **Science, Epistemology of.**

KNOX, JOHN (c. 1514–1572), Scottish Protestant preacher who had a major impact on the course of the British Reformations. Born of humble parents in the village of Haddington, near Edinburgh, Knox was educated at Saint Andrews University, which, while not untouched by humanist and reforming influences, was dominated in the 1530s by the Scholasticism of the distinguished logician and theologian John Major (1469–1550). Knox's later writings show obvious signs of his early training in Scholastic method; but whether he was also touched by the humanist or evangelical opinions current in Saint Andrews is unclear. More certain is the fact that he was ordained a Catholic priest in 1536 and, unable to obtain a benefice, initially made his living as a notary public and tutor to the children of the gentry.

The circumstances of his conversion to Protestantism are obscure, but it must have occurred in the early 1540s as Knox first came to prominence as an associate of the Protestant preacher George Wishart (c. 1513–1546), who returned to Scotland from England and the Continent in 1543 and embarked on a preaching mission that led to his arrest by the Catholic authorities on the orders of the archbishop of Saint Andrews, Cardinal David Beaton (c. 1494–1546). Wishart's martyrdom in Saint Andrews in 1546 was immediately followed by the retaliatory murder of Beaton. The cardinal's assassins were subsequently besieged in Saint Andrews Castle and it was there that Knox, fearful for his own safety, joined them in April 1547, and where he was first called to the Protestant ministry. Although initially reluctant to heed the call, Knox became convinced that his public summons in the face of the congregation was a "lawful vocation" that came directly from God. Thereafter, closely identifying with the Old Testament prophets, Knox constantly referred to himself as God's "trumpet" and "messenger," legitimizing his public actions and utterances in terms of his calling as God's prophet.

In summer 1547, however, Knox's future as a prophet looked decidedly bleak. In July, Saint Andrews Castle fell to the French, and he spent the next nineteen months serving as a galley slave. Released in March 1549, he chose to settle in Protestant England rather than return to Catholic Scotland and, licensed to preach by Edward VI's reforming privy council, he initially ministered to congregations at Berwick and Newcastle before his powerful preaching brought him to the attention of the duke of Northumberland and led to his appointment as a royal chaplain and the offer (which he declined) of the bishopric of Rochester. Already noted for his rig-

John Knox. Facsimile after a copper engraving by Hendrik Hondius the Younger. CORBIS/BETTMANN

orous adherence to the paramount authority of scripture, Knox's biblical literalism, typified by his opposition to kneeling at communion as unscriptural, led to the inclusion of the "black rubric" in the Book of Common Prayer of 1552, a late addition to the text that denied that kneeling at communion was idolatrous. While effectively a victory for the archbishop of Canterbury, Thomas Cranmer, rather than Knox, the arguments over the Prayer Book served to establish Knox's radical credentials, while leaving him deeply skeptical of the temporizing world of the lay and clerical politicians who dominated England's magisterial Reformation.

In January 1554, following the accession to the English throne of the Catholic Mary Tudor, Knox fled to the Continent, initially ministering to the English exile community at Frankfurt. His views on the liturgy, however, split the congregation there, forcing him to move to Calvin's Geneva. From there he not only observed events in England with rising frustration, but also embarked on a clandestine mission to Scotland in 1555–1556, which enabled him to reestablish contact with the leaders of the underground Protestant movement in his native land. Now concerned as much with the fate of Protestantism in Scotland as in England, Knox began to seek means of justifying armed resistance to "ungodly" rulers. The result was a series of pamphlets published in Geneva in 1558, including his infamous diatribe against female rule, *The First Blast of the Trumpet against the Monstrous Regiment of Women,* and two open letters to the Scots, *The Appellation to the Nobility and Estates* and *The Letter to the Commonalty,* in which he developed a limited theory of aristocratic resistance to tyranny. While more complex and less radical than is often assumed, the coruscating biblical rhetoric in which the 1558 tracts are couched immediately established Knox's European reputation as a firebrand revolutionary.

It also ensured that, on Elizabeth's accession to the English throne in November 1558, Knox was barred from reentering England. Instead, he returned to Scotland where, in May 1559, his iconoclastic preaching triggered a Protestant rebellion against the queen regent, Mary of Guise, whose daughter Mary, queen of Scots, had in April 1558 married the dauphin, Francis, and aligned Scotland with French Catholic interests. The success of the rebellion resulted, under Knox's influence, in the adoption in 1560 of a Protestant *Confession of Faith* and the drawing up of what was to become known as *The First Book of Discipline*. However, the Protestant settlement of 1560 was jeopardized by the return to Scotland in 1561 of the widowed and Catholic Mary, queen of Scots.

Knox, as minister of Edinburgh, used his influential position to denounce her "idolatry" from the pulpit and had several celebrated interviews with the young queen during which he tried unsuccessfully to convert her to Protestantism. In fact, in political terms, Knox was increasingly marginalized and he played no significant role in the events that led to Mary's deposition and exile from Scotland in 1567–1568. Dogged by failing health, Knox devoted his later years to compiling and revising his most enduring memorial, *The History of the Reformation of Religion in Scotland* (published in 1586), a brilliant Protestant polemic that has become a prime historical source. He died in Edinburgh on 24 November 1572. Never a systematic theologian, and leaving no significant body of theological works, Knox's importance stemmed from the power of his pulpit oratory, the pungency of his polemical writings, and his deep-felt conviction that he was indeed a prophet of God called to proclaim the divine will.

See also **Protestant Reformation; Scotland.**

BIBLIOGRAPHY

Primary Works

Knox, John. *John Knox's History of the Reformation in Scotland.* 2 vols. Edited by William Croft Dickinson. Edinburgh and London, 1949.

Knox, John. *On Rebellion.* Edited by Roger A. Mason. Cambridge, U.K., 1994.

Knox, John. *The Works of John Knox.* Edited by David Laing. 6 vols. Edinburgh, 1846–1864.

Secondary Works

Kyle, Richard G. *The Mind of John Knox.* Lawrence, Kans., 1984. The fullest study of Knox's theology and ecclesiology.

Mason, Roger A., ed. *John Knox and the British Reformations.* Aldershot, U.K., 1998. A wide-ranging collection of essays on Knox's career and thought.

Ridley, Jasper. *John Knox.* Oxford, 1968. The standard biography of Knox.

ROGER A. MASON

KOCHANOWSKI, JAN (Cochanovius Joannes; 1530–1584), Polish and neo-Latin poet. Kochanowski was born in Sycyna, to a wealthy landowner, Piotr, and a well-educated mother, Anna. Kochanowski began his education at the Jagiellonian University in Cracow in the mid-1540s and continued his studies abroad in Prussia and Italy in the 1550s. He acquired a solid knowledge of Greek and Roman literature at the University of Padua. These works strongly influenced Kochanowski's views on moral, aesthetic, and political questions.

Back in Poland, Kochanowski was employed by the *voyvode* (palatine, a lord exercising sovereign power) of Lublin, Jan Firlej, then by two church dignitaries, and finally by King Sigismund II Augustus.

After 1570 Kochanowski began spending most of his time in Czarnolas, a small village of which he was the squire. He devoted himself to literary work and public life. He had close and friendly relationships with contemporary Polish intellectuals. Kochanowski began his literary work with Latin poetry and continued to write epigrams, elegies, and odes. These were published in *Elegiarum libri IV, eiusdem foricoenia sive epigrammatum libellus* (Cracow; 1584). His odes were collected in the *Lyricorum libellus* (Cracow; 1580).

Kochanowski's knowledge of the ancient pagan and biblical traditions strongly influenced his Polish poetry. His main achievement is in Polish lyric poetry, particularly two books of *Pieśni* (Songs; 1585) and the series of nineteen funeral laments, *Treny.* Kochanowski was master of the Anacreontic form. His *Fraszki* (from Italian, "frasca," twig, trifle) collected in three books (1584) became a model of Polish lyric epigram for future generations. His magnum opus was a poetic paraphrase of the Psalms of David, *Psałterz Dawidów* (1579) that summarized all his aesthetic, philosophical, and religious experience. The psalms, reshaped into the form of stanzas, were widely popular. They were also sung to the tunes of Mikolaj Gomółka (*Melodie na psałterz polski;* 1580) up to the present.

Like many of his contemporaries, Kochanowski was also a political writer. His tragedy *Odprawa posłów greckich* (The dismissal of the Grecian envoys; 1578), was modeled on the works of Euripides, Aeschylus, Seneca, and Italian Renaissance tragedy. The drama deals with moral problems and with political implications faced by statesmen and by society in general. Kochanowski's main achievement was the introduction of new poetic forms, genres, themes, and imagery into Polish literary culture. His influence continued into the seventeenth century, making him the outstanding representative of Polish poetry.

Kochanowski died on 22 August 1584 in Lublin. He was buried in the parish church in Zwoleń (in the modern province of Radom). It is here that one could still see the epitaph and the bust of Jan Kochanowski that was made by an unknown sculptor (c. 1610). The bust seems to be the only authentic picture of the poet.

BIBLIOGRAPHY

Primary Works

Kochanowski, Jan. *The Dismissal of the Grecian Envoys.* Translated by George Rapall Noyes and put in English verse by Ruth Earl Merrill. Berkeley, Calif., 1918. Translation of *Odprawa posłów greckich.*

Kochanowski, Jan. *Laments.* Translated by Dorothea Prall. Berkeley, Calif., 1920. Translation of *Treny.*

Kochanowski, Jan. *Laments.* Translated by Seamus Heaney and Stanisław Baranczak. London, 1995. Translation of *Treny.*

Kochanowski, Jan. *Treny.* Translated by Adam Czerniawski. Foreword by Donald Davie. Edited and annotated by Piotr Wilczek. Katowice, Poland, 1996.

Secondary Works

Fiszman, Samuel, ed. *The Polish Renaissance in Its European Context.* Foreword by Czeslaw Milosz. Bloomington and Indianapolis, Ind., 1988. See part 6, "Jan Kochanowski," pp. 303–429.

Korolko, Miroslaw, ed. *Kochanowski: Z dziejów badań i recepcji twórczości.* Warsaw, Poland, 1980. A chronicle of the poet's life together with a well-chosen collection of essential articles on Kochanowski's life and work.

Pelc, Janusz. *Jan Kochanowski: Szczyt renesansu w literaturze polskiei.* Warsaw, Poland, 1980. A monograph.

Pirie, Donald, ed. *Jan Kochanowski in Glasgow. Papers and Materials from the Jan Kochanowski Anniversary Symposium.* Glasgow, Scotland, 1985.

Weintraub, Wiktor. "Kochanowski's Renaissance Manifesto." *Slavonic and East European Review* 30 (1952): 412–424.

Welsh, David. *Jan Kochanowski.* New York, 1974.

ANDRZEJ BOROWSKI

KRISTELLER, PAUL OSKAR. *See* **Renaissance, Interpretations of the,** *subentry on* **Paul Oskar Kristeller.**

KRZYCKI, ANDRZEJ (Cricius, Andreas; 1482–1537), Polish poet, diplomat, statesman, Roman Catholic bishop. Born to a noble family and orphaned as a child, Krzycki remained under the protection of his relatives, Piotr Tomicki and others. He studied in Bologna under the humanists Antonio Urceo, called Codro, and Filippo Beroaldo the Elder. He was appointed secretary of the king (1515), bishop of Przemyśl (1522) and Płock (1527), and archbishop of Gniezno, which made him primate of Poland (1535). He played an important role in diplomatic missions to Hungary (1524, 1526) and negotiations about the secularization of the Teutonic Knights Order (1525).

One of the most distinguished Latin poets in Poland, Krzycki was highly esteemed by contemporaries. Desiderius Erasmus mentioned him in *Ciceronianus* as the only Pole among well-known Latin authors and in his eight letters to Krzycki praised his works and compared his prose to Cicero's. In 1525 Krzycki unsuccessfully attempted to invite Erasmus to Poland as a professor of the Cracow Academy. After 1530 he tried also to invite Philipp Melanchthon in order to separate him from Martin Luther. These efforts were criticized by Erasmus and Johannes Cochlaeus.

Krzycki was an uncompromising opponent of the Reformation. His poems "In imaginem Lutheri" (On Luther's image) and "Condiciones boni Lutherani" (Commandments of a good Lutheran) were published in the collective volume *Encomia Lutheri* (The praise of Luther; 1524), one of the first anti-Lutheran satirical works in Europe. Because of the title, which is an obvious allusion to Erasmus's *Encomium moriae* (The praise of folly), the book was included by mistake in the *Index librorum prohibitorum* (Index of prohibited books).

Krzycki's literary output consists mainly of occasional verse devoted to church and state celebrations and court events: epigrams, epithalamia (poems in celebration of weddings), epinicia (triumphal odes), eulogies, epitaphs, and threnodies. His most important political poem is *Religionis et Reipublicae querimonia* (Complaint of the religion and republic;

1522), a satire on the political activities of the gentry. An allegorical figure of a complaining Republic would be imitated later in numerous poems written in Poland in both Latin and Polish. Krzycki also wrote conventional love elegies imitating Ovid, Propertius, and Tibullus. He is especially known as the author of satirical poems in which he ridicules the most distinguished figures of the political establishment, including the queen Bona Sforza. These poems support a common opinion of him as a cynical, malicious, and revengeful intriguer and careerist. A known patron of the arts, Krzycki has special merit as the protector of Klemens Janicki.

Although he was regarded as one of the greatest Latin writers of the period in Poland, his Latin did not imitate the patterns of Augustan poetry and prose. It was lively and unconventional, influenced both by ancient Roman comedies and the medieval popular lyric. He wrote many satirical poems that parodied church hymns and popular religious verse.

Most of his literary output, especially the erotic poems, remained unpublished and survived in manuscript copies assembled by other authors. Scholars have questioned the authorship of up to half of the contents of the only critical edition, published in 1888.

See also **Poland**.

BIBLIOGRAPHY

Primary Work
Cricius, Andreas. *Carmina* (Songs). Edited by Kazimierz Morawski. Cracow, Poland, 1888.

Secondary Works
Backvis, Claude. "Un poete latin de la Pologne humaniste. André Krzycki–Andreas Cricius." *Latomus* 6 (1947): 45–67.
Gruchała, Janusz S. "Zmarnowany talent-Andrzej Krzycki." In Vol. 1 of *Pisarze staropolscy: Sylwetki.* Edited by Stanisław Grzeszczuk. Warsaw, 1991. Pages 256–305.
Zabłocki, Stefan. "Krzycki Andrzej." *Polski słownik biograficzny.* 15 (1970): 544–549.

PIOTR WILCZEK

LABÉ, LOUISE (c. 1520–1566), French writer. A daughter and wife of prosperous Lyons rope makers (she was nicknamed "La Belle Cordière"—the beautiful rope maker), Louise Labé was given an unusually rich classical education for a woman and welcomed into the Italianized humanist circles of France's second largest city. As she began writing poetry, she met Olivier de Magny, an established translator and Pléiade poet, who was traveling through Lyons on his way to Rome. Nothing is clear about the relationship between Labé and Magny except their common passion for love poetry.

Labé's *Oeuvres* (Works) were published in 1555 by Jean de Tournes, a well-known printer. They included a prefatory epistle in the form of a "feminist" manifesto, dedicated to a female friend, Clémence de Bourges; a mythological dialogue in prose (*Débat de Folie et d'Amour* [Debate between folly and love]), depicting the tragic consequences of Love's blindness in the lighthearted mood of a *facetia,* a literary genre long debated by Renaissance theorists, which relies heavily on surprise and cunning reversal; three elegies in verse about a destructive passion, which show familiarity with Catullus's and Ovid's evocation of Sappho (Labé was also called the "Sapho lyonnaise" by her friends); and finally, twenty-four love sonnets (the first in Italian) moving from close imitation of the Neoplatonic mode (cosmic harmony) and Petrarchan imagery (an idealized portrait of the lover) to an ironic commentary on the male-coded language of love. As a female writer, Labé claims to work within the Renaissance tradition of lyrical and satirical discourse, while asserting her intellectual freedom through female-inspired patterns of daring revisionism.

BIBLIOGRAPHY

Primary Works

Labé, Louise. *The Debate between Folly and Love.* Translated and edited by Edwin Marion Cox. London, 1925.

Labé, Louise. *Oeuvres complètes de Louise Labé.* Edited by François Rigolot. Paris, 1986.

Labé, Louise. *The Sonnets.* Translated and edited by Bettina L. Knapp. Paris, 1964.

Secondary Works

Baker, Deborah Lesko. *The Subject of Desire: Petrarchan Poetics and the Female Voice in Louise Labé.* Lafayette, Ind., 1996.

Harvey, L. E. *The Aesthetics of the Renaissance Love Sonnet: An Essay on the Art of the Sonnet in the Poetry of Louise Labé.* Geneva, 1962.

Jones, Ann Rosalind. *The Currency of Eros: Women's Love Lyric in Europe, 1540–1620.* Bloomington, Ind., 1990. Pages 155–200.

Rigolot, F. "Gender vs. Sex Difference in Louise Labé's Grammar of Love." In *Rewriting the Renaissance: The Discourses of Sexual Difference in Early Modern Europe.* Edited by M. W. Ferguson, M. Quilligan, and N. J. Vickers. Chicago, 1986. Pages 287–298.

Rigolot, F. *Louise Labé Lyonnaise, ou la Renaissance au féminin.* Paris, 1997.

FRANÇOIS RIGOLOT

LA BODERIE, GUY LE FÈVRE DE (1541–1598), French biblical translator, poet. Guy Le Fèvre de La Boderie was chosen, along with his brother Nicolas, to work on the ambitious Polyglot Bible because of his background in Eastern languages: Greek, Hebrew, Arabic, Chaldean, and Syrian, among others. The brothers were recommended to Christopher

Plantin by the great humanist Guillaume Postel, and Postel's influence on La Boderie's work can be seen in the attention paid to divination, prophesy, and the Kabbalah. While engaged in working on the Polyglot Bible in Antwerp, La Boderie lived among the members of the Family of Love (*la Famille de la Charité*) but also worked with the Jesuits in Louvain, to whom he dedicated several poems in his *L'encyclie des secrets de l'eternité* (Compendium of the secrets of eternity; Antwerp, 1571).

In 1578 he published his translations of Marsilio Ficino's *Diverses meslanges poétiques* (Diverse poetic miscellany), *Hymnes ecclesiastiques, cantiques spirituelz & autres meslanges poëtiques* (Ecclesiastic hymns, spiritual songs, and other poetic miscellanies), as well as *La galliade ou De la revolution des arts et sciences* (The galliad or On the revolution of the arts and sciences). D. P. Walker views this last work as the most critical source for the poetical and musical theories of Jean-Antoine de Baïf's Academy of Poetry and Music.

La Boderie also translated Giovanni Pico della Mirandola's *Oration on the Dignity of Man* (1578). Perhaps because of his early contact with the Family of Love and the Jesuits, his absorption in the natural, mathematical, and astronomical sciences is tempered by his desire to reconcile wisdom grasped by human intelligence with divine revelation. One of the Renaissance poets most engaged in the Prisca Theologia and curious about the mysticism of the Druids, La Boderie sought to blend his belief in the superiority of divine wisdom and revelation over revealed science with his curiosity about the planets and the ties between music, mathematics, and astronomy in the music of the spheres.

La galliade takes us through a mystical tour of the origins of culture and traces its beginnings across five spheres: astronomy/astrology, architecture, magic, music, and poetry. The scientific thrust of La Boderie's exploration of the cosmos, including a thorough discussion of acoustics, is always tempered by his spiritual orientation, his belief that the immense potential of the human mind and spirit can be reached only within the context of God's revealed truth. In dedicating his *Hymnes ecclesiastiques* to Henry III, La Boderie states that through the merging of music and spiritual songs, he hopes to inspire good Catholics in their faith in an era when the Protestants were winning converts through the appeal of their hymns.

La Boderie's erudition is at once a great gift, in that it makes him an extraordinary reader and translator of ancient and humanist texts, and an obstacle.

His use of obscure, etymological references constrains his poetic flights of fancy. His muse is most apparent as he evokes the natural surroundings of his Norman youth or the ineffable music of the spheres that so inspired his predecessors: Maurice Scève, Pontus de Tyard, and Pierre de Ronsard.

BIBLIOGRAPHY

Primary Works

Biblia sacra hebraice, chaldaice, graece et latine. 8 vols. Antwerp, Netherlands, 1570–1572.

Le Fèvre de la Boderie, Guy. *Diverses meslanges poétiques.* Edited by Rosanna Gorris. Geneva, 1993.

Le Fèvre de la Boderie, Guy. *La galliade ou De la revolution des arts et sciences.* Edited by François Roudaut. Paris, 1993.

Secondary Works

Secret, François. *L'ésotérisme de Guy le Fèvre de la Boderie.* Geneva, 1969.

Walker, D. P. *The Ancient Theology: Studies in Christian Platonism from the Fifteenth to the Eighteenth Century.* London, 1972.

Walker, D. P. *Music, Spirit, and Language in the Renaissance.* London, 1985.

Yates, Frances Amelia. *The French Academies of the Sixteenth Century.* London, 1947.

DEBORAH N. LOSSE

LA BOÉTIE, ÉTIENNE DE (1530–1563), French political writer, poet, translator, and magistrate. Étienne de La Boétie is chiefly remembered as Michel de Montaigne's closest friend. In his own time, La Boétie was considered a gifted humanist and magistrate, an active controversialist and political writer. He was trained as a lawyer and admitted as a judge in the Bordeaux parlement. In 1560 Chancellor Michel de L'Hôpital assigned him the task of explaining and implementing the official royal policies of the Bordeaux municipal government. In 1562 La Boétie was given command of a company of Bordeaux soldiers.

La Boétie is known especially for his connection with Montaigne, his colleague and editor, who published twenty-nine of La Boétie's sonnets in his *Essais* (1580). Their friendship was immortalized in Montaigne's "De l'amitié" (On friendship; in *Essais*) and in the detailed account that Montaigne wrote concerning La Boétie's premature death. La Boétie translated Plutarch's *Lettre de consolation* (Letter of consolation; 1571) and the *Règles de mariage* (Precepts of marriage; 1571), as well as Xenophon's *Oeconomicus,* which he entitled *La mesnagerie de Xenophon* (Xenophon's household management; 1571). La Boétie's political conservatism is evident in his *Mémoire sur la pacification des troubles* (Memoir on the pacification of the civil wars), formerly known as *Mémoire touchant l'Édit de janvier 1562* (Memoir on the edict of January 1562), first published 1922: while he condemns using force against intellectual dissidence, he stresses that since Protestantism and Catholicism cannot coexist peacefully, Catholicism must be the only official religion. In his *Discours de la servitude volontaire* (Discourse on voluntary servitude; 1574), La Boétie argues for submission to the laws under which one is born, and in the process he analyzes and condemns tyrannicide. Montaigne, however, refused to publish this work because the Huguenots had pirated it and used it to support their cause.

See also biography of Michel de Montaigne.

BIBLIOGRAPHY

Primary Works

La Boétie, Étienne de. *Discours de la servitude volontaire.* Edited by Françoise Bayard. Paris, 1992.

La Boétie, Étienne de. *Oeuvres complètes.* 2d ed. Edited by Louis Desgraves. 2 vols. Bordeaux, France, 1991. Originally published in Bordeaux in 1892, edited by Paul Bonnefon.

La Boétie, Étienne de. *Slaves by Choice.* Edited and translated by Malcolm Smith. Egham, U.K., 1988. A translation of *Discours de la servitude volontaire.*

Secondary Work

Cocula, Anne-Marie. *Étienne de La Boétie.* Bordeaux, France, 1985.

ANNE R. LARSEN

LADINO LITERATURE AND LANGUAGE.

Evolving like other major Jewish languages that emerged in the Jewish Diaspora, such as Yiddish (Judeo-German), Judeo-Arabic, or Judeo-Persian, Ladino (Judeo-Spanish) developed during three centuries as the oral and written language among the Jewish communities of Andalusia, Castile, and Aragon, before the expulsion of the Jews from Spain in 1492.

Ladino Language. In communicating among themselves both orally and in written transactions (community ordinances, legal and commercial matters), as well as in translations of biblical, ethical, and philosophical works, using almost exclusively the Hebrew alphabet, the Jews of Spain interspersed their local dialects with Hebrew and Aramaic words or expressions, particularly terms and concepts relating to religious beliefs and ritual practices. Ladino also preserved archaic Hispanic words and forms, many of which have disappeared from use in modern Spanish or changed their original meaning among the Sephardic exiles. Except for those who

went to Italy and Morocco, most of the Jews expelled from Spain settled all over the Ottoman Empire. Putting aside some minor phonetic and morphological differences between the so-called oriental Ladino (as used, for example, in Constantinople, Smyrna, and Rhodes) and western Ladino (as used in Salonika, Bosnia, Serbia, Macedonia, and Romania), the oral and written Ladino between the sixteenth and nineteenth centuries essentially preserved all the characteristics of the Spanish language before 1492, the year Antonio de Nebrija articulated the first grammar of the Castilian language in *Gramatica sobre la lengua castellana.* However, from the 1700s onward, the Sephardic speakers and writers replaced hundreds of words, either forgotten or unfamiliar, with parallel ones borrowed from the local languages with which they came in contact in the Ottoman Empire: Turkish, Greek, Arabic, Italian, and, after the 1850s, French.

Ladino Literature. Whereas some Ladino translations in Latin script of the scriptures and of a few philosophical and ethical treatises—mainly destined for Christian patrons or conversos (forced converts) and predating the 1492 expulsion—have survived the public burning of Hebrew manuscripts, only three fifteenth-century Ladino manuscript texts in Hebrew script are presently known: Valladolid's community ordinances, a three-hundred-stanza poem on Joseph and his brethren, and a "Woman's Prayer Book." Some works in Ladino, such as Moses Almosnino's *Hanhagat ha-hayyim* (Regimen of life) or the Ladino translation of Bahya ibn Paquda's eleventh-century pietistic treatise *Hovot ha-levavoth* (Duties of the heart), both printed in the 1560s, were so sophisticated in content, language, and style that they were destined to a very limited Sephardic readership. Ladino literature from the mid-sixteenth century to the 1800s comprises translated versions of the scriptures and of prayer books, books on ritual practices, ethical treatises, and adaptations of medieval Hebrew chronicles and religious legal codes, as well as some rare original poetic works on biblical figures associated with festive days such as Purim and Passover.

The earliest Ladino translations of the scriptures in the sixteenth century were published according to the most pressing needs in the synagogues and the religious schools: the Psalms and Pentateuch (Constantinople, 1540, 1547); Prophets (two editions; Salonika, 1569–1572 and 1583–1585); the Five Scrolls, read during specific holidays, probably printed in small volumes, of which no copy has survived; and the Later Prophets (Joshua to 2 Kings), translated in Constantinople (1580), which has been preserved in a single manuscript. Due to the scarcity of the above editions, a popular biblical glossary (*Heshek Shelomo*), first printed between 1572 and 1587, was twice reprinted in Venice (1588, 1617). The first and most influential complete Ladino translation of the scriptures was the work of Abraham Assa (Constantinople, 1739–1745). Assa was the translator of many ethical and historical works, among them *Sefer Bin Gorion* (Book of Bin Gorion; 1743), the Ladino version of the *Book of Yosippon,* a late tenth-century Hebrew epic chronicle derived from the writings of Flavius Josephus. Another Hebrew epic chronicle, *Sefer ha-yashar* (Book of the righteous; printed in 1550), was translated into Ladino but not printed, and has survived in a single seventeenth-century manuscript.

The culminating achievement in the field of Ladino religious prose, which was to have the deepest influence on the mentality and culture of the Ottoman Sephardim, was without doubt the multivolume series conceived by Jacob Khuli (1689–1732), *Me'am Lo'ez* (People of a foreign tongue; in Ladino, *puevlo ladinan*), an encyclopedic compendium of Jewish religious tradition, wisdom, and lore, couched in a language and style accessible to the widest readership. It draws its commentaries and exempla from the Talmud, the Mishnah, and the Midrash, as well as from medieval rabbinic exegetes and Kabbalists, illustrating the comments with sayings and proverbs, anecdotes and tales. Khuli published the first volume on Genesis (Constantinople, 1730) and the second one on Exodus (posthumously, 1732). Isaac Magriso and Isaac Argueti completed the task in publishing their own volumes on Leviticus-Deuteronomy between 1732 and 1773. Later volumes by ten different rabbis on other biblical books, published between 1849 and 1901, never achieved the perfection and the success of the earlier ones, which were frequently reprinted.

BIBLIOGRAPHY

Lazar, Moshe. *The Sephardic Classical Library.* Culver City, Calif., 1989–1999.

Lazar, Moshe. *Sefarad in My Heart. A Ladino Reader.* Lancaster, Calif., 1999.

Levy, Avigdor, ed. *The Jews of the Ottoman Empire.* Princeton, N.J., 1994.

Romero, Elena. *La creación literaria en lengua sefardí.* Madrid, 1992.

Shaw, Stanford J. *The Jews of the Ottoman Empire and the Turkish Republic.* New York, 1991.

MOSHE LAZAR

LANDINO, CRISTOFORO (c. 1424–1498), Florentine poet, humanist, and professor of literature and rhetoric. Born into a family of modest means, Landino studied law at Volterra. He despised the subject, however, and in 1439 he returned to Florence to attend humanities lectures, especially those of Carlo Marsuppini, but probably also those of Leonardo Bruni and Poggio Bracciolini. During this time he also wrote verse, where his success led him to the circle of Leon Battista Alberti. In 1459 Landino married Lucrezia di Alberto di Adovardo degli Alberti.

In 1453 Landino's teacher at the University of Florence, Carlo Marsuppini, died, and after a prolonged battle Marsuppini's duties were divided among three lecturers, with Landino, who had received the support of the Medici, obtaining the appointment in rhetoric and poetics in 1458. He lectured on Dante, Petrarch's *Canzoniere* (Song Book), Cicero's *Tusculan Disputations* and *Familiar Letters,* Horace's *Odes* and *Ars poetica* (Art of poetry), Virgil's *Aeneid,* and the satires of Juvenal and Persius. He became the academic authority in the humanities for almost forty years in Florence, numbering among his pupils such figures as Marsilio Ficino and Lorenzo de' Medici and receiving an annual salary that rose to three hundred florins—generous by the standards of the day—in 1485.

With the aid of the Medici, Landino also obtained several political appointments. He became chancellor of the Guelph party in 1467, then in 1483 received the chancery secretaryship that he held until his death.

The literary, academic, and political parts of Landino's career cannot be separated from one another. He praised Cosimo, Piero, and Lorenzo de' Medici in the highest terms in his published books, and his major work of Latin scholarship, the *Disputationes Camaldulenses* (Camaldulensian disputations; c. 1472), marks Landino's effort to integrate Florentine intellectuals like himself into the passage from republican city-state to Medici principate.

Landino was pensioned in 1497, and shortly before his death he returned to Borgo alla Collina, a small village near his ancestral home of Pratovecchio, where he died on 24 September 1498.

Works. Among the works of Landino's youth, what stands out is the *Xandra* (completed before 1460), a collection of vernacular poems invoking the Roman elegists and Petrarch's *Canzoniere.* The appearance of his major dialogues after 1470 marks a more serious engagement with philosophical concerns, probably under the influence of Ficino. These dialogues include *De anima* (On the soul; early 1470s), on the nature, operation, and immortality of the soul; *Disputationes Camaldulenses,* on the relationship of the active and contemplative lives; and *De vera nobilitate* (On true nobility; after 1487), on the nature of nobility as seen through the Neoplatonic gradation of virtues.

Although his university career focused on Latin authors, Landino also devoted significant attention to Italian as a language for serious literary expression. He produced an important translation of Pliny's *Natural History* (1476), a collection of model letters (1485), and a translation from Latin into the vernacular of Giovanni Simonetta's *Sforziade* (1490) that detailed the history of Milan in the 1460s. His masterwork in this area is undoubtedly the Dante edition with text and commentary. Landino's text leaves much to be desired by modern standards, and the commentary, in spite of its borrowings from previous scholars, often fails to identify key persons and events in the poem. Nevertheless this commentary was very influential in its day, and it was the logical consequence of Landino's belief that as culture once moved from Greece to Rome, so it later moved from Rome to Florence.

Landino's lectures followed the usual humanist practice of providing linguistic, historical, and mythological analysis of each word in the text, and he prepared commentaries on Horace (1482), Virgil (1488), and Juvenal and Persius (extant in manuscript). However, he also posits a methodological division within his works, suggesting that his Virgil commentary, for example, functions on the level of grammar and rhetoric while the *Disputationes Camaldulenses* unveils the higher, allegorical truth in the *Aeneid*. Indeed, Landino believed that all great literature conveyed essentially the same truth, which he alluded to in reference to Homer and developed in detail in reference to Virgil and Dante. In a scheme derived from Neoplatonic authors, the literary hero passes through a hierarchy of moral values, beginning with the civic virtues of life on earth, proceeding to the purgatorial virtues by which we pass from earth to heaven, and ending with the virtues of a purified spirit, which concerns itself only with the divine. All three grades of virtue are good, but they are arranged in a hierarchy, so that moral growth should involve passage from the earthly to the divine. As the hero progresses toward the *summum bonum* (highest good), he encounters a series of moral impediments along the way: *voluptas* (pleasure), *avaritia* (greed), and *ambitio* (striving after

Cristoforo Landino. Illustration from the title page of Landino's *Formulaio di lettore e di oratione vulgari* (Florence, 1492).

honors). In the *Aeneid, voluptas* was represented by the city of Troy, Anchises, and Scylla; *avaritia* was represented by Thrace, the Harpies, and Charybdis; and *ambitio* by Polyphemus and Dido. In the *Divine Comedy,* the vices are represented by the three beasts of canto 1, the panther, lion, and she-wolf. Both poems reach a climax of sorts in the hero's descent to the underworld, where he gains the intellectual understanding he needs to complete his moral journey. Landino did not originate all the details of this interpretive pattern; his originality lies in the effort to uncover the same truth in both the *Aeneid* and the *Divine Comedy,* and to incorporate the details of allegorical interpretation into a sustained drive toward the truth.

Influence. Landino's Dante commentary was the most influential treatment of that text in the Italian Renaissance, and his Virgil commentary became an instant best-seller whose importance can be documented well into the next century. At that point it was still influential enough to structure fresco cycles of the *Aeneid* and to be cited in the notes to Gavin Douglas's English rendering of the poem. Landino's reliance on allegory, however, passed out of fashion, and his philological achievements were superseded by those who came after him. He remains a figure of unusual complexity and interest, but of a second, rather than a first, level of importance.

BIBLIOGRAPHY

Primary Works

Landino, Cristoforo. *Disputationes Camaldulenses.* Edited by Peter Lohe. Florence, 1980. Landino's most important work from a modern perspective. Partial translation available in Thomas H. Stahel, "Cristoforo Landino's Allegorization of the *Aeneid:* Books 3 and 4 of the *Camaldolese Disputations.*" Ph.D. diss., Johns Hopkins University, 1968.

Landino, Cristoforo. *Scritti critici e teorici.* Edited by Roberto Cardini. 2 vols. Rome, 1974. A collection of prefaces and lectures chosen to illustrate Landino's views on literature.

Secondary Works

Bandini, A. M. *Specimen literaturae Florentinae saeculi XV, in quo . . . Christophori Landini gesta enarrantur. . . .* 2 vols. Florence, 1747–1751. Still the basic source on Landino's life and works.

Field, Arthur. "The *Studium Florentinum* Controversy, 1455." *History of Universities* 3 (1983): 31–59. An interesting exploration of Landino's early career.

Kallendorf, Craig. " 'You Are My Master': Dante and the Virgil Criticism of Cristoforo Landino." In his *In Praise of Aeneas: Virgil and Epideictic Rhetoric in the Early Italian Renaissance.* Hanover, N.H., 1989. Pages 129–165. Study of Landino's literary theory as applied to Virgil and Dante.

Lentzen, Manfred. *Studien zur Dante-Exegese Cristoforo Landinos.* Cologne, Germany, and Vienna, 1971. The best single study of Landino's famous Dante commentary.

CRAIG KALLENDORF

LA NOUE, FRANÇOIS DE (1531–1591), French soldier and author of several works of historical and military interest. Born into an old Breton noble family, La Noue began his military career in Italy before 1558. Returning to France, he embraced Calvinism and became a key Huguenot leader in the religious wars after 1562. An able soldier, La Noue seized Orléans in 1567 with just fifteen horsemen and led the Calvinist rear guard at the battle of Jarnac (March 1569). Captured at Moncontour seven months later but soon released, he lost his left arm while besieging Fontenay-le-Comte (1570). The limb subsequently was replaced with an iron hook; hence his nickname, "Bras de Fer" (iron arm). After the peace of 1570, La Noue fought in the Spanish Netherlands until recalled to France following the Saint Bartholomew's Day massacre of Huguenots on 24 August 1572. At that time he agreed reluctantly to bring Calvinist La Rochelle to an accommodation with Charles

IX, only to lead the Huguenots in a new rebellion in 1573.

With peace restored in 1577, La Noue returned to Flanders, where he was captured in 1580. While incarcerated, he wrote his *Discours politiques et militaires* (Political and military discourses; first published in 1587), which combine moral and military reflections with a commentary on the state of France. His account of the religious wars from 1562 to 1570 constitutes his "memoirs," often issued separately. Released in 1585, La Noue rallied to Henry IV in 1589, and distinguished himself in the battles at Senlis (1589), Arques (1589), and Ivry (1590). Dubbed the "Huguenot Bayard," La Noue died on 4 August 1591 from wounds received at the siege of Lamballe.

BIBLIOGRAPHY

Primary Works

A modern edition of La Noue's *Discours* was published by F. E. Sutcliffe in Geneva, in 1967; the first English translation appeared in 1587. A good version of his *Memoires* is found in volume 9 of the *Nouvelle collection des mémoires relatifs à l'histoire de France,* edited by Joseph F. Michaud and Jean Joseph Poujoulat (Paris, 1854). His correspondence was published in 1854 by P. Kervyn de Volkaersbeke. La Noue also wrote *Déclaration de Monsieur de La Noue, sur sa prise d'armes, pour la juste défence des villes de Sedan et de Jamets* (Verdun, France, 1588); the two-volume book *Observations politiques et morales sur l'histoire de Guicciardini* (1593); and an unpublished work, "Abrégé des vies de Plutarque avec des annotations."

Secondary Works

Hauser, Henri. *François de La Noue.* Paris, 1892.

Taboureau, J. *Un moraliste militaire du seizième siècle: François de La Noue (1531–1591).* Paris, 1908.

RONALD S. LOVE

LANYER, AEMILIA (1569–1645), English poet. The daughter of Venetian-born court musician Baptista Bassano and Margaret Johnson, Aemilia Bassano grew up around the Elizabethan court and was educated in the household of Susan Bertie, dowager countess of Kent. Her father died when she was seven, her mother when she was eighteen, and sometime thereafter she became the mistress of Queen Elizabeth's cousin and Lord Chamberlain, Henry Carey, Lord Hunsdon. In October 1592 she was pregnant by him and was promptly married to Alfonso Lanyer, a court musician who accepted fatherhood of the son, Henry. From May to September 1597 Aemilia paid visits to the popular astrologer Simon Forman, whose casebooks provide a record of her nostalgia for life at court and her longing to be a lady; she hoped that Alfonso's adventure with the earl of Essex on the Islands voyage (an attack against Spain in 1597) would result in a knighthood. It did not, though he became a captain and was eventually awarded a hay- and grain-weighing patent.

Sometime during the first decade of the seventeenth century Aemilia spent time at the crown manor of Cookham with Margaret Russell Clifford, dowager countess of Cumberland, and her daughter, Anne Clifford. From this relationship came the book of poems that has established Lanyer as a major figure among early women writers in English. It apparently did not garner her financial success, however, because she taught school from 1617 to 1619, litigated to receive more income from her husband's patent after his death in 1613 until the mid-1630s, and ended her life in the household of her son's family in the London suburb of Clerkenwell, where she died in April 1645.

Lanyer's book, *Salve deus rex judaeorum* (Hail God, king of the Jews), was published in 1611. *Salve deus,* prefaced by eleven dedications, all to women, is centered by the long title poem on the subject of Christ's Passion told entirely from women's points of view. The book concludes with the first country-house poem published in English (preceding Ben Jonson's "To Penshurst" by five years).

The eleven dedicatory pieces are addressed to James's consort, Queen Anne; Princess Elizabeth; "all vertuous Ladies in generall"; Arbella Stuart (James's cousin and sometime rival); Susan, countess dowager of Kent; the countess of Pembroke (Mary Sidney, sister of Sir Philip and a recognized author in her own right); Lucie, countess of Bedford (an important patron of Jonson and Donne); Margaret (Clifford), countess dowager of Cumberland (Lanyer's principal dedicatee); Katherine, countess of Suffolk; Anne, countess of Dorset (Margaret's daughter, who at the time was fighting to inherit her late father's lands); and "the Vertuous Reader" (in prose).

Subtle and complex, the title poem is 1,840 lines of ottava rima iambic pentameter. It tells the story of the Passion of Christ but is surrounded by lines that praise and comfort the countess dowager of Cumberland, who is pictured as a suffering saint and the exemplary bride of Christ, and provides a woman's commentary on the stories of Cleopatra, Solomon and Sheba, Lucrece, and Rosamond, among others. At several points the Passion story contrasts the virtues of women (Pilate's wife, the tearful daughters of Jerusalem, the Virgin Mary, the countess of Cumberland) with the wickedness of men (Caiphas, Pontius Pilate, even the thrice-denying Peter). The section titled "Eve's Apology," told in the voice of Pilate's wife, audaciously argues for women's liberty.

The volume's concluding poem, "The Description of Cooke-ham," shows evidence that Lanyer was aware of country-house poems by Horace and Martial and that she was writing in the Augustan tradition of contrasting the idyllic natural order with a fallen human civilization—a tradition that Jonson, Thomas Carew, Robert Herrick, and Andrew Marvell later exploited. A valedictory to an Edenic world, Lanyer's poem is also an overt criticism of the British class structure.

BIBLIOGRAPHY

Primary Work
Lanyer, Aemilia. *The Poems of Aemilia Lanyer: Salve deus rex judaeorum.* Edited by Susanne Woods. New York, 1993.

Secondary Works
Grossman, Marshall, ed. *Aemilia Lanyer: Gender, Genre, and The Canon.* Lexington, Ky., 1998. Studies by a variety of prominent scholars of English Renaissance literature.
Lewalski, Barbara K. "Imagining Female Community: Aemilia Lanyer's Poems." In *Writing Women in Jacobean England.* Cambridge, Mass., 1993. Excellent summary of the poems in their Renaissance context.
Woods, Susanne. *Lanyer: A Renaissance Woman Poet.* New York, 1999. Situates Lanyer among her contemporaries, including Spenser, Shakespeare, Jonson, and Donne.

SUSANNE WOODS

LA RAMÉE, PIERRE DE. *See* **Ramus, Petrus.**

LASCARIS, CONSTANTINE (c. 1434–1501), Greek scholar and teacher. Little is known about Constantine Lascaris's life before he arrived in Italy. He was born in Constantinople and studied under John Argyropoulos before the fall of the city to the Ottoman Turks in 1453. Ransoming himself, he made his way to Rhodes and then to Venetian-controlled Crete before turning up in Milan in 1458 as a private teacher and Greek scribe. He eventually became the Greek tutor of Duke Francesco Sforza's daughter Ippolita and in 1463 ascended Milan's municipal chair of Greek. During these years in Milan the humanist Giorgio Valla studied with him. Lascaris accompanied Ippolita to Naples in 1465 and was given the chair of Greek at the university. In 1466 he was on his way back to Greece when he stopped in Messina and agreed to teach Greek there at the monastery of the Holy Savior. He remained there until his death, attracting students from all over Italy, the most important of whom was the Venetian Pietro Bembo.

Lascaris cemented his fame as a teacher first through his Greek grammar, the *Erotemata,* which in 1476 became the first book ever printed by a Greek (Demetrius Damilas with Dionysius Paravisinus in Milan), and then through his full Greek grammar in three books, which first appeared 1500–1503. He published *Lives* of the ancient Greek philosophers of Sicily in 1499 in Messina. He also collected Greek proverbs, was an early enthusiast for the collection of classical epigrams called the Greek Anthology, and left behind work in manuscript on Orphic literature, Greek historiography, Greek metrics, Greek astronomy, and individual literary and scientific texts.

BIBLIOGRAPHY

Legrand, Émile. *Bibliographie hellénique des XVe et XVIe siècles.* 4 vols. Paris, 1855–1906. Reprint, Paris, 1962. See vol. 1, pp. lxxi–lxxxvii, and vols. 2–4, passim. A bit dated but invaluable for its bibliographical and textual material.

Manzano, Teresa Martínez. *Konstantinos Laskaris: Humanist, Philologe, Lehrer, Kopist.* Hamburg, Germany, 1994.

JOHN MONFASANI

LASCARIS, JANUS (c. 1445–1534), Greek diplomat, scholar, educator. Baptized John and born in Constantinople into a family of the Byzantine high nobility, Lascaris changed his name to the more classical Janus after he emigrated to western Europe. He was eight years old when Constantinople fell to the Turks. His family took refuge in the Peloponnesus and later Crete, whence he arrived in 1463 at the University of Padua to study under Demetrius Chalcondyles with the financial support of Cardinal Bessarion. After Bessarion's death in 1472, Lascaris traveled to Florence with Chalcondyles, who had received a professorship at the University of Florence.

In Florence he established a successful private school, counting among his pupils Marcus Musurus (c. 1470–1517), who would become one of the greatest Greek scholars of the Renaissance. Lascaris became well known for the various classical Greek authors he edited for the press in Florence, including Homer, the Greek Anthology (a collection of classical epigrams first compiled in the tenth century), Euripides, and Lucian. He also found a patron in the Florentine leader Lorenzo de' Medici (Lorenzo the Magnificent), who sent him on two important journeys through Greece collecting Greek manuscripts.

Lascaris moved to Paris in 1496, where he became a royal adviser. In 1503 he took up the post of French emissary in Venice. There, along with Erasmus, he became active in the circle of Greek scholars around Aldo Manuzio. In the following year, Lascaris was appointed French ambassador. In 1513, when Giovanni de' Medici, Lorenzo the Magnificent's son, be-

came Pope Leo X, Lascaris took up residence in Rome and established, with the pope's support, a Greek College for Uniate Greeks. Lascaris, however, moved to Milan in 1518 to set up another Greek College; it failed after a few years because the promised support of King Francis I of France never materialized. In 1525 he returned to papal service under the Medici pope Clement VII and undertook embassies to the imperial court in Spain and the royal court in France before retiring to Rome, where he eventually died. In 1527, in Paris, a disciple published a collection of his Greek epigrams, which would be reprinted in three more editions during the Renaissance.

In an extraordinarily long career as a teacher, editor, collector of manuscripts, scholar, poet, and diplomat, Lascaris became one of the most conspicuous representatives of Greek culture in the Renaissance, influencing the general reading public, scholars, secular rulers, and popes across a wide range of issues.

BIBLIOGRAPHY

Primary Works

Lascaris, Janus. *Epigrammi greci.* Edited by Anna Meschini. Padua, Italy, 1976.

Pontani, Anna Meschini. "Paralipomeni dei *Turcica*: Gli scritti di Giano Lascaris per la crociata contro i turchi." *Römische historische Mitteilungen* 27 (1985): 213–338.

Secondary Works

Knös, Börje. *Un ambassadeur de l'hellénisme—Janus Lascaris—et la tradition greco-byzantine dans l'humanisme français.* Uppsala, Sweden, and Paris, 1945. Not definitive because of various flaws, but the only book-length study.

Legrand, Émile. *Bibliographie hellénique des quinzième et seizième siècles.* 4 vols. Paris, 1855–1906. Reprint, Paris, 1962. See vol. 1, pp. cxxxi–clxii; and vols. 2–4, passim.

JOHN MONFASANI

LAS CASAS, BARTOLOMÉ DE (1474–1566), Spanish author and activist in defense of American Indian rights. Fray Bartolomé de Las Casas is known principally for his work denouncing the Spanish colonization of the Americas and its cruel treatment of the indigenous peoples.

After settling in Hispaniola in 1502 and participating in the pacification of Cuba in 1512, Las Casas came to see the oppressive character of the *encomienda* system, by which Indians were assigned to labor for colonists who ostensibly would Christianize them. His experience of the cruelties of the conquest of the Indies coincided with the protest initiated by the Dominicans who had come to Hispaniola in 1510. This movement had a significant influence on Las Casas. In 1514 he gave up his *encomienda,* freed the Indians, and charged that the Spanish conquest was responsible for the decimation of the indigenous people. Las Casas defended the project of evangelizing Indians but condemned those who supported evangelization by war. In 1515 he and other friars met with the king and other high officials in Spain to present the Dominicans' plea for a radical reform and constructive redress of injustice.

In condemning Spanish colonization, Las Casas took pains to offer constructive alternative solutions to the encounter between the indigenous peoples of the Americas and Spaniards. In 1516 he proposed to Cardinal Francisco Jiménez de Cisneros a new community project where Indians would be free; he inspired the Hieronymite mission of three friars to investigate the treatment of Indians and to determine whether they could govern themselves; and in 1520 he received permission to establish a self-sufficient community in Venezuela. All these efforts ended in failure, in large part because of the opposition of the colonists. In 1523 he joined the Dominican convent in Hispaniola, where he developed the ideas that grew out of his experience. He began *Del único modo de atraer a todos los pueblos a la verdadera religión* (The only way to bring all peoples to the true religion; 1537); he also began work on his *Apologética historia* (In defense of the Indians) and his *Historia de las Indias* (History of the Indies).

In 1530 he set out for Mexico, Guatemala, and Nicaragua, criticizing the Spanish officials wherever he found the Indians unjustly treated. He now experienced some successes. Pope Paul III issued a papal bull, *Sublimis Deus* (1537), declaring that American Indians were rational people whose lives and property should be protected. Shortly after, Las Casas successfully established a mission community by peaceful means in hostile Indian villages in Guatemala. Back in Spain, where he was preparing the first version of his *Brevíssima relación de la destruyción de las Indias* (Very brief account of the destruction of the Indies; published 1552), Las Casas persuaded Emperor Charles V to publish the New Laws in 1542, which outlawed Indian slavery and sought to abolish the *encomienda* system within a generation. He returned to Mexico as bishop of Chiapas in 1544, preferring the poor community in the Yucatán to a rich one in Cuzco, Peru. Colonists' opposition to Las Casas and the new legislation was so formidable that, fearing a revolt, Charles V revoked some sections of the New Laws. In response, Las Casas went to a conference of bishops in Mexico City and persuaded them to support a resolution defending Indian rights. He wrote the *Confesionario*, a manual

for confessors that said that all Spaniards must free their Indians and make restitution in order to receive the last rites. Las Casas was summoned to Spain and all copies of the *Confesionario* were ordered confiscated.

The intellectual opposition to Las Casas was led by the Spanish humanist Juan Ginés de Sepúlveda, who argued in his *Democrates secundus* that it was legitimate to use war to bring the Indians to Christianity. The Council of the Indies convened a meeting of jurists and theologians at Valladolid in 1550 to judge the arguments of Las Casas and Sepúlveda. The council seemed to support Las Casas but reached no judgment. Las Casas retired to the Dominican convent at Valladolid but still found time to be active in American politics, intervening, for example, when the issue of the *encomienda* was raised in Peru in 1555.

Critics have charged Las Casas with writing inaccurate history and creating the Black Legend of Spain by exaggerating Spanish atrocities. They also accused him of introducing African slavery in America. Recent studies on the demographic decline of the Indies have in the main supported Las Casas. His works were written in the context of the struggle for justice for the indigenous people. There were African slaves in the Indies before Las Casas recommended that they be used in 1518 to alleviate the forced labor of American Indians. But in *Historia de las Indias* he confessed that he was wrong and that African slavery was as unjust as Indian slavery. Las Casas remains a powerful representative of the struggle for human rights.

BIBLIOGRAPHY

Works by Las Casas

Brevísima relación de la destrucción de las Indias. Edited and translated by Nigel Griffen, with an introduction by Anthony Pagden. London, 1992.

De unico vocationis. Edited by Helen Rand Parish. Translated by Francis Patrick Sullivan. New York, 1992.

Historia de las Indias. Translated and edited by Andrée Collard. New York, 1971.

In Defense of the Indians. Translated, edited, and annotated by Stafford Poole. DeKalb, Ill., 1974. Translation of *Apologética historia.*

Obras completas. Edited by Paulino Cataneda Delgado. Madrid, 1988.

Secondary Works

Friede, Juan, and Benjamin Keen, eds. *Bartolomé de Las Casas in History.* DeKalb, Ill., 1971.

Gibson, Charles. *The Black Legend: Anti-Spanish Attitudes in the Old World and the New.* New York, 1971.

Gutiérrez, Gustavo. *Las Casas: In Search of the Poor of Jesus Christ.* Translated by Robert R. Barr. Maryknoll, N.Y., 1993.

Hanke, Lewis. *All Mankind Is One.* DeKalb, Ill., 1970.

Markus, G. *Bartolomé de Las Casas: The Gospel of Liberation*. Dublin, Ireland, 1988.

Wagner, Henry Raup, and Helen Rand Parish. *The Life and Writings of Bartolomé de Las Casas*. Albuquerque, N. Mex., 1967.

DAVID M. TRABOULAY

ŁASKI FAMILY. A prominent Polish family, the Łaskis were diplomats, churchmen, champions of Renaissance humanism. Jan Łaski (1455–1531) was the most eminent Polish churchman and diplomat in the first half of the sixteenth century. Enjoying the support of the royal chancellor, Krzesław of Kurozwęki, he entered the service of the king in 1496 and received canonries at Poznan (1484) and Gniezno (1487). He rose to the office of grand chancellor of the crown under King Aleksander Jagielłończyk and in 1510 was appointed archbishop of Gniezno and primate of Poland. He took part in the Lateran Council in Rome (1513–1515) and visited Jerusalem on a pilgrimage. Jan Łaski was an expert in contemporary European political matters, particularly in the relationship between Poland and the Teutonic Order, as well as in the internal issues of the Polish state system. An advocate of political and legal reforms, Łaski initiated the publication of *Commune incliti Poloniae regni privilegium* (General legal privileges of the illustrious kingdom of Poland; 1506), the set of Polish laws and Seym (parliamentary) enactments—hence its commonly used name, *Statut Łaskiego*. Like all other family members, Jan Łaski offered his support for the king of Hungary, Janos Zapolya, which exposed him to a severe reprimand from Pope Clement VII. Toward the end of his life Łaski fought against the first Lutheran influences in Poland. He also extended patronage to talented young people, such as the distinguished humanist Andrzej Frycz Modrzewski and a Spanish poet living in Poland, Peter Roysius (Pedro Ruiz de Moroz).

Łaski provided for the education of his nephews: Hieronim (1496–1542), later palatine of Sieradz and Transylvania, and a political supporter of Janos Zapolya, the king of Hungary; Stanisław (c. 1500–c. 1550), later a palatine of Sieradz, and a courtier and official of Francis I of France; and Jan Łaski the Younger (1499–1560). Stanisław Łaski was active as a diplomat in the service of Sigismund I and Sigismund II Augustus but also had significant literary gifts. He was the author of a pamphlet, circulating anonymously, entitled *Dialogus de asiana diaeta* (Dialogue on the Asian meeting), and a military treatise, as well as the translator into Polish of Erasmus's *Querela pacis* (Complaint of peace; 1545).

Jan Łaski the Younger, who with Hieronim had accompanied his uncle to the Lateran Council at

Jan Łaski. Portrait from Théodore de Bèze's *Icones,* 1580. BIBLIOTHÈQUE NATIONALE, PARIS

Rome, studied abroad in Vienna, Bologna, and Padua. He also engaged in scholarly work while on diplomatic missions as the king's secretary (appointed 1521). In 1524 he visited Erasmus in Basel, returning the next year for a stay of six months in Erasmus's house. Łaski purchased Erasmus's famous library but left him the use of it for life. After his return to Cracow in 1526, he held several ecclesiastical offices. For a few years he supported his brother Hieronim in his work for Janos Zapolya and thus visited Vienna, Germany, and Hungary. And he gathered around himself a circle of young humanists devoted to the ideas of the Christian humanism and the teaching of Erasmus.

In the 1520s Jan became interested in the ideas of the Reformers. He rejected Luther's radical methods, however, and favored Philipp Melanchthon's moderate approach. When the family's involvement in Hungarian politics led to their political ruin in Poland, Jan retired to his brother Hieronim's estate. In 1539 he left Poland and settled in Louvain, attracted by the *philosophia Christi* of the Brethren of the

Common Life. In Louvain he married the daughter of a merchant, thereby forfeiting his ecclesiastical benefices in Poland. He moved to Emden in Friesland, where he worked for the introduction of public education. Returning to Poland in 1541 to meet with his ailing brother, he swore a solemn oath that he was an orthodox Catholic. Back in Emden after his brother's death, he again broke with the Catholic Church, and in 1543 he was appointed superintendent of the church of East Friesland. Unwilling to adopt the Augsburg Interim (1548), he went to England, where he was invited by the archbishop, Thomas Cranmer, to help him in setting up the Church of England. In 1550 he became a superintendent of the so-called foreign congregations of London. He stayed there until 1553, when the persecution of the Protestants under Queen Mary made him return to Emden. After being forced to leave Emden in 1555 and settling for a while in Germany, Łaski found his last refuge in his homeland in 1556.

During the last years of his life Łaski took an active part in the efforts to unify different factions of Polish Protestants. An initiator and author of the Calvinist translation of the Bible into Polish (the so-called Biblia Brzeska), he also participated in the creation of an academy for non-Catholics in Królewiec (Königsberg). He authored numerous theological works and had a rich correspondence with eminent humanists and important leaders of the Reformation. Together with his friend the Flemish Reformer Jan Utenhove, he wrote *Simplex et fidelis narratio de instituta as demum dissipata Belgarum aliorumque peregrinorum in Anglia ecclesia* (Simple and faithful account of the foundation and ultimate destruction of the church of the Belgians and other foreigners in England), which was published in Basel in 1560 under Utenhove's name. In the same year he died in Pińczów, the famous center of Polish Protestantism.

Jan Łaski the Younger had a considerable impact on various representatives of the Reformation in Poland, especially on his nephew Olbracht (Albrecht) Łaski (1536–1605), a son of Hieronim. Olbracht became a Calvinist and participated in the Reformation. A courtier and a diplomat, Olbracht Łaski was one of the most famous and colorful figures of his age. He was a model for one of the characters in Shakespeare's comedy *Love's Labors Lost*.

See also **Poland**.

BIBLIOGRAPHY

Primary Works

Erasmus, Desiderius. *Collected Works of Erasmus*. Edited by R. J. Schoeck. 86 vols. Toronto, 1974–. See correspondence between Erasmus and members of the Łaski family.

Łaski, Jan. *Opera: Tam edita quam inedita*. Edited by Abraham Kuyper. Amsterdam, 1866.

Melanchthon, Philipp. *Melanchthons Briefwechsel*. Edited by Heinz Scheible. Vol. 2. Stuttgart, Germany, 1977.

Secondary Works

Bartel, Oskar. *Jan Łaski*. Warsaw, 1955. Reprint, Berlin, 1981.

Cytowski, Maria. Articles on Hieronim Łaski, Jan I Łaski, Jan II Łaski, and Stanisław Łaski. In *Contemporaries of Erasmus: A Biographical Register of the Renaissance and Reformation*. Edited by Peter G. Bietenholz and Thomas B. Deutscher. Vol. 2. Toronto and Buffalo, N.Y., 1986. Pages 294–302.

Dalton, Hermann. *John a Lasco: His Earlier Life and Labours*. London, 1886. Translation of *Johannes a Lasco: Beitrag zur Reformationsgeschichte Polens, Deutschlands und Englands* (1881).

Hall, Basil. *John à Lasco, 1499–1560: A Pole in Reformation England*. London, 1971.

Kowalska, Halina. *Działalność reformatorska Jana Łaskiego w Polsce 1556–1560*. Wrocław, Poland, 1969.

ANDRZEJ BOROWSKI

LASSO, ORLANDO DI (Roland or Orlande de Lassus; c. 1530–1594), Franco-Flemish composer. Born in Mons, Lasso received his earliest musical training there and was kidnapped three times because of his beautiful voice. The third time his parents let him remain in the service of Ferrante I Gonzaga, viceroy of Sicily, in whose retinue he traveled in 1544 to Palermo. During the next ten years he also resided in Milan, Naples, and Rome, where he became choirmaster at Saint John Lateran in 1552. Lasso's Italian years were crucial for his musical development and even for the italianized form of his name that he preferred through the rest of his life (his original name and birthdate are undocumented). In 1554 he was summoned home but arrived only after his parents had died. He then settled in Antwerp until 1556, when he was engaged as a singer in the court chapel of Duke Albert V of Bavaria in Munich. He became head of the chapel in 1562 and held that position until his death, serving Albert (ruled 1550–1579) and his successor William V (ruled 1579–1597) for over thirty years as director of one of Europe's leading musical establishments.

In his more than one thousand compositions Lasso excelled in all of the musical genres of his day except instrumental music, which he did not compose. Settings of Latin texts are most numerous, including over five hundred motets, about sixty Masses, over one hundred Magnificats, other liturgical music such as Lamentations for Holy Week, and some of his most famous works, especially the *Penitential Psalms* and *Prophetiae sibyllarum* (Sibylline prophecies). The motets have predominantly sacred texts, and they may have been intended variously

Orlando di Lasso. ART RESOURCE

for liturgical use, public ceremony, or private devotions. Smaller numbers of them celebrate secular occasions or personages, while a few others are humorous or didactic or set classical texts. His Italian madrigals are his most numerous and important settings of vernacular texts; he also composed a smaller number of *villanelle* and *moresche* (Italian songs with rustic texts). Lasso's over 150 chansons set texts by some of the most noted sixteenth-century French poets, while his polyphonic Lieder bring an international style to the vernacular music of his adopted homeland.

In his time Lasso was the most famous and admired composer in Europe, hailed early in his career as "prince of music" and "le divin Orlande." His first biographer, Samuel Quickelberg, praised his ability to "place the object almost alive before the eyes," to express in music the content of the words, and expression of the text is an essential element in all of Lasso's music. He accomplished this by a variety of means, sometimes through sudden changes in rhythm, melody, or harmony, sometimes through subtleties that can easily escape a modern listener. He was always a consummate technician, fundamentally a conservative who only infrequently used an extravagantly chromatic style, notably in the *Sibylline Prophecies*. The texture of his music varies frequently, with much chordal declamation, free counterpoint, and dialogue within the ensemble, and rather less often strict imitation or canon. Old-fashioned compositional devices like cantus firmus and ostinato may occasionally be seen. By the end of his life his style had been overtaken by newer currents, but his command of musical rhetoric was considered exemplary in Germany well into the seventeenth century. His music is so wedded to its texts that it can be completely understood only in conjunction with the words it presents so vividly.

Lasso was the first great composer whose fame was spread by printed music. During and soon after his lifetime over six hundred publications contained his music; that is, between 1555 and 1595 something by Lasso appeared in print on average once a month in France, Italy, the Low Countries, or the German empire.

BIBLIOGRAPHY

Primary Works

Lasso, Orlando di. *The Complete Motets.* Edited by Peter Bergquist. Madison, Wis., 1995–. A new edition of the motets; *SW*'s edition of them is frequently unsatisfactory. 11 vols. of a projected 21 published by 1999.

Lasso, Orlando di. *Sämtliche Werke (SW).* Edited by Franz Xaver Haberl, Carl Proske, and Adolf Sandberger. 21 vols. Leipzig, Germany, 1894–1927. Reprint, New York, 1973. The standard collected edition, though its texts are not always reliable.

Lasso, Orlando di. *Sämtliche Werke.* 2d rev. ed. Edited by Horst Leuchtmann. Wiesbaden, Germany, 1968–. A revision of *SW* in the light of current research; 8 vols. published by 1998.

Lasso, Orlando di. *Sämtliche Werke, neue Reihe.* Edited by Siegfried Hermelink et al. 26 vols. Kassel, Germany, 1956–1995. A continuation of the collected edition that includes all the music not published in *SW*.

Secondary Works

Bergquist, Peter, ed. *Orlando di Lasso Studies.* Cambridge, U.K., 1999. A collection of research on Lasso by eleven international scholars.

Boetticher, Wolfgang. *Orlando di Lasso und seine Zeit.* Kassel, Germany, 1958. The most comprehensive study of Lasso and his music. Still valuable for its bibliography of Lasso sources, but its biographical and critical observations must be used with caution.

Crook, David. *Orlando di Lasso's Imitation Magnificats for Counter-Reformation Munich.* Princeton, N.J., 1994. The most extensive study in English of any part of Lasso's music. Valuable discussions of liturgy in Munich and the Bavarian court.

Erb, James. *Orlando di Lasso: A Guide to Research.* New York, 1990. A comprehensive bibliography of Lasso research up to its publication date.

Haar, James. "Lassus [Lasso], Orlande." In *The New Grove Dictionary of Music and Musicians.* Edited by Stanley Sadie. London, 1980. Vol. 10, pp. 480–501. Revised reprint in *The New Grove High Renaissance Masters*. New York, 1984. The best short survey of Lasso's life and works in English.

Leuchtmann, Horst. *Orlando di Lasso: I. Sein Leben; II. Briefe*. Wiesbaden, Germany, 1976–1977. The most complete and authoritative biography of Lasso and a collection of his letters with German translation.

PETER BERGQUIST

LATERAN V, COUNCIL OF (1512–1517). Held in the Lateran Basilica in Rome at the height of the Renaissance, the eighteenth general council was convoked by Julius II (1503–1513) on 18 July 1511 to countermand the Council of Pisa (1511–1512) called by the pope's enemies, political (Emperor Maximilian I and King Louis XII) and ecclesiastical (disgruntled cardinals). The pope set as the goals for his council the restoration of church unity, peace among Christians and a crusade against the infidels, the extirpation of heresy, and a reform of church and society. The council opened on 3 May 1512, held five sessions under Julius II, and was continued by Leo X (1513–1521) who presided over seven sessions, the last on 13 March 1517.

In addition to the reform proposals submitted by Ferdinand II of Aragon and the Spanish bishops, a number of Italian humanists, clergymen, and one prince wrote reform treatises and orations addressed to the pope and/or council. Among the twelve preachers at the council's sessions were such noted humanists as the general of the Augustinians, Egidio Antonini di Viterbo (1469–1532), and the disciple of Bessarion, Alexios Celadenus (1450–1517), and such theologians as the Dominican general Tommaso de Vio (Cajetan) (1469–1534) and the Venetian patrician Cristoforo Marcello (d. 1527). The most famous literary work occasioned by the council was the satirical dialogue *Dialogus, Julius exclusus e Coelis* (Julius excluded from Heaven) attributed to Erasmus (c. 1466–1536).

Attendance at the council varied. Over 280 prelates of episcopal rank or higher attended the council (the average per session was about 115). The majority came from Italy. Julius II's commission of twenty-four prelates Leo X replaced with three deputations (faith, unity-peace-crusade, and reform), each composed of eight bishops elected by their peers and of eight cardinals and four prelates appointed by him. Unofficially the council members were divided on the issues: they were either pro- or anti-French partisans and either wanted a restoration of episcopal rights and dignity or were opposed (cardinals, religious, exempt clerics, curial officials, and so on).

The problems with France lasted for much of the council. Not until the eighth session did the French abandon their schismatic Pisan Council and adhere to the Lateran. Following the meeting at Bologna in December of 1515 between Leo X and the French king Francis I and the conclusion of detailed negotiations, the Lateran Council at its penultimate session in 1516, but with the French ambassadors absent, approved the Concordat of Bologna and abrogated the Pragmatic Sanction of Bourges (1438), the so-called charter of Gallican liberties.

The bishops' efforts to restore their dignity and power produced modest results. Exemptions from episcopal authority enjoyed by various diocesan and curial officials and by nuns were curtailed, appeals from episcopal courts restricted, and interference from lay patrons forbidden. Curbs were placed on the exemptions of the mendicant friars. Due to the opposition of the cardinals, the bishops failed to secure the establishment at Rome of a college of bish-

Fifth Lateran Council. Woodcut published in Rome by Marcello Silber, c. 1514.

ops to advance their interests. The council also enacted traditional reform measures, but these had little effect. To promote a crusade the pope and council sent legates to Catholic princes to urge them to make peace with one another and to the Bohemians to encourage reconciliation with the church. A campaign against the Turks was ordered and the recent crusade tax on the clergy noted.

On issues related to Renaissance culture, the council fathers expressed a discerning acceptance. They generally agreed that many areas of church life needed to be reformed according to ancient norms. The council decreed that preachers should preach the Gospel according to the interpretations of the approved fathers and doctors of the church. The council fathers noted that although printing made scholarship less expensive, some books also disseminated errors and encouraged immorality. To eliminate this problem the council ordered preventive censorship by local bishops. School teachers were to include religion in their instruction; university professors of philosophy were commanded to defend with convincing arguments the truths of the Catholic faith on such topics as the soul's immortality and multiplicity, the unity of truth, and the creation of the world. Clerics studying at universities were not to devote themselves to philosophy and poetry for longer than five years without also studying theology or canon law so as to cleanse and heal infection coming from these sources. While continuing to condemn the practice of usury, the Medici pope and the council approved credit organizations for the poor that charged fees only to cover expenses.

If Lateran V failed to win wide acceptance, it did nonetheless leave a legacy beyond its decrees. Its failed efforts to reform the calendar may have led Nicolaus Copernicus to make his observations and calculations that revolutionized astronomy. While there is no direct major artistic representation of the council, Raphael seems to have made allusions to its goals in the frescos of the *Stanza dell'incendio* (Room of the fire) in the Vatican and the seated bishops in the fresco of Charlemagne's coronation may have been sketched at a conciliar ceremony.

See also Conciliarism; Leo X.

BIBLIOGRAPHY

De la Brosse, Olivier. "Latran V." In Olivier de la Brosse et al., *Latran V et Trente.* Paris, 1975. Vol. 1, pp. 13–114.

Hergenröther, Joseph. "Le dix-huitième concile général, cinquième de Latran." In Charles-Joseph Hefele et al., *Histoire des conciles d'après les documents originaux.* Revised and translated by Henri Leclercq. Vol. 8, Pt. 1. Paris, 1917. Pages 239–565.

Landi, Aldo. *Concilio e papato nel Rinascimento (1449–1516): Un problema irrisolto.* Turin, Italy, 1997.

Minnich, Nelson H. *The Catholic Reformation: Council, Churchmen, Controversies.* Aldershot, U.K., 1993.

Minnich, Nelson H. *The Fifth Lateran Council (1512–17): Studies on Its Membership, Diplomacy, and Proposals for Reform.* Aldershot, U.K., 1993.

NELSON H. MINNICH

LATIN LITERATURE AND LANGUAGE. *For discussion of classical Latin poets, see* **Poetry,** *subentry on* **Classical Poetry; Ovid; Virgil.** *For discussion of the Renaissance discovery and criticism of ancient Latin literature and language, see* **Classical Scholarship.** *For discussion of Latin works written in the Renaissance, see* **Neo-Latin Literature and Language.**

LAW. The Renaissance inherited from the Middle Ages a highly developed and complex system of legal training and procedure, and a variety of law codes. Much of this inheritance remained intact throughout the Renaissance. But the period also saw the spread of Roman law to parts of northern Europe previously little touched by it, as well as the development of humanistic jurisprudence. Modern international law began in the seventeenth century. Law affected all aspects of human existence and it especially regulated the position of women.

Legacy of Medieval and Canon Law. The twelfth century marked a watershed in the development of law in Italy and Europe as a whole. In that century, to which the term "renaissance" has also been applied, stimulated by continuing tensions between emperors and popes, study of Roman law was revived and alongside it developed the related study of ecclesiastical canon law. Feudal law and Lombard law also received attention. The main, but not sole, early center for the study of law was Bologna, from which derived the establishment of a school at Padua in the early thirteenth century by dissident students.

Studies of law were text-based. Those of Roman law had been compiled at the behest of the emperor Justinian (527–565), including the *Codex* of existing laws, the *Institutes* as a textbook, and the *Digest,* a collection of snippets from the Roman jurisconsults, arranged according to legal topics. It was above all the rediscovery of the *Digest* tracts (c. 1089) that animated both rhetorical and substantive investigations of the law, reviving the very image of the legal expert teaching and advising. Roman civil law, however, was largely about matters that in the twentieth century would be termed private law—that is, kinship and status, inheritance, property, and obligations. Public law, criminal law, and judicial procedure received much less attention. These areas, especially procedure, were further developed in canon law.

Canon law was based on a work compiled around 1140 by a shadowy figure, the monk Gratian, who collected segments from disparate sources to form what was entitled *Concordia discordantium canonum* (The concordance of discordant canons) but is and was better known as the *Decretum.* Canon law, in contrast to Roman, was used, interpreted, and applied in courts ranging from Rome to remote dioceses on the fringes of western Christendom, and problems were appealed to Rome. Thus, papal decretal letters in response to legal problems also served as a source of law; these included important rulings regarding marriage and other matters. In 1234 Gregory IX (1227–1241) issued the *Liber extra,* which organized decretals by topic in five books, and superseded all previous compilations. Boniface VIII (1294–1303) issued a sixth book (*Liber Sextus*) in 1298. The age of canonical legislation ended with small additions, by the Avignon popes John XXII (1316–1334) and Clement V (1305–1314), which refined the so-called romano-canonical civil procedure.

Learned jurists who taught and studied at Bologna or elsewhere were intent on harmonizing the collections of textual fragments. It was they (not the ancient Romans or Byzantines) who saw these texts as forming a single body of law, animated and informed by a single standard of reason and justice (*ratio scripta,* written reason); hence the titles *Corpus iuris* (Body of laws) of Justinian and *Corpus iuris canonici* (Body of canonical laws). As such, the *Corpus* was an unchanging model, beyond textual criticism. The jurists' intellectual apparatus did not call for philological or historical techniques, rather "their sole concern was the need to consult a reliable and authoritative text" (M. Bellomo, *The Common Legal Past of Europe,* p. 68). The predominant mode of inquiry and instruction was the textual gloss, a brief annotation to explain terms, highlight principles, or refer to other portions of the *Corpus.* These were rendered in the margins or interlinearly in the pages of the authoritative texts, and they were themselves gathered and expanded over time. All the texts thus acquired a standard or "ordinary" gloss in the course of the thirteenth century. These glosses were the basic apparatus from which students learned to apply and extend the *ius commune,* "common" universal laws—civil and canon. If they chose, students could pursue a degree as *utriusque iuris doctor* (doctor of both laws).

Instruction in the medieval law schools also involved lectures on the texts, public presentations, and debates on *quaestiones disputatae* (disputed matters). These reflected the involvement of jurists in ongoing political and legal affairs and an interest on the part of rulers, courts, and civic bodies in having the jurists' determinations and the input of legal scholarship. The impact of learned jurisprudence on legal practices was immense, if often indirect or gradual.

By the mid-thirteenth century a number of Italian communes, some quite small, had books of statutes covering matters like communal offices and public places, crimes, procedures, dowry, and inheritance. Frederick II (d. 1250) gave his kingdom of Sicily its own laws in 1231; and parallel developments occurred in Iberia and France. These statutes and customs were the *iura propria* (laws peculiar to a given place), in contrast to the *ius commune. Ius commune* contained rules that were not found in local law, as well as the terms and standards for interpretation of local laws. Thus *ius commune* served as a secondary source of rules on the local level and had an intellectual if not jurisdictional priority. Furthermore, local laws were notorious for changing with annoying frequency (to judge from complaints on that score), whereas the "common law" seemed a fixed and imposing force.

A related dimension of this process of refinement was a shift from oral to written law and the proliferation of notaries, and of standards for their education. *Scriptores* (scribes) who made written records of transactions are found in Italy since the Lombard era of the sixth through the eighth centuries, but their level of training in Latin and law was minimal. As legal science developed and local laws took written form, the level of sophistication of notaries had to increase. Formulary books arose and ultimately an *ars notariae* (art of the notary) developed from the *ars dictaminis* (art of letter writing), as found in the *Summa artis notariae* of Rolandino Passaggieri (c. 1234–1300). Notaries formed guilds that set and enforced standards, and from whose ranks, it must be added, came many of the first humanists—Petrarch (1304–1374) and Giovanni Boccaccio (1313–1375), and later Coluccio Salutati (1331–1406) and Leon Battista Alberti (1404–1472)—who first confronted study of the ancients in the form of Roman law.

Ius commune in the Fourteenth and Fifteenth Centuries. By the end of the thirteenth century changes were taking place in the law that later had a great impact. Two related forms of legal writing stand out—the commentary on legal texts and the *consilium* (advice) on legal cases or problems.

Commentators. Following the formulation of standard glosses, a new form of learned inquiry and pedagogy arose that directed attention to explicating the glosses themselves; these *commentaria* (commentaries) were personal meditations on the materials and problems accumulated around a text. Cino da Pistoia (c. 1270–1336), also notable as a lyric poet in vernacular Tuscan, employed Aristotelian logic in his commentaries. Aristotelian dialectic was well suited to discerning internal connections between legal precepts and giving reality to the "body" of law. It had already entered legal science in France, where it was dominant in scholastic theology, but Cino was the first to use dialectic to resolve contradictions between *ius commune* and various *iura propria*. His *Lectura in Codicem,* composed between 1312 and 1314, ranged beyond the *Codex* and its glosses to consider norms arising in statutes and to pose them against the equity of *ius commune*. But it was Bartolus of Sassoferrato (Bartolo da Sassoferrato) who left the most imposing legacy in late medieval jurisprudence.

Bartolus was born in a little hamlet in the region of Ancona in 1313; and he died while teaching law in Perugia in 1357. His brief life was enormously productive of commentaries, treatises, and *consilia* containing hundreds of original doctrinal constructions based on his mastery of dialectic and his imposing knowledge of the *Corpus,* feudal law, statutes, and jurisprudence. In his hands law became more open and flexible than it had been in the rather abstract and closed harmonies of the earlier glossators. He accommodated Justinianian formulas to practices and realities of his day. In one famous formulation, for example, he equated statute-giving cities to the emperor, calling them *sibi princeps* (emperor to themselves), which both gave their norms validity and posed them in relation to the overarching imperial law. The jurist became the necessary interpreter of social acts and living norms, bringing the logic of learned law and its principles to bear to determine where justice lay. Bartolus kept an eye open to contemporary issues and to the use of jurisprudence to resolve them. This is most evident in his treatises (also a new legal genre) on tyranny, reprisals, coats of arms, and other topics to which he turned after completing his masterly commentaries.

In the next generation it was Baldus de Ubaldis (Baldo da Ubaldis, 1327–1400), of a noble Perugian family, who carried on and also modified Bartolus's work. Productive for almost half a century, Baldus left complete commentaries on civil law as well as a commentary on the decretals, feudal law, and roughly 3,000 *consilia*. Baldus has been characterized as both more philosophical and also more accepting of the realities of contemporary norms and practices than Bartolus. As aware as he was of the differences between his own age and the ancient world that gave him the legal texts, his energies were concentrated on accommodating the present. Thus, in contrast to Bartolus, who saw grants of citizenship by city-states to foreigners as fully contractual, Baldus argued that citizenship not conferred by descent arose not just by legal convention but also by a habit of acting that became a second nature, and made the new citizen, in this sense, a "natural" citizen of his new *patria* (fatherland). He maintained some distance between "true" citizenship and acquired forms of it. His more abstract approach to the corporate character of the city-state similarly made him more accepting of the realities of rule by *signori* (lords) in Italian cities than had been Bartolus, who denounced their "tyranny" and investigated its legal effects.

Bartolus and Baldus became obligatory points of reference to those who followed them. Commentaries of fifteenth-century jurists, including men of considerable talent like Paolo di Castro (1360–1441) and Alessandro Tartagni of Imola (1424–1477), took their teachings into account systematically, even when they rejected or modified their illustrious predecessors' arguments. For that reason it has been customary among legal historians to speak in terms of intellectual decline. No equally imposing legal minds arose. Bartolus and Baldus were endlessly cited—and some works falsely attributed to them were smuggled into circulation—to the extent that humanists saw all jurists as bartolists (*nemo jurista nisi bartolista;* no one is a jurist unless he is a bartolist). But at least some of this sense of decline is countered if one looks past the academic commentary at *consilia,* where learned law informed practical problems.

***Consilia** and practical jurisprudence.* *Consilia* were the written opinions of legal *doctores* rendered in cases. After the parties to a suit had introduced evidence and legal rules, each for his own side, the problem of *quid iuris?* (what law applies? or, what is the legal right in this case?) emerged and could be handed to a trained jurist. Jurists addressed legal problems that arose, offering resolution in line with texts of *ius commune* or rules of *iura propia* as they saw fit. A *consilium* could be authored by a single jurist or, increasingly, signed by two or more linked sequentially with several *consilia* of others advancing similar lines of argument. *Consilia* first appeared in the twelfth century, but by the end of the fourteenth they had become so regular a feature of judicial practice that communes devised statutes to regulate them, even as they also employed jurists to help in revising statutes. *Consilia* could be given to aid the judge (not himself always a legal expert) or to bolster the arguments of one of the parties to a suit. In general, judges were expected to follow *consilia* they had commissioned, and a *consilium* produced by one of the parties was seen to carry great decisory weight unless counterbalanced by a *consilium* on the other side. Arguments in *consilia* that overturned local statutes were especially bothersome to governments, so that they attempted to rule that judges not follow such decisions. The authority of *consilia* rested on the impartiality and expertise of the learned jurist(s) who composed them, who could also be made accountable for them according to local statutes. These *consilia* were truly creative documents. They resolved contradictory material and symbolic interests in original ways, using legal texts as authoritative points of reference. However, their authority was fleeting, as there was no law of precedent in civil law or statutes. In *consilia, ius commune* and *iura propria* truly met, case by case.

Consilia became the growth area of legal writing in the fifteenth century. Those of authoritative jurists especially were collected, and published after the onset of print. Jurists mined them for arguments and citations for their own *consilia,* just as they did glosses and commentaries. In cities of Italy, producing practical opinions became a major activity and source of income for jurists, who wrote *consilia* singly or in groups. As the century progressed *consilia* became longer, and incorporated more and more citations on each point. While this led to denunciations by humanists and others, jurists were able to build up a wealth of *communes opiniones* (common opinions) on legal points. In essence they became a form of judicial precedent or jurisprudential law.

When rulers lost tolerance for such juristic independence, which sometimes led to the overturn of their own laws, they found ways to use legal expertise against itself. Culminating a century of gradual replacement of trained foreign jurists by citizens in

A Professor of Law. Francesco Alvarotti giving legal instruction. From the frontispiece of his *Consilia et allegationes,* copied by Jacopo de' Ruberiis. BIBLIOTECA CLASSENSE, RAVENNA

a succession of new courts, the Florentine *ruota* (the name copied from a papal court, invoking an image of a wheel of justice) was established in 1502. It was to be staffed by trained jurists (but local as well as foreign), and it was their sentence, rather than the opinions of advocates given before them, that came to matter in practice, as these judges were every bit as versed in the law as were those who put their *consilia* before them. The jurist lost the operating space of the scholar; academic and practical law split. Rulers also intervened to rewrite laws and overturn rulings. One of the factors at play here was legal humanism and its critique of law.

Humanistic Jurisprudence. Legal professionals were a strong presence in the cultural life of early-fourteenth-century cities. Cities moved to found law schools and attract teachers and students. The growing practical importance of legal knowledge and of legal Latin along with the increasingly dense and sophisticated terminology coming from the schools enhanced the social standing of notaries as well as lawyers. Throughout the fourteenth and fifteenth centuries, the expansive and aggressive state structures of cities like Milan and Florence continued to rely on jurists and notaries, whose visibility increased. They became indispensable in redacting statutes, in drafting legislation, and in carrying out diplomatic missions. Humanists, as rhetoricians and moralists wedded to classical texts and possessed of a view of the past, found their path to social and cultural influence impeded by these legal professionals.

Humanistic jurisprudence had its roots in fourteenth-century humanists' historicizing of classics. Petrarch decried jurists' lack of historical sensibility; and both Boccaccio and Salutati offered criticisms of legal practice and teaching. Such men opened up the question of the moral position of law in human knowledge. In his *De nobilitate legum et medicinae* (On the nobility of law and medicine; 1399), Salutati linked "good" law to general public welfare, from which point he could then offer Roman examples and draw implicit criticisms of prevailing patterns that obfuscated the law. This theme persisted with his humanist successors as chancellors of Florence— Poggio Bracciolini (1380–1459), Bartolomeo Scala (1430–1497), and even Benedetto Accolti (1415– 1466). A jurist himself, Accolti's dislike of legal practice spurred him to attempt to reorganize the Florentine chancery, taking up Poggio's attacks on law for verbosity, conflicting opinions, and lack of stylistic refinements. Along the same lines, in 1432, Ambrogio Traversari (1386–1439) urged a young associate to study the Justinianian texts themselves and not the glosses and commentaries.

Fifteenth-century Italy.
By the fifteenth century humanists had earned a separate status from the law and were freer to criticize it, and to indulge prejudices and misunderstandings. No one was more critical than Lorenzo Valla (1407–1457). His well-known philological deconstruction of the Donation of Constantine as a forgery (*De falso credito et ementita Constantini donation* [On the falsely believed and forged Donation of Constantine]) was an attack on jurists like Baldus who had defended the emperor's grant of spiritual authority to the pope as a valid gift or a prescribed right. Valla's criticisms of editing errors held the danger of attacking the very authoritative texts themselves; and he did not hesitate to take on imposing figures like Gratian and Bartolus. The latter he attacked in March 1433 in a letter excoriating a long list of errors in the treatise on coats of arms, as well as poor latinity and grammar. In fact, the portion of the treatise most heavily battered by Valla's rhetorical thrusts was not written by Bartolus, it now turns out, but was hastily assembled after his death by his son-in-law. Still, as it was widely accepted as Bartolus's work, Valla's criticisms carried

weight. Valla even attacked the sixth-century jurist Tribonian, commissioned by Justinian to oversee the *Digest,* for editing methods that did not respect textual integrity.

Valla's scathing parodies of professional legal jargon could not form the basis of a positive legal method. What contributed powerfully to a humanistic jurisprudence was specific textual criticism. When Florence annexed Pisa in 1406 there emerged an old copy of the Justinianian *corpus,* the so-called *littera florentina* or *pisana* (Florentine or Pisan text), as contrasted to the vulgate *littera bononiensis* (Bolognese text) that had served as the basis of legal study since the twelfth century. Revered almost as a relic, the *florentina* was first approached philologically by Angelo Poliziano (1454–1494). His death cut short his work, but the process was carried on by others.

The Frenchman Guillaume Budé (1467–1540) made two trips to Italy to consult the *florentina* and, inspired by Valla's 1444 *Elegantiae linguae latinae* (Elegances of the Latin Language), in 1508 produced his *Annotationes in quattuor et viginti Pandectarum libros,* which carefully laid out textual problems in the first twenty-four books of the *Digest* (also known as Pandects, a compilation). Andrea Alciato (1492– 1550), who had both a humanist background and a conventional legal education from the esteemed Milanese jurist Giasone del Maino (1435–1519), authored his first humanistic work in 1515; and the German Ulrichs Zasius (1461–1535) wrote in 1518.

The implication of their work was that Roman law had been the positive law of a particular social and political context in the past. It was not an eternal standard—certainly not when riddled with textual corruptions and interpretive errors. Humanist scholarship proposed to correct these errors, but in doing so it also rejected bartolist accommodations of law to society. Just as humanism's preference for classical Latin hastened the demise of Latin as a living, evolving language, it rendered Roman law a mere relic of the past—useful perhaps, but not necessarily and systematically so. Thus, to a number of legal historians especially, legal humanism was a regrettable episode or, at best, "no more than a new episode in the long history of assimilation of ancient law" (R. C. van Caenegem, *Historical Introduction to Private Law,* p. 33).

Mention of a Frenchman and a German in this context indicates another facet of law in the Renaissance. Like humanism and artistic styles, Italian jurisprudence spread in this era, which is known for the "reception" of Roman law. Even England felt the influence of civil-law-inspired notions of equity in chancery proceedings, and the possibility of the learned law supplementing royal common law was debated. Henry VIII (ruled 1509–1547) founded the regius, that is, royal, chairs of civil law at Oxford and Cambridge. The law faculties of German universities founded in the fifteenth century adopted Italian pedagogical and consultative techniques. A class of jurists arose. Their activities on behalf of litigating parties helped gain influence for academic jurisprudence and Roman law principles in municipal and princely courts.

The consequent confusion of traditional trial procedures spurred the intervention of governments. In the absence of a strong central government, German principalities and cities were free to adapt *ius commune* and use its practitioners. Statutes were rewritten into legal Latin and procedures were changed. An imperial court, proposed as a reform in 1495, was to require participation of trained jurists, but the emperor Charles V (ruled 1519–1556) ended these developments by publishing a reform of criminal law. Thus Roman law entered Germany at the same time as humanism and, for all that humanists decried law's technical Latin and crabbed dialectic, humanism aided law's reception as ancient in origin, superior to German. Both were part of a secularization of learning; both were in demand from a segment of the population that took them as insightful and useful.

The sixteenth century. The late fifteenth- and early sixteenth-century Holy Roman Empire prized the practical rationality of the law developed in Italy. This included the use of judge-run inquisitional procedure rather than an accusatorial arraignment, which was already being abandoned by governments that saw defendants less as someone's enemy and more as a "criminal" who had breached a law. In the accusatory procedure parties lodged their accusations or their defense against the charges, taking turns producing evidence, testimony, and legal arguments in their behalf. In the inquisitional procedure the judge ran the case and questioned witnesses, following initial accusation or even acting on anonymous denunciation of certain serious types of cases. The judge was to ensure that all transpired according to law, but especially in criminal cases there was a tendency to see substance in the charges that truly put the defendant on the defensive.

In France the more philological approach of humanist jurisprudence found a favorable political climate. There humanistic law was seen as a *mos gallicus* (French style or custom) in opposition to a bartolist *mos italicus* (Italian style or custom). French jurists, less entrenched in social and cultural life than were their Italian counterparts, linked their social and legal standing to a centralizing sovereign and took a nationalistic turn. Roman law or Italian method was rejected as foreign. Imposing as it was, Roman law was seen as unsuitable for the French, and therefore surpassable. Thus, while many legal historians have characterized the *mos italicus* as practical and contemporary and the *gallicus* as scholarly, historical, even antiquarian, the latter had practical resonance in France.

François Hotman's (1524–1590) *Antitribonianus* of 1567 (first published in French in 1603) argued forcefully that Justinian's text was not usable in France, that historicized Roman law was not superior to French customs. Philological approaches had opened up two questions—the validity of positive law (and the role of the king in forming it), and the restoration of Roman norms to their original state (revealing the distance from prevailing custom). French councillors and advocates could utilize the categories and logic of Roman law, but they had to go by local custom. The first academic chair for the teaching of specifically French law, however, was not set up until 1679. Criticisms of the *ius commune* as complex and of its proceedings as secretive and lengthy also received more play in France. Yet even in France inquisitional procedure spread at the expense of accusatorial or jury modes of trial.

A similar development was not so apparent in Spain because the monarchy was more transnational in orientation and because Spanish universities, especially Salamanca, became centers of the so-called Second Scholasticism. There figures like Francisco de Vitoria (1486–1546) and Domingo de Soto (1494–1560) retained a strong faith in an eternal standard of justice contained in natural law, as well as a sense of state sovereignty. Natural law was taken as a divinely instituted rational standard of rules and behavior applicable to all human societies, and it became a more pressing and practical matter as the Spanish encountered increasingly diverse populations around the globe. Academic debates on natural law, which had potential practical influence on the treatment of native American peoples, illustrated the powerful attraction of a single standard of right reason as opposed to a system built on a false sense of superiority rooted in Christianity but not in history.

Natural Law. Arguments exist as to whether notions of individual subjective rights, rooted in some sense of a natural law, first arose with the medieval canonists or only after the appearance of nominalist philosophy with William of Ockham (c. 1285–1349). These arguments are important, but not easily resolved. What seems certain is that discussion of natural law deepened considerably in the seventeenth century. Humanistic jurisprudence and textual criticism took their toll on Roman law, as did the desire of rulers to control legislative and judicial processes and to reduce legal experts to functionaries.

Roman law, in corrupt or uncorrupted texts, could not pose as a universal standard after humanism, nor could canon law after Protestantism and the Council of Trent (1545–1563), as there was no longer a single church whose law it was, and even within the Anglican church, where canon law continued to function, the changes of Trent were never accepted. As early as 1553 there appeared a printed edition of the *Institutes* based on the *littera florentina* and without glosses. Luther's criticisms and the problems that arose at Trent propelled the establishment of an official commission to undertake a careful reediting of the *Decretum*. After the early seventeenth century, printed editions of the *Corpus iuris civilis* omitted the *glossa ordinaria,* and around that time reprints of the great commentaries of Bartolus, Baldus, and others, which had been in steady demand through the sixteenth century, also ceased.

Existing legislation, custom, and court rulings became the stuff of legal publication, and proposals to codify existing laws were made. Needs of practical jurisprudence were broached even within Italy by figures such as the cardinal Giovan Battista de Luca (1614–1683), who, in his *Il Dottore Volgare* (The Italian doctor of law) wrote in Italian and proposed "reasonable" reorganizations of private law to aid practicing lawyers. In Germany the *usus modernus Pandectarum* (Modern use of the Pandects) arose after the 1495 official reception of Roman law. Figures such as Samuel Stryk (1640–1710) and Hermann Conring (1606–1681) pointed to ways to reorganize and use the ancient law and *ius commune* in the new terrain of Germany's commercial growth. Conring also wrote convincingly to destroy the myth that Roman law had been officially received as the law of the Holy Roman Empire by an act of 1135.

Hugo Grotius (1583–1645) inaugurated the modern era of international law with his *De iure belli ac pacis* (The law of war and peace) of 1625. In an era of colonies and growing transatlantic trade, Grotius turned to Spanish legal writings of the sixteenth century and grounded legal institutions in natural law, rather than Justinianian patterns, though he remained in line with many teachings of *ius commune.* At his hands nature became less the imprint of divine will that it had been for Spanish theologians and jurists, and more an extension of human reason as its highest expression. The success of his work in inspiring legal reform and the growth of international law can be gauged by a publishing history that saw twenty-six Latin editions of his famous book by 1700, as well as translations into Dutch, English, French, and German. In his 1631 treatise on Dutch law, *Inleiding tot de Hollandsche Rechtsgellertheyd* (Introduction to Dutch jurisprudence), Grotius placed Roman law, in the absence of specific written laws, as the standard of equity and wisdom and even of allowed custom.

Law and Women.   By the time of Justinian in ancient Rome, women faced surprisingly few disabilities in Roman law; guardianship was minimal and inheritance rights were substantially equal to those of men. The disabilities that remained, however, were not negligible, as women were still forbidden to hold offices and they could not be *patres* (fathers) and hold the *patria potestas* (paternal power) from which agnatic relationships (kinship traced exclusively through males), inheritance, and so much else flowed.

The situation was different in Germanic customs, where women had restricted inheritance rights (at least to real property) and were under a perpetual form of male guardianship. Church law further complicated matters, both extending rights of consent to marriage and a role for mothers as guardians of their children, for example, while also restricting women's access to courts and the altar. By the Renaissance each locality had customs and statutes that variously restricted women's control of property and access to legal actions. One common feature of many of these codes was that if her husband died without a valid will, a woman could not inherit beyond her dowry if there were also close male agnates.

The development of learned law was neither uniformly positive nor negative for women. Jurists shared the gendered prejudices and assumptions of their society, but they also were committed to the *ius commune* as a standard of justice. Just as some men used the device of the testament (itself revived by civil and canon law) to protect their wives and daughters and extend their claims on family property, jurists invoked the law to protect women. For example, the device of *consignatio dotis* (delivery of dowry) to safeguard dowry from a husband's bankruptcy, was itself based on a tacit claim the dowry had on the husband's goods prior to all other creditors' claims.

While these devices played a role in an escalation of dowry amounts, the freedom of women to dispose of any such property as they saw fit was extremely limited, in practice if not in law. Legislators and jurists looked at women not as right-bearing subjective individuals but as members of family groups, whose dominant figure was the male head of household. Women's legal visibility and activity were related to the contribution they could make to the group's welfare, which was most apparent in widowhood. Then, in the guise of guardian to children and owner of the dowry, they might enter into transactions, possibly with the advice of men, to pursue family interests. The Florentine widow Alessandra Macinghi negli Strozzi (c. 1410–1471), whose correspondence with her exiled sons survives, is an outstanding example of such a widow.

Humanistic jurisprudence did nothing to improve the situation of women; instead it licensed local customs as it historicized Roman law. The Counter-Reformation moves to cloister nuns more strictly and to govern their spiritual impulses (or their obverse in witchcraft) similarly restricted legal access for women; and much the same occurred in Protestant lands. Extension of agnatic lines by primogeniture and entail (*fideicommissum* in Italy and *mayorazgo* in Spain) steered more property to and through men; but these practices also placed some women in the position of heiresses to be sought by ambitious men. Nineteenth-century codifications, in their rejection of the form and much of the content of the jurisprudential *ius commune,* in their assertion of the basic law as legislation, gave very little legal or public role to women.

Law in Historical Context. As Europe moved in the late 1990s toward economic union, which entails a great deal of legal uniformity, interest was renewed in the late medieval *ius commune* and humanist and other reactions to it. The fact that Europe—with the major exception of England, and that only partial—had a substantial legal heritage could be taken as a basis for the future as well. Yet that "common" law always had as its correlative the particular laws of localities, frequently an obstacle for the professional caste of jurists. It is as likely that, were Europe to find a new Bartolus to shape contemporary legal realities, it would also find a new Valla to recall the differing historical realities in play. It is certain only that knowledge of legal history will play a large role in European debates and, in consequence, for those areas like the United States that will be vitally implicated in European developments.

See also **Bologna, University of; Humanism; Monarchy; Sumptuary Laws; Women,** *subentry on* **Women in the Renaissance;** *and biographies of figures mentioned in this essay.*

BIBLIOGRAPHY

Abbondanza, Roberto. "Jurisprudence: The Methodology of Andrea Alciato." In *The Late Italian Renaissance, 1525–1630.* Edited by Eric Cochrane. New York, 1970; Magnolia, Mass., 1983. Pages 77–90.

Ascheri, Mario, Ingrid Bäumgartner, and Julius Kirshner, eds. *Legal Consulting in the Civil Law Tradition.* Berkeley, Calif., 1999.

Bellomo, Manlio. *The Common Legal Past of Europe, 1000–1800.* Translated by Lydia G. Cochrane. Washington, D.C., 1995. Polemical and presentist, but a good survey of technical developments.

Black, Robert. *Benedetto Accolti and the Florentine Renaissance.* Cambridge, U.K., 1985.

Caenegem, Raoul C. van. *An Historical Introduction to Private Law.* Cambridge, U.K., 1992.

Canning, Joseph. *The Political Thought of Baldus de Ubaldis.* Cambridge, U.K., 1987.

Cavallar, Osvaldo. *Francesco Guicciardini giurista: I ricordi degli onorari.* Milan, 1991. Study of cases and fees, as well as legal thought.

Cavallar, Osvaldo, Susanne Degenring, and Julius Kirshner. *A Grammar of Signs: Bartolo da Sassoferrato's "Tract on Insignia and Coats of Arms."* Berkeley, Calif., 1994. In addition to fine analysis contains translation of Bartolus and Valla.

Gilmore, Myron. *Humanists and Jurists: Six Studies in the Renaissance.* Cambridge, Mass., 1963.

Kelley, Donald. *Foundations of Modern Historical Scholarship: Language, Law, and History in the French Renaissance.* New York, 1970.

Kirshner, Julius. "*Ars imitatur naturam:* A Consilium of Baldus on Naturalization in Florence." *Viator* 5 (1974): 289–331.

Kirshner, Julius. "Materials for a Gilded Cage: Non-Dotal Assets in Florence (1300–1500)." In *The Family in Italy from Antiquity to the Present.* Edited by David I. Kertzer and Richard P. Saller. New Haven, Conn., 1991. Pages 184–207.

Kuehn, Thomas. *Law, Family, and Women: Toward a Legal Anthropology of Renaissance Italy.* Chicago, 1991.

Lombardi, Luigi. *Saggio sul diritto giurisprudenziale.* Milan, 1967. Powerful argument regarding the role of jurists in fashioning law.

Maclean, Ian. *Interpretation and Meaning in the Renaissance: The Case of Law.* Cambridge, U.K., 1992.

Maffei, Domenico. *Gli inizi dell'umanesimo giuridico.* Milan, 1956. Classic examination of the topic.

Martines, Lauro. *Lawyers and Statecraft in Renaissance Florence.* Princeton, N.J., 1968. Monumental study of lawyers at work.

Mazzacane, Aldo. "Law and Jurists in the Formation of the Modern State in Italy." In *The Origins of the State in Italy, 1300–1600.* Edited by Julius Kirshner. Chicago, 1996. Pages 62–73.

Pennington, Kenneth. *The Prince and the Law, 1200–1600: Sovereignty and Rights in the Western Legal Tradition.* Berkeley, Calif., 1993.

Rowan, Steven. *Ulrich Zasius: A Jurist in the German Renaissance, 1461–1535.* Frankfurt, Germany, 1987.

Strauss, Gerald. *Law, Resistance, and the State: The Opposition to Roman Law in Reformation Germany.* Princeton, N.J., 1986.

Tierney, Brian. *The Idea of Natural Rights: Studies on Natural Rights, Natural Law, and Church Law, 1150–1625.* Atlanta, Ga., 1997.

THOMAS KUEHN

LAW COURTS. *See* **Crime and Punishment.**

LEAGUE, FRENCH CATHOLIC. *See* **Wars of Religion.**

LEFÈVRE D'ÉTAPLES, JACQUES (Faber Stapulensis, Jacobus; c. 1455–1536), French humanist. Jacques Lefèvre d'Étaples (Lefèvre) was born in Étaples in Picardy and died in Nérac in the kingdom of Navarre. He was an Aristotelian humanist who was also interested in the church fathers, medieval mystical writings, translations and editions of the Psalms and New Testament, and monastic and ecclesiastical reform. A major shift in the balance of his intellectual life seems to have occurred around 1508, when he became less the quiet university scholar and more the public monastic and diocesan reformer. It should be noted, however, that he had shown sympathy for

Jacques Lefèvre d'Étaples.

evangelical Christianity before that date and continued his Aristotelian interests after it.

Before 1508, Lefèvre taught in the collège du Cardinal Lemoine in the University of Paris. There he instructed scholars from his native Picardy in the new learning of the Renaissance, the "humanities" (*studia humanitatis*). He was particularly interested in the metaphysical works of Aristotle, as well as mathematical and astronomical works such as Euclid's *Elements* and Johannes de Sacrobosco's *Sphere.* However, he also valued the writings of the Greek fathers, whom he claimed he and his fellow humanists had rescued from the obscurity of monastic libraries where they had lain unread for centuries.

In 1508, Lefèvre retired from his university position and joined the Abbey of Saint-Germain-des-Prés under the abbot Guillaume Briçonnet. There Lefèvre said that he found the religious life of the monks devoid of spirituality and felt that they did not know how to pray with devotion. (This assessment was not unlike other humanist diatribes against monastic culture throughout Europe at this time.) In 1509, Lefèvre published his *Quincuplex psalterium* (Five-fold Psalter). This work contrasted five versions of the Book of Psalms and provided brief introductions to the spiritual meaning of each psalm. In his introduction to the Psalter, Lefèvre asserted that the literal-historical meanings of the psalms, made so popular a century and a half earlier by Nicolaus of Lyra (c. 1270–1349), were to blame for the lackluster spirituality of the monks. Lefèvre continued his work at Saint-Germain (publishing his commentary on the Pauline Epistles in 1512) until Briçonnet was made bishop of Meaux. In 1521, the new bishop called Lefèvre to his diocese and put him in charge of the reform of the clergy and laity of the region. It was at Meaux that Lefèvre's greatest work was done. He worked with a group of Old and New Testament scholars who, together, engaged in a great scriptural publication industry. Lefèvre himself translated into French and published the Gospels (1522), the Catholic Epistles (1524) (comprising James; 1 and 2 Peter; 1, 2, and 3 John; and Jude), and the French New Testament (1523), followed by the entire Bible (1530). These works were aimed at educating the secular clergy and the laity and once again engaging parish priests in their appropriate ecclesiastical roles.

At the behest of the Franciscans, who were losing their role as dispensers of the sacraments in Meaux as the parish priests began once again to perform these as well as their homiletic duties, the Faculty of Theology at the University of Paris accused the Lefèvrian circle of Lutheran heresy. Their reform activities and insistence on making scripture available in the vernacular seemed similar to Luther's work in Germany. Indeed, Lefèvre himself had read some of the early Protestant Reformers and was not entirely opposed to their views. However, a careful reading of Lefèvre's writings, especially his comments on the passages in Paul's Epistle to the Romans that deal with justification (central to Luther's contention that man is saved by faith and God's grace alone), shows that Lefèvre still held to the Catholic formulation that man is saved by faith and good works. Lefèvre's group was dispersed because of the charges brought against them, and he himself fled to the protection of Margaret of Navarre in Nérac.

Lefèvre's work in Saint-Germain and his group's work in Meaux indicate the presence of a lively reform movement in France in the early sixteenth century that was supported by nobility (for example, the Briçonnet) and the royal family (François I and Margaret of Navarre). However, this support waned when the king was taken prisoner at the battle of Pavia in 1525, and the reform movement was never able to complete its work in Meaux or extend its reform throughout France. Lefèvre himself is best viewed as a Renaissance humanist of intense spirituality who tried to bring about reform through the study of the classic works of early Christianity.

See also **Humanism,** *subentry on* **France.**

BIBLIOGRAPHY

Primary Works

Bedouelle, Guy, and Franco Giacone. *Lefèvre d'Étaples et ses disciples, Épistres et Évangiles pour les cinquante et deux dimenches de l'an.* Leiden, Netherlands, 1976. Suggested sermon topics for clergy of Meaux by Lefèvre and his associates.

Lefèvre d'Étaples, Jacques. *Quincuplex Psalterium. Fac-similé de l'édition de 1513.* Geneva, 1979. Lefèvre's 1509 work on the Psalms with which he intended to reinvigorate monastic spiritual life.

Rice, Eugene F., Jr., ed. *The Prefatory Epistles of Jacques Lefèvre d'Étaples and Related Texts.* New York, 1972. Critical edition of the dedicatory letters for all of Lefèvre's works; shows his goals therein, and also indicates the patronage for these works.

Secondary Works

Bedouelle, Guy. *Lefèvre d'Étaples et l'intelligence des Écritures* Geneva, 1976. Discusses Lefèvre's method of interpreting the Bible.

Bedouelle, Guy. *Le Quincuplex Psalterium de Lefèvre d'Étaples: Un guide de lecture.* Geneva, 1979.

Gosselin, Edward A. "Two Views of the Evangelical David: Lefèvre d'Étaples and Theodore Beza." In *The David Myth in Western Literature.* Edited by Raymond-Jean Frontain and Jan Wojcik. West Lafayette, Ind., 1980. Pages 56–67. Discusses differences between Lefèvre's and Bèze's David as an evangelical figure.

Gosselin, Edward A. "Lefèvre d'Étaples." In *The King's Progress to Jerusalem: Some Interpretations of David during the Reformation Era and Their Patristic and Medieval Background.* Malibu, Calif., 1976. Pages 49–63. Discussion of Lefèvre's method of interpreting the figure of David and the variety of spiritual meanings attached to him.

Heller, Henry. "The Evangelicism of Lefèvre d'Étaples: 1525." *Studies in the Renaissance* 19 (1972): 42–77. Shows how Lefèvre's work in Meaux related to evangelical reform.

Jacques Lefèvre d'Étaples (1450?–1536). Actes du Colloque d'Étaples les 7 et 8 novembre 1992 organisé à l'initiative de la ville d'Étaples-sur-Mer avec la collaboration de l'Association des Professeurs d'Histoire et de Géographie sous la direction de Jean-François Pernot, Maître de Conférences au Collège de France. [Papers from the Conference on Lefèvre at Étaples, 7–8 November 1992, Organized on the Initiative of the Association of History and Geography Professors under the Direction of Jean-François Pernot, Master of Conferences at the Collège de France]. Paris, 1995. Series of papers dealing with the relation of Picardy to France in the sixteenth century and Lefèvre's intellectual and literary influences.

Renaudet, Augustin. *Préréforme et humanisme à Paris pendant les premières guerres d'Italie (1494–1517).* 2d ed. Paris, 1953. Still the major study of Parisian intellectual life in the early sixteenth century and Lefèvre's role in it.

Rice, Eugene F., Jr. "The Humanist Idea of Christian Antiquity: Lefèvre d'Étaples and His Circle." In *French Humanism, 1470–1600.* Edited by Werner L. Gundersheimer. New York, 1969. Pages 163–180. Discussion of Lefèvre's and his associates' understanding and evaluation of the church fathers.

EDWARD A. GOSSELIN

LEGISLATURES. *See* **Representative Institutions.**

LEIDEN. The prosperity of the town of Leiden (Leyden) in Holland chiefly depended upon its cloth industry, which employed about half the population. During an industrial boom in the third quarter of the fifteenth century, the number of inhabitants tripled to 14,000, which made Leiden the most populous town of the county. After the death of Charles the Bold in 1477, a century-long period of economic and demographic stagnation and social unrest set in, the worst local and regional conflict coming in the 1480s. The Dutch Revolt against the lord of the Netherlands, King Philip II of Spain, marked a turning point. Leiden's relief on 3 October 1574, after a one-year siege by Spanish troops, led to the foundation of a Protestant university by William of Orange in 1575. (Ironically, the founding charter was issued in the name of King Philip II.) In addition, the town welcomed Protestant refugees from the southern Netherlands, who modernized the cloth industry. The population rose to 45,000 by 1622 and to 50,000 by 1640.

Until 1575, cultural life in Leiden was mainly of regional importance. The chapter of the Church of St. Pancras owned the library left by the fourteenth-century lawyer Philips of Leiden; two nearby Augustinian monasteries, Engelendaal and Lopsen, were the chief producers of manuscripts. Latin humanism is perhaps best represented by the schoolmaster Engelbrecht Schut (c. 1410–c. 1503); Dutch literature flowered in the chambers of rhetoric (fraternities having literature as their main activity; first documented in 1493). The earliest surviving printed book dates from 1483; Jan Seversz (fl. 1502–1524) was probably the most important printer in Holland in his day. The painter Cornelis Engebrechtsz (1468–1533), a follower of Rogier van der Weyden, had two notable disciples, Aert Claesz (1498–1564) and most notably Lucas van Leiden (1494–1533), but they did not establish a lasting tradition.

Many of Leiden's rhetoricians sympathized with Protestantism. One of them, Jan Beukelsz (or Boekelsz), or Jan of Leiden (1509–1536), founded the Anabaptist Kingdom of Sion in Münster (1534–1535). In 1572 the town turned to Calvinism. A controversy on predestination between two university theologians, Jacobus Arminius (or Jacob Harmensen; 1560–1609) and Franciscus Gomarus (or Franciscus Gommer; 1563–1641), escalated into a politico-religious conflict that divided the Dutch republic and was forcefully solved in 1619 by Maurice of Nassau in favor of strict orthodoxy (the predestinarian position); all Remonstrants (followers of Arminius) were removed from office and from university posts. But as a rule a more tolerant climate prevailed. Thus, John Robinson could organize his Separate Church in Leiden from 1609; his followers numbered about three hundred. Two of those, William Brewster and Thomas Brewer, established a printshop in Leiden which produced twenty titles, mostly militant Puritan treatises, between 1617 and 1619. It is Robinson's community that started the English colonization of New England. William Bradford organized the departure of the first group of Pilgrims from Leiden in 1620; the others followed in several waves until 1630. (John Robinson himself died in Leiden in 1625).

Leiden's university—which admitted non-Protestant students within a few years after its founding—quickly gained fame, not so much in theology as in the other disciplines, especially in literary studies. Justus Lipsius (1547–1606), teaching in Leiden from 1578 to 1591, and Joseph Justus Scaliger (1540–1609), teaching from 1593, ranked among Europe's most eminent philologists. Three other renowned

scholars were Janus Dousa senior (1545–1604), politician, historian, and the university's first curator; Daniël Heinsius (1580–1655), philologist and a Latin and Dutch poet; and Gerardus Vossius (1577–1649), regent of the Estates College for theology (1615–1619) and professor of rhetoric, history, and Greek at the university (1622–1631). Rudolph and Willebrord Snellius (1546–1613, 1580–1626) were outstanding mathematicians, and Everhardus van Bronchorst (1554–1627) was a celebrated jurist.

But intellectual life also flowered outside the university, in men like the genial mathematician and engineer Simon Stevin (1548–1620), who settled in Leiden in 1581 and became Prince Maurice's tutor in 1583, and the political theorist Pieter de la Court (c. 1618–1685); moreover, mathematician and philosopher René Descartes (1596–1650) regularly stayed in Leiden during his Dutch residence from 1629 to 1649. Famous printers sustained the output of intellectual life. Christophe Plantin transferred his activities to Leiden in 1583 to 1585; his former employee, Lodewijk Elzevier (c. 1540–1617), founded a press in 1580, continued by his descendants, which was highly reputed for its editions of classics, contemporary scholarship, and (after 1625) oriental books.

Leiden played only a secondary role in the Golden Age of Dutch literature and painting. The chambers of rhetoric, outlawed in 1567, were reactivated from 1577 by Jan van Hout (1542–1609), poet and secretary of town and university, who tried to introduce modern forms of poetry. In the beginning of the seventeenth century many chambers were active, but the renewal of Dutch literature was brought about outside the chambers, in Amsterdam. A state-appointed committee of Calvinist theologians and ministers worked in Leiden from 1626 to 1635 on the official (Estates) Dutch translation of the Bible (first published in Leiden in 1637), which was to exercise a major influence on the Dutch language. As for painting, Leiden produced many talented individuals who, however, often settled elsewhere. Rembrandt spent only his first active years in his native Leiden (1625–1631/2), sharing his workshop with Jan Lievensz (1607–1674), who left the town shortly afterward; likewise, Jan van Goyen (1596–1656) left Leiden in 1532. The latter's pupil and son-in-law, Jan Steen (1626–1679), was to remain in Leiden, as did Rembrandt's pupil Gerard Dou (1613–1675), whose school of "smooth finish" painting was to flower for several generations. Gabriel Metsu (1629–1667) was among his disciples.

The most impressive examples of ecclesiastical architecture are late Gothic (St. Peter's, St. Pancras's).

Renaissance architecture was introduced only at the end of the sixteenth century. Representative examples are the elaborate facades of the Town Hall (1596–1598) by Claes Cornelisz van Es and Lieven de Key, and the residence of the regional board of water economy (1598, Gemeenlandhuis Rijnland) by Jacob Quirijnsz van Banchem and Jan Dircksz. Arent van's-Gravensande (1600–1662), the town architect from 1638 to 1655, built Mare Church (1639–1649) and the Cloth Hall (1639–1640). A typical feature of Leiden are the numerous almshouses or "hofjes" (literally "little courtyards") founded by private benefactors from the late Middle Ages until the beginning of the twentieth century. Almost twenty examples from the late medieval and Renaissance period survive today, including the Cornelis Sprongh or Holy Ghost almshouse.

See also **Netherlands,** *subentry on* **The Netherlands and the Renaissance,** *and biographies of Justus Lipsius, Maurice of Nassau, Joseph Justus Scaliger, and Gerardus Vossius.*

BIBLIOGRAPHY

Blok, Petrus Johannes. *Geschiedenis eener Hollandsche stad.* 4 vols. The Hague, Netherlands, 1910–1918. Survey of Leiden's history. Outdated, incomplete, but not yet replaced.

Brinkman, Herman. *Dichten uit liefde: Literatuur in Leiden aan het einde van de Middeleeuwen.* Hilversum, Netherlands, 1997. Study of Dutch literary life in Leiden, from about 1450 to 1550.

Dröge, Jan, Evelyn de Regt, and Pieter Vlaardingerborek, eds. *Architectuur- en monumentengids Leiden.* Leiden, the Netherlands, 1996. Survey of architectural history.

Harris, Rendel, and Steven K. Jones. *The Pilgrim Press: A Bibliographical and Historical Memorial of the Books Printed at Leyden by the Pilgrim Fathers.* 1922. Partial reprint with new contributions, edited by R. Breugelmans, Nieuwkoop, Netherlands, 1987.

Kleibrink, Herman, and Ruud Spruit. *Hofjes in Leiden.* Leiden, Netherlands, 1979. On the almshouses.

Lunsingh Scheurleer, T. H., and G. H. M. Posthumus Meyjes, eds. *Leiden University in the Seventeenth Century: An Exchange of Learning.* Leiden, Netherlands, 1975.

Waite, Gary K. "Popular Drama and Radical Religion: The Chambers of Rhetoric and Anabaptism in the Netherlands." *Mennonite Quarterly Review* 65 (1991): 227–255.

ISTVÁN BEJCZY

LEIPZIG. Situated on a small plateau at the conjuncture of the Elster, Pleisse, and Parthe Rivers, Leipzig emerged as a commercial and academic center during the fifteenth and sixteenth centuries. Medieval Leipzig was an important regional economic center. Its annual trade fairs, at Easter and in September, attracted merchants from throughout Germany and other parts of Europe. By 1400 Leipzig had a population of approximately six thousand.

In 1409, with the encouragement of Friedrich the Warlike (duke of Saxony, 1382–1428; Elector, 1423–1428), and in response to the Hussite controversies, approximately two thousand German students and masters left the University of Prague to found the University of Leipzig. During the fifteenth and sixteenth centuries, the university offered degrees in philosophy, law, medicine, and theology and enrolled approximately two thousand students per year. Humanism was introduced during the 1460s, but not until the 1530s did courses on classical literature, Greek, and Hebrew become part of the official curriculum. The university's presence helped make Leipzig an important publishing center, with no fewer than eleven printing houses in the early 1500s.

Leipzig experienced impressive economic growth during the fifteenth and sixteenth centuries. Its merchants benefited from the development of the mining industry in the nearby regions of Erzgebirge and Mansfeld and by the establishment in 1456 of a third trade fair, held every January. Major commercial houses such as the Welsers and Fuggers established offices and warehouses in the city, and by the 1560s Leipzig's fairs were attracting merchants from as far away as Russia.

Protestantism attracted a strong following among Leipzig's citizens, many of whom were impressed with Martin Luther (1483–1546) and his colleague Andreas Karlstadt (c. 1480–1541) when they debated Ingolstadt's Johann Eck (1486–1543) in Leipzig in 1519. But Duke George the Rich of Saxony (ruled 1500–1539), whose line had received Leipzig when Wettin lands had been divided in 1485, suppressed Lutheranism until his death in 1539, when his brother Heinrich the Pious (ruled 1539–1541) became duke and instituted the Reformation. Under Heinrich's son Maurice (ruled 1541–1553), Catholic lands and buildings were confiscated. Although Calvinism gained adherents in Leipzig during the late sixteenth century, from the 1540s onward Leipzig remained firmly Lutheran.

Leipzig's prosperity combined with the windfall of confiscated church property to accelerate a building boom that had begun in the late 1400s. Several municipal building projects were undertaken under the direction of Hieronymus Lotter, a Nürnberger who as a young man came to Leipzig on business, married into the Leipzig patriciate, and served as city architect and mayor. His most impressive project, the Alte Rathaus (old town hall), was begun in 1556 and became a model of the Renaissance style in German cities. Lotter also was responsible for the design and construction of the Alte Waage (old weighing station), where goods to be sold at the trade fairs were weighed and registered.

At the close of the Reformation era, Leipzig's fortunes temporarily declined as a result of the gradual exhaustion of nearby mines and the damage to trade caused by the outbreak of the Thirty Years' War in 1618. Beginning in the late 1620s, Leipzig itself was placed under siege no fewer than five times and was occupied four times by contending armies. After the Treaty of Westphalia (1648), Leipzig regained its commercial and cultural prominence and reestablished itself as Saxony's leading city.

See also **Saxony.**

BIBLIOGRAPHY

Bieber, Ingrid, and Katharina Walch. *Leipzig und seine Geschichte.* Leipzig, Germany, 1991.

Czok, Karl, and Horst Thieme. *Leipzig: Geschichte der Stadt in Wort und Bild.* Berlin, 1978.

Grosse, Karl. *Geschichte der Stadt Leipzig von der ältesten bis auf die neueste Zeit.* Leipzig, Germany, 1839.

JAMES H. OVERFIELD

LEO X (Giovanni Romolo Damaso de' Medici; 1475–1521), pope (1513–1521). Born in Florence, the second son of Lorenzo ("il Magnifico") de' Medici and of Clarice Orsini, Giovanni de' Medici was destined for a clerical career. He studied Latin and Italian literature under the direction especially of Angelo Ambrogini ("Politian"; 1454–1494) and Bernardo Michelozzi (c. 1450–1519), and he also studied Greek and music. On 24 February 1489 he was ordained a deacon. On 9 March 1489 he was appointed a cardinal by his sister's father-in-law Innocent VIII. He went to Pisa (1489–1492) where he studied under some of the most eminent jurists of his day and on 1 February 1492 received from the university a doctorate in canon law.

When he went to Rome a month later to join the college of cardinals, he served as legate to the Patrimony of St. Peter (1492) and to Florence (1492). In 1499–1500 he traveled for pleasure and education incognito through Germany, the Low Countries, and France, finally settling in Rome in time for the Jubilee. Erasmus, whom he met in the Low Countries, enjoyed his hospitality while visiting Rome (1509) and later dedicated to him the *Novum Instrumentum* (1 February 1516), his Greek and Latin edition of the New Testament. Under Julius II, Giovanni de' Medici served as governor of Perugia (1506) and legate to Romagna and the papal army (1511–1512).

Elected pope on 9 March 1513, he was ordained a priest on the fifteenth, consecrated bishop on the seventeenth, and crowned on the nineteenth. As ruler of the Papal States he continued many of the policies of his predecessor Julius II. He managed to assert greater control over his territory by keeping the Bentivoglio family out of power in Bologna and executing in 1520 Gianpaolo Baglioni, lord of Perugia. Lesser tyrants in the Marches and Ancona were forced to submit. He absolved duke Alfonso I d'Este (ruled 1505–1534) of Ferrara, but removed from power for insubordination after a costly war (1516–1517) Gianfrancesco Maria della Rovere of Urbino and installed in his place his nephew Lorenzo de' Medici (ruled 1516–1519).

In external affairs Leo presented himself as the promoter of peace among Christians but worked behind the scenes to lessen foreign influence in Italy. Initially he joined Spain and the empire to drive the French out of Italy (1513), but reached accommodations with the French on their victorious return in 1515. Having failed to prevent the election in 1519 of Charles Habsburg as emperor, and needing the emperor's help to repress the Lutherans, Leo renewed his Habsburg alliance (1521) and helped to drive the French from Milan and restore to the papacy Parma and Piacenza. Although the pope's efforts to promote his family's interests were frustrated by the untimely deaths of his brother Giuliano (1479–1516) and nephew Lorenzo, who both ruled Florence and for whom he had negotiated marriages to members of the French royal family, he retained control of Florence through his first cousin Giulio de' Medici (1478–1534). His intervention in Sienese affairs provoked a conspiracy to poison him led by Cardinal Alfonso Petrucci (1492–1517) whom Leo then had executed. His cardinal co-conspirators were forced to pay enormous fines for their freedom, and the college of cardinals was intimidated into agreeing to the creation of thirty-one new members, among whom were relatives and clients of the pope.

Leo X brought to a successful conclusion the Fifth Lateran Council (1512–1517) by means of which he formally ended the Pisan Schism, condemned Averroistic teachings on the soul's unicity and mortality, ordered the reform of morals and curial practices, approved credit organizations for the poor that charged a management fee, confirmed the Concordat of Bologna, rescinded the Pragmatic Sanction of Bourges, and restored some episcopal authority. Having failed to silence or secure Luther's retraction or to take prompt, firm action against him for political reasons, Leo finally threatened him with penalties (*Exsurge Domine* of 15 June 1520) and excommunicated him (*Decet Romanum Pontificem* of 3 Jan-

Pope Leo X. Portrait of Leo with two cousins by Raphael. The prelate at the left is Giulio de' Medici, who became Pope Clement VII in 1523; at the right is Luigi de Rossi. GALLERIA PALATINA, FLORENCE/ANDERSON/ALINARI/ART RESOURCE

uary 1521). He rewarded King Henry VIII of England for writing against Luther by assigning him the title *Defensor fidei* (Defender of the faith). To encourage the propagation of the faith, Leo granted special privileges to the Portuguese and approved the ordination of native clergy, agreeing to the consecration as bishop of the son of the king of the Congo (1518). He increasingly acceded to the wishes of secular rulers in the appointment of prelates, and in his own selection of cardinals he promoted three first cousins and three nephews. His cousin Giulio, whom he appointed archbishop of Florence and car-

dinal vice-chancellor of the church, became his chief adviser and eventually his successor as de facto ruler of Florence and as pope (Clement VII). Leo promoted the cause of observant reform among religious orders. His failure to enforce reforms of the Roman Curia was often due to the loss of revenues that would necessarily follow such reforms.

During Leo's pontificate Rome experienced a "golden age" of Renaissance culture. He made the University of Rome an intellectual center with the appointment of distinguished professors and founding of a Greek college and press. He increased the holdings of the Vatican library. As his domestic secretaries Leo employed the humanists Pietro Bembo (1470–1547) and Jacopo Sadoleto (1477–1547). The humanist Paolo Giovio (1483–1552), whom Leo appointed as professor of moral philosophy at the University of Rome, wrote a famous biography of the pope. The most important artists patronized by Leo were Michelangelo (1475–1564), whom he commissioned to carve the tombs of Giuliano and Lorenzo de' Medici, and Raphael (1483–1520), his favorite, who among other things continued work on the *stanze* of the papal apartments, designed the tapestries for the Sistine Chapel, took charge of the construction of St. Peter's, and painted the pontiff's portrait.

To finance his military operations, splendid court, and patronage of writers and artists Leo pushed to new limits the sale of offices, dispensations, and indulgences. He borrowed heavily. Only with difficulty could money be found to give him a proper funeral after his sudden death from pneumonia. He was buried initially in St. Peter's, but then was reinterred in Santa Maria sopra Minerva.

See also **Medici, House of; Papacy.**

BIBLIOGRAPHY

Falconi, Carlo. *Leone X: Giovanni de' Medici.* Milan, 1987.

Ferrajoli, Alessandro. *Il ruolo della corte di Leone X (1514–1516).* Edited by Vincenzo de Caprio. Rome, 1984. A collection of journal studies.

Pastor, Ludwig von. *The History of the Popes from the Close of the Middle Ages.* 2d ed. Translated by Amabel Kerr. Edited by Ralph Francis Kerr. St. Louis, Mo., 1923. See vols. 7 and 8.

Picotti, Giovanni Battista. *La giovinezza di Leone X: Il papa del rinascimento.* Preface by Massimo Petrocchi, introduced by Cinzio Violante. Rome, 1981. Classic study of the family, education, and early career of Giovanni de' Medici.

Mitchell, Bonner. *Rome in the High Renaissance: The Age of Leo X.* Norman, Okla., 1973.

NELSON H. MINNICH

LEÓN, LUIS DE (c. 1527–1591), Spanish poet and biblical scholar. Born in Belmonte (Cuenca) into a prosperous and well-connected family of lawyers and churchmen, Fray Luis's life is intimately associated with the University of Salamanca, where he is commemorated by a statue. There he studied philosophy and theology, as well as biblical languages, and went on to occupy a series of chairs, culminating in the prestigious prime chair of sacred scripture, which he held from 1579 until his death. But his was also a life of controversy. He spent almost five years, from 1572 to the end of 1576, in solitary confinement in the inquisitorial prison in Valladolid, accused by

Luis de León. Portrait from *Descripcio de verdaderos retratos* (1599). INSTITUT AMATLLER D'ART HISPÀNIC, BARCELONA

his largely Dominican opponents of holding unorthodox views about the Vulgate (the Latin translation of the Bible attributed to Jerome), and of "Judaizing," preferring rabbinical to Christian interpretations of the Old Testament.

His trial represents a moment of real intellectual crisis within the Roman Catholic church in sixteenth-century Spain. The controversy centered around two issues that the Council of Trent had not sufficiently resolved: the precise authority of the Vulgate and its relationship with the Greek and especially the Hebrew originals. Fray Luis, following at least a century of textual scholarship, questioned the Vulgate's accuracy at certain points in the light of Hebrew readings. The accusations of Judaizing were the more pointed as several of his ancestors had been brought before the Inquisition on charges of relapsing into their ancestral faith. Fray Luis conducted his defense with great vigor and clarity, despite the intense frustrations and delays of inquisitorial procedures. That he emerged with only the lightest of warnings was a sign that the defenders of the infallibility of the Vulgate had lost the battle.

Fray Luis wrote many works both in Spanish and Latin. His original poems, published in 1631, after circulating widely before that in manuscript, are remarkable for their formal perfection and for their beauty and elegance of diction. Using primarily the *lira* (stanzaic) form, introduced into Spain by Garcilaso de la Vega, they betray at many points the influence of Horace. They give new and memorable expression to many traditional philosophical ideas, especially of a neo-Stoic or Neoplatonic kind, and rework a range of poetic commonplaces of the age. Symbols such as music and the night sky awaken the soul to ascend to the region of the music of the spheres and everlasting light; nature, in its simplicity, offers peace and contentment that the thirst for riches and power can never attain. However, Fray Luis is not a mystic in the fullest sense, since the soul can rarely sustain its flight and must return to its earthbound state, painfully longing for release. He also made fine translations of many Psalms and of Greek and Latin classical poets. He was the first editor of the complete works of Teresa of Ávila (1588), and his preface speaks movingly of her writing and her communities, whose rights he vigorously defended.

In an age in which people were forbidden to read the Bible in the vernacular, Fray Luis produced a number of Spanish works imbued with scripture and intended, as he controversially stated, to make up for this lack of vernacular texts; most notable was his magisterial dialogues, *De los nombres de Cristo* (On the names of Christ), which reached its final form posthumously in 1595. The Christ of *Los Nombres* is a Pauline, cosmic Christ, whose redemptive work is discussed in an idyllic natural setting by three friends through a series of fourteen "names" or biblical images for Christ, taken largely from Old Testament prophecy. Fray Luis displays an unusually wide range of learning in a prose style the order and harmony of which reflect his own sense of the larger harmony of God's creation. His vernacular treatise, *La perfecta casada* (The perfect wife), now perhaps something of a period piece, is an exposition of Proverbs 31; his ambitious commentary in Spanish on Job was not published until 1779.

During his lifetime he published Latin commentaries on Psalm 27 (Vulgate 26), Obadiah, Galatians, and 2 Thessalonians, but his crowning achievement was a threefold commentary on the Song of Songs, which held his interest as early as the 1560s. In its final form (1589) the Latin commentary offers a literal, allegorical, and mystical exposition of each chapter, with frequent references back to the Hebrew text and to previous commentators. One of the interesting features of his commentaries, especially on Obadiah and Job, is his view that the biblical text contains prophecies of the Spaniards' arrival in the New World. In addition, several volumes of his Latin works were published at the end of the nineteenth century, mostly transcripts of his lectures at Salamanca on a range of topics in scholastic theology. During the second half of the twentieth century, still more works were discovered and published.

The most famous anecdote about Fray Luis—that he began his first lecture following his release by the Inquisition with the words "*Dicebamus hesterna die*" (As we were saying yesterday)—has no independent corroboration, but the story says a lot about the spirit of the man. He has remained one of the towering figures of the golden age of Spain: a great scholar, a man of courage who was prepared to stand by his views, an original thinker, and the begetter of some of the era's most beautiful, accomplished, and intellectually satisfying prose and poetry.

BIBLIOGRAPHY

Primary Works

Fray Luis de León: Obras completas castellanas. Edited by Félix García. 5th ed. Madrid, 1991.

Luis de León: The Names of Christ. Translated by Manuel Durán and William Kluback. London, 1984.

El proceso inquisitorial de fray Luis de León. Edited by Ángel Alcalá. Valladolid, Spain, 1991.

Secondary Works

Bell, Aubrey F. G. *Luis de León.* Oxford, 1925.

Guy, Alain. *El pensamiento filosófico de fray Luis de León.* Madrid, 1960.

Rivers, Elias L. *Fray Luis de León: The Original Poems.* London, 1983.

Thompson, C. P. *The Strife of Tongues: Fray Luis de León and the Golden Age of Spain.* Cambridge, U.K., and New York, 1988.

C. P. THOMPSON

LEONARDO DA VINCI (1452–1519), Tuscan painter, sculptor, draftsman, theorist, designer, architect, scientist, and civil and military engineer. He is, without doubt, one of the best-known personalities of the Renaissance and, due to the spectacular range of his interests and accomplishments, has come to represent the supreme example of the universal genius. An innovator in the fields of both art and science, Leonardo uniquely combined these two activities as he investigated the truths of the world around him. Although he completed relatively few paintings, he played a crucial role in creating and

Leonardo da Vinci. *Virgin of the Rocks.* Painted for the church of San Francesco Grande, Milan. Oil on canvas; 1480s; 199 × 122 cm (78 × 48 in.). MUSÉE DU LOUVRE, PARIS/ALINARI/ART RESOURCE

shaping the art of the high Renaissance, and his achievements were admired by Raphael and recognized, if more reluctantly, by Michelangelo.

Vinci and Florence, 1452–1482.

Born 15 April 1452 in Anchiano (near Vinci), Leonardo was the illegitimate son of Piero da Vinci, a successful notary, and Caterina, a peasant girl. He was brought up in the house of his paternal grandfather, but he was living in Florence by 1472, the year he joined the Compagnia di San Luca, or painters guild. Leonardo, as Giorgio Vasari recorded, was apprenticed to the versatile Florentine artist Andrea del Verrocchio (c. 1435–1488), in whose shop he would have had the opportunity to develop his interests in painting as well as sculpture, metal-casting, drawing, and the study of nature. A precocious ability in these last two areas shines through in his early drawing *Tuscan Landscape* (Florence, Uffizi; dated 1473), where there is a convincing rendering of a landscape with atmospheric effects. Leonardo's earliest surviving painting is thought to be the *Annunciation* (Florence, Uffizi; from the convent of Monte Oliveto; c. 1473), in which the influence of Verrocchio is evident in the sculptural forms of the drapery, the style of the Virgin's lectern, and the meticulous detail of the physiognomies. From the subtlety of the light on the faces to the botanical accuracy of the vegetation, this work is filled with a wide variety of natural effects that betray the young Leonardo's interest in attempting to understand and re-create natural phenomena.

In 1478 Leonardo recorded in his notes that he was at work on two designs of the Madonna. Today some Virgin and Child pictures associated with him are dated to this year or shortly after, and the paintings themselves display his efforts to create an integrated composition of mother and child that takes account of the physical and emotional links between two figures. Throughout this fertile period of experimentation and innovation in design, the painter's style evolved from the early *Virgin and Child with a Vase of Flowers* (Munich, Alte Pinakothek; c. 1474–1476), which is indebted to Verrocchio, to the later *Benois Madonna* (St. Petersburg, Hermitage; c. 1480/85), which exhibits a more coordinated interplay of expression and gesture, a more confident use of light, and a greater awareness of the rhythmic movements of the drapery.

In 1476 Leonardo still worked in Verrocchio's studio, and it may have been around this time or shortly after that he contributed to or repainted aspects of Verrocchio's *Baptism of Christ* (Florence, Uffizi; c. 1475/80) for San Salvi, Florence. [See the entry on Verrocchio in volume 6 for an image of the *Baptism of Christ*.] Leonardo's intervention is visible in the relaxed posture of the angel (far left), whose face is defined by a gentle modeling and whose eyes reveal a sense of emotional vitality. Leonardo also painted the landscape above the angel, and in his rendering of the expanse of water framed by rocky precipices and bathed in a misty atmosphere, he reveals yet again his profound interest in nature as well as an ability to record its effects. Not too different in style is the portrait of *Ginevra de' Benci* (Washington, National Gallery of Art; c. 1475/76; see the color plates in this volume), which once almost certainly included the sitter's hands, as in a marble portrait bust of a woman (Florence, Bargello) by Verrocchio. The drawing *Woman's Arms and Hands* (Windsor, Royal Library; c. 1475/76) is generally thought to be a preparatory study for the missing hands in the *Ginevra,* which exhibits a proficient handling of the paint to expose the delicate luminosity of the complexion, the highlights in the hair, and the amospheric recession of the landscape.

The only securely datable painting to survive from Leonardo's early years in Florence is the unfinished *Adoration of the Magi* (Florence, Uffizi; ca. 1481), which was commissioned for an altar of the monastery of San Donato a Scopeto outside Florence, and is now considered to be the masterpiece of Leonardo's early years. Highly innovative, the *Adoration* displays a carefully articulated composition in which the pyramidal group of foreground figures of the Virgin and the Magi is set within a great arc of adoring onlookers. Leonardo, furthermore, paid great attention to every gesture, emotion, and facial expression within the scene, and despite his investing of these figures with a distinct individuality, the composition achieves a unified and integrated effect. The unfinished state of the painting highlights the artist's concerns with the interplay of light and shade, or chiaroscuro, to convincingly re-create a real sense of form, substance, and weight for figures and objects. A similar approach is adopted in the unfinished panel *Saint Jerome* (Rome, Pinacoteca Vaticana; c. 1481). The stylistic affinities are brought out not only in the expressive modeling in light and shade, but also in the emotional charge and carefully orchestrated movements and gestures of the penitent saint.

Milan, 1483–1499.

The *Adoration* and perhaps the *Saint Jerome* were left unfinished when Leonardo abandoned Florence around 1482. The artist is mentioned in Milan in 1483, the year that he and

Leonardo da Vinci. *Head of an Old Man.* Thought to be a self-portrait. Drawn in 1512. National Gallery, Turin, Italy/Alinari/Art Resource

the brothers Ambrogio and Evangelista de' Predis received a commission from the Confraternity of the Immaculate Conception for a great altarpiece to be placed in the confraternity's chapel in San Francesco Grande, Milan. The commission has a complicated history involving a lengthy legal dispute over price, and the painting was not completed until 1508. Today two versions of the *Virgin of the Rocks,* the central panel of the altarpiece by Leonardo, survive. On account of style, the earlier version (Paris, Louvre) is thought to date to the 1480s. The composition comprises a carefully planned and fully integrated pyramidal group of figures in which glance, movement, and gesture reinforce unity. Working with two sources of light—one behind the cave and the other in front of it—Leonardo manipulated light and atmosphere so that figures and forms are defined by soft gradations of tone and gentle modeling.

Leonardo's move to Milan appears to have been prompted by a desire to work for Ludovico Sforza,

to whom Leonardo addressed a now famous draft of a letter that was written before 1489, the year when the artist is first recorded in the service of the ruler of Milan. In his petition Leonardo outlined his competence as a civil and military engineer, and these details testify to his broad range of interests, especially in designing military devices for use on sea and land. Leonardo also mentioned his sculpting ability, and by 1489 he had set to work on a colossal equestrian monument to Ludovico's father, Francesco Sforza, that was to be cast in bronze. Having discarded his first dramatic design of a rearing horse and gesturing rider, Leonardo executed a full-scale clay model (1491/1492; destroyed) of a horse and rider in quiet movement in the tradition of Donatello's and Verrocchio's equestrian works. In preparation for this project, he made studies of the anatomy and movement of horses from life, and he also considered the technical problems of casting bronze for such a vast monument, which, due to Ludovico's expulsion from Milan (1499), was never completed.

As a painter to the Sforza, Leonardo was involved in decorating the Sala delle Asse (c. 1498) in the Castello Sforzesco in Milan; the design includes intertwined tree branches, depicted with a vibrant naturalism, and gold cord. The artist, furthermore, had an important role in designing stage sets and costumes for the many allegorical and theatrical representations at the Sforza court, whose sophisticated society is reflected in a group of portraits also associated with Leonardo. The most important is *Portrait of a Lady with an Ermine* (Cracow, Czartoryski Collection; c. 1490), believed to represent one of Ludovico Sforza's mistresses, Cecilia Gallerani. The work is pervaded with a psychological suggestiveness resulting from the sitter's turning toward an unseen figure. Besides attention to surface details of form and texture, the painter displays an interest in the graceful position of the hands as a means of communicating something of the refined inner spirit of the sitter. A similar interest in psychological introspection and keenly observed surface details is found in three other portraits sometimes associated with Leonardo's first Milanese period: *Portrait of a Musician* (1480s), *Portrait of a Woman in Profile* (c. 1485–1495; both Milan, Ambrosiana), and *La belle ferronnière* (1490s; Paris, Louvre).

Leonardo's greatest project of these years was the fresco of the *Last Supper* (c. 1495–1497; see the color plates in this volume) for the refectory of Santa Maria delle Grazie, a Milanese convent protected by the Sforza. Owing to the painter's experimental technique, which came close to painting in tempera *a secco* (egg-based medium on dry plaster; this process resembled panel painting rather than *buon fresco*) on a primed wall surface, the work now suffers from a poor state of preservation; centuries of repainting have added to the problem. Nevertheless, the measured dignity of a carefully balanced composition, which presents a subtle interaction of grandiose figures, can still be discerned. Generally considered to be an early monument to high Renaissance classicism, the design includes a virtuoso handling of perspective that expands the space of the refectory. The restoration campaign completed in 1999 has done much to remove later overpainting and expose the vibrant illusionism of Leonardo's treatment of the objects on the table and the intense luminosity of the white linen cloth. Of equal importance is Leonardo's attention to glance, expression, and gesture in the figures who respond to Christ's imminent betrayal; the painter considered the inward disposition of everyone around the table.

In the draft of his letter to Ludovico, Leonardo mentions his experience as an architect, and during his first Milanese stay he was asked for advice on technical aspects of construction. He entered the competition for the design of the dome of Milan cathedral (1487–1488) but withdrew before the judges had reached a decision. On the basis of surviving studies in his notebooks, the artist's proposal would have combined a system of Gothic ribs with a freestanding dome in the tradition of Filippo Brunelleschi's double-shell construction in Florence. Leonardo's concern with theoretical architectural problems is manifested in a series of church designs that display his thoughts on centralized plans (Paris, Bibliothèque de l'Institut de France; c. 1488); Donato Bramante, an architect in the service of the Sforza at this same time, may well have come into contact with Leonardo's ideas. Other drawings in Leonardo's notebooks testify to his interest in urban planning, and although he may never have constructed anything, his ideas were reflected in the Sforza planning of Vigevano.

Florence and Elsewhere, 1500–1508. In 1499 Ludovico Sforza fled Milan, and the French under Louis XII took control of the city. In the following year Leonardo set off for Venice and subsequently made his way to Florence via Mantua, where he draw a portrait of Isabella d'Este (Paris, Louvre). Upon his return to Florence in 1500, Leonardo was offered accommodation in the monastery of Santissima Annunziata and was involved with the commission for an altarpiece for the church, but he pro-

duced nothing. Two other projects occupied the painter at this time: a cartoon of the *Virgin and Child with Saint Anne and a Lamb* (lost; probably independent of the SS. Annunziata commission), and the *Virgin of the Yarn Winder,* known from copies and studio versions (for example, the version in the collection of the duke of Buccleuch). Judging from the surviving evidence, in both compositions the painter attempted to create a fully integrated group of figures in which each form retains a dynamic and organic relationship to the others. Of equal importance for both works was the degree of psychological interplay within the groups and the effective use of symbols—a lamb and a yarn winder—that have been effortlessly inserted into the designs.

By 1502 Leonardo had left Florence for the employ of Cesare Borgia. Traveling through much of the Romagna and the surrounding area, he worked as architect and engineer to the condottiere, and he also designed for him city plans and topographical maps that unified pictorial and planimetric representation. In his design of the map of Imola (Windsor, Royal Library; c. 1502). Leonardo combined measured distances on the ground with measured angles from a centrally located building in Imola.

Back in Florence in 1503, Leonardo was invited to paint a large-scale fresco that celebrated a military victory of the Florentine Republic over the Milanese in 1440 for the walls of the newly built Council Chamber of the Republic in the Palazzo della Signoria. His *Battle of Anghiara* (c. 1503/06; lost) was executed in an experimental technique that was more idiosyncratic than that of the *Last Supper* and involved painting *a secco* with an oil-based medium on a primed wall surface; this process proved to be unsatisfactory because the paint did not dry. The central section of the composition, which was destroyed in 1565 in the course of Giorgio Vasari's restoration and is now known through numerous copies of the sixteenth and seventeenth centuries, focused on the desperate struggle for a standard. As Rubens's copy (Paris, Louvre; c. 1615) indicates, Leonardo presented the extreme physical exertion of man and horse engaged in furious battle. On the evidence of the copies and Leonardo's surviving preparatory sketches, the tight group of central figures displayed faces distorted by rage or pain; even the heads of the horses, with flaring nostrils and gnashing teeth, were treated in this expressive manner. On a formal level the figural composition exhibited a complex interplay of forms to create a rhythmic union of parts. In 1504, when work on the *Battle of Anghiari* had commenced, Michelangelo, Leonardo's younger rival, was commissioned to paint another celebrated military victory of the Republic, the *Battle of Cascina,* for the same chamber.

While work was progressing on the *Anghiari* project, Leonardo started the portrait of *Mona Lisa* (Paris, Louvre; c. 1503; see the color plates in this volume), the wife of the important Florentine citizen Francesco del Giocondo (the painting's other name is *La Gioconda*). Investing the category of portraiture with an increased sense of monumentality, the painter carefully positioned the sitter between framing columns and before a wall. The ample form of the woman, whose torso and head are enlivened with a gentle spiraling motion, is gently modeled with sfumato painting, or smoky gradations of tones. The sitter, or rather her personality, is inextricably linked to the surrounding landscape that is also bathed in shadowy atmosphere. In the process Leonardo has united the elusive expression of the woman with the mood evoked by the landscape to create a poetic fusion between the forces of man and nature.

In this second Florentine period Leonardo started work on a now lost painting, *Leda and the Swan,* whose composition, probably not completed until after 1513, can be discerned from later copies after Leonardo (for example, one by Cesare del Sesto; Salisbury, Wilton House) and the artist's own preparatory drawings (including those in the Royal Library at Windsor Castle). Starting with a kneeling pose, the painter later developed the design into a standing figure whose slow contrappostal movements create a gentle spiral effect. Raphael evidently saw this work because he copied it before leaving Florence in 1508. Another lost composition from these years is *Angel of the Annunciation,* in which the archangel Gabriel confronts the spectator, who therefore takes the place of the Virgin.

Milan, 1508–1513. Between 1506 and 1508 Leonardo traveled frequently between Florence and Milan, perhaps on account of the dispute concerning the altarpiece for San Francesco Grande. By 1508, however, the painter had received payments and had delivered the second version of the *Virgin of the Rocks* (London, National Gallery; c. 1495/1508). Despite showing signs of studio assistance, the later version is characterized by a more harmonious unity of color and tone, and a graver, more introspective mood throughout.

By 1508 Leonardo had abandoned the *Anghiari* project in Florence and was in the service of the French rulers of Milan, working for the governor of

the city, Charles d'Amboise. The latter made full use of Leonardo's wide-ranging abilities, employing him on a variety of projects. Following the death of Charles in 1511, Gian Giacomo Trivulzio, a mercenary who had come to prominence by helping the French forces take control of Milan in 1499, was appointed joint governor of the city. In the period 1508–1511 Leonardo planned a funerary monument, which included an equestrian group set upon an ornate architectural base, for Trivulzio's family chapel. The series of drawings associated with the project (Windsor, Royal Library) reveals that Leonardo, building on his experience of life studies of man and horse for the *Anghiari* project, focused on the question of motion and movement for horse and rider. Like the Sforza monument, the Trivulzio project was never completed.

At the same time Leonardo was engaged in scientific investigation, but he was also active as a painter, and he is known to have worked on at least two Virgin and Child compositions for the king of France. His *Saint John the Baptist* (Paris, Louvre) is generally thought to have been executed during this second Milanese period as well, and since the paintings for Louis XII cannot be traced with absolute certainty, it indicates just how the painter's style evolved in his late career. The *Baptist,* a reworking of the pose of the earlier *Angel of the Annunciation,* exhibits an expressive use of sfumato modeling with the figure emerging from darkness; the forms of the saint, therefore, are not rendered by means of hard outlines, but are instead defined through soft gradations of tones. The painting also reveals Leonardo's interest in coordinating gesture and movement with the inward disposition or spirit of the subject. So, in this picture, the figure's elusive smile and engaging expression are in place to convey something of the power of divine will and knowledge.

In 1512 the French lost control of Milan when the combined forces of Spain, the papacy, and Venice invaded. In this unstable political climate Leonardo spent time at the family villa of his assistant, Francesco Melzi, at Vaprio d'Adda, outside Milan; by the autumn of 1513, Leonardo had abandoned Milan.

Rome and France, 1513–1519. Leonardo headed for Florence and then Rome, where he was provided with accommodation at the Vatican Belvedere by the pope's brother Giuliano de' Medici. At this time he dedicated himself to scientific research, but he may also have worked on the painting *Virgin and Child with Saint Anne and a Lamb*

Leonardo da Vinci. *Vitruvian Man.* Study of proportions for Vitruvius's *De architectura* (1492). GALLERIA DELL'ACCADEMIA, VENICE/ALINARI/ART RESOURCE

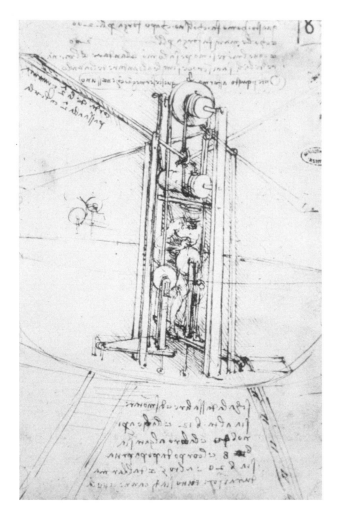

Leonardo da Vinci. *Study for Flying Machine with Man Standing Upright.* Codex Atlanticus, MS. B, Biblioteca Ambrosiana, Milan, c. 1485–1490. INSTITUT DE FRANCE, PARIS/SCALA/ART RESOURCE

(Paris, Louvre; c. 1515; see the frontispiece to this volume), his third known attempt at a full-scale composition on this subject (that is, after the lost 1501 cartoon, and the cartoon in the National Gallery, London, c. 1505–1507). This latest design displays a tightly packed group of overlapping figures arranged in a pyramid; Leonardo also studied the counterposition of movements and psychological interplay within the group. Nonetheless, his artistic achievements in Rome are difficult to assess, and in comparison with Michelangelo, Raphael, and Bramante, Leonardo appears to have contributed little to the otherwise vibrant artistic scene at the time of Pope Leo X, who is reported to have questioned whether Leonardo was capable of ever completing anything.

By 1517 Leonardo had accepted the invitation of the new French king, Francis I, to go to France, where he was given lodgings at the manor house of Clos-Lucé, Amboise. He is thought to have taken with him the paintings *Mona Lisa, John the Baptist, Leda,* and *Virgin with St. Anne;* some of these may have been altered or finished there. At the French court he performed a wide range of duties, including furnishing designs for courtly ephemera and, of greater importance, planning a huge royal palace at Romorantin. The latter project was never realized because Leonardo died on 2 May 1519, after only two years at the French court.

Scientific Studies. For Leonardo art theory and scientific investigation were inextricably linked. He thought that the artist, before anyone else in society, had the ability and power to scrutinize reality and to convey his perceptions of it to others. As a result Leonardo embraced scientific investigation throughout most of his life, and the areas he researched ranged from anatomy to geology, mechanics to mathematics. Building on the foundation of medieval and classical thinking, Leonardo's theories were greatly enriched by experience and by his own immense powers of observation and perception.

Leonardo's investigation of anatomy was initially tied to his desire—perhaps inherited from Verrocchio but in tune with artistic practices in Florence— to understand the structure of human form. This developed into an overwhelming passion that led him to dissect the human body so that he could attempt to understand, for example, the function of muscles or the process of vocal production. From his first stay at Milan in the 1490s to his stay in Rome about 1515, Leonardo made extensive notes on the subject, including analytical drawings for scientific illustration, which were intended for a treatise on anatomy (never realized).

Alongside the workings of the body Leonardo explored the endless possibilities of the machine as a mechanically functioning organism. His qualities as an inventive engineer were established early in his career, and he had taken great care to stress his talents as a military engineer in his draft letter to the Sforza. His Codex Atlanticus (Milan, Biblioteca Ambrosiana) and Codex Madrid I (Madrid, Biblioteca Nacional) are particularly rich in carefully planned drawings or technical studies that have, in some instances, been translated into working models in recent times; these demonstrate Leonardo's ability to design a range of mechanical devices from a screw jack to a two-wheeled hoist, from an "armored car" to a gun with three racks of barrels. His best-known activity as an artist-inventor however, is in the area of human-powered flight. Numerous sheets of mechanical studies survive, and these bear witness to the range and intensity of his thoughts on flying. In his attempt to construct a flying machine, Leonardo studied in careful detail the dynamics of bird flight and the motions of air.

Central to much of Leonardo's scientific thought was the study of mathematics. This science enabled him to analyze the structure of elements in nature, as well as to develop perspective arrangements and to create a sense of order—through geometry and proportion—in his artistic compositions. His study of optics and many of his theories of vision also were translated into mathematical terms. In addition Leonardo was preoccupied with geological questions, and in this area his astonishing powers of observation were used to great effect. He investigated a wide range of issues, from the origin of fossils to the role of water as a vital force of the earth, through his own firsthand experience and research into physical geography.

Conclusion. Leonardo exercised a considerable influence on artists of his own day and later times. Some of his views on art, which had been in circulation since the sixteenth century, were published in 1651 in the *Trattato della pittura* (Treatise on painting), a posthumous collection of writings taken from his many manuscripts. His small corpus of surviving paintings confirms the magnitude of his achievements as an artist; from portraiture to religious narrative, Leonardo enriched every artistic category with fresh insights into figural grouping, space, individual characterization, and light and shade. Many of his designs inspired copies, especially in the Milanese artistic milieu, where his ideas and technical innovations were keenly taken up by his pupils or collaborators Andrea Solario, Bernardino Luini, the brothers de' Predis, Cesare da Sesto, and Giovanni Boltraffio. In Florence his compositions were carefully studied by Raphael, whose designs of the Virgin and Child of 1504–1508 adopt Leonardo's pyramidal arrangement of figures. Alongside Michelangelo's *Cascina* cartoon, Leonardo's *Battle of Anghiari* was, Benvenuto Cellini reported, the "school for the world." Even in the nineteenth century, long after Leonardo's cartoon had perished and his fresco had disappeared, aspects of its design continued to intrigue the minds of artists throughout Europe, as shown in the work of Eugène Delacroix.

See also **Florence,** *subentries on* **Art of the Fifteenth Century** *and* **Art of the Sixteenth Century;** *and biographies of figures mentioned in this entry.*

BIBLIOGRAPHY

Works by Leonardo

The Complete Paintings of Leonardo da Vinci. Introduction by D. Ettlinger and with notes and catalog by Angela Ottino della Chiesa. Harmondsworth, U.K., and New York, 1985.

The Drawings of Leonardo da Vinci. Introduced and with notes by Arthur E. Popham. London, 1946.

The Drawings of Leonardo da Vinci and His Circle in America. Arranged and produced by Carlo Pedretti; catalog by Patricia Trutty-Coohill. 2 vols. Florence, 1993. A register of drawings held in American collections.

Leonardo da Vinci: One Hundred Drawings from the Collection of Her Majesty the Queen. Compiled by Martin Clayton. London, 1996.

Leonardo on Painting: An Anthology of Writings. Edited and translated by Martin Kemp and Margaret Walker. New Haven, Conn., and London, 1989.

The Literary Works of Leonardo da Vinci. Compiled and edited by Jean Paul Richter, with commentary by Carlo Pedretti. 2 vols. Oxford and Berkeley, Calif., 1977.

Secondary Works

Ahl, Diane Cole, ed. *Leonardo da Vinci's Sforza Monument Horse: The Art and the Engineering.* Bethlehem, Pa., and London, 1995.

Brown, David Alan. *Leonardo da Vinci: Origins of a Genius.* New Haven, Conn., 1998.

Clark, Kenneth. *Leonardo da Vinci: An Account of His Development as an Artist.* Cambridge, U.K., and New York, 1939. Reprinted many times.

Galluzzi, Paolo. *Mechanical Marvels: Invention in the Age of Leonardo.* Florence, 1997.

Gould, Cecil. *Leonardo: The Artist and the Non-Artist.* London and Boston, 1975.

Kemp, Martin. *Leonardo da Vinci: The Marvellous Works of Nature and Man.* London and Cambridge, Mass., 1981. 2d ed., revised, 1988.

Marani, Pietro C. *Leonardo da Vinci.* Milan, 1994.

Monti, Raffaele. *Leonardo da Vinci: From the* Adoration of the Magi *to the* Annunciation. Livorno, Italy, 1998.

Turner, A. Richard. *Inventing Leonardo.* New York, 1993.

Zwijnenberg, Robert. *The Writings and Drawings of Leonardo da Vinci: Order and Chaos in Early Modern Thought.* Cambridge, U.K., and New York, 1999.

FLAVIO BOGGI

LEONE EBREO (Judah ben Isaac Abrabanel; c. 1460–c. 1521), Iberian philosopher, physician, writer. Judah ben Isaac Abrabanel, better known as Leone Ebreo, was born in Lisbon to Isaac Abrabanel, an important exegete, philosopher, and statesman of the Portuguese kingdom. In 1483 Isaac was forced to leave Portugal; Leone followed him and they lived at the court of the Spanish kings. When the Jews were expelled from Spain in 1492 the Abrabanels left for Italy. It is still a matter of doubt whether Leone first settled in Florence, where he would have met Giovanni Pico della Mirandola (1463–1494); had they met, the latter, according to the sixteenth-century physician Amatus Lusitanus (1511–1568), would have committed to Leone a philosophical treatise on the harmony of heavens (*De coeli harmonia*), no longer extant. Leone left Naples in 1495 for Genoa at the time of the French invasion of the Kingdom of Naples. In 1501 he was back in Naples, where he was appointed chief physician to the Spanish viceroy, Gonzalo Fernandez de Córdoba.

His literary works date mostly to the first years of the sixteenth century. The *Dialoghi d'amore* (Dialogues on love) were probably composed around 1502. In 1503 he wrote an elegy (*Telunah al ha-Zeman;* Complaint against the time) in which he regrets that his son Isaac had been obliged by the king of Portugal, John II, to convert to Christianity; in 1504 he composed three short poems in which he praises his father's works; around 1520 he wrote fifty-two stanzas commemorating his father and his exegetical commentaries. The poems were first published with the *Dialoghi*. At the time of the first edition (Rome, 1535), Leone was certainly dead. It has been supposed, on the basis of the title pages of the second (1541) and third (1545) editions of the *Dialoghi,* that he had converted to Christianity, but this can hardly be proved, since in the same work he frequently refers to himself as a Jew.

Aesthetic, psychological, and metaphysical theories derived by Leone from Greek, medieval Arabic, and Jewish, as well as contemporary Western sources, transposed in a Renaissance frame, render the *Dialoghi d'amore* one of the most interesting literary works of the Renaissance, as well as an excellent example of Italian Platonic speculation. The three *Dialoghi* are clearly reminiscent of Plato's dialogues from a stylistic viewpoint as well. The names of the two main characters, Filone and Sofia, express the central theme of the whole work—the supreme role of love in the achievement of humanity's highest level of knowledge. Love is the connecting medium of all creation and the catalyzing factor of the relationship between individuals and God. The meanings of love vary according to the different levels of nature, the highest form of love being the intellectual love of God, which allows people to reunite their divine souls with the source, thus completing a circular process from God to the individual to God. Leone's love theory was partly founded on Jewish medieval philosophy (in particular, affinities between Hasdai Crescas's [1340–c. 1410] and Leone's views have been observed); however, the importance of love in Leone's system has closer connec-

tions with Greek and early medieval Platonic sources.

This new approach to original Greek texts was possibly the result of the relationship between Leone and the Neoplatonic Florentine Academy, where he might have also learned the theories on intellectual love expressed by Tuscan thirteenth-century poets adhering to the *dolce stil novo* (literally, sweet new style). Love and beauty are closely connected and, since love has its origin in God, the Supreme Being could be conceived of as the source of beauty as well. From the *Dialoghi* a strong feeling of universal unity emerges, extraneous to Jewish thought and derived from the cosmic pantheist attitude of the Italian Renaissance. However, Leone never gave up his strongly monotheistic principles, including the concept that the universe was fashioned by a God who created, from nothing, a series of worlds, the present world being just one out of the many (this theory had already appeared in the Talmud and in Leone's father's writings). However, instead of a medieval static universe ruled over by an Aristotelian unmoved mover, Leone described a dynamic world whose discrete elements were animated by a lively tendency toward movement. The medieval Jewish Kabbalah in its Italian fifteenth-century Platonic interpretation was influential in the articulation of Leone's fluid and interrelated universe. This dynamic system also relies on the superior forms of astrological and magical knowledge described by Marsilio Ficino (1433–1499). Leone interpreted pagan myths according to Jewish biblical, rabbinic, and kabbalistic tradition, thus creating a syncretism in which Jewish faith represented the original religious wisdom, and perpetuating the humanist theory of *prisca theologia* (ancient theology), adapted to Judaism. In this sense the unification of kabbalistic tradition with the Platonic doctrines as formulated by Ficino and his Academy was not completely original: a few years earlier, in the same Florentine milieu, Yohanan ben Isaac Alemanno (c. 1435–after 1504) had already developed such a syncretism.

The decision to write his treatise in Tuscan literary language instead of medieval Hebrew certainly depended on Leone's will to address those humanists who were increasingly using Italian, instead of Latin, as their cultural language. The *Dialoghi d'amore* exercised a profound influence on sixteenth-century and later European philosophic thought and mysticism as well as literature. However, neither Leone nor other Jewish Platonic philosophers, with the exception of Spinoza, exerted a considerable influence on Judaism.

BIBLIOGRAPHY

Primary Works

Leone Ebreo. *Dialoghi d'amore.* Edited by Santino Caramella. Bari, Italy, 1929. Not completely reliable.

Leone Ebreo. *Dialoghi d'amore.* Edited by Giacinto Manuppella. 2 vols. Lisbon, Portugal, 1983. Philologically the best, but difficult to find.

Leone Ebreo. *The Philosophy of Love.* Translated by F. Friedeberg-Seeley and Jean H. Barnes. London, 1937. Translation of *Dialoghi d'amore.*

Secondary Works

Damiens, Suzanne. *Amour et intellect chez León l'Hébreu.* Toulouse, France, 1971.

Idel, Moshe. "Kabbalah ve-Philosopheeya Kadumah etzel R'Yitzchak ve-Yehudah Abravanel." In *Filosofyat Ha-Ahavah Shel Yehudah Abravanel.* Edited by Menahem Dorman and Zeev Levy. Tel Aviv, Israel, 1985. Pages 73–112.

Kodera, Sergius. *Filone und Sofia in Leone Ebreo's* Dialoghi d'amore: *Platonische Liebesphilosophie der Renaissance und Judentum.* Frankfurt am Main, Germany, and New York, 1995. Pages 1–147.

Lesley, Arthur. "The Place of the *Dialoghi d'amore* in Contemporaneous Jewish Thought." In *Ficino and Renaissance Neoplatonism.* Edited by Konrad Eisenbichler and Olga Zorzi Pugliese. Ottawa, Canada, 1986. Pages 69–86.

Pines, Shlomo. "Medieval Doctrines in Renaissance Garb? Some Jewish and Arabic Sources of Leone Ebreo's Doctrines." In *Jewish Thought in the Sixteenth Century.* Edited by Bernard Dov Cooperman. Cambridge, Mass., 1983. Pages 365–398.

Soria Olmedo, Andrés. *Los "Dialoghi d'amore" de Léon Hebreo: Aspectos literários y culturales.* Granada, Spain, 1984.

FABRIZIO LELLI

LEPANTO, BATTLE OF

(7 October 1571). No Renaissance battle matches the victory of the Christian Holy League at Lepanto over the Muslim Ottoman Turks in the quantity of art, literature, and music it engendered. It occurred during the War of Cyprus that erupted in 1570 when Venice refused the demand of Ottoman Sultan Selīm II to surrender Cyprus.

Venice appealed for help to Pope Pius V, who thundered for a crusade and forged a Holy League. It included the papacy; Venice; Philip II of Spain; his dominions of Naples, Sicily, and Milan; his Genoese allies; and Savoy, Tuscany, Parma, and Mantua. France and the Catholic states of the Holy Roman Empire for various reasons remained aloof. Philip agreed to pay half the costs, Venice a third, and the pope a sixth. When Emmanuel Philibert of Savoy refused the office of commander in chief, Venice reluctantly agreed to the appointment of Don John of Austria, Philip's younger half-brother and commander

of Spain's Mediterranean galleys. The League's first task was to save Cyprus. Afterward, its armada might operate in the eastern Mediterranean, as Venice wished, or against Algiers, Philip's preference. Negotiations proved difficult, and not until May 1571 was the League ratified in Rome.

In July 1570 the Turks invaded Cyprus and by autumn had confined the Venetians to Famagusta. An allied armada commanded by papal admiral Marcantonio Colonna achieved nothing and left the Venetians frustrated.

Not until early September 1571 did the entire League armada assemble at Messina. Though some thought the season late, Don John insisted that the armada weigh anchor. The fate of Famagusta was still unknown. The Turkish fleet had screened Cyprus all summer, done mischief in the Adriatic, and then anchored at Lepanto (Návpaktos), where the Gulf of Corinth meets the Gulf of Patras. The Turks prepared to winter and began to discharge people. When they learned the allies were at sea, they scrambled to get ready.

On Sunday, 7 October, the two fleets met in the Gulf of Patras. The League deployed more than two hundred galleys, preceded by six galleasses with guns in broadsides. Don John, Captain General Sebastiano Venier of Venice, and Colonna served in the center; Agostino Barbarigo of Venice commanded the left; and the Genoese Gian Andrea Doria, the right. Three days earlier they had received certain news of the fall of Famagusta on 1 August and the cruel fate of its defenders. The near three hundred galleys and smaller galliots of the Turkish fleet formed what seemed a vast crescent, its tips stretched to outflank the allies, its center closely backed by a second line of galliots. Between sailors, fighting men, and slave, convict, and pressed rowers, some 140,000 people were involved. The battle, its terrible drama afterward caught in Andrea Vicentino's mural for the Doge's Palace, raged from late morning to late afternoon, with the League's bigger guns decisive. The Turkish fleet was virtually annihilated. Among the Christian wounded was Miguel de Cervantes.

Though the victory saved Crete, Venice lost Cyprus and made a humiliating peace in 1573. The Turks tightened their hold on Barbary and in 1578 got a favorable truce with Philip, who turned his attention to the Atlantic world. Yet Lepanto revived the allies' faith that they could beat the Turks in battle, and for years it was celebrated throughout Catholic Europe. Paintings that glorify Lepanto include Tin-

The Battle of Lepanto. Paolo Veronese's painting of the battle, depicting the intercession of the Virgin Mary. Oil on canvas; 1571; 169 × 137 cm (67 × 54 in.). Galleria dell'Accademia, Venice/The Bridgeman Art Library

toretto's heroic portrait of Venier, Titian's portrayal of Philip II with his son Don Fernando giving thanks to God, El Greco's *Adoration of the Name of Jesus* [see the color plates in volume 5], Veronese's depiction that credits the intercession of the Virgin Mary, and Vasari's stylized treatment for the Vatican's Sala Regia.

See also **John of Austria.**

BIBLIOGRAPHY

Braudel, Fernand. *The Mediterranean and the Mediterranean World in the Age of Philip II.* 2 vols. Translated by Sian Reynolds. London and New York, 1972. Translation of *La Méditerranée et le monde méditerranéen dans l'époque de Philippe II* (1966). A masterpiece of historiography.

Lesure, Michael. *Lépante: La crise de l'empire ottoman.* Paris, 1972. For the Turkish side.

Pierson, Peter. "Lepanto." *MHQ: Quarterly Journal of Military History* 9, no. 2 (1997): 6–19. Based on the latest research, including underwater archaeology.

PETER PIERSON

LERMA, DUKE OF. *See* **Sandoval y Rojas, Francisco de.**

LE ROY, LOUIS (c. 1510–1577), French translator, writer, historical theorist. After Jacques Amyot (1513–1593), Louis Le Roy (sometimes called Regius) is arguably the most famous translator of the French Renaissance. Born in Normandy of poor parents, Le Roy received a humanistic and legal education with the aid of an aristocratic patron. In 1540 he attached himself in some minor capacity to the king's court in Paris, where he hoped to establish a literary reputation. Although he penned numerous orations and eulogies, as well as political and religious pamphlets, he became known by his contemporaries chiefly as a translator of works by Plato, Aristotle, Xenophon, Isocrates, and Demosthenes. In recognition of this activity, he was named royal professor of Greek in 1572, a position that did little to offset his chronic penury.

In addition to his translations, Le Roy authored a number of political and historical treatises, among them *De l'excellence du gouvernement royal* (On the excellence of royal government; 1575) and a well-known commentary on Aristotle's *Politics* (1568). But his most famous work remains *De la vicissitude ou variété des choses* (Of the vicissitude or variety of things; 1575), a universal history of civilization from the Egyptians to his own day. His approach to this vast subject is less chronological than comparative. The initial chapters of *Vicissitude* describe the distinctive features of civilized life—language, the arts,

knowledge, and military power—and trace them from their rude beginnings to the present. Later chapters follow the course of specific civilizations—chiefly Greek, Roman, Islamic, and contemporary European—whose rise and fall Le Roy attributes to the waxing and waning of two confluent factors: learning and military prowess. Ending with the Renaissance revival of learning and the emergence of powerful European kingdoms, *Vicissitude* is sometimes interpreted as a harbinger of the eighteenth-century idea of progress, but one should not forget that Le Roy's title implies a future of ups and downs.

BIBLIOGRAPHY

Gundersheimer, Werner L. *The Life and Works of Louis Le Roy.* Geneva, 1966. Still the standard account.

Huppert, George. *The Idea of Perfect History: Historical Erudition and Historical Relativism in Renaissance France.* Urbana, Ill., 1970. See chapter 6.

Manuel, Frank E. *Shapes of Philosophical History.* London, 1965. See chapter 3.

ZACHARY S. SCHIFFMAN

LETO, POMPONIO (1428–1498), Roman humanist teacher, antiquarian, founder of the Roman Academy. The illegitimate son of Giovanni Sanseverino, a count in the southern Italian province of Salerno, Giulio Pomponio Leto early distanced himself from his family and cast off his birth name in favor of the classicized form, Iulius Pomponius. To this he added the agnomen Laetus (cheerful), later changing it to Infortunatus and then Fortunatus to reflect his condition. In the 1450s he went to Rome, where he studied Latin under Lorenzo Valla and then Pietro Odi da Montopoli, whom Pomponio later succeeded as professor of rhetoric at the University of Rome. At his home on the Quirinal hill, Pomponio hosted gatherings of intellectuals interested in antiquity. Members of this group, known as the Roman or Pomponian Academy, took latinized names and referred to Pomponio as their *pontifex maximus* (chief priest). Together they discussed ancient history, made archaeological expeditions, revived the Palilia (an annual feast commemorating the founding of Rome, celebrated on 20 or 21 April), enacted plays by Plautus and Terence, and critiqued one another's Latin compositions.

In 1467 Pomponio began a trip east to learn Greek and Arabic, stopping in Venice, where he earned money tutoring noblemen's sons. There he was accused of sodomy and arrested. In February 1468 he was extradited to Rome, where, along with other members of his academy including Platina (Bartolomeo Sacchi), he was imprisoned in the Castel

Sant'Angelo and charged with sodomy, conspiracy against the pope, and heresy. Two trials ensued (1468, 1469), with Pope Paul II himself presiding over the latter. While some of the academicians may have practiced sodomy, ridiculed the clergy, and held heterodox beliefs, there probably was no elaborate conspiracy, and ultimately all charges were dropped. Around 1470 Pomponio was reinstated in his university post, and in 1479, under Pope Sixtus IV (reigned 1471–1484), he refounded the academy, this time prudently making it a religious sodality, or association. Again it celebrated the Palilia, but simultaneously honored saints Fortunatus, Genesius, and Victor, whose feast days conveniently fell on 20 April. While renewing their studies of classical Rome, the academicians now also explored Christian antiquities and composed poems praising saints and popes. Rather than suppress them, Sixtus IV encouraged their efforts to dignify him with comparisons to the emperor Augustus.

Beyond founding the Roman Academy, which provided a model for the sodalities of Paolo Cortesi, Johann Küritz, and Angelo Colocci, Pomponio furthered classical studies through pedagogy, textual criticism, and antiquarianism. Renowned as an inspiring teacher, Pomponio had many prominent students, including Ermolao Barbaro the Younger, Pietro Marsi, and Marc Antonio Sabellico. Around 1479 Pomponio married, and his daughter Nigella eventually assisted her father in copying manuscripts. His editorial efforts included editions of Festus, *De verbum significatione* (On the meaning of words); Pliny, *Epist. libri 1–9* (Letters, books 1–9); Silius Italicus; Terence; and Varro, *De lingua Latina* (On the Latin language). Surviving notes from his lectures reveal that he also commented upon Cicero, Horace, Lucan, Lucretius, Martial, Ovid, and Quintilian. The notes confirm his interest in studying texts in combination with physical monuments, the two kinds of sources illuminating each other and the ancient culture that had produced them.

BIBLIOGRAPHY

Primary Work

Valeriano, Pierio. *Pierio Valeriano on the Ill-Fortune of Learned Men: A Renaissance Humanist and His World.* Edited by Julia Haig Gaisser. Ann Arbor, Mich., 1999. Translation and critical edition of *De litteratorum infelicitate* with extensive documentation and commentary. Includes an important biographical sketch of Leto.

Secondary Works

D'Amico, John F. *Renaissance Humanism in Papal Rome: Humanists and Churchmen on the Eve of the Reformation.* Baltimore, Md., and London, 1983. See esp. chap. 4, "The Roman Academies."

D'Onofrio, Cesare. *Visitiamo Roma nel Quattrocento: La città degli umanisti.* Rome, 1989. Includes (pp. 271–290) a student's transcription of the itinerary of Leto's walking tours of Rome.

Lee, Egmont. *Sixtus IV and Men of Letters.* Vatican City, Italy, 1978.

Zabughin, V. *Giulio Pomponio Leto.* 2 vols. Rome, 1909; Grottaferrata, 1910–1912.

KENNETH GOUWENS

LETTERBOOKS. Letterbooks were collections of epistles that had several purposes. Usually with documents they served as archival registers for secular or ecclesiastical administrations. Letterbooks were also formularies or collections of real or fictional public or private model letters used in teaching or for reference. Collections of private letters as literary works of art were compiled for personal use or as memorials for lifetime activities or tributes for one's attainment.

The earliest letterbooks were compiled in ancient Greece for the study of rhetoric and philosophy. In Rome Cicero, Seneca, and Pliny the Younger composed letters on daily life and thought that were gathered in letterbooks. Letter collections of this kind were also compiled in late Roman antiquity and the early Middle Ages. After the rise of medieval civilization in the eleventh century, the major branch of rhetoric, the *ars dictaminis*—the art of letter writing, with its many treatises and manuals on epistolography as well as *dictamina,* form-letter collections that adhered to the rigid rules and procedures of epistolary composition—flourished and continued to be found through the Renaissance.

The largest category of Renaissance letterbooks was the collections of the humanists, whose compilations of private letters were a major achievement in the literature of the period. Intended to appeal to patrons, these letterbooks were to provide evidence of the letter writer's learning, latinity, and links to society. Petrarch (1304–1374), the first humanist, discovered the ancient correspondence of Cicero and ushered in a new era for epistolography that imitated classical letters, abandoning the strict dictaminal rules for ordinary and daily speech in private letters. Besides *Epistolae familiares* (Letters on familiar matters) and *Epistolae sine nomine* (Nameless letters), he wrote *Epistolae seniles* (Letters of old age), which were to represent his autobiography for posterity. Johann von Neumarkt (c. 1310–1380), the chancellor in the court of Emperor Charles IV who met Petrarch and made the first contacts with humanism in central Europe, wrote *Summa cancellariae* (Compendium of the chancellery), a collection of over three hundred public form letters. Poggio Bracciolini (1380–1459), an apostolic secretary in the papal Curia and late in life the chancellor of the Republic of Florence, compiled *Epistolae,* 558 private letters that described personal affairs and humanistic activities. Another collection of autobiographical letters, *Epistolae familiares,* was made by Laura Cereta (1469–1499), who supported a woman's right to learning. Almost all of her letters related to the loss of her husband.

Desiderius Erasmus (1466?–1536), the most renowned northern humanist, compiled *Opus epistolarum* (A work of letters), which advanced humanists' doctrines for educational and religious reforms. Another eminent Dutch humanist, Justus Lipsius (1547–1606), wrote *Centuriae epistolarum* (Hundreds of letters) and corresponded with intellectuals across Europe. In the sixteenth century many French epistolographers, including Étienne DuTronchet (c. 1510–c. 1585), Marc-Antoine Muret (1526–1585), and Étienne Pasquier (1529–1615), left letterbooks that were autobiographical and showed an awareness of individualism. Johann Reuchlin (1455–1522), a German Hebraist, assumed another purpose in compiling his *Clarorum virorum epistolae* (Letters of famous men; 1514). This letterbook supported intellectual freedom and specifically defended him as an author of Hebrew studies. In response, a collection of satirical letters by unknown clergy and scholars, *Epistolae obscurorum virorum* (Letters of obscure men), was published in two volumes. In Spain Pietro Martire d'Anghiera (1457–1526), the first historian of America, compiled *Opus epistolarum,* many of whose 813 letters concern the discovery of America and events in the New World from 1488 to 1525. In England, Robert Joseph (c. 1500–1569) composed not only an official monastic letterbook covering business, legal, and administrative matters for the monastery at Evesham but also a collection of personal letters that revealed his activities and thoughts as a monk and as a scholar with humanistic interests at Oxford.

Letterbooks, which were among the greatest contributions of the civilization of the Renaissance, have historical, autobiographical, rhetorical, and literary importance. Initially in Latin manuscripts and gradually in vernaculars as well as in print, they served governments, the church, and individuals in the humanistic culture of Europe.

See also **Commonplace Books; Petrarch.**

BIBLIOGRAPHY

Primary Works

Butler, Kathleen T. B. *"The Gentlest Art" in Renaissance Italy: An Anthology of Italian Letters, 1459–1600.* Cambridge, U.K., 1954.

Cereta, Laura. *Collected Letters of a Renaissance Feminist.* Translated and edited by Diana Robin. Chicago, 1997.

Joseph, Robert. *The Letter Book of Robert Joseph.* Edited by Hugh Aveling and W. A. Pantin. Oxford, 1967.

Petrarca, Francesco. *Letters of Old Age.* Translated by Aldo S. Bernardo, Saul Levin, and Reta A. Bernardo. Baltimore, 1992. 2 vols. Translation of *Rerum senilium libri I–XVIII.*

Secondary Works

Clough, Cecil H. "The Cult of Antiquity: Letters and Letter Collections." In *Cultural Aspects of the Italian Renaissance: Essays in Honor of Paul Oskar Kristeller.* Edited by Cecil H. Clough. Manchester, U.K., and New York, 1976. Pages 33–67.

Poster, Carol, and Linda Mitchell, eds. *Letter-Writing Manuals from Antiquity to the Present.* Columbia, S. C., 2000.

Taylor, John. *English Historical Literature in the Fourteenth Century.* Oxford, 1987. See chapter 11, "Letters and Letter Collections," pp. 217–235.

EMIL J. POLAK

L'HÔPITAL, MICHEL DE (1505?–1573), chancellor of France. As chancellor from 1560 to 1568, L'Hôpital pursued a policy of peaceful coexistence between Catholics and Protestants during the French Wars of Religion (1562–1598). L'Hôpital favored granting limited toleration to Protestants as the only means to maintain the unity of the state, and he has often been deemed a precursor of the Politique party.

L'Hôpital was the eldest child of Jean de L'Hôpital, a personal physician of Charles de Bourbon, the constable of France. When his father was exiled in Italy following his complicity in Bourbon's rebellion against Francis I (1523), Michel joined him and studied law at the universities of Padua and Bologna. Following his return to France in 1533, L'Hôpital began his public career in 1537 when his wife, Marie Morin, brought as dowry the office of *conseiller* (judge) at the Parlement of Paris. Soon his scholarship drew the attention of Margaret of Valois, Henry II's sister, who appointed him chancellor of her duchy in Berry in 1550. L'Hôpital owed his subsequent rapid rise in the royal government to the generous patronage of the Guise family. Under the protection of Charles de Guise, the cardinal of Lorraine, L'Hôpital obtained the office of *maître des requêtes* (master of requests) in 1553, the presidency at the *chambre des comptes* (chamber of accounts) in 1555, and finally the chancellorship of France in 1560.

The royal court's religious policy in the early 1560s sought a kind of forced religious concord between Catholics and Protestants. But the fiasco of the Colloquy of Poissy (1561) finally brought to an end the hope that the restoration of religious unity in the kingdom could be achieved by doctrinal compromise, and it convinced L'Hôpital that limited toleration of Protestants was the only way to escape a civil war. The Edict of January (1562) and the Edict of Amboise (March 1563) legalized Protestant worship. L'Hôpital declared in a speech to the extended assembly of the royal council at Saint-Germain-en-Laye in 1562 that "many can be citizens who will not be Christians," and "even the excommunicated does not cease to be a citizen" (*Oeuvres complètes de Michel de L'Hospital,* vol. 1, p. 452). These bold statements dramatically revealed L'Hôpital's wish to stop the religious hostilities that were endangering the unity of the kingdom. L'Hôpital asserted that only a powerful prince with absolute sovereignty, capable of carrying out judicial reforms and providing impartial administration of justice, would spare France from further calamities of civil war. His attempts to create a reformed judicial structure, epitomized in the Ordinance of Orléans (1561), the Edict of Roussillon (1564), and the Ordinance of Moulins (1566), thus foreshadowed many later absolutist policies.

L'Hôpital was too pragmatic a mind to rank among Erasmian humanists, because he considered the matter of religious differences mainly in the context of the state's interests. At the same time, however, his uphill battle for religious moderation in the 1560s represented a fundamentally idealistic belief that religious coexistence could work in France, when all the evidence suggested otherwise. In particular, his apology for unchallenged royal authority and his crusade for judicial reforms revealed an indelible trace of idealism. L'Hôpital fell out of favor in 1568, and this marked the ultimate failure of his religious policy. Yet his advocacy of toleration revealed a vision that went beyond the sixteenth-century settlement of religious conflict.

See also **Toleration; Wars of Religion.**

BIBLIOGRAPHY

Primary Works

L'Hôpital, Michel de. *Discours pour la majorité de Charles IX et trois autres discours.* Edited by Robert Descimon. Paris, 1993. An annotated edition of the four major political discourses of L'Hôpital.

L'Hôpital, Michel de. *Oeuvres complètes de Michel de L'Hospital.* Edited by P. J. S. Duféy. 3 vols. Paris, 1824–1825. Reprint, Geneva, 1968. Duféy also published *Traité de la réformation de la justice* in the two-volume *Oeuvres inédites de Michel de L'Hospital* (1826), but L'Hôpital's authorship of *Traité* remains questionable. See Neely's article below.

L'Hôpital, Michel de. *Poésies complètes du chancelier Michel de L'Hospital.* Translated by Louis Bandy de Nalèche. Paris, 1857. Translation of L'Hôpital's Latin verses, first published in 1585.

Secondary Works

Buisson, Albert. *Michel de L'Hospital.* Paris, 1950.

Dupré-Lasale, Émile. *Michel de L'Hospital avant son élévation au poste de chancelier de France.* 2 vols. Paris, 1875–1899.

Kim, Seong-Hak. *Michel de L'Hopital: The Vision of a Reformist Chancellor during the French Religious Wars.* Kirksville, Mo., 1997.

Neely, Sylvia. "Michel de L'Hospital and the *Traité de la Réformation de la Justice:* A Case of Misattribution." *French Historical Studies* 14 (1986): 339–366. Refutes L'Hôpital's authorship of *Traité.*

Taillandier, A. H. *Nouvelles recherches historiques sur la vie et les ouvrages du chancelier de L'Hospital.* Paris, 1861.

MARIE SEONG-HAK KIM

LIBERTINISM. According to René Pintard's classic study of 1943, libertinism refers to an Italian and French erudite, cultural, and philosophical movement of the late sixteenth and seventeenth century that established reason and nature as the criteria for morality, law, and politics—thus challenging, if not frequently dismantling, transcendental sources of truth and authority. Learned libertinism provides an important intellectual bridge between the late Renaissance and the Enlightenment.

The terms *libertin* and *libertinage* were first used in a religious context by both Protestants and Catholics, beginning with the Reformer John Calvin (1509–1564). He attacked religious dissenters within his own church who wanted freedom of conscience in matters of faith and morals, and in their interpretation of the Bible. Calvinists and libertines opposed each other in political and communal life in Holland up to 1620, with the eventual triumph of the Calvinist Dutch Reformed Church. It was nevertheless possible for religious libertines to reject both Catholic and Protestant authority and live within tolerant communities that allowed diverse religious practices.

In the early seventeenth century, however, French Catholic theologians called "libertine" those they accused of irreligion and atheism. The term was extended to those who behaved as if they had no moral principles, especially in sexual matters, and who, it was inferred, embraced Epicurean, materialist beliefs, displaying no fear of divine retribution in the next life. (After his death in 1556, the work of the Italian writer Pietro Aretino acquired an ever-increasing reputation for libertine debauchery; and fear of libertine moral values lies at the origins of the

Don Juan/Don Giovanni figure as well as the "rake.")

Lists of libertine "libraries" identified particular authors and texts as belonging to a tradition dating back to Greek antiquity. In 1623, the French Jesuit François Garasse drew up a list of atheists and materialists; he denounced the Italians Niccolò Machiavelli (1469–1527), Pietro Pomponazzi (1462–1525), Girolamo Cardano (1501–1576), and Giulio Cesare Vanini (1584–1619) for subverting belief in the divine foundations of Christianity, providential intervention in history, and moral absolutes. Marin Mersenne also drew up similar lists in 1623, and his *Impieté des déistes, athées et libertins de ce temps* (The irreligion of deists, atheists and libertines of our age; 1624) added the French skeptic Pierre Charron (1541–1603), a disciple of Michel de Montaigne (1533–1592) to the Italians, and tarred them all with the brush of Epicurean atomism. (Note that Deism, belief in a divinity based on reason alone, was considered just as dangerous as were atheism and libertinism.)

The metaphor of a library supplied a sense of a coherent tradition to the libertines themselves, who looked upon the same authors and texts with admiration. Gabriel Naudé composed his *Advis pour dresser une bibliothèque* (Advice on building a library; 1627), extolling Charron in particular, and sweeping into the skeptical libertine fold Francis Bacon (1561–1626), Pierre Gassendi (1592–1655), Giordano Bruno (1548–1600), and Tommaso Campanella (1568–1639). François de La Mothe Le Vayer (1588–1672), author of dialogues published under the name of Orasius Tubero in 1630 and 1631–1632, chose the same books. But erudite libertines like Le Vayer also made classical Greek and Latin authors appear critical of pagan religion, doubtful of the powers of reason, and supportive of a purely natural law and morality: Sextus Empiricus, Epicurus, Lucian, and Plutarch among the Greeks; and Lucretius, some of Cicero's dialogues, and Pliny the Elder among the Romans. The most highly articulated expression of atheism is found in the anonymous *Theophrastus redivivus* (Theophrastus born again), a work whose title page tells us is "composed from the opinions of philosophers [ancient and modern], and designed to overthrow theologians [Catholic, Protestant, Jewish, and Mohammedan]." The names of fifteen ancient and four modern atheists surround the title itself; the latter are Pomponazzi, Cardano, Jean Bodin (1530–1596), and Vanini. Not all libertines were atheists; but all held to Pomponazzi's mutual exclusion of the realms of faith and reason, on the grounds that religious dogma should not impinge on the findings of rational investigation.

A socially diverse group, including poets, scholars, librarians, lawyers, philosophers, and moralists, libertines lived and wrote in a climate of intolerance and persecution. Some were imprisoned, tortured, and executed for antiauthoritarian opinions, both in Italy and France. Libertines often employed playful and satirical genres to hide serious points. Charles Sorel, in a preface to a comic work of 1626, said he resorted to fables, dreams, and other fictions to speak truths that those in authority did not want to hear. The Venetian Academy of the Incogniti (the Disguised, so named because its members often disguised their true opinions) founded in 1627 by the patrician and patron Giovan Francesco Loredan (1607–1661) produced novels, epistolary satires, and Boccaccian *novelle* that exposed papal corruption and the abuse of political power. In large measure, the academy kept alive the success of Traiano Boccalini's *Ragguagli di Parnasso* (Dispatches from Parnassus; 1613), witty and subversive observations on tyranny, hypocrisy, and censorship in Italy and elsewhere, from a utopian court where liberty and the voice of reason ruled. Loredan's favorite satirist, Ferrante Pallavicino (1615–1644), even more corrosive than Boccalini, was put to death on papal orders before he was thirty years old. Anonymous, clandestine publications allowed libertine writings to circulate; and widespread correspondences all over Europe disseminated opinions too dangerous to publish.

Although they were not organized as a system or school, libertines shared some common concerns. In addition to cultivating doubt, they defended religious and political liberty, plurality of beliefs and opinions, and practiced tolerance. They believed that natural causes, as opposed to supernatural ones, could provide explanations of all phenomena, including miracles and prophecies; implicit in this belief is a validation of pleasure as a gift of nature that should not be suppressed. Fantastic journeys to unknown societies, from Thomas More's *Utopia* (1516), to Campanella's *City of the Sun* (1602) and Cyrano de Bergerac's *Voyages to the States and Empires of the Moon,* were means to entertain the possibility of laws, political and social institutions, and cultural values that were very different from those established in Europe.

Libertines made a central issue of the human, historical fabrication of all religions, a doctrine fueled by an anonymous, clandestine tract of uncertain origins, *The Three Imposters*—the title refers to Christ,

Moses, and Mohammed—and also by reflections on Machiavelli, who had advanced the view that religion was used by rulers to enhance their own and the state's authority, and to control their subjects. Libertines reevaluated paganism, which led them to deny that belief in the immortality of the soul, with the attendant rewards and punishments after death, was necessary for leading a moral life. It was possible to have a virtuous atheist citizen. Vanini, Naudé, and the *Theophrastus redivivus* added doses of Lucretius to their expositions of the savage origins of a society held together by force with hardly a divine construct. Naudé in particular exposed rulers as governing in their own interest and justifying their actions by the principle of *raison d'état* (reason of state). The movement petered out after 1650, though echoes reverberated in England, in the writings of Thomas Hobbes, Robert Burton, Charles Blount, and John Toland.

See also Bacon, Francis; Campanella, Tommaso; Cardano, Girolamo; Charron, Pierre; Pomponazzi, Pietro; Skepticism.

BIBLIOGRAPHY

Gregory, Tullio. " 'Libertinisme érudit' in Seventeenth-Century France and Italy: The Critique of Ethics and Religion." *Journal of the British Society for the History of Philosophy* 6, no. 3 (1998): 323–349.

Gregory, Tullio. *Theophrastus redivivus: erudizione e ateismo nel Seicento.* Naples, Italy, 1979.

Gregory, Tullio, et al., eds. *Ricerche su letteratura libertina e letteratura clandestina nel Seicento.* Florence, 1981. Twenty-two contributions covering Italian, French, and English aspects of libertinism.

Pintard, René. *Le libertinage érudit dans la première moitié du dix-septième siècle.* Paris, 1943. Reprint, Geneva and Paris, 1983.

Spink, John S. *French Free-Thought from Gassendi to Voltaire.* London, 1960.

LETIZIA PANIZZA

LIBRARIES. The cultural history of the Renaissance is inextricably entwined with the fortune of its libraries. From the discovery of forgotten classical texts in neglected medieval collections to contemporary foundations established to preserve newfound spoils, Renaissance libraries were important sites of learning, patronage, and prestige. More than simple collections of texts, Renaissance libraries often prized books as much for their beauty as for their content. They furnished materials for close philological scrutiny of ancient texts and provided the opportunity to encounter forgotten literary and scientific traditions. Many libraries incorporated cabinets of antiquities, natural and man-made curiosities, and mathematical and scientific instruments. And whether modest private collections or court marvels, many formed the nucleus for local circles of learning as well as far-flung networks of scholars.

Early Humanist Libraries. Francesco Petrarch (1304–1374), the fourteenth-century scholar most closely associated with the birth of humanism, viewed books and collecting as an "insatiable passion," amassing a private collection of some two hundred volumes. The majority were works of Latin antiquity and the church fathers. His collection originated in the shadow of the papal library at Avignon, and traveled with him between Provence, Milan, and the Veneto. His surviving books bear evidence of a close, questioning reading. This was also the case with other early humanist libraries. In Florence, both Coluccio Salutati and Niccolò Niccoli amassed collections of around eight hundred volumes. Salutati, as had Petrarch, densely annotated, cross-referenced, and indexed the texts in his collection. Niccoli's library was available to his friends and was intended, after his death in 1437, to "be brought to the common good, to the public service, to a place open to all." Through the patronage of Cosimo de' Medici, Niccoli's books provided the foundation for the Dominican library of San Marco in Florence. Opened in 1444 as a public library, the San Marco collection was part of wider Medici patronage of scholars and learning. By the end of the fifteenth century, the private collection of Lorenzo de' Medici (il Magnifico) contained some one thousand manuscripts, later kept in the cloister at San Lorenzo in Florence and normally open to scholars known to the family. One of the most spectacular private humanist libraries was that of Giovanni Pico della Mirandola (1463–1494), comprising over one thousand volumes. Pico's library contained over one hundred Hebrew manuscripts, one of the largest hordes in Italy. It encompassed both works of contemporary literature and manuscripts bearing on classical antiquity, reflecting contemporary humanist culture on the one hand, and volumes on theology and scholastic philosophy and Latin scientific texts, indicative of Pico's engagement with the medieval legacy, on the other. Pico's library, emblematic of the interests of his generation of humanists, reveals no great rupture with previous traditions of learning.

Perhaps the most exceptional of the early humanist libraries was that of Bessarion (1403–1472), a Greek monk who became a cardinal in the Latin church. Bessarion's library contained more than one thousand volumes, and was particularly strong in

Pope Sixtus IV Visits the Vatican Library. The pope is greeted by his nephew Giuliano; the librarian, Bartolomeo Sacchi, called il Platina is third from right. Painting from the school of Melozzo da Forli in the Ospedale di S. Spirito, Rome. [For a portrayal of Sixtus and Platina by Melozzo, see the color plates in volume 4.] D. ANDERSON/ALINARI/ART RESOURCE

Greek manuscripts. After the fall of Constantinople in 1453, his collection of Greek texts came to function as an archive for the cultural patrimony of Greek learning; his Latin collection constituted a voyage of personal discovery of the Western intellectual tradition. In order to preserve the legacy of a collection made freely available to his circle of friends, Bessarion donated it to the city of Venice, where it was intended to serve the "public use" and "the utility of scholars." It eventually become the Biblioteca Marciana.

Cardinals' Libraries. While unique, Bessarion's library was part of a distinct fifteenth-century model of a working professional and scholarly library that emerged in Rome around a College of Cardinals active in ecclesiastical and cultural affairs. The rise in importance of cardinalate libraries was

prior to the foundation of the Vatican Library in the 1470s by Pope Sixtus IV, for which they were an important precedent. Cardinalate collections were made possible through the economic opportunities that the cardinal's office afforded, and fueled by contact many cardinals enjoyed with humanist circles, fostering interest in the recovery of ancient texts from both pagan and Christian traditions. Fifteenth-century cardinals' libraries demonstrate a decided predeliction for legal and patristic works, revealing the mixed professional and intellectual orientation of their owners. They ranged in size from the very modest to relatively large (388 volumes in one such collection), to Bessarion's enormous collection. In the sixteenth century, collections such as Guglielmo Sirleto's were closely keyed to Sirleto's patristic interests and the demands of a Counter-Reformation cardinal. That of Alessandro Farnese marked a new initiative of cardinalate patronage of scholarship on a grand scale, with more universal patterns of acquisition and a more precocious presence on the Roman cultural landscape. This was continued by the library founded in 1628 by Cardinal Federico Barberini, nephew of Pope Urban VIII, destined to become the richest in Rome after the Vatican Library. Even the library founded in Paris in 1643 by Cardinal Jules Mazarin, the first public library in France, owed a good deal to the cardinalate model. Rome itself would continue to witness the formation of important cardinalate collections into the eighteenth century.

Court Libraries. Cardinals' libraries came to embody many aspects of the traditional court library. The earliest major court collection in Italy was at Naples. Dating to the thirteenth century, it grew extensively in the mid-fifteenth century under the patronage of King Alfonso of Aragon and Naples. Court libraries were among the richest in Italy. The Gonzaga collection at Mantua held 300 Latin manuscripts in 1407; the Visconti in Milan, 998 manuscripts in 1426; and that of Federico da Montefeltro at Urbino, in the same period, 772 manuscripts. At the end of the century, the d'Este library at Ferrara held 512 volumes. Developed partly as archives of estate accounts and legal documents and partly in pursuit of the humanist interests of their owners, such libraries were also important centers of humanist patronage.

While in France the early court collection of Emperor Charles V was dispersed in 1435, King Francis I entrusted the foundation of a new royal library at Fontainebleau to the humanist Guillaume Budé in 1520. By 1544 the collection held some 2,686 volumes. While the library grew only incrementally over the course of the next century, leading humanists would always be associated with it. By the end of the sixteenth century the collection was no longer the personal library of the king, but led an itinerant life in Paris. One of the most ambitious court libraries of the period was the Escorial near Madrid, a unique amalgamation of humanist scholarship, Counter-Reformation arsenal, and personal spiritual retreat for King Philip II of Spain. The library grew quickly under Philip's patronage and the librarianship of the Christian humanist Arias Montano. In addition to its books the library also possessed a leading collection of mathematical and scientific instruments.

It was in Germany and central Europe where the court library had its most profound and enduring impact. At Augsburg in the late fifteenth and early sixteenth centuries, the banker Jakob Fugger deliberately set out to imitate Italian models, employing Italian book agents and having one of them, the architect Jacobo Strada, design his library. The Fugger library, among other collections, later provided a foundation for the library instituted at Munich by Duke Albrecht V of Bavaria. In Protestant Germany, late-sixteenth-century courts such as Gottorp in Holstein or Wolfenbüttel in Lower Saxony built up rich libraries out of the spoils of dispersed monastic collections and the explosion of printed books. By the middle of the following century, Wolfenbüttel would be the largest library in Europe with over 100,000 titles, eventually claiming the philosopher G. W. Leibnitz as librarian. By contrast, and despite its obvious prestige, the imperial library at Vienna always remained a modest collection. It had a fine tradition of sixteenth-century humanist librarians: Conrad Celtis (1459–1508) early in the century, followed by Wolfgang Lazius (1514–1565), who built up the library as an archive of imperial historical records. Slightly later Hugo Blotius (1533–1608) attempted to broaden the humanist vision of the library, a project eventually fulfilled by Peter Lambeck (1628–1680), imperial librarian at the end of the seventeenth century. In the baroque courts of northern and central Europe, the Renaissance court library model would endure well into the eighteenth century.

Ecclesiastical Libraries. Alongside such frequently dramatic secular initiatives, ecclesiastical libraries in much of Europe retained their vitality through much of the Renaissance. Fourteenth-century private clerical, legal, and medical libraries were, in many ways, adaptions of the great study libraries of religious houses attached to the universities. Such ecclesiastical libraries were also important models for the establishment of college libraries in university centers during the fourteenth century. With the exception of the Sorbonne at Paris, which housed a sizable collection, university libraries were relatively unimportant before the early seventeenth century. In urban centers such as Rome, Venice, and Paris, ecclesiastical libraries were quasi-public institutions. In Protestant lands in the sixteenth century, rich monastic libraries were dispersed, their holdings passing into private hands or secular city, court, or university collections. Elsewhere in Catholic Europe, particularly in Italy, southern Germany, and Austrian lands, monastic libraries gained a new mandate as instruments of Catholic renewal. At Rome, the Vallicelliana Library of the new Congregation of the Oratory not only amassed collections of manuscripts and printed books, but also served as the scholarly workshop for the production of the vast Counter-Reformation ecclesiastical history of Cardinal Cesare Baronio (1538–1607) (for a time also Vatican librarian). Yet there were important local initiatives as well, seeing both new foundations and the renewal of older centers. In France, ecclesiastical collections that had suffered greatly during the Wars of Religion experienced a remarkable revival, growing to become among the best in Europe over the course of the seventeenth century.

Private Libraries. Most private libraries in the period tended to be quasi-technical collections closely linked to the professional interests of their owners; size is more a factor of economic possibility than interest or intensity of use. In sixteenth-century Venice, a handful of patrician libraries held one thousand or so books, while other patricians and merchants possessed more modest collections of around one hundred volumes. Lawyers and particularly physicians had considerable collections, while many other libraries held between a dozen and fifty volumes, mostly works concerning commercial affairs and piety. Devotional texts remained dominant into the middle of the sixteenth century in inventoried Florentine private libraries, which rarely numbered more than one hundred volumes.

Scientific libraries, particularly medical libraries, were of great importance. The collection of Nicolò Leoniceno (1428–1524), physician and teacher of medicine at the University of Ferrara at the end of the fifteenth century, was closely allied to his program of medical reform. In his desire to overcome medieval Latin medicine, Leoniceno sought direct contact with Greek sources of scientific learning in philosophy, medicine, botany, and mathematics. His collection of 345 volumes was overwhelmingly scientific in character. It contained 117 Greek volumes, the majority manuscripts, representing every significant text of the Greek scientific corpus now extant. Libraries such as Leoniceno's were important for the rise of medical humanism in general and the revival of Galen in medicine in particular. Similarly, the renaissance of mathematics in the sixteenth century was largely the product of collections of Greek mathematical manuscripts established the previous century. At Venice, libraries of physicians tended to be larger than those of lawyers, and even apothecaries possessed significant collections. Private collections of physicians and professors of medicine were also important in Paris in the sixteenth and seventeenth centuries. Particularly in northern Europe, private professional libraries were used both for teaching and scholarship across a variety of disciplines.

The second half of the sixteenth century witnessed a proliferation of such private collections representing a confluence of historical, political, and scientific interests. In Italy, this tradition is best represented by the libraries of Fulvio Orsini (1529–1600) at Rome and Gian Vincenzo Pinelli (1535–1601) at Padua. Orsini, librarian to Cardinal Alessandro Farnese (collecting art and antiquities as well as books for the cardinal) and corrector of Greek texts at the Vatican Library, assembled his own collection of manuscripts largely out of the debris of those of earlier generations of humanists. He actively collected manuscripts annotated by earlier humanists and as with them, his undertaking was largely a philological enterprise. Variant readings encountered in other libraries or in the works of friends were entered into the margins of his own books. Extraordinarily for a late humanist library, Orsini owned more manuscripts than printed books (more than 500 manuscripts, of which there were more Greek than Latin, compared to around 230 printed books). Such was not the case with his fellow collector Pinelli, whose collection included 6,428 printed books and 738 manuscripts. Unlike Orsini, Pinelli published nothing himself, more a patron and facilitator of learning than a scholar. His house at Padua was both museum and library, serving as a meeting place for local and visiting scholars; it was here, for example, that Galileo wrote his first lectures for the University of Padua.

In Paris, this was the generation of the great collections of the robe nobility: those of Claude Dupuy (1545–1594), of Henri de Mesmes (1532–1596), of Jacques-Auguste de Thou (1553–1617). These were at once collections emblematic of humanist learning (Dupuy, like Orsini, filled the margins of his books with variant readings; de Mesmes employed a Greek copyist) and cabinets of legal documents and political papers bearing on the immediate French political crisis. These French collections found echos in England in the scientific and historical collections of John Dee (1527–1608) and Sir Robert Cotton (1571–1631). Dee enjoyed close relationships with continental scholars and bibliophiles. His collection of scientific manuscripts not only fueled his own scholarship, but also formed the basis for the museum and academy run from his home and provided a focal point for a wide network of scholars. Cotton's library, more closely tied to contemporary political expedients, contained copies of rare archival documents. Such private libraries of the late Renaissance arbitrated between often overlapping worlds of classical and historical scholarship, scientific learning, and politics. They functioned equally as sites of intellectual and political exchange and store-houses of books.

Public Libraries. Throughout the Renaissance, many collections hovered between a private and semi-public status. The very end of the period witnessed the rise of libraries that declared themselves to be public in something approximating the modern sense. These new public libraries incorporated elements of the Renaissance library tradition while heralding developments of the century to follow. The new university library founded at Oxford by Thomas Bodley (1545–1613) opened to readers in 1602. Bodley's first librarian, Thomas James (1573–1629), launched a virulently anti-Catholic campaign from the library, a confessional program mirrored in the portraits of continental and English reformers gracing the library's walls. Francis Bacon (1561–1626) evinced a slightly different view, expressing the hope that the new library would serve as "an ark of learning." The Angelica Library, founded by Angelo Rocca (1545–1620) in 1604, complemented a host of cardinalate and ecclesiastical libraries in Rome. Rocca had been the principal assistant of Pope Sixtus V (reigned 1585–1590) in refounding the Vatican Library in the 1580s, and the library itself was housed in the Augustinian convent at Rome. It was Rome's first public library. The Ambrosiana Library at Milan, founded by Cardinal Federico Borromeo (1564–1631) in 1607, can be placed within the tradition of earlier cardinalate libraries and the Vallicelliana and Vatican Libraries at Rome. Graced with a museum and a college of scholars, the Ambrosiana was intended both to support the Counter-Reformation in Milan and to furnish an autonomous "institute" of learning. It was by means of such new institutions, at a moment when the new science had yet to replace the new learning, that the textual and intellectual legacy of the Renaissance would be preserved, evaluated, and communicated to subsequent generations.

See also **Vatican Library.**

BIBLIOGRAPHY

Bianca, Concetta, et al. "Materiale e ipotesi per le biblioteche Cardinalizie." In *Scrittura, biblioteche, e stampa a Roma nel quattrocento. Aspetti e problemi.* Edited by Concetta Bianca et al. Pp. 73–84. Vatican City, 1980. This volume includes other important articles on cardinalate libraries.

Dadson, Trevor J. *Libros, lectores y lecturas: Estudios sobre bibliotecas particulares españolas del Siglo de Oro.* Madrid, 1998.

With an essential bibliography on Spanish libraries and the book trade in Spain.

Delatour, Jérôme. *Une bibliothèque humaniste au temps des guerres de religion: Les livres de Claude Dupuy.* Paris, 1998.

Fabian, Bernhard, ed. *Handbuch der historischen Buchbestände in Deutschland.* New York; Hildesheim, Germany, 1991–. A comprehensive historical and bibliographical guide to German collections.

Fehrenbach, Robert J., and E. S. Leedham-Green, eds. *Private Libraries in Renaissance England: A Collection and Catalogue of Tudor and Early Stuart Book-lists.* 5 vols. Binghamton, N.Y., 1992–1998. A collection of inventories of private collections.

Grendler, Marcella. "A Greek Collection in Padua: The Library of Gian Vincenzo Pinelli (1535–1601)." *Renaissance Quarterly* 33 (1980): 386–416.

Hobson, Anthony. *Great Libraries.* London, 1970. A magnificently illustrated survey, with bibliography, of major Renaissance collections.

Kibre, Pearl. *The Library of Pico della Mirandola.* New York, 1936.

Nelles, Paul. "The Library As an Instrument of Discovery: Gabriel Naudé and the Uses of History." In *History and the Disciplines. The Reclassification of Knowledge in Early Modern Europe.* Edited by Donald R. Kelley. Rochester, N.Y., 1997. Pages 41–57.

Nolhac, Pierre de. *La bibliothèque de Fulvio Orsini.* 1887. Reprint, Geneva, 1976.

Robathan, Dorothy M. "Libraries of the Italian Renaissance." In *The Medieval Library.* Edited by James Westfall Thompson. 1939. Reprint, New York, 1957. Pages 509–588.

Rose, Paul Lawrence. "Humanist Culture and Renaissance Mathematics: The Italian Libraries of the *Quattrocento.*" *Studies in the Renaissance* 20 (1973): 46–105.

Serrai, Alfredo. *Storia della bibliografia.* 6 vols. Rome, 1984–1995. A richly documented study of the genesis of the bibliographical disciplines in the Renaissance period, with much information on contemporary libraries.

Sherman, William H. *John Dee: The Politics of Reading and Writing in the English Renaissance.* Amherst, Mass., 1995.

Ullman, Berthold L., and Philip A. Stadter. *The Public Library of Renaissance Florence: Niccolò Niccoli, Cosimo de' Medici, and the Library of San Marco.* Padua, Italy, 1972.

Vernet, André, ed. *Histoire des bibliothèques françaises.* 4 vols. Paris, 1988–1992. The first two volumes are on medieval and Renaissance libraries, with essential bibliography.

Zorzi, Marino. "La circolazione del libro a Venezia nel cinquecento: Biblioteche private e pubbliche." *Ateneo veneto* 177 (1990): 117–189. A model study of local library culture.

PAUL NELLES

LIFE STAGES. Defining periods of life common to everyone serves at least two purposes: it provides expectations by which to measure performance, and it tells people of different ages what society permits them to do.

Traditional Concepts. The life stages defined in Roman law were *infantia* (infancy and early childhood), *pueritia* (childhood), and *pubertas* (adulthood). This tripartite scheme persisted through the Middle Ages. However, writers and artists tended to depict more than three stages. A common number was seven. A woodcut of 1491, for example, shows a swaddled infant in a cradle; a little child in skirts with a walker; an older child, also in skirts, on a hobby horse; a boy in a scholar's robe; a young man in doublet and hose with a sword at his side; a bearded man sitting in a chair; and another bearded man with a wrinkled face holding a staff.

Conventional ages were assigned to life stages. The age of seven marked the end of *infantia,* and succeeding stages were usually marked off by sevens. Seven to fourteen was childhood, fourteen to twenty-one was youth, and so on. These ages acquired a certain authority. Fourteen was thought of as the normal age to begin apprenticeship, which was normally expected to last seven years. A conventional age for the end of active life was sixty.

Life Stages in Practice. People's expectations of the stages they would go through varied considerably according to region, class, and sex. In addition, the contradiction between social life stages and biological development created ambivalences. All men shared the experience of a first stage of life spent in the company of women, when they wore clothing that was not distinctively masculine. At some point, not necessarily the age of seven, they started to move into the world of men. For most of them youth was an important stage, terminated when they entered marriage. Women started life the same way, but continued to wear the same sort of clothing. Their next major stage was marriage, and a third stage, that of widowhood, was highly likely. Almost all men and women in the lower classes went through a stage of being servants away from home. Upper-class men and some upper-class women might also go through an analogous stage, as pages, gentlemen servants, maids of honor, or merchant apprentices. In addition, some youths spent several years in school.

In a sense, there were only two life stages: the period before adulthood and the period of adulthood. With the exception of celibate clergy, whose entrance into their vocations was considered a passage to a new life stage, adulthood was usually entered by marriage. However, only the head of a household could function as a full adult. Thus, marriage was in a sense not a sufficient requirement for adulthood for sons living in joint-family households headed by fathers. Widows who headed households were the only fully adult women, since women were otherwise dependent on fathers or husbands.

See also **Childhood; Family and Kinship.**

BIBLIOGRAPHY

Ariès, Philippe. *Centuries of Childhood: A Social History of Family Life.* Translated by Robert Baldick. New York, 1962. Translation of *L'enfant et la vie familiale sous l'ancienne régime* (1960). This groundbreaking work on family history starts with the chapter "The Ages of Life" and reverts to the concept throughout the book.

Kett, Joseph F. *Rites of Passage: Adolescence in America, 1790 to the Present.* New York, 1977. In spite of the title, the first chapter, "The Stages of Life," is a larger historical overview.

BEATRICE GOTTLIEB

LIGORIO, PIRRO (1513–1583), Italian painter, architect, and antiquarian. Ligorio was born in Naples to a noble family probably linked with the Carafa family, who probably educated him and sent him to Rome around 1534.

Early Career. Ligorio is known primarily as a painter of palace facades, which he decorated with frescoes in a yellow chiaroscuro reminiscent of Polidoro da Caravaggio and Baldassare Peruzzi. This activity is confirmed by a contract of 1542 for the palace of the archbishop of Benevento located in Via Lata, and by his only extant fresco (c. 1544), representing the *Dance of Salome* (in the oratory of San Giovanni Decollato, where another little panel is also preserved). Two years later Ligorio contracted to paint a banner for the Confraternity of Santa Maria of Rieti (lost). In 1549 he painted a fresco for the palace of Cardinal Ippolito II d'Este at Monte Giordano. Ligorio was proposed for membership in the Confraternity of the Virtuosi al Pantheon in 1548.

During archaeological investigations in and around Rome in 1545 Ligorio collected and transcribed Latin inscriptions and other antiquities. He also studied the topography of ancient Rome, which he discussed with antiquarians of the Farnese circle, including Onofrio Panvinio, Fulvio Orsini, Antonio Agustín, Jean Matal, Gabriele Faerno, Girolamo Mercuriale, Benedetto Egio, and the Stampa brothers.

In 1549 Ligorio entered the service of Cardinal Ippolito II d'Este for six years. In 1550 he worked for the cardinal at Tivoli, excavating Hadrian's villa and laying out the extraordinary gardens of the Villa d'Este. He decorated several villas with statues and grottoes (Villa Medici, Giulia, and Carafa at Monte Cavallo), and gardens (Pio Carpi on the Quirinal) with antique statues, which were found during his archaeological investigations.

Architect in the Vatican. The year 1549 also marks Ligorio's appointment in the Vatican as overseer of St. Peter's fountain. The major results of his investigations on Roman architecture and ancient

Pirro Ligorio. Casino of Pius IV. Ligorio built the casino—a summer house—in the Vatican gardens, in 1560. The exuberant stucco decoration is by Ligorio and Rocco di Silvestro da Montefiascone. ALINARI/ART RESOURCE

literary sources were published in the 1550s. He produced three maps of Rome (1552, 1553, 1561), the last of which exerted considerable influence until the nineteenth century. He published a treatise on theaters and circuses, *Delle antichità di Roma* (Antiquities of Rome, 1553), and issued reconstructions of the Circus Maximus, the thermal baths of Diocletian and Maximinian, and the Aviary of Varro (1552–1558). He provided illustrations for Faerno's edition of *Aesop's Fables* (1563).

During the exile of Ippolito II d'Este (1555–1559), Ligorio entered the service of Pope Paul IV, a member of the Carafa family, as a *disegnator* (draftsman), and in 1558 he was appointed architect of the Vatican Palace. He painted and executed projects of reparation and decoration for different rooms in the Vatican Palace, including the chapel in the new papal apartment in the Belvedere Court. His main projects as papal architect were a revised design for the Belvedere Court and the design of the wonderful Casino of Pius IV in the Vatican gardens. Both were decorated with antique statues. Construction was completed in 1562. Ligorio was commissioned to construct the Palazzina of Pius IV, which he built on the Via Flaminia above the fountain of Julius III (1561–1564).

In 1564 Ligorio had several commissions outside the Vatican Palace to work on the facade of San Giovanni in Laterano, the Palazzo della Sapienza, Torres-Lancellotti, and Capodiferro. Outside Rome he designed gardens, fountains, and grottoes at Bomarzo, Papacqua, and Bagnaia. His most important achievement, however, was his appointment to succeed Michelangelo as architect of St. Peter's, along with Jacopo Vignola. In 1565 he was imprisoned for three weeks after having been accused of larceny. Following his release Ligorio returned to work in the Sistine Chapel. The following year he helped decorate the Vatican for the coronation of Pius V. His final important commissions for the Vatican (1566) were to design a new Palace of the Holy Office and the tomb of Pope Paul IV (in the Church of Santa Maria sopra Minerva).

In 1567 Ligorio was replaced in the Vatican, and he left Rome for Tivoli with his family after selling the first manuscripts of his *Delle antichità di Roma* and his collection of medals to Cardinal Alessandro Farnese.

Late Career and Reputation. In 1568 Ligorio was appointed antiquarian in the court of Duke Alfonso II d'Este, nephew of the cardinal, and he moved to Ferrara in 1569. Later that year he created for Ippolito a series of drawings (for tapestries) illustrating the life of Hippolytus, and in the following years he designed the *XII Dei Consentes* (twelve ancient gods of agriculture) for Farnese (Archivio Borromeo) and the illustrations of body exercises for the second edition of the *De arte gymnastica* of Girolamo Mercuriale (1573). The same figures appeared in the frescoes of the Sala dei Giochi in the Castello Estense. Other designs were made for the Sala dell'Aurora. Ligorio made a series of genealogical drawings of the Este family in the courtyard of the Castello. In 1573 he was commissioned to design the tomb of Ludovico Ariosto.

During these years Ligorio was curator of the duke's library and collection of antiquities. He worked as an engineer and an architect with Giovanni Battista Aleotti, especially on the reconstruction of the Castello after the earthquake of 1570. He was involved in the organization of the famous *cavallerie ferraresi* (allegorical tournaments) with Cornelio Bentivoglio in 1569, and he designed six triumphal arches for the royal entry of Henry III of

France in 1574. At his death Ligorio left a wife and several children. He also left thirty volumes of a new encyclopedia of antiquities and more than five thousand drawings. Ligorio's *Delle antichità di Roma* enjoyed enormous success during his life and in the following centuries. Copies are found in the Codex Ursinianus (Vat. lat. 3439) and in the Museo Cartaceo of Cassiano Dal Pozzo (Windsor Castle and British Museum). Although scholars of the nineteenth century demonstrated that these books are full of archaeological and epigraphical forgeries, the *Antichità di Roma* is an important representation of antiquarian research conducted by one of the most fascinating architects of the Renaissance.

BIBLIOGRAPHY

Coffin, David R. "Ligorio, Pirro." In *Dictionary of Art*. Edited by Jane Turner. Vol. 19. London, 1996. Pages 370–373.

Mandowsky, Erna, and Charles Mitchell. *Pirro Ligorio's Roman Antiquities.* London, 1963.

Rausa, Federico. *Pirro Ligorio. Tombe e mausolei dei Romani.* Rome, 1997.

Vagenheim, Ginette. "Some Newly Discovered Works by Pirro Ligorio." *Journal of the Warburg and Courtauld Institutes* 51 (1988): 242–245.

Vagenheim, Ginette. "Las falsification chez Pirro Ligorio. À la lumière des *Fasti Capitolini* et des inscriptions de Préneste." *Eutopia* 3 (1994): 67–113.

Volpi, Caterina. *Il libro dei disegni di Pirro Ligorio: all'Archivio di Stato di Torino.* Rome, 1994.

GINETTE VAGENHEIM

LINACRE, THOMAS (c. 1460–1524), English humanist, physician, medical writer. Linacre was the first humanist scholar to bring knowledge of ancient medical practice to England. While he is often said to have been born at Linacre Hall in Derbyshire, it is more likely that he grew up in Canterbury. He was educated at Oxford and then in Italy; between 1487 and 1493 he studied Greek and Latin with Demetrius Chalcondyles and Angelo Poliziano in Florence. He received the M.D. degree from Padua in 1496 and was invited to join the distinguished faculty there, but he decided to return to England. Before doing so he assisted the Venetian printer Aldus Manutius with a Greek edition of Aristotle and a Latin translation of Proclus's *De sphaera* (On spheres).

Following the accession of Henry VIII in 1509, Linacre was appointed physician to the king and tutor to Princess Mary. He lectured on medicine at Oxford and in 1518 founded the Royal College of Physicians, which soon obtained a monopoly on the practice of medicine, originally limited to London but later running throughout the realm.

Linacre's chief importance lies in his efforts to make the ideas of the classical Greek and Roman physicians available in England. His translation of the works of Galen of Pergamum from Greek into Latin appeared between 1517 and 1523. Linacre did not produce English versions of these treatises because he did not want ordinary persons to attempt to diagnose and treat their own illnesses; he believed that trained doctors could read the Latin texts but not the Greek. It was largely as a result of Linacre's efforts that the theory of the humors and complexions became a part of the Tudor worldview. Much of the imagery of Shakespeare and the seventeenth-century metaphysical poets derives ultimately from his work.

Many humanists knew Linacre and corresponded with him. These included Sir Thomas More, John Colet, William Latimer, William Lily, Erasmus, and Guillaume Budé. He probably instructed Sir Thomas Elyot in medical matters; Elyot later popularized the teachings of Galen and Linacre in his book *The Castel of Helth* (1539). In addition to his works on medicine, Linacre wrote a Latin grammar, originally intended for use by Mary Tudor, and he founded lectureships in medicine at both Oxford and Cambridge. His religious views are unknown—indeed, he does not appear to have been much interested in the church—but he accumulated profitable ecclesiastical livings, using the revenues to subsidize his scholarly activities.

See also Medicine.

BIBLIOGRAPHY

Dowling, Maria. *Humanism in the Age of Henry VIII.* London, 1986.

Maddison, Francis, Margaret Pelling, and Charles Webster, eds. *Essays on the Life and Works of Thomas Linacre.* Oxford, 1977.

STANFORD E. LEHMBERG

LIPPI, FILIPPINO. *See* **Florence,** *subentry on* **Art of the Fifteenth Century.**

LIPPI, FILIPPO. *See* **Florence,** *subentry on* **Art of the Fifteenth Century.**

LIPSIUS, JUSTUS (Joost Lips; 1547–1606), Netherlandish humanist. Lipsius's life and works were profoundly affected by the religious and political divisions of his time, especially the Revolt of the Netherlands against their overlord, the king of Spain, and the widening breach between Protestants and Catholics.

Lipsius was born into a prosperous family in a village in the province of Brabant, where his father was bailiff. He received an excellent education at a Jesuit college at the University of Cologne, where he became a novice to the order but soon opted out. He continued his studies at Louvain and found his first job in Rome, as secretary to Antoine Perrenot, Cardinal Granvelle (1517–1586), diplomat in the service of Spain. There he moved in an international and stimulating circle of humanists and published his first book, *Variae lectiones* (Various texts; 1569), critical comments on texts by various Latin authors, especially Cicero. He returned to Louvain in 1570 but soon left again, probably frightened by the Revolt, like so many Netherlandish humanists and artists. After vainly trying to find patronage at the imperial court in Vienna, in 1572 he accepted a professorship in history and rhetoric at the University of Jena, which meant that, at least outwardly, he had to accept Lutheranism. In 1573 he married Anna van den Calstere from Louvain, with whom he had boarded as a student, and in the following year he returned via Cologne to Louvain. There he received his licentiate in law and started to teach. In Cologne he had prepared editions of Tacitus's *Historiae* and *Annales* which, together with a second volume of comments on classical Latin texts, made him famous.

Lipsius was appointed professor of history and law at the newly founded Protestant (but not Calvinist) University of Leiden in 1578 and left his native Brabant for the rebellious provinces in the northern Netherlands. During his Leiden years he was able to publish a large number of works and some of his correspondence, although he found his administrative duties extremely onerous (he was twice rector of the university). In 1591 he traveled to Germany, where he made his peace with the Roman Catholic Church. His decision to leave Leiden was mainly inspired by his longing for a place where he could work untroubled by war and religious dissension. After spending a year at Liège he received a professorship in history and Latin at the University of Louvain (1592) and was also appointed historiographer to the king of Spain (1595), who ruled the southern Netherlands. In Louvain he wrote and edited numerous works, mainly on Roman history and political philosophy. There he also published a few devotional treatises and expurgated editions of some of his books, as well as continuing to publish his letters, revising a number of them to make them fit his position as a devout son of the church and a faithful subject of the king.

Lipsius was above all a philologist of genius. His critical editions of Tacitus and Seneca remained authoritative for over three centuries. His reputation

Justus Lipsius. Portrait by Théodor de Bry from *Thesaurus virtutis et gloriae* by J. J. Boissart (Frankfurt, 1598–1632). BY PERMISSION OF THE FOLGER SHAKESPEARE LIBRARY, WASHINGTON, D.C.

also rests on his commentaries on classical Latin and to a lesser degree Greek authors, and on his own Latin style. Lipsius's Latin resembled the concise language of Tacitus, but it also incorporated difficult turns of phrase and unusual words to show off his immense learning, making it appear as far removed as possible from the Ciceronian style used by most humanists. Closely connected with his philological work are his numerous historical studies of the Roman world, on such subjects as the gladiatorial combats, the amphitheater, the vestal virgins, and crucifixion as a criminal punishment. A number of these studies concerned the Roman art of war and possibly influenced sixteenth- and seventeenth-century changes in warfare. His historical work culminated in a book about the grandeur of the Roman Empire, presented as an example for contemporary social and political life.

Lipsius's long-lasting fame was also founded on his promotion of ancient Stoicism as a political philosophy eminently suited to a contemporary Europe torn apart by strife. The individual citizen was instructed how to cope with the troubles besetting Europe in the immensely popular book *De constantia* (1584). The scarcely less popular *Politica* (1589) was a manual for princes. Both books were intended to propagate a Christian philosophy derived from the Stoics as an alternative to the combative spirit based on theological dissension which could be found among Catholics and Protestants alike. Consequently, Lipsius was often attacked from—but also appreciated in—all religious camps.

See also **Humanism,** *subentry on* **Germany and the Low Countries; Stoicism.**

BIBLIOGRAPHY

Primary Works

Lipsius, Justus. *Iusti Lipsi epistolae.* Edited by A. Gerlo, M. A. Nauwelaerts, and H. D. L. Vervliet. 6 vols. Brussels, 1978–.

Lipsius, Justus. *Opera Omnia.* 4 vols. Wesel, Germany, 1675.

Secondary Works

Enenkel, Karl, and Chris Heesakkers, eds. *Lipsius in Leiden: Studies in the Life and Works of a Great Humanist.* 4th ed. Voorthuizen, Netherlands, 1997.

Haeghen, Ferdinand van der. *Bibliographie lipsienne. Oeuvres de Juste Lipse.* 3 vols. Ghent, Belgium, 1886–1888.

Morford, Mark. *Stoics and Neostoics: Rubens and the Circle of Lipsius.* Princeton, N.J., 1991.

Oestreich, Gerhard. *Neostoicism and the Early Modern State.* Cambridge, U.K., 1982.

NICOLETTE MOUT

LISBON. Portugal's royal capital since 1256, Lisbon naturally played a key role in the sudden rise and equally sudden fall of the nation's economy and culture during the Renaissance. In the fourteenth century King Dinis improved Lisbon's port facilities, strengthening trade with northern and Mediterranean cities. The enlarged city walls built under Ferdinand in 1375 helped unify the city, preparing it for the consolidation of the monarchy begun by João I with his victory over Castile in the 1380s. In the 1400s and early 1500s the successive voyages of crusade and coastal conquest in Africa and then Asia caused considerble change within Lisbon. The influx of West African gold and slaves at first, and then the pepper, gems, camphor boxes, silks, porcelains, and other exotica from Asia, and Brazilian dyewood by mid-century, provoked reorganization of city and society. King Manuel I ("the Fortunate"; ruled 1495–1521) moved his residence in 1505 from the old Christian Moorish hilltop fortress, São Jorge, to a newly built palace by the Tagus River estuary, signaling a shift from a local, medieval outlook to that of empire and commerce. Customhouses, a granary, an arsenal, and many other public and private buildings were quickly constructed by the monarchy, no-

ble families, and ever-more-numerous Genoese, Florentine, and German merchants and bankers, flush with sudden wealth and slave labor. Peasants streamed into the city, becoming sailors or working the new industries and markets at portside.

Yet public services poorly served this new, mobile city: water supplies remained unreliable; bread commonly contained sand from central supplies of unsifted flour; and few streets were paved. As the slave population grew to about one-tenth of Lisbon's approximately 90,000 people in 1551, and the lure of quick riches held strong in Lisbon, some writers lamented the decay of discipline and the work ethic. One declared Lisbon's empire a poor version of Rome's. In fact, the city led the nation into economic decline during the sixteenth century. The royal trade monopoly fostered deep corruption far from Lisbon and a penchant for short-term gains in bullion. The great complexities—and profits—of currency trading and the transshipment of incoming goods to Antwerp and then their marketing were left largely in foreign hands, both in Lisbon and abroad. Many capable Jewish administrators had been persecuted and driven out of Lisbon from 1496 to 1498, while those who stayed in Portugal as "New Christians" suffered during the 1504, Dominican-inspired massacres. The Inquisition was established at the Rossio Square in 1536; the first Jesuits arrived in 1540; and Portugal's unreserved reception of the restrictions of the Council of Trent (1545–1563) furthered the Church's influence within society. With the collapse of the monarchy in 1578, Portugal was subsumed into the reign of Spain's King Philip II in 1580. Lisbon retained its status as capital of Portugal, but, like the country itself, now owed taxes to the Habsburg rulers in Madrid. The "Invincible Armada" sailed from Lisbon to its destruction in 1588. After sixty years of Habsburg rule the monarchy was restored in the city, and with it, Portuguese independence.

Literature and humanist writing in Lisbon were stimulated through contacts with Italy, France, Spain, and the northern European cultures, rising to a peak of intensity during the 1530s and 1540s, then fading with the restrictions of the Counter-Reformation.

As with literature, painting in the Portuguese court responded to Italian models (for example, Francisco de Holanda's contacts with Michelangelo), as well as to Flemish painters resident there. Notable Portuguese artists included Nuno Gonçalves and Gregório Lopes. Painting and architecture were somewhat resistant to Renaissance innovations, conserving medieval tendencies. The royally sponsored Manueline style of building produced two masterpieces in Lis-

Lisbon. Woodcut view from Pedro Medina, *Libro de grandezas de Espana* (1548). By permission of the British Library. C62F18

bon, the Jerónimos monastery and cathedral (finished 1551) and the Tower of Belém fortress (1515–1521). This late Gothic style featured marine motifs (twisted ropes, anchors, nets, shells, and the ever-present royal armillary sphere), and was succeeded toward the mid-1500s by Italianate styles, especially those of Filippo Terzi. The Bairro Alto neighborhood was laid out in 1513; in 1598 a detailed, bird's-eye view of all of Lisbon was published by Braun and Hogenberg in the collection *Civitatis Orbis Terrarum*. Painted and geometric tile work was imported from Andalusia from the fifteenth century (still seen at the Sintra palace west of Lisbon) and took root as a local art industry. Tiles from the Renaissance and later remain today as one of the most attractive and visible features of high and low architecture throughout Lisbon. Few buildings of note survived the catastrophic earthquake of 1755; those that did include the Casa dos Bicos, the Jerónimos and Tower of Belém structures, and the pre-Renaissance Castle of São Jorge and part of the Carmo cathedral.

See also **Humanism,** *subentry on* **Portugal.**

BIBLIOGRAPHY

Góis, Damião de. *Lisbon in the Renaissance.* Translated by Jeffrey S. Ruth. New York, 1996. Translation of *Urbis Olisiponis Descriptio,* 1554.

Moita, Irisalva, ed. *O livro de Lisboa.* Lisbon, Portugal, 1994.

Wohl. Helmutt. "Recent Studies in Portuguese Post-Medieval Architecture." *Journal of the Society of Architectural Historians* 34, no. 1 (1975): 67–73.

JEFFREY S. RUTH

LITERACY. Literacy (or literacies) involves skills in reading and writing. Beyond this vague notion, scholars have not agreed upon a single definition of literacy, or on one method for determining rates of literacy. At the same time, no clear predictor, such as extent of schooling or particular economic trends, offers an uncontested explanation for rising or falling literacy rates. Given this situation therefore, it is not surprising to find no clear-cut relationship between the Renaissance and literacy or between humanism and literacy, although the Renaissance evolved in an urban context of growing European literacy. Nevertheless, it is possible to describe developments in literacy during the Renaissance and to link aspects of literacy with the humanist use of books, teaching initiatives, and with the advent of printing that occurred during the Renaissance.

Definition. Literacy has been defined as the ability to write or, commonly, as the ability to write one's signature. Some scholars consider reading ability a crucial index for a better understanding of literacy. In either case, literacy skill levels can vary significantly from person to person and from context to context. Studies of Inquisition registers from sixteenth- and seventeenth-century Spain describe an enormous range of literacy levels. Historians talk of pragmatic and functional literacy, literacy that allowed people to carry out business or other practical tasks. They contrast this with, for example, scholarly, or religious literacy. Some religious uses of the written word, as in particular prayers or liturgical responses, may be learned by rote (without learning either to read or to write), or they may be the first step toward a fuller literacy. Some scribes or signatories have little understanding of what they have written or subscribed to. Literacy in one language does not necessarily translate into literacy in the dominant social language. Nor do literacy skills, particularly private reading and writing, displace oral culture, which remained rich throughout the Renaissance. All these varieties and stages of literacy or relations between use of the spoken word and mastery of the written word have their own difficulties for historians who seek to discover and analyze evidence of their practice. Reading literacy, in particular, is notoriously difficult for the historian to study or quantify. In assessing the subtle differences in literacy skills, the historian also looks to variations by region, language, status, and gender.

Literacy Rates. Harvey Graff gives an overall literacy figure among European males, on the eve of the Renaissance, of 5 to 10 percent literacy, varying by class and by region, with perhaps as much as 40 percent literacy among merchants in some urban areas. The city of Florence in the 1330s, at a time when Giovanni Villani suggested that up to 45 percent of all children were learning to read, may have had an overall literacy rate of 25 to 35 percent, with sharp differences by sex, status, wealth, and occupation. Male literacy in Venice by the late fifteenth century may have been as high as 40 percent. The Low Countries likely had similar levels of literacy, while in most parts of Europe literacy rates were significantly lower. In parts of the north, particularly Germany and England, numbers of elementary, grammar, and vernacular schools grew, particularly in the fifteenth century. No effort has been made to determine levels of literacy rates for Germany on the eve of the impact of humanism and the beginnings of the Reformation. In England literacy levels by 1530 may have reached 20 to 25 percent male literacy overall and higher in London. Literacy rates rose for various reasons. They include the increased availability of manuscripts and then printed books through professional scribes, printers, and booksellers; the manufacture and dissemination of paper; and the growing use of the vernacular for literary, business, administrative, and legal purposes. At the same time, church and local lay leaders were making efforts to found schools. A favorable economic climate (with rising per capita income) may have been another factor; others include greater demand for clergy and for better educated clergy; the larger numbers of universities (for training schoolmasters, among other things); rising demands of civil and ecclesiastical bureaucracies; and changing patterns of philanthropy. Indirect indicators for a growth in literacy rates include the increased number of schools and extant books and manuscripts, as well as the growing size of library collections and numbers of libraries. Increasingly, books were mentioned in wills and inventories. The evidence suggests a rise of individual, private reading (particularly in the production of books of hours), and even architectural changes in churches that allowed for seating and increased light for reading.

From this basis of rising but limited literacy, a variety of indices suggest that literacy rates continued to climb throughout the Rennaissance period. This increase was not uniform, nor was it linear over all of Europe, and it may mask significant urban-rural divisions and growing differences among classes. Literacy rates among women were generally much lower than among men, and geographical differences could be extreme, even within the radius of a few miles. Various factors explain these differences. In England, for example, between 1500 and 1700, illiteracy rates dropped sharply in general, particularly in the sixteenth century. This broad increase, however, had variations among groups. Literacy did not increase among those in the lowest social classes, among women, or among those in some northern parishes. Yeomen and craftsmen benefited the most from the larger number of opportunities for schooling, but significant periods of disruption occurred in education and literacy levels were affected accordingly, particularly during the civil wars of the seventeenth century. Venice in 1586 educated perhaps 33 percent of all males, while Florence schooled 28 to 33 percent of its boys in 1480. This, plus more informal learning, may have produced what Paul Grendler calls "functional literacy among a broad part of the masculine population in Italy during the High Renaissance." Studies of sixteenth-century Spain show that reading spread into the lower classes, and that levels of literacy were high relative to other parts of Europe. From 1601–1650,

62 percent of men in Toledo could sign their names, while 54 percent of men born in Cuenca between 1571 and 1590 were literate—a significant improvement from the 25 percent literacy rate among those born from 1511 to 1530. These rates were socially stratified. In Languedoc, France, toward the end of the sixteenth century, nearly all merchants were literate, while two-thirds of artisans, one-tenth of farmers and one in one hundred laborers could sign their names. Over time, and much later than the Renaissance, these social differences smoothed out. Some countries, most notably Sweden, achieved reading literacy for the entire population by 1800.

Schools. Renaissance Europe saw an impressive variety of schools. There were petty or ABC schools, where small children learned their alphabet and beginning prayers, elementary vernacular or Latin schools, and secondary, normally Latin, schools. Within this basic hierarchy were commercial schools (called *abbaco* schools in Italy because they taught commercial arithmetic, or abaco), almonry schools in monasteries (which distributed alms), song schools (where children learned the liturgy), separate writing schools, or schools where writing was taught alongside reading and reciting. There were town schools, cathedral schools, parish schools, guild schools, chantry schools, household schools (in noble, merchant, and clerical households), private schools, and dame schools, where women used their own homes to teach small children rudimentary skills. These names referred more to the auspices under which education was conducted than the level of learning conveyed. Some schools charged fees; others were privately endowed or supported by religious orders, or by ecclesiastical or state authorities and were tuition-free. Some were boarding schools, particularly at the Latin grammar level; others were within walking distance, a prerequisite for elementary education in the eyes of the English educator, Richard Mulcaster (c. 1531–1611). Some scholars might be instructed privately by tutors (particularly among the more affluent), while apprentices were often taught literacy skills on the job. Not everyone who became literate did so through formal education. The evidence from Spanish Inquisition records suggests that significant numbers learned to read and write on their own or from friends and relatives. Lutheran campaigns for literacy in the sixteenth and seventeenth centuries often depended upon learning at home.

In general, as one moved into secondary schooling, education became more uniform. By the six-teenth century, even the children of aristocratic families were more likely to attend a formal grammar school than to have private tutors. There, education in Latin grammar and literature was the norm; Greek and Hebrew were honored more in the breach, at least until the late sixteenth century when some grammar schools could hire competent teachers in these languages. Although Latin remained dominant for many years, vernacular education at the secondary level eventually prevailed, in France by the early seventeenth century and in the English academies by the Restoration (after 1660). Developments at the secondary school level illuminate the study of literacy as it pertains to Latin literacy; one can also measure social mobility from first letters to Latin learning. It is in the expansion of humanist education at the secondary school level that the Renaissance was to have its greatest impact on literacy—mostly Latin literacy.

Humanism and Literacy. For Italy, the humanist motivation for learning—to educate boys in the wisdom and virtues of the classics as part of a program for promoting civic values, Christian piety, and service to the state—unquestionably contributed to the expansion of secondary schooling from the mid-fifteenth century forward. In addition, the modern educational historians Richard Kagan and George Huppert have linked the development of a humanist curriculum with the growth of urban grammar schools in Spain and France respectively. This development, however, did not last beyond the end of the sixteenth century. Joan Simon has made a similar connection between humanism and the foundation of grammar education for England, but David Cressy's work shows that, from the 1540s to the 1560s, when humanism was at its height, literacy levels, in fact, deteriorated. Further, in those cases where the number of schools being established increased, there is no clear connection to humanist motivations.

The great humanist pedagogue, Erasmus (c. 1466–1536), whose educational goals were based on Latin and whose writings were widely influential, did not determine the growth of educational resources either in England or the Low Countries, although his textbooks considerably lightened the burden for students doing Latin grammar. Like Erasmus, the Spanish grammarian Antonio de Nebrija (1441–1522) linked the spread of literacy in both Latin and Spanish with the *studia humanitatis* or humanistic studies. His Spanish grammar, however, was to far outreach the influence of his Latin grammar. Even the

Jesuits, who used Nebrija's Latin grammar to spread Latin literacy in Mexico, eventually switched to teaching in Spanish. In Germany, where a humanist curriculum became embedded in the grammar schools of the sixteenth century, the expansion of elementary and vernacular schools, as well as parish schools devoted to catechetical learning, was a product of Reformation and religious goals that were far removed from Renaissance ideals. Insofar as humanist curricula began to dominate the grammar schools of Europe, humanism may have contributed to a greater degree of elitism, with Latin learning increasingly out of reach of the middle and lower classes and, certainly, of women. It did contribute to greater prestige for grammar education and a curriculum that was lay-oriented. Grammar education, as it emerged in the fifteenth and sixteenth centuries, was increasingly separated from the institutional needs of the church, although it was never divorced from the religious and moral concerns of state and society. At the elementary level, a specifically humanist curriculum was less in evidence. What strengthened access to literacy skills for those who could afford the time and the modest investment in school fees was an integration of reading and writing in the curriculum (usually taught separately in the Middle Ages); and the growing availability of books.

Despite these changes at the elementary level (and Thomas More's utopian vision of mass education), humanists were rarely directly concerned with elementary education (except as a prelude to Latin learning) or with popular literacy. The influence of the Renaissance on literacy is less quantitative and more qualitative; it is linked with the value given to reading over speaking, what could be seen over what could be heard, the private over the collective, and, finally, the impact of the printed book. Although much of the product of the printing press was not humanist in content, nonetheless, the inextricable fact that the Renaissance and the printing press grew up together, each promoting the other, makes it difficult to separate out the causes for certain shifts in approaches toward learning, literacy, and books.

Renaissance humanists were enthusiastic book collectors, both before and after the invention of the printing press. A growing number of libraries came into being in the fourteenth century (in friaries, cathedrals, parishes, guildhalls, and in universities and schools). It was, however, the public library envisioned by Petrarch in 1362 and the libraries established in Florence under Medici auspices in the fifteenth century that resulted in newer, more accessible, more global collections of books and manuscripts. These model libraries were to influence all of Europe, particularly as they inspired princes and sovereigns to create state libraries. Such libraries that people could consult, as well as the expansion of private studies in lay households, contributed to growing habits of private reading and study. They did not, however, destroy habits of collective reading that were to migrate from courts to coffeehouses over the sixteenth and seventeenth centuries.

Humanists were also instrumental in changing the format of manuscripts and printed books by moving the experience of reading out of the lecture hall and removing the apparatus of glosses, divisions, abbreviations, and even the Gothic hand in which they were written. This was replaced with the Carolingian-derived minuscule, a calligraphy that was the ancestor of roman type and far easier to read than the Gothic. Armando Petrucci argues that these innovations liberated the text, making it more accessible to private reading and no longer guided by the need for scholastic commentary. During this same time, however, Eugene Kintgen and others argue that reading, for those trained by humanist pedagogues, was a matter of recovering and reinforcing what they already knew, rather than discovering new thoughts.

Humanists were also instrumental in developing the pocket-size book, particularly from the Venetian press of Aldo Menuzio. The reading public, however, did not favor humanist works for its pocket-size books, but preferred almanacs, romances, books of hours, and religious writings.

Humanist pedagogues, most notably Erasmus, the Valencian scholar Juan Luis Vives (1492–1540), and Philipp Melanchthon (1497–1560) in Germany, contributed to the development of commonplace books—books that allowed readers to look up and reproduce quotations from a variety of (primarily classical) sources on many topics. This humanist practice of compiling excerpts into a notebook (creating a kind of portable library) was to determine classroom practice and preaching strategies throughout Renaissance Europe. The construction of commonplace notebooks carried over from Latin pedagogy to vernacular readers by the seventeenth century, providing a memory-store even for those with little formal education. These books influenced the mental habits of early modern European readers and writers, possibly promoting the decline of memorization that the printed book portended.

The printing press also made available, in very large quantities, beginning reading books (primers) and grammar texts, most of which were destined for schoolboys and schools, but some permitted the unschooled to teach themselves. Presses in Spain, England, France, and Germany published more books in the vernacular than in Latin (Lyon and Venice tended to dominate the publication of Latin works). Those scholars who have looked at inventories, wills, and booksellers' lists have documented the impressive range of books printed, but they cannot, from these, tell us the extent of the reading public. It is the lesser publications—the catechisms, pamphlets, placards, and the *bibliothèque bleue* (collections of chivalric romances, heroic tales, and saints' lives) or the small books and pleasant histories that reveal a popular market for printed texts that reached into the lower classes. Because of their content, these texts, dismissed by the elites of the seventeenth century, have their roots in the medieval world rather than that of the Renaissance.

In the final analysis, the growth of literacy throughout sixteenth- and seventeenth-century Europe was based less on the impact of the Renaissance and more on the competing demands of religious confessionalism (and the catechisms on which they were based); on economic, bureaucratic, and mercantile needs; and on efforts to impose linguistic models (for example, English against Gaelic in Scotland). Nevertheless, the humanists helped shape the instruments of this growth—the schools and their curricula, the schoolmasters, books themselves, their method of collection, and the manner in which they might read. In all of this the printing press was instrumental in extending the written word.

BIBLIOGRAPHY

Berger, Philippe. *Libro y lectura en la Valencia del Renacimiento.* 2 vols. Valencia, Spain, 1987.

Cressy, David. *Literacy and the Social Order: Reading and Writing in Tudor and Stuart England.* Cambridge, U.K., 1980.

Eisenstein, Elizabeth L. *The Printing Press as an Agent of Change.* 2 vols. Cambridge, U.K., and New York, 1979.

Furet, François, and Jacques Ozouf. *Reading and Writing: Literacy in France from Calvin to Jules Ferry.* Cambridge, U.K., and New York, 1977. Vol. 1 of *Lire et écrire: L'alphabétization des français de Calvin à Jules Ferry.*

Graff, Harvey J. *The Legacies of Literacy.* Bloomington, Ind., 1987.

Grendler, Paul. *Schooling in Renaissance Italy: Literacy and Learning, 1300–1600.* Baltimore, 1989.

Houston, R. A. *Literacy in Early Modern Europe: Culture and Education 1500–1800.* New York, 1988.

Houston, R. A. *Scottish Literacy and the Scottish Identity.* Cambridge, U.K., and New York, 1985.

Huppert, George. *Public Schools in Renaissance France.* Urbana, Ill., 1984.

Johansson, Egil. *The History of Literacy in Sweden* (Educational Reports Umeå, no. 12). Umeå, Sweden, 1977.

Kagan, Richard. *Students and Society in Early Modern Spain.* Baltimore, 1974.

Kintgen, Eugene. *Reading in Tudor England.* Pittsburgh, Pa., 1996.

Moran, Jo Ann Hoeppner. *The Growth of English Schooling, 1340–1548.* Princeton, N.J., 1985.

Moss, Ann. *Printed Commonplace-Books and the Structuring of Renaissance Thought.* Oxford and New York, 1996.

Nalle, Sara. "Literacy and Culture in Early Modern Castile." *Past and Present,* no. 125 (1989): 65–96

Petrucci, Armando. *Writers and Readers in Medieval Italy.* Edited and translated by Charles M. Radding, New Haven, Conn., 1995.

Simon, Joan. *Education and Society in Tudor England.* Cambridge, U.K., 1966.

Spufford, Margaret. *Small Books and Pleasant Histories: Popular Fiction and Its Readership in Seventeenth-Century England.* Athens, Ga., 1982.

JO ANN HOEPPNER MORAN CRUZ

LITERARY THEORY, RENAISSANCE. The Renaissance saw an extraordinarily rich output of literary theory and criticism, first on the Continent and subsequently in England, ranging from the publication of classical texts (most notably Aristotle's *Poetics*) to the use of these texts and imagined extrapolations from them to explain, justify, or deplore post-antique literary products and trends. A survey of Renaissance literary theory is in large measure a survey of the major cultural phenomena and anxieties of the period.

The (Re)discovery of the Antique. The fall of Constantinople in 1453 accelerated a movement of Greek manuscripts and scholars to western Europe, where the invention of printing (and its fostering of a reading public eager for the novel and the exotic) would quickly facilitate a lively market in classical texts, in the original language and in translation, and in both plain and lavishly annotated versions. Aristotle's *Poetics* had previously been known only through a garbled Arabic commentary written by Averroes (Ibn Rushd) in the twelfth century and translated into Latin by Hermannus Alemanus in the thirteenth; it was first published in 1481. In 1498, however, Giorgio Valla was able to publish a Latin translation of the Greek text of the *Poetics,* based on a manuscript in the Biblioteca Estense, Modena. Ten years later, the Greek original was published by Aldo Manuzio in Venice; but it was not until 1536, with the appearance of Alessandro de' Pazzi's parallel Greek and Latin texts (the latter a more accurate and readable version than Valla's), and 1548, with Francesco Robortello's extensive commentary, that the full importance of Aristotle's work began to be felt, and the author was able to emerge from a prejudicial cloud of association with medieval Scholasticism.

Similarly influential editions of other classical theorists appeared as well. Robortello brought out the Greek text of Longinus's *On the Sublime* in 1554. Among Latin authors, the complete text of Quintilian's *Institutes* had been discovered by Poggio Bracciolini in the monastery of St. Gall in 1417, and an edition appeared in 1470. In general, the emergence of a complete and coherent body of classical texts, most notably those published by Manuzio in Venice during this period, pointed the way toward an enhanced sense of antique models and cultural values. Horace's *Art of Poetry,* which had been available through the Middle Ages, took on the status of a familiar text that seemed newly useful to the concerns of Renaissance readers. It provided a rhetorical view of poetry—emphasizing as it did an imaginative work's effect on an audience, the audience's sense of the work's meaning and impact—that the added knowledge of Cicero, Quintilian, or Aristotle's *Rhetoric* would enhance, as may be seen in the commentaries by Cristoforo Landino (1482) and Jodocus Badius Ascensius (1500). By the early sixteenth century, the stage had been set for theoretically informed debates over the major issues of the day.

The Question(s) of Language. Knowledge of the ancients could be used by both sides in debates over the relative merits of Latin and vernacular literatures. As early as 1300, Dante had written a defense (albeit in Latin) of his native language's capacity for eloquence and legitimacy, in his *De vulgari eloquentia* (On vernacular eloquence). The emergence of distinct national literatures in the Renaissance would produce comparable defenses, most notably Joachim du Bellay's *Deffence et illustration de la langue francoyse* of 1549, where "illustration" carries the sense of making the tongue more lustrous, by careful attention to the development of a learned, "polished" style; the later emergence of the French Academy would be consistent with such notions of purity and correctness. Where a nation's language was less plausibly or simply derived from its classical, Latinate origins, as with English, the grounds for such a defense of the native literature would be different. The anonymous "E. K." argues in his notes to Edmund Spenser's *Shepheardes Calender* (1579) that the language of poetry can be enriched by borrowings from rustic dialect that would be anathema to continental purists. Spenser's deliberate embrace of medieval romance and native idiom would remain controversial to his contemporaries, as seen in Sir Philip Sidney's qualms ("That same framing of his style to an old rustic language I dare not allow," *Defence of Poesie* [1595]), or Ben Jonson's claim that Spenser "writ no language."

Another question of language that was exacerbated by the new awareness of classical literature involved prosody. If vernacular verse was to be rendered lustrous by approaching classical norms of diction and rhetorical coloring, should it not also emulate the quantitative measures of Latin, much as Latin itself had shunned its native, accentual origins by imitating Greek models during the classical period? Vigorous attempts at quantitative vernacular meters appear in Italy and France during the period, and in England among the members of the "Areopagus," a somewhat mysterious society, probably informal if not largely fictitious, that included both Sidney and even Spenser himself, for all his identification with the demotic elements in poetic language. Although these efforts to impose an alien prosody on the vernacular were probably doomed from the start, they do seem to have afforded an opportunity to look closely, and to listen even more closely, to the sounds of the native tongue, and so in the end to have enabled more subtly modulated rhythms, with echoes of the Latin models if not a direct reproduction of them.

Finally, a clearer sense of the shape and substance of Latin literature enabled the emergence of a new, neo-Latin culture, the "Republic of Letters" that flourished during the Renaissance but is virtually unknown today as a result of the total victory (finally realized during the eighteenth century) of national languages and literatures. The late-medieval Latin of church and state documents gave way, among educated people, to a reformed and purified version of the language that emulated the usages of the classical period, most notably (and even notoriously) those of Cicero. Educated persons could communicate with one another, across national and to some extent social and religious boundaries, in a classical or classicizing Latin that was felt to be truly "republican" in that it avoided the hegemony of any single nation's language over another. At the same time, "Ciceronian" became (as in Desiderius Erasmus's comic *Ciceronianus* dialogue of 1528) a term of ironic mockery, much like "Puritan" in Protestant England or "politically correct" in postliberal America, recognizing the sterile absurdities to which a self-consciously reformed discourse could easily extend, while not denying that reform of corrupt medieval practices was both necessary and desirable. Neither Latin nor the vernacular would be the same again, once the corpus of classical texts could be viewed clearly and comprehensively.

Defenses of Poetry and of Specific Poems.

In the arena of formal "arts of poetry" a contrast is to be seen between the relaxed, chatty *Art* of Horace (cast as an epistle to his friend Piso) and more systematic, exhaustive treatises like Aristotle's *Poetics* or Quintilian's *Institutes*. The Horatian model anticipates versified essays like Nicolas Boileau's *Art poétique* of 1674 or Alexander Pope's *Essay on Criticism* of 1711; but the mid-sixteenth century was given rather to more substantial and often polemical works. In France, Julius Caesar Scaliger composed the most extensive and strict of these, his *Poetices libri septem* (Seven books of poetics; 1561) in Latin; in Italy, Marco Girolamo Vida's *De arte poetica* of 1527 was followed by Antonio Minturno's six-book Latin treatise on the poet (1559) and his Italian *Arte poetica* (1564). Borrowing from both traditions is the substantial but witty *Defence of Poesie* (published 1595) that Sir Philip Sidney composed around 1583 in response to moralists' attacks on poetry, most notably Stephen Gosson's *Schoole of Abuse* (1579, with a doubtless unwelcome dedication to Sidney). A gracious, relaxedly "amateur" essay in the Horatian mode, it courteously demurs from the strictly logical (or moral) objections to poetic feigning and the amoral pleasures of the aesthetic, while conceding that poetry can indeed be abused and do harm. Sidney's response to the charge (going back to Plato) that a poet tells lies is his famous, if finally rather bland, remark that in fact the poet "nothing affirmeth, and therefore never lieth." Although the *Defence* summarizes with great bravura a century of critical theory, as scholars have studied its sources, it is quintessentially a product of its Elizabethan setting, keeping puritan strictness at bay while hewing to a via media of English Reformed thought and practices.

The vast bulk of critical writings in Italy during the sixteenth century were addressed to specific problems of reconciling contemporary poetic practice with the explicit or implied teachings of the ancients. As Bernard Weinberg has shown in great detail, Aristotle's *Poetics* were mined for a theory of genres that would enable the acceptance or rejection of major Italian works. Jacopo Mazzoni's *Discorso difesa della Comedia del divino poeta Dante* (Defense of Dante's *Commedia;* 1572 and 1587) defends his nation's, or better, his language's, masterpiece by means of a frequently confusing blend of Aristotelian and Platonic arguments, not always distinct from the medieval allegorical defenses of pagan fables: teaching delightfully, the poet should aim for the plausible, the credible, the edifying, and not for the literally or tediously true.

Like his contemporary defenders of the romance epics of Ludovico Ariosto and Tonquato Tasso, and of the new genre of pastoral tragicomedy, Mazzoni is confronting not only the theoretical definitions of genre and imitation he finds in the ancients but also the example of the great epic of his land, Virgil's *Aeneid*. Italian critics of the late sixteenth century are greatly exercised by the startling contrasts between the classical harmonies and teleology of Virgil's poem and the sprawling works that their own Christian and postmedieval culture has produced. Tasso's *Discorsi del poema eroico* (Discourses on the heroic poem; published 1594) were begun prior to the composition of his *Gerusalemme liberata* (Jerusalem delivered) and not completed until shortly before he died. Like Giambattista Cinzio Giraldi's treatise defending Ariosto's variety of romance plot lines, *Discorsi intorno al comporre dei romanzi* (On the composition of romances; 1554), and Giovanni Battista Guarini's defense of his *Pastor fido* (1590; trans. *The Faithful Shepherd*) in his *Compendio della poesia tragicomica* (Compendium of tragicomic poetry; 1601), Tasso is at once practicing and theorizing his practice.

The lively debate in the latter part of the century over the relative merits of Ariosto and Tasso occupies far more bulk, and undergoes far more convolutions, than readers today can easily digest, but it was of considerable interest to an England that was confronting its own sprawling romance epic, Edmund Spenser's *Faerie Queene,* with its similarly scandalous departures from classical norms—"Hobgoblin runne away with the Garland from Apollo," as Spenser's friend Gabriel Harvey phrased it. When Sir John Harington published his translation of *Orlando Furioso* in 1591, he appended *A Preface, or rather a Briefe Apologie of Poetrie, and of the Author and Translator,* in which he ranges at length over the by now familiar arguments for the delightful and edifying variety of Ariosto's poem. He concludes his "triple apologie" (for poetry, Ariosto, and himself) by confessing that he has added notes of his own to the end of each canto, "even as if some of my frends and my selfe reading it together (and so it fell out indeed many times) had after debated upon them what had bene most worthie consideration in them."

Harington's involvement of himself as reader and contributor to the meaning of Ariosto's text shows a typical Renaissance motif, found in the visual arts and in literature alike: the introduction of participatory or interpretive secondary figures who are used to comment on the action and to legitimize it. Here, his comments both echo and embody the major themes of the literary theories of his time; they show the reading, for both pleasure and profit, that justifies the work of art. His "apologie," like Sidney's, is itself an imaginative work, a "poem" as the word was used embracingly in the Renaissance.

See also **Aristotle and Cinquecento Poetics**; and biographies of figures mentioned in this entry.

BIBLIOGRAPHY

Primary Works

Smith, G. Gregory, ed. *Elizabethan Critical Essays*. 2 vols. London, 1904.

Spingarn, J. E., ed. *Critical Essays of the Seventeenth Century*. 3 vols. Oxford, 1908.

Tasso, Torquato. *Discourses on the Heroic Poem*. Translated with notes by Mariella Cavalchini and Irene Samuel. Oxford, 1973.

Weinberg, Bernard, ed. *Trattati di poetica e retorica del cinquecento*. 4 vols. Bari, Italy, 1970–1974.

Secondary Works

Cave, Terence. *The Cornucopian Text: Problems of Writing in the French Renaissance*. Oxford, 1979.

Colie, Rosalie L. *The Resources of Kind: Genre-Theory in the Renaissance*. Berkeley, Calif., 1973.

Kinney, Arthur F. *Humanist Poetics: Thought, Rhetoric, and Fiction in Sixteenth-Century England*. Amherst, Mass., 1986.

Lewalski, Barbara K., ed. *Renaissance Genres: Essays on Theory, History, and Interpretation*. Cambridge, Mass., 1986.

Montgomery, Robert L. *The Reader's Eye: Studies in Didactic Theory from Dante to Tasso*. Berkeley, Calif., 1979.

Quint, David. *Origin and Originality in Renaissance Literature: Versions of the Source*. New Haven, Conn., 1983.

Weinberg, Bernard. *A History of Literary Criticism in the Italian Renaissance*. 2 vols. Chicago, 1961.

Wimsatt, William K., Jr., and Cleanth Brooks. *Literary Criticism: A Short History*. New York, 1959. Especially Chapter 9, "The Sixteenth Century," pp. 155–173.

DONALD CHENEY

LITHUANIA. *See* **Poland-Lithuania.**

LITURGY. The term "liturgy" (from Greek *laos,* people, and *ergon,* work) originally meant a "public work." By the Renaissance the term was used exclusively and restrictively in the Orthodox Church to refer to an official ritual, especially the Eucharist, but also the Office and other sacraments. The public quality of the rituals in which the entire church participated had changed gradually, and liturgical functions were firmly in the control of clerics without any regard for lay participation. From the Middle Ages onward, priests presided over the liturgy for the benefit of the laity, who were passive spectators.

Mass. The Mass of the Latin rite, used from 1570 until the Second Vatican Council (1962), is the codification and synthesis of the eucharistic rite used in the Middle Ages. Mandated by the Council of Trent, the rituals of the Mass and the sacraments were revised in response to the Protestant Reformation. The Low Mass signaled a change in the execution of the eucharistic liturgy, with the priest taking over all the parts formerly performed by the deacon, lector, choir, and people. The Ordinary parts (Kyrie eleison, Gloria, Credo, Sanctus, Benedictus, and Agnus Dei) were recited, whereas in the High Mass these would be sung by a choir or a *schola cantorum*. Much musical activity in the Renaissance centered on polyphonic settings of the Mass.

The word Mass comes from the final dismissal, "ite missa est" ("go, it is concluded"). The book that governed the correct performance of the eucharistic liturgy was therefore called the missal. To understand the genesis and use of the Roman Missal is to appreciate how the Roman rite enjoyed such great stability while suffering liturgical stagnation for almost four hundred years. The earlier Middle Ages was very fertile in liturgical production, and new and diverse prayers proliferated throughout the Middle Ages. Popular devotional elements as well as prayers to accompany the feasts of different saints found their place in the Roman Missal. Piety was nourished by liturgical allegory, whereby invented and often fanciful meanings were overlaid upon the liturgical actions and words. On the other hand, the Middle Ages witnessed the development of a strongly sacrificial eucharistic theology, which made the priest the sacerdotal offerer of the sacrifice. This development rendered the Eucharist an exercise of private devotion by the priest and stressed that each mass was a good and holy work and a new act of Christ, through which he applies his sacrificial redemption. Medieval theology thus accentuated the privileged place of the priest who reenacted the words and actions of Christ.

During the Renaissance until the mid-sixteenth century in Italy, dramatic performances called *sacre rappresentazioni* were inspired by the liturgy and corresponded to the mystery and morality plays of northern Europe. As the laity could not participate directly in the official liturgy, these popular forms of devotion mimicked the liturgy and provided for their spiritual needs. The subjects of these performances

Ordo Missae (Order of the Mass) of 1570

Preparation (prayers at the foot of the altar)
- Sign of the cross
- *Introibo ad altare Dei* (Psalm 43; Psalm 42 in the Vulgate)
- *Confiteor* (said first by priest and repeated by servers) and Absolution
- Greeting to the altar

I. Mass of the Catechumens

Introit Antiphon
Kyrie
Gloria (except in Advent and Lent)
Salutation (greeting)
Collect
Epistle
Gradual and Alleluia (or Tract during Lent)
Sequence
Gospel
Credo (only on Sundays and major feasts)

II. Mass of the Faithful

Offertory (preparation and incensing of eucharistic elements)
- Uncovering of chalice and paten
- Offering of host on paten
- Mingling of water and wine in chalice
- Incensing of eucharistic elements, altar, ministers, and congregation (for solemn masses)
- *Lavabo* (washing of hands)
- *Orate fratres* (request to congregation to pray for a worthy sacrifice)
- *Secreta* or *Super oblata* (prayer over the gifts)

Canon
- Introductory dialogue
- Preface (variable according to the feast or liturgical season)
- *Sanctus* and *Benedictus*
- Canon of the Mass (eucharistic prayer)
  - *Te igitur* (plea for acceptance of the gifts)
  - *Memento* (for those offering)
  - *Communicantes* (for those deceased)
  - *Hanc igitur* (call for God to accept the offering)
  - *Quam oblationem* (final plea for the sanctification of the oblation)
  - *Qui pridie* (consecration of bread and elevation of host)
  - *Simili modo* (consecration of wine and elevation of chalice)
  - *Unde et memores* (*anamnesis,* or offering prayer)
  - *Supra quae* (plea for acceptance of the offering)
  - *Supplices* (pleas for the bestowal of grace)
  - *Memento* (remembrance of the dead)
  - *Nobis quoque peccatoribus* (prayer for those offering)
  - *Per ipsum* (concluding doxology)

Communion
- *Pater noster* (Our Father)
- *Pax* (the peace; shared between the clergy)
- *Commixtio* (commingling of consecrated bread and wine)
- Priest's communion (three prayers and reception of the elements by the priest)
- Communion of the faithful
- Communion antiphon

Concluding Rites
- Postcommunion
- *Ite missa est* or *Benedicamus Domino* (dismissal)
- Blessing (solemn form, first appearing in the fourteenth century)
- Last Gospel (prologue to the Gospel of John; John 1:1–14)

were taken from biblical stories, legends, and lives of the saints, and they underscored moral themes.

Liturgical Reform. The need for liturgical reform, especially of the Roman Missal, was recognized from the time of Pope Pius II (reigned 1458–1464). During the pontificate of Sixtus IV (1471–1484), several feeble attempts at reform were enacted, particularly in the area of chant at the celebrated Sistine Chapel (1473). For many historical reasons, most notably the Protestant Reformation, it was necessary to wait for the Council of Trent in the sixteenth century for the long-needed liturgical reform.

When Martin Luther initiated the Reformation in 1517, he did so as an Augustinian friar in good standing. By 1520 he composed his *De captivitate Babylonica ecclesiae* (Babylonian captivity of the church), his first major statement on liturgical matters. Three years later the *Formula missae et communionis* (Formula of the Mass and Communion) appeared, asking for moderate reform of the Mass, especially the suppression of the sacrificial language that had long dominated the medieval understanding of the Eucharist. Other Reformers, such as Huldrych Zwingli and John Calvin, were pushing for more radical liturgical reform. Luther found himself in a simultaneously conservative and radical position, fending off the extreme demands of the radical Reformers while advocating the purification of the historic Mass from "the wretched accretions which corrupted it." In 1526 he produced his *Deutsche Messe* (German Mass), a vernacular liturgy intended as a rite for "unlearned lay folk."

Encouraged by Pope Leo X (1513–1521) and Clement VII (1523–1534), the liturgical reformers, such as Zaccaria Ferreri and the early Theatines, first revised the hymns, having determined that this area had been impoverished by music of a popular nature. They produced a work that was almost completely new and brought about the flowering of the great age of polyphony. Beyond the musical dimension, several reforms were introduced to improve the liturgy: the legislation in liturgical matters was clarified through the use of rubrics; the Sunday cycle was reformed; all the texts of the Mass were reviewed, eliminating historical accretions to the liturgy of dubious origin and value; and certain historical additions were simplified, allowing a better execution of the liturgy.

Various synods and regional councils sought still more changes that would touch fundamental questions of liturgical reform. Partially in response to these requests as well as to the demands of the Re-formers north of the Alps and later of the German emperor Ferdinand I (1558–1564) and the French king Charles IX (1560–1574), the Council of Trent in its first period (1545–1547) undertook a larger reform of the liturgy. Elements of this program were approved during the second period (1547–1552), but it was not fully developed until the last period (1562–1563). The general tenets of Trent called for liturgical uniformity, while upholding the rights for individual diocesan usages which were historically verifiable.

Authorized by the twenty-fifth session of the council, Pope Pius IV (1559–1565) promulgated the necessary decrees to insure the Tridentine reforms. A liturgical commission formed in 1564 was soon suspended, later to be reestablished in 1566. The next pope, Pius V (1566–1572), completed the work of Trent. The newly revised missal appeared in 1570 and contained several important points: simplification of the feasts of saints in order to reemphasize the Sunday cycle; suppression of numerous octaves (periods of observances beginning with a festival day and lasting eight days); and clarification of the rubrics. Trent signified the end to the liturgical development in the Latin church for the next four centuries. In the interest of liturgical order, objectivity, and stability, diversity was sacrificed for uniformity.

Diffusion. In the fifteenth century, the invention of the printing press aided widespread diffusion of the Roman Missal, leading also to the disappearance of many liturgical elements which formerly had been conserved in the independent ancient rites. Prior to the printing press, the liturgical books had been copied by hand, a slow and costly process, allowing for regional differences in the contents of the missal. The first printed missal (that of Constance) appeared in 1457 in Mainz, the production center for the Rhenish region. The first Roman Missal was published in Milan in 1474 and in Rome the following year. Other European printing centers, like Paris, Lyon, Strasbourg, and Venice, followed suit and undertook the task of printing and distributing the new missal, contributing to even more widespread uniformity.

Structure of the Mass. The Tridentine missal delineated a number of parts of the eucharistic liturgy, yet one can broadly discern four parts: Mass of the Catechumens, the Offertory, the Canon, and the Communion. The Mass of the Catechumens derives its name from the liturgy of the early church, when catechumens underwent a lengthy period of preparation for Christian initiation called the catechumenate. This term in the Renaissance was anachronistic since the catechumenate had fallen into disuse since the fifth century. The second part of the Mass, called the Offertory, reflected a eucharistic theology based on sacrifice. The priest first recited an offertory verse over the Oblation, underscoring the sacrificial notion of the Mass. The purpose of these verses was to make a transition from the Liturgy of the Catechumens to the Eucharistic Prayer. The choice of scriptural texts heightened the sense of offering the paschal victim for the salvation of the whole human race as well as offering the Christian people together with Christ, the principal victim. In the Canon, the priest raises the elements of bread and wine individually, reciting prayers which underline the action of a propitiatory offering for sins. The attitude of priest and people is twofold: they offer themselves with Christ, the eternal victim, and they herald the great sacrificial action itself. The double communion in the Tridentine liturgy remains as a vestige of the earlier eucharistic practice, where the priest would first receive, but the second communion for the faithful was not always carried out. The Council of Trent reiterated the legislation of Lateran IV (1215) requiring at least an annual reception of Holy Communion. The strong sacrificial and penitential piety left its trace on the eucharistic devotion whereby the faithful envisaged themselves as making acts of self-offering, which could be accomplished in adoration as well as reception of the Host.

The Mass was enacted on three levels. First, in the sanctuary of the church, the priest and servers engaged in a fixed form of liturgical prayer, the only variations in the order being the predetermined variable prayers. All gestures and words were carefully governed by the Roman Missal. Second, in the body or nave of the church, the faithful participated passively as spectators of this heavenly event. Third, in the choir, music to accompany the action was produced, musicians being careful to take their cues from bells, gestures, or certain key words. The principle of progressive solemnity determined the setting of the Mass in accordance with the liturgical feasts and season. A musical setting of a mass became a part of the standard repertory of most composers. Since the Ordinary parts were fixed texts, composers took great liberties. Music was a key element stimulating the proper feeling and attitude. In addition to musical styles, architecture and the visual arts reflected the spiritual and cultural modes of humanism characteristic of the Renaissance.

The Papal Liturgy. Between 1570 and 1580 some reforms enacted by the Council of Trent were implemented within the papal court and Curia. For the bishop of Rome special pontifical rites were prescribed by the *Caeremoniale episcoporum* (The ceremonial of bishops), published in 1600, which indicated a more complex liturgy. The normative text for the performance of the rites of the papal court wherever it assembled for worship was based on the papal ceremonial of the Sistine Chapel. Although the eucharistic liturgy of the universal church was reformed by the Council of Trent, only moderate liturgical reform was introduced into the papal court, which still followed a pontifical ceremonial compiled by Agostino Patrizzi (c. 1435–1494) and dating to 1488. Engravings of the papal mass in the Sistine Chapel by Etienne Dupérac dating to 1578 and diaries of the papal master of ceremonies written between 1572 and 1590 testify to the modifications in liturgical practice.

See also **Christianity,** *subentry on* **The Western Church; Drama,** *subentry on* **Religious Drama; Music,** *subentry on* **Sacred Vocal Music; Trent, Council of.**

BIBLIOGRAPHY

Primary Works

Catholic Church. *Missale romanum ex decreto sacrosancti concilii Tridentini restitutum, S. Pii V. pontificis maximi jussu editum, Clementis VIII. et Urbani VIII. auctoritate recognitum, et Novis missis ex indulto apostolico hucusque concessis auctum.* Mechlin, Belgium, 1862.

Biblioteca Apostolica Vaticana. *Liturgia in figura: Codici liturgici rinascimentali della Biblioteca apostolica Vaticana.* Vatican City, 1995.

Secondary Works

Jungmann, Josef A. *The Mass of the Roman Rite, Its Origins and Development.* Translated by Francis A. Brunner. New York, 1959. Translation of *Missarum sollemnia, eine genetische Erklarung der romischen Messe* (1948).

Klauser, Theodor. *A Short History of The Western Liturgy.* Translated by John Halliburton. 2d ed. New York, 1979.

Library of Congress. *Medieval and Renaissance Manuscript Books in the Library of Congress: A Descriptive Catalog.* Washington, D.C., 1989–.

Rasmussen, Niels Krogh. "Liturgy and Liturgical Arts." In *Catholicism in Early Modern History: A Guide to Research.* Edited by John O'Malley. Saint Louis, Mo., 1988. Pages 277–303.

Rasmussen, Niels Krogh. *Maiestas Pontificia: A Liturgical Reading of Etienne Dupérac's Engraving of the Capella Sixtina from 1578.* Rome, 1983.

MICHAEL S. DRISCOLL

LIVES OF THE SAINTS. *See* **Hagiography.**

LIVORNO. The port city of Livorno (called Leghorn in English) on the Mediterranean coast of Tuscany was a creation of the Renaissance. In the fourteenth

Livorno. A panoramic view of the city; pen-and-ink drawing by Petrus Tola (1613–after 1699). PHILLIPS AUCTIONEERS, UK/ THE BRIDGEMAN ART LIBRARY

century, Livorno was a fortified coastal hamlet in the Pisan territory, best known for a painting of the Virgin said to have been miraculously transported in 1345 from Negroponte in Greece to the nearby hilltop of Montenero. By the seventeenth century Livorno had become one of the most important ports of Europe.

In 1405, with the political collapse of Pisa, Livorno passed to the French, who in 1407 sold it to the Genovese for 26,000 gold *ducats.* Florence, however, saw greater possibilities in Livorno, and it purchased the town from the Genovese for the much higher sum of 100,000 *florins* in 1421. When the duke of Milan criticized the Florentines for paying such a huge price, the Florentine statesman Niccolò da Uzzano replied that Livorno "was worth far more than it cost" for the convenience it would bring to Florentine trade. The principal reason for the growth of Livorno lay in the steady silting of Pisa's chief harbor at the mouth of the Arno, the Porto Pisano. As anchorage at Pisa disappeared, neighboring Livorno gradually became Tuscany's chief outlet to the sea. Although Livorno was not a natural harbor, an indentation in the coastline made possible the construction of a protective breakwater, a project first achieved under Pisan rule. Proximity to Pisa meant that ships could anchor at either port. The Florentine magistracies that supervised maritime commerce, such as the Sea Consuls, were active in both places. By the second half of the fifteenth century, Livorno was regularly visited by English and Flemish merchant ships.

The revolt of Pisa from 1494 to 1509 further increased the town's strategic importance, and Livorno was the object of a fruitless siege by the emperor Maximilian I in 1496. But the sizable state investments needed to realize Livorno's potential did not occur until the second half of the sixteenth century. Malarial marshes, moreover, kept the population in check. Only 413 inhabitants were recorded in the 1427 *catasto,* and the population remained at between 400 and 700 residents through most of the 1500s. Relegation to Livorno was one of the most common punishments for sixteenth-century Tuscan criminals.

The situation changed dramatically under Grand Duke Ferdinand I, who in 1590 and 1591 issued invitations to "people of every nation" to come to Livorno. As enticements he offered privileges that included safe-conduct, the nullification of debts, and pardon for criminal offenses. The town's population jumped to 1,140 in 1592 alone, and it continued to grow thereafter. In 1593 the grand duke's invitation was extended explicitly to Jews, who, along with other privileges, were promised freedom of residence and religious practice, protection at sea by the Tuscan fleet, equal treatment under the law, easy terms of credit, and the right to construct a synagogue. Outfitted with new harbor works and a canal connecting the port to Arno commerce, Livorno grew to more than three thousand inhabitants in 1601 and to more than eighteen thousand in 1674.

See also **Pisa**; **Tuscany**.

BIBLIOGRAPHY

Primary Work
Vigo, Pietro, ed. *Statuti e provvisioni del castello e comune di Livorno (1421–1581).* Livorno, Italy, 1892.

Secondary Works
Braudel, Fernand, and Ruggiero Romano. *Navires et marchandises à l'entrée du port de Livourne (1547–1611).* Paris, 1951.

Livorno: Progetto e storia di una città tra il 1500 e il 1600. Pisa, Italy, 1980.

Matteoni, Dario. *Livorno.* Bari, Italy, 1985.

Toaff, Renzo. *La nazione ebrea a Livorno e a Pisa (1591–1700).* Florence, 1990.

WILLIAM J. CONNELL

LIVY. *See* **Historiography,** *subentry on* **Classical Historians.**

LODI, PEACE OF. Agreed to on 9 April 1454, the treaty known as the Peace of Lodi ended the War of the Milanese Succession (1452–1454). It was negotiated in secret by the duke of Milan, Francesco Sforza, and Venice through an intermediary. The lack of legitimate heirs to the preceding duke, Filippo Maria Visconti (d. 1447), and the failure of Milan to create a permanent change of government with its Ambrosian Republic (1447–1450), led to the surrender in 1450 of the republic to Sforza, the leading condottiere and claimant to the ducal throne through his wife, Bianca Maria Visconti, illegitimate daughter of Filippo Maria. The resulting war to dislodge Sforza was fought by two coalitions: Venice, King Alfonso of Naples, Savoy-Piedmont, and Monferrat against Sforza, Florence, Genoa, Mantua, and King Charles VII of France. The fall of Constantinople to the Turks (29 May 1453), the inconclusiveness and devastating effects of the hostilities, Sforza's exhausted treasury, and Florence's reluctance to supply additional funding, together with Pope Nicholas V's peace congress in Rome (November 1453–March 1454) to promote unity against the Turks, all led to a desire for compromise and peace. With the Rome congress failing to produce results, the principal contestants, Sforza and Venice, tried bilateral secret talks at Lodi, near Milan. Neither side had achieved its goals: Venice did not dislodge Sforza, but regained Bergamo, Brescia, and Crema, while the duke retained the contested Ghiaradadda and had his title recognized by Venice. Secret clauses gave Sforza a free hand in recovering certain lands on the duchy's western frontier which had been lost to Savoy and Monferrat. Allies of both sides, all of whom except Cosimo de' Medici of Florence had been ignorant of the negotiations, accepted the peace terms, more or less reluctantly.

The expected dissatisfaction by allies of both sides prompted Venice and Sforza to conclude a league with Florence on 30 August 1454 to consolidate the peace with an open invitation to the pope and Alfonso to join, provided they accepted the territorial status quo established at Lodi. In the mind of the negotiators there were other threats to peace in the Italian peninsula—the threat of a Turkish invasion; the claims of the houses of Anjou and Orléans over Naples and Milan, respectively; the machinations of exiles and of unemployed mercenary captains such as Jacopo Piccinino—all of which they hoped to deter through a general alliance of the five regional states (Venice, Milan, Florence, papal Rome, and Naples), with the other Italian states serving as secondary members. Thus the Italian League gradually took shape with the stipulated duration of twenty-five years. Alfonso was the last to accept the treaty of Lodi and the Italian League, only after some modifications were made to the latter (26 January 1455) which gave him a free hand to prosecute his claims against Genoa and the lords Malatesta and Manfredi in Romagna. The Peace of Lodi and the Italian League became inseparable in the minds of contemporaries. Together they promoted the birth of modern diplomacy by generating an organization of sovereign states to preserve peace; the evolution of the simple resident embassy into a permanent embassy to serve as first line of defense against threats to peace; and a more sophisticated system of balance of power as the League failed in its peacekeeping efforts. This was the system exported to the rest of Europe in the following century.

BIBLIOGRAPHY

Primary Works

Virtually the entire documentation regarding the Peace of Lodi as well as the formation and operation of the Italian League for the second half of the fifteenth century, as extant in archives and libraries in Italy and western Europe, has been assembled on microfilm in *The Ilardi Microfilm Collection of Renaissance Diplomatic Documents ca. 1450–ca. 1500,* Sterling Memorial Library, Yale University. The index to the collection is available for consultation and downloading from the Internet at http://www.library.yale.edu/Ilardi/il-home.htm. A printed version is included in *The French Descent into Renaissance Italy, 1494–95: Antecedents and Effects,* edited by David Abulafia (Aldershot, U.K., 1995), pp. 405–483. The films can be borrowed worldwide on interlibrary loan.

Secondary Works

Antonino, Federico. "La pace di Lodi ed i segreti maneggi che la prepararono." *Archivio storico lombardo.* 6th ser., 57 (1930): 233–296. With documents from the state archives of Milan and Venice.

Canetta, Carlo. "La pace di Lodi (9 aprile 1454)." *Rivista storica italiana* 2 (1885): 516–564. With many documents on the negotiations.

Fossati, Felice. "Francesco Sforza e la pace di Lodi." *Archivio veneto.* 5th ser., 60–61 (1957): 15–34.

Ilardi, Vincent. "Fifteenth-Century Diplomatic Documents in Western European Archives and Libraries (1450–1494)." *Studies in the Renaissance* 9 (1962): 64–112. The only general description to date of archival collections for the diplomacy of the age.

Soranzo, Giovanni. *La lega italica (1454–1455).* Milan, 1924. The standard monograph on the subject with discussion of the evolution of the League from the peace negotiations at Lodi.

VINCENT ILARDI

LOGIC. Logic is an instrumental habit directing operations of the intellect in the attainment of knowledge. In the Renaissance its basic content was that of Aristotle's *Organon,* to which were commonly added preparatory materials from Porphyry's *Isagoge* (Introduction) and Peter of Spain's *Summulae logicales* (Summaries on logic). Aristotle's *Rhetoric* and *Poetics* were sometimes appended to this list, following the practice of Greek and medieval commentators.

Historians of logic give brief treatment to Renaissance logic because of their exclusive interest in formal logic, to which few contributions were made during the Renaissance. The Renaissance development was mainly in material or "content" logic, as typified in Aristotle's *Posterior Analytics, Topics,* and *Rhetoric,* the first devoted to scientific reasoning, the second to dialectical or probable reasoning, and the third to persuasive reasoning. Following a usage dating back to Alexander of Aphrodisias (fl. c. 200), the whole of Renaissance logic (*logica*) was frequently called dialectics (*dialectica*). Humanist contributions to the discipline were twofold: the recovery of the Greek text of the *Organon,* together with Greek commentaries on the text; and the development of simplified logics that restricted their scope to probable and persuasive argumentation. These are treated in what follows under traditional logic and humanist logic respectively.

Traditional Logic. The most extensive development of Aristotelian logic was achieved in the writings of Jacopo Zabarella (1533–1589). Some idea of the importance of this logic in education may be gathered from the teaching notes of the Jesuit Ludovicus Rugerius, who taught the three-year philosophy course at the Collegio Romano from 1590 to 1592. Fortunately Rugerius numbered all his lectures on philosophy, reaching a grand total of 1,088. The first year he devoted to logic, on which he gave 304 lectures, accompanied by repetitions and disputations. Here he expounded the text of Aristotle with care, making use of commentaries by Greeks, Arabs, and Latins, including contemporaries such as Zabarella. The breakdown of his logic lectures (by number) was as follows: *Summulae,* or introduction to

dialectics (29); the nature of logic (30); *Isagoge,* on modes of predicating (32); *Categories,* on modes of being (65); *On Interpretation,* on propositions (23); *Prior Analytics,* on syllogisms (31); and *Posterior Analytics* (94), divided into tracts on demonstration (49), definition (12), and science (33). Such extensive coverage was similar to that of another Jesuit, Paolo della Valle (Paulus Vallius), who taught logic at the Collegio in 1587–1588 and whose lecture notes on demonstration were appropriated by Galileo Galilei (1564–1642) in 1589.

It was the recovery of texts that made this achievement possible. Aristotle's *Organon* came to the Latin West in three stages: first the "Old Logic," the *Categories* and *On Interpretation,* plus Porphyry's *Isagoge,* translated by Boethius from the Greek in the sixth century; then the "New Logic," the *Prior* and *Posterior Analytics, Topics,* and *Sophistical Refutations,* translated from Greek and Arabic in the high Middle Ages, to about 1280; and finally in the original Greek, edited by Aldus Manutius from 1495 to 1498, who followed this with editions of the Greek commentators to the sixth century. The commentaries of Averroes (Ibn Rushd; 1126–1198) on all these works appeared in the Giunti Press edition of Aristotle (1550–1552). Those of Thomas Aquinas (1225–1274) on the *Posterior Analytics* and *On Interpretation* first appeared in print in 1477 and 1497 respectively, and each had gone through twenty-four editions by 1594.

Developments at Padua. The history of material logic in the period has yet to be written, but two lines of development may be sketched. The first occurred mainly at the University of Padua, where problems related to methods of demonstration were debated intensely for more than a century in commentaries on the *Posterior Analytics.* The main difficulty was the relation of demonstration of the fact (*quia*) to demonstration of the reasoned fact (*propter quid*), and how some combination of the two can produce scientific knowing (*scientia*)—the problem of the demonstrative regress. This originated with Galen (c. 130–c. 200) in his discussions of methodology, and was focused by Themistius (c. 317–c. 388) and Averroes in their analyses of texts of Aristotle bearing on its solution.

The first phase took place in the late fifteenth century. Pietro d'Abano (1257–c. 1315) conciliated Galen's account of the regress with that of Aristotle in *Posterior Analytics* (1. 13), and Urban the Averroist (fl. 1334) reinforced this interpretation using the three types of demonstration advanced by Averroes.

Paul of Venice (c. 1370–1428/29) then explained the regressive process in detail and showed how no circularity was involved in its reasoning. Ugo Benzi of Siena (1376–1439) argued similarly, while pointing out that only the first or *quia* stage is truly one of discovery.

The next phase reached into the mid-sixteenth century. It began with Francisco Securo di Nardo, who was professor of Thomistic metaphysics at the University of Padua from 1464 until his death in 1489 and taught Thomas de Vio Cajetan (1469–1534), Gasparo Contarini (1483–1542), and Pietro Pomponazzi (1462–1525). Di Nardo attacked the second or *propter quid* stage of the regress, arguing that it is not truly demonstrative. Pomponazzi reacted against his mentor, maintaining that the second stage actually constitutes a *demonstratio potissima* (most powerful demonstration). Agostino Nifo (c. 1470–1538) then took up the debate and showed how difficulties could be avoided by introducing an intermediate stage between the first and the second, a work (*negotiatio*) of the intellect that assures causal validity to the reasoning process. Nifo's position was reinforced by Marcantonio Zimara (1460–1532), who offered many texts from Averroes in its support. Finally, another Averroist, Girolamo Balduino (fl. 1550), gave a comprehensive account of all three stages of the regress, justifying them in terms of Averroes's three types of demonstration.

The culmination of the argument came with Zabarella, who in 1578 offered the definitive solution in his *Liber de regressu* (Book on the regress). This was prepared for by Balduino, but also by Zabarella's logic teacher, Bernardino Tomitano (1517–1576), who identified the first stage of the regress as an inductive process, and by a professor at Bologna, Ludovico Boccaferro (1482–1545), who differentiated this demonstrative induction from that used in dialectics and rhetoric, which work on the plane of the contingent and do not arrive at universal or scientific knowledge.

Paris, Salamanca, and Rome. A different line of development began at the University of Paris in the early sixteenth century. The main difference was the influence there of Nominalism, as opposed to Averroism, and an increasing concern with mathematics and with applications of logic to philosophy and theology rather than to Galenic medicine. This development can be seen in the work of three Spaniards studying at Paris in the early sixteenth century. All three taught the formal logic of Peter of Spain's *Summulae* but later wrote commentaries on Aristotle's *Analytics* as well as treatises on mathematics. Pedro Ciruelo (1470–1554) edited *De sphaera* (On spheres) of Johannes de Sacrobosco (d. 1244/56) and produced a complete course in mathematics, while Juan Martínez Silíceo (1486–1557) wrote a treatise on the astrolabe along with a complete course in logic. Gaspar Lax (1487–1560), who taught Juan Luis Vives (1492–1540), turned out so many tomes on terminist logic he became known as the prince of Parisian *sophistae*. Later all three gave up schoolboy dialectics for more serious scientific and philosophical pursuits.

Associated with them were other "summulists" studying at Paris with John Major (1469–1550). These included Peter Crockaert of Brussels (1465?–1514), Jean Dullaert of Ghent (1470–1513), Juan de Celaya (1490–1558), and Domingo de Soto (1495–1560). Crockaert studied under Major and first taught nominalism, then became a Thomist and wrote commentaries on Aristotle's *Organon, Physics,* and *On the Soul.* Dullaert also studied under Major, taught Silíceo, Celaya, and Vives, and was working on the *Analytics* at his death. Celaya wrote important questions on Aristotle's *Physics* (1517) and a commentary on the *Posterior Analytics* (1521) "according to the threefold way of St. Thomas, the realists, and the nominalists."

Soto returned to Spain, completed his theology studies at Alcalá under Ciruelo, and published his own *Summulae* at Burgos in 1529. He then taught at the University of Salamanca, where in 1539 he published a second, simplified edition of the *Summulae,* which had eight more editions to 1582. After this he composed his commentaries *In dialecticam Aristotelis* (On Aristotle's dialectic), all in one folio volume, including a brief introduction to logic, Porphyry's predicables, Aristotle's *Categories,* and both books of the *Analytics.* That appeared in 1543 and was followed by twelve more editions to 1598. Soto's favorite student at Salamanca was a young priest, Franciscus Toletus (1532–1596), who became a Jesuit in 1558 and, while still a novice, was sent to Rome to set up the philosophy course at the newly founded Collegio Romano.

By 1561 Toletus had published his *Introductio in dialecticam Aristotelis* (Introduction to Aristotle's dialectic) in Rome, with seventeen more editions to 1621. Then in 1572 he produced his *Commentaria una cum quaestionibus in universam Aristotelis logicam* (Commentaries, with questions, on all of Aristotle's logic), also in Rome, with twenty more editions to 1616. These formed the backbone of Jesuit teaching in logic to the end of the century. As amplified by successive Jesuits at the Collegio Romano, they produced the versions of Rugerius's and Valle's lectures noted at the beginning of this section.

Humanist Logic. The humanists repudiated traditional logic with its formal arguments based on syllogisms as sterile and not useful. In its place they created a new logic that emphasized persuasion and the links of logic to grammar and eloquence.

Vives left Paris for Bruges in 1512 and in 1520 published his *Adversus pseudodialecticos* (Against pseudo-dialecticians), an attack on Lax and Dullaert, who probably agreed with much of his diatribe. More significant attempts to provide an alternative logic based on humanism were those of Lorenzo Valla (1407–1457), Rudolph Agricola (1443/44–1485), and Petrus Ramus (1515–1572).

Ordained a priest in 1431, Valla taught eloquence at the University of Pavia, served as secretary of King Alfonso V (c. 1435), then as apostolic secretary to Pope Nicholas V (1448). He translated Greek authors, detected the forgery of the Donation of Constantine, composed notes on the New Testament, and wrote learned treatises on pleasure, the beauties of the Latin language, free will, and the true good. Though untrained in philosophy, in 1439 he wrote a polemic against Aristotelian logic, *Dialecticae disputationes* (Dialectical disputations), for which he substituted categories of his own devising. He rejected concerns over formal validity and sought instead apt and sound arguments, those that are simply good from the viewpoint of grammar and eloquence. Demonstrative inference, for Valla, was not to be privileged over the nondemonstrative. Yet he was inconsistent in the system he elaborated and subsequently had little effect on philosophy.

More respected as a logician was the Dutch humanist Agricola. Having studied at Erfurt and Louvain until 1465, Agricola traveled in Italy and studied intermittently at Pavia and Ferrara, returning to north Europe in 1479, where, for his last three years, he lectured informally at Heidelberg. He wrote commentaries on Boethius and Seneca the Elder, humanist orations, and poems, and translated works from the Greek. In 1479 he completed his most influential work, *De inventione dialectica* (On dialectical invention). This builds on Boethius's *Topics* to propose a logic based on topics rather than on terms, and substitutes the probabilities of dialectics (and even rhetoric) for the ideal of demonstrative certitude. Syllogisms, for Agricola, are of limited use in debate; rather, one should practice the art of influencing, involve opponents in debate, skirmish for

position, and aim at likelihood and plausibility, not certainty. His Latin *"probabile,"* normally translated as "probable," took on the connotation of "provable" and effectively eliminated the need for Aristotle's *Analytics*.

Ramus, the French humanist, is known more as an educator and a popularizer than as a logician. He studied at Paris from 1527 to 1536, wrote commentaries on Euclid, and then in 1543 his *Aristotelicae animadversiones* (Aristotelian animadversions), a polemic against Aristotelian logic that went through many revisions and reeditions to 1560. He became involved in a prolonged dispute with the Aristotelian Jacques Charpentier (1521–1574), who published his own *Animadversiones* in 1554. Ramus's was a topics-logic like Agricola's, placing emphasis on rules of natural reasoning, dichotomous divisions, and tabular methods of displaying subject matters so as to proceed from more to less general concepts. Ramus then composed textbooks for teaching logic, metaphysics, physics, and politics. These had a fantastic publication record and were extremely popular in northern Europe. There his new way of presenting knowledge was received enthusiastically and imitated in the great number of textbooks on all subjects produced to the end of the sixteenth century.

See also **Aristotle and Aristotelianism; Rhetoric; Scholasticism.**

BIBLIOGRAPHY

Primary Works

Aristotle. *The Complete Works of Aristotle.* Edited by Jonathan Barnes. Vol. 1. Princeton, N.J., 1984.

Galilei, Galileo. *Galileo's Logical Treatises: A Translation, with Notes and Commentary, of His Appropriated Latin Questions on Aristotle's* Posterior Analytics. Translated by William A. Wallace. Dordrecht, Netherlands; Boston; and London, 1992.

McNally, J. R. "Rudolph Agricola's *De inventione dialectica:* A Translation of Selected Chapters." *Speech Monographs* 34 (1967): 393–422.

Secondary Works

Ashworth, E. J. *Language and Logic in the Post-Medieval Period.* Dordrecht, Netherlands, and Boston, 1974. Mainly on formal logic.

Ashworth, E. J., ed. "Late Scholastic Philosophy." *Vivarium* 33 (1995): 1–112. See especially pages 76–97.

Camporeale, Salvatore. *Lorenzo Valla: Umanesimo e teologia.* Florence, 1972.

Kretzmann, Norman, et al., eds. *The Cambridge History of Later Medieval Philosophy.* Cambridge, U.K., 1982. See especially pages 273–299, 787–807, and 818–837.

Mack, Peter. *Renaissance Argument: Valla and Agricola in the Tradition of Rhetoric and Dialectic.* Leiden, Netherlands; New York; and Cologne, Germany, 1993.

Ong, Walter J. *Ramus: Method, and the Decay of Dialogue.* Cambridge, Mass., 1958.

Schmitt, Charles B., et al., eds. *The Cambridge History of Renaissance Philosophy.* Cambridge, U.K., 1988. See especially pages 143–198 and 685–711.

Wallace, William A. *Galileo's Logic of Discovery and Proof: The Background, Content, and Use of His Appropriated Treatises on Aristotle's* Posterior Analytics. Dordrecht, Netherlands; Boston; and London, 1992.

WILLIAM A. WALLACE

LOMBARDY. *See* **Milan.**

LONDON. During the era of the Renaissance London consisted of two separate areas, the City of London and Westminster, together with some suburbs. The City proper was a small but densely populated area originally developed and walled by the Romans. It was dominated by Saint Paul's Cathedral, the Guildhall, the shops of rich merchants and their livery halls, docks, and warehouses. London Bridge gave access to Southwark and other areas south of the Thames. Several miles upstream, a second center of population had grown up around Westminster

Abbey and the Palace of Westminster. No longer a royal residence, the palace included Westminster Hall, where the law courts still met, and Saint Stephen's Chapel, adapted in the mid-sixteenth century as a meeting place for the House of Commons in Parliament. Smaller buildings for the Exchequer and the Star Chamber crowded up against the palace, creating an administrative complex where most of the realm's business was conducted.

These two areas were connected by the Strand, the principal street paralleling the river. Here there were palaces or town houses for a number of bishops, including York Place, the residence of the archbishops of York. Following the fall of Thomas Wolsey, who held the archbishopric along with several other offices, York Place was taken over by the monarch and converted into Whitehall Palace, which became the king's chief lodging. Henry VIII also built Saint James's Palace nearby as a subsidiary home for some members of his family and court.

Southwark, across the river from the City, held some of the principal entertainment sites, including the Globe Theatre, built in 1599, and the Bear Gar-

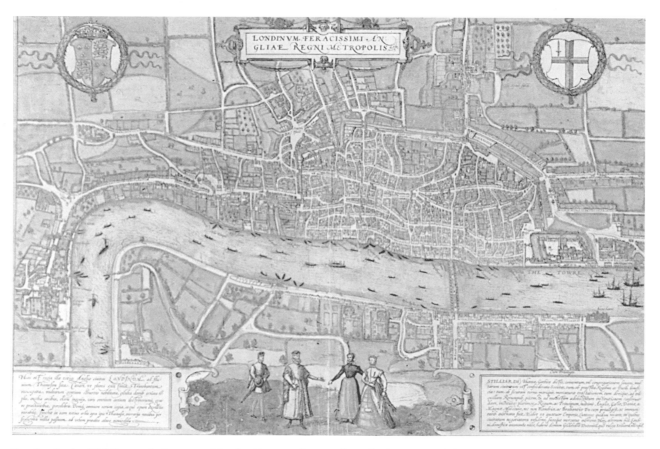

London in the Mid-Sixteenth Century. Map by Bauerand Hogenberg (Cologne, 1550). THE GRANGER COLLECTION

The Tower of London. The city of London and London Bridge appear in the background. From a fifteenth-century manuscript. BY PERMISSION OF THE TRUSTEES OF THE BRITISH LIBRARY

den in Bankside. Lambeth Palace, opposite Westminster, had been the residence of the archbishops of Canterbury since the twelfth century. There was no bridge between Lambeth and Westminster—Westminster Bridge was not constructed until 1750—but ferries and barges regularly plied the Thames.

London under the Tudors. The principal changes in London during the sixteenth century came as a result of the Reformation. The dissolution of the monasteries and other religious houses between 1536 and 1540 had a great impact. Westminster Abbey itself was too important to be touched, since it was the site of coronations and royal funerals and housed the tombs of most of the medieval monarchs. It was originally secularized as a cathedral, and for a decade Westminster had its own bishop. A few monks returned under Mary Tudor; Elizabeth ejected them a second time and turned the Abbey into a "royal peculiar" exempt from episcopal jurisdiction though similar in other respects to a cathedral. The rest of the religious houses fell, their sites often being acquired for commercial development

or as residences for members of the aristocracy. The lands later developed as Bloomsbury, Soho, and Piccadilly had also been held by religious houses prior to the Reformation. Covent Garden, as the name implies, was originally a pasture or garden for the monks of Westminster. Following the dissolution it was acquired by John Russell, first earl of Bedford, whose descendants constructed Bedford House just north of the Strand.

Many bishops lost their town houses at about the same time. Protector Somerset razed the houses of five bishops to make space for Somerset House, one of the earliest English structures to show the influence of the Renaissance and to incorporate elements of classical architecture. Medieval hospitals were often operated by religious orders, and there was fear that these would be closed in the 1540s, but shortly before his death Henry VIII granted five of the principal institutions to the City of London so that they might continue under secular auspices. These included Saint Bartholomew's and Saint Thomas's. Bethlehem Hospital (the madhouse that gave rise to the name Bedlam) was also spared, as well as Greyfriars, which was converted into the orphanage and school of Christ's Hospital.

London under the Stuarts. The appearance of London changed dramatically during the seventeenth century. Development along the Thames and Strand continued, the most notable instance being the earl of Bedford's building at Covent Garden. Russell called in the renowned architect Inigo Jones, who designed a great square or piazza, based on those he had seen in France and Italy, surrounded by elegant town houses for members of the aristocracy who more and more felt the need of a London residence as well as a country estate. Although Bedford had obtained a license for this development, he was later fined for violating proclamations going back to Elizabeth's reign that prohibited further building in the capital—the queen had justifiably been concerned about crowding, pollution, unsanitary conditions, and the spread of disease and social unrest occasioned by the growth of the metropolis. The prosecution was ironic, since Jones's scheme had produced some of the finest houses in the capital and had established a pattern that would be widely emulated as the West End of London came to be developed in succeeding centuries. The new church of Saint Paul's Covent Garden was part of Jones's plan.

Inigo Jones also worked for the royal family. It was here that his love of classical and Renaissance

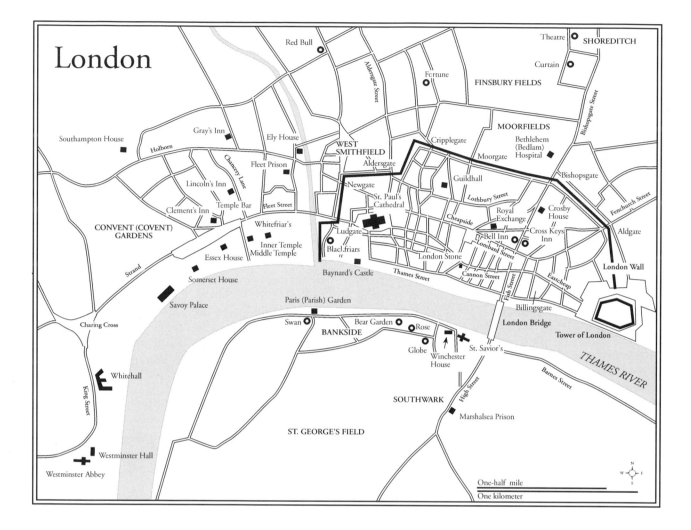

architecture became most apparent. He drew plans for the reconstruction of Whitehall Palace, but money was never forthcoming and only the Banqueting House was built. It was of great importance, however, in establishing the pure classical style of architecture in England.

Population. The number of people in London grew enormously during the early modern period. In 1500 London was not yet one of the world's largest cities. Paris was much bigger, and Milan, Florence, Venice, and Naples also exceeded it in size. But London grew from perhaps 100,000 in 1500 to about 200,000 in 1600 and 400,000 in 1650. By the middle of the seventeenth century London had nearly twenty times more inhabitants than the next largest English town; it held a tenth of the nation's people, as opposed to a seventieth in the late Middle Ages. Indeed, London had become the largest city in western Europe. Throughout this period mortality in London was very high, and the increase in population was the result of continuing migration from the provinces.

See also **England** *and biography of Inigo Jones.*

BIBLIOGRAPHY

Beier, A. L., and Roger Finlay, eds. *London 1500–1700: The Making of the Metropolis.* London, 1986.

Brigden, Susan. *London and the Reformation.* Oxford, 1989.

Pearl, Valerie. *London and the Outbreak of the Puritan Revolution.* London, 1961.

Porter, Roy. *London: A Social History.* Cambridge, Mass., 1995.

Rappaport, Steven. *Worlds Within Worlds: Structures of Life in Sixteenth-Century London.* Cambridge, U.K., 1989.

Saunders, Ann. *The Art and Architecture of London.* Oxford, 1984.

Weinreb, Ben, and Christopher Hibbert, eds. *The London Encyclopaedia.* 2d ed. London, 1993.

STANFORD E. LEHMBERG

LOPE DE VEGA, FELIX. *See* **Vega Carpio, Lope Félix de.**

LÓPEZ DE ZÚÑIGA, DIEGO. *See* **Stunica, Jacobus Lopis.**

LORENZETTI FAMILY. *See* **Siena,** *subentry on* **Art in Siena.**

LOTTO, LORENZO. *See* **Venice,** *subentry on* **Art in Venice.**

LOUIS XI (1423–1483), king of France (1461–1483). Often called the Spider King or the Universal Spider, Louis XI is regarded as having strengthened and centralized the French monarchy through the suppression of the great independent nobles and the integration into France of such regions as Anjou, Artois, and Provence.

Born at Bourges, Louis XI was the son of Charles VII and Mary of Anjou. He spent much of his early life at the forbidding château of Loches, conceiving there an animosity toward his father that would last until the end of Charles VII's life. Indeed, at the age of seventeen Louis led a coalition of discontented nobles in a rebellion known La Praguerie. After its failure, Charles VII sent his wayward son to Dauphiné, which Louis proceeded to administer competently but with pretensions of sovereignty. When in 1456 the king's patience finally wore out and he determined to bring the disobedient dauphin to heel, Louis fled to Burgundy to seek the protection of his uncle, Philip the Good. Louis remained there until the death of Charles VII in 1461.

Upon his succession to the throne, Louis XI reshuffled the royal administration, depriving many nobles of their offices and redistributing them, in many cases, to men of considerably lower rank. The loss of both the prestige and the lucrative income associated with such offices alienated a sizable portion of the political elite, who were consequently easily convinced by several of the great lords to rise up against the king. Led by the dukes of Brittany and Alençon, the comte de Charolais (later the duke of Burgundy, known as Charles the Bold), and the king's own brother, Charles de Berry, the League of the Public Weal went to war against Louis XI. Although it was often interpreted by subsequent generations of writers critical of the centralizing mon-

Louis XI. Portrait attributed to Colin d'Amiens, 1482. GIRAUDON/ART RESOURCE

archy as a great struggle on behalf of the French people against royal tyranny, in fact the League seems to have been primarily motivated by the particularist aims of its leaders.

After the only major pitched battle of the War of the Public Weal ended inconclusively at Montlhéry in 1465, Louis XI opened negotiations with the rebellious nobles. The treaties of Conflans and St.-Maur-des-Fossés provided considerable pensions for the leading nobles, as well as granting the province of Normandy as an appanage to the heir presumptive, the king's brother Charles. In 1468 the Estates General was assembled in Tours to ratify the treaties, but, under Louis XI's approving eye, it refused to allow the alienation of the valuable province of Normandy. Conflict flared up again between the king and the great nobles and continued intermittently throughout the 1470s, encouraged by the English king Edward IV, but the nobles were never again united enough to pose a significant challenge to Louis XI.

His preoccupation with domestic problems left Louis XI little time to pursue aggressive foreign policies. He did, however, succeed in detaching Roussillon from Spain, and he was actively involved in northern Italian politics, especially after his sister Yolande became the regent of Savoy. His relations with the pope were strained, due in part to Louis's inconsistent policy on the Pragmatic Sanction (1438), which had established the virtual autonomy of the Gallican church over ecclesiastical appointments within France. Although he had abolished the Pragmatic Sanction almost immediately upon his succession to the throne, by 1464 Louis XI had restored it, but with the significant change that he, not the French church, controlled higher ecclesiastical offices.

In contrast to his troubled relationship with the first and second estates, Louis XI found a wellspring of support in the towns. Indeed, nineteenth-century historians often called him the Bourgeois King, on account of both his purported affinity with wealthy but non-noble urban dwellers (with whom he often dined, garbed in plain wool clothing) and, more importantly, his efforts to stimulate industry and commerce. He helped establish the silk industry in Lyon and promoted trade with England and the Hanseatic cities.

Although not known for his patronage of artists or writers, Louis XI did have at his court Philippe de Commynes (c. 1447–1511), whose *Mémoires* were extremely popular during the early modern period. The *Mémoires* is both a historical narrative of Louis XI's reign and a thoughtful analysis of the nature of kingship, wherein at times Commynes advocates the hard-nosed political pragmatism later associated with Machiavelli.

Toward the end of his reign, Louis XI's lifelong tendency to suspicion, even paranoia, intensified, making him a virtual recluse at the château of Plessis-les-Tours, where he died on 30 August 1483. In his will he chose his daughter Anne de Beaujeu and her husband, Pierre, to act as coregents for his son, Charles VIII, who was still a minor. The pent-up discontent of the nobles who had never fully reconciled with Louis XI was manifested in the demand for an Estates General. Held at Tours in 1484, the assembly was characterized by acrimonious debates over taxation and the composition of the regency council, attacking by implication the character of Louis XI's reign and laying the groundwork for the dark portrait of the king endorsed and embellished upon by later writers.

BIBLIOGRAPHY

Bakos, Adrianna E. *Images of Kingship in Early Modern France: Louis XI in Political Thought, 1560–1789.* London, 1997.

Champion, Pierre. *Louis XI.* 2 vols. Paris, 1927.

Cleugh, James. *Chant Royal: The Life of King Louis of France (1423–1483).* New York, 1970.

Kendall, Paul Murray. *Louis XI: The Universal Spider.* New York, 1971.

ADRIANNA E. BAKOS

LOUIS XII (1462–1515), king of France (1498–1515). The son of Charles of Orléans and Mary of Cleves, Louis did not expect to gain the throne since he was several degrees of blood distant from the ruling family. Louis XI coerced him into marrying his deformed daughter, Jeanne, who was regarded as incapable of bearing children. He spent his early adulthood seeking an annulment for the marriage. When he failed to become regent for his underage

Louis XII of France. Anonymous portrait. THE ROYAL COLLECTION © HER MAJESTY QUEEN ELIZABETH II

cousin Charles VIII (ruled 1483–1498), he led the "Fools War" against the monarchy. Defeated at Saint-Aubin in 1488, he was imprisoned for three years. He was released in time to join Charles in the first French invasion of Italy in 1494 to make good a claim to the kingdom of Naples. Because Charles's only child died at age three, Louis gained the throne when Charles died. He immediately received an annulment from Pope Alexander VI and married Charles's widow, Anne of Brittany, with whom he had two daughters, Claude and Renée.

Louis had a claim to the duchy of Milan through his grandmother Valentina Visconti, and he sought to make good his Italian rights in the second French invasion of Italy in 1499. Concentrating on Milan, he agreed to divide Naples with Ferdinand of Aragon, but Ferdinand expelled the French from the entire realm in 1503. For the next several years France was largely at peace. Louis dramatically reduced taxes, which, along with the era's broad prosperity, prompted the Estates General to name him "Father of the People" in 1506.

Although his tastes still ran largely to the medieval, Louis took an interest in Renaissance culture, which he saw on several trips to Italy. He patronized the Italian humanists John Lascaris and Girolama Aleandro, who taught Greek in France, and supported Guillaume Budé at the beginning of his career. Prominent at court were the *rhétoriqueurs,* writers of poetry and prose in classical Latin, of whom the best known was Jean Lemaire de Belges. In 1499 Louis brought Italian architects and artists to France to rebuild the château of Blois, although the principal architect was probably a French mason, Colin de Briart. The rebuilt château introduced the concept that a king need not live in a gloomy fortified stronghold but could live in a place with open spaces and pleasant gardens for gracious living.

Louis allowed Pope Julius II to persuade him to join an anti-Venetian league, bringing him back into the thick of Italian politics. After defeating the Venetians at Agnadello in 1509, he found that Julius had organized the Holy League to drive him out. Louis attempted to counter Julius by convoking the schismatic Council of Pisa in 1511, but it drew only a few French bishops. Julius excommunicated Louis and promised parts of France to Switzerland, Aragon, England, and the Holy Roman Empire, which had joined his alliance. Ferdinand of Aragon seized southern Navarre, and Henry VIII invaded northern France. The French army failed in Italy, and in 1513 it retreated back to France, leaving Milan to the Swiss. The death of Julius in 1513 allowed Louis to make peace with the papacy. He reconciled with Henry VIII and, after the death of Anne of Brittany, married Henry's sister Mary. The excitement of the wedding and his young bride probably hastened his death on 1 January 1515. His cousin, Francis I, succeeded him. Jean Perréal painted Louis's best-known portrait.

BIBLIOGRAPHY

Baumgartner, Frederic J. *Louis XII.* New York, 1994.

Bridge, John. *A History of France from the Death of Louis XI to 1515.* 5 vols. Oxford, 1921–1936.

Quilliet, Bernard. *Louis XII, père du peuple.* Paris, 1986.

FREDERIC J. BAUMGARTNER

LOUIS XIII (1601–1643), king of France (1610–1643). Born at Fontainebleau on 27 September 1601, Louis was the first son of Henry IV and his second wife, Marie de Médicis. The birth of the dauphin consolidated at last the Bourbon hold on the French throne. The much-awaited heir was closely monitored, and the smallest details of his daily life were controlled and recorded by the physician Jean Héroard. Until the age of eight, he was raised by a governess, Madame de Montglat; in 1609 Louis was

Louis XIII of France. Engraving by J. Morin after a portrait by Philippe de Champagne (1602–1674). GIRAUDON/ART RESOURCE

turned over to the marquis de Souvré. Louis was a shy child who grew into a mistrustful adult.

Louis XIII succeeded to the throne following the assassination of his father, Henry IV, by the "mad monk" François Ravaillac in May 1610. During Louis XIII's minority, Marie de Médicis assumed control of the government as regent. She quickly alienated the counselors and friends of her late husband, relying in their stead on her Italian compatriots, Leonora Galigaï and her husband, Concino Concini. Concini's influence in the government grew: he became marquis d'Ancre in 1611 and was named maréchal of France in 1613.

In the first few years of her regency, Marie was able to keep the nobility relatively quiescent by paying them large pensions. By 1614, however, tensions had mounted between the crown and the great Huguenot nobles. Led by the prince de Condé, the nobles were opposed to the proposed marriage of Louis to Anne of Austria, the daughter of Philip III of Spain. They raised a revolt against the crown in January of 1614. Although the conflict amounted to little from a military standpoint, the nobles did convince Marie to call an assembly of the Estates General. The treaty of Sainte-Ménehould, signed in May 1614, provided that the Estates General would meet at Sens on 25 August. Marie managed to postpone the assembly until late October, however, after Louis XIII's majority had been officially declared by the Parlement of Paris.

In his address to the Estates General, Louis XIII endorsed the continued control of his government by Marie. Nevertheless, the subsequent years saw increasing estrangement between the queen mother and her son. While Marie continued to place her trust in Concini, Louis promoted his own favorite, Charles d'Albert, duc de Luynes. The rift between Marie and Louis grew wider as the latter sought greater control over his own kingdom. In a well-orchestrated coup, Concino Concini was assassinated on 24 April 1617. Upon hearing the news, Louis XIII ostensibly appeared on one of the balconies of the Louvre, crying, "My great thanks to all! From now on, I am king!"

When Louis XIII decided that he truly was king, he ended the French Renaissance monarchy, which since 1461 had struggled through great difficulties and opportunities. The French monarchy of Louis XIII and Louis XIV would be a different government, one with expanded powers and its own cultural program.

See also **Marie de Médicis.**

BIBLIOGRAPHY

Hayden, J. Michael. *France and the Estates General of 1614.* Cambridge, U.K., 1974.

Marvick, Elizabeth W. *Louis XIII. The Making of a King.* New Haven, Conn., 1986.

Moote, A. Lloyd. *Louis XIII, the Just.* Berkeley, Calif., 1989.

Tapié, Victor L. *France in the Age of Louis XIII and Richelieu.* Translated by D. M. Lockie. Cambridge, U.K., 1984.

ADRIANNA E. BAKOS

LOUISE OF SAVOY (1476–1531), mother of Francis I, king of France. Louise of Savoy was the daughter of Philip, comte de Bresse, who became duc de Savoy in 1496, and his first wife, Marguerite de Bourbon. After her mother's death in 1483, Louise of Savoy was brought up by her aunt, Anne de Beaujeu, daughter of Louis XI, who married her off in 1487 to Charles, comte d'Angoulême, the impoverished first cousin of the future Louis XII. Charles died in 1495, leaving his young widow to bring up their two children, Margaret and Francis. She provided well for their education, employing notable tutors like Fran-

Louise of Savoy. Miniature from a book of hours belonging to Catherine de Médicis. CLICHÉ BIBLIOTHEQUE NATIONALE DE FRANCE, PARIS. NAL 82, FOL. 2v

çois Dumoulin, and set her heart on her son's becoming king of France. This duly happened in 1515 following Louis XII's death.

Louise was rewarded by her son with the duchies of Angoulême and Anjou and the counties of Maine and Beaufort. She served him as regent in 1515–1516, during his first military campaign in Italy, and again in 1525–1526 during his Spanish captivity. On this occasion she fended off a foreign invasion of his kingdom and attacks on his authority by the Parlement of Paris. For the rest of her life Louise played a significant role in public affairs. If her influence was sometimes malign, as in the affair of the treason of Charles, duc de Bourbon, and the condemnation of the finance minister, Jacques de Beaune-Semblançay, she also gained a reputation as an international peacemaker, which she confirmed in 1529 by negotiating the so-called Ladies' Peace at Cambrai. She died of plague at Grez-sur-Loin in 1531.

BIBLIOGRAPHY

Primary Work

Lefranc, Abel, and J. Boulanger, eds. *Comptes de Louise de Savoie et de Marguerite d'Angoulême (1512–39)*. Paris, 1905.

Secondary Works

Jacqueton, G. *La politique extérieure de Louise de Savoie*. Paris, 1892.

Knecht, Robert Jean. *Renaissance Warrior and Patron: The Reign of Francis*. Cambridge, U.K., 1994.

Mayer, Dorothy Moulton. *The Great Regent: Louise of Savoy, 1476–1531*. London, 1966.

R. J. KNECHT

LOUVAIN, UNIVERSITY OF. The University of Louvain was founded on the initiative of Duke John IV of Brabant in 1425. A bull from Pope Martin V authorized the establishment of faculties of arts, canon and civil law, and medicine. In 1432 Pope Eugene IV granted permission for the establishment of a faculty of theology, turning the institution into a full-fledged university, or *studium generale*.

Like all medieval universities, the institution at Louvain was a privileged body, governed by the rector. Its members were exempted from all outside jurisdiction and enjoyed fiscal immunity. Between 1446 and 1453 general statutes were drafted, to which amendments were added in the second half of the century. Following the examples of Paris, Cologne, and Vienna, they established rules governing the organization, institutions, curriculum, and discipline of the university.

Rectors were elected—originally four times a year, but after 1445 on a semestral basis—by electors from among the doctors and masters of each of the five faculties. The rector, by university law an ecclesiastic, was the highest official, presiding over judicial matters. The chancellor conferred academic degrees and the right to teach (*licentia docendi*). The conservators of privileges protected the university against spiritual or temporal authorities, whereas the delegates (*deputati*) administered the university faculties, nominating their own officers (dean, bedel, receiver).

The town provided the university with premises and buildings for teaching—in 1426 the Vicus Artrium (arts quarter), and in 1432 the still-existing Cloth Hall—and paid for the repair, maintenance, and extension of the four pedagogies (residential houses): Porcus (pig), Lilium (lily), Falco (falcon), and Castrum (castle). The university also benefited from several residential colleges and other (private) foundations intended for needy students. Between 1442 and 1625 forty-one residential colleges were established, some of them specifically intended for students of theology, civil law, and arts.

By the sixteenth century the university had acquired a solid reputation for learning. The faculty of theology was frequently consulted in the confessional debate, and one of its members was elected pope in 1522 (Adrian VI). Humanistic studies became the focal point of the Collegium Trilingue, established in 1517 through a legacy of Jerome de Busleyden for the promotion of studies in Hebrew, Greek, and Latin. Erasmus, then living at Louvain, was one of the college's foremost champions. Among its professors were a number of well-known humanists, including Adrianus Barlandus, Petrus Nannius, Conradus Goclenius, and Erycius Puteanus. Eminent scholars were teaching in every faculty: Andreas Vesalius, Hieremias Triverius, and Adrianus Romanus in medicine; Gabriel Mudaeus and Elbertus Leoninus in civil law; Joannes Wamesius and Petrus Peckius in canon law; Jacques Masson and Michael Baius in theology; Gemma Frisius and Gerardus Mercator in cartography; and Rembert Dodoens in botany.

Humanism was promoted in the 1460s and 1470s by the Louvain printers Jan van Westfalen and Dirk Martens and at the university by Carolus Viruli, Maarten van Dorp, and Erasmus (who had been co-opted into the university). It was attacked, however, by members of the faculty of theology, who regarded Erasmus and Luther as kindred spirits and defended the scholastic method and the traditional doctrine of the church.

The second half of the sixteenth century was a period of decline. Civil authorities began to interfere in the university's affairs. Wars, sieges, and pillaging afflicted the town. All but one (Johannes Viringus) of the professors of medicine succumbed to the plague of 1578–1579. Peace and order, which were restored under the archdukes Albert and Isabella, gave a new impetus to intellectual and cultural life at the university (Justus Lipsius, Erycius Puteanus). The seventeenth century was dominated by Cartesianism (Gerard van Gutschoven, Arnold Geulincx), but failed to supplant the Aristotelian system. At the insistence of theologians such as Libert Froidmont, the university officially rejected Cartesianism in 1662.

See also **Universities.**

BIBLIOGRAPHY

Eijl, Edmond J. M. van, ed. *Facultas S. Theologiae Lovaniensis 1432–1797. Bijdragen tot haar geschiedenis (Contribution to Its history. Contributions à son histoire).* Louvain, Belgium, 1977. With bibliography on pp. 495–551.

History of Universities. Avebury and Oxford, U.K., 1977–. An annual publication.

Ijsewijn, Jozef, and Jacques Paquet, eds. *The Universities in the Late Middle Ages.* Louvain, Belgium, 1978.

Lamberts, Emiel, and Jan Roegiers, eds. *Leuven University, 1425–1985.* Louvain, Belgium, 1990.

Vocht, Henry de. *History of the Foundation and the Rise of the Collegium Trilingue Lovaniense, 1517–1550.* 4 vols. Louvain, Belgium, 1951–1955.

JAN PAPY

LOVE. As a synonym for sexual attraction, love has existed everywhere and at all times. Its significance in people's lives can, however, vary greatly from culture to culture. Long regarded as important in Western culture, it was shaped during the Renaissance in ways that lasted for centuries.

Love in Literature. Much of Renaissance literature took love as its subject. This was also true of literature in the immediately preceding centuries, when romantic love was supposedly invented. Dante (1265–1321) and Petrarch (1304–1374), the towering giants of Italian literature, developed a theme from earlier courtly-love literature when they focused their vernacular poetry on the idealization of the loved one. The Beatrice of Dante and the Laura of Petrarch appeared in their verse as objects of veneration, muselike inspirations, and symbols of female perfection. The stream of European lyric poetry in the succeeding centuries followed the lead of Petrarch in particular. Love was treated as a transcendent experience, whether or not it involved overt sexual desire. Ambiguity about sexuality was one of the legacies of the courtly-love tradition. The poet was as likely to pride himself on self-denial and selfless devotion as he was to plead with his beloved to gratify his desire. In either case love was an overwhelming emotion that could be an ennobling force.

Similar themes were pursued in the chivalric narratives of the Renaissance, which evolved from medieval romances. Great warriors were almost always true lovers, spurred by the remarkable power of love to perform their feats of bravery. Love was depicted as a quest, not unlike the quest for an object like the Holy Grail. Cervantes's Don Quixote in the early seventeenth century had thoroughly absorbed the message that no knight could be worthy of the name who did not have a lady love. Printed versions of prose romances, translated into many languages, were widely circulated. Even an ambitious verse epic like Torquato Tasso's *Gerusalemme liberata* (Jerusalem delivered; 1575), written in the vernacular, owed more to this tradition than to Homer and Virgil.

The most elevated concept of love in the Renaissance was so-called Platonic love. Based on Neoplatonic thought, it treated love as a path to the divine, the source from which the beauty of the beloved emanated. The locus classicus for the concept is the description by Pietro Bembo (1470–1547) in the fourth book of Castiglione's *Il cortegiano* (1528; trans. *The Book of the Courtier*).

Pastoral poetry dealt with love somewhat differently. The world of shepherds and nymphs that the poets imagined as free of artifice and false ambition was a place where honest feelings and simple pleasures abounded. In works such as Battista Guarini's *Il pastor fido* (1590; trans. *The Faithful Shepherd*), love was a delight, somehow both carnal and pure. Pastoral literature, with protagonists who had Greek names and lived in Greek settings, was a distinctive Renaissance genre.

Medieval countercurrents to these versions of love continued to flow throughout the Renaissance. They appeared in bawdy stories and in misogynistic attacks on women, whose sexuality supposedly tempted men to shame and sinfulness. One work of the thirteenth century, *Le roman de la rose* (The romance of the rose), that encompassed a variety of opposing attitudes was still being read in the fifteenth and sixteenth centuries. A literary oddity from its beginning, it was started as an allegory of courtly love by one poet, Guillaume de Lorris, and completed in a different spirit by another, Jean de Meun (c. 1240–c. 1305), and in the early fifteenth century was the focus of a literary debate about morality in poetry. What was in question was the morality of the opinions on carnal love, adultery, and seduction expressed by Jean de Meun's large cast of characters, one of whom, for example, heartily approves of unrestrained sexuality and ridicules the conventions of courtly love. The debate was set in motion by the French poet Christine de Pisan (1364–c. 1430). She attacked the poem's sexual explicitness and coarseness and what she considered its denigrating view of women. The French theologian Jean de Gerson (1363–1429) joined her in the debate, attacking all love literature as immoral. Christine did not go that far, although she saw that love could threaten virtue, especially when unscrupulous seducers cloaked themselves in the conventions of courtly love.

Most of *The Decameron* (1353) of Boccaccio (1313–1375) consists of tales about love, some of them about deep devotion, most of them rambunctious accounts of coarse adulteries. The many Italian and French story collections (called *novelle* in Italian) that appeared in the next two centuries tended to have the same mixture. In *The Heptameron* (1558) of Margaret of Navarre (1492–1549) conversations among the storytellers are explorations of the meaning of love, its effect on Christian virtue, and its relationship to marriage.

Love and Marriage. It was generally agreed that marriage had little to do with love. The perfect love described by Bembo was incompatible with the mundane concerns of marriage. In the realm of theory, at least, the values of love were simply irrelevant to marriage.

In the real world the situation was more complex. When a marriage was arranged in the higher ranks of society the sentiments of the couple were rarely taken into account, unless either party expressed a strong antipathy. Lower down on the social scale some suitors paid court to women whom they either chose for themselves or who were chosen for them. In some peasant communities, young unmarried people socialized fairly freely. There is far more plentiful evidence about those at the top than about those at the bottom. It was only from the rare cases of contested betrothals that were brought to court that we learn what may have happened to individuals in the lower strata. Arranged marriages seem to have been fairly common in peasant communities, especially if there were property and power to be concerned about, but on all levels of society some rebels insisted on marrying for love, exploiting every loophole in a very complicated and flexible system of marriage law. They were apparently oblivious to the theoretical incompatibility of love and marriage.

Although most people who thought seriously about marriage did not think falling in love was a sound basis for getting married, young people were influenced by ideas of romantic love, especially if they had the opportunity to go through a period of courtship. The language of courtship often came from the literature of love, from romances, and from widely circulated songs and ballads. Such courtship was tolerated, perhaps even encouraged, as long as sensible choices were made, preferably by parents. In any case, courtship behavior was to be dropped once the couple was married. The love of husband and wife was a subject for moralists rather than poets and romancers. They warned against infatuation and sensuality and stressed harmony, companionship, and the maintenance of a pious household.

See also **Chivalry**, *subentry on* **Romance of Chivalry**; **Pastoral**, *subentry on* **Pastoral on the Continent**; **Plato and Platonism**.

BIBLIOGRAPHY

Primary Work

Lorris, Guillaume de, and Jean de Meun. *The Romance of the Rose.* Translated by Charles Dahlberg. Princeton, N.J., 1971. Translation of *Le roman de la rose* (c. 1236 and c. 1275). A good prose translation with an interesting introduction.

Secondary Works

Febvre, Lucien. *Amour sacré, amour profane: Autour de l'Heptaméron.* Paris, 1971; first published 1944. Discusses the ideas of Margaret of Navarre in the context of her time. See especially chapters 5 and 6.

Goode, William J. *Explorations in Social Theory.* New York, 1973. See "The Theoretical Importance of Love," pp. 245–260.

Houlbrooke, Ralph A. *The English Family 1450–1700.* London and New York, 1984. Mainly about ordinary people.

Huizinga, Johan. *The Autumn of the Middle Ages.* Translated by Rodney J. Payton and Ulrich Mammitzsch. Chicago, 1996. Translation of *Herfsttij der Middeleeuwen* (1919). Its insights are still valuable. For love, see especially chapters 5, 6, 8, and 9.

BEATRICE GOTTLIEB

LOW COUNTRIES. *See* **Netherlands.**

LOYOLA, IGNATIUS. *See* **Ignatius Loyola.**

LUCA DELLA ROBBIA. *See* **Della Robbia, Luca.**

LUCCA. Lucca is a city of northwestern Tuscany, situated ten miles (sixteen kilometers) northeast of Pisa and thirty-eight miles (sixty-one kilometers) west of Florence. It was a city of some fifteen thousand inhabitants before the Black Death of 1348. Plague and warfare reduced Lucca's population to

Lucca. The complex geometrical design of Lucca's walls was intended to force attackers into areas that could be more efficiently defended. COLLECTION, THE VISUAL CONNECTION

perhaps ten thousand by the late fourteenth century. By the early 1540s the population had recovered to almost nineteenth thousand.

Lucca dominated a state that, under the rule of Castruccio Castracani from 1316 to 1328, had included the Lunigiana and the Valdarno regions, extending as far east as Pistoia. By the fifteenth century the Lucchese state had been greatly reduced as a result of warfare and the encroaching ambitions of more powerful neighbors. Changing borders, together with broader demographic vicissitudes, produced a Lucchese state of perhaps 62,000 inhabitants by the 1540s. In a world dominated by the larger and more structured political entities of the Renaissance, Lucca survived the sixteenth century as an old-style city-state with control over surrounding castles and villages—the area of the city's traditional jurisdiction.

Between 1400 and 1430 Lucca was ruled by Paolo Guinigi, member of an ancient Lucchese family that had been prescribed as noble in 1308. When the republican government was abolished Lucca became more open to the Renaissance-inspired values of the Italian principalities and Guinigi's court saw a modest flourishing of humanist studies. Guinigi himself was a noted builder and collector of jewels. And the new court culture encouraged the writing of a number of histories in verse and prose, including that of Giovanni Sercambi (c. 1347–1424), chronicler, writer of short stories, and bibliophile.

Republican government was restored in 1430 and was to endure until 1799. Throughout these centuries executive authority rested with a Council of Ten, legislative power with a General Council sometimes consisting of 90, sometimes of 120 members. Unlike in Florence, the guilds played no part in determining political eligibility. Government after 1430 was more oligarchic than in the late fourteenth century, when the General Council comprised 180 members. Political eligibility was restricted further by legislation after 1556. Power was increasingly concentrated in the hands of a small number of families, some of feudal origins, with extensive landed, mercantile, and banking interests. Lucca's political tranquillity was disturbed, albeit briefly, by the revolt of the *straccioni* (silk workers) in 1531.

Lucca's traditional silk manufacture revived from the fifteenth century, and the city remained well served by its highly mobile, international merchants. Widely dispersed merchant colonies introduced into Lucca precious objects from Paris and Flanders. Within the city, conspicuous displays of wealth entrenched Lucca's reputation as the producer of the finest cloths of silk and gold. Urban palaces and rural villas built in the fourteenth century were reconstructed and elaborated in the sixteenth. In Matteo Civitali (1436–1501), Lucca produced a sculptor of more than local repute. Angelo Puccinelli (late fourteenth century) and Francesco Anguilla (1386–1440) were painters of some local significance. Generally, the Lucchese patriciate, encased within their city's walls, were more preoccupied with the preservation of Lucca's fragile independence.

Interest in Lucca lies not with Renaissance patronage or humanist studies, although the city was insulated from neither. Rather the city was a highly inventive social, economic, and political community, a distinctiveness highlighted in the sixteenth century when Lucca became the Italian city most markedly affected by Protestant influences.

BIBLIOGRAPHY

Bratchel, M. E. *Lucca 1430–1494: The Reconstruction of an Italian City-Republic.* Oxford, 1995.

Meek, Christine. *Lucca 1369–1400: Politics and Society in an Early Renaissance City-State.* Oxford, 1978.

Paoli, Marco. *Arte e committenza privata a Lucca nel trecento e nel quattrocento: Produzione artistica e cultura libraria.* Lucca, Italy, 1986.

M. E. BRATCHEL

LUCIAN (c. 120–180), Greek satirist. A native of Samosata in Syria, Lucian early mastered Greek letters, and his extant works, numbering about eighty, bear witness to his career as a successful *rhetor,* or itinerant public speaker. Lucian's most influential writings belong to four genres noted for their comic and satirical elements: dialogues of the dead (such as *Menippus* and *The Downward Journey*), dialogues of the gods (*Icaromenippus, Charon*), the paradoxical encomium (*The Fly, The Parasite*), and the fantastic voyage (*The True Story*). After his death Lucian's fame soon declined, but his works enjoyed a revival in the late Byzantine period. In 1397, when Manuel Chrysoloras began to teach Greek in Florence, Lucian was among the first Greek authors taught and translated in the Renaissance classroom. The earliest extant Latin translations—an anonymous *Charon* and a *Timon* attributed to one Bertholdus—were made by Chrysoloras's students, who no doubt valued Lucian for his humorous moralism couched in lively Attic conversation.

After 1400, texts by Lucian spread to other Italian cities. As Chrysoloras's guest in Constantinople (1403–1408), Guarino da Verona translated Lucian's *Slander* and *The Fly* and soon began a version of *The Parasite.* When Giovanni Aurispa returned to Italy from Constantinople in 1423, his 238 Greek codices included Lucian's complete works. Under Pope Nicholas V (1447–1455), the Vatican Library owned four manuscripts of Lucian.

By 1450 many of Lucian's best works had been translated into Latin: *True Story* by Lilius Tifernas; *Toxaris* and *Dialogue of the Dead* 25 by Aurispa; *Zeus Catechized* and *The Ass* by Poggio Bracciolini; *Charon, Philosophies for Sale,* and *Dialogue of the Dead* 20 by Rinuccio da Castiglione; and *On Funerals, The Dream, Octogenarians, My Native Land, Demonax, Slander, On Sacrifices,* and *The Tyrannicide* by Lapo da Castiglionchio.

Imitators of Lucian kept pace with the translators. Foremost among them was Leon Battista Alberti, whose *Intercenales* (Dinner pieces; 1430–1440) often borrow from Lucian. As a dialogue of the gods, Alberti's *Virtus dea* (Virtue; c. 1441–1443) passed as a work by Lucian for centuries, and his mock encomia *Musca* (The fly; 1441) and *Canis* (My dog; 1441) pointed the way toward Desiderius Erasmus's *Encomium moriae* (Praise of folly; 1509). Alberti's compositions soon inspired others, such as Maffeo Vegio's *Philalethes* (1444) and *Palinurus* (c. 1445) and Pandolfo Collenuccio's *Apologues* (1496). Later in the century, Lucian also provided more eclectic inspiration for dialogues like Giovanni Pontano's *Charon* (1467) and Antonio Galateo's *Eremita* (1496).

With the introduction of printing, the diffusion of Lucianic literature accelerated. A volume of selected Latin translations appeared in Rome in 1470, and Janus Lascaris published the editio princeps (first printed edition) of the Greek text in Florence in 1496. By 1500 the taste for Lucian was spreading beyond the Alps. In his Latin dialogues titled *Colloquia,* the Dutch humanist Erasmus often imitated Lucian, and in 1506 he and Thomas More published selected works of Lucian in Latin translation. In 1538 the German scholar Jacobus Micyllus (Jakob Moltzer; 1503–1558) published a complete Greek-Latin edition of Lucian's works in Frankfurt.

To varying degrees, Lucian inspired Renaissance masterpieces as diverse as Erasmus's *Praise of Folly,* More's *Utopia* (1516), Ludovico Ariosto's *Orlando Furioso* (1516), and François Rabelais's *Pantagruel* (1532). In an age of religious dissent, however, Lucian's often irreverent tone—especially in his dialogues—made his name synonymous with "atheist." Erasmus was repeatedly called a "Lucianist," and some of Lucian's works ended up on the Index of Prohibited Books.

Although Lucian is not considered a writer of the first order, his wit and originality distinguish him from most of the Greek authors in the Roman Empire that make up the the Second Sophistic, and after 1400 his literary influence pervades Western literature. His dialogues of the dead offered Renaissance readers imaginative allegories of human transience, and the outspoken Cynic, represented by Menippus, inspired a series of iconoclastic outsiders in Western letters. His dialogues of the gods created a vogue for mythological fictions in which the dilemmas of Olympian deities often parody the contemporary politics of earthly rulers. His paradoxical encomiums inspired countless Renaissance exercises in adoxography, or the praise of ignoble topics. Alberti's praise of the vagabond influenced the Spanish picaro, while the hedonism of Lucian's *Parasite* found its apotheosis in the Gargantuan appetites of Rabelais's fiction. His *True Story,* with its undermining of

Odyssean epic and Herodotean history, led to the absurd quests of the Rabelaisian hero and the Spanish picaro. Not surprisingly, the age of exploration made Lucian's voyage of discovery a central genre of Western fiction.

See also **Satire**.

BIBLIOGRAPHY

Lauvergnat-Gagnière, Christiane. *Lucien de Samosate et le lucianisme en France au XVIe siècle: Athéisme et polémique.* Geneva, 1988.

Marsh, David. *Lucian and the Latins: Humor and Humanism in the Early Renaissance.* Ann Arbor, Mich., 1998.

Robinson, Christopher. *Lucian and His Influence in Europe.* London, 1979.

Tomarken, Annette. *The Smile of Truth: The French Satirical Eulogy and Its Antecedents.* Princeton, N.J., 1990.

DAVID MARSH

LURIA, ISAAC (also known by his cognomen, HaAri, the lion; 1534–1572), Jewish Kabbalist. Luria's theories influenced many trends in Jewish thinking from his time to this day. Some of his theological concepts can be found, though very often not in their original meaning, in Shabbetaianism, Hasidism—as well as among the latter's opponents—and even in the contemporary American Jewish Reform movement. He was also a halakist (codifier of the Jewish law) and a poet. Three Sabbath hymns of his, infused with kabbalistic symbolism, have remained popular. Luria was born in Jerusalem. His father came from an Ashkenazic family, his mother, as legend has it, from a wealthy Sephardic family who lived in Egypt. Several surviving documents show that throughout his life he made his living as a merchant. By 1554 Luria had moved to Egypt, where he soon became the peer of the halakic authorities David ibn Zimra and Bezalel Ashkenazi, being appointed as a judge in the Ashkenazic religious court.

Education and Move to Safed. In Jerusalem Luria studied some Kabbalah with an Ashkenazic Kabbalist, Kalonymus. In Egypt he may have studied Kabbalah with David ibn Zimra, who was also a Kabbalist, although Luria hardly ever followed his teaching; in general he seems to have been self-taught. He delved into various kabbalistic sources but considered the *Safer ha-Zohar* (Book of splendor; written in Spain in the thirteenth century, attributed to Simeon bar Yohai of the second century) to be the most authoritative one. He was also acquainted with the writings of the leading authority of his time, Moses Cordovero, who lived in Safed.

In 1569 Luria moved to Safed, probably in expectation of a more intense spiritual life in the Holy Land, an expectation that was largely fulfilled. He had a reputation both as a halakist and as a bold and charismatic Kabbalist—he even dared argue with the great Cordovero about the correct interpretation of the *Zohar*. He brought with him a grant large enough to support a yeshiva of Kabbalists for ten years, including personal support for the students. By the time of his death of the plague about two and a half years later, the yeshiva had some forty students. Outstanding among them were Hayyim Vital, Joseph ibn Tabul, Moses Yona, and Israel Saruq.

Luria's Theories. Luria wrote very little. Most of what he wrote (largely commentaries on the *Zohar*) was incorporated into Vital's writings. Luria explained his reluctance to write by saying that he was "suffocated" by too much inspiration from the holy spirit. He suggested that each of his disciples should write down what he had heard. In consequence we have several versions of Luria's teaching, with many contradictions. Moreover, many internal contradictions are to be found in what Vital wrote in the name of his master. The contradictions were explained either as stemming from misunderstandings on the part of the disciples, or as variants typical of a mythical way of thinking. Later researchers explained them in terms of Luria's own development—Yosef Avivi by greater skills in interpreting the *Zohar*, Yehuda Liebes by his inner development, and Ronit Meroz by inner spiritual and intellectual developments leading him to compose more and more sophisticated, yet more consistent, theories.

The first stages of Luria's thought were developed in Egypt. They did not reveal unusual creativity or innovation. From the beginning Luria's ideas exhibit an extremely anthropomorphic notion of the divinity. At quite an early stage of his development he espoused the notion of a catastrophe within the divine realm that created a cleavage between the forces of evil and the holy forces. Following a similar zoharic notion, he called it "the death of the primordial kings."

After he moved to Safed his theories about the inner structures of the divinity became more and more sophisticated. His innovative thinking did not lie so much in creating novel notions but rather in using known ones in multifaceted structures—he seems to have combined a vivid visual imagination with an interest in technical details. Like most Safadian scholars, he was not a typical Renaissance thinker but rather saw himself as a faithful successor of an ancient as well as a medieval heritage.

While always clinging to the basic notion of a catastrophe within the divine world, Luria was nevertheless doubtful about the reason for it. Was it God's free will that brought the catastrophe upon itself for the sake of creating evil in the world, so that punishment of and retribution to mankind would become possible? This idea implied that the catastrophe happened because of God's goodness. Or was there a flaw within the divinity, the catastrophe being not only a means for creating evil and retribution but a necessary act of self-purification? And if so, where in the divinity did the flaw lie? At some point his ideas went so far as to speak almost in terms of dualism: in the beginning infinity contained, for reasons unknown, not only goodness but also the "seeds of evil." His insistence on the existence of such a catastrophe within the divinity and his pessimistic notion of this world led him toward dualism; his fear of heresy drew him back to monism.

Luria gradually added further ideas concerning the divinity. First, he proposed the idea of contraction (in Hebrew, *zimzum*): in the beginning Infinity caused itself to contract in order to leave room, free of itself, for the creation of the world. Second, he described the catastrophe within the divinity in terms of the "breaking of the (divine) vessels" (Shevirat ha-kelim) of light. The broken and fallen vessels turned into evil shells capturing sparks of uncontaminated light. It is the duty of mankind to mend them through keeping the commandments, performing good deeds, and through mystical techniques, thereby helping the divinity gain its sought-for harmony (Tikkun). Third, Luria added multiple anthropomorphic worlds to earlier kabbalistic theories about the divinity, calling them the "primordial man" (Adam Kadmon).

Luria showed great interest in the inner world of the soul and in techniques of approaching the holy spirit. He is renowned for developing a technique for communicating with the souls of the righteous, practiced with some variations to this day, as well as techniques for the moral purification of the soul (*yihudim*). He also developed a theory about the structure of the soul and its reincarnations, intended, for example, to explain psychological traits as well as historical events, but unlike what we would expect of a Renaissance figure, he did not leave room for individuality or for any humanistic values.

In private, Luria nurtured messianic expectations concerning himself. It seems that Vital became his faithful disciple (probably in January or February 1571) only after Luria made room for Vital's personality in the messianic scheme. (Before Luria arrived in Safed Vital had had his own messianic expectations.) Two factors seem to have played an important role in the development of Luria's messianic theory: the zoharic messianic notion of representing the sexual aspects of the divinity, and the specific characters and lives of Luria and Vital and their relationship.

See also **Jewish Messianism; Kabbalah.**

BIBLIOGRAPHY

Primary Work
Vital, Hayim. *Eight Gates* [in Hebrew]. Jerusalem, 1960. A comprehensive version of Luria's teaching compiled from Vital's writings.

Secondary Works
Idel, Moshe. "On the Concept of Zimzum in Kabbalah and Its Research" [in Hebrew]. *Jerusalem Studies in Jewish Thought* 10 (1992): 59–112. Discusses the origins of Luria's ideas about "the contraction"; argues with Scholem about the extent of innovation.
Liebes, Yehuda. "New Directions in the Study of the Kabbalah" [in Hebrew]. *Pe'amim* 50 (1992): 150–170. Sets Liebes's direction of research in relation to Luria.
Meroz, Ronit. *Redemption in the Lurianic Teaching* [in Hebrew]. Ph.D. diss., Hebrew University, Jerusalem, 1988. Describes five different phases of Luria's development of thought.
Scholem, Gershom G. "Isaac Luria and His School." *Major Trends in Jewish Mysticism*. New York, 1961. A lucid description of the spirit of Luria's thought, though some points are no longer thought valid today.
Tishby, Isaiah. *The Doctrine of Evil and the "Kelippah" in Lurianic Kabbalism* [in Hebrew]. Jerusalem, 1942. Best research of Luria's theory of evil. The basic assumption, though, is that variants in what is known about Luria's teaching derives from the disciples' misunderstandings.

RONIT MEROZ

LUTHER, MARTIN (1483–1546), German religious reformer.

Early Life and Career. Martin's father, Hans Luther, a restless Saxon miner who moved often, recognized the brilliance of his second son, saw to it that he went to good schools, and sent him off to the University of Erfurt in 1501. After Martin took his M.A. in the spring of 1505, Hans had intended him to study law and had planned a good marriage for him. But on 2 July on his way back to Erfurt from a visit home, Martin was knocked down by lightning during a storm, and in his terror before death he vowed to become a monk. Against Hans's will, he entered the Augustinian monastery at Erfurt, where he was ordained in 1507.

The young Luther soon attracted the attention of John von Staupitz, the vicar of the Augustinians in Germany and a childhood friend of the elector Frederick the Wise of Saxony. Frederick had founded a

Luther Preaching. Detail from a triptych by Lucas Cranach the Elder (1472–1553). Painted 1547. CHURCH OF ST. MARIEN, WITTENBERG/THE BRIDGEMAN ART LIBRARY

university in his capital, Wittenberg, and Luther went there to teach for a year in 1508. In the winter of 1510 Luther was sent to Rome to represent his monastery in a dispute within the order. Later he told harrowing tales of the immorality and unbelief that he found among the Roman clergy. In 1512 he went back to Wittenberg, took his doctorate, and began lecturing on the Bible. For him, all the Bible was explained by the New Testament epistles of Paul, with their emphasis on Christ as victor over death and the grave.

Luther stepped onto the world stage as a consequence of Pope Leo X's plans to build the basilica of Saint Peter over the supposed grave of the apostle in the Vatican. Leo sanctioned a sale of indulgences to raise money for the construction. Indulgences offered remission of temporal penalty in purgatory or cleansed the penalty for any previous sin of a living beneficiary so long as the sinner was penitent. In Luther's time indulgences often were hawked by unscrupulous "pardoners" whose motives were purely mercenary. When in 1517 an experienced indulgence salesman, a Dominican friar named Johan Tetzel, showed up in a town not far from Wittenberg, Luther wrote a Latin letter of protest to his archbishop, Albrecht von Brandenburg, archbishop of Mainz—who was sharing the profits with the pope. Luther appended ninety-five propositions for debate to his letter, questioning the value of indulgences and excoriating the papal curia for its financial exploitation of Germany. Contrary to legend, Luther did not nail these ninety-five theses to the door of the castle church in Wittenberg. After someone translated them into German, they were printed and quickly circulated all over Germany.

Luther the Reformer. From the beginning the battleground was papal authority. Luther attacked the papacy and Catholics defended it. At Leipzig in the summer of 1519 he debated Johann Eck, a theologian from Ingolstadt, and Eck drove him to claim that the Council of Constance had erred in its condemnation of the Bohemian dissident Jan Hus a century earlier. Constance was the darling of conciliar thinkers who wanted to limit papal authority. Constance had decreed the absolute superiority of a general council over the pope. Luther refused to accept the decision of any council unless it conformed to his reading of scripture, and in effect his movement—that grew out of his position—brought about the death of conciliarism.

For years Luther was tormented by melancholy doubts about his ability to meet the demands of a righteous God. In a preface to an edition of his Latin works in 1545, a few months before he died, he wrote that studying the Psalms in 1519 after the Leipzig debate brought him the joyful assurance that God did not demand righteousness from human beings but made them righteous by his gift in Christ to be accepted by faith. Earlier on he had taught that Christians who feared death were guilty of unbelief. How could one be a Christian and doubt that God could raise the dead? But after 1519 Luther taught that horror before death was part of the human condition because death was the penalty for sin. Paradoxically, the Christian could be terrified of death and yet trust

God's graciousness despite this doubting and imperfect attitude.

In 1520 Luther wrote powerful assaults on the papacy. In his *An den christlichen Adel deutscher Nation* (Appeal to the Christian nobility of the German nation), he asked the princes to take over from the pope the duty of church reform. In *De captivitate Babylonica ecclesiae* (Babylonian captivity of the church), he represented the sacramental system of the church as a papal conspiracy to enslave Christians. He rejected the sacramental status of confirmation, marriage, ordination, and extreme unction, changed penance to a mutual assurance of divine forgiveness beween Christians, and kept only baptism and the Eucharist as they were practiced in the old system. There was considerable controversy among the reformers about the idea of a real presence of the body and blood of Christ in the bread and the wine. Luther advocated a belief in consubstantiation (the body and blood of Christ are combined with the substance of the bread and wine) over transubstantiation (the wine and bread are transformed into the actual body and blood). In *Von der Freiheit eines Christenmenschen* (The freedom of the Christian), he held that the true Christian did good works not out of a desire for reward but out of spontaneous gratitude to God for salvation.

In 1520 Pope Leo X issued a bull called *Exsurge domine,* threatening Luther with excommunication if he did not recant, and on 3 January 1521 the pope formally excommunicated him. But fearing public opinion, the new emperor, Charles V (also king of Spain) agreed to give Luther a hearing at the Diet of Worms. Luther expected to debate. Instead, when he appeared before the emperor in April, he was asked only if he would recant. In his answer he managed to make a rhetorically powerful defense of his books, but the emperor was unmoved, and in the Edict of Worms he was declared an outlaw.

Charles was, however, occupied by threats from the Turks, the French, and rebels against his rule in Spain. Agents of Frederick the Wise spirited Luther away to the Wartburg Castle, where he hid for almost a year, writing prodigiously. His treatise *De votis monasticis* (On monastic vows) renounced the binding quality of such vows and with them a medieval ideal of solitude and contemplation. In solitude, Luther thought, the Christian was open to dangerous attacks by Satan. In the Wartburg, Luther began translating the New Testament into German. The first edition appeared in September 1522 with prefaces explaining each book according to Luther's views. His Old Testament translation was not completed for another decade. His German Bible became one of the commanding influences in shaping the modern German language.

Unrest in Wittenberg made Luther return there in March 1522. The unrest was caused by men who pushed to the limit Luther's teaching that all religious authority came from the Bible. God spoke directly to people in the Bible, condemning worship of images and raising up prophets to destroy images and those who served them. Why not believe that God spoke now to tell Christians to destroy crucifixes and images of saints? The violence of this destruction threatened the social order, and supported by Frederick, Luther put a stop to it. Some institutional framework was required to contain the movement he had begun. Since most Christians remained loyal to the papacy, and social reformers condemned his conservatism, he would have to create a church of his own.

In the mid-1520s, Germany experienced a series of peasant uprisings. Oppressed by increasing restrictions imposed on them by the nobility, peasants combined demands for social justice with gospel slogans that reflected the language of the reformers. Initially, Luther supported their aspirations. Once they proceeded to armed resistance, however, he published a scorching tirade, calling on the authorities to suppress the "thieving and murdering hordes of peasants."

In 1525 Luther married Katherine von Bora (1499–1552), a former nun. In the same year he answered Erasmus's treatise *De libero arbitrio* (Concerning free will; 1524). Erasmus had written reluctantly in response to the clamor of Catholic friends that he write against Luther and clarify his own position vis-à-vis the reformer. He argued that the Bible was not clear on the concept of free will. However, he accepted the concept on the authority of the church. Luther's vehement reply, *De servo arbitrio* (Concerning the bondage of the will; 1525), is an uncompromising declaration of predestination, coupled with accusations that Erasmus was an infidel. The ugly tone of the work is in keeping with the molten anger Luther poured out on everyone who contested his opinions. His last years were filled with hateful denunciations of enemies, especially Jews. His last sermon, preached a few days before he died, was a cruel attack on them.

Luther and the Renaissance. Although Luther's significance as a reformer is uncontested, his life seems almost a rebellion against the Renaissance. He knew that many classical philosophers had rejected belief in the immortality of the soul. He denounced their reasoning, calling reason a "whore" when it tried to understand the ways of God with men. Whereas Giovanni Pico della Mirandolo and Marsilio Ficino in Italy could extol the "dignity of man" and proclaim the freedom of the will, Luther saw human nature helpless under the curse of Adam.

Nor was Luther a humanist. Although he used Erasmus's editions of the Greek New Testament in translating the Bible into German, he never professed to be expert in Greek himself. He acquired a rudimentary knowledge of Hebrew, but he depended on Jerome's Latin Vulgate in his translations of both the Old and New Testaments. He could follow Erasmus in rejecting the apostolic authorship of New Testament books such as the Apocalypse, James, and Hebrews. But he refused to consider the larger implications of Erasmus's historical critique of the New Testament text. He cared nothing for the visual arts, and although he wrote the words and music to stirring hymns (most famously, "Ein' feste Burg ist unser Gott"; English version, "A Mighty Fortress Is Our God") and required students at Wittenberg to become proficient in Hebrew, Greek, and Latin, his aim was not to teach them to enjoy literature for itself. He was much more likely to quote proverbs than poetry.

Though Luther lived in a haunted world, he rarely spoke of hell and in his commentary on Jonah in 1526 he denied that hell is a place. Here he followed his beloved Paul, who in none of his New Testament epistles mentions hell. Satan, Luther said, was not in hell but in the air, and he believed himself surrounded by demons and witches. A German scholar has said that a "melody of death" runs through all Luther's work, and his horror at death recalls the stark iconography of death and corruption during the Renaissance. But whereas many scholars have said that the late medieval fear of death drove some to enjoy earthly life all the more, Luther's reaction was to shape a faith to allow him the assurance that death was not the end—an assurance never complete for him.

Luther may have been a Renaissance "individual" as Jakob Burckhardt described individualism—complete with the superstitions that Burckhardt also noted. But if the Renaissance was born of appreciation for classical antiquity and inspired by a spirit of rational inquiry, artistic innovation, historical relativism, and imaginative literature, it is difficult to find a place for Luther there.

See also Bible, *subentry on* German Translations;
  Christianity, *subentry on* The Western Church;

German Literature and Language; Protestant Reformation.

BIBLIOGRAPHY

Primary Works

Luther, Martin. *D. Martin Luthers Werke: Kritische Gesamtausgabe.* Edited by J. K. F. Knaake et al. Weimar, Germany, 1883–.

Luther, Martin. *Luther's Works.* 55 vols. Edited by Jaroslav Pelikan and Helmut T. Lehmann. St. Louis, Mo., 1955–1986.

Luther, Martin. *Sämtliche Schriften.* 24 vols. Edited by Johann George Walch. Halle, Germany, 1739–1753. Reprint St. Louis, Mo., 1881–1910.

Secondary Works

Bainton, Roland H. *Here I Stand: A Life of Martin Luther.* New York, 1950.

Bornkamm, Heinrich. *Luther in Mid-Career, 1521–1530.* Translated by E. Theodore Bachmann. Philadelphia, 1983.

Brecht, Martin. *Martin Luther.* Translated by James L. Schaaf. 3 vols. Philadelphia, 1985–1992.

Marius, Richard. *Martin Luther: The Christian between God and Death.* Cambridge, Mass., 1999.

Oberman, Heiko A. *Luther: Man between God and the Devil.* Translated by Eileen Walliser-Schwarzbart. New Haven, Conn., 1989

Todd, John M. *Luther: A Life.* London, 1982.

RICHARD MARIUS

LUZZATTO, SIMONE (Simha; c. 1582–1663), Venetian rabbi. Relatively little biographical material has been preserved regarding Simone Luzzatto, one of the leading rabbis of Venice for several decades. Highly respected by his Jewish contemporaries, he was also esteemed by Christians for his learning and eloquence. Unpublished documents preserved in the Venetian State Archives reveal that he represented the Jewish community in its dealings with the Venetian government regarding matters such as charter renewals, disputes over housing in the Venetian ghetto, and the age under which Jewish minors were not to be baptized without parental consent. He also served as the official public translator of documents from Hebrew into Italian.

Luzzatto's Hebrew rabbinic writings remain dispersed, for the most part in various manuscript collections, and he is remembered primarily for two books written in Italian for non-Jewish readers. His *Discorso circa il stato de gl'Hebrei et in particolar dimoranti nell'inclita Città di Venetia* (Discourse concerning the state of the Jews and in particular those living in the noble city of Venice; Venice, 1638), written to avert a possible expulsion of the Jews from Venice as a result of the bribery of Venetian judges through Jewish intermediaries, sought to convince the Venetian government that in accordance with the principles of justice and equity, only the guilty Jews ought to be expelled. He then justified the residence of the Jews in Venice on the basis of their fiscal and commercial utility, primarily in the sphere of international maritime commerce but also in moneylending. He also attempted to create a more favorable climate of opinion toward Jews by refuting traditional anti-Jewish charges current at the time and by presenting a brief account of their schools of thought, especially pointing out similarities to Catholicism. In addition, he described their geographic distribution, demonstrating that they were allowed to reside in many countries.

In the course of his presentation, Luzzatto displayed a keen understanding of the economic and commercial situation in Venice, combined with a thorough acquaintance with classical Greco-Roman literature and an awareness of contemporary intellectual trends, especially in philosophical and political thought, as well as of new scientific discoveries in mathematics and astronomy. He was successful in that no expulsion took place and his *Discorso* subsequently exerted a a major influence on the *Humble Addresses* (London, 1655) of Menasseh ben Israel and the *Reasons for Naturalizing the Jews in Great Britain and Ireland* (London, 1714) of John Toland. The *Discorso* was also invoked at least once in a speech presumably delivered in the Venetian Senate against a later proposal to expel the Jews.

Luzzatto's other major work, *Socrate overo dell'humano sapere* (Socrates, or concerning human knowledge; Venice, 1651), is virtually unstudied. It appears to endorse a somewhat skeptical approach to dogmatism. Written in Italian and dedicated to the leaders of the Venetian government, it presents an erudite discussion among various members of the ancient Athenian Delphic Academy assembled to liberate reason, which had been imprisoned and oppressed by human authority, and to put Socrates on trial for the subversion of human science, ultimately acquitting him. Although it is unclear what Luzzatto's real views were, his *Discorso* and *Socrate* are significant not only in themselves but also as indications of the extent to which the rich external culture of early modern Venice was known to and utilized by members of the traditional leadership of the Jewish ghetto community of Venice.

BIBLIOGRAPHY

Cozzi, Gaetano. *Giustizia "Contaminata": Vicende giudiziarie di nobili ed ebrei nella Venezia del Seicento.* Venice, 1996.

Ravid, Benjamin C. I. *Economics and Toleration in Seventeenth-Century Venice: The Background and Context of the* Discorso *of Simone Luzzatto.* Jerusalem, Israel, 1977.

Ruderman, David. *Jewish Thought and Scientific Discovery in Early Modern Europe.* New Haven, Conn., 1995.

BENJAMIN C. I. RAVID

LYLY, JOHN (1554–1606), English writer. John Lyly was the grandson of William Lily, pioneer humanist, headmaster of the first English grammar school (Saint Paul's School in London), and author of the long-lived standard Latin grammar. George Lyly, John's uncle, was secretary to Reginald Pole, the last English cardinal. The family history thus recapitulates the cultural history of the nation, as it moved out of the commonwealth of Christian principalities, sharing a common culture of Catholic humanism, into a vernacular and secular separateness.

In consequence, Lyly's Oxford education pointed not to the church but to the new definer of cultural understanding—the court. His first publication, the prose romance *Euphues: The Anatomy of Wit* (1578), is a fable of the delights and dangers of secular wit and of the kinds of company where wit flourishes. The hero, Euphues—the word means "endowed with good parts"—leaves Athens (Oxford) and goes to Naples (London), where his wit makes him loved and admired. But such societies are essentially unstable, and so Euphues must escape into a quasi-monastic solitude, from which he issues letters of moral advice to his former companions.

The combination of morality and playfulness in the story is obviously germane to the cultural situation of the time. But the runaway success of the book was due more to the writing style than the subject matter. The editor of the 1632 edition of Lyly's plays notes that in the Elizabethan court "all our ladies were then his scholars, and that Beauty in court who could not parley Euphuism was as little regarded as she which now speaks not French." This appreciation of a fashionable dialect leaves unnoted, however, the appropriateness of the style to the subject matter, its use of a *sic et non* (yes and no) technique from scholastic logic to show the instability of mind and world at a semicomic distance, aided in this by the quaint unreality of the correspondences it employs, "talking of stones, stars, plants, of fishes, flies" (Michael Drayton, "Epistle to Reynolds").

Today Lyly is most easily appreciated as a dramatist. But he may have become a dramatist by accident, when in about 1583 his patron, the "Italianate" seventeenth earl of Oxford, gave him control of a company of choirboys used to acting at court. No doubt both Lyly and Oxford appreciated the access to the queen provided by plays presented before her. The themes of Lyly's plays remain, however, the same as in *Euphues:* conflicts between love and duty, social propriety and individual will. But now the wit belongs less to the person than the plotting, set out in triangles and quadrilaterals of argumentative positions: mortals set against gods, shepherds and nymphs against sovereigns and courtiers, and all these against soldiers and scholars, the relations being presented by the speakers with a witty ceremoniousness, but shown as inherently absurd in the commentaries of the pages and servants. Lyly seems to have hoped that his theatrical success would lead to some court appointment (such as the mastership of the Revels), but he was destined to go on hoping until the queen was dead and he himself was a mere relic. He died, neglected, in 1606. But in the modern literary-critical world he lives again in the dramatic structures that Shakespeare borrowed to create his more complex and humanized comedies.

BIBLIOGRAPHY

Primary Works

Lyly, John. *The Complete Works of John Lyly.* Edited by R. Warwick Bond. 3 vols. Oxford, 1902.

Lyly, John. *Euphues: The Anatomy of Wit; Euphues and His England.* Edited by Morris William Croll and Harry Clemons. London, 1916.

Secondary Works

Feuillerat, Albert. *John Lyly: Contribution à l'histoire de la Renaissance en Angleterre.* Cambridge, U.K., 1910.

Hunter, G. K. *John Lyly: The Humanist as Courtier.* London, 1962.

G. K. HUNTER

LYON. The city of Lyon was Renaissance France's greatest money market and commercial hub, an important printing center, and a hotbed of literary and intellectual activity. From roughly 20,000 inhabitants in the mid-fifteenth century, it grew to about 41,000 in 1515 and 58,000 in 1550. The civil wars of the last four decades of the century hit Lyon hard; the population in 1597 stood at 30,000 to 35,000.

Economy. Lyon's prosperity derived from its location at the intersection of land and water routes between the Paris basin, the Mediterranean, and Italy, in an age when much of Europe's most lucrative commerce passed overland between the Italian peninsula and northern Europe. No less important were the city's four annual two-week-long trade fairs. Established between 1420 and 1463, these were granted extensive privileges by Louis XI in 1463 in an effort to draw business away from Geneva. With the restoration of peace after the Hundred Years' War, Lyon attracted many Italian merchants who had previously made Geneva the center for their dealings across the Alps. The Medici, for instance, shifted their operations from Geneva to Lyon in 1466. By 1502, forty-six Florentine merchant and banking families had representatives there. Lucchese, Milanese, and Genoese merchants were scarcely less numerous. A few Swiss and south German merchants also made Lyon a base of operations.

The richest part of the city's commerce involved the importation of fine cloth from Italy. The trade fairs were important occasions for exchanging and speculating upon bills of credit. The Italian wars brought France's kings to Lyon often and led them to rely on the city's merchant-bankers to finance their military operations; this in turn gave the city a central role in tax collecting and financial operations. Francis I also encouraged the establishment of the silk industry in Lyon in 1536. It took root rapidly and employed thousands by midcentury. Lyon's first printing press was established in 1473, and a series of enterprising printers soon made the city Europe's fourth-greatest center of book production, after Venice, Antwerp, and Paris. In the middle of the sixteenth century, Lyon's presses produced 100 to 150 books annually and gave work to 500 to 600 people.

The rapid growth of new industries gave rise to considerable social unrest. On 25 April 1529, crowds sacked the Franciscan convent and the houses of several prominent officials in anger over hoarding and high grain prices. Tensions were particularly high in the printing trade; the protracted industry-wide strike of an association of journeymen printers in 1539 led Francis I to outlaw all such labor associations, in vain.

Municipal Government. Lyon had a municipal government (Consulat) composed of twelve consuls. Each year six were elected for a two-year term by representatives of the city's crafts and a restricted group of wealthy bourgeois. Major decisions were taken in larger Assemblées de Ville, attended by all those with voting privileges. Judicial authority over the city was exercised by the archbishop and his cathedral chapter until 1562, when it was taken over by the royal *sénéchaussée* court, which also helped oversee sanitation, markets, and public health. In 1595, Henry IV replaced the Consulat with a smaller body of four councillors and a *prévôt des marchands* (merchant's provost), whom he frequently named directly. In 1527 the municipality established an important secondary school, the Collège de la Trinité, which adopted a humanist curriculum. Another celebrated initiative in 1534 created the Aumône Générale, which became a national model for the reform of poor relief.

Intellectual and Artistic Life.

The most prominent local intellectual of the early sixteenth century was the physician and consul Symphorien Champier (c. 1472–c. 1540), whose writing about medical and philosophical subjects helped transmit Florentine Neoplatonism to France. In 1520 the printer Sébastian Gryphius began to produce elegant editions of the classical authors. Among the learned men who worked for him correcting proofs was Étienne Dolet (1509–1546), who subsequently founded a press of his own and earned fame as a humanist grammarian and notoriety as an outspoken advocate of Protestant ideas, for which he was executed.

Literary circles gained luster from two of the greatest French poets of the Renaissance, Maurice Scève (1501–1560) and Louise Labé (c. 1520–1566). François Rabelais worked as a doctor at Lyon's Hôtel-Dieu from 1532 to 1535 and returned frequently in subsequent years to oversee the printing of his books. The book trade also engendered a local school of printmakers and book illustrators around Bernard Salomon (c. 1508–c. 1561). The celebrated portrait painter Corneille de Lyon (c. 1510–1575) worked for most of his career in the city.

Reformation and Wars of Religion.

Lyon was an important center of evangelical and Calvinist sentiments and even housed a small group around 1563 who gained notoriety as "deists"—the first Europeans to be so labeled. More conventional Protestant sentiments circulated underground for decades and gained an institutional basis when a Reformed church was established in the 1550s. It quickly grew to encompass roughly a third of the population. The Protestants seized control of Lyon in April 1562 and retained the city until the 1563 Peace of Amboise.

The Catholics subsequently regained control of the Consulat and promoted an energetic Counter-Reformation. The Jesuits were put in charge of the College de la Trinité in 1565. One of the bloodiest of the provincial sequels to the Parisian Saint Bartholomew's Day massacre broke out on 31 August 1572, claiming hundreds of victims and prompting many more Protestants to flee or return to the Catholic church. The greatest economic hardships of the era of the Wars of Religion came in the last years of these conflicts, after the city was secured by supporters of the French Catholic League on 23 February 1589. As warfare paralyzed trade in the region, many leading Italian banking families fled. Between 1592 and 1594, Lyon's fairs ceased. On 7–8 February 1594 Lyon recognized Henry IV as king, ending the worst of the fighting.

The city subsequently regained some of its old commercial prosperity, but most of those engaged in financial dealings with the crown now wanted to reside in Paris, which superseded Lyon as France's banking and financial capital. The seventeenth century was a new period of growth for Lyon, but the silk industry was now the prime mover of the local economy.

See also **Printing and Publishing; Wars of Religion.**

BIBLIOGRAPHY

Davis, Natalie Zemon. *Society and Culture in Early Modern France*. Stanford, Calif., 1975. Several essays in this collection explore aspects of Lyon's history.

Gascon, Richard. *Grand commerce et vie urbaine au seizième siècle. Lyon et ses marchands*. Paris, 1971.

Latreille, André, et al. *Histoire de Lyon et du Lyonnais*. Toulouse, France, 1975.

PHILIP BENEDICT